World Business Resources.com

A Directory of 8,000+ Business Resources on the Internet

Garrett Wasny

McGraw-Hill

New York   San Francisco   Washington, D.C.   Auckland   Bogotá
Caracas   Lisbon   London   Madrid   Mexico City   Milan
Montreal   New Delhi   San Juan   Singapore
Sydney   Tokyo   Toronto

McGraw-Hill

*A Division of The **McGraw·Hill** Companies*

1 2 3 4 5 6 7 8 9 0   DOC/DOC   0 9 8 7 6 5 4 3 2 1 0

ISBN 0-07-136072-7

This book was previously published under the title *How to Conquer the World*.

Printed and bound by R. R. Donnelley and Sons Company.

This publication is designed to provide accurate and authoritative information in regard to the subject matter covered. It is sold with the understanding that the publisher is not engaged in rendering legal, accounting, or other professional service. If legal advice or other expert assistance is required, the services of a competent professional person should be sought.
—From a declaration of principles jointly adopted by a committee of the American Bar Association and a committee of publishers.

 This book is printed on recycled, acid-free paper containing a minimum of 50% recycled de-inked fiber.

McGraw-Hill books are available at special quantity discounts to use as premiums and sales promotions, or for use in corporate training programs. For more information, please write to the Director of Special Sales, Professional Publishing, McGraw-Hill, Two Penn Plaza, New York, NY 10121. Or contact your local bookstore.

Never in human history have the barriers between nations been so few, the bridges between countries so abundant, and the opportunities for global commerce so promising. The time has come to conquer the world.

CONTENTS

CHAPTER 10
FAR EAST POWER PORTALS: 1,500+ ASIA PACIFIC BUSINESS RESOURCES ON THE INTERNET 533

ACKNOWLEDGMENTS

Thanks to the excellent team at Government Institutes for their assistance, particularly Russ Bahorsky, Doug English, Tom Ehart, and Janet Wolfe. Special thanks to my family for their constant support, especially my mother and father, Valerie and Joseph Wasny, my brothers, Brett and Lance, my sister-in-law, Sharon, my two nephews, Cameron and Cole, my aunt and uncle, Pearl and Ed Evertoski, and my uncle, Charlie Wazney. Most of all, thanks to Marie-Josée (Jos) Landry for her editorial advice and love throughout this project.

INTRODUCTION

World Business Resources.com is a directory of international business resources on the Internet. From export manuals to automatic translators and online shipment trackers to virtual consultants, the directory spotlights more than 8,000 of the best export information and tools online. Global in scope, the index covers 230 countries and territories, and profiles the leading trade applications and services on the web in each of the 50 American states and 10 Canadian provinces. The publication also provides 200+ Internet tips for global businesspeople, and reviews the leading web-trade tools in 20 functional areas including training, sales, purchasing, banking, accounting, law, customs brokerage, and shipping.

20 Reasons Why You Should Read This Book

Information-packed, jargon-free, and easy-to-use, the directory has been created to help you succeed in the online global marketplace. This book will help you:

Save money. Find out where to get top-notch international trade information for free—like market reports, procurement notices, company directories, electronic commerce manuals, export software, and trade finance documentation. This material would normally cost you thousands of dollars from a consultant or retailer.

Save time. If you've surfed the Internet, you know the frustrations of searching online for information. Endless links. Ads everywhere. Questionable content. This book shows you how to cut through all the cyber junk and gain instant access to the top trade sites, benefiting immediately.

Discover buried e-treasures. According to the journal *Science*, popular search engines cover only 10% or less of the electronic universe. That means millions of pages are unreachable to anyone lacking the specific web address. Like a virtual treasure map, this directory gives you the precise locations of thousands of little-known but highly valuable global business sites that would be virtually impossible to find using regular search engines.

Boost cross-border sales. Discover where to find prime prospects in overseas markets at the click of a mouse. Learn about underrated e-services that will market your products and services to international buyers, and automatically match you with potential overseas partners and suppliers at no charge.

Expand buying power. Find out how to work the Internet to find new international suppliers, and attract more and better bidders from the world over for your inputs, contracts, and outsourcing needs.

Check out foreign competition. See what organizations and companies all around the world—from Argentina to Andorra, China to Canada—are doing online to promote trade and attract investment.

Go global. According to the World Trade Organization, 25% of global output is now exported, up from 7% in 1950. Even with the recent Asian slowdown, exports of merchandise and commercial services surged from $U.S. 4.6 trillion in 1993 to more than $U.S. 7 trillion in 1998. That translates into worldwide exports of nearly $U.S. 20 billion a day, and $800 million an hour. If you're new to exporting, this book will show you how to access this exploding universe of trade prospects online. If you already export, uncover new markets and offshore prospects—prospects that may have been unfeasible to target using traditional marketing methods but are now a snap to reach on the web.

See the world. Doing random searches for international business resources online is like traveling in a foreign city without a map. You'll go in circles and waste valuable time and money. Like a first-class ticket on a luxury tour, the directory takes the guesswork out of your online experience and shows you exactly where to find the best and freshest information on seven continents.

Increase productivity. Learn how to access virtual trade teams—websites that provide free how-to advice on everything from exhibiting at a trade show to recruiting overseas to arranging an international trip. You'll transform your desktop into an international trade service center at no charge.

Build smarter. Find out easy ways you can globalize your website, flag your page to international customers, get free webspace, and add interactive features such as message boards, chat rooms, counters, and e-mail lists at zero expense.

Tap cross-border networks. Discover the free trade services and information offered by thousands of Embassies, Consulates, trade offices, bilateral business associations, and other offices online.

Learn new competitive intelligence techniques. Find out how the web introduces scores of new intelligence sources onto the research radar screen. Discover how to gather and distill this previously inaccessible information into high-magnification reports on international market opportunities.

Smash barriers. Asked why they don't export, businesspeople often cite "lack of information and capital," and a belief that exporting is "too complicated" and "only for big manufacturing firms." This book shows you how the Internet blows away these barriers and levels the global playing field for even the tiniest of operations.

Rethink old assumptions. Find out why you must revisit old assumptions about what is—and what is not—a potentially exportable good or service. Your organization may have services or products long thought of as "for internal use only" or "strictly for a local, domestic market." On the Internet, these seemingly unexportable offerings could be converted into a cross-border revenue stream.

Upgrade skills. This book is a wise investment for your career. In today's digital jungle, cyber-trade skills and intelligence will give you an important edge, especially with the growing importance of the Internet and global trade in virtually all sectors of the economy.

Beat the 404 blues. Most surfers have encountered the time-wasting "404 error" or "unable to locate server" messages when looking for a particular website. Learn simple browsing techniques that can help you bypass these errors and quickly find sites you're seeking even with no forwarding address.

Search deeper and farther. Find out how to use regional search engines, company directories, and product databases to uncover new global contacts, customers, suppliers, and partners that would be impossible using popular search tools.

Learn from past experience. Discover the preferred portals, proven tactics, and street-wise solutions used by successful global businesspeople online. Know which strategies to follow and which pitfalls to avoid when pursuing new cross-border markets on the web.

Gain comfort. Feel secure in the knowledge that you're preparing yourself and your organization for the digital age and charting your course in a single electronic market moving at the speed of light.

See the big picture. Pinpoint the key Internet trade trends that are now revolutionizing global business, and what simple and inexpensive things you can do—right here, right now—to leapfrog to the front of the digital pack.

50 Professional Groups Who Should Read This Book

World Business Resources.com was developed for people who conduct international business. You have customers, suppliers, or partners in other countries. You export, import, or assist those that do. The assumption is that you have at least a basic knowledge of the Internet and know how to navigate on the web. You may have logged online a few times during an Internet training course or a quick tutorial from a colleague or family member. You may have already visited some trade websites and used cyberspace web for international market research. You may have even developed your own webpage, however modest. Still, you have many unanswered questions on how to use the web for exporting and importing and don't have the time or expertise to search out the top global sites on your own. Whatever your level of web experience, this directory will show you the cyber hotspots of international business and how to go global online.

While the directory has applications in virtually every industry, it was especially designed for executives, management, and staff in 50 professional groups involved in cross-border commerce. These groups are:

- Exporters
- Importers
- Trading houses
- Export management companies
- Export financiers
- Export trainers
- Customs brokers
- Freight forwarders
- Airport and seaport managers
- Air, rail, and ocean carriers
- Diplomats
- Embassy and Consulate commercial officers
- Government export promotion officers
- Trade policy analysts
- Trade mission organizers
- Government customs officers
- Government investment promotion officers
- Government business advisors
- Local economic development officers
- Bilateral chambers of commerce personnel
- International financial institution professionals
- Trade show organizers
- Market researchers
- Consultants
- Salespeople
- Agents and representatives

- Distributors
- Franchisers
- Wholesalers and retailers
- Purchasing managers
- Bankers
- Venture capitalists
- Credit reporting professionals
- Accountants
- Insurers
- Lawyers
- Industrial park managers
- Free trade zone managers
- Technology incubator and transfer professionals
- Utility business development officers
- Travel agents
- Translators
- Employment counselors
- Webmasters and other information technology professionals
- Industry association personnel
- Civic chambers of commerce personnel
- Business school professors
- Business school students
- Reference librarians
- Business editors and journalists

All of these global players require the latest and best information for their long-term planning and day-to-day operations. The directory reveals exactly where to go on the web to gather this intelligence. It reveals where and how to hunt for opportunities, develop contacts, identify customers, and locate new suppliers. If you are new to exporting or importing, the book gives you a jump-start on the exploding world of global trade. It provides information on every step of cross-border commerce, and was also written to be a companion for export training and international business courses.

How This Book Is Organized

World Business Resources.com is divided into 10 chapters, and covers virtually every geographic market from Andorra to Zimbabwe, and every global business function from market research to air cargo. The chapters are:

Chapter 1: Border-Buster Toolkit: 200+ Web Tips for Global Businesspeople. A virtual toolkit of web strategies and tactics for international businesspeople, the chapter provides proven success secrets and time-saving tricks on everything from browsers to competitive intelligence, and website design to online research nodes.

Chapter 2: All-World E-Champions: 20 Virtual Trade Teams for Your Desktop. Virtual trade teams refer to a series of websites that provide functional trade information normally obtained from export service providers. This chapter spotlights some 450 of these resources in 20 international business professions: trainer, researcher, consultant, reporter, pollster, marketer, presenter, salesperson, purchaser, banker, accountant, lawyer, diplomat, customs broker, travel agent, shipper, translator, employment counselor, webmaster, and bargain hunter.

Chapter 3: American Web-Ports: 1,100+ United States Business Resources on the Internet. First in a series of geographic-based chapters, this chapter profiles more than 1,100 leading international trade websites that focus on the United States. Along with national sites, the chapter reviews the top resources and online trade promotion initiatives in each of the 50 American states.

Chapter 4: Maple Leaf Cyber-Stations: 340+ Canadian Business Resources on the Internet. This chapter reviews over 340 web resources that focus on Canada, including search tools, media, market guides, trade assistance, and representative offices. The chapter showcases the leading national sites, along with the top resources in each of the 10 provinces and two territories.

Chapter 5: Digital Negocios: 900+ Latin American and Caribbean Business Resources on the Internet. This chapter highlights some 900 international business websites which focus on 47 Latin American and Caribbean countries and territories. These are Anguilla, Antarctica, Antigua and Barbuda, Argentina, Aruba, Bahamas, Barbados, Belize, Bermuda, Bolivia, Brazil, British Virgin Islands, Cayman Islands, Chile, Colombia, Costa Rica, Cuba, Dominica, Dominican Republic, Ecuador, El Salvador, French Guiana, Grenada, Guadeloupe, Guatemala, Guyana, Haiti, Honduras, Jamaica, Martinique, Mexico, Montserrat, Netherlands Antilles, Nicaragua, Panama, Paraguay, Peru, Puerto Rico, Saint Kitts and Nevis, Saint Lucia, Saint Vincent and the Grenadines, Suriname, Trinidad and Tobago, Turks and Caicos Islands, United States Virgin Islands, Uruguay, and Venezuela.

Chapter 6: Euro E-Hotspots: 1,300+ Western Europe Business Resources on the Internet. This chapter previews over 1,300 global trade resources that focus on 31 Western European countries and territories. These are Andorra, Austria, Belgium, Corsica, Denmark, Faroe Islands, Finland, France, Germany, Gibraltar, Greece, Greenland, Guernsey, Iceland, Ireland, Isle of Man, Italy, Jersey, Liechtenstein, Luxembourg, Malta, Monaco, Netherlands, Norway, Portugal, San Marino, Spain, Sweden, Switzerland, United Kingdom, and Vatican City.

Chapter 7: Slavic Cyber-Centers: 700+ Eastern Europe and Newly Independent States Business Resources on the Internet. This chapter profiles over 700 trade websites that focus on 27 Eastern European countries and territories. These are Albania, Armenia, Azerbaijan, Belarus, Bosnia and Herzegovina, Bulgaria, Croatia, Czech Republic, Estonia, Georgia, Hungary, Kazakhstan, Kyrgyzstan, Latvia, Lithuania, Macedonia, Moldova, Poland, Romania, Russia, Serbia and Montenegro, Slovakia, Slovenia, Tajikistan, Turkmenistan, Ukraine, and Uzbekistan.

Chapter 8: Arabian Sea E-Marts: 800+ Middle East and Southcentral Asia Business Resources on the Internet. This chapter reviews more than 800 global webpages that focus on 24 Middle Eastern countries. These are Afghanistan, Bahrain, Bangladesh, Bhutan, Cyprus, Egypt, India, Iran, Iraq, Israel, Jordan, Kuwait, Lebanon, Libya, Oman, Pakistan, Palestinian Authority, Qatar, Saudi Arabia, Sri Lanka, Syria, Turkey, United Arab Emirates, and Yemen.

Chapter 9: Sub-Sahara Web-Hubs: 850+ Africa Business Resources on the Internet. Along with a roundup of regional trade sites, the chapter profiles more than 850 e-commerce hotspots that focus on 55 African countries and territories. These are Algeria, Angola, Benin, Botswana, Burkina Faso, Burundi, Cameroon, Cape Verde, Central African Republic, Chad, Comoros, Côte d'Ivoire, Democratic Republic of Congo, Djibouti, Equatorial Guinea, Eritrea, Ethiopia, Gabon, Gambia, Ghana, Guinea, Guinea-Bissau, Kenya, Lesotho, Liberia, Madagascar, Malawi, Mali, Mauritania, Mauritius, Mayotte, Morocco, Mozambique, Namibia, Niger, Nigeria, Republic of Congo, Reunion, Rwanda, Saint Helena, São Tomé and Príncipe,

Senegal, Seychelles, Sierra Leone, Somalia, South Africa, Sudan, Swaziland, Tanzania, Togo, Tunisia, Uganda, Western Sahara, Zambia, and Zimbabwe.

Chapter 10: Far East Power Portals: 1,500+ Asia Pacific Business Resources on the Internet. This chapter highlights more than 1,550 international trade cyber-ports that focus on 44 Asia Pacific countries and territories. These are American Samoa, Australia, Brunei Darussalam, Cambodia, China, Cook Islands, Fiji, French Polynesia, Guam, Indonesia, Japan, Kiribati, Laos, Macau, Malaysia, Maldives, Marshall Islands, Micronesia, Mongolia, Myanmar, Nauru, Nepal, New Caledonia, New Zealand, Niue, Norfolk Island, North Korea, Northern Mariana Islands, Palau, Papua New Guinea, Philippines, Pitcairn Islands, Singapore, Solomon Islands, South Korea, Tahiti, Taiwan, Thailand, Tonga, Tuvalu, Vanuatu, Vietnam, Wallis and Futuna, and Western Samoa.

Appendices. The Appendices provide an assortment of questionnaires, exercises, action plans, templates, and checklists to assist in your online global business prospecting. Appendices A-C offer fill-in-the-bank exercises and instructions on how to identify and contact new customers, suppliers, and partners online around the world. Appendix D provides three sample e-mails that can be used as templates when writing correspondence to online prospects. Appendix E provides a checklist of 65 global business online research nodes—a unique web-scanning program—that can be used to gather information, identify contacts, and uncover opportunities in virtually any international market. Appendix F offers a Navigation Checklist, a 23-point system for troubleshooting broken links. Appendix G is a directory of Internet Country Codes, a two-letter coding system that identifies the country location of websites and e-mail services around the world.

How the Resources Were Selected

The Internet trade resources were selected based on five criteria:

Know-how. The site provides key market information and insight on how to conduct business in a particular geographic area or export function.

Know-who. The site lists leading business contacts and decision-makers in a particular geographic area or export function.

Freshness. The site is continually updated and offers the most current information available.

Design. The site is easy to use and navigate and is relatively quick to download.

Cost. The site is free to access or is available at minimal cost.

The sites and tips were compiled over three years of research, both on and off the Internet. Tens of thousands of international websites and newsgroups were reviewed. Interviews were conducted with hundreds of export and import professionals, from front-line staff to Chief Executive Officers. Forums were held in chat rooms, bulletin boards, trade shows, international business missions, export training sessions, and boardrooms around the world. The goal: find out what global business information international traders needed most, which sites they liked best, and how they used the web to develop cross-border sales, and then distill all this intelligence into one source. The directory delivers all this and much more. It reflects the real-world information needs of international trade personnel at all levels, from a shipping clerk to the Chairman—or Chairwoman—of the Board.

While all provide key international trade information and contacts, the resources vary widely in size and design. Some sites are short and simple. For example, the Checklist for Evaluating Potential Export Markets at http://www.tradeport.org/ts/planning/marketlist.html is a one-page, text-only, 25-line checklist on assessing target markets. Other sites are mammoth virtual libraries with interactive tools and multimedia features. An example is Strategis at http://strategis.ic.gc.ca/, a huge archive of international market reports, trade statistics, and global business tools. Although size and design vary, all the sites offer excellent content and can lead you to new cross-border prospects and business online.

In the vast majority of cases, the resources are free to access. No subscription or transaction fees are required to use the online services. A small proportion—less than three percent—require registration, but are free to access once a user has completed the necessary forms. A tiny share—less than half of one percent—are subscription or pay-for-view sites, and are indicated as such in the site description.

How the Resources Are Classified

In Chapters 1 and 2, the functional-based sections, the trade resources and tips are grouped by export-related professions and activities such as customs brokerage, shipping, and translation. In Chapters 3 to 10, the geographic-based sections, the trade resources are divided into five categories:

Search tools. These are web navigation services that provide browsable directories of online resources for a particular geographic area. Infoseek at http://www.infoseek.com and Yahoo at http://www.yahoo.com are examples.

Media. These are leading newspaper, magazine, television, and radio websites in a particular area, or a link page of such sites. The homepages of the *U.S.A. Today* newspaper at http://www.usatoday.com/ and *Business Week* magazine at http://www.businessweek.com/ are examples.

Market guides. These are webpages that provide fact sheets and reports on the economy, government, industry sectors, companies, business regulations, consumers, and other market segments and players in a particular area. Examples include the American Community Network at http://www.acn.net/ and the Thomas Register of American Manufacturers at http://www.thomasregister.com/.

Trade assistance. These are websites that provide export guides, import primers, and other information and online services related to international trade in a specific area. Examples include the American Export Register at http://www.aernet.com/english/, and the United States International Trade Administration at http://www.ita.doc.gov/.

Representative offices. These are the homepages of bilateral chambers of commerce, Embassies, Consulates, and other diplomatic posts based in an area. Examples include European Union in the United States at http://www.eurunion.org/, and the Embassy of Vietnam in Washington, D.C. at http://www.vietnamembassy-usa.org/.

In the case of representative offices, the resources are classified according to the physical location of the server, not the country of origin. Example: the Embassy of Vietnam in Washington, D.C.—which is physically located in the United States—is listed as a United States resource, even though the site provides Vietnamese information. Other examples: the United States Embassy in Tokyo at http://www.usia.gov/posts/japan/—which is based in Japan—is classified as a Japanese resource, and listed in Chapter 10: Asia Pacific Trade Resources. The British Embassy in Mexico City at http://www.embajadabritanica.com.mx/—located in Mexico—is classified as a Latin American resource, and listed in Chapter 5: Latin American and Caribbean Trade Resources. The lesson is that the trade resources of a particular country—the United States, for example—are not strictly confined to its corresponding chapter. The resources are dispersed throughout all the other geographic-based sections. In both the real and virtual worlds, nationalities are intermixed and information is borderless.

Not all countries or geographic areas have resources in all five categories. The Yukon Territory in Canada, for example, has websites listed in the media and market guides categories, but none indicated for the search tools, trade assistance, and representative offices categories. This is because no such resources were online in those categories at this writing. The same applies to other geographic areas: if no resources are listed for one or more of the five categories, no sites were available in that category.

While over 8,100 international business resources are included in the directory, many thousand more had to be excluded for deadline and space considerations. This book is intended to be a snapshot of the leading online resources in 1999 and is not intended to be a complete listing of every global trade site on the web. Everyday online, thousands of websites appear and disappear, and keeping precise track of every webpage related to international trade is impossible at this time.

How to Find Broken Links

While all URLs cited in this directory were accurate at the time of writing, some website addresses will have changed by the time you read this book. In such cases, refer to Appendix F, Navigation Checklist, a 23-point guide to finding websites that may have moved or changed. Of all the tips, perhaps the easiest and quickest is slash after the slash, a simple yet effective navigation technique. Whenever you encounter a "404: File Not Found" or another outdated link prompt, place your cursor at the end—that's the end, not the beginning—of the URL in the location window. Delete the portion of the URL from this point back to the first forward-slash (/) you encounter. Hit enter. If nothing happens, delete that portion of the URL to the next forward-slash (/). Hit enter again. Repeat until you access the site or delete the entire URL. If you access the site, you're in luck. This means the particular page you sought within the site has moved, not the entire site. Now, scan the index and contents of the site. Often, you'll find the page in a new spot. If you still cannot connect to the resource, the website has moved, and you should employ the other search techniques listed in the navigation checklist. Using these tips, you should track down most of the broken links or find alternative e-sources that provide the information you are seeking.

Companion Website

For additional global business e-resources and tips, visit the *World Business Resources.com* companion website at http://www.howtoconquertheworld.com. An international trade webcast center, the site features book excerpts, a free newsletter, cyber-seminars, PowerPoint® templates, and dozens of interviews with leading e-commerce and cross-border professionals from around the world. Guests to date have included:

- **Richard Fursland**, Executive Director, British-American Business Council in New York City, New York.
- **Joseph Grasmick**, U.S. Business Immigration Lawyer in Buffalo, New York.
- **Gary Klein**, Editor, Business Librarians' Discussion Group in Salem, Oregon.
- **Barney Lehrer**, Webmaster, Federation of International Trade Organizations in Reston, Virginia.
- **Michael White**, International Trade Journalist in Irvine, California.
- **Paul Gerbino**, Publisher, American Export Group in New York City, New York.
- **Frank Baia**, CEO, Globalspeak in Atlanta, Georgia.
- **Greg Secker**, Producer, Virtual Trading Desk in Toronto, Canada.
- **Barry Siskind**, President, International Training and Management Company in Toronto, Canada.
- **Ken Anderberg**, Publisher and Editor, InterTrade and Investment in Atlanta, Georgia.
- **Paula Murphy**, Director, Massachusetts Export Center in Boston, Massachusetts.
- **Glenn Zagoren**, Chairman, ProNetLink, in New York City, New York.
- **Mary Pyle**, Director of International Development, Greater Kansas City Chamber of Commerce in Kansas City, Missouri.
- **John Passalacqua**, President, ExpoWorld.net in Toronto, Canada.
- **Laura Thieme**, President, Business Research International in Columbus, Ohio.
- **Tunga Kiyak**, Webmaster, Michigan State University Center for International Business Education and Research.
- **Gary Hayward**, Vice President, International Channel Development, Network Solutions, in Herndon, Virginia.
- **Paul Oliva**, Executive Director, BayTrade in Oakland, California.
- **Shuzhen Liu**, Deputy Director General, Economic Information Department, China Council for the Promotion of International Trade in Beijing, People's Republic of China.
- **Martin Duggan**, President, Small Business Exporters Association in McLean, Virginia.

- **Sam Kaplan**, Deputy Director, Trade Development Alliance of Greater Seattle in Seattle, Washington.
- **Bill Dunlap**, Managing Director, Euro-Marketing Associates in Paris, France.
- **Browning Rockwell**, President, Trade Compass in Washington, D.C.
- **Guy Tozzoli**, President, World Trade Centers Association in New York City, New York.
- **Robert L. Lapides**, President and CEO, TSCentral in Wellesley, Massachusetts.
- **Ray Gabriel**, Managing Director, Association for International Business in Salida, Colorado.
- **Mike O'Donnell**, Executive Director, University of Kansas International Business Resource Connection in Lawrence, Kansas.
- **Daniel Stafford**, Senior Technical Writer/Editor, U.S. International Trade Administration in Washington, D.C.
- **Dean Petruk**, Director, CMS Company Limited in Vancouver, Canada.
- **Steve Perrault**, New Market Specialist, Great Outdoors Marketing in Vancouver, Canada.

With new interviews and features added weekly, the *World Business Resources.com* companion website is a must-see multimedia treasure chest of international trade tools. The resource transforms your computer into a virtual presentation center and delivers expert advice from leading cross-border deal-makers in their own words.

How This Book Gives You Global Power at Your Fingertips

Along with the companion website, *World Business Resources.com* gives you unprecedented global power—the power to reach thousands of key web resources in 230 countries and territories in mere seconds. It shows you how to network with thousands of leading trade organizations and decision-makers around the planet from any web-connected desktop. It reveals how you can scout markets, research opportunities, and gather prime intelligence at virtually zero cost. It explains how you can access potentially thousands of fresh, new trade leads every day. It gives you the power to blast through borders and zoom digitally around the planet without having to endure crowded airports, flight delays, or customs line-ups.

Using this book as a guide, challenge yourself and your organization to extend your geographic reach.

Think big. View the whole world, not just your own country or local area, as your home market and base of operations.

Check the controls. Familiarize yourself with the many web-based tools that can help you do more, better, faster, at less cost in the world marketplace.

Train the web-nauts. Spread the word in your organization, and inform your colleagues—especially the corporate planners, researchers, and salespeople—about the border-busting potential of the Internet.

Build your cyber-space ship. Construct your own world-beater website and suite of online services to communicate your message and attract attention in as many countries and cultures as possible.

Blast off. Unleash your global power and target new customers, seek out new suppliers, and develop new partners around the planet.

At the dawn of a new millennium, the time has come to ready your desktop, chart your e-course, and go for launch.

Godspeed and let your global cyber-adventure begin.

## CHAPTER 1

BORDER-BUSTER TOOLKIT: 200+ WEB TIPS FOR GLOBAL BUSINESSPEOPLE

The World Wide Web offers international businesspeople a wide array of performance-boosting tools. From online calculators to presentation templates to tariff schedules, the Internet is teeming with information and e-gadgets that can transform even the tiniest operation into a global player. This chapter highlights over 200 of these world-beater resources in 12 areas: browsing, personal management, navigation, research nodes, cyber strategy, competitive intelligence, e-networking, website design, trade finance, logistics, on the road, and presentations. Use this toolkit to save time and money, search smarter, uncover new prospects, and turbo-charge your cross-border clout.

Browsing Tools

Use two browsers. For backup and variety, download and use the two major browsers, Navigator and Explorer. Netscape International at http://home.netscape.com/intl/home.html offers 14 international versions of the Netscape surfing software. The site includes Australian, French, German, Japanese, Spanish, and United Kingdom editions of the surf software. Microsoft offers a free copy of Internet Explorer at http://www.microsoft.com/worldwide/. The site provides special downloads and computer information for over 50 countries from Argentina to Zimbabwe.

Asian Flew. If you read Chinese, Japanese, or Korean, try out AltaVista Asian Search at http://www.altavista.com/av/oneweb/. Using the web navigation tool, you can type Chinese, Japanese, or Korean characters directly into the search box, and scan for webpages in these languages.

Get Real. A must-have program for web browsers is RealPlayer at http://www.real.com/international/index.html, a free Internet audio and video player. Written in eight languages including French, German, Japanese, and Spanish, the program allows a user to tune in to web-based business briefings, multimedia presentations, and radio shows.

Follow the Guide. After you download the RealPlayer, check out RealGuide at http://www.real.com/realguide/index.html. Updated daily, the site is a directory of web-based audio and video programming in seven categories including live events, business, and news.

Fly with Acrobat. Many websites post reports and information in PDF format, an image-rich text and graphic display format. To view such reports, you need special software, the Acrobat Reader, which may be downloaded for free at http://www.adobe.com/prodindex/acrobat/readstep.html.

Personal Management

Mail Call. Don't have e-mail or need another account? E-mail Category at http://www.freeindex.com/email/index.html is a directory of over 200 free online e-mail services in 13 languages including French, German, and Japanese.

Message Instantly. Want to track colleagues online? The Instant Messenger Service at http://www.newaol.com/aim/netscape/adb00.html lets you know when selected colleagues anywhere in the world who also have the service go online. You can also send and receive private text messages.

Turn on the E-Pager. Want to know instantly when new e-mail arrives? Yahoo Pager at http://pager.yahoo.com/pager/ allows a user to send private messages, receive alerts for new messages, and see when colleagues are online.

Check Your E-Calendar. Looking for a zero-cost personal organizer? Yahoo Calendar at http://edit.my.yahoo.com/config/login?.src=yc&.done=http://calendar.yahoo.com/?v=20 is a free online scheduling system. Data from the service can be exported to a personal digital assistant and other computer devices.

Tool Time. Need help with cash budgets? Balance sheets? Benchmarking? The Interactive Toolbox at http://www.edgeonline.com/main/toolbox/interact.shtml is a directory of self-calculating worksheets. The tools can help you do everything from preparing a cash budget to calculating profit ratios to benchmarking your company's information technology capabilities.

Penny Wise. Planning an overseas move? Salary Calculator at http://www2.homefair.com/calc/salcalc.html?NETSCAPE_LIVEWIRE.src=altavista

provides cost-of-living comparisons for hundreds of cities across the United States and around the world. To use the tool, input your current salary in your country's currency. If you live in the United States, for example, list your salary in American dollars. Assuming you wanted to move to France, the calculator then tells you how many American dollars you need to maintain your standard of living in France. According to the calculator, if you make $100,000 in Minneapolis you would need to make $154,014 to live at the same level in Paris.

Speak in Tongues. Need a quick translation? AltaVista Translation at http://babelfish.altavista.com/cgi-bin/translate? and Comprende at http://www.globalink.com/ are free virtual translators. The services translate English from and into French, German, Italian, Portuguese, and Spanish.

Try Before You Buy. Interested in trying out new business software at no cost? Check out BizProWeb's Business & Professional Shareware at http://www.bizproweb.com/pages/shareware/shareware.html. The site links to hundreds of business-related shareware programs online including employment tools, personal information managers, and text editors.

Plan to Meet. Need to arrange a phone or conference call with an associate on another continent? Use the World Clock Meeting Planner at http://www.timeanddate.com/worldclock/meeting.html to arrange a convenient time, and avoid middle-of-the-night meetings.

Deploy the Robot. No time to scan the web? Use the Informant at http://informant.dartmouth.edu/, a personal search agent. Free to use, the service will search the web for key words you designate, and e-mail you when matching pages are found.

Shop Lift. If you use the Internet to shop, visit Compare Net at http://www.compare.net/. The site is a searchable database of product information, comparisons, and side-by-side charts in seven categories including electronics, services, computing, and home office.

Navigation

You may attempt to locate a website listed in this or other Internet guides only to find that you are unable to connect to the page. You may receive messages such as "unable to locate server," or

"server busy," or "404: File Not Found." Unfortunately, website access problems are a normal and frequent part of the Internet experience. The web is highly fluid and in a constant state of flux. Overnight, existing sites move or vanish. Even the freshest web guides, search engines, and link pages have dead links—links that don't work. While some access difficulties are unavoidable, the following 404-busting techniques can help you overcome initial connectivity problems, and track down pages that may have moved.

Check Own Connection. When a site doesn't load, the first instinct is to blame the equipment or people at the other end. "Their problem," you might say. "Faulty website or server." Before pointing the finger, ensure that you are properly connected to your own Internet Service Provider. To check, try sending a quick e-mail to yourself, and see if the message is sent and received. If it doesn't go through, your own Internet Service Provider could be the source of the disruption, and may have their server temporarily down for repairs or upgrades. You could also be the culprit. You may have not connected to the service properly because of a misdial, time-out, or faulty equipment. If so, fix what you can on your own computer, and wait for your Internet Service Provider to get back online. Usually, the interruptions are brief, a few hours at a time at most. Continue trying to e-mail yourself, say every half hour or so, until the connection is properly restored. Then you can begin browsing.

Be a Copy Cat. Ensure that the universal resource locator or URL that you type in the location toolbar of your browser is typed exactly as it is written in the directory. The key word is *exactly*. Every letter, every forward slash, every number, every period, and every other character must be included—in precisely the right order—or the address will not work. All it takes is one alphanumeric to be off—say, a missing period or two w's instead of three—and the connection will fail. For many websites in this directory, the URL is relatively long—70 characters or more—and reading and typing mistakes are easy to make. If you can't connect to the site on your first attempt, review the URL—character by character—to ensure that what's written in the directory is identical to what's typed in the location toolbar of your browser.

Watch One's and L's. Confusing the number one character—as in you're number 1—with the letter l character—as in L for Larry—is a common mistake. If you're having trouble connecting to a site, look for the number one and letter l characters in the URL. Double-check to see that the number one's and letter l's are in fact where they should be and haven't been reversed or incorrectly typed. This is a simple error, but is all it takes to block access to a webpage.

Watch Zero's and O's. Another frequent error is confusing the number zero character—as in 2 minus 2 equals 0—with the capital O character—as in O for Oscar. While they look similar to our eyes, they are totally different characters from the perspective of a computer. When inputting all web addresses, take special care to not mix up the zero and O to ensure a successful connection.

Fiddle with the Ending. Sometimes, a directory may list a URL with a period at the end. In some instances, this is misleading because the period refers to the end of the sentence, and was not meant to be included in the web address. In such cases, omit the period to complete the connection.

Wait it Out. After you've typed in the correct address, and hit enter, just sit and wait. Depending on the speed of your Internet connection, linking to a website—particularly to a page in a distant country with unreliable or slow telecommunication networks—can take a full 90 seconds or more.

Try Again. After waiting more than three minutes with either no result or a "can't connect" message, hit the enter key a second time. The first attempt may have been aborted by a failed connection en route, a busy server, or some other network error. In some cases, a second attempt will do the trick.

Use Another Window. Still no luck? Go to the top left-hand corner of your browser and select File, New, New Window. This will create a new browser window on your desktop. Retype the URL in the location toolbar, and verify that the address is correct. Now, hit enter and watch. In some instances, trying an address again using another window will make the connection.

Use a Different Browser. If you're using Netscape Navigator, fire up Microsoft's Internet Explorer. Reenter the web address, and see if you can connect with a different browser. Similarly, if you're using Explorer and can't connect to a site, try the URL again using Navigator. In some cases, websites were developed on or for

exclusively one browser, say Netscape Navigator. When you try accessing it with a different browser, say Internet Explorer, connection problems may arise. On occasion, switching browsers may do the trick and connect you to a site.

Beat the Rush Hour. Like any highway, the Internet has its own rush-hour. During certain peak periods, particularly in the early evening, millions jam the digital freeways of cyberspace. The congestion slows down online traffic, and may cause disruptions or failures. In certain cases, the site you're trying to access may be highly popular. If the traffic to this particular site exceeds a certain limit, access to the page may be temporarily suspended. In such cases, wait an hour or two for the traffic to subside. Try again and you may connect. To beat the rush hour altogether, you could also access the site during low usage periods, usually between 6:00 am and noon, and improve your chances of connecting to a site.

Try Again Next Week. In some instances, a site you're attempting to access may be undergoing extensive repairs or upgrades. The server may be down for days, weeks, and even months. In many cases, servers are fixed outside regular working hours in the late evening, and on Saturday and Sunday, to minimize disruptions to employees. If you can't access a particular site, try again tomorrow, next week, and even next month, preferably during regular business hours. By then, repairs may be completed, and access restored.

Slash After the Slash. When you encounter a "404: File Not Found" prompt, try this simple but effective trick. Place your cursor at the end—that's the end, not the beginning—of the URL in the location window. Delete the portion of the URL from this point back to the first forward-slash (/) you encounter. Hit enter. If nothing happens, delete that portion of the URL to the next forward-slash (/). Hit enter again. Repeat until you access the site or delete the entire URL. If you still cannot connect to the resource, move on. The website has moved. If you do access the site, it means the particular page you sought within the site has moved, not the entire site. Now, scan the index and contents of the site. Often, you'll find the page in a new spot.

Search Dogpile. If none of these techniques works, chances are the website has moved or been discontinued. But don't give up the search just yet. Call up Dogpile at http://www.dogpile.com/, a multi-engine search tool. Enter the name of the site you're seeking in the Dogpile window and hit enter. The service will scan a dozen or so of the leading search engines including InfoSeek, Lycos, and Yahoo at the same time. This sweeping search may yield the new address of the site.

Search Regional Search Engines. If the site you seek is based outside North America, scan one or more regional search engines that focus on that particular global region or country. While the site may not be listed on a popular United States search service, the page could be posted on another non-North American search listing. Visit Virtual International Search at http://www.dreamscape.com/frankvad/search.international.html for a directory of regional search engines around the world.

Search on Altavista. If still no results, call up AltaVista at http://www.altavista.com/, one of the Internet's largest and most powerful search services. Enter the name of the site and hit enter. If no matches are found on the first result page, scan at least the next five result pages. The address information you seek may be buried further down in the search results.

Do General Search with Quotes. Still on AltaVista, reenter the name of the site you seek. Only this time, put the name in quotation marks. Say you were looking for Swedish Trade Council International. In the AltaVista search window, type "Swedish Trade Council International" and include the quotation (") marks. These instruct the engine to look for sites with that exact phrase.

Search Title. Say you're still looking for the Swedish Trade Council International. In the AltaVista search window, type title:Swedish Trade Council International. This would scan for pages that contain this particular phrase in the title bar of the browser, the blue bar at the very top of the screen. What other scans may have missed, this title search may detect.

Search Text. Continue on with AltaVista. In the search window, type text:Swedish Trade Council International. This looks for pages that contain this phrase in the actual text of the website, excluding image tags, links, or the URL.

Search URL. Refer to the original URL of the website you seek. In this case, the address of the Swedish Trade Council International is http://www.swedishtrade.com/. In the AltaVista search form, type url: http://www.swedishtrade.com/. This looks for pages that contain the specific phrase http://www.swedishtrade.com/ in the URL. This may uncover new information and links.

Search Link. Try one final scan with AltaVista. In the search form, type link: http://www.swedishtrade.com/. This finds pages that link to this particular URL. Visit these linked pages and look for information about the site you seek. In some cases, a linked page may be that of an affiliate, parent, or subsidiary organization, and may provide updates about the site's new location and status.

Search DejaNews. If none of these tactics is successful, visit DejaNews at http://www.dejanews.com, a database of some 80,000 discussion groups. Enter the name of the site in the DejaNews search window and hit enter. The service will scan through millions of discussion group postings for the phrase. This may uncover new information about the whereabouts of the site, and its administrators.

Do a Post. Still in DejaNews, visit the Power Search features at http://www.dejanews.com/home_ps.shtml. In the Forum window, type in the name of the organization you seek. This will return a list of online discussion forums related to the topic area. For example, typing in the phrase Swedish Trade Council International yielded five newsgroup matches. These included alt.business, alt.business.export.import, and biz.market. Of these, select one or two that appear to be the best match, or use the Power Search feature to look for other related discussion forums. Using DejaNews, post a message to these newsgroups, and inquire if anyone in the newsgroup knows of the site and its new location. Someone in the forum may know, and pass along the information.

Contact Other Nationals. If all else fails, try contacting a leading government organization, industry association, or source from the same country. Assuming you wished to contact the Swedish Trade Council International, review the Sweden trade resources listed in this directory. In Sweden's case, over 60 resources are listed, from search tools to market guides to export assistance. Look among these sources and scan for related organizations and sites. In this case, they could include the Swedish Export

Directory at http://www.swedishtrade.se/sed/index.htm, and Sweden Trade Profiles at http://www.swedishtrade.se/tradeprofiles/index.htm. These or other organizations could provide a status report on the site, or suggest alternative ways to get the information or contacts you seek.

Research Nodes

Prior to the Internet, international trade research was often conducted from a single-node, unilateral perspective. Typically, an exporter, say from New York, who wanted to export to Japan would gather information on Japanese market opportunities from a local business library. In many cases, much of this information was published by an American federal government agency such as the United States Department of Commerce. Exporters in other countries around the world were in a similar situation. From the United Kingdom to South Africa to Malaysia, businesspeople relied heavily on their own national governments for international trade information.

While valuable, this information was often written solely from a single-country perspective, and influenced by a variety of political and economic factors. Assume that country A—where you live—had positive political relations with country B but chilly relations with country C. In general, the country A market reports on country B would generally be more favorable in tone, substantive in content, and frequent in number than market reports on country C. Even among the market reports on country B, however well-researched and numerous, other issues would be at play. To placate special interests and even the personal whims of senior government officials, country A would often promote the export of certain industries—say aerospace and machinery—over others—say food and beverage products—even though the latter offered more and better opportunities than the former. The lesson is that much of the international trade information prepared by national governments worldwide was—and still is—filtered and biased in varying degrees to meet the political and economic development priorities of the day.

The web changes all this. For the first time ever, an exporter has the opportunity to transcend his or her nationality. International traders no longer have to rely primarily on information and contacts pre-screened by their own government. They can now triangulate and process information from many governments and sources from a multi-nodal, multinational perspective.

Let's return to the example of a New York-based exporter seeking new business in Japan. While a United States export scenario is used here, the lessons apply equally to exporters in Paris, Bangalore, Kuala Lumpur, or any other center. No matter where you live, cyberspace offers an explosion of new options and sources for collecting international business information that would have been too impractical, time-consuming, or expensive to gather offline. While by no means complete, what follows is a sample of key online sources that could be tapped by the New York exporter interested in the Japanese market, and a research checklist to guide you in your own information gathering on the Internet.

The nodes are divided into three categories: home nation, target market, and third country. Home nation nodes refer to organizations and websites that represent the international trade interests of the exporter's country or region. In this example, the home nation is the United States. Target market nodes refer to organizations and websites that represent the export and import interests of businesspeople in the target market. In this instance, the target market is Japan. Third country nodes refer to organizations and websites that represent the global business interests of businesspeople in other countries apart from the home nation and target market. In this case, third countries refer to all countries in the world except for the United States and Japan.

Home Nation Nodes

National Trade Agencies. These are national government trade promotion agencies that provide export information, counseling, trade mission support, and other services. In many Western, industrial countries, normally one organization is the official lead organization for export development, but up to dozens more provide additional information and services, usually with a special sectoral or geographic focus. In the case of the United States, the International Trade Administration at http://www.ita.doc.gov/ is the lead export agency. Numerous other agencies provide export support including:

- United States Department of State at http://www.state.gov/,
- United States Small Business Administration at http://www.sba.gov/oit/, and
- United States Trade Representative at http://www.ustr.gov/.

State/Provincial Trade Agencies. These are export promotion agencies at the state or provincial level. Similar to national export agencies, they offer export information, counseling, and trade mission support, although with a specific state or provincial focus. In this example, the lead state agency in New York is Empire State Development Export Assistance at http://www.empire.state.ny.us/international/exportassistance/index.html

City Trade Agencies. These are export and investment promotion services offered at a local or municipal level. Many larger cities with populations of a million or more provide selected export services to local exporters. These include the development of trade missions and sister-city relationships with metropolitan areas in other countries. In many cases, they also provide business incentive information and services to international investors. In this example, the New York City Commission for International Business at http://www.ci.nyc.ny.us/html/mcp/html/ib.html promotes both export and investment promotion services.

Trade Training Programs. These are export training courses or programs offered as part of a university business school or technical college curriculum, or a government export education initiative. In New York, examples include New York University's International Business Area at http://www.stern.nyu.edu/ib/ and the New York State Small Business Development Center at http://www.sbdc.rockland.ny.us/international.htm.

Trade Mentor Programs. These offer export counseling services from experienced traders. In New York and across the United States, popular mentor programs include:

- National District Export Council at http://www.ita.doc.gov/usfcs/usf/dec/, and
- Service Corps of Retired Executives at http://www.score.org/, a network of small business and export advisors.

Export Guides. These provide general tutorials and tips on how to export and conduct interna-

tional business. In the United States, some guides are prepared by the federal government, such as:

- Breaking Into the Trade Game at http://www.tradeport.org/cgi-bin/banner.pl/ts/t_expert2/infobase/breaking/index.html, and
- Small Business Guide to Exporting at http://www.sbaonline.sba.gov/gopher/Business-Development/International-Trade/Guide-To-Exporting.

Other guides are developed by universities and consultants, such as:

- Export Guide at http://sys1.tpusa.com/dir01/exprtgui/t_of_c.shtml, and
- Export Tutor at http://www.miep.org/tutor/.

Geographic Guides. Developed by the home nation government, these provide primers on how to export to a particular global region or country. In the United States, leading guide databases include:

- Big Emerging Markets Home Page at http://www.ita.doc.gov/bems/index.html, and
- Country Commercial Guides at http://www.ita.doc.gov/uscs/ccglist.html,
- Country Reports on Economic Policy and Trade Practices at http://www.state.gov/www/issues/economic/trade_reports/index.html,
- Library of Congress Country Studies at http://lcweb2.loc.gov/frd/cs/cshome.html.

Trade Finance Organizations. These are banking organizations that provide financing and risk management services for home nation exporters. In the United States, a leading trade finance agency is the Export-Import Bank at http://www.exim.gov/.

National Representative Offices in Target Market. These are diplomatic and representative offices of a federal government in another country. The offices provide a range of consular and commercial services such as issuing visas, arranging trade missions, and reporting on local business conditions and opportunities in a particular market. In this example, the United States federal government maintains at least nine offices in Japan including:

- United States Agricultural Trade Service in Tokyo at http://www.usato.or.jp/.

- United States Embassy in Tokyo at http://www.usia.gov/posts/japan/, and
- United States Trade Center in Tokyo at http://www.csjapan.doc.gov/ustc/.

National Representative Offices in Target Market Regions. These are representative offices of a home nation national government in a particular region in the target market. In Japan, examples include:

- American Consulate in Nagoya at http://www.japan-net.or.jp/~amconngo/,
- American Consulate General in Osaka-Kobe at http://www.senri-l.or.jp/amcon/usa_01.htm, and
- American Consulate General in Sapporo at http://plaza12.mbn.or.jp/~AmConGenSapporo/.

State/Provincial Offices in Target Market. These are representative offices of a state or provincial government in another country. Normally, the offices provide investment promotion services to businesspeople in the host country, and export assistance services to traders from its own state or province. In the case of Japan, some 40 American states maintain a trade office in Japan. This includes the State of New York Trade Office in Tokyo at http://www.venture-web.or.jp/asoa/e-directory.html#1.

City Offices in Target Market. These are representative offices of a particular city in another country. In this case, the office is the Port Authority of New York and New Jersey Trade Office in Tokyo http://www.venture-web.or.jp/asoa/e-directory.html#1. Similar to state and provincial posts, this and other offshore-based civic offices offer export and investment promotion services.

National Export Associations. These are national export organizations that provide international trade information, counseling, and networking services to clients nationwide. In the United States, these include the National Association of Export Companies at http://www.imex.com/nexco/nexcohom.html and the United States Council for International Business at http://www.uscib.org/.

National Sector-Focused Export Associations. These are national export organizations that focus on international trade opportunities in a particular sector. In the United States, an example

is the Environmental Export Council at http://www.eec.org/.

National Geographic-Focused Export Associations. These are nationwide export organizations that focus on international trade opportunities in a particular geographic region or country. In the United States, an example is the United States Business Council for Southeastern Europe at http://www.usbizcouncil.org/.

State/Provincial Export Associations. These are regionally based export alliances that provide trade services to members in a particular state, province, or major region therein. In New York, examples include the Long Island Import Export Association at http://www.liiea.org/, the Southern Tier World Commerce Association at http://www.stwca.org/, and the Western New York International Trade Council at http://www.wnyitc.org/.

City Export Associations. These are civic-based export organizations that provide international trade information and services to members in a particular city. In New York, an example is the International Business Network of Greater New York at http://www.ibnogny.org/.

Bilateral Chambers of Commerce. These are organizations based in the home nation that promote bilateral trade and relations with the target market. In New York, an example is the Japan Society of New York at http://www.jpnsoc.com/.

Industry Associations. The are national, state, or local organizations based in the home country which promote the interests of a particular industry group. In many cases, the association offers international marketing information and services to its members. In some instances, associations organize their own trade missions to foreign markets, or invite buyers from other countries to visit their home country.

Outgoing Trade Missions to Target Market. These are trade missions from the home nation to the target market. Normally, exporters from the home nation make a brief—usually a three to seven day—visit to the target market. There, they attend briefings, meet potential customers and partners, and participate in trade shows. In this example, Trade Events Calendar at http://infoserv2.ita.doc.gov/epc.nsf/

By+Country?OpenView&Start=30&Count=30& Expand=32#32 provides a list of upcoming trade missions from the United States to Japan.

Incoming Trade Missions from Target Market. These are trade missions composed of businesspeople from the target market who visit the home nation. Trade Events Calendar at http:// infoserv2.ita.doc.gov/epc.nsf/ Main+Navigator?OpenNavigator provides a directory of incoming trade missions into the U.S. from around the world.

Business Events on Target Market. These are seminars, conferences, or other events in a home market on business opportunities in the target market. In the United States, Trade Events Hub at http://www.fita.org/conferences.shtml delivers a directory of upcoming American-based events on Japan and other markets around the world.

Export Directories. These provide a database of exporters and international trade organizations in the home nation. In the United States, an example is the American Export Register at http:// www.aernet.com/english/.

International Trade Statistics. These provide data on home nation exports and imports. The leading United States trade databases are Office of Trade and Economic Analysis at http:// www.ita.doc.gov/tradestats, Foreign Trade Statistics at http://www.census.gov/foreign-trade/ www/, and Trade Data Online at http:// strategis.ic.gc.ca/sc_mrkti/tdst/engdoc/ tr_homep.html which features data on the United States, Canada, and the European Union.

Media. These are magazines, newspapers, television stations, and radio services that report on international business in general, and bilateral trade between the home nation and the target market. In the United States, MediaINFO Links at http://www.mediainfo.com/emediajs/ links-geo.htm?location=us provides a directory of American media sites online. Plus, Real Guide Business at http://www.real.com/realguide/ business/index.html lists business-related live events, streaming sites, and other multimedia presentations on the web in the United States.

Target Market Nodes

National Trade Agencies. These are national government trade promotion agencies that provide trade information and counseling in the target market. In Japan, these include the Ministry of International Trade and Industry at http:// www.miti.go.jp/index-e.html, and the Japan External Trade Organization at http:// www.JETRO.go.jp/top/.

Customs Agency. This agency administers customs laws in the target market. In Japan, the lead organization is Japan Customs at http:// www.mof.go.jp/~customs/conte-e.htm.

State/Province Economic Development Agencies. These are organizations that promote economic development, trade, and investment in specific states or provinces in the target market. In Japan, Japan's Local Governments at http:// www.JETRO.go.jp/HOMEPAGE/02.html provides a directory of Prefectures—state equivalents—in Japan.

City Economic Development Agencies. These are organizations that promote economic development in a particular city in the target market. In Japan, an example is the Tokyo Metropolitan Government at http:// www.metro.tokyo.jp/.

National Representative Offices in Home Nation. These are diplomatic and representative offices of the target market national government in the home nation. In this case, an example is the Embassy of Japan in Washington, D.C. at http:// www.embjapan.org/ and Japan External Trade Organization U.S.A. at http://www.JETRO.org/.

National Representative Offices in Home Region/State/Province. These are representative offices of a target market national government in a particular region in the home nation. In the United States, an example is the Consulate General of Japan in New York at http:// www.embjapan.org/ny/. The Consulate serves states in the American Northeast including Connecticut, Delaware, Pennsylvania, Maryland, New Jersey, and New York.

National Representative Offices in Home City. These are representative offices of a target market national government in a specific city in the home nation. In the United States, an example is Japan External Trade Organization New York at http://www.JETRO.org/newyork/, a Japanese trade promotion office that focuses exclusively on the New York area.

National Representative Offices in Third Countries. These are diplomatic and representative offices of a target market national government in third countries. In the case of Japan, examples include the Embassy of Japan in Ottawa at http://www.embjapan.can.org/, the Embassy of Japan in London at http://www.embjapan.org.uk/, and the Consulate General of Japan in Hong Kong at http://www.japan.org.hk/.

State/Provincial Representative Offices in Home Nation. These are representative offices of target market states or provincial governments in the home nation. In the United States, an example is the Fukui Prefecture New York Office at http://www.fukui-in-usa.org/.

City Representative Offices in Home Nation. These are representative offices of target market cities in the home nation. In the United States, an example is Yokohama Business Online in New York at http://www.coyokohama.org/.

Export Associations. These are organizations that promote the interests of target market exporters. In Japan, an example is the Chambers Information Network at http://www.jcci.or.jp/home-e.html.

Bilateral Chambers of Commerce. These are associations in the target market that promote bilateral trade and relations between the home nation and the target market. In Japan, an example is the American Chamber of Commerce in Japan at http://www.accj.or.jp/.

Industry Associations. These are organizations of companies that promote their industry interests in the target market. In Japan, examples include Keidanren at http://www.keidanren.or.jp/, the Japan Federation of Economic Organizations.

Statistical Agency. This agency collects and disseminates census data, economic statistics, and other information in the target market. In Japan, the Statistics Bureau at http://www.stat.go.jp/1.htm is the lead statistics agency.

Credit Agencies. These provide credit information on organizations in the target market. Credit Reporting Agencies at http://www.creditworthy.com/us/providers/agency.html is a directory of leading credit firms in Japan and around the world.

Stock Exchanges. These provide financial statements and other information on public companies in the target market. Stock Exchanges at http://www.creditworthy.com/us/credit/stock.html is a database of leading stock exchanges in Japan and around the world.

Patent and Trademark Authority. These organizations manage the administration of patents, trademarks, and other intellectual property in the target market. In Japan, the leading authority is the Japan Patent Office at http://www.jpo-miti.go.jp/.

Business Events. These are trade shows, industry conferences, seminars, and other business events in the target market. Trade Shows in Japan at http://www.expoguide.com/shows/data/loc_30.htm provides a directory of leading events in the Japanese market.

Company Directories. These provide searchable directories of companies in the target market. In Japan, examples include Business of Japan at http://www.iijnet.or.jp/press/boj/index.e.html, Nihongo Yellow Pages at http://www.nyp.com/, and Small and Medium Enterprises in Japan at http://www.sme.ne.jp/japane.html.

Internet Newsgroups. These are online discussion groups that focus on business, culture, and other issues in a particular target market. For a list of newsgroups on Japan and other countries, visit the DejaNews Interest Finder at http://www.dejanews.com/home_if.shtml, a searchable database of online discussion forums. As of January 1999, the Internet Finder noted that 32 forums focus on Japan.

Employment Databases. These are databases of job postings and resumes in the target market. They provide information on which companies are hiring, which jobs and activities are in demand, and what talent is available. In Japan, a leading job database is Career Mosaic Japan at http://www.careermosaic.or.jp/.

Procurement Agencies. These are organizations that provide information on government procurement opportunities in the target market. In Japan, the Japanese Government Procurement Database at http://www.JETRO.go.jp/cgi-bin/gov/govinte.cgi provides a searchable database of Japanese procurement notices in over 70 categories.

Business and Investment Guides. Normally prepared by a target market national government, these provide tutorials on how to start a business and invest in the target market. Invest in Japan at http://www.JETRO.go.jp/INVEST/index.html offers Japanese start-up and investment information.

Trade Leads. These are databases of buy and sell offers and other business opportunities in a particular target market. In Japan, a leading trade lead database is Venture-Web at http://www.venture-web.or.jp/.

Search Engines. These are web navigation services that focus on Internet resources based in a particular target market. In Japan, leading search engines include EasySearch at http://www.aist.go.jp/NIBH/~honda/EasySEARCH/, and Yahoo Japan at http://www.yahoo.co.jp/.

Media. These are newspapers, magazines, and other media sources that report on business in the target market. Japan Media at http://www.mediainfo.com/emediajs/specific-geo.htm?region=japan provides a directory of business and other media outlets in Japan.

Third Country Nodes

National Trade Agencies. These are national government trade promotion agencies that provide trade information and counseling in their respective countries. Examples include:

- Austrade Online in Australia at http://www.austrade.gov.au/,
- Department of Trade and Industry in the United Kingdom at http://www.dti.gov.uk/, and
- Foreign Affairs and International Trade in Canada at http://www.dfait-maeci.gc.ca/menu-e.asp

National Representative Offices in Target Market. These are the Embassies, Consulates, and Trade offices of third countries in the target market. In Japan, examples include:

- Embassy of Britain in Tokyo at http://www.gate-uk.co.jp/embassy/top.html,
- Embassy of Chile in Tokyo at http://www.oficom-chile.gol.com/, and
- Embassy of Mexico in Tokyo at http://embassy.kcom.ne.jp/mexico/index.htm.

Export Guides. Normally prepared by a national government export agency for businesspeople in their own country, these provide general primers on how to export and conduct international business. Examples include:

- Export Source in Canada at http://exportsource.gc.ca/,
- Getting Ready to Export in Australia at http://www.austrade.gov.au/GettingReadyToExport/index.asp, and
- Joint Action Groups in New Zealand at http://www.tradenz.govt.nz/coopetition/jag/index.html.

Geographic Guides. Usually developed by a national export agency for businesspeople in their own country, these provide market reports on a particular global region or country. Examples include:

- Barclays Country Reports from the United Kingdom at http://www.offshorebanking.barclays.com/services/economic/yearly/contents.html?(none)
- Business Reports from Italy at http://italchambers.net/BusinessReports.html,
- Countries and Regions from the World Bank at http://www.worldbank.org/html/extdr/regions.htm,
- Country Profiles from New Zealand at http://www.tradenz.govt.nz/intelligence/profiles/,
- Market Reports from Canada at http://www.infoexport.gc.ca/section2/market-e.asp,
- Observatory from France at http://www.france-companies.com/fc/observatoire/us/index_obser.html, and
- Overseas Trade Services from the United Kingdom at http://www.dti.gov.uk/ots/.

Trade Finance Organizations. These are trade banks and agencies that provide trade finance and risk management services for exporters in their respective countries. Examples include:

- Export Credit Guarantee Corporation in India at http://www.nic.in/commin/AUTOBODI.HTM#ECGCIL,
- Export Credits Guarantee Department in the United Kingdom at http://www.open.gov.uk/ecgd/,
- Export Development Corporation in Canada at http://www.edc.ca, and
- Export Finance and Insurance Corporation in Australia at http://www.efic.gov.au/.

Export Associations. These are organizations of exporters in third countries. Examples include:

- Danish Export Group at http://www.dega.dk/,
- Federation of Indian Export Organizations at http://www.fieo.com/, and
- Korea International Trade Association at http://www.kita.or.kr/.

Bilateral Chambers of Commerce in Target Market. These are associations in the target market that promote trade between the target market and a third country. In Japan, examples include:

- Australian and New Zealand Chamber of Commerce in Japan at http://www2.gol.com/users/anzccj/,
- Canadian Chamber of Commerce in Japan at http://www.cccj.or.jp/, and
- French Chamber of Commerce and Industry in Japan at http://www.ccifj.or.jp/.

Bilateral Chambers of Commerce. These are associations in third countries that promote trade between the target market and a third country. Such organizations may provide valuable information and contacts on how to do business in the target market. Examples include:

- Japan Business Association of Geneva at http://www.jetroge.ch/~jetroi/japonais2/jbag.html, and
- Japanese Chamber of Commerce and Industry in Singapore at http://www.jcci.org.sg/.

Industry Associations. These are organizations that promote the business interests of a particular industry group in a third country. While not focused on your target market, related associations in other countries may provide key marketing, technology, or research tools and information that may be applicable to your own firm, and help you in the global marketplace.

Outgoing Trade Missions to Target Market. These are trade missions organized by a third country to the target market. An example is Export Related Activities and Events at http://strategis.ic.gc.ca/SSG/bi18091e.html, a database of upcoming Canadian trade missions to Japan, and incoming buyer missions from Japan to Canada.

Incoming Trade Missions from Target Market. These are trade missions from the target market to a third country. Export Related Activities and Events at http://strategis.ic.gc.ca/SSG/bi18091e.html also provides a list of upcoming Japanese trade missions to Canada. If the third country is close to your own, you should consider contacting organizers and inquiring if you may participate. If you're based in the U.S., for example, making arrangements to meet an incoming delegation of Japanese businesspeople in Canada is far less expensive and time-consuming than traveling to Japan from the United States.

Business Events on Target Market. These are trade shows, conferences, seminars, and other events on the target market organized in third countries. Online examples include Austrade Events from Australia at http://www.austrade.gov.au/Toolbar/events.asp, and Overseas Trade Services from the United Kingdom at http://www.dti.gov.uk/ots/. Both provide a database of business events planned in their country on doing business in Japan and other countries around the world.

Trade Leads. These are databases of buy and sell offers and other business opportunities. The services are often targeted by geographic region and by sector. International Trade Leads at http://ciber.bus.msu.edu/busres/tradlead.htm lists dozens of trade lead services worldwide.

Media. These are newspapers, magazines, and other media online that report on business conditions and opportunities in the target market. Directories of media sites on the web include:

- MediaINFO Links at http://www.mediainfo.com/emedia/,
- News 365 at http://www.News365.com/, and
- Web Wombat Online Newspapers at http://www.webwombat.com.au/intercom/newsprs/index.htm.

Cyber-Strategy

Change the Frequency. According to Michael Goldberg, a Vancouver economist, global executives need to change from an "AM" frequency to an "FM" frequency when filtering information about the world marketplace. AM refers to traditional economic measurements such as manufacturing output and merchandise exports. While valuable for tracking resource and goods-producing firms, these AM channels are not good at monitoring FM transmissions such as Internet business and service industries. On AM stations, these FM signals cannot be seen or tracked by normal customs and statistical procedures. Lesson: switch from an AM to FM transmission, and tune in the new and exploding cyber-business channels.

Survey the Surveys. Three excellent sources for tracking Internet trends are CyberAtlas at http://www.cyberatlas.com/, NUA Internet Surveys at http://www.nua.ie/surveys/, and Internet World at http://www.iw.com/. All offer breaking news and statistics on cyber developments around the world.

Quiz Show. Is your organization export-ready? Find out at Am I Ready? at http://exportsource.gc.ca/nonframe/engdoc/1.2.3.htm, Export Readiness Diagnostic at http://www.infoexport.gc.ca/section2/diagnos-e.asp, and Online Assessment at http://www.infoexport.gc.ca/businesswomen/assess-e4.asp. All are interactive quizzes that test your level of export preparedness based on management commitment, competitiveness, and other variables.

Center the Web. New to e-commerce and don't know where to start? Visit the Web Marketing Info Center at http://www.wilsonweb.com/webmarket/ for hundreds of free introductory articles and a free, monthly e-mail newsletter on Internet business. This is a must-see resource for any businessperson new to the web.

Cover the World. Need some help developing a global web strategy for your business? Marketing Internationally Via the Web at http://www.webmarketingtoday.com/webmarket/global.htm and Euro-Marketing Editorial Material at http://euromktg.com/eng/ed.html offer dozens of case studies and tutorials on selling online to world markets.

Foreign Service. Exporting a service? Take a World View at http://strategis.ic.gc.ca/SSG/sc01071e.html provides a 12 step guide to exporting consulting, construction, engineering, architectural and other services. Modules include acquiring export skills, operating abroad, and expanding into new markets.

Master Plan. Developing an export business plan? Review International Business Plan at http://www.sbaonline.sba.gov/gopher/Business-Development/International-Trade/Guide-To-Exporting/trad6.txt and Creating an International Business Plan at http://www.ded.state.nh.us/oic/trade/plan/index.htm. Both provide free export plan writing tips and templates.

Learn from the Best. For a state-of-the-art example of how the web can be used as a global business development tool, check out the Trading Process Network at http://www.tpn.geis.com/. Launched in 1995 by General Electric, the site is an Internet-based trading network that enables buyers and sellers world-wide to conduct business-to-business electronic commerce and transactions.

Saddle Up, Partner. Just as you look for promising customers online in international markets, you should also scan the web for potential partners. Online or off, a cross-border alliance can provide you with instant connections and a key beachhead in a particular country. Working together, you can spread risks, share costs, and boost your competitive clout.

Y2K OK. For advice and information on the millennium bug, visit Year 2000 Bookmarks at http://pw1.netcom.com/~ggirod/bookmark.html. The site lists hundreds of Y2K online fixes, diagnostics, tools, and organizations.

Euro Dinero. The phase-in of the Euro, the European Union's new single currency, began on January 1, 1999. To learn more on how the new currency will impact business inside and outside of Europe, review Euro Information at http://www2.euroinformation.com/eu/eu.html, the Exporter's Guide to the Euro at http://www.mac.doc.gov/euro/index.html by the U.S. Department of Commerce, and Welcome to the Euro at http://europa.eu.int/euro/html/entry.html by the European Commission. All provide Euro conversion information and advice.

Globalize Windows. Developing computers or softwares for PCs? Going Global at http://www.microsoft.com/globaldev/ provides free tips and information on globalizing Windows applications and components. The site includes European, Far Eastern, and Middle Eastern modules.

Trade Parade. Do you promote exports for a country, state, or city? If so, check out the Canadian Exporters Catalogue at http://www.worldexport.com/ and Thai Trade Fair at http://www.thaitradefair.com/. Featuring a host of company profiles and product catalogs, the sites illustrate how trade promotion agencies can combine substance with style. Both use the web to showcase their products and services to customers worldwide.

Virtual Reality. Virtual Trade Mission at http://www.vtmission.com/ provides valuable lessons for export promotion agencies everywhere, and offers a glimpse of how trade missions will be conducted in the future. Developed by a private-public sector alliance from Canada, Malaysia, and the United States, the site was created as part of an initiative to promote trade between women entrepreneurs in the three countries. During July and August 1998, businesswomen from the three nations were invited to register on the e-service. Site administrators then matched registrants with compatible business interests, and encouraged online exchanges through e-mail, chat sessions, and video-conferencing. After two months of electronic networking, selected participants from the three countries were invited to attend in-person meetings in September 1998 to talk face-to-face and finalize deals. In the coming years, look for more of these pre-event websites to be established as part of international trade missions. The e-service encourages more and better networking prior to an event, and expedites the discussion and negotiation process. When participants from different countries actually do meet in person following a period of initial e-networking, the groundwork has been covered. This allows precious trade mission time to be spent discussing deals in progress with people they've already met online. With no initial contact, much trade mission time is spent on hit-or-miss introductions between businesspeople who may or may not have complementary trade interests.

Competitive Intelligence

Don't Judge a Book by Its Cover. At first glance, many international websites may not look like much, especially those based in areas such as Africa, Latin America, and the Middle East where the Internet is still in its infancy. Don't let the basic design and the odd spelling and grammatical errors fool you. To post a simple website, however crude, in these cyber-neophyte cultures is a major undertaking. In these locales, even the most basic telecommunications infrastructure is

lacking and computer equipment sparse and antiquated. Often, the only businesspeople capable of such a venture are the key movers and shakers who have the know-who and know-how in their particular market. That's why the best thing about such websites is not the actual website content, but the simple e-mail link or street address of the businessperson who created the page or runs the organization. To take full advantage of this resource, manage your expectations about the site design and content, and focus instead on the people behind it. If you're interested in that particular market, e-mail or write the administrators and start a dialogue. However plain their webpage, they may have valuable insights and door-opening clout, and may be useful guides and partners for you in that country.

There's No Place Like Home. While the web provides access to valuable trade resources worldwide, it also connects to key local trade contacts that many businesspeople have traditionally overlooked or underestimated. This directory, for example, lists approximately 1,100 trade resources based in the United States. Of these, some 500 or 43% are representative offices—Embassies, Consulates, Trade Offices, and bilateral chambers of commerce. When gathering information about international markets, be sure to include a sweep of these representative offices in your own country and city. Virtually all provide business information and assistance, and can help you connect with partners and customers in their home country. In some cases, the best online contacts and information on a particular market—especially those from Africa, Latin America, and the Middle East—are not based in the actual country. Rather, they are on the website of that country's Embassy in North America or Western Europe. This is because the representative offices in these highly developed regions have access to the latest and best Internet technologies and computer equipment, while government and business organizations in the home market do not.

Be Specific. When e-mailing Embassy and Consulate officials to seek advice about a particular market, be as specific as possible with your questions. Avoid open-ended queries such as "what are the best trade opportunities this year," "how is the economy doing," or other general questions that could be easily answered with a quick Internet search. Instead, zero-in on specific companies, products, and places. Ask questions like "which companies are the leading distributors of wooden furniture in Mexico City" or "which consulting engineers in Monterrey have experience in wastewater treatment." The more focused your query, the greater your chances of a quality response. Commercial officers receive thousands of requests for information every year, many of which are unfocused inquiries from businesspeople with no serious game-plan or commitment to a particular export market. These submissions generally go to the bottom of the pile. The inquiries that receive top priority and the most attention are those which focus on a specific product or service, and identify clear cross-border business goals.

Search for RFPs. When using the major search engines, key in the terms "request for proposal" and "request for information" along with the names of your product or service categories, and your geographic target markets. A management consultant interested in, say, the United Kingdom market, should key in the phrase "request for proposal AND management consulting AND United Kingdom." Experiment with different keywords in different combinations. This may uncover new sales leads and supply opportunities.

Get Smart. Looking for industry-specific Internet resources? The Internet Intelligence Index at http://www.fuld.com/i3/index.html provides a directory of leading online resources in over 20 industries including aerospace, construction, pharmaceuticals, and retailing.

Track Invisibles. To gather tough-to-find data on commercial services trade, visit World Trade Organization Trade Statistics at http://www.wto.org/wto/statis/stat.htm. Along with statistics on world merchandise trade, the webpage delivers data on the world trade of commercial services by region and selected economies for the years 1985 to 1997.

See the Wizard. For customs purposes, every international trader should know the harmonized system or HS tariff number of every product they buy and sell. To find out the numbers of your particular products, visit the Tariff Wizard at http://207.245.213.146/services/twiz98/twiz98e.cfm. Developed by Revenue Canada, the site has a database of harmonized system tariff descriptions searchable by keywords and tariff number.

Letter Perfect. Get international trade information delivered to your desktop for free. Check out newsletters such as the Daily Brief at http://brief.tradecompass.com/ and Global Business Newsletter at http://www.gbw.net/. Both provide global trade headlines and industry reports at no charge.

Back to School. An underrated source of market information is business school cases, studies conducted by business school professors and graduate students on countries, sectors, companies, executives, and management strategies. For case availability and pricing, check out the MBA Program Information Site at http://www.mbainfo.com/. With links to more than 1,700 MBA programs in 115 countries, the site is an excellent starting point to investigate business school research resources.

Patent the Search. An often-overlooked source of business intelligence is patents, the grant of a property right by a government to an inventor. Among other information, patent searches can tell you the latest developments in a technical field, and how products you may plan to commercialize stack up against state-of-the-art inventions. Check out Patent and Trademark Offices Worldwide at http://www.uspto.gov/web/menu/other.html for a directory of patent databases in over 30 countries including Canada, France, Germany, and the United States.

E-Networking

Use Traditional Channels. Display your webpage and e-mail addresses on all your business cards, brochures, catalogs, ads, signage, packaging, and giveaways. You'll show the world you're ready to do business online.

Take It to the Bank. Interested in doing business with international financial institutions such as the World Bank and the Asian Development Bank? Check out:

- Development Business Team from the United Kingdom at http://www.dti.gov.uk/ots/dbt/,
- IFINet from Canada at http://www.dfait-maeci.gc.ca/ifinet/menu-e.htm, and
- Multilateral Development Bank Operations Homepage from the United States at http://www.ita.doc.gov/mdbo/.

All provide tutorials and insider tips on how to access contracts at multilateral development banks.

Expat on the Back. Network with businesspeople on international assignments at Expat Exchange at http://www.expatexchange.com/. The site is an online community of some 75,000 people relocating to, living in, or returning from over 140 overseas locations.

Hitch a Ride. Don't have time or the money to go on a trade mission to, say, the Netherlands? No sweat. E-mail your national and state export promotion agencies, and even those of other countries. Ask who's responsible for promoting trade with the Netherlands—or whatever international market you're targeting. Inquire if any trade missions have been organized recently to the market. If so, ask for a copy of the mission report—a little-known government document that normally provides a list of the participating companies, contacts made, and deals done on the mission. Often, the reports are a gold mine of information, and will alert you to key players and opportunities in a particular market. You can also e-mail those companies that attended, and ask for their insights on the trip. In many cases, businesspeople love to talk about their international travel experiences, and are delighted to share what they learned on the mission. A few simple but strategically placed e-mails can glean you as much, sometimes more, market intelligence than if you had actually gone on the trip.

Thanks for the Megabytes. If you visit a government-run international trade site you find especially helpful, take 20 seconds to write a quick thank-you note. You may reap rewards. Government organizations worldwide crave positive feedback from business clients, and often deliver preferred service and inside information to those who take the time to write.

Procure for Sure. Seeking government procurement contracts? The International Procurement Jumpstation at http://www.fedmarket.com/international.html links to dozens of government procurement agencies across North and South America, Europe, the Middle East, and Asia. Scan these for tender information and supply opportunities.

Create Your E-Signature. Advertise yourself and your company with every e-mail you send. Use an electronic signature, a brief virtual business card that appears at the bottom of your e-mail messages. Visit Your Electronic Signature as a Marketing Tool at http://www.penmark.com/chic/signature.htm for details on how to create your own at no charge.

Play Your Card. Send virtual greeting cards to clients around the world to say thanks, celebrate special holidays or anniversaries, or just stay in touch. Your simple e-gesture—which costs nothing to send and arrives in an instant—will be remembered and appreciated. Visit CardCentral at http://www.cardcentral.net/ for a directory of hundreds of virtual postcard sites in multiple languages and dozens of card categories including congratulations, thank you, and good luck.

E-Invite. For your next trade show, product demonstration, or other special event, don't send invitations in the mail—send them over the Internet. Cyber Invitations at http://www.cardcentral.net/invite.mv lists dozens of electronic invitation services that can be used to send e-invitations to anyone online.

Talk to the Coach. New to international business? The Association for International Business at http://earthone.com/projects.html offers a free export mentoring program. Applicants are matched with an experienced trade professional, and the two correspond by e-mail on specific export topics and international markets.

Hear Me Roar. The male-dominated world of global business can sometimes be an intimidating place for women, especially for those just starting out. On the Internet, support for women traders is only a mouse-click away at Businesswomen in Trade at http://www.infoexport.gc.ca/businesswomen/menu-e.asp, Women in International Trade at http://www.embassy.org/wiit/, and Women's International Shipping and Trading Association at http://web.ukonline.co.uk/wista/wista1.htm. All provide travel tips, surveys, export bulletins, and online networking opportunities for female globetrotters.

Website Design

Start from Scratch. Are you a complete website design novice? If so, a must-read is A Beginner's Guide to HTML at http://www.ncsa.uiuc.edu/General/Internet/WWW/HTMLPrimer.html. Developed by the University of Illinois, the site provides an easy-to-read primer on HTML or hypertext markup language, the coding program used to create Webpages.

Find a Home. Need a webpage for your organization? The Free Homepage Guide at http://www.freeindex.com/webspace/index.html is a directory of 100 homepage providers who offer free websites. Most provide between five and 25 megabytes of space at no charge.

Spread the News. Create your own free online newsletters and mailing lists with ListBot at http://www.listbot.com/. The service offers three types of mailing lists: announcement, discussion, and moderated discussion.

Chat It Up. Interested in a chat room for your website? Chatrooms Online at http://www.freeindex.com/chat/index.html provides a directory of free chat software that can be added to virtually any webpage. After your chatroom is up and running, schedule regular chat sessions, say once a month, and invite customers to participate. Appoint a moderator and have a different company representative each month as a guest to discuss a particular product or business segment of your business. For more details, visit How to Make Business Chat Work at http://www.samizdat.com/events.html for a free tutorial on how to run a chat session.

Grab a Surf-Board. Messageboards Online at http://www.freeindex.com/mess/index.html is a directory of free message board services on the web. Add one to your site and run your own virtual discussion forum.

Count Your Hits. Counters and Trackers at http://www.freeindex.com/count/index.html provides a directory of online counters, which count the number of visitors to your site. It also lists trackers, which monitor how many visitors you get, when they came, and other information.

Get a Sponsor. Sponsors Online at http://www.freeindex.com/sponsor/index.html is an index of companies which sponsor websites, and pay an amount based on the number of clicks on a banner or link on a site.

Pop the Question. Add a quizlet—a pop informal survey—on your website. BeSeen at http://www.beseen.com/quiz/qr-index.html offers the quizlet service at no charge.

Go to the Polls. Add a little fun and interactivity on your site with a web poll, a multi-choice question and answer feedback tool. Free Web Polls at http://pollit.com/?clicktrade=46630 allows you to create full customizable polls at no charge.

Watch Your Expressions. Familiar expressions in one culture may be confusing or even offensive in other cultures. To avoid misunderstandings, remove ethnocentric idioms from your web content. According to Dave Zielinski, an international business consultant, the word piggybacking can be inflammatory in Israel, where the pig is considered a lowly animal. Other idioms such as "dog-and-pony-show" or "shotgun approach" may be common in North America, but unknown in Middle Eastern and Latin American countries.

Mind Your Metaphors. Minimize golf, football, and baseball metaphors in your web content. While popular in North America, these sports are less known in other regions of the world. If you must use a sports analogy, talk about soccer or the World Cup, which are universally understood.

Axe the Acronyms. Avoid acronyms on your website. Many of your online visitors will not speak English as their first language and will be confused by the abbreviations. When in doubt, spell the phrase out.

Dab Your Palette. Be aware that colors have different connotations around the world. Green is considered a religious color in Islamic countries. Purple is the color of funerals in Latin America. A liberal use of red still carriers a negative stigma in some Eastern European countries. Check out The Web of Culture at http://www.webofculture.com/ for details on which colors are appropriate for which cultures.

Hit the Links. When you link to another page from your site, you are making an implicit recommendation, and effectively saying "this is a good page: check it out." Regularly inspect and update links to ensure they are of the highest quality. Overnight, content and competence can change, and reflect poorly on you.

Eyeball the Icons. While icons and other symbols on a website can improve communication and navigation, used incorrectly they can be confusing and even insulting to the intended audience. Review Monitoring Your Cultural Presence in Cyberspace at http://www.webofculture.com/home/analysis.html for advice on taboo-proofing your website visuals and icons.

Don't Play Hide and Seek. Make it easy for visitors to know what's on your website. On your front page, list all the major sections and key content with clearly marked hyper-links, buttons, or other navigation tools. In all too many cases, valuable material is buried within websites, and difficult to find. In one instance, a bilateral trade association in Canada posted an excellent newsletter deep within their site, but made no mention of it on the front page, or even on their second or third level section pages. Unless a surfer stumbled upon the newsletter by accident, they most certainly would have missed it. Don't make the same mistake. Similar to a department store window, highlight your best material on your front page, and encourage visitors to come in and browse.

Leave Forwarding Address. Moving your website? Switching servers? Reorganizing your content? If so, list the URL of the new location on the old pages for at least six months after the change of address. Also re-register the new addresses with the leading search engines. This will minimize frustrations for online visitors who want to reach you, but can't using your outdated URLs.

Post RFPs. Planning a major purchase for your organization? Looking to cut costs? Post requests-for-proposals and requests-for-information on your site for the major goods and services you buy. You may be surprised at the results. In virtually all product and service categories, vendors worldwide—sometimes from a place you'd least expect—are constantly scanning the Internet for such opportunities, and may be able to deliver superior price, service, or delivery.

Detect with Inspect. Quickly inspect the quality of your site with Site Inspector at http:// siteinspector.linkexchange.com/. Offered by Link Exchange, the free service will check the browser compatibility, spelling, popularity, and load time of your website. Simply type in your URL in the designated form and hit the Inspect button. Wait 30 or so seconds for the service to conduct a diagnostic test of your site, and—presto—an overall rating and detailed performance report is provided for your webpage at no charge.

Lose the Logo Intro. On some websites, the opening page shows only the logo of the organization, and the instructions "Click on Logo to Enter." Scrap this. Turn this into your true opening page, and save your visitors the hassle of an extra click. Depending on connection speeds, the logo can take up to 30 seconds or more to load, and will frustrate your visitors who want immediate access.

Be Upfront. Make it easy for visitors to know what you do and how to contact you. Somewhere on your homepage, list your organization name, street address, city and country, phone and fax numbers, and web and e-mail addresses. Also provide a brief description—no more than 20 words—of your product or service offering. On many homepages, this basic contact information is omitted. This frustrates users who are forced to either dig around the site for contact details, or simply move on to the next webpage. The listing of the web address is especially important. In some instances, visitors connect to a webpage through a framed site that does not show the web address of a site within the frame. If a web address is shown on the homepage, a surfer can key in the URL on the location toolbar, escape the frame, and connect to the site directly. Otherwise, they will have to go through the framed site to access the site they really want.

Break the Code. When listing your telephone and fax numbers, be sure to list your country code and area code. International callers may not know how to call overseas, or dial your particular country. Check out International Dialing Codes at http://www.construction-site.com/int_dial.htm for a directory of country codes around the world.

Mark Time. Do you have customer service hours? If so, consider that countries around the world mark time differently. Some use a 12-hour clock (such as 2:00 PM) and others a 24-hour clock (14H00). For international customers, spell it out. List your office hours using both a 12-hour and 24-hour clock, and also their relation to Greenwich Mean Time, an international time system. Example: say you're based in Los Angeles in the Pacific Time Zone. On your website, write "Office Hours 9:00 AM to 5:00 PM Pacific Standard Time (9H00-19H00 GMT -8)". Calculate your time zone's offset from Greenwich Mean Time at World Time at http://www.cnn.com/ WEATHER/worldtime/.

Get a Date. Just as time is expressed in different countries, so are dates. Some express dates in month-day-year or day-month-year. A date written as 11/5/98 can mean either November 5 or May 11. To avoid confusion, write out dates in full such as November 5, 1999 or 5-Nov-99, which are universally understood.

Forget Frames. High-priced web designers may love them, but web surfers for the most part loathe them. They are framed sites: sites partitioned off into two or more separate scrollable screens. In many instances, framed sites are crash-prone and difficult to navigate, bookmark, print, and search. Don't use them on your site. If management powers beyond your control insist on a framed site, at least give visitors a choice and offer a no-frames version of your webpage.

Start the Presses. When you design a webpage, you naturally look at how the site will look on a screen. You should also consider how the page will look when printed out in black and white. Many surfers print out paper copies of websites to share with colleagues and include in reports. If possible, avoid dark background and colored text combinations that may look fine on a color screen, but wash-out in black and white and make the text illegible when printed.

Speak in Tongues. For ideas on how to translate your site, check out Global AMP at http://www.amp.com/about/global_amp.html. Homepage of a Pennsylvania-based electrical supplier, the award-winning webpage features special online services and language options for customers in some 50 countries.

Talk the Same Language. An easy way to show consideration for international visitors on your website is to say welcome in different languages. Somewhere on your homepage, say Bienvenue (French), Willkommen (German), Benvenuto (Italian), Boa vinda (Portuguese), and Bienvenida (Spanish). While simple, the gesture shows you're at least thinking about prospects in other cultures. As a next step, prepare a 100- to 200-word report in English on your organization. Briefly describe who you are, what you do, and the goods and services you provide. Translate this summary in the five languages using resources such as AltaVista Translation at http://babelfish.altavista.com/cgi-bin/translate? and Free Translation Services at http://rivendel.com/~ric/resources/dictad-2.html#freetrans. On your homepage, create active links from the one-word greetings to the translated summaries. Don't worry if the translations aren't perfect. You'll still win points for your effort, and set your site apart from the millions of English-only webpages. In time, add other languages such as Arabic, Chinese, Japanese, and Russian to further expand your global reach.

Parlez Vous Internet? When you create any non-English pages for your website, register those pages in an appropriate international search engine. Non-English speakers search for keywords in their own language, and may not even use English web navigation services to scan the web. When shopping online for, say, shirts, French consumers type in the word "chemise"—French for shirt—not the English word. In this case, shirt manufacturers targeting the French market should register in French search engines such as Voila at http://www.voila.fr/ and Weborama at http://www.weborama.fr/. Similarly, if you plan to sell to Germany, register your pages in a German search engine. Register your Spanish pages in Latin American and Spanish web navigation tools, and so on. Check this directory for a list of leading online search tools in your target markets.

Cut and Paste. Spice up your site with everything from forms to calendars to clocks at the JavaScript Source at http://javascript.internet.com/. The site is a collection of hundreds of free JavaScripts that are available for use on your webpage at no charge.

Know Your Limitations. If you wish to restrict offers to customers in certain countries or don't wish to ship overseas, say so up front. Note "we don't export" or "this offer good only in the continental United States and Canada." This will save time and aggravation for your non-resident visitors.

Think Metric. List the dimensions and descriptions of all your merchandise in imperial and metric measurements. List weights in pounds and kilos, dimensions in inches and centimeters, and temperatures in Fahrenheit and Centigrade. While the United States still uses the imperial system, the rest of the world is largely metric. Visit Metric Internet Links at http://ts.nist.gov/ts/htdocs/200/202/mpo_reso.htm for a directory of measurement conversion tools and calculators online.

Provide Details. Sell electrical items? Plugs? Wires? Phone jacks? Stationery goods? Consider that standards for these and other products vary around the world. Provide as much information as possible on the size, shape, thickness, color, weight, voltage and other details. You'll minimize misunderstandings and surprises, and let the buyers know exactly what they're ordering.

Make Global Comparisons. Budget a morning or afternoon to search the web for products and offerings similar to your own. How does your offering stack up in terms of quality? Price? After-sales service? Prospects online are doing just that, and couldn't care less if the supplier is in Canada or China or Chile. If the right product is offered at the right price, they'll buy. To keep pace, start comparing yourself against your competition on the web, not just in your home city or region. You'll gain a big-picture perspective on your strengths and weaknesses, and opportunities and threats in the digital marketplace.

Highlight Success Stories. Received any thank-you letters or glowing e-mails from satisfied customers? Share this with the world. On your website, consider developing a "success stories" section that highlights the benefits gained, savings achieved, and profits made as a result of your products or services. If you've received praises from customers in different countries, make a special effort to post this positive feeback. Testimonials are powerful marketing tools in any culture.

Show a Human Face. In both the real and virtual worlds, people like to know who they're dealing with, and how a vendor is qualified to deliver a product or service. Address this need by posting pictures of your senior management on your website, along with brief biographies. You'll improve your credibility and rapport with online visitors.

Pay Up. Even if you accept payments online, also invite payments by traditional methods such as fax, telephone, and even snail-mail. While web-based payment systems are highly secure and confidential, old buying habits are tough to break. Many web users are still hesitant to transfer money over the Internet, and prefer traditional payment options.

Improve Your Form. When designing online forms for ordering or capturing data, make the lines long and the fields plentiful. Around the world, contact information—names, titles, street addresses, phone and fax numbers, and zip codes—can vary widely. Provide lots of text-room to ensure visitors have space to write out their complete address and other key data in full. Visit Nancy Hickman's Internationalizing Your Web Site at http://www.webtechniques.com/features/1998/03/junk/junk.shtml for a tutorial on developing forms for international customers.

Do Your Duty. On any order form, clarify who will be responsible for any customs duties, value-added taxes, transportation costs, and other fees when shipping across borders. If it's you, factor these expenses into your final price. If it's the customer, let them know upfront. Say "shipping and customs charges not included." This will minimize misunderstandings over tariffs and freight costs.

Aim High. Gain and maintain high placement for your website on search engines. Visit the Webmaster's Guide to Search Engines at http://www.searchenginewatch.com/webmasters/index.html) for tutorials on how search engines work, and how to improve your site's ranking on web navigation services.

Take a Load Off. Keep the load time of all your website pages to less than 20 seconds each using a 28.8 modem, the current speed of most Internet connections. To speed up downloads, cut or minimize graphics and overly complex Javascripts. With so many choices online, surfers demand rapid access, and will skip over slow-loading sites.

Submission Hold. Use SiteOwner at http://www.siteowner.com/ to announce your webpage to seven search engines including AltaVista, Excite, HotBot, Infoseek, and Lycos. Simply type in your URL and e-mail address, hit the submit button, and your entry is complete.

Trade Finance

Crash Course. New to trade finance? Review the Crash Course in International Trade at http://www.tdbank.ca/business/trade_services/crash/crash.html. The online presentation highlights global business risk issues, payment methods, financial guarantees, and key definitions.

Highs and Lows. Uncertain how to control the risks of fluctuating exchange rates? Foreign Exchange Management at http://www.tdbank.ca/tdbank/bizexch/fmfe.html provides tutorials on foreign exchange management tools such as spot contracts, forward contracts, and foreign currency options.

Take Credit. Preparing an export letter of credit? The Export Letters of Credit Kit at http://www.bankamerica.com/corporate/corp_intltradekit_ov.html provides letters of credit issuance guidelines, checklists, and preparation guides.

Money Talks. Need help with the terminology of international finance? Consult the International Financial Encyclopaedia at http://www.euro.net/innovation/Finance_Base/Encyclopaedia/TNumbers.Symbols.html. The site is a directory of key words, phrases, acronyms, and codes used in cross-border trade and finance.

Milk the Cash Cows. Seeking financing for an export project or other business venture? Review:

- Business Cashfinder at http://www.cashfinder.com/,
- Commercial Finance Online at http://www.cfol.com/FrameHome.htm, and
- MoneyHunter at http://www.moneyhunter.com.

Along with business matchmaking and networking services, all provide searchable databases of bankers, venture capitalists, and other financial professionals around the world.

Under the Counter. Learn more on the tax and accounting implications of doing business in another country. International Tax at http://www.taxsites.com/international.html is an archive of tax and accounting guides, bulletins, and resources online around the world.

Reach to the Converted. Converting foreign exchange? Use the Universal Currency Converter at http://www.xe.net/currency/full/, a free virtual worksheet. The service calculates exchange rates on 180 currencies from the Afghanistan Afghani to the Zimbabwe dollar.

Get a Desk Job. Looking to manage international payments online? The Thomas Cook Virtual Trading Desk at http://www.fx4business.com/ provides real-time foreign exchange over the Internet. The service allows international drafts and wire transfers to be sent and received from any Internet-ready computer anywhere in the world.

Alternative Walk. Eager to complete a trade deal, but can't get the financing? Review Alternative Trade Finance at http://infoserv2.ita.doc.gov/Tradebase/Finance.nsf/7521754277cb208a852565a8006c1c9e?OpenView. The site links to alternative sources of trade financing online including counter trade organizations, credit reporting services, and financial consulting agencies.

The Price Is Right. Unsure how to price in foreign currencies? The Export Pricing System at http://currency.xe.net/eps/ is a free online tool that can help you determine what to charge your customer in their currency. Interactive and customizable, the service provides pricing recommendations based on the customer's credit period, foreign exchange bank charges, exchange rates, and other variables.

Paper Tiger. Doing export paperwork? Global Business Model at http://www.qualitylc.com/gbm.html provides downloadable templates of nearly 20 key export documents including a shipping order, packing list, certificate of origin, and bill of lading.

Logistics

Ship Shape. Sending a package? Find the best rate with Smart Ship at http://www.smartship.com/, an online guide to express delivery rates. Based on the destination, timing, and weight of your shipment, the free service compares the Airborne, FedEx, UPS, and United States Postal Service rates for your package.

Terms of Reference. Preparing shipping documents? Visit Incoterms at http://ananse.irv.uit.no/trade_law/documents/sales/incoterms/nav/inc.html. A dictionary of international trade terms, the site explains phrases such as ex works, free alongside ship, cost and freight, delivered ex ship, and other terminology used in cross-border business.

Lay Down the Law. Need information on international shipping law? Carriage of Goods at http://itl.irv.uit.no/trade_law/nav/carriage.html is a directory of leading air, sea, road, rail, and multimodal conventions, protocols, uniform rules and minimum standards around the world.

Carry On. Seeking freight suppliers or partners? Freightworld at http://www.freightworld.com/ provides a database of hundreds of cargo and freight operations worldwide from airlines to seaports to truckers.

Match Maker. Shopping last-minute for air cargo space? Cargo Load Matching at http://www.cargo-online.com/ provides a searchable directory of aircraft seeking cargo, and cargo seeking aircraft worldwide. The service includes air cargo news and a database of aircraft for lease and sale.

Track Record. Exporting products by air cargo? Track the status of your shipments at Air Cargo Tracking at http://www.tradecompass.com/lms/free/air/tracking.html. The service provides free tracking information for seven airlines including American Airlines, British Airways, and United Airlines.

Forward Motion. Need a quote for freight forwarding services? Use the Freight Forwarders General Rate Inquiry Form at http://www.cargolog.com/ to submit a rate inquiry to a select group of freight forwarders in one easy step. Quotes are provided based on the origin and destination of the goods, the dimensions and weight of the items, and other variables.

Sail Away. If you're using an ocean carrier to transport your products, visit Sea Cargo Tracking at http://www.schednet.com/schedule/seacargo/index.htm. The service provides real-time shipment tracking for nine ocean carriers including Maersk Line, OOCL, and Sea-Land.

Time Traveler. If you ship products by ocean carrier, check out Shipcards Online at http://www.joc.com/shipcards/. The site is a searchable directory of shipping schedules for over 100 ocean carriers around the world. The service includes departure and arrival dates, and transit times.

Moving Experience. For tips on how to ship products overseas, visit Shipping the Product at http://www.tradeport.org/ts/t_expert2/details/ship/index.html. The service features primers on freight forwarders, documentation, packing, labeling, and insurance.

On the Road

Reserve With Verve. Become your own travel agent. Use services such as:
- Biztravel.com at http://www.biztravel.com/,
- Microsoft Expedia at http://expedia.msn.com/,
- TheTrip.com at http://www.thetrip.com/, and
- Travelocity at http://www.travelocity.com/ to

All enable you to check fares, book flights, and reserve hotels worldwide online.

Map It Out. Need a map for your cross-border travels? Mapquest at http://www.mapquest.com/ offers maps on dozens of cities across the United States and around the world. Free to download and print, the maps can be customized to list places of interest such as hotels and automatic teller machines, and even zoom in on particular city sections and streets.

State of the City. For country and city guides, check out:

- Click City at http://www.clickcity.com/,
- Excite Travel at http://www.city.net/, and
- Lonely Planet at http://www.lonelyplanet.com/

All provide free profiles and travel tips for thousands of destinations worldwide.

Miles and Miles. Take control of your frequent flyer programs with bizMiles at http://bizmiles.biztravel.com/ and Mileage Miner at http://www.maxmiles.com/itn/. The services provide account summaries of your frequent flyer programs, highlight how to get more points, and report when miles expire.

Stay Alert. Never be late for a flight again with bizAlerts at http://www.biztravel.com/V4/newhome.cfm, an online paging service. Use the tool to receive pre-departure pager alerts before your flight, and updates on flight status, gate information and even weather conditions.

Landing Party. Want to let family or colleagues know when your flight will land? Using real-time flight data, E-Mail Flight Notification at http://www.thetrip.com/usertools/enotify/login/0,1445,1-1,00.html can notify up to three people for you via e-mail when your plane arrives at a destination.

Under the Weather. Check out the latest weather information on hundreds of locations around the world at:

- Rain or Shine Weather at http://www.rainorshine.com/,
- Weather Channel at http://www.weather.com/homepage.html, and
- World Climate at http://www.worldclimate.com/.

The services include satellite photos, Doppler radar images, weather forecasts, and climate data.

Hot Bed. Traveling to a political hotspot? Get the latest situation reports from Travel Warnings and Consular Information Sheets at http://travel.state.gov/travel_warnings.html. A service of the United States Department of State, the site reports on unusual immigration practices, health conditions, political disturbances, unusual currency and entry regulations, and crime and security conditions in over 100 countries around the world.

Go to Town. You've just landed in an unfamiliar city and need to go downtown. What's the best way? Terminally Hip at http://travel.epicurious.com/travel/c_planning/06_airports/intro.html may have the answer. The service lists travel distances and times, and taxi and bus fares from the airport to downtown for more than 100 airports worldwide.

Chart Your Course. Need road directions for a trip? Use Driving Directions at http://www.expediamaps.com/DrivingDirections.asp for North American travel and EuroShell Route Planner at http://www.euroshell.com/base_routeue.html for European trips. Both provide point-to-point driving directions and maps.

Stake Your Claim. Need help with international travel expenses? Visit the Travel Expenses Calculator at http://www.xe.net/currency/expenses/, a free online worksheet. The service automatically calculates your cross-border travel expenses based on credit card charges, foreign exchange rates, and other variables.

Far and Away. Need to calculate distances between two cities? How Far is It? at http://www.indo.com/distance/ measures the distance in kilometers and miles between any two points on the globe.

Presentations

Present Tense. Planning a big presentation in front of an overseas audience? International Presentations at http://www.presentations.com/deliver/audience/1998/10/18_f1_go_01.html provides a series of articles and tips on how to prepare for presentations in foreign cultures.

Presentation U. Need help crafting a presentation? Check out:

- Effective Public Speaking at http://www.la.psu.edu/speech/100a/,
- Presenters University at http://www.presentersuniversity.com, and
- Virtual Presentation Assistant at http://strategis.ic.gc.ca:80/SSG/mi04456e.html.

All provide tutorials on how to select and research a topic, analyze your audience, and deliver a presentation.

Spiff it Up. Add color and style to your presentations with free PowerPoint Templates at http://www.presentersuniversity.com/library/ppt.htm?link_to=ppt?link_to=ppt. Professionally designed, the templates are divided into six categories including general business, marketing, and industry specific.

Show Off. Looking for events to showcase your company and products? See ExpoGuide at http://www.expoguide.com/ and Trade Show Central at http://www.tscentral.com/. Both offer searchable databases of trade shows and conferences around the world.

Cast Your Web. Use the power of the web to make live presentations to prospects worldwide. Visit NetSeminar at http://www.netseminar.com/ and Webcast Center at http://ww2.tscentral.com/WebcastCenter/ for webcast examples and tutorials.

Color Your World. Make screen captures and custom graphics for your presentations. Download Paint Shop Pro at http://www.jasc.com/psp5.html, a painting and image manipulation package. The tool includes free tutorials on file formats, color optimization, animations, and other design elements.

Sound Idea. Add sound effects, soundtracks, and other audio to your presentations using Goldwave at http://www.goldwave.com/. The shareware program is a digital audio editor that can open and play sounds in different sound formats. The tool can also combine audio files, and add special effects such as distortion, echo, and pitch to create new sounds.

## CHAPTER 2

ALL-WORLD E-CHAMPIONS: 20 VIRTUAL TRADE TEAMS FOR YOUR DESKTOP

Imagine if you had your own A-team of international trade experts on call 24 hours a day. Every time you had an export question you could hit a buzzer and a training specialist would race through your office door. Need help with export financing? Flick a switch and the world's top trade financier would rush to your aid. Want global business legal advice? Press a button and an impeccably dressed, briefcase-toting attorney would appear in a flash.

In the physical world, only a few elite organizations could afford such high-priced counsel. In the digital world, virtually any businessperson located anywhere can access this same trade expertise and experience in seconds using virtual trade teams, and all at no-charge. Virtual trade teams refer to a series of websites that provide functional trade information normally obtained from export service providers such as customs brokers, shippers, and translators. While no substitute for professional advice, the resources are the next best thing. They can help you save money on professional trade services and information, and conduct global transactions on your desktop that were unthinkable even months ago. This chapter spotlights some 450 of these resources in 20 international business professions: trainer, researcher, consultant, reporter, pollster, marketer, presenter, salesperson, purchaser, banker, accountant, lawyer, diplomat, customs broker, travel agent, shipper, translator, employment counselor, webmaster, and bargain hunter.

Trainer

Trainer websites provide online instruction and tutorials related to international trade.

Association for International Practical Training
http://www.aipt.org/
Based in Maryland, the Association offers opportunities for American citizens to receive on-the-job training abroad and offers non-American citizens the chance to receive on-the-job training and experiential education in the United States. The site includes newsletters, press releases, and success stories.

Basic Guide to Exporting
http://www.tradeport.org/cgi-bin/banner.pl/ts/ t_expert2/infobase/basic/index.html
A primer on international trade basics, the site covers topics such as international market research, channels of distribution and technology licensing.

Business Netiquette International
http://www.bspage.com/1netiq/Netiq.html
A guide to e-mail etiquette, the site offers tips on e-mail headings, signatures, and language, and how best to correspond with global contacts whose first language is not English.

Breaking into the Trade Game
http://www.tradeport.org/cgi-bin/banner.pl/ts/ t_expert2/infobase/breaking/index.html

An export guide developed by the U.S. Department of Commerce, the site features modules on how to identify international opportunities, finance exports, and transport goods around the world.

Checklist for Evaluating Potential Export Markets
http://www.tradeport.org/cgi-bin/banner.pl/ts/ planning/marketlist.html
A one-page rating system, the site highlights key export opportunity variables in international markets. Categories include market size, growth, accessibility, and stability.

Commonly Used Export Documents
http://www.ded.state.nh.us/oic/trade/assist/ forms.htm#top
An export dictionary, the site explains common international trade terms such as a certificate of origin, commercial invoice, and export packing list.

Creating an International Business Plan
http://www.ded.state.nh.us/oic/trade/plan/ index.htm
Created by the New Hampshire International Trade Resource Center, the site lists fundamental questions and issues that should be addressed in any cross-border marketing strategy.

Developing an Export Plan
http://www.tradeport.org/cgi-bin/banner.pl/ts/ t_expert2/getting/plan/index.html
A service of the Los Angeles-based TradePort,

the site explains how to develop an international business strategy. A one-page export plan template is provided as an example.

Entrepreneurial Edge Business Builders
http://edgeonline.com/main/bizbuilders/bb2.shtm
A virtual training center, the site offers a series of 40+ free modules on how to market, manage and grow a business. Topics include sales savvy, financial management, and personnel development.

Evaluating Your Target Markets
_http://www.tradeport.org/cgi-bin/banner.pl/ts/t_expert2/market/evaluate/index.html_
A tutorial on how to pick international markets, the site reviews how to spot opportunities and threats in a particular area, and how to modify a product or service to address local tastes and requirements.

Export Beginners Tutorial
http://www.teleport.com/~iexportc/tutorial.htm
Prepared by an Oregon trade consultant, the site provides a nine-step guide to starting an export business. Key success factors include culture knowledge, overseas connections, a marketing plan, and patience.

Export Guide
_http://sys1.tpusa.com/dir01/exprtgui/t_of_c.shtml_
A service of Trade Point U.S.A. in Columbus, Ohio, the site explains how to develop an export strategy and manage the international trade process.

Export Institute
http://www.exportinstitute.com/
Based in Minneapolis, the site offers a number of export manuals for sale, although a variety of free services and reports are available. These include an "Ask the Export Institute" feature and a 10-step guide on how to become an export agent.

Export Process Assistant
http://citm.cob.ohio-state.edu:1111/expadocs/
A service of Ohio State University, the site provides tutorials on establishing export relationships, foreign contracts, and other international trade topics.

Export Readiness Diagnostic
http://www.infoexport.gc.ca/section2/diagnos-e.asp
Developed by Industry Canada, the site offers two

tools—one for products and one for services—that test an organization's export readiness for a new foreign market.

Export Source
http://exportsource.gc.ca/
Posted in French and English, the site provides tutorials on preparing for trade shows, business trips, and international project bids.

Export Tutor
http://www.miep.org/tutor/
A product of the Michigan State University International Business Center, the site provides a 10-step roadmap to success in foreign markets. Steps include preparing a company profile, conducting a global opportunity assessment, and planning and budgeting for international expansion.

Exporting Basics
_http://www.tradeport.org/cgi-bin/banner.pl/ts/t_expert2/infobase/exportbasics/index.html_
Divided into four modules, the site explores the fundamentals of exporting, and how to assess export readiness, develop overseas markets, and make export sales.

Finding Buyers
http://www.tradeport.org/cgi-bin/banner.pl/ts/buyers/index.html
A service of TradePort, the site spotlights how to find trade leads, overseas representatives and international bid opportunities.

First Steps
http://www.moimpact.com/export/firstste.htm
Written by Ann Lambert, a Missouri export counselor, the site provides a 10-step guide to investigating your export potential. Steps include learning from other exporters, finding your market niche, and setting goals.

Forum for International Trade Training
http://www.fitt.ca/
Based in Ottawa, the Forum for International Trade Training or FITT is a not-for-profit export training organization. FITT programs are delivered in community colleges and other education institutions across Canada, and provide courses on export-related subjects such as international research, logistics and financing.

Free Export and Import Primers
http://www.exportimportlaw.com/guidesTOC.html
Developed by the law firm of Braumiller &

Rodriguez, the site provides international trade tutorials. Topics include tariff classification, customs audits, export and import compliance programs, exporting encryption technology, and information technology agreements.

Getting Ready to Export

http://www.austrade.gov.au/ GettingReadyToExport/index.asp
A service of Australia's Austrade, the site includes an online export readiness test, a glossary of export terms, and primers on steps for successful exporting and financial assistance for exporters.

Getting Through Customs

http://www.getcustoms.com/omnibus.html
The site features a grab-bag of articles on international business etiquette. Topics include dress, introductions, gift-giving, gestures and drinking.

How to Become a Successful Export Agent

http://www.exportinstitute.com/planp3.htm
Written by John Jagoe, a Minnesota trade consultant, the site outlines how to start an export business. Tips include how to develop a plan, make business contacts every day, and use outside business expertise.

How to Plan for Global Growth

http://www.dbisna.com/global/hglobal2.htm
Developed by Dun & Bradstreet, the site explores how to identify strategic markets, compare capabilities, choose channels of entry, set performance targets, and monitor progress in global business ventures.

Inc. Online's Guide to International Business

http://www.inc.com/international/
A library of trade reports, the site features tips on international business travel, banking, sourcing, and marketing. The service includes two bulletin boards: the International Business Advice board where users may ask export questions and give advice, and the Business Networking board where users may view and post global partnering opportunities.

Institute for Small Business

http://www.bmo.com/smallbiztips/
A Bank of Montreal service, the site provides entrepreneurial quizzes and financial management tutorials for small businesspeople.

International Business Plan Workbook

http://www.massport.com/trade/busplan.html
Developed by Boston-based Massport, the workbook provides an outline for an international trade business plan. Key sections include an export policy commitment statement, company export objectives, marketing preparation, and tactics and strategies.

International Import-Export Institute

http://www.intlimport-export.com/
Based in Arizona, the Institute operates an international trade certification program, and offers memberships to corporations, educational institutions, and students.

International Trade Center

http://www.intracen.org/
Based in Geneva, the International Trade Center provides trade promotion assistance to developing and transition economies. The site provides background information on Center programs and training services related to export packaging, quality management, financing and supply management, and other international trade functions.

Is Exporting for Me?

http://www.moimpact.com/export/exportready.html
Written by Brian Gauler, a Missouri export counselor, the online report outlines why companies export, how to develop export readiness, and how to explore your global market potential.

Learn About Import/Export

http://www.wbenet.com/guest4.htm
An online training tool, Learn About Import/Export explains how to start an import/export business from home using the Internet. Modules include export pricing, documentation, and methods of payment.

Moving the Goods

http://www.tradeport.org/cgi-bin/banner.pl/ts/ transport/index.html
A TradePort service, the site provides a beginner's guide to shipping products around the world. Modules include insurance, packing and documentation.

National Association of Small Business International Trade Educators

http://www.nasbite.dcccd.edu/
Based in Dallas, NASBITE promotes the involvement and competitiveness of U.S. small busi-

nesses in international trade. Key programs include an annual training conference, the International Trade Educator of the Year awards, and on online trade training discussion group.

Obtaining Financing
http://www.tradeport.org/cgi-bin/banner.pl/ts/ financing/index.html
Sponsored by Bank of America, the site explains how to obtain export financing in the U.S., and links to leading trade finance programs and organizations.

Online Business Workshop
http://www.sb.gov.bc.ca/smallbus/workshop/ workshop.html
Developed by the Canada-British Columbia Business Service Centre in Vancouver, the site provides tutorials on how to build a business from scratch. The workshop is divided into five sessions: starting with a good idea, marketing basics, financing your business, planning fundamentals, and basic regulations for getting started.

Preparing Your Export Plan
http://www.infoexport.gc.ca/section2/plan-e.asp
Developed by Industry Canada, the site explores how to prepare an export plan. The steps include planning and preparation, trial run, and imple-mentation.

Small Business Guide to Exporting
http://www.sbaonline.sba.gov/gopher/Business-Development/International-Trade/Guide-To-Exporting
Posted by the U.S. Small Business Administra-tion, the site is a global business primer for small and upstart companies. Lessons include foreign market entry, the export transaction, export financing, international transportation, and strategic alliances.

Smart Business Supersite
http://www.smartbiz.com/
A virtual business library, the site features business news, trade shows listings, job openings, tips of the day, and a free newsletter.

Take a World View
http://strategis.ic.gc.ca/SSG/sc01071e.html
Developed by Industry Canada, the site features a 12-step tutorial on how to export services around the world. Modules include assessing export readiness, developing the export plan,

delivering services, and expanding into new markets.

Tips to Help You Export More Successfully
http://www.dbisna.com/global/hglobal.htm
A Dun & Bradstreet service, the site explains how to assess business risk by country, understand export regulations, create an export document checklist, select a freight forwarder, and under-stand export financing.

Trade and Development Centre
http://www.itd.org/
A joint venture of the World Bank and the World Trade Organization, the Centre offers trade policy courses, seminars, discussion forums, and workshops to international trade professionals around the world.

Trade Expert
http://www.tradeport.org/ts/t_expert2/index.html
A service of California-based TradePort, the site features tutorials on how to research markets, develop an export strategy, understand the rules of trade, and finance exports.

Tradewinds
http://www.tradewinds-tv.com/idxnode.html
Part of a television series on global business, the site features tutorials on international trade strategies, and a directory of trade specialists across Canada.

TrainingNet
http://www.trainingnet.com/
An online hub for trainers, the site features teleforums, distance learning, and free software for training and human resource professionals.

Researcher

Researcher websites provide studies and data on regions, countries, industries, markets, and companies around the world.

Central Intelligence Agency World Factbook
http://www.odci.gov/cia/publications/factbook/ index.html
Developed by the Central Intelligence Agency with contributions from dozens of other U.S. govern-ment agencies, the site profiles the geography, people, government, economy, communications, and transportation infrastructure of all the countries in the world.

CEO Express
http://www.ceoexpress.com/
A service of Boston-based Express Company, the site is a directory of leading business resources online. Categories include news, magazines, statistics, and international business.

Corporate Information
http://www.corporateinformation.com/
Organized by country, the site provides a directory of websites that provide information on publicly traded and privately held companies around the world.

Global Business Web
http://www.gbw.net/
A hub of global trade information, the site features discussion groups, articles, newsletters, and a directory of online resources by subject and world region.

Global Information Network
http://www.ginfo.net/
Developed by Washington, D.C.-based Trade Compass, the site features international business news, trade leads, currency rates, industry profiles, and career opportunities. The service includes *The Daily Brief*, a free e-mail newsletter on international trade that's delivered each business day.

E-Journal
http://www.edoc.com/ejournal/
A searchable directory of online journals, the site is divided into ten sections including academic and reviewed journals, e-mail newsletters, print magazines, and business and finance journals.

Economist Intelligence Unit
http://www.eiu.com/
A branch of *The Economist* magazine organization, the site features a directory of upcoming conferences, and a catalog of Economist information products. A pay-per-view database includes a searchable archive of past issues.

ForWorld International Business Web Center
http://www.forworld.com/marketinfo.htm
A portal of international trade information online, the site provides global business news, software, bulletin boards, and web guides.

Geographically Specific Search Engines
http://www.beaucoup.com/1geoeng.html
A directory of search engines, the site lists the leading search engines in the Americas, Europe, the Middle East, Africa, and Asia.

Global 500
http://www.pathfinder.com/fortune/global500/
A searchable directory of the world's largest corporations, the site reports the revenues, profits, assets, and number of employees for global giants such as General Motors, Nike, and Mitsubishi.

Global Business Centre
http://www.euromktg.com/gbc/
Organized by language, the site links to leading international business resources, travel guides, shopping hubs, and electronic magazines online.

Global Economic Forum
http://www.ms.com/GEF/index.html
Prepared by Morgan Stanley Dean Witter Economists, the site features breaking news and special studies on the global economy and industrialized countries.

Ideas
http://ideas.uqam.ca/ideas/data/JEL/F.html
Hosted by the University of Québec in Montreal, the site is a catalog of international economics research papers from around the world. While all the papers are briefly summarized, only a fraction of the reports can be downloaded in full.

Institute for International Economics
http://www.iie.com/
Based in Washington, the site provides speeches, testimony, essays, and working papers related to international economics. Recent working papers include the costs and benefits of Korean unification, a NAFTA four-year review, and the lessons learned from the General Agreement on Tariffs and Trade and the World Trade Organization.

International Business Resources on the World Wide Web
http://ciber.bus.msu.edu/busres.htm
Developed by the University of Michigan International Business Center, the site is a huge library of international trade links, reviews and articles. The service features the latest periodicals, regional and country specific information, statistical data, international trade leads, company directories, international trade shows, mailing lists, and many other business tools from around the world. If you visit only one international trade site, this should be it.

International Chamber of Commerce
http://www.iccwbo.org/
Based in Paris, the Chamber promotes international trade, investment and the market economy system worldwide, and makes rules that govern the conduct of business across borders. The site spotlights a variety of Chamber services including the International Court of Arbitration, and the Commercial Crime Bureau.

International Database
http://www.census.gov/ipc/www/idbprint.html
A service of the U.S. Census Bureau, the site is a customizable and searchable database of global demographic and economic information. Variables include total population, fertility rates, net number of migrants, and population by religious and ethnic groups.

International Development Research Centre
http://www.idrc.ca/
Based in Ottawa, the Centre researches economic and environmental problems in developing countries. The site features a virtual library, an online magazine, and a directory of research initiatives.

International Directories
http://www.infobel.be/inter/world.asp
A service of Belgian-based Kapitol, the site provides a searchable directory of telephone and company directories in over 150 countries from Algeria to Zimbabwe.

International Monetary Fund Staff Country Reports
http://www.imf.org/external/pubs/CAT/scr.cfm
Prepared by International Monetary Fund economists, the site features economic reports and statistics on over 20 countries including China, Czech Republic and Vietnam. The reports are in PDF format, and must be viewed using an Adobe Acrobat Reader which is available free online at http://www.adobe.com/.

International Small Business Consortium
http://www.isbc.com/
Based in Norman, Oklahoma, the site offers funding sources, discussion groups, awards, and online marketing tips for small business owners in the U.S. and around the world.

International Trade Abstracts
http://econwpa.wustl.edu/alllistings/it/all
The site is a directory of research abstracts related to international trade. Topics include the World Trade Organization, European monetary union, and ethical issues in trade policy. The full papers are not available for download, although e-mail links to the authors are provided along with ordering information.

International Trade Centre Infobases
http://www.intracen.org/infobase/itcinfb.htm
Co-sponsored by the World Trade Centre, the site is a directory of international trade resources online. Categories include trade contacts, trade statistics, and services.

International Trade and Transport Advisor
http://www.itds.treas.gov/itdssitemap.html
A trade advisory service, the site features tariff schedules and databases, and tutorials on how to export and import.

IPANet
http://www.ipanet.net/
Sponsored by the Multilateral Investment Guarantee Agency of the World Bank, the site provides country and sector reports, and directories of international investment opportunities, organizations, and professionals.

Nations of the World
http://www.intergov.gc.ca/world/index.html
A service of the Canadian government, the site is a directory of international organizations and country resources online in Africa, the Americas, Asia, and Europe.

News, Views and Trends
http://www.dbisna.com/newsview/menu.htm#global
Developed by Dun & Bradstreet, the site reports on global economic trends, country risks, industry outlooks, corporate purchasing, and outsourcing.

North American Industry Classification System
http://www.census.gov/epcd/www/naics.html
Posted by the U.S. Census Bureau, the site explains the North American Industry Classification System, an economic data classification system that replaced the U.S. Standard Industrial Classification (SIC) system in January 1997. The service includes NAICS-SIC conversion tables.

OECD Online Trade Documents
http://www.oecd.org/ech/tradedoc.htm
Based in Paris, this Organization for Economic Cooperation and Development site provides papers on international trade topics such as trade relations with developing countries, trade and the environment, and export credits.

Pangaea
http://www.pangaea.net/
An online service of Pangaea International Consultants, the site features trade leads, business contacts, interactive meeting rooms, international news, and country profiles.

Patent and Trademark Offices Online
http://www.uspto.gov/web/menu/other.html
A service of the U.S. Patent and Trademark Office, the site links to leading intellectual property organizations around the world.

Patscan
http://www.patscan.ubc.ca/
A service of the University of British Columbia, the site provides guides to researching patents, trademarks, industrial designs, and other intellectual property online.

Privatization Link
http://www.privatizationlink.com/
A service of the World Bank Group, the site reports on privatization initiatives in developing countries. The service includes a directory of privatization opportunities, contacts, and events in transition economies.

Privatization News
http://www.privatization.net/
Updated weekly, the electronic magazine spotlights privatization opportunities in developing and transition economies such as Argentina, Brazil and Egypt.

PRS Online
http://www.countrydata.com/
A pay-per-view service, the site has ten years of economic statistics for 100 key countries, single-currency comparisons, and risk forecasts.

Reference Maps
http://www.odci.gov/cia/publications/factbook/ref-frame.html
Part of the Central Intelligence Agency World Factbook, the site displays color maps of nearly 20 global regions including North America, Central and South America, Middle East, Africa and Asia.

Resources for Economists on the Internet
http://econwpa.wustl.edu/EconFAQ/EconFAQ.html
A service of the University of Southern Mississippi Economics Department, the site links to hundreds of economics-related resources online.

Organized by subject, key topics include consulting and forecasting, financial markets, and societies and associations.

Search Engine Watch
http://www.searchenginewatch.com/
A search engine directory and resource page, the site features search tool reviews, tutorials, and news.

Search Engines on the Net
http://www.advocacy-net.com/searchmks.htm
The site links to some 100 search engine links and guides. The list includes specialty search engines that focus on a particular subject or geographic area.

Search Page
http://www.accesscom.com/~ziegler/search.html
A compendium of search links and information, the site explains how to best use search engines to scan for information on people, business, education, news, software and other subjects.

Society of Competitive Intelligence Professionals
http://www.scip.org/
Based in Alexandria, Virginia, the Society is a non-profit organization that provides education and networking opportunities for competitive intelligence professionals. The site features information on the competitive intelligence industry, discussion forums, and a code of ethics.

Special Search Engines
http://www.leidenuniv.nl/ub/biv/specials.htm
Based in the Netherlands, the site is a directory of specialized search engines in dozens of categories including agriculture, business, and trademarks.

Tools for Searching the Web
http://web.ntu.ac.sg/library/searchw3.htm
A search engine resource center, the site spotlights general, regional, specialty, e-mail, software and newsgroup search tools from around the world.

Trade Data Online
http://strategis.ic.gc.ca/sc_mrkti/tdst/engdoc/tr_homep.html
A database of trade statistics from the U.S. Department of Commerce and Statistics Canada, the site contains export and import information on over 200 countries, 500 industries, and 5,000 products. The free service creates custom

reports and graphs, and generates trade data at a national level and by U.S. state and Canadian province.

Tradeport
http://www.tradeport.org/
Managed by the Bay Area Economic Forum and Los Angeles Trade, the site is a virtual library of trade information. Features include trade events, a global company directory, world news, newsgroups and mailing lists, and job opportunities in international trade.

Transparency International
http://www.transparency.de/
Based in Berlin, Transparency International promotes accountability in international business transactions, and lobbies governments of the world to implement anti-corruption programs. The site offers free annual reports, newsletters, press releases, and advice on how to combat corruption.

Virtual International Search Engines
http://www.dreamscape.com/frankvad/search.international.html
A search tool center, the site links to dozens of regional search engines, and over 1,000 specialized engines in 50 categories including government, business, and money.

Wall Street Journal
http://interactive.wsj.com/edition/current/summaries/front.htm
Updated daily, the site provides breaking news on the global marketplace, money and investing, and technology. The headlines are free to access, but a paid subscription is required to view the full articles.

Weekly International Economic Briefing
_http://www.bankamerica.com/capmkt/brief_intl.html_
A service of Bank of America, the site provides a weekly international economic briefing on financial markets and economic indicators around the world. Short-term economic forecasts are also provided.

World Bank International Trade Division Working Papers
http://www.worldbank.org/html/iecit/archive.html
A service of the World Bank, the site is a library of recent working papers written by the Bank's International Trade Division. Key themes include

regional groupings, developing countries in the World Trade Organization, and foreign investment.

World Business Conference
http://www.worldbusiness.net/conference/
A service of the World Business Network, the site posts conference papers that have been delivered by international trade professionals at recent global business events. Titles include _India Market Entry Strategy, Venture Capital in the 21st Century_, and _Russia's Place in the Global Economy_.

World Class
http://web.idirect.com/~tiger/
Created by Vancouver-based Mike Kuiack and Associates, the service reviews over 1,000 international business sites from some 100 countries. The site is divided into seven categories: reference, news, learning, money, trade, networking, and world beaters.

World Competitiveness Online
_http://www.imd.ch/wcy/wcy_online.html_
Prepared by the Geneva-based International Institute for Management Development, the site features excerpts from the Institute's annual World Competitiveness report. The service features country profiles, statistical tables, and rankings of variables such as infrastructure, management, and science and technology.

World Development Sources
http://www-wds.worldbank.org/
Developed by the World Bank Group, the site is a virtual archive of over 6,000 World Bank reports on a variety of economic, development and trade issues. Updated daily, the searchable archive contains over 500,000 pages.

World Merchant
http://aaatrading.com/
A resource center for exporters and importers, the site provides a directory of country reports, international business courses, and other global trade information online.

World Opinion
http://www.worldopinion.com/home.qry
A service of Survey Sampling Inc., the site provides a directory of over 6,600 research organizations in some 100 countries. The service also features a calendar of research events, job database, and newsstand.

World Trade Centers Association On-Line
http://iserve.wtca.org/
Based in New York, the World Trade Centers Association promotes international trade around the world. The site links to Association affiliates in some 300 cities, and provides a free trade opportunities bulletin board.

World Wide Web Servers
http://vlib.stanford.edu/Servers.html
Developed by Stanford University, the site is a directory of World Wide Web servers around the world. The servers are listed alphabetically by continent, country and state.

World Wide Web Virtual Library
http://vlib.stanford.edu/Overview.html
Based at Stanford University, the site is a catalog of Web-based information on topics ranging from agriculture to society. The service is operated by an informal confederation of volunteers who compile pages of key links for particular subject and geographic areas in which they are expert or specialists.

Consultant

Consultant websites provide interactive and advisory tools to help businesspeople in domestic and global markets.

America Online International Trade Forum
aol://4344:690.intrade.6168268.518551597
Available only on America Online, the Forum is an online discussion group that meets regularly to discuss trade issues ranging from search tips to fast track to customs paperwork. The virtual meetings feature guest speakers and experts from all areas of international trade.

Assist International
http://www.assist-intl.com/
Based in New York, Assist International publishes international trade reference materials and databases. The site features global business reports, event directories, and guides. Access is free with registration.

Association for International Business
http://earthone.com/international-list.html
Home page of the International Business Discussion Group, the site provides reports and analysis on all aspects of international trade including marketing, law, exporting, importing and education. The service includes a free mentoring program which matches experienced traders with new exporters.

Barclays Country Reports
http://www.offshorebanking.barclays.com/services/economic/yearly/contents.html?(none)
A service of Barclays Offshore Banking, the site profiles over 50 countries from Argentina to Zimbabwe. Each profile reviews recent trends in politics, economic policy, foreign trade and debt.

Business Reports
http://italchambers.net/BusinessReports.html
A service of the Italian Chamber of Commerce, the site provides ten sector reports and nearly 30 business profiles of countries such as Argentina, Belgium, Canada, India, and the United States.

Business Resource Center
http://www.morebusiness.com/
A virtual library of business information, the site features marketing checklists, templates, sample agreements, discussion groups, shareware, and interactive questionnaires to help small businesspeople.

Country Commercial Guides
http://www.ita.doc.gov/uscs/ccglist.html
A service of the U.S. International Trade Administration, the site provides economic and trade reports on countries around the world. The reports discuss key market issues and trends, the leading prospects for U.S. firms, and other business topics.

Country Commercial Guides
http://www.state.gov/www/about_state/business/com_guides/index.html
Developed by the U.S. State Department, the site is a library of country reports that are prepared annually by commercial officers and researchers in U.S. embassies and trade offices around the world.

Country Profiles
http://www.tradenz.govt.nz/intelligence/profiles/
A service of the New Zealand Trade Development Board, the site provides economic indicators, geographical information, market surveys, people and society profiles, and leading business prospects for some 70 countries around the world.

Country Reports on Economic Policy and Trade Practices
http://www.state.gov/www/issues/economic/trade_reports/index.html
Prepared by the U.S. Department of State, the site profiles over 70 countries, customs territories,

and customs unions. Each report contains nine sections including key economic indicators, general policy framework, exchange rate policies, significant barriers to U.S. exports and investment, export subsidies policies, and worker rights.

Doing Business In
http://www.doingbusinessin.com/
A service of Ernst & Young, the site is a virtual library of business guides and tax information for over 140 countries and seven industries.

EMUNet
http://www.euro-emu.co.uk/
Based in London, the site provides news, editorials and advice on European monetary union and the Eurodollar. The service includes an online forum and a directory of events.

Ernie
http://ernie.ey.com/
Developed by Ernst and Young, the site is a virtual business consultant. The site includes case studies, self-service advisory tools, and a business-question answering service.

Expanding Internationally
http://www6.americanexpress.com/ smallbusiness/segments/ expand_intl.asp?aexp_nav=sbs_hp_id3
A service of American Express, the site provides country profiles, export and import guides, a directory of international trade shows, and an "ask the trade expert" feature.

Expert Marketplace
http://expert-market.com/index-alta.html
A virtual directory of consultants, the searchable site lists over 200,000 consulting operations around the world. The service includes business case studies, information on how to select and manage consultants, and an "ask the expert" forum in which users may pose brief business-related questions to expert consultants.

Export Hotline Online
http://www.exporthotline.com/
A service of Boston-based International Strategies, the site offers country and industry studies, trade statistics and shows, shipment tracking, and export contacts. The service is free to access with registration.

Export and International Trade
http://www.stat-usa.gov/BEN/subject/trade.html

Developed by Stat-U.S.A., the site is a virtual library of trade leads, market research reports, export and import statistics, press releases, and articles on global business. The service is available through subscription only, although users may take a free online test drive.

Idea Café: The Small Business Channel
http://www.ideacafe.com/
An online center for small business, the site features free software, chat rooms, financing advice, Internet guides, and presentation tips for start-up and growing companies.

Inc. Online Virtual Consultant
http://www.inc.com/virtualconsult/
Developed by *Inc.* magazine, the site offers searchable databases, a software library, interactive worksheets and surveys, and over 300 business ideas for new and growing firms.

Interactive Business Planner
http://www.sb.gov.bc.ca/smallbus/cbcbsc/ibp.html
Using interactive templates and fill-in-the-blank prompts, the site guides a user through the preparation of a three-year, bank-ready business plan. The service includes a financial projection tool and business plan tutorials.

International Comparisons
http://strategis.ic.gc.ca/sc_mrkti/ibin/ compare.html
A service of Industry Canada in Ottawa, the site is a custom report generator. Users select a country or topic from the menu, press a button, and a market research study is automatically generated.

International Council of Management Consulting Institutes
http://www.mcninet.com/icmci/cmcHome.html
A global association of management consultants, the Council promotes professional development and networking in the consulting industry. The site provides a directory of member institutes, an online discussion forum, and a searchable database of management consultants worldwide.

International Organization for Standardization
http://www.iso.ch/
Based in Geneva, the ISO is a worldwide federation of national standards agencies. The site provides information on the organization's international standards and quality management certification program.

Journal of Management Consulting
http://www.jmcforum.com/
An online management consulting journal, the site features free papers, downloads, and an index of past authors, subjects, and articles.

Library of Congress Country Studies
http://lcweb2.loc.gov/frd/cs/cshome.html
Developed by the Federal Research Division of the Library of Congress, the site features reports on some 80 countries. The reports profile political institutions, economy, culture, and national security.

Management Consulting Network International
http://www.mcni.com/home.cfm
A meeting point for consultants worldwide, the site offers a classified ads service, directories of consulting firms and professionals, discussion forums, conference listings, and reports on best practices.

Management Consulting Online
http://www.cob.ohio-state.edu/~opler/cons/mco.html
A resource center for management consultants, the site features a company directory, career guides, job listing, interactive quizzes, and articles on the consulting profession.

Market Reports
http://www.infoexport.gc.ca/section2/market-e.asp
Compiled by Canada's Department of Foreign Affairs and International Trade in Ottawa, the site is a library of geographic and sectoral market studies from around the world. The site is free to access with registration.

Market Research
http://strategis.ic.gc.ca/sc_mrkti/ibinddc/engdoc/1a1.html
Developed by Industry Canada, the site is an archive of over 100 market research reports on countries and industries from around the world.

Observatory
http://www.france-companies.com/fc/observatoire/us/index_obser.html
Sponsored by the France Ministry of the Economy, Finance and Industry, the site provides international trade statistics, investment primers, sectoral studies, company directories, economic forecasts, and employment opportunities for 70 countries around the world.

SOS 2000
http://strategis.ic.gc.ca/sc_mangb/y2k/engdoc/homepage.html
A service of Industry Canada, the site provides resources and tutorials for Canadian companies on how to address the Y2K issue. While written for Canadians, the lessons are applicable to virtually any business located anywhere.

Trade Compass
http://www.tradecompass.com
Based in Washington, D.C., the site is a virtual library of trade information and interactive business tools. The service includes trade leads, cargo tracking, a virtual campus, trade statistics, regulation and compliance systems, and a news bureau. Trade Compass is a subscription service, although new users may try out the site free for seven days.

Year 2000 Bookmarks
http://pw1.netcom.com/~ggirod/bookmark.html
A directory of Year 2000 resources, the site links to hundreds of vendors, government organizations, software tools, and discussion groups that address the Y2K issue.

Year 2000 and Euro: IT Challenges of the Century
http://www.ispo.cec.be/y2keuro/
Sponsored by the European Commission, the site is a compendium of Internet resources on the Y2K issue and the introduction of the Euro, the single European currency. The service features case studies, tutorials and online workshops.

Reporter

Reporter websites provide the latest news about a particular geographic area, industry, or subject.

AJR NewsLink
http://www.newslink.org/news.html
Developed by the American Journalism Review, the site is a directory of over 3,600 online newspapers. U.S. and Canadian papers are indexed by category, state, and province.

Business Wire
http://www.businesswire.com
A news distribution service, the site posts full-text news releases from companies and organizations around the world. Updated hourly, the site

features special sections on high tech, health, banking, energy, automotive, entertainment, sports and retail sectors.

Electronic Newsstand
http://www.enews.com/
Based in Washington, D.C., the site is a searchable database of over 3,000 magazines worldwide. The service includes online channels, discussion forums, and subscription discounts.

Export Today
http://www.exporttoday.com/
The Washington, D.C.-based site reports the latest export news, and provides a directory of trade development professionals in the United States. A key feature is the Matchmakers Spot Market, an interactive meeting area for buyers and sellers.

The Exporter
http://www.exporter.com/
Based in New York, the site provides international trade discussion forums, a glossary of export terms, and tutorials on numerous global business subjects including export pricing, shipments, and payments.

International Business Online
http://www.internationalbusiness.com/
Based in Austin, Texas, the site reports on global trade, economic development, foreign investment, and international logistics. The service includes an editorial calendar, and full-text articles from the current issue.

International Herald Tribune
http://www.iht.com/
Edited in Paris, the site reports the latest business, travel, and fashion news from around the world. With 14 bureaus in North America, Europe and Asia, the service includes classified ads, stock market updates, and special reports.

Internet News Bureau
http://www.newsbureau.com/
An Internet press release service, the Bureau writes and distributes press releases to some 2,000 media professionals around the world.

Journal of Commerce
http://www.joc.com/web_indx.htm
A leading international trade information service, the site reports on global finance, trade, imports, exports, transportation, foreign investments and markets, logistics, energy, insurance and other subjects related to cross-border business.

Media Finder
http://www.mediafinder.com/index.cfm
Developed by New York-based Oxbridge Communications, the site is a database of nearly 100,000 publications and catalogs from around the world. Categories include North American catalogs, British catalogs, German catalogs, newsletters, newspapers, and mailing lists.

MediaNFO Links
http://www.mediainfo.com/emedia/
A service of Editor & Publisher, the site is a searchable database of over 10,000 media sites online. The directory is divided by geographic locations such as Canada, Europe and the U.S., and by media type such as magazines, newspapers, and television.

News 365
http://www.News365.com/
The site is a database of some 10,000 news sites. Categories include business, markets, computers, industries, health, and science and technology.

News Tracker
http://nt.excite.com/ntd.gw?page=create
Developed by Excite, the site retrieves the latest online news articles about a particular subject area as specified by a user. The service is free with registration.

PR Newswire
http://www.prnewswire.com
A news distribution service, the site provides breaking news and information on private and public organizations around the world. Stories are searchable by industry, company, stock symbol or state, as well as by keywords and concept.

Pointcast
http://www.pointcast.com
A free Internet news service, Pointcast broadcasts personalized news and information to your computer screen. Content suppliers include *CNN*, *The Wall Street Journal*, *The New York Times*, and the *Washington Post*.

RealGuide
http://www.real.com/realguide/index.html
A guide to video and audio programs online, the

site lists hundreds of interviews, live concerts, sporting events, and television and radio programs that are available on the Internet.

Tips on Press Release Writing
http://www.newsbureau.com/tips/
A service of the Internet News Bureau, the site links to tutorials on media relations. Guides include *How to Get the Press on Your Side*, *Press Release Tips*, and *A Publicity Primer*.

Web Wombat Online Newspapers
http://www.webwombat.com.au/intercom/newsprs/index.htm
Hosted by Web Wombat, an Australian Internet search service, the site is a directory of 3,000 online newspapers in over 100 countries including Afghanistan, Iran, and Slovenia.

World Trade Magazine
http://www.worldtrademag.com/
Based in Irvine, California, the site reports the latest international trade trends, and profiles global business organizations and professionals. Priority industries include cargo transportation, global marketing, and trade finance.

Pollster

Pollster websites provide the results of public opinion surveys and online discussion groups.

AC Nielsen
http://acnielsen.com/
Homepage of the global survey giant, the site lists the firm's research services, news releases, and publications from over 50 countries. Most reports are priced between $1,000 and $30,000 each, but a few are free. Check the site for details.

American Demographics Marketing Tools
http://www.demographics.com/
Homepage of *American Demographics* magazine, the site contains a full-text archive of past issues dating back to January 1995. The service includes back issues of *Marketing Tools*, an e-zine for marketers, and *Forecast*, a newsletter of demographic trends and business forecasts.

APT Strategies
http://www.aptstrategies.com.au/default.htm
Based in Australia, the site features surveys, online focus groups, case studies, and statistics on Internet commerce.

DejaNews
http://www.dejanews.com
An Internet discussion network, the site archives some 50,000 online discussion groups. Using the free service, a user can read, search, and join any of the forums.

Forum One
http://www.forumone.com/
A database of online discussion forums, the site catalogs over 210,000 topics including current events, business and finance, and international. The service includes a step-by-step tutorial on how to build and promote your own online discussion group.

Jupiter Communications
http://www.jup.com/
Homepage of a new media research firm, the site provides reports and case studies on online consumers, digital commerce, and Internet advertising. The service includes *Digital Digest*, a free bi-monthly e-mail newsletter on Jupiter's latest research.

NetRatings
http://www.netratings.com/
A web audience measurement service, the site reports on viewer profiles and audience interaction with websites and banner ads. Features include the *Online Observer Report*, a free weekly newsletter.

NUA Internet Surveys
http://www.nua.ie/surveys/
Based in Ireland, the site is a database of articles and information on Internet trends. Products include *NUA Internet Surveys*, a weekly newsletter that summarizes the findings of recent Internet studies and reports from around the world.

Reference.Com
http://www.reference.com/
A newsgroup research service, the site enables a user to find, browse, search, and join more than 150,000 newsgroups, mailing lists, and web forums.

Tile.Net
http://www.tile.net/
A newsgroup reference center, the site provides searchable directories of online discussion lists, newsgroups, computer-product vendors, and web-design companies.

Marketer

Marketer websites provide information about marketing strategies, advertising tactics, and promotion events.

Advertising Age
http://adage.com/interactive/
A service of Ad Age Group publishers, the site reports on breaking news in online advertising in the U.S. and global markets. Content includes website reviews, editorials, and a directory of advertising-related conferences and events.

Advertising World
http://advertising.utexas.edu/world/
Developed by the University of Texas Department of Advertising, the site is an index of advertising-related links on the web. Subjects include account planning, direct marketing, sweepstakes and contests, and website promotion.

All4One Submission Machine
http://www.all4one.com/all4submit/
A free website promotional tool, the site registers a website address with the leading search engines with one submission. The machine submits to six search engines: AltaVista, Excite, Hotbot, Lycos, Infoseek and Webcrawler.

Business to Business
http://www.business2business.on.ca/
welcome.html
An electronic magazine on Internet business, the site reports on marketing, sales, security and tax strategies for companies online.

Channel Seven
http://www.channelseven.com/index.html
A networking resource for advertising executives, the site offers advertising case studies, agency profiles, and special e-commerce reports. The service includes *NarrowCast*, a free newsletter on advertising news and research.

CIO WebBusiness
http://webbusiness.cio.com/
Homepage of *Chief Information Officer (CIO)* magazine, the site provides an archive of past articles, a web business forum, a directory of technology job openings, and a directory of upcoming Internet-related conferences.

ClickZ
http://www.clickz.com/
A guide for online publishers, the site features a

daily column on web marketing written by an industry expert, as well as weekly interviews with Internet business leaders.

Direct Marketing Online
http://www.directmarketing-online.com/features/
archives/
A resource for direct marketers, the site provides tutorials and articles on how translate traditional direct marketing methods to the Internet. The service includes software tools, online chat rooms, web-based forums, and a calendar of events.

DM News
http://www.dmnews.com/web_marketing.html
A direct marketing hub, the site features industry news, a searchable directory of employment and business opportunities, an event calendar, and a back issues archive.

E-Business
http://www.hp.com/Ebusiness/main1.html
Homepage of *E-Business* magazine, the site provides news, case-studies, checklists, and software tools for Internet marketing professionals.

E-Marketer
http://www.emarketer.com/
A library of web marketing information, the site features Internet usage statistics, discussion forums, and *eMarketer*, a free weekly e-mail newsletter.

First Steps Marketing and Design Daily
http://www.interbiznet.com/nomad.html
Edited by John Sumser, CEO of the Internet Business Network, the site provides tutorials on online marketing and design. Articles from the past four years are available free in an indexed archive.

Global Promote
http://www.globalpromote.com/
A resource for international marketing online, the site features discussion lists, global Internet statistics, and *Global Promoter*, a free newsletter on website promotion techniques for world markets.

Guerrilla Tactics
http://www.gmarketing.com/tactics/weekly.html
Updated weekly, the site provides articles on a variety of marketing issues. Topics include how to

spread word-of-mouth, break through sales resistance, and write classified ads.

International Advertising Resource Center
http://www.getbiz.com/~louisaha/home.htm
Updated bi-weekly, the site is an archive of information on international advertising. Sections include global media, advertising research, and international advertising awards.

Internet Advertising Discussion List
http://www.internetadvertising.org/
The site is the homepage of the Internet Advertising Discussion List, a newsgroup on online marketing, banner advertising, and website promotions. Users may subscribe to the list on the site, and view archives of discussions for the past three months.

Internet Sales Discussion
http://www.mmgco.com/isales.html
Developed by the Multimedia Marketing Group, the site is the homepage of Internet-Sales, a discussion group on online marketing. Topics include payment methods, order forms, and success stories. Users may subscribe to the list on the site.

Journal of International Marketing
http://www.ama.org/pubs/jim/index.html
A service of the American Marketing Association, the site provides summaries and full-text articles on international marketing subjects. Topics include collaborating with international business partners, trends in global executive education, and U.S.-Japanese buyer-seller interactions.

Link Exchange
http://www.linkexchange.com/
An Internet advertising network, the site provides tools and tutorials for website promotion, quality inspection, online selling, and audience measurement.

Marketing One to One
http://www.1to1.com/index.html
Homepage of a Stamford, Connecticut consulting firm, the site provides free spreadsheet downloads, discussion forums, Internet articles and *Inside 1to1*, a newsletter on web marketing.

Marketing Resource Center
http://comfind.com/mrc.html
Developed by ComFind, a Los Angeles Internet company, the site provides articles and primers on how to sell and network on the web.

Marketing Tools
http://www.demographics.com/Publications/MT/index.htm
Homepage of *Marketing Tools* magazine, the site provides information and guides for marketing professionals. The service includes Conference Call, a directory of marketing conferences and trade shows.

Marketing Tools Directory
http://www.marketingtools.com/directory/default.htm
A guide to finding customers online, the site features modules on demographics, direct selling, ethnic marketing, market research, and psychographics.

Narrowline
http://www.narrowline.com
An electronic exchange for Net advertising, the site brings together media buyers with websites looking to sell available ad space.

NetMarketing
http://www.netb2b.com/
A meeting place for Internet professionals, the site provides a guide to website pricing, online forums and bulletin boards, rankings of top business sites, and a list of webpage developers in major cities.

Net Profits
http://www.netprofits-mag.com/
An e-zine for Internet entrepreneurs, the site features U.S. and international case studies, success stories, and e-commerce news.

Publicity.Com
http://www.publicity.com/
Developed by Minneapolis-based Media Relations Inc., the site provides news, stories and tutorials on online public relations, publicity, and marketing.

RepLink
http://www.replink.com/
Based in Newmarket, Ontario, the site is a matchmaking service for sales agents, manufacturers, representatives and distributors.

Submit It
http://www.submit-it.com/
A website announcement service, the site explains how to list a site on Internet search engines, issue a press release, participate in e-mail lists, and issue an electronic newsletter.

Web Digest for Marketers

http://wdfm.com/
Developed by Larry Chase, a New York Internet consultant, the service reviews leading websites and reports on Internet marketing trends. The current issue is available free online, but back issues are available by subscription only.

Website Banner Advertising

*http://www.markwelch.com/bannerad/*Developed by Mark Welch, a California attorney, the site is a directory of website banner advertising resources. The service includes directories of advertising networks and brokers, commission and partner programs, banner exchange services, and reciprocal link exchanges.

Who's Marketing Online

http://www.wmo.com/
A marketing e-zine, the site offers reports and editorials on all aspects of Internet marketing. Topics include banner campaigns, creative content, and pricing models.

Presenter

Presenter websites provide resources for trade shows and presentations.

ExhibitorNet

http://www.exhibitornet.com/
Developed by *Exhibitor* magazine, the site includes a show directory, discussion groups, exhibiting tips, and a supplier directory.

ExpoBase

http://www.expobase.com/E/ebhpfram.htm
A database of exhibition resources, the site features directories of trade show consultants, decorators, associations, facilities, and job opportunities.

ExpoGuide

http://www.expoguide.com/
Based in Stamford, Connecticut, the site is a searchable directory of trade shows and conferences around the world. Features include a lead generation program and a directory of event organizers and associations.

ExpoWorld

http://www.ExpoWorld.net/
A directory of directories, the site is a browsable database of trade show resources online. The service includes a design gallery, career centre, and chat room.

Hot Exhibiting Tips

http://www.exhibitornet.com/text/hottips/index.html-ssi
A service of Exhibitor Net, the site provides trade show strategies and tactics. Key tips: arrive early, listen first, and always follow-up.

NetSeminar

http://www.netseminar.com
Sponsored by the Education News and Entertainment Network, the service delivers live seminars over the Internet. The virtual seminars include video, audio, and closed captioning.

Presentations.Com

http://www.presentations.com/
Homepage of *Presentations* magazine, the site provides presentation news, equipment reviews, delivery tips, and an ask-the-expert feature.

Presenters University

http://www.presentersuniversity.com/
A service of Proxima, the site features free presentation templates and tutorials, along with links to clip art resources, famous quotations, and sound files.

Presenting Solutions

http://www.presentingsolutions.com/
A directory of presentation services, the site offers product guides, a glossary of presenting terms, projector price lists, and primers on communicating effectively.

Selling at Trade Shows

http://strategis.ic.gc.ca/SSG/mi03842e.html
Compiled by Industry Canada, the site provides a tutorial on how to sell at trade shows. Topics include planning for the event, approaching visitors, and following up on leads.

TechCalendar

http://www.techweb.com/calendar/
A searchable directory of technology-related trade shows and events, the site features free downloads, job opportunities, show passes, and a speaker database.

Trade Show Central

http://www.tscentral.com/
Based in Wellesley, Massachusetts, Trade Show Central provides information on some 50,000 trade shows and events, 5,000 service providers, and 8,000 venues and facilities around the world. Features include the Broadcast Center, a guide to trade show broadcasts on the Internet, and

Career Center, a directory of employment opportunities.

Trade Show Exhibiting
http://www.cmarket.net/FEATURES/Fea_ts.htm
A service of the Construction Marketing Network, the site provides trade show tips and trends. Primers include how to quickly capture a prospect's attention, and how to sell to buying teams.

Trade Show News Network
http://www.tsnn.com/
A trade show search service, the site profiles and compares thousands of trade shows, exhibitors, industry suppliers, and convention facilities around the world.

Trade Show Tips and Pointers
http://www.gapent.com/seminars/
trade_shows_FAQ.htm
A service of GAP Enterprises, the site provides tips and tactics for exhibiting successfully at trade shows.

Trade Show Week Magazine on the Web
http://www.tradeshowweek.com/
Homepage of *Trade Show Week* magazine, the site includes tradeshow reports, buyer's guides, classified ads, and articles from past issues.

Salesperson

Salesperson websites provide trade leads and listings of offers to buy and sell internationally.

Access Business Online
http://www.bizwiz.com/
A database of business opportunities, the site includes company profiles, requests for proposals, discount products, and an import/export exchange.

DigiLead
http://www.digilead.com/
A searchable directory of international trade leads, the site is divided into some 20 industry categories including medical and health, electronic and electrical, lumber and wood, and paper and allied products.

Free Classified Sites
http://www.magpage.com/~rispoli/free.html
Organized alphabetically, the webpage connects to over 100 online resources that provide free classified ad posting services.

Golden Trade
http://www.golden-trade.com/
A bulletin board of import and export opportunities, the site features posting services, a build-your-own-site feature and the *Golden Trade* newsletter, a trade e-zine.

Global Trade Center
http://www.tradezone.com/
Developed by the Mellinger Company, the site provides free trade leads, classified advertising, company profiles, and a trader bulletin board.

IFINet
http://www.dfait-maeci.gc.ca/ifinet/menu-e.htm
Developed by Canada's Department of Foreign Affairs and International Trade, the site provides information on projects financed by International Financial Institutions such as the World Bank, the Inter-American Development Bank, and the Asian Development Bank. The website features business guides, and lists procurement opportunities in some 20 emerging sectors and developing economies. Registration is required to access the service.

IMEX Exchange
http://www.imex.com/
Based in New York, the site features international trade leads, company profiles, a trade event calendar, a trade association directory, and global business news.

Import-Export Bulletin Board
http://www.iebb.com/welcome.html
A database of trade leads, the service is divided into offers to buy, offers to sell, and success stories. The site includes live chats and a business matchmaker forum.

International Business Forum
http://www.ibf.com/
A global business hub, the site provides directories of international trade opportunities, associations, events, and executive development programs.

International Business Opportunities
http://www.tradezone.com/busops.htm
A bulletin board of international trade leads, the site features a free banner exchange and the TradeSites Home Page Creator, a tool that creates an instant corporate webpage. The service is free with registration.

International Export Connections
http://www.teleport.com/~iexportc/dewaniah.shtml
Based in Seattle, the site is a directory of international business opportunities. Sections include offers to buy, offers to sell, agents wanted, suppliers wanted, and joint ventures.

International Procurement Jumpstation
http://www.fedmarket.com/international.html
A directory of government procurement agencies online, the site lists leading public sector buyers in Latin America, Europe, the Middle East, and Asia.

International Trade Leads
http://ciber.bus.msu.edu/busres/tradlead.htm
Compiled by the Michigan State University Center for International Business, the site profiles dozens of trade lead services and international business bulletin boards from around the world.

Internet Card Central
http://www.cardcentral.net/
A directory of virtual greeting card services online, the site is divided into ten categories, including art, other languages, popular occasions, and scenery. Similar to birthday and thank you cards, virtual greeting cards allow a user to send an image along with an attached message to anyone with an e-mail address. Most services are free.

I-Trade
http://www.i-trade.com/
A service of Trade Point U.S.A., the site explains how to trade, develop a business plan, take advantage of NAFTA, market your company, and find trading partners.

NAFTALink
http://naftalink.web.com.mx/
Written in three languages, the site provides NAFTA-related news, company directories, and links to leading government trade promotion agencies and industry associations in Canada, Mexico and the United States.

NAFTAnet
http://www.nafta.net/
A directory of NAFTA-related business information, the service includes news, bulletin boards, success stories, buy/sell lists, and tutorials on electronic commerce and electronic data interchange.

NetSource
http://www.netsource-asia.com/trade.htm
A trade lead database, the site lists hundreds of global business opportunities in dozens of industries including agriculture, automotive, fashion, fish and seafood, footwear, and furniture.

On-Line Tenders
http://www.explorer-software.com/tender.htm
A database of international tenders and bids, the site links to dozens of government and business organizations around the world that list procurement opportunities online.

Partnerbase
http://www.partnerbase.com/
An online matching service, the site provides a database of company profiles. From this list, users may select a potential business partner, customer, or supplier.

Planet Business
http://www.planetbiz.com/
An online marketplace for traders, the site features trade leads from industries such as chemicals, electronics, fashion, machinery, and food and beverage.

Telephone Directories on the Web
http://www.contractjobs.com/tel/
A database of telephone directories online, the site links to the leading Yellow and White page directories in North America, Latin America, Europe, Africa and Asia Pacific.

Trade Book
http://www.tradebook.com/
Based in Seoul, Korea, the site is a directory of offers to buy and sell. Features include a patent exchange, a distribution-wanted service, and an international trade discussion group.

Trade Bulletin Board
http://www.intl-trade.com/wwwboard/index.html
A trade lead clearinghouse, the site features four forums: an offers forum for posting leads, an immediate-demands forum for posting wholesale or large lot commodities needed immediately, a discussion forum for asking and answering global business questions, and a trade leads forum that features numerous postings and bulletins from government procurement agencies.

Trade Channel

http://www.tradechannel.nl/
Developed by Netherlands-based Trade Channel Organization, the site is a directory of international business opportunities. The database is searchable by product and by company.

Trade Express

http://www.trade-express.com/
Based in Melbourne, Australia, the site is a bulletin board of export and import opportunities in industries such as food and beverage, medical and health, and transportation equipment. The webpage includes a trade matchmaking service and a trade law library.

TradeMatch

http://www.expo.co.uk/
Based in the United Kingdom, the site provides a database of exporters, importers, and international trade service-providers seeking global partners and alliances.

TradeNet World Service

http://www.TradeNet.org/
An online international business exchange, the site is a directory of trade leads in 15 categories including agents and representatives, consumer hard goods, currencies and metals, garments and textiles, and industrial machinery.

Trader's City

http://www.teleport.com/~iexportc/TradersCity.htm
Based in Seattle, the site provides free Internet pages for exporters, importers and companies involved in international trade. The service is open to companies from all countries.

Trading Floor

http://trading.wmw.com/
A subscription trading service, the site provides an exchange for traders to offer, bid, and negotiate real-time. Other features include private business chat rooms, a trade lead directory, and a tariff rate database that lists the duty for every commodity imported into the U.S. from any country.

Trading House

http://www.tradinghouse.com/
A virtual marketplace, the site is a directory of export offers, import demands, and businesses for sale from around the world. Categories include aerospace, consumer electronics, medical equipment, plastics, and transportation.

Venture Web

http://www.venture-web.or.jp/
Based in Japan, the site provides information on international business opportunities in the cities of Osaka and Yokohama.

World Access Network Directory

http://www.wand.com/
Posted in 12 languages, the site is a searchable directory of international trade companies around the world. The service includes country profiles and a trade lead database.

World Trade Markets

http://www.wtm.com/
Based in New York, the site is a directory of global trade opportunities. The leads are searchable by date, country, and product.

World Trade Opportunities

http://www.sgn.com/4sale/4_trade.html
Developed by Rockville, Maryland-based SGN Inc., the site features export and import leads in industries such as aircraft, beverages, electrical, fashion, grains, pipes, wood and lumber.

World Trade Resources

http://www.worldtraderesources.com/
Based in New York, the site is a mergers and acquisitions deal network. Sections include acquisitions wanted, companies for sale, investments needed, and merger and joint venture opportunities.

World Wide Expo

http://www.worldwideexpo.com/expo/
A virtual trade show, the site provides digital booths and pavilions similar to a physical trade show. Modules include business and marketing, education and publishing, medical, import and export, and safety and health.

Worldwide Business Club

http://www.wbc.com/
Based in Washington, D.C., the site is a global trade lead directory. Written in ten languages, the service includes offers to buy and sell, and a database of international representatives.

Purchaser

Purchaser websites provide information and advice on how to search for suppliers and procure goods and services online.

Corporate Purchasing Alliance and Exchange
http://www.cpax.com/
Developed by an alliance of U.S. companies and industry associations, the New York-based site is a buyer's network that negotiates discounts on business supplies and consumer products.

Global Procurement and Supply Chain Benchmarking
http://gebn.bus.msu.edu/
Developed by the Michigan State University School of Management, the site reports on corporate procurement and supply chain strategies. Sections include conference proceedings, corporate profiles, and benchmarking studies.

Journal of Internet Purchasing
http://www.arraydev.com/commerce/jip/current.htm
Based in Ottawa, the site is an e-zine on electronic purchasing. The service includes a discussion forum, a directory of Internet commerce initiatives, and an archive of back issues.

National Association of Purchasing Management
http://www.napm.org/
Based in Tempe, Arizona, the Association promotes the purchasing and supply management profession. The site includes back issues of *Purchasing Today*, the monthly association publication, and *InfoEdge Online*, a tutorial on purchasing management.

Purchasing Management Association of Canada
http://www.pmac.ca/ehome.htm
Based in Toronto, the site provides reports on procurement benchmarking, electronic data interchange, salary surveys, and purchasing law in Canada.

Purchasing Manager's Forum
http://www.execforum.com/
An online community of purchasing professionals, the site features discussion forums, supplier and market directories, a digital library, and reports on purchasing best practices.

Purchasing Online
http://www.manufacturing.net/magazine/purchasing/
Homepage of *Purchasing Magazine*, the site provides buying news, salary surveys, and tutorials on supply chain issues such as requests for proposals and freight billing.

Purchasing Station
http://management.bus.okstate.edu/faculty/christensen/
Based at the Oklahoma State University Department of Management, the site is a global sourcing resource page. The service includes a directory of purchasing management organizations, consultants, and job opportunities.

Purchasing and Supply Sites
http://www.ipsera.org/links.htm
A service of the International Purchasing and Supply Education and Research Association in the United Kingdom, the site links to dozens of purchasing management resources online worldwide. Categories include vendors, industry associations, software, and publications.

Banker

Banker websites provide information and services related to international trade financing and foreign exchange.

Alternative Trade Finance
http://infoserv2.ita.doc.gov/Tradebase/Finance.nsf/7521754277cb208a852565a8006c1c9e?OpenView
Developed by the U.S. International Trade Administration, the site is a database of alternative sources of trade financing. These include counter trade organizations, credit reporting services, and financial consulting agencies.

Business Cashfinder
http://www.cashfinder.com/
A service of Quicken, the site provides a database of financing and credit opportunities from participating lenders including American Express, Citibank, and Chase.

Central Banking Resource Center
http://patriot.net/~bernkopf/
Based in Arlington, Virginia, the site is a directory of central banks on the web. The listings include ministries of finance, multilateral financial institutions, banking associations, and mints.

Commercial Finance Online
http://www.cfol.com/FrameHome.htm
A business finance resource center, the site is a searchable database of organizations seeking capital and commercial financial professionals seeking new clients. The service includes financial news, articles, press releases, events, and employment opportunities.

Credit Reporting Agencies
http://www.creditworthy.com/us/providers/
agency.html
A service of Oregon-based Credit Management Information and Support, the site profiles dozens of credit reporting organizations in North America, Latin America, Europe, the Middle East, and Asia Pacific.

Currency Resources
http://www.uta.fi/~ktmatu/rate-curres.html
A virtual library of currency and financial resources online, the site links to dozens of currency converters, foreign exchange rate calculators, and financial analysis charts on the Internet.

Electronic Banker
http://www.euro.net/innovation/FinanceHP.html
A toolkit of virtual banking resources, the site features the *Encyclopedia of Financial Products*, a financial industry guide, and *the International Financial Encyclopedia*, a dictionary of financial terms.

Export Letters of Credit Kit
http://www.bankamerica.com/corporate/
corp_intltradekit_ov.html
A free tutorial by Bank of America, the site explains how to use a letter of credit. The service includes tips on preparing export documents such as a commercial invoice, bill of lading, packing list, and certificate of origin.

Export Trade Financing Information
http://infoserv2.ita.doc.gov/Tradebase/Finance.nsf
Developed by the U.S. International Trade Administration, the site is a directory of trade financing organizations in the United States. The index is searchable by name and by U.S. state.

FinanceHub
http://financehub.com/
Based in Gainesville, Florida, the site links to leading venture capital, banking, stock market, and small business resources online. The venture capital section features special tutorials and business plan templates.

Financial Information Link Library
http://www.mbnet.mb.ca/~russell/
Based in Winnipeg, Manitoba, the site is a directory of leading banks, currency traders, investment dealers, stock exchanges and other financial-related organizations around the world.

Financing News
http://www.datamerge.com/financingnews/
index.html
A virtual library of financial information, the site provides tips and tutorials on commercial mortgages, venture capital, initial public offerings, and small business loans.

Foreign Exchange Management
http://www.tdbank.ca/tdbank/bizexch/fmfe.html
A service of the Toronto Dominion Bank, the site provides tutorials on foreign exchange management. Topics include spot contracts, forward contracts, option dated forward contracts, foreign currency options, and zero cost range forwards.

Foreign Exchange Rates
http://www.dna.lth.se/cgi-bin/kurt/rates
Based on rates provided by the Federal Reserve Bank of New York, the site provides the latest foreign exchange rates for over 20 currencies. These include the Austrian schilling, the Irish pound, and the U.S. dollar.

FundLine
http://www.worldbank.org/html/fpd/psd/fundline/
index.html
A service of the World Bank's Private Sector Development Department, the site is a directory of investment funds and equity resources in Eastern Europe and the former Soviet Union.

Global Business Forms
http://www.qualitylc.com/gbm.html
A service of Quality Letters of Credit Inc., the site provides trade finance forms and templates. The documents include a pro forma invoice, shipping order, packing list, certificate of origin, inspection certificate, and bill of lading.

International Buying and Selling
http://www.tdbank.ca/trade/
A service of the Toronto Dominion Bank, the site provides a foreign exchange calculator, trade finance glossaries, and a crash course in international trade.

International Reciprocal Trade Association
http://www.irta.net/
Headquartered in Chicago, the Association promotes the interests of the commercial barter industry in the U.S. and around the world. The site features barter statistics, a barter exchange checklist, and a directory of barter consultants.

International Trade Desk Manual
http://www.island-metro.com/trade/
An export reference guide developed by Island-Metro Publications in Plainview, New York, the site provides tutorials and reports on export strategies, markets, technology, finance, and law.

Mastercard ATM Locator
http://www.mastercard.com/atm/
A service of Mastercard, the site lists the locations of automatic teller machines around the world which accept the Mastercard credit card.

MoneyHunter
http://www.moneyhunter.com
The online companion to the MoneyHunt television program, the site is a finance resource center. Features include business plan templates, a financial mentor service, an investor's directory, venture capital news, and a start-up capital bulletin board.

NVST
http://www.nvst.com/
A virtual investment network, the site offers financial forums, an investment capital database, venture capital journals, business valuation news, and a mergers and acquisitions newsletter.

Owens Online
http://www.owens.com/about.htm
Homepage of an international credit reporting agency, the site provides free trade leads, company directories, and country fact sheets.

Today's Business Briefing
http://www.mcs.com/~tryhardz/tmp.html
A service of the Product Management Group, the site provides reports on interest rates, foreign exchange, government bonds, and stock markets in the U.S. and around the world.

Trade Card
http://trade-card.com/
A service of the World Trade Centers Association, the site explains the Trade Card, an electronic payment system for international trade transactions. The webpage includes Trade Card software, bulletins, and a frequently asked questions feature for exporters, importers, and freight forwarders.

Universal Currency Converter
http://www.xe.net/currency/full/
An interactive foreign exchange tool, the site performs instant conversions of some 180 currencies such as the Albanian lek, the Mexican peso, and the Zimbabwe dollar.

Venture Capital Marketplace
http://www.v-capital.com.au/
Based in Sydney, Australia, the site is a venture capital exchange. The service lists private companies seeking equity capital for expansionary purposes. Listings are grouped into six geographic areas: Australia, Canada, Europe, Asia, U.S. and Other.

Visa ATM Locator
http://www.visa.com/cgi-bin/vee/main.html
A service of Visa, the site lists the locations of automatic teller machines around the world that accept the Visa credit card.

World Bank Group
http://www.worldbank.org/
Based in Washington, D.C., the World Bank Group is a consortium of five international financial institutions: the International Bank for Reconstruction and Development, International Development Association, International Centre for Settlement of Investment Disputes, International Finance Corporation, and Multilateral Investment Guarantee Agency. The site profiles each agency, reports on Group activities around the world, and provides tutorials on how to do business with the Bank.

Accountant

Accountant websites provide accounting and taxation information and resources.

Accounting Network
http://www.csu.edu.au/anet/
Based at Charles Sturt University in New South Wales, Australia, the site provides a digital forum for the discussion of accounting, auditing, and related disciplines.

AccountingNet
http://www.accountingnet.com/
A resource for accounting professionals, the site features accounting news, tax and financial data, online tutorials, and a discussion forum.

International Tax Resources
http://www.taxsites.com/international.html
Compiled by Dennis Schmidt, a professor of accounting at the University of Northern Iowa, the site is a directory of accounting firms, newslet-

ters, bulletins, guides and software in over 40 countries.

Introduction to International Taxation
http://www.intltaxlaw.com/
Developed by Bradley Smith, a San Diego accountant, the site is an international taxation primer. Topics include taxation of foreign persons with U.S. activities, taxation of U.S. persons with foreign activities, income tax treaties, and civil penalties.

KPMG International Tax
http://www.tax.kpmg.net/
Developed by KMPG, the site provides international tax news, a directory of tax authorities worldwide, taxation surveys, and country tax facts.

Tax and Accounting Sites Directory
http://www.taxsites.com/
A taxation link center, the webpage is a directory of leading tax and accounting sites in the U.S. and around the world. Categories include federal tax law, state taxes, auditing and fraud.

Tax News Network
http://www.taxnews.com/tnn_public/index.shtml
Hosted by Price Waterhouse Coopers, the site features tax updates, Internal Revenue Service forms and publications, global tax communiqués, and an event calendar.

Tax Resources
http://shell5.ba.best.com/~ftmexpat/html/taxsites/foreign.html
An online tax resources hub, the site features global tax news, country tax reports, guides, and codes for dozens of countries around the world.

Taxman International
http://www.xs4all.nl/~edvisser/taxman.html
A collection of tax and customs administration resources on the Internet, the site links to sites in over 60 countries including Argentina, Costa Rica, France, Germany and the United Kingdom.

World Tax
http://www.eyi.com/ITAX/
A service of Ernst & Young, the site reports on transfer pricing, offshore financial centers, and executive immigration. The service includes country profiles and tax guides for corporations and executives.

Lawyer
Lawyer websites provide information and advice on international trade law.

ABA Network
http://www.abanet.org/
Homepage of the American Bar Association, the site provides a lawyer locator, event calendar, legal conference reports, and a directory of the Association's hundreds of standing and special committees, forums and task forces.

CataLaw
http://www.catalaw.com/
A catalog of law resources online, the site is searchable by global region and legal topics such as information technology law, trademark law, and natural resources law.

Center for International Legal Studies
http://www.cils.org/
Based in Salzburg, Austria, the site features a directory of leading law firms in the world, legal discussion forums, book reviews, conference updates, and law school profiles.

Copyright Website
http://www.benedict.com/index.html
An archive of copyright resources, the site features copyright law tutorials, lessons on fair use and public domain, reports on the development and distribution of copyrighted software on the Internet, examples of famous copyright infringements, and a copyright discussion group.

Counsel Connect
http://www.counsel.com/en/bin/login?Tag=/&URI=/lawlinks/world.html
An online service for lawyers, the site provides a searchable directory of attorneys, a database of employment opportunities for lawyers, and primers on managing a legal practice.

Export Legal Assistance Network
http://www.miep.org/elan/
Sponsored by the U.S. Small Business Administration, the Export Legal Assistance Network is an alliance of international trade attorneys from the Federal Bar Association who provide free initial consultations to small businesses interested in starting export operations.

FindLaw International Trade
http://www.findlaw.com/01topics/25interntrade/index.html
Part of the FindLaw online database, the site links to leading international trade resources online. These include legal journals, newsletters, articles, mailing lists, message boards, and news services.

FindLaw: Internet Legal Resources
http://www.findlaw.com
A virtual law library, the site is a searchable directory of Internet legal resources. Categories include cases and codes, legal practice materials, law firms and lawyers, legal organizations, professional development, and law schools.

Foreign and International Law
http://www.law.indiana.edu/law/v-lib/non-us.html
Sponsored by the Indiana University of School Law Library, the site is a directory of international legal databases on the Internet. Listed alphabetically, the resources range from Alabama international lawyers to the Zambia Legal Information Institute.

Hieros Gamos
http://www.hg.org/hg.html
Written in five languages, the site is a hub of legal and government information. Features include country legal guides, law journals, online seminars, law firm directories, and a database of some 200 legal discussion groups.

Indiana Journal of Global Legal Studies
http://www.law.indiana.edu/glsj/glsj.html
Published by the Indiana University School of Law, the site features full-text articles written by legal experts on international trade law issues. Topics include international law and private foreign investment, foundations of law on the Internet, and globalization and privatization.

Information Resources for Law
http://www.library.ucsb.edu/subj/law.html
A legal link page, the site links to leading law database on the Internet. Categories include general law sites, criminal justice, dispute resolution, courts and court decisions, legislation, statutes, and law journals.

International Centre for Commercial Law
http://www.icclaw.com/
Based in the United Kingdom, the site is a guide to the top commercial law firms in the United Kingdom, Europe and Asia. The service also

reports on law developments in a variety of commercial areas such as banking, consumer law, licensing, and dispute resolution.

International Guide to Trademarks and Copyright
http://ttdomino.thomson-thomson.com/www/links.NSF/NVIS?OpenNavigator
A service of Thomson and Thomson, the site provides primers on international trademark and copyright laws and organizations.

International Law Center
http://www.ljextra.com/practice/internat/
Sponsored by Netherlands-based Kluwer Law International, the site features global law news, columns, forums, links and job listings. The service includes *International Law Express*, a free e-mail newsletter on global legal developments.

International Trade Law Library
http://www.tradepoint.org/library.html
A service of Trade Winds Publishing, the site links to leading international trade treaties, tariff schedules, and newsletters on the Internet.

International Trade Law Monitor
http://itl.irv.uit.no/trade_law/
Based at the University of Tromso Law Faculty in Norway, the award-winning site features a subject index of law resources online, and a directory of international trade law treaties, conventions and rules. Categories include customs, dispute settlement, insurance, and payment mechanisms.

Internet Law Library
http://law.house.gov/
Developed by the U.S. House of Representatives Law Revision Council, the site features a searchable database of current public laws and amendments enacted by U.S. Congress. Other features include a database of U.S. federal laws, U.S. state and territorial laws, and international treaties and laws.

Law Lounge
http://lawlounge.com/
Based in London, England, the site provides legal news, law reports, attorney directories, and discussion forums. Topics include Internet law, corporate law, and criminal law.

Law Office
http://www.thelawoffice.com/
A legal networking center, the site has lawyer

directories, ask-a-lawyer bulletin boards, and discussion forums on U.S. legal topics such as business, maritime, environmental, and intellectual property law.

Laws of Other Nations
http://law.house.gov/52.htm
Part of the U.S. House of Representatives Internet Law Library, the site profiles the legal systems of more than 100 countries. Resources include fundamental laws, banking statutes, international treaties, human rights practices, and legal profession directories.

Legal Dictionary
http://www.wwlia.org/diction.htm
A service of the World Wide Legal Information Association, the site provides definitions of legal terms in plain language.

Legal dot Net
http://www.legal.net/
A virtual legal network, the site features an attorney registry, legal articles and columns, a legal chat service, and intellectual property tutorials.

Seamless Website: Law and Legal Resources
http://seamless.com/
Owned and operated by Kevin Lee Thomason, a San Francisco lawyer, the site contains legal news, attorney directories, and bulletin boards on a variety of law topics. These include business law and venture capital, cyberspace law, labor law, and trade secrets.

Trade Law Tips
http://www.exportingcanadaonline.com/MainMenu/ExportT/Legal.htm
Sponsored by Vancouver-based Bogle & Gates, the site answers a number of frequently asked questions related to U.S.-Canada trade. Topics include U.S. litigation, lawsuits, and patent and trademark protection.

Trade Secrets Home Page
http://www.execpc.com/~mhallign/
Developed by Mark Halligan, a Chicago attorney, the site is a trade secrets resource page. Features include a case archive, trade secret developments, and tutorials on protection programs, investigations, disclosure doctrine, and licensing.

Western Hemisphere Trade Agreements
http://www.sice.oas.org/root/tradee.stm

A service of the Washington, D.C.-based Organization of American States, the site features full-texts of trade agreements and treaties in the Western Hemisphere. The pacts include the Treaty of Montevideo, the Protocol of Trujillo, the G-3 Free Trade Agreement, the North American Free Trade Agreement, and the Final Act of the Uruguay Round.

World Intellectual Property Association
http://www.wipo.org/
Headquartered in Geneva, the Association promotes the protection of intellectual property throughout the world. The site features intellectual property tutorials, newsletters, conference proceedings, and international agreement texts.

World Trade Organization
http://www.wto.org/
Homepage of the Geneva-based global trade authority, the site is a virtual library of international trade reports and statistics. Features include legal texts, press releases, export and import data tables, global trade forecasts, and *Focus*, the official World Trade Organization newsletter.

Diplomat

Diplomat websites provide information on government embassies, consulates, and trade offices around the world.

Electronic Embassy
http://www.embassy.org/
A service of Arlington, Virginia-based TeleDiplomacy, the site is a directory of foreign embassies in Washington, D.C. on the Internet. Features include an international business center, a press release clearinghouse, and a list of recommended readings on diplomacy and international affairs.

EmbassyWeb
http://www.embpage.org/
Developed by infoCatch in Arlington, Virginia, the site is a database of embassies, consulates, and trade missions worldwide. The service includes *Embassy Web*, a free e-mail newsletter on diplomatic post news, events, and webpage design trends.

Escape from America Embassy and Consulate Directory
http://www.escapeartist.com/embassy1/embassy1.htm
A diplomatic post resource guide, the site links to embassies and consulates online around the

world including American embassies overseas and foreign embassies in the United States.

Output Embassies for Links
http://webserver.tagish.co.uk/embassy1b/
A service of U.K.-based Tagish Ltd., the site lists United Kingdom embassies abroad, delegations to the European Union, and the diplomatic posts of more than 100 countries.

Web of Culture
http://www.webofculture.com/
A source for cross-cultural information, the site features country profiles, culture guides, expert articles, and tutorials on body language and foreign phrases.

Yahoo Government: Embassies and Consulates
*http://www.yahoo.com/Government/
Embassies_and_Consulates/*
Part of the Yahoo search engine, the site is a directory of diplomatic posts around the world that are registered with the Yahoo search service.

Customs Broker
Customs broker websites provide tips and reports on border regulations, tariff classifications, and customs clearance procedures.

APEC Tariff Database
http://www.apectariff.org/apeccgi.cgi
A service of Asia Pacific Economic Cooperation, the site provides tariff information on APEC member countries. The database includes duty rates, customs guides, and a searchable index of harmonized system code numbers and product descriptions.

Canadian Importing and Exporting
http://www.rc.gc.ca/menu/EmenuHLA.html
Developed by Revenue Canada, the site is a primer on Canadian exporting and importing. The service provides fact sheets on automated export declarations, customs tariff classifications, North American Free Trade Agreement rules of origin, electronic data interchange, and other trade topics.

Customs Guide to the Americas
http://americas.fiu.edu/customs/
Developed by the Florida-based Summit of the Americas Center, the site summarizes key trade pacts in the Western Hemisphere such as Mercosur, the North American Free Trade Agreement, and the Caribbean Community and Common Market. The service also spotlights customs regulations in selected countries in North and South America.

Customs Tips
*http://www.exportingcanadaonline.com/MainMenu/
ExportT/Customs.htm*
Developed by Mississauga, Ontario-based J.W. Smith Customs Brokers, the site provides a tutorial on Canadian customs brokerage. The service defines key terms such as duties, harmonized system code, Canada Customs Invoice, Goods and Services Tax, B3, and electronic data interchange.

International Federation of Customs Brokers Associations
http://www.ifcba.org/
Based in Ottawa, the Federation promotes the development of the customs brokerage industry around the world. The site features news, an association directory, online forum, event calendar, and training contacts.

Market Access Database
http://mkaccdb.eu.int/
A service of the European Commission, the site reviews the trade policies of more than 30 countries around the world including Canada, the U.S., and South Africa. The database catalogs the leading trade barriers in each country such as tariff rates, other import duties, documentation, customs procedures, import prohibitions, licensing, export restrictions, and subsidies.

NAFTA: A Guide to Customs Procedures
http://www.i-trade.com/dir05/customs/
Developed by Trade Point U.S.A., the site is a tutorial on North American Free Trade Agreement customs rules. Topics include rules of origin, certificate of origin, entry procedures, origin verification, advance ruling procedures, and country of origin marking.

Virtual Customs Office
http://207.245.213.146/home.htm
A Revenue Canada pilot project in Vancouver, the site features a variety of Canadian customs guides and interactive tools. The service provides downloadable customs forms, exchange rates, tariff rulings, trade news, and the Tariff Wizard, a searchable directory of Canadian tariff rates.

U.S. Customs Service
http://www.customs.ustreas.gov/index.htm
Homepage of the U.S. Customs Service, the site

provides traveler information, customs forms, a directory of U.S. customs office locations, and an overview of American border laws and regulations.

U.S. Importing/Exporting

http://www.customs.ustreas.gov/imp-exp1/index.htm

A directory of U.S. customs resources, the site provides tutorials on U.S. exporting and importing. Topics include rulings and regulations, informed compliance, automated systems, import quotas, and customs broker licensing requirements.

World Customs Organization

http://www.wcoomd.org/

Based in Brussels, the Organization promotes the effectiveness and efficiency of customs administrations around the world. The site features reports on the harmonized system code, customs reform and modernization, and customs information technology.

World Tariff Online

http://www.fritz.com/world-tariff/wtintro.htm

Developed by Fritz Companies, the subscription service is a searchable database of commodity duty and tax information for countries around the world.

Travel Agent

Travel agent websites provide travel information and reservation services.

Air Travel Pro

http://www.dfw.net/~morris/

An online travel resource center, the site features directories of airlines, airports, bed and breakfasts, car rental agencies, and automated teller machines worldwide.

Airports International

http://www.airportsintl.com/

Developed by Mobius Technology Group, the site profiles over 5,000 airports around the world. The service reports on airport operations, communications, and runways.

Asia Tour

http://www.asiatour.com/

A database of Asian travel resources, the site features maps, photos, video clips, country profiles, immigration regulations, and attractions for seven countries: Cambodia, China, Laos, Malaysia, Myanmar, Vietnam and Thailand.

Biztravel.com

http://www.biztravel.com/V4/newhome.cfm

An online travel planning service, the site allows a user to book flights, cars, and hotels. Features include bizMiles, a frequent flyer program tracking tool, and bizCityInfo, a virtual library of information on hotels, restaurants, and weather.

Business Traveler Info Network

http://www.ultranet.com/~mes/sharware.htm

A directory of business travel shareware and freeware, the site includes programs for travel planning, expense reporting, remote access, and frequent flyer point tracking.

Checklist for Your Overseas Trip

http://www.tradeport.org/cgi-bin/banner.pl/ts/planning/travlist.html

Developed by Minneapolis-based trade consultant John Jagoe, the site provides an international trip checklist. Items include travel documents, medical, target markets, potential sales representatives, and company information and supplies.

ClickCity

http://www.clickcity.com/

A virtual library of city information, the site provides news, profiles, travel tips, and entertainment guides for over 1,600 cities worldwide.

Culture Finder

http://www.culturefinder.com/

Updated daily, the site provides a searchable database of theater, opera, music, visual arts, dance, and film events across the United States.

Excite Travel

http://www.city.net/

Updated daily, the site features country profiles, city guides, maps, cruise and tour information, and farefinders for more than 5,000 destinations worldwide.

Expat Exchange

http://www.expatexchange.com/

The site is an online community of some 75,000 people relocating to, living in, or returning from over 140 overseas locations. Launched in 1997 by Betsy Burlingame as part of a New York University thesis project, the service has grown into a major networking portal for businesspeople on international assignments.

Fodor's Travel Service

http://www.fodors.com/

A service of Fodor's Travel Publications, the site offers online forums, travel planning tools, a hotel index, and restaurant directory for 99 destinations.

Homebuyer's Fair
http://www.homefair.com/
An online relocation toolkit, the site features free city reports, special moving discounts, and virtual gadgets. Tools include the Salary Calculator which computes the cost-of-living differences between hundreds of cities, the Lifestyle Optimizer which selects the best places to live based on your criteria, and the Relocation Wizard which prepares a customized relocation "to do" list.

International Business Kiosk
http://www.webcom.com/one/world/
A reference page for doing business around the world, the site is a guide to duty free shopping, national flags, subway and train systems, translators and other services related to global trade and travel.

International Travel Information
http://www.go-global.com/homepage.shtml
A world travel guide, the site features reports on global weather, time zones, dialing codes, power voltage, distances, and holidays.

Internet Travel Network
http://www.itn.net/
Based in Palo Alto, California, the site allows a user to book air, car and, hotel reservations, search for low fares, and manage frequent flyer programs. The service includes travel discussion forums and a driving directions feature which provides door-to-door road directions to a destination.

Landseer Online
http://www.landseer.com/
Based in Essex, Connecticut, the site links to world facts, destination profiles, travel advisories, currency converters, and local time information worldwide.

Lonely Planet
http://www.lonelyplanet.com/
Updated daily, the site features country guides, city profiles, photo galleries, travel writing, health advisories, and special on-the-road reports.

Microsoft Expedia
http://expedia.msn.com/
A service of the Microsoft Network, the site enables a user to book and buy flights, hotels,

and rental cars, and shop for cruises, vacation packages, and charters online.

Moving and Storage Knowledge Database
http://www.avatar-moving.com/kbframes/kb.html
Created by Chris Noblit of New York-based Avatar Moving Systems, the online service includes primers on moving household goods, business and office equipment, sensitive electronics, and trade show exhibition materials.

Outspoken Encyclopedia of Travel
http://www.frommers.com/
Developed by Arthur Frommer's *Budget Travel Magazine*, the site is a directory of bargain-priced trips, vacations, hotels and charters worldwide. The service includes an ask-the-travel-expert feature, and dozens of message boards on international travel.

QuickAid
http://www.quickaid.com/
A resource for airport information, the site provides terminal maps and fact sheets on ground transportation, shops and services for U.S. and international air terminals.

Rain or Shine Weather
http://www.rainorshine.com/
Sponsored in part by the Old Farmer's Almanac, the site provides 24-hour weather forecasts and satellite photos for over 900 cities worldwide.

TaxiNetwork
http://www.taxinetwork.com/cgi-bin/webc/home.html
Developed by the International Taxicab and Livery Association, the site provides searchable directories of taxicab, limousine and livery services around the world.

TheTrip.com
http://www.thetrip.com/
Based in Englewood, Colorado, the site features flight availability reports, reservation services, real-time flight tracking, airport maps and guides, hotel reviews, ground transportation directories, interactive maps, and low fare notification.

Travel Warnings and Consular Information Sheets
http://travel.state.gov/travel_warnings.html
Developed by the U.S. State Department, the site provides consular information sheets, public announcements, and travel warnings.

TravelNow

http://www.travelnow.com/

A global reservation service, the site allows a user to search for the lowest price airfares, book hotels, rent a car, and order a cruise or package vacation online.

Travelocity

http://www.travelocity.com/

A web-based travel service, the site allows a user to shop and reserve airplanes, hotels and car rentals on the Internet. Features include hotel maps and photos, a low fare search engine, departure and arrival information, airplane diagrams, destination guides, travel news, and a flight paging service.

Weather Channel

http://www.weather.com/homepage.html

A resource page for weather information, the site provides interactive maps, weather safety tips, a glossary of weather terms, severe weather alerts, and forecasts for U.S. and international cities.

WebFlyer

http://www.webflyer.com/

Based in Colorado Springs, Colorado, the site offers resources and interactive tools for frequent flyers. Features include frequent flyer program comparisons, program enrollment services, account checkers, program news, flight trackers, and air miles bonus bulletins.

World Climate

http://www.worldclimate.com/

An online climate database, the site provides key climate information for tens of thousands of locations worldwide. The data include average temperature, rainfall, sea-level pressure, and station-level pressure.

World Clock

http://www.stud.unit.no/USERBIN/steffent/ verdensur.pl

Updated every five minutes, the site provides the local times for hundreds of cities and locations around the world.

World Travel Guide

http://www.wtgonline.com/navigate/default.asp

Developed by London-based Columbia Press, the site provides travel guides for hundreds of countries, states, and provinces around the world. Topics include area size, population, population density, geography, and local time.

Shipper

Shipper websites offer freight services and cargo information online.

Air Cargo Newsgroup

http://www.mta-ic.com/

Homepage of the Air Cargo online discussion group, the site provides subscription information, forum archives, an air cargo resource list, and a directory of airline tracking sites.

Air Cargo Online

http://www.cargo-online.com/

Based in the Isle of Man, United Kingdom, the site provides a variety of air cargo resources and matching services. Features include a daily-updated list of aircraft seeking cargo and cargo seeking aircraft, a directory of aircraft for sale and lease, an event calendar, conference transcripts, and air cargo news. A six-month free trial is available with registration.

Air Cargo Tracking

http://www.tradecompass.com/lms/free/air/ tracking.html

A Trade Compass service, the site allows a user to track air cargo on some 20 airlines including American, British Airways, Cathay Pacific, and Delta. An air waybill prefix and air waybill number are needed to use the online tool and track an air shipment.

Airlines of the Web

http://www.itn.net/cgi/get?itn/cb/aow/index:XX-AIRLINES

Developed by the Internet Travel Network, the site links to hundreds of airline homepages world-wide. The service includes directories of airport codes, city codes, duty free shops, and aviation organizations.

CargoConnect

http://www.ccx.com/

Based in the United Kingdom, the site allows users to get immediate tracking status information from seven airlines: American, British Airways, Canadian, Emirates, Qantas, TWA and United. The service includes real-time updates on cargo flight availability and scheduling.

CargoLog

http://www.cargolog.com/

An online cargo costing service, the site allows a user to submit a rate inquiry to a select group of freight forwarders. The service includes cargo news, press releases, job opportunities, and a searchable database of cargo and freight operations.

CargoWeb
http://www.cargoweb.com/
A directory of online cargo resources, the site provides industry news, cargo fact sheets, and a searchable directory of road, air, sea, rail, inland and intermodal cargo carriers worldwide.

ClearFreight
http://www.clearfreight.com/
Homepage of Clearfreight, a Los Angeles-based freight forwarder, the site provides air waybill tracking, a shipping news bureau, export declaration information, trade and shipping glossaries, a currency converter, and other online cargo tools and directories.

Electronic Shipping Guide
http://www.shipguide.com/
An ocean cargo resource center, the site features ocean carrier and port news, discussion forums, a searchable database of ocean carrier voyages, and a directory of ocean services by departure port, arrival port, and by carrier.

FreightNet
http://www.freightnet.com/
A directory of freight forwarders worldwide, the site provides the names, addresses, phone and fax numbers, and, where available, the web and e-mail addresses of freight companies in Africa, Asia, Australasia, Europe, North America, and South America.

Freightworld
http://www.freightworld.com
Based in Clayton, California, the site is a directory of freight and cargo resources on the Internet. Categories include airlines, airports, freight forwarders, logistics providers, maritime, moving and warehousing, package express, railroads, seaports and trucking.

Logistics World
http://www.logisticsworld.com/
Developed by Dayton, Ohio-based Logistics World, the site is a worldwide directory of transportation and logistics resources. Categories include freight, employment, supply chain, import/export, technology, manufacturing and services.

Maritime Global Net
http://www.mglobal.com/

Based in Bristol, Rhode Island, the site is an online network for the maritime community. Features include maritime news, job opportunities, discussion groups, and a broker's exchange where maritime professionals post buy and sell offers related to dry cargo, liquid cargo, vessels, and equipment.

Ocean Transit Analyzer
http://ota.tradecompass.com/
A Trade Compass subscription service, the site tracks routing options for container shipments, the competitors sharing space on the same ship, and the on-time reliability of different ocean carriers.

SchedNet
http://www.schednet.com/schedule/
A global shipping database, the site includes shipping news, a database of schedules for sailings to and from Asian ports, airfreight schedules, and a directory of shipping employment opportunities.

Seaports Infopages
http://www.seaportsinfo.com/
Based in Coral Gables, Florida, the site provides seaport news, directories, and reports. Features include U.S. port rankings by import and export, and links to leading industry associations and ocean carriers.

TruckNet
http://www.truck.com
Based in Lebanon, Missouri, the site is an online resource center for the trucking industry. The service includes trucking news, employment opportunities, freight matching, discussion forums, vendor directories, and truckstop guides.

World Shipping Directory
http://wsd.world.no/
Based in Hønefoss, Norway, the site is a searchable directory of shipping services worldwide. The resource includes a job centre, parts exchange, and software library.

Translator

Translator websites provide translation services and language dictionaries.

AltaVista Translation Service
http://babelfish.altavista.digital.com/cgi-bin/translate?
A service of AltaVista, the site provides instant translations in six languages: English, French,

German, Italian, Portuguese, and Spanish. The service includes translation tips and frequently asked questions.

Eurodicautom

http://www2.echo.lu/edic/
Developed by the European Commission Translation Service, the site allows a user to translate terms and abbreviations in 12 languages including Danish, Dutch, English, and Finnish.

Online Language Dictionaries

http://rivendel.com/~ric/resources/dictionary.html
Created by Rivendell International Communications in Hyattsville, Maryland, the site features dozens of online dictionaries and translation tools. Categories include multilingual dictionaries, free online translation, free online language courses, language chat sites, and language software.

Travlang's Translating Dictionaries

http://dictionaries.travlang.com/
A directory of free online translating resources, the site provides dictionaries and tools for 16 languages including Afrikaans, Czech, Danish, English, Hungarian, German, Dutch, Finnish, French, Italian, Norwegian, Spanish, and Portuguese.

Employment Counselor

Employment counselor websites feature employment opportunities and career resources.

America's Job Bank

http://www.ajb.dni.us/
Developed by the U.S. Department of Labor, the site is a searchable database of U.S. job opportunities. The free service allows employers to post job vacancies, and job seekers to post resumes and search for employment openings online. Features include wage reports, geographic profiles, occupational trends, and a career library.

Best Jobs U.S.A.

http://www.bestjobsusa.com/
Created by Employment Review magazine, the site offers career guides, human resources directories, salary surveys, corporate profiles, and full-text articles from Employment Review magazine.

Career City

http://www.careercity.com/
A career resource center, the site provides a job database searchable by profession and city. Features include industry reports, salary comparisons, career planning tutorials, and primers on how to start a business.

Career Magazine

http://www.careermag.com/
Based in Boulder, Colorado, the site features job openings, employer profiles, career articles, a resume database, discussion forums, and relocation resources.

Career Mosaic

http://www.careermosaic.com/
Updated daily, the site provides a searchable job database, a recruiting-event calendar, and tutorials on employment and salary negotiation strategies. The service features a number of industry-specific career centers for food manufacturing, healthcare, and pharmaceuticals.

Career Mosaic International Gateway

http://www.careermosaic.com/cm/gateway/gateway1.html
A global job network, the site links to Career Mosaic employment resources in 11 geographic areas: Association of South East Asian Nations, Australia, Canada, France, Hong Kong, Japan, Korea, New Zealand, Québec, the United Kingdom, and the United States.

Career Path

http://www.careerpath.com/res/owa/rb_applicant.display_rblogin?
Based in Los Angeles, the site is a directory of job listings posted in more than 50 leading newspapers from all regions of the United States. The listings are searchable by industry, data and keyword.

Careers

http://careers.wsj.com/
A service of the *Wall Street Journal*, the site features career columnists, salary surveys, employer profiles, job-hunting tips, executive recruiter databases, and tutorials on how to find a job overseas.

E.Span

http://www.espan.com/
Based in Indianapolis, the site offers job listings and resume services for employment seekers,

and hiring tools and job ads for employers. A career library includes discussion forums and job hunting tips.

Going On-Line to Locate Overseas Opportunities
http://www.nbew.com/current/intljobs.html
A service of the *National Business Employment Weekly*, the site provides advice on using the Internet to find international employment opportunities. Tips include isolating country sites and checking Embassies.

Headhunter.Net
http://www.headhunter.net/
A resource for employers and job seekers, the site is a searchable database of job openings, resumes, company profiles, and headhunting news.

International Organizations with Job Openings on the Internet
http://www.psc-cfp.gc.ca/intpgm/epb6.htm
Developed by the Public Service Commission of Canada, the site is a database of vacancy notices posted by international organizations such as the Asian Development Bank, International Monetary Fund, Organization of American States, World Bank, and World Trade Organization.

Monster Board
http://www.monster.com/
Based in Maynard, Massachusetts, the site is a U.S. and international job database. Features include online recruitment seminars, a job search agent, employer profiles, a resume builder, and industry employment reports.

Online Career Center
http://www.occ.com/
Featuring daily-updated job news, the site offers an employment database browsable by U.S. city, state, company and industry. An international job directory lists employment opportunities in Africa, Asia, Australasia, Canada, Central America, Europe, Mexico, Middle East, and South America.

Personal Search Agent
http://findjob.internet.com/psainfo.html
Developed by Mecklermedia, the site searches job postings online that meet your criteria. When a match is found, the service sends you an e-mail with a job summary and the Internet address of the employment posting.

Positionwatch
http://www.positionwatch.com/
An information technology job search service, the site features high-tech employer profiles, recruiting tutorials, a searchable database of information technology jobs, and job-alert, an e-mail notification system.

Riley Guide
http://www.dbm.com/jobguide/
Developed by Margaret Riley, an Internet consultant in Rockville, Maryland, the site is a virtual library of online employment resources. Features include reviews of Internet job services, career tutorials, job-hunting checklists, resume databases, and employment directories for specific occupational areas such as sales, health, engineering, manufacturing, and law enforcement.

Resources for International Job Opportunities
http://www.dbm.com/jobguide/internat.html
Part of the Riley Guide, the page is a directory of leading employment databases in Australia, Canada, China, Germany, India, Japan, Russia, South Africa, Thailand, and the United Kingdom.

Webmaster
Webmaster websites provide tools and tutorials for developing webpages.

A Beginner's Guide to HTML
http://www.ncsa.uiuc.edu/General/Internet/WWW/HTMLPrimer.html
Developed by the National Center for Supercomputing Applications at the University of Illinois, the site provides a primer on HTML (hypertext markup language), the coding program used to create webpages.

Computer Information Centre
http://www.compinfo.co.uk/index.htm
A computer resource center, the site provides information technology news, downloadable software, equipment comparison reports, and directories of hardware and software manufacturers and suppliers worldwide.

FindMail
http://www.findmail.com/index.html
Based in San Francisco, the site is a free e-mail list hosting service. Using the system, a webmaster can add a form to a website that

allows users to enter their e-mail address and subscribe to the e-mail list directly from the web.

Free E-mail Address Directory
http://www.emailaddresses.com/
A guide to free e-mail online, the site provides tutorials on e-mail etiquette, and a list of mail forwarding and web-based e-mail services worldwide.

Free E-mail Providers
http://www.yahoo.com/Business_and_Economy/Companies/Internet_Services/Email_Providers/Free_Email/
A service of Yahoo, the site is a directory of free e-mail sites and mail forwarding services on the Internet.

Free Index
http://www.freeindex.com/
A directory of free webmaster resources online, the site spotlights no-cost homepages, e-mail services, chatrooms, HTML guides, statistics, message boards, and banner rotation services on the Internet.

Going Global
http://www.microsoft.com/globaldev/
A service of the Microsoft Developer Network, the site provides tips and information on globalizing Windows applications and components.

InfoWorld Electric
http://www.infoworld.com/
Developed by InfoWorld Media Group, the site is an information technology forum. The service features discussion groups, guest columnists, a hardware and software test center, and career resources.

Internet.Com
http://www.internet.com
A service of Westport, Connecticut-based Mecklermedia, the site is an Internet information center. Offerings include Internet news, online shopping catalogs, webmaster tutorials, job databases, free newsletters and bulletins, trade show information, and a computer glossary.

Internet and Webpage Tools
http://mirror.direct.ca/tucows/window95.html
Compiled by Tucows Interactive, the site is a directory of web-based software. Tools include browsers, e-mail services, image mappers and viewers, HTML guides, news readers, and security software.

Internet World
http://www.internetworld.com/
Updated daily, the site provides opinion and breaking news on electronic commerce, web development, technology infrastructure, and internet service providers. Features include *Internet World Weekly Digest*, a free weekly newsletter on Internet developments, and *Internet World Daily*, a free daily bulletin on cyber-commerce.

The List
http://thelist.internet.com/
A buyer's guide to Internet services, the site provides a searchable directory of Internet Service Providers—ISPs—around the world. The database is browsable by area code and country code.

NetLingo
http://www.netlingo.com/
A searchable dictionary of technology terms, the site provides definitions of hundreds of Internet and computer-related words and phrases. The service includes a pocket dictionary that lists all the words in a floating window.

Web Design and Review
http://www.graphic-design.com/Web/
An electronic magazine for webmasters, the site provides design tips, tools, interviews, and tutorials on everything from page creation software to search engines.

Web Developer.Com
http://www.webdeveloper.com/
A resource for web technicians, the site profiles authoring tools, security software, multimedia technologies, and graphics packages. The service includes a how-to section that provides instructions on basic HTML and Java programming.

Web Developers Journal
http://webdevelopersjournal.com/
A webmaster resource center, the site offers web columns and commentary, tutorials, software and book reviews, and discussion groups. The service includes free browsers, HTML editors, graphics utilities, and site management tools.

Web Marketing Info Center
http://www.wilsonweb.com/webmarket/
Based in Rocklin, California, the site is an online archive of Internet marketing information. The service provides hundreds of articles and

tutorials on everything from banner ad design to justifying website expenses to targeted e-mail lists. Features include *Web Marketing Today*, a free, monthly e-mail newsletter on Internet marketing.

Web Review
http://webreview.com/wr/pub/List_Issues
An electronic magazine for webmasters, the site provides web design tips, software reviews, and guides on HTML, fonts, graphics, navigation, networks, security, and servers.

Web Techniques
http://www.webtechniques.com/
A primer on webpage development, the site features Internet news, commentary, an event calendar, and a web tools buyer's guide. A free subscription is offered to *Web Techniques* magazine, the hard-copy version, with registration.

Webmaster's Resource Center
http://jdante.hypermart.net/wmrc/
A directory of free webpage tools, the site profiles no-cost websites, hit counters, chat rooms, HTML guides, e-mail forwarding, banner exchanges, java scripts, graphics, and other services and software for webmasters.

World Wide Web Consortium
http://www.w3.org/
A library of web information and primers, the site provides web news, technical reports, sample codes, mailing lists, tutorials, style sheets, fonts and experimental software.

Bargain Hunter

Bargain hunter websites feature shareware, freeware, and discount purchasing opportunities.

BizProWeb's Business & Professional Shareware
http://www.bizproweb.com/pages/shareware/shareware.html
A resource page for small business owners, the site links to hundreds of business-related shareware programs online. Categories include employment and job searching tools, personal information managers, and text editors.

Bottom Dollar
http://www.bottomdollar.com/
A price search service, the site scans the Internet

for the lowest price on selected products. To use the tool, a user picks from one of six product categories such as hardware and videos. The user types in the name of the product, clicks a go button, and the service returns a list of product descriptions and prices, along with the Internet addresses of the online vendors.

Comprehensive List of Freeware, Shareware and Software Sites
http://pilot.msu.edu/user/heinric6/soft.htm
Based in East Lansing, Michigan, the site is a directory of freeware and shareware sites online. The resources are organized by operating system such as Windows 95, Windows NT, DOS, OS2, Unix and Mac.

FileWorld
http://www.pcworld.com/fileworld/
A service of *PC World Online*, the site reviews leading shareware and trial-ware software programs. Categories include antivirus, business and office, desktop utilities, graphics, programming, and sound and audio.

FinanceNet
http://www.financenet.gov/financenet/
A primer on buying from public agencies, the site reports on government asset sales, auctions and surplus purchasing opportunities in the U.S. and around the world.

Financial and Business Shareware Archive
http://www.schco.com/software.htm
A service of New York City-based Skelton Carter Hall Investment Bankers, the site provides free business and financial software downloads. The tools include business plan templates, money manager programs, employee attendance tracker, and project management utility.

Jumbo Shareware
http://www.jumbo.com/
Based in New York City, the site provides a searchable archive of software downloads. Categories include business, multimedia, desktop, developer, home and hobbies, and utilities.

Microsoft Free Downloads
http://www.microsoft.com/msdownload/
A service of Microsoft, the site provides free browsers, add-ons, publishing tools, server software, viewers, templates, tutorials, fonts, and utilities.

Online Auctions

http://www.yahoo.com/Business_and_Economy/
Companies/Auctions/Online_Auctions/
Compiled by Yahoo, the site is a directory of
online auction services worldwide. The virtual
auctions sell everything from computer equipment to audio systems to aircraft.

SBA Shareware Library

http://www.sba.gov/library/sharewareroom.html
Compiled by the U.S. Small Business Administration, the site is a directory of shareware for
starting, financing, managing and marketing a
business. Tools include a day planner, money
manager, inventory control program, and a form
generator.

Shareware.Com

http://www.shareware.com/
An online shareware library, the site offers a
database of some 15,000 business, multimedia,
and Internet programs. Business categories
include finance, inventory systems, legal,
presentation tools, and word processing.

Shareware for the PC

http://shareware.netscape.com/computing/
shareware/
A service of Netscape, the site is a directory of
shareware in 11 categories including business,
development tools, drivers, education, home and
personal, Internet, multimedia, and design.

Small Business Software Library

http://www.hotfiles.com/business.html
Developed by ZDNet, the site is a shareware and
software library. Categories include employee
management, math and engineering, personal
information managers, and spreadsheets.

CHAPTER 3

AMERICAN WEB-PORTS: 1,100+ UNITED STATES BUSINESS RESOURCES ON THE INTERNET

This chapter spotlights more than 1,100 of the top international business resources online that focus on the United States. The section profiles national websites and online hubs for each of the 50 U.S. states. Home to 270 million people, the United States is an $8 trillion annual market, the world's largest. From Silicon Valley laboratories to Iowa cornfields to Wall Street investment banks, the U.S. is the most highly diverse and technology-advanced economy on the planet. Leading business and trade opportunities include computing technologies, environmental equipment, professional services, biotechnology, and telecommunications. According to NUA Internet Surveys, an estimated 90 million Americans—one out every three—were online as of January 1999. Every day, approximately 60,000 more in the United States log on for the first time.

National Sites

United States Search Tools

All-in-One
http://www.albany.net/allinone/
Created by William Cross, the site is a directory of search tools online. Categories include specialized interest, images, people, news, weather, technical reports, and desk reference.

AltaVista
http://www.altavista.digital.com
Developed by Digital Equipment Corporation, the site is an Internet search service with an index of some 125 million unique webpages. Features include an instant translation service, content zones, and a multi-lingual capability that allows users to scan the Internet in some 25 languages including Chinese, English, French, German, and Japanese.

Ask Jeeves
http://www.askjeeves.com/
Based in Berkeley, California, the search service consists of thousands of question templates and millions of researched answer links to websites. A user types in a question in plain English and the service returns a pre-researched answer to the query.

ComFind
http://comfind.com/
Based in Los Angeles, the search service is a global business and product directory. The site is browsable by subjects such as employment, entertainment, personal finance, real estate, software, and travel.

Direct Hit
http://www.directhit.com/
Launched in 1998, the web navigation service is a "popularity" engine that lists the ten most-visited sites for any query.

Dogpile
http://www.dogpile.com
A search engine of search engines, the site scans 12 search services including Excite, InfoSeek, and Yahoo at the same time. With one query, the tool returns a consolidated list of documents and responses from numerous web navigation tools.

Excite
http://www.excite.com
Based in Redwood City, California, the search service is a personalized web start page. Localized versions of Excite are available in France, Germany, the United Kingdom, Netherlands, Sweden, Japan and Australia.

Four11
http://www.four11.com
Written in seven languages including French, Italian, and Norwegian, the site provides a searchable database of individuals and companies online. Features include a net phone search feature and a custom map generator.

Hotbot
http://www.hotbot.com
Operated by San Francisco-based Wired Digital, the search service provides directories of domain names, news sites, stocks, and jobs and resumes. Categories include computers and Internet, business and finance, entertainment and media, and people and chat.

Atlas
http://www.iatlas.com/
A subscription web navigation service, the site provides a browsable database of domain and

business information and filtering technology. The service helps users focus their searches on specific types of businesses, geographic locations, and industry sectors.

Informant
http://informant.dartmouth.edu/
A personal search agent, the site saves a user's favorite search engine queries and websites. The service periodically checks these keywords and pages online, and notifies the user by e-mail when new information is found and webpages are updated.

Infoseek
http://www.infoseek.com
Based in Sunnyvale, California, the service provides searches of the web, business listings, residential addresses, and over 12 million e-mail addresses from around the world. The service includes searchable databases for ten countries including Brazil, Germany, Japan, and the United Kingdom.

Infospace
http://www.infospace.com/
An online content aggregator, the site provides searches of yellow and white page directories, classified listings, weather forecasts, news, and electronic commerce. The service features interactive maps, city guides, and a door-to-door directions generator.

iSleuth
http://isleuth.com/
Along with business news and shopping guides, the site features a searchable index of Internet resources and web navigation tools in 18 categories including business, computers, and employment.

Livelink Pinstripe
http://pinstripe.opentext.com/
A browsable index of business resources online, the site is divided into some 20 categories including agriculture and forestry, construction, manufacturing, mining, and retail trade.

Locate.com
http://www.locate.com/
An all-in-one search page, the site is a compilation of 15 web navigation services including Dejanews, Excite, Hotbot, Infoseek, Lycos, Webcrawler, and Yahoo.

Lycos
http://www.lycos.com

Based in Waltham, Massachusetts, the site is a customizable Internet navigation resource and online information hub. The service includes road maps, website reviews, classifieds, shopping guides, and chat forums.

Northern Light
http://www.nlsearch.com
Based in Cambridge, Massachusetts, the site allows a user to search the web, along with a special collection of some four million articles and over 3,400 journals, magazines, and other databases.

Magellan
http://www.mckinley.com/
A browsable Internet guide, the site provides web searches, free e-mail, stock quotes, and a people and product finder. The service reviews websites in 16 categories including business, investing, shopping, news, and reference.

Profusion
http://www.profusion.com/
A web navigation service, the site sends queries to multiple search engines at the same time, and returns combined results.

SavvySearch
http://www.cs.colostate.edu/~dreiling/ smartform.html
A meta search tool, the site simultaneously sends a query to multiple Internet search engines and returns the complete set of results. Options include searching people, technical reports, news, software, reference, and image resources.

Starting Point
http://www.stpt.com/
A customizable web search service, the site is divided into 12 sections including business, computing, entertainment, health, and investing. Features include free e-mail, search software, product information, and stock quotes.

Webcrawler
http://www.webcrawler.com
An Internet search and directory service, the site provides news, website reviews, technology tutorials, classifieds, business listings, and a host of virtual tools such as mortgage calculators, calorie counters, and debt reduction planners.

Whowhere
http://www.whowhere.com

Based in Mountain View, California, the site features searchable directories of telephone listings, e-mail addresses, personal home pages, and business URLs. Features include free e-mail, personal homepage, and personal guide services.

Yahoo
http://www.yahoo.com
Headquartered in Santa Clara, California, the site is a network of web navigation and programming services. Features include Internet searching, news, a web-based calendar, a virtual pager, message boards, and an online store creator.

World Pages
http://www.worldpages.com/
A San Francisco-based Internet search service, the site is a browsable directory of e-mail addresses, white and yellow page listings, and webpages worldwide.

United States Media

BusinessWeek Online
http://www.businessweek.com/index.html
Homepage of *Business Week* magazine, the site provides business news, daily briefings, article excerpts, a searchable archive of past issues from the hard-copy publication, and special web content.

United States MedialNFO Links
http://www.mediainfo.com/emediajs/links-geo.htm?location=us
A service of New York City-based Editor and Publisher Interactive, the site provides a browsable directory of thousands of American media sites such as online newspapers, magazines, radio, and television services.

U.S.A. Today
http://www.usatoday.com/
Based in Arlington, Virginia, the site provides breaking U.S. and world news, money reports, sports scores, lifestyle features, and weather information.

United States Market Guides

Agriculture Online
http://www.agriculture.com
An online agriculture network, the service provides U.S. and world agricultural news, farming guides, technology tips, machinery

reviews, discussion groups, classified ads, and auction calendars and results.

American Community Network
http://www.acn.net/
A tool for corporate and site selection, the site is a searchable database of statistical information for over 3,100 counties and 315 metropolitan statistical areas in the United States. The service provides custom profiles and comparisons of population, workforce, transportation, education, taxes, incentives, and other variables.

Barclays Country Report: U.S.A.
http://www.offshorebanking.barclays.com/ services/economic/yearly/usaapr97/usacont.html
A service of Barclays Bank, the site reports on U.S. market trends, politics, monetary and fiscal policy, and foreign trade.

Big Yellow
http://www.bigyellow.com/
Containing some 16 million U.S. business listings, the site is a browsable database of American companies and organizations in over 7,000 industry categories from abdominal supports to zoos.

Business Cycle Indicators
http://www.tcb-indicators.org/
A service of the Conference Board, the site features news releases and reports on leading economic indicators in the U.S. such as manu-facturing new orders, vendor performance, building permits, stock prices, interest rate spread, and consumer expectations.

Commerce Business Daily Net
http://cbdnet.access.gpo.gov/
A service of the U.S. Department of Commerce, the site lists notices of proposed U.S. govern-ment procurement actions, contract awards, sales of government property, and other informa-tion. Published every business day, each edition contains approximately 500-1,000 new notices.

Companies Online
http://www.companiesonline.com
Sponsored by Dun & Bradstreet, the site is an online database of U.S. companies on the web. Browsable by industry categories such as natural resources and industrial technology, the service profiles over 100,000 public and private firms.

Data Web Sites for the 50 States
http://www.prb.org/news/stateweb.htm
A service of the Population Reference Bureau, the

site provides a directory of U.S. state data sources online in six categories including population, economy, lifestyles, and resources.

Doing Business in the United States
http://www.com/mmm/mmmDOBUS.html
Written by Atlanta-based attorneys Charles R. Beaudrot, Jr. and Evelyn A. Ashley, the site is a legal primer on doing business in the United States. Topics include contract principles, franchising, forms of business entities, taxation, intellectual property protection, immigration, labor law, and environmental protection laws.

Edgar Database
http://www.sec.gov/edgarhp.htm
A service of the Securities and Exchange Commission, Edgar—the Electronic Data Gathering, Analysis and Retrieval system—is a searchable database of filings by U.S. public companies to the SEC.

Federal Marketplace Procurement Data Warehouse
http://www.fedmarket.com/
An Internet procurement gateway, the site is a database of federal, state and local government purchasing agencies online in the U.S. and around the world. The service lists contracting opportunities, procurement regulations, procurement forms, and information on how to do business with the federal government.

Fedworld
http://www.fedworld.gov/index.html
A U.S. federal government information network, the site provides a searchable database of U.S. federal agencies, reports, laws, and job announcements.

Fortune 500
http://www.pathfinder.com/fortune/fortune500/
A service of *Fortune* magazine, the site is a searchable database of the Fortune 1000 and the Global 500, rankings of leading U.S. and international companies. The service lists the Chief Executive Officer, headquarters address and web address of the firms, along with data on corporate revenues, assets, profits, stock prices, and other variables.

Hoover's Online
http://www.hoovers.com/
An archive of company profiles, the site provides information on more than 13,000 public and private operations in the U.S. and around the

world. The service includes links to web homepages and stock quotes.

Industry.Net
http://www.industry.net/
An interactive marketplace for manufacturing professionals, the site features industry and regional news, online discussions, a shareware library, software demos, and a directory of manufacturing organizations and associations.

IndustrySearch
http://industrysearch.com/
Developed by Lexington, Kentucky-based Industrial Marketing Inc., the site is a browsable directory of U.S. manufacturers and industrial suppliers. Searchable by keyword and by U.S. state, the database profiles companies in over 100 industrial categories from abrasive products to zinc.

InfoExport United States
http://www.infoexport.gc.ca/continent-e.asp?continent=Usa
A service of Foreign Affairs and International Trade Canada, the site provides economic fact sheets and business guides for 11 American metro areas including Atlanta, Detroit, New York, and Seattle.

MapQuest
http://www.mapquest.com/
Based in Denver, Colorado, the site is an interactive atlas service. A user may zoom and browse maps on more than 3 million locations worldwide, obtain city-to-city and door-to-door driving directions, and create and save personalized maps.

Relocation Central
http://www.relocationcentral.com/
An online guide for businesspeople moving to or within the U.S., the site provides state profiles, city guides, relocation checklists, and a directory of moving services nationwide.

Stat-U.S.A.
http://www.stat-usa.gov/
A subscription service of the U.S. Department of Commerce, the site features statistics on U.S. economic indicators, housing and construction, employment, manufacturing and industry, money supply, economic policy, and international trade.

Thomas Register of American Manufacturers
http://www3.thomasregister.com/

An online database of U.S. and Canadian companies, the service profiles some 155,000 operations in 60,000 product headings. Access is free with registration.

Trading Process Network
http://tpn.geis.com
A service of General Electric, the site is a web-based trading network that allows buyers and sellers worldwide to conduct business-to-business electronic commerce.

United States Business Briefs
http://www.austrade.gov.au/IOOM/DETROIT/
A service of Austrade, the site provides fact sheets on United States business etiquette, foreign investment, corporate taxation, marketing, and visas.

United States Business Report
http://italchambers.net/BusinessReports.html
Prepared by the Italian Chamber of Commerce and written in Italian, the site provides United States fact sheets, market reports, and commercial guides.

United States Country Profile
http://www.tradenz.govt.nz/intelligence/profiles/united_states_of_america.html
A service of the New Zealand Trade Development Board, the site provides United States economic statistics, market information, and business tips.

United States Department of Commerce
http://www.doc.gov/
Based in Washington, D.C., the site spotlights Commerce Department programs and services. Features include a searchable index of Commerce e-mail addresses and phone numbers, a directory of small business opportunities, and primers on the department's numerous bureaus and agencies.

United States InfoExport
http://www.infoexport.gc.ca/continent-e.asp?continent=Usa
A service of Foreign Affairs and International Trade Canada, the site provides United States commercial guides and market reports.

United States Market Access Database
http://mkaccdb.eu.int/mkdb/mkdb.pl?METHOD=COUNTRY
A service of the European Commission, the site delivers briefs on United States trade policy, tariff barriers, non-tariff barriers, investment-related measures, and financial services regulations.

United States Market Information
http://dtiinfo1.dti.gov.uk/ots/usa/
A service of the London-based Department of Trade and Industry, the site delivers country fact sheets, maps, and trade show information.

United States Patent and Trademark Office
http://www.uspto.gov/
Homepage of the U.S. Patent and Trademark Office, the site provides a searchable database of U.S. patents, along with patent and trademark tutorials, statistics, public hearing transcripts, notices, and proposed legislative changes.

United States Telephone Directories
http://www.contractjobs.com/tel/us/
Written by Robert Hoare, the site reviews leading U.S. yellow and white pages, fax, toll-free, and regional directories on the web.

Wall Street Journal Annual Reports Service
http://www.icbinc.com/cgi-bin/wsj.pl
A free service of the *Wall Street Journal*, the site allows a user to order annual reports from a selection of hundreds of U.S. and international companies.

Wall Street Research Net
http://www.wsrn.com/cgi-bin/EDB/today
A searchable catalog of U.S. and Canadian company information, the site links to press releases, Securities and Exchange Commission filings, company home pages, stock charts, quotes and annual reports.

United States Trade Assistance

ACEC International Program
http://www.intl.acec.org/
A service of the American Consulting Engineers Council, the site provides project leads, matchmaking services, a monthly international business newsletter, and a directory of United States consulting engineers.

Advocacy Center
http://www.ita.doc.gov/advocacy
A unit of the International Trade Administration, the Center provides assistance to U.S. companies competing for international government contracts. The agency assists firms that are improperly treated by foreign government decision-makers, have tenders unduly delayed, or face unfair foreign competition.

Airlines in the U.S.
http://www.freightworld.com/airl_geo.html#3
A service of Freightworld, the site links to U.S. airline homepages on the web from Alaska Airlines to World Airways.

Airports in the U.S.
http://www.freightworld.com/airptgeo.html#3
A service of Freightworld, the site links to U.S. airport homepages on the Internet from Atlanta Hartsfield to Washington National.

American Export Register
http://www.aernet.com/english/
Based in New York City, the site is a searchable directory of some 45,000 U.S. exporters in 5,000 product categories. The service includes three monthly e-mail newsletters—*Buying American, Exporting from America*, and *What's New at American Export Register*. All are free with registration.

American Foreign Service Association
http://www.afsa.org/
Based in Washington, D.C., the Association represents the interests of 23,000 active and retired Foreign Service employees. The site features foreign service reports, tutorials and discussion forums.

ATA Carnet Export Service
http://www.uscib.org/frame5a.htm
A service of the U.S. Council for International Business, the site provides a primer on the ATA Carnet, a special international customs document which may be used for temporary imports and exports. The carnet is issued instead of the usual customs documents and eliminates value-added taxes, duties, and temporary import bonds.

Big Emerging Markets Home Page
http://www.ita.doc.gov/bems/index.html
A service of the International Trade Administration, the site highlights trade opportunities in 11 areas deemed by the U.S. Department of Commerce to hold the greatest potential for increases in U.S. exports. These include Argentina, Brazil, China, and India.

Business America: Magazine of International Trade
http://www.ita.doc.gov/bizam/
A service of the U.S. International Trade Administration, the site is the homepage of *Business America*, a monthly paper publication on U.S.

trade policies and programs. The site features U.S. trade news, website reviews, and a calendar of Commerce-approved trade promotion events around the world.

Commercial News U.S.A.
http://www.cnewsusa.com/index.html
An online export catalog, the site promotes U.S. products and services to international buyers. The searchable directory profiles hundreds of American exporters in dozens of sectors from advertising to water purification.

Commercial Service
http://www.ita.doc.gov/uscs/forweb.html
Part of the U.S. Department of Commerce, the Commercial Service operates offices in nearly 80 countries, and promotes U.S. exports and interests. The service supports U.S. business vying for international contracts, organizes trade missions and events, hosts business delegations, researches market conditions and trade leads, and conducts credit checks of potential overseas business partners. The site links to Commercial Service offices online around the world from Argentina to Vietnam.

Consumers for World Trade
http://www.cwt.org/
Based in Washington, D.C., Consumers for World Trade represents the interests of consumers in international trade. The site includes news, testimony, a member's directory, and reports on Congressional trade activities.

Council on International Educational Exchange
http://www.ciee.org/
A directory of international education exchanges and job opportunities for students, the site profiles leading programs in the U.S., Europe and Asia.

Environmental Export Council
http://www.eec.org/
Based in Washington, D.C., the Council promotes the export of environmental goods and services. The site provides member profiles and links, success stories, job opportunities, an event calendar, and reports on Council trade agreements with environmental business associations in Brazil, Costa Rica, Guatemala, Panama, and Singapore.

Export Education Events Nationwide
http://infoserv2.ita.doc.gov/Tradebase/Educate.nsf
A searchable database of trade education events

in the U.S., the service lists initiatives by country, industry, state, and date.

Export-Import Bank
http://www.exim.gov/
Headquartered in Washington, D.C., the Export-Import Bank or Ex-Im Bank is a U.S. government agency that helps finance the overseas sales of American goods and services. The site features country fact sheets, trade finance handbooks, and program information.

Exporter's Guide to the Euro
http://www.mac.doc.gov/euro/index.html
Prepared by the U.S. Department of Commerce, the site provides Euro glossaries, checklists, and preparation materials for American exporters.

Federation of International Trade Associations
http://www.fita.org/
An alliance of 300 international trade organizations in Canada, U.S. and Mexico, the service features a database of international trade leads, events, and employment opportunities.

Food Online
http://www.foodonline.com
A food processing resource center, the site offers food industry news, live chat, discussion forums, an event calendar, buyer's guides, free software, and product and supplier directories.

Framework for Global Electronic Commerce
http://www.iitf.nist.gov/eleccomm/ecomm.htm/
A service of the Information Infrastructure Task Force, a White House-appointed board of U.S. federal information and technology specialists, the site outlines the Clinton Administration's strategy for developing electronic commerce.

Freight Forwarders in the U.S.
http://www.freightworld.com/forw_geo.html#3
A service of Freightworld, the site links to over 100 freight forwarders online in the United States.

Global Infrastructure Projects Database
http://infoserv2.ita.doc.gov/td/Infrastr.nsf
A service of the International Trade Administration Infrastructure Division, the site provides a searchable directory of power, transportation, water, environmental, and industrial projects worldwide. Projects are browsable by project name, country, and industry.

Global Technology Network
http://www.usgtn.org/
A trade-lead matching service, the site links U.S. products and services with U.S. Agency for International Development buyers and projects worldwide. Opportunities are organized by sector such as agriculture and health and by region such as Eastern Europe and Latin America.

Intermodal Carriers in the U.S.
http://www.freightworld.com/intmod_geo.html#3
A service of Freightworld, the site links to leading intermodal carriers across the United States.

International Data Base
http://www.census.gov/ipc/www/idbnew.html
Developed by the U.S. Census Bureau, the site is a database of demographic and socioeconomic statistics for over 100 countries. The service includes interactive tables, population pyramids, and downloadable spreadsheets.

Maritime Carriers in the U.S.
http://www.freightworld.com/mari_geo.html#3
A service of Freightworld, the site links to U.S. maritime carriers online.

Market Development Cooperator Program
http://www.ita.doc.gov/industry/opcrm/mdcp.html
A competitive matching grants program, the service provides federal assistance to states, trade associations, Chambers of Commerce, world trade centers, and other nonprofit industry groups to help underwrite the start-up costs of creative export marketing ventures.

Metric Program
http://ts.nist.gov/ts/htdocs/200/202/ mpo_home.htm
Based in Gaithersburg, Maryland, the site provides metric fact sheets, Internet tools, and conversion information for U.S. federal agencies and organizations.

Multilateral Development Bank Operations Homepage
http://www.ita.doc.gov/mdbo/
A unit of the International Trade Administration, the service provides information on contracts in developing countries financed by Multilateral Development Banks such as the African Development Bank, the Caribbean Development Bank, and the European Bank for Reconstruction and Development.

National Association of Export Companies
http://www.imex.com/nexco/nexcohom.html
Based in New York, the service provides North American Free Trade Agreement updates, export tutorials, and a calendar of international trade shows and events.

National Association of Foreign Trade Zones
http://www.imex.com/naftz.html
Based in Washington, D.C., the site features free trade zone tutorials, statistics, case studies, web resources, and a member directory.

National District Export Council
http://www.ita.doc.gov/usfcs/usf/dec/
An association of U.S. business leaders with international trade experience, the Council provides counseling and mentoring services to new or aspiring U.S. exporters. The site features case studies, an event calendar, discussion forum, and business guides.

Office of Export Trading Company Affairs
http://www.ita.doc.gov/export_admin/sox3.html
Part of the International Trade Administration, the service promotes the use of export trade intermediaries and the development of export joint ventures. Programs include the Export Trade Certificate of Review, an antitrust immunity plan, and the Contact Facilitation Service, a matching service for U.S. exporters and trading houses.

Office of Trade and Economic Analysis
http://www.ita.doc.gov/tradestats
Part of the U.S. International Trade Administration, the site is a virtual library of U.S. trade data and information. Features include U.S. foreign trade highlights, industry sector data, state export data, and metropolitan area exports.

Overseas Private Investment Corporation
http://www.opic.gov/
Based in Washington, D.C., the service provides political risk insurance and financing for U.S. business projects worldwide. The site features OPIC handbooks, press releases, application forms, and an executive and staff directory.

Package Carriers in the U.S.
http://www.freightworld.com/exp_geo.html#3
A service of Freightworld, the site links to U.S. package express operations online.

Postal Services in the U.S.
http://www.freightworld.com/postal.html#3
Developed by Freightworld, the service links to U.S. postal services online.

Railroads in the U.S.
http://www.freightworld.com/railroads.html#3
Compiled by Freightworld, the page links to U.S. railroads online from the Aberdeen and Rockfish Railway Company to the Wisconsin and Southern Railroad Company.

SABIT Online
http://www.mac.doc.gov/sabit/sabit.html
Managed by the U.S. Department of Commerce, SABIT—the Special American Business Internship Training Program—provides financial assistance to eligible U.S. companies to train executives and managers from the former Soviet Union.

Seaports in the U.S.
http://www.freightworld.com/port_geo.html#3
Prepared by Freightworld, the site links to U.S. seaports online from the Port of Baltimore to the Port of Wilmington.

Service Corps of Retired Executives
http://www.score.org/
A network of U.S. small business advisors, the service features free e-mail counseling, financial management guides, success stories, and business start-up tutorials.

Standards Information Program
http://ts.nist.gov/ts/htdocs/210/217/217.htm
A service of the National Institute of Standards and Technology, the site reports on U.S. and international standards, technical regulations, and conformity assessment procedures.

Top Targets for Trade Promotion
http://infoserv2.ita.doc.gov/Tradebase/TOPTAR.NSF
A service of the International Trade Administration, the service highlights leading export opportunities for U.S. firms between 1998 and 2000. Viewable by country, industry and world rank, the targets were based on U.S. export capabilities and international market demand forecasts.

Tracking U.S. Trade
http://www.lanic.utexas.edu/cswht/tradeindex/index.html
Developed by the Center for the Study of Western Hemispheric Trade at the University of Texas, the site is a database of U.S. export and import statistics from 1995 to the latest available.

Trade Compliance Center
http://www.mac.doc.gov/tcc/index.html
A unit of the International Trade Administration, the site provides a database of U.S. trade agreements, commercial guides, and trade policy summaries. The service includes global economic reports, success stories, tutorials, and a trade complaint hotline for U.S. businesspeople who encounter trade barriers.

Trade Event calendar

http://infoserv2.ita.doc.gov/epc.nsf
Compiled by the International Trade Administration, the site is a browsable database of trade promotion events organized by U.S. government agencies. The events are organized by industry, country, and event type such as a trade mission, reverse trade mission, or matchmaker.

Trade Events Hub

http://www.fita.org/conferences.shtml
A service of the Federation of International Trade Association, the site is a browsable database of seminars, conferences and trade shows related to international business. The directory is searchable by topic, sponsor, location, and date.

Trade Information Center

http://www.ita.doc.gov/tic/
An online guide to U.S. federal export assistance, the site features country guides, trade leads, financing tutorials, foreign tariffs, and customs information. The service includes a directory of federal and state government trade offices nationwide.

Trade U.S.

http://www.tradeus.com/
A virtual primer on exporting to the U.S., the U.K.-based site provides U.S. trade leads, labeling and packaging fact sheets, technical standards information, and electronic business guides.

Trucking and Motor Carriers in the U.S.

http://www.freightworld.com/truc_geo.html#3
Developed by Freightworld, the site links to U.S. trucking and motor carriers online from Alaska West Express to Yellow Freight System.

U.S. Agency for International Development

http://www.info.usaid.gov/about/
Established in 1961 by President John F. Kennedy, the Agency provides economic development and humanitarian assistance worldwide. The site includes U.S. AID policy papers, movie clips, country information, and procurement bulletins.

U.S.-Asia Environmental Partnership

http://www.usaep.org/
Based in Washington, D.C., the Partnership links Asian environmental needs with U.S. environmental products and services. The service provides trade leads, exchange programs, business partnerships, country assessments, and environmental management reports.

U.S. Association of Importers of Textiles and Apparel

http://www.usaita.com/
Based in New York, the Association promotes the interests of U.S. textile and apparel importers. The site features trade publications, job classifieds, and links to member sites.

U.S. Bureau of Export Administration

http://www.bxa.doc.gov/
Based in Washington, D.C., the Bureau controls U.S. exports for national security, foreign policy, and short supply reasons. The site provides Bureau press releases, speeches, testimony, and export control lists.

U.S. Business Advisor

http://www.business.gov/
A one-stop resource center for U.S. federal government information, the service provides primers on the International Trade Administration, Federal Communications Commission, Small Business Administration, Social Security, U.S. Postal Service, Environmental Protection Agency, Internal Revenue Service and other federal agencies that assist or regulate American business.

U.S. Business Council for Southeastern Europe

http://www.usbizcouncil.org/
Based in New York City, the Council promotes U.S. trade with Albania, Bosnia, Bulgaria, Croatia, Macedonia, Romania, Slovenia, and the Former Republic of Yugoslavia. The site features country profiles, an event calendar, and membership information.

U.S. Council for International Business

http://www.uscib.org/
Headquartered in New York City, the Council advances the global trade interests of U.S. business. The site includes news, press releases, policy papers, committee profiles, member directories, electronic commerce tutorials, and ATA Carnet services.

U.S. Department of State

http://www.state.gov/
Homepage of the U.S. Department of State, America's lead foreign affairs agency, the site offers senior official biographies, annual reports, an online telephone directory, and electronic magazines. The service includes directories of Foreign Service officers, U.S. missions online, Foreign Consular offices in the U.S., country offices, and diplomatic staff of foreign governments in Washington.

U.S. Diplomatic Posts Abroad
http://www.usia.gov/regional/posts/posts.htm#AF
A service of the U.S. Information Agency, the site is a directory of U.S. diplomatic posts online. The links are divided into seven sections: Africa, American Republics, East Asia and Pacific, Europe, Near East and North Africa, South Asia, and International Organizations.

U.S. Export Assistance Directory
http://www.ita.doc.gov/uscs/domfld.html
Developed by the U.S. Department of Commerce, the site is a directory of Export Assistance Centers in each U.S. state from Alaska to West Virginia. The Centers provide export counseling and trade finance services to American companies.

U.S. Exporter Search
http://www.tradecompass.com/mktplace/company.html
A service of Trade Compass, the site is a U.S. exporters database searchable by product, standard industrial code, company, state, city, and zip code.

U.S. Foreign Agricultural Service
http://www.fas.usda.gov/
An agency of the U.S. Department of Commerce, the Service promotes U.S. agricultural exports. The site features agricultural trade circulars, world market forecasts, commodity statistics, country pages, buyer alerts, export counseling, and satellite imagery.

U.S. Foreign Agricultural Service Hot Country Pages
http://www.fas.usda.gov/hotpages/
A service of the U.S. Foreign Agricultural Service, the site provides attaché reports, and import and export statistics for over 100 countries from Afghanistan to Zimbabwe. Features include a searchable trade-leads database that generates custom reports by country, date, and commodity.

U.S. Government Electronic Commerce Policy
http://www.ecommerce.gov/
Maintained by the U.S. Department of Commerce, the site features U.S. government policy papers and documents on electronic commerce.

U.S. Import Administration
http://www.ita.doc.gov/import_admin/records/
A branch of the U.S. Department of Commerce, the U.S. Import Administration enforces laws and agreements to prevent unfairly traded imports. The site offers Federal Register notices, a trade

remedies tutorial, policy bulletins, statistics, an import document library, and a list of foreign cases against U.S. firms.

U.S. Imports/Exports History
http://govinfo.kerr.orst.edu/impexp.html
Posted by Oregon State University, the site is a browsable database of U.S. import and export statistics from 1993 to 1997. The database generates custom reports by commodity, country of export or import, and U.S. city of export or import.

U.S. Information Agency International
http://www.usia.gov/usis.html
With more than 200 posts in 143 countries, the U.S. Information Agency provides U.S. information and education programs. Along with primers on American history, politics, geography, culture and media, the site delivers U.S. foreign policy news, electronic journals, regional reports, and international exchange and training information.

U.S. International Trade Administration
http://www.ita.doc.gov/
A branch of the U.S. Department of Commerce, the International Trade Administration or ITA promotes U.S. exports and regulates unfair trade practices. The site provides trade news, statistics, program directories, and reports on global business opportunities by region and by industry.

U.S. International Trade Commission
http://www.usitc.gov/
Based in Washington, D.C., the Commission studies U.S. international trade issues and takes action against unfair trade practices. The site includes news releases, recent petitions and complaints, a monthly calendar of hearings, antidumping and countervailing duty handbooks, summaries of past investigations, and Federal Register notices and rules of procedure.

U.S. International Trade Statistics
http://www.census.gov/foreign-trade/www/
A service of the U.S. Census Bureau, the site contains commodity level trade data, export classification assistance, trade balances with partner countries, a profile of U.S. exporting companies, and a browsable directory of commodity classifications by keyword and 10-digit identification code.

U.S. Small Business Administration Office of International Trade
http://www.sba.gov/oit/
Based in Washington, D.C., the Office provides

programs and information for new exporters, small business, and trade financiers in the United States. The site includes contact information and an event calendar.

U.S. Trade Center
http://www.ustradecenter.com/
With offices in Buffalo, New York and Seattle, Washington, the U.S. Trade Center provides information and assistance to Canadian companies exporting to the United States. Along with American trade news and tax advice, the site provides tutorials on choosing a distribution channel, finding customers, and establishing a corporation in the United States.

U.S. Trade and Development Agency
http://www.tda.gov
Based in Arlington, Virginia, the Agency provides financial assistance to eligible U.S. companies to conduct feasibility studies, orientation visits, and other activities as part of bids for infrastructure and industrial projects worldwide. The site includes trade news, an event calendar, and a searchable library of Agency-funded studies by international trade consultants.

U.S. Trade Representative
http://www.ustr.gov/
Based in Washington, D.C., the United States Trade Representative develops and negotiates U.S. international trade and investment policy. The site provides complete versions of major international agreements, declarations, and statements related to trade such as the Summit of the Americas, the Multilateral Agreement on Investment, and the Information Technology Agreement. The service also includes U.S.T.R. speeches and testimony, biographies of agency officials, and dozens of reports such as Global Electronic Commerce proposals, World Trade Organization reviews, and foreign trade barrier studies.

Women in International Trade
http://www.embassy.org/wiit/
Based in Washington, D.C., Women in International Trade promotes the role of women in international trade. The site includes trade news, an event calendar, job bank, directory of executives, and a 1998 member survey on international trade.

United States Representative Offices

Foreign Trade Offices Database
http://infoserv2.ita.doc.gov/FTOHomeP.nsf
Developed by the U.S. Department of Commerce, the site is a searchable directory of foreign customs authorities around the world, and foreign chambers of commerce and embassies in the United States.

Afghanistan

Islamic State of Afghanistan Online Embassy
http://www.afghan-government.com/
Based in Washington, D.C., the site features Afghanistan news, links, Embassy and visa information, and a directory of leading government Ministers.

Angola

Embassy of the Republic of Angola in Washington, D.C.
http://www.angola.org/
An official website of the Republic of Angola, the site features Angolan news, fast facts, trade and investment guides, a business bulletin board, bimonthly newsletter, and an event calendar.

U.S. Angola Chamber of Commerce
http://ourworld.compuserve.com/homepages/usacc/
Based in Washington, D.C., the Chamber promotes U.S.-Angola trade. The site includes a mission statement, news, event information, publications list, and member directory.

Argentina

Embassy of Argentina in Washington, D.C.
http://emb-eeuu.mrecic.gov.ar/
The virtual Embassy reports on Argentina news, agriculture, consular affairs, foreign policy, science and technology, and international trade. The service includes directories of Argentine Consulates in the U.S., Argentine companies in the U.S., and U.S. companies in Argentina.

Armenia

Armenian Embassy in the U.S.
http://www.armeniaemb.org/
Home page of the Armenian Embassy, the site provides Armenian news, country reports, visa regulations, government contacts, and fact sheets on travel, foreign relations, and investment opportunities.

Association of Southeast Asian Nations

United States-ASEAN Business Council
http://www.us-asean.org/
Based in Washington, D.C., the Council promotes trade between the United States and the member countries of the Association of Southeast Asian Nations including Brunei Darussalam, Indonesia, Laos, and Malaysia. The site includes testimony, speeches, press releases, and event information.

Australia

Austrade in Washington, D.C.
http://www.austrade.gov.au/washington/
Based in Washington, D.C., the service promotes Australian products and services to World Bank procurement agencies.

Australian New Zealand American Chambers of Commerce
http://www.austemb.org/aacchead.htm
With offices in Canberra, Sydney, Auckland, Christchurch, and Washington, D.C., the Chambers promote Australian-New Zealand-U.S. Trade. The site provides a directory of Chamber offices and executives in the three countries.

Embassy of Australia in Washington, D.C.
http://www.austemb.org/
Featuring greetings from Prime Minister John Howard, the site features primers on Australian business and investment, visas and immigration, flora and fauna, geography and history, travel and tourism, and people and culture.

Austria

Austrian Trade Commission in Washington, D.C.
http://www.austriantrade.org/AustrianTrade/offices/ahst_was.htm
Part of the Austrian Trade Commission network, the site lists the names, addresses, phone and fax numbers, and e-mail addresses of the Austrian Embassy Trade Commissioner and Deputy Trade Commissioner.

Austrian Trade Commissions in the U.S. and Canada
http://www.webhost.net/AustrianTrade/
An Austrian trade promotion service, the site features Austrian economic facts, business leads, links, a worldwide office directory, tutorials on exporting to Austria, and a calendar of Commission-sponsored events in Canada and the United States.

Azerbaijan

Embassy of Azerbaijan in Washington, D.C.
http://azembassy.com/
The virtual Embassy provides Azerbaijan news, fact sheets, political briefing papers, visa and passport information, and a calendar of events.

U.S.-Azerbaijan Chamber of Commerce
http://www.usacc.com/
Based in Washington, D.C., the Chamber promotes U.S.-Azerbaijan trade and relations. The site includes Chamber news, a member directory, investment guides, and contact information.

U.S. Azerbaijan Council
http://ourworld.compuserve.com/homepages/usazerb/
Based in Washington, D.C., the service features Azerbaijan news, an event calendar, a key contacts directory, and two business webzines, *Caspian Crossroads* and *Caspian Business Report*.

Bangladesh

Bangladesh Embassy in Washington, D.C.
http://members.aol.com/banglaemb/main.htm
With an introduction by Ambassador K.M. Shehabuddin, the site provides a Bangladesh country profile, photo archive, and directory of Embassy services.

Belgium

Belgian-American Chamber of Commerce
http://www.belgium-emb.org/usa/representatives/usa_chamber_of_commerce.html
Based in New York, the service offers Road Show, a trade promotion initiative that helps Belgian exporters either attend or distribute

marketing materials at selected U.S. trade shows.

Embassy of Belgium in Washington, D.C.
http://www.belgium-emb.org/usa/
Developed by the Belgian Ministry of Foreign Affairs, the site features Belgian news, business memos, general country information, travel tips, and trade and investment guides. The service includes directories of Belgian representatives in the U.S. and Belgians worldwide.

Bosnia and Herzegovina

Embassy of Bosnia and Herzegovina in Washington, D.C.
http://www.bosnianembassy.org/
An archive of Bosnian country and business information, the site provides searchable directories of Bosnian government ministries, reconstruction projects, investment opportunities, banks, construction and engineering companies, and diplomatic offices.

Brazil

Brazilian American Chamber of Commerce
http://www.brazilcham.com/
Based in New York, the service delivers Brazilian trade news, leads, contacts, sectoral bulletins, and an events directory.

Brazilian Embassy in Washington, D.C.
http://www.brasil.emb.nw.dc.us/
Written in English and Portuguese, the site reports on Brazilian business, foreign policy, consular services, science and technology, and eco-tourism.

Brunei Darussalam

Embassy of Brunei Darussalam in Washington, D.C.
http://www.brunet.bn/homepage/gov/bruemb/govemb.htm
The site provides contact information for the Brunei Darussalam Embassy in Washington, D.C.

Bulgaria

Embassy of Bulgaria in Washington, D.C.
http://www.bulgaria.com/embassy/wdc/
Homepage of the Bulgarian Embassy, the site includes Bulgarian news, country primers, foreign investment reports, web links, and a directory of consular services.

U.S.-Bulgaria Trade Council
http://www.internationalcenter.com/bulgaria.htm
Based in Washington, D.C., the site delivers Bulgarian news, commercial guides, and tutorials on marketing U.S. products and services in Bulgaria.

Cambodia

Embassy of Cambodia in Washington, D.C.
http://www.embassy.org/cambodia/
Homepage of the Royal Embassy, the site reports on Cambodian news, government, education, business, investment, tourism, visa requirements, and consular services.

Canada

Canadian Embassy in Washington, D.C.
http://www.cdnemb-washdc.org/
Written in English and French, the service provides Canadian news, fact sheets, travel and passport information, and a directory of business development officers in the Embassy.

Can-Am Border Trade Alliance
http://www.rrtrade.org/can-am/
Based in Lewiston, New York, the service promotes U.S.-Canada trade and investment. The site includes an event calendar, member directory, and a list of working committees.

International Center for Canadian-American Trade
http://www.iccat.org/
Based in Port Huron, Michigan, the service reports on Canada-U.S. trade, non-tariff trade barriers, environmental and labor standards, and cross-border paperwork. Features include a Canadian-American Business Research Guide, editorials on Canada-U.S. trade disputes, and *Seamless Trader*, a free trade webzine.

China

China Council for the Promotion of International Trade in Washington, D.C.
http://www.ccpit.org/engVersion/cp_about/cp_over/cp_over.html
A Chinese export promotion service, the site provides contact information for the China Council for the Promotion of International Trade Office in Washington, D.C.

Chinese Embassy in Washington, D.C.
http://www.china-embassy.org/
Featuring a welcome by Li Zhaoxing, Chinese Ambassador to the U.S., the site features Chinese news, fact sheets, issue statements, regional profiles, visa and passport information, and a directory of Chinese scholars abroad.

Colombia

Embassy of Colombia in Washington, D.C.
http://www.colombiaemb.org/
Homepage of the Colombian Embassy, the site profiles Colombian trade, culture, education, tourism, and business. A monthly bulletin provides breaking economic and political news.

Croatia

Embassy of Croatia in Washington, D.C.
http://www.croatiaemb.org/
An online service of the Croatian government, the site features Croatian fact sheets, press releases, economic statistics, foreign investment reports, and business guides.

Czech Republic

Czech Companies in the U.S.
http://www.czech.cz/washington/ekon/eco-23.htm
A service of the Czech Embassy, the site is a directory of Czech companies in the United States.

Embassy of the Czech Republic in Washington, D.C.
http://www.czech.cz/washington/
Written in English and Czech, the site provides Czech news, fact sheets, business guides, company directories, visa information, and a listing of cultural and trade promotion events at the Embassy.

Denmark

Embassy of Denmark in Washington, D.C.
http://www.denmarkemb.org/
Homepage of the Royal Danish Embassy, the site provides Danish news, fact sheets, bulletin boards, visa information, and web links. The service includes two free webzines, *Invest in Denmark* and *Denmark Investment News Update.*

Dominican Republic

Embassy of the Dominican Republic in Washington, D.C.
http://www.domrep.org/
Based in Washington, D.C., the site reports on Dominican Republic free trade zones, business associations, shipping, investments, and consular services.

Ecuador

Embassy of Ecuador in Washington, D.C.
http://www.ecuador.org/
Written in English and Spanish, the site features Ecuadorian news, fact sheets, business guides, international trade reports, travel and tourism information, cultural lessons, and government directories.

Egypt

American Egyptian Chamber of Commerce
http://www.aceus.org/
Based in Washington, D.C., the Chamber promotes American-Egyptian trade. The site includes a mission statement, event calendar, and contact information.

Estonia

Estonian Embassy in Washington, D.C.
http://www.estemb.org/pages/tere.htm
A hub of country information, the site includes Estonian news, maps, fact sheets, travel and visa information, business guides, and government directories.

Ethiopia

Embassy of Ethiopia in Washington, D.C.
http://www.nicom.com/~ethiopia/
A virtual guide to Ethiopia, the site features Ethiopian daily news, a monthly newsletter, fact sheets, travel guides, economic profiles, and directories of the leading exporters and importers.

European Union

European-American Business Council
http://www.eabc.org/
Headquartered in Washington, D.C., the Council

promotes European-American trade. The site features Council press releases, public statements, staff profiles, a member directory, and a calendar of events.

European Union in the U.S.
http://www.eurunion.org/
Based in Washington, D.C., the site delivers European Union news, fact sheets, member state profiles, legislative bulletins, and reports on European Union-U.S. trade and relations.

Fiji

Embassy of Fiji in Washington, D.C.
http://fiji.gov.fj/core/fj_mis.html
The site provides contact information for the Fiji Embassy in Washington, D.C.

Finland

Embassy of Finland in Washington, D.C.
http://www.finland.org/
A service of the Finnish government, the site includes Finnish daily news, press releases, country facts, an event calendar, media links, bulletin boards, and a RealAudio English radio service.

Finnish American Chamber of Commerce
http://www.finlandtrade.com/
Based in New York, the site offers a directory of key Finnish government and corporate contacts, an event calendar, and *Headlines*, a quarterly electronic magazine on Finnish-American trade.

France

French Embassy in Washington, D.C.
http://www.info-france-usa.org/
Part of the largest French diplomatic mission in the world, the website offers a daily press briefing, French profiles, trade reports, government directories, media links, research fact sheets, and cultural information.

Germany

German American Business Association
http://www.psii-worldwide.com/gabaus/
Based in Alexandria, Virginia, the Association promotes German-American trade. The site provides an event calendar, membership information, and business matchmaking services.

German Embassy in Washington, D.C.
http://www.germany-info.org/
An online German information center, the site delivers German news, weather bulletins, socioeconomic statistics, government directories, and streaming video and radio services.

Ghana

Embassy of Ghana in Washington, D.C.
http://www.ghana-embassy.org/
An online Ghana resource page, the site provides Ghana news, country profiles, tourism information, business guides, and a directory of upcoming events.

Greece

Embassy of Greece in Washington, D.C.
http://www.greekembassy.org/
The Hellenic Republic site reports on Greek news, culture, history, and government. A business and economy section provides investment guides, tax tips, and tutorials on how to establish a company in Greece.

Guatemala

Embassy of Guatemala in Washington, D.C.
http://www.mdngt.org/agremilusa/embassy.html
Written in English and Spanish, the site provides Guatemala travel guides, contact information, and a directory of consular staff.

Guatemalan Military Attaché
http://www.mdngt.org/agremilusa/
Part of the Guatemalan Embassy, the site provides Guatemalan country profiles, armed forces information, and peace accord reports.

Guyana

Embassy of Guyana in Washington, D.C.
http://www.wam.umd.edu/~swi/embassy.htm
Posted by Safraz W. Ishmael, the site lists the address, phone and fax numbers, and e-mail address of the Embassy of Guyana in Washington, D.C.

Haiti

Embassy of Haiti in Washington, D.C.
http://www.haiti.org/embassy/
Written in English and French, the site provides

Haitian country fact sheets, government directories, business resources, travel tips, and visa information.

Hungary

Embassy of Hungary in Washington, D.C.
http://www.hungaryemb.org/
Featuring an audio message from Ambassador György Bánlaki, the site provides Hungarian news, country fact sheets, visa information, travel guides, and a directory of Hungarian representative offices in the United States.

Hungary American Chamber of Commerce
http://www.hungaryemb.org/
HunAmChamCom.htm
A service of the Embassy of Hungary, the site provides contact information for Hungarian-American Chamber of Commerce offices in the states of California, Florida, Hawaii, Illinois, New Jersey, Pennsylvania, and Washington.

Iceland

Embassy of Iceland in Washington, D.C.
http://www.iceland.org/
A country information hub, the site features Iceland daily news, visa regulations, tourism guides, business primers, cultural bulletins, foreign policy statements, and an online bulletin board.

Icelandic American Chamber of Commerce
http://www.icelandtrade.com/
Based in New York, the site offers Icelandic-American trade news, event information, and business matchmaking services.

India

Embassy of India in Washington, D.C.
http://www.indianembassy.org/
Posted by the Embassy's Press, Information and Culture Wing, the site provides Indian press releases, newsletters, policy statements, event listings, visa and passport information, government directories, and U.S.-India trade reports.

U.S.-India Business Council
http://www.usibc.com/
Based in Washington, D.C., the Council promotes U.S.-India trade. The site includes a mission statement, member directory, staff profiles, event information, and Indian news.

Indonesia

Embassy of Indonesia in Washington, D.C.
http://www.kbri.org/
Written in English and Indonesian, the site offers Indonesian news, country profiles, cost of living facts, agricultural import regulations, visa information, and a directory of Indonesia trade promotion centers around the world.

United States-Indonesia Society
http://www.usembassyjakarta.org/usindo.html
Formed in 1994, the Society promotes United States-Indonesia relations. The site includes a mission statement, program directory, and contact information.

Iran

Iran Office in Washington, D.C.
http://www.daftar.org/default_eng.htm
The Islamic Republic of Iran website provides Iranian customs information, exit permits, visa application forms, passport requirements, and conference schedules.

Israel

Association of American-Israel Chambers of Commerce
http://www.israeltrade.org/
With offices in 15 cities across the U.S., the Association promotes U.S.-Israel trade. The site includes a member directory, event information, Israeli business guides, and reports on U.S. trade missions to Israel.

Embassy of Israel in Washington, D.C.
http://www.israelemb.org/
The Israeli Embassy homepage provides Israeli news, country guides, economic reports, visa and travel information, government directories, and video clips.

Guide to Promoting Israel-U.S. Trade
http://www.std.com/neicc/read.html
Developed by the New England-Israel Chamber of Commerce, the site provides Israeli business guides, investment information, and a directory of leading trade associations and economic development programs.

U.S. Israel Biotechnology Council
http://www.usibc.org/
Based in Bethesda, Maryland, the Council promotes U.S.-Israel collaboration in biotechnol-

ogy research and development. The site includes a mission statement, newsletter, member directory, and strategic partnering opportunities.

Italy

Embassy of Italy in Washington, D.C.
http://www.italyemb.org/
The site delivers Italian news, country and regional profiles, travel tips, economic and trade statistics, a discussion forum, and a directory of Italian diplomatic posts and organizations in the United States.

Italy-America Chamber of Commerce
http://www.italian-chamber.com/
Written in English and Italian, the site includes a member directory, business opportunities, trade news, and event calendar.

Jamaica

Embassy of Jamaica in Washington, D.C.
http://www.caribbean-online.com/jamaica/embassy/washdc/
Featuring a welcome from the Ambassador, the webpage features Jamaican news, fact sheets, entry and work requirements, economic reports, and a directory of trade and investment incentives.

Japan

Embassy of Japan in Washington, D.C.
http://www.embjapan.org/
The Embassy service provides Japanese news, country profiles, visa information, a local event calendar, reports on Japan-U.S. relations, and links to Japanese government organizations.

JETRO U.S.A.
http://www.JETRO.org/
Based in New York, JETRO U.S.A.—the Japan External Trade Organization U.S. office—is a Japanese government agency that promotes Japan-U.S. trade. The site includes JETRO news, press releases, an event calendar, and export product showcase.

Jordan

Embassy of Jordan in Washington, D.C.
http://www.jordanembassyus.org/
The Hashemite Kingdom of Jordan service offers Jordanian press releases, Embassy events,

frequently asked questions and answers about the country, and *Jordan Issues and Perspectives*, a free electronic newsletter on Jordanian politics and business.

Kenya

Embassy of Kenya in Washington, D.C.
http://www.embassyofkenya.com/
Featuring a welcome by Ambassador Dr. Benjamin E. Kipkorir, the site provides briefs on Kenyan education, tourism, politics, foreign policy, business, and immigration. A government section lists key Kenyan executives, ministries, and addresses.

Kuwait

Kuwait Information Office in Washington, D.C.
http://www.kuwait.info.nw.dc.us/
Developed by the Kuwait Ministry of Information, the site features Kuwaiti news, fact sheets, industry profiles, education reports, government directories, and a list of Kuwaiti antiquities and museums.

Kyrgyzstan

Embassy of the Kyrgyz Republic in Washington, D.C.
http://www.kyrgyzstan.org/
The Kyrgyz Republic website reports on Kyrgyz travel, business, events, politics, history, culture, current affairs, and consular services.

North American Kyrgyz Business Council
http://www.kyrgyzstan.org/council.html
Based in Falls Church, Virginia, the website provides a member directory and Kyrgyz business reports.

Laos

Embassy of Laos in Washington, D.C.
http://www.laoembassy.com/
Updated daily, the site offers Laos news, country profiles, travel guides, and a directory of leading government officials.

Latvia

Embassy of Latvia in Washington, D.C.
http://www.virtualglobe.com/latvia/
Featuring a message from Ambassador Ojars Kalnins, the site provides Latvian fact sheets,

visa information, customs regulations, business guides, and travel tips.

Lebanon

Embassy of Lebanon in Washington, D.C.
http://www.embofleb.org/
The Embassy homepage provides Lebanon news, business primers, travel guides, visa and passport information, demographic and economic statistics, and an employment and business bulletin board.

Liberia

Embassy of Liberia in Washington, D.C.
http://www.liberiaemb.org/
The Republic of Liberia service offers Liberian country fact sheets, visa and consular information, business guides, and reports on health and education services.

Madagascar

Embassy of Madagascar in Washington, D.C.
http://www.embassy.org/madagascar/
The online service provides Madagascan news, fact sheets, tourism information, and a directory of foreign organizations in Madagascar.

Malaysia

Embassy of Malaysia in Washington, D.C.
http://www.mnet.com.my/klonline/www/missions/ malmiss/musa1.htm
The site provides contact information for the Malaysian Embassy in Washington, D.C.

Marshall Islands

Embassy of the Marshall Islands in Washington, D.C.
http://www.rmiembassyus.org/usemb.html
The Marshall Islands diplomatic site lists available intern positions, cultural bulletins, and a directory of Embassy staff.

Mauritania

Embassy of Mauritania in Washington, D.C.
http://embassy.org/mauritania/
The online service features Mauritania news, fact sheets, a photo gallery, weather bulletins, and travel guides.

Mauritius

Embassy of Mauritius in Washington, D.C.
http://www.idsonline.com/usa/embasydc.html
Featuring greetings by Ambassador Chitmansin Jesseramsing, the site reviews Mauritius passport regulations, visa and entry requirements, and consular services.

Micronesia

Embassy of Micronesia in Washington, D.C.
http://www.fsmembassy.org/
The virtual Embassy provides Micronesia news, country profiles, press releases, a photo gallery, investment guides, job announcements, visa information, and an Embassy staff directory.

Moldova

Moldova Online
http://www.moldova.org/
Homepage of the Moldova Embassy in Washington, D.C., the site provides Moldova fact sheets, news, economic bulletins, and trade mission reports.

Mongolia

Embassy of Mongolia in Washington, D.C.
http://www.mongolnet.com/monemb.htm
The diplomatic service provides Mongolian news, country profiles, economic reports, trade guides, foreign investment policies, visa information, and a directory of Mongolian companies.

U.S.-Mongolia Business Council
http://www.internationalcenter.com/mongolia.htm
Based in Washington, D.C., the Council promotes U.S.-Mongolian trade. The site includes a mission statement, membership information, and intern opportunities.

Namibia

Embassy of Namibia in Washington, D.C.
http://www.republicofnamibia.com/adress.htm
Along with a directory of Namibian companies and government agencies, the site provides contact information for the Namibian Embassy in Washington, D.C.

Nepal

Embassy of Nepal in Washington, D.C.
http://www.newweb.net/nepal_embassy/
A service of the Royal Nepalese Embassy, the
site provides information on Nepali passports,
visas, publications, international trade, and
consular services.

Netherlands

Embassy of the Netherlands in Washington, D.C.
http://www.netherlands-embassy.org/
The digital Embassy delivers Dutch news,
country profiles, business guides, sectoral
reports, government links, and visa and passport
information.

New Zealand

Embassy of New Zealand in Washington, D.C.
http://www.emb.com/nzemb/
Featuring the New Zealand national anthem in
streaming audio, the site provides New Zealand
country facts, travel guides, visa and immigration
information, and a directory of New Zealand
Embassies and Chambers of Commerce online.

Norway

Embassy of Norway in Washington, D.C.
http://www.norway.org/
Developed by Team Norway U.S.A., the site offers
Norwegian news, business guides, government
directories, tourism information, an event
calendar, and culture and history fact sheets.

Norwegian American Chamber of Commerce
http://www.norway.org/NACC/
Based in New York City, the Chamber promotes
Norwegian-American trade. The site provides a
mission statement, event calendar, membership
information, and directory of Chamber offices in
the United States.

Norwegian Trade Council in Washington, D.C.
http://www.norway.org/trade/mainbod3.html#wdc
The site lists the street address, phone and fax
numbers, e-mail links, and staff profiles of the
Norwegian Trade Council in Washington, D.C.

Pakistan

Embassy of Pakistan in Washington, D.C.

http://www.pakistan-embassy.com/
Developed by the Embassy Information Division,
the site provides Pakistani news, press releases,
foreign affairs statements, government directories, passport and visa information, and product
catalogs.

Paraguay

Paraguayan-American Chamber of Commerce
http://www.vimc.com/pacc/
Based in Miami, the site lists the Chamber's
mission statement, board of directors, recent
activities, and membership categories.

Philippines

Philippine Embassy in Washington, D.C.
http://www.sequel.net/RPinUS/WDC/
The Embassy service features Philippine
business opportunities, tourist guides, an event
calendar, and consular information.

Philippine Trade and Investment Promotion Office in Washington, D.C.
http://www.dti.gov.ph/WDC/
The site provides a mission statement, service
directory, and contact information for the Philippine Trade Office in Washington, D.C.

Poland

Embassy of Poland in Washington, D.C.
http://www.polishworld.com/polemb/
Written in English and Polish, the site delivers
Polish news, country facts, business guides,
travel tips, scientific developments, consular
information, and a list of Polish Cabinet members.

Polish American Chamber of Commerce
http://inglot.com/polcom.html
Based in Chicago, the site features Chamber
news, press releases, admission requirements,
a member directory, and contact information.

Portugal

Portuguese Trade and Investment Office in Washington, D.C.
http://www.portugal.org/geninfo/abouticep/newyork.html
The site lists the staff, street address, phone and
fax numbers, and e-mail link of the Portuguese
Trade and Investment Office in Washington, D.C.

Romania

Embassy of Romania in Washington, D.C.
http://www.embassy.org/romania/
The Embassy page offers Romanian news, travel tips, trade guides, economic statistics, investment opportunities, and cultural fact sheets.

Romanian American Chamber of Commerce
http://www.romamcc.org/
Based in Washington, D.C., the site provides Romanian business guides, executive profiles, speeches, sector profiles, and trade reports.

Romanian American Enterprise Fund
http://www.raef.com/
Established in 1994 by the U.S. Congress, the Fund provides financing to Romanian small business. The site lists the Fund's loan programs, eligibility requirements, board of directors, and major projects.

Russia

Embassy of Russia in Washington, D.C.
http://www.russianembassy.org/
Updated daily, the site provides Russian news, country facts, business reports, travel guides, and visa information.

Russian American Chamber of Commerce
http://www.rmi.net/racc/
Based in Aurora, Colorado, the Chamber promotes Russian-American trade. The site includes Russian business news, activity reports, an events directory, corporate profiles, visa information, and interactive maps.

Rwanda

Embassy of Rwanda in Washington, D.C.
http://www.rwandemb.org/
The Embassy service delivers Rwandan news, country profiles, travel guides, business reports, judicial briefings, visa information, and an online bulletin board.

Saint Kitts and Nevis

Embassy of Saint Kitts and Nevis in Washington, D.C.
http://www.stkittsnevis.net/offices.html
The site provides contact information for the Saint Kitts and Nevis Embassy in Washington, D.C.

Saudi Arabia

Royal Embassy of Saudi Arabia in Washington, D.C.
http://www.saudi.net/
Featuring a message from Ambassador Prince Bandar Bin Sultan, the site features Saudi news, country profiles, travel information, a monthly newsletter, a quarterly electronic magazine, multimedia presentations, and reports on Saudi-U.S. relations.

U.S.-Saudi Arabian Business Council
http://www.us-saudi-business.org/
Based in New York City, the Council promotes U.S.-Saudi trade and investment. The site provides a member directory, export documentation, and contact information.

Serbia and Montenegro

Embassy of Former Yugoslavia in Washington, D.C.
http://ourworld.compuserve.com/homepages/yuembassy/
The diplomatic website features former-Yugoslavia news, maps, country facts, and a directory of consular services.

Singapore

Embassy of Singapore in Washington, D.C.
http://www.gov.sg/mfa/consular/mww_u.htm
The site provides contact information for the Singapore Embassy in Washington, D.C.

Slovakia

Embassy of Slovakia in Washington, D.C.
http://www.slovakemb.com/
The virtual Embassy features Slovak country fact sheets, economic data, travel guides, consular and visa information, and a directory of Slovak organizations in the United States.

South Africa

South African Embassy Staff and Functions
http://www.southafrica.net/welcome.html
Featuring a welcome by Ambassador Franklin Sonn, the site provides South African news, tourism information, an event calendar, arts and culture guides, sector profiles, and a trade opportunities bulletin board.

South Africa Foreign Trade Office in Washington, D.C.
http://wwwdti.pwv.gov.za/dtiwww/
foreign_offices.htm
A service of the South Africa Department of Trade and Industry, the site provides contact information for the South Africa Trade Office in Washington, D.C.

South Korea

Korean Embassy in Washington, D.C.
http://korea.emb.washington.dc.us/new/frame/
core.htm
The Embassy site delivers South Korean news, press releases, an event calendar, and economic reports.

Korean International Trade Association in Washington, D.C.
http://www.kita.or.kr/eng/national.html
The site provides contact information for the Korean International Trade Association in Washington, D.C.

Spain

Embassy of Spain in Washington, D.C.
http://www.spainemb.org/information/indexin.htm
The online diplomatic service provides Spanish daily news, press releases, country facts, and government directories.

Sri Lanka

Embassy of Sri Lanka in Washington, D.C.
http://piano.symgrp.com/srilanka/
The virtual Embassy features Sri Lankan news, country facts, travel guides, passport and visa information, and a database of investment opportunities in industries such as electronics, textiles, and mineral processing.

Sweden

Embassy of Sweden in Washington, D.C.
http://www.swedenemb.org/
The diplomatic site delivers Swedish country facts, visa regulations, an event calendar, tourism guides, trade matchmaking services, an online bulletin board, and Radio Sweden in streaming audio.

Swedish-American Interactive Marketplace
http://www.saim.com

Based in Chicago, the site is a searchable database of Swedish companies, subsidiaries, distributors and other affiliates in the United States. The directory is browsable by industry, location and company.

Switzerland

Embassy of Switzerland in Washington, D.C.
http://www.swissemb.org/
The virtual Embassy features Swiss news, country fact sheets, tourism guides, science and technology briefs, culture and education primers, and export directories.

Taiwan

Taiwan Government Information Office in Washington, D.C.
http://www.gio.gov.tw/info/ngio/usa-f.html
Posted in Chinese and English, the site lists the street address, phone and fax numbers, and e-mail link of the Taiwan Government Information Office in Washington, D.C.

Tanzania

Embassy of Tanzania in Washington, D.C.
http://www.tanzania-online.gov.uk/visa/
envoys.html
The site provides contact information for the Tanzania Embassy in Washington, D.C.

Thailand

Royal Thai Embassy in Washington
http://www.thaiembdc.org/
A Thailand resource page, the site provides Thai press releases, country fact sheets, economic reports and data, foreign affairs policy statements, and background information on Thailand's monarchy.

Thailand Office of Commercial Affairs in Washington, D.C.
http://www.thaitrade.com/thcoaf.html
The site lists the street address, phone and fax numbers, and e-mail link of the Thailand Office of Commercial Affairs in Washington, D.C.

Turkey

Embassy of the Republic of Turkey in Washington, D.C.
http://www.turkey.org/turkey/

Written in English and Turkish, the site offers Turkish news, tourism information, business guides, an event calendar, a virtual reference library, and primers on Turkish politics.

Turkmenistan

Embassy of Turkmenistan in Washington, D.C.
http://www.dc.infi.net/~embassy/
The digital Embassy provides Turkmenistan news, maps, travel tips, sector profiles, culture and history lessons, visa information, trade statistics, and business guides.

Uganda

Embassy of Uganda in Washington, D.C.
http://www.ugandaweb.com/ugaembassy/
The virtual Embassy delivers Ugandan news, press releases, an event calendar, travel advice, trade and investment reports, and a directory of diplomatic officers.

Ukraine

Trade Commission of Ukraine
http://www.brama.com/ua-trade-mission/
Based in New York, the site provides Ukrainian country and regional profiles, legal guides, investment opportunities, and trade leads.

United Kingdom

Britain in the U.S.A.
http://britain-info.org/
Based in New York City, the site provides British news, passport and visa information, trade and investment guides, foreign policy statements, sector profiles, and an event calendar.

British American Business Council
http://www.babc.org/
Based in New York City, the Council promotes British-American trade and investment. The site features a member directory, event calendar, online bulletin board, and list of affiliated organizations in the U.S. and Canada.

British American Chamber of Commerce
http://www.bacc.org/
With offices in New York City and London, the Chamber promotes British-American transatlantic business. The site provides British trade and investment guides, passport and visa information, and corporate matchmaking services.

British Commercial Offices in the U.S.
http://britain-info.org/bis/bto/map_txt.stm
A service of Britain in the U.S.A., the site is a directory of British Commercial offices in the United States.

British Embassy in Washington, D.C.
http://britain-info.org/bis/embassy/embassy.htm
Featuring an audio message from Ambassador Sir Christopher Meyer, the site provides British news, press releases, trade guides, transportation policies, and science and technology reports. The service includes a directory of British Consulates in the U.S., and a virtual tour of the Ambassador's residence.

Uruguay

Embassy of Uruguay in Washington, D.C.
http://www.embassy.org/uruguay/
The virtual Embassy provides Uruguay press releases, country profiles, business guides, economic reports, travel tips, and a directory of government ministers.

Uzbekistan

Embassy of Uzbekistan in Washington, D.C.
http://www.uzbekistan.org/
The Central Asian republic site offers Uzbekistan news, press releases, country fact sheets, visa regulations, foreign investment guides, and travel advice.

Venezuela

Embassy of Venezuela in Washington, D.C.
http://www.embavenez-us.org/
The virtual Embassy features Venezuelan economic statistics, trade and investment reports, tourism information, and an event calendar.

Vietnam

Embassy of Vietnam in Washington, D.C.
http://www.vietnamembassy-usa.org/
An online resource center, the site provides Vietnamese news, country facts, business guides, foreign investment reports, tourism information, and foreign policy statements.

U.S.-Vietnam Trade Council
http://www.internationalcenter.com/vtc.htm
Based in Washington, D.C., the Council pro-

motes U.S.-Vietnam bilateral trade. The site provides a mission statement, membership application form, and a list of intern opportunities.

Western Samoa

Embassy of Western Samoa in New York
http://www.interwebinc.com/samoa/missus.html
The site lists the street address, and phone and fax numbers of the Western Samoa Embassy in New York.

Zimbabwe

Embassy of Zimbabwe in Washington, D.C.
http://www.zimweb.com/Embassy/Zimbabwe/
Developed by ZimWeb, the site provides Zimbabwe fact sheets, investment opportunities, travel guides, and a directory of Embassy staff.

State Sites

Alabama

Alabama Media

Alabama Media
http://www.mediainfo.com/emediajs/specific-geo.htm?region=alabama
A service of New York City-based Editor and Publisher Interactive, the site provides a browsable directory of web-based media sites in Alabama including online city guides, magazines, and newspapers.

Alabama Market Guides

Alabama Development Office
http://www.ado.state.al.us/
Based in Montgomery, the site provides primers on Alabama industrial recruitment, international trade, research and communications, small business advocacy, and film production.

Alabama Economy
http://www.state.al.us/econ-m.html
A service of the Alabama Finance Department, the site is a directory of Alabama businesses, news organizations, economic development agencies, and employment opportunities online. The page includes a primer on how to apply to the state vendor list and compete in the state procurement process.

AlaWeb
http://alaweb.asc.edu/
Featuring an audio and video message from the Governor, AlaWeb is the official state government website. Modules include tourism, education, economy, what's new, and frequently asked questions.

Business Council of Alabama
http://www.bcatoday.org/
Based in Montgomery, the site features *Alabama Today*, a Council webzine, and directories of state legislative, congressional and Chamber of Commerce members.

Alabama Trade Assistance

Commercial Service in Alabama
http://www.ita.doc.gov/uscs/al/
A service of the U.S. Department of Commerce, the site is a directory of international trade statistics, leads, events, services, and contacts in Alabama.

International Trade Division
http://www.ado.state.al.us/#International Trade
A unit of the Alabama Development Office, the Division promotes the export of Alabama products and services, and organizes trade development activities for state companies.

North Alabama International Trade Association
http://www.naita.org/
Based in Huntsville, the Association promotes international trade in Northern Alabama. The site features a newsletter, event calendar, member index, and directory of international business programs and services in the area.

Trade Shows in Alabama
http://www.expoguide.com/shows/data/loc_al.htm
A service of Expoguide, the site provides a directory of trade shows in Birmingham, Huntsville, Mobile, Montgomery, Orange Beach, Point Clear, and other Alabama centers.

Alaska

Alaska Media

Alaska Media
http://www.mediainfo.com/emediajs/specific-geo.htm?region=alaska
A service of Editor and Publisher Interactive, the site provides a browsable directory of web-based

media sites in Alaska including magazines, newspapers, and television stations.

Alaska Market Guides

Alaska Department of Commerce
http://www.state.ak.us/local/akpages/COMMERCE/dced.htm
Based in Anchorage, the site is a directory of state business promotion, research, regulatory, and financing agencies including the Seafood Marketing Institute, Science and Technology Foundation, and Division of Investments.

Alaska High-Tech Business Council
http://www.ahtbc.org/
Developed by a coalition of Alaska high technology companies, the site provides a member directory, event calendar, and e-mail discussion group.

Great Alaskan Mall
http://www.alaskan.com/
A virtual mall of Alaskan companies, the site is divided into six categories: Business Listings, Community Information, Lodging, Outdoors, Real Estate, and Trip Planner.

Local Area Economic Information
http://www.state.ak.us/local/akpages/LABOR/research/relocate/relocmap.htm
A service of the Alaska Department of Labor, the site is a virtual library of Alaskan relocation resources. Categories include general information, cost of living, employment opportunities, and travel.

State of Alaska Online
http://www.state.ak.us/
The official State of Alaska homepage, the site provides state news, fact sheets, event information, job bulletins, and government directories.

Alaska Trade Assistance

Alaska Export Assistance Center
http://www.alaska.net/~export/
A service of the U.S. Department of Commerce, the site is a directory of U.S. federal government international trade programs, specialists, and events in Alaska. Offerings include export credit insurance, working capital, and loan guarantees.

Alaska Industrial Development and Export Authority
http://www.alaska.net/~aidea/

Developed by the Alaskan state government, the site provides economic development and export promotion press releases, fact sheets, project directories and financial information. Key initiatives include the Development Finance Program, Business and Export Assistance Program, and City-State Partner Program.

Commercial Service in Alaska
http://www.ita.doc.gov/uscs/ak/
A service of the International Trade Administration, the site is a directory of international trade statistics, leads, events, services, and contacts in Alaska.

Office of International Trade
http://www.state.ak.us/local/akpages/COMMERCE/oit.htm
Based in Anchorage, the Office serves as a commercial liaison for the Alaskan state government and private business. The site provides contact information for the agency, and the name of the Acting Director.

Trade Shows in Alaska
http://www.expoguide.com/shows/data/loc_ak.htm
A service of Expoguide, the site provides a directory of trade shows in Anchorage, Juneau, and other Alaskan centers.

Alaska Representative Offices

Japan

Consulate General of Japan in Anchorage
http://www.embjapan.org/anchorage/
A service of the Ministry of Foreign Affairs of Japan, the site provides Japanese Consulate speeches, an event calendar, reports on Japan-Alaska relations, and a directory of consular services.

Arizona

Arizona Media

Arizona Media
http://www.mediainfo.com/emediajs/specific-geo.htm?region=arizona
A service of Editor and Publisher Interactive, the site provides a browsable directory of web-based media sites in Arizona including online city guides, magazines, and newspapers.

Arizona Market Guides

Arizona Department of Commerce
http://www.commerce.state.az.us/
Homepage of the Arizona Commerce Department, the site delivers community profiles, economic updates, incentive information, and a directory of business services across the state.

Arizona Small Business Resource
http://www.azresource.com/
A resource for Arizona small business owners, the site provides primers on business planning, marketing, international trade, finance, and electronic commerce.

Arizona State Website
http://www.state.az.us/
The state of Arizona homepage, the site provides event information, weather updates, a trip planner, and a legislative information system. A key feature is the Arizona Procurement Information Exchange, the online purchasing network for the over 400 state agencies, colleges and universities, counties, cities, school districts, and qualified not-for-profit organizations.

Guide to Establishing and Operating a Business in Arizona
http://www.abgnews.com/bizbook/ smbizmain.html
Posted by the Arizona Business Gazette, the site explains how to start and run a company in Arizona. Topics include preliminary planning, business structure, regulatory information, demographics, marketing, and financial information.

Arizona Trade Assistance

Arizona International Trade Division
http://www.commerce.state.az.us/fr_itrad.shtml
Part of the Arizona Department of Commerce, the site provides NAFTA updates, event information, export primers, a directory of state export services, and e-mail links to the Division's foreign trade offices in London, Munich, Mexico City, Hermosillo, Taipei, and Tokyo.

Commercial Service in Arizona
http://www.ita.doc.gov/uscs/az/
A service of the International Trade Administration, the site is a directory of international trade statistics, leads, events, services, and contacts in Arizona.

Trade Shows in Arizona
http://www.expoguide.com/shows/data/loc_az.htm
A service of Expoguide, the site provides a directory of trade shows in Litchfield Park, Mesa, Phoenix, Scottsdale, Tuscon, and other Arizona centers.

Arizona Representative Offices

United Kingdom

Consulate of Britain in Phoenix
http://www.fco.gov.uk/directory/posts.asp?US
The site provides contact information for the British Consulate in Phoenix.

Arkansas

Arkansas Media

Arkansas Media
http://www.mediainfo.com/emediajs/specific-geo.htm?region=arkansas
A service of Editor and Publisher Interactive, the site provides a browsable directory of web-based media sites in Arkansas including online magazines, newspapers, and radio stations.

Arkansas Market Guides

Arkansas Business Climate
http://www.aedc.state.ar.us/climate/index.html
Developed by the Arkansas Economic Development Commission, the site is a directory of state business incentives. Offerings include income tax credits, tax refunds, and training programs.

Arkansas Economic Development Commission
http://www.aedc.state.ar.us/
The site provides tutorials on Arkansas business services, incentives, communities and sites, natural resources, education, financing, utilities, human resources, quality of life, and international business.

Development Information Network of Arkansas
http://www.aiea.ualr.edu/dina/
A network of state economic information, the site provides Arkansas regional profiles, sector fact sheets, business primers, and tourism guides.

Institute for Economic Advancement
http://www.aiea.ualr.edu/
Based at the University of Arkansas at Little Rock, the site is a virtual library of state economic

information on everything from county population to per capita income to manufacturing earnings.

Arkansas Trade Assistance

Arkansas International Offices
http://www.aedc.state.ar.us/business_services/int-offices.html
Developed by the Arkansas Industrial Development Commission, the site profiles the state's foreign trade offices in Mexico City, Kuala Lumpur, Brussels, and Yokohama. The offices provide export promotion and matchmaking services for Arkansas companies.

Commercial Service in Arkansas
http://www.ita.doc.gov/uscs/ar/
A service of the International Trade Administration, the site is a directory of international trade statistics, leads, events, services, and contacts in Arkansas.

Trade Development Assistance
http://www.aedc.state.ar.us/business_services/export.html
Based in Little Rock, the site describes the Trade Development Program, an export promotion and global business training service offered by the Arkansas Economic Development Commission.

Trade Shows in Arkansas
http://www.expoguide.com/shows/data/loc_ar.htm
A service of Expoguide, the site provides a directory of trade shows in Little Rock and other Arkansas centers.

California

California Media

California Media
http://www.mediainfo.com/emediajs/specific-geo.htm?region=california
A service of Editor and Publisher Interactive, the site provides a searchable directory of web-based media sites in California including city guides, magazines, and newspapers.

California Market Guides

California Business Report
http://italchambers.net/BusinessReports.html
Prepared by the Italian Chamber of Commerce and written in Italian, the site provides California fact sheets, market reports, and commercial guides.

California Chamber of Commerce
http://www.calchamber.com/
Based in Sacramento, the site provides California business news, commentary, legislative reports, labor law tutorials, corporate start-up kits, employee management software, and environmental compliance handbooks.

California ChamberLink
http://www.saratoga-ca.com/link/index.htm
Sponsored by the Saratoga Chamber of Commerce, the site is a directory of California Chambers of Commerce online from Acton to Manhattan Beach to West Lake Village.

California Trade and Commerce Agency
http://commerce.ca.gov/index.html
A virtual library of economic development information, the site provides California relocation news, site location opportunities, incentive guides, financing tutorials, training reports, and enterprise zone fact sheets.

Doing Business in California
http://www.ca.gov/s/business/
A service of the California state government, the site features California fact sheets, permit and license guides, corporate codes, environmental regulations, labor law guides, and a directory of business support programs.

California Trade Assistance

Agri-Food Trade Leads
http://coho.atinet.org/scripts/atinet/tradelead/tradelead1.asp
A service of the California Advanced Technology Information Network, the site is a searchable directory of agri-food trade leads around the world. The leads are searchable by agri-food product and country.

Baytrade
http://www.abag.ca.gov/bayarea/commerce/baytrade.html
Based in Oakland, Baytrade is a consortium of the U.S. Department of Commerce, the California Trade and Commerce Agency, the Bay Area Economic Forum, and the cities of San Francisco, San Jose, and Oakland. The partners provide international trade information and services online for Bay area exporters.

California Council for International Trade
http://www.ccit.net
A business advocacy group, the Council promotes the international trade and investment

interests of California companies. The site features trade policy updates, newsletters, editorials, fact sheets, e-mail action alerts, and membership information.

California International Offices
http://commerce.ca.gov/agency/org-iti-fieldoffices.html
A service of the California Trade and Commerce Agency, the site is a directory of California Offices of Trade and Investment in Hong Kong, Tokyo, London, Frankfurt, Mexico City, Taipei, Johannesburg, Jerusalem, Jakarta, and Seoul.

California Southeast Asia Business Council
http://www.calsea.org/
Based in Oakland, the Council promotes California-Asian trade and investment. The site features a newsletter, country profiles, member directory, and event information.

California Trade Event calendar
http://www.tradeport.org/cgi-bin/tradenet/tradebase-form
A service of Tradeport, the site provides a searchable directory of trade events in California. Events are browsable by location, date, and keyword.

Center for International Trade Development
http://www.discover.net/~trading/
Based in Glendora, California, the Center provides international trade research and advisory services. Businesspeople located in Los Angeles County or Western San Bernardino County are eligible to receive free export counseling and logistics assistance from Center trade professionals at no charge upon request.

Commercial Service in California
http://www.ita.doc.gov/uscs/ca/
A service of the International Trade Administration, the site is a directory of international trade statistics, leads, events, services, and contacts in California.

Commercial Service in the Inland Empire
http://www.ieeac.com/
Serving San Bernardino and Riverside counties and a portion of eastern Los Angeles County, the Inland Empire Commercial Service provides export counseling to southern California companies. The site features a newsletter, trade leads, and event calendar.

Export Forecast
http://www.bankamerica.com/corporate/trade_exportfore.html
Prepared by Bank of America Trade Services, the site provides growth forecasts for California exporters in Latin American markets such as Argentina, Brazil, Chile, Colombia, Ecuador, Mexico, Peru, and Venezuela.

Export Small Business Development Center
http://www.exportsbdc.org/
Headquartered in El Segundo, California, the Center counsels California companies on exporting and global business. The site provides an export primer, event calendar, and free e-mail advisory services.

Foreign Trade Association of Southern California
http://www.csz.com/foreigntrade/
Based in Los Angeles, the Association promotes the growth of international trade in Southern California. The site features a mission statement, calendar of events, directory of Association officers, and membership information.

Going Global
http://commerce.ca.gov/international/
A service of the California International Trade and Investment Division, the site offers California export success stories, a trade finance guide, event calendar, export fact sheets, and interviews with leading global businesspeople.
A key publication is *Meridian*, a quarterly newsletter on state trade activities.

Greater Oakland International Trade Center
http://www.tradeport.org/ts/partners/oitc.html
Part of a regional trade development partnership, the Center provides export assistance to Oakland area companies. The site provides contact information, an e-mail directory of key personnel, and a list of trade services provided.

Inland Empire Small Business Development Center
http://www.iesbdc.org/index.html
Based in Riverside, California, the Center provides export counseling to Southern California companies. The site provides contact information and a list of services provided.

LA Trade
http://www.tradeport.org/cgi-bin/banner.pl/ts/partners/latrade.html
A cooperative venture of Los Angeles, Orange,

Riverside, San Bernardino and Ventura counties, LA Trade promotes exporting in the Greater Los Angeles area. The site provides contact information, an e-mail directory of key personnel, and a list of export counseling services provided.

Los Angeles Women in International Trade

http://www.pacificcoasthwy.com/wit-la/
The Los Angeles branch of the Organization of Women in International Trade, the organization provides professional development for women exporters and importers. The site includes a job bank, executive directory, event calendar, and membership information.

Monterey Bay International Trade Association

http://www.mbita.org/
Based in Santa Cruz, California, the Association promotes international trade in the Monterey Bay area. The site features export news, a membership roster, event calendar, and directory of government partners.

Monterey Park and International Trade

http://www.montereypark.com/trade/trade.html
Developed by the Monterey Park Chamber of Commerce, the site provides export fact sheets on Monterey Park City, and the Ports of Long Beach and Los Angeles.

Office of Export Development

http://commerce.ca.gov/international/oed/
A unit of the California Trade and Commerce Agency, the Office provides export marketing services to California companies. The site includes a newsletter, trade leads, program information, an event calendar, and export primers.

Professional Association of Exporters and Importers

http://www.paei.org/
An organization of California international trade professionals, the Association provides global business education and networking services. The site provides a newsletter, event calendar, contact information, and a list of job opportunities.

Santa Clara Export Assistance Center

http://www.ita.doc.gov/uscs/ca/santaclara/
Developed by the International Trade Administration, the site features a directory of Center staff, local event calendar, and list of export services provided.

Silicon Valley Export Resource Center

http://tradeport.org/cgi-bin/banner.pl/ts/partners/sjoed.html
Based in San Jose, the Center provides export counseling to Silicon Valley area companies. The site includes contact information, an e-mail directory of key personnel, and a list of trade services offered.

Trade Point Los Angeles

http://www.tradepointla.org/
Part of the United Nations Global Trade Point Network, the site provides Los Angeles trade leads, market bulletins, and contact information.

Trade Shows in California

http://www.expoguide.com/shows/data/loc_ca.htm
A service of Expoguide, the site provides a directory of trade shows in Anaheim, Bakersfield, Beverly Hills, Fresno, Long Beach, Los Angeles, Pasadena, Sacramento, San Diego, San Francisco, San Jose, Santa Clara and other California centers.

California Representative Offices

Armenia

Consulate General of Armenia in Beverly Hills

http://www.armeniaemb.org/forrel/embas2.htm
The site provides contact information for the Armenia Consulate General in Beverly Hills.

Australia

Austrade in Los Angeles

http://www.austrade.gov.au/losangeles/
A service of the Australian government, Austrade provides export promotion and business matchmaking services for Australian companies doing business in California.

Austrade in San Francisco

http://www.austrade.gov.au/sanfrancisco/
The virtual office of Austrade in San Francisco, the site provides contact information, export primers, and a list of trade services offered.

Australian American Chamber of Commerce

http://www.anzacc.com/
Based in Los Angeles, the site provides contact information, a member directory, and Australian-American business matchmaking services.

Austria

Austrian Trade Commission in Los Angeles
http://www.austriantrade.org/AustrianTrade/offices/ahst_lax.htm
An Austrian trade promotion service, the site lists the trade officers, street and e-mail address, and phone and fax numbers of the Austrian Trade Commission in Los Angeles.

Belgium

Belgian Club of Northern California
http://www.bcnc.com/
Based in Palo Alto, the Club provides networking services for Belgians living or traveling in the Bay area. The site includes a newsletter, event calendar, and executive e-mail directory.

Belgica: Association of Belgians at Stanford
http://www.stanford.edu/group/belgica/
Based at Stanford University, the site is a directory of Belgian students at Stanford, and Belgian Stanford alumni. The service includes a newsletter, mailing list, and event calendar.

Belgium Consulate General in Los Angeles
http://www.belgium-emb.org/usa/representatives/usa_los_angeles.html
Developed by the Belgian Ministry of Foreign Affairs, the site provides Belgian news and trade reports, and contact information for the Belgian Consulate General in Los Angeles.

Wallonia Trade Office in San Francisco
http://www.wco.com/~sfwallon/
A service of the Belgian Trade Commission, the site delivers fact sheets, sector profiles and a list of investment incentives in Wallonia, a Belgian region.

Brazil

Consulate General of Brazil in San Francisco
http://www.crl.com/~brazil/index.htm
Written in English and Portuguese, the site provides Brazilian fact sheets, visa application forms, and Consulate contact information.

Canada

Canadian Consulate General in Los Angeles
http://www.cdnconsulat-la.com/
Written in English and French, the site profiles the trade, passport, tourism, immigration and political services of Canada's Los Angeles Consulate.

Canadian Consulate Trade Office in San Francisco
http://www.cdntrade.com/
Part of a worldwide network of Canadian trade posts, the site features an information technology newsletter, software marketing primer, and U.S. business tutorial.

Province of Québec Trade Office in Los Angeles
http://www.mri.gouv.qc.ca/dans_le_monde/etats_unis/antennes_us_an.html#Los Angeles
A service of the Québec government, the site lists the Commercial Attaché and contact information for the Québec Trade Office in Los Angeles.

China

Hong Kong Association of Northern California
http://www.hkanc.com/
Based in San Francisco, the Association promotes Northern California-Hong Kong trade and cultural ties. The site features a newsletter, event calendar, member roster, and program directory.

Hong Kong Association of Southern California
http://www.hkasc.org/
Based in Los Angeles, the Association promotes Hong Kong-Southern California trade. The site includes a newsletter, event calendar, and membership information.

Hong Kong Economic and Trade Office in San Francisco
http://www.hongkong.org/
Created in 1986, the Office promotes California-Hong Kong trade. The site includes Hong Kong news, business reports, government speeches, and procurement bulletins.

Colombia

Colombia Consulate General in Los Angeles
http://www.colombiaemb.org/consular/consus.html#los angeles
A service of the Colombian government, the site lists the staff and street address of the Colombia Consulate General in Los Angeles.

Colombia Consulate General in San Francisco
http://www.drcomputer.com/colombia/
Written in English and Spanish, the site provides Colombian fact sheets, drug enforcement reports, and a directory of Colombian exporters.

Czech Republic

Consulate General of the Czech Republic in Los Angeles
http://www.czechemb.net/
scroll_of_embassies.html
Along with a directory of diplomatic offices in the Czech Republic, the site provides contact information for the Czech Consulate General in Los Angeles.

Denmark

Consulate General of Denmark in Los Angeles
http://www.danishconsulate.com/english/
A service of the Royal Danish Consulate, the site features Danish visa information, business guides, investment reports, event information, and a staff directory.

Finland

Finland Consulate General in Los Angeles
http://www.finlandla.org/
Written in English and Finnish, the site delivers Finnish news, fact sheets, economic statistics, tourism guides, a calendar of cultural events, and a staff directory.

Finland Trade Center
http://www.ftcla.com/
Based in Los Angeles, the site provides primers on selling to and sourcing from Finland, and a directory of Finnish trade activities in Southern California.

France

Consulate General of France in Los Angeles
http://www.etats-unis.com/consulat-la/
Posted in French, the site features a message from the Consul General, a directory of Consulate services, and an event calendar.

Consulate General of France in San Francisco
http://www.accueil-sfo.org/
Written in English and French, the site provides general information on France, and a directory of Consulate staff and departments such as the Office for Science and Technology.

French-American Chamber of Commerce of San Francisco
http://www.faccsf.com/
Part of an international French commercial network, the site includes contact information, a mission statement, event bulletins, and an online membership application form.

French American Chamber of Commerce of Southern California
http://www.tradepointla.org/facc.htm
Based in Los Angeles, the Chamber promotes French-South California trade. The site includes a mission statement, member directory, and contact information.

French Trade Commission in Los Angeles/San Francisco
http://www.dree.org/usa/InfoGene/PEE/
SanFrancisco/index.htm
A French trade promotion service, the Commission delivers export counseling and market intelligence for French companies. The site lists priority sectors for French exporters in the Los Angeles and San Francisco metro areas.

Germany

German American Chamber of Commerce in Los Angeles
http://www.ahk.net/en/us/LosAngeles/
The site lists the Chief Executive Officer, Chairpersons, street address and e-mail address of the Chamber office in Los Angeles.

German American Chamber of Commerce in San Francisco
http://www.ahk.net/en/us/LosAngeles/
The page lists the Chief Executive Officer, street address and e-mail address of the Chamber office in San Francisco.

German American Chamber of Commerce of the Western United States
http://www.gaccwest.org/
With offices in Los Angeles and San Francisco, the Chamber promotes German-U.S. trade. The site features industry reports, job opportunities, a staff directory, event calendar, publications directory, and a list of business development services.

Greece

Consulate General of Greece in Los Angeles
http://www.hellas-info.org/
A virtual Consulate, the site provides Greek fact sheets, cultural information, business primers, a staff directory, and a list of consular services.

Guyana

Honorary Consul of Guyana in Inglewood
http://www.guyana.org/TRADEREP.htm
The site provides contact information for the Guyana Honorary Consul in Inglewood.

Hungary

Consulate General of Hungary in Los Angeles
http://www.hungaryemb.org/ConsulatesGen.htm
The page lists the Consul General, street address, and phone and fax numbers for the Hungarian Consulate in Los Angeles.

Iceland

Consulate General of Iceland in Los Angeles
http://www.iceland.org/list1n.htm#CONS
The site lists the Consul General, street address, phone and fax numbers, and e-mail link of the Icelandic Consulate in Los Angeles.

India

Consulate General of India in San Francisco
http://www.indianconsulate-sf.org/
A Consulate homepage, the site features Indian business primers, tourism guides, visa forms, online passport renewals, and contact information.

Silicon Valley Indian Professionals Association
http://www.sipa.org/
Based in Santa Clara, the Association promotes U.S.-India high technology trade and networking. The site provides online message boards, an events directory, speeches, workshop and seminar proceedings, and membership information.

Indonesia

Consulate General of Indonesia in Los Angeles
http://www.kjri-la.com/
The site includes contact information and a directory of Indonesia news services, magazines, and journals.

Iran

Iranian Trade Association
http://www.iraniantrade.org/
Based in La Jolla, California, the Association promotes U.S.-Iran trade. The site provides a member directory, event information, Iranian business guides, and an online discussion forum.

Ireland

Enterprise Ireland in Campbell
http://www.irish-trade.ie/office_network/office_locate01.html#campbell
The site lists the Manager, street address, and phone and fax numbers of the Enterprise Ireland office in Campbell.

Enterprise Ireland in Palo Alto
http://www.irish-trade.ie/office_network/office_locate01.html#palo alto
The site lists the Manager, street address, and phone and fax numbers of the Enterprise Ireland office in Palo Alto.

Israel

Consulate General of Israel in Los Angeles
http://www.israelemb.org/la/index.htm
The digital Consulate features Israeli news, daily and weekly e-mail newsletters, fact sheets, a staff roster, and interactive maps.

Consulate General of Israel in San Francisco
http://www.israelemb.org/sanfran/index.htm
Serving Northern California, Alaska, Idaho, Montana, Oregon, and Washington states, the Consulate provides Israeli news, business primers, speeches, and a local event calendar.

Italy

Consulate General of Italy in Los Angeles
http://www.italyemb.org/italcons.htm#losang
The site provides the street address, e-mail link, and phone and fax numbers for the Italian Consulate in Los Angeles.

Consulate General of Italy in San Francisco
http://www.icsi.berkeley.edu/~diporto/consolato.html
Posted in Italian, the site provides Italian fact sheets, sector profiles, and passport information.

Japan

Consulate General of Japan in Los Angeles
http://www.embjapan.org/la/
Posted in English and Japanese, the site

delivers Japanese country profiles, visa information, customs fact sheets, and directories of educational opportunities and sister city associations.

Consulate General of Japan in San Francisco
http://www.embjapan.org/sf/
A country information center, the site provides Japanese visa information, research reports, and an event calendar.

JETRO Los Angeles
http://www.JETRO.org/losangeles/
JETRO—the Japan External Trade Organization—provides information on Japanese trade and investment opportunities. A resource for businesspeople in Arizona, Hawaii, New Mexico, Nevada, Southern California and Utah, the site features an event calendar, a free Japanese language test, and a list of Japanese assistance programs for U.S. companies.

JETRO San Francisco
http://www.JETRO.org/sanfrancisco/
Serving businesspeople in Alaska, Idaho, Montana, Northern California, Oregon, and Washington, the site delivers Japanese fact sheets, press releases, success stories, and an event calendar.

United States-Japan Technology Management Center
http://fuji.stanford.edu/
Based at the Stanford University School of Engineering in Stanford, California, the Center researches American and Japanese technology trends. The site includes a staff roster, project profiles, and event information.

Malaysia

Consulate General of Malaysia in Los Angeles
http://www.mnet.com.my/klonline/www/missions/malmiss/musa3.htm
The site provides contact information for the Malaysia Consulate General in Los Angeles.

Trade Commission of Malaysia in Los Angeles
http://www.mnet.com.my/klonline/www/missions/malmiss/musa8.htm
The site provides contact information for the Malaysia Trade Commission in Los Angeles.

Mexico

Consulate General of Mexico in Sacramento

http://www.quiknet.com/mexico/
Posted in Spanish, the site offers Mexican fact sheets, economic reports, and passport information.

Trade Commission of Mexico in Los Angeles
http://www.mexico-businessline.com/ingles/ofrepmu3.html#angeles
The site lists the street address, phone and fax numbers, and e-mail link of the Trade Commission of Mexico in Los Angeles.

Netherlands

Netherlands Foreign Investment Agency in San Mateo
http://www.nfia.com/html/contact/index.html
The site lists the street address, phone and fax numbers, and e-mail link of the Netherlands Foreign Investment Agency in San Mateo.

New Zealand

New Zealand Consulate in Los Angeles
http://www.emb.com/nzemb/offices/consul~1.htm#la
A service of the New Zealand government, the site provides the street address, phone and fax numbers, and office hours of the Consulate in Los Angeles.

New Zealand Consulate in San Diego
http://www.emb.com/nzemb/offices/consul~1.htm#sd
The webpage lists the street address, and phone and fax numbers of the New Zealand Consulate in San Diego.

New Zealand Consulate in San Francisco
http://www.emb.com/nzemb/offices/consul~1.htm#sf
The site lists the street address and phone and fax numbers of the New Zealand Consulate in San Francisco.

Trade New Zealand in Los Angeles
http://www.tradenz.govt.nz/contact/northam.html
An export promotion service, the site provides contact information for the Trade New Zealand office in Los Angeles.

Norway

Norwegian Trade Commission in San Francisco
http://www.norway.org/trade/mainbod3.html#sf
The site lists the street address, phone and fax

numbers, e-mail links, and staff profiles of the Norwegian Trade Commission in San Francisco.

Panama

Consulate General of Panama in San Francisco
http://www.drcomputer.com/panama/
Written in English and Spanish, the site includes a message from the Consul General, a list of consular services, and a profile of the Panamanian merchant marine.

Philippines

Consulate General of the Philippines in Los Angeles
http://www.philconsul-la.org/
A service of the Philippine government, the site provides fact sheets on Philippine passports, visas, laws, and income tax.

Philippine Trade and Investment Promotion Office in Los Angeles
http://www.dti.gov.ph/LA/
The site provides a mission statement, service directory, and contact information for the Philippine Trade Office in Los Angeles.

Poland

Consulate General of Poland in Los Angeles
http://www.pan.net/konsulat/
The virtual Consulate features Polish fact sheets, legal primers, passport information, economic bulletins, and a cultural event calendar.

Portugal

Portuguese Chamber of Commerce of California
http://www.portugal.org/pccsj/
Based in San Jose, the site provides a Chamber newsletter, event calendar, member directory, and contact information.

Portuguese Trade and Investment Office in San Francisco
http://www.portugal.org/geninfo/abouticep/newyork.html
The site lists the staff, street address, phone and fax numbers, and e-mail link of the Portuguese Trade and Investment Office in San Francisco.

Russia

Consulate General of Russia in San Francisco
http://www.vldbros.com/consul/rfcons.html
The digital Consulate delivers Russian visa information, business primers, and a biography of the Consul General.

Singapore

Consulate General of Singapore in Los Angeles
http://www.gov.sg/mfa/consular/mww_u.htm
The site provides contact information for the Singapore Consulate General in Los Angeles.

Consulate General of Singapore in San Francisco
http://www.gov.sg/mfa/consular/mww_u.htm
The site provides contact information for the Singapore Consulate General in San Francisco.

South Africa

Consulate General of South Africa in Los Angeles
http://www.link2southafrica.com/
A service of the South African government, the site features South African news, economic reports, sector profiles, visa information, and travel guides.

Spain

Consulate General of Spain in Los Angeles
http://www-bcf.usc.edu/~ravera/
Written in English and Spanish, the site reports on U.S.-Spain school exchanges. A key feature is *LA Voz*, a newsletter for Spanish teachers in California.

Spanish Commercial Office in Los Angeles
http://www.icex.es/openURL.html#openURL=/english/infoproyem/ofcomes/ofcomes.html#AM
The site lists the staff, street address, phone and fax numbers, and e-mail link of the Spanish Commercial Office in Los Angeles.

Sweden

Consulate General of Sweden in Los Angeles
http://www.webcom.com/swedcons/
The virtual Consulate provides Swedish passport

information and a directory of Swedish organizations, translators, and classes in the Los Angeles area.

Consulate General of Sweden in San Francisco
http://www.scandinavius.com/sweden/seconsl.html
The site features a Swedish event calendar, and a directory of Scandinavian companies, artists, cultural organizations, and language training in the San Francisco area.

Switzerland

Consulate General of Switzerland in Los Angeles
http://www.swissconla.org/
The digital service offers Swiss news, editorials, fact sheets, a database of science and technology jobs, and a California-Switzerland economic comparison.

Swiss-American Chamber of Commerce in Los Angeles
http://www.amcham.ch/usa/losangel/index.htm
The Chamber promotes California-Swiss trade and relations. The site includes an executive directory, event calendar, and contact information.

Swiss-American Chamber of Commerce in San Francisco
http://www.amcham.ch/usa/sanfranc/index.htm
Along with a mission statement, the site provides an executive directory, event calendar, and contact information.

Swiss Trade Office in San Francisco
http://www.swissemb.org/biz/html/san_francisco.html
The site lists the Director, street address, e-mail link, and phone and fax numbers for the Swiss Trade Office in San Francisco.

Taiwan

China External Trade Development Council Office in San Francisco
http://www.cetra.org.tw/english/o_office/indexset.htm
A Taiwanese trade promotion service, the site lists the mission statement and e-mail link of the China External Trade Development Council Office in San Francisco.

Taiwan Government Information Office in Los Angeles
http://www.gio.gov.tw/info/ngio/usa-f.html
Posted in Chinese and English, the site lists the street address, phone and fax numbers, and e-mail link of the Taiwan Government Information Office in Los Angeles.

Taiwan Government Information Office in San Francisco
http://www.gio.gov.tw/info/ngio/usa-f.html
Posted in Chinese and English, the site lists the street address, phone and fax numbers, and e-mail link of the Taiwan Government Information Office in San Francisco.

Thailand

Royal Thai Consulate in Los Angeles
http://www.mfa.go.th/Embassy/detail/22.htm
A service of the Royal Thai government, the site lists the Consul General, street address, and phone and fax numbers of the Thai Consulate in Los Angeles.

Thai Trade Center in Los Angeles
http://www.thaitrade.com/wwtto.html
A service of the Thailand Department of Export Promotion, the site lists the street address, phone and fax numbers, and e-mail address of the Thai Trade Center in Los Angeles.

Turkey

Consulate General of Turkey in Los Angeles
http://www.turkiye.net/lacg/
Along with Turkish passport information and a visa application form, the site lists the street address, e-mail link, and office hours of the Consulate.

United Kingdom

British American Chamber of Commerce in Los Angeles
http://home.earthlink.net/~baccla/Main/index_html.html
An online forum for United States-United Kingdom networking, the site offers an event calendar, staff directory, and membership information.

British American Chamber of Commerce of Orange County
http://www.baccoc.org/
Based in Irvine, the Chamber promotes United

Kingdom-Orange County trade. The site features a newsletter, member directory, calendar of events, job postings, and an online bulletin board.

British American Chamber of Commerce in San Francisco
http://www.baccsf.org/
An American-British networking forum, the site offers an event calendar, a directory of Chamber executives, and primers on British and European product standards.

Consulate of Britain in San Diego
http://www.fco.gov.uk/directory/posts.asp?US
The site provides contact information for the British Consulate in San Diego.

Consulate General of Britain in Los Angeles
http://britain-info.org/bis/dipoff/la.sTM
The site provides British fact sheets, press releases, business guides, investment primers, and a directory of commercial services.

Consulate General of Britain in San Francisco
http://britain-info.org/bis/dipoff/sf.STM
The site provides British press releases, trade information, investment primers, and a directory of commercial services.

Uruguay

Consulate General of Uruguay in Los Angeles
http://www.primenet.com/~urula/
Posted in English and Spanish, the site provides the street address, office hours, and phone and fax numbers of the Consulate, along with Uruguay passport and visa information.

Venezuela

Consulate General of Venezuela in San Francisco
http://venezuela.mit.edu/consulado.sfo/
Written in English and Spanish, the site delivers Venezuelan cultural guides, visa information, exchange rates, travel primers, and a directory of consular services.

Colorado

Colorado Media

Colorado Media
http://www.mediainfo.com/emediajs/specific-geo.htm?region=colorado
A service of Editor and Publisher Interactive, the site provides a searchable directory of web-based media sites in Colorado including city guides, magazines, and newspapers.

Colorado Market Guides

Business Information
http://governor.state.co.us/business_dir/businessmenu.html
A service of the Colorado state government, the site features state business guides, demographic statistics, company reports, and a directory of economic development agencies.

Colorado Association of Commerce and Industry
http://www.businesscolorado.com/
Based in Denver, the site provides Colorado government guides, legislative agendas, and a directory of Association programs and publications.

Colorado Business Development Guide
http://www.scan.org/clg/
A resource page for Colorado businesspeople, the site offers regional maps, an online entrepreneurial test, amortization worksheet, and a searchable directory of economic development assistance by city.

Market Colorado
http://www.marketcolorado.com/
A virtual product catalog, the site profiles Colorado companies and products in 12 categories including apparel, automotive and manufacturing. The service includes a newsletter, event calendar, and list of job opportunities.

State of Colorado Homepage
http://governor.state.co.us/
Homepage of the state government, the site provides Colorado fact sheets, county profiles, press releases, meeting notices, a government telephone directory, job banks, tax forms, and visitor information.

Colorado Trade Assistance

Colorado International Trade Directory
http://www.coloradotrade.com/
Developed by World Trade Center Denver, the site is a browsable database of Denver exporters. The service is searchable by keyword and company name.

Colorado International Trade Office
http://www.state.co.us/gov_dir/intl_trade_gov.html
A service of the state government, the site provides export primers, press releases, a list of advisory board members, and directories of Office services, internship appointments, Colorado offices abroad, and Colorado sister cities.

Commercial Service in Colorado
http://www.ita.doc.gov/uscs/co/
A service of the International Trade Administration, the site is a directory of international trade statistics, leads, events, services, and contacts in Colorado.

Trade Shows in Colorado
http://www.expoguide.com/shows/data/loc_co.htm
Developed by Expoguide, the site is a directory of trade shows in Colorado Springs, Denver, Keystone, and other Colorado centers.

World Trade Center Denver
http://www.wtcdn.com/
Part of a global network of World Trade Center offices, the site features an event calendar, and a directory of export counseling programs and services.

Colorado Representative Offices

Australia

Australian American Chamber of Commerce
http://www.aussiedenver.com/
Part of a national network of Chamber offices, the site provides a member directory, event calendar, and U.S.-Australia business matchmaking service.

Australian Office in Denver
http://www.aussiedenver.com/
The site delivers Australian passport and citizenship fact sheets, employment opportunities, and contact information.

Japan

JETRO Denver
http://www.sni.net/jetrodenver/
Serving the states of Colorado, Nebraska and Wyoming, JETRO Denver offers free information and consultation services to U.S. businesspeople interested in doing business in Japan or with Japanese companies.

Mexico

Consulate General of Mexico in Denver
http://www.terapath.com/~mexico/
The virtual Consulate provides Mexican news, economic statistics, federal government directories, tourism guides, cultural information, and a list of Mexican universities and colleges.

Connecticut

Connecticut Media

Connecticut Media
http://www.mediainfo.com/emediajs/specific-geo.htm?region=connecticut
A service of Editor and Publisher Interactive, the site provides a searchable directory of web-based media sites in Connecticut including magazines, newspapers, and television stations.

Connecticut Market Guides

Connecticut Economic Information System
http://www.state.ct.us/ecd/research/ceis/
Developed by the Connecticut state government, the site is a database of Connecticut economic and demographic information. Categories include housing, defense, income, employment, population, exports, and taxes.

Connecticut Economic Resource Center
http://www.cerc.com/cerc/cercweb.nsf/frmHome?OpenForm
Based in Rocky Hill, the site is a virtual library of Connecticut business information. Tools include state fact sheets, export guides, a licensing database, business plan templates, event calendar, and a site-finder service.

Connecticut Technology Council
http://www.ctcweb.org/
Based in Hartford, the site provides Connecticut technology news, fact sheets, an event calendar, and a member directory.

CT Business
http://www.ctbusiness.com/
An online business directory, the site links to leading Connecticut companies online in industries such as food processing, tourism, and architecture.

Department of Economic and Community Development
http://www.state.ct.us/ecd/
The state agency provides press releases, business incentive guides, enterprise zone fact sheets, sector reports, city and town profiles, and a directory of the top 100 companies headquartered in Connecticut.

Connecticut Trade Assistance

Commercial Service in Connecticut
http://www.ita.doc.gov/uscs/ct/
Developed by the International Trade Administration, the site is a directory of international trade statistics, leads, events, services, and contacts in Connecticut.

Connecticut International Division
http://www.state.ct.us/ecd/international/index.html
Part of the Department of Economic and Community Development, the Division provides export counseling services to Connecticut companies. The site features a trade event calendar, export fact sheets, a staff roster, and a directory of Connecticut trade offices abroad in Argentina, Brazil, China, and Mexico.

Connecticut World Trade Association
http://www.imex.com/cwta.html
Based in Bridgeport, the site features an international trade event calendar, members roster, and directory of services.

International Trade Advisor
http://www.state.ct.us/ecd/international/ita.htm
Developed by the Connecticut International Division, the International Trade Advisor is an export counseling service. Using checklists and questionnaires, Division trade specialists prepare a brief customized report summarizing a particular company's strengths, weaknesses, opportunities and threats in the international marketplace.

Middletown Export Assistance Center
http://www.ita.doc.gov/uscs/ct/middletown/
Developed by the U.S. Department of Commerce, the site provides a directory of international trade programs, seminars and export counselors in the Middletown area.

Trade Shows in Connecticut
http://www.expoguide.com/shows/data/loc_ct.htm
Compiled by Expoguide, the site is a directory of trade shows in Danbury, Hartford, New Haven, New London, West Springfield, and other Connecticut centers.

Connecticut Representative Offices

Puerto Rico

Puerto Rico Federal Affairs Administration in Hartford
http://www.prfaa-govpr.org/connecticut.htm
The site lists the street address, phone and fax numbers, and e-mail link of the Puerto Rico Federal Affairs Administration regional office in Hartford.

Delaware

Delaware Media

Delaware Media
http://www.mediainfo.com/emediajs/specific-geo.htm?region=delaware
A service of Editor and Publisher Interactive, the site provides a searchable directory of web-based media sites in Delaware including magazines, newspapers, and radio stations.

Delaware Market Guides

Delaware Business Research
http://www.state.de.us/dedo/research.htm
A service of the Delaware Economic Development Office, the site features Delaware family tax comparisons, property tax rates, and fact sheets on state site selection, municipal permits, construction costs, education, training, and financing.

Delaware Economic Development Office
http://www.state.de.us/dedo/index.htm
Based in Dover, the site delivers primers on Delaware business development, international trade, workforce development, corporate finance, tourism, and public/private partnerships.

Delaware State Chamber of Commerce
http://www.inetcom.net/dscc/
Based in Wilmington, the site reports on Delaware government affairs, education, public policy, small business, tourism and international trade.

Delaware State Data Center
http://www.state.de.us/dedo/dsdc/dsdc.htm
The Delaware government site is a searchable database of state census data. Categories

include demographics, economics, geography, snapshots, and quick facts.

State of Delaware
http://www.state.de.us/
Homepage of the state government, the site provides Delaware fact sheets, census information, an event calendar, tourism guides, regulatory handbooks, employment opportunities, and a directory of state agencies.

Delaware Trade Assistance

Commercial Service in Delaware
http://www.ita.doc.gov/uscs/de/
Developed by the International Trade Administration, the site is a directory of international trade statistics, leads, events, services, and contacts in Delaware.

Delaware Exporter
http://www.inet.net/export/
Sponsored by the Delaware State Chamber of Commerce, the site is a database of Delaware exporters in dozens of industry categories.

International Trade Section
http://www.state.de.us/dedo/intntl/intntl.htm
A unit of the Delaware Economic Development Office, the International Trade Section provides export counseling to Delaware companies. The site features an event calendar, mission statement, and contact information.

Trade Shows in Delaware
http://www.expoguide.com/shows/data/loc_de.htm
Compiled by Expoguide, the site is a directory of trade shows in Dover, Wilmington, and other Delaware centers.

District of Columbia

District of Columbia Media

District of Columbia Media
http://www.mediainfo.com/emediajs/specific-geo.htm?region=districtofcolumbia
A service of Editor and Publisher Interactive, the site provides a searchable directory of web-based media sites in the District of Columbia including city guides, magazines, and newspapers.

District of Columbia Market Guides

Greater Washington Board of Trade
http://www.bot.org/
A regional service for the District of Columbia, Northern Virginia, and Suburban Maryland, the site delivers press releases, a membership directory, policy statements, and ad-hoc studies.

Washington, D.C. Online
http://www.dchomepage.net/
An online city guide, the site includes local news, and reports on District of Columbia business, education, tourism, and entertainment.

District of Columbia Trade Assistance

D.C. Office of International Business
http://www.dchomepage.net/dcmain/ibo.html
Homepage of the D.C. Office of International Business, the site provides a mission statement, e-mail link, and directory of Office programs and services.

International Business Council
http://www.tradecompass.com/mktplace/country/namerica/usa/dc/ibc.html
A branch of the Greater Washington Board of Trade, the site features an international trade event calendar for the District of Columbia area, and a list of key tasks for the Council.

International Economy of Greater Washington
http://www.bot.org/IntBusinessStudy.html
Posted by the Greater Washington Board of Trade, the site delivers *The International Economy of Greater Washington*, a consultant's report on the economic impact of global business activities on the District of Columbia area.

Trade Shows in the District of Columbia
http://www.expoguide.com/shows/data/loc_dc.htm
Compiled by Expoguide, the site is a directory of trade shows in the District of Columbia.

Washington International Trade Association
http://www.wita.org/
Based in the Ronald Reagan International Trade Center, the Association is an international trade education and networking forum. The site includes an event calendar, member directory, member surveys, job and resume bulletins, and *Trade Trends*, a quarterly newsletter.

District of Columbia Representative Offices

United Kingdom

British American Business Association of Washington, D.C.
http://www.baba-dc.org/
Part of an American-British business network, the site delivers Association news, contact information, and an event calendar.

Florida

Florida Media

Florida Media
http://www.mediainfo.com/emediajs/specific-geo.htm?region=florida
A service of Editor and Publisher Interactive, the site provides a searchable directory of web-based media sites in Florida including city guides, magazines, and newspapers.

Florida Market Guides

Bizport Florida
http://bizport.com/fldirectory/
An interactive marketplace, the site is a directory of nearly 2,000 Florida companies and organizations online. Categories include communications and media, construction and real estate, health care services, manufacturing, and wholesaling.

Enterprise Florida
http://www.floridabusiness.com/default.html
Written in nine languages including Arabic, Chinese and French, the site provides Florida news, fact sheets, interactive maps, company profiles, and primers on finance, international trade, minority business, technology, and wages.

Florida Business Resources
http://www.floridabusiness.com/resources/default.html
A service of Enterprise Florida, the site is a virtual library of Florida business information. Topics include start-ups, international trade and economic development, capital, technology, and workforce.

Florida Chamber of Commerce
http://www.flchamb.com/home.html
Based in Tallahassee, the site provides Chamber news, annual reports, a member directory, event calendar, and publications catalog.

Guide to Florida's Chamber of Commerce
http://www.floridaguide.com/chambers/f-index.html
Developed by the Florida Internet Real Estate Guide, the site provides a searchable directory of Florida economic development organizations such as the Cocoa Beach Chamber of Commerce and the Miami-Dade Chamber of Commerce.

Florida Trade Assistance

AmericasNet
http://americas.fiu.edu/americas/americas-frames-noblue.html
A service of Florida International University, the site provides fact sheets and progress reports on Summit of the Americas, Free Trade Agreement of the Americas, and hemispheric integration.

Association of Bi-National Chambers of Commerce in South Florida
http://www.abicc.org/
The Association provides shared office space and advocacy services for a consortium of bi-national business organizations in Southern Florida. The site includes news, a member directory, and an event calendar.

Central Florida Women in International Trade
http://www.crossoceans.com/owit/
Based in Goldenrod, the organization promotes the advancement of Florida women in international trade. The site provides contact information and a list of the Board of Directors.

Commercial Service in Florida
http://www.ita.doc.gov/uscs/fl/
Developed by the International Trade Administration, the site is a directory of international trade statistics, leads, events, services, and contacts in Florida.

Enterprise Florida International Offices
http://www.flatrade.org/cgi-dos/efii.exe
The site is a directory of Enterprise Florida overseas trade offices in Brazil, Canada, Germany, Japan, Korea, Mexico, Taiwan, and the United Kingdom.

Export Miami
http://www.exportmiami.com/
The site is an online directory of Miami exporters

in over 20 industries including aerospace, automotive, electronics, transportation, and medical equipment.

Florida Trade Data Center
http://www.flatrade.org/
Based in Miami, the site features Florida export facts, statistics, trade leads, global business classifieds, event calendar, mailing lists, a chat line, a discussion group, and a searchable database of international trading partners.

International Trade and Economic Development
http://www.floridabusiness.com/ITED/default.html
Part of the Enterprise Florida economic development agency, the International Trade and Economic Development program promotes Florida exports and international investment. The site includes export primers, sector profiles, and event information.

Miami Women in International Trade
http://www.wit-miami.com/
Part of a national network, the organization promotes the role of women in international trade. The site includes a member directory, event calendar, and meeting photos.

Polk County International Trade and Investment
http://www.cfdc.org/trade/
Written in English, Spanish, German and Japanese, the site provides Polk County demographic data, a directory of manufacturers, a land and building database, and an international trade mailing list.

Team Florida Trade Network
http://www.floridabusiness.com/ITED/targeted_market_pilot.html
A partnership of industry associations and economic development organizations, the Network provides export counseling and financing to small and medium-sized exporters in Florida.

Trade Shows in Florida
http://www.expoguide.com/shows/data/loc_fl.htm
Compiled by Expoguide, the site is a directory of trade shows in Fort Lauderdale, Jacksonville, Miami, Orlando, Tampa, West Palm Beach, and other Florida centers.

Florida Representative Offices

Bahamas

Consulate of Bahamas in Miami
http://flamingo.bahamas.net.bs/government/gov8.html
The site provides contact information for the Bahamas Consulate in Miami.

Belgium

Belgian Club of Florida
http://www.shadow.net/~pjaspar/belclub/0001.html
Based in Fort Lauderdale, the site features Belgian news, an event calendar, and contact information.

Brazil

Brazil Trade Miami
http://www.brtrademiami.org/
A service of the Brazilian Consulate General, the site features Brazilian news, exchange rates, economic statistics, privatization reports, trade bulletins, an event calendar, and an online business matchmaking service.

Brazilian American Chamber of Commerce of Florida
http://www.brazilchamber.org/
Based in Miami, the Chamber promotes Brazil-Florida trade. The site includes Brazil and Florida fact sheets, an event calendar, membership information, committee reports, and a list of the Board of Directors.

Consulate General of Brazil in Miami
http://www.brazilmiami.org/
Written in English and Portuguese, the site features Brazilian profiles, cultural bulletins, tourism guides, visa information, and legal primers.

U.S. Brazil
http://www.usbrazil.com/
Based in Florida, the English and Portuguese language site provides U.S.-Brazil trade bulletins, monthly newsletters, and business opportunities.

Canada

Canadian American Business Alliance of South Florida
http://canamtrade.badm.sc.edu/caba.htm
Based in Pompano Beach, the Alliance promotes Canada-South Florida trade. The site delivers a mission statement, program directory, and membership information.

Canadian American Business Association of Orlando
http://canamtrade.badm.sc.edu/orlando.htm
The Orlando-based Association promotes Canada-Florida trade. The site provides a mission statement and membership information.

Canadian American International Business Council
http://www.floridacanadatrade.com/
Based in Tampa Bay, the Council promotes Canada-Florida trade and investment. The site features Council news, a membership roster, program directory, and event calendar.

Chile

Chile-U.S. Chamber of Commerce
http://www.chileus.org/
Based in Miami, the site features Chile fact sheets, a member directory, event calendar, company profiles, and online bulletin board.

Colombia

Colombian American Chamber of Commerce of Miami
http://www.colombiachamber.com/
Based in Coral Gables, the Chamber promotes Colombia-U.S. trade. The site provides a Chamber newsletter, member directory, legal primers, economic reports, event calendar, and Colombian importing guide.

Consulate General of Colombia in Miami
*http://www.colombiaemb.org/consular/
consus.html#miami*
A service of the Colombian government, the site lists the Consul General, street address, and phone and fax numbers of the Colombian Consulate in Miami.

Ecuador

Ecuador Trade Center
http://www.miamiweb.com/etc/
Based in Miami, the site features Ecuadorian economic statistics, fact sheets, export and import reports, business opportunities, and a directory of Ecuador resources online.

Ecuadorian American Chamber of Commerce of Greater Miami
http://www.ecuachamber.com/
The Chamber promotes Ecuadorian-U.S. commercial ties. The site provides Ecuador news, fact sheets, and a list of Chamber directors.

France

French Trade Commission in Miami
*http://www.dree.org/usa/InfoGene/PEE/Miami/
index.htm*
A French trade promotion service, the Commission delivers export counseling to French companies. Written in French, the site lists priority sectors for French exporters in the Florida area.

Germany

German-American Trade Council
http://www.gatc.org/
Based in Miami, the Council promotes commercial relations between South Florida and German speaking countries. The site includes a mission statement, member directory, and an online information exchange.

Guyana

Honorary Consul of Guyana in Fort Lauderdale
http://www.guyana.org/TRADEREP.htm
The site provides contact information for the Guyana Honorary Consul in Fort Lauderdale.

Hungary

Hungarian-American Chamber of Commerce of Miami
http://www.abicc.org/hungary/
The Chamber promotes Hungary-United States trade. The site contains a newsletter, member directory, and event calendar.

Iceland

Consulate General of Iceland in Tallahassee
http://www.iceland.org/list1n.htm#CONS
The site lists the Consul General, street address, phone and fax numbers, and e-mail link of the Icelandic Consulate in Tallahassee.

Israel

Consulate General of Israel in Miami
http://www.gate.net/~israelmi/
Targeting Florida and Puerto Rico, the service includes a staff directory, visa and passport information, and Israel economic reports.

Florida-Israel Institute
http://www.fau.edu/other/flisrael/
Sponsored by Florida Atlantic University, the Institute promotes Florida-Israel cultural and economic exchanges. The site includes contact information and a list of directors.

Italy

Consulate General of Italy in Miami
http://www.italconsmiami.com/
Posted in English and Italian, the site provides a welcome from the Consul General, passport and visa information, and a directory of consular services.

Italy America Chamber of Commerce Southeast
http://www.italian-chamber-miami.com/
Written in English and Italian, the site provides a Chamber newsletter, member directory, event calendar, and a directory of business opportunities in the United States and Italy.

Japan

Consulate General of Japan in Miami
http://www.embjapan.org/miami/
Along with Japanese fact sheets and market reports, the site provides Consulate speeches, contact information, and an event calendar.

Japan Society of South Florida
http://www.fl-news.com/
Posted in Japanese, the Miami-based site provides Japanese news, fact sheets, and business reports.

Mexico

Trade Commission of Mexico in Miami
http://www.mexico-businessline.com/ingles/ofrepmu3.html#miami
The site lists the street address, phone and fax numbers, and e-mail link of the Trade Commission of Mexico in Miami.

Peru

Consulate General of Peru in Miami
http://www.heuristika.com/consulado-peru/
Written in Spanish, the site provides Peru business primers, government directories, legal guides and Consulate contact information.

Poland

Polish American Chamber of Commerce of Florida and the Americas
http://www.wwdir.com/polishcc.html
Based in Miami Springs, the Chamber promotes Poland-Florida trade. The site includes a mission statement, member directory, and contact information.

Puerto Rico

Puerto Rico Federal Affairs Administration in Coral Gables
http://www.prfaa-govpr.org/southflorida.htm
The site lists the street address of the Puerto Rico Federal Affairs Administration regional office in Coral Gables.

Puerto Rico Federal Affairs Administration in Orlando
http://www.prfaa-govpr.org/florida.htm
Featuring greetings from the Regional Director, the site lists the street address, phone and fax numbers, and e-mail link of the Puerto Rico Federal Affairs Administration regional office in Orlando.

Russia

Former Soviet Union Florida Chamber of Commerce
http://www.lati.net/fsuf/
Based in Miami, the Chamber promotes trade between Florida and independent countries in the former Soviet Union. The site features a Chamber mission statement, member directory, and event calendar.

South Africa

South African Trade Center in Orlando
http://www.satcis.com/011.satc_orlando/
001.intro_to_satc_orlando.html
A South Africa trade promotion service, the site provides contact information and a directory of Center services including export counseling, international banking, and transportation assistance.

Spain

Spanish Commercial Office in Miami
http://www.icex.es/openURL.html#openURL=/
english/infoproyem/ofcomes/ofcomes.html#AM
The site lists the staff, street address, phone and fax numbers, and e-mail link of the Spanish Commercial Office in Miami.

Sweden

Swedish American Chamber of Commerce in Florida
http://207.237.124.120/florida/
Based in Coral Gables, the site provides a Chamber newsletter, member directory, event calendar, and Sweden fact sheets.

Swedish American Trade Center
http://www.swedeamtrade.com/
Sponsored by the Swedish Trade Council, the Center provides information and advice to Swedish exporters and distributors. The site features Swedish business opportunities and trade primers.

Switzerland

Swiss-American Chamber of Commerce Florida Division
http://www.amcham.ch/usa/losangel/index.htm
Based in Winter Park, the Division promotes Florida-Switzerland trade and relations. The site includes an executive directory, event calendar, and contact information.

Taiwan

China External Trade Development Council Office in Miami
http://www.cetra.org.tw/english/o_office/
indexset.htm

A Taiwanese trade promotion service, the site lists the mission statement and e-mail link of the China External Trade Development Council Office in Miami.

Thailand

Thai Trade Center in Miami
http://www.thaitrade.com/wwtto.html
A service of the Thailand Department of Export Promotion, the site lists the street address, phone and fax numbers, and e-mail link of the Thai Trade Center in Miami.

United Kingdom

British American Chamber of Commerce of Central Florida
http://www.btrg.com/bacccf/
Based in Orlando, the site provides a Chamber member directory, event calendar, and contact information.

British American Chamber of Commerce of Greater Fort Lauderdale
http://www.babc.org/ft_lauderdale/
With a membership of approximately 100 people, the Chamber promotes U.S.-British trade. The site includes the Chamber mission statement and history, and lists key executives and directors.

British American Chamber of Commerce of Tampa
http://www.babc.org/tampa/
The site includes Chamber news, an event calendar, member directory, and contact information.

Consulate of Britain in Miami
http://britain-info.org/bis/bto/BTO_FL.sTM
Along with contact information, the site provides British fact sheets, business guides, and investment primers.

Vice Consulate of Britain in Orlando
http://britain-info.org/bis/dipoff/DIPOFFFL.HTM
The site provides contact information for the British Vice Consulate in Orlando.

Venezuela

Venezuelan American Chamber of Commerce of Florida
http://www.venezuelanchamber.org/
Based in Coral Gables, the site features Venezuelan news, fact sheets, event information, and a directory of Chamber staff and committees.

Georgia

Georgia Media

Georgia Media
http://www.mediainfo.com/emediajs/specific-geo.htm?region=georgia
A service of Editor and Publisher Interactive, the site provides a searchable directory of web-based media sites in Georgia including city guides, magazines, and newspapers.

Georgia Market Guides

Business Location and Assistance
http://www.georgia.org/itt/recruitment/index.html
A service of Georgia Industry, Trade and Tourism, the site provides Georgia fact sheets, success stories, incentives, and a directory of business services.

Georgia Business and Economic Development
http://www.state.ga.us/index/topic_pages.cgi?topic_id=1
The site lists key economic development agencies and resources in Georgia such as the Georgia Procurement Registry, Department of Banking and Finance, and Small Business Resource Guide.

Georgia Chamber of Commerce
http://www.gachamber.org/
Based in Atlanta, the site provides Georgia newsletters, press releases, legislative bulletins, a member directory, and event information.

Georgia County Snapshots
http://www.dca.state.ga.us/snapshots/default.asp
A service of the Georgia Department of Community Affairs, the site provides demographic and economic snapshots of the state's 159 counties.

How to Do Business with the State of Georgia
http://www2.state.ga.us/Departments/DOAS/PROCURE/procbuff.html
Posted by the Georgia Department of Administrative Services, the site provides primers on how to conduct business with Georgia procurement agencies. The service includes vendor manuals, purchasing contacts, requests for proposals, and an online supply catalog.

Georgia Trade Assistance

Atlanta International Magazine's International Marketplace
http://www.aimlink.com/marketpl.html
A service of *Atlanta International* magazine, the site is a directory of U.S. southeastern manufacturers who are seeking overseas sales opportunities and business partners.

Commercial Service in Georgia
http://www.ita.doc.gov/uscs/ga/
Developed by the International Trade Administration, the site is a directory of international trade statistics, leads, events, services, and contacts in Georgia.

Department of Agriculture International Trade Section
http://www.agr.state.ga.us/html/international_trade.html
A unit of the Georgia Department of Agriculture, the International Trade Section provides export counseling to Georgia agri-food companies. Online publications include the *International Advertiser*, a newsletter for European food buyers, and *International Update*, a newsletter for Georgia agri-food exporters on international trade opportunities.

Georgia Export Assistance
http://www.georgia.org/itt/export/index.html
A service of Georgia Industry, Trade and Tourism, the site features export primers, importing tutorials, and a searchable directory of Georgia exporters and products.

Guia Export Online
http://www.guiaexport.bellsouth.com/
Written in English and Spanish, the site is a browsable database of Georgia exporters. The service includes a glossary of trade terms, U.S. trade statistics by commodity and country, and a directory of international trade events.

Trade Shows in Georgia
http://www.expoguide.com/shows/data/loc_ga.htm
Compiled by Expoguide, the site is a directory of trade shows in Atlanta, Moultrie, Savannah, and other Georgia centers.

Georgia Representative Offices

Australia

Austrade in Atlanta
http://www.austrade.gov.au/Atlanta/
A service of the Australian government, Austrade provides export promotion and business matchmaking services for Australian companies doing business in the United States Southwest..

Austria

Austrian Trade Commission in Atlanta
http://www.austriantrade.org/AustrianTrade/offices/ahst_atl.htm
The site lists the Trade Commissioner, address, e-mail link, and phone and fax numbers of the Austrian Trade Commission in Atlanta. The territories covered include Alabama, Arkansas, Florida, and Georgia.

Belgium

Belgium Consulate General in Atlanta
http://www.belgium-emb.org/usa/representatives/usa_atlanta.html
The virtual Consulate provides Belgium fact sheets, tourism guides, business bulletins, and sector profiles.

Canada

Canadian American Society of Georgia
http://canamtrade.badm.sc.edu/newgeorg.html
Based in Atlanta, the Society promotes Canada-U.S. trade. The site delivers a mission statement, program directory, and membership information.

Canadian Consulate General in Atlanta
http://www.sesoft.org/directry/members/canad_en.htm
The Consulate represents Canada and promotes Canadian interests in the Southeast U.S., Puerto Rico and the U.S. Virgin Islands. Posted in English and French, the site explains the Consulate's export counseling and business matching services.

Province of Québec Trade Office in Atlanta
http://www.mri.gouv.qc.ca/dans_le_monde/etats_unis/antennes_us_an.html#Atlanta
A service of the Québec government, the site lists the Commercial Attaché and contact information for the Québec Trade Office in Atlanta.

Colombia

Colombian Consulate in Atlanta
http://www.colombiaemb.org/consular/consus.html#atlanta
The site lists the Consul General, street address, phone and fax numbers, and geographic jurisdiction for the Colombian Consulate in Atlanta.

France

French Trade Commission in Atlanta
http://www.dree.org/usa/InfoGene/PEE/Atlanta/index.htm
A French trade promotion service, the Commission delivers export counseling to French companies. Written in French, the site lists priority sectors for French exporters in Alabama, Georgia, Mississippi, North Carolina, South Carolina, and Tennessee.

Germany

German American Chamber of Commerce in Atlanta
http://www.ahk.net/en/us/Atlanta/
Part of a worldwide network of German Chamber offices, the German American Chamber promotes German-U.S. trade. The site lists the Chief Executive Officer, street address, phone and fax numbers, and e-mail link of the Chamber office in Atlanta.

Iceland

Consulate General of Iceland in Atlanta
http://www.iceland.org/list1n.htm#CONS
The site lists the Consul General, street address, phone and fax numbers, and e-mail link of the Icelandic Consulate in Atlanta.

Israel

Consulate General of Israel in Atlanta
http://www.israelemb.org/atlanta/atlanta.htm
Serving Alabama, Georgia, Mississippi, North Carolina, South Carolina, and Tennessee, the site provides Israeli fact sheets, cultural reports, academic directories, and Consulate contact information.

Japan

Consulate General of Japan in Atlanta
http://cgjapanatlanta.org/

Targeting Alabama, Georgia, North Carolina, South Carolina, and Virginia, the site delivers Japanese fact sheets, speeches, an event calendar, visa information, and study opportunities.

JETRO Atlanta
http://www.JETRO.org/atlanta/
Serving businesspeople in the U.S. Southeast, the site delivers Japanese fact sheets, press releases, success stories, and an event calendar.

Mexico

Consulate General of Mexico in Atlanta
http://www.enespanol.com/atlanta/mexconsulate/
Posted in English and Spanish, the site includes Mexican news, press releases, fact sheets, international trade reports, and policy bulletins.

Trade Commission of Mexico in Atlanta
http://www.mexico-businessline.com/ingles/ ofrepmu3.html#atlanta
The site lists the street address, phone and fax numbers, and e-mail link of the Trade Commission of Mexico in Atlanta.

Switzerland

Swiss-American Chamber of Commerce Southeast United States Chapter
http://www.amcham.ch/usa/southeas/index.htm
Based in Atlanta, the Chapter promotes Southeastern United States-Switzerland trade and relations. The site includes an executive directory, event calendar, and contact information.

Swiss Trade Office in Atlanta
http://www.swissemb.org/biz/html/atlanta.html
Serving Alabama, Florida, Mississippi, North Carolina, South Carolina, and Tennessee, the site lists the street address, phone and fax numbers, and e-mail link of the Swiss Trade Office in Atlanta.

Taiwan

Taiwan Government Information Office in Atlanta
http://www.gio.gov.tw/info/ngio/usa-f.html
Posted in Chinese and English, the site lists the street address, phone and fax numbers, and e-mail link of the Taiwan Government Information Office in Atlanta.

United Kingdom

Consulate General of Britain in Atlanta
http://britain-info.org/bis/dipoff/atlanta.sTM
The site provides British fact sheets, business guides, investment primers, press releases, and a directory of commercial services.

Hawaii

Hawaii Media

Hawaii Media
http://www.mediainfo.com/emediajs/specific-geo.htm?region=hawaii
A service of Editor and Publisher Interactive, the site provides a searchable directory of web-based media sites in Hawaii including city guides, magazines, and newspapers.

Hawaii Market Guides

Business Hawaii
http://www.hcc.hawaii.edu/hspls/hbiz.html
A hub of state information, the site is a directory of leading economic development agencies, industry associations and business resources online in Hawaii.

Department of Business, Economic Development and Tourism
http://www.hawaii.gov/dbedt/index.html
Based in Honolulu, the site provides Hawaii news releases, county profiles, business primers, tourism guides, economic reports, and census data.

Hawaii Small Business Development Center Network
http://www.hawaii-sbdc.org/
Sponsored by the U.S. Small Business Administration, the site is a directory of small business support centers, libraries, workshops, and programs in Hawaii.

Starting a Business in Hawaii
http://www.hawaii.gov/dbedt/start/starting.html
An entrepreneurial road map, the site explains how to start a business in Hawaii. Topics include feasibility studies, marketing strategies, legal forms, licenses and permits, work force, and tax climate.

State of Hawaii Data Book
http://www.hawaii.gov/dbedt/db96/index.html
A service of the Hawaii state government, the site

is a virtual library of Hawaii statistics. Categories include population, health, education, land use, recreation and travel, social insurance, transportation, and agriculture.

Hawaii Trade Assistance

Commercial Service in Hawaii
http://www.ita.doc.gov/uscs/hi/
Developed by the International Trade Administration, the site is a directory of international trade statistics, leads, events, services, and contacts in Hawaii.

International Trade Hawaii
http://www.hawaii.gov/dbedt/trade/greg4.html
A service of the State of Hawaii, the site features trade leads, foreign trade zone reports, export and import guides, and an international trade financing primer.

Trade/Invest Hawaii's Monthly Bulletin
http://www.hawaii.gov/dbedt/trade/newsltr.html
Updated monthly, the site provides international trade news, procurement notices, market reports, and book reviews.

Trade Shows in Hawaii
http://www.expoguide.com/shows/data/loc_hi.htm
Compiled by Expoguide, the site is a directory of trade shows in Honolulu, Maui, Oahu, and other Hawaii centers.

Hawaii Representative Offices

China

Hong Kong Business Association of Hawaii
http://www.hkbah.org/
An online forum for the promotion of Hawaii-Hong Kong trade, the site provides a mission statement, newsletter, press releases, and event information.

Japan

Consulate General of Japan in Honolulu
http://www.embjapan.org/honolulu/
The Japanese government site posts Consulate contact information and Japan fact sheets.

Marshall Islands

Consulate of the Marshall Islands in Honolulu
http://www.rmiembassyus.org/address.html

The site lists the street address, phone and fax numbers, and e-mail link of the Marshall Islands Consulate in Honolulu.

Micronesia

Consulate General of Micronesia in Honolulu
http://www.fsmembassy.org/honolu~1.htm
The site provides the street address, phone and fax numbers, and e-mail directory of the Micronesian Consulate in Honolulu.

Western Samoa

Consulate General of Western Samoa in Waipahu
http://www.interwebinc.com/samoa/ missus.html#hawaii
The site lists the street address, and phone and fax numbers of the Western Samoan Consulate General in Waipahu.

Idaho

Idaho Media

Idaho Media
http://www.mediainfo.com/emediajs/specific-geo.htm?region=idaho
A service of Editor and Publisher Interactive, the site provides a searchable directory of web-based media sites in Idaho including city guides, magazines, and newspapers.

Idaho Market Guides

Business Information
http://www.idoc.state.id.us/pages/ businesspage.html
An Idaho business resource page, the site offers primers on Idaho quality of life, workers, education, utilities, agriculture, high technology, training, and taxation.

Idaho Department of Commerce
http://www.idoc.state.id.us/
Homepage of the state Commerce Department, the site provides Idaho business guides, travel tips, statistics, county profiles, relocation handbooks, and discussion forums.

Idaho Small Business Development Centers
http://www.idbsu.edu/isbdc/
Sponsored in part by the U.S. Small Business Administration, the Centers provide small

business assistance and training to Idaho entrepreneurs. Services include financing and marketing workshops.

Starting a Business in Idaho
http://www.idoc.state.id.us/information/quickinfo/start.html
Posted in English and Spanish, the site explains how to start and operate a business in Idaho. Chapters include product and service protection, business organization, state and federal taxes, employee requirements, and occupational licenses.

Idaho Trade Assistance

Commercial Service in Idaho
http://www.ita.doc.gov/uscs/id/
Developed by the International Trade Administration, the site is a directory of international trade statistics, leads, events, services, and contacts in Idaho.

Idaho International Business
http://www.idoc.state.id.us/Pages/EXPORTPAGE.html
A service of the Idaho Department of Commerce, the site delivers Idaho export news, event bulletins, and program information. The page also lists Idaho's overseas trade offices in Japan, Korea, Mexico, and Taiwan.

Trade Shows in Idaho
http://www.expoguide.com/shows/data/loc_id.htm
Compiled by Expoguide, the site is a directory of trade shows in Boise, Pocatello, Sun Valley, and other Idaho centers.

Illinois

Illinois Media

Illinois Media
http://www.mediainfo.com/emediajs/specific-geo.htm?region=illinois
Developed by Editor and Publisher Interactive, the site provides a browsable directory of web-based media sites in Illinois including city guides, magazines, and newspapers.

Illinois Market Guides

Economic Facts and Figures
http://www.commerce.state.il.us/dcca/menus/pdpr/pdpr_hme.htm

A service of the State Office of Planning and Research, the site is a browsable database of Illinois statistics. Categories include economic indicators, population projections, and interesting Illinois facts.

Illinois Business Report
http://italchambers.net/BusinessReports.html
Prepared by the Italian Chamber of Commerce and written in Italian, the site provides Illinois fact sheets, market reports, and commercial guides.

Illinois Department of Commerce and Community Affairs
http://www.commerce.state.il.us/
Based in Springfield, the site features Illinois fact sheets, business guides, population statistics, energy and recycling reports, press releases, and a Department staff directory.

Illinois Manufacturers Association
http://www.ima-net.org/
Headquartered in Springfield, the site provides a newsletter, executive memos, government bulletins, an online bulletin board, and a directory of Illinois manufacturers.

Illinois Trade Assistance

Central Illinois Exporters' Association
http://www.conted.ceps.uiuc.edu/ceps/IA/Exporters_Assn.html
Based in Champaign, the Association promotes Central Illinois exports. The site includes an Association mission statement and contact information.

Commercial Service in Illinois
http://www.ita.doc.gov/uscs/il/
Developed by the International Trade Administration, the site is a directory of international trade statistics, leads, events, services, and contacts in Illinois.

International Business Division
http://www.commerce.state.il.us/dcca/menus/int'l/int_home.htm
A unit of the Illinois Department of Commerce, the International Business Division provides export counseling and assistance to Illinois companies. The site includes an event calendar, trade leads, program directory, and contact information for Illinois trade offices in Belgium, Hong Kong, Hungary, Japan, Mexico, and Poland.

International Economic Development
http://www.siu.edu/~econdev/intecdev.html
A service of Southern Illinois University, the site provides information on exporting, importing, trade finance, global business research, and the Illinois Consortium for International Education.

International Trade Association of Greater Chicago
http://www.itagc.org/
An export promotion service for Chicago area companies, the site delivers trade news, an event calendar, membership information, and a directory of programs and services.

International Trade Association of Southern Illinois
http://www.siu.edu/~econdev/intl_trade.html
Based in Carbondale, the Association offers export assistance to Southern Illinois companies. The site includes a program directory and contact information.

International Trade Shows and Missions
http://www.commerce.state.il.us/dcca/files/int'l/missions.htm
A service of the Illinois International Business Division, the site is a directory of upcoming Illinois trade missions and product showcases in countries such as China, England, Hungary, and South Africa.

Trade Shows in Illinois

http://www.expoguide.com/shows/data/loc_il.htm
Developed by Expoguide, the site is a directory of trade shows in Chicago, Oak Brook, Peoria, Rosemont, Springfield, and other Illinois centers.

U.S. Export Assistance Center in Chicago
http://www.ita.doc.gov/useacchicago/
A service of the International Trade Administration, the site provides international marketing guides, trade finance primers, and contact information.

Illinois Representative Offices

Argentina

Consulate General of the Republic of Argentina in Chicago
http://www.uic.edu/orgs/argentina/
The virtual Consulate delivers Argentina news, fact sheets, economic profiles, tourism guides, an event calendar, and visa and passport information.

Austria

Austrian Trade Commission in Chicago
http://www.austriantrade.org/AustrianTrade/offices/ahst_chi.htm
Targeting businesspeople in Illinois, Indiana, Iowa, Kansas, Kentucky, Michigan, Minnesota, Missouri, Nebraska, North Dakota, Ohio, South Dakota, and Wisconsin, the site lists the Trade Commissioners, street address, phone and fax numbers, and e-mail link of the Austrian Trade Commission in Chicago.

Belgium

Belgium Consulate General in Chicago
http://www.belgium-emb.org/usa/representatives/usa_chicago.html
Serving businesspeople in the U.S. Midwest, the site lists the address, phone and fax numbers, and e-mail link of the Belgian Consulate in Chicago.

Canada

Canadian Consulate General in Chicago
http://www.canadaonlinechicago.net/
Posted in English and French, the site features Canadian news, tourism guides, trade reports, strategic alliance primers, and investment studies.

Province of Québec Trade Office in Chicago
http://www.mri.gouv.qc.ca/dans_le_monde/etats_unis/antennes_us_an.html#Chicago
A service of the Québec provincial government, the site lists the Commercial Attachés and contact information for the Québec Trade Office in Chicago.

Colombia

Colombia Consul in Chicago
http://www.colombiaemb.org/consular/consus.html#chicago
The site lists the Consul General, street address, phone and fax numbers, and geographic jurisdiction for the Colombian Consulate in Chicago.

Denmark

Consulate General of Denmark in Chicago
http://www.consulatedk.org/
Along with a directory of consular services, the English and Danish language site provides United States market information, and Danish product catalogs.

France

French Trade Commission in Chicago
http://www.dree.org/usa/InfoGene/PEE/Chicago/index.htm
A French trade promotion service, the site lists priority sectors for French exporters in 13 U.S. Midwestern states including Illinois, Indiana, and Iowa.

Germany

German American Chamber of Commerce in Chicago
http://www.ahk.net/en/us/Chicago/
Part of a worldwide network of German Chamber offices, the site lists the Chairperson, street address, phone and fax numbers, and e-mail link of the Chamber office in Chicago.

Haiti

Consulate General of Haiti in Chicago
http://www.chrd.org/Cons.html
The online service provides Haitian fact sheets, passport information, legal guides, business opportunities, travel tips, and a directory of government agencies.

India

Consulate General of India in Chicago
http://chicago.indianconsulate.com/
The digital Consulate delivers India news, press releases, visa and passport information, and a directory of leading Indian trade shows.

Israel

Consulate General of Israel in Chicago
http://www.israelemb.org/chicago/index.htm
The virtual Consulate delivers Israel news, articles, interviews, tourism information, a staff directory, and event calendar.

Italy

Consulate General of Italy in Chicago
http://www.italyemb.org/italcons.htm#chicago
Serving businesspeople in the U.S. Midwest, the site lists the street address, phone and fax numbers, and e-mail link of the Italian Consulate in Chicago.

Japan

Consulate General of Japan in Chicago
http://www.embjapan.org/chicago/
A Japanese information center, the site provides Japanese fact sheets, visa information, research reports, and an event calendar.

Japanese Chamber of Commerce and Industry of Chicago
http://www.japanlink.com/jccchome.html
A service for Japanese businesses located in the Chicago area and American companies doing business with Japan, the site includes a mission statement, member directory and contact information.

JETRO Chicago
http://www.JETROcgo.org/
Serving companies in the U.S. Midwest, the site provides Japanese newsletters, success stories, trade reports, and business matchmaking services in industries such as electronics, fasteners, forging and stamping, and casting and tooling.

Mexico

State of Guanajuato Trade Office in Chicago
http://www.guanajuato.gob.mx/cofoce/offices.htm
The site lists the street address, phone and fax numbers, and e-mail link of the Mexican state of Guanajuato Trade Office in Chicago.

Trade Commission of Mexico in Chicago
http://www.mexico-businessline.com/ingles/ofrepmu3.html#chicago
The site lists the street address, phone and fax numbers, and e-mail link of the Trade Commission of Mexico in Chicago.

Netherlands

Netherlands Foreign Investment Agency in Chicago
http://www.nfia.com/html/contact/index.html

The site lists the street address, phone and fax numbers, and e-mail link of the Netherlands Foreign Investment Agency in Chicago.

New Zealand

New Zealand Consulate in Chicago
http://www.emb.com/nzemb/offices/consul~1.htm#chicago
The site lists the street address, and phone and fax numbers of the New Zealand Consulate in Chicago.

Philippines

Philippine Trade and Investment Promotion Office in Chicago
http://www.dti.gov.ph/chi/
The site provides a mission statement, service directory, and contact information for the Philippine Trade Office in Chicago.

Poland

Consulate General of Poland in Chicago
http://homepage.interaccess.com/~comconpl/
The virtual Consulate provides Poland news, fact sheets, investment guides, business primers, and a directory of consular program and services.

Puerto Rico

Puerto Rican Chamber of Commerce of Illinois
http://www.prcci.com/
Based in Chicago, the Chamber promotes Puerto Rico trade and investment. The site includes the Chamber mission statement, member directory, and e-mail link.

Puerto Rico Federal Affairs Administration in Chicago
http://www.prfaa-govpr.org/chicago.htm
Featuring greetings from the Regional Director, the site lists the street address, phone and fax numbers, and e-mail link of the Puerto Rico Federal Affairs Administration regional office in Chicago.

Russia

American-Russia Chamber of Commerce and Industry
http://www.uic.edu/orgs/arcci/
Based in Chicago, the Chamber promotes United States-Russia trade and relations. The

site includes a mission statement, membership directory, and event information.

Spain

Spanish Commercial Office in Chicago
http://www.icex.es/openURL.html#openURL=/english/infoproyem/ofcomes/ofcomes.html#AM
The site lists the staff, street address, phone and fax numbers, and e-mail link of the Spanish Commercial Office in Chicago.

Sweden

Swedish Trade Council in Chicago
http://www.swedentrade.com/index.htm
An online trade center, the site features Sweden fact sheets, business news, economic statistics, an interactive marketplace, event calendar, and Internet primers.

Switzerland

Swiss Trade Office in Chicago
http://www.swissemb.org/biz/html/chicago.html
The site lists the Director, street address, e-mail link, and phone and fax numbers of the Swiss Trade Office in Chicago.

Taiwan

China External Trade Development Council Office in Chicago
http://www.cetra.org.tw/english/o_office/indexset.htm
A Taiwanese trade promotion service, the site lists the mission statement and e-mail link of the China External Trade Development Council Office in Chicago.

Taiwan Government Information Office in Chicago
http://www.gio.gov.tw/info/ngio/usa-f.html
Posted in Chinese and English, the site lists the street address, phone and fax numbers, and e-mail link of the Taiwan Government Information Office in Chicago.

Thailand

Royal Thai Consulate General in Chicago
http://www.mfa.go.th/Embassy/detail/23.htm
The site lists the Consul General, street address, and phone and fax numbers of the Thai Consulate in Chicago.

Thai Trade Center in Chicago
http://www.thaitrade.com/wwtto.html
A service of the Thailand Department of Export Promotion, the site lists the street address, phone and fax numbers, and e-mail link of the Thai Trade Center in Chicago.

United Kingdom

British American Chamber of Commerce for the Midwest
http://www.babc.org/midwest/
Based in Chicago, the site provides United States-United Kingdom trade news, an event calendar, and a directory of member services such as teleconferencing, translation, and business matchmaking.

Consulate General of Britain in Chicago
http://britain-info.org/bis/dipoff/chicago.sTM
The site provides British fact sheets, business guides, investment primers, and a directory of consular and commercial services.

Indiana

Indiana Media

Indiana Media
http://www.mediainfo.com/emediajs/specific-geo.htm?region=indiana
Developed by Editor and Publisher Interactive, the site provides a browsable directory of web-based media sites in Indiana including city guides, magazines, and newspapers.

Indiana Market Guides

Indiana Business Development
http://www.ai.org/bdev/index.html
Based in Indianapolis, the service features Indiana profiles, taxation reports, cost of living comparisons, and a directory of business incentives.

Indiana County Profiles
http://www.iupui.edu/it/ibrc/PROFILES/SIFT/sift_overview.html
A service of the Indiana University School of Business, the site is a browsable database of statistics on Indiana counties. Categories include economy and jobs, people and households, and health and vital statistics.

Indiana Small Business Development Corporation
http://www.isbdcorp.org/
A support service for small and medium-sized companies, the site highlights Corporation programs for entrepreneurs, and women and minority business owners.

Indiana State Information Center
http://www.ai.org/sic/
Part of the Access Indiana online network, the site delivers Indiana fact sheets, relocation primers, consumer assistance, travel tips, and a business owner's guide to state government.

Indiana Trade Assistance

Commercial Service in Indiana
http://www.ita.doc.gov/uscs/in/
A service of the International Trade Administration, the site is a directory of international trade statistics, leads, events, services, and contacts in Indiana.

Indianapolis Export Assistance Center
http://www.ita.doc.gov/uscs/in/indeac.htm
An online service for Indianapolis area exporters, the site includes a newsletter, regional reports, sector profiles, staff directory, and calendar of events.

International Assistance
http://www.ai.org/bdev/html/ass_iia.html
Posted by Access Indiana, the site is a directory of Indiana export assistance services and programs. Offerings include international trade counseling, export loan guarantees, and trade show financing.

International Business Website
http://www.indychamber.com/intl/INTLST.HTM
A service of the Indianapolis Chamber of Commerce, the site provides a nine-step international trade plan, trade finance primer, and a directory of key federal and state contacts.

Trade Shows in Indiana
http://www.expoguide.com/shows/data/loc_in.htm
Developed by Expoguide, the site is a directory of trade shows in Fort Wayne, Indianapolis, South Bend, and other Indiana centers.

World Trade Club of Indiana
http://www.surf-ici.com/wtc/
Based in Indianapolis, the Club promotes

Indiana international trade. The site delivers an event calendar, member directory, presentation transcripts, and a list of job openings.

Iowa

Iowa Media

Iowa Media
http://www.mediainfo.com/emediajs/specific-geo.htm?region=iowa
A service of Editor and Publisher Interactive, the site provides a browsable directory of web-based media sites in Iowa including magazines, newspapers, and radio stations.

Iowa Market Guides

Iowa Business Network
http://www.iabusnet.org/
Updated daily, the site provides Iowa business news, editorials, government bulletins, an event calendar, employer's handbook, and an ask-the-expert feature.

Iowa Department of Economic Development
http://www.state.ia.us/government/ided/index.html
Based in Des Moines, the site delivers Iowa news, site selection primers, economic statistics, travel information, and a directory of business assistance programs.

Iowa Economic Trends
http://www.state.ia.us/trends/index.html
A service of the Iowa Department of Economic Development, the site provides state statistics on housing permits, home sales, employment, factory and farm exports, personal income, and other economic indicators.

Iowa—Smart State for Business
http://www.smart.state.ia.us/index.html
An online relocation resource, the site offers Iowa economic development news, a business climate overview, an executive guide to site selection, and a directory of available buildings and sites.

Iowa Trade Assistance

Commercial Service in Iowa
http://www.ita.doc.gov/uscs/ia/
Developed by the International Trade Administration, the site is a directory of international trade statistics, leads, events, services, and contacts in Iowa.

Export Stats and Facts
http://www.state.ia.us/international/Stats.htm
A service of the Iowa state government, the site provides Iowa export facts and statistics.

International Division
http://www.state.ia.us/international/
A unit of the Iowa Department of Economic Development, the Division promotes Iowa exports and attracts foreign investment to the state. The site includes an event calendar, program directory, and exporter profiles.

Trade Shows in Iowa
http://www.expoguide.com/shows/data/loc_ia.htm
Compiled by Expoguide, the site is a directory of trade shows in Ames, Cedar Rapids, Davenport, Des Moines, Dubuque, and other Iowa centers.

Kansas

Kansas Media

Kansas Media
http://www.mediainfo.com/emediajs/specific-geo.htm?region=kansas
A service of Editor and Publisher Interactive, the site provides a browsable directory of web-based media sites in Kansas including city guides, magazines, and newspapers.

Kansas Market Guides

Kansas Department of Commerce and Housing
http://www.kansascommerce.com/
Based in Topeka, the site delivers Kansas press releases, job opportunities, fact sheets, tourism information, business guides, quality of life comparisons, and product directories.

State of Kansas
http://www.state.ks.us/
Developed by the Information Network of Kansas, the site offers Kansas fact sheets, business contacts, professional directories, city profiles, and government bulletins.

Kansas Trade Assistance

Commercial Service in Kansas
http://www.ita.doc.gov/uscs/ks/
Developed by the International Trade Administration, the site is a directory of international trade statistics, leads, events, services, and contacts in Kansas.

International Business
http://www.kansascommerce.com/0306international.html
A service of the Kansas Department of Commerce and Housing, the site provides Kansas export news and a directory of export workshops, trade show financing, and other state-sponsored international trade programs.

International Business Resource Center
http://www.ibrc.bschool.ukans.edu/
Developed by the University of Kansas Center for International Business, the site features world news, trade leads, export statistics, country profiles, and a Midwest trade database.

Kansas International
http://www.ksintl.org/
Based in Lawrence, Kansas International promotes Kansas exports and global partnering. The site includes news, an event calendar, a membership directory, and contact information.

Why Come to Kansas
http://www.kansascommerce.com/0306-04why.html#WE WELCOME
The state government site provides a directory of Kansas foreign trade and investment offices in Australia, Belgium, and Japan.

Trade Shows in Kansas
http://www.expoguide.com/shows/data/loc_ks.htm
A service of Expoguide, the site is a directory of trade shows in Lawrence, Topeka, Wichita, and other Kansas centers.

Kentucky

Kentucky Media

Kentucky Media
http://www.mediainfo.com/emediajs/specific-geo.htm?region=kentucky
A service of Editor and Publisher Interactive, the site provides a browsable directory of web-based media sites in Kentucky including magazines, newspapers, and television stations.

Kentucky Market Guides

Business Incentives
http://www.state.ky.us/edc/incen.htm
A service of the Kentucky state government, the site provides a directory of Kentucky business incentives. Programs include income tax credits, enterprise zone assistance, industrial revenue bonds, loans, and job recruitment and training services.

Commonwealth of Kentucky
http://www.state.ky.us/
Homepage of the state government, the site delivers state fact sheets, sector profiles, government directories, tourism guides, vital statistics information, and business filing forms.

Kentucky Cabinet for Economic Development
http://www.state.ky.us/edc/cabmain.htm
Based in Frankfort, the site includes Kentucky news, county profiles, job opportunities, relocation primers, sector reports, and quality of life fact sheets.

Kentucky Chamber of Commerce
http://www.kychamber.com/
The site provides Chamber news, press releases, business bulletins, a member directory, and policy position papers on issues such as government efficiency, healthcare insurance, and transportation.

Kentucky Trade Assistance

Commercial Service in Kentucky
http://www.ita.doc.gov/uscs/ky/
A service of the International Trade Administration, the site is a directory of international trade statistics, leads, events, services, and contacts in Kentucky.

Kentucky Export Directory
http://promarket.com/ky-pg1.htm
Sponsored by Western Kentucky University, the site provides a browsable directory of Kentucky exporters.

Kentucky Export Message Board
http://promarket.com/disc1_toc.htm
Part of the Kentucky Export Directory, the site is an online international trade message board. Users can post global business questions, provide answers, and search for information.

Kentucky International Trade Office
http://www.state.ky.us/edc/ito.htm
A unit of the state government, the Office provides export counseling and business matchmaking services to Kentucky companies. The site includes contact information for the Kentucky foreign trade offices in Belgium, Mexico, and Japan.

Trade Shows in Kentucky
http://www.expoguide.com/shows/data/loc_ky.htm
Compiled by Expoguide, the site is a directory of trade shows in Lexington, Louisville, and other Kentucky centers.

Louisiana

Louisiana Media

Louisiana Media
http://www.mediainfo.com/emediajs/specific-geo.htm?region=louisiana
A service of Editor and Publisher Interactive, the site provides a searchable directory of web-based media sites in Louisiana including magazines, newspapers, and television stations.

Louisiana Market Guides

Entergy Louisiana Economic Development
http://www.entergy.com/retserv/econ/la/index.htm
A service of Entergy Corporation, the site delivers Louisiana company profiles, a building and site database, and a directory of state seaports.

Louisiana Department of Economic Development
http://www.lded.state.la.us/
Based in Baton Rouge, the site provides Louisiana fact sheets, relocation primers, sector profiles, and a directory of tax and business incentives.

Louisiana Trade Assistance

Commercial Service in Louisiana
http://www.ita.doc.gov/uscs/la/
A service of the International Trade Administration, the site is a directory of international trade statistics, leads, events, services, and contacts in Louisiana.

International Trade Division
http://www.lded.state.la.us/int_trade_assist.html
A unit of the Louisiana Department of Economic Development, the Division promotes Louisiana exports. Services include export counseling, and international business matchmaking.

Southern United States Trade Association
http://www.susta.org/
Based in New Orleans, the Association promotes the export of agri-food products in 15 U.S. southern states. The site includes a newsletter, staff directory, and program information.

Trade Shows in Louisiana
http://www.expoguide.com/shows/data/loc_la.htm
Compiled by Expoguide, the site is a directory of trade shows in Baton Rouge, Lafayette, New Orleans, Shreveport, and other Louisiana centers.

Louisiana Representative Offices

Colombia

Consulate General of Colombia in New Orleans
http://www.colombiaemb.org/consular/consus.html#new orleans
The site lists the Consul General, street address, phone and fax numbers, e-mail link, and geographic jurisdiction for the Colombian Consulate in New Orleans.

Japan

Consulate General of Japan in New Orleans
http://www.embjapan.org/neworleans/
A Japanese resource center, the site provides Japanese fact sheets, visa and passport information, an event calendar, and reports on Japanese trade with Arkansas, Kentucky, Louisiana, Mississippi, and Tennessee.

United Kingdom

Consulate of Britain in New Orleans
http://www.fco.gov.uk/directory/posts.asp?US
The site provides contact information for the British Consulate in New Orleans.

Maine

Maine Media

Maine Media
http://www.mediainfo.com/emediajs/specific-geo.htm?region=maine
A service of Editor and Publisher Interactive, the site provides a searchable directory of web-based media sites in Maine including city guides, magazines, and newspapers.

Maine Market Guides

Maine Business Online
http://www.mainebusiness.com/
Updated daily, the site features Maine news, business leads, economic statistics, consumer

trends, market surveys, a municipal directory, census data, and retail trade area analysis.

Maine Economic and Community Development
http://www.econdevmaine.com/
Featuring welcoming remarks by the Maine governor, the state government site provides primers on Maine business, tourism, and government.

Maine Trade Assistance

Commercial Service in Maine
http://www.ita.doc.gov/uscs/me/
A service of the International Trade Administration, the site is a directory of international trade statistics, leads, events, services, and contacts in Maine.

Maine International Trade Center
http://www.mitc.com/
With offices in Bangor and Portland, the Center promotes Maine exports. The site includes state export statistics, an event calendar, member directory, and an ask-the-trade-guru service.

Trade Shows in Maine
http://www.expoguide.com/shows/data/ loc_me.htm
Developed by Expoguide, the site is a directory of trade shows in Augusta, Bangor, Portland, and other Maine centers.

Maryland

Maryland Media

Maryland Media
http://www.mediainfo.com/emediajs/specific-geo.htm?region=maryland
A service of Editor and Publisher Interactive, the site provides a searchable directory of web-based media sites in Maryland including city guides, magazines, and newspapers.

Maryland Market Guides

Maryland Chamber Online
http://www.mdchamber.org/index.htm
Homepage of the Maryland Chamber of Commerce, the site features Maryland business news, press releases, an event calendar, legislative updates, and a directory of business assistance programs in the state.

MD Business
http://www.mdbusiness.state.md.us/
An online information network, the site provides Maryland company profiles, sector reports, regulatory primers, county demographic information, a business opportunities forum, and a directory of business assistance programs.

Maryland Trade Assistance

Commercial Service in Maryland
http://www.ita.doc.gov/uscs/md/
A service of the International Trade Administration, the site is a directory of international trade statistics, leads, events, services, and contacts in Maryland.

Maryland Goes Global
http://www.mdisglobal.org/
A service of the Maryland Office of International Business, the site features a global business newsletter, event calendar, and Maryland investment and plant relocation news.

Maryland Services for Exporters
http://www.mdbusiness.state.md.us/GovSvcs/ exp_serv.html
Compiled by the Maryland Business Information Network, the site is a directory of state export assistance. Programs include an exporter's hotline, financial assistance, global business primers, and a network of Maryland foreign trade offices in China, Japan, and the Netherlands.

Suburban Maryland International Trade Association
http://www.smita.org/
Based in Montgomery Village, the Association is an international business forum for Maryland companies and organizations. The site provides news, an event calendar, and membership information.

Trade Shows in Maryland
http://www.expoguide.com/shows/data/ loc_md.htm
Compiled by Expoguide, the site is a directory of trade shows in Annapolis, Baltimore, Ocean City, Timonium, and other Maine centers.

Massachusetts

Massachusetts Media

Massachusetts Media
http://www.mediainfo.com/emediajs/specific-

geo.htm?region=massachusetts
A service of Editor and Publisher Interactive, the site provides a searchable directory of web-based media sites in Massachusetts including magazines, newspapers, and television stations.

Massachusetts Market Guides

Business Report
http://italchambers.net/BusinessReports.html
Prepared by the Italian Chamber of Commerce and written in Italian, the site provides Boston fact sheets, market reports, and commercial guides.

Office of Business Development
http://www.state.ma.us/mobd/mobdhome.htm
An online business assistance center, the site offers Massachusetts legal guides, economic statistics, sector profiles, and primers on starting a business and bidding on state contracts.

Statewide and Local Data
http://www.state.ma.us/mobd/data.htm
A service of the Massachusetts Office of Business Development, the site provides a virtual library of market information including census data, municipal guides, employment statistics, and municipal tax rates.

Massachusetts Trade Assistance

Boston Center for International Visitors
http://www.tiac.net/users/bciv/
A global networking service, the Center arranges professional and social meetings between Boston citizens and prominent government and industry leaders from around the world. The site features a member database, event calendar, online bulletin board, and contact information.

Boston International Trade and Business Development
http://www.ci.boston.ma.us/International/index.htm
A branch of the Boston Mayor's Office, the organization promotes Boston as a global business center. The site includes a mission statement, case studies, and a directory of international trade contacts in over 20 countries including Australia, Sweden and Taiwan.

Commercial Service in Massachusetts
http://www.ita.doc.gov/uscs/ma/
A service of the International Trade Administration, the site is a directory of international trade

statistics, leads, events, services, and contacts in Massachusetts.

Global Business Alliance of New England
http://www.gbane.org/
An online trade forum, the site provides Massachusetts export news, an event calendar, a list of the executive committee, and membership information.

Massachusetts Export Center
http://www.state.ma.us/export/
Based in Boston, the Center is a one-stop resource for Massachusetts exporters. The site delivers export primers, newsletters, event information, and a staff directory.

Massachusetts Office of International Trade and Investment
http://www.magnet.state.ma.us/moiti/
A state government agency, the Office provides export counseling, trade mission reports and other global business services for Massachusetts companies. The site features a staff directory, event calendar, and program directory.

Massport
http://www.massport.com/trade/partners.html
Based in Boston, Massport organizes export workshops and training programs for Boston area companies. The site includes an international business plan workbook, trade statistics, and an event calendar.

New England Latin America Business Council
http://www.nelabc.org/
Founded in 1991, the Council promotes New England-Latin American trade and investment. The site provides a mission statement and membership information.

Trade Shows in Massachusetts
http://www.expoguide.com/shows/data/loc_ma.htm
Compiled by Expoguide, the site is a directory of trade shows in Andover, Boston, Marlborough, West Springfield, Worcester, and other Massachusetts centers.

Women in World Trade Boston
http://www.capecod.net/wwt-boston/
Part of a national network, the organization promotes the advancement of women in international trade. The site includes an event calendar, membership information, and an executive directory.

World Affairs Council
http://www.worldaffairs.org/
Based in Boston, the Council promotes public awareness of global issues. The site includes an event calendar, program directory, and contact information.

Massachusetts Representative Offices

Belgium

Belgian American Society of New England
http://www.tiac.net/users/steger/BAS/
Based in Watertown, the site provides Society news, membership information, and an event calendar.

Canada

Canadian Consulate General in Boston
http://www.dfait-maeci.gc.ca/~boston/
Posted in English and French, the site provides Canada fact sheets, business guides, visa and immigration information, and a directory of trade and investment services for New England companies.

Province of Québec Trade Office in Boston
http://www.mri.gouv.qc.ca/dans_le_monde/etats_unis/antennes_us_an.html#Boston
A service of the Québec government, the site lists the Commercial Attachés and contact information for the Québec Trade Office in Boston.

Colombia

Colombian Consul in Boston
http://www.colombiaemb.org/consular/consus.html#boston
The site lists the Consul General, street address, phone and fax numbers, and geographic jurisdiction for the Colombian Consulate in Boston.

Germany

German-American Council for Business
http://www.gacb.org/
Based in Plymouth, the site provides Council news, an event calendar, member directory, and contact information.

Hungary

Honorary Consulate of Hungary in Boston
http://www.hungary.com/boston-consul/

The virtual Consulate delivers Hungarian fact sheets, visa and passport information, business guides, and legal primers.

Hungarian American Chamber of Commerce of New England
http://www.net.hu/haccne/
Based in Boston, the Chamber promotes New England-Hungarian trade. The site posts Hungarian news, country profiles, investment guides, and Chamber events.

Ireland

Irish American Partnership
http://www.adnet.ie/iap/
With offices in Dublin and Boston, the Partnership promotes the economic development of Ireland through investment in job creation and education. The site provides event schedules, a membership application form, and contact information.

Israel

Consulate General of Israel in New England
http://www.israelemb.org/boston/index.htm
Targeting Maine, Massachusetts, New Hampshire, Rhode Island, and Vermont, the site provides Israeli news, event information, and a directory of consular services.

New England-Israel Chamber of Commerce
http://www.israeltrade.com/
Based in Boston, the Chamber promotes New England-Israeli trade. The site features a directory of Chamber services and a database of Israeli export assistance and information resources.

Italy

Consulate General of Italy in Boston
http://www.reference.it/cgboston/
Posted in English and Italian, the site delivers Italian fact sheets, visa and passport information, an event calendar, education reports, and legal guides.

Italy-New England Chamber of Commerce
http://www.italchambers.net/boston/
Based in Boston, the site provides membership information, an event calendar, and a database of Italian trade opportunities in apparel, food processing, agricultural machinery, and other industries.

Japan

Consulate General of Japan in Boston
http://www.embjapan.org/boston/
Written in English and Japanese, the site provides Japanese fact sheets, visa and passport information, and a directory of New England cities and states with Japanese sister cities.

Japan Society of Boston
http://www.us-japan.org/japanboston/
A non-profit organization, the Society promotes Japan-Massachusetts relations through cultural activities, public affairs seminars, social gatherings, and Japanese language classes. The site features a member directory and event calendar.

Poland

U.S. Poland Chamber of Commerce of Boston
http://www.ultranet.com/~uspcc/
The site delivers Polish fact sheets, business primers, and job opportunities. The service includes Chamber news, an event calendar, and member directory.

Puerto Rico

Puerto Rico Federal Affairs Administration in Boston
http://www.prfaa-govpr.org/boston.htm
Featuring greetings from the Regional Director, the site lists the street address, and phone and fax numbers of the Puerto Rico Federal Affairs Administration regional office in Boston.

Romania

Honorary Consulate of Romania in Boston
http://world.std.com/~ff/romania/
The digital Consulate provides Romanian news, business guides, job opportunities, a directory of consular services, and *Foaia*, a newsletter for Romanians in New England.

Sweden

Sweden American Chamber of Commerce in New England
http://www.sacc-ne.org/
A New England-Nordic business gateway, the site features membership information, a list of upcoming trade events, and a directory of Chamber business matchmaking services.

Taiwan

Taipei Economic and Cultural Office
http://www.ifor.com/teco/
Based in Boston, the Office provides business matchmaking and export counseling for New England companies doing business in Taiwan. The site provides Taiwan fact sheets, economic statistics, and a directory of Office services and upcoming events.

Taiwan Chamber of Commerce in New England
http://www.epartner.com/tccne/
A Taiwan-New England trade promotion service, the site features Chamber news, a member directory, staff roster, and contact information.

Taiwan Government Information Office in Boston
http://www.gio.gov.tw/info/ngio/usa-f.html
Posted in Chinese and English, the site lists the street address, phone and fax numbers, and e-mail link of the Taiwan Government Information Office in Boston.

United Kingdom

British American Business Council of New England
http://www.babc.org/New_England/
The Council is a consortium of some 150 New England companies involved in transatlantic trade. The site provides program information and a calendar of events.

Consulate General of Britain in Boston
http://britain-info.org/bis/dipoff/DIPOFFMA.HTM
The site provides contact information for the British Consulate General in Boston.

Michigan

Michigan Media

Michigan Media
http://www.mediainfo.com/emediajs/specific-geo.htm?region=michigan
A service of Editor and Publisher Interactive, the site provides a searchable directory of web-based media sites in Michigan including city guides, magazines, and newspapers.

Michigan Market Guides

Business Services
http://www.state.mi.us/mjc/ceo/business/business.htm
A service of the Michigan Jobs Commission, the site provides primers on Michigan relocation incentives, venture capital, business roundtables, and licensing requirements.

Michigan Chamber of Commerce
http://www.michamber.com/
Based in Lansing, the site provides Chamber news, a member directory, calendar of events, employment opportunities, legal handbooks, health and safety guides, and a directory of policy committees.

Michigan Information Center
http://www.state.mi.us/dmb/mic/
A database of state statistics, the site delivers Michigan census data, maps, migration information, population projections, and county business patterns.

Michigan Live
http://www.mlive.com/
Updated daily, the site is a virtual library of Michigan information. Categories include news, business, classifieds, forums, travel, employment opportunities, and advertising.

Michigan Trade Assistance

Business to Business International Videoconferencing
http://www.ita.doc.gov/uscs/mi/videocon.htm
Developed by the Pontiac Export Assistance Center, the site provides rate and schedule information for international video-conferencing. The service is available for over 30 countries including Australia, England, Malaysia, Sweden and Turkey.

Commercial Service in Michigan
http://www.ita.doc.gov/uscs/mi/
A service of the International Trade Administration, the site is a directory of international trade statistics, leads, events, services, and contacts in Michigan.

International and National Business Development Office
http://www.state.mi.us/mjc/ceo/business/inbd.htm
A branch of the Michigan Jobs Commission, the Office promotes Michigan exports and international investment. The site provides contact

information, and a directory of Michigan foreign trade offices in Belgium, Canada, China, England, Germany, Japan, Mexico, and South Africa.

Pontiac Export Assistance Centre
http://www.ita.doc.gov/uscs/mi/pontiac/
Developed by the U.S. Department of Commerce, the site is a database of international trade specialists, programs, and events in the Pontiac area.

Trade Shows in Michigan
http://www.expoguide.com/shows/data/loc_mi.htm
Developed by Expoguide, the site is a directory of trade shows in Dearborn, Detroit, Grand Rapids, Jackson, Lansing, Pontiac, Traverse City, and other Michigan centers.

Michigan Representative Offices

Australia

Austrade in Detroit
http://www.austrade.gov.au/Detroit/
Part of a global network of Australian trade offices, Austrade Detroit provides export promotion and business matchmaking services for Australian companies doing business in Detroit and the U.S. Midwest.

Canada

Canadian Consulate General in Detroit
http://www.dfait-maeci.gc.ca/~detroit/
Posted in English and French, the site features Canadian export primers, sector profiles, visa and passport information, a staff directory, and a calendar of cultural and academic events.

France

French Trade Commission in Detroit
http://www.dree.org/usa/InfoGene/PEE/SanFrancisco/index.htm
Part of an international network of French export offices, the French-language site provides market intelligence and sector profiles for French companies doing business in the U.S. Midwest.

Italy

Consulate General of Italy in Detroit
http://www.italyemb.org/italcons.htm#detroit
Serving businesspeople in Indiana, Kentucky, Michigan, Ohio, and Tennessee, the site lists the

street address, phone and fax numbers, and e-mail link of the Italian Consulate in Detroit.

Japan

Consulate General of Japan in Detroit
http://www.embjapan.org/detroit/
The virtual Consulate provides Japan fact sheets, Consul General speeches, visa and passport information, a calendar of events, and Japan-Michigan trade reports.

Mexico

Trade Commission of Mexico in Southfield
http://www.mexico-businessline.com/ingles/ofrepmu3.html#detroit
The site lists the street address, phone and fax numbers, and e-mail link of the Trade Commission of Mexico in Southfield.

Minnesota

Minnesota Media

Minnesota Media
http://www.mediainfo.com/emediajs/specific-geo.htm?region=minnesota
A service of Editor and Publisher Interactive, the site provides a searchable directory of web-based media sites in Minnesota including city guides, magazines, and newspapers.

Minnesota Market Guides

Compare Minnesota
http://www.dted.state.mn.us/mnecon/compare/compa-96.html
A virtual library of Minnesota information, the site provides national and international comparisons of Minnesota in over a dozen categories including demographics, personal income, government, and labor.

Minnesota Chamber of Commerce
http://www.mnchamber.com/
Based in St. Paul, the site features Minnesota business news, a staff directory, event calendar, government bulletins, and a directory of Chamber committees and task forces.

Minnesota Department of Trade and Economic Development
http://www.dted.state.mn.us/
The state government site delivers Minnesota

business news, economic statistics, community profiles, site selection primers, travel guides, and a directory of business incentives and assistance programs.

Minnesota Trade Assistance

Commercial Service in Minnesota
http://www.ita.doc.gov/uscs/mn/
A service of the International Trade Administration, the site is a directory of international trade statistics, leads, events, services, and contacts in Minnesota.

Red River Trade Corridor
http://www.rrtrade.org/
Based at the University of Minnesota, the Red River Trade Corridor is a regional development organization serving Minnesota, North Dakota, South Dakota, and the Canadian province of Manitoba. The site includes a staff directory, event calendar, and membership information.

Minnesota Trade Office
http://www.dted.state.mn.us/intl/intl.html
Based in St. Paul, the site provides a directory of Trade Office services including export counseling, global business workshops, trade finance assistance, and investment prospecting.

Trade Shows in Minnesota
http://www.expoguide.com/shows/data/loc_mn.htm
Developed by Expoguide, the site is a directory of trade shows in Bloomington, Minneapolis, Rochester, St. Paul, and other Minnesota centers.

Minnesota Representative Offices

Canada

Canadian Consulate General in Minneapolis
http://www.dfait-maeci.gc.ca/minneapolis/
Posted in English and French, the site provides Canada fact sheets, visa and immigration information, sector profiles, tourism guides, U.S. state reports, and a directory of manufacturing representative associations in the U.S. Midwest.

Guyana

Honorary Consul of Guyana in Minneapolis
http://www.guyana.org/TRADEREP.htm
The site provides contact information for the Guyana Honorary Consul in Minneapolis.

United Kingdom

Consulate of Britain in Minneapolis
http://www.fco.gov.uk/directory/posts.asp?US
The site provides contact information for the British Consulate in Minneapolis.

Mississippi

Mississippi Media

Mississippi Media
http://www.mediainfo.com/emediajs/specific-geo.htm?region=mississippi
A service of Editor and Publisher Interactive, the site provides a searchable directory of web-based media sites in Mississippi including city guides, magazines, and newspapers.

Mississippi Market Guides

Mississippi Business Journal
http://www.msbusiness.com/
Based in Jackson, the site provides Mississippi business reports, editorials, interviews with leading state entrepreneurs and government officials, and a past issues archive dating back to 1995.

Mississippi: Your Business Connection
http://www.decd.state.ms.us/ecd/Main.htm
The state government service provides primers on Mississippi business incentives, infrastructure, technology, quality of life, human resources, and foreign trade zones.

Mississippi Trade Assistance

Commercial Service in Mississippi
http://www.ita.doc.gov/uscs/ms/
An International Trade Administration service, the site is a directory of international trade statistics, leads, events, services, and contacts in Mississippi.

International Business Assistance
http://www.decd.state.ms.us/ecd/Assistance_International.htm
Developed by the Mississippi Department of Economic and Community Development, the site provides Mississippi trade and investment facts and statistics. The service includes a directory of Mississippi international offices in Chile, England, and Singapore.

Trade Shows in Mississippi
http://www.expoguide.com/shows/data/loc_ms.htm
Developed by Expoguide, the site is a directory of trade shows in Biloxi, Jackson, Laurel, and other Mississippi centers.

Missouri

Missouri Media

Missouri Media
http://www.mediainfo.com/emediajs/specific-geo.htm?region=missouri
A service of Editor and Publisher Interactive, the site provides a searchable directory of web-based media sites in Missouri including city guides, magazines, and newspapers.

Missouri Market Guides

Missouri Department of Economic Development
http://www.ecodev.state.mo.us/ded/
Based in Jefferson City, the site features Missouri press releases, business guides, community profiles, job opportunities, an online finance network, professional licensing primers, and motor carrier and safety information.

Missouri Impact
http://www.moimpact.com/
A virtual database of business and technology information, the site offers Missouri news, education and training reports, interviews, government bulletins, and business directories.

Missouri Trade Assistance

Commercial Service in Missouri
http://www.ita.doc.gov/uscs/mo/
An International Trade Administration service, the site is a directory of international trade statistics, leads, events, services, and contacts in Missouri.

Export Opportunities
http://www.moimpact.com/export/opportunities.html
Developed by Missouri Impact, the site offers three export primers: *Is Exporting for Me?*, *First Steps*, and *Developing Exporting in Small Business in Missouri*.

International Trade Club of Greater Kansas City
http://www.itckc.org/itc/
A global business forum for Kansas City compa-

nies, the site features a mission statement, calendar of events, member directory, and a membership application form.

Kansas City U.S. Export Assistance Center
http://pw2.netcom.com/~kcdeac/small.html
A service of the U.S. Department of Commerce, the site provides contact information for the Center and an e-mail form for submitting export-related questions.

Missouri Office of International Marketing
http://www.ecodev.state.mo.us/intermark/
Based in Jefferson City, the Office provides trade show reports, foreign company background checks, and other export counseling services. The site features an event calendar, staff roster, a list of Missouri sister city relationships, and a directory of Missouri foreign trade offices around the world.

St. Louis U.S. Export Assistance Center
http://www.ita.doc.gov/uscs/mo/stlouis.html
Sponsored in part by the U.S. Department of Commerce, the Center provides export assistance and information to St. Louis area companies. The site features a staff e-mail directory and program information.

Trade Shows in Missouri
http://www.expoguide.com/shows/data/ loc_mo.htm
Developed by Expoguide, the site is a directory of trade shows in Kansas City, Springfield, St. Louis, and other Missouri centers.

Missouri Representative Offices

Guyana

Honorary Consul of Guyana in Hazelwood
http://www.guyana.org/TRADEREP.htm
The site provides contact information for the Guyana Honorary Consul in Hazelwood.

Japan

Consulate General of Japan in Kansas City
http://www.embjapan.org/kansascity/
Featuring a message from the Consul General, the site delivers Japan fact sheets, speeches, an event calendar, a directory of consular services, and reports on Japanese trade with Iowa, Kansas, Missouri, Nebraska, North Dakota, and South Dakota.

United Kingdom

Consulate of Britain in St. Louis
http://www.fco.gov.uk/directory/posts.asp?US
The site provides contact information for the British Consulate in St. Louis.

Montana

Montana Media

Montana Media
http://www.mediainfo.com/emediajs/specific-geo.htm?region=montana
A service of Editor and Publisher Interactive, the site provides a searchable directory of web-based media sites in Montana including city guides, magazines, and newspapers.

Montana Market Guides

Montana Economic Development
http://commerce.state.mt.us/economic/index.htm
A service of the state government, the site is a directory of business assistance programs in Montana. Categories include regional development, licensing, site selection, census data, and manufacturing technologies.

Montana Online
http://www.mt.gov/
Homepage of the State of Montana, the site provides state factsheets, employment opportunities, government directories, education bulletins, and travel guides.

Montana Trade Assistance

Commercial Service in Montana
http://www.ita.doc.gov/uscs/mt/
An International Trade Administration service, the site is a directory of international trade statistics, leads, events, services, and contacts in Montana.

Montana Trade Program
http://commerce.state.mt.us/economic/trade.htm
A service of the Montana Department of Commerce, the Program provides export and international business assistance to Montana companies. The site delivers contact and program information.

Trade Shows in Montana
http://www.expoguide.com/shows/data/loc_mt.htm
Compiled by Expoguide, the site is a directory of

trade shows in Billings, Kalispell, and other Montana centers.

Nebraska

Nebraska Media

Nebraska Media
http://www.mediainfo.com/emediajs/specific-geo.htm?region=nebraska
A service of Editor and Publisher Interactive, the site provides a searchable directory of web-based media sites in Nebraska including city guides, magazines, and newspapers.

Nebraska Market Guides

A Guide to Doing Business in Nebraska
http://assist.ded.state.ne.us/guide/guide.html
The state government site provides tutorials on incorporating a business, job training programs, business licensing agencies, and financing in Nebraska.

Information for Startup and Existing Businesses
http://assist.ded.state.ne.us/index.html
An online business toolkit, the site features start-up guides, site selection information, financing primers, intellectual property reports, and tax information.

Nebraska BusinessLink Directory
http://www.nebraska.org/
A virtual business library, the site contains a browsable directory of Nebraska companies, and research reports on Nebraska small business, education, and high technology.

Nebraska Department of Economic Development
http://www.ded.state.ne.us/
Based in Lincoln, the site features state news, press releases, government bulletins, community profiles, and economic reports. The service includes the *Nebraska Databook*, a virtual library of population, business, and tourism statistics.

Nebraska Trade Assistance

Agricultural Products Trade Directory
http://www.agr.state.ne.us/tradedir/title.htm
Compiled by the Nebraska Department of Agriculture, the site is a browsable database of Nebraska agri-food products for export. Catego-ries include bulk commodities, livestock, meat products, and special services.

Commercial Service in Nebraska
http://www.ita.doc.gov/uscs/ne/ne.htm
Developed by the International Trade Administration, the site is a directory of international trade statistics, leads, events, services, and contacts in Nebraska.

International Assistance and Resource List
http://international.ded.state.ne.us/iarl.htm
The site is a telephone directory of international bankers, attorneys, customs brokers, freight forwarders, credit reporting agencies, and transportation companies in Nebraska.

Nebraska International Trade Directory
http://www.ded.state.ne.us/trade/tr-home.htm
The online service is a browsable database of Nebraska exporters in over 30 industries including agricultural production, chemicals, transportation equipment, and wholesale trade.

Office of International Trade and Investment
http://international.ded.state.ne.us/
A branch of the Nebraska Department of Economic Development, the Office provides export counseling and global business assistance to state companies. The site features export primers, an event calendar, and a staff directory.

Trade Shows in Nebraska
http://www.expoguide.com/shows/data/loc_ne.htm
Compiled by Expoguide, the site is a directory of trade shows in Lincoln, Omaha, South Sioux City, and other Nebraska centers.

Nevada

Nevada Media

Nevada Media
http://www.mediainfo.com/emediajs/specific-geo.htm?region=nevada
A service of Editor and Publisher Interactive, the site provides a searchable directory of web-based media sites in Nevada including magazines, newspapers, and radio stations.

Nevada Market Guides

Nevada Business and Industrial Directory
http://nevadadata.com/nid/
A service of Gold Hill Publishing, the site is a searchable database of some 6,500 Nevada

companies. The directory is browsable by standard industrial code, company, city, zip code, county, and keyword.

Nevada Business Information Network
http://www.state.nv.us/binn/
The state government site features primers on business start-ups, license requirements, incorporations, finance and incentive programs, chambers of commerce, and development authorities.

Nevada Department of Business and Industry
http://www.state.nv.us/b&i/index.htm
With offices in Las Vegas and Carson City, the Department promotes business growth in Nevada. The site provides information on the agency's nearly 30 agencies, boards, and commissions.

Nevada State Data Center
http://www.clan.lib.nv.us/docs/NSLA/SDC/sdc.htm
An archive of state statistics, the site provides a newsletter, population forecasts, and technical articles.

Nevada Trade Assistance

Commercial Service in Nevada
http://www.ita.doc.gov/uscs/nv/
A service of the International Trade Administration, the site is a directory of international trade statistics, leads, events, services, and contacts in Nevada.

Nevada Export Assistance
http://www.i-trade.com/states/nevada/itp/expass.html
The site describes the Nevada International Trade Program, an export promotion initiative which includes trade missions, seminars, counseling, and foreign buyer delegations.

Trade Shows in Nevada
http://www.expoguide.com/shows/data/loc_nv.htm
Compiled by Expoguide, the site is a directory of trade shows in Las Vegas and other Nevada centers.

New Hampshire

New Hampshire Media

New Hampshire Media
http://www.mediainfo.com/emediajs/specific-geo.htm?region=newhampshire
A service of Editor and Publisher Interactive, the site provides a searchable directory of web-based media sites in New Hampshire including city guides, magazines, and newspapers.

New Hampshire Market Guides

New Hampshire Economic Development Resources
http://www.state.nh.us/subject/ecodev.html
The site provides a directory of economic development agencies and programs in the state including the Division of Economic Development, Office of Business and Industrial Development, and the Vendor Matching Program.

Webster
http://webster.state.nh.us/
Homepage of the New Hampshire state government, the site provides state fact sheets, county profiles, government bulletins, employment opportunities, procurement primers, and a directory of state businesses and organizations.

New Hampshire Trade Assistance

Commercial Service in New Hampshire
http://www.ita.doc.gov/uscs/nh/
A service of the International Trade Administration, the site is a directory of international trade statistics, leads, events, services, and contacts in New Hampshire.

International Trade Resource Center
http://www.ded.state.nh.us/oic/trade/
A global business service of the New Hampshire state government, the site provides international business news, export primers, an event calendar, sector profiles, country bulletins, shipping tips, and a guide to export documents.

New Hampshire International Trade Association
http://www.nhita.org/
Based in Portsmouth, the Association promotes New Hampshire exports. The site includes a mission statement, member directory, event calendar, and contact information.

Trade Shows in New Hampshire
http://www.expoguide.com/shows/data/loc_nh.htm
Developed by Expoguide, the site is a directory of trade shows in Manchester and other New Hampshire centers.

New Jersey

New Jersey Media

New Jersey Media
http://www.mediainfo.com/emediajs/specific-geo.htm?region=newjersey
A service of Editor and Publisher Interactive, the site provides a searchable directory of web-based media sites in New Jersey including city guides, magazines, and newspapers.

New Jersey Market Guides

Business News
http://www.bnjol.com/
Updated daily, the site features New Jersey business news, investment reports, article archives, online discussion groups, and a directory of New Jersey companies online.

Business Sources
http://www.state.nj.us/business.htm
A service of the state government, the site is a virtual library of New Jersey business information. Categories include tax, financial assistance, statistics, and doing business with the State of New Jersey.

New Jersey Business and Industry Association
http://www.njbia.org/
Serving some 16,000 member companies throughout the state, the Association promotes the interests of New Jersey business. The site provides state business news, legislative briefs, and an event calendar.

New Jersey Trade Assistance

Commercial Service in New Jersey
http://www.ita.doc.gov/uscs/nj/
A service of the International Trade Administration, the site is a directory of international trade statistics, leads, events, services, and contacts in New Jersey.

New Jersey International Trade Assistance
http://www.state.nj.us/commerce/trade.htm
The site describes the international trade services offered by the New Jersey state government. Programs include trade missions, export counseling, financial assistance, and a network of international trade offices in Argentina, England, Germany, Israel, and Japan.

Trade Shows in New Jersey
http://www.expoguide.com/shows/data/loc_nj.htm
Developed by Expoguide, the site is a directory of trade shows in Atlantic City, Edison, Secaucus, Whippany, and other New Jersey centers.

World Trade Association of New Jersey
http://www.inc.com/users/wtanj.html
Based in Springfield, the Association is an international trade forum for New Jersey companies. Along with a mission statement, the site provides contact and membership information.

New Jersey Representative Offices

Israel

New Jersey-Israel Commission
http://www.state.nj.us/commerce/israel.htm
Established in 1989, the Commission promotes New Jersey-Israel trade. The site posts Israel fact sheets, a directory of trade events, and contact information.

Italy

Consulate General of Italy in Newark
http://www.italyemb.org/italcons.htm#newark
The site lists the street address, phone and fax numbers, e-mail link, and geographic jurisdiction of the Italian Consulate in Newark.

Puerto Rico

Puerto Rico Federal Affairs Administration in Trenton
http://www.prfaa-govpr.org/newjersey.htm
Featuring greetings from the Regional Director, the site lists the street address, phone and fax numbers, and e-mail link of the Puerto Rico Federal Affairs Administration regional office in Trenton.

New Mexico

New Mexico Media

New Mexico Media
http://www.mediainfo.com/emediajs/specific-geo.htm?region=newmexico
A service of Editor and Publisher Interactive, the site provides a searchable directory of web-based media sites in New Mexico including city guides, magazines, and newspapers.

New Mexico Market Guides

New Mexico Business Resources
http://www.edd.state.nm.us/ECONOMIC/index.html
A guide to New Mexico business development, the site delivers economic research reports, demographic statistics, training guides, financing information, and site selection primers.

New Mexico Economic Development Department
http://www.edd.state.nm.us/
The state government site provides fact sheets on New Mexico economic development, space commercialization, science and technology, and border development.

New Mexico Trade Assistance

American Business Women International
http://www.abwiworld.com/
Based in Corrales, the organization promotes the role of women in global business. The site features world news, an executive roster, and a directory of upcoming trade missions and events.

Border Issues
http://www.edd.state.nm.us/TRADE/ISSUES/ border.htm
A service of the New Mexico state government, the site features primers on foreign trade zones, maquiladoras, the North American Free Trade Agreement, and New Mexico-Mexico border crossings.

Commercial Service in New Mexico
http://www.ita.doc.gov/uscs/nm/
A service of the International Trade Administration, the site is a directory of international trade statistics, leads, events, services, and contacts in New Mexico.

International Site Selection Solution
http://www.edd.state.nm.us/FACTBOOK/ch7.htm
Part of a site selection handbook, the service reports on New Mexico foreign trade zones, international banking, and state export programs.

International Trade Council of New Mexico
http://www.itcnm.org/
The Council promotes international trade and investment in New Mexico. The site includes a member directory and contact information.

New Mexico Trade Division
http://www.edd.state.nm.us/TRADE/index.html
A unit of the New Mexico Economic Development Department, the Division promotes New Mexico exports. The site delivers state export statistics, international trade primers, and border issue reports.

Trade Shows in New Mexico
http://www.expoguide.com/shows/data/ loc_nm.htm
Developed by Expoguide, the site is a directory of trade shows in Albuquerque, Santa Fe, and other New Mexico centers.

New Mexico Representative Offices

Japan

New Mexico U.S.-Japan Center
http://www.nmjc.org/
Based in Albuquerque, the Center organizes New Mexico-Japan exchange programs and cultural events such as film festivals, drama presentations, and history lectures.

New York

New York Media

New York Media
http://www.mediainfo.com/emediajs/specific-geo.htm?region=newyork
A service of Editor and Publisher Interactive, the site provides a searchable directory of web-based media sites in New York including city guides, magazines, and newspapers.

New York Market Guides

Business Council of New York State
http://www.bcnys.org/
An association of more than 4,000 state businesspeople, the Council represents the interests of New York small and big business. The site delivers news releases, government bulletins, a staff directory, corporate surveys, and economic reports.

Empire State Development
http://www.empire.state.ny.us/
Headquartered in Albany and New York, Empire State Development is New York's lead business promotion agency. The site includes New York fact sheets, press releases, a site selection database, tourism guides, and a directory of business assistance programs.

New York Business Report
http://italchambers.net/BusinessReports.html
Prepared by the Italian Chamber of Commerce and written in Italian, the site provides New York fact sheets, market reports, and commercial guides.

New York State Data Center
http://www.empire.state.ny.us/nysdc/
A service of Empire State Development, the site is a virtual library of New York population and economic data. Categories include population estimates, census profiles, migration, employment, wages, county business patterns, and gross state product.

New York Trade Assistance

BorderNet
http://www.bordernet.org/
A partnership of the Buffalo, New York and Hamilton, Ontario Chambers of Commerce, BorderNet is a business matchmaking service that promotes alliances between New York and Ontario companies. The site provides a strategic alliance application form and contact information.

Commercial Service in New York
http://www.ita.doc.gov/uscs/ny/
A service of the International Trade Administration, the site is a directory of international trade statistics, leads, events, services, and contacts in New York.

Export Assistance
http://www.empire.state.ny.us/international/ exportassistance/index.html
A service of Empire State Development, the site features trade news, leads, an export dictionary, travel tips, and primers on tariff rates, export licenses, and other international trade topics.

International Business Network of Greater New York
http://www.ibnogny.org/
Serving companies in Rockland and the greater New York area, the Network is an international trade forum for New York exporters. The site includes news, an event calendar, and contact information.

International Offices
http://www.empire.state.ny.us/newphone3.htm
The state government site provides a directory of New York international offices in Canada, Germany, Japan, and the United Kingdom.

Long Island Import Export Association
http://www.liiea.org/
A global business networking forum, the site provides international trade news, editorials, articles, an event calendar, member directory, product showcase, and a service-provider database.

New York District Export Council
http://www.imex.com/goexport/nyeac.html
Part of a national network of volunteer export advisors, the Council provides international business counseling and training services to new exporters in the New York City area.

New York State Small Business Development Center
http://www.sbdc.rockland.ny.us/international.htm
Located at Rockland Community College, the Center provides export advisory and research services for New York area companies. The site includes contact information and a list of the resources available such as country reports, export primers, and business guides.

Southern Tier World Commerce Association
http://www.stwca.org/
Based in Binghamton, the Association promotes international trade in southern New York. The site includes an event calendar, member profiles, and contact information.

Trade Shows in New York
http://www.expoguide.com/shows/data/loc_ny.htm
Developed by Expoguide, the site is a directory of trade shows in Buffalo, New York City, Rochester, Syracuse, Uniondale, White Plains, and other New York centers.

Trading Hub
http://www.imex.com/goexport/nyeac/ hubhome.html
Sponsored by the New York Export District Council, the site features export news, primers, and events. A key feature is the Visitors' Center, a resource for businesspeople who live outside New York who wish to develop business contacts in the area. The resource includes New York business guides and maps.

Western New York International Trade Council
http://www.wnyitc.org/
Based in Buffalo, the Council promotes exporting and global business in Western New York. The site provides an event calendar, publications list, and contact information.

New York Representative Offices

Australia

Austrade New York
http://www.austrade.gov.au/NewYork/
Part of a global network of Australian trade offices, Austrade New York provides export promotion and business matchmaking services for Australian companies doing business in New York and the U.S. Northeast.

Austria

Austrian Trade Commission New York
http://www.austriantrade.org/AustrianTrade/offices/ahst_nyc.htm
An Austrian export promotion service, the site lists the Trade Commissioners, street address, phone and fax numbers, and e-mail link of the Office in New York.

Bahamas

Consul General of the Bahamas
http://flamingo.bahamas.net.bs/government/gov8.html
The site provides contact information for the Bahamas Consul General in New York.

Belgium

Belgium Consulate General in New York
http://www.belgium-emb.org/usa/representatives/usa_new_york.html
The virtual Consulate lists the street address, office hours, e-mail links, geographic jurisdiction, and phone and fax numbers of the Belgium Consulate in New York.

Brazil

Trade Bureau of Brazil in New York
http://www.braziltradeny.com/
A service of the Government of Brazil, the site provides Brazil news, fact sheets, export statistics, tourism guides, investment primers, and a directory of leading Brazilian exporters.

Canada

Canadian Consulate General in Buffalo
http://www.canadianconsulatebuf.org/
Posted in English and French, the site provides Canada news, fact sheets, visa and immigration information, tourism guides, an event calendar, and primers on how to select a manufacturer's representative and distributor.

Canadian Consulate General in New York
http://www.canada-ny.org/
The virtual Consulate features Canadian economic news, job postings, government reports, cultural guides, travel information, business opportunities, and a directory of Canadian organizations in New York.

Province of Québec Government House in New York
http://www.mri.gouv.qc.ca/dans_le_monde/etats_unis/dg_quebec_ny_an.html
A service of the Québec government, the site provides contact information, and a directory of consular services for the Québec office in New York City.

China

Consulate General of China in New York
http://www.nyconsulate.prchina.org/
The digital Consulate features China news, academic directories, job opportunities, student handbooks, foreign policy statements, and visa and passport information.

Hong Kong Economic and Trade Office in New York
http://www.hketony.org/
A Hong Kong trade promotion service, the site includes Hong Kong fact sheets, investment primers, and business guides.

Colombia

Colombia Consulate General in New York
http://www.colombiaemb.org/consular/nyc/homenyc.html
Written in Spanish, the site provides Colombia fact sheets, visa and passport information, legal guides, and a directory of consular services.

Cyprus

Cyprus Embassy Trade Center in New York
http://www.cyprustradeny.org/
A country business guide, the site provides Cyprus fact sheets, export primers, import tips, sector profiles, and a publication directory.

Czech Republic

Czech Center in New York
http://www.czech.cz/new_york/
The Center provides Czech news, an event calendar, travel information, and a database of trade opportunities in industries such as cosmetics, glass, and engineering. A key feature is *Export U.S.A.*, an export guide written in Czech for Czech companies doing business in the United States.

Denmark

Consulate General of Denmark in New York
http://www.denmark.org/index.html
The virtual Consulate reports on Denmark weather, economic trends, exchange rates, government, manufacturing, international trade, education, and culture.

Dominican Republic

Consulate General of the Dominican Republic in New York
http://www.consudom-ny.do/
Posted in English and Spanish, the site features Dominican Republic fact sheets, news, tourism guides, international trade reports, business opportunities, and a directory of consular services and staff.

Finland

Consulate General of Finland in New York
http://www.finlandfolio.org/frconsulate.html
The digital Consulate provides Finland fact sheets, travel guides, visa information, and a directory of consular staff, services and e-mail links.

France

French Trade Commission in New York
http://www.dree.org/usa/InfoGene/PEE/NewYork/index.htm
A French trade promotion service, the site lists priority sectors for French exporters in five U.S. northeastern states: Connecticut, Massachusetts, New Jersey, New York, and Virginia.

Germany

German American Chamber of Commerce in New York

http://www.ahk.net/en/us/NewYork/
The site provides German fact sheets, key contacts and a directory of Chamber services which include business matchmaking, internship programs, and value-added tax refunds.

Guyana

Consul General of Guyana in New York
http://www.guyana.org/TRADEREP.htm
The site provides contact information for the Guyana Consul General in New York.

Hungary

Hungary Economic and Trade Office in New York
http://www.hungaryemb.org/OffEcoTraRep.htm
A service of the Hungarian government, the site lists the staff, street address, phone and fax numbers, and e-mail link of the Hungarian Office in New York.

India

Consulate General of India in New York
http://www.indiaserver.com/cginyc/
The virtual Consulate provides Indian press releases, visa and passport information, travel guides, and directories of Indian Chambers of Commerce, exporters, and banks.

Iran

Center for Iranian Trade and Development
http://www.neda.net/ibr/citad.html
Based in New York, the Center promotes Iranian international trade and investment. The service includes Iranian fact sheets, business news, company directories, and travel information.

Ireland

Enterprise Ireland in New York
http://www.irish-trade.ie/office_network/office_locate01.html#anchor1409791
The site lists the Manager, street address, and phone and fax numbers of the Enterprise Ireland office in New York.

Israel

Consulate General of Israel in New York
http://www.newyork.israel.org/consulate/default.htm

The site provides Israeli news, press releases, fact sheets, cultural reports, visa and passport information, foreign affairs statements, and a directory of consular services and staff.

Italy

Consulate General of Italy in New York
http://www.italconsulnyc.org/
Featuring a message from the Consul General, the site provides passport information, visa application forms, legal primers, language training guides, and a directory of Italian scientists and technology organizations in Connecticut, New Jersey, and New York.

Italian Trade Commission in New York
http://www.italtrade.com/ice/New_York.htm
Part of an international network of Italian trade promotion offices, the site lists the staff, street address, phone and fax numbers, e-mail link, and priority products of the Italian Trade Commission in New York City.

Japan

Consulate General of Japan in New York
http://www.embjapan.org/ny/
Written in English and Japanese, the site features Japanese news, speeches, policy statements, tax primers, research guides, and a directory of consular services and staff.

Fukui Prefecture New York Office
http://www.fukui-in-usa.org/
Posted in Japanese, the site provides Fukui Prefecture fact sheets, business guides, investment primers, and contact information.

Japanese Chamber of Commerce and Industry in New York
http://www.jcciny.org/
Launched in 1932, the Chamber promotes Japanese-American trade and relations. The site includes a mission statement, economic bulletins, and membership information.

JETRO New York
http://www.JETRO.org/newyork/
Serving the U.S. northeast, the site delivers Japanese press releases, fact sheets, an event calendar, a monthly newsletter, staff roster, and a directory of Japanese importers and procurement agencies.

Yokohama Business Online in New York
http://www.coyokohama.org/

Developed by the City of Yokohama, the site provides Yokohoma fact sheets, business guides, maps, real estate information, and a directory of support programs for foreign companies.

Malaysia

Consulate General of Malaysia in New York
http://www.mnet.com.my/klonline/www/missions/malmiss/musa2.htm
The site provides contact information for the Malaysia Consulate General in New York.

Trade Commission of Malaysia in New York
http://www.mnet.com.my/klonline/www/missions/malmiss/musa8.htm
The site provides contact information for the Malaysia Trade Commission in New York.

Mexico

Consulate General of Mexico in New York
http://www.quicklink.com/mexico/ingles/ing.htm
The virtual Consulate delivers Mexico newsletters, economic statistics, government profiles, state of the nation reports, political bulletins, legal primers, and a directory of consular services.

State of Guanajuato Trade Office in New York
http://www.guanajuato.gob.mx/cofoce/offices.htm
The site lists the street address, phone and fax numbers, and e-mail link of the Mexican state of Guanajuato Trade Office in New York.

Trade Commission of Mexico in New York
http://www.mexico-businessline.com/ingles/ofrepmu3.html#new
The site lists the street address, phone and fax numbers, and e-mail link of the Trade Commission of Mexico in New York.

Netherlands

Netherlands Foreign Investment Agency in New York
http://www.nfia.com/html/contact/index.html
The site lists the street address, phone and fax numbers, and e-mail link of the Netherlands Foreign Investment Agency in New York.

New Zealand

New Zealand Consulate General in New York
http://www.emb.com/nzemb/offices/consul~1.htm#ny

The site lists the street address, and phone and fax numbers of the New Zealand Consulate in New York.

Norway

Norwegian Trade Office in New York
http://www.ntcusa.org/
The site lists the street address, phone and fax numbers, e-mail links, and staff profiles of the Norwegian Trade Office in New York.

Philippines

Consulate General of the Philippines in New York
http://www.sequel.net/RPinUS/NYC/
Serving the U.S. northeast and mid-Atlantic states, the site provides an event calendar, and a directory of consular services and personnel.

Philippine Trade and Investment Promotion Office in New York
http://www.dti.gov.ph/NY/
Along with a mission statement and program directory, the site provides contact information for the Philippine Trade Office in New York.

Poland

Polish Commercial Office in New York
http://pw1.netcom.com/~brhusa/index.html
Posted in English and Polish, the site offers Polish news, sector profiles, business guides, and investment primers. The service includes a Polish company directory, and a list of U.S. companies and investors in Poland.

Portugal

Portuguese Trade and Investment Office in New York
http://www.portugal.org/geninfo/abouticep/newyork.html
The site lists the staff, street address, phone and fax numbers, and e-mail link of the Portuguese Trade and Investment Office in New York.

Puerto Rico

Puerto Rico Federal Affairs Administration in New York
http://www.prfaa-govpr.org/newyork.htm
Featuring greetings from the Regional Director,

the site lists the street address, phone and fax numbers, and e-mail link of the Puerto Rico Federal Affairs Administration regional office in New York City.

Saint Kitts and Nevis

Consulate General of Saint Kitts and Nevis in New York
http://www.stkittsnevis.org/
The digital Consulate features Saint Kitts and Nevis press releases, fact sheets, visa and passport information, tourism guides, economic citizenship information, and investment primers.

Saint Vincent and the Grenadines

Saint Vincent and the Grenadines Office in New York
http://www.freenet.hamilton.on.ca/~aa462/svgref.html#svgmtd
The site provides contact information for the Saint Vincent and the Grenadines Office in New York.

South Africa

South Africa Consulate General in New York
http://www.southafrica-newyork.net/
The virtual Consulate General provides fact sheets on South African telecommunications, mining, health, and other industries.

South Korea

Korean International Trade Association in New York
http://www.kita.or.kr/eng/national.html
The site provides contact information for the Korean International Trade Association in New York.

Spain

Consulate General of Spain in New York
http://www.spainconsul-ny.org/
Written in English and Spanish, the site provides Spanish fact sheets, cultural reports, visa and passport information, tourism guides, and a directory of consular services and staff.

Spanish Commercial Office in New York
http://www.icex.es/openURL.html#openURL=/english/infoproyem/ofcomes/ofcomes.html#AM
The site lists the staff, street address, phone and

fax numbers, and e-mail link of the Spanish Commercial Office in New York.

Sweden

Swedish Information Service in New York
http://www.webcom.com/sis/welcome.html
A virtual library of Swedish information, the site reports on Swedish history, geography, business, international trade, education, media, travel and events.

Switzerland

Swiss-American Chamber of Commerce in New York
http://www.amcham.ch/usa/losangel/index.htm
The Chamber promotes New York-Swiss trade and relations. The site includes an executive directory, event calendar, and contact information.

Swiss Trade Office in New York
http://www.swissemb.org/biz/html/new_york.html
Serving the U.S. northeast, the site posts the street address, phone and fax numbers, e-mail link, and geographic jurisdiction of the Swedish Trade Office in New York City.

Taiwan

China External Trade Development Council Office in New York
http://www.cetra.org.tw/english/o_office/indexset.htm
A Taiwanese trade promotion service, the site lists the mission statement and e-mail link of the China External Trade Development Council Office in New York.

Taipei Economic and Cultural Office in New York
http://www.taipei.org/
A service of the Republic of China on Taiwan, the site offers Taiwanese news, speeches, policy statements, electronic magazines, economic statistics, visa and passport information, travel information, sector profiles, and an event calendar.

Taiwan Government Information Office in New York
http://www.gio.gov.tw/info/ngio/usa-f.html
Posted in Chinese and English, the site lists the street address, phone and fax numbers, and e-mail link of the Taiwan Government Information Office in New York.

Taiwan Trade Center in New York
http://www.taipei.org/cetra/ttcny.htm
A branch of the Taipei-based China External Trade Development Council, the Center promotes trade between Taiwan and the U.S. northeastern states. The site provides a monthly newsletter and a directory of consular services.

Tanzania

Consulate of Tanzania in New York
http://www.tanzania-online.gov.uk/visa/envoys.html
The site provides contact information for the Tanzania Consulate in New York.

Thailand

Royal Thai Consulate General in New York
http://www.mfa.go.th/Embassy/detail/229.htm
The site lists the Consul General, street address, and phone and fax numbers of the Thai Consulate in New York City.

Thai Trade Center in New York City
http://www.thaitrade.com/wwtto.html
A service of the Thailand Department of Export Promotion, the site lists the street address, phone and fax numbers, and e-mail link of the Thai Trade Center in New York City.

Ukraine

Consulate General of Ukraine in New York
http://www.brama.com/ua-consulate/
The site provides Ukraine legislative bulletins, visa and passport information, and a directory of consular and commercial services.

Trade Mission of Ukraine in New York
http://www.brama.com/ua-trade-mission/index.html
The site delivers Ukraine fact sheets, economic and trade policy reports, legal guides, and a directory of investment and business opportunities.

United Kingdom

British Consulate General in New York
http://www.britain-info.org/bis/dipoff/dipoffco.htm
The virtual office lists the street address, and phone and fax numbers of the British Consulate in New York City.

North Carolina

North Carolina Media

North Carolina Media
http://www.mediainfo.com/emediajs/specific-geo.htm?region=northcarolina
Compiled by Editor and Publisher Interactive, the site provides a searchable directory of web-based media sites in North Carolina including city guides, magazines, and newspapers.

North Carolina Market Guides

North Carolina Business Information
http://www.state.nc.us/business/
A service of the state government, the site provides information on North Carolina corporations, land records, procurement opportunities, waste management, land resources, and business licenses.

North Carolina Department of Commerce
http://www.commerce.state.nc.us/commerce/commhome.html
Based in Raleigh, the site provides North Carolina economic statistics, investment primers, company directories, sector profiles, travel guides, county profiles, and small business information.

North Carolina Trade Assistance

Appalachian International Business Center
http://www.bibd.appstate.edu/aibc/
Based at Appalachian State University, the Center officers training and information services to North Carolina exporters. The site includes trade leads, a publication database, and online discussion forums.

Carolinas U.S. Export Assistance Center
http://www.ita.doc.gov/uscs/carolinas/
Sponsored in part by the U.S. Small Business Administration, the site includes export primers, a trade event calendar, and a directory of international trade service providers in the Carolinas.

Charlotte Council for International Visitors
http://www.charweb.org/organizations/international/ih/cciv/
In cooperation with the United States Information Agency, the Council arranges visits and exchanges of foreign representatives in the Charlotte-Mecklenburg area. The site provides

contact information and a directory of hosting and volunteer opportunities.

Charlotte International Trade Bulletin Board
http://www.charweb.org/organizations/international/wwwboard/wwwboard.html
Updated daily, the site is a browsable archive of some 19,000 buy and sell offers from across the state and around the world. Postings are searchable by date and keyword.

Charlotte World Trade Association
http://www.charweb.org/organizations/international//cwta/
The second largest World Trade Association in the U.S., the organization promotes North Carolina exports. The site includes a newsletter, members roster, and program directory.

Charlotte's International Resources
http://www.charweb.org/organizations/international/
A service of the Mayor's International Cabinet of Charlotte, the site features an event calendar, an interactive trade board, and a directory of translators and interpreters.

Commercial Service in North Carolina
http://www.ita.doc.gov/uscs/nc/
A service of the International Trade Administration, the site is a directory of international trade statistics, leads, events, services, and contacts in North Carolina.

International Visitors Council
http://www.ivc-rtp.org/
In cooperation with the United States Information Agency, the Council arranges international visits and exchanges in the Raleigh, Durham and Chapel Hill areas. The site features an arrivals list, executive directory, and membership information.

Mayor's International Cabinet
http://www.charweb.org/organizations/international/mic/
The Cabinet promotes Charlotte as a global business center. The site provides a mission statement, meeting minutes, member profiles, and international reports.

North Carolina Furniture Export Office
http://www.commerce.state.nc.us/commerce/itd/furni.html
A unit of the North Carolina International Trade Division, the Office promotes the export of North

Carolina furniture and wood products. The site lists the staff, street address, and phone and fax numbers of the Office.

North Carolina International Trade Division
http://www.commerce.state.nc.us/commerce/itd/
Based in Raleigh, the site provides fact sheets on North Carolina export events, programs, and foreign trade zones. The service includes a directory of North Carolina foreign trade offices in China, Germany, Japan, Mexico, the United Kingdom.

Trade Shows in North Carolina
http://www.expoguide.com/shows/data/loc_nc.htm
Compiled by Expoguide, the site is a directory of trade shows in Charlotte, Greensboro, High Point, Raleigh, and Winston-Salem.

North Carolina Representative Offices

France

Honorary Consul of France in North Carolina
http://www.charweb.org/organizations/international/frc.html
Based in Charlotte, the site provides contact information, tourism tips, and a directory of North Carolina-France sister cities.

Germany

Honorary Consul of Germany in North Carolina
http://www.charweb.org/organizations/international/grc.html
Based in Charlotte, the site lists the name, street address, and phone and fax numbers of the Honorary Consul of Germany in North Carolina.

Mexico

Honorary Consul of Mexico in North Carolina
http://www.charweb.org/organizations/international/mxc.html
The site provides the name, address, and functions of the Mexican Honorary Consul in Charlotte.

Switzerland

Swiss-American Chamber of Commerce Carolina Division
http://www.amcham.ch/usa/carolina/index.htm
Based in Charlotte, the Division promotes trade and relations between the Carolinas and

Switzerland. The site includes an executive directory, event calendar, and contact information.

United Kingdom

Consulate of Britain in Charlotte
http://www.fco.gov.uk/directory/posts.asp?US
The site provides contact information for the British Consulate in Charlotte.

Honorary British Consulate in North Carolina
http://www.britain-info.org/nc.stm
Opened in 1994, the Consulate represents British interests in North Carolina. The site provides the name, street address, and e-mail link of the British Honorary Consul in Charlotte.

North Dakota

North Dakota Media

North Dakota Media
http://www.mediainfo.com/emediajs/specific-geo.htm?region=northdakota
A service of Editor and Publisher Interactive, the site provides a searchable directory of web-based media sites in North Dakota including city guides, magazines, and newspapers.

North Dakota Market Guides

Get the Details
http://www.growingnd.com/details/edf_details_2.html
The state government site provides primers on North Dakota labor, education, productivity, wages, training, infrastructure, site selection, telecommunications, environmental standards, taxes, and quality of life.

North Dakota Economic Development and Finance
http://www.growingnd.com/
Based in Bismarck, the site delivers North Dakota press releases, program descriptions, relocation guides, education reports, and a staff directory.

North Dakota Trade Assistance

Commercial Service in North Dakota
http://www.ita.doc.gov/uscs/nd/
A service of the International Trade Administration, the site is a directory of international trade

statistics, leads, events, services, and contacts in North Dakota.

North Dakota International Trade Program
http://www.growingnd.com/itp_prog.html
A service of North Dakota Economic Development and Finance, the Program provides export counseling and training for North Dakota companies. The site includes contact information and an event calendar.

Trade Shows in North Dakota
http://www.expoguide.com/shows/data/loc_nd.htm
Prepared by Expoguide, the site is a directory of trade shows in Bismarck, Fargo, Grand Forks, Minot and other North Dakota centers.

Ohio

Ohio Media

Ohio Media
http://www.mediainfo.com/emediajs/specific-geo.htm?region=ohio
A service of Editor and Publisher Interactive, the site provides a searchable directory of web-based media sites in Ohio.

Ohio Market Guides

Connect Ohio
http://www.connectohio.com/
An Ohio e-commerce hub, the site delivers Ohio news, job opportunities, product catalogs, and searchable databases of state companies, government agencies, and media organizations online.

Discover Ohio
http://www.oplin.lib.oh.us/OHIO/
A service of the Ohio Public Library, the site provides Ohio fact sheets, legal guides, county profiles, travel information, biographies, agricultural statistics, and education resources.

Showcase Ohio
http://www.i-trade.com/ooed/showcase/welcome.html
Created by the Ohio Department of Development, the site is a virtual showcase of Ohio products in a dozen categories including automotive, apparel, office products, beverages, sporting goods, and specialty foods.

Ohio Trade Assistance

Agriculture International Trade Program
http://www.state.oh.us/agr/intprog.html
A service of the Ohio Department of Agriculture, the Program provides export counseling and assistance to Ohio agri-food companies. The site includes a staff directory, and contact information for Ohio's international offices in Belgium, Canada, China, Japan, Mexico, and Israel.

Cleveland World Trade Association
http://www.cwta.org/
Founded in 1915, the Association promotes international trade in northeastern Ohio. The site provides news, conference information, technical papers, country profiles, and meeting agendas.

Commercial Service in Ohio
http://www.ita.doc.gov/uscs/oh/
A service of the International Trade Administration, the site is a directory of international trade statistics, leads, events, services, and contacts in Ohio.

Ohio International Trade Division
http://ohiotrade.tpusa.com/
Based in Columbus, the site features trade leads, export primers, and online discussion forums. The site spotlights Division programs including export counseling, trade missions, and export tax credits.

Ohio On-Line Export Directory
http://www.i-trade.com/exhibit/search/search_ohio.html
The site is a searchable directory of Ohio exporters in over 25 industries including vegetable products, plastics and rubber, footwear and headgear, machinery, and optical and medical equipment.

Trade Shows in Ohio
http://www.expoguide.com/shows/data/loc_oh.htm
Prepared by Expoguide, the site is a directory of trade shows in Akron, Cincinnati, Cleveland, Columbus, Dayton, Toledo and other Ohio centers.

Ohio Representative Offices

United Kingdom

British American Chamber of Commerce in the Great Lakes Region
http://www.baccgl.org/
Based in Cleveland, the Chamber promotes trade between Britain and the Great Lakes region. The site includes a mission statement, member profiles, export primers, patent information, travel guides, and an event calendar.

Consulate of Britain in Cleveland
http://britain-info.org/bis/dipoff/DIPOFFOH.HTM
The site provides contact information for the British Consulate in Cleveland.

Oklahoma

Oklahoma Media

Oklahoma Media
http://www.mediainfo.com/emediajs/specific-geo.htm?region=oklahoma
A service of Editor and Publisher Interactive, the site provides a searchable directory of web-based media sites in Oklahoma including city guides, magazines, and newspapers.

Oklahoma Market Guides

Oklahoma Commerce Demographic Information Forum
http://www.odoc.state.ok.us/homepage/dglib.nsf/main?openview
A virtual library of state statistics, the site includes data on population, housing units, personal income, wage levels, school enrollment, educational attainment, and ancestry.

Oklahoma Department of Commerce
http://www.odoc.state.ok.us/
Based in Oklahoma City, the site provides Oklahoma press releases, fact sheets, community profiles, site selection databases, labor and training information, and a directory of business and tax incentives.

Oklahoma Trade Assistance

Commercial Service in Oklahoma
http://www.ita.doc.gov/uscs/ok/
A service of the International Trade Administration, the site is a directory of international trade statistics, leads, events, services, and contacts in Oklahoma.

Global Marketplace
http://www.odoc.state.ok.us/index.html
A unit of the Oklahoma Department of Commerce, the International Trade and Investment Division promotes Oklahoma as an international business center. The Global Marketplace site provides a trade question and answer forum, sector profiles, and a directory of international business services.

Oklahoma's International Marketing Offices
http://www.odoc.state.ok.us/homepage/internat.nsf/pages/imo
The site provides contact information for Oklahoma's international trade offices in Belgium, China, Mexico, Singapore, South Korea, Taiwan, and Vietnam.

Tulsa World Trade Association
http://www.webtek.com/worldtrade/
Created in 1969, the Association provides international trade training in the Tulsa area. The site includes a mission statement, member directory, and contact information.

Trade Shows in Oklahoma
http://www.expoguide.com/shows/data/loc_ok.htm
Compiled by Expoguide, the site is a directory of trade shows in Oklahoma City, Tulsa and other Oklahoma centers.

Oregon

Oregon Media

Oregon Media
http://www.mediainfo.com/emediajs/specific-geo.htm?region=oregon
A service of Editor and Publisher Interactive, the site provides a searchable directory of web-based media sites in Oregon including magazines, newspapers, and television stations.

Oregon Market Guides

Oregon Economic Development Department
http://www.econ.state.or.us/DEPT.HTM
The state government site delivers Oregon fact sheets, regional profiles, community and port reports, and a directory of site selection and business finance services.

Oregon Marketplace
http://www.oregonmarketplace.com/

Administered by the Organization for Economic Initiatives, the site is a browsable database of Oregon companies. Categories include apparel, computers, health and fitness, seafood, and sporting goods.

Oregon Trade Assistance

Commercial Service in Oregon
http://www.ita.doc.gov/uscs/or/
A service of the International Trade Administration, the site is a directory of international trade statistics, leads, events, services, and contacts in Oregon.

Export Oregon
http://www.exportoregon.org/
Based in Portland, the site features export primers, a trade missions calendar, sector profiles, country reports, and a directory of Oregon trade services.

Latin American Trade Council of Oregon
http://www.latco.org/
Based in Lake Oswego, the site provides an Oregon export calendar, job opportunities, and directories of exporters in forestry, agri-food, software, transportation, and other industries.

Oregon International Resource Center
http://www.econ.state.or.us/INTL/IT.HTM
A service of the Oregon Economic Development Department, the site delivers Oregon export statistics, primers, glossaries, country profiles, transportation tutorials, and business etiquette briefings.

Trade Shows in Oregon
http://www.expoguide.com/shows/data/loc_or.htm
Developed by Expoguide, the site is a directory of trade shows in Eugene, Portland, Salem and other Oregon centers.

Oregon Representative Offices

China

Northwest China Council
http://www.exportoregon.org/nwchina/
Based in Portland, the Council organizes China seminars and events in Oregon. The site contains a staff directory, program directory, and contact information.

Japan

Consulate General of Japan in Portland
http://www.embjapan.org/portland/
The virtual Consulate provides Japan fact sheets, a directory of consular services, and reports on Japan-Oregon relations and sister city agreements.

United Kingdom

Consulate of Britain in Portland
http://www.fco.gov.uk/directory/posts.asp?US
The site provides contact information for the British Consulate in Portland.

Pennsylvania

Pennsylvania Media

Pennsylvania Media
http://www.mediainfo.com/emediajs/specific-geo.htm?region=pennsylvania
A service of Editor and Publisher Interactive, the site provides a searchable directory of web-based media sites in Pennsylvania including city guides, magazines, and newspapers.

Pennsylvania Market Guides

Business Resource Network
http://www.dced.state.pa.us/PA_Exec/DCED/business/busres.htm
A service of Team Pennsylvania, the site features primers on Pennsylvania business assistance, real estate, education, workforce, infrastructure, regulations and permits, taxation, and quality of life.

Doing Business in Pennsylvania
http://www.dced.state.pa.us/PA_Exec/DCED/business/doingbusiness.htm
Developed by the Department of Community and Economic Development, the site provides Pennsylvania quick facts, entrepreneur guides, port profiles, a directory of state technology centers, and a list of recent business expansions and relocations in the state.

Pennsylvania State Data Center
http://www.hbg.psu.edu/psdc/psdchome1.1.html
Based in Middletown, the site is a virtual library of Pennsylvania statistics. Categories include economy and business, employment, housing,

occupation, income, population, transportation, and education.

Pennsylvania Trade Assistance

Bucks County International Trade Council
http://www.buckscounty.com/tradecouncil/
Based in Doylestown, the site features an international trade newsletter, member directory, event calendar, and contact information.

Commercial Service in Pennsylvania
http://www.ita.doc.gov/uscs/pa/
A service of the International Trade Administration, the site is a directory of international trade statistics, leads, events, services, and contacts in Pennsylvania.

Export Activity in Pennsylvania
http://www.pitt.edu/~wpaintl/activity.html
Developed by the University of Pittsburgh, the site is a directory of Pennsylvania export statistics and graphs. Data includes state exports by country and sector.

Exporting Your Product
http://www.dced.state.pa.us/PA_Exec/DCED/ business/international/exporting.htm
A service of the Department of Community and Economic Development, the site features Pennsylvania export success stories, a trade mission calendar, a list of foreign trade zones, and a directory of international trade programs and services.

International Business Center
http://www.pitt.edu/~ibcmod/
Based at the University of Pittsburgh, the site is a directory of international business services, foreign language instruction, and joint-degree programs offered by the Joseph M. Katz Graduate School of Business and the University Center for International Studies.

Southcentral Pennsylvania International Network
http://www.spinworld.org/
Based in York, the Network promotes Pennsylvania exporting and global business. The site includes news, a member directory, event calendar, and contact information.

Trade Shows in Pennsylvania
http://www.expoguide.com/shows/data/loc_pa.htm
Developed by Expoguide, the site is a directory of trade shows in Fort Washington, Harrisburg, King of Prussia, Philadelphia, Pittsburgh and other Pennsylvania centers.

Western PA International BusinessNet
http://www.pitt.edu/~wpaintl/
Sponsored in part by the Western Pennsylvania District Export Council, the site provides export primers, trade mission calendars, and a directory of international trade assistance centers throughout the state.

World Affairs Council of Philadelphia
http://www.libertynet.org/wac/
The Council hosts speakers and arranges tours to promote public awareness of global issues. The site includes an event calendar, program directory, and contact information.

Pennsylvania Representative Offices

Italy

Consulate General of Italy in Philadelphia
http://www.italyemb.org/italcons.htm#philly
The site lists the street address, phone and fax numbers, e-mail link, and geographic jurisdiction of the Italian Consulate in Philadelphia.

Puerto Rico

Puerto Rico Federal Affairs Administration in Philadelphia
http://www.prfaa-govpr.org/philadelphia.htm
Featuring greetings from the Regional Director, the site lists the street address, phone and fax numbers, and e-mail link of the Puerto Rico Federal Affairs Administration regional office in Philadelphia.

Russia

Pennsylvania-Russia Business Council
http://www.fita.org/prbc/
Based in Philadelphia, the Council promotes Russia-Pennsylvania trade. The site includes U.S.-Russia trade statistics, an event calendar, and membership information.

United Kingdom

British American Business Council of Greater Philadelphia
http://www.babc.org/philadelphia/
An American-British networking forum, the site includes a mission statement, member directory, and contact information.

Consulate of Britain in Pittsburgh
http://www.fco.gov.uk/directory/posts.asp?US
The site provides contact information for the British Consulate in Pittsburgh.

Rhode Island

Rhode Island Media

Rhode Island Media
http://www.mediainfo.com/emediajs/specific-geo.htm?region=rhodeisland
A service of Editor and Publisher Interactive, the site provides a searchable directory of web-based media sites in Rhode Island including city guides, magazines, and newspapers.

Rhode Island Market Guides

Rhode Island Economic Development Corporation
http://www.riedc.com/atoz.html
Based in Providence, the site delivers fact sheets on Rhode Island business incentives, enterprise zones, financial assistance, job training, licenses and permits, taxation, utilities, and site locations.

RI Business
http://www.state.ri.us/submenus/buslink.htm
An online information kiosk, the site provides primers on Rhode Island business assistance, financing, taxation, new incorporations, and environmental regulations.

Rhode Island Trade Assistance

Commercial Service in Rhode Island
http://www.ita.doc.gov/uscs/ri/
A service of the International Trade Administration, the site is a directory of international trade statistics, leads, events, services, and contacts in Rhode Island.

District Export Assistance Center
http://www.riedc.com/growth/export/US%20Commerce.html
Based in Providence, the Center provides export counseling to Rhode Island companies. The site includes program descriptions and contact information.

Rhode Island Export Assistance Center
http://www.state.ri.us/bus/RIEX.HTM
Based at Bryant College, the site features a directory of Center export counseling programs and information products such as country reports, trade leads, and global business statistics.

Trade Shows in Rhode Island
http://www.expoguide.com/shows/data/loc_ri.htm
Compiled by Expoguide, the site is a directory of trade shows in Providence, Warwick, and other Rhode Island centers.

South Carolina

South Carolina Media

South Carolina Media
http://www.mediainfo.com/emediajs/specific-geo.htm?region=southcarolina
A service of Editor and Publisher Interactive, the site provides a searchable directory of web-based media sites in South Carolina including city guides, magazines, newspapers, and radio stations.

South Carolina Market Guides

Office of Research and Statistics
http://www.state.sc.us/drss/
A service of the State Budget and Control Board, the site is a virtual library of South Carolina population statistics.

South Carolina Department of Commerce
http://www.state.sc.us/commerce/index.html
The state government site delivers South Carolina press releases, employment opportunities, research and development reports, quality of life comparisons, and directories of industrial site locations and business incentives.

South Carolina Trade Assistance

Commercial Service in South Carolina
http://www.ita.doc.gov/uscs/sc/
A service of the International Trade Administration, the site is a directory of international trade statistics, leads, events, services, and contacts in South Carolina.

South Carolina's International Trade Page
http://www.state.sc.us/commerce/internat.htm
Developed by the South Carolina Department of Commerce, the site provides export leads, a trade event calendar, a directory of state trade promotion programs, and contact information for the South Carolina trade offices in Germany and Japan.

Trade Shows in South Carolina
http://www.expoguide.com/shows/data/loc_sc.htm
Developed by Expoguide, the site is a directory of trade shows in Charleston, Columbia, Greenville, Myrtle Beach, and other South Carolina centers.

South Carolina Representative Offices

Canada

Canadian American Society of South Carolina
http://canamtrade.badm.sc.edu/cassc.htm
Based in Columbia, the Society promotes Canada-South Carolina trade. The site includes a mission statement, contact information, and a membership application form.

Canadian American Trade Site
http://canamtrade.badm.sc.edu
A service of the University of South Carolina College of Business Administration, the site provides Canada-U.S. fact sheets and a directory of Canadian-American Societies in the U.S. southeast.

South Dakota

South Dakota Media

South Dakota Media
http://www.mediainfo.com/emediajs/specific-geo.htm?region=southdakota
A service of Editor and Publisher Interactive, the site provides a searchable directory of web-based media sites in South Dakota including city guides, magazines, and newspapers.

South Dakota Market Guides

Doing Business in South Dakota
http://www.state.sd.us/state/executive/oed/oed.html
Based in Pierre, the site features primers on South Dakota companies, products, buildings, communities, labor, tourism, agriculture, manufacturing, population, and quality of life.

South Dakota Trade Assistance

Commercial Service in South Dakota
http://www.ita.doc.gov/uscs/sd/
A service of the International Trade Administration, the site is a directory of international trade statistics, leads, events, services, and contacts in South Dakota.

South Dakota International Business Institute
http://sdibi.northern.edu/sdibi.html
Based at Northern State University, the Institute provides export counseling to state companies. The site delivers South Dakota trade statistics, foreign trade zone reports, export primers, and a trade event calendar.

South Dakota International Trade Directory
http://sdibi.northern.edu/sdibi/trad-dir/page1.htm
Developed by the South Dakota International Business Institute, the site is a searchable directory of South Dakota exporters in over 80 product areas including bearings, medical equipment, trailers and trucks, and vending and gaming machines.

Trade Shows in South Dakota
http://www.expoguide.com/shows/data/loc_sd.htm
Compiled by Expoguide, the site is a directory of trade shows in Aberdeen, Rapid City, Sioux Falls, and other South Dakota centers.

Tennessee

Tennessee Media

Tennessee Media
http://www.mediainfo.com/emediajs/specific-geo.htm?region=tennessee
A service of Editor and Publisher Interactive, the site provides a searchable directory of web-based media sites in Tennessee including city guides, magazines, and newspapers.

Tennessee Market Guides

Tennessee Economic and Community Development
http://www.state.tn.us/ecd/
Based in Nashville, the site offers primers on Tennessee business advantages, economic development incentives, and industrial buildings and sites.

Tennessee Economic Development Guide
http://www.jnlcom.com/tedg/
A state resource page, the site provides Tennessee sector profiles, country statistics, success stories, company profiles, investment reports, and business guides.

Tennessee Trade Assistance

Commercial Service in Tennessee
http://www.ita.doc.gov/uscs/tn/
A service of the International Trade Administration, the site is a directory of international trade statistics, leads, events, services, and contacts in Tennessee.

Export Kit
http://www.state.tn.us/ecd/export/contents.htm
An online export primer, the site provides tutorials on preparing for export, trade planning, and selling internationally. The service includes a database of Tennessee's leading export markets and products.

Global Commerce
http://www.mtsu.edu/~berc/global/gcmain.html
An international business e-journal, the site reports on Tennessee trade and investment flows, state exporters, and global export opportunities and challenges.

Tennessee Export Office
http://www.state.tn.us/ecd/export.htm
A unit of the Department of Economic and Community Development, the Office provides export assistance to Tennessee companies. The site includes contact information and a program directory.

Trade Shows in Tennessee
http://www.expoguide.com/shows/data/loc_tn.htm
Compiled by Expoguide, the site is a directory of trade shows in Chattanooga, Knoxville, Nashville and other Tennessee centers.

Tennessee Representative Offices

United Kingdom

British American Business Association of Tennessee
http://www.telalink.net/~babat/
Based in Nashville, the Association promotes British-Tennessee trade. The site provides an event calendar, member directory, and contact information.

Consulate of Britain in Nashville
http://www.fco.gov.uk/directory/posts.asp?US
The site provides contact information for the British Consulate in Nashville.

Texas

Texas Media

Texas Media
http://www.mediainfo.com/emediajs/specific-geo.htm?region=texas
A service of Editor and Publisher Interactive, the site provides a searchable directory of web-based media sites in Texas.

Texas Market Guides

Commerce Connection
http://www.Instar.com/mall/main-areas/chamber/chambers.htm
The site is directory of Texas Chambers of Commerce online. Listed cities include Austin, Dallas, Galveston, El Paso, Fort Worth, Laredo, and San Antonio.

Expanding or Locating Your Business in Texas
http://www.tded.state.tx.us/expand.htm
A service of the state government, the site provides Texas county profiles, success stories, business check lists, maps, census data, foreign trade zone reports, and tourism guides.

Texas Business Report
http://italchambers.net/BusinessReports.html
Prepared by the Italian Chamber of Commerce and written in Italian, the site provides Texas fact sheets, market reports, and commercial guides.

Texas Marketplace
http://www.texas-one.org/
Developed by the Texas Department of Economic Development, the site features a Texas company directory, a database of state procurement opportunities, and an online buy/sell exchange for agricultural commodities, building supplies, medical equipment, and other products.

Texas Trade Assistance

Commercial Service in Texas
http://www.ita.doc.gov/uscs/tx/
A service of the International Trade Administration, the site is a directory of international trade statistics, leads, events, services, and contacts in Texas.

Greater Dallas Chamber of Commerce International Trade Department
http://www.gdc.org/

Part of the Greater Dallas Chamber of Commerce, the Department promotes Dallas as a global business center. The site includes a quarterly trade newsletter, trade finance success stories, a calendar of events, and a directory of export programs and services.

Texas International Trade Initiative
http://www.bus.utexas.edu/~ciber/busgov/DEC.htm
A service of the Texas District Export Council, the site provides bulletins on trade legislation, export loan guarantees, foreign language instructions, and other export issues in Texas.

Trade Shows in Texas
http://www.expoguide.com/shows/data/loc_tx.htm
Compiled by Expoguide, the site is a directory of trade shows in Amarillo, Austin, Corpus Christi, Dallas, Houston, San Antonio, and other Texas centers.

Texas Representative Offices

Canada

Canadian Consulate General in Dallas
http://www.canada-dallas.org/
Posted in English and French, the site provides Canadian fact sheets, passport and visa information, tourism guides, southwest state profiles, and Canada-U.S. southwest trade statistics.

China

Hong Kong Association of Northern Texas
http://www.hongkong.org/htm/hkant.htm
Based in Dallas, the Association promotes Hong Kong-Texas trade. The site includes a mission statement, executive roster, event calendar, and membership information.

Colombia

Consulate General of Colombia in Houston
http://members.aol.com/ConsulbiaH/
Posted in English and Spanish, the site provides Colombia fact sheets, visa and passport information, legal guides, an event calendar, and contact information.

Ecuador

Ecuadorian American Chamber of Commerce in Houston
http://www.eacc.org/
An online fact sheet, the site provides primers on Ecuador geography, climate, currency, literacy, population, qualify of life, international trade, finance, and infrastructure.

Finland

Finland Trade Center in Houston
http://www.exports.finland.fi/tradecen.htm
The site lists the staff, street address, phone and fax numbers, and e-mail link of the Finland Trade Center in Houston.

France

French Trade Commission in Houston
http://www.dree.org/usa/InfoGene/PEE/Houston/index.htm
Representing French interests in Arkansas, Louisiana, Oklahoma, and Texas, the Commission provides export counseling to French companies doing business in the U.S. south. Written in French, the site delivers U.S. sector profiles and French export plans.

Germany

German American Chamber of Commerce in Houston
http://www.ahk.net/en/us/Atlanta/
Part of a global network of German trade promotion offices, the site lists the Chairperson, Chief Executive Officer, street address, phone and fax numbers, and e-mail link of the German Chamber in Houston.

Guyana

Honorary Consul of Guyana in Houston
http://www.guyana.org/TRADEREP.htm
The site provides contact information for the Guyana Honorary Consul in Houston.

India

Consulate General of India in Houston
http://www.indianembassy.org/cgi/cgi.htm
A service of the Embassy of India, the site lists the street address and e-mail link of the Indian Consulate in Houston.

Israel

Consulate General of Israel in Houston
http://www.israelemb.org/houston.htm
Posted by the Embassy of Israel in Washington, D.C., the site lists the Consul Generals, street address, phone and fax numbers, e-mail link, and geographic jurisdiction of the Israeli Consulate in Houston.

Italy

Consulate General of Italy in Houston
http://www.italyemb.org/italcons.htm#houst
Serving Arkansas, Louisiana, Oklahoma, and Texas, the site lists the street address, phone and fax numbers, and geographic jurisdiction of the Italian Consulate in Houston.

Japan

Consulate General of Japan in Houston
http://www.embjapan.org/houston/
Featuring greetings from the Consul General, the site provides Japanese fact sheets, speeches, a staff directory, an event calendar, and a directory of Japan-related organizations in Texas and Oklahoma.

JETRO Houston
http://www.JETRO.org/houston/Default.htm
Targeting Arkansas, Louisiana, Mississippi, Oklahoma, and Texas, the site provides resources for companies doing business in Japan. Features include a trade mission calendar, export program directory, and *Impetus Japan*, a quarterly newsletter on Japan-Texas trade trends.

Mexico

Bancomext Dallas
http://bancomextdallas.com/noframeindex.htm
A Mexico trade promotion service, the site features Mexican trade news, staff profiles, a frequently asked questions and answers page, and a directory of foreign investment and business matchmaking programs.

Consulate General of Mexico in Austin
http://www.onr.com/consulmx/austin_english.html
Posted in English and Spanish, the site provides Mexican news, fact sheets, visa and passport information, business guides, investment primers, and a directory of consular services.

State of Guanajuato Trade Office in Dallas
http://www.guanajuato.gob.mx/cofoce/offices.htm
The site lists the street address, phone and fax numbers, and e-mail link of the Mexican state of Guanajuato Trade Office in Dallas.

Texas Association of Mexican American Chambers of Commerce
http://www.tamacc.org/
Based in Austin, the Association promotes Hispanic business in Texas. The site provides a mission statement, member directory, and event calendar.

Trade Commission of Mexico in San Antonio
http://www.mexico-businessline.com/ingles/ofrepmu3.html#san
The site lists the street address, phone and fax numbers, and e-mail link of the Trade Commission of Mexico in San Antonio.

Netherlands

Netherlands Foreign Investment Agency in Dallas
http://www.nfia.com/html/contact/index.html
The site lists the street address, phone and fax numbers, and e-mail link of the Netherlands Foreign Investment Agency in Dallas.

New Zealand

New Zealand Consulate in Houston
http://www.emb.com/nzemb/offices/consul~1.htm#houston
A service of the New Zealand government, the site lists the street address, and phone and fax numbers of the New Zealand consulate in Houston.

Norway

Norwegian Trade Council in Houston
http://www.ntchouston.com/
Along with Norwegian fact sheets, the site provides Houston business guides, trade leads, sector profiles, travel information, and an event calendar.

Puerto Rico

Puerto Rico Federal Affairs Administration in San Antonio
http://www.prfaa-govpr.org/texas.htm
Featuring greetings from the Regional Director,

the site lists the street address, phone and fax numbers, and e-mail link of the Puerto Rico Federal Affairs Administration regional office in San Antonio.

Saint Vincent and the Grenadines

Saint Vincent and the Grenadines Office in Dallas
http://www.freenet.hamilton.on.ca/~aa462/svgref.html#svgmtd
The site provides contact information for the Saint Vincent and the Grenadines Office in Dallas.

Switzerland

Swiss Trade Office in Houston
http://www.swissemb.org/biz/html/houston.html
Serving Texas, Arkansas, Colorado, Kansas, Louisiana, New Mexico, and Oklahoma, the site lists the Director, street address, phone and fax numbers, and e-mail link of the Swiss Trade Office in Houston.

Taiwan

Taipei Economic and Cultural Office in Houston
http://www.tecocd.org/
An international office of the Republic of China on Taiwan government, the site provides Taiwan investment guides, development reports and contact information.

Taiwan Government Information Office in Houston
http://www.gio.gov.tw/info/ngio/usa-f.html
Posted in Chinese and English, the site lists the street address, phone and fax numbers, and e-mail link of the Taiwan Government Information Office in Houston.

United Kingdom

British American Business Association in Houston
http://www.babc.org/houston/
Founded in 1982, the Association promotes British-Houston trade. The site includes an event calendar, member directory, and contact information.

British American Commerce Association in Dallas
http://www.bacadallas.org/
A British-Dallas business networking forum, the

site provides a member directory, event calendar, and contact information.

Consulate of Britain in Dallas
http://www.fco.gov.uk/directory/posts.asp?US
The site provides contact information for the British Consulate in Dallas.

Consulate General of Britain in Houston
http://britain-info.org/bis/dipoff/houston.sTM
The site provides British fact sheets, press releases, business guides, investment primers, and a directory of commercial services.

Utah

Utah Media

Utah Media
http://www.mediainfo.com/emediajs/specific-geo.htm?region=utah
A service of Editor and Publisher Interactive, the site provides a searchable directory of web-based media sites in Utah including city guides, magazines, and newspapers.

Utah Market Guides

Directory of Business and Industry
http://www.ce.ex.state.ut.us/busdev/bizdir.htm
Published by the Utah Division of Business and Economic Development, the site is a browsable database of more than 9,800 employers in Utah. Categories include agriculture, mining, construction, manufacturing, trade, finance, insurance, real estate, and services.

Doing Business in Utah
http://www.ce.ex.state.ut.us/NAV/library/bizutah/title.htm
Developed by eight federal and state agencies, the site is a primer on doing business in Utah. Key steps include assessing your business idea, preparing a written business plan, financing your business, and selecting a business structure.

Utah Department of Community and Economic Development
http://www.ce.ex.state.ut.us/welcome.htm
Based in Salt Lake City, the site provides Utah news, fact sheets, investment guides, enterprise zone reports, staff profiles, and a directory of business development programs and services.

Utah Trade Assistance

Center for International Management
http://msm.byu.edu/c&i/cim/
Part of the Provo-based Marriot School of Management, the Center provides international business training. The site includes faculty profiles, course directories, and contact information.

Commercial Service in Utah
http://www.ita.doc.gov/uscs/ut/
A service of the International Trade Administration, the site is a directory of international trade statistics, leads, events, services, and contacts in Utah.

State of Utah International Business Development Office
http://www.ce.ex.state.ut.us/international/welcome.htm
Based in Salt Lake City, the site features Utah export news, primers, an event calendar, country profiles, market research reports, trade leads, and staff profiles.

Trade Shows in Utah
http://www.expoguide.com/shows/data/loc_ut.htm
Compiled by Expoguide, the site is a directory of trade shows in Ogden, Salt Lake City and other Utah centers.

Utah Export Directory
http://www.ce.ex.state.ut.us/international/Companies/search.htm
A service of the Utah International Business Development Office, the site is a searchable database of Utah exporters. The Directory is searchable by company and keyword.

Utah Representative Offices

New Zealand

New Zealand Consulate in Salt Lake City
http://www.emb.com/nzemb/offices/consul~1.htm#slc
The site lists the street address, and phone and fax numbers of the New Zealand Consulate in Salt Lake City.

United Kingdom

Consulate of Britain in Salt Lake City
http://www.fco.gov.uk/directory/posts.asp?US

The site provides contact information for the British Consulate in Salt Lake City.

Vermont

Vermont Media

Vermont Media
http://www.mediainfo.com/emediajs/specific-geo.htm?region=vermont
A service of Editor and Publisher Interactive, the site provides a searchable directory of web-based media sites in Vermont including city guides, magazines, and newspapers.

Vermont Market Guides

Vermont Chamber of Commerce
http://www.vtchamber.com/
Based in Montpelier, the site provides Vermont business guides, travel tips, legislative report cards, an events directory, and membership information.

Vermont Department of Economic Development
http://www.state.vt.us/dca/economic/developm.htm
Featuring greetings from the Governor, the site delivers Vermont fact sheets, quality of life comparisons, business guides, an event calendar, and a directory of economic development programs and services.

Vermont Trade Assistance

Commercial Service in Vermont
http://www.ita.doc.gov/uscs/vt/
A service of the International Trade Administration, the site is a directory of international trade statistics, leads, events, services, and contacts in Vermont.

Trade Shows in Vermont
http://www.expoguide.com/shows/data/loc_vt.htm
Developed by Expoguide, the site is a directory of trade shows in Burlington, Richmond and other Vermont centers.

Vermont Export Council
http://www.vtchamber.com/development/export.html
The international marketing unit of the Vermont Chamber of Commerce, the Council promotes Vermont exports. The site reports on Council trade promotion initiatives in Africa, Russia, Switzerland, and Taiwan.

Vermont World Trade Office
http://www.bsad.emba.uvm.edu/wto/index.html
Located in Burlington and Montpelier, the Office provides export counseling and information to Vermont companies. The site includes international trade primers, newsletters, exporter profiles, frequently asked questions and answers, and a trade event calendar.

Virginia

Virginia Media

Virginia Media
http://www.mediainfo.com/emediajs/specific-geo.htm?region=virginia
A service of Editor and Publisher Interactive, the site provides a searchable directory of web-based media sites in Virginia including magazines, newspapers, and television stations.

Virginia Market Guides

Virginia Chamber of Commerce
http://www.vachamber.com/
Based in Richmond, the site offers Virginia business bulletins, publication lists, an event calendar, meeting reports, a staff directory, and membership information.

Virginia Economic Development Partnership
http://www.YesVirginia.org/index2.html
This state government site delivers fact sheets on Virginia business, labor, infrastructure, transportation, site selection, education, research and development, population, and quality of life.

Virginia Trade Assistance

Commercial Service in Virginia
http://www.ita.doc.gov/uscs/va/
A service of the International Trade Administration, the site is a directory of international trade statistics, leads, events, services, and contacts in Virginia.

International Trade Association of Northern Virginia
http://www.itanv.org/
Founded in 1979, the Association promotes international trade in Northern Virginia. The site includes a workshop schedule, member directory, and contact information.

Trade Shows in Virginia
http://www.expoguide.com/shows/data/loc_va.htm
Compiled by Expoguide, the site is a directory of trade shows in Arlington, Chantilly, Norfolk, Richmond, and other Virginia centers.

Virginia International Trade Development
http://www.YesVirginia.org/profile/divisions.html
A service of the Virginia Economic Development Partnership, the site describes the export counseling assistance offered by the state government. Programs include one-on-one consulting, trade missions, catalog shows, and incoming buyer missions.

Washington

Washington Media

Washington Media
http://www.mediainfo.com/emediajs/specific-geo.htm?region=washington
A service of Editor and Publisher Interactive, the site provides a searchable directory of web-based media sites in Washington including city guides, magazines, and newspapers.

Washington Market Guides

Washington Business and Industry
http://www.econd.org/info/busind/index.htm
A service of the Washington State Economic Development Network, the site features primers on doing business with the state government, relocating or expanding a business, and other economic development topics.

Washington State Business Development Homepage
http://www.busdev.wa.gov/
Based in Olympia, the site provides fact sheets on Washington business, transportation, utilities, labor force, education, taxation, research and development, and quality of life.

Washington Trade Assistance

Commercial Service in Washington
http://www.ita.doc.gov/uscs/wa/
A service of the International Trade Administration, the site is a directory of international trade statistics, leads, events, services, and contacts in Washington state.

Impact
http://impact.wsu.edu/
A service of the Washington State University College of Agriculture, Impact is the International Marketing Program for Agricultural Commodities and Trade. The site provides success stories, project updates, agricultural studies, and market reports.

International Business Card Directory
http://www.pan.ci.seattle.wa.us/business/tda/listing2.htm
Developed by the Trade Development Alliance of Greater Seattle, the site is a browsable directory of Seattle area exporters, importers, and multinationals. The Directory is searchable by company name, industry and keyword.

Trade Development Alliance of Greater Seattle
http://www.pan.ci.seattle.wa.us/business/tda/tda.htm
A collaboration of the Port of Seattle, the Greater Seattle Chamber of Commerce and other agencies, the Alliance promotes international trade in the Seattle area. Posted in ten languages including Chinese, Russian, and Portuguese, the site delivers Seattle sector profiles, visitor guides, international market reports and statistics, and relocation primers.

Trade Shows in Washington
http://www.expoguide.com/shows/data/loc_wa.htm
Developed by Expoguide, the site is a directory of trade shows in Bellevue, Seattle, Spokane, Tacoma, and other Washington centers.

U.S. Export Assistance Center
http://www.pan.ci.seattle.wa.us/business/tda/eac.htm
An alliance of the U.S. Commercial Service, the Export Finance Assistance Center of Washington, and the U.S. Small Business Administration, the Center provides export counseling and assistance to Washington companies. The site includes a program directory and contact information.

Washington Council on International Trade
http://www.eskimo.com/~wcit/
Based in Seattle, the site provides Washington international trade news, issue papers, annual reports, export primers, teaching guides, and an event calendar.

Washington Overseas Offices
http://www.trade.wa.gov/overseas.htm
A service of the Washington State International Trade Division, the site provides a directory of Washington overseas offices in China, France, Japan, Russia, and Taiwan.

Washington State International Trade Division
http://www.trade.wa.gov/
Based in Seattle, the site delivers Washington international trade news, export primers, trade policy alerts, foreign trade zone reports, employment opportunities, and an event calendar.

Washington State International Trade Fair
http://www.wsitf.org/
Established in 1951, the Fair promotes Washington exports through exhibitions and trade shows. The site includes press releases, an events schedule, and member directory.

Washington State Office of the Special Trade Representative
http://www.wa.gov/wstr/
A representative of the State Governor, the Office represents the state in international trade discussions, and promotes the state's global business interests in Washington, D.C. The site includes trade policy statements, trade mission summaries, and export and import statistics.

World Trade Club of Seattle
http://www.businesscity.com/worldtradeclub/
An association of international trade professionals, the Club provides global business networking and education. The site includes a member directory, event calendar, and the *World Trader*, a monthly newsletter on export topics.

Washington Representative Offices

Australia

Australia-New Zealand-American Society of Seattle
http://anzas.com/
The Society represents the interests of expatriate Australians and New Zealanders living in the Pacific Northwest. The site delivers a mission statement, member directory, and event calendar.

Canada

Canadian Consulate General in Seattle
http://www.canada-seattle.org/
Posted in English and French, the site provides Canadian fact sheets, visa and passport informa-

tion, sector profiles, a staff directory, Pacific northwest reports, and an online strategic alliance center.

Japan

Consulate General of Japan in Seattle
http://www.embjapan.org/seattle/
The virtual Consulate provides Japanese fact sheets, visa and passport information, culture guides, and reports on Washington-Japan trade, relations, and sister cities.

Japan-America Society of the State of Washington
http://www.us-japan.org/jassw/
Based in Seattle, the Society promotes Japan-Washington communication. The site includes news, an annual report, event calendar, and contact information.

Mexico

Trade Commission of Mexico in Seattle
http://www.mexico-businessline.com/ingles/ofrepmu3.html#seattle
The site lists the street address, phone and fax numbers, and e-mail link of the Trade Commission of Mexico in Seattle.

New Zealand

New Zealand Consulate in Seattle
http://www.emb.com/nzemb/offices/consul~1.htm#seattle
The site lists the street address, and phone and fax numbers of the New Zealand Consulate in Seattle.

Philippines

Philippine Trade and Investment Promotion Office in Seattle
http://www.dti.gov.ph/sea/
The site provides a mission statement, service directory, and contact information for the Philippine Trade Office in Seattle.

Russia

Consulate General of Russia in Seattle
http://www.russia.net/travel/visas.html
The digital Consulate provides Russian visa information, and a directory of Russian embassies and consulates in the U.S. and Canada.

United Kingdom

British American Chamber of Commerce of the Pacific Northwest
http://www.babc.org/seattle/
Based in Seattle, the Chamber promotes British-Pacific Northwest trade. The site features news, a member directory, and calendar of events.

Consulate of Britain in Seattle
http://britain-info.org/bis/dipoff/seattle.sTM
The site provides British fact sheets, press releases, business guides, event information, and a directory of consular and commercial services.

West Virginia

West Virginia Media

West Virginia Media
http://www.mediainfo.com/emediajs/specific-geo.htm?region=westvirginia
A service of Editor and Publisher Interactive, the site provides a searchable directory of web-based media sites in West Virginia including city guides, magazines, and newspapers.

West Virginia Market Guides

Going into Business in West Virginia
http://www.mountain.net/Pinnacle/wv/business/handbook/toc.html
A virtual entrepreneur's handbook, the site provides primers on West Virginia business incentives, licensing requirements, taxation, employment programs, labor legislation, and financing.

West Virginia Chamber of Commerce
http://www.wvchamber.com/
Based in Charleston, the site features Chamber news, policy statements, legislative bulletins, tourism guides, education reports, a member directory, and event information.

West Virginia Development Office
http://www.wvdo.org/
Based in Charleston, the site delivers West Virginia fact sheets, news, press releases, an industrial properties database, event calendar, and a directory of state business incentives.

West Virginia Economic Development
http://wvweb.com/www/wvedc/
A service of the West Virginia Economic Develop-

ment Council, the site provides information on West Virginia counties, business incentives, tax credits, workforce, transportation, and real estate.

West Virginia Trade Assistance

Commercial Service in West Virginia
http://www.ita.doc.gov/uscs/wv/
A service of the International Trade Administration, the site is a directory of international trade statistics, leads, events, services, and contacts in West Virginia.

West Virginia International Development
http://www.wvdo.org/international/index.htm
A branch of the West Virginia Development Office, the service promotes West Virginia exports and international investment. The site features West Virginia trade news, events, a staff roster, and contact information for West Virginia offices in Japan and Taiwan.

Trade Shows in West Virginia
http://www.expoguide.com/shows/data/loc_wv.htm
Compiled by Expoguide, the site is a directory of trade shows in Charleston, White Sulphur Springs, and other West Virginia centers.

Wisconsin

Wisconsin Media

Wisconsin Media
http://www.mediainfo.com/emediajs/specific-geo.htm?region=wisconsin
A service of Editor and Publisher Interactive, the site provides a searchable directory of web-based media sites in Wisconsin including city guides, magazines, and newspapers.

Wisconsin Market Guides

Business Journal
http://www.amcity.com/milwaukee/
A business e-zine, the site provides Wisconsin commercial news, editorials, small business strategies, an event calendar, sector profiles, and financial guides.

Taking Care of Business
http://badger.state.wi.us/agencies/commerce/
Based in Madison, the site provides Wisconsin fact sheets, community profiles, business incentives, a site and building database, planning checklists, and relocation primers.

Wisconsin Trade Assistance

Commercial Service in Wisconsin
http://www.ita.doc.gov/uscs/wi/
A service of the International Trade Administration, the site is a directory of international trade statistics, leads, events, services, and contacts in Wisconsin.

International Business Programs
http://badger.state.wi.us/agencies/commerce/html/inttrade.html
A service of the Wisconsin Department of Commerce, the site delivers Wisconsin export primers, statistics, program information, and a trade show calendar. A key program is Wisconsin Individualized Services for Exporters or WISE, a suite of international trade planning, research and networking services for Wisconsin companies.

Starting an Import/Export Business
http://badger.state.wi.us/agencies/dod/html/imexb923.html
A beginner's guide to international trade, the site provides tutorials on export and import planning, and licensing. The service includes a directory of export assistance programs in Wisconsin.

Trade Shows in Wisconsin
http://www.expoguide.com/shows/data/loc_wi.htm
Developed by Expoguide, the site is a directory of trade shows in La Crosse, Madison, Milwaukee, and other Wisconsin centers.

Wisconsin World Trade Center
http://www.execpc.com/~wistrade/wis.htm
Based in Milwaukee, the Center provides international trade information to Wisconsin companies. The site includes state fact sheets and a member directory.

Wyoming

Wyoming Media

Wyoming Media
http://www.mediainfo.com/emediajs/specific-geo.htm?region=wyoming
A service of Editor and Publisher Interactive, the site provides a searchable directory of web-based media sites in Wyoming including city guides, magazines, and newspapers.

Wyoming Market Guides

Welcome to the State of Wyoming
http://www.state.wy.us/business.html
A service of the state government, the site provides Wyoming fact sheets, statistics, labor market information, economic forecasts, business incentives, taxation guides, and employment opportunities.

Wyoming Business Guide
http://www.nwwyo.com/index.cfm
A searchable database of Wyoming companies, the site is browsable by city, industry, or keyword. Categories include banking, footwear, hotels, mining, and repair shops.

Wyoming Trade Assistance

Commercial Service in Wyoming
http://www.ita.doc.gov/uscs/wy/
A service of the International Trade Administration, the site is a directory of international trade statistics, leads, events, services, and contacts in Wyoming.

Trade Shows in Wyoming
http://www.expoguide.com/shows/data/loc_wy.htm
Developed by Expoguide, the site is a directory of Wyoming trade shows.

## CHAPTER 4

MAPLE LEAF CYBER-STATIONS: 340+ CANADIAN BUSINESS RESOURCES ON THE INTERNET

This chapter profiles more than 340 of the leading international business resources online that focus on Canada. The section reviews national websites and online hubs for each of the ten provinces and two territories. One of the richest and most developed countries in the world, Canada has a population of 30 million people and a diverse industrial base including agriculture, mining, forestry, manufacturing, and professional services. The U.S. Department of Commerce reports that the top business prospects in Canada include computers and peripherals, computer software, telecommunications equipment, automotive parts and service, and pollution control equipment. According to a survey by Comquest Research in December 1998, over 6.3 million Canadians access the Internet on a weekly basis. Over 26 percent of the adult population is now online, up from 4.6 million or 19 percent of adults in November 1997.

National Sites

Canada Search Tools

AltaVista Canada
http://www.altavistacanada.com/
Part of the AltaVista search network, the site is an index of more than 14 million pages of Canadian web content.

Canada.Com
http://www.canada.com/
A Canadian web navigation service, the English and French language site features news, shopping guides, and free e-mail services.

Canadian Online Explorer
http://www.canoe.com/
Based in Toronto, the site is a Canadian online search service. Categories include news, newspapers, business, and entertainment.

Infospace Canada
http://in-105.infospace.com/_1_34407537__info/cansvcs.htm
An online search service, the site includes Canadian business and people finders, home listings, personals, city profiles, and travel guides for all of the Canadian provinces and territories.

Yahoo Canada
http://www.yahoo.ca/
Part of the Yahoo network, the site is a Canadian and global online search service. Features include news, weather, stock quotes, reference, and Internet guides.

Canada Media

Canada Media
http://www.mediainfo.com/emediajs/links-geo.htm?location=canada
A service of Editor and Publisher Interactive, the site provides a browsable directory of hundreds of Canadian media sites including online newspapers, magazines, and television services.

Financial Post
http://www.canoe.com/FP/home.html
Based in Toronto, the online newspaper provides Canadian news, business reports, editorials, investment primers, a mutual funds database, and a directory of leading Canadian companies.

Globe and Mail
http://www.theglobeandmail.com/
Updated daily, the online newspaper features Canadian news, business reports, editorials, book reviews, sector profiles, mutual fund bulletins, and employment opportunities.

Canada Market Guides

Barclays Country Report: Canada
http://www.offshorebanking.barclays.com/services/economic/yearly/canmar98/canconts.html
Prepared by Barclays Bank, the site reports on Canadian economic trends, politics, monetary and fiscal policy, international trade, and U.K.-Canada merchandise trade and investment flows.

Canada Business Briefs

http://www.austrade.gov.au/IOOM/CANADA/
A service of Austrade, the site offers fact sheets on Canadian culture, business etiquette, marketing, transportation, travel, and visas.

Canada Business Reports

http://italchambers.net/BusinessReports.html
Prepared by the Italian Chamber of Commerce and written in Italian, the site provides Canada fact sheets, market reports, and commercial guides.

Canada Business Service Centers

http://www.cbsc.org/main.html
With 12 offices nationwide, the Centres provide fact sheets and guides for Canadian business. The site includes government directories and web navigation services.

Canada Country Profile

http://www.tradenz.govt.nz/intelligence/profiles/canada.html
A service of the New Zealand Trade Development Board, the site provides Canadian economic statistics, market information, and business tips.

Canada Country Report

http://www.state.gov/www/issues/economic/trade_reports/europe_canada97/canada97.html
Prepared by the U.S. Department of State, the site profiles Canadian economic policy and trade practices. Sections include economic indicators, exchange rate policy, debt management policies, significant barriers to U.S. exports, export subsidies policies, protection of U.S. intellectual property, and worker rights.

Canada: An Introduction

http://www.apecsec.org.sg/member/apeccan.html
A service of the Asia Pacific Economic Cooperation, the site provides fact sheets on Canadian geography, climate, population, language, religion, and government.

Canada Market Access Database

http://mkaccdb.eu.int/mkdb/mkdb.pl?METHOD=COUNTRY
A service of the European Commission, the site delivers briefs on Canada trade policy, tariff barriers, non-tariff barriers, investment-related measures, and financial services regulations.

Canada Market Information

http://dtiinfo1.dti.gov.uk/ots/canada/
A service of the London-based Department of Trade and Industry, the site delivers country fact sheets, maps, and trade-show information.

Canada Market Research

http://strategis.ic.gc.ca/sc_mrkti/ibinddc/engdoc/1a1e1.html
A service of Industry Canada, the site is a virtual library of reports on Canadian commerce, politics, investment, international trade, regulations, and business travel.

Canada NewsWire

http://www.newswire.ca/
Posted in French and English, the site is a searchable database of Canadian news releases. The directory is searchable by category, date, industry, keyword, organization, stock symbol, and subject.

Canada Telephone Directories

http://www.contractjobs.com/tel/ca/
A directory of Canadian online phone books, the site includes the Yellow Pages for British Columbia, Manitoba, Québec, Saskatchewan, and other Canadian provinces and areas.

Canadian Business

http://www.canbus.com/
Homepage of *Canadian Business* magazine, the site provides Canadian business news, sector reports, company profiles, Internet guides, and special features on Canadian businesspeople and leaders.

Canadian Business Map

http://strategis.ic.gc.ca/scdt/bizmap/nav.html
A service of Industry Canada, the site provides a directory of Canadian online resources in six categories: investing, exporting, research and development, company directories, industry statistics, and aboriginal business.

Canadian Company Capabilities

http://strategis.ic.gc.ca/sc_coinf/ccc/engdoc/homepage.html
Developed by Industry Canada, the site is a browsable database of over 35,000 Canadian companies and 200,000 products and services. The information is searchable by company name, product, province, and keyword.

Canadian Corporate News

http://www.cdn-news.com/
A media distribution service, the site is a data-

base of Canadian news releases from companies and government organizations. The directory is browsable by keyword, stock symbol, company name, and industry.

Canadian Intellectual Property Office
http://cipo.gc.ca/
The Canadian Intellectual Property Office provides information on Canadian intellectual property such as patents, trademarks, copyrights, industrial designs and integrated circuit topographies. The service includes intellectual property primers, and a searchable database of patents and trademarks.

Canadiana: Canadian Resource Page
http://www.cs.cmu.edu/Unofficial/Canadiana/
Developed by Stewart Clamen, a Carnegie Mellon University graduate student, the site is a directory of Canadian information online. Categories include news and information, facts and figures, travel and tourism, government services, and technology and commerce.

Career Mosaic Canada
http://canada.careermosaic.com/
Part of the Career Mosaic global network, the site provides a searchable database of Canadian employment opportunities, employer profiles, resume posting services, online job fairs, and career primers.

Country Commercial Guide
http://www.state.gov/www/about_state/business/com_guides/1998/europe_canada/canada98.html
Prepared by the U.S. Embassy in Ottawa, the site reviews the Canadian business climate. Topics include business, politics, marketing U.S. products and services, and leading sectors for U.S. exports and investments.

Doing Business in Canada
http://www.dbic.com/global-cgi-bin/quote.cgi?file=/guide.html
Sponsored by Smith Lyons Barristers, the site is a Canadian business primer. Topics include marketing, establishing a business, money matters, social issues, working with government, human resources, and site selection.

Government of Canada Homepage
http://Canada.GC.CA/
Written in English and French, the site provides Canada fact sheets, an overview of government institutions and legislation, and a directory of federal government departments, boards, corporations, banks, museums, and other entities.

Guide for Canadian Small Business
http://www.rc.gc.ca/~paulb/rc4070/english/rc4070e1.htm#Table of contents
A free business primer by Revenue Canada, the guide explains Canadian business structures, income tax reporting and payment, importing and exporting, payroll deductions, and audits.

MERX
http://www.merx.cebra.com/
A Canadian electronic tendering service, the site is a searchable directory of procurement opportunities posted by Canadian federal, provincial, territorial, and municipal governments, along with academic institutions, school boards, and hospitals.

Micro-Economic Research and Statistical Analysis
http://strategis.ic.gc.ca/sc_ecnmy/engdoc/homepage.html
A service of Industry Canada, the site provides Canadian economic reports and statistics such as Gross Domestic Product, consumer spending, business investment, housing, employment, commodity prices, exchange rates, and other key indicators.

National Technology Index
http://strategis.ic.gc.ca/sc_innov/nti/engdoc/search.html
A virtual registry of advanced technologies, the site lists leading Canadian scientists, organizations, and commercialization opportunities in industries such as biotechnology, electronics, and aerospace.

Report on Business
http://www.robmagnet.com/html/contents.html
Homepage of *Report on Business* magazine, the site features Canadian business articles, editorials, technology guides, employment opportunities, and market reports.

Statistics Canada
http://www.statcan.ca
Posted in English and French, the site provides statistics on Canadian economic performance, land area, population traits, education, culture, and government finances and employment.

Strategis
http://strategis.ic.gc.ca
Developed by Industry Canada, the site is a virtual library of Canadian business information. Modules include company information, international business opportunities, micro-economic research, business support and services, marketplace laws and regulations, and human resources and training.

Virtual Library
http://www.kpmg.ca/main/vl.htm
Prepared by KPMG Canada, the site provides newsletters, surveys and articles on biotechnology, health care, hospitality, transportation, insurance, electronic commerce, and other industries in Canada.

Canada Trade Assistance

Agri-Food Trade Service Online
http://atn-riae.agr.ca/public/atnnf-e.htm
A service of Agriculture and Agri-Food Canada, the site provides trade news, event calendars, market reports, country profiles, export start-up kits, financing primers, and regulatory guides for agri-food exporters.

Airlines in Canada
http://www.freightworld.com/airl_geo.html#3
A service of Freightworld, the site is a database of Canadian airline homepages on the web such as Air Canada, Canadian Airlines, and Skyward Aviation.

Airports in Canada
http://www.freightworld.com/airptgeo.html#3
Compiled by Freightworld, the site is a directory of Canadian airports online including the Edmonton, Montreal, Toronto, and Vancouver airports.

Alliance of Manufacturers and Exporters Canada
http://www.palantir.ca/the-alliance/
Based in Toronto, the Alliance promotes Canadian competitiveness and exports. The site includes a newsletter, events calendar, and member directory.

Asia Pacific Foundation of Canada
http://www.apfnet.org/apfc/foundation/index.html
Headquartered in Vancouver, the Foundation provides programs and consulting services related to Asian education, research, and media.

The site includes business briefings, country backgrounders, and a staff directory.

Association for the Export of Canadian Books
http://www.aecb.org/index.html
Based in Ottawa, the site provides Canadian publishing news, business opportunities, book catalogs, a list of publishing workshops, and a directory of assistance programs for Canadian book publishers.

Business Development Bank of Canada
http://www.bdc.ca/
Based in Montreal, the Bank provides financial and export consulting services to Canadian business. The site includes news, press releases, program information, and executive profiles.

Businesswomen in Trade
http://www.infoexport.gc.ca/businesswomen/ menu-e.asp
Developed by Foreign Affairs and International Trade, the site is a resource page for women exporters. The service includes success stories, press releases, an export readiness quiz, events calendar, and studies on women entrepreneurship.

Canada Agriculture Online
http://www.agcanada.com/
An information center for Canadian food growers and processors, the site provides agri-food reports, crop bulletins, production reports, cattle inventories, and online forums for buying, selling, and trading machinery, livestock, and commodities.

Canada Beef Export Federation
http://www.cbef.com/
Based in Calgary, the Federation promotes Canadian beef exports. The site includes beef product catalogs, a grading menu, meat inspection primers, a membership directory, and reports on feedlot finishing, the cattle cycle, and cow productivity.

Canada Customs Procedures
http://americas.fiu.edu/customs/canada.htm
A service of Florida International University, the site reviews Canada customs regulations, entry procedures, documentation, and taxes.

Canada Housing Export Centre
http://www.cmhc-schl.gc.ca/chec-cceh/en/ home.html

A service of Canada Mortgage and Housing Corporation, the site provides a virtual help desk, event information, market studies, and trade leads for building product exporters.

Canada Pork International
http://www.cfta.ca/cpi/cpi.html
Based in Ottawa, Canada Pork International is the export promotion agency for the Canadian pork industry. The site includes reports on Canadian hog production and processing, animal health, meat hygiene, pork marketing, and nutrition facts.

Canada's Action Plan for Japan
http://www.dfait-maeci.gc.ca/ni-ka/business/actnplan1998/menu-e.asp
Developed by the Department of Foreign Affairs and International Trade, the site highlights Canada's export strategy for the Japanese market. Priority sectors include agri-food, building products, furniture, giftware, sporting goods, medical devices, and tourism.

Canada's International Business Strategy
http://strategis.ic.gc.ca/SSG/bi17964e.html
The site is a directory of international trade action plans developed by the Canadian federal and provincial governments for 27 industries including aerospace, chemicals, and plastics, and six global regions such as Asia Pacific, Europe, and Latin America.

CanadExport Online
http://www.dfait-maeci.gc.ca/english/news/newsletr/canex/
An electronic magazine on Canadian exporting, the site features international trade news, exporter of the month profiles, business opportunities, trade fair reports, and interviews with leading government trade officials.

Canadian Association of Fish Exporters
http://www.seafood.ca/
Based in Ottawa, the Association promotes the export of Canadian fish and seafood products. Along with contact information, the site provides a directory of Canadian suppliers of lobster, scallop, shrimp, Pacific salmon and other seafood products.

Canadian Association of Mining Equipment and Services for Export
http://www.camese.org/
Founded in 1981, the Association promotes the export of Canadian mining equipment and services. The site provides over 230 profiles of Canadian mining suppliers, and a directory of mining trade shows worldwide.

Canadian Commercial Corporation
http://www.ccc.ca/index-e.htm
A crown corporation established in 1946, the Canadian Commercial Corporation is an international trade facilitator that helps Canadian companies sell to foreign buyers and international organizations. The site provides press releases, program information, and staff profiles.

Canadian Council for the Americas
http://www.infoexport.gc.ca/team_canada/profiles/on-counamer-e.asp
Based in Toronto, the Canadian Council for the Americas promotes Canadian trade with Latin American and Caribbean countries. The site provides a mission statement and a list of Council offices across Canada.

Canadian Council for International Business
http://www.ccib.org/
Based in Ottawa, the Council promotes Canadian interests in international policy development. The site includes a mission statement, publications list, committee directory, and membership information.

Canadian Exporters Catalogue
http://www.worldexport.com/
Posted in seven languages including Arabic, Chinese, and German, the site is a searchable directory of Canadian exporters in over 15 industry categories including agriculture, engineering, forestry, building products, health care, and transportation.

Canadian Food Trade Alliance
http://www.cfta.ca/
Based in Ottawa, the Alliance promotes the export of Canadian food products. The site includes a directory of member organizations such as the Canadian Poultry and Egg Processors Council, the Canadian Council of Grocery Distributors, and the Canadian Association of Specialty Foods.

Canadian Importers Association
http://www.importers.ca/
Based in Toronto, the Association promotes the interests of Canadian importers. The site includes a mission statement, activity reports, and event information.

Canadian Industrial Innovation Centre
http://www.innovationcentre.ca/
Based in Waterloo, Ontario, the Centre provides
assistance and financing to Canadian inventors.
The site includes a newsletter, success stories,
program information, and a calendar of events.

Canadian International Development Agency
http://www.acdi-cida.gc.ca/index.htm
Canada's lead player in development assistance, the Agency supports foreign aid projects in
more than 100 of the poorest countries in the
world. The site includes news releases, newsletters, program information, regional profiles, and
staff telephone directories.

Canadian International Trade Tribunal
http://www.citt.gc.ca/
Based in Ottawa, the Tribunal investigates
dumped or subsidized imports in Canada. Along
with annual reports, the site provides investiga-
tion notices and determinations.

Canadian Trade Index
*http://www.exportingcanadaonline.com/MainMenu/
Assoc/index.htm*
A service of Exporting Canada Online, the site is
a directory of international trade associations and
publications across Canada.

Canadian Transportation Web
http://www.cteam.ca/ctw/
Developed by C-Team Systems, the site is a
database of Canadian transportation resources
online. Categories include air carriers, customs
brokers, freight forwarders, ocean, rail, software,
and technology.

Direct Canada Exports
http://www.canadex.com/
Posted in English and Japanese, the site is a
directory of Canadian building supply exporters.
Featured products include windows, doors,
hardwood floors, furniture, and lumber.

Embassies and Missions Online
*http://www.dfait-maeci.gc.ca/english/missions/
menu.htm*
A service of the Department of Foreign Affairs and
International Trade, the site is a directory of
Canadian Embassies, Consulates, and Trade
Offices on the web. Posts online include Bonn,
Dallas, Johannesburg, New York City, and
Seattle.

Export Canada.Com
http://www.exportcanada.com/
A Québec-based subscription service, the site
matches Canadian exporters with international
buyers. Searchable by product and company, the
database contains profiles on Canadian exporters in industries such as biotechnology, hospitality, telecommunications, and water treatment. A
registration fee is required to be listed on the site,
although visitors may search the database at no
charge.

Export Development Corporation
http://www.edc.ca
Based in Ottawa, the Export Development
Corporation provides export financing to Canadian companies. The site includes program
information, newsletters, export primers, country
risk assessments, and Canadian international
trade forecasts.

Export Related Activities and Events
http://strategis.ic.gc.ca/SSG/bi18091e.html
A service of Industry Canada, the site is a
searchable database of international trade
missions and events across Canada. The
directory is browsable by sector, keyword, and
geographic region of interest such as Europe,
Latin America, and the Middle East.

Export Risk Profiler
http://www.edc.ca/risk/index.html
A service of the Export Development Corporation,
the site will prepare a customized list of international business web links based on your export
needs and targets.

Exporting Canada Online
http://exportingcanadaonline.com/
A virtual library of Canadian exporting information,
the site includes international trade primers, a
database of U.S. importers and buyers, and a
directory of Canadian export service firms such
as air carriers, freight forwarders, and customs
brokers.

Foreign Affairs and International Trade Canada
http://www.dfait-maeci.gc.ca/menu-e.asp
Homepage of Canada's lead export promotion
agency, the site provides Canadian fact sheets,
passport information, investment primers, travel
reports, global business guides, foreign policy
statements, and a directory of Canadian Embassies and Consulates around the world.

Freight Forwarders in Canada
http://www.freightworld.com/forw_geo.html#3
A service of Freightworld, the site is a database of Canadian freight forwarders online from Ag Logisitcs Inc. to Worldwide Shipping and Forwarding Ltd.

Health Canada International Business Development
http://www.hc-sc.gc.ca/datapcb/iad/coordina.htm
A service of Health Canada, the program promotes the export of Canadian health care products and medical equipment. The site provides program guides, health business opportunities, and contact information.

Importing/Exporting
http://www.rc.gc.ca/~paulb/rc4070/english/ rc4070e3.htm#Chapter 5: Importing/Exporting
Developed by Revenue Canada, the site is an importing and exporting primer. Modules include introduction to importing, accounting for goods, trade incentives, assessment and appeals, and exporting.

Importing and Exporting in Canada
http://www.dbic.com/global-cgi-bin/ quote.cgi?file=/guide/m3-1.html
Sponsored by Smith Lyons Barristers and Solicitors, the site is a beginner's guide to exporting and importing in Canada. Topics include the North American Free Trade Agreement, Canada Customs, warehousing, and packaging and labeling.

InfoExport
http://www.infoexport.gc.ca/menu-e.asp
A service of Foreign Affairs and International Trade Canada, the site provides export primers, statistics, checklists, market guides, interactive quizzes, and program directories for Canadian exporters.

Intermodal Carriers in Canada
http://www.freightworld.com/intmod_geo.html#3
Compiled by Freightworld, the site is a database of Canadian intermodal carriers online such as Global Forwarding Company Ltd. and Trimac Transportation System.

International Business Information Network
http://strategis.ic.gc.ca/SSG/bi18087e.html
Developed by Industry Canada, the site is a directory of Canadian international trade advisors, fact sheets, export programs, events, market studies, country profiles, and procurement opportunities.

International Business Opportunities Centre
http://www.dfait-maeci.gc.ca/iboc-coai/ menuen_a.htm
Based in Ottawa, the Centre matches Canadian companies with international trade leads provided by Canadian Trade Commissioners and Commercial Officers around the world. The site posts a selection of global business opportunities, and explains where to register to receive the trade leads.

Maritime Carriers in Canada
http://www.freightworld.com/mari_geo.html#3
Developed by Freightworld, the site is a database of Canadian maritime carriers online such as Algoma Central Marine, Canada Steamship Lines, and Montreal Shipping.

NAFTA Secretariat
http://www.nafta-sec-alena.org/english/index.htm
Posted in English, French, and Spanish, the site delivers North American Free Trade Agreement status reports, and dispute settlement decisions.

Northstar Trade Finance
http://www.northstar.ca/
Headquartered in Richmond, British Columbia, Northstar provides export financing services to Canadian exporters. The site includes a newsletter, program information, and an export problem solver service.

OnTRAC
http://www.ontractrade.com/
An online marketplace, the site is a searchable directory of business opportunities and trade leads from across Canada and around the world. The service includes country backgrounders, market reports, and export tutorials.

Package Carriers in Canada
http://www.freightworld.com/exp_geo.html#3
A service of Freightworld, the site is a directory of Canadian package carriers online such as Air World Express and Loomis Courier Service.

Postal Services in Canada
http://www.freightworld.com/postal.html#3
Developed by Freightworld, the site is a database of Canadian postal services online such as Canada Post Corporation and Key Mail International Mail Service.

Railroads in Canada
http://www.freightworld.com/railroads.html#3
A service of Freightworld, the site is a registry of

Canadian railroads online such as BC Rail, Canadian National Railway, and Canadian Pacific Railway.

Royal Bank of Canada International Trade
http://www.royalbank.com/trade/index.html
Developed by the Royal Bank of Canada, the site provides an international trade newsletter, currency exchange tables, a trade terms glossary, and a directory of trade finance services including electronic letters of credit and import documentary collections.

Scotiabank International
http://www.scotiabank.ca/TradeExpress.html
A unit of Scotiabank, a leading Canadian financial institution, the site provides an Internet letter of credit service, and other electronic trade services.

Seaports in Canada
http://www.freightworld.com/port_geo.html#3
Prepared by Freightworld, the site is a database of Canadian seaports online such as Charlottetown, Halifax, Saint John, Sydney, Toronto, and Vancouver.

Team Canada
http://www.infoexport.gc.ca/team_canada/menu-e.asp
A partnership of federal, provincial and municipal trade organizations across Canada, Team Canada provides export counseling and organizes overseas trade missions for Canadian exporters. The site includes success stories, mission reports, and a directory of upcoming international trade activities.

Trade Facilitation Office Canada
http://www.tfoc.ca/tfoc.htm
Based in Ottawa, the Office assists exporters from developing countries, and Canadian importers who wish to locate new sources of products from over 130 countries. The site includes program information, and a list of client countries.

Trade Shows in Canada
http://www.expoguide.com/shows/data/loc_can.htm
Developed by Expoguide, the site is a directory of trade shows across Canada from Victoria, British Columbia to St. John's, Newfoundland.

Tradenet Canada
http://www.tradenet.ca/
Posted in eight languages including German, French, and Italian, the site is a searchable directory of international organizations and business opportunities in Canada. Categories include manufacturers, joint ventures, importers, exporters, real estate, and economic development corporations.

Trucking and Motor Carriers in Canada
http://www.freightworld.com/truc_geo.html#3
A service of Freightworld, the site is a registry of Canadian trucking and motor carriers online such as Arnold Brothers Transport, Fillmore Trucking, and Yellow Freight Canadian Coverage.

Virtual Market Place
http://www.virtualmarketplace.com/
Written in English and French, the site is a browsable catalog of Canadian export products and services. Categories include aviation, rail, biotechnology, information technology, language, and cultural industries.

U.S. Opportunities for Canadian Firms
http://209.82.43.25/
A service of the Canadian Commercial Corporation, the site is a browsable database of U.S. government procurement opportunities. Categories include fuels and lubricants, containers and packaging, and cleaning equipment and supplies.

Virtual Trade Mission
http://www.vtmission.com/
Sponsored in part by the CanAsian Businesswomen's Network, the site is an online networking forum for businesswomen in Canada, Malaysia, and Singapore. The service includes press releases and a membership application form.

Women's Business Directory Import and Export
http://www.cdnbizwomen.com/directory/import.shtm
A service of the Canadian Women's Business Network, the site is a registry of trading houses, import-export agents, and freight forwarders across Canada.

Canada Representative Offices

Armenia

Embassy of Armenia in Ottawa
http://www.armeniaemb.org/forrel/embas2.htm
The site provides contact information for the Embassy of Armenia in Ottawa.

Bahamas

High Commission of the Bahamas in Ottawa
*http://flamingo.bahamas.net.bs/government/
gov8.html*
The site provides contact information for the High
Commission of Bahamas in Ottawa.

Brunei Darussalam

High Commission of Brunei Darussalam in
Ottawa
*http://www.brunet.bn/homepage/gov/bruemb/
govemb.htm*
The site provides contact information for the
Brunei Darussalam High Commission in Ottawa.

Chile

Chile's Business Update
http://www.chiletrade.cl/newslttr/index.htm
Published by the Consulate General of Chile in
Toronto, the site provides Chilean fact sheets, a
calendar of events, Canada-Chile trade reports,
and a directory of trade and investment opportunities in Chile.

China

Canada China Business Council
http://www.ccbc.com/
Based in Toronto, the Council promotes Canada-
China trade. The site includes a member
directory, program information, and a directory of
Canada-China events and activities.

Embassy of China in Ottawa
http://www.buildlink.com/embassy/
Posted in English and Chinese, the site provides
Chinese newsletters, visa and passport application forms, cultural bulletins, an investment
guide, political statements, and employment
opportunities.

Hong Kong-Canada Business Association
http://www.hkcba.com/
Formed in 1984, the Association promotes
commercial ties between Canada and Hong
Kong. Posted in Chinese, English, and French,
the site includes a mission statement, events
calendar, and Hong Kong market bulletins.

Colombia

Embassy of Colombia in Ottawa
http://www.travel-net.com/~embcolot/
Posted in English and Spanish, the site features
Colombian news, product catalogs, visa and
passport information, business guides, and
government bulletins.

Czech Republic

Embassy of Czech Republic in Ottawa
*http://www.czechemb.net/
scroll_of_embassies.html*
Along with a directory of diplomatic offices in the
Czech Republic, the site provides contact
information for the Czech Embassy in Ottawa.

Ecuador

Embassy of Ecuador in Ottawa
*http://www.ncf.carleton.ca:12345/freeport/govern-
ment/embassies/south.am/ecuador/menu*
The virtual Embassy provides fact sheets on
Ecuadorian business, government, infrastructure,
geography, climate, people, history, language,
culture, environment, and travel.

Ethiopia

Embassy of Ethiopia in Ottawa
http://www.ethiopia.ottawa.on.ca/
Featuring a welcome message from the Ambassador, the site provides Ethiopian news, press
releases, country profiles, economic reports,
tourism guides, investment information, and an
online visa application form.

European Union

European Union in Canada
http://www.eudelcan.org/
Posted in English and French, the site provides
European Union news, fact sheets, country
profiles, and interactive tests. The service
includes an overview of European Union-Canada
relations, a directory of European Union-Canada
trade agreements, and a list of upcoming
European Union events in Canada.

European Union Chamber of Commerce

http://www.euro-chamber.ca/
Based in Toronto, the Chamber promotes Canada-European Union business and cultural exchanges. The site includes European Union fact sheets, country profiles, a member directory, and reports on Canada-European Union trade and relations.

Finland

Embassy of Finland in Ottawa

http://www.finemb.com/
The virtual Embassy delivers information on Finnish visas, tourism, culture, exchange programs, customs, international trade, and investment.

France

Embassy of France in Ottawa

http://www.amba-ottawa.fr/
Posted in English and French, the site delivers French news, press releases, cultural bulletins, scientific reports, and a directory of consular and business matchmaking services.

French Trade Commission in Ottawa

http://www.dree.org/canada/francais/services/ottawa/presenta.htm
The site lists the staff, street address, phone and fax numbers, and e-mail links of the French Trade Commission in Ottawa.

Germany

Embassy of Germany in Ottawa

http://www.germanembassyottawa.org/
Featuring a welcome from the Ambassador, the site delivers German fact sheets, speeches, tourism guides, event calendars, legal primers, election results, and reports on German-Canada relations and trade.

Ghana

High Commission of Ghana in Ottawa

http://www.juntung.com/ghana-consul-hk/2misabo.htm
The site provides contact information for the Ghanaian High Commission in Ottawa.

Hungary

Embassy of Hungary in Ottawa

http://www.DocuWeb.ca/Hungary/
The digital Embassy offers Hungarian news, fact sheets, travel guides, business primers, economic bulletins, privatization reports, and a directory of diplomatic, consular and commercial representatives in Canada.

India

Canada-India Business Council

http://www.canada-indiabusiness.ca/
Based in Toronto, the Council promotes Canada-India trade. The site features Indian facts, an events calendar, and a directory of sector programs in environment, agri-business, telecommunications, and financial services.

Focus India

http://www.dfait-maeci.gc.ca/focus_india/
A service of Foreign Affairs and International Trade Canada, the site delivers Indian news, weekly reports, business primers, travel guides, a directory of key industry players, and reports on Canada-India trade and relations.

High Commission of India in Ottawa

http://www.DocuWeb.ca/India/
The Commission service provides India news, maps, travel guides, and primers on Indian politics, business, geography, people, agriculture, rural development, and culture.

Indo-Canada Chamber of Commerce

http://www.iccc.org/
Based in North York, Ontario, the Chamber promotes Canada-India trade. The site includes a newsletter, events calendar, and membership information.

Indonesia

Canada Indonesia Business Development Office

http://www.prica.org/CIBDO.htm
In cooperation with the Alliance of Manufacturers and Exporters Canada, the office promotes Canadian investment and technology transfer to Indonesia. The site provides program information and a list of priority sectors including forestry, mining, and agriculture.

Embassy of Indonesia in Ottawa
http://www.prica.org/
The virtual Embassy provides Indonesian news, economic bulletins, investment information, tourism guides, and tutorials on Indonesian geography, history, culture, and government.

Iran

Embassy of the Islamic Republic of Iran in Ottawa
http://www.salamiran.org/Embassy/
The Islamic Republic site features Iranian news, visa and passport information, legal guides, travel tips, cultural bulletins, economic strategies, free trade zone fact sheets, and Canada-Iran trade reports.

Israel

Embassy of Israel in Ottawa
http://www.israelca.org/
Posted in English and French, the site provides Israeli news, fact sheets, tourism guides, cultural reports, and business and investment opportunities.

Italy

Embassy of Italy in Ottawa
http://www.trytel.com/~italy/
Posted in English and Italian, the site provides contact information for the Embassy, and a directory of Italian commercial, consular, and cultural resources online.

Italian Chamber of Commerce of Toronto
http://www.italchamber-tor.on.ca/
Part of a global network of Italian Chambers, the site features a staff directory, events calendar, and reports on key Italian companies and sectors such as automotive, electronics, agri-food, and apparel.

Japan

Canada-Japan Trade Council
http://infoweb.magi.com/~cjtc/
Based in Ottawa, the Council promotes Canada-Japan trade. The site includes membership information, a program directory, and a bi-monthly newsletter on Canada-Japan trade issues and opportunities.

Directory of Canadian Business in Japan
http://www.dcbj.com/
An online directory of Canadian companies doing business in Japan, the site is searchable by keyword and company name. Categories include agriculture, biotechnology, forest products, and high technology.

Embassy of Japan in Ottawa
http://www.embjapan.can.org/
An online Japanese resource center, the site delivers Embassy press releases, bulletins, Japan visa information, leader profiles, economic fact sheets, and Canada-Japan trade reports.

Kuwait

Embassy of Kuwait in Ottawa
http://www.EmbassyOfKuwait.com/
The virtual Embassy provides Kuwaiti news, telephone and fax directories, education bulletins, weather forecasts, visa information, business and investment guides, and travel primers.

Latvia

Embassy of Latvia in Ottawa
http://www2.magmacom.com/~latemb/
The virtual diplomatic service delivers Latvian news, visa information, exchange rates, government contacts, and a directory of consular staff and services.

Lebanon

Embassy of Lebanon in Ottawa
http://www.synapse.net/~emblebanon/
Featuring a welcome from the Ambassador, the site provides Lebanese news, quick facts, travel guides, visa and passport information, legal documents, investment bulletins, and business primers.

Madagascar

Embassy of Madagascar in Ottawa
http://www.madagascar-contacts.com/us/ adresse.htm#alext
Along with a directory of Madagascar government agencies, the site provides contact information for the Madagascar Embassy in Ottawa.

Malaysia

High Commission of Malaysia in Ottawa
http://www.mnet.com.my/klonline/www/missions/ malmiss/mcanada1.htm
The site provides contact information for the Malaysia High Commission in Ottawa.

Mexico

Embassy of Mexico in Ottawa
http://www.embamexcan.com/
The online service delivers information on Mexican politics, business, education, culture, human rights, agriculture, technology, and Canada-Mexico relations. A trade module provides a database of Canada-Mexico export and import statistics.

Export I
http://www.dfait-maeci.gc.ca/exporti/
A service of Foreign Affairs and International Trade Canada, the site provides Mexican market profiles, business primers, and economic statistics. The service is free with registration.

Mexican Business Association of Canada
http://www.interam.com/asocmex/index.html
Posted in English, French and Spanish, the site includes a mission statement, member directory, and contact information.

New Zealand

High Commission of New Zealand in Ottawa
http://www.nzhcottawa.org/
The virtual High Commission provides New Zealand fact sheets, press releases, foreign policy statements, travel guides, visa information, and tutorials on New Zealand geography, education, and culture.

Norway

Norwegian Canadian Chamber of Commerce
http://www.ntc-can.com/NCCC/NCCC-Alex.htm
The Toronto-based Chamber promotes Canada-Norway trade. The site provides the street address, phone and fax numbers, e-mail link, and mission statement of the Chamber.

Norwegian Trade Council in Canada
http://www.ntc-can.com/NTC/NTC.html
Based in Toronto, the Council promotes Norway exports to Canada and countries worldwide. The site includes Canada-Norway trade news, a staff directory, and database of Norway companies and business opportunities.

Royal Norwegian Embassy in Ottawa
http://www.ntc-can.com/Embassy/NRE.html
Written in English, French and Norwegian, the site offers Norwegian fact sheets, residence and work permit information, education bulletins, and a directory of Norwegian Consulates in Canada.

Organization of Eastern Caribbean States

High Commission of the Organization of Eastern Caribbean States in Ottawa
http://www.stkittsnevis.net/offices.html
The site provides contact information for the Organization of Eastern Caribbean States in Ottawa.

Paraguay

Embassy of Paraguay in Ottawa
http://www.magmacom.com/~embapar/
Posted in English and Spanish, the site provides Paraguayan maps, fact sheets, tourist attractions, export and investment opportunities, sector profiles, and a directory of consular staff and services.

Peru

Embassy of Peru in Ottawa
http://www.cyberus.ca/~sudameris/emb-peru.htm
The virtual diplomatic service includes Peruvian news, visa information, travel guides, economic bulletins, regional profiles, education reports, and a directory of key government agencies and contacts.

Philippines

Philippines-Canada Trade Council
http://www.geocities.com/~pctc/
Based in Vancouver, the Council promotes Philippine-Canadian trade and relations. The site features a mission statement, member directory, and contact information.

Poland

Embassy of Poland in Ottawa
http://www.polonianet.com/eng/embassy

Posted in English and Polish, the site provides Poland passport and visa information, exchange rate reports, and a customs guide.

Poland Canada
http://www.Poland-Canada.org/
Homepage of the Polish Trade Commissioner in Canada, the site is a directory of Polish business development services and diplomatic offices in Ottawa, Montreal, Regina, Toronto, and Vancouver.

Russia

Canada-Russia Business Forum
http://www.canada-russia.com/
Based in Toronto, the Forum promotes Canada-Russia trade. The site includes press releases, an event calendar, membership directory, and a business-opportunity newsletter.

South Africa

Canada-South Africa Chamber of Business
http://www.DocuWeb.ca/SouthAfrica/ chamber1.html
A Canada-South Africa trade promotion service, the site provides the contacts, street address, phone and fax numbers, and e-mail links of the Chamber offices in Toronto and Vancouver.

High Commission of South Africa in Ottawa
http://www.DocuWeb.ca/SouthAfrica/
The High Commission service provides fact sheets on South Africa travel, education, and politics. A business section includes a database of South African exporters and investment opportunities.

Spain

Embassy of Spain in Ottawa
http://www.DocuWeb.ca/SpainInCanada/
Posted in English, French, and Spanish, the site delivers Spanish news, fact sheets, tourism guides, scholarship information, an online bulletin board, and a directory of Canadian companies in Spain, and Spanish companies in Canada.

Sri Lanka

High Commission of Sri Lanka in Ottawa
http://infoweb.magi.com/~lankacom/

The online service includes Sri Lankan news, press releases, maps, tourism guides, history lessons, government bulletins, and Canada-Sri Lanka trade statistics and reports.

Sweden

Embassy of Sweden in Ottawa
http://www.sweden-suede-can.org/
Written in English and French, the site delivers Swedish fact sheets, visa information, tourist guides, government directories, and product catalogs.

Swedish Canadian Chamber of Commerce
http://www.sccc.ca/
A Canada-Sweden networking service, the site provides news, an events calendar, meeting reports, and a member directory.

Taiwan

Canada-Taiwan Trade Association
http://www.jurock.com/ctta/
Based in Vancouver, the Association promotes Canada-Taiwan trade. The site includes news, meeting minutes, membership information, an event calendar, and a directory of business opportunities.

Taiwan Government Information Office in Ottawa
http://www.gio.gov.tw/info/ngio/cana-f.html
Posted in Chinese and English, the site lists the street address, phone and fax numbers, and e-mail link of the Taiwan Government Information Office in Ottawa.

Tanzania

Embassy of Tanzania in Ottawa
http://www.tanzania-online.gov.uk/visa/ envoys.html
The site provides contact information for the Tanzanian Embassy in Ottawa.

Thailand

Thailand Office of Commercial Affairs in Ottawa
http://www.thaitrade.com/thcoaf.html
The site lists the street address, phone and fax numbers, and e-mail link of the Thailand Office of Commercial Affairs in Ottawa.

Trinidad and Tobago

High Commission of Trinidad and Tobago in Ottawa
http://www.travel-net.com/~tthcotta/
The digital High Commission features Trinidadian and Tobagonian fact sheets, travel guides, history lessons, an events calendar, and contact information.

Ukraine

Canada-Ukraine Monitor
http://home.istar.ca/~monitor/
An electronic business magazine, the site reports on key Canada-Ukraine trade events, projects, players, and business opportunities in industries such as agri-food, machinery, electronics, and biotechnology.

Trade and Economic Mission of Ukraine in Canada
http://www3.sympatico.ca/tem-ukraine/
A service of the Ukrainian Embassy in Ottawa, the site features Ukrainian news, fact sheets, regional profiles, tax guides, investment primers, exchange rate reports, legal information, and Canada-Ukraine trade bulletins.

United Kingdom

British Canadian Chamber of Trade and Commerce
http://www.bcctc.ca/
Based in Markham, Ontario, the site delivers a British-Canadian trade newsletter, events calendar, meeting reports, membership information, and board member profiles.

British Trade and Investment Office
http://www.uk-canada-trade.org/
A service of the United Kingdom government, the site provides British fact sheets, an events calendar, and a database of over 300 United Kingdom companies seeking Canadian agents, distributors and customers.

High Commission of Britain in Ottawa
http://www.bis-canada.org/
Featuring a greeting from the High Commissioner, the site provides British fact sheets, visa and passport information, and a directory of consular and commercial services.

United States

Canada-United States Relations Homepage
http://www.dfait-maeci.gc.ca/geo/usa/menu-e.htm
A service of Foreign Affairs and International Trade Canada, the site provides fact sheets and reports on Canada-United States trade and relations.

Commercial Service of the United States Embassy in Canada
http://www.ita.doc.gov/cscanada/
The U.S. government site features Canadian fact sheets, a trade events calendar, a list of Canadian markets with high export potential for U.S. companies, and a directory of U.S. Consulates in Canada.

United States Embassy in Ottawa
http://www.usembassycanada.gov/
The virtual Embassy provides United States news, fact sheets, travel guides, and issue papers. The service includes reports on U.S.-Canada trade, Clinton-Chrétien meetings, the North American Free Trade Agreement, and the Free Trade Area of the Americas.

Uruguay

Embassy of Uruguay in Ottawa
http://www.iosphere.net/~uruott/
The virtual Embassy provides Uruguayan fact sheets, business guides, investment primers, travel information, visa application forms, and a directory of staff and consular services.

Venezuela

Embassy of Venezuela in Ottawa
http://www.trade-venezuela.com/EMBVENG.HTM
The site lists the street address, phone and fax numbers, and e-mail link of the Venezuelan Embassy in Ottawa.

Zimbabwe

High Commission of Zimbabwe in Ottawa
http://www.docuweb.ca/Zimbabwe/
The High Commission service includes Zimbabwe news, tourism guides, and an events calendar. A key feature is *Doing Business in Zimbabwe*, a virtual primer on international trade, investment, exchange controls, taxation, and export processing zones in the African country.

Provincial and Territorial Sites

Alberta

Alberta Media

Alberta Media
http://www.mediainfo.com/emediajs/specific-geo.htm?region=alberta
A service of Editor and Publisher Interactive, the site provides a browsable directory of Alberta media sites including online newspapers, magazines, and radio services.

Alberta Market Guides

Alberta Advantage
http://www.gov.ab.ca/edt/adv.htm
The online service delivers primers on Alberta business, manufacturing, natural resources, taxation, utilities, labor force, standard of living, and investment.

Alberta Chamber of Commerce
http://www.abchamber.ab.ca/
Based in Edmonton, the site includes a mission statement, staff e-mail directory, and contact numbers for the Chamber office.

Alberta Industry Sector Profiles
http://www.gov.ab.ca/edt/ind.htm
Developed by Alberta Economic Development, the site provides a searchable database of Alberta high-technology companies. The service includes reports on the Alberta biotechnology, electronics, telecommunications, geomatics, and heath care industries.

Business Link
http://www.cbsc.org/alberta/index.html
A virtual business center, the site includes a business start-up kit, inventor's guide, small business statistics, and primers on how to write a proposal, buy a business, and conduct marketing research.

Alberta Trade Assistance

Alberta World Trade Centre
http://www.wtcab.com/
Based in Edmonton, the Centre provides international trade information and training. The site includes an events calendar, members database, and directory of export counseling and travel assistance programs.

International Business Information Service
http://www.gov.ab.ca/edt/ibis/index.htm
An online export resource library, the site provides Alberta international trade news, leads, primers, events, competitive intelligence, and program directories. The service includes fact sheets on Trade Team Alberta, a partnership of federal, provincial and industry organizations that work together to promote provincial exports.

Investment Matching Service of Alberta
http://www.gov.ab.ca/edt/imsa/index.htm
Developed by Alberta Economic Development, the site is a searchable database of business and investment opportunities in Alberta. Categories include electronics, forestry, environment, medical, advanced technology, and retail.

Petro-Trade
http://www.petro-trade.ab.ca/
Based in Calgary, Petro-Trade promotes the export of Canadian oil and gas equipment and supplies. The site includes a mission statement, member directory, and a list of products and services including pipe and tube manufacturing, production testing, and electronic monitoring equipment.

Western Economic Diversification Canada
http://www.wd.gc.ca/eng/content/inter/index.html
Headquartered in Edmonton, Western Economic Diversification Canada promotes economic development in the four western provinces of Canada: Manitoba, Saskatchewan, Alberta, and British Columbia. The site provides a database of Western Canadian export and international trade statistics, and a directory of export counseling, training, and financing programs.

Alberta Representative Offices

Japan

Consulate General of Japan in Edmonton
http://www.embjapan.can.org/Edmon/edmon2.htm
The virtual Consulate lists the Consul General, street address, office hours, contact information, and events calendar for the Japanese Consulate in Edmonton.

United States

U.S. Consulate General in Calgary
http://www.ita.doc.gov/cscanada/locate.html
A service of the U.S. Embassy in Ottawa, the site lists the Commercial Specialist, street address, phone and fax numbers, and e-mail link of the U.S. Consulate General in Calgary.

British Columbia

British Columbia Media

British Columbia Media
http://www.mediainfo.com/emediajs/specific-geo.htm?region=britishcolumbia
A service of Editor and Publisher Interactive, the site provides a browsable directory of British Columbia media sites including online city guides, newspapers, and magazines.

British Columbia Market Guides

British Columbia Chamber of Commerce
http://www.bcchamber.org/
Based in Vancouver, the site features a mission statement, membership information, policy handbook, legislative bulletins, opinion polls, an event calendar, and reports on trade, transportation, and tourism issues.

British Columbia Investment Climate
http://www.ei.gov.bc.ca/directory/bctio/IC98/
A service of the British Columbia Ministry of Employment and Investment, the site provides fact sheets on British Columbia business, international trade, labor, government, taxation, infrastructure, environment, quality of life, and economic development incentives.

British Columbia Stats
http://www.bcstats.gov.bc.ca/
Based in Victoria, the site provides fact sheets and statistics on British Columbia people, geography, climate, health care, education, labor, and business.

British Columbia Wood Specialties Group
http://www.bcwood.com/
A consortium of British Columbia wood companies, the Group promotes the export of British Columbia wood products. The site provides a newsletter, issue papers, an event calendar, and education guides.

Canada/British Columbia Business Service Centre
http://www.sb.gov.bc.ca/smallbus/sbhome.html
Based in Vancouver, the site delivers an interactive business planner, and an online small business workshop. Modules include marketing basics, business financing, planning fundamentals, and basic regulations for getting started.

Canada West Telecom Group
http://www.ei.gov.bc.ca/directory/bctio/alliance/cwtg/index.htm
Based in Vancouver, the Group promotes the export of Canadian telecommunications equipment and services. The site includes a mission statement and contact information for the Group office in Vancouver.

Hanford Alliance
http://www.ei.gov.bc.ca/directory/bctio/alliance/hanford/index.htm
Based in Vancouver, the Alliance promotes the export of environmental products and services to the U.S. Energy and Defense Departments, and other markets. The site provides a directory of members in five categories: robotics and sensing technologies, remediation equipment, instrumentation and control, engineering companies, and custom equipment.

T-Net British Columbia
http://www.bctechnology.com/
Sponsored in part by the Vancouver Enterprise Forum, the site provides British Columbia high technology news, editorials, stock bulletins, employment opportunities, an event calendar, and a directory of advanced technology operations in the province.

British Columbia Trade Assistance

British Columbia Trade Network
http://bc-trade.net/bctrade/
Based in Victoria, the Network is an online export promotion service for British Columbia companies. The site features trade leads, export primers, a free e-mail newsletter, opinion surveys, and a searchable database of British Columbia exporters.

British Columbia International Training
http://www.bcit.bc.ca/international_home.htm
A service of the British Columbia Institute of Technology, the site provides a directory of international trade training courses and programs for students and businesspeople.

British Columbia Trade and Investment Office
http://www.ei.gov.bc.ca/directory/bctio/
A branch of the British Columbia Ministry of Employment and Investment, the Office promotes British Columbia exports and international investment. The site provides British Columbia fact sheets, sector profiles, and a directory of British Columbia trade offices in China, Japan, Taiwan, and the United Kingdom.

Latin America Marketing Group
http://www.nifcosynergy.com/Partners/lamg/lamghp.htm
Based in Vancouver, the Group promotes the export of engineering, geomatics and urban development consulting services to Latin America. The site includes a mission statement, member profiles, and contact information.

British Columbia Representative Offices

Australia

Austrade Canada in Vancouver
http://www.austrade.gov.au/canada/
An Australian trade promotion service, the site provides Australian fact sheets, market reports, and the street address, staff directory, and e-mail links of the Austrade office in Vancouver.

Austria

Austrian Trade Commission in Vancouver
http://www.austriantrade.org/AustrianTrade/offices/ahst_van.htm
The site lists the Trade Commissioners, street address, phone and fax numbers, and e-mail link for the Austrian Trade Commission in Vancouver.

France

Consulate General of France in Vancouver
http://www.consulfrancevancouver.org/
Posted in English and French, the site features French fact sheets, visa and passport information, travel guides, government directories, and a message from the Consul General.

French Chamber of Commerce in Vancouver
http://www.consulfrancevancouver.org/cdcfsumm.htm
Part of a national network of offices, the Chamber promotes Canada-France trade. The site provides a mission statement, events calendar, and membership information.

French Trade Commission in Vancouver
http://www.dree.org/canada/francais/services/vancouve/presenta.htm
A French export promotion service, the site provides a directory of Commission services, and a list of export opportunities for French exporters in the Vancouver area and province of British Columbia.

Germany

Canadian German Chamber of Industry and Commerce
http://www.germanchambervan.org/
Part of a global network of German Chamber offices, the site delivers a mission statement, a list of Canadian market studies for sale, and contact information for the Chamber in Vancouver.

Iceland

Consulate General of Iceland in Vancouver
http://www.iceland.org/list1n2.htm
The site lists the Consul General, street address, phone and fax numbers, and e-mail link of the Icelandic Consulate in Vancouver.

India

Indian Commercial Mission in Vancouver
http://www.nic.in/commin/ICM.HTM
The site lists the street address, phone and fax numbers, and e-mail link of the Indian Commercial Mission in Vancouver.

Japan

Canada-Japan Society of British Columbia
http://www.embjapan.can.org/Van/vancjsoc.htm
Based in Vancouver, the Society promotes Canada-Japan relations. The site features a mission statement, program guide, and contact information.

Consulate General of Japan in Vancouver
http://www.embjapan.can.org/Van/vanc.htm
The virtual Consulate provides a staff e-mail directory, events calendar, a guide to local Japanese television and radio programs, and a list of consular services.

JETRO Vancouver
http://www.canadex.com/JETROvan/
A Japanese trade promotion service, the site features Japanese fact sheets, an event calen-

dar, and list of publications such as Japanese market studies and business primers available for viewing in the JETRO Vancouver office.

Malaysia

Consulate General of Malaysia in Vancouver
http://www.mnet.com.my/klonline/www/missions/malmiss/mcanada2.htm
The site provides contact information for the Malaysian Consulate General in Vancouver.

Mexico

Trade Commission of Mexico in Vancouver
http://www.mexico-trade-van.com/
The virtual office provides staff profiles, sector reports, an events calendar, and a directory of Mexican exporters and international trade and investment opportunities in industries such as agri-food, mining, and apparel.

New Zealand

Trade New Zealand in Vancouver
http://www.tradenz.govt.nz/contact/northam.html
An export promotion service, the site provides contact information for the Trade New Zealand office in Vancouver.

Poland

Consulate General of Poland in Vancouver
http://www.polonia-online.com/Konsulat/
Posted in English and Polish, the site provides visa and passport information, travel guides, business primers, and a directory of consular services and staff.

South Africa

Canadian-South African Chamber of Business
http://www.bridgerecruit.com/chamber/
Based in Vancouver, the site provides a directory of Canadian and South African business opportunities.

Singapore

Consulate General of Singapore in Vancouver
http://www.gov.sg/mfa/consular/mww_c.htm
The site provides contact information for the Singapore Consulate General in Vancouver.

Switzerland

Swiss-Canadian Chamber of Commerce in Vancouver
http://swisstrade.com/xicodes2.asp?P1=3&lvl=3&cid=B01
The site lists the street address, phone and fax numbers, and e-mail link of the Swiss Chamber of Commerce in Vancouver.

Taiwan

China External Trade Development Council Office in Vancouver
http://www.cetra.org.tw/english/o_office/indexset.htm
A Taiwanese trade promotion service, the site lists the mission statement and e-mail link of the China External Trade Development Council Office in Vancouver.

Taiwan Government Information Office in Vancouver
http://www.gio.gov.tw/info/ngio/cana-f.html
Posted in Chinese and English, the site lists the street address, phone and fax numbers, and e-mail link of the Taiwan Government Information Office in Vancouver.

Thailand

Royal Thai Consulate General in Vancouver
http://www.thaicongenvancouver.org/
Featuring a message from the Consul General, the site includes Thai fact sheets, visa and passport information, and a directory of consular services and staff.

Thai Trade Center in Vancouver
http://www.thaitrade.com/wwtto.html
A service of the Thailand Department of Export Promotion, the site lists the street address, phone and fax numbers, and e-mail link of the Thai Trade Center in Vancouver.

United Kingdom

Consulate General of Britain in Vancouver
http://www.bis-canada.org/Contact/
The site provides contact information for the British Consulate General in Vancouver.

United States

U.S. Commercial Service in Vancouver
http://www.ita.doc.gov/cscanada/locate.html
A service of the U.S. Embassy in Ottawa, the site lists the Commercial Specialist, street address, phone and fax numbers, and e-mail link for the U.S. Consulate General in Vancouver.

Manitoba

Manitoba Media

Manitoba Media
http://www.mediainfo.com/emediajs/specific-geo.htm?region=manitoba
A service of Editor and Publisher Interactive, the site provides a browsable directory of Manitoba media sites including online newspapers, magazines, and city guides.

Manitoba Market Guides

Manitoba Advantage
http://www.gov.mb.ca/itt/advantage/index.html
Written in English and French, the site delivers backgrounders on Manitoba business, government, workforce, population, natural resources, infrastructure, and call centre opportunities.

Manitoba Companies Database
http://db.itt.gov.mb.ca/ITT/CIMIS/CIMISWeb.nsf
A service of Manitoba Industry, Trade and Tourism, the site is a searchable database of Manitoba companies. Categories include aerospace, building products, health, and information technology.

Manitoba Trade Assistance

Canada/Manitoba Business Service Centre
http://www.cbsc.org/manitoba/index.html
Part of a national network of Canadian business support centres, the Winnipeg-based site provides primers on exporting, importing, financing, and starting a new business.

Manitoba Trade and Investment Corporation
http://www.gov.mb.ca/itt/trade/index.html
Based in Winnipeg, the Corporation promotes Manitoba exports and international investment. The site includes a Manitoba business calendar, staff profiles, and a directory of export promotion programs and services.

Manitoba Representative Offices

Iceland

Consulate General of Iceland in Winnipeg
http://www.iceland.org/list1n2.htm
The site lists the Consul General, street address, phone and fax numbers, and e-mail link of the Icelandic Consulate in Winnipeg.

Sri Lanka

Sri Lankan Association of Manitoba
http://www.winnipeg.freenet.mb.ca/iphome/s/slam/
Based in Winnipeg, the Association promotes Manitoba-Sri Lankan trade and relations. The site includes Sri Lankan news, fact sheets, business guides, and contact information.

New Brunswick

New Brunswick Media

New Brunswick Media
http://www.mediainfo.com/emediajs/specific-geo.htm?region=newbrunswick
A service of Editor and Publisher Interactive, the site provides a browsable directory of New Brunswick media sites on the web including newspapers, magazines, and radio stations.

New Brunswick Market Guides

Canada-New Brunswick Business Service Centre
http://www.cbsc.org/nb/index.html
Based in Fredericton, the site delivers New Brunswick sector profiles and primers on training, finance, intellectual property, research and development, taxation, and other business topics.

New Brunswick Manufacturers and Selected Services to Industry
http://www.gov.nb.ca/edt_det/nbmfsv/search.htm
Posted in English and French, the site is a searchable directory of New Brunswick manufacturers. The database is browsable by company name, contact, location, and product.

New Brunswick Organizations on the Web
http://www.gov.nb.ca/edt/infohigh/biz/index.htm
The site is a browsable database of New Brunswick organizations online. Categories

include manufacturing, wholesale and retail trade, education, communications, and tourism.

New Brunswick: Your Profit Center
http://www.gov.nb.ca/NBFirst/
An online relocation guide, the site provides New Brunswick fact sheets, business primers, incentive information, and reports on information technology, metal fabrication, plastics, textiles, warehousing, and other industries.

New Brunswick Trade Assistance

Atlantic Canada Opportunities Agency
http://www.acoa.ca/
Based in Moncton, the site provides international trade toolkits for exporters in New Brunswick, Newfoundland, Nova Scotia, and Prince Edward Island. The toolkits include primers on international trade research, planning, and logistics.

New Brunswick Trade Winds
http://www.gov.nb.ca/cnb/trade.htm
A global business electronic magazine, the site features New Brunswick export success stories, company profiles, and interviews with leading entrepreneurs in the province.

Newfoundland

Newfoundland Media

Newfoundland Media
http://www.mediainfo.com/emediajs/specific-geo.htm?region=newfoundland
A service of Editor and Publisher Interactive, the site provides a browsable directory of Newfoundland media sites online including newspapers and radio stations.

Newfoundland Market Guides

Ambassador
http://www.success.nfld.net/ambassador/index.html
A Newfoundland and Labrador promotion service, the site includes a newsletter, a list of upcoming conventions and trade shows, and a directory of incentives such as tax abatements and site selection assistance.

Canada Business Service Centre in Newfoundland
http://www.cbsc.org/nfld/index.html
Based in St. John's, the site delivers infoguides

on starting a small business. Modules include boat tour operation, restaurant, microbrewery, daycare, hair salon, convenience store, and garage.

Newfoundland and Labrador Online Business Directory
http://www.nfbusiness.com/
A database of Newfoundland and Labrador companies, the site is searchable by company name, location, and industry such as accountants, retail grocers, janitor supplies, and woodworking.

Newfoundland Trade Assistance

Newfoundland and Labrador Department of Industry Trade and Technology
http://www.success.nfld.net/
Based in St. John's, the site provides Newfoundland news, business incentives, cost comparisons, key government contacts, a list of provincial export award winners, and profiles of companies in petroleum, engineering, biotechnology, and mining industries.

Trade Team Newfoundland
http://www.netfx.iom.net/ttn/
A service of Industry Canada, the site provides regional trade plans, business success stories, an event calendar, and a directory of government assistance programs.

Northwest Territories

Northwest Territories Media

Northwest Territories Media
http://www.mediainfo.com/emediajs/specific-geo.htm?region=northwestterritories
A service of Editor and Publisher Interactive, the site provides a browsable directory of Northwest Territories online newspapers.

Northwest Territories Market Guides

Canada/Northwest Territories Business Service Centre
http://www.cbsc.org/nwt/index.html
Posted in English and French, the Yellowknife-based site features contact information for the Centre, and a primer on how to start a small business in the Northwest Territories.

Government of the Northwest Territories
http://www.gov.nt.ca/
Homepage of the Northwest Territories government, the site provides local news, fact sheets, tourism guides, government bulletins, an event calendar, and a directory of investment and business opportunities.

Nova Scotia

Nova Scotia Media

Nova Scotia Media
http://www.mediainfo.com/emediajs/specific-geo.htm?region=novascotia
A service of Editor and Publisher Interactive, the site provides a browsable directory of Nova Scotia online newspapers and radio stations.

Nova Scotia Market Guides

Canada-Nova Scotia Business Service Centre
http://www.cbsc.org/ns/index.html
Based in Halifax, the Centre provides assistance and information to Nova Scotia companies. The site lists the street address, phone and fax numbers, and e-mail link of the Centre.

Nova Scotia Economy and Business
http://www.gov.ns.ca/econ-bus.htm
The online service provides Nova Scotia fact sheets, business guides, a registry of joint stock companies, a public tenders notice system, and a directory of business assistance resources in the province.

Virtual Nova Scotia
http://explore.gov.ns.ca/business/bus.htm
A service of the Nova Scotia Marketing Agency, the site features primers on Nova Scotia business, workers, transportation, ports, convention facilities, and tourism.

Nova Scotia Trade Assistance

InNOVAcorp
http://www.innovacorp.ns.ca/
Based in Dartmouth, InNOVAcorp promotes Nova Scotia high-technology exports. The site includes a staff directory, and a list of commercialization, engineering, and scientific programs and services.

Trade Team Nova Scotia
http://ttns.gov.ns.ca/

A partnership of government agencies and industry interests, the Team promotes Nova Scotia exports. The site includes news, a member directory, and calendar of events.

Nova Scotia Representative Offices

United States

U.S. Commercial Service in Halifax
http://www.ita.doc.gov/cscanada/locate.html
A service of the U.S. Embassy in Ottawa, the site lists the Commercial Specialist, street address, phone and fax numbers, and e-mail link for the U.S. Consulate General in Halifax.

Ontario

Ontario Media

Ontario Media
http://www.mediainfo.com/emediajs/specific-geo.htm?region=ontario
A service of Editor and Publisher Interactive, the site provides a browsable directory of Ontario media online.

Ontario Market Guides

Business Ontario
http://www.gov.on.ca/MBS/english/business/index.html
Developed by the Government of Ontario, the site is a directory of business assistance programs and services in the province. Resources include business primers, economic statistics, consumer information, and electronic tendering.

Canada-Ontario Business Call Centre
http://www.cbsc.org/ontario/index.html
Based in Toronto, the Centre provides Ontario sector profiles, and primers on human resources, intellectual property, marketing, regulations, research and development, training, strategic alliances, and other business topics.

Ontario Business Opportunities
http://204.101.2.101/bizop/home.html
Developed by the Government of Ontario, the site is a searchable database of Ontario business and investment opportunities. The listings are divided into six categories: seeking to invest, available for sale, seeking an investor, new ventures, licensing opportunities, and joint ventures.

Ontario Canada
http://www.ontario-canada.com/
A service of the Ontario Ministry of Economic Development, Trade and Tourism, the site delivers Ontario news, fact sheets, business guides, travel tips, investment reports, and electronic postcards.

Ontario Chamber of Commerce
http://www.occ.on.ca/
Based in Toronto, the site provides Chamber news, policy statements, executive profiles, legislative bulletins, opinion surveys, and a list of business achievement award winners.

Ontario Trade Assistance

Canada-Ontario Export Forum
http://www.cobsc.org/ICGC/events.nsf/CAN-ONT-ExportForum?OpenNavigator
Posted in English and French, the Forum provides a searchable database of international trade events and activities in Ontario. The directory is browsable by organization, sector, country of interest, and event type such as an outgoing mission, conference, or trade show.

Ontario International Trade Corporation
http://www.ontario-canada.com/trade
Based in Toronto, the Corporation promotes Ontario exports and international investment. The site features news releases, trade mission reports, export primers, global marketing studies, staff profiles, and fact sheets on Ontario suppliers.

Ontario Representative Offices

Australia

Austrade Canada in Toronto
http://www.austrade.gov.au/canada/
An Australian trade promotion service, the site provides Australian fact sheets, market reports, and the street address, staff directory, and e-mail links of the Austrade office in Toronto.

Austria

Austrian Trade Commission in Toronto
http://www.austriantrade.org/AustrianTrade/offices/ahst_trt.htm
The site lists the trade commissioners, street address, phone and fax numbers, and e-mail link of the Austrian Trade Commission in Toronto.

Argentina

Consulate General of Argentina in Toronto
http://www.consargtoro.org/
Posted in English and Spanish, the site delivers Argentine fact sheets, a newsletter, visa and passport information, international trade reports, investment primers, and a directory of business opportunities and public tenders.

Chile

Trade Commission of Chile in Toronto
http://www.chiletrade.cl/prochile/
The virtual trade mission provides background information on ProChile, Chile's export promotion agency. The service also lists the Consul General, Assistant Trade Commissioner, street address, phone and fax numbers, and e-mail link of the Chilean Trade Commission in Toronto.

China

China Council for the Promotion of International Trade in Toronto
http://www.ccpit.org/engVersion/cp_about/cp_over/cp_over.html
A Chinese export promotion service, the site provides contact information for the China Council for the Promotion of International Trade office in Toronto.

Hong Kong Economic and Trade Office in Toronto
http://www.hketo.ca/
A Hong Kong trade promotion service, the site provides Hong Kong fact sheets, legislative reports, and business bulletins.

Denmark

Consulate General of Denmark in Toronto
http://www.tradecomm.com/danish/english/indexeng.htm
Written in English and Danish, the site provides Danish export guides, import primers, travel tips, visa and passport information, and a directory of consular services and staff.

Finland

Finland Trade Center in Toronto
http://www.ftctor.com/~pkoning/
A service of the Finnish Foreign Trade Association, the site features staff profiles, a directory of

trade opportunities in Finland, and export primers for Finnish companies doing business in the Toronto area and North America.

France

Consulate General of France in Toronto
http://web.idirect.com/~fsltto/
Written in French, the site provides French news, visa and passport information, a calendar of events, legal primers, and a directory of consular services and staff.

French Trade Commission in Toronto
http://www.dree.org/canada/francais/services/ toronto/presenta.htm
A French export promotion service, the site provides a directory of Commission services, and a list of export opportunities for French exporters in Toronto and the province of Ontario.

Germany

Germany Chamber of Commerce in Toronto
http://www.ahk.net/en/ca/Toronto/
Part of a global network of German Chamber offices, the site lists the Chairperson, Chief Executive Officer, street address, phone and fax numbers, and e-mail link of the German Chamber in Toronto.

Iceland

Consulate General of Iceland in Toronto
http://www.iceland.org/list1n2.htm
The site lists the Consul General, street address, phone and fax numbers, and e-mail link of the Icelandic Consulate in Toronto.

Israel

Consulate General of Israel in Toronto
http://www.israelca.org/toronto/
Featuring a welcome message from the Consul General, the site delivers Israeli news, fact sheets, business reports, investment bulletins, tourism guides, cultural primers, and a virtual cookbook.

Italy

Consulate General of Italy in Toronto
http://www.toronto.italconsulate.org/
Posted in English and Italian, the site provides primers on Italian citizenship, passports, visas, vital records, social assistance for Italian emi-

grants, and assistance for Italian citizens in transit.

Italian Trade Commission in Toronto
http://www.italcomm.com/
The virtual office delivers an Italian trade newsletter, events calendar, program directory, and contact information for the Commission in Toronto.

Japan

Consulate General of Japan in Toronto
http://www.embjapan.can.org/Tron/tron.htm
The site lists the Consul General, street address, phone and fax numbers, office hours, and services of the Japanese Consulate in Toronto.

JETRO Toronto
http://www.toronto.JETRO.org/JETRO.html
A branch of the Japan External Trade Organization or JETRO in Tokyo, the site provides Japanese fact sheets, international trade success stories, a local events calendar, and reports on Canada-Japan investment.

Malaysia

Trade Commission of Malaysia in Toronto
http://www.mnet.com.my/klonline/www/missions/ malmiss/mcanada5.htm
The site provides contact information for the Malaysia Trade Commission in Toronto.

Mexico

Consulate General of Mexico in Toronto
http://www.quicklink.com/mexico/toronto/ consulado.htm
Written in English and Spanish, the site provides Mexican news, fact sheets, visa and passport information, a directory of consular services, and contact information.

Trade Commission of Mexico in Toronto
http://www.bancomext-can.com/
Part of a global network of Mexican trade promotion offices, the site features Mexican export primers, import guides, trade-show directories, international trade statistics, and travel tips.

Norway

Norwegian Trade Council in Toronto
http://www.norway.org/trade/ mainbod3.html#toronto

The site lists the street address, phone and fax numbers, e-mail links, and staff profiles of the Norwegian Trade Council in Toronto.

Philippines

Consulate General of the Philippines in Toronto
http://www.philcongen-toronto.com/
The virtual Consulate provides Philippine maps, fact sheets, international trade reports, investment primers, tourism guides, visa and passport information, and a directory of consular services.

Philippine Trade and Investment Promotion Office in Toronto
http://www.dti.gov.ph/tor/
The site provides a mission statement, service directory, and contact information for the Philippine Trade Office in Toronto.

Portugal

Consulate General of Portugal in Toronto
http://www.consulportugaltoronto.com/home.htm
Posted in English and Portuguese, the site delivers Portuguese visa and passport information, citizenship registration forms, cultural bulletins, and a directory of consular services.

Portuguese Trade and Investment Office in Toronto
http://www.portugal.org/geninfo/abouticep/ toronto.html
The site lists the staff, street address, phone and fax numbers, and e-mail link of the Portuguese Trade and Investment Office in Toronto.

Saint Vincent and the Grenadines

Saint Vincent and the Grenadines Office in Toronto
http://www.freenet.hamilton.on.ca/~aa462/ svgref.html#svgmtd
The site provides contact information for the Saint Vincent and the Grenadines Office in Toronto.

South Africa

South Africa Foreign Trade Office in Toronto
http://wwwdti.pwv.gov.za/dtiwww/ foreign_offices.htm
A service of the South Africa Department of Trade and Industry, the site provides contact information for the South Africa Trade Office in Toronto.

South Korea

Consulate General of Korea in Toronto
http://www.consulatekorea-tor.org/
The digital Consulate provides Korean fact sheets, press releases, newsletters, visa application forms, entry and departure information, business primers, travel tips, and frequently asked questions and answers.

Spain

Spanish Commercial Office in Ottawa
http://www.icex.es/openURL.html#openURL=/ english/infoproyem/ofcomes/ofcomes.html#AM
The site lists the staff, street address, phone and fax numbers, and e-mail link of the Spanish Commercial Office in Ottawa.

Spanish Commercial Office in Toronto
http://www.icex.es/openURL.html#openURL=/ english/infoproyem/ofcomes/ofcomes.html#AM
The site lists the staff, street address, phone and fax numbers, and e-mail link of the Spanish Commercial Office in Toronto.

Switzerland

Swiss Chamber of Commerce in Etobicoke
http://swisstrade.com/ xicodes2.asp?P1=3&lvl=3&cid=B01
The site lists the street address, phone and fax numbers, and e-mail link of the Swiss Chamber of Commerce in Etobicoke.

Taiwan

Taiwan Government Information Office in Toronto
http://www.gio.gov.tw/info/ngio/cana-f.html
Posted in Chinese and English, the site lists the street address, phone and fax numbers, and e-mail link of the Taiwan Government Information Office in Toronto.

United Kingdom

British Trade and Investment Office in Toronto
http://www.bis-canada.org/Trade/
A British trade promotion service, the site provides British sourcing information, investment guides, and a directory of commercial services.

Consulate General of Britain in Toronto
http://www.bis-canada.org/Contact/
The site provides contact information for the British Consulate General in Toronto.

United States

Council of Great Lakes Governors Canada Trade Liaison Office in Toronto
http://www.cglg.org/projects/trade/
Funded by the States of Indiana, Pennsylvania, and Wisconsin, the Office assists small to mid-size companies from the three states seeking to do business in Canada. The site provides contact information and a directory of trade mission and export counseling services.

State of Michigan Office in Toronto
http://www.state.mi.us/mjc/ceo/business/inbd.htm
A service of the Michigan Jobs Commission, the site lists the street address, and phone and fax numbers of the State of Michigan Office in Toronto.

State of Ohio Canadian Trade Office
http://www.state.oh.us/agr/outstate.html
A service of the Ohio Department of Commerce, the site lists the street address, phone and fax numbers, and e-mail link of the State of Ohio Trade Office in Toronto.

U.S. Commercial Service in Toronto
http://www.ita.doc.gov/cscanada/locate.html
A service of the U.S. Embassy in Ottawa, the site lists the Commercial Specialist, street address, phone and fax numbers, and e-mail link for the U.S. Consulate General in Toronto.

Prince Edward Island

Prince Edward Island Media

Prince Edward Island Media
http://www.mediainfo.com/emediajs/specific-geo.htm?region=princeedwardisland
A service of Editor and Publisher Interactive, the site provides a browsable directory of Prince Edward Island media online such as magazines, newspapers, and radio stations.

Prince Edward Island Market Guides

Canada-Prince Edward Island Business Service Centre
http://www.cbsc.org/pei/index.html
Based in Charlottetown, the site delivers company start-up guides, and primers on business opportunities in Prince Edward Island agriculture, construction, forestry, manufacturing, mining, tourism, transportation, and other industries.

Enterprise PEI
http://www.gov.pe.ca/edt/epei/index.asp
Updated daily, the site provides Prince Edward Island fact sheets, staff e-mail links, an online store, and a directory of business assistance programs and services for agriculture, aquaculture, manufacturing, and tourism operations.

Prince Edward Island Information Center
http://www.gov.pe.ca/
Homepage of the Prince Edward Island government, the site features tourism guides, an event calendar, population statistics, interactive maps, weather information, driving charts, and economic reports.

Prince Edward Island Trade Assistance

Prince Edward Island Trade Development Centre
http://www.gov.pe.ca/edt/epei/tradectr/index.asp
Based in Charlottetown, the Centre promotes Prince Edward Island exports. The site includes a staff roster, e-mail links, contact information, and a directory of Centre programs and services.

Québec

Québec Media

Québec Media
http://www.mediainfo.com/emediajs/specific-geo.htm?region=quebec
A service of Editor and Publisher Interactive, the site provides a browsable directory of Québec media online such as magazines, newspapers, and radio stations.

Québec Market Guides

Business in Québec
http://www.gouv.qc.ca/affaires/indexa.htm
The site provides fact sheets on starting a business and investing in Québec, and doing business with the Québec government.

Info Entrepreneurs
http://www.infoentrepreneurs.org/eng/index.html
Based in Montreal, the site provides primers on starting a business, financial assistance programs, permits and licenses, employment and training programs, self-employment, and multimedia in Québec.

Investment Québec
http://invest-quebec.com/
Posted in English and French, the site features Québec press releases, corporate success stories, a list of business incentives, and a directory of multinationals in Québec such as General Motors, Kraft, Bayer, and Siemens.

Québec Chamber of Commerce
http://cciqm.megatoon.com/
The online service lists the street address, phone and fax numbers, and e-mail link of the Québec Chamber of Commerce in Québec City.

Québec Trade Assistance

Gourmet Export
http://www.profil-cdi.qc.ca/export/int_repe.htm
Sponsored in part by the Québec provincial government, the site is a searchable directory of Québec agri-food exporters. The database is browsable by company name, product, service, current market, and target market.

Ministry of International Relations
http://www.mri.gouv.qc.ca/
Written in four languages, the site delivers Québec news, history lessons, business primers, tourism guides, cultural bulletins, legal reports, university profiles, and a directory of Québec departments, secretariats and agencies.

Québec Association of Export Trading Houses
http://www.amceq.org/
Posted in English and French, the site provides trade house primers, a database of Québec export trading houses, and contact information.

Québec International Trade Office
http://www.micst.gouv.qc.ca/menu/commerce.html
A unit of the Québec Ministry of Industry, Science and Technology, the Office promotes Québec exports. The site delivers a trade event calendar, and a menu of export counseling and trade mission services for Québec companies.

Québec Representative Offices

Argentina

Consulate General of Argentina in Montreal
http://www.consargenmtl.com/
Posted in English, French, and Spanish, the site provides fact sheets on Argentine international trade, investment, privatization, tourism, and culture. The service includes Canada-Argentina

trade statistics, and a database of Canadian companies established in Argentina.

Austria

Austrian Trade Commission in Montreal
http://www.austriantrade.org/AustrianTrade/offices/ahst_mtr.htm
The online service lists the Trade Commissioner, street address, phone and fax numbers, e-mail link, and geographic jurisdiction of the Austrian Trade Commission in Montreal.

Bulgaria

Québec-Bulgaria Trade Council
http://www.accent.net/cacqb/cacqb.htm
Written in French, the site provides a mission statement, program and service directory, and contact information for the Trade Council in Montreal.

France

Consulate General of France in Québec City
http://www.consulat-france-qc.org/
Posted in French, the site delivers French news, press releases, an events calendar, visa and passport information, legal primers, a Consul General message, and a directory of consular staff and services.

French Trade Commission in Montreal
http://www.dree.org/canada/francais/services/montreal/presenta.htm
A French export promotion service, the site provides a directory of Commission services, and a list of export opportunities for French exporters in Québec and Atlantic Canada.

Greece

Consulate General of Greece in Montreal
http://www.citenet.net/grconsulate/
Posted in English and French, the site provides Greek news, fact sheets, visa and passport information, tourism guides, cultural bulletins, business primers, and a directory of consular services.

Israel

Consulate General of Israel in Montreal
http://www.israelca.org/francais/fm-index.htm
Written in French, the site provides Israeli news, fact sheets, economic statistics and reports,

investment primers, tourism guides, cultural bulletins, and a list of education and exchange opportunities.

Japan

Consulate General of Japan in Montreal
http://www.embjapan.can.org/Mtl/mont.htm
The site lists the Consul General, street address, phone and fax numbers, office hours, and geographic jurisdiction of the Japanese Consulate in Montreal.

Mexico

Trade Commission of Mexico in Montreal
http://bancomext-mtl.com/bancomext/
A Mexican trade promotion service, the site includes a mission statement, contact information, and a Mexican textile and apparel online showroom.

Pakistan

Pakistan Trade Office in Montreal
http://www.jamal.com/epb/ptoa.htm
The site provides contact information for the Pakistan Trade Office in Montreal.

Poland

Consulate General of Poland in Montreal
http://www.poloniaweb.com/konsulat/
Written in English, French, and Polish, the site lists the street address, phone and fax numbers, office hours, and e-mail link of the Polish Consulate in Montreal.

Portugal

Portuguese Trade and Investment Office in Montreal
http://www.portugal.org/geninfo/abouticep/toronto.html
The site lists the staff, street address, phone and fax numbers, and e-mail link of the Portuguese Trade and Investment Office in Montreal.

Spain

Consulate General of Spain in Montreal
http://www.total.net:8080/~consular/
Posted in English, French, and Spanish, the site provides fact sheets on Spanish geography, history, language, business, international trade,

infrastructure, health, media, travel and government.

Switzerland

Swiss Chamber of Commerce in Montreal
http://swisstrade.com/xicodes2.asp?P1=3&lvl=3&cid=B01
The site lists the street address, phone and fax numbers, and e-mail link of the Swiss Chamber of Commerce in Montreal.

Taiwan

China External Trade Development Council Office in Montreal
http://www.cetra.org.tw/english/o_office/indexset.htm
A Taiwanese trade promotion service, the site lists the mission statement and e-mail link of the China External Trade Development Council Office in Montreal.

United Kingdom

Consulate General of Britain in Montreal
http://www.bis-canada.org/Contact/
The site provides contact information for the British Consulate General in Montreal.

United States

U.S. Commercial Service in Montreal
http://www.ita.doc.gov/cscanada/locate.html
A service of the U.S. Embassy in Ottawa, the site lists the Principal Commercial Officer, street address, phone and fax numbers, and e-mail link of the U.S. Consulate General in Montreal.

U.S. Commercial Service in Québec City
http://www.ita.doc.gov/cscanada/locate.html
The U.S. online service lists the Commercial Assistant, street address, phone and fax numbers, and e-mail link for the U.S. Consulate General in Québec City.

Saskatchewan

Saskatchewan Media

Saskatchewan Media
http://www.mediainfo.com/emediajs/specific-geo.htm?region=saskatchewan
A service of Editor and Publisher Interactive, the site provides a browsable directory of

Saskatchewan media online such as magazines, newspapers, and radio stations.

Saskatchewan Market Guides

Canada-Saskatchewan Business Service Centre
http://www.cbsc.org/sask/index.html
The virtual resource center provides Saskatchewan start-up guides, an events calendar, frequently asked questions and answers, online discussion groups, a directory of government programs, and info-sheets on Saskatchewan agriculture, forestry, manufacturing, and other industries.

Locating in Saskatchewan
http://www.gov.sk.ca/econdev/locating/default.shtml
A service of Saskatchewan Economic and Co-operative Development, the site delivers Saskatchewan quick facts, business primers, workforce reports, cost of living comparisons, lifestyle indicators, and health care and education facts.

Saskatchewan Economic and Co-operative Development
http://www.gov.sk.ca/econdev/
Based in Regina, the site features Saskatchewan economic statistics, business news, news releases, a guide to provincial manufacturers, and a directory of investment opportunities in agri-food, forestry, mining, energy, and other industries.

Saskatchewan Trade Assistance

Provincial Exporters
http://saskexport.com/
A service of the Provincial Exporters Association, the site is a browsable directory of Saskatchewan exporters. Categories include construction, manufacturing, agriculture, mining, management consultants, and transportation and shipping.

Saskatchewan Opportunities Corporation
http://www.gov.sk.ca/soco/
Based in Regina, the Corporation provides economic development financing in Saskatchewan. The site includes news releases, a mission statement, annual reports, executive profiles, program information, and a directory of provincial offices.

Saskatchewan Trade and Export Partnership
http://www.sasktrade.sk.ca/
With offices in Regina and Saskatoon, the Partnership promotes Saskatchewan exports. The site provides news, an event calendar, and a showcase of member products and services in agricultural equipment, biotechnology, energy, mining, education, and other industries.

Trade and Export
http://www.cbsc.org/sask/trade.html
A service of the Canada-Saskatchewan Business Service Center, the site reports on Trade Team Saskatchewan, a consortium of public and private sector organizations that promote provincial exports.

Yukon Territory

Yukon Territory Media

Klondike Sun
http://www.yukonweb.com/community/dawson/klondike_sun/
Published bi-weekly, the Dawson City-based newspaper reports on current events, business, and entertainment in the Yukon. The site includes an online archive dating back to March 1996.

Yukon News
http://www.yukonweb.com/community/yukon-news/
Based in Whitehorse, the site provides Yukon area news and editorials. The service includes a newspaper archive dating back to 1995.

Yukon Territory Market Guides

Canada/Yukon Business Service Centre
http://www.cbsc.org/yukon/index.html
Posted in English and French, the site lists the street address, phone and fax numbers, and e-mail link of the Business Centre in Whitehorse.

Government of Yukon
http://www.gov.yk.ca/
Based in Whitehorse, the site provides Yukon news, fact sheets, travel guides, government directories, budget highlights, task force reports, and employment opportunities.

## CHAPTER 5

DIGITAL NEGOCIOS: 900+ LATIN AMERICAN AND CARIBBEAN BUSINESS RESOURCES ON THE INTERNET

This chapter reviews more than 900 of the top international business resources online that focus on Latin America and the Caribbean. The section profiles regional websites and online hubs for 47 countries and territories including Argentina, Brazil, Chile, and Mexico. With a population of some 500 million, the region is rich in agricultural, forestry, fishing, mineral, and energy resources, although economic development is uneven. A key initiative is the Free Trade Area of the Americas, a plan to unite the economies of the Western Hemisphere into a single free trade arrangement. Negotiations are now underway, and a tentative agreement is scheduled for 2005.

Leading business opportunities in the region include informatics and telecommunications, agriculture and food products, oil and gas machinery, urban and rail transportation networks, environmental equipment, and forestry machinery. According to NUA Internet Surveys, an estimated 4.5 million people in the region—about one percent of the total—were online as of January 1999. Although cyber development has been impeded by high telephone costs and slow bandwidth, Internet Service Providers throughout the region are investing millions in upgrades, and the online population is expected to more than triple over the next two years.

Regional Sites

Latin American and Caribbean Search Tools

AltaVista Latin America
http://www.altavista.magallanes.net/jump.html
Part of the AltaVista search network, the site is a Latin American online search service. The database is browsable by keyword, language, and country.

America's Trade Search Engine
http://www.atradesource.com/html/search.html
Developed by New Jersey-based Synapse International, the site is a browsable database of Latin American products and international traders. The directory is searchable by keyword, country, and industry.

Bienvenido a AltaVista
http://www.altavista.magallanes.net/
Part of the AltaVista network, the site is a browsable index of online resources in some 20 Latin American countries including Brazil, Chile, Mexico, and Peru.

IPL Trade Directory
http://www.latinmarkets.com/
Posted in English and Spanish, the site is a browsable database of some 40,000 companies in Central America, Mexico, and the United States. The service is searchable by keyword and country.

The Spanish Connection
http://www.spanishconnection.com/
Posted in English and Spanish, the site is a directory of search engines in over 20 Spanish speaking countries including Argentina, Bolivia, Chile, Colombia, and Mexico.

Latin American and Caribbean Media

Caribbean Media
http://www.mediainfo.com/emediajs/links-geo.htm?location=caribbean
The service is a database of online media in 15 Caribbean countries including the Bahamas, Cuba, Jamaica, Puerto Rico, and the West Indies.

Latin America Media
http://www.mediainfo.com/emediajs/links-geo.htm?location=samerica
Compiled by Editor and Publisher Interactive, the site is a directory of Latin American online media such as newspapers, magazines, and radio stations. The service provides databases for 20 Latin American countries including Argentina, Colombia, Peru, and Venezuela.

Latin America and Caribbean Market Guides

La Asociación Latinoamericana de Integración
http://www.aladi.org/
Based in Montevideo, Uruguay, ALADI is an

economic cooperation organization with 11 member countries: Argentina, Bolivia, Brazil, Chile, Colombia, Ecuador, Mexico, Paraguay, Peru, Uruguay, and Venezuela. Written in Spanish, the site includes ALADI fact sheets, economic databases, and country profiles.

Association of Caribbean States

http://www.acs-aec.org/
Headquartered in Port of Spain, Trinidad and Tobago, the Association promotes Caribbean economic development. The site includes a mission statement, legal documents, country profiles, meeting minutes, a statistics database, a calendar of events, and special committee reports.

Bureau of Inter-American Affairs

http://www.state.gov/www/regions/ara/index.html
A service of the U.S. State Department, the site provides U.S. press statements, testimony, briefings, issue reports, and travel information on the region and countries of Latin America.

Caribbean Islands: A Country Study

http://lcweb2.loc.gov/frd/cs/cxtoc.html
A service of the U.S. Library of Congress, the site provides economic and political profiles of selected Caribbean Islands including Barbados, Jamaica, and Trinidad and Tobago.

Caricom

http://www.caricom.org/expframes.htm
Based in Georgetown, Guyana, Caricom promotes economic cooperation among member states in the Caribbean including Belize, Grenada, Jamaica, and Suriname. The site includes news, project profiles, country reports, and employment opportunities.

Center for the Study of Western Hemispheric Trade

http://lanic.utexas.edu/cswht/
Trade.Insight.Papers2.html
A service of the University of Texas, the site provides Latin American trade statistics, a trade experts directory, North American Free Trade Agreement reports, a calendar of events, and a series of research papers on hemispheric trade, peso devaluation, and other regional business topics.

Central and South America International Trade Resources

http://ciber.bus.msu.edu/busres/samerica.htm
A service of Michigan State University, the site provides a directory of Latin American international trade resources online including business guides, investment primers, and company databases.

CiberCentro

http://www.cibercentro.com/
Posted in English and Spanish, the site is a database of Latin American country and business information. Categories include government, maps, newspapers, classifieds, reference, and universities.

Freight Forwarders in Central America

http://www.freightworld.com/forw_geo.html#2
A service of Freightworld, the site is a directory of Central American freight forwarders online including APA World Wide Movers in Costa Rica, and Paramar Import and Export in Panama.

Freight Forwarders in South America

http://www.freightworld.com/forw_geo.html#4
Compiled by Freightworld, the site is a database of South American freight forwarders online including Tiger Cargo in Argentina, Ocean Express in Brazil, and Click Cargo in Venezuela.

Global Net

http://www.bolsadetrabajo.com/
Posted in Spanish, the site is a Latin American employment and resume database. Job postings are listed in over a dozen industry categories including medical, tourism, government, transportation, media, education, and oil and gas.

InfoExport Latin America and Caribbean

http://www.infoexport.gc.ca/continent-e.asp?continent=Latin
A service of Foreign Affairs and International Trade Canada, the site provides economic fact sheets and business guides for over 40 Latin America and Caribbean countries.

Inter-American Development Bank

http://www.iadb.org/exr/english/index_english.htm
Created in 1959, the Washington, D.C.-based Bank promotes economic and social development in Latin America and the Caribbean. The site includes press releases, business opportunities, project profiles, and a database of economic and trade statistics.

Latin American and Caribbean Business Bulletin

http://www.ita.doc.gov/region/latinam/
Developed by the International Trade Administration, the site provides bulletins on Latin American export, sourcing, and investment opportunities.

The service includes a directory of upcoming events, and trade mission reports.

Latin America and the Caribbean: Selected Economic and Social Data
*http://www.info.usaid.gov/regions/lac/sesd/
index.html*
Developed by U.S. AID, the site is a database of Latin American socioeconomic statistics and indicators for Latin America and the Caribbean. Categories include health, education, environment, economy, trade, and investment.

Latin America Infrastructure Center
http://www.laic.com/
A service of Washington, D.C.-based CG/LA Infrastructure, the site provides bulletins on infrastructure projects in Argentina, Brazil, Chile, Colombia, Mexico, Peru, and other Latin American countries.

Latin American Network Information Center
http://lanic.utexas.edu/
Developed by the University of Texas, the site is a browsable database of Latin American resources online. The directory provides information on over 30 countries and nearly 50 subject areas including government, economy, trade, maps, and finance.

Latin and South America Market Research
*http://strategis.ic.gc.ca/sc_mrkti/ibinddc/engdoc/
1a1c.html*
A service of Industry Canada, the site is a database of fact sheets and market studies on over 30 Latin American and Caribbean countries.

Latin World
http://www.latinworld.com/
Posted in English and Spanish, the site is a directory of Latin American and Caribbean Internet resources. Categories include economy and finance, education and research, and government and politics.

Mercosur
http://www.rau.edu.uy/mercosur/
Created in 1991, Mercosur—also known as the Southern Cone Common Market—is a free trade pact between Argentina, Brazil, Paraguay, and Uruguay. The site delivers Mercosur fact sheets, legal documents, and country reports.

Mercosur Information
*http://www.idrc.ca/lacro/investigacion/
mercosur.html*
Developed by the Ottawa-based International

Development Research Centre, the site provides Mercosur news, statistics, country profiles, business opportunities, and research papers on Mercosur trade liberalization and competition policy.

Mercosur: South America's Common Market
*http://www.americasnet.com/mauritz/mercosur/
english/*
The online service provides primers on Mercosur free trade zones, safeguards, dispute settlement, investment regulations, taxation treaties, origin rules, and tariff reductions.

Multilateral Investment Guarantee Agency in Latin America and the Caribbean
http://www.ipanet.net/region/mil.htm
A service of the World Bank, the site reports on the activities of the Multilateral Investment Guarantee Agency in Latin America and the Caribbean.

North American Development Bank
http://www.nadbank.org/
Based in San Antonio, the Bank provides financing for environmental infrastructure projects in the U.S.-Mexico border region. The site features news, program information, project fact sheets, and a directory of procurement and employment opportunities.

Tips
http://www.redtips.org/tips/eng/index.html
Posted in English and Spanish, the site provides Latin American company profiles, market studies, Mercosur reports, trade leads, travel information, and an event calendar.

World Bank Group Latin America and the Caribbean
*http://www.worldbank.org/html/extdr/offrep/lac/
lac.htm*
A database of World Bank projects in Latin America and the Caribbean, the site provides press releases, speeches, mission statements, country profiles, and regional economic reports.

Latin America and Caribbean Trade Assistance

Airlines in Latin America and the Caribbean
http://www.freightworld.com/airl_geo.html#2b
Compiled by Freightworld, the site is a directory of Latin American and Caribbean airlines online such as ALM Antillean Airlines in Antilles, Air Aruba in Aruba, and Aero Costa Rica in Costa Rica.

Foreign Trade Information System
http://www.sice.oas.org/
Developed by the Organization of American States, the site provides primers on Western Hemispheric trade agreements, investment treaties, and dispute settlement mechanisms. The service includes trade statistics, a calendar of trade events, articles and opinions, and progress reports on the Free Trade Area of the Americas initiative.

Free Trade Area of the Americas
http://www.ftaa-alca.org/
Posted in four languages, this is the official homepage of the Free Trade Agreement of the Americas process or FTAA. The service includes official documents and negotiation updates.

Intermodal Carriers in South America
http://www.freightworld.com/intmod_geo.html#4
Developed by Freightworld, the site is a database of South American intermodal carriers online such as Alianca in Brazil, and Servicios Marítimos Paraguayos in Paraguay.

Latin America and the Caribbean Regional Perspectives
http://www.dfait-maeci.gc.ca/latin/menu-e.asp?continent=Latin
A service of the Department of Foreign Affairs and International Trade, the site provides fact sheets and reports on Canadian trade and relations with over 40 Latin America and Caribbean countries.

Latin Export
http://www.latinexport.com/
A portal of information on Latin business, the site includes a buy and sell bulletin board and a directory of Latin exporters searchable by product, company name, and standard industrial code.

Market Access and Compliance Office of Latin America and the Caribbean
http://www.ita.doc.gov/olac/
A service of the U.S. International Trade Administration, the site provides Latin America and Caribbean market access reports, country profiles, and economic statistics.

Maritime Carriers in Latin America
http://www.freightworld.com/mari_geo.html#2
The site is a registry of Latin American maritime carriers online such as Antilles Freight Corporation in Antilles, and Seaboard Marine in Panama.

Mercosur Export
http://www.mercosurexport.com/

Posted in Spanish, the site is a directory of business and trade opportunities in the four Mercosur countries: Argentina, Brazil, Paraguay and Uruguay. Categories include agriculture, automotive, cargo and freight, electronics, textiles, and tourism.

Railroads in South America
http://www.freightworld.com/railroads.html#4
Compiled by Freightworld, the site is a directory of South American railroads online in Bolivia, Brazil, Chile, Paraguay, and Peru.

Seaports in Latin America
http://www.freightworld.com/port_geo.html#2
A database of Latin American seaports online, the site includes port information from Jamaica, Panama, and Puerto Rico.

Trucking and Motor Carriers in Latin America
http://www.freightworld.com/truc_geo.html#2
A database of Latin American trucking operations online, the site links to motor carriers in Argentina, Brazil, Costa Rica, Paraguay, and Puerto Rico.

National Sites

Anguilla

Anguilla Media

The Light
http://www.thelight-anguilla.com/
Updated daily, the online newspaper reports on Anguillan current events, lifestyles, business, entertainment, and sports. The service includes a back issues archive.

Anguilla Market Guides

Anguilla Guide
http://net.ai/
Homepage of the Anguilla Tourist Board, the service includes primers on Anguillan history, currency, climate, entry and visa requirements, taxation, work permits, and tourism.

Anguilla InfoExport
http://www.infoexport.gc.ca/country-e.asp?continent=Latin&country=1
A service of Foreign Affairs and International Trade Canada, the site provides fact sheets and statistics on Anguillan geography, business and politics.

Anguilla Information Page

http://www.offshore.com.ai/anguilla/
An Anguilla resource page, the site features economic reports, sector profiles, history lessons, navigational charts, cultural information, and a directory of Anguillan magazines and newspapers.

Anguilla Market Research

http://strategis.ic.gc.ca/sc_mrkti/ibinddc/engdoc/ 1a1c1.html
A service of Industry Canada, the site posts fact sheets on Anguillan geography, people, government, economy, communications, and transportation.

Antarctica

Antarctica Media

New South Polar Times

http://205.174.118.254/nspt/home.htm
Written by the staff of the Amundsen-Scott South Pole Station, the site provides South Pole news, frequently asked questions and answers, Antarctic exploration reports, teaching primers, and a directory of other Antarctica research stations.

Antarctica Market Guides

Antarctica Market Research

http://strategis.ic.gc.ca/sc_mrkti/ibinddc/engdoc/ 1a1a3.html
A service of Industry Canada, the site posts information on Antarctica geography, people, government, economy, communications, and transportation.

Antarctica Visitor Centre

http://www.iceberg.co.nz/
Based in Christchurch, New Zealand, the site provides Antarctica news, teaching programs, and expedition information.

South Pole Adventure

http://www.southpole.com/
Homepage of the Center for Astrophysical Research in Antarctica, the site delivers South Pole news, weather information, mission reports, scientific data, and a picture of the day.

Antigua and Barbuda

Antigua and Barbuda Market Guides

Antigua and Barbuda Country Brief

http://www.worldbank.org/cgi-bin/ sendoff.cgi?page=%2Fhtml%2Fextdr%2Foffrep%2 Flac%2Fag.htm
A service of the World Bank Group, the site provides Antiguan population statistics, financial data, development reports, and economic forecasts.

Antigua and Barbuda InfoExport

http://www.infoexport.gc.ca/country- e.asp?continent=Latin&country=2
A service of Foreign Affairs and International Trade Canada, the site provides fact sheets and statistics on Antiguan geography, business and politics.

Antigua and Barbuda: Investing in Paradise

http://antigua-barbuda.com/
The government service delivers primers on Antiguan business, finance, taxation, investment incentives, offshore banking, tourism, and immigration.

Antigua and Barbuda Market Research

http://strategis.ic.gc.ca/sc_mrkti/ibinddc/engdoc/ 1a1c2.html
Posted by Industry Canada, the site provides backgrounders on Antiguan geography, people, government, economy, communications, and transportation.

Antigua and Barbuda Official Travel Guide

http://www.interknowledge.com/antigua-barbuda/
Homepage of the Antigua and Barbuda Department of Tourism, the site features Antiguan news, press releases, travel tips, accommodation directories, entertainment guides, and a calendar of events.

Antigua Banking and Investment

http://www.access.digex.net/~warlock/ecin/anu/ anubnk.htm
The online service delivers Antiguan banking and investment reports. Topics include free trade processing zones, merchant shipping regulations, permanent resident tax programs, and offshore banking.

Investing in Antigua
http://kpmgantigua.com/
Written by KPMG, the site provides an Antiguan investment profile. Topics include geography and climate, history and government, language, currency, tourism, agriculture, and manufacturing.

Antigua and Barbuda Trade Assistance

Antigua and Barbuda Customs Procedures
http://americas.fiu.edu/customs/antigua.htm
A service of Florida International University, the site reviews Antiguan customs regulations, entry procedures, documentation, tariffs, and taxes.

Argentina

Argentina Media

Argentina Media
http://www.mediainfo.com/emediajs/specific-geo.htm?region=argentina
A service of Editor and Publisher Interactive, the site provides a browsable directory of Argentine media sites online such as magazines, newspapers, radio and television stations.

Buenos Aires Herald
http://www.buenosairesherald.com/
An electronic newspaper, the site provides Argentine news, editorials, business reports, Mercosur bulletins, classifieds, travel tips, and cargo and freight information.

Argentina Market Guides

Argentina: Big Emerging Markets Home Page
http://www.ita.doc.gov/bems/argent.htm
Developed by the United States Department of Commerce, the site delivers Argentine fact sheets, economic forecasts, export and import statistics, sector profiles, and international trade guides.

Argentina Business
http://www.invertir.com/
Created by the Buenos Aires-based Argentina Investment Bureau, the site provides primers on Argentine business law, labor, currency and foreign exchange, taxation, marketing, and transportation. The service includes *Argentina Monthly*, a free monthly e-mail newsletter.

Argentina Business Briefs
http://www.austrade.gov.au/IOOM/Argentina/

A service of Austrade, the site offers fact sheets on Argentine business etiquette, foreign investment, corporate taxation, marketing, and visas.

Argentina Business Reports
http://italchambers.net/BusinessReports.html
Prepared by the Italian Chamber of Commerce and written in Italian, the site provides Argentine fact sheets, market reports, and commercial guides.

Argentina Chamber of Commerce
http://www.cac.com.ar/menu_inicio.htm
Based in Buenos Aires, the Chamber promotes Argentina business and international trade. The site provides Argentina business news, a member directory, and program information.

Argentina Company Directory
http://argentina.tpusa.com/menu8.htm
A service of Trade Point U.S.A., the site is a searchable directory of Argentina companies involved in international trade. Categories include importers, exporters, and service providers.

Argentina Country Brief
http://www.worldbank.org/cgi-bin/sendoff.cgi?page=%2Fhtml%2Fextdr%2Foffrep%2Flac%2Far.htm
A service of the World Bank Group, the site provides Argentine population statistics, financial data, development reports, and economic forecasts.

Argentina Country Profile
http://www.tradenz.govt.nz/intelligence/profiles/argentina.html
A service of the New Zealand Trade Development Board, the site provides Argentine economic statistics, market information, and business tips.

Argentina Country Report
http://www.state.gov/www/issues/economic/trade_reports/latin_america97/argentina97.html
Developed by the U.S. Department of State, the service reports on Argentine exchange rates, debt management, trade barriers, and intellectual property protection.

Argentina Economic and Financial Data
http://www.mecon.ar/progeco/dsbb.htm
A service of the International Monetary Fund, the site is a database of Argentine economic statistics. Topics include employment rates, wages and earnings, consumer prices, public sector revenues and expenditures, balance of payments, and population.

Argentina InfoExport
http://www.infoexport.gc.ca/country-e.asp?continent=Latin&country=33
A service of Foreign Affairs and International Trade Canada, the site provides Argentine commercial guides and market reports.

Argentina Market Access Database
http://mkaccdb.eu.int/mkdb/mkdb.pl?METHOD=COUNTRY
A service of the European Commission, the site offers briefs on Argentine trade policy, tariff barriers, non-tariff barriers, investment-related measures, and financial services regulations.

Argentina Market Information
http://dtiinfo1.dti.gov.uk/ots/argentina/
A service of the London-based Department of Trade and Industry, the site delivers Argentine fact sheets, maps, and trade-show information.

Argentina Market Research
http://strategis.ic.gc.ca/sc_mrkti/ibinddc/engdoc/1a1c3.html
A service of Industry Canada, the site provides a virtual library of Argentine market reports prepared by the U.S. Department of Commerce. Topics include economic trends, trade regulations and standards, investment climate, trade and project financing, and business travel.

Argentina Reference Desk
http://lanic.utexas.edu/la/argentina/
Developed by the University of Texas, the site is a directory of Argentine resources online. Categories include discussion groups, economy and finance, government, magazines and periodicals, science and technology, and travel and tourism.

Argentina Yellow Pages
http://www.paginas-doradas.com.ar/
A service of Telefonica de Argentina, the site is a searchable database of Argentine and Mercosur telephone numbers, addresses, companies, and individuals.

Barclays Country Report: Argentina
http://www.offshorebanking.barclays.com/services/economic/yearly/argmar98/contents.html
Prepared by Barclays Bank, the site reports on Argentine economic trends, politics, monetary and fiscal policy, international trade, foreign debt, merchandise trade, and investment flows.

Country Commercial Guide
http://www.state.gov/www/about_state/business/com_guides/1998/latin_america/argentina98.html
Prepared by the U.S. Embassy in Buenos Aires, the site delivers primers on Argentine business, politics, trade regulations and standards, investment climate, trade and project financing, and business travel.

Ministry of Economy and Public Works and Services
http://www.mecon.ar/default.htm
A department of the Argentine federal government, the Ministry promotes economic development. The site includes Argentine economic news, socioeconomic statistics, and program information.

Argentina Trade Assistance

Argentina Customs Procedures
http://americas.fiu.edu/customs/argentin.htm
A service of Florida International University, the site reviews Argentine customs regulations, entry procedures, documentation, tariffs, and taxes.

Argentine Exporters Directory
http://www.arexport.com.ar/inicio.htm
Posted in English and Spanish, the site is a searchable directory of Argentine exporters in categories such as agriculture, medical equipment, and wood products. The service includes a database of international trade leads and employment opportunities.

Argentina Importers and Exporters Association
http://www.aiera.org.ar/quienes.htm#in
Based in Buenos Aires, the Association promotes Argentine international trade. The site lists the street address, and phone and fax numbers of the organization.

Externa Argentina
http://www.externa.com.ar/
Written in English and Spanish, the subscription site is a browsable database of companies and international business opportunities in Argentina and Brazil. A 15-day free trial is available with registration.

National Commission of Foreign Trade
http://www.mecon.ar/cnce/default.htm
An Argentine federal government agency based in Buenos Aires, the Commission studies the impact of international trade on the Argentine economy. The site includes fact sheets, legislation, and anti-dumping and countervail reports.

Trade Leads On-Line
http://www.tradeline.com.ar/
The online service is a browsable database of international business opportunities in Argentina. Categories include exports available, imports wanted, representatives wanted, representatives available, and joint ventures.

Trade Point Cordoba
http://www.untpdc.org/incubator/arg/tpcor/tpc.htm
Part of the United Nations Global Trade Point Network, the site provides Cordoba trade leads, market bulletins, and contact information.

Trade Point La Plata
http://www.tplaplata.com.ar/
Part of the United Nations Global Trade Point Network, the site provides La Plata trade leads, market bulletins, and contact information.

Trade Point Santa Fe
http://www.untpdc.org/incubator/arg/tpsan/
Part of the United Nations Global Trade Point Network, the site provides Santa Fe trade leads, market bulletins, and contact information.

Trade Shows in Argentina
http://www.expoguide.com/shows/data/loc_1.htm
Compiled by Expoguide, the site is a directory of upcoming trade shows in Argentina.

World Business
http://www.bacoweb.com/worbus/index2.html
Posted in English and Spanish, the site is a directory of Argentine international trade events, associations, and companies in over 30 industries including automotive, electronics, mining, textiles, and transportation.

Argentina Representative Offices

Armenia

Embassy of Armenia in Buenos Aires
http://www.armeniaemb.org/forrel/embas2.htm
The site provides contact information for the Armenian Embassy in Buenos Aires.

Australia

Austrade in Buenos Aires
http://www.austrade.gov.au/Argentina/
An Australian trade promotion service, the site provides a mission statement, market reports, and contact information for Austrade in Buenos Aires.

Embassy of Australia in Buenos Aires
http://www.hq.satlink.com/ausemba/
The virtual Embassy provides Australian fact sheets, visa and passport information, tourism guides, immigration primers, and a directory of consular programs and staff.

Austria

Austrian Trade Commission in Buenos Aires
http://aw.wk.or.at/awo/ahst-buenosaires.htm
The site lists the staff, street address, phone and fax numbers, e-mail link, and office hours of the Austrian Trade Commission in Buenos Aires.

Canada

Canadian Embassy in Buenos Aires
http://www.dfait-maeci.gc.ca/bairs/
Posted in English, French, and Spanish, the site delivers Canadian fact sheets, visa and immigration information, and primers on how to develop a business plan, identify opportunities, and find potential buyers or partners in the Argentine market.

European Union

Delegation of the European Union in Argentina
http://delarg.mailcom.net/
Written in Spanish, the site posts European fact sheets, and reports on Argentina-European Union trade and relations.

Finland

Embassy of Finland in Buenos Aires
http://www.finembue.com.ar/
The virtual Embassy provides Finnish profiles, government information, a list of Honorary Consuls in Argentina, and a directory of consular commercial services.

France

French Trade Commission in Buenos Aires
http://www.dree.org/argentine/
A French trade promotion service, the site delivers Argentine business news, border and customs reports, and a directory of international trade and investment opportunities for French exporters and multinationals.

Germany

German-Argentina Chamber of Commerce
*http://www.ahk.net/en/ar/BuenosAires/
chamber.contact.html*
The site lists the Chairperson, Chief Executive Officer, street address, phone and fax numbers, and e-mail link of the German-Argentina Chamber of Commerce in Buenos Aires.

German Embassy in Buenos Aires
http://www.embalemana.com.ar/
Posted in English and German, the virtual Embassy provides German fact sheets, press releases, business reports, and contact information.

Israel

Embassy of Israel in Buenos Aires
http://www.israel-embassy.org.ar/
Posted in Spanish, the site delivers Israeli news, business guides, press releases, a calendar of events, cultural and education bulletins, and travel tips.

Italy

Consulate General of Italy in Mendoza
http://www.consitalia-mendoza.com.ar/
Written in Italian and Spanish, the site provides contact information, Italian government guides, and a directory of consular services and staff.

Embassy of Italy in Buenos Aires
http://www.ambitalia-bsas.org.ar/
Written in Italian, the site posts Italian business guides, scientific bulletins, contact information, and a directory of consular staff and services.

Italian Chamber of Commerce in Buenos Aires
http://www.ice.it/estero/buenos/
Part of a global network of Italian Chamber offices, the site delivers Italian business reports, investment guides, economic statistics, travel tips, and a directory of Chamber services.

Malaysia

Embassy of Malaysia in Buenos Aires
*http://www.mnet.com.my/klonline/www/missions/
malmiss/margenti1.htm*
The site provides contact information for the Malaysian Embassy in Buenos Aires.

Mexico

Trade Commission of Mexico in Buenos Aires
*http://www.mexico-businessline.com/ingles/
ofrepmu3.html#argentina*
The site lists the street address, phone and fax numbers, and e-mail link of the Mexican Trade Commission in Buenos Aires.

New Zealand

Trade New Zealand in Buenos Aires
http://www.tradenz.govt.nz/contact/southam.html
An export promotion service, the site provides contact information for the Trade New Zealand office in Buenos Aires.

Singapore

Consulate General of Singapore in Buenos Aires
http://www.gov.sg/mfa/consular/mww_a.htm
The site provides contact information for the Singapore Consulate General in Buenos Aires.

South Africa

Embassy of South Africa in Buenos Aires
http://www.sicoar.com/saemba/
Written in Spanish, the site provides South African visa and passport information, telephone directories, tourism guides, and a directory of consular services.

South Africa Foreign Trade Office in Buenos Aires
*http://wwwdti.pwv.gov.za/dtiwww/
foreign_offices.htm*
A service of the South Africa Department of Trade and Industry, the site provides contact information for the South Africa Trade Office in Buenos Aires.

Spain

Spanish Commercial Office in Buenos Aires
*http://www.icex.es/openURL.html#openURL=/
english/infoproyem/ofcomes/ofcomes.html#AM*
The site lists the staff, street address, phone and fax numbers, and e-mail link of the Spanish Commercial Office in Buenos Aires.

Sweden

Embassy of Sweden in Buenos Aires

http://www.ud.se/english/mfa/ambassad/ argentin.htm
The site lists the staff, street address, phone and fax numbers, and e-mail link of the Swedish Embassy in Buenos Aires.

Taiwan

Taiwan Government Information Office in Buenos Aires

http://www.gio.gov.tw/info/ngio/arg-f.html
Posted in Chinese and English, the site lists the street address, phone and fax numbers, and e-mail link of the Taiwan Government Information Office in Buenos Aires.

Thailand

Royal Thai Embassy in Buenos Aires

http://www.mfa.go.th/Embassy/detail/186.htm
The site lists the Ambassador, street address, and phone and fax numbers of the Thai Embassy in Buenos Aires.

United Kingdom

Embassy of Britain in Buenos Aires

http://www.fco.gov.uk/directory/posts.asp?AA
The site provides contact information for the British Embassy in Buenos Aires.

United States

Embassy of the U.S. in Argentina

http://www.usia.gov/abtusia/posts/AR1/ wwwh0100.html
The virtual Embassy provides consular information and primers on the Argentine economy and food industry. The service includes Argentine consumer profiles, and a list of leading market trends and business opportunities.

State of Utah Office in Buenos Aires

http://www.ce.ex.state.ut.us/international/reps/ reps.htm
A service of the Utah International Business Development Office, the site lists the street address, phone and fax numbers, and e-mail link of the State of Utah Office in Buenos Aires.

United States Information Service in Buenos Aires

http://www.usia.gov/abtusia/posts/AR1/ wwwh0001.html
Along with U.S. news and state visit reports, the online service delivers Argentine cultural bulletins, conference highlights, and a directory of education exchange programs.

Venezuela

Embassy of Venezuela in Buenos Aires

http://www.trade-venezuela.com/EMBVENG.HTM
The site lists the street address, phone and fax numbers, and e-mail link of the Venezuelan Embassy in Buenos Aires.

Aruba

Aruba Market Guides

Aruba Central Bureau of Statistics

http://www.arubastatistics.com/Index.htm
Homepage of Aruba's statistics agency, the site features labor force surveys, a business census, and foreign trade statistics for 21 industries including footwear, textiles, and base metals.

Aruba Foreign Investment Agency

http://www.arubaforeigninvestment.com/
The Agency attracts and retains international investment in Aruba. Along with globalization reports, the site profiles leading airports, seaports, free trade zones, and other infrastructure in Aruba.

Aruba InfoExport

http://www.infoexport.gc.ca/country-e.asp?continent=Latin&country=3
A service of Foreign Affairs and International Trade Canada, the site provides fact sheets and statistics on Aruban geography, business and politics.

Aruba Market Research

http://strategis.ic.gc.ca/sc_mrkti/ibinddc/engdoc/ 1a1c4.html
Posted by Industry Canada, the site provides fact sheets on Aruban geography, people, government, economy, communications, and transportation.

Aruba Reference Desk

http://lanic.utexas.edu/la/ca/other/aruba/
Developed by the University of Texas at Austin,

the site is a directory of leading Aruban news, government, and travel resources online.

Ministry of Economic Affairs and Tourism
http://www.arubaeconomicaffairs.com/
The online service provides primers on Aruban labor, social security, financial services, intellectual property, utilities, business incentives, tourism, currency, manufacturing, and entry requirements.

Aruba Trade Assistance

Aruba Trade
http://www.arubaeconomicaffairs.com/trade.htm
A service of the Aruba Ministry of Economic Affairs and Tourism, the site reports on Aruban foreign trade, rules of origin, preferential tariff treatment, the Generalized System of Preferences, and the Caribbean Basin Initiative.

Bahamas

Bahamas Media

Bahamas Media
http://www.mediainfo.com/emediajs/specific-geo.htm?region=bahamas
The site provides a directory of Bahamian media sites online including newspapers and magazines.

Bahamas Market Guides

Bahamas Country Report
http://www.state.gov/www/issues/economic/trade_reports/latin_america97/bahamas97.html
Prepared by the U.S. State Department, the site reviews Bahamian economic policy and trade practices. Sections include key economic indicators, exchange rate policy, debt management policies, significant barriers to U.S. exports, export subsidies policies, protection of U.S. intellectual property, and worker rights.

Bahamas InfoExport
http://www.infoexport.gc.ca/country-e.asp?continent=Latin&country=4
A service of Foreign Affairs and International Trade Canada, the site provides fact sheets and statistics on Bahamian geography, business and politics.

Bahamas Market Research
http://strategis.ic.gc.ca/sc_mrkti/ibinddc/engdoc/

1a1c5.html
Posted by Industry Canada, the site reports on Bahamian business, politics, trade regulations and standards, investment climate, trade and project financing, and business travel.

Bahamas Reference Desk
http://lanic.utexas.edu/la/cb/bahamas/
Developed by the University of Texas at Austin, the site is a directory of Bahamian news, culture, business, and government resources online.

Government of the Bahamas
http://flamingo.bahamas.net.bs/government/
The online service provides backgrounders on the Bahamian constitution, judiciary, parliament, Cabinet Ministers, Ministers of State, Members of the House of Assembly, and the Senate.

Bahamas Trade Assistance

Bahamas Customs Procedures
http://americas.fiu.edu/customs/bahamas.htm
A service of Florida International University, the site reviews Bahamian customs regulations, entry procedures, documentation, tariffs, and taxes.

Bahamas Overseas Representatives
http://flamingo.bahamas.net.bs/government/gov8.html
The site lists the Consul Generals and High Commissioners, street addresses, and phone and fax numbers of the Bahamas representative offices in Canada, the United Kingdom, and the United States.

Bahamas Representative Offices

Canada

High Commission of Canada in Nassau
http://www.dfait-maeci.gc.ca/english/missions/rep-can1e.htm#bahamas
The site provides contact information for the Canadian High Commission in Nassau.

Sweden

Consulate General of Sweden in Nassau
http://www.ud.se/english/mfa/ambassad/bahamas.htm
The site lists the staff, street address, and phone and fax numbers of the Swedish Consulate in Nassau.

United Kingdom

High Commission of Britain in Nassau
http://www.fco.gov.uk/directory/posts.asp?BH
The site provides contact information for the British High Commission in Nassau.

Barbados

Barbados Media

Barbados Media
http://www.mediainfo.com/emediajs/specific-geo.htm?region=barbados
A service of Editor and Publisher Interactive, the site is a registry of Barbadian media sites online including magazines and newspapers.

Barbados Market Guides

Barbados Background Notes
http://www.state.gov/www/background_notes/barbados_398_bgn.html
Prepared by the U.S. Department of State, the site provides reports and statistics on Barbadian geography, people, government, economy, history, political conditions, and U.S.-Barbadian relations.

Barbados InfoExport
http://www.infoexport.gc.ca/country-e.asp?continent=Latin&country=5
A service of Foreign Affairs and International Trade Canada, the site provides fact sheets and statistics on Barbadian geography, business and politics.

Barbados Investment and Development Corporation
http://www.bidc.com/
The online service delivers Barbadian fact sheets, success stories, infrastructure reports, business incentive guides, work force data, and a directory of high technology and manufacturing companies in the country.

Barbados Market Research
http://strategis.ic.gc.ca/sc_mrkti/ibinddc/engdoc/1a1c6.html
A service of Industry Canada, the site reports on Barbadian business, politics, trade regulations and standards, investment climate, trade and project financing, and business travel.

Barbados: Recent Economic Developments
http://www.imf.org/external/pubs/CAT/
longres.cfm?sk=2548.0
Prepared by the International Monetary Fund, the site reports on recent developments in Barbadian tax reform, trade policy, financial networks, and labor markets.

Barbados Reference Desk
http://lanic.utexas.edu/la/cb/barbados/
Developed by the University of Texas at Austin, the site is a directory of Barbadian news, culture, business, and government resources online.

Barbados Trade Assistance

Barbados Customs Procedures
http://americas.fiu.edu/customs/barbados.htm
A service of Florida International University, the site reviews Barbadian customs regulations, entry procedures, documentation, tariffs, and taxes.

Caribbean Export Development Agency
http://www.carib-export.com/
Based in St. Michael, Barbados, the Agency promotes the export of Caribbean products and services. The site features a mission statement, country profiles, and guides to Caribbean tariffs, price controls, technical requirements, and border documentation.

Barbados Representative Offices

Canada

High Commission of Canada in Bridgetown
http://www.dfait-maeci.gc.ca/english/missions/rep-can1e.htm#barbados
The site provides contact information for the Canadian High Commission in Bridgetown.

Sweden

Consulate of Sweden in Bridgetown
http://www.ud.se/english/mfa/ambassad/barbados.htm
The site lists the staff, street address, phone and fax numbers, and e-mail link of the Swedish Consulate in Bridgetown.

United Kingdom

High Commission of Britain in Bridgetown
http://www.fco.gov.uk/directory/posts.asp?BB
The site provides contact information for the British High Commission in Bridgetown.

United States

United States Embassy in Bridgetown
*http://www.usia.gov/abtusia/posts/BB1/
wwwhmain.html*
The virtual Embassy provides U.S. news, fact
sheets, press releases, U.S.-Caribbean Summit
reports, and a directory of Embassy services and
staff.

Venezuela

Embassy of Venezuela in Bridgetown
http://www.trade-venezuela.com/EMBVENG.HTM
The site lists the street address, phone and fax
numbers, and e-mail link of the Venezuelan
Embassy in Bridgetown.

Belize

Belize Media

Belize Media
*http://www.mediainfo.com/emediajs/specific-
geo.htm?region=belize*
Compiled by Editor and Publisher Interactive, the
site is a directory of Belizean sites online including magazines and newspapers.

Belize Market Guides

Belize Chamber of Commerce and Industry
http://www.belize.org/
Based in Belize City, the site features a newsletter, calendar of events, business primers, an
online message board, and contact information.

Belize Country Brief
*http://www.worldbank.org/cgi-bin/
sendoff.cgi?page=%2Fhtml%2Fextdr%2Foffrep%2
Flac%2Fbz.htm*
A service of the World Bank Group, the site
provides Belizean population statistics, financial
data, development reports, and economic
forecasts.

Belize: A Country Study
http://lcweb2.loc.gov/frd/cs/bztoc.html
A service of the U.S. Library of Congress, the site
delivers fact sheets on Belizean business,
government institutions, foreign economic
relations, transportation, and communications.

Belize InfoExport
http://www.infoexport.gc.ca/country-

e.asp?continent=Latin&country=6
A service of Foreign Affairs and International
Trade Canada, the site provides fact sheets and
statistics on Belizean geography, business,
trade, and politics.

Belize Investment Guide
http://AmbergrisCaye.com/economics/
Featuring a welcome from the Prime Minister, the
site delivers Belizean fact sheets, maps, visa and
immigration information, investment primers,
foreign exchange bulletins, and a directory of site
selection and business assistance programs.

Belize Investment Guide
http://www.belize.org/html/big/toc.html
Developed by the Belize Chamber of Commerce
and Industry, the site provides primers on
Belizean tax policy, investment opportunities,
labor, social security, immigration, land, and
income tax.

Belize Market Research
*http://strategis.ic.gc.ca/sc_mrkti/ibinddc/engdoc/
1a1c7.html*
A service of Industry Canada, the site reports on
Belizean business, politics, trade regulations and
standards, investment climate, and project
financing.

Belize Online
http://www.belize.com/
Homepage of the Belize Tourism Industry
Association, the site provides Belizean news,
maps, business reports, cultural bulletins,
tourism guides, and accommodation directories.

Belize Reference Desk
http://lanic.utexas.edu/la/ca/belize/
Developed by the University of Texas at Austin,
the site is a directory of Belizean news, government, tourism, and Internet resources online.

Business Directory
http://www.belize.org/html/busdir.html
Prepared by the Belize Chamber of Commerce
and Industry, the site is a searchable directory of
Belizean companies. The database is browsable
by company name, contact, or product.

Offshore Belize: Investing in Belize
http://www.belize.com/business.html
The online service provides primers on Belizean
investment opportunities, business incentive
programs, economic citizenship, offshore trusts,
asset protection, and bank accounts.

Belize Trade Assistance

Belize Customs Procedures
http://americas.fiu.edu/customs/belize.htm
A service of Florida International University, the site reviews Belizean customs regulations, entry procedures, documentation, tariffs, and taxes.

Belize Embassies, High Commissions and Consulates Abroad
http://AmbergrisCaye.com/economics/directory.html
The site lists the street addresses, office hours, and phone and fax numbers of Belizean diplomatic posts in Canada, China, Guatemala, Mexico, the United Kingdom, and the United States.

Belize Representative Offices

Canada

High Commission of Canada in Belize
http://www.dfait-maeci.gc.ca/english/missions/rep-can1e.htm#belize
The site provides contact information for the Canadian High Commission in Belize.

Sweden

Consulate General of Sweden in Belize
http://www.ud.se/english/mfa/ambassad/belize.htm
The site lists the staff, street address, phone and fax numbers, and e-mail link of the Swedish Consulate in Belize.

United Kingdom

High Commission of Britain in Belize
http://www.fco.gov.uk/directory/posts.asp?BZ
The site provides contact information for the British High Commission in Belize.

United States

United States Embassy in Belize
http://www.usemb-belize.gov/
The virtual Embassy provides U.S. fact sheets and background reports on Belizean economic trends, investment climate, trade regulations and standards, and business travel.

Bermuda

Bermuda Media

Bermuda Media
http://www.mediainfo.com/emediajs/specific-geo.htm?region=bermuda
Compiled by Editor and Publisher Interactive, the site is a directory of Bermudian media sites online including magazines and newspapers.

Bermuda Market Guides

Bermuda Chamber of Commerce
http://www.bermudacommerce.com/
Based in Hamilton, the site features a member directory, sales permit information, and fact sheets on Bermudian infrastructure, taxation, regulation, financial services, and incorporation.

Bermuda InfoExport
http://www.infoexport.gc.ca/country-e.asp?continent=Latin&country=7
A service of Foreign Affairs and International Trade Canada, the site provides fact sheets and statistics on Bermudian geography, business, and politics.

Bermuda Market Research
http://strategis.ic.gc.ca/sc_mrkti/ibinddc/engdoc/1a1c8.html
A service of Industry Canada, the site delivers fact sheets on Bermudian geography, people, government, economy, communications, and transportation.

Bermuda Online
http://www.bermuda-online.com/
Posted by the Royal Gazette, the site is a Bermudian virtual library. Sections include news, business and economy, government and politics, history and culture, and travel and tourism.

Bermuda Yellow Pages
http://www.bermudayp.com/
A telephone directory of Bermuda companies, the site is searchable by business name, keyword, phone and fax number, and hundreds of categories such as advertising agencies, marine equipment, and wholesale distributors.

Bermuda's Economy
http://www.bermuda-online.com/economy.htm
A fact sheet on the Bermuda Economy, the site

reports on Bermudian international business, tourism, government, gross domestic product, employment, home ownership, income, and social security.

Bermuda Trade Assistance

Bermuda International Business Association
http://biba.org/cgi-win/bermuda-inc.exe/biba
Based in Hamilton, the Association promotes Bermuda as an international business center. The site includes a mission statement, calendar of events, sector profiles, business guides, legal primers, and a membership directory.

Bermuda: A World Leader in International Business
http://www.biba.org/documents/bibabro.htm
Prepared by the Bermuda Monetary Authority, the site provides primers on Bermudian banking, trusts, mutual funds, foreign sales corporations, shipping registration, international arbitration, and other business topics.

Bermuda Representative Offices

Canada

Canadian Commission to Bermuda
http://www.Canada-Bermuda.org/
Posted in English and French, the site provides Canadian fact sheets, visa and passport information, government and political bulletins, and a directory of Bermuda business resources online.

Bolivia

Bolivia Media

Bolivia Media
http://www.mediainfo.com/emediajs/specific-geo.htm?region=bolivia
Compiled by Editor and Publisher Interactive, the site is a directory of Bolivian media sites online including newspapers, radio, and television.

Bolivia Market Guides

Bolivia Business Online
http://www.boliviabiz.com/index.htm
A virtual library of Bolivian business information, the site includes socioeconomic statistics, travel guides, a photo gallery, company directories, and a list of industry and trade associations.

Bolivia Chamber of Commerce
http://www.bolivia-industry.com/index.html
Based in La Paz, the site provides Bolivian fact sheets, business guides, sector profiles, economic statistics, company directories, and contact information.

Bolivia Country Brief
http://www.worldbank.org/cgi-bin/ sendoff.cgi?page=%2Fhtml%2Fextdr%2Foffrep%2 Flac%2Fbo.htm
A service of the World Bank Group, the site provides Bolivian population statistics, financial data, development reports, and economic forecasts.

Bolivia Country Profile
http://www.tradenz.govt.nz/intelligence/profiles/ bolivia.html
A service of the New Zealand Trade Development Board, the site provides Bolivian economic statistics, market information, and business tips.

Bolivia Country Report
http://www.state.gov/www/issues/economic/ trade_reports/latin_america97/bolivia97.html
Prepared by the U.S. State Department, the site reviews Bolivian economic policy and trade practices. Sections include key economic indicators, exchange rate policy, debt management policies, and barriers to U.S. exports.

Bolivia: A Country Study
http://lcweb2.loc.gov/frd/cs/botoc.html
A service of the U.S. Library of Congress, the site delivers fact sheets on Bolivian geography, population, agriculture, mining, manufacturing, and foreign economic relations.

Bolivia InfoExport
http://www.infoexport.gc.ca/country-e.asp?continent=Latin&country=34
A service of Foreign Affairs and International Trade Canada, the site provides Bolivian commercial guides and market reports.

Bolivia Market Research
http://strategis.ic.gc.ca/sc_mrkti/ibinddc/engdoc/ 1a1c9.html
A service of Industry Canada, the site reports on Bolivian business, politics, trade regulations and standards, investment climate, and project financing.

Bolivia Reference Desk
http://lanic.utexas.edu/la/sa/bolivia/

Developed by the University of Texas at Austin, the site is a directory of Bolivian news, business, government, and education resources online.

Bolivian Company Directory
http://www.boliviabiz.com/business/company.htm
Posted in English and Spanish, the site is a searchable directory of Bolivian companies. Categories include agri-business, banking, energy, mining, and transportation.

Bolivia Trade Assistance

CADEX
http://www.cadex.org/
Based in Santa Cruz, CADEX is the National Chamber of Exporters of Santa Cruz. Written in Spanish, the site includes a mission statement, Bolivian fact sheets, business primers, and contact information.

Customs Procedures
http://americas.fiu.edu/customs/bolivia.htm
A service of Florida International University, the site reviews Bolivian customs regulations, entry procedures, documentation, tariffs, and taxes.

Ministry of External Trade and Investment
http://www.mcei-bolivia.com/
Based in La Paz, the site provides Bolivian news, press releases, business primers, investment information, export tutorials, international trade statistics, and a directory of export counselors and services.

Bolivia Representative Offices

Canada

Office of Canadian Cooperation in La Paz
http://www.dfait-maeci.gc.ca/english/missions/rep-can1e.htm#bolivia
The site provides contact information for the Canadian Cooperation Office in La Paz.

France

French Trade Commission in La Paz
http://www.dree.org/bolivie/
The site lists the street address, phone and fax numbers, and e-mail link of the French Trade Commission in La Paz.

Germany

German Chamber of Commerce in La Paz
http://www.ahk.net/en/bo/La_Paz/
The site posts the Chairperson, Chief Executive Officer, street address, phone and fax numbers, and e-mail link of the German Chamber in La Paz.

Mexico

Trade Commission of Mexico in La Paz
http://www.mexico-businessline.com/ingles/ofrepmu3.html#bolivia
The site lists the street address, phone and fax numbers, and e-mail link of the Mexican Trade Commission in La Paz.

Sweden

Embassy of Sweden in La Paz
http://www.ud.se/english/mfa/ambassad/bolivia.htm
The site lists the staff, street address, phone and fax numbers, and e-mail link of the Swedish Embassy in La Paz.

United Kingdom

Embassy of Britain in La Paz
http://www.fco.gov.uk/directory/posts.asp?BL
The site provides contact information for the British Embassy in La Paz.

United States

American Chamber of Commerce of Bolivia
http://www.megalink.com/amcham/welcome.html
The online service delivers Bolivian fact sheets, Chamber contact information, and a member directory.

United States Embassy in La Paz
http://www.megalink.com/usemblapaz/
Written in Spanish, the site provides U.S. fact sheets, passport information, commercial bulletins, agricultural reports, and a directory of consular services.

United States Information Service in La Paz
http://www.megalink.com/usemblapaz/wwwusis.htm
Posted in Spanish, the site features U.S. news,

Voice of America information government bulletins, and a directory of U.S.-Bolivia exchange and education programs.

Brazil

Brazil Search Tools

Infoseek Brasil
http://www.infoseek.com/ Home?pg=Home.html&sv=BR
Part of the Infoseek search network, the site is a browsable database of Brazilian resources online.

Brazil Media

Brazil Media
http://www.mediainfo.com/emediajs/specific-geo.htm?region=brazil
Compiled by Editor and Publisher Interactive, the site is a directory of Brazilian media sites online including magazines, newspapers, and city guides.

Gazeta Mercantil
http://www.gazeta.com.br/gazasp/index.asp
Written in English, Portuguese, and Spanish, the online service provides Brazilian investment news, money information, and sector reports.

Brazil Market Guides

Barclays Country Report: Brazil
http://www.offshorebanking.barclays.com/ services/economic/yearly/brajan98/bracont.html
Prepared by Barclays Bank, the site reports on Brazilian economic trends, politics, monetary and fiscal policy, international trade, foreign debt, merchandise trade, and investment flows.

Brazil: Big Emerging Markets Home Page
http://www.ita.doc.gov/bems/brazil.html
Developed by the U.S. Department of Commerce, the site delivers Brazilian fact sheets, economic forecasts, export and import statistics, sector profiles, and international trade guides.

Brazil & Biz
http://www.brazilbiz.com/
Posted in English and Portuguese, the site features Brazilian company directories, technology guides, market bulletins, and classified ads.

Brazil Biz2Biz
http://www.brazilbiz.com.br/
Posted in English and Portuguese, the site is a searchable directory of Brazilian companies. Categories include aerospace, automotive, electronics, mining, textiles, marketing, engineering, franchising, telecommunications, and transportation.

Brazil Business Briefs
http://www.austrade.gov.au/IOOM/Brazil/
A service of Austrade, the site offers fact sheets on Brazilian business etiquette, foreign investment, corporate taxation, marketing, and visas.

Brazil Business Reports
http://italchambers.net/BusinessReports.html
Prepared by the Italian Chamber of Commerce and written in Italian, the site provides Brazilian fact sheets, market reports, and commercial guides.

Brazil Country Brief
http://www.worldbank.org/cgi-bin/ sendoff.cgi?page=%2Fhtml%2Fextdr%2Foffrep%2 Flac%2Fbr.htm
A service of the World Bank Group, the site provides Brazilian population statistics, financial data, development reports, and economic forecasts.

Brazil Country Profile
http://www.tradenz.govt.nz/intelligence/profiles/ brazil.html
A service of the New Zealand Trade Development Board, the site provides Brazilian economic statistics, market information, and business tips.

Brazil Country Report
http://www.state.gov/www/issues/economic/ trade_reports/latin_america97/brazil97.html
Prepared by the U.S. Department of State, the site delivers information on Brazil exchange rates, debt management, barriers to U.S. trade, export subsidies, protection of U.S. intellectual property, and worker rights.

Brazil InfoExport
http://www.infoexport.gc.ca/country-e.asp?continent=Latin&country=35
A service of Foreign Affairs and International Trade Canada, the site provides Brazilian commercial guides and market reports.

Brazil Information Services

http://www.brasil.emb.nw.dc.us/embing6.htm
A virtual library of market information, the site features Brazilian news, fact sheets, economic reports, science and technology bulletins, government directories, and foreign policy statements.

Brazil Market Access Database

http://mkaccdb.eu.int/mkdb/
mkdb.pl?METHOD=COUNTRY
A service of the European Commission, the site offers briefs on Brazilian trade policy, tariff barriers, non-tariff barriers, investment-related measures, and financial services regulations.

Brazil Market Information

http://dtiinfo1.dti.gov.uk/ots/brazil/
A service of the London-based Department of Trade and Industry, the site delivers country fact sheets, maps, and trade-show information.

Brazil Market Research

http://strategis.ic.gc.ca/sc_mrkti/ibinddc/engdoc/
1a1c10.html
A service of Industry Canada, the site provides U.S. Department of Commerce reports on Brazilian business, politics, trade regulations and standards, investment climate, trade and project financing, business travel, and market opportunities.

Brazil Network

http://www.brazilnetwork.com/directory/dir2_0.htm
Written in English and Portuguese, the site is a searchable database of Brazilian companies in some 50 industries including automotive, finance, marketing, medical, publishing, retail, and transportation.

Brazil: Recent Economic Developments

http://www.imf.org/external/pubs/CAT/
longres.cfm?sk=2562.0
Prepared by the International Monetary Fund, the site reports on Brazilian macroeconomic trends, balance of payments, monetary policy, debt restructuring, foreign direct investment, and privatization.

Brazil Reference Desk

http://lanic.utexas.edu/la/brazil/
Developed by the University of Texas at Austin, the site is a directory of leading Brazilian media, business, government, and travel resources online.

Brazil Special Report

http://www.usbrazil.com/report/
An electronic magazine on Brazilian business, the site features economic and company news, political analysis, video e-mail, and business matchmaking services.

Brazil Telephone Directories

http://www.contractjobs.com/tel/br/
Written by Robert Hoare, the site is a database of online telephone directories for selected Brazilian states and cities.

Brazil Trends

http://www.amcham.com.br/boston/indexe.html
A service of BankBoston, the site provides Brazilian news summaries, political scenarios, policy reviews, and economic forecasts. Updated monthly, the service is available in English and Portuguese.

Doing Business with Brazil

http://www.demon.co.uk/Itamaraty/dbwb.html
Written by the National Confederation of Brazilian Industry, the site delivers primers on the Brazilian economy, foreign investment, intellectual property rights, and shipping and port facilities.

A Guide for the Foreign Investor

http://www.demon.co.uk/Itamaraty/gfi.html
The online service provides tutorials on Brazilian business law, taxation, international contracts, environmental regulations, foreign arbitration, investment promotion, and technology transfer.

Brazil Trade Assistance

Brazil Customs Procedures

http://americas.fiu.edu/customs/brazil.htm
A service of Florida International University, the site reviews Brazilian customs regulations, entry procedures, documentation, tariffs, and taxes.

Brazil Exporters

http://www.brazilexporters.com/
Developed by De Paula Publishing, the site delivers Brazilian news, business primers, company profiles, product catalogs, and a directory of Brazilian exporters and importers in over 50 industries including aerospace, furniture, and wood products.

Brazil InfoNet

http://www.brazilinfo.net/index.html
An online trade network, the site features Brazilian news, business guides, and classifieds. A

trade leads service allows a user to post buy or sell offers in some 30 categories including agri-food, apparel, metal products, and transportation.

Brazil Trade Fairs
http://www.brasil.emb.nw.dc.us/secom/fairs.htm
The online service is a browsable database of Brazilian industry fairs and international trade shows in agri-food, construction, environmental technology, packaging, and other industries.

Brazil Trade Net
http://www.dpr.mre.gov.br/e/default-e.htm
The site is the homepage of the Brazilian Trade Promotion Network, a government export promotion agency. Posted in English, Portuguese, and Spanish, the service includes Brazilian trade-show reports, and a directory of trade and investment opportunities.

Brazilian Business Development Program
http://www.bbd.com.br/
Written in four languages, the site is a database of Brazilian export and import opportunities in industries such as automotive, electronics, textiles, beverages, and advertising.

Brazilian Marketplace
http://www.brasil.emb.nw.dc.us/secom/tutorial.htm
Published by the Trade Promotion Section of the Brazilian Embassy in Washington, D.C., the site provides information on how to find Brazilian suppliers and products.

Trade Point Belo Horizonte
http://www.tradebhz.com.br/ingles/index.htm
Part of the United Nations Global Trade Point Network, the site provides Belo Horizonte trade leads, market bulletins, and contact information.

Trade Point Curitiba
http://www.cits.br/tpcuritiba/hometp-in/homepage.html
Part of the United Nations Global Trade Point Network, the site provides Curitiban trade leads, market bulletins, and contact information.

Trade Point Porto Alegre
http://prefpoa.com.br/TP_Portoalegre/
Part of the United Nations Global Trade Point Network, the site provides Porto Alegre trade leads, market bulletins, and contact information.

Trade Point Salvador
http://www.tpsalvador.com.br/
Part of the United Nations Global Trade Point Network, the site provides Salvador trade leads, market bulletins, and contact information.

Trade Point Sao Paulo
http://www.tpsaopaulo.com.br/
Posted in four languages, the site provides Sao Paulo trade leads, market bulletins, and contact information.

Trade Shows in Brazil
http://www.expoguide.com/shows/data/loc_6.htm
Compiled by Expoguide, the site is a directory of upcoming trade shows in Brazil.

Brazil Representative Offices

Argentina

Embassy of Argentina in Brazil
http://www.tba.com.br/embarg/
Written in Portuguese, the site features Argentina-Brazil trade reports, discussion papers, a calendar of events, and a directory of Embassy staff and services.

Australia

Austrade in Sao Paulo
http://www.austrade.gov.au/Brazil/
An Australian trade promotion service, the site provides a mission statement, market reports, and contact information for Austrade in Sao Paulo.

Austria

Austrian Trade Commission in Rio de Janeiro
http://www.austria.org.br/
Along with Austrian business guides and fact sheets, the site lists the street addresses, phone and fax numbers, and e-mail links of the Austrian Trade Offices in Rio de Janeiro and Sao Paulo.

Austrian Trade Commission in Sao Paulo
http://aw.wk.or.at/awo/ahst-saopaulo.htm
The site lists the staff, street address, phone and fax numbers, e-mail link, and office hours of the Austrian Trade Commission in Sao Paulo.

Canada

Consulate General of Canada in Sao Paulo
http://www.dfait-maeci.gc.ca/english/missions/rep-can1e.htm#brazil
The site provides contact information for the Canadian Consulate in Sao Paulo.

Embassy of Canada in Brasilia
http://www.dfait-maeci.gc.ca/english/missions/rep-can1e.htm#brazil
The site provides contact information for the Canadian Embassy in Brasilia.

Denmark

Consulate General of Denmark in Sao Paulo
http://www.denmark.org.br/
Posted in English and Portuguese, the site provides Danish fact sheets, visa and passport information, and a directory of consular and commercial services.

Finland

Embassy of Finland in Brasilia
http://www.tba.com.br/finlandia/
Along with Finnish fact sheets and trade guides, the virtual Embassy delivers Brazilian economic reports, an event calendar, and a directory of consular staff and services.

Finland Trade Center in Sao Paulo
http://www.exports.finland.fi/tradecen.htm
The site lists the staff, street address, phone and fax numbers, and e-mail link of the Finland Trade Center in Sao Paulo.

France

Embassy of France in Brasilia
http://www.ambafrance.org.br/
Posted in French and Portuguese, the site offers French fact sheets, science and technology bulletins, trade primers, a calendar of events, and Brazilian news.

French Trade Commission in Brasilia
http://www.dree.org/bresil/
A French trade promotion service, the Commission provides export counseling and market research services for French companies in Brazil. Written in French, the site delivers French fact sheets, contact information, and a directory of Trade Commission staff.

Germany

German Chamber of Commerce in Sao Paulo
http://www.ahk.net/en/br/saopaulo/
The site lists the Chairperson, Chief Executive Officer, street address, phone and fax numbers, and e-mail link of the German Chamber in Sao Paulo.

Ghana

Embassy of Ghana in Brasilia
http://www.juntung.com/ghana-consul-hk/2misabo.htm
The site provides contact information for the Ghanaian Embassy in Brasilia.

Israel

Consulate General of Israel in Rio de Janeiro
http://www.israelrio.org.br/
The virtual Consulate provides Israeli news, fact sheets, an event calendar, travel guides, contact information, Israel-Brazil trade reports, and a directory of consular services.

Italy

Consulate General of Italy in Rio de Janeiro
http://www.alternex.com.br/~conrio/
Written in Italian, the site delivers Italian fact sheets, visa and passport information, and a directory of consular programs and services.

Japan

Consulate General of Japan in Rio de Janerio
http://www.rio.com.br/cccjapao/
Featuring messages from the Japanese Ambassador and Consul General, the site provides Japanese news, sector profiles, and reports on Brazil-Japan relations.

Malaysia

Embassy of Malaysia in Brasilia
http://www.mnet.com.my/klonline/www/missions/malmiss/mbrazil1.htm
The site provides contact information for the Malaysian Embassy in Brasilia.

Trade Commission of Malaysia in Sao Paulo
http://www.mnet.com.my/klonline/www/missions/malmiss/mbrazil3.htm
The site provides contact information for the Malaysian Trade Commission in Sao Paulo.

Mexico

Trade Commission of Mexico in Sao Paulo
http://www.mexico-businessline.com/ingles/ofrepmu3.html#brazil
The site lists the street address, phone and fax

numbers, and e-mail link of the Mexican Trade Commission in Sao Paulo.

New Zealand

Trade New Zealand in Sao Paulo
http://www.tradenz.govt.nz/contact/southam.html
An export promotion service, the site provides contact information for the Trade New Zealand office in Sao Paulo.

Norway

Norwegian Trade Council in Sao Paulo
http://www.ntc.com.br/
The online service provides Norwegian fact sheets, export guides, reports on Brazilian-Norwegian trade, and a directory of Council programs and services.

Pakistan

Pakistan Trade Office in Sao Paulo
http://www.jamal.com/epb/ptoa.htm
The site provides contact information for the Pakistani Trade Office in Sao Paulo.

Paraguay

Consulate General of Paraguay in Sao Paulo
http://www.paraguaysp.com.br/
The digital Consulate delivers Paraguayan fact sheets, Mercosur reports, a directory of consular staff and services, and the Paraguayan national anthem in streaming audio.

Peru

Consulate General of Peru in Sao Paulo
http://www.geocities.com/CapitolHill/Lobby/5428/
The online service features Peruvian news, fact sheets, cultural bulletins, contact information, and a directory of consular services.

Portugal

Portuguese Trade and Investment Office in Sao Paulo
http://www.portugal.org/geninfo/abouticep/spaulo.html
The site lists the staff, street address, phone and fax numbers, and e-mail link of the Portuguese Trade and Investment Office in Sao Paulo.

Romania

Consulate General of Romania in Rio de Janeiro
http://www.cons-gen-romania-rio.com/
The virtual Consulate provides Romanian news, sector profiles, reports on Brazil-Romania relations, and a directory of consular staff and services.

Russia

Embassy of Russia in Brasilia
http://www.brnet.com.br/pages/embrus/
Written in Portuguese, the site features primers on Russian geography, government, people, history, and business.

Singapore

Consulate General of Singapore in Sao Paulo
http://www.gov.sg/mfa/consular/mww_b.htm
The site provides contact information for the Singapore Consulate General in Sao Paulo.

South Africa

South Africa Foreign Trade Office in Sao Paulo
http://wwwdti.pwv.gov.za/dtiwww/foreign_offices.htm
A service of the South Africa Department of Trade and Industry, the site provides contact information for the South Africa Foreign Trade Office in Sao Paulo.

Spain

Spanish Commercial Office in Brasilia
http://www.icex.es/openURL.html#openURL=/english/infoproyem/ofcomes/ofcomes.html#AM
The site lists the staff, street address, phone and fax numbers, and e-mail link of the Spanish Commercial Office in Brasilia.

Spanish Commercial Office in Rio de Janeiro
http://www.icex.es/openURL.html#openURL=/english/infoproyem/ofcomes/ofcomes.html#AM
The site lists the staff, street address, phone and fax numbers, and e-mail link of the Spanish Commercial Office in Rio de Janeiro.

Spanish Commercial Office in Sao Paulo
http://www.icex.es/openURL.html#openURL=/english/infoproyem/ofcomes/ofcomes.html#AM
The site lists the staff, street address, phone and

fax numbers, and e-mail link of the Spanish Commercial Office in Sao Paulo.

Sweden

Embassy of Sweden in Brasilia
http://www.ud.se/english/mfa/ambassad/ brasilie.htm
The site lists the staff, street address, phone and fax numbers, and e-mail link of the Swedish Embassy in Brasilia.

Switzerland

Swiss Chamber of Commerce in Sao Paulo
http://swisstrade.com/ xicodes2.asp?P1=3&lvl=3&cid=C02
The site lists the street address, phone and fax numbers, and e-mail link of the Swiss Chamber of Commerce in Sao Paulo.

Taiwan

China External Trade Development Council Office in Sao Paulo
http://www.cetra.org.tw/english/o_office/ indexset.htm
A Taiwanese trade promotion service, the site lists the mission statement and e-mail link of the China External Trade Development Council Office in Sao Paulo.

Taiwan Government Information Office in Brasilia
http://www.gio.gov.tw/info/ngio/brazil-f.html
Posted in Chinese and English, the site lists the street address, phone and fax numbers, and e-mail link of the Taiwan Government Information Office in Brasilia.

Thailand

Royal Thai Embassy in Brasilia
http://www.mfa.go.th/Embassy/detail/34.htm
The site lists the Ambassador, street address, and phone and fax numbers of the Thai Embassy in Brasilia.

Thai Trade Center in Sao Paulo
http://www.thaitrade.com/wwtto.html
A service of the Thailand Department of Export Promotion, the site lists the street address, phone and fax numbers, and e-mail link of the Thai Trade Center in Sao Paulo.

Turkey

Embassy of Turkey in Brasilia
http://www.turkey.org/madres.htm
As part of a directory of Turkish diplomatic offices around the world, the site lists the e-mail link of the Turkish Embassy in Brasilia.

United Kingdom

Consulate General of Britain in Rio de Janeiro
http://www.fco.gov.uk/directory/posts.asp?BI
The site provides contact information for the British Consulate General in Rio de Janeiro.

Consulate General of Britain in Sao Paulo
http://www.fco.gov.uk/directory/posts.asp?BI
The site provides contact information for the British Consulate General in Sao Paulo.

Embassy of Britain in Brasilia
http://www.fco.gov.uk/directory/posts.asp?BI
The site provides contact information for the British Embassy in Brasilia.

United States

AmChamNet
http://www.amcham.com.br/indexe.html
Homepage of the American Chamber of Commerce in Brazil, the site provides Chamber news, Brazil and United States fact sheets, articles on the Brazilian business climate, and *Amcham Green Pages*, a directory of environmental operations in Brazil.

American Chamber of Commerce of Rio de Janeiro
http://www.amchamrio.com.br/
Posted in Portuguese, the site provides Brazilian business news, an event calendar, international trade reports, and a directory of Chamber staff and services.

United States Commercial Center in Sao Paulo
http://www.ita.doc.gov/uscs/ccsnpaul.html
A service of the United States Department of Commerce, the Center provides office services and export counseling to American companies doing business in the Sao Paulo area. The site lists the mission statement, street address, phone and fax numbers, and e-mail link of the Center.

United States Consulate in Rio De Janeiro
http://www.consulado-americano-rio.org.br/rio.htm
Posted in English and Portuguese, the site
provides a biography of the Consul General, a
directory of consular sections and services, and
fact sheets on the United States.

United States Embassy in Brasilia
http://www.embaixada-americana.org.br/
The virtual Embassy features U.S. fact sheets,
government bulletins, reports on United States-
Brazil relations, and a library of discussion
papers on electronic commerce, intellectual
property, the Free Trade Area of the Americas,
and other economic issues.

United States Information Service in Sao Paulo
http://www.geocities.com/CapitolHill/7722/
The online service delivers United States news,
press releases, fact sheets, product catalogs,
and a directory of Embassy and consular
services in Brazil.

Venezuela

Embassy of Venezuela in Brasilia
http://www.trade-venezuela.com/EMBVENG.HTM
The site lists the street address, phone and fax
numbers, and e-mail link of the Venezuelan
Embassy in Brasilia.

British Virgin Islands

British Virgin Islands Media

Island Sun
http://www.islandsun.com/
An online newspaper, the site features British
Virgin Islander editorials, classifieds, tourism
guides, and local, Caribbean and world news.

British Virgin Islands Market Guides

British Virgin Islands Homepage
http://www.britishvirginislands.com/
The online service provides British Virgin Islander
fact sheets, accommodation directories, dining
information, a calendar of events, and an electronic bulletin board.

British Virgin Islands InfoExport
_http://www.infoexport.gc.ca/country-
e.asp?continent=Latin&country=8_
A service of Foreign Affairs and International
Trade Canada, the site provides fact sheets and

statistics on British Virgin Islander geography,
business and politics.

British Virgin Islands Market Research
_http://strategis.ic.gc.ca/sc_mrkti/ibinddc/engdoc/
1a1c11.html_
Posted by Industry Canada, the site provides U.S.
Central Intelligence Agency fact sheets on British
Virgin Islander geography, people, government,
economy, and transportation.

Government of the British Virgin Islands
http://www.bvigovernment.org/
Homepage of the British Virgin Islands government, the site delivers news, fact sheets, tourism
guides, an event calendar, education bulletins,
history lessons, legal primers, and a government
e-mail directory.

British Virgin Islands Trade Assistance

**British Virgin Islands Trade and Investment
Guide**
http://www.bviguide.com/trade/
A virtual library of British Virgin Islander business
information, the site features sector profiles,
maps, tourism guides, taxation information,
investment primers, and a directory of business
opportunities in agri-food, manufacturing and
other industries.

**International Financial Services Information
Center**
http://www.bviibc.com/
Developed by Hewlett Beck and Arad, an international law firm, the site provides primers on
British Virgin Islander financial services, international business company legislation, and
incorporation procedures.

Cayman Islands

Cayman Islands Market Guides

Cayman Islands
http://www.caymanislands.ky/
Homepage of the Cayman Islands Department of
Tourism, the site features fact sheets, tourism
guides, accommodation directories, and contact
information.

Cayman Islands E-mail Directory
http://cayman.com.ky/email.htm
Developed by Cayman Web World, the site is an
e-mail database of individuals and companies in

the Cayman Islands, and Caymanians living overseas.

Cayman Islands InfoExport

http://www.infoexport.gc.ca/country-e.asp?continent=Latin&country=9

A service of Foreign Affairs and International Trade Canada, the site provides Caymanian commercial guides and market reports.

Cayman Islands Market Research

http://strategis.ic.gc.ca/sc_mrkti/ibinddc/engdoc/1a1c12.html

Posted by Industry Canada, the site provides U.S. Central Intelligence Agency fact sheets on Caymanian geography, people, government, economy, communications, and transportation.

Cayman Islands Reference Desk

http://lanic.utexas.edu/la/ca/other/ci/

Developed by the University of Texas at Austin, the site is a directory of leading Caymanian news, business, government, and travel resources online.

Chile

Chile Media

Chile Media

http://www.mediainfo.com/emediajs/specific-geo.htm?region=chile

Compiled by Editor and Publisher Interactive, the site is a directory of Chilean media sites online including city guides, magazines, and newspapers.

Chile Market Guides

Barclays Country Report: Chile

http://www.offshorebanking.barclays.com/services/economic/yearly/chileaug97/chicont.html

Prepared by Barclays Bank, the site reports on Chilean economic trends, politics, monetary and fiscal policy, international trade, foreign debt, merchandise trade, and investment flows.

Chile Business Briefs

http://www.austrade.gov.au/IOOM/Chile/

A service of Austrade, the site offers fact sheets on Chilean business etiquette, foreign investment, corporate taxation, marketing, and visas.

Chile Business Directory

http://www.chilnet.cl/

Based in Santiago, the site is a directory of Chilean companies in hundreds of categories including accounting, marine electronics, packaging, pharmaceuticals, textiles, and wood products.

Chile Business Reports

http://italchambers.net/BusinessReports.html

Prepared by the Italian Chamber of Commerce and written in Italian, the site provides Chilean fact sheets, market reports, and commercial guides.

Chile Country Brief

http://www.worldbank.org/cgi-bin/sendoff.cgi?page=%2Fhtml%2Fextdr%2Foffrep%2Flac%2Fcl.htm

A service of the World Bank Group, the site provides Chilean population statistics, financial data, development reports, and economic forecasts.

Chile Country Profile

http://www.tradenz.govt.nz/intelligence/profiles/chile.html

A service of the New Zealand Trade Development Board, the site provides Chilean economic statistics, market information, and business tips.

Chile Country Report

http://www.state.gov/www/issues/economic/trade_reports/latin_america97/chile97.html

Prepared by the U.S. Department of State, the site delivers information on Chilean exchange rates, debt management, barriers to U.S. trade, export subsidies, protection of U.S. intellectual property, and worker rights.

Chile: A Country Study

http://lcweb2.loc.gov/frd/cs/cltoc.html

A service of the U.S. Library of Congress, the site delivers fact sheets on Chilean geography, population, agriculture, mining, manufacturing, and foreign economic relations.

Chile InfoExport

http://www.infoexport.gc.ca/country-e.asp?continent=Latin&country=36

A service of Foreign Affairs and International Trade Canada, the site provides Chilean commercial guides and market reports.

Chile: An Introduction
http://www.apecsec.org.sg/member/apecchil.html
A service of the Asia Pacific Economic Cooperation, the site provides fact sheets on Chilean geography, climate, population, language, religion and government.

Chile Market Access Database
http://mkaccdb.eu.int/mkdb/
mkdb.pl?METHOD=COUNTRY
A service of the European Commission, the site offers briefs on Chilean trade policy, tariff barriers, non-tariff barriers, investment-related measures, and financial services regulations.

Chile Market Information
http://dtiinfo1.dti.gov.uk/ots/chile/
A service of the London-based Department of Trade and Industry, the site delivers country fact sheets, maps, and trade-show information.

Chile Market Research
http://strategis.ic.gc.ca/sc_mrkti/ibinddc/engdoc/
1a1c13.html
A service of Industry Canada, the site provides U.S. Department of Commerce reports on Chilean business, politics, trade regulations and standards, investment climate, trade and project financing, business travel, and market opportunities.

Chile Reference Desk
http://lanic.utexas.edu/la/chile/
Developed by the University of Texas at Austin, the site is a directory of leading Chilean arts, business, education, government, media, technology, and tourism resources online.

Chile: Selected Issues
http://www.imf.org/external/pubs/CAT/
longres.cfm?sk=2563.0
Prepared by the International Monetary Fund, the site reports on Chilean output, prices, competitiveness, exchange rates, export performance, and other fiscal and policy issues.

Country Commercial Guide
http://www.state.gov/www/about_state/business/
com_guides/1998/latin_america/chile98.html
Prepared by the U.S. Embassy in Santiago, the site delivers primers on the Chilean economy, political environment, trade regulations and standards, investment climate, trade and project financing, and business travel.

Chile Trade Assistance

Chile Customs Procedures
http://americas.fiu.edu/customs/chile.htm
A service of Florida International University, the site reviews Chilean customs regulations, entry procedures, documentation, tariffs, and taxes.

Chile Import/Export
http://www.beachnet.org/chiletrade/export.htm
A searchable directory of Chilean exporters and importers, the site includes legal primers, company profiles, and contact information for hundreds of operations.

Chile Trade
http://www.chiletrade.cl/
A Chilean export promotion service, the site provides Chilean business news, a trade newsletter, North American Free Trade Agreement reports, company profiles, and cultural bulletins.

Chile Trade and Investment Guide
http://journal.chilnet.cl/
The online service delivers Chilean news, maps, fact sheets, sector profiles, business travel tips, investment primers, an event calendar, and a directory of Chilean industry associations.

Chilean Trade Shows
http://journal.chilnet.cl/shows.htm
A database of Chilean trade shows, the site lists hundreds of events in 20 categories including agriculture, construction, environment, information technology, telecommunications, tourism, and transportation.

Embassies and Consulates Abroad
http://www.minrel.cl/direct/frampais.htm
Developed by the Chilean Ministry of Foreign Affairs, the site lists the Ambassadors, Consul Generals, street addresses, phone and fax numbers, and e-mail links of Chilean Embassies and Consulate Generals around the world.

International Trade Book of Chile
http://www.dicom.cl/inter/trade.html
Written in Spanish, the site is a directory of leading Chilean exporters and importers in hundreds of categories including agri-food, textiles, metal fabrication, construction, plastics, and hospitality.

ProChile
http://www.prochile.cl/
Based in Santiago, ProChile promotes Chilean exports and international investment. The site includes Chilean export news, catalogs, events, and a directory of international trade programs and services.

Trade Shows in Chile
http://www.expoguide.com/shows/data/loc_7.htm
Compiled by Expoguide, the site is a directory of upcoming trade shows in Chile.

Chile Representative Offices

Austria

Austrian Trade Commission in Santiago
http://aw.wk.or.at/awo/ahst-santiago.htm
The site lists the staff, street address, phone and fax numbers, e-mail link, and office hours of the Austrian Trade Commission in Santiago.

Bolivia

Consulate General of Bolivia in Chile
http://www.microweb.cl/bolivia/
Written in Spanish, the site delivers Bolivian fact sheets, visa and passport information, tourism guides, business primers, and a directory of consular staff and services.

Canada

Embassy of Canada in Santiago
http://www.dfait-maeci.gc.ca/santiago/
Posted in English, French, and Spanish, the site provides Canadian fact sheets and Chilean market studies. Priority industries include mining, information technology, energy, environmental equipment, building products, and transportation systems.

Pro Business Connections Canada-Chile
http://www.interlog.com/~chile97/chile.htm
A primer on Chilean business opportunities, the site features Chilean fact sheets, sector profiles, investment guides, and Canada-Chile trade reports.

Finland

Finland Trade Center in Santiago
http://www.exports.finland.fi/tradecen.htm

The site lists the staff, street address, phone and fax numbers, and e-mail link of the Finland Trade Center in Santiago.

France

French Trade Commission in Santiago
http://www.dree.org/chili/ftcny/wwwroot/chili/sommaire.htm
Written in French, the site provides Chilean sector profiles, and a directory of export programs and services for French companies doing business in Chile and Santiago.

Germany

German Chamber of Commerce in Santiago
http://www.ahk.net/chambers/cl/
Posted in German, the site lists the Chairperson, street address, phone and fax numbers, and e-mail link of the German Chamber in Santiago.

Malaysia

Embassy of Malaysia in Santiago
http://www.mnet.com.my/klonline/www/missions/malmiss/mchile1.htm
The site provides contact information for the Malaysian Embassy in Santiago.

Trade Commission of Malaysia in Santiago
http://www.mnet.com.my/klonline/www/missions/malmiss/mchile2.htm
The site provides contact information for the Malaysian Trade Commission in Santiago.

Mexico

Trade Commission of Mexico in Santiago
http://www.mexico-businessline.com/ingles/ofrepmu3.html#chile
The site lists the street address, phone and fax numbers, and e-mail link of the Mexican Trade Commission in Santiago.

New Zealand

Trade New Zealand in Santiago
http://www.tradenz.govt.nz/contact/southam.html
An export promotion service, the site provides contact information for the Trade New Zealand office in Santiago.

Singapore

Consulate General of Singapore in Santiago
http://www.gov.sg/mfa/consular/mww_c.htm
The site provides contact information for the Singapore Consulate General in Santiago.

Spain

Spanish Commercial Office in Santiago
http://www.icex.es/openURL.html#openURL=/ english/infoproyem/ofcomes/ofcomes.html#AM
The site lists the staff, street address, phone and fax numbers, and e-mail link of the Spanish Commercial Office in Santiago.

Sweden

Embassy of Sweden in Santiago
http://www.ud.se/english/mfa/ambassad/chile.htm
The site lists the staff, street address, phone and fax numbers, and e-mail link of the Swedish Embassy in Santiago.

Taiwan

Taiwan Government Information Office in Santiago
http://www.gio.gov.tw/info/ngio/chile-f.html
Posted in Chinese and English, the site lists the street address, phone and fax numbers, and e-mail link of the Taiwan Government Information Office in Santiago.

Thailand

Royal Thai Embassy in Santiago
http://www.mfa.go.th/Embassy/detail/36.htm
The site lists the street address, and phone and fax numbers of the Thai Embassy in Santiago.

Thailand Office of Commercial Affairs in Santiago
http://www.thaitrade.com/thcoaf.html
The site lists the street address, phone and fax numbers, and e-mail link of the Thailand Office of Commercial Affairs in Santiago.

United Kingdom

Embassy of Britain in Santiago
http://www.fco.gov.uk/directory/posts.asp?CL
The site provides contact information for the British Embassy in Santiago.

United States

State of Utah Office in Santiago
http://www.ce.ex.state.ut.us/international/reps/ reps.htm
A service of the State of Utah International Business Development Office, the site lists the name, street address, phone and fax numbers, and e-mail link of the state representative in Santiago.

United States Embassy in Chile
http://www.rdc.cl/~usemb/index.htm
Posted in English and Spanish, the site provides United States news, fact sheets, press releases, Summit of the Americas bulletins, Chilean market reports, and a directory of Embassy programs and commercial services.

United States Information Service in Santiago
http://www.rdc.cl/~usemb/usis/usis.htm
Part of a global network of United States Information Service offices online, the site features United States news, fact sheets, cultural bulletins, Summit of the Americas reports, electronic journals, and contact information.

Venezuela

Embassy of Venezuela in Santiago
http://www.cmet.net/emvenchi/
Along with Venezuelan news summaries, the virtual Embassy posts the street address, phone and fax numbers, and e-mail link of the Venezuelan Embassy in Santiago.

Colombia

Colombia Media

Colombia Media
http://www.mediainfo.com/emediajs/specific-geo.htm?region=colombia
Compiled by Editor and Publisher Interactive, the site is a directory of Colombian media sites online including magazines, newspapers, and radio stations.

Colombia Market Guides

Colombia Business Reports
http://italchambers.net/BusinessReports.html
Prepared by the Italian Chamber of Commerce and written in Italian, the site provides Colombian fact sheets, market reports, and commercial guides.

Colombia Country Brief

http://www.worldbank.org/cgi-bin/
sendoff.cgi?page=%2Fhtml%2Fextdr%2Foffrep%2
Flac%2Fco.htm
A service of the World Bank Group, the site provides Colombian population statistics, financial data, development reports, and economic forecasts.

Colombia Country Profile

http://www.tradenz.govt.nz/intelligence/profiles/
colombia.html
A service of the New Zealand Trade Development Board, the site provides Colombian economic statistics, market information, and business tips.

Colombia Country Report

http://www.state.gov/
www/issues/economic/trade_reports/
latin_america97/colombia97.html
Prepared by the U.S. Department of State, the site delivers information on Colombian exchange rates, debt management, barriers to U.S. trade, export subsidies, protection of U.S. intellectual property, and worker rights.

Colombia: A Country Study

http://lcweb2.loc.gov/frd/cs/cotoc.html
A service of the U.S. Library of Congress, the site delivers fact sheets on Colombian geography, population, agriculture, mining, manufacturing, and foreign economic relations.

Colombia InfoExport

http://www.infoexport.gc.ca/country-
e.asp?continent=Latin&country=37
A service of Foreign Affairs and International Trade Canada, the site provides Colombian commercial guides and market reports.

Colombia Market Access Database

http://mkaccdb.eu.int/mkdb/
mkdb.pl?METHOD=COUNTRY
A service of the European Commission, the site offers briefs on Colombian trade policy, tariff barriers, non-tariff barriers, investment-related measures, and financial services regulations.

Colombia Market Information

http://dtiinfo1.dti.gov.uk/ots/colombia/
A service of the London-based Department of Trade and Industry, the site delivers Colombian fact sheets, maps, and trade-show information.

Colombia Market Research

http://strategis.ic.gc.ca/sc_mrkti/ibinddc/engdoc/
1a1c14.html
A service of Industry Canada, the site provides

U.S. Department of Commerce reports on Colombian business, politics, trade regulations and standards, investment climate, trade and project financing, business travel, and market opportunities.

Colombia Passport System

http://www.getcustoms.com/col.html
A primer on Colombia business etiquette, the site explains how to negotiate, entertain, and arrange appointments in Colombia. The service includes Colombian quotations, travel guides, and a cultural quiz.

Colombia Reference Desk

http://lanic.utexas.edu/la/colombia/
Developed by the University of Texas at Austin, the site is a directory of leading Colombian arts, business, government, media, and travel resources online.

Colombian Economic Statistics

http://www.access.digex.net/~coltrade/2.htm
A service of the Colombian Government Trade Bureau, the site features Colombian sector profiles, investment guides, and a database of statistics on foreign trade, price indexes, exchange rates, and other economic indicators.

Colombian Organizations on the Web

http://www.access.digex.net/~coltrade/73.htm
Compiled by the Colombia Government Trade Bureau, the site is a directory of leading Colombian industry associations, government agencies, and companies on the Internet.

Colombian Yellow Pages

http://www.quehubo.com/
Posted in English and Spanish, the site is a searchable directory of Colombian telephone and fax numbers, cellular phones, and e-mail addresses.

Country Commercial Guide

http://www.state.gov/www/about_state/business/
com_guides/1998/latin_america/
colombia98.html
Prepared by the U.S. Embassy in Bogota, the site delivers primers on the Colombian economy, political environment, trade regulations and standards, investment climate, trade and project financing, and business travel.

Daily Investment Reporter

http://www.coinvertir.org.co/i/main.html
Updated daily, the site provides Colombian investment guides, sector profiles, economic

statistics, and primers on Colombian taxation, foreign exchange, labor law, and free zones.

Information Guide: Colombia
_http://www.i-trade.com/infosrc/pw//col/ col_menu.html_
Prepared by Price Waterhouse, the site provides primers on Colombian investment incentives, banking and finance, business entities, labor relations and social security, partnerships and joint ventures, and taxation.

Latinexpo
_http://www.latinexpo.com/latinexp/english/ home_e.htm_
Posted in English and Spanish, the site is a searchable database of Colombian companies in over 50 categories including books, clothing, electronics, footwear, machinery, plastics, and steel.

Paginas Amarillas
http://www.paginasamarillas.com/prototip/ princol.htm
An online telephone directory, the site provides listings from a dozen Colombian cities including Bogota, Bolívar, Boyaca, Bucaramanga, Caqueta, Girardot, Magdalena, and Medellín.

Colombia Trade Assistance

Colombia Customs Procedures
http://americas.fiu.edu/customs/colombia.htm
A service of Florida International University, the site reviews Colombian customs regulations, entry procedures, documentation, tariffs, and taxes.

Colombian Exporters
http://www1.colombiaexport.com/export/
An electronic directory of Colombian exporters and importers, the site profiles some 3,000 companies. The database is searchable by product, location, company name, target market, and harmonized system tariff code.

Colombian Government Trade Bureau
http://www.coltrade.org/
A government trade promotion service, the site provides Colombian export news, sector profiles, and primers on rules of origin, tariff schedules, and inspection certificates.

Guide to Imports in Colombia
http://www.colombiachamber.com/ guideimport.htm

Developed by the Colombian-American Chamber of Commerce, the site explains how to import into Colombia. Modules include the import process, documentation procedures, payment methods, and frequently asked questions.

Trade Point Cartagena
http://www.axisgate.com/trade/
Part of the United Nations Global Trade Point Network, the site provides Colombian trade leads, market bulletins, and contact information.

Trade Shows in Colombia
_http://www.expoguide.com/shows/data/loc_8.htm_
Compiled by Expoguide, the site is a directory of upcoming trade shows in Colombia.

Colombia Representative Offices

Austria

Austrian Trade Commission in Bogota
http://aw.wk.or.at/awo/ahst-bogota.htm
The site lists the staff, street address, phone and fax numbers, e-mail link, and office hours of the Austrian Trade Commission in Bogota.

Canada

Embassy of Canada in Bogota
http://www.dfait-maeci.gc.ca/english/missions/rep-can1e.htm#colombia
The site provides contact information for the Canadian Embassy in Bogota.

France

French Trade Commission in Bogota
http://www.dree.org/colombie/
Written in French, the site provides Colombian sector profiles, and a directory of export programs and services for French companies doing business in Colombia and Bogota.

Germany

German-Colombian Chamber of Commerce in Bogota
http://www.ahk-colombia.com/de/Colombia.htm
Written in German, the site provides German fact sheets, German-Colombian trade reports, and Chamber contact information.

Italy

Italian Trade Commission in Bogota
http://www.ice.it/estero/bogota/
Posted in Italian, the site delivers Italian fact sheets, visa and passport information, and a directory of Italian trade promotion programs and services.

Mexico

Trade Commission of Mexico in Bogota
http://www.mexico-businessline.com/ingles/ofrepmu3.html#colombia
The site lists the street address, phone and fax numbers, and e-mail link of the Mexican Trade Commission in Bogota.

Spain

Spanish Commercial Office in Bogota
http://www.icex.es/openURL.html#openURL=/english/infoproyem/ofcomes/ofcomes.html#AM
The site lists the staff, street address, phone and fax numbers, and e-mail link of the Spanish Commercial Office in Bogota.

Sweden

Embassy of Sweden in Bogota
http://www.ud.se/english/mfa/ambassad/colombia.htm
The site lists the staff, street address, phone and fax numbers, and e-mail link of the Swedish Embassy in Bogota.

United Kingdom

Embassy of Britain in Bogota
http://www.fco.gov.uk/directory/posts.asp?CO
The site provides contact information for the British Embassy in Bogota.

United States

United States Embassy in Bogota
http://www.usia.gov/abtusia/posts/CO1/wwwhmain.html
The virtual Embassy provides Colombian fact sheets and U.S. news, visa guides, sector profiles, business bulletins, government directories, and contact information.

United States Information Service in Bogota
http://www.usia.gov/abtusia/posts/CO1/wwwhusis.html
The online service delivers U.S. news, fact sheets, cultural bulletins, electronic journals, contact information, and reports on U.S.-Colombia trade.

Costa Rica

Costa Rica Media

Costa Rica Media
http://www.mediainfo.com/emediajs/specific-geo.htm?region=costarica
Compiled by Editor and Publisher Interactive, the site is a directory of Costa Rican media sites online such as magazines and newspapers.

Costa Rica Market Guides

Costa Rica Country Brief
http://www.worldbank.org/cgi-bin/sendoff.cgi?page=%2Fhtml%2Fextdr%2Foffrep%2Flac%2Fcr.htm
A service of the World Bank Group, the site provides Costa Rican population statistics, financial data, development reports, and economic forecasts.

Costa Rica Country Report
http://www.state.gov/www/issues/economic/trade_reports/latin_america97/costarica97.html
Prepared by the U.S. Department of State, the site delivers information on Costa Rican exchange rates, debt management, barriers to U.S. trade, export subsidies, protection of U.S. intellectual property, and worker rights.

Costa Rica InfoExport
http://www.infoexport.gc.ca/country-e.asp?continent=Latin&country=10
A service of Foreign Affairs and International Trade Canada, the site provides Costa Rican commercial guides and market reports.

Costa Rica Investment and Trade
http://www.cinde.or.cr/
Prepared by the Costa Rica Investment and Trade Development Board, the site features primers on Costa Rican infrastructure opportunities, environmental projects, and business incentive programs.

Costa Rica Market Research
_http://strategis.ic.gc.ca/sc_mrkti/ibinddc/engdoc/_
1a1c15.html
A service of Industry Canada, the site provides U.S. Department of Commerce reports on Costa Rican business, politics, trade regulations and standards, investment climate, trade and project financing, business travel, and market opportunities.

Costa Rica Reference Desk
http://lanic.utexas.edu/la/ca/cr/
Developed by the University of Texas at Austin, the site is a directory of leading Costa Rican arts, business, government, media, language, and travel resources online.

Costa Rican Company and Institutions Directory
http://www.cinde.or.cr/cindecgi/owa/main
Compiled by the Costa Rica Investment and Trade Development Board, the site is a searchable database of Costa Rican companies. Categories include agriculture, construction, manufacturing, retail, and transportation.

Government of Costa Rica
http://www.casapres.go.cr/
Written in Spanish, the site is a directory of Costa Rican government ministries and agencies online including the Departments of Foreign Trade, Energy, and Housing.

Paginas Blancas
http://200.9.47.5/buscarpf.htm
An online telephone directory, the site provides listings from Costa Rica's seven provinces: Alajuela, Cartago, Guanacaste, Heredia, Limon, Puntarenas, and San Jose.

Costa Rica Trade Assistance

Costa Rica Customs Procedures
http://americas.fiu.edu/customs/costaric.htm
A service of Florida International University, the site reviews Costa Rican customs regulations, entry procedures, documentation, tariffs, and taxes.

Procomer
http://www.procomer.com/english/
An export promotion service of the Costa Rican government, the site delivers Costa Rican business guides, economic statistics, and sector profiles. The service includes a database of

Costa Rican international companies in 20 categories including agri-food, plastics, chemicals, and building materials.

Trade Shows in Costa Rica
_http://www.expoguide.com/shows/data/loc_9.htm_
Compiled by Expoguide, the site is a directory of upcoming trade shows in Costa Rica.

Costa Rica Representative Offices

Canada

Embassy of Canada in San Jose
http://www.dfait-maeci.gc.ca/english/missions/rep-
can1e.htm#costa rica
The site provides contact information for the Canadian Embassy in San Jose.

Chile

Consulate General of Chile in San Jose
http://www.infoweb.co.cr/chile/
The virtual Consulate provides Chilean fact sheets, product catalogs, business guides, a calendar of events, Chile-Costa Rica trade reports, and contact information.

Italy

Embassy of Italy in San Jose
http://www.ambitcr.com/
Written in Italian, the site provides Italian fact sheets and statistics, Costa Rican sector profiles and consular information, and Belizian situation reports and economic bulletins.

Mexico

Trade Commission of Mexico in San Jose
http://www.mexico-businessline.com/ingles/
ofrepmu3.html#costa
The site lists the street address, phone and fax numbers, and e-mail link of the Mexican Trade Commission in San Jose.

Sweden

Consulate General of Sweden in San Jose
http://www.ud.se/english/mfa/ambassad/
costaric.htm
The site lists the staff, street address, phone and fax numbers, and e-mail link of the Swedish Consulate General in San Jose.

Taiwan

Taiwan Government Information Office in San Jose
http://www.gio.gov.tw/info/ngio/costa-f.html
Posted in Chinese and English, the site lists the street address, phone and fax numbers, and e-mail link of the Taiwan Government Information Office in San Jose.

United Kingdom

Embassy of Britain in San Jose
http://www.fco.gov.uk/directory/posts.asp?CB
The site provides contact information for the British Embassy in San Jose.

United States

Costa Rican-American Chamber of Commerce
http://www.crica.com/amcham.html
Based in San Jose, the Chamber promotes Costa Rica-America business. The site includes an electronic magazine, online bulletin board, membership directory, and a calendar of events.

United States Embassy in San Jose
http://usembassy.or.cr/
Along with United States fact sheets, the virtual Embassy provides Costa Rican market reports, commercial guides, bilateral trade bulletins, and updates on the Free Trade Area of the Americas.

Venezuela

Embassy of Venezuela in San Jose
http://www.trade-venezuela.com/EMBVENG.HTM
The site lists the street address, phone and fax numbers, and e-mail link of the Venezuelan Embassy in San Jose.

Cuba

Cuba Media

Cuba Media
http://www.mediainfo.com/emediajs/specific-geo.htm?region=cuba
Compiled by Editor and Publisher Interactive, the site is a directory of Cuban media sites online including magazines, newspapers, and news syndicates.

Cuba Market Guides

Business Tips on Cuba
http://www.tips.cu/
Posted in eight languages including Arabic and Russian, the site provides Cuban headlines, editorials, interviews, business opportunities, market bulletins, and legislative news.

Cuba InfoExport
http://www.infoexport.gc.ca/country-e.asp?continent=Latin&country=11
A service of Foreign Affairs and International Trade Canada, the site provides Cuban commercial guides and market reports.

Cuba Market Information
http://dtiinfo1.dti.gov.uk/ots/cuba/
A service of the London-based Department of Trade and Industry, the site delivers Cuban fact sheets, maps, and trade-show information.

Cuba Market Research
http://strategis.ic.gc.ca/sc_mrkti/ibinddc/engdoc/1a1c16.html
Posted by Industry Canada, the site provides U.S. Central Intelligence Agency fact sheets on Cuban geography, people, government, economy, communications, and transportation.

Cuba Reference Desk
http://lanic.utexas.edu/la/cb/cuba/
Developed by the University of Texas at Austin, the site is a directory of leading Cuban arts, business, government, media, and travel resources online.

CubaWeb
http://www.cubaweb.com/eng/index.html
A Cuban virtual library, the site features news, maps, editorials, classifieds, cultural bulletins, an event calendar, economic statistics, investment guides, and reports on Cuban and U.S. legislation.

Cuba Trade Assistance

Trade Shows in Cuba
http://www.expoguide.com/shows/data/loc_10.htm
Compiled by Expoguide, the site is a directory of upcoming trade shows in Cuba.

Cuba Representative Offices

Canada

Embassy of Canada in Havana
http://www.dfait-maeci.gc.ca/english/missions/rep-can1e.htm#cuba
The site provides contact information for the Canadian Embassy in Havana.

Ghana

Embassy of Ghana in Havana
http://www.juntung.com/ghana-consul-hk/2misabo.htm
The site provides contact information for the Ghanaian Embassy in Havana.

Laos

Embassy of Laos in Havana
http://www.laoembassy.com/news/embassyabroad.htm
The site provides contact information for the Embassy of Laos in Havana.

Namibia

Embassy of Namibia in Havana
http://www.republicofnamibia.com/adress.htm
Along with a directory of Namibian companies and government agencies, the site provides contact information for the Namibian Embassy in Havana.

Spain

Spanish Commercial Office in Havana
http://www.icex.es/openURL.html#openURL=/english/infoproyem/ofcomes/ofcomes.html#AM
The site lists the staff, street address, phone and fax numbers, and e-mail link of the Spanish Commercial Office in Havana.

Sweden

Embassy of Sweden in Havana
http://www.ud.se/english/mfa/ambassad/cuba.htm
The site lists the staff, street address, phone and fax numbers, and e-mail link of the Swedish Embassy in Havana.

United Kingdom

Embassy of Britain in Havana
http://www.fco.gov.uk/directory/posts.asp?CU
The site provides contact information for the British Embassy in Havana.

United States

United States Information Service in Havana
http://www.usia.gov/abtusia/posts/CU1/wwwhmain.html
The site features U.S. fact sheets, policy statements and legislation on Cuba, migration reports, human rights bulletins, and updates on the Summit of the Americas.

Venezuela

Embassy of Venezuela in Havana
http://www.trade-venezuela.com/EMBVENG.HTM
The site lists the street address, phone and fax numbers, and e-mail link of the Venezuelan Embassy in Havana.

Dominica

Dominica Media

The Chronicle
http://www.delphis.dm/chron.htm
An online newspaper, the site provides news, editorials, business reports and entertainment bulletins from the Commonwealth of Dominica.

Dominica Market Guides

Dominica: The Basics
http://www.delphis.dm/basics.htm
Sponsored by Nature Island Destinations, the site features Dominican news, maps, nature guides, accommodation directories, cultural bulletins, and tourism information.

Dominica Country Brief
http://www.worldbank.org/cgi-bin/sendoff.cgi?page=%2Fhtml%2Fextdr%2Foffrep%2Flac%2Fdm.htm
A service of the World Bank Group, the site provides Dominican population statistics, financial data, development reports, and economic forecasts.

Dominica InfoExport
http://www.infoexport.gc.ca/country-e.asp?continent=Latin&country=12
A service of Foreign Affairs and International Trade Canada, the site provides fact sheets and statistics on Dominican geography, business and politics.

Dominica Market Research
http://strategis.ic.gc.ca/sc_mrkti/ibinddc/engdoc/1a1c18.html
Posted by Industry Canada, the site provides U.S. Central Intelligence Agency fact sheets on Dominican geography, people, government, economy, communications, and transportation.

Dominica Trade Assistance

Dominica Customs Procedures
http://americas.fiu.edu/customs/dominica.htm
A service of Florida International University, the site reviews Dominican customs regulations, entry procedures, documentation, tariffs, and taxes.

International Promotions for Dominica
http://www.domini-inc.com/
Based in Roseau, the site delivers Dominican fact sheets, real estate listings, investment opportunities, sector profiles, and primers on economic citizenship, offshore trusts, and international ship registration.

Dominica Representative Offices

Sweden

Consulate of Sweden in Roseau
http://www.ud.se/english/mfa/ambassad/dominica.htm
The site lists the staff, street address, and phone and fax numbers of the Swedish Consulate in Roseau.

United Kingdom

High Commission of Britain in Roseau
http://www.fco.gov.uk/directory/posts.asp?DO
The site provides contact information for the British High Commission in Roseau.

Dominican Republic

Dominican Republic Media

Dominican Republic Media
http://www.mediainfo.com/emediajs/specific-geo.htm?region=dominicanrepublic
Compiled by Editor and Publisher Interactive, the site is a directory of Dominican Republic media sites online including magazines, newspapers, and radio stations.

Dominican Republic Market Guides

Central Bank of the Dominican Republic
http://www.bancentral.gov.do/
Written in Spanish, the site provides Dominican Republic sector profiles, price indexes, international trade reports, economic statistics, and government budgetary information.

Dominican Republic Country Brief
http://www.worldbank.org/cgi-bin/sendoff.cgi?page=%2Fhtml%2Fextdr%2Foffrep%2Flac%2Fdo.htm
A service of the World Bank Group, the site provides Dominican Republic population statistics, financial data, development reports, and economic forecasts.

Dominican Republic Country Report
http://www.state.gov/www/issues/economic/trade_reports/latin_america97/dominican97.html
Prepared by the U.S. Department of State, the site delivers information on Dominican Republic exchange rates, debt management, barriers to U.S. trade, export subsidies, and intellectual property protection.

Dominican Republic: A Country Study
http://lcweb2.loc.gov/frd/cs/dotoc.html
A service of the U.S. Library of Congress, the site delivers fact sheets on Dominican Republic geography, population, agriculture, mining, manufacturing, and foreign economic relations.

Dominican Republic InfoExport
http://www.infoexport.gc.ca/country-e.asp?continent=Latin&country=13
A service of Foreign Affairs and International Trade Canada, the site provides Dominican Republic commercial guides and market reports.

Dominican Republic Market Research
http://strategis.ic.gc.ca/sc_mrkti/ibinddc/engdoc/
1a1c17.html
A service of Industry Canada, the site provides U.S. Department of Commerce reports on Dominican business, politics, trade regulations and standards, investment climate, trade and project financing, business travel, and market opportunities.

Dominican Republic One
http://209.41.4.222/index.shtml
An online information service, the site features Dominican Republic daily news, travel information, a resort database, classifieds, relocation primers, and an electronic message board.

Dominican Republic Reference Desk
http://lanic.utexas.edu/la/cb/dr/
Compiled by the University of Texas at Austin, the site is a directory of leading Dominican Republic arts, business, government, media, and travel resources online.

Santo Domingo Chamber of Commerce
http://ccpsd.org.do/
Written in Spanish, the site provides a Chamber mission statement, event calendar, member directory, and calendar of events.

Dominican Republic Trade Assistance

Dominican Republic Customs Procedures
http://americas.fiu.edu/customs/domrep.htm
A service of Florida International University, the site reviews Dominican Republic customs regulations, entry procedures, documentation, tariffs, and taxes.

Itabo Industrial Park
http://www.piisa.com/
Situated ten miles west of Santo Domingo, the Park is a manufacturing facility and free trade zone. The website provides fact sheets about the operation, and a directory of services and staff.

Dominican Republic Representative Offices

Canada

Embassy of Canada in Santo Domingo
http://www.dfait-maeci.gc.ca/english/missions/rep-
can1e.htm#dominican republic
The site provides contact information for the Canadian Embassy in Santo Domingo.

China

China Council for the Promotion of International Trade in Santo Domingo
http://www.ccpit.org/engVersion/cp_about/cp_over
/cp_over.html
A Chinese export promotion service, the site provides contact information for the China Council for the Promotion of International Trade office in Santo Domingo.

Spain

Spanish Commercial Office in Santo Domingo
http://www.icex.es/openURL.html#openURL=/
english/infoproyem/ofcomes/ofcomes.html#AM
The site lists the staff, street address, phone and fax numbers, and e-mail link of the Spanish Commercial Office in Santo Domingo.

Sweden

Consulate General of Sweden in Santo Domingo
http://www.ud.se/english/mfa/ambassad/
domrep.htm
The site lists the staff, street address, phone and fax numbers, and e-mail link of the Swedish Consulate General in Santo Domingo.

Taiwan

Taiwan Government Information Office in Santo Domingo
http://www.gio.gov.tw/info/ngio/domin-f.html
Posted in Chinese and English, the site lists the street address, phone and fax numbers, and e-mail link of the Taiwan Government Information Office in Santo Domingo.

United Kingdom

Embassy of Britain in Santo Domingo
http://www.fco.gov.uk/directory/posts.asp?DM
The site provides contact information for the British Embassy in Santo Domingo.

United States

American Chamber of Commerce of the Dominican Republic
http://www.amcham.org.do/
Based in Santo Domingo, the site promotes American-Dominican Republic trade. The site includes a Dominican Republic commercial directory, taxation reports, and legislative bulletins.

Ecuador

Ecuador Media

Ecuador Media
http://www.mediainfo.com/emediajs/specific-geo.htm?region=ecuador
Compiled by Editor and Publisher Interactive, the site is a directory of Dominican Republic media sites online such as magazines and newspapers.

Ecuador Market Guides

Country Commercial Guide
http://www.state.gov/www/about_state/business/com_guides/1998/latin_america/ecuador98.html
Prepared by the U.S. Embassy in Quito, the site delivers primers on the Ecuadorian economy, political environment, trade regulations and standards, investment climate, trade and project financing, and business travel.

Ecuador Country Brief
http://www.worldbank.org/cgi-bin/sendoff.cgi?page=%2Fhtml%2Fextdr%2Foffrep%2Flac%2Fec.htm
A service of the World Bank Group, the site provides Ecuadorian population statistics, financial data, development reports, and economic forecasts.

Ecuador Country Profile
http://www.tradenz.govt.nz/intelligence/profiles/ecuador.html
A service of the New Zealand Trade Development Board, the site provides Ecuadorian economic statistics, market information, and business tips.

Ecuador Country Report
http://www.state.gov/www/issues/economic/trade_reports/latin_america97/ecuador97.html
Prepared by the U.S. Department of State, the site delivers information on Ecuadorian exchange rates, debt management, barriers to U.S. trade, export subsidies, and intellectual property protection.

Ecuador: A Country Study
http://lcweb2.loc.gov/frd/cs/ectoc.html
A service of the U.S. Library of Congress, the site delivers fact sheets on Ecuadorian geography, population, agriculture, mining, manufacturing, and foreign economic relations.

Ecuador InfoExport
http://www.infoexport.gc.ca/country-e.asp?continent=Latin&country=38
A service of Foreign Affairs and International Trade Canada, the site provides Ecuadorian commercial guides and market reports.

Ecuador Market Research
http://strategis.ic.gc.ca/sc_mrkti/ibinddc/engdoc/1a1c19.html
A service of Industry Canada, the site provides U.S. Department of Commerce reports on Ecuadorian business, politics, trade regulations and standards, investment climate, trade and project financing, business travel, and market opportunities.

Ecuador Reference Desk
http://lanic.utexas.edu/la/ecuador/
Developed by the University of Texas at Austin, the site is a directory of leading Ecuadorian arts, business, government, media, and travel resources online.

EcuaNet
http://www3.ecua.net.ec/
Written in Spanish, the site provides Ecuadorian business primers, tourism guides, education reports, arts and culture bulletins, online chat services, and a directory of industry associations.

Information Guide: Ecuador
http://www.i-trade.com/infosrc/pw/ecu/TOC.htm
Prepared by Price Waterhouse, the site reviews Ecuadorian investment incentives, banking and finance, labor relations and social security, audit requirements, taxation regulations, partnerships, and joint ventures.

Ecuador Trade Assistance

Ecuador Customs Procedures
http://americas.fiu.edu/customs/ecuador.htm
A service of Florida International University, the site reviews Ecuadorian customs regulations, entry procedures, documentation, tariffs, and taxes.

Ecuador Embassies Online
http://www.mmrree.gov.ec/mreini/webs1.htm
A service of the Ecuador Ministry of Foreign Affairs, the site is a directory of Ecuadorian Embassies online in Austria, El Salvador, Japan, Sweden, and the United States.

Ecuador Ministry of Foreign Affairs
http://www.mmrree.gov.ec/
Posted in English and Spanish, the site provides Ecuadorian news, foreign policy statements, tourism guides, history lessons, and a directory of Ministry programs and services.

Ecuadorian Foreign Trade
http://www.eacc.org/trade.html
Developed by the Ecuadorian-American Chamber of Commerce, the site delivers Ecuadorian export and import statistics, airport and port profiles, and a directory of government agencies and industry associations that promote international trade.

Exports
http://www.ecuador.org/trdinv2.htm
The online service reports on Ecuadorian commodity exports including bananas, cocoa, coffee, flowers, fruits, gold, sea products, vegetables, wood and timber.

Trade and Investment
http://www.ecuador.org/trade.htm
A service of the Ecuadorian Embassy in Washington, the site delivers Ecuadorian trade fact sheets, policy statements, investment guides, and a directory of international trade contacts.

Ecuador Representative Offices

Canada

Embassy of Canada in Quito
http://www.dfait-maeci.gc.ca/english/missions/rep-can2e.htm#ecuador
The site provides contact information for the Canadian Embassy in Quito.

France

French Trade Commission in Quito
http://www.dree.org/equateur/
Written in French, the site provides Ecuadorian sector profiles, and a directory of export programs and services for French companies doing business in Ecuador.

Germany

German Chamber of Commerce in Quito
http://www.ahk.net/chambers/ec/
Posted in German and Spanish, the site provides Ecuadorian fact sheets, German-Ecuador trade reports, and contact information for the German Chamber in Quito.

Mexico

Trade Commission of Mexico in Quito
http://www.mexico-businessline.com/ingles/ofrepmu3.html#ecuador
The site lists the street address, phone and fax number, and e-mail link of the Mexican Trade Commission in Quito.

Spain

Spanish Commercial Office in Quito
http://www.icex.es/openURL.html#openURL=/english/infoproyem/ofcomes/ofcomes.html#AM
The site lists the staff, street address, phone and fax numbers, and e-mail link of the Spanish Commercial Office in Quito.

Sweden

Consulate General of Sweden in Quito
http://www.ud.se/english/mfa/ambassad/ecuador.htm
The site lists the staff, street address, phone and fax numbers, and e-mail link of the Swedish Consulate General in Quito.

United Kingdom

Embassy of Britain in Quito
http://www.fco.gov.uk/directory/posts.asp?EC
The site provides contact information for the British Embassy in Quito.

United States

United States Embassy in Ecuador
http://www.usis.org.ec/
Posted in English and Spanish, the site delivers U.S. news, fact sheets, government bulletins, travel information, and a directory of Embassy programs and services.

El Salvador

El Salvador Media

El Salvador Media
http://www.mediainfo.com/emediajs/specific-geo.htm?region=elsalvador
Compiled by Editor and Publisher Interactive, the

site is a directory of Salvadoran media sites online.

El Salvador Market Guides

Economy and Business
http://www.el-salvador.org.il/ecobus.htm
A service of the Salvadoran Embassy in Washington, D.C., the site is a directory of leading international companies, product catalogs, free trade zones, and business contacts in El Salvador.

El Salvador Country Brief
http://www.worldbank.org/cgi-bin/ sendoff.cgi?page=%2Fhtml%2Fextdr%2Foffrep%2 Flac%2Fsv.htm
A service of the World Bank Group, the site provides Salvadoran population statistics, financial data, development reports, and economic forecasts.

El Salvador Country Report
http://www.state.gov/www/issues/economic/ trade_reports/latin_america97/elsalvador97.html
Prepared by the U.S. Department of State, the site delivers information on Salvadoran exchange rates, debt management, barriers to U.S. trade, export subsidies, and intellectual property protection.

El Salvador: A Country Study
http://lcweb2.loc.gov/frd/cs/svtoc.html
A service of the U.S. Library of Congress, the site delivers fact sheets on Salvadoran geography, population, agriculture, mining, manufacturing, and foreign economic relations.

El Salvador InfoCenter
http://www.elsalvador.nu/
Posted in Spanish, the site features Salvadoran business primers, tourism guides, education bulletins, weather reports, government directories, and history lessons.

El Salvador InfoExport
http://www.infoexport.gc.ca/country-e.asp?continent=Latin&country=14
A service of Foreign Affairs and International Trade Canada, the site provides Salvadoran commercial guides and market reports.

El Salvador Market Research
http://strategis.ic.gc.ca/sc_mrkti/ibinddc/engdoc/ 1a1c20.html

A service of Industry Canada, the site provides U.S. Department of Commerce reports on Salvadoran business, politics, trade regulations and standards, investment climate, trade and project financing, business travel, and market opportunities.

El Salvador On-line Resources
http://www.nortropic.com/el_salvador/index.html
The online service provides a directory of Salvadoran news, weather, tourism, business, and education resources on the web.

El Salvador Reference Desk
http://lanic.utexas.edu/la/ca/salvador/
Developed by the University of Texas at Austin, the site is a directory of leading Salvadoran arts, business, government, media, and travel resources online.

El Salvador Trade Assistance

El Salvador Customs Procedures
http://americas.fiu.edu/customs/elsal.htm
A service of Florida International University, the site reviews Salvadoran customs regulations, entry procedures, documentation, tariffs, and taxes.

El Salvador Ministry of Foreign Affairs
http://www.rree.gob.sv/sitio/sitio.nsf
The federal government site delivers Salvadoran press releases, foreign policy statements, visa and passport information, economic reports, and cultural bulletins.

El Salvador Representative Offices

Brazil

Embassy of Brazil in San Salvador
http://www.netcomsa.com/embbrasil/
Posted in English and Portuguese, the site includes Brazilian news, fact sheets, Brazil-El Salvador trade reports, and a directory of Embassy programs and services.

Canada

Embassy of Canada in San Salvador
http://www.dfait-maeci.gc.ca/english/missions/rep-can2e.htm#el salvador
The site provides contact information for the Canadian Embassy in San Salvador.

Mexico

Trade Commission of Mexico in San Salvador
_http://www.mexico-businessline.com/ingles/
ofrepmu3.html#salvador_
The site lists the street address, phone and fax
numbers, and e-mail link of the Mexican Trade
Commission in San Salvador.

Spain

Spanish Commercial Office in San Salvador
_http://www.icex.es/openURL.html#openURL=/
english/infoproyem/ofcomes/ofcomes.html#AM_
The site lists the staff, street address, phone and
fax numbers, and e-mail link of the Spanish
Commercial Office in San Salvador.

Sweden

Consulate General of Sweden in San Salvador
_http://www.ud.se/english/mfa/ambassad/
elsalvad.htm_
The site lists the staff, street address, phone and
fax numbers, and e-mail link of the Swedish
Consulate General in San Salvador.

Taiwan

Taiwan Government Information Office in San Salvador
http://www.gio.gov.tw/info/ngio/salva-f.html
Posted in Chinese and English, the site lists the
street address, phone and fax numbers, and e-
mail link of the Taiwan Government Information
Office in San Salvador.

United Kingdom

Embassy of Britain in San Salvador
http://www.fco.gov.uk/directory/posts.asp?EL
The site provides contact information for the
British Embassy in San Salvador.

United States

United States Embassy in San Salvador
http://www.usinfo.org.sv/
Along with U.S. fact sheets and consular information, the site delivers Salvadoran commercial
guides, legislative bulletins, sector profiles,
economic forecasts, and investment reports.

Venezuela

Embassy of Venezuela in San Salvador
http://www.trade-venezuela.com/EMBVENG.HTM
The site lists the street address, phone and fax
numbers, and e-mail link of the Venezuelan
Embassy in San Salvador.

French Guiana

French Guiana Market Guides

Destination French Guiana
http://www.lonelyplanet.com.au/dest/sam/fgu.htm
Developed by Lonely Planet, the site features
French Guianese maps, quick facts, economic
profiles, history lessons, cultural bulletins, and
tourism guides.

French Guiana Economy
_http://www.theodora.com/wfb/
french_guiana_economy.html_
A fact sheet on the French Guiana economy, the
site provides information and data on gross
domestic product, unemployment, budget
revenues and expenditures, exports and imports,
and exchange rates.

French Guiana InfoExport
_http://www.infoexport.gc.ca/country-
e.asp?continent=Latin&country=40_
A service of Foreign Affairs and International
Trade Canada, the site provides fact sheets and
statistics on French Guianese geography,
business and politics.

French Guiana Reference Desk
http://lanic.utexas.edu/la/ca/other/fg/
Developed by the University of Texas at Austin,
the site is a directory of leading French Guianese
information and travel resources online.

French Guiana Trade Assistance

French Guiana Essential Information
_http://www.gcc.net/commerce/chamber/caribe/
frengian.htm_
A service of the Global Chamber of Commerce,
the site provides French Guianese fact sheets,
and directories of leading business associations
and international trade organizations.

Grenada

Grenada Media

Grenadian Voice
http://www.spiceisle.com/homepages/gvoice/
Updated weekly, the online newspaper provides Grenadian news, editorials, business features, political reports, entertainment bulletins, and a four-month news archive.

Grenada Market Guides

Grenada Country Brief
http://www.worldbank.org/cgi-bin/ sendoff.cgi?page=%2Fhtml%2Fextdr%2Foffrep%2 Flac%2Fgd.htm
A service of the World Bank Group, the site provides Grenadian population statistics, financial data, development reports, and economic forecasts.

Grenada InfoExport
http://www.infoexport.gc.ca/country-e.asp?continent=Latin&country=15
A service of Foreign Affairs and International Trade Canada, the site provides fact sheets and statistics on Grenadian geography, business and politics.

Grenada Market Research
http://strategis.ic.gc.ca/sc_mrkti/ibinddc/engdoc/ 1a1c23.html
Posted by Industry Canada, the site provides U.S. Central Intelligence Agency fact sheets on Grenadian geography, people, government, economy, communications, and transportation.

Grenada: Recent Economic Developments
http://www.imf.org/external/pubs/CAT/ longres.cfm?sk=2464.0
Prepared by the International Monetary Fund, the site reports on labor market developments, poverty alleviation programs, environmental protection, tourism trends, and external debt in Grenada.

Grenada Trade Assistance

Grenada Customs Procedures
http://americas.fiu.edu/customs/grenada.htm
A service of Florida International University, the site reviews Grenadian customs regulations, entry procedures, documentation, tariffs, and taxes.

Grenada Representative Offices

Sweden

Consulate of Sweden in St. George's
http://www.ud.se/english/mfa/ambassad/ grenada.htm
The site lists the staff, street address, phone and fax numbers, and e-mail link of the Swedish Consulate in St. George's.

Taiwan

Taiwan Government Information Office in St. George's
http://www.gio.gov.tw/info/ngio/grena-f.html
Posted in Chinese and English, the site lists the street address, phone and fax numbers, and e-mail link of the Taiwan Government Information Office in St. George's.

United Kingdom

High Commission of Britain in St. George's
http://www.fco.gov.uk/directory/posts.asp?GN
The site provides contact information for the British High Commission in St. George's.

United States

United States Embassy in St. George's
http://www.spiceisle.com/homepages/usemb_gd/
The virtual Embassy provides U.S. visa information, an event calendar, and a directory of Embassy services and staff.

Guadeloupe

Guadeloupe Market Guides

Data for Guadeloupe
http://www.antilles-info-business.com/ guadeloupe/busfragb.htm
The online service delivers Guadeloupe fact sheets, maps, company directories, a calendar of events, sector profiles, international trade reports, and demographic information.

Guadeloupe InfoExport
http://www.infoexport.gc.ca/country-e.asp?continent=Latin&country=16
A service of Foreign Affairs and International Trade Canada, the site provides fact sheets and statistics on Guadeloupe geography, business and politics.

Guadeloupe Market Research
http://strategis.ic.gc.ca/sc_mrkti/ibinddc/engdoc/1a1c24.html
Posted by Industry Canada, the site provides U.S. Central Intelligence Agency fact sheets on Guadeloupe geography, people, government, economy, communications, and transportation.

Guadeloupe Reference Desk
http://lanic.utexas.edu/la/ca/other/guad/
Compiled by the University of Texas at Austin, the site is a directory of leading Guadeloupe arts, business, government, media, and travel resources online.

Guadeloupe Trade Assistance

World Trade Center in Guadeloupe
http://www.antilles-info-business.com/guadeloupe/wtc-us.htm
Posted in English and French, the site provides fact sheets and contact information for the Guadeloupe World Trade Center.

Guatemala

Guatemala Media

Guatemala Media
http://www.mediainfo.com/emediajs/specific-geo.htm?region=guatemala
Compiled by Editor and Publisher Interactive, the site is a directory of Guatemalan media sites online including magazines, newspapers, and radio stations.

Guatemala News Watch
http://www.quetzalnet.com/newswatch/
Updated monthly, the electronic magazine provides Guatemalan news summaries, sector profiles, and economic statistics.

Guatemala Market Guides

Country Commercial Guide
http://www.state.gov/www/about_state/business/com_guides/1998/latin_america/guatemala98.html
Prepared by the U.S. Embassy in Guatemala City, the site delivers primers on Guatemalan business, politics, trade regulations and standards, investment climate, trade and project financing, and business travel.

Guatemala Business Guidebook
http://www.quetzalnet.com/quetzalNET/Bus_Guide.html
Prepared by the Guatemalan Development Foundation, the site delivers primers on Guatemalan taxation, business entities, labor laws, environmental legislation, and trademark and patent rules.

Guatemala Country Brief
http://www.worldbank.org/cgi-bin/sendoff.cgi?page=%2Fhtml%2Fextdr%2Foffrep%2Flac%2Fgt.htm
A service of the World Bank Group, the site provides Guatemalan population statistics, financial data, development reports, and economic forecasts.

Guatemala Country Report
http://www.state.gov/www/issues/economic/trade_reports/latin_america97/guatemala97.html
Prepared by the U.S. Department of State, the site delivers information on Guatemalan exchange rates, debt management, barriers to U.S. trade, export subsidies, and intellectual property protection.

Guatemala InfoExport
http://www.infoexport.gc.ca/country-e.asp?continent=Latin&country=17
A service of Foreign Affairs and International Trade Canada, the site provides Guatemalan commercial guides and market reports.

Guatemala Market Research
http://strategis.ic.gc.ca/sc_mrkti/ibinddc/engdoc/1a1c25.html
A service of Industry Canada, the site provides U.S. Department of Commerce reports on Guatemalan business, politics, trade regulations and standards, investment climate, trade and project financing, business travel, and market opportunities.

Guatemala Online
http://www.quetzalnet.com/default.html
The online service provides Guatemalan fact sheets, sector profiles, economic statistics, company directories, investment guides, and tourism bulletins.

Guatemala Reference Desk
http://lanic.utexas.edu/la/ca/guatemala/
Developed by the University of Texas at Austin, the site is a directory of leading Guatemalan arts,

business, education, government, media, language, and travel resources online.

Guatemala Trade Assistance

AGEXPRONT
http://www.quetzalnet.com/gexpront/default.html
Homepage of the Non Traditional Products Exporters Association of Guatemala, the site features company directories, sector profiles, international trade statistics, and a database of international market prices for fruits, vegetables and flowers.

Exporters in Guatemala
http://www.infoguate.com/business/exporters.htm
A service of Infoguate, the site posts a list of Guatemalan agri-food and handicraft exporters.

Guatemala Customs Procedures
http://americas.fiu.edu/customs/guatemal.htm
A service of Florida International University, the site reviews Guatemala customs regulations, entry procedures, documentation, tariffs, and taxes.

One-Step Export Bureau
http://www.quetzalnet.com/quetzalNET/Bus_Guide.html#27
Prepared by the Guatemalan Development Foundation, the site provides backgrounders on Guatemalan tariff exemptions, tax abatements, and free trade zones.

Trade Point Guatemala
http://www.tradepoint.org.gt/indexe.html
Based in Guatemala City, the site delivers Guatemalan news, statistics, business primers, company directories, customs information, tourism guides, and a buy and sell message board.

Guatemala Representative Offices

Canada

Embassy of Canada in Guatemala City
http://www.dfait-maeci.gc.ca/english/missions/rep-can2e.htm#guatemala
The site provides contact information for the Canadian Embassy in Guatemala City.

France

French Trade Commission in Guatemala City
http://www.dree.org/guatemala/

Written in French and Spanish, the site provides Guatemalan market studies, and a directory of export programs and services for French companies doing business in Central America and Guatemala.

Mexico

Trade Commission of Mexico in Guatemala City
http://www.mexico-businessline.com/ingles/ofrepmu3.html#guatemala
The site lists the street address, phone and fax numbers, and e-mail link of the Mexican Trade Commission in Guatemala City.

Spain

Spanish Commercial Office in Guatemala City
http://www.icex.es/openURL.html#openURL=/english/infoproyem/ofcomes/ofcomes.html#AM
The site lists the staff, street address, phone and fax numbers, and e-mail link of the Spanish Commercial Office in Guatemala City.

Sweden

Embassy of Sweden in Guatemala
http://www.ud.se/english/mfa/ambassad/guatemal.htm
The site lists the staff, street address, phone and fax numbers, and e-mail link of the Swedish Embassy in Guatemala City.

Taiwan

Taiwan Government Information Office in Guatemala City
http://www.gio.gov.tw/info/ngio/guat-f.html
Posted in Chinese and English, the site lists the street address, phone and fax numbers, and e-mail link of the Taiwan Government Information Office in Guatemala City.

United Kingdom

Embassy of Britain in Guatemala City
http://www.fco.gov.uk/directory/posts.asp?GU
The site provides contact information for the British Embassy in Guatemala City.

United States

American Chamber of Commerce of Guatemala
http://www.guatenet.com/amcham/
Based in Guatemala City, the Chamber promotes

United States-Guatemala trade. The site includes news, contact information, a staff directory, a calendar of events, and employment opportunities.

Venezuela

Embassy of Venezuela in Guatemala City
http://www.trade-venezuela.com/EMBVENG.HTM
The site lists the street address, phone and fax numbers, and e-mail link of the Venezuelan Embassy in Guatemala City.

Guyana

Guyana Media

Stabroek News
http://www.stabroeknews.com/
Based in Georgetown, the site delivers Guyanese news, editorials, letters, business features, and tourism information.

Guyana Market Guides

Guyana Country Brief
http://www.worldbank.org/cgi-bin/sendoff.cgi?page=%2Fhtml%2Fextdr%2Foffrep%2Flac%2Fgy.htm
A service of the World Bank Group, the site provides Guyanese population statistics, financial data, development reports, and economic forecasts.

Guyana: A Country Study
http://lcweb2.loc.gov/frd/cs/gytoc.html
A service of the U.S. Library of Congress, the site delivers fact sheets on Guyanese geography, population, agriculture, mining, manufacturing, and foreign economic relations.

Guyana Economy and Investment
http://www.guyana.org/Economy/economy.htm
The online service provides Guyanese business news, socioeconomic data, commercial guides, investment primers, foreign aid reports, and legislative bulletins.

Guyana InfoExport
http://www.infoexport.gc.ca/country-e.asp?continent=Latin&country=41
A service of Foreign Affairs and International Trade Canada, the site provides Guyanese commercial guides and market reports.

Guyana Market Research
http://strategis.ic.gc.ca/sc_mrkti/ibinddc/engdoc/1a1c26.html
A service of Industry Canada, the site provides U.S. Department of Commerce reports on Guyanese economic trends, politics, trade regulations and standards, investment climate, trade and project financing, business travel, and market opportunities.

Guyana News and Information
http://www.guyana.org/
A virtual library of information, the site features Guyanese news, maps, a virtual handbook, photo gallery, community announcements, political reports, speeches, press releases, and an online discussion forum.

Guyana Reference Desk
http://lanic.utexas.edu/la/sa/guyana/
Developed by the University of Texas at Austin, the site is a directory of leading Guyanese arts, business, government, media, and travel resources online.

Guyana: Statistical Appendix
http://www.imf.org/external/pubs/CAT/longres.cfm?sk=2498.0
Prepared by the International Monetary Fund, the site provides data on Guyanese output, savings and investments, price movements, population, employment, and public sector finances.

Guyana Trade Assistance

Export Products of Guyana
http://www.guyana.org/Economy/guyana_exports.htm
Compiled by the Guyana Export Promotion Council, the site is a directory of Guyanese export products including rice, fish, sugar, gold, furniture, electrical appliances, chemicals, pharmaceuticals, and wood products.

Government of Guyana Offices in the U.S.
http://www.guyana.org/TRADEREP.htm
The site is a directory of Guyanese diplomatic posts in California, Florida, Minnesota, Missouri, New York, Texas, and Washington, D.C.

Guyana Customs Procedures
http://americas.fiu.edu/customs/guyana.htm
A service of Florida International University, the site reviews Guyanese customs regulations, entry procedures, documentation, tariffs, and taxes.

Guyana Representative Offices

Canada

Embassy of Canada in Georgetown
http://www.dfait-maeci.gc.ca/english/missions/rep-can2e.htm#guyana
The site provides contact information for the Canadian Embassy in Georgetown.

Sweden

Consulate of Sweden in Georgetown
http://www.ud.se/english/mfa/ambassad/guyana.htm
The site lists the staff, street address, phone and fax numbers, and e-mail link of the Swedish Consulate in Georgetown.

United Kingdom

High Commission of Britain in Georgetown
http://www.fco.gov.uk/directory/posts.asp?GY
The site provides contact information for the British High Commission in Georgetown.

Venezuela

Embassy of Venezuela in Georgetown
http://www.trade-venezuela.com/EMBVENG.HTM
The site lists the street address, phone and fax numbers, and e-mail link of the Venezuelan Embassy in Georgetown.

Haiti

Haiti Media

Haiti Media
http://www.mediainfo.com/emediajs/specific-geo.htm?region=haiti
Compiled by Editor and Publisher Interactive, the site is a directory of Haiti media sites online including magazines and television stations.

Haiti Market Guides

Business and Economy
http://www.haiti.org/embassy/business.htm
A service of the Haitian Embassy in Washington, D.C., the site delivers Haitian investment guides, company directories, market profiles, and economic statistics.

Country Commercial Guide
http://www.state.gov/www/about_state/business/com_guides/1998/latin_america/haiti98.html
Prepared by the U.S. Embassy in Port-au-Prince, the site delivers primers on Haitian business, politics, trade regulations and standards, investment climate, trade and project financing, and business travel.

Guide to Investing in Haiti
http://www.haiti.org/embassy/invest.htm
A service of the Haitian Embassy in Washington, D.C., the site provides fact sheets on Haitian business incentives, taxation, and labor codes.

Haiti Country Brief
http://www.worldbank.org/cgi-bin/sendoff.cgi?page=%2Fhtml%2Fextdr%2Foffrep%2Flac%2Fht.htm
A service of the World Bank Group, the site provides Haitian population statistics, financial data, development reports, and economic forecasts.

Haiti Country Report
http://www.state.gov/www/issues/economic/trade_reports/latin_america97/haiti97.html
Prepared by the U.S. Department of State, the site delivers information on Haitian exchange rates, debt management, barriers to U.S. trade, export subsidies, and intellectual property protection.

Haiti: A Country Study
http://lcweb2.loc.gov/frd/cs/httoc.html
A service of the U.S. Library of Congress, the site delivers fact sheets on Haitian geography, population, agriculture, mining, manufacturing, and foreign economic relations.

Haiti InfoExport
http://www.infoexport.gc.ca/country-e.asp?continent=Latin&country=50
A service of Foreign Affairs and International Trade Canada, the site provides fact sheets and statistics on Haitian geography, business and politics.

Haiti Market Research
http://strategis.ic.gc.ca/sc_mrkti/ibinddc/engdoc/1a1c27.html
Developed by Industry Canada, the site provides U.S. Department of Commerce reports on Haitian business, politics, trade regulations and standards, investment climate, trade and project financing, business travel, and market opportunities.

Haiti Reference Desk
http://lanic.utexas.edu/la/cb/haiti/
Created by the University of Texas at Austin, the site is a directory of leading Haitian arts, business, government, human rights, media, and travel resources online.

Haitian Development Network *http://www.hdn.org/*
A hub of Haitian information, the site features Haitian news, market guides, investment primers, an event calendar, and a directory of business associations and lending institutions.

Haiti Trade Assistance

Haiti Customs Procedures
http://americas.fiu.edu/customs/haiti.htm
A service of Florida International University, the site reviews Haitian customs regulations, entry procedures, documentation, tariffs, and taxes.

Haiti Essential Data
http://www.gcc.net/commerce/chamber/caribe/haiti.htm
A service of the Global Chamber of Commerce, the site provides Haitian fact sheets, and directories of leading business associations and international trade organizations.

Haiti Trade
http://www.hdn.org/pages/tradedit.htm
Posted by the Haitian Development Network, the site provides Haitian international trade news and editorials.

Haiti Representative Offices

Canada

Embassy of Canada in Port-au-Prince
http://www.dfait-maeci.gc.ca/english/missions/rep-can2e.htm#haiti
The site provides contact information for the Canadian Embassy in Port-au-Prince.

Sweden

Consulate of Sweden in Port-au-Prince
http://www.ud.se/english/mfa/ambassad/haiti.htm
The site lists the staff, street address, phone and fax numbers, and e-mail link of the Swedish Consulate in Port-au-Prince.

United Kingdom

Consulate of Britain in Port-au-Prince
http://www.fco.gov.uk/directory/posts.asp?HA
The site provides contact information for the British Consulate in Port-au-Prince.

Honduras

Honduras Media

Honduras Media
http://www.mediainfo.com/emediajs/specific-geo.htm?region=honduras
Compiled by Editor and Publisher Interactive, the site is a directory of Honduran media sites online including magazines, newspapers, and radio stations.

Honduras Market Guides

Honduras Country Brief
http://www.worldbank.org/cgi-bin/sendoff.cgi?page=%2Fhtml%2Fextdr%2Foffrep%2Flac%2Fhn.htm
A service of the World Bank Group, the site provides Honduran population statistics, financial data, development reports, and economic forecasts.

Honduras Country Report
http://www.state.gov/www/issues/economic/trade_reports/latin_america97/honduras97.html
Prepared by the U.S. Department of State, the site delivers information on Honduran exchange rates, debt management, barriers to U.S. trade, export subsidies, and intellectual property protection.

Honduras: A Country Study
http://lcweb2.loc.gov/frd/cs/hntoc.html
A service of the U.S. Library of Congress, the site delivers fact sheets on Honduras geography, population, agriculture, mining, manufacturing, and foreign economic relations.

Honduras InfoExport
http://www.infoexport.gc.ca/country-e.asp?continent=Latin&country=19
A service of Foreign Affairs and International Trade Canada, the site provides fact sheets and statistics on Honduran geography, business and politics.

Honduras Market Research
http://strategis.ic.gc.ca/sc_mrkti/ibinddc/engdoc/1a1c28.html
A service of Industry Canada, the site provides U.S. Department of Commerce reports on Honduran business, politics, trade regulations and standards, investment climate, trade and project financing, business travel, and market opportunities.

Honduras Reference Desk
http://lanic.utexas.edu/la/ca/honduras/
Developed by the University of Texas at Austin, the site is a directory of leading Honduran arts, business, government, human rights, media, and travel resources online.

Honduras Resources
http://www.honduras-resources.com/
A directory of Honduran Internet resources, the site is divided into seven sections: business, economic development, government, news, tourism, contacts, and computers.

Honduras Trade Assistance

Honduras Customs Procedures
http://americas.fiu.edu/customs/honduras.htm
A service of Florida International University, the site reviews Honduran customs regulations, entry procedures, documentation, tariffs, and taxes.

Honduras Representative Offices

Canada

Embassy of Canada in Tegucigalpa
http://www.dfait-maeci.gc.ca/english/missions/rep-can2e.htm#honduras
The site provides contact information for the Canadian Embassy in Tegucigalpa.

Sweden

Consulate General of Sweden in Tegucigalpa
http://www.ud.se/english/mfa/ambassad/honduras.htm
The site lists the staff, street address, phone and fax numbers, and e-mail link of the Swedish Consulate General in Tegucigalpa.

Taiwan

Taiwan Government Information Office in Tegucigalpa
http://www.gio.gov.tw/info/ngio/gua-f.html
Posted in Chinese and English, the site lists the street address, phone and fax numbers, and e-mail link of the Taiwan Government Information Office in Tegucigalpa.

United Kingdom

Embassy of Britain in Tegucigalpa
http://www.fco.gov.uk/directory/posts.asp?HN
The site provides contact information for the British Embassy in Tegucigalpa.

Venezuela

Embassy of Venezuela in Tegucigalpa
http://www.trade-venezuela.com/EMBVENG.HTM
The site lists the street address, phone and fax numbers, and e-mail link of the Venezuelan Embassy in Tegucigalpa.

Jamaica

Jamaica Media

Go-Jamaica
http://www.jamaica-gleaner.com/
Featuring the latest Jamaican news, editorials, and business reports, the site includes telephone directories and tourism guides.

Jamaica Market Guides

Jamaica Country Brief
http://www.worldbank.org/cgi-bin/sendoff.cgi?page=%2Fhtml%2Fextdr%2Foffrep%2Flac%2Fjm.htm
A service of the World Bank Group, the site provides Jamaican population statistics, financial data, development reports, and economic forecasts.

Jamaica Country Report
http://www.state.gov/www/issues/economic/trade_reports/latin_america97/jamaica97.html
Prepared by the U.S. Department of State, the site delivers information on Jamaican exchange rates, debt management, barriers to U.S. trade, export subsidies, and intellectual property protection.

Jamaica: Everything You Need to Know
http://www.jamaicans.com/jam.htm
A virtual library of country information, the site provides Jamaican fact sheets, weather informa-

tion, cultural bulletins, language tutorials, and people profiles.

Jamaica InfoExport
http://www.infoexport.gc.ca/country-e.asp?continent=Latin&country=20
A service of Foreign Affairs and International Trade Canada, the site provides Jamaican commercial guides and market reports.

Jamaica Market Research
http://strategis.ic.gc.ca/sc_mrkti/ibinddc/engdoc/1a1c29.html
A service of Industry Canada, the site provides U.S. Department of Commerce reports on Jamaican business, politics, trade regulations and standards, investment climate, trade and project financing, business travel, and market opportunities.

Jamaica Reference Desk
http://lanic.utexas.edu/la/cb/jamaica/
Developed by the University of Texas at Austin, the site is a directory of leading Jamaican arts, business, government, media, and travel resources online.

Jamaica: Statistical Annex
http://www.imf.org/external/pubs/CAT/longres.cfm?sk=2421.0
A service of the International Monetary Fund, the site provides data on Jamaican gross domestic product, consumer prices, central government finance, banking accounts, and exports and imports.

Jamaica Trade Assistance

Export Jamaica Home Page
http://www.exportjamaica.org/
Based in Kingston, the site provides Jamaican export primers, sector profiles, and a directory of Jamaican exporters in 15 categories including automotive, electronics, pharmaceuticals, and textiles.

Jamaica Customs Procedures
http://americas.fiu.edu/customs/jamaica.htm
A service of Florida International University, the site reviews Jamaican customs regulations, entry procedures, documentation, and taxes.

Trade Shows in Jamaica
http://www.expoguide.com/shows/data/loc_29.htm
Compiled by Expoguide, the site is a directory of upcoming trade shows in Jamaica.

Jamaica Representative Offices

Canada

Embassy of Canada in Kingston
http://www.dfait-maeci.gc.ca/english/missions/rep-can3e.htm#jamaica
The site provides contact information for the Canadian Embassy in Kingston.

France

French Trade Commission in Kingston
http://www.dree.org/jamaique/contents.htm#top
Written in English and French, the site provides market reports and a directory of export programs and services for French companies doing business in Jamaica.

Sweden

Consulate of Sweden in Kingston
http://www.ud.se/english/mfa/ambassad/jamaica.htm
The site provides contact information for the Swedish Consulate in Kingston.

United Kingdom

High Commission of Britain in Kingston
http://www.fco.gov.uk/directory/posts.asp?JA
The site provides contact information for the British High Commission in Kingston.

Martinique

Martinique Market Guides

Martinique Market Research
http://strategis.ic.gc.ca/sc_mrkti/ibinddc/engdoc/1a1c30.html
Posted by Industry Canada, the site provides U.S. Central Intelligence Agency fact sheets on Martiniquais geography, people, government, economy, communications, and transportation.

Martinique Reference Desk
http://lanic.utexas.edu/la/ca/other/martin/
Developed by the University of Texas at Austin, the site is a directory of leading Martiniquais arts, language, and travel resources online.

Martinique Trade Assistance

Martinique Business and Industry
http://www.gcc.net/commerce/caribe/martinic.htm
A service of the Global Chamber of Commerce, the site provides a directory of Martiniquais business and tourism resources on the web.

Mexico

Mexico Search Tools

Mexico Web Guide
http://mexico.web.com.mx/
Written in Spanish, the site is a Mexican web search service. Categories include arts and culture, science and technology, education, business, entertainment, and government.

MexWeb
http://www.mexweb.com.mx/
A directory of Mexican resources online, the site is searchable by keyword or categories such as business, government, news, reference, and entertainment.

Mexico Media

Mexico Media
http://www.mediainfo.com/emediajs/specific-geo.htm?region=mexico
Compiled by Editor and Publisher Interactive, the site is a directory of Mexican media sites online, including magazines, newspapers, and radio stations.

Mexico Market Guides

Barclays Country Report: Mexico
http://www.offshorebanking.barclays.com/services/economic/yearly/mexjan98/mexcont.html
Prepared by Barclays Bank, the site reports on Mexican economic trends, politics, monetary and fiscal policy, international trade, foreign debt, merchandise trade, and investment flows.

Country Commercial Guide
http://www.state.gov/www/about_state/business/com_guides/1998/latin_america/mexico98.html
Prepared by the U.S. Embassy in Mexico City, the site delivers primers on Mexican business, politics, trade regulations and standards, investment climate, trade and project financing, and business travel.

Doing Business in Mexico
http://www.abcnews.com/sections/travel/DailyNews/biztrav1024.html
A service of ABC News, the site explains Mexican business etiquette. The service includes two brief audio messages by Christopher Payne, a Mexican executive, on business relationships in Mexico.

Finance Secretariat
http://www.shcp.gob.mx/english/
Homepage of Mexico's Finance Secretariat, the site delivers Mexican government press releases, speeches, economic policy statements, and public finance statistics.

Freight Forwarders in Mexico
http://www.freightworld.com/forw_geo.html#3
Compiled by Freightworld, the site is a directory of Mexican freight forwarders online including Calberson Overseas Network, Koramex Forwarding, and Mex Transport.

Information Mexico
http://www.mexicosi.com:80/business/business.htm
Developed by Soluciones Internet, the site features Mexican business primers, company directories, a calendar of events, currency converter, and economic statistics.

Mexican Companies
http://www.mexicosi.com/business/busdir/company.htm
A database of Mexican companies, the site profiles some 100 firms in 18 categories including metals and mining, publishing, transportation, building materials, construction, retail, banks, and tourism.

Mexican Industrial Directory
http://telesur.acnet.net/cgi-bin/AIEM_busca.pl
A database of Mexican companies, the site profiles firms in 15 categories including agri-food, automotive, construction, electronics, metal fabrication, and transportation.

Mexican Institute of Industrial Property
http://www.impi.gob.mx/
Written in Spanish, the site delivers Mexican patent and trademark information, and primers on Mexican intellectual property law.

Mexican Investment Board
http://www.mib.org.mx/
Based in Mexico City, the site provides Mexican investment guides, country profiles, fact sheets,

company directories, a business event calendar, and a directory of investment opportunities in telecommunications, petrochemicals, railroads, and other industries.

Mexico: Big Emerging Markets Home Page
http://www.ita.doc.gov/bems/Mexico.html
Developed by the U.S. Department of Commerce, the site delivers Mexican fact sheets, economic forecasts, export and import statistics, sector profiles, and international trade guides.

Mexico Business
http://www.nafta.net/mexbiz/
An electronic business magazine, the site provides Mexican sectoral profiles, business cases, language guides, company profiles, and tips on managing a maquiladora and Mexican workers.

Mexico Country Brief
http://www.worldbank.org/cgi-bin/ sendoff.cgi?page=%2Fhtml%2Fextdr%2Foffrep%2 Flac%2Fmx.htm
A service of the World Bank Group, the site provides population statistics, financial data, development reports, and economic forecasts.

Mexico Country Profile
http://www.tradenz.govt.nz/intelligence/profiles/ mexico.html
A service of the New Zealand Trade Development Board, the site provides Mexican economic statistics, market information, and business tips.

Mexico Country Report
http://www.state.gov/www/issues/economic/ trade_reports/latin_america97/mexico97.html
Prepared by the U.S. Department of State, the site delivers information on Mexican exchange rates, debt management, barriers to U.S. trade, export subsidies, and intellectual property protection.

Mexico InfoExport
http://www.infoexport.gc.ca/country- e.asp?continent=Latin&country=48
A service of Foreign Affairs and International Trade Canada, the site provides Mexican commercial guides and market reports.

Mexico Information Center
http://www.mexico-trade.com/
A one-stop Mexico information center, the site features Mexican company directories, investment primers, trade leads, legal primers, North American Free Trade Agreement reports, and regional and state information.

Mexico: An Introduction
http://www.apecsec.org.sg/member/apecmex.html
A service of the Asia Pacific Economic Cooperation, the site provides fact sheets and statistics on Mexican geography, climate, population, language, business, and international trade.

Mexico Market Access Database
http://mkaccdb.eu.int/mkdb/ mkdb.pl?METHOD=COUNTRY
A service of the European Commission, the site offers briefs on Mexican trade policy, tariff barriers, non-tariff barriers, investment-related measures, and financial services regulations.

Mexico Market Information
http://dtiinfo1.dti.gov.uk/ots/mexico/
A service of the London-based Department of Trade and Industry, the site delivers Mexican fact sheets, maps, and trade-show information.

Mexico Market Research
http://strategis.ic.gc.ca/sc_mrkti/ibinddc/engdoc/ 1a1e3.html
A service of Industry Canada, the site provides U.S. Department of Commerce reports on Mexican business, politics, trade regulations and standards, investment climate, trade and project financing, business travel, and market opportunities.

Mexico Reference Desk
http://lanic.utexas.edu/la/mexico/
Developed by the University of Texas at Austin, the site is a directory of leading Mexican academic, business, government, media, North American Free Trade Agreement, travel, and state and city resources online.

MexPlaza
http://mexplaza.udg.mx/
Posted in Spanish, the site is a database of Mexican companies and products in over 50 categories including agri-food, automotive, construction, education, publishing, and plastics.

Mexico Trade Assistance

BANCOMEXT
http://www.mexico-businessline.com/
Based in Mexico City, BANCOMEXT promotes Mexican exports and international investment. The site includes Mexican fact sheets, sector profiles, and a directory of Mexican trade offices around the world.

Directory of Mexican Exporters

http://www.mexico-trade.com/directory.html
A database of some 2,000 Mexican exporters, the site divides firms into 18 categories including agri-food, pharmaceuticals, machinery, transportation, plastics, electronics, and textiles.

Fairs and Exhibitions in Mexico

http://www.mexicosi.com/business/fairs/fairs.htm
A service of Information Mexico, the site is a database of Mexican business fairs and exhibitions. The directory is searchable by date and by industries such as automotive, chemicals, construction, and machinery.

Guanajuato World Trade Commission

http://www.guanajuato.gob.mx/cofoce/index2.htm
The Commission promotes exports from Guanajuato, a Mexican state. The site includes a mission statement, investment primers, sector profiles, and contact information.

Maritime Carriers in Mexico

http://www.freightworld.com/mari_geo.html#3
A service of Freightworld, the site is a database of Mexican maritime carriers online such as Agencia Maritima Fermorol, Calberson Overseas Network, and Transpac.

Mexico Customs Procedures

http://americas.fiu.edu/customs/mexico.htm
A service of Florida International University, the site reviews Mexican customs regulations, entry procedures, documentation, tariffs, and taxes.

Mexico Embassies and Consulates

http://www.undp.org/missions/mexico/embassys.htm
A service of the Permanent Mission of Mexico to the United Nations, the site is a directory of Mexican Embassies online in 12 countries including Canada, Denmark, Germany, Japan, the United Kingdom, and the United States.

Mexico Trade Monitor

http://www.mextrademonitor.com.mx/
An international business database, the site features Mexican trade leads, business guides, product catalogs, investment information, company directories, and a registry of export and import advisers.

MexTrade

http://www.mextrade.com/
Based in Mexico City, MexTrade is an Internet service provider and international business matchmaker. The site features the *Mexican Trade Bulletin*, a free daily e-mail newsletter on Mexican business opportunities.

Ministry of Foreign Affairs

http://www.sre.gob.mx/
Written in Spanish, the site provides Mexican fact sheets, foreign policy statements, international trade reports, and a directory of Mexican Embassies and Consulates abroad.

Queretaro Exporta

http://www.queretaroexporta.com.mx/
Queretaro Exporta promotes exports from Queretaro, a Mexican state. The site includes Queretaro fact sheets, company directories, an event calendar, an online business billboard, and contact information.

Trade Shows in Mexico

http://www.expoguide.com/shows/data/loc_mex.htm
A service of Expoguide, the site is a directory of trade shows in Guadalajara, Mexico City, Monterrey, and other Mexican centers.

Trucking and Motor Carriers in Mexico

http://www.freightworld.com/truc_geo.html#3
Compiled by Freightworld, the site is a directory of Mexican trucking and motor carriers online including Torres Trucking, Transportes Comandos Del Norte, and Transportes Especializados Jeomara.

Mexico Representative Offices

Australia

Austrade in Mexico City

http://www.austrade.gov.au/Mexico/
An Australian trade promotion service, the site provides a mission statement, market reports, and contact information for Austrade in Mexico City.

Austria

Austrian Trade Commission in Mexico City

http://aw.wk.or.at/awo/ahst-mexiko.htm
The site lists the staff, street address, phone and fax numbers, e-mail link, and office hours of the Austrian Trade Commission in Mexico City.

Canada

Canadian Consulate in Guadalajara

*http://www.canada.org.mx/trade/english/
guadalaj.htm*
The site lists the Trade Commissioners, street
address, phone and fax numbers, and e-mail link
of the Canadian Consulate in Guadalajara.

Canadian Consulate in Monterrey

*http://www.canada.org.mx/trade/english/
monterre.htm*
The site lists the Trade Commissioners, street
address, phone and fax numbers, and e-mail link
of the Canadian Consulate in Monterrey.

Canadian Embassy in Mexico City

http://www.canada.org.mx/
Along with Canadian fact sheets and tourism
guides, the site features Mexican market guides,
a business event calendar, privatization reports,
and a database of Canada-Mexico trade statistics.

Québec General Delegation in Mexico City

*http://www.mri.gouv.qc.ca/dans_le_monde/
ame_latine_antilles/mexico_an.html*
A Québec trade promotion service, the site lists
the street address, phone and fax numbers, and
e-mail link of the Québec General Delegation in
Mexico City.

China

China Council for the Promotion of International Trade in Mexico City

*http://www.ccpit.org/engVersion/cp_about/
cp_over/cp_over.html*
A Chinese export promotion service, the site
provides contact information for the China
Council for the Promotion of International Trade
office in Mexico City.

Finland

Finland Trade Center in Mexico City

http://www.exports.finland.fi/tradecen.htm
The site lists the staff, street address, phone and
fax numbers, and e-mail link of the Finland Trade
Center in Mexico City.

France

French Trade Commission in Mexico City

http://www.dree.org/mexique/
Posted in French and Spanish, the site provides

Mexican sector profiles, and a directory of export
programs and services for French companies
doing business in Mexico.

Italy

Embassy of Italy in Mexico City

http://www.pentanet.com.mx/Embitaly/
Posted in Italian, the site provides Italian fact
sheets, Mexican market reports, an event
calendar, contact information, and a directory of
Embassy services.

Italian Trade Commission in Mexico City

http://www.pentanet.com.mx/Italytrade/Default.htm
Written in English and Spanish, the site lists the
street address, phone and fax numbers, and e-
mail links of the Italian Trade Commission in
Mexico City.

Mexico-Italy Chamber of Commerce

http://www.pentanet.com.mx/Camcom/Default.htm
Posted in English, Italian and Spanish, the site
provides an event calendar and e-mail link to the
Mexico-Italy Chamber of Commerce.

Japan

Embassy of Japan in Mexico City

http://www.internet.com.mx/embjapon/
Written in Spanish, the site provides Japanese
news, reports on Mexico-Japan trade and
relations, and a directory of consular services
and staff.

Japan External Trade Organization in Mexico City

http://www.jetro.org.mx/
Posted in Spanish, the site provides Japanese
business bulletins, event information, and
reports on Japan-Mexico trade and relations.

Malaysia

Embassy of Malaysia in Mexico City

*http://www.mnet.com.my/klonline/www/missions/
malmiss/mmexico1.htm*
The site provides contact information for the
Malaysian Embassy in Mexico City.

New Zealand

Trade New Zealand in Mexico City

http://www.tradenz.govt.nz/contact/northam.html
An export promotion service, the site provides

contact information for the Trade New Zealand office in Mexico City.

Singapore

Consulate General of Singapore in Mexico City
http://www.gov.sg/mfa/consular/mww_m.htm
The site provides contact information for the Singapore Consulate General in Mexico City.

South Africa

South Africa Foreign Trade Office in Mexico City
http://wwwdti.pwv.gov.za/dtiwww/
foreign_offices.htm
A service of the South Africa Department of Trade and Industry, the site provides contact information for the South Africa Trade Office in Mexico City.

Spain

Spanish Commercial Office in Mexico City
http://www.icex.es/openURL.html#openURL=/
english/infoproyem/ofcomes/ofcomes.html#AM
The site lists the staff, street address, phone and fax numbers, and e-mail link of the Spanish Commercial Office in Mexico City.

Sweden

Embassy of Sweden in Mexico City
http://www.ud.se/english/mfa/ambassad/
mexico.htm
The site provides contact information for the Sweden Embassy in Mexico City.

Switzerland

Swiss Chamber of Commerce in Mexico City
http://swisstrade.com/
xicodes2.asp?P1=3&lvl=3&cid=C06
The site lists the street address, phone and fax numbers, and e-mail link of the Swiss Chamber of Commerce in Mexico City.

Taiwan

China External Trade Development Council Office in Mexico City
http://www.cetra.org.tw/english/o_office/
indexset.htm
A Taiwanese trade promotion service, the site lists the mission statement and e-mail link of the

China External Trade Development Council Office in Mexico City.

Thailand

Royal Thai Embassy in Mexico City
http://www.mfa.go.th/Embassy/detail/206.htm
The site lists the Ambassador, street address, and phone and fax numbers of the Thai Embassy in Mexico City.

United Kingdom

British Embassy in Mexico City
http://www.embajadabritanica.com.mx/
Posted in Spanish, the site provides United Kingdom news, fact sheets, tourism guides, education bulletins, an event calendar, and reports on United Kingdom-Mexico trade and relations.

Consulate of Britain in Guadalajara
http://www.fco.gov.uk/directory/posts.asp?MK
The site provides contact information for the British Consulate in Guadalajara.

Trade Office of Britain in Monterrey
http://www.fco.gov.uk/directory/posts.asp?MK
The site provides contact information for the British Trade Office in Monterrey.

United States

American Chamber in Mexico City
http://www.amcham.com.mx/
Posted in English and Spanish, the site provides Mexican news, business guides, contact information, and data on interest rates, employment, imports, exports, and other economic indicators.

Commercial Service of the United States Embassy in Mexico City
http://uscommerce.org.mx/
Part of the U.S. Embassy in Mexico City, the Commercial Service promotes U.S. exports and interests in Mexico. The site provides a mission statement, export guides, frequently asked questions and answers, and contact information.

State of Arizona Trade Office in Hermosillo
http://www.commerce.state.az.us/itrade/
offices.shtml
A service of the Arizona Department of Commerce, the site lists the Trade Representative, street address, and phone and fax numbers of the Arizona Trade Office in Hermosillo.

State of Arizona Trade Office in Mexico City
http://www.commerce.state.az.us/itrade/
offices.shtml
The site lists the Trade Representative, street address, phone and fax number, and e-mail link of the Arizona Trade Office in Mexico City.

State of California Trade Office in Mexico City
http://commerce.ca.gov/international/
it_off.html#mexico
A service of the California Office of Trade and Investment, the site lists the Director, street address, phone and fax numbers, and e-mail link of the California Trade Office in Mexico City.

State of Colorado Trade Office in Guadalajara
http://governor.state.co.us/gov_dir/govnr_dir/ITO/
abroad.htm#mexico
Developed by the Colorado International Trade Office, the site lists the mission statement and program directory of the Colorado Trade Office in Guadalajara.

State of Idaho-Jalisco Sister State Page
http://www.idoc.state.id.us/Information/exportinfo/
index.htm
Developed by the Idaho Department of Commerce, the site provides fact sheets on the Idaho-Jalisco Sister State agreement. The pact promotes trade and economic cooperation between the two states.

State of Idaho Trade Office in Guadalajara
http://www.idoc.state.id.us/Information/exportinfo/
overseas.html
A service of the Idaho Department of Commerce, the site posts the street address, phone and fax numbers, and e-mail link of the Idaho Trade Office in Guadalajara.

State of Illinois Trade Office in Mexico City
http://www.commerce.state.il.us/dcca/files/int'l/
mexico.htm
The site lists the Managing Director, street address, phone and fax numbers, and e-mail link of the Illinois Trade Office in Mexico City.

State of Missouri Latin American Office in Guadalajara
http://www.ecodev.state.mo.us/intermark/latin.html
A service of the Missouri Department of Economic Development, the site provides staff profiles and contact information for the Missouri Latin American Office in Guadalajara.

State of New Mexico Trade Office in Mexico City
http://www.edd.state.nm.us/TRADE/other.htm

The site lists the Director, street address, phone and fax numbers, and e-mail link of the New Mexico Trade Office in Mexico City.

State of Ohio Trade Office in Mexico City
http://ohiotrade.tpusa.com/offices.htm
Developed by the Ohio Department of Development, the site lists the street address and e-mail link of the Ohio Trade Office in Mexico City.

State of Texas Trade Office in Mexico City
http://www.tded.state.tx.us/commerce/busdev/
trade/mxfyi.htm
Developed by the Texas Department of Economic Development, the Office promotes Texas-Mexico trade. The site lists the Office mission statement, programs, Director, street address, and phone and fax numbers.

State of Utah Trade Office in Mexico City
http://www.ce.ex.state.ut.us/international/reps/
reps.htm#Mexico
Prepared by the State of Utah International Business Development Office, the site lists the Representative, street address, phone and fax numbers, and e-mail link of the Utah Trade Office in Mexico City.

United States Consulate in Ciudad Juarez
http://www.usia.gov/abtusia/posts/MX2/
wwwhmain.html
A service of the U.S. State Department, the site provides contact information, U.S. immigrant and non-immigrant visa application instructions, and a directory of consular programs.

United States Consulate in Monterrey
http://www.usembassy.org.mx/Monterrey.html
Written in English and Spanish, the site provides Mexican news, visa and border crossing information, business guides, and a directory of assistance programs for U.S. citizens.

United States Embassy in Mexico
http://www.usembassy.org.mx/
Along with U.S. fact sheets and visa information, the site features U.S.-Mexico business guides, environmental bulletins, and a directory of the 17 U.S. Consulates and U.S. Consular Agencies in Mexico.

U.S. Trade Center in Mexico City
http://uscommerce.org.mx/com3000.html
Developed by the U.S. Department of Commerce, the U.S. Trade Center provides office space and trade promotion services for U.S. exporters in

Mexico. The site includes contact information and the floor plan for the Center.

Montserrat

Montserrat Market Guides

Montserrat InfoExport
http://www.infoexport.gc.ca/country-e.asp?continent=Latin&country=22
A service of Foreign Affairs and International Trade Canada, the site provides fact sheets and statistics on Montserratian geography, business and politics.

Montserrat Information Site
http://www.clark.net/pub/innanen/montserrat/touristboard/index.html
A service of the Montserrat Tourist Board, the site provides accommodation directories, restaurant guides, transportation information, and an event calendar.

Montserrat Market Research
http://strategis.ic.gc.ca/sc_mrkti/ibinddc/engdoc/1a1c31.html
Posted by Industry Canada, the site provides U.S. Central Intelligence Agency fact sheets on Montserratian geography, people, government, economy, communications, and transportation.

Montserrat Trade Assistance

Montserrat Economic Development Unit
http://www.mninet.com/devunit/
A service of the Government of Montserrat, the site delivers Montserratian fact sheets, sector reports, economic statistics, and a sustainable development plan.

Montserrat Useful Addresses
http://www.caribisles.org/add-05.htm
The site provides the street addresses, phone and fax numbers, and e-mail links of key organizations in Montserrat including the Office of the Chief Minister and the Government Information Service.

Netherlands Antilles

Netherlands Antilles Media

Netherlands Antilles Media
http://www.mediainfo.com/emediajs/specific-geo.htm?region=netherlandsantilles

Compiled by Editor and Publisher Interactive, the site is a directory of Netherlands Antilles media sites online including city guides, newspapers, and radio stations.

Netherlands Antilles Market Guides

Curacao Chamber of Commerce
http://www.curacao-chamber.an/ChamberWeb/
The Chamber represents the interests of Curacao business. The site includes a mission statement, e-mail link, and a directory of Curacao resources online.

Netherlands Antilles InfoExport
http://www.infoexport.gc.ca/country-e.asp?continent=Latin&country=23
A service of Foreign Affairs and International Trade Canada, the site provides fact sheets and statistics on Netherlands Antillean geography, business and politics.

Netherlands Antilles Market Research
http://strategis.ic.gc.ca/sc_mrkti/ibinddc/engdoc/1a1c32.html
Posted by Industry Canada, the site provides U.S. Central Intelligence Agency fact sheets on Netherlands Antillean geography, people, government, economy, communications, and transportation.

Netherlands Antilles On-Line
http://gov.an/
The site provides Netherlands Antillean news, maps, fact sheets, government directories, tourism guides, and transportation information.

Netherlands Antilles Trade Assistance

Trade Point Curacao
http://www.tpcuracao.com/
Part of a global network of Trade Point offices, the site features Netherlands Antillean investment primers, export guides, a company directory, and a database of international trade opportunities.

Nicaragua

Nicaragua Media

Nicaragua Media
http://www.mediainfo.com/emediajs/specific-geo.htm?region=nicaragua
Developed by Editor and Publisher Interactive, the site is a directory of Nicaraguan media sites

online including magazines, newspapers, and television stations.

Nicaragua Market Guides

Country Commercial Guide
http://www.state.gov/www/about_state/business/ com_guides/1998/latin_america/ nicaragua98.html
Prepared by the U.S. Embassy in Managua, the site delivers primers on the Nicaraguan economy, political environment, trade regulations and standards, investment climate, trade and project financing, and business travel.

Foreign Investment Promotion Committee
http://www.economia.gob.ni/inver/inicio/espanol/ html/inicio.htm
Developed by the Nicaragua Ministry of Economy, the site features Nicaraguan backgrounders, investment guides, sector profiles, and a directory of economic development programs and contacts.

Nicaragua Country Brief
http://www.worldbank.org/cgi-bin/ sendoff.cgi?page=%2Fhtml%2Fextdr%2Foffrep%2 Flac%2Fni.htm
A service of the World Bank Group, the site provides Nicaraguan population statistics, financial data, development reports, and economic forecasts.

Nicaragua Country Report
http://www.state.gov/www/issues/economic/ trade_reports/latin_america97/nicaragua97.html
Prepared by the U.S. Department of State, the site delivers information on Nicaraguan exchange rates, debt management, barriers to U.S. trade, export subsidies, and intellectual property protection.

Nicaragua: A Country Study
http://lcweb2.loc.gov/frd/cs/nitoc.html
A service of the U.S. Library of Congress, the site delivers fact sheets on Nicaraguan geography, population, agriculture, mining, manufacturing, and foreign economic relations.

Nicaragua InfoExport
http://www.infoexport.gc.ca/country- e.asp?continent=Latin&country=24

A service of Foreign Affairs and International Trade Canada, the site provides Nicaraguan commercial guides and market reports.

Nicaragua Market Research
http://strategis.ic.gc.ca/sc_mrkti/ibinddc/engdoc/ 1a1c33.html
A service of Industry Canada, the site provides U.S. Department of Commerce reports on Nicaraguan business, politics, trade regulations and standards, investment climate, trade and project financing, business travel, and market opportunities.

Nicaragua Ministry of Economy
http://www.economia.gob.ni/
Written in Spanish, the site provides Nicaraguan fact sheets, science and technology reports, sector profiles, economic statistics, and contact information.

Nicaragua Reference Desk
http://lanic.utexas.edu/la/ca/nicaragua/
Developed by the University of Texas at Austin, the site is a directory of leading Nicaraguan arts, business, government, media, language, and travel resources online.

Nicaragua Trade Assistance

National Commission for Export Promotion
http://www.economia.gob.ni/expor/inicio/html/ inicio.htm?40,8
A branch of the Nicaragua Ministry of Economy, the site delivers Nicaraguan product catalogs, export reports, international trade statistics, and contact information.

Nicaragua Customs Procedures
http://americas.fiu.edu/customs/nicaragu.htm
A service of Florida International University, the site reviews Nicaraguan customs regulations, entry procedures, documentation, tariffs, and taxes.

Trade Information Nicaragua
http://www.usia.gov/abtusia/posts/NU1/ wwwhcom.html
The online service features Nicaraguan commercial guides, taxation primers, market studies, sector profiles, U.S.-Nicaraguan trade statistics, tourism information, and a directory of local Internet service providers.

Nicaragua Representative Offices

Taiwan

Taiwan Government Information Office in Managua

http://www.gio.gov.tw/info/ngio/nica-f.html
Posted in Chinese and English, the site lists the street address, phone and fax numbers, and e-mail link of the Taiwan Government Information Office in Managua.

United Kingdom

Embassy of Britain in Managua

http://www.fco.gov.uk/directory/posts.asp?NC
The site provides contact information for the British Embassy in Managua.

United States

United States Embassy in Managua

http://www.usia.gov/abtusia/posts/NU1/ wwwhemb.html
Written in English and Spanish, the site features U.S. news, fact sheets, Nicaraguan market information, and a directory of Embassy services and staff.

U.S. Information Service Nicaragua

http://www.usia.gov/abtusia/posts/NU1/ wwwhusis.html
Written in Spanish, the online service provides American news, cultural bulletins, scholarship information, and government bulletins.

Panama

Panama Media

Panama Media

http://www.mediainfo.com/emediajs/specific-geo.htm?region=panama
Prepared by Editor and Publisher Interactive, the site is a directory of Panamanian media sites online, including newspapers and news services.

Panama Market Guides

Panama Chamber of Commerce

http://www.panacamara.com/
Written in English and Spanish, the site features

Panamanian company directories, business guides, an online message board, economic fact sheets, and contact information.

Panama Country Brief

http://www.worldbank.org/cgi-bin/ sendoff.cgi?page=%2Fhtml%2Fextdr%2Foffrep%2 Flac%2Fpa.htm
A service of the World Bank Group, the site provides Panamanian population statistics, financial data, development reports, and economic forecasts.

Panama: A Country Study

http://lcweb2.loc.gov/frd/cs/patoc.html
A service of the U.S. Library of Congress, the site delivers fact sheets on Panamanian geography, population, agriculture, mining, manufacturing, and foreign economic relations.

Panama InfoExport

http://www.infoexport.gc.ca/country-e.asp?continent=Latin&country=25
A service of Foreign Affairs and International Trade Canada, the site provides fact sheets and statistics on Panamanian geography, business and politics.

Panama Market Research

http://strategis.ic.gc.ca/sc_mrkti/ibinddc/engdoc/ 1a1c34.html
A service of Industry Canada, the site provides U.S. Department of Commerce reports on Panama business, politics, trade regulations and standards, investment climate, trade and project financing, business travel, and market opportunities.

Panama Reference Desk

http://lanic.utexas.edu/la/ca/panama/
Developed by the University of Texas at Austin, the site is a directory of leading Panamanian arts, business, government, media, Panama Canal, and travel resources online.

Panama: Statistical Annex

http://www.imf.org/external/pubs/CAT/ longres.cfm?sk=2495.0
Prepared by the International Monetary Fund, the site reports on Panamanian output, expenditure, employment, wages, prices, public sector finances, banking, and international trade.

Panama Today
http://www.segumar.com/PANAMA_TODAY/
index.html
The virtual library provides fact sheets on Panamanian geography, business, international trade, tourism, labor force, banking, living costs, taxation, and communications.

Panama Trade Assistance

Panama Customs Procedures
http://americas.fiu.edu/customs/panama.htm
A service of Florida International University, the site reviews Panamanian customs regulations, entry procedures, documentation, tariffs, and taxes.

Panama Directorate General of Consular and Maritime Affairs
http://www.segumar.com/
The online service provides Panamanian ship registry information, and a directory of Panamanian consulates and lawyers.

Panama Exporters
http://www.latinworld.com/centro/panama/
business/exporters.html
Prepared by Latinworld, the site is a database of Panamanian exporters online. Categories include electronics, apparel, and trading houses.

Panamanian Consulates
http://www.segumar.com/CONSULATES/
consulates.html
A service of the Panama Directorate General of Consular and Maritime Affairs, the site is a directory of Panamanian consulates in North America, Latin America, Africa, Europe, the Middle East, and Asia Pacific.

Panama Representative Offices

Canada

Embassy of Canada in Panama City
http://www.dfait-maeci.gc.ca/english/missions/rep-can3e.htm#panama
The site provides contact information for the Canadian Embassy in Panama.

Spain

Spanish Commercial Office in Panama City
http://www.icex.es/openURL.html#openURL=/

english/infoproyem/ofcomes/ofcomes.html#AM
The site lists the staff, street address, phone and fax numbers, and e-mail link of the Spanish Commercial Office in Panama City.

Taiwan

Taiwan Government Information Office in Panama City
http://www.gio.gov.tw/info/ngio/pan-f.html
Posted in Chinese and English, the site lists the street address, phone and fax numbers, and e-mail link of the Taiwan Government Information Office in Panama City.

United Kingdom

Embassy of Britain in Panama City
http://www.fco.gov.uk/directory/posts.asp?PN
The site provides contact information for the British Embassy in Panama City.

Paraguay

Paraguay Media

Paraguay Media
http://www.mediainfo.com/emediajs/specific-geo.htm?region=paraguay
Prepared by Editor and Publisher Interactive, the site is a directory of Paraguayan newspapers and other media sites online.

Paraguay Market Guides

Paraguay Business Report
http://italchambers.net/BusinessReports.html
Prepared by the Italian Chamber of Commerce and written in Italian, the site provides Paraguayan fact sheets, market reports, and commercial guides.

Paraguay Country Brief
http://www.worldbank.org/cgi-bin/
sendoff.cgi?page=%2Fhtml%2Fextdr%2Foffrep%2
Flac%2Fpy.htm
A service of the World Bank Group, the site provides Paraguayan population statistics, financial data, development reports, and economic forecasts.

Paraguay Country Profile

http://www.tradenz.govt.nz/intelligence/profiles/paraguay.html
A service of the New Zealand Trade Development Board, the site provides Paraguayan economic statistics, market information, and business tips.

Paraguay: A Country Study

http://lcweb2.loc.gov/frd/cs/pytoc.html
A service of the U.S. Library of Congress, the site delivers fact sheets on Paraguayan geography, population, agriculture, mining, manufacturing, and foreign economic relations.

Paraguay InfoExport

http://www.infoexport.gc.ca/country-e.asp?continent=Latin&country=42
A service of Foreign Affairs and International Trade Canada, the site provides fact sheets and statistics on Paraguayan geography, business, and politics.

Paraguay Market Access Database

http://mkaccdb.eu.int/mkdb/mkdb.pl?METHOD=COUNTRY
A service of the European Commission, the site offers briefs on Paraguayan trade policy, tariff barriers, non-tariff barriers, investment-related measures, and financial services regulations.

Paraguay Market Information

http://dtiinfo1.dti.gov.uk/ots/paraguay/
A service of the London-based Department of Trade and Industry, the site delivers Paraguayan fact sheets, maps, and trade-show information.

Paraguay Market Research

http://strategis.ic.gc.ca/sc_mrkti/ibinddc/engdoc/1a1c35.html
A service of Industry Canada, the site provides U.S. Department of Commerce reports on Paraguayan business, politics, trade regulations and standards, investment climate, trade and project financing, business travel, and market opportunities.

Paraguay Reference Desk

http://lanic.utexas.edu/la/sa/paraguay/
Developed by the University of Texas at Austin, the site is a directory of leading Paraguayan arts, business, government, education, media, and travel resources online.

Paraguay: Selected Issues

http://www.imf.org/external/pubs/CAT/longres.cfm?sk=2500.0
Prepared by the International Monetary Fund, the site reports on Paraguayan privatization, and the implications of the Southern Cone Common Market, or Mercosur, on Paraguayan agriculture, manufacturing, and international trade.

Paraguayan Links

http://www.vimc.com/pypags.html
Written in Spanish, the site is a directory of Paraguayan resources online. Categories include media, government, education, and business.

Paraguay Trade Assistance

Paraguay Customs Procedures

http://americas.fiu.edu/customs/paraguay.htm
A service of Florida International University, the site reviews Paraguayan customs regulations, entry procedures, documentation, tariffs, and taxes.

ProParaguay

http://www.pla.net.py/proparaguay/html/ques1.html
A service of the Asuncion-based Paraguay Ministry of Foreign Affairs, ProParaguay promotes Paraguayan exports and international investment. The site features Paraguayan news, trade leads, country information, an event calendar, and business guides.

Paraguay Representative Offices

Argentina

Embassy of Argentina in Asuncion

http://www.pla.net.py/embarpy/
Written in Spanish, the site provides Argentine fact sheets, tourism guides, business information, Paraguay-Argentina trade reports, and a directory of Embassy services.

Brazil

Embassy of Brazil in Asuncion

http://www.uninet.com.py/parbrem/
Written in Portuguese, the site provides Brazilian news, fact sheets, and business reports on Paraguay and Mercosur.

France

French Trade Commission in Asuncion
http://www.dree.org/paraguay/
Posted in French and Spanish, the site provides Paraguayan market reports, and a directory of export programs for French companies doing business in Paraguay.

Germany

German Chamber of Commerce in Asuncion
http://www.ahk.net/en/py/Asuncion/
The site lists the Chairperson, Chief Executive Officer, street address, phone and fax numbers, and e-mail link of the German Chamber of Commerce in Asuncion.

German Embassy in Asuncion
http://www.pla.net.py/embalem/
Written in German and Spanish, the site features German news, fact sheets, German-Paraguay trade reports, bilateral cultural bulletins, and a directory of Embassy programs.

Spain

Spanish Commercial Office in Asuncion
http://www.icex.es/openURL.html#openURL=/ english/infoproyem/ofcomes/ofcomes.html#AM
The site lists the staff, street address, phone and fax numbers, and e-mail link of the Spanish Commercial Office in Asuncion.

Taiwan

Taiwan Government Information Office in Asuncion
http://www.gio.gov.tw/info/ngio/par-f.html
Posted in Chinese and English, the site lists the street address, phone and fax numbers, and e-mail link of the Taiwan Government Information Office in Asuncion.

United Kingdom

Embassy of Britain in Asuncion
http://www.fco.gov.uk/directory/posts.asp?PG
The site provides contact information for the British Embassy in Asuncion.

United States

United States Embassy in Asuncion
http://www.usembparaguay.gov.py/
Written in Spanish, the site provides United States fact sheets, visa and passport information, Paraguayan commercial guides, and a directory of Embassy programs and services.

Venezuela

Embassy of Venezuela in Asuncion
http://www.trade-venezuela.com/EMBVENG.HTM
The site lists the street address, phone and fax numbers, and e-mail link of the Venezuelan Embassy in Asuncion.

Peru

Peru Media

Peru Media
http://www.mediainfo.com/emediajs/specific-geo.htm?region=peru
Compiled by Editor and Publisher Interactive, the site is a directory of Peruvian media sites online, including magazines, newspapers, and radio stations.

Peru Market Guides

Country Commercial Guide
http://www.state.gov/www/about_state/business/ com_guides/1998/latin_america/peru98.html
Prepared by the U.S. Embassy in Lima, the site delivers primers on the Peruvian economy, political environment, trade regulations and standards, investment climate, trade and project financing, and business travel.

How to Set Up a Company in Peru
http://www.rree.gob.pe/i-defaul.htm
A service of the Peru Ministry of Foreign Affairs, the site is a primer on starting a business in Peru. Topics include new companies, joint ventures and partnerships, and useful addresses for investors.

Paginas Amarillas
http://paginasamarillas.telefonica.com.pe/
A service of Telefonica del Peru, the site is a browsable database of business telephone numbers in Peru. Categories include law, medical, electronics, agri-food, and wood processing.

Paginas Blancas
http://paginasblancas.telefonica.com.pe/
Written in Spanish, the online service is a

searchable white pages directory of Peruvian telephone numbers.

Peru Country Brief

http://www.worldbank.org/cgi-bin/ sendoff.cgi?page=%2Fhtml%2Fextdr%2Foffrep%2 Flac%2Fpe.htm

A service of the World Bank Group, the site provides Peruvian population statistics, financial data, development reports, and economic forecasts.

Peru Country Profile

http://www.tradenz.govt.nz/intelligence/profiles/ peru.html

A service of the New Zealand Trade Development Board, the site provides Peruvian economic statistics, market information, and business tips.

Peru Country Report

http://www.state.gov/www/issues/economic/ trade_reports/latin_america97/peru97.html

Prepared by the U.S. Department of State, the site delivers information on Peru exchange rates, debt management, barriers to U.S. trade, export subsidies, and intellectual property protection.

Peru: A Country Study

http://lcweb2.loc.gov/frd/cs/petoc.html

A service of the U.S. Library of Congress, the site delivers fact sheets on Peruvian geography, population, agriculture, mining, manufacturing, and foreign economic relations.

Peru InfoExport

http://www.infoexport.gc.ca/country- e.asp?continent=Latin&country=43

A service of Foreign Affairs and International Trade Canada, the site provides Peruvian commercial guides and market reports.

Peru Intellectual Property Office

http://www.indecopi.gob.pe/

Based in Lima, the site provides information on Peruvian patents, trademarks, copyrights, and other intellectual property.

Peru Market Access Database

http://mkaccdb.eu.int/mkdb/ mkdb.pl?METHOD=COUNTRY

A service of the European Commission, the site offers briefs on Peruvian trade policy, tariff barriers, non-tariff barriers, investment-related measures, and financial services regulations.

Peru Market Information

http://dtiinfo1.dti.gov.uk/ots/peru/

A service of the London-based Department of Trade and Industry, the site delivers Peruvian fact sheets, maps, and trade-show information.

Peru Market Research

http://strategis.ic.gc.ca/sc_mrkti/ibinddc/engdoc/ 1a1c36.html

A service of Industry Canada, the site provides U.S. Department of Commerce reports on Peruvian business, politics, trade regulations and standards, investment climate, trade and project financing, business travel, and market opportunities.

Peru Online

http://www.peruonline.com/

Written in English and Spanish, the site is a directory of Peruvian resources online. Categories include news, arts, business, government, tourism, and education.

Peru Reference Desk

http://lanic.utexas.edu/la/peru/

Developed by the University of Texas at Austin, the site is a directory of leading Peruvian arts, business, government, education, language, media, and travel resources online.

Peruvian Business Directory

http://www.denperu.com/

Developed by Peru Virtual, the site is a searchable database of Peruvian companies and business opportunities. Written in English and Spanish, the service includes an electronic bulletin board of buy and sell offers.

Peru Trade Assistance

ADEX

http://www.adexperu.org.pe/

An association of Peruvian exporters, ADEX promotes international business in Peru. The site includes trade leads, a member directory, event calendar, and export and import statistics.

Ministry of Foreign Affairs

http://www.rree.gob.pe/i-defaul.htm

A branch of the Peruvian federal government, the Ministry represents and promotes the interests of Peruvians abroad. The site includes Peruvian fact sheets, maps, and economic reports.

Peru Customs Procedures

http://americas.fiu.edu/customs/peru.htm

A service of Florida International University, the site reviews Peruvian customs regulations, entry procedures, documentation, tariffs, and taxes.

Peruvian Exportable Offer
http://perubusiness.com.pe/proy/menuing.htm
Written in English and Spanish, the online service features Peruvian export primers, sector profiles, investment guides, product catalogs, an event calendar, and a directory of Peruvian exporters.

Peruvian Exporters Association
http://ekeko.rcp.net.pe/SNE/
Written in English and Spanish, the site offers Peruvian fact sheets, a trade event calendar, and a directory of Peruvian exporters in categories such as food and beverage, textiles and apparel, and mining and oil.

Peru Representative Offices

Canada

Embassy of Canada in Lima
http://www.dfait-maeci.gc.ca/english/missions/rep-can3e.htm#peru
The site provides contact information for the Canadian Embassy in Lima.

France

French Trade Commission in Lima
http://www.dree.org/perou/
Posted in French and Spanish, the site provides Peruvian market reports, and a directory of export programs for French companies doing business in Peru.

Peru-France Chamber of Commerce
http://www.samerica.net/amcham/#francesa
The site lists the President, General Manager, street address, and phone and fax numbers of the Peru-France Chamber of Commerce in Lima.

Germany

Peru-Germany Chamber of Commerce
http://www.samerica.net/amcham/#alemana
The site posts the President, General Manager, street address, and phone and fax numbers of the Peru-Germany Chamber of Commerce in Lima.

India

Embassy of India in Lima
http://ekeko.rcp.net.pe/INDIA/

Written in Spanish, the site provides Indian news, fact sheets, economic statistics, reports on India-Peru trade and relations, and a directory of Embassy services.

Italy

Peru-Italy Chamber of Commerce
http://www.samerica.net/amcham/#italiana
The site lists the President, General Secretary, street address, and phone and fax numbers of the Peru-Italy Chamber of Commerce in Lima.

Japan

Peru-Japan Chamber of Commerce
http://www.samerica.net/amcham/#JAPONESA
The service posts the President, Vice Presidents, street address, and phone and fax numbers of the Peru-Japan Chamber of Commerce in Lima.

Malaysia

Embassy of Malaysia in Lima
http://www.mnet.com.my/klonline/www/missions/malmiss/mperu.htm
The site provides contact information for the Malaysian Embassy in Lima.

Mexico

Trade Commission of Mexico in Lima
http://www.mexico-businessline.com/ingles/ofrepmu3.html#peru
The site lists the street address, phone and fax numbers, and e-mail link of the Mexican Trade Commission in Lima.

Netherlands

Peru-Netherlands Chamber of Commerce
http://www.samerica.net/amcham/#holandesa
The site lists the President, Vice President, street address, and phone and fax numbers of the Peru-Netherlands Chamber of Commerce in Lima.

Spain

Peru-Spain Chamber of Commerce
http://www.samerica.net/amcham/#espana
The site lists the President, Vice President, street address, and phone and fax numbers of the Peru-Spain Chamber of Commerce in Lima.

Spanish Commercial Office in Lima
*http://www.icex.es/openURL.html#openURL=/
english/infoproyem/ofcomes/ofcomes.html#AM*
The site lists the staff, street address, phone and
fax numbers, and e-mail link of the Spanish
Commercial Office in Lima.

Switzerland

Peru-Switzerland Chamber of Commerce
http://www.samerica.net/amcham/#suiza
The site lists the President, General, street
address, and phone and fax numbers of the
Peru-Switzerland Chamber of Commerce in
Lima.

Taiwan

Taiwan Government Information Office in Lima
http://www.gio.gov.tw/info/ngio/peru-f.html
Posted in Chinese and English, the site lists the
street address, phone and fax numbers, and e-
mail link of the Taiwan Government Information
Office in Lima.

United Kingdom

Embassy of Britain in Lima
http://www.fco.gov.uk/directory/posts.asp?PE
The site provides contact information for the
British Embassy in Lima.

Peru-Britain Chamber of Commerce
http://www.samerica.net/amcham/#britancia
The site lists the President, street address, and
phone and fax numbers of the Peru-Britain
Chamber of Commerce in Lima.

United States

American Chamber of Commerce of Peru
http://www.amcham.org.pe/
Based in Lima, the Chamber promotes Peru-U.S.
trade. The site includes a mission statement,
staff profiles, a program directory, event calendar,
and Peruvian business primers.

United States Embassy in Lima
http://ekeko.rcp.net.pe/usa/wwwhmain.htm
Along with U.S. fact sheets, the site provides
Peruvian commercial guides, a trade event
calendar, and a directory of programs and
services for U.S. companies doing business in
Peru.

United States Information Service in Lima
http://ekeko.rcp.net.pe/usa/usis.htm
Posted in Spanish, the site delivers U.S. news,
fact sheets, government bulletins, and information on U.S.-Peru scholarships and exchange
programs.

Venezuela

Embassy of Venezuela in Lima
http://www.trade-venezuela.com/EMBVENG.HTM
The site lists the street address, phone and fax
numbers, and e-mail link of the Venezuelan
Embassy in Lima.

Puerto Rico

Puerto Rico Media

Puerto Rico Media
*http://www.mediainfo.com/emediajs/specific-
geo.htm?region=puertorico*
Compiled by Editor and Publisher Interactive, the
site is a directory of Puerto Rican media sites
online including the *El Dia* and *El Nuevo Dia*
newspapers.

Puerto Rico Market Guides

Puerto Rico Business Links
http://www.latinworld.com/countries/puertorico/
A service of Latinworld, the site is a directory of
Puerto Rican resources online. Categories
include news, business, culture, education, and
government.

Puerto Rico Federal Affairs Administration
http://www.prfaa-govpr.org/
Based in Washington, D.C., the Administration
represents Puerto Rican interests in the United
States. The site includes a mission statement,
Puerto Rican fact sheets, and contact information.

Puerto Rico Market Information
http://dtiinfo1.dti.gov.uk/ots/puerto_rico/
A service of the London-based Department of
Trade and Industry, the site delivers Puerto Rican
fact sheets, maps, and trade-show information.

Puerto Rico Market Research
*http://strategis.ic.gc.ca/sc_mrkti/ibinddc/engdoc/
1a1c37.html*
Posted by Industry Canada, the site provides U.S.
Central Intelligence Agency fact sheets on Puerto

Rican geography, people, government, economy, communications, and transportation.

Puerto Rico Reference Desk
http://lanic.utexas.edu/la/ca/other/pr/
Developed by the University of Texas at Austin, the site is a directory of leading Puerto Rican academic, arts, business, environment, government, and media resources online.

Puerto Rico Trade Assistance

Commercial Service in Puerto Rico
http://www.ita.doc.gov/uscs/pr/
A service of the International Trade Administration, the site is a directory of international trade statistics, leads, events, services, and contacts in Puerto Rico.

Trade Shows in Puerto Rico
http://www.expoguide.com/shows/data/loc_pr.htm
Compiled by Expoguide, the site is a directory of trade shows in Hato Rey, San Juan, and other Puerto Rican centers.

Puerto Rico Representative Offices

Colombia

Colombia Consulate General in Hato Rey
http://www.colombiaemb.org/consular/consus.html#san juan
The site lists the Consul, street address, phone and fax numbers, and geographic jurisdiction of the Colombia Consulate General in Hato Rey.

Spain

Spanish Commercial Office in San Juan
http://www.icex.es/openURL.html#openURL=/english/infoproyem/ofcomes/ofcomes.html#AM
The site lists the staff, street address, phone and fax numbers, and e-mail link of the Spanish Commercial Office in San Juan.

United Kingdom

Consulate of Britain in San Juan
http://britain-info.org/bis/bto/BTO_PR.sTM
The site provides contact information for the British Consulate in San Juan.

Saint Kitts and Nevis

Saint Kitts and Nevis Market Guides

Accenting Saint Kitts and Nevis
http://www.stkitts-nevis.com/
Developed by InterKnowledge, the site provides fact sheets on Kittsian geography, history, climate, and tourism.

Government of Saint Kitts and Nevis
http://www.stkittsnevis.net/index.html
Homepage of the Saint Kitts and Nevis government, the site delivers press releases, budget bulletins, tourism guides, and a directory of government ministries.

Saint Kitts and Nevis Country Brief
http://www.worldbank.org/cgi-bin/sendoff.cgi?page=%2Fhtml%2Fextdr%2Foffrep%2Flac%2Fkn.htm
A service of the World Bank Group, the site provides Kittsian population statistics, financial data, development reports, and economic forecasts.

Saint Kitts and Nevis Economic Affairs
http://www.stkittsnevis.org/econ.html
Featuring a message from the Prime Minister, the site provides Kittsian fact sheets, investment guides, and a directory of business incentives such as tax rebates and tariff exemptions.

Saint Kitts and Nevis InfoExport
http://www.infoexport.gc.ca/country-e.asp?continent=Latin&country=27
A service of Foreign Affairs and International Trade Canada, the site provides fact sheets and statistics on Kittsian geography, business and politics.

Saint Kitts and Nevis Trade Assistance

Investment Trade and Tourism
http://www.stkittsnevis.net/investment.html
A service of the Saint Kitts and Nevis government, the site delivers information on the Citizenship by Investment Program, an immigration and business development initiative.

Saint Kitts and Nevis Customs Procedures
http://americas.fiu.edu/customs/stkitts.htm
A service of Florida International University, the site reviews Kittsian customs regulations, entry procedures, documentation, tariffs, and taxes.

Saint Kitts and Nevis Offices Abroad
http://www.stkittsnevis.net/offices.html
The site lists the High Commissioners, street address, and phone and fax numbers of Kittsian foreign offices in Belgium, Canada, the United Kingdom, and the United States.

Saint Kitts and Nevis Representative Offices

United Kingdom

High Commission of Britain in Basseterre
http://www.fco.gov.uk/directory/posts.asp?SO
The site provides contact information for the British High Commission in Basseterre.

Saint Lucia

Saint Lucia Market Guides

Official Guide to Saint Lucia
http://www.interknowledge.com/st-lucia/
Homepage of the Saint Lucia Tourist Board, the site provides Saint Lucian fact sheets, maps, accommodation directories, restaurant guides, and travel tips.

Saint Lucia Country Brief
http://www.worldbank.org/cgi-bin/ sendoff.cgi?page=%2Fhtml%2Fextdr%2Foffrep%2 Flac%2Flc.htm
A service of the World Bank Group, the site provides Saint Lucian population statistics, financial data, development reports, and economic forecasts.

Saint Lucia Government Information Service
http://www.stlucia.gov.lc/gis/gishome.htm
The online service provides Saint Lucian news, press releases, sector reports, employment opportunities, government bulletins, economic forecasts, and a calendar of events.

Saint Lucia InfoExport
http://www.infoexport.gc.ca/country-e.asp?continent=Latin&country=28
A service of Foreign Affairs and International Trade Canada, the site provides Saint Lucian commercial guides and market reports.

Saint Lucia Market Research
http://strategis.ic.gc.ca/sc_mrkti/ibinddc/engdoc/ 1a1c38.html
Posted by Industry Canada, the site provides U.S.

Central Intelligence Agency fact sheets on Saint Lucian geography, people, government, economy, communications, and transportation.

Saint Lucia Reference Desk
http://lanic.utexas.edu/la/cb/stlucia/
Developed by the University of Texas at Austin, the site is a directory of leading Saint Lucian arts, business, government, media, and travel resources online.

Saint Lucia Trade Assistance

Saint Lucia Customs Procedures
http://americas.fiu.edu/customs/stlucia.htm
A service of Florida International University, the site reviews Saint Lucian customs regulations, entry procedures, documentation, tariffs, and taxes.

Saint Lucia Representative Offices

United Kingdom

High Commission of Britain in Castries
http://www.fco.gov.uk/directory/posts.asp?SP
The site provides contact information for the British High Commission in Castries.

Saint Vincent and the Grenadines

Saint Vincent and the Grenadines Media

The Herald
http://www.heraldsvg.com/
Updated daily, the site provides Saint Vincentian news, business reports, government bulletins, tourism guides, and accommodation directories.

Saint Vincent and the Grenadines Media
http://www.mediainfo.com/emediajs/specific-geo.htm?region=saintvincent
Compiled by Editor and Publisher Interactive, the site is a directory of Saint Vincent and the Grenadines media sites online.

Saint Vincent and the Grenadines Market Guides

Saint Vincent and the Grenadines Country Brief
http://www.worldbank.org/cgi-bin/ sendoff.cgi?page=%2Fhtml%2Fextdr%2Foffrep%2 Flac%2Fvc.htm
A service of the World Bank Group, the site provides Saint Vincentian population statistics,

financial data, development reports, and economic forecasts.

Saint Vincent and the Grenadines: Economic Conditions
http://www.imf.org/external/pubs/CAT/longres.cfm?sk=2496.0
Developed by the International Monetary Fund, the site delivers data on Saint Vincentian production, economic activity, energy consumption, prices, wages, government operations, and balance of payments.

Saint Vincent and the Grenadines Homepage
http://vincy.com/svg/
The online service features Saint Vincentian fact sheets, photographs, travel guides, an event calendar, and accommodation directories.

Saint Vincent and the Grenadines InfoExport
http://www.infoexport.gc.ca/country-e.asp?continent=Latin&country=29
A service of Foreign Affairs and International Trade Canada, the site provides Saint Vincentian commercial guides and market reports.

Saint Vincent and the Grenadines Links
http://www.freenet.hamilton.on.ca/~aa462/svgref.html
Developed by Russ Filman, the site is a directory of Saint Vincentian resources online. Categories include business, tourism, and government.

Saint Vincent and the Grenadines Trade Assistance

Saint Vincent and the Grenadines Customs Procedures
http://americas.fiu.edu/customs/stvince.htm
A service of Florida International University, the site reviews Saint Vincentian customs regulations, entry procedures, documentation, tariffs, and taxes.

Saint Vincent and the Grenadines Government Offices
http://www.freenet.hamilton.on.ca/~aa462/svgref.html#svgmtd
The site is a directory of Saint Vincentian government offices and travel bureaus in Kingstown and around the world.

Suriname

Suriname Market Guides

Complete Guide to Suriname
http://www.surinam.net/
Developed by KC Multimedia, the site features Surinamese news, business information, company directories, travel guides, classifieds, and online discussion forums.

Suriname Country Brief
http://www.worldbank.org/cgi-bin/sendoff.cgi?page=%2Fhtml%2Fextdr%2Foffrep%2Flac%2Fsr.htm
A service of the World Bank Group, the site provides Surinamese population statistics, financial data, development reports, and economic forecasts.

Suriname InfoExport
http://www.infoexport.gc.ca/country-e.asp?continent=Latin&country=44
A service of Foreign Affairs and International Trade Canada, the site provides fact sheets and statistics on Surinamese geography, business and politics.

Suriname Market Research
http://strategis.ic.gc.ca/sc_mrkti/ibinddc/engdoc/1a1c41.html
A service of Industry Canada, the site provides U.S. Department of Commerce reports on Surinamese business, politics, trade regulations and standards, investment climate, trade and project financing, business travel, and market opportunities.

Suriname Reference Desk
http://lanic.utexas.edu/la/sa/suriname/
Developed by the University of Texas at Austin, the site is a directory of leading Surinamese business, government, media, and travel resources online.

Suriname Trade Assistance

Embassies and Consulates in Suriname
http://www.sr.net/srnet/InfoSurinam/embassy.html
The site is a directory of Surinamese Embassies and Consulates in 27 countries including Belgium, Brazil, Canada, Chile, China, Colombia, Denmark, France, Germany, and Guyana.

International Business Practices in Suriname
http://www.smartbiz.com/sbs/arts/bpr94.htm
A service of the University of Missouri at St. Louis, the site provides primers on Surinamese import regulations, commercial policies, investment incentives, and intellectual property.

Suriname Representative Offices

United Kingdom

Consulate of Britain in Paramaribo
http://www.fco.gov.uk/directory/posts.asp?ST
The site provides contact information for the British Consulate in Paramaribo.

Venezuela

Embassy of Venezuela in Paramaribo
http://www.trade-venezuela.com/EMBVENG.HTM
The site lists the street address, phone and fax numbers, and e-mail link of the Venezuelan Embassy in Paramaribo.

Trinidad and Tobago

Trinidad and Tobago Media

Trinidad and Tobago Media
http://www.mediainfo.com/emediajs/specific-geo.htm?region=trinidad
Compiled by Editor and Publisher Interactive, the site is a directory of Trinidadian media sites online such as magazines and newspapers.

Trinidad and Tobago Market Guides

Doing Business in Trinidad and Tobago
http://www.trinidadlaw.com/
A service of M. Hamel-Smith & Co. Attorneys-at-Law, the site provides fact sheets on Trinidadian business, taxation, intellectual property, real estate, commercial disputes, and company law.

Trinidad and Tobago Chamber of Industry and Commerce
http://www.trinidad.net/chambers/ttcic/
Based in Port of Spain, the site features a Chamber mission statement, member directory, event calendar, and a dispute resolution center.

Trinidad and Tobago Company Database
http://tradepoint.tidco.co.tt/ttcdbase/
A browsable directory of Trinidadian organiza-

tions, the site is searchable by keyword, industry, product, company name, and harmonized system code.

Trinidad and Tobago Country Brief
http://www.worldbank.org/cgi-bin/sendoff.cgi?page=%2Fhtml%2Fextdr%2Foffrep%2Flac%2Ftt.htm
A service of the World Bank Group, the site provides Trinidadian population statistics, financial data, development reports, and economic forecasts.

Trinidad and Tobago Country Report
http://www.state.gov/www/issues/economic/trade_reports/latin_america97/trinidad97.html
Prepared by the U.S. Department of State, the site delivers information on Trinidadian exchange rates, debt management, barriers to U.S. trade, export subsidies, and intellectual property protection.

Trinidad and Tobago InfoExport
http://www.infoexport.gc.ca/country-e.asp?continent=Latin&country=30
A service of Foreign Affairs and International Trade Canada, the site provides Trinidadian commercial guides and market reports.

Trinidad and Tobago Manufacturers Association
http://www.ttma.com/
Based in Port of Spain, the site features Association news, a member directory, trade mission reports, an event calendar, and updates on the Free Trade Area of the Americas negotiations.

Trinidad and Tobago Market Information
http://dtiinfo1.dti.gov.uk/ots/trinidad/
A service of the London-based Department of Trade and Industry, the site delivers Trinidadian fact sheets, maps, and trade-show information.

Trinidad and Tobago Market Research
http://strategis.ic.gc.ca/sc_mrkti/ibinddc/engdoc/1a1c42.html
A service of Industry Canada, the site provides U.S. Department of Commerce reports on Trinidadian business, politics, trade regulations and standards, investment climate, trade and project financing, business travel, and market opportunities.

Trinidad and Tobago Reference Desk
http://lanic.utexas.edu/la/cb/tt/
Developed by the University of Texas at Austin,

the site is a directory of leading Trinidadian arts, business, government, media, and travel resources online.

Trinidad and Tobago Trade Assistance

Trade Point Port of Spain
http://tradepoint.tidco.co.tt/
Part of a global network of Trade Point offices, the site includes Trinidadian trade statistics, company directories, investment guides, sector profiles, an event calendar, and online marketplace.

Trade Shows in Trinidad and Tobago
http://www.expoguide.com/shows/data/loc_62.htm
Compiled by Expoguide, the site is a directory of upcoming trade shows in Trinidad and Tobago.

Trinidad and Tobago Customs Procedures
http://americas.fiu.edu/customs/trinidad.htm
A service of Florida International University, the site reviews Trinidadian customs regulations, entry procedures, documentation, tariffs, and taxes.

Trinidad and Tobago Representative Offices

Canada

High Commission of Canada in Port of Spain
http://www.dfait-maeci.gc.ca/english/missions/rep-can4e.htm#trinidad and tobago
The site provides contact information for the Canadian High Commission in Port of Spain.

Sweden

Consulate General of Sweden in Port of Spain
http://www.ud.se/english/mfa/ambassad/trinitob.htm
The site provides contact information for the Swedish Embassy in Port of Spain.

United Kingdom

High Commission of Britain in Port of Spain
http://www.fco.gov.uk/directory/posts.asp?TT
The site provides contact information for the British High Commission in Port of Spain.

United States

American Chamber of Commerce of Trinidad and Tobago
http://www.trinidad.net/chambers/acchome/acchome.htm
Based in Port of Spain, the Chamber promotes U.S.-Trinidad and Tobago trade. The site provides Chamber speeches, member profiles, an event calendar, and contact information.

Venezuela

Embassy of Venezuela in Port of Spain
http://www.trade-venezuela.com/EMBVENG.HTM
The site lists the street address, phone and fax numbers, and e-mail link of the Venezuelan Embassy in Port of Spain.

Turks and Caicos Islands

Turks and Caicos Islands Market Guides

Investment Opportunities in the Turks and Caicos Islands
http://www.turksandcaicos.tc/InvestmentOpportunities/invest.htm
The government site provides primers on Turks and Caicos investment incentives, immigration policy, business incorporation, and licensing. An Input Costs feature provides cost comparisons of electricity, water, waste, and telephone services throughout the Islands.

Turks and Caicos Gateway
http://www.turksandcaicos.tc/
The online service delivers fact sheets on Turks and Caicos geography, history, tourism, real estate, banks, investment, accommodations and restaurants, and transportation.

Turks and Caicos InfoExport
http://www.infoexport.gc.ca/country-e.asp?continent=Latin&country=31
A service of Foreign Affairs and International Trade Canada, the site provides fact sheets and statistics on Turks and Caicos geography, business and politics.

Turks and Caicos Market Research
http://strategis.ic.gc.ca/sc_mrkti/ibinddc/engdoc/1a1c43.html
Posted by Industry Canada, the site provides U.S.

Central Intelligence Agency fact sheets on Turks and Caicos geography, people, government, economy, communications, and transportation.

Welcome to Turks and Caicos
http://www.interknowledge.com/turks-caicos/
Homepage of the Turks and Caicos Tourist Board, the site features Turks and Caicos fact sheets, accommodation directories, restaurant guides, newsgroups, and contact information.

Turks and Caicos Islands Trade Assistance

Turks and Caicos Customs Information
http://www.turksandcaicos.tc/InvestmentOpportunities/invest8.htm
A service of the Turks and Caicos government, the site provides information on Turks and Caicos border regulations, customs clearance procedures, and tariff rates.

U.S. Virgin Islands

U.S. Virgin Islands Market Guides

Complete Guide to the U.S. Virgin Islands
http://www.usviguide.com/
The online service delivers U.S. Virgin Islander general information, real estate directories, relocation guides, online classifieds, mailing lists, history lessons, and cultural bulletins.

Government of the U.S. Virgin Islands
http://www.gov.vi/
The online service explains the missions and functions of the U.S. Virgin Islands Executive, Legislative and Judicial Branches of government. The site includes a directory of independent agencies such as the U.S. Virgin Islands Housing Authority, Water and Power Authority, and Agricultural Experiment Station.

Network Virgin Islands
http://www.networkvirginislands.com/
An online travel and community guide, the site provides information on U.S. Virgin Islander arts and entertainment, business, government, hotels and accommodations, shopping, and weather.

U.S. Virgin Islands Market Research
http://strategis.ic.gc.ca/sc_mrkti/ibinddc/engdoc/1a1c45.html
Posted by Industry Canada, the site provides U.S. Central Intelligence Agency fact sheets on U.S. Virgin Islander geography, and transportation.

U.S. Virgin Islands Reference Desk
http://lanic.utexas.edu/la/ca/other/vi/
Developed by the University of Texas at Austin, the site is a directory of leading U.S. Virgin Islander arts, government, media, and travel resources online.

U.S. Virgin Islands Trade Assistance

Virgin Islands Port Authority
http://www.gov.vi/html/list.html#vipa
Posted by the U.S. Virgin Islands government, the site lists the Executive Director, mission statement, street address, and phone and fax numbers of the Virgin Islands Port Authority.

Uruguay

Uruguay Media

Uruguay Media
http://www.mediainfo.com/emediajs/specific-geo.htm?region=uruguay
Compiled by Editor and Publisher Interactive, the site is a directory of Uruguayan magazine, newspaper, and other media sites online.

Uruguay Market Guides

Country Commercial Guide
http://www.state.gov/www/about_state/business/com_guides/1998/latin_america/uruguay98.html
Prepared by the U.S. Embassy in Montevideo, the site delivers primers on the Uruguayan economy, political environment, trade regulations and standards, investment climate, trade and project financing, and business travel.

Doing Business in Uruguay
http://www.embassy.org/uruguay/pwaterhouse/pw.htm
A service of Price Waterhouse, the site provides primers on Uruguayan investment incentives, banking and financing, labor relations, audit requirements, taxation, and partnerships and joint ventures.

Infrastructure Project Homepage
http://www.embassy.org/uruguay/bopportunities/index.htm
Developed by the Embassy of Uruguay in Washington, D.C., the site profiles major infrastructure projects in Uruguay. Initiatives include new seaports, airports, bridges, water and sanitation, rail, highway, and power generation systems.

Uruguary Country Brief
*http://www.worldbank.org/cgi-bin/
sendoff.cgi?page=%2Fhtml%2Fextdr%2Foffrep%2
Flac%2Fuy.htm*
A service of the World Bank Group, the site
provides Uruguayan population statistics,
financial data, development reports, and economic forecasts.

Uruguay Country Profile
*http://www.tradenz.govt.nz/intelligence/profiles/
uruguay.html*
A service of the New Zealand Trade Development
Board, the site provides Uruguayan economic
statistics, market information, and business tips.

Uruguay Country Report
*http://www.state.gov/www/issues/economic/
trade_reports/latin_america97/uruguay97.html*
Prepared by the U.S. Department of State, the site
delivers information on Uruguayan exchange
rates, debt management, barriers to U.S. trade,
export subsidies, and intellectual property
protection.

Uruguay: A Country Study
http://lcweb2.loc.gov/frd/cs/uytoc.html
A service of the U.S. Library of Congress, the site
delivers fact sheets on Uruguayan geography,
population, agriculture, mining, manufacturing,
and foreign economic relations.

Uruguay InfoExport
*http://www.infoexport.gc.ca/country-
e.asp?continent=Latin&country=45*
A service of Foreign Affairs and International
Trade Canada, the site provides Uruguayan
commercial guides and market reports.

Uruguay Market Access Database
*http://mkaccdb.eu.int/mkdb/
mkdb.pl?METHOD=COUNTRY*
A service of the European Commission, the site
offers briefs on Uruguayan trade policy, tariff
barriers, non-tariff barriers, investment-related
measures, and financial services regulations.

Uruguay Market Research
*http://strategis.ic.gc.ca/sc_mrkti/ibinddc/engdoc/
1a1c44.html*
A service of Industry Canada, the site provides
U.S. Department of Commerce reports on
Uruguayan business, politics, trade regulations
and standards, investment climate, trade and
project financing, business travel, and market
opportunities.

Uruguay Reference Desk
http://lanic.utexas.edu/la/uruguay/
Developed by the University of Texas at Austin,
the site is a directory of leading Uruguayan arts,
business, education, government, media,
technology, and travel resources online.

Uruguay Trade Assistance

Exporting to Uruguay
*http://www.embassy.org/uruguay/pwaterhouse/
chapter8.htm*
An export resource guide, the site features
primers on Uruguayan import restrictions,
custom duties, taxes, documentation procedures,
port of entry, and inland transportation.

Foreign Investment and Trade Opportunities
*http://www.embassy.org/uruguay/pwaterhouse/
chapter3.htm*
An online investment primer, the site provides fact
sheets on Uruguayan trade policy, foreign
investment, business incentives, taxation, labor,
financing, and profit repatriation.

Trade Point Montevideo
*http://www.untpdc.org/incubator/ury/tpmon/
trade.htm*
Part of the United Nations Global Trade Point
Network, the site provides Uruguayan trade
leads, market bulletins, and contact information.

Uruguay Customs Procedures
http://americas.fiu.edu/customs/uruguay.htm
A service of Florida International University, the
site reviews Uruguayan customs regulations,
entry procedures, documentation, tariffs, and
taxes.

Uruguay Representative Offices

Argentina

Embassy of Argentina in Montevideo
http://emb-uruguay.mrecic.gov.ar/
Written in Spanish, the site delivers Argentine fact
sheets, cultural bulletins, visa information,
reports on Argentina-Uruguay trade and relations,
and a directory of Embassy programs and
services.

Canada

Embassy of Canada in Montevideo
http://www.dfait-maeci.gc.ca/english/missions/rep-can4e.htm#uruguay
The site provides contact information for the Canadian Embassy in Montevideo.

Germany

German Chamber of Commerce in Montevideo
http://www.ahk.net/en/uy/Montevideo/
The site lists the Chairperson, Chief Executive Officer, street address, phone and fax numbers, and e-mail link of the German Chamber in Montevideo.

Italy

Embassy of Italy in Montevideo
http://www.netgate.com.uy/~uffcomit/
Posted in Italian, the site provides contact information, Mercosur reports, Italian tourism and commercial guides, and a directory of Embassy services.

Mexico

Embassy of Mexico in Montevideo
http://www.rau.edu.uy/embamex/
The virtual Embassy delivers Mexican fact sheets, business guides, travel primers, reports on Mexico-Uruguay trade and relations, and a directory of Embassy services.

South Africa

South Africa Foreign Trade Office in Montevideo
http://wwwdti.pwv.gov.za/dtiwww/foreign_offices.htm
A service of the South Africa Department of Trade and Industry, the site provides contact information for the South Africa Trade Office in Montevideo.

Spain

Spanish Commercial Office in Montevideo
http://www.icex.es/openURL.html#openURL=/english/infoproyem/ofcomes/ofcomes.html#AM
The site lists the staff, street address, phone and fax numbers, and e-mail link of the Spanish Commercial Office in Montevideo.

Sweden

Consulate General of Sweden in Montevideo
http://www.ud.se/english/mfa/ambassad/uruguay.htm
The site provides contact information for the Swedish Consulate General in Montevideo.

United Kingdom

Embassy of Britain in Montevideo
http://www.fco.gov.uk/directory/posts.asp?UR
The site provides contact information for the British Embassy in Montevideo.

United States

American Chamber Uruguay
http://www.zfm.com/amchamuru/
Based in Montevideo, the Chamber promotes U.S.-Uruguay trade. The site includes a Chamber mission statement, member directory, Uruguayan country profile, and Mercosur reports.

United States Embassy in Montevideo
http://www.embeeuu.gub.uy/
Along with U.S. fact sheets and visa information, the site features Uruguayan business guides, travel primers, Mercosur bulletins, and government directories.

United States Information Service in Montevideo
http://www.embeeuu.gub.uy/usismont.htm
Part of the U.S. Embassy in Montevideo, the site includes U.S. press releases, briefings, Voice of America broadcast information, cultural bulletins, and reports on U.S.-Uruguay student exchanges.

Venezuela

Embassy of Venezuela in Montevideo
http://www.trade-venezuela.com/EMBVENG.HTM
The site lists the street address, phone and fax numbers, and e-mail link of the Venezuelan Embassy in Montevideo.

Venezuela

Venezuela Media

Venezuela Media
http://www.mediainfo.com/emediajs/specific-geo.htm?region=venezuela
Compiled by Editor and Publisher Interactive, the

site is a directory of Venezuelan media sites online including magazines, newspapers, and television stations.

Venezuela Market Guides

Barclays Country Report: Venezuela
*http://www.offshorebanking.barclays.com/
services/economic/yearly/vennov97/index.html*
Prepared by Barclays Bank, the site reports on Venezuelan economic trends, politics, monetary and fiscal policy, international trade, foreign debt, merchandise trade, and investment flows.

Venezuela Business Report
http://italchambers.net/BusinessReports.html
Prepared by the Italian Chamber of Commerce and written in Italian, the site provides Venezuelan fact sheets, market reports, and commercial guides.

Venezuela Country Brief
*http://www.worldbank.org/cgi-bin/
sendoff.cgi?page=%2Fhtml%2Fextdr%2Foffrep%2
Flac%2Fve.htm*
A service of the World Bank Group, the site provides Venezuelan population statistics, financial data, development reports, and economic forecasts.

Venezuela Country Profile
*http://www.tradenz.govt.nz/intelligence/profiles/
venezuela.html*
A service of the New Zealand Trade Development Board, the site provides Venezuelan economic statistics, market information, and business tips.

Venezuela Country Report
*http://www.state.gov/www/issues/economic/
trade_reports/latin_america97/venezuela97.html*
Prepared by the U.S. Department of State, the site delivers information on Venezuelan exchange rates, debt management, barriers to U.S. trade, export subsidies, and intellectual property protection.

Venezuela: A Country Study
http://lcweb2.loc.gov/frd/cs/vetoc.html
A service of the U.S. Library of Congress, the site delivers fact sheets on Venezuelan geography, population, agriculture, mining, manufacturing, and foreign economic relations.

Venezuela InfoExport
*http://www.infoexport.gc.ca/country-
e.asp?continent=Latin&country=46*
A service of Foreign Affairs and International

Trade Canada, the site provides Venezuelan commercial guides and market reports.

Venezuela Market Information
http://dtiinfo1.dti.gov.uk/ots/venezuela/
A service of the London-based Department of Trade and Industry, the site delivers Venezuelan fact sheets, maps, and trade-show information.

Venezuela Market Research
*http://strategis.ic.gc.ca/sc_mrkti/ibinddc/engdoc/
1a1c46.html*
A service of Industry Canada, the site provides U.S. Department of Commerce reports on Venezuelan business, politics, trade regulations and standards, investment climate, trade and project financing, business travel, and market opportunities.

Venezuela Reference Desk
http://lanic.utexas.edu/la/venezuela/
Developed by the University of Texas at Austin, the site is a directory of leading Venezualan arts, business, government, state and municipal, media, and travel resources online.

Venezuela Trade Assistance

Trade Shows in Venezuela
http://www.expoguide.com/shows/data/loc_68.htm
Compiled by Expoguide, the site is a directory of upcoming trade shows in Venezuela.

Trade Venezuela
http://www.trade-venezuela.com/
A directory of Venezuelan products and services for export, the site features Venezuelan fact sheets, company profiles, and an online message board. The service includes a database of international business opportunities in ten categories including automotive, construction, pharmaceuticals, and food and beverage.

Venezuela Customs Procedures
http://americas.fiu.edu/customs/venezuel.htm
A service of Florida International University, the site reviews Venezuelan customs regulations, entry procedures, documentation, tariffs, and taxes.

Venezuela Export Directory
http://www.ddex.com.ve/
Posted in English and Spanish, the site provides a browsable directory of Venezuelan exporters. Categories include agri-food, electronics, and transportation equipment.

Venezuelan Diplomatic Offices Worldwide
http://www.trade-venezuela.com/EMBVENG.HTM
A service of Trade Venezuela, the site is a database of Venezuelan Embassies and Consulates in Africa, the Americas, Asia, and Europe.

Venezuela Representative Offices

Austria

Austrian Trade Commission in Caracas
http://www.internet.ve:80/austria/
Written in Spanish, the site provides Austrian fact sheets, economic statistics, contact information, reports on Austria-Venezuela trade and relations, and a directory of Embassy commercial services.

Canada

Canadian Chamber of Commerce in Venezuela
http://www.cancham.com.ve/
Representing over 100 members, the Chamber promotes Canada-Venezuela trade. The site includes a mission statement, news, and event information.

Embassy of Canada in Caracas
http://www.dfait-maeci.gc.ca/caracas/
Posted in English, French, and Spanish, the site provides Canadian fact sheets, tourism guides, visa and immigration information, reports on Canada-Venezuela trade and relations, and Venezuelan business primers.

Denmark

Embassy of Denmark in Caracas
http://www.dinamarca.com/
Posted in Danish, English, and Spanish, the site delivers Danish maps, fact sheets, tourism guides, company profiles, and a directory of Danish Embassy programs and services.

France

French Trade Commission in Caracas
http://www.dree.org/venezuela/
Written in French and Spanish, the site provides Venezuelan market reports, and a directory of export programs for French companies doing business in Venezuela.

Germany

German Chamber of Commerce in Caracas
http://www.cavenal.com/
Posted in German and Spanish, the site delivers German fact sheets, business guides, reports on Germany-Venezuela trade and relations, a Chamber event calendar, and member directory.

Iceland

Consulate General of Iceland in Caracas
http://www.iceland.org/list1n2.htm#latin
The site lists the Consul General, street address, phone and fax numbers, and e-mail link of the Icelandic Consulate in Caracas.

Italy

Consulate of Italy in Maracaibo
http://www.conmara.com/
Posted in Italian and Spanish, the site features a message from the Consul General, Italian visa and passport information, a list of Italian and Venezuelan business contacts, and a directory of consular services.

Malaysia

Embassy of Malaysia in Caracas
http://www.mnet.com.my/klonline/www/missions/malmiss/mvenezue1.htm
The site provides contact information for the Malaysian Embassy in Caracas.

Mexico

Trade Commission of Mexico in Caracas
http://www.mexico-businessline.com/ingles/ofrepmu3.html#venezuela
The site lists the street address, phone and fax numbers, and e-mail link of the Mexican Trade Commission in Caracas.

Portugal

Portuguese Trade and Investment Office in Caracas
http://www.portugal.org/geninfo/abouticep/venezuela.html
The site lists the staff, street address, and phone and fax numbers of the Portuguese Trade and Investment Office in Caracas.

Spain

Spanish Commercial Office in Caracas
http://www.icex.es/openURL.html#openURL=/
english/infoproyem/ofcomes/ofcomes.html#AM
The site lists the staff, street address, phone and
fax numbers, and e-mail link of the Spanish
Commercial Office in Caracas.

Sweden

Embassy of Sweden in Caracas
http://www.ud.se/english/mfa/ambassad/
venezuel.htm
The site provides contact information for the
Swedish Embassy in Caracas.

Switzerland

Swiss Chamber of Commerce in Caracas
http://swisstrade.com/
xicodes2.asp?P1=3&lvl=3&cid=C09
The site lists the street address, phone and fax
numbers, and e-mail link of the Swiss Chamber
of Commerce in Caracas.

Taiwan

China External Trade Development Council Office in Caracas
_http://www.cetra.org.tw/english/o_office/_
indexset.htm
A Taiwanese trade promotion service, the site
lists the mission statement and e-mail link of the
China External Trade Development Council Office
in Caracas.

Taiwan Government Information Office in Caracas
http://www.gio.gov.tw/info/ngio/ven-f.html
Posted in Chinese and English, the site lists the
street address, phone and fax numbers, and e-
mail link of the Taiwan Government Information
Office in Caracas.

United Kingdom

British Venezuelan Chamber of Commerce
http://www.britcham.com.ve/
A forum for promoting British-Venezuelan trade,
the site includes Chamber news, event information, and Venezuelan business guides.

Embassy of Britain in Caracas
http://www.fco.gov.uk/directory/posts.asp?VZ
The site provides contact information for the
British Embassy in Caracas.

United States

United States Embassy in Caracas
http://www.usia.gov/posts/caracas/
Along with United States fact sheets and visa
information, the site features Venezuelan country
guides, Summit of the Americas reports, and
Organization of American States bulletins.

VenAmCham
http://www.venamcham.org/
Based in Caracas, the Chamber promotes
Venezuela-United States trade. The site features
Chamber news, committee information, a
member directory, and an event calendar.

Venezuelan American Partnership
http://www.vap.c-com.net/
Founded in 1996, the Partnership promotes
Venezuela-Texas trade. The site includes a
mission statement, a list of upcoming events,
and a directory of member services.

## CHAPTER 6

EURO E-HOTSPOTS: 1,300+ WESTERN EUROPE BUSINESS RESOURCES ON THE INTERNET

This chapter highlights more than 1,300 global business resources online that focus on Western Europe. The section profiles regional websites and online hubs for 31 countries and territories including France, Germany, Italy, Spain, and the United Kingdom. Home to some 390 million people, the region is among the largest, richest, and most sophisticated markets in the world. A key development now underway is monetary union. On January 1, 1999, a new currency—the Euro—was introduced in 11 Western European countries. By July 1, 2002, the Euro will be in full circulation, and national currencies will no longer be legal tender. Leading business opportunities in the region include advanced technology, agrifood products, biotechnology and health products, business and educational services, environmental equipment, and consumer products. As of January 1999, NUA Internet Surveys reported that an estimated 30 million people in the region—about eight percent of the total—were online. According to Datamonitor, the number of Western Europeans with Internet access is expected to increase to 43 million by 2003.

Regional Sites

Western Europe Search Tools

AltaVista Northern Europe
http://www.altavista.telia.com/
Posted in more than 20 languages including Italian, Polish, and Swedish, the site is a searchable directory of online resources in nearly 30 Northern European countries including France, Germany, and Russia.

European Search Engines and Directories
http://www.netmasters.co.uk/ european_search_engines/page2.html
Based in the United Kingdom, the site is a directory of online search engines in 45 European countries including Bulgaria, Finland, Ireland, Portugal, Sweden, and the Ukraine.

EuroSeek
http://www.euroseek.net/
Posted in some 40 languages, the site is a European online search engine. The service is browsable by keyword or categories such as business and economy, news and media, and science and technology.

YellowWeb Europe Directory
http://www.yweb.com/home-en.html
Written in seven languages, the site is a browsable index of European online resources. The service includes industrial directories, telecommunications guides, and transportation fact sheets.

Western Europe Media

European Union Business
http://www.eubusiness.com/
Based in Luxembourg, the site provides daily European and world business news, sector reports, country profiles, and a searchable directory of European Union procurement opportunities.

Western Europe Media
http://www.mediainfo.com/emediajs/links-geo.htm?location=europe
Compiled by Editor and Publisher Interactive, the site is a directory of European online media including newspapers, magazines, and radio stations. The service provides databases for some 45 European countries including Belgium, Sweden, and the United Kingdom.

Western Europe Market Guides

API Online
http://www.api.se/
Based in Sweden, this subscription site provides a searchable database of public sector contracts open to tender in the European Community.

Bureau of European Affairs
http://www.state.gov/www/regions/eur/index.html
Developed by the U.S. State Department, the site provides U.S. press statements, testimony, briefings, issue reports, and travel information on Europe.

Business Europe
http://www.businesseurope.com/
A virtual library of European business information, the site delivers European investment guides, legal primers, market reports, trade leads, and a regional conference calendar.

Council of the European Union
http://ue.eu.int/
Based in Brussels, the Council coordinates the activities of the 15 member states of the European Community. The site includes Council press releases, legislative bulletins, and fact sheets.

EmuNet
http://www.euro-emu.co.uk/
An online gateway to Europe's single currency, the site provides news, fact sheets, and discussion forums on Europe's economic and monetary union.

Eurobarometer
http://europa.eu.int/en/comm/dg10/infcom/epo/eb.html
A service of the European Commission, the site provides the results of European public opinion surveys on political, economic, and consumer issues.

Europa
http://europa.eu.int/index-en.htm
Along with primers on European Union policies and institutions, the site provides European official documents, legal texts, publications and databases.

Europages
http://www.europages.com/
A searchable database of 500,000 European countries in 30 countries, the site is browsable by keyword, company, and sectors such as agriculture and livestock, rubber and plastics, and information technology and telecommunications.

Europe Business Briefs
http://www.austrade.gov.au/IOOM/Europe/
A service of Austrade, the site offers fact sheets on European business etiquette, foreign investment, trade shows, investment opportunities, and venture capital funds.

Europe International Business Resources
http://ciber.bus.msu.edu/busres/europe.htm
A service of Michigan State University, the site provides a directory of European international

trade resources online including business guides, investment primers, and company databases.

Europe Market Research
http://strategis.ic.gc.ca/sc_mrkti/ibinddc/engdoc/1a1b.html
A service of Industry Canada, the site is a database of fact sheets and market studies on over 30 European countries.

European Commission Host Organization
http://www2.echo.lu/echo/en/menuecho.html
Posted in five languages including French, German, and Spanish, the site is a database of European news, country profiles, government procurement opportunities, and information technology reports.

European Documentation Center
http://www.uni-mannheim.de/users/ddz/edz/eedz.html
A virtual library of European Union information, the site provides European law guides, environmental reports, exchange rate bulletins, company profiles, and government procurement opportunities.

European Economic Information
http://www.europages.com/business-info-en.html
A service of Europages, the site delivers European business guides, sector studies, country profiles, economic forecasts, market surveys, and patent information.

European Investment Bank
http://www.eib.org/
Created in 1958, the Bank is the European Union's financing institution. The site includes Bank news, press releases, project reports, loan information, and tender guides.

European Patent Office
http://www.european-patent-office.org/index.htm
Based in Munich, the European Patent Office administers European patents and other intellectual property. The site includes news, annual reports, facts and figures, and a searchable database of European patents and patent attorneys.

European Procurement Information Network
http://epin1.epin.ie/
Based in Dublin, the subscription site is a searchable database of contract notices from public sector organizations and utilities in

Europe, the U.S., and other countries around the world.

European Union Country Report
http://www.state.gov/www/issues/economic/trade_reports/europe_canada97/eu.html
Prepared by the U.S. Department of State, the site reports on European Union exchange rates, debt management, barriers to U.S. trade, export subsidies, and intellectual property protection.

Eurostat
http://europa.eu.int/en/comm/eurostat/eurostat.html
Homepage of the European Community Statistical Office, the site is a database of European socioeconomic data and indicators. Categories include national accounts, external trade, balance of payments, prices, industry, labor market, and public finance.

Exporters Guide to the Euro
http://www.ita.doc.gov/media/euro/exporting.htm
A service of the U.S. International Trade Administration, the site provides European monetary union fact sheets, preparation guides, and event information.

InfoExport Europe
http://www.infoexport.gc.ca/continent-e.asp?continent=Europe
A service of Foreign Affairs and International Trade Canada, the site provides economic fact sheets and business guides for nearly 40 European countries.

Showcase Europe
http://www.sce.doc.gov/
A service of the U.S. Department of Commerce, the site provides European business news, commercial guides, sector reports, a trade event calendar, and a directory of U.S. Commercial Service Offices in Europe.

Welcome to the Euro
http://europa.eu.int/euro/html/entry.html
A service of the European Community, the site provides fact sheets, press releases, speeches, publications, statistics, and guides to the Euro, the European single currency.

Western Europe Trade Assistance

Airlines in Europe
http://www.freightworld.com/airl_geo.html#7
A service of Freightworld, the site is a directory of

European Airlines online including Austrian Airlines, Finnair, Air France, Air Greece, and Virgin Atlantic.

Airports in Europe
http://www.freightworld.com/airptgeo.html#7
A directory of European airports online, the site links to leading air transport facilities in Vienna, Brussels, Copenhagen, Frankfurt, and London.

Electronic Commerce and the European Union
http://www.ispo.cec.be/Ecommerce/
A service of the European Union, the site provides electronic commerce primers, project reports, best practice guides, and bulletins on security, intellectual property, translation, and other e-commerce issues.

European Trade Promotion Organization
http://www.wk.or.at/wk/aw/etpo/index.htm
Formed in 1996, the Organization is a consortium of European government agencies responsible for promoting exports and international investment. The site provides a mission statement, contact information, and a directory of member organizations.

Freight Forwarders in Europe
http://www.freightworld.com/forw_geo.html#7
A registry of European freight forwarders online, the site links to operations in 25 countries including Belgium, Bulgaria, Czech Republic, France, Germany, and the United Kingdom.

Intermodal Carriers in Europe
http://www.freightworld.com/intmod_geo.html#7
Compiled by Freightworld, the site is a directory of European intermodal carriers including TAB in France, NS Cargo in the Netherlands, and Sea Containers in the United Kingdom.

International Fairs in Europe
http://www.europages.com/fairs-en.html
A service of Europages, the site is a directory of European trade fairs in nearly 30 industries including mechanical engineering, electronics, textiles and clothing, and printing and publishing.

Maritime Carriers in Europe
http://www.freightworld.com/mari_geo.html#7
A directory of European maritime carriers online, the site links to operations in 18 countries including Estonia, Denmark, Iceland, and Italy.

Package Carriers in Europe
http://www.freightworld.com/exp_geo.html#7
Developed by Freightworld, the site is a registry of

European package carriers online including RGW Express in Germany, Express Fly in Greece, and Parcelforce in the United Kingdom.

Postal Services in Europe
http://www.freightworld.com/postal.html#7
A directory of European postal services online, the site links to organizations in five countries including Germany, Iceland, Norway, Russia, and Sweden.

Railroads in Europe
http://www.freightworld.com/railroads.html#7
A directory of European railroads on the Internet, the site links to operations in 11 countries including Belgium, the Czech Republic, Finland, and Italy.

Seaports in Europe
http://www.freightworld.com/port_geo.html#7
A service of Freightworld, the site is a database of European seaports online including Antwerp in Belgium, Bremen in Germany, and Rotterdam in the Netherlands.

Trucking and Motor Carriers in Europe
http://www.freightworld.com/truc_geo.html#7
A directory of European trucking and motor carriers online, the site links to operations in 11 countries including Belarus, Estonia, Finland, Spain, and the Ukraine.

Western Europe Representative Offices

Austria

Austrian Trade Commission Delegation to the European Union
http://aw.wk.or.at/awo/ahst-eubruessel.htm
Based in Brussels, the site lists the staff, street address, phone and fax numbers, e-mail link, and office hours of the Austrian Trade Commission Delegation to the European Union.

Canada

Canada-Europe Country Specific
http://www.dfait-maeci.gc.ca/english/geo/europe/index.htm
A service of Foreign Affairs and International Trade Canada, the site provides fact sheets and reports on Canadian trade and relations with over 30 European countries.

Canadian Mission to the European Union
http://www.dfait-maeci.gc.ca/eu-mission/
Posted in English and French, the site provides Canadian Mission press releases, publications, reports on Canada-European Union trade and relations, and a directory of official institutions in Canada and the European Union.

Finland

Representation of Finland to the European Union
http://www.uunet.be/perm-rep-finland/index.html
Posted in Finnish, the site delivers press releases, business bulletins, and reports on Finland-European Union trade and relations.

South Africa

South Africa Mission to the European Union in Brussels
http://wwwdti.pwv.gov.za/dtiwww/foreign_offices.htm
A service of the South Africa Department of Trade and Industry, the site provides contact information for the South Africa Mission to the European Union in Brussels.

Sweden

Permanent Mission of Sweden to the European Union
http://www.ud.se/english/mfa/ambassad/belgien.htm
The site lists the staff, street address, phone and fax numbers, and e-mail link of the Permanent Mission of Sweden to the European Union.

Thailand

Royal Thai Embassy in Brussels
http://www.waw.be/rte-be/
Posted in English, French, and Flemish, the site provides Thai visa and consular information, tourism guides, trade and investment bulletins, and reports on Thai-European Union relations.

United Kingdom

United Kingdom Representation to the European Union
http://ukrep.fco.gov.uk/
Based in Brussels, the site features a United Kingdom Representative newsletter, sector profiles, and a directory of European Union

agencies and United Kingdom government departments.

United States

Council of American States in Europe
http://www.case-europe.com/
Comprised of the European representative offices of individual American state governments, the Council promotes U.S.-European trade. The site includes a mission statement, state profiles, and contact information.

European Institute
http://www.europeaninstitute.org/
Located in Washington, D.C., the site is a U.S.-European networking forum. The site includes a mission statement, program directory, speeches, articles, and *Europe in Washington*, a newsletter on Europe-U.S. affairs.

European Union Committee of the American Chamber of Commerce
http://www.eucommittee.be/
Based in Brussels, the Committee represents American companies operating in Europe. The site includes Committee news, press releases, position papers, and an event calendar.

TransAtlantic Business Dialogue
http://www.tabd.com/index.html
With offices in Brussels and Washington, D.C., the Dialogue is a Europe-U.S. networking and policy forum. The site delivers press releases, speeches, background papers, and an event calendar.

United States Business Navigator
http://www.uscom.ch/main.htm
A service of the U.S. Department of Commerce, the site provides U.S.-European trade news, event information, sector profiles, and business opportunities in aerospace, energy, health care, telecommunications, and information technology.

United States Mission to the European Union
http://www.useu.be/
Based in Brussels, the Mission represents U.S. interests in the European Union. The site includes news, issue bulletins, speeches, fact sheets, and statistics on European Union-U.S. trade and investment flows.

National Sites

Andorra

Andorra Media

Andorra Media
http://www.mediainfo.com/emediajs/specific-geo.htm?region=andorra
Compiled by Editor and Publisher Interactive, the site is a directory of Andorra media sites online.

Andorra Market Guides

All About Andorra
http://www.xmission.com/~dderhak/andorra.htm
Posted in four languages, the site provides Andorran fact sheets, photos, tourism guides, shopping directories, and cultural bulletins.

Andorra Chamber of Commerce
http://www.andorra.ad/ccis/index.html
The online service delivers Andorran background information, business bulletins, annual reports, a member directory, and a calendar of events.

Andorra InfoExport
http://www.infoexport.gc.ca/country-e.asp?continent=Europe&country=2
A service of Foreign Affairs and International Trade Canada, the site provides fact sheets and statistics on Andorran geography, business and politics.

Andorra Market Research
http://strategis.ic.gc.ca/sc_mrkti/ibinddc/engdoc/1a1b2.html
Posted by Industry Canada, the site provides U.S. Central Intelligence Agency fact sheets on Andorran geography, people, government, economy, communications, and transportation.

Govern D'Andorra
http://www.andorra.ad/govern/governuk.html
Homepage of the Andorran government, the site features Andorran backgrounders, government directories, and legislative bulletins.

Andorra Representative Offices

United Kingdom

Consulate of Britain in Andorra
http://www.fco.gov.uk/directory/posts.asp?AD
The site provides contact information for the British Consulate in Andorra.

Austria

Austria Search Tools

Austria Annotated
http://harvest.Austria.EU.net/Server-in-AT/categories.html
Browsable by keyword, the site is an index of Austrian resources online. Categories include media and news, events, finance, education, sciences, and health.

Infospace Austria
http://in-100.infospace.com/_1_110041712__info/index_int.htm
A service of Infospace, the Austrian search engine includes a travel guide, e-mail directory, and business and people finders.

Austria Media

Austria Media
http://www.mediainfo.com/emediajs/specific-geo.htm?region=austria
Compiled by Editor and Publisher Interactive, the site is a directory of Austrian media sites online.

Austria Market Guides

Austria Business Reports
http://italchambers.net/BusinessReports.html
Prepared by the Italian Chamber of Commerce and written in Italian, the site provides Austrian fact sheets, market reports, and commercial guides.

Austria Country Profile
http://www.tradenz.govt.nz/intelligence/profiles/austria.html
A service of the New Zealand Trade Development Board, the site provides Austrian economic statistics, market information, and business tips.

Austria Country Report
http://www.state.gov/www/issues/economic/trade_reports/europe_canada97/austria97.html
Prepared by the U.S. Department of State, the site delivers information on Austrian exchange rates, debt management, trade barriers, export subsidies, and intellectual property protection.

Austria: A Country Study
http://lcweb2.loc.gov/frd/cs/attoc.html
A service of the U.S. Library of Congress, the site delivers fact sheets on Austrian geography, population, agriculture, mining, manufacturing, and foreign economic relations.

Austria InfoExport
http://www.infoexport.gc.ca/country-e.asp?continent=Europe&country=3
A service of Foreign Affairs and International Trade Canada, the site provides Austrian commercial guides and market reports.

Austria Market Information
http://dtiinfo1.dti.gov.uk/ots/austria/
A service of the London-based Department of Trade and Industry, the site delivers Austrian fact sheets, maps, and trade-show information.

Austria Market Research
http://strategis.ic.gc.ca/sc_mrkti/ibinddc/engdoc/1a1b3.html
A service of Industry Canada, the site provides U.S. Department of Commerce reports on Austrian business, politics, trade regulations and standards, investment climate, trade and project financing, business travel, and market opportunities.

Austria Virtual Library
http://www.pitt.edu/~wwwes/austria.nhp.html
A service of the University of Pittsburgh Center for West European Studies, the site is a directory of Austrian online resources. Categories include government, education, and culture.

Austria Press and Information Service
http://www.austria.org/
Based in Washington, D.C., the site provides Austrian news, fact sheets, visa information, tourism guides, culture and science bulletins, international trade contacts, and Radio Austria broadcasts in streaming audio.

Austrian Business Agency
http://www.aba.gv.at/english/main_s.htm
A virtual library of Austrian business information, the site delivers Austrian economic profiles, cultural bulletins, political briefings, success stories, and bilateral trade reports.

Barclays Country Report: Austria
http://www.offshorebanking.barclays.com/
services/economic/yearly/auzfeb98/index.html
Prepared by Barclays Bank, the site reports on
Austrian economic trends, politics, monetary and
fiscal policy, international trade, and U.K.-Austria
merchandise trade and investment flows.

Economic News from Austria
http://www.austria.org/econ11.shtml
Published by the Austrian Press and Information
Service in Washington, D.C., the site delivers
Austrian news headlines, economic forecasts,
and travel information.

How to Do Business in Austria
http://www.wk.or.at/aw/aw_intl/business/home.htm
Developed by the Austrian Foreign Trade Organization, the site is an Austrian business primer.
Topics include the European Union, marketing,
legal information, and investment.

Österreichischen Patentamt
http://www.at-patent.co.at/patent/
The online service provides information about
Austrian patents, trademarks, and other intellectual property.

Post and Telekom Austria
http://www.etb.at/
A service of Telekom Austria, the site provides a
searchable directory of Austrian business and
residential telephone numbers.

Austria Trade Assistance

Austrian Federal Economic Chamber
http://www.wk.or.at/aw/aw_intl/
Based in Vienna, the site provides Austrian fact
sheets, business guides, sector profiles,
international trade statistics, and a directory of
Austrian importers and exporters.

Austrian Foreign Trade by Main Sectors
http://www.wk.or.at/wk/aw/whis/awstate/ahat.htm
Posted in English and German, the site is a
database of Austrian import and export statistics.
The service includes trade data on over 100
countries from Algeria to Venezuela.

Austrian Importing and Exporting Companies
http://www.vttz.at/cgi-bin/
interhost.sh?ID=0&ACTION=LOGIN&NAME=EFA&
PASSWORD=EFA
A searchable directory of Austrian importers and
exporters, the site lists the key contacts, street
address, phone and fax numbers, e-mail link,

and web address of hundreds of Austrian
companies involved in international trade.

Trade Shows in Austria
http://www.expoguide.com/shows/data/loc_3.htm
Compiled by Expoguide, the site is a directory of
upcoming trade shows in Austria.

Austria Representative Offices

Armenia

Embassy of Armenia in Vienna
http://www.armeniaemb.org/forrel/embas2.htm
The site provides contact information for the
Embassy of Armenia in Vienna.

Canada

Embassy of Canada in Vienna
http://www.dfait-maeci.gc.ca/english/missions/rep-
can1e.htm#austria
The site provides contact information for the
Canadian Embassy in Vienna.

Colombia

Embassy of Colombia in Vienna
http://www.embcol.or.at/home/home.htm
Written in Spanish, the site delivers Colombian
fact sheets, business guides, reports on Colom-
bia-Austria trade and relations, and a directory of
Embassy services.

Cyprus

Cyprus Trade Center in Vienna
http://www.cyprustradeny.org/cyny5.html
The site lists the street address, and phone and
fax numbers of the Cyprus Trade Center in
Vienna.

Finland

Embassy of Finland in Vienna
http://www.finlandemb.at/
Posted in German, the site delivers Finnish fact
sheets, visa and passport information, and a
directory of consular and commercial services.

Finland Trade Center in Vienna
http://www.exports.finland.fi/tradecen.htm
The site lists the staff, street address, phone and
fax numbers, and e-mail link of the Finland Trade
Center in Vienna.

France

French Trade Commission in Vienna
http://www.dree.org/autriche/
Posted in French and German, the site provides Austrian market reports, and a directory of export programs for French companies doing business in Austria.

Germany

German-Austria Chamber of Commerce
http://www.ahk.net/en/at/Wien/
The site lists the street address, phone and fax numbers, and e-mail links of the German Chambers in Salzburg and Vienna.

Indonesia

Embassy of Indonesia in Vienna
http://indag.dprin.go.id/INGG/trade/atache.HTM
The site provides contact information for the Indonesian Embassy in Vienna.

Ireland

Enterprise Ireland in Vienna
http://www.irish-trade.ie/office_network/ office_locate01.html#vienna
The site lists the Manager, street address, and phone and fax numbers of the Enterprise Ireland office in Vienna.

Italy

Italian Trade Commission in Vienna
http://www.ice.it/estero/vienna/
Posted in German and Italian, the site features Italian fact sheets, business guides, reports on Austria-Italy trade and relations, and a directory of Commission services.

Japan

Embassy of Japan in Vienna
http://www.embjapan.at/embjapan/
Written in German, the site delivers Japanese news, sector profiles, visa and passport information, bulletins on Austria-Japan trade, and contact information.

Malaysia

Embassy of Malaysia in Vienna
http://www.mnet.com.my/klonline/www/missions/ malmiss/maustria1.htm
The site provides contact information for the Malaysian Embassy in Vienna.

Trade Commission of Malaysia in Vienna
http://www.mnet.com.my/klonline/www/missions/ malmiss/maustria2.htm
The site provides contact information for the Malaysian Trade Commission in Vienna.

Philippines

Philippine Trade and Investment Promotion Office in Vienna
http://www.dti.gov.ph/vnn/
The site provides a mission statement, service directory, and contact information for the Philippine Trade Office in Vienna.

Poland

Embassy of Poland in Vienna
http://www.brh-gov-pl.or.at/
Posted in English and German, the site provides Polish fact sheets, duty free zone reports, company profiles, visa and passport information, and a directory of Embassy services.

Portugal

Portuguese Trade and Investment Office in Vienna
http://www.portugal.org/geninfo/abouticep/ viena.html
The site lists the staff, street address, phone and fax numbers, and e-mail link of the Portuguese Trade and Investment Office in Vienna.

Singapore

Consulate General of Singapore in Vienna
http://www.gov.sg/mfa/consular/mww_a.htm
The site provides contact information for the Singapore Consulate General in Vienna.

South Africa

South Africa Foreign Trade Office in Vienna
http://wwwdti.pwv.gov.za/dtiwww/ foreign_offices.htm
A service of the South Africa Department of Trade and Industry, the site provides contact information for the South Africa Trade Office in Vienna.

Spain

Spanish Commercial Office in Vienna
http://www.icex.es/openURL.html#openURL=/
english/infoproyem/ofcomes/ofcomes.html#EU
The site lists the staff, street address, phone and fax numbers, and e-mail link of the Spanish Commercial Office in Vienna.

Sweden

Embassy of Sweden in Vienna
http://www.ud.se/english/mfa/ambassad/
osterrik.htm
The site lists the staff, street address, phone and fax numbers, and e-mail link of the Swedish Embassy in Vienna.

Switzerland

Swiss-Austrian Chamber of Commerce in Vienna
http://swisstrade.com/
xicodes2.asp?P1=3&lvl=3&cid=A10
The site lists the street address, phone and fax numbers, and e-mail link of the Swiss Austrian Chamber of Commerce in Vienna.

Taiwan

Taiwan Government Information Office in Vienna
http://www.gio.gov.tw/info/ngio/aust-f.html
Posted in Chinese and English, the site lists the street address, phone and fax numbers, and e-mail link of the Taiwan Government Information Office in Vienna.

Thailand

Royal Thai Embassy in Vienna
http://www.mfa.go.th/Embassy/detail/33.htm
The site lists the Ambassador, street address, and phone and fax numbers of the Thai Embassy in Vienna.

Thailand Office of Commercial Affairs in Vienna
http://www.thaitrade.com/thcoaf.html
The site lists the street address, phone and fax numbers, and e-mail link of the Thailand Office of Commercial Affairs in Vienna.

United Kingdom

Embassy of Britain in Vienna
http://www.fco.gov.uk/directory/posts.asp?AS
The site provides contact information for the British Embassy in Vienna.

United States

State of Utah Trade Office in Vienna
http://www.ce.ex.state.ut.us/international/reps/
reps.htm#Austria
A service of the Utah International Business Development Office, the site lists the Representative, street address, phone and fax numbers, and e-mail link of the Utah Trade Office in Vienna.

United States Department of Agriculture Office in Vienna
http://www.usia.gov/abtusia/posts/AU1/
wwwhusda.html
Part of the United States Embassy, the Office promotes United States agricultural exports to Western Europe. The site includes agricultural trade leads, market reports, and agri-food inspection information.

United States Embassy in Vienna
http://www.usia.gov/abtusia/posts/AU1/
wwwhmain.html
Along with United States fact sheets, consular information, and speeches, the site includes information on the Organization for Security and Cooperation in Europe, and United Nations organizations in Vienna.

United States Information Service in Vienna
http://www.usia.gov/abtusia/posts/AU1/
wwwhusis.html
The online service features United States press releases, electronic journals, history and literature guides, and a directory of educational exchange programs between the United States and Austria.

Venezuela

Embassy of Venezuela in Vienna
http://www.trade-venezuela.com/EMBVENG.HTM
The site lists the street address, phone and fax numbers, and e-mail link of the Venezuelan Embassy in Vienna.

Belgium

Belgium Search Tools

Infospace Belgium
http://pic2.infospace.com/_1_34407537_info/
intldb/intl-be.html
Part of the Infospace search service, the site includes a Belgian travel guide, e-mail directory, and business and people finder.

Lycos Belgium
http://www.be.lycos.de/
A country search engine, the site features a Belgian map and a browsable index of Belgian resources online. Categories include business, computers, automotive, and entertainment.

Roadhouse
http://www.roadhouse.be/rh/
A searchable directory of Belgian resources online, the site is divided into 15 major sections including business, education, government and politics, industry, media, and regional information.

WebWatch
http://www.webwatch.be/
A Belgian search service, the site features chat rooms, translation tools, and employment opportunities.

Belgium Media

Belgium Media
http://www.mediainfo.com/emediajs/specific-geo.htm?region=belgium
Compiled by Editor and Publisher Interactive, the site is a directory of Belgian media sites online.

Belgium Market Guides

Barclays Country Report: Belgium
http://www.offshorebanking.barclays.com/
services/economic/yearly/belaug97/belcont.html
Prepared by Barclays Bank, the site reports on Belgian economic trends, politics, monetary and fiscal policy, international trade, and U.K.-Belgium merchandise trade and investment flows.

Belgian Federal Government Online
http://belgium.fgov.be/
An information guide to the Belgian federal government, the site features Belgian press releases, fact sheets, cultural guides, socioeco-nomic statistics, and profiles of government Ministers and State Secretaries.

Belgian Patent Office
http://www.european-patent-office.org/patlib/
country/belgium/
Based in Brussels, the site provides information on Belgian and European patents and intellectual property. The service includes a primer on the use of patent searches for competitive intelligence.

Belgium Business Reports
http://italchambers.net/BusinessReports.html
Prepared by the Italian Chamber of Commerce and written in Italian, the site provides Belgian fact sheets, market reports, and commercial guides.

Belgium Country Profile
http://www.tradenz.govt.nz/intelligence/profiles/
belgium.html
A service of the New Zealand Trade Development Board, the site provides Belgian economic statistics, market information, and business tips.

Belgium Country Report
http://www.state.gov/www/issues/economic/
trade_reports/europe_canada97/belgium97.html
Prepared by the U.S. Department of State, the site delivers information on Belgian exchange rates, debt management, barriers to U.S. trade, export subsidies, and intellectual property protection.

Belgium InfoExport
http://www.infoexport.gc.ca/country-e.asp?continent=Europe&country=5
A service of Foreign Affairs and International Trade Canada, the site provides Belgian commercial guides and market reports.

Belgium Market Information
http://dtiinfo1.dti.gov.uk/ots/belux/
A service of the London-based Department of Trade and Industry, the site delivers Belgian fact sheets, maps, and trade-show information.

Belgium Market Research
http://strategis.ic.gc.ca/sc_mrkti/ibinddc/engdoc/
1a1b4.html
A service of Industry Canada, the site provides U.S. Department of Commerce reports on Belgian business, politics, trade regulations and standards, investment climate, trade and project financing, business travel, and market opportunities.

Belgium Virtual Library
http://www.pitt.edu/~wwwes/belgium.nhp.html
A service of the University of Pittsburgh Center for West European Studies, the site is a directory of Belgian online resources. Categories include government, education, and culture.

Digital Chamber Network
http://www.cci.be/
Based in Brussels, the Chamber represents the interests of some 30,000 Belgian companies. The site includes Belgian business news, press releases, information technology surveys, and a directory of Chamber programs and services.

Federation of Belgian Companies
http://www.vbo-feb.be/
Headquartered in Brussels, the Federation represents the interests of Belgian firms in some 50 industries. The site provides press releases, a member directory, weekly newsletter, press releases, an event calendar, and guides on the introduction of the Euro, the European single currency.

Infobel
http://www.infobel.be/
A browsable database of Belgian addresses and telephone numbers, the site includes Belgian maps, travel guides, classifieds, employment opportunities, and electronic shopping.

Invest in Belgium
http://www.ib.be/invest-belgium/
A service of the Belgium Ministry of Economic Affairs, the site delivers primers on Belgian investment opportunities, business entities, taxation, labor, work permits, and visas.

Setting Up in Belgium
http://www.belgium-emb.org/usa/business/pocket96.html
Developed by the Belgian Embassy in Washington, D.C., the site is a guide to establishing a Belgian business. Topics include choice of business entities, tax questions, work and residency permits, and real estate issues.

TIJD
http://www.tijd.be/tijd/
The website of publishing company Uitgeversbedrijf Tijd, the service features Belgian news, business guides, investment primers, cultural bulletins, shopping directories, and an event calendar.

Belgium Trade Assistance

Belgian Exports
http://www.belgiumexports.com/
Developed by ABC Business Information Services, the site is a searchable directory of Belgian and Luxembourg exporters and export products. The database is browsable by product, company, and keyword.

Belgium Customs and International Trade
http://www.ib.be/invest-belgium/trade.htm
A service of the Belgium Federal Agency for Foreign Investments, the site provides tutorials on Belgian custom duties, preferential agreements, customs facilities, and tax and tariff abatement programs.

Belgian Diplomatic Posts
http://www.ib.be/invest-belgium/embassy.htm
Written in French, the site is a directory of the street addresses, phone and fax numbers, and geographic jurisdictions of Belgian Embassies and Consulates around the world.

Belgian Foreign Trade Board
http://www.obcebdbh.be/en/obce/index.html
Based in Brussels, the Board promotes Belgian exports and international investment. The site provides Belgian export news, economic statistics, investment guides, market surveys, and travel tips.

Belgian and Luxembourg Exporters
http://www.obcebdbh.be/exp/en/exp.html
A service of the Belgian Trade Board, the site is a searchable directory of Belgian exporters. Categories include manufacturers, general contractors, consultants, services, and wholesalers.

Belgium Trade Area
http://www.duportail.be/belgiumtrade/
Developed by Guy Duportail, the site is a free Belgian trade lead service. Users may post and sell offers, and requests for distributors, strategic alliances, and joint ventures.

Belgium Trade and Investment
http://www.belgium-emb.org/usa/business/business.html
A service of the Belgian Embassy in Washington, D.C., the site provides Belgian business bulletins, market guides, and a directory of Belgian international trade resources online.

Export Services
http://www.cci.be/services/rendering.htm#export
The site describes the export services of the Digital Chamber Network, a Belgian business association.

Made in Belgium
http://www.madeinbelgium.be/
A Belgian investment guide, the site provides Belgian maps, fact sheets, business opportunities, regional profiles, and a directory of leading Belgian operations in agri-food, construction, pharmaceuticals, and transportation.

Trade Point Brussels
http://www.obcebdbh.be/tradepoint/welcome.html
Part of the United Nations Global Trade Point Network, the site provides Brussels trade leads, market bulletins, and contact information.

Trade Shows in Belgium
http://www.expoguide.com/shows/data/loc_5.htm
Compiled by Expoguide, the site is a directory of upcoming trade shows in Belgium.

Belgium Representative Offices

Armenia

Embassy of Armenia in Brussels
http://www.armeniaemb.org/forrel/embas2.htm
The site provides contact information for the Armenian Embassy in Brussels.

Australia

Embassy of Australia in Belgium
http://ourworld.compuserve.com/homepages/Australian_Embassy_Brussels/
The virtual Embassy provides Australian fact sheets, press releases, customs information, travel guides, reports on Australia-Belgium trade, and a directory of consular services.

Austria

Austrian Trade Commission in Brussels
http://aw.wk.or.at/awo/ahst-bruessel.htm
The site lists the staff, street address, phone and fax numbers, e-mail link, and office hours of the Austrian Trade Commission in Brussels.

Brunei Darussalam

Embassy of Brunei Darussalam in Brussels
http://www.brunet.bn/homepage/gov/bruemb/govemb.htm
The site provides contact information for the Brunei Darussalam Embassy in Brussels.

Canada

Embassy of Canada in Brussels
http://www.dfait-maeci.gc.ca/english/missions/rep-can1e.htm#belgium
The site provides contact information for the Canadian Embassy in Brussels.

Québec Delegation in Brussels
http://www.mri.gouv.qc.ca/dans_le_monde/europe/bruxelles_an.html
A service of the Québec Department of International Relations, the site lists the street address, phone and fax numbers, and e-mail link of the Québec Delegation in Brussels.

Quebel
http://www.quebel.org/
A Québec-Belgium networking service, the site provides contact information and business matchmaking tools for Québec and Belgium operations.

China

China Council for the Promotion of International Trade in Brussels
http://www.ccpit.org/engVersion/cp_about/cp_over/cp_over.html
A Chinese export promotion service, the site provides contact information for the China Council for the Promotion of International Trade office in Brussels.

Cyprus

Cyprus Trade Center in Brussels
http://www.cyprustradeny.org/cyny5.html
The site lists the street address, and phone and fax numbers of the Cyprus Trade Center in Brussels.

Fiji

Embassy of Fiji in Brussels
http://fiji.gov.fj/core/fj_mis.html
The site provides contact information for the Fijian Embassy in Brussels.

Finland

Finland Trade Center in Brussels
http://www.exports.finland.fi/tradecen.htm
The site lists the staff, street address, phone and fax numbers, and e-mail link of the Finland Trade Center in Brussels.

France

French Trade Commission in Brussels
http://www.dree.org/belgique/
A French trade promotion service, the site provides Belgian market reports, and a directory of export programs for French companies doing business in Belgium.

Ghana

Embassy of Ghana in Brussels
http://www.juntung.com/ghana-consul-hk/2misabo.htm
The site provides contact information for the Ghana Embassy in Brussels.

India

Indian Commercial Mission in Brussels
http://www.nic.in/commin/ICM.HTM
The site lists the street address, phone and fax numbers, and e-mail link of the Indian Commercial Mission in Brussels.

Ireland

Enterprise Ireland in Brussels
http://www.irish-trade.ie/office_network/office_locate01.html#anchor1413331
The site lists the Manager, street address, and phone and fax numbers of the Enterprise Ireland office in Brussels.

Italy

Consulate General of Italy in Brussels
http://www.euronet.be/consitbxl/
Posted in Italian, the site provides Italian news, fact sheets, market guides, education bulletins, visa and passport information, and a directory a consular services.

Embassy of Italy in Brussels
http://www.pi.cnr.it/ambitbe/
Along with Italian economic and tourism information, the site features Belgian fact sheets, investment guides, city profiles, and government directories.

Japan

Embassy of Japan in Brussels
http://www.amb-jpn.be/
A Japanese information center, the site provides Japanese press releases, speeches, economic fact sheets, an event calendar, and reports on Japan-European Union trade.

Gateway to Japan
http://www.cci.be/japan/default.htm
A service of the Digital Chamber Network, the site features Japanese business primers, an event calendar, and reports on Belgium-Japan bilateral trade and relations.

Madagascar

Embassy of Madagascar in Brussels
http://www.madagascar-contacts.com/us/adresse.htm#alext
Along with a directory of Madagascar government agencies, the site provides contact information for the Madagascar Embassy in Brussels.

Malaysia

Embassy of Malaysia in Brussels
http://www.mnet.com.my/klonline/www/missions/malmiss/mbelgium1.htm
The site provides contact information for the Malaysian Embassy in Brussels.

Trade Office of Malaysia in Brussels
http://www.mnet.com.my/klonline/www/missions/malmiss/mbelgium2.htm
The site provides contact information for the Malaysian Trade Office in Brussels.

Mexico

Embassy of Mexico in Brussels
http://www.embamexbel.be/
Posted in three languages, the site provides Mexican fact sheets, political bulletins, economic

statistics, travel guides, and a directory of Embassy services.

Mongolia

Embassy of Mongolia in Brussels
http://users.skynet.be/mongolia/body.htm
Featuring a welcome address by the Ambassador, the site delivers country fact sheets, visa and passport information, and reports on Mongolian agriculture, mining, manufacturing, energy, international trade, and transportation.

Namibia

Embassy of Namibia in Brussels
http://www.republicofnamibia.com/adress.htm
Along with a directory of Namibian companies and government agencies, the site provides contact information for the Namibian Embassy in Brussels.

Nepal

Embassy of Nepal in Brussels
http://www.info-nepal.com/members/fips/contacts/nepalese.html
The site provides contact information for the Nepalese Embassy in Brussels.

Norway

Embassy of Norway in Brussels
http://www.ntc.no/cgi-bin/wbch.exe?html=../templates/utekontor2.html&profile=1103
The site lists the staff, street address, phone and fax numbers, and e-mail link of the Norwegian Embassy in Brussels.

Organization of Eastern Caribbean States

High Commission of the Organization of Eastern Caribbean States in Brussels
http://www.stkittsnevis.net/offices.html
The site provides contact information for the Organization of Eastern Caribbean States in Brussels.

Pakistan

Pakistan Trade Office in Brussels
http://www.jamal.com/epb/ptoa.htm
The site provides contact information for the Pakistan Trade Office in Brussels.

Philippines

Embassy of the Philippines in Brussels
http://embassy.belgamedia.be/philippines/
Featuring greetings from the Ambassador, the virtual Embassy provides Philippine maps, business guides, investment incentive information, industrial park reports, and tourism bulletins.

Philippine Trade and Investment Promotion Office in Brussels
http://www.dti.gov.ph/belg/
The site provides a mission statement, service directory, and contact information for the Philippine Trade Office in Brussels.

Portugal

Portuguese Trade and Investment Office in Brussels
http://www.portugal.org/geninfo/abouticep/bruxelas.html
The site lists the staff, street address, phone and fax numbers, and e-mail link of the Portuguese Trade and Investment Office in Brussels.

Singapore

Consulate General of Singapore in Brussels
http://www.gov.sg/mfa/consular/mww_b.htm
The site provides contact information for the Singapore Consulate General in Brussels.

South Africa

Embassy of South Africa in Brussels
http://www.ambassade.net/southafrica/
The online service delivers South African news, maps, and regional profiles. The site includes primers on South African banking, foreign investment, patents, infrastructure, and international trade.

South Africa Foreign Trade Office in Brussels
http://wwwdti.pwv.gov.za/dtiwww/foreign_offices.htm
A service of the South Africa Department of Trade and Industry, the site provides contact information for the South Africa Trade Office in Brussels.

South Korea

Korean International Trade Association in Brussels
http://www.kita.or.kr/eng/national.html

The site provides contact information for the Korean International Trade Association in Brussels.

Spain

Spanish Commercial Office in Brussels
http://www.icex.es/openURL.html#openURL=/
english/infoproyem/ofcomes/ofcomes.html#EU
The site lists the staff, street address, phone and fax numbers, and e-mail link of the Spanish Commercial Office in Brussels.

Sweden

Embassy of Sweden in Brussels
http://www.ud.se/english/mfa/ambassad/
belgien.htm
The site lists the staff, street address, phone and fax numbers, and e-mail link of the Swedish Embassy in Brussels.

Taiwan

Taiwan Government Information Office in Brussels
http://www.gio.gov.tw/info/ngio/bel-f.html
Posted in Chinese and English, the site lists the street address, phone and fax numbers, and e-mail link of the Taiwan Government Information Office in Brussels.

Tanzania

Embassy of Tanzania in Brussels
http://www.tanzania-online.gov.uk/visa/
envoys.html
The site provides contact information for the Tanzanian Embassy in Brussels.

Thailand

Royal Thai Embassy in Brussels
http://www.waw.be/rte-be/
Posted in English, Flemish, and Thai, the site features Thai news, visa and passport information, socioeconomic statistics, government development plans, trade and investment guides, tourism bulletins, and an opinion box.

Thailand Office of Commercial Affairs in Brussels
http://www.thaitrade.com/thcoaf.html
The site lists the street address, phone and fax numbers, and e-mail link of the Thailand Office of Commercial Affairs in Brussels.

United Kingdom

British Embassy in Brussels
http://www.british-embassy.be/
A British information service, the site provides British news, visa and passport information, export guides, investment primers, cultural bulletins, and reports on Belgium-British trade and relations.

Consulate General of Britain in Antwerp
http://www.fco.gov.uk/directory/posts.asp?BE
The site provides contact information for the British Consulate General in Antwerp.

United States

American Chamber of Commerce in Belgium
http://www.amcham.be/
Based in Brussels, the Chamber promotes Belgium-United States trade. The site includes Chamber news, member profiles, committee reports, and a directory of programs and upcoming events.

Office of Agricultural Affairs
http://www.useu.be/agri/usda.html
Part of the United States Department of Agriculture, the Office promotes United States agricultural exports to the European Union. The site provides current issue reports and contact information.

Port Authority of New York and New Jersey in Antwerp
http://www.case-europe.com/States/nj.htm
Along with New Jersey fact sheets, the site lists the staff, street address, phone and fax numbers, and e-mail link of the Port Authority of New York and New Jersey in Antwerp.

State of Arkansas European Trade Office in Brussels
http://www.case-europe.com/States/ar.htm
Along with Arkansas fact sheets, the site lists the Managing Director, street address, phone and fax numbers, and e-mail link of the State of Arkansas European Trade Office in Brussels.

State of Georgia Trade Office in Brussels
http://www.case-europe.com/States/ga.htm
Along with Georgia fact sheets, the site lists the Managing Director, street address, phone and fax numbers, and e-mail link of the State of Georgia Trade Office in Brussels.

State of Illinois European Office in Brussels

http://www.commerce.state.il.us/dcca/files/int'l/belgium.htm
A service of the Illinois Department of Commerce and Community Affairs, the site lists the Managing Director, street address, phone and fax numbers, and e-mail link of the Illinois Trade Office in Brussels.

State of Kansas European Office in Brussels

http://www.kansascommerce.com/0306-04why.html#WE WELCOME
Developed by the Kansas Department of Commerce and Housing, the site lists the Director, street address, phone and fax numbers, and e-mail link of the Kansas European Office in Brussels.

State of Kentucky European Office in Brussels

http://www.state.ky.us/edc/foreign.htm
Prepared by the Kentucky Cabinet for Economic Development, the site lists the Director, street address, phone and fax numbers, and e-mail link of the Kentucky European Office in Brussels.

State of Michigan Trade Office in Brussels

http://www.case-europe.com/States/mi.htm
Along with Michigan fact sheets, the site lists the staff, street address, phone and fax numbers, and e-mail link of the Michigan Trade Office in Brussels.

State of Ohio European Office in Brussels

http://www.state.oh.us/agr/outstate.html
The site lists the street address, phone and fax numbers, and e-mail link of the Ohio European Office in Brussels.

State of Oklahoma Trade Office in Antwerp

http://www.case-europe.com/States/ok.htm
Along with Oklahoma fact sheets, the site lists the staff, street address, phone and fax numbers, and e-mail links of the Oklahoma Trade Office in Antwerp.

State of Utah European Office in Brussels

http://www.ce.ex.state.ut.us/international/reps/reps.htm
A service of the Utah International Business Development Office, the site lists the Trade Executive, regional responsibilities, street address, phone and fax numbers, and e-mail link of the Utah European Office in Brussels.

United States Embassy in Belgium

http://www.usinfo.be/
The digital Embassy delivers United States news, government bulletins, press releases, position papers, meeting transcripts, visa and passport information, and reports on Belgium-United States trade and relations.

Venezuela

Embassy of Venezuela in Brussels

http://www.trade-venezuela.com/EMBVENG.HTM
A service of the Venezuelan federal government, the site lists the street address, phone and fax numbers, and e-mail link of the Venezuelan Embassy in Brussels.

Western Samoa

Embassy of Western Samoa in Belgium

http://www.interwebinc.com/samoa/missbe.html
The site lists the street address and phone and fax numbers of the Western Samoan Embassy in Belgium.

Corsica

Corsica Market Guides

Invest in Corsica
http://www.netcorse.tm.fr/investir/us_index.htm
A virtual investment guide, the site provides Corsican fact sheets, photos, government bulletins, business incentive information, and a directory of leading Corsican companies online.

Corsica Trade Assistance

Free Zone in Corsica
http://www.netcorse.tm.fr/investir/zone_franche/us_zone_franche.htm
Written in English, French, and Italian, the site profiles the Corsican Free Zone, a business enclave that provides special tax and tariff abatements.

Denmark

Denmark Search Tools

Infoseek Denmark
http://www.infoseek.com/Home?pg=Home.html&sv=DK
Part of the Infoseek international search network, the site provides personalized news, browsing tips, and web scans of Denmark resources online.

Yahoo Denmark

http://www.yahoo.dk/
A service of Yahoo, the site provides Danish news, web-based personal management tools, and Internet searching.

Denmark Media

Denmark Media

http://www.mediainfo.com/emediajs/specific-geo.htm?region=denmark
Compiled by Editor and Publisher Interactive, the site is a directory of Danish media sites online including city guides, magazines, newspapers, radio, and television stations.

Denmark Market Guides

Barclays Country Report: Denmark

http://www.offshorebanking.barclays.com/services/economic/yearly/denjun97/index.html
Prepared by Barclays Bank, the site reports on Danish economic trends, politics, monetary and fiscal policy, international trade, and U.K.-Denmark merchandise trade and investment flows.

Business and Economy

http://www.denmarkemb.org/trade.htm
A service of the Danish Embassy in Washington, D.C., the site features Danish investment news, company profiles, socioeconomic statistics, and a directory of Danish government resources online.

Business Guide to Denmark

http://www.krak.dk/export/default.asp
Sponsored by the Danish Chamber of Commerce, the site provides Danish fact sheets, travel guides, sector profiles, and reports on Denmark-European Union trade and relations.

Copenhagen Capacity

http://www.copcap.dk/
A Copenhagen investment guide, the site delivers primers on Copenhagen air links, telecommunications, transportation, warehousing, taxation, business incentives, and companies.

Denmark Book

http://www.um.dk/danmark/denmark/
Developed by the Danish Ministry of Foreign Affairs, the site provides fact sheets on Danish history, geography, business, culture, environment, and quality of life.

Denmark Business Briefs

http://www.austrade.gov.au/IOOM/Denmark/
A service of Austrade, the site offers fact sheets on Danish business etiquette, foreign investment, corporate taxation, marketing, and visas.

Denmark Country Profile

http://www.tradenz.govt.nz/intelligence/profiles/denmark.html
A service of the New Zealand Trade Development Board, the site provides Danish economic statistics, market information, and business tips.

Denmark Country Report

http://www.state.gov/www/issues/economic/trade_reports/europe_canada97/denmark97.html
Prepared by the U.S. Department of State, the site delivers information on Denmark exchange rates, debt management, barriers to U.S. trade, export subsidies, and intellectual property protection.

Denmark in Figures

http://www.denmarkemb.org/tal95.htm
A service of the Danish Embassy in Washington, D.C., the site provides facts and statistics on Danish elections, referendums, education, standard of living, employment, income, and environmental protection.

Denmark InfoExport

http://www.infoexport.gc.ca/country-e.asp?continent=Europe&country=10
A service of Foreign Affairs and International Trade Canada, the site provides Danish commercial guides and market reports.

Denmark Market Information

http://dtiinfo1.dti.gov.uk/ots/denmark/
A service of the London-based Department of Trade and Industry, the site delivers Danish fact sheets, maps, and trade-show information.

Denmark Market Research

http://strategis.ic.gc.ca/sc_mrkti/ibinddc/engdoc/1a1b10.html
A service of Industry Canada, the site provides U.S. Department of Commerce reports on Danish business, politics, trade regulations and standards, investment climate, trade and project financing, business travel, and market opportunities.

Denmark Patent Office

http://www.dkpto.dk/
Posted in Danish and English, the site provides information on Danish patents, industrial

designs, and other intellectual property. The service includes a directory of Denmark Patent Office staff and programs.

Industry and Economy
http://www.denmarkemb.org/indust.htm
A primer on the Danish economy, the site delivers fact sheets on the Danish agri-food, apparel, energy, environment, financial services, and tourism industries.

Invest in Denmark
http://www.investindk.com/
Based in Copenhagen, the site features Danish business news, maps, socioeconomic statistics, investment guides, productivity comparisons, sector studies, and company profiles.

Ministry of Business and Industry
http://www.em.dk/engvers.htm
Along with a mission statement and program directory, the government site provides position papers on Danish transportation, technology, logistics, and resource development.

Denmark Trade Assistance

Danish Diplomatic Missions Abroad
http://www.um.dk/english/organisation/links.html
A service of the Royal Ministry of Foreign Affairs, the site is a directory of Danish Embassies and Consulates online around the world.

Danish Export Group Association
http://www.dega.dk/
Based in Silkeborg, the Association promotes the exports of Danish member companies. The site includes news, contact information, and a member directory.

Danish Exporters
http://www.danish-exporters.dk/
Published by Tele Danmark Forlag, the site is a searchable directory of some 6,000 Danish exporters. The database is browsable by product, company name, number of employees, and target export market.

Export Promotion Denmark
http://www.ees.dk/expopromo.html
A Danish export promotion service, the site lists the street address, phone and fax numbers, and e-mail link of the Export Promotion Denmark office in Copenhagen.

Made in Denmark
http://www.made-in-denmark.dk/indexny.htm
A browsable directory of Danish products and companies, the site profiles firms in over 20 categories including agriculture, investment banking, waste technology, and fish processing.

Royal Danish Ministry of Foreign Affairs
http://www.um.dk/
Written in English and Danish, the site provides Danish news, fact sheets, press releases, foreign policy statements, and a directory of consular services.

Trade Shows in Denmark
http://www.expoguide.com/shows/data/loc_13.htm
Compiled by Expoguide, the site is a directory of upcoming trade shows in Denmark.

Denmark Representative Offices

Foreign Representations in Denmark
http://www.geocities.com/CapitolHill/Lobby/8593/index.html
The online service provides a directory of Danish diplomatic offices online, and a list of embassies, consulates-general, consulates, trade offices and other representation offices in Denmark.

Australia

Austrade Scandinavia in Copenhagen
http://www.austrade.gov.au/Scandinavia/
An Australian export promotion service, the site features business guides, investment primers, and a directory of trade assistance programs for Australian exporters in Denmark and Scandinavia.

Austria

Austrian Trade Commission in Copenhagen
http://aw.wk.or.at/awo/ahst-kopenhagen.htm
The site lists the staff, street address, phone and fax numbers, e-mail link, and office hours of the Austrian Trade Commission in Copenhagen.

Canada

Canadian Embassy in Copenhagen
http://www.canada.dk/
Posted in English and French, the site provides Canadian fact sheets, business guides, visa and passport information, travel bulletins, and reports

on Canada-Denmark and Canada-European Union trade and relations.

Finland

Embassy of Finland in Copenhagen
http://www.finamb.dk/
Written in four languages, the site delivers Finnish news, press releases, cultural bulletins, export guides, visa and working permit information, and a directory of Embassy programs.

Finland Trade Center in Copenhagen
http://www.exports.finland.fi/tradecen.htm
The site lists the staff, street address, phone and fax numbers, and e-mail link of the Finland Trade Center in Copenhagen.

France

Embassy of France in Copenhagen
http://www.amba-france.dk/
Posted in Danish and French, the site provides French fact sheets, business guides, reports on Denmark-France trade and relations, and a directory of Embassy services.

French Trade Commission in Copenhagen
http://www.dree.org/danemark/
A French trade promotion service, the site provides Danish market reports, and a directory of export programs for French companies doing business in Denmark.

Germany

German Chamber of Commerce in Copenhagen
http://www.ahk.net/en/dk/Boersen/
The site lists the Chairperson, Chief Executive Officer, street address, and phone and fax numbers of the German Chamber in Copenhagen.

Ghana

Embassy of Ghana in Copenhagen
http://www.juntung.com/ghana-consul-hk/2misabo.htm
The site provides contact information for the Ghana Embassy in Copenhagen.

India

Indian Commercial Mission in Copenhagen
http://www.nic.in/commin/ICM.HTM

The site lists the street address, phone and fax numbers, and e-mail link of the Indian Commercial Mission in Copenhagen.

Indonesia

Embassy of Indonesia in Copenhagen
http://indag.dprin.go.id/INGG/trade/atache.HTM
The site provides contact information for the Indonesian Embassy in Copenhagen.

Ireland

Enterise Ireland in Copenhagen
http://www.irish-trade.ie/office_network/office_locate01.html#anchor1414868
The site lists the Manager, street address, and phone and fax numbers of the Enterprise Ireland office in Copenhagen.

Israel

Embassy of Israel in Copenhagen
http://www.pip.dknet.dk/~pip3028/
The virtual Embassy delivers Israeli news, press releases, cultural bulletins, tourism guides, passport information, an event calendar, and a directory of business and investment opportunities in Israel.

Japan

Embassy of Japan in Copenhagen
http://www.embjapan.dk/
The online service provides Japanese visa information, cultural bulletins, a directory of Japanese-related organizations in Denmark, and a list of Japanese national holidays.

Mexico

Embassy of Mexico in Copenhagen
http://www.mexican-embassy.dk/
Posted in English and Spanish, the site features Mexican news, press releases, state of the nation reports, Chiapas updates, government bulletins, and cultural guides.

Norway

Embassy of Norway in Copenhagen
http://www.norsk.dk/
The site provides Norwegian fact sheets, visa and passport information, government directories, cultural bulletins, and travel information.

Pakistan

Pakistan Trade Office in Copenhagen
http://www.jamal.com/epb/ptoa.htm
The site provides contact information for the Pakistan Trade Office in Copenhagen.

Portugal

Portuguese Trade and Investment Office in Copenhagen
http://www.portugal.org/geninfo/abouticep/denmark.html
The site lists the staff, street address, phone and fax numbers, and e-mail link of the Portuguese Trade and Investment Office in Copenhagen.

Singapore

Consulate General of Singapore in Copenhagen
http://www.gov.sg/mfa/consular/mww_d.htm
The site provides contact information for the Singapore Consulate General in Copenhagen.

Spain

Spanish Commercial Office in Copenhagen
http://www.mcx.es/copenhague/
Posted in Danish and English, the site provides Spanish fact sheets, economic bulletins, investment primers, event information, and product catalogs.

Sweden

Embassy of Sweden in Copenhagen
http://www.ud.se/english/mfa/ambassad/danmark.htm
The site lists the staff, street address, phone and fax numbers, and e-mail link of the Swedish Embassy in Copenhagen.

Taiwan

Taiwan Government Information Office in Copenhagen
http://www.gio.gov.tw/info/ngio/den-f.html
Posted in Chinese and English, the site lists the street address, phone and fax numbers, and e-mail link of the Taiwan Government Information Office in Copenhagen.

Thailand

Royal Thai Embassy in Copenhagen
http://www.mfa.go.th/Embassy/detail/77.htm
The site lists the Ambassador, street address, and phone and fax numbers of the Thai Embassy in Copenhagen.

Thailand Office of Commercial Affairs in Copenhagen
http://www.thaitrade.com/thcoaf.html
The site lists the street address, phone and fax numbers, and e-mail link of the Thailand Office of Commercial Affairs in Copenhagen.

Turkey

Embassy of Turkey in Copenhagen
http://www.turkembassy.dk/
Posted in English and Turkish, the site provides a staff roster, Turkish visa and passport information, and a directory of Embassy programs.

United Kingdom

Embassy of Britain in Copenhagen
http://www.britishembassy.dk/
The site delivers British fact sheets, visa and passport information, and a directory of consular and commercial services.

United States

United States Embassy in Denmark
http://www.usis.dk/
Featuring a welcome message from the Ambassador, the site delivers United States news, government bulletins, press releases, position papers, and a directory of Embassy services.

Faroe Islands

Fareo Islands Media

Fareo Islands Media
http://www.mediainfo.com/emediajs/specific-geo.htm?region=faeroeislands
Compiled by Editor and Publisher Interactive, the site is a directory of Fareo Islands media sites online.

Faroe Islands Market Guides

Companies in the Faroe Islands
http://randburg.com/fa/index.html
A service of Maryland-based Randburg Corporation, the site provides a directory of Faroese resources and companies online. Categories

include transportation, agri-food, electronics, and machinery.

Faroe Islands Business Environment
http://www.denmarkemb.org/faroebusi/ffibe.html
Developed by the Faroe Islands Development Office, the site delivers fact sheets on Faroese geography, culture, climate, transportation, construction, telecommunications, education, taxation, foreign relations, and politics.

Faroe Islands Links and Statistics
http://www.framtak.com/info/links.html
A virtual library of Faroe Islands information, the site includes Faroese news, socioeconomic statistics, photos, travel guides, company directories, business primers, and employment opportunities.

Faroe Islands Market Research
http://strategis.ic.gc.ca/sc_mrkti/ibinddc/engdoc/ 1a1b14.html
Posted by Industry Canada, the site provides U.S. Central Intelligence Agency fact sheets on Faroese geography, people, government, economy, communications, and transportation.

Government of the Faroe Islands
http://www.randburg.com/fa/governme.html
The online service provides an overview of the Faroe Islands government and economic base, a list of Faroe Islands representative offices in Denmark and Scotland, and a directory of Faroese resources online.

Finland

Finland Search Tools

Haku.Net
http://www.haku.net/
Written in Finnish, the site is a web navigation service and Finnish link directory. A frequently asked question page is provided in English.

Finland Media

Finland Media
http://www.mediainfo.com/emediajs/specific- geo.htm?region=finland
Compiled by Editor and Publisher Interactive, the site is a directory of Finland media sites online.

NewsRoom Finland
http://virtual.finland.fi/nr/index.html
A service of the Finnish Ministry for Foreign

Affairs, the site provides Finnish daily news, press releases, speeches, and arts and sports weekly reports.

Finland Market Guides

Barclays Country Report: Finland
http://www.offshorebanking.barclays.com/ services/economic/yearly/finfeb98/finconts.html
Prepared by Barclays Bank, the site reports on Finnish economic trends, politics, monetary and fiscal policy, international trade, and U.K.-Finland merchandise trade and investment flows.

Confederation of Finnish Industry and Employers
http://www.tt.fi/english/index.shtml
Established in 1992, the Confederation represents the interests of Finnish manufacturing, construction and service sector employers. The site includes a mission statement, committee directory, Finnish fact sheets, and economic forecasts.

Country Commercial Guide
http://www.state.gov/www/about_state/business/ com_guides/1998/europe_canada/finland98.html
Prepared by the U.S. Embassy in Helsinki, the site delivers primers on the Finnish economy, political environment, trade regulations and standards, investment climate, trade and project financing, and business travel.

Finland Business Briefs
http://www.austrade.gov.au/IOOM/Finland/
A service of Austrade, the site offers fact sheets on Finnish business etiquette, foreign investment, corporate taxation, marketing, and visas.

Finland Country Profile
http://www.tradenz.govt.nz/intelligence/profiles/ finland.html
A service of the New Zealand Trade Development Board, the site provides Finnish economic statistics, market information, and business tips.

Finland Country Report
http://www.state.gov/www/issues/economic/ trade_reports/europe_canada97/finland97.html
Prepared by the U.S. Department of State, the site delivers information on Finnish exchange rates, debt management, trade barriers, export subsidies, and intellectual property protection.

Finland: A Country Study
http://lcweb2.loc.gov/frd/cs/fitoc.html
A service of the U.S. Library of Congress, the site

delivers fact sheets on Finnish geography, population, agriculture, mining, manufacturing, and foreign economic relations.

Finland InfoExport
http://www.infoexport.gc.ca/country-e.asp?continent=Europe&country=13
A service of Foreign Affairs and International Trade Canada, the site provides Finnish commercial guides and market reports.

Finland Market Information
http://dtiinfo1.dti.gov.uk/ots/finland/
A service of the London-based Department of Trade and Industry, the site delivers Finnish fact sheets, maps, and trade-show information.

Finland Market Research
http://strategis.ic.gc.ca/sc_mrkti/ibinddc/engdoc/1a1b15.html
A service of Industry Canada, the site provides U.S. Department of Commerce reports on Finnish business, politics, trade regulations and standards, investment climate, trade and project financing, business travel, and market opportunities.

Finland Patent Office
http://www.prh.fi/
Written in English, Finnish and Swedish, the site provides information on Finnish patents, trademarks, layout designs of integrated circuits, and other intellectual property.

Finland Virtual Library
http://www.pitt.edu/~wwwes/finland.nhp.html
A service of the University of Pittsburgh Center for West European Studies, the site is a directory of Finnish online resources. Categories include government, education, and culture.

Invest in Finland Bureau
http://www.investinfinland.fi/
A virtual investment primer, the site provides Finnish fact sheets, cost comparisons, business guides, case histories, and a directory of Finnish investment opportunities in electronics, agri-food, medical technology, and other industries.

Research Institute of the Finnish Economy
http://www.etla.fi/
Based in Helsinki, the Institute conducts Finnish socioeconomic research. The site delivers Finnish financial surveys, economic forecasts, and sector profiles.

Statistics Finland
http://www.stat.fi/sf/home.html
Posted in English, Finnish, and Swedish, the site provides the latest statistics on Finnish gross national product, industrial output, employment, unemployment, international trade, and other economic indicators.

Virtual Finland
http://virtual.finland.fi/
Developed by the Finland Ministry for Foreign Affairs, the site delivers Finnish news, satellite photos, parliamentary guides, cultural primers, government directories, and company profiles.

Finland Trade Assistance

Finland Exports
http://www.exports.finland.fi/
Developed by the Finnish Foreign Trade Association, the site provides Finnish product directories, sector profiles, and Northern Europe market reports. The service includes a directory of Finnish export networks—consortiums of Finnish businesspeople who work together to target a particular export market.

Finland Trade Centers
http://www.exports.finland.fi/tradecen.htm
A service of the Finnish Foreign Trade Association, the site lists the Trade Commissioners, street addresses, phone and fax numbers, and e-mail links of the Finland Trade Centers in some 50 countries around the world.

Finnish Missions on the Web
http://virtual.finland.fi/ministry/english/emba.html
Prepared by the Finland Ministry for Foreign Affairs, the site is a directory of Finnish diplomatic offices online from Abu Dhabi to Windhoek to Vilnius.

Trade Finland
http://www.trade-finland.com/
Posted in English and Finnish, the site is a browsable directory of Finnish export companies. The database is searchable by keyword, company name, product, industry, and number of employees.

Trade Point Finland
http://www.tradepoint.fi/
Part of the United Nations Global Trade Point Network, the site provides Finnish trade leads, market bulletins, and contact information.

Trade Shows in Finland
http://www.expoguide.com/shows/data/loc_17.htm
Compiled by Expoguide, the site is a directory of upcoming trade shows in Finland.

Finland Representative Offices

Australia

Austrade Scandinavia
http://www.austrade.gov.au/Scandinavia/
An Australian export promotion service, the site features business guides, investment primers, and a directory of trade assistance programs for Australian exporters in Finland and Scandinavia.

Austria

Austrian Trade Commission in Helsinki
http://aw.wk.or.at/awo/ahst-helsinki.htm
The site lists the staff, street address, phone and fax numbers, e-mail link, and office hours of the Austrian Trade Commission in Helsinki.

Canada

Embassy of Canada in Helsinki
http://www.canada.fi/
Along with Canadian fact sheets and passport information, the site features market reports on selected Finnish industries including biotechnology, pharmaceuticals, aerospace, transportation, consumer goods, and agri-food.

Estonia

Embassy of Estonia in Helsinki
http://www.estemb.fi/
The virtual Embassy delivers Estonian fact sheets, visa information, reports on Estonia-Finland trade and relations, and a directory of Embassy programs and staff.

France

Embassy of France in Helsinki
http://www.hrsk.edu.fi/ambafrance/
Posted in Finnish and French, the site provides French background information, education reports, an event calendar, and a directory of Embassy programs.

French Trade Commission in Helsinki
http://www.dree.org/finlande/
A French trade promotion service, the site

provides Finnish market reports, and a directory of export programs for French companies doing business in Finland.

Germany

German Embassy in Helsinki
http://www.germanembassy.fi/
Written in German, the site delivers German news, fact sheets, government guides, cultural bulletins, contact information, and a directory of consular services.

Greece

Embassy of Greece in Finland
http://www.personal.eunet.fi/pp/grembfi/
Written in English, Finnish, and Greek, the site features Greek press releases, fact sheets, foreign policy statements, business guides, tourist information, and cultural reports.

Iceland

Embassy of Iceland in Helsinki
http://www.islanti.fi/
Written in Icelandic, the site provides Icelandic news, press releases, fact sheets, business guides, travel information, and cultural bulletins.

Indonesia

Embassy of Indonesia in Helsinki
http://www.iit.edu/~syafsya/finland/helsinki1.html
Along with a directory of Indonesian resources online, the site lists the street address, phone and fax numbers, and e-mail link of the Indonesian Embassy in Helsinki.

Norway

Norwegian Trade Council in Helsinki
http://www.ntc.no/cgi-bin/wbch.exe?html=../templates/utekontor2.html&profile=1062
The site lists the staff, street address, phone and fax numbers, and e-mail link of the Norwegian Trade Council in Helsinki.

Portugal

Portuguese Trade and Investment Office in Helsinki
http://www.portugal.org/geninfo/abouticep/finland.html
The site lists the staff, street address, phone and

fax numbers, and e-mail link of the Portuguese Trade and Investment Office in Helsinki.

Singapore

Consulate General of Singapore in Helsinki
http://www.gov.sg/mfa/consular/mww_f.htm
The site provides contact information for the Singapore Consulate General in Helsinki.

Spain

Spanish Commercial Office in Helsinki
http://www.icex.es/openURL.html#openURL=/ english/infoproyem/ofcomes/ofcomes.html#EU
The site lists the staff, street address, phone and fax numbers, and e-mail link of the Spanish Commercial Office in Helsinki.

Sweden

Embassy of Sweden in Helsinki
http://www.ud.se/english/mfa/ambassad/ finland.htm
The site lists the staff, street address, phone and fax numbers, and e-mail link of the Swedish Embassy in Helsinki.

United Kingdom

British Embassy in Helsinki
http://www.ukembassy.fi/
The site lists the street address, phone and fax numbers, e-mail link, and office hours of the British Embassy in Helsinki.

United States

United States Embassy in Helsinki
http://www.usis.fi/
Along with a Finnish commercial guide, the site provides U.S. news, press releases, fact sheets, electronic commerce reports, and a directory of consular services.

United States Information Service in Helsinki
http://www.usembassy.fi/usishki/usis00.htm
A branch office of the U.S. Information Service, the site features information on American teacher exchange programs, Fulbright scholarships, and Voice of America broadcasts.

France

France Search Tools

Excite France
http://fr.excite.com/
A personalized web start page, the site features French news, e-mail directories, maps and directions, and event finders.

France on the Internet
http://www.france.net.au/fr_links/index.html
Posted in English and French, the site is a browsable index of French websites. Categories include economy and business, history and geography, government, education and research.

Francite
http://www.francite.com/
A French language search engine, the site is divided into 14 categories including economics, culture and society, education, government, and science and technology.

Indexa
http://www.indexa.fr/
Written in French, the site is an index of French resources on the web. The service is divided into over 30 categories including aerospace, commerce, culture, and government.

Infoseek France
http://www.infoseek.com/ Home?pg=Home.html&sv=FR
Written in French, the site provides web navigation, browsing tips, city guides, and a searchable directory of French resources online.

Lokace
http://www.lokace.com/
A French-language web browsing service, the site is divided into 15 categories including culture, media, research, science, tourism, and health.

Lycos France
http://www.lycos.fr/
Posted in French, the search service includes road maps, website reviews, classifieds, shopping guides, and chat forums.

Nomade

http://www.nomade.fr/
A browsable index of French online resources, the site is divided into ten categories including arts and culture, economic and business, and science and technology.

Voila

http://www.voila.fr/
A web navigation service, the site is a searchable directory of French resources online. Categories include media, politics, business, and science and technology.

Weborama

http://www.weborama.fr/
Posted in French, the site offers web navigation services, online discussion groups, and media guides.

Yahoo France

http://www.yahoo.fr/
A service of Yahoo, the site provides French news, web-based personal management tools, and Internet searching.

France Media

France Media

http://www.mediainfo.com/emediajs/specific-geo.htm?region=france
Prepared by Editor and Publisher Interactive, the site is a directory of French media sites online including city guides, magazines, and newspapers.

France Market Guides

Barclays Country Report: France

http://www.offshorebanking.barclays.com/services/economic/yearly/fraoct97/index.html
Prepared by Barclays Bank, the site reports on French economic trends, politics, monetary and fiscal policy, international trade, and U.K.-France merchandise trade and investment flows.

Delegation for Industrial Establishment

http://www.business-in-france.com/ukdii/index.htm
A service of France Electricity, the site provides fact sheets on French small and medium-sized exporters, economic development, and rural electrification.

France Business Briefs

http://www.austrade.gov.au/IOOM/France/

A service of Austrade, the site offers fact sheets on French business etiquette, foreign investment, corporate taxation, marketing, and visas.

France Business Reports

http://italchambers.net/BusinessReports.html
Prepared by the Italian Chamber of Commerce and written in Italian, the site provides French fact sheets, market reports, and commercial guides.

France Companies

http://www.france-companies.com/
Developed by the Center for International Affairs and Economic Studies, the site features French business news, company profiles, international job opportunities, trade leads, and a database of global market reports.

France Country Profile

http://www.tradenz.govt.nz/intelligence/profiles/france.html
A service of the New Zealand Trade Development Board, the site provides French economic statistics, market information, and business tips.

France Country Report

http://www.state.gov/www/issues/economic/trade_reports/europe_canada97/france97.html
Prepared by the U.S. Department of State, the site delivers information on French exchange rates, debt management, trade barriers, and intellectual property protection.

France InfoExport

http://www.infoexport.gc.ca/country-e.asp?continent=Europe&country=14
A service of Foreign Affairs and International Trade Canada, the site provides French commercial guides and market reports.

France Market Information

http://dtiinfo1.dti.gov.uk/ots/france/
A service of the London-based Department of Trade and Industry, the site delivers French fact sheets, maps, and trade-show information.

France Market Research

http://strategis.ic.gc.ca/sc_mrkti/ibinddc/engdoc/1a1b16.html
A service of Industry Canada, the site provides U.S. Department of Commerce reports on French business, politics, trade regulations and standards, investment climate, trade and project financing, business travel, and market opportunities.

France Patent Office
http://www.evariste.anvar.fr/inpi/
Posted in French, the site is a directory of French patent, trademark, industrial design, and other intellectual property resources online.

France: Selected Issues
http://www.imf.org/external/pubs/CAT/longres.cfm?sk=2486.0
Prepared by the International Monetary Fund, the site reports on French accounting frameworks, demographic developments, expenditure trends, and economic forecasts.

France Virtual Library
http://www.pitt.edu/~wwwes/france.nhp.html
A service of the University of Pittsburgh Center for West European Studies, the site is a directory of France online resources. Categories include government, education, and culture.

French Economic Report
http://www.actufax.com/
Posted in English and French, the site provides the latest French economic statistics, company news, government bulletins, sector profiles, and regional reports.

French Trade and Science
http://www.info-france-usa.org/ftrade.htm
A service of the French Embassy in Washington, D.C., the site features French news, press releases, position papers, travel guides, business reports, and investment information.

Invest in France
http://www.investinfrance.com/index.html
A French investment guide, the site delivers French fact sheets, business guides, regional profiles, and market reports.

Ministry of Economy and Finance
http://www.finances.gouv.fr/
Homepage of the France Ministry of Economy and Finance, the site offers French commercial guides, sector profiles, industrial policy statements, and international trade bulletins.

National Institute of Industrial Property
http://www.inpi.fr/
Based in Paris, the site provides French intellectual property primers, statistics, and contacts. The service includes the Institute's mission statement, annual report, and staff directory.

France Trade Assistance

Club France
http://www.france-companies.com/fc/clubfr/us/index_clubfr.html
Part of the France Companies website, the service is a searchable directory of French exporters and importers. Categories include agriculture and food, distribution, fashion and apparel, transportation, and printing and publishing.

France Companies: International Trade Leads Center
http://www.france-companies.com/fc/tradezone/us/index_tradezo.html
A service of the Center for International Affairs and Economic Studies, the site is a database of trade leads in four categories: buying, selling, distributors and partners wanted, and distributor and partner offers. The leads are searchable by country, product, and keyword.

France Export
http://franceexport.com/
An online export showcase, the site spotlights French export products and companies in 11 categories including fashion, agri-food, communications, health, and art.

French Customs and Excise Service
http://info-france-usa.org/america/embassy/customs/cover.htm
Based in Paris, the Service collects revenue, fights fraud and crime, and regulates French trade. The site features primers on customs clearance procedures, intra-European Community clearances, and automated customs systems.

French Trade Commission
http://www.commerce-exterieur.gouv.fr/Sommaire.htm
A branch of the France Ministry of Economy, Finance, and Industry, the site provides French export guides, international trade statistics, regional trade reports, position papers, and a directory of Commission staff and services.

French Trade Commission International Posts
http://www.dree.org/pee/
Posted in French, the site is a directory of French Trade Commission offices in North America, Latin America, Western Europe, Eastern Europe, Middle East, Africa, and Asia Pacific.

Registered International Correspondents for Exporting

http://www.cci-oise.fr/rice/index.html
Based in Beauvais, the organization promotes French-Asian trade and joint ventures. The site provides a newsletter, member directory, and contact information.

Trade Shows in France

http://www.expoguide.com/shows/data/loc_18.htm
Compiled by Expoguide, the site is a directory of upcoming trade shows in France.

France Representative Offices

Armenia

Embassy of Armenia in Paris

http://www.armeniaemb.org/forrel/embas2.htm
The site provides contact information for the Embassy of Armenia in Paris.

Australia

Austrade in Paris

http://www.austrade.gov.au/Paris_eng/
An Australian export promotion service, the site features business guides, investment primers, and a directory of trade assistance programs for Australian exporters in France.

Embassy of Australia in Paris

http://www.austgov.fr/
Posted in French, the site delivers Australian fact sheets, visa and immigration information, cultural bulletins, and a directory of consular and commercial services.

Austria

Austrian Embassy in Paris

http://www.wk.or.at/aw/atc/france/
Written in French, the site features Austrian economic reports, bulletins on Austria-France trade and relations, and a directory of Embassy staff and services.

Austrian Trade Commission in Paris

http://aw.wk.or.at/awo/ahst-paris.htm
The site lists the staff, street address, phone and fax numbers, e-mail link, and office hours of the Austrian Trade Commission in Paris.

Austrian Trade Commission in Strasbourg

http://aw.wk.or.at/awo/ahst-strassburg.htm
The site lists the staff, street address, phone and fax numbers, e-mail link, and office hours of the Austrian Trade Commission in Strasbourg.

Brazil

Embassy of Brazil in Paris

http://www.axidia.fr/bresil/
Along with reports on Brazil-France trade, the site provides primers on Brazilian history, geography, politics, education, science and technology, and the environment.

Brunei Darussalam

Embassy of Brunei Darussalam in Paris

http://www.brunet.bn/homepage/gov/bruemb/govemb.htm
The site provides contact information for the Brunei Darussalam Embassy in Paris.

Canada

Canadian Embassy in Paris

http://www.dfait-maeci.gc.ca/~paris/
Posted in English and French, the site provides Canadian fact sheets, Canada-France comparisons, and French economic forecasts, market reports, and sector profiles.

France-Canada Chamber of Commerce

http://www.ccfc-france-canada.com/
Based in Paris, the bilateral organization promotes Canada-France trade. The site lists the Chamber mission statement, street address, phone and fax numbers, and e-mail link.

Québec Delegation in Paris

http://www.mri.gouv.qc.ca/dans_le_monde/france/paris_an.html
A service of the Québec Department of International Relations, the site lists the street address, phone and fax numbers, and e-mail link of the Québec Delegation in Paris.

China

China Council for the Promotion of International Trade in Paris

http://www.ccpit.org/engVersion/cp_about/cp_over/cp_over.html
A Chinese export promotion service, the site provides contact information for the China Council for the Promotion of International Trade office in Paris.

Cyprus

Cyprus Trade Center in Paris
http://www.cyprustradeny.org/cyny5.html
The site lists the street address, and phone and fax numbers of the Cyprus Trade Center in Paris.

Denmark

Consulate General of Denmark in Marseille
http://www.webmax.fr/dkconsul/
Written in Danish, the site provides Danish fact sheets, visa and passport information, reports on Denmark-France relations, and a directory of consular programs and staff.

Embassy of Denmark in Paris
http://www.webmax.fr/dkconsul/amb0.html
Posted in Danish, the virtual Embassy provides Danish business primers, tourism guides, visa and passport information, and a directory of Embassy services.

Finland

Embassy of Finland in Paris
http://pages.pratique.fr/~finlande/index.html
Written in Finnish, the online service delivers Finnish visa and passport information, business guides, and a directory of consular and commercial services.

Finland Trade Center in Paris
http://www.exports.finland.fi/tradecen.htm
The site lists the staff, street address, phone and fax numbers, and e-mail link of the Finland Trade Center in Paris.

Germany

German Chamber of Commerce in Paris
http://www.ahk-ccifa.fr/
Posted in French and German, the site features French fact sheets, German business guides, Germany-France trade reports, an event calendar, and contact information.

German Embassy in France
http://www.amb-allemagne.fr/
Written in French, the site delivers German news, fact sheets, press releases, reports on Germany-France trade and relations, and a directory of Embassy programs and staff.

Ghana

Embassy of Ghana in Paris
http://www.juntung.com/ghana-consul-hk/2misabo.htm
The site provides contact information for the Ghanaian Embassy in Paris.

Greece

Consulate of Greece in Grenoble
http://perso.wanadoo.fr/consulat.grece.grenoble/
Along with a directory of consular programs and staff, the site provides fact sheets on Greek geography, history, government, business, and investment.

India

Indian Commercial Mission in Paris
http://www.nic.in/commin/ICM.HTM
The site lists the street address, phone and fax numbers, and e-mail link of the Indian Commercial Mission in Paris.

Indonesia

Embassy of Indonesia in Paris
http://indag.dprin.go.id/INGG/trade/atache.HTM
The site provides contact information for the Indonesian Embassy in Paris.

Ireland

Enterprise Ireland in Paris
http://www.irish-trade.ie/office_network/office_locate01.html#paris
The site lists the Manager, street address, and phone and fax numbers of the Enterprise Ireland office in Paris.

Israel

Embassy of Israel in Paris
http://www.amb-israel.fr/
The online service provides Israeli news, business guides, travel tips, culture and science bulletins, reports on France-Israel trade and relations, and a directory of Israeli resources online.

Italy

Consulate General of Italy in Toulouse
http://wwwperso.hol.fr/~tconsula/
Posted in French and Italian, the site delivers information on Italian tourism, culture, and business. The service includes a directory of Italian government agencies and chambers of commerce.

Japan

Embassy of Japan in Paris
http://www.amb-japon.fr/
The online service provides Japanese fact sheets, sector profiles, an event calendar, Ambassador speeches, and reports on France-Japan trade and relations.

Laos

Embassy of Laos in Paris
http://www.laoembassy.com/news/
embassyabroad.htm
The site provides contact information for the Embassy of Laos in Paris.

Madagascar

Embassy of Madagascar in Paris
http://www.madagascar-contacts.com/us/
adresse.htm#alext
Along with a directory of Madagascar government agencies, the site provides contact information for the Madagascar Embassy in Paris.

Malaysia

Embassy of Malaysia in Paris
http://www.mnet.com.my/klonline/www/missions/
malmiss/mfrance1.htm
The site provides contact information for the Malaysian Embassy in Paris.

Trade Commission of Malaysia in Paris
http://www.mnet.com.my/klonline/www/missions/
malmiss/mfrance3.htm
The site provides contact information for the Malaysian Trade Commission in Paris.

Mexico

Trade Commission of Mexico
http://www.mexico-businessline.com/ingles/
ofrepmu3.html#france

A service of Bancomext, the site lists the street address, phone and fax numbers, and e-mail link of the Mexican Trade Commission in Paris.

Namibia

Embassy of Namibia in Paris
http://www.republicofnamibia.com/adress.htm
Along with a directory of Namibian companies and government agencies, the site provides contact information for the Namibian Embassy in Paris.

Nepal

Embassy of Nepal in Paris
http://www.info-nepal.com/members/fips/contacts/
nepalese.html
The site provides contact information for the Embassy of Nepal in Paris.

Netherlands

Embassy of the Netherlands in Paris
http://myweb.worldnet.fr/~nlgovpar/intro.shtml
The site lists the street address, phone and fax numbers, and e-mail link of the Netherlands Embassy in Paris.

New Zealand

Trade New Zealand in Paris
http://www.tradenz.govt.nz/contact/europe.html
An export promotion service, the site provides contact information for the Trade New Zealand office in Paris.

Nicaragua

Embassy of Nicaragua in Paris
http://www.blue-brain.com/embassy/nicaragua/
Posted in English, French, and Spanish, the site features primers on Nicaraguan history, geography, tourism, and commerce. The service includes a staff directory and contact information.

Norway

Norwegian Trade Council in Paris
http://www.ntc.no/cgi-bin/wbch.exe?html=../
templates/utekontor2.html&profile=1123
The site lists the staff, street address, phone and fax numbers, and e-mail link of the Norwegian Trade Council in Paris.

Pakistan

Pakistan Trade Office in Paris
http://www.jamal.com/epb/ptoa.htm
The site provides contact information for the
Pakistan Trade Office in Paris.

Paraguay

Embassy of Paraguay in Paris
http://www.univercom.fr/paraguay/
Along with Mercosur reports, the site provides
Paraguayan visa and passport information,
economic bulletins, and a directory of Embassy
programs and staff.

Philippines

**Philippine Trade and Investment Promotion
Office in Paris**
http://www.dti.gov.ph/par/
The site provides a mission statement, service
directory, and contact information for the Philippine Trade Office in Paris.

Poland

Consulate General of Poland in Strasbourg
*http://ourworld.compuserve.com/homepages/
KGStrasburg/*
Posted in four languages, the site lists the street
address, and phone and fax numbers of the
Polish Consulate in Strasbourg. The service
includes a directory of Polish business and
tourism resources online.

Portugal

Embassy of Portugal in Paris
http://www.embaixada-portugal-fr.org/
Posted in French and Portuguese, the site
delivers Portuguese socioeconomic statistics,
cultural bulletins, travel tips, business opportunities, and reports on France-Portugal trade and
relations.

**Portuguese Trade and Investment Office in
Paris**
*http://www.portugal.org/geninfo/abouticep/
paris.html*
The site lists the staff, street address, phone and
fax numbers, and e-mail link of the Portuguese
Trade and Investment Office in Paris.

Singapore

Embassy of Singapore in Paris
http://www.gov.sg/mfa/consular/mww_f.htm
The site provides contact information for the
Singapore Embassy in Paris.

South Africa

South Africa Foreign Trade Office in Paris
*http://wwwdti.pwv.gov.za/dtiwww/
foreign_offices.htm*
A service of the South Africa Department of Trade
and Industry, the site provides contact information
for the South Africa Trade Office in Paris.

Spain

Spanish Commercial Office in Paris
*http://www.icex.es/openURL.html#openURL=/
english/infoproyem/ofcomes/ofcomes.html#EU*
The site lists the staff, street address, phone and
fax numbers, and e-mail link of the Spanish
Commercial Office in Paris.

Sweden

Embassy of Sweden in Paris
http://www.amb-suede.fr/
Featuring a welcome message from the Ambassador, the site provides Swedish visa and
passport information, tourism guides, cultural
bulletins, and reports on France-Sweden trade
and business opportunities.

Switzerland

Swiss-French Chamber of Commerce in Paris
*http://swisstrade.com/
xicodes2.asp?P1=3&lvl=3&cid=A07*
The site lists the street address, phone and fax
numbers, and e-mail link of the Swiss French
Chamber of Commerce in Paris.

Taiwan

**China External Trade Development Council
Office in Paris**
*http://www.cetra.org.tw/english/o_office/
indexset.htm*
A Taiwanese trade promotion service, the site
lists the mission statement and e-mail link of the
China External Trade Development Council Office
in Paris.

Taiwan Government Information Office in Paris
http://www.gio.gov.tw/info/ngio/fra-f.html
Posted in Chinese and English, the site lists the street address, phone and fax numbers, and e-mail link of the Taiwan Government Information Office in Paris.

Taiwan Trade Office in Paris
http://france.roc-taiwan.org.uk/
Written in Chinese, English and French, the site delivers Taiwanese news, speeches, trade leads, an event calendar, and *ROC Today*, a newsletter on Taiwanese economic development.

Tanzania

Embassy of Tanzania in Paris
http://www.tanzania-online.gov.uk/visa/envoys.html
The site provides contact information for the Tanzanian Embassy in Paris.

Thailand

Royal Thai Embassy in Paris
http://www.mfa.go.th/Embassy/detail/38.htm
The site lists the Ambassador, street address, and phone and fax numbers of the Thai Embassy in Paris.

Thailand Office of Commercial Affairs in Paris
http://www.thaitrade.com/thcoaf.html
The site lists the street address, phone and fax numbers, and e-mail link of the Thailand Office of Commercial Affairs in Paris.

Turkey

Embassy of Turkey in Paris
http://www.turkey.org/madres.htm
Part of a directory of Turkish diplomatic offices around the world, the site lists the e-mail link of the Turkish Embassy in Paris.

United Kingdom

Consulate General of Britain in Bordeaux
http://www.fco.gov.uk/directory/posts.asp?FR
The site provides contact information for the British Consulate General in Bordeaux.

Embassy of Britain in Paris
http://www.amb-grandebretagne.fr/
Written in French, the site provides British fact sheets, press releases, visa and immigration information, education and cultural bulletins, investment primers, and French market guides.

United States

American Chamber of Commerce in France
http://www.amchamfr.com/
An alliance of Franco-American business interests, the Chamber promotes France-United States trade. The site includes a mission statement, membership information, a calendar of events, publications list, and a directory of Chamber staff and committees.

State of Washington Trade Office in Paris
http://www.trade.wa.gov/overseas.htm
A service of Washington State Community, Trade and Economic Development, the site lists the street address, phone and fax numbers, and e-mail link of the Washington Trade Office in Paris.

United States Embassy in Paris
http://www.amb-usa.fr/
Posted in English and French, the site features United States news, press releases, diplomat profiles, investment guides, French trade leads, and French-American trade reports.

Venezuela

Embassy of Venezuela in Paris
http://www.embavenez-paris.com/
Posted in French and Spanish, the site provides Venezuelan fact sheets, visa and passport information, reports on France-Venezuela trade and relations, and a directory of Embassy programs and staff.

Germany

Germany Search Tools

DINO
http://www.dino-online.de/
Along with web navigation, the site provides news, chat services, browsing tips, and a directory of German resources online.

Excite Germany
http://www.excite.de/
A personalized web start page, the site features German news, e-mail directories, maps and directions, and event finders.

Infoseek Germany
http://www.infoseek.com/
Home?pg=Home.html&sv=DE
Written in German, the site provides web navigation, browsing tips, and a searchable directory of German resources online.

Infospace Germany
http://in-132.infospace.com/_1_34407537__info/
intldb/intl-de.html
A service of Infospace, the German search engine includes a travel guide, e-mail directory, and business and people finders.

Kolibri Online
http://www.kolibri.de/
The German search tool provides chat services, web hosting, website reviews, and Internet guides.

LEO
http://www.leo.org/
Posted in English and German, the site is a browsable directory of information technology guides, software reviews, and operating system reports.

Lycos Germany
http://www.lycos.de/
Posted in German, the search service includes road maps, website reviews, classifieds, shopping guides, and chat forums.

Yahoo Deutschland
http://www.yahoo.de/
A service of Yahoo, the site provides German news, web-based personal management tools, and Internet searching.

Germany Media

Germany Media
http://www.mediainfo.com/emediajs/specific-geo.htm?region=germany
Prepared by Editor and Publisher Interactive, the site is a directory of German media sites online.

Handelsblatt
http://www.handelsblatt.de/englishsum/index.html
A German electronic magazine, the site provides German business news, company profiles, money and market reports, and a news archive.

Germany Market Guides

Barclays Country Report: Germany
http://www.offshorebanking.barclays.com/
services/economic/yearly/gerapr97/index.html
Prepared by Barclays Bank, the site reports on German economic trends, politics, monetary and fiscal policy, international trade, and U.K.-Germany merchandise trade and investment flows.

Branchenbuch
http://english.branchenbuch.com/
Posted in English, German, and Spanish, the site is a searchable directory of German companies. The database is browsable by keyword, company name, geographic region, and industry.

Country Commercial Guide
http://www.state.gov/www/about_state/business/
com_guides/1998/europe_canada/
germany98.html
Prepared by the U.S. Embassy in Bonn, the site delivers primers on German business, politics, trade regulations and standards, investment climate, trade and project financing, and business travel.

Expo 2000
http://www.expo2000.de/
Posted in ten languages, the site provides fact sheets on the upcoming World Exposition in Hannover from June 1 to October 31, 2000. The service includes press kits, an events program, and ticket information.

German Business Net
http://www.german-business.de/
Written in German, the site is a searchable directory of German companies online in 15 categories including banking, hardware, software, and communications.

German Electronic Business
http://www.e-business.iao.fhg.de./
Posted in German, the site provides German e-commerce fact sheets, business guides, market studies, and company profiles.

German Government
http://www.bundesregierung.de/english/01/
newsf.html
A service of the German Press and Information Office, the site provides German news, press releases, photos, sector profiles, education and science bulletins, and culture reports.

German Institute for Economic Research
http://www.diw-berlin.de/
Based in Berlin, the site delivers German economic bulletins, discussion papers, statistics, Eastern Europe reports, an event calendar, and a database of researchers and projects.

Germany Business Briefs
http://www.austrade.gov.au/IOOM/Germany/
A service of Austrade, the site offers fact sheets on German business etiquette, foreign investment, corporate taxation, marketing, and visas.

Germany Business Reports
http://italchambers.net/BusinessReports.html
Prepared by the Italian Chamber of Commerce and written in Italian, the site provides German fact sheets, market reports, and commercial guides.

Germany Country Profile
http://www.tradenz.govt.nz/intelligence/profiles/germany.html
A service of the New Zealand Trade Development Board, the site provides German economic statistics, market information, and business tips.

Germany Country Report
http://www.state.gov/www/issues/economic/trade_reports/europe_canada97/germany97.html
Prepared by the U.S. Department of State, the site delivers information on German exchange rates, debt management, trade barriers, and intellectual property protection.

Germany InfoExport
http://www.infoexport.gc.ca/country-e.asp?continent=Europe&country=15
A service of Foreign Affairs and International Trade Canada, the site provides German commercial guides and market reports.

Germany Market Information
http://dtiinfo1.dti.gov.uk/ots/germany/
A service of the London-based Department of Trade and Industry, the site delivers German fact sheets, maps, and trade-show information.

Germany Market Research
http://strategis.ic.gc.ca/sc_mrkti/ibinddc/engdoc/1a1b18.html
A service of Industry Canada, the site provides U.S. Department of Commerce reports on German business, politics, trade regulations and standards, investment climate, trade and project

financing, business travel, and market opportunities.

Germany Patent Office
http://www.deutsches-patentamt.de/
Posted in German, the site provides information on German patents, industrial designs, and other intellectual property.

Germany: Selected Issues
http://www.imf.org/external/pubs/CAT/longres.cfm?sk=2417.0
Prepared by the International Monetary Fund, the site reports on German unification, unemployment, wage gaps, taxation, and pension reform.

Germany: Statistical Appendix
http://www.imf.org/external/pubs/CAT/longres.cfm?sk=2418.0
A service of the International Monetary Fund, the site provides data on German output, income, demand, consumption, saving, wages, prices, government finances, interest rates, trade flows, and other economic indicators.

Germany Virtual Library
http://www.pitt.edu/~wwwes/germany.nhp.html
A service of the University of Pittsburgh Center for West European Studies, the site is a directory of German online resources. Categories include government, education, and culture.

Germany Trade Assistance

Foreign Office
http://www.auswaertiges-amt.de/1_fremsp/english/index.htm
Posted in seven languages, the site is a directory of German government foreign offices online in eight countries including Canada, Egypt, Singapore, and the United States.

German Chambers Abroad
http://www.globalguide.de/country1.htm
The site lists the street addresses, phone and fax numbers, and website addresses of German Chambers of Commerce in over 60 countries including Albania, El Salvadar, Ukraine, and Yemen.

Trade Shows in Germany
http://www.expoguide.com/shows/data/loc_19.htm
Compiled by Expoguide, the site is a directory of upcoming trade shows in Germany.

Germany Representative Offices

Armenia

Embassy of Armenia in Bonn
http://www.armeniaemb.org/forrel/embas2.htm
The site provides contact information for the Embassy of Armenia in Bonn.

Australia

Austrade in Frankfurt
http://www.austrade.gov.au/Frankfurt/
An Australian export promotion service, the site features business guides, investment primers, and a directory of trade assistance programs for Australian exporters in Germany.

Austria

Austrian Trade Commission in Berlin
http://www.oesterreich.org/offices/ahst_ber.htm
The site lists the staff, street address, phone and fax numbers, and e-mail link of the Austrian Trade Commission in Berlin.

Austrian Trade Commission in Düsseldorf
http://www.oesterreich.org/offices/ahst_dus.htm
The site lists the staff, street address, phone and fax numbers, and e-mail link of the Austrian Trade Commission in Düsseldorf.

Austrian Trade Commission in Dresden
http://aw.wk.or.at/awo/ahst-dresden.htm
The site lists the staff, street address, phone and fax numbers, and office hours of the Austrian Trade Commission in Dresden.

Austrian Trade Commission in Frankfurt
http://www.oesterreich.org/offices/ahst_fra.htm
The site lists the staff, street address, phone and fax numbers, and e-mail link of the Austrian Trade Commission in Frankfurt.

Austrian Trade Commission in Germany
http://www.oesterreich.org/
An Austrian export promotion service, the site provides Austrian business primers, contact information, German market bulletins, and reports on Austria-Germany trade.

Austrian Trade Commission in Hamburg
http://www.oesterreich.org/offices/ahst_ham.htm
The site lists the staff, street address, phone and fax numbers, and e-mail link of the Austrian Trade Commission in Hamburg.

Austrian Trade Commission in Munich
http://www.oesterreich.org/offices/ahst_mun.htm
The site lists the staff, street address, phone and fax numbers, and e-mail link of the Austrian Trade Commission in Munich.

Belgium

Belgium Embassy in Bonn
http://diplobel.org/germany/
Posted in four languages, the site provides Belgian fact sheets, visa and passport information, German market guides, and reports on Belgium-Germany trade.

Brunei Darussalam

Embassy of Brunei Darussalam in Bonn
http://www.brunet.bn/homepage/gov/bruemb/govemb.htm
The site provides contact information for the Brunei Darussalam Embassy in Bonn.

Canada

Canadian Embassy in Bonn
http://www.dfait-maeci.gc.ca/~bonn/
Posted in English, French, and German, the site delivers Canadian fact sheets, speeches, tourism guides, an event calendar, German market studies, and bulletins on Canada-Germany trade.

Consulate of Canada in Düsseldorf
http://www.dfait-maeci.gc.ca/english/missions/rep-can2e.htm#germany
The site provides contact information for the Canadian Consulate in Düsseldorf.

Consulate of Canada in Hamburg
http://www.dfait-maeci.gc.ca/english/missions/rep-can2e.htm#germany
The site provides contact information for the Canadian Consulate in Hamburg.

Consulate of Canada in Munich
http://www.dfait-maeci.gc.ca/english/missions/rep-can2e.htm#germany
The site provides contact information for the Canadian Consulate in Munich.

Québec Government Office in Munich
http://www.mri.gouv.qc.ca/dans_le_monde/europe/munich_an.html
A service of the Québec Department of Interna-

tional Relations, the site lists the street address, phone and fax numbers, and e-mail link of the Québec Government Office in Munich.

China

China Council for the Promotion of International Trade in Frankfurt
_http://www.ccpit.org/engVersion/cp_about/ cp_over/cp_over.html_
A Chinese export promotion service, the site provides contact information for the China Council for the Promotion of International Trade office in Frankfurt.

Cyprus

Cyprus Trade Center in Cologne
http://www.cyprustradeny.org/cyny5.html
The site lists the street address, and phone and fax numbers of the Cyprus Trade Center in Cologne.

Denmark

Consulate General of Denmark in Munich
http://www.daenemark.org/muenchen/
Posted in Danish, the site provides Danish fact sheets, visa and passport information, and a directory of consular and commercial services.

Embassy of Denmark in Bonn
http://www.daenemark.org/
Posted in Danish and German, the site provides Danish fact sheets, visa and passport information, German export guides, and reports on Denmark-Germany trade.

Finland

Embassy of Finland in Bonn
http://www.finlandemb.de/
Written in Finnish and German, the site delivers Finnish news, press releases, fact sheets, tourism information, and reports on Finland-Germany trade and relations.

Finland Trade Center in Berlin
http://www.exports.finland.fi/tradecen.htm
The site lists the staff, street address, phone and fax numbers, and e-mail link of the Finland Trade Center in Berlin.

Finland Trade Center in Bonn
http://www.ftc.de/index.htm

A Finnish export promotion service, the site offers Finnish business news, company directories, and a virtual catalog of Finnish software and telecommunications products.

Finland Trade Center in Frankfurt
http://www.exports.finland.fi/tradecen.htm
The site lists the staff, street address, phone and fax numbers, and e-mail link of the Finland Trade Center in Frankfurt.

Finland Trade Center in Hamburg
http://www.exports.finland.fi/tradecen.htm
The site lists the staff, street address, phone and fax numbers, and e-mail link of the Finland Trade Center in Hamburg.

Finland Trade Center in Munich
http://www.exports.finland.fi/tradecen.htm
The site lists the staff, street address, phone and fax numbers, and e-mail link of the Finland Trade Center in Munich.

France

French Embassy in Bonn
http://www.botschaft-frankreich.de/
Posted in German, the site delivers French business guides, fact sheets, visa and passport information, German market bulletins, and France-Germany trade reports.

French Trade Commission in Bonn
http://www.dree.org/allemagne/
A French trade promotion service, the site provides German market studies, and a directory of export programs for French companies doing business in Germany.

Ghana

Embassy of Ghana in Bonn
http://www.juntung.com/ghana-consul-hk/ 2misabo.htm
The site provides contact information for the Ghanaian Embassy in Bonn.

Greece

Embassy of Greece in Bonn
http://www.griechische-botschaft.de/
The virtual Embassy delivers Greek backgrounders, visa and passport information, tourism guides, contact information, and a directory of Embassy programs.

Iceland

Embassy of Iceland in Bonn
http://www.geysir.com/Botschaft/
Posted in German and Icelandic, the site offers Icelandic fact sheets, visa application forms, business guides, frequently asked questions and answers, and a directory of Embassy programs.

India

Embassy of India in Bonn
http://www.k.shuttle.de/essente-eoi/
Featuring a greeting from the Ambassador, the site delivers Indian news, maps, fact sheets, business primers, investment guides, science and technology bulletins, and reports on Indo-German relations.

Indian Commercial Mission in Frankfurt
http://www.nic.in/commin/ICM.HTM
The site lists the street address, phone and fax numbers, and e-mail link of the Indian Commercial Mission in Frankfurt.

Indian Commercial Mission in Hamburg
http://www.nic.in/commin/ICM.HTM
The site lists the street address, phone and fax numbers, and e-mail link of the Indian Commercial Mission in Hamburg.

Indonesia

Embassy of Indonesia in Bonn
http://indag.dprin.go.id/INGG/trade/atache.HTM
The site provides contact information for the Indonesian Embassy in Bonn.

Iran

Iran Trade Center in Hamburg
http://www.neda.net/ibr/tcc.html
An Iranian trade promotion service, the site lists the street address and phone and fax numbers of the Iran Trade Center in Hamburg.

Ireland

Enterprise Ireland in Berlin
http://www.irish-trade.ie/office_network/office_locate01.html#anchor1412883
The site lists the Manager, street address, and phone and fax numbers of the Enterprise Ireland office in Berlin.

Enterprise Ireland in Düsseldorf
http://www.irish-trade.ie/office_network/office_locate01.html#anchor1415358
The site lists the Manager, street address, and phone and fax numbers of the Enterprise Ireland office in Düsseldorf.

Enterprise Ireland in Munich
http://www.irish-trade.ie/office_network/office_locate01.html#munich
The site lists the Manager, street address, and phone and fax numbers of the Enterprise Ireland office in Munich.

Israel

Embassy of Israel in Bonn
http://www.israel.de/
The virtual Embassy offers Israeli visa and passport information, business guides, travel primers, reports on Germany-Israel trade, and a directory of Embassy services.

Israel Trade Center in Cologne
http://www.israel.de/tradecenter/
An Israeli trade promotion service, the site lists the mission statement, street address, phone and fax numbers, and e-mail link of the Israel Trade Center in Cologne.

Israel Trade Center in Munich
http://www.israel.de/tradecenter/muenchen.html
Along with Israeli business news and German market reports, the site spotlights Israeli capabilities in a dozen industries including biotechnology, electronics, encryption, and telecommunications.

Italy

Embassy of Italy in Bonn
http://www.iei.pi.cnr.it/BONN/AMBASCIATA/ITALIA/
Posted in Italian, the site provides Italian fact sheets, business guides, and a directory of consular and commercial services.

Italian Trade Commission in Düsseldorf
http://www.ice.it/estero/dusseldorf/
Along with Italian fact sheets, sector profiles, and company directories, the site lists the street address, phone and fax numbers, and e-mail link of the Italian Trade Commission in Düsseldorf.

Italian Trade Commission in Leipsic
http://www.ice.it/estero/germania/lipsia/
Posted in Italian, the site delivers Italian sector

profiles, economic statistics, contact information, and a directory of consular programs and staff.

Japan

Embassy of Japan in Bonn
http://www.embjapan.de/
Posted in German, the site provides Japanese business guides, visa and passport information, travel primers, reports on German-Japan trade and relations, and a directory of Embassy programs.

Madagascar

Embassy of Madagascar in Bonn
http://www.madagascar-contacts.com/us/ adresse.htm#alext
Along with a directory of Madagascar government agencies, the site provides contact information for the Madagascar Embassy in Bonn.

Malaysia

Embassy of Malaysia in Bonn
http://www.mnet.com.my/klonline/www/missions/ malmiss/mgermany1.htm
The site provides contact information for the Malaysian Embassy in Bonn.

Trade Commission of Malaysia in Cologne
http://www.mnet.com.my/klonline/www/missions/ malmiss/mgermany3.htm
The site provides contact information for the Malaysian Trade Commission in Cologne.

Mexico

Embassy of Mexico in Bonn
http://www.inf.fu-berlin.de/~mexico/
Written in German, the site features Mexican news, press releases, fact sheets, Germany-Mexico trade reports, and a directory Embassy services.

Trade Commission of Mexico in Bonn
http://www.mexico-businessline.com/ingles/ ofrepmu3.html#germany
The site lists the street address, phone and fax numbers, and e-mail link of the Mexican Trade Commission in Bonn.

Namibia

Embassy of Namibia in Bonn
http://www.republicofnamibia.com/adress.htm
Along with a directory of Namibian companies and government agencies, the site provides contact information for the Namibian Embassy in Bonn.

Nepal

Embassy of Nepal in Bonn
http://www.info-nepal.com/members/fips/contacts/ nepalese.html
The site provides contact information for the Nepalese Embassy in Bonn.

New Zealand

Trade New Zealand in Hamburg
http://www.tradenz.govt.nz/contact/europe.html
An export promotion service, the site provides contact information for the Trade New Zealand office in Hamburg.

Norway

Consulate General of Norway in Düsseldorf
http://www.ntc.no/cgi-bin/wbch.exe?html=../ templates/utekontor2.html&profile=1105
The site lists the staff, street address, phone and fax numbers, and e-mail link of the Norwegian Consulate General in Düsseldorf.

Embassy of Norway in Bonn
http://www.norwegen.org/
Posted in English and Norwegian, the site provides Norwegian fact sheets, press releases, government directories, and contact information.

Pakistan

Pakistan Trade Office in Bonn
http://www.jamal.com/epb/ptoa.htm
The site provides contact information for the Pakistan Trade Office in Bonn.

Paraguay

Honorary Counsel of Paraguay in Munich
http://www.paraguay.spacenet.de/
Posted in German, the site features Paraguayan fact sheets, market reports, company profiles, contact information, and a directory of consular services.

Philippines

Philippine Trade and Investment Promotion Office in Cologne
http://www.dti.gov.ph/ger/
The site provides a mission statement, service directory, and contact information for the Philippine Trade Office in Cologne.

Poland

Embassy of Poland in Bonn
http://www.pol-bot.com/
The virtual Embassy provides Polish backgrounders, business guides, culture bulletins, reports on Germany-Poland trade, and a directory of Embassy programs.

Portugal

Portuguese Trade and Investment Office in Berlin
http://www.portugal.org/geninfo/abouticep/germany.html
The site lists the staff, street address, phone and fax numbers, and e-mail link of the Portuguese Trade and Investment Office in Berlin.

Portuguese Trade and Investment Office in Düsseldorf
http://www.portugal.org/geninfo/abouticep/germany.html
The site lists the staff, street address, phone and fax numbers, and e-mail link of the Portuguese Trade and Investment Office in Düsseldorf.

Portuguese Trade and Investment Office in Frankfurt
http://www.portugal.org/geninfo/abouticep/germany.html
The site lists the staff, street address, phone and fax numbers, and e-mail link of the Portuguese Trade and Investment Office in Frankfurt.

Singapore

Consulate General of Singapore in Hamburg
http://www.gov.sg/mfa/consular/mww_g.htm
The site provides contact information for the Singapore Consulate General in Hamburg.

Embassy of Singapore in Bonn
http://www.gov.sg/mfa/consular/mww_g.htm
The site provides contact information for the Singapore Embassy in Bonn.

South Africa

South Africa Foreign Trade Office in Bonn
http://wwwdti.pwv.gov.za/dtiwww/foreign_offices.htm
A service of the South Africa Department of Trade and Industry, the site provides contact information for the South Africa Trade Office in Bonn.

Spain

Spanish Commercial Office in Berlin
http://www.icex.es/openURL.html#openURL=/english/infoproyem/ofcomes/ofcomes.html#EU
The site lists the staff, street address, phone and fax numbers, and e-mail link of the Spanish Commercial Office in Berlin.

Spanish Commercial Office in Bonn
http://www.icex.es/openURL.html#openURL=/english/infoproyem/ofcomes/ofcomes.html#EU
The site lists the staff, street address, phone and fax numbers, and e-mail link of the Spanish Commercial Office in Bonn.

Spanish Commercial Office in Düsseldorf
http://www.icex.es/openURL.html#openURL=/english/infoproyem/ofcomes/ofcomes.html#EU
The site lists the staff, street address, phone and fax numbers, and e-mail link of the Spanish Commercial Office in Düsseldorf.

Sudan

Embassy of Sudan in Bonn
http://home.t-online.de/home/sudan-embassy.bonn/
Posted in Arabic and German, the site delivers Sudanese news, press releases, investment guides, cultural bulletins, and Germany-Sudan trade updates.

Sweden

Consulate General of Sweden in Hamburg
http://www.ud.se/english/mfa/ambassad/tyskland.htm
The site lists the staff, street address, phone and fax numbers, and e-mail link of the Swedish Consulate General in Hamburg.

Embassy of Sweden in Bonn
http://www.schweden.org/
Posted in German, the site delivers Swedish fact sheets, visa and passport information, and a directory of consular and commercial services.

Switzerland

Swiss-German Chamber of Commerce
http://swisstrade.com/
xicodes2.asp?P1=3&lvl=3&cid=A04
The site lists the street address, phone and fax numbers, and e-mail link of the Swiss-German Chamber of Commerce in Bonn.

Taiwan

China External Trade Development Council Office in Berlin
http://www.cetra.org.tw/english/o_office/
indexset.htm
A Taiwanese trade promotion service, the site lists the mission statement and e-mail link of the China External Trade Development Council Office in Berlin.

China External Trade Development Council Office in Düsseldorf
http://www.cetra.org.tw/english/o_office/
indexset.htm
A Taiwanese trade promotion service, the site lists the mission statement and e-mail link of the China External Trade Development Council Office in Düsseldorf.

Düsseldorf Design Center
http://www.cetra.org.tw/english/o_office/
indexset.htm
A Taiwanese trade promotion service, the site lists the mission statement and e-mail link of the Düsseldorf Design Center.

Taiwan Government Information Office in Bonn
http://www.gio.gov.tw/info/ngio/ger-f.html
Posted in Chinese and English, the site lists the street addresses, phone and fax numbers, and e-mail links of the Taiwan Government Information Offices in Bonn, Berlin, Hamburg, and Munich.

Tanzania

Embassy of Tanzania in Bonn
http://www.tanzania-online.gov.uk/visa/
envoys.html
The site provides contact information for the Tanzanian Embassy in Bonn.

Thailand

Royal Thai Consulate General in Berlin
http://www.mfa.go.th/Embassy/detail/14.htm

The site lists the Consul General, street address, and phone and fax numbers of the Thai Consulate General in Berlin.

Royal Thai Embassy in Bonn
http://www.mfa.go.th/Embassy/detail/39.htm
The site lists the Ambassador, street address, and phone and fax numbers of the Thai Embassy in Bonn.

Thai Trade Center in Frankfurt
http://www.thaitrade.com/wwtto.html
A service of the Thailand Department of Export Promotion, the site lists the street address, phone and fax numbers, and e-mail link of the Thai Trade Center in Frankfurt.

Thailand Office of Commercial Affairs in Berlin
http://www.thaitrade.com/thcoaf.html
The site lists the street address, phone and fax numbers, and e-mail link of the Thailand Office of Commercial Affairs in Berlin.

Turkey

Embassy of the Republic of Turkey in Bonn
http://www.tcbonnbe.de/
Posted in German and Turkish, the site provides Turkish fact sheets, government directories, tourism guides, cultural bulletins, and reports on Germany-Turkey trade and relations.

United Kingdom

Consulate General of Britain in Düsseldorf
http://www.british-dgtip.de/
Written in German, the site offers British fact sheets, business guides, investment primers, visa and passport information, product catalogs, and contact information.

Consulate General of Britain in Frankfurt
http://www.fco.gov.uk/directory/posts.asp?GD
The site provides contact information for the British Consulate General in Frankfurt.

Consulate General of Britain in Hamburg
http://www.fco.gov.uk/directory/posts.asp?GD
The site provides contact information for the British Consulate General in Hamburg.

Consulate General of Britain in Munich
http://www.fco.gov.uk/directory/posts.asp?GD
The site provides contact information for the British Consulate General in Munich.

Consulate General of Britain in Stuttgart
http://www.fco.gov.uk/directory/posts.asp?GD
The site provides contact information for the British Consulate General in Stuttgart.

Grobbritainnien Online
http://www.britbot.de/h
A British information service for Germans, the site features British news, cultural updates, sector profiles, and reports on British-German trade and relations.

Helping U.K. Firms in Germany
http://www.british-dgtip.de/export.htm
Along with German market reports, the site provides contact information for the British Consulates General in Düsseldorf, Hamburg, Frankfurt, Stuttgart, Munich, Berlin, and Leipzig.

Trade Office of Britain in Leipzig
http://www.fco.gov.uk/directory/posts.asp?GD
The site provides contact information for the British Trade Office in Leipzig.

United States

Agricultural Trade Office in Hamburg
http://www.usembassy.de/atohamburg/index.htm
Part of the U.S. Foreign Agricultural Service, the Office promotes U.S. agricultural exports in Europe. The site includes market briefs, trade leads, buyer alerts, an event calendar, and international trade contacts.

Office of Defense Cooperation
http://www.usembassy.de/odc/index.htm
A service of the American Embassy, the Office promotes U.S. defense product exports to Europe. The site includes an International Armaments Cooperation Handbook, and a directory of Office programs and key personnel.

State of Alabama Trade Office in Stuttgart
http://www.case-europe.com/States/al.htm
The site lists the Director, street address, and phone and fax numbers of the Alabama Trade Office in Stuttgart.

State of California Trade Office in Frankfurt
http://commerce.ca.gov/international/ it_off.html#frankfurt
A service of the California Office of Export Development, the site lists the Director, street address, phone and fax numbers, and e-mail link of the California Trade Office in Frankfurt. The geographic responsibility of the Office includes

Germany, Italy, Switzerland, Austria, Central and Eastern Europe.

State of Florida Trade Office in Hamburg
http://www.case-europe.com/States/fl.htm
Along with Florida fact sheets, the site lists the Trade Specialist, street address, phone and fax numbers, and e-mail link of the Florida Trade Office in Hamburg.

State of Iowa Trade Office in Frankfurt
http://www.case-europe.com/States/ia.htm
Along with Iowa fact sheets, the site lists the Director, street address, phone and fax numbers, and e-mail link of the Iowa Trade Office in Frankfurt.

State of Louisiana European Office in Herborn
http://www.case-europe.com/States/la.htm
Along with Louisiana fact sheets, the site lists the Director, phone and fax numbers, and e-mail link of the Louisiana European Office in Herborn.

State of Massachusetts Trade Office in Berlin
http://www.case-europe.com/States/ma.htm
Along with Massachusetts fact sheets, the site lists the Director, street address, phone and fax numbers, and e-mail link of the Massachusetts Trade Office in Berlin.

State of Missouri Trade Office in Düsseldorf
http://www.ecodev.state.mo.us/intermark/ europe.html
Hosted by the Missouri Department of Economic Development, the site lists the mission statement, Manager, and street address of the Missouri Trade Office in Düsseldorf.

State of New York Trade Office in Frankfurt
http://www.case-europe.com/States/ny.htm
Along with New York fact sheets, the site lists the Director, street address, phone and fax numbers, and e-mail link of the New York Trade Office in Frankfurt.

State of North Carolina Trade Office in Düsseldorf
http://www.commerce.state.nc.us/commerce/itd/ foreign.html
A service of the North Carolina International Trade Division, the site lists the Trade Specialist, street address, phone and fax numbers, and e-mail link of the North Carolina Trade Office in Düsseldorf.

State of Pennsylvania Trade Office in Frankfurt
http://www.case-europe.com/States/pa.htm

Along with Pennsylvania fact sheets, the site lists the staff, street address, phone and fax numbers, and e-mail link of the Pennsylvania Trade Office in Frankfurt.

State of South Carolina Trade Office in Frankfurt
http://www.state.sc.us/commerce/trade2.htm
A branch office of the South Carolina Department of Commerce, the site lists the Director, street address, phone and fax numbers, and e-mail link of the South Carolina Trade Office in Frankfurt.

State of Utah Trade Office in Dortmund
http://www.ce.ex.state.ut.us/international/reps/ reps.htm#Germany
A service of the State of Utah International Business Development Office, the site lists the Representative, street address, phone and fax numbers, and e-mail link of the Utah Trade Office in Dortmund.

State of Utah Trade Office in Stuttgart
http://www.ce.ex.state.ut.us/international/reps/ reps.htm#Germany
Prepared by the State of Utah International Business Development Office, the site lists the Representative, street address, phone and fax numbers, and e-mail link of the Utah Trade Office in Stuttgart.

State of Virginia Central Europe Office
http://www.case-europe.com/States/va.htm
Along with Virginia fact sheets, the site lists the staff, street address, phone and fax numbers, and e-mail link of the Virginia Central Europe Office.

State of West Virginia Trade Office in Munich
http://www.case-europe.com/States/wv.htm
Along with West Virginia fact sheets, the site lists the Director, street address, phone and fax numbers, and e-mail link of the West Virginia Trade Office in Munich.

State of Wisconsin Trade Office in Frankfurt
http://badger.state.wi.us/agencies/commerce/ html/EurOff/index.htm
Along with Wisconsin state profiles, tourism guides, and investment primers, the site provides European market news, socioeconomic statistics, and a directory of trade promotion services for Wisconsin firms doing business in Europe.

United States Consulate in Düsseldorf
http://www.usembassy.de/consular/dusseldorf/ rechts.htm

The site lists the street address, phone and fax numbers, and commercial and consular services of the United States Consulate in Düsseldorf.

United States Consulate in Frankfurt
http://www.usembassy.de/consular/frankfurt/ rechts.htm
The site lists the street address, phone and fax numbers, and commercial and consular services of the United States Consulate in Frankfurt.

United States Consulate in Hamburg
http://www.usembassy.de/consular/hamburg/ rechts.htm
The site lists the street address, phone and fax numbers, and commercial and consular services of the United States Consulate in Hamburg.

United States Consulate in Leipzig
http://www.usembassy.de/consular/leipzig/ right.htm
Along with U.S. fact sheets and visa information, the site provides German market reports, legal guides, green card chat sessions, an event calendar, and a directory of German-United States sister cities in the Leipzig area.

United States Consulate in Munich
http://www.usembassy.de/consular/munchen/ right.htm
Along with United States fact sheets and visa information, the site provides German market reports, legal guides, green card chat sessions, an event calendar, and a directory of German-American sister cities in the Munich area.

United States Embassy in Germany
http://www.usia.gov/abtusia/posts/GE1/ wwwh0000.html
Written in English and German, the site offers United States fact sheets, cultural primers, visa and passport information, an event calendar, and German market reports and business guides.

Uzbekistan

Embassy of Uzbekistan in Bonn
http://www.uzbekistan.de/
Written in German, the site provides Uzbekistan news, fact sheets, business guides, cultural primers, visa and passport information, and event information.

Venezuela

Embassy of Venezuela in Bonn
http://www.trade-venezuela.com/EMBVENG.HTM
The site lists the street address, phone and fax numbers, and e-mail link of the Venezuelan Embassy in Bonn.

Western Samoa

Honorary Consulate of Western Samoa in Hamburg
http://www.interwebinc.com/samoa/missde.html
The site lists the street address, and phone and fax numbers of the Honorary Consulate of Western Samoa in Hamburg.

Gibraltar

Gibraltar Media

The M@G
http://www.gibnynex.gi/info/mag/
A Gibraltar electronic magazine, the site features Gibraltar news, features, photos, and a virtual buy and sell exchange.

Gibraltar Market Guides

About Gibraltar
http://www.deloitte.gi/aboutgib.htm
Developed by Deloitte Touche, the site provides quick facts on Gibraltar geography, population, history, government, legal system, economy, currency, communications, and cost of living.

Financial Services Commission
http://www.gibnet.gi/~fsc/home.htm
The online service provides fact sheets on Gibraltar banking, insurance, and investment. The site includes a directory of Gibraltar investment advisors, professional trustees, insurance managers, and other financial professionals.

Gibraltar Home Page
http://www.gibraltar.gi/
A virtual library of information, the site features primers on Gibraltar business, tourism and leisure, history and politics, and nature and wildlife.

Gibraltar Market Research
http://strategis.ic.gc.ca/sc_mrkti/ibinddc/engdoc/1a1b19.html
Posted by Industry Canada, the site provides U.S.

Central Intelligence Agency fact sheets on Gibraltar geography, people, government, economy, communications, and transportation.

Gibraltar Trade Assistance

Port of Gibraltar
http://www.gibraltar.gi/port/
Along with tourism and yachting guides, the site delivers information on pilotage fees, tonnage dues, berthing charges, and customs regulations at the Port of Gibraltar.

Greece

Greece Search Tools

Greek Indexer
http://www.gr-indexer.gr/
Posted in English and Greek, the site is a searchable index of Greek resources online. Categories include business, economy, government, media, organizations, and regional.

THEA
http://www.powernet.gr/thea/
A browsable directory of Greek resources on the web, the site is divided into 12 categories including business, computers, education, government, media, news, and society.

Greece Media

Athens News Agency
http://www.hri.org/ana/
Based in Athens, the online newspaper provides daily bulletins on Greek business, politics, and society. The site includes editorials, and a news archive and search service.

Greece Media
http://www.mediainfo.com/emediajs/specific-geo.htm?region=greece
Prepared by Editor and Publisher Interactive, the site is a directory of Greek media sites online.

Greece Market Guides

Barclays Country Guide: Greece
http://www.offshorebanking.barclays.com/services/economic/yearly/gremay97/index.html
Prepared by Barclays Bank, the site reports on Greek economic trends, politics, monetary and fiscal policy, international trade, and U.K.-Greece merchandise trade and investment flows.

Country Commercial Guide

http://www.state.gov/www/about_state/business/ com_guides/1998/europe_canada/ greece98.html

Prepared by the U.S. Embassy in Athens, the site delivers primers on Greek business, politics, trade regulations and standards, investment climate, trade and project financing, and business travel.

Greece Country Profile

http://www.tradenz.govt.nz/intelligence/profiles/ greece.html

A service of the New Zealand Trade Development Board, the site provides Greek economic statistics, market information, and business tips.

Greece Country Report

http://www.state.gov/www/issues/economic/ trade_reports/europe_canada97/greece97.html

Prepared by the U.S. Department of State, the site delivers information on Greek exchange rates, debt management, trade barriers, and intellectual property protection.

Greece InfoExport

http://www.infoexport.gc.ca/country- e.asp?continent=Europe&country=17

A service of Foreign Affairs and International Trade Canada, the site provides Greek commercial guides and market reports.

Greece Market Information

http://dtiinfo1.dti.gov.uk/ots/greece/

A service of the London-based Department of Trade and Industry, the site delivers Greek fact sheets, maps, and trade-show information.

Greece Market Research

http://strategis.ic.gc.ca/sc_mrkti/ibinddc/engdoc/ 1a1b20.html

A service of Industry Canada, the site provides U.S. Department of Commerce reports on Greek business, politics, trade regulations and standards, investment climate, trade and project financing, business travel, and market opportunities.

Greece Virtual Library

http://www.pitt.edu/~wwwes/greece.nhp.html

A service of the University of Pittsburgh Center for West European Studies, the site is a directory of Greek online resources. Categories include government, education, and culture.

Greek Economy

http://www.greekembassy.org/busin-econ/ index.html

Developed by the Greek Embassy in Washington, D.C., the site provides Greek fact sheets, business guides, investment primers, taxation information, and European Union reports.

Hellas Home Page

http://www.greece.org/hellas/root.html

The webpage of a Greek discussion group, the site features Greek news, articles, cultural bulletins, travel guides, Cyprus information, and a directory of Hellenic communities around the world.

Greece Trade Assistance

ExpoHellas

http://www.expohellas.com/

An online trade show, the site features virtual exhibits from exporters in some 20 categories including agri-food, chemicals, apparel, furniture, and plastics. The service includes Greek export news, trade leads, and a help desk.

Hellenic Embassies and Consulates

http://www.hepogreektrade.com/htmldocs/ offices.htm

A service of the Hellenic Foreign Trade Board, the site lists the street addresses and phone and fax numbers of Greek Embassies and Consulates around the world.

Hellenic Foreign Trade Board

http://www.hepogreektrade.com/

Based in Athens, the Board promotes Greek exports. The site features Greek export guides, investment primers, and a directory of Board programs and services.

Hellenic Ministry of Foreign Affairs

http://www.mfa.gr/

Along with government directories and executive biographies, the site provides Greek news, press releases, fact sheets, foreign policy statements, and regional economic reports.

Trade Shows in Greece

http://www.expoguide.com/shows/data/loc_20.htm

Compiled by Expoguide, the site is a directory of upcoming trade shows in Greece.

Greece Representative Offices

Armenia

Embassy of Armenia in Athens
http://www.armeniaemb.org/forrel/embas2.htm
The site provides contact information for the
Embassy of Armenia in Athens.

Austria

Austrian Trade Commission in Athens
http://aw.wk.or.at/awo/ahst-athen.htm
The site lists the staff, street address, phone and
fax numbers, e-mail link, and office hours of the
Austrian Trade Commission in Athens.

Canada

Embassy of Canada in Athens
http://www.dfait-maeci.gc.ca/english/missions/rep-can2e.htm#greece
The site provides contact information for the
Canadian Embassy in Athens.

Cyprus

Cyprus Trade Center in Athens
http://www.cyprustradeny.org/cyny5.html
The site lists the street address, and phone and
fax numbers of the Cyprus Trade Center in
Athens.

Finland

Finland Trade Center in Athens
http://www.exports.finland.fi/tradecen.htm
The site lists the staff, street address, phone and
fax numbers, and e-mail link of the Finland Trade
Center in Athens.

France

French Trade Commission in Athens
http://www.dree.org/grece/
A French trade promotion service, the site
provides Greek market studies and a directory of
export programs for French companies doing
business in Greece.

Germany

German Chamber of Commerce in Athens
http://www.german-chamber.gr/
Written in Greek, the site provides German fact
sheets, Greek market reports, contact information, and a directory of Chamber programs and
services.

India

Indian Commercial Mission in Athens
http://www.nic.in/commin/ICM.HTM
The site lists the street address, phone and fax
numbers, and e-mail link of the Indian Commercial Mission in Athens.

Italy

Consulate General of Italy in Athens
http://www.forthnet.gr/iic/
Written in Italian, the site delivers Italian fact
sheets, business guides, cultural bulletins, visa
and passport information, and a directory of
consular services.

Consulate General of Italy in Salonicco
http://users.forthnet.gr/the/italcons/
Posted in Italian, the site offers Italian fact sheets,
visa and passport information, education and
cultural bulletins, and a directory of consular
programs.

Netherlands

Royal Netherlands Embassy in Athens
http://www.dutchembassy.gr/
The virtual Embassy provides Dutch news,
business guides, trade leads, tender information,
cultural bulletins, and an event calendar.

Norway

Norwegian Trade Council in Athens
*http://www.ntc.no/cgi-bin/wbch.exe?html=../
templates/utekontor2.html&profile=1099*
The site lists the staff, street address, phone and
fax numbers, and e-mail link of the Norwegian
Trade Council in Athens.

Singapore

Consulate General of Singapore in Athens
http://www.gov.sg/mfa/consular/mww_g.htm
The site provides contact information for the Singapore Consulate General in Athens.

Spain

Spanish Commercial Office in Athens
http://www.icex.es/openURL.html#openURL=/
english/infoproyem/ofcomes/ofcomes.html#EU
The site lists the staff, street address, phone and fax numbers, and e-mail link of the Spanish Commercial Office in Athens.

Sweden

Embassy of Sweden in Athens
http://www.ud.se/english/mfa/ambassad/
grekland.htm
The site lists the staff, street address, phone and fax numbers, and e-mail link of the Swedish Embassy in Athens.

Thailand

Royal Thai Embassy in Athens
http://www.mfa.go.th/Embassy/detail/40.htm
The site lists the Ambassador, street address, and phone and fax numbers of the Thai Embassy in Athens.

United Kingdom

British Council in Greece
http://www.britcoun.gr/
A gateway to Britain, the site provides primers on British arts, economics, management, education, government, publishing, and science and technology. The service includes reports on British-Greek relations and cultural exchanges.

British Embassy in Athens
http://www.british-embassy.gr/
Written in English and Greek, the site features British fact sheets, passport information, reports on the Britain and Greece Festival, and a directory of British organizations in Greece.

British Hellenic Chamber of Commerce
http://www.british-embassy.gr/institut.htm
Based in Athens, the Chamber promotes British-Greek trade. The site includes a mission statement, membership directory, and contact information.

Consulate of Britain in Corfu
http://www.fco.gov.uk/directory/posts.asp?GC
The site provides contact information for the British Consulate in Corfu.

United States

American Hellenic Chamber of Commerce
http://www.usisathens.gr/chamber.html
Based in Athens, the Chamber promotes Greek-American trade. The site features a mission statement, program directory, and contact information.

United States Embassy in Greece
http://www.usisathens.gr/
Posted in English and Greek, the site features U.S. fact sheets, speeches, press releases, legislative bulletins, issue reports, visa and passport information, and a directory of commercial services.

Venezuela

Embassy of Venezuela in Athens
http://www.trade-venezuela.com/EMBVENG.HTM
The site lists the street address, phone and fax numbers, and e-mail link of the Venezuelan Embassy in Athens.

Greenland

Greenland Market Guides

Greenland Business Development Corporation
http://www.sulisa.gl/
Established in 1993 by the Greenland Home Rule Authority, the Corporation provides business counseling services to Greenlandic companies. The site features a mission statement and contact information.

Greenland Government
http://www.gh.gl/
Written in English and Danish, the site delivers Greenlandic news, fact sheets, government guides, international trade reports, and an event calendar.

Greenland Guide
http://www.greenland-guide.dk/default.htm
Developed by the national tourist board, the site provides Greenlandic travel information, accommodation directories, community profiles, press kits, virtual postcards, and a free screen saver.

Greenland Market Research
*http://strategis.ic.gc.ca/sc_mrkti/ibinddc/engdoc/
1a1e2.html*
Posted by Industry Canada, the site provides U.S.
Central Intelligence Agency fact sheets on
Greenlandic geography, people, government,
economy, communications, and transportation.

Greenland Trade Assistance

Greenland Trade Directory
http://www.greentrade.gl/
Posted in English and Danish, the site is a
directory of Greenlandic exporters, products,
business organizations, trade shows, investment
programs, and international offices.

Guernsey

Guernsey Market Guides

Doing Business in Guernsey
http://www.guernsey-ey.com/dbigg/index.htm
A service of Ernst & Young, the site is a Guernsey
business guide. Topics include foreign investment, structure of business entities, labor force,
taxation, and financial reporting and auditing.

Guernsey Tourism Information Centre
http://www.guernsey.net/~tourism/index.html
Homepage of the Guernsey Tourist Board, the
site provides Guernsey maps, community
profiles, accommodation directories, weather
information, and a calendar of events.

Iceland

Iceland Media

Daily News from Iceland
http://www.centrum.is/icerev/daily1.html
Updated daily, the site provides Icelandic news,
business reports, maps, fact sheets, community
profiles, shopping directories, weather bulletins,
and satellite pictures.

Iceland Media
*http://www.mediainfo.com/emediajs/specific-
geo.htm?region=iceland*
Prepared by Editor and Publisher Interactive, the
site is a directory of Icelandic media sites online
including magazines, newspapers, and television stations.

Iceland Market Guides

Iceland Business
http://www.centrum.is/icerev/ib/
Based in Reykjavík, the site provides Icelandic
company profiles, sector bulletins, global
business reports, and interviews with senior
government officials.

Iceland General Information
http://www.iceland.org/general.html
A service of the Icelandic Embassy in Washington, D.C., the site delivers fact sheets on Iceland-
dic government, population, language, education,
business, and weather.

Iceland InfoExport
*http://www.infoexport.gc.ca/country-
e.asp?continent=Europe&country=21*
A service of Foreign Affairs and International
Trade Canada, the site provides fact sheets and
statistics on Icelandic geography, business, and
politics.

Iceland Market Information
http://dtiinfo1.dti.gov.uk/ots/iceland/
A service of the London-based Department of
Trade and Industry, the site delivers Icelandic fact
sheets, maps, and trade-show information.

Iceland Market Research
*http://strategis.ic.gc.ca/sc_mrkti/ibinddc/engdoc/
1a1b22.html*
Posted by Industry Canada, the site provides U.S.
Central Intelligence Agency fact sheets on
Icelandic geography, people, government,
economy, communications, and transportation.

Invest in Iceland
http://www.invest.is/
An Icelandic investment primer, the service
delivers fact sheets on Icelandic infrastructure,
logistics, energy, food production, labor, education, health care, and business opportunities.

Islandia
http://islandia.nomius.com/
A web-based guide to Iceland, the site includes
Icelandic news, history lessons, fact sheets,
tourism information, education reports, economic
profiles, and a list of Icelandic holidays.

Welcome to Islandia
http://www.arctic.is/islandia/
A digital library of Icelandic information, the service delivers fact sheets on Icelandic history, geography, language, culture, religion, business, weather, and tourism.

Iceland Trade Assistance

Iceland Export Directory
http://www.midlun.is/export/
Developed by the Reykjavik-based Midlun Group, the site is a searchable database of Icelandic exporters. The directory is browsable by company, product, and industries such as export financing institutions, shipping agents, and fish processors.

Iceland Export Index
http://www.arctic.is/Practical/Export/
Prepared by Iceland Internet Service, the site is a browsable database of Icelandic exporters. Categories include beverages, fish processing, plastics, and paper products.

Icelandic Companies in the Americas
http://www.iceland.org/fyrirta.htm
A service of the Icelandic Embassy in Washington, D.C., the site is a directory of Icelandic companies in Canada, the U.S., and Latin America. Categories include airlines and travel, computers and software, and food and beverages.

Icelandic Export
http://export.is/
A directory of Icelandic exporters, the site is searchable by keyword, company name, product, and senior executive.

Icelandic Government Offices Abroad
http://www.iceland.org/list1n.htm
Developed by the Icelandic Embassy in Washington, D.C., the site is a database of Icelandic Embassies, Consulates and other government offices in Canada, the U.S., and Latin America.

Ministry for Foreign Affairs
http://brunnur.stjr.is/interpro/utanr/utn-eng.nsf/pages/front
Along with Ministry fact sheets, the site delivers primers on Icelandic business, tourism, culture, and foreign relations. The service includes a directory of Icelandic Embassies and Consulates abroad, and international Embassies and Consulates in Iceland.

Trade Council of Iceland
http://www.icetrade.is/
Based in Reykjavik, the Council promotes Icelandic exports and international investment. The site features Icelandic export directories, company profiles, and trade-show information.

Iceland Representative Offices

Canada

Consulate General of Canada in Reykjavik
http://www.dfait-maeci.gc.ca/english/missions/rep-can2e.htm#iceland
The site provides contact information for the Canadian Consulate General in Reykjavik.

Sweden

Embassy of Sweden in Reykjavik
http://www.ud.se/english/mfa/ambassad/island.htm
The site lists the staff, street address, phone and fax numbers, and e-mail link of the Swedish Embassy in Reykjavik.

United Kingdom

Embassy of Britain in Reykjavik
http://www.fco.gov.uk/directory/posts.asp?IC
The site provides contact information for the British Embassy in Reykjavik.

United States

United States Embassy in Reykjavik
http://www.itn.is/america/mainemb.html
Along with staff profiles, the site provides contact information, a directory of consular and commercial services, and reports from the Iceland-U.S. Educational Commission.

United States Information Service in Reykjavik
http://www.itn.is/america/mainusis.html
A virtual library of U.S. information, the site provides U.S. news, press releases, electronic journals, economic articles, and foreign policy statements.

Ireland

Ireland Search Tools

Finfacts
http://www.finfacts.ie/
An Irish web gateway, the site provides Internet searching, daily business news, salary surveys, information technology reports, employment opportunities, and e-commerce bulletins.

Yahoo U.K. and Ireland
http://www.yahoo.co.uk/
A service of Yahoo, the site provides Irish news, web-based personal management tools, and Internet searching.

Ireland Media

Ireland Media
http://www.mediainfo.com/emediajs/specific-geo.htm?region=ireland
Prepared by Editor and Publisher Interactive, the site is a directory of Irish media sites online.

Irish Times
http://www.irish-times.ie/
A Dublin-based electronic newspaper, the site provides Irish news, editorials, discussion forums, employment opportunities, business guides, and a news archive.

Ireland Market Guides

Barclays Country Guide: Ireland
http://www.offshorebanking.barclays.com/services/economic/yearly/iredec97/index.html
Prepared by Barclays Bank, the site reports on Irish economic trends, politics, monetary and fiscal policy, international trade, and U.K.-Ireland merchandise trade and investment flows.

Doing Business in Ireland
http://www.itw.ie/binirl.html
A service of Irish Trade Web, the site is a guide to selling and investing in Ireland. Topics include distribution and sales channels, trade regulations, taxation, employment, and travel.

Enterprise Ireland
http://www.irish-trade.ie/
Posted in six languages, the site provides Irish business news, company profiles, sector reports, success stories, employment opportunities, economic data, and supplier directories.

Ireland Country Profile
http://www.tradenz.govt.nz/intelligence/profiles/ireland.html
A service of the New Zealand Trade Development Board, the site provides Irish economic statistics, market information, and business tips.

Ireland Country Report
http://www.state.gov/www/issues/economic/trade_reports/europe_canada97/ireland97.html
Prepared by the U.S. Department of State, the site delivers information on Irish exchange rates, debt management, trade barriers, and intellectual property protection.

Ireland InfoExport
http://www.infoexport.gc.ca/country-e.asp?continent=Europe&country=22
A service of Foreign Affairs and International Trade Canada, the site provides Irish commercial guides and market reports.

Ireland Market Information
http://dtiinfo1.dti.gov.uk/ots/republic_of_ireland/
A service of the London-based Department of Trade and Industry, the site delivers Irish fact sheets, maps, and trade-show information.

Ireland Market Research
http://strategis.ic.gc.ca/sc_mrkti/ibinddc/engdoc/1a1b23.html
A service of Industry Canada, the site provides U.S. Department of Commerce reports on Irish business, politics, trade regulations and standards, investment climate, trade and project financing, business travel, and market opportunities.

Ireland Virtual Library
http://www.pitt.edu/~wwwes/ireland.nhp.html
A service of the University of Pittsburgh Center for West European Studies, the site is a directory of Irish online resources. Categories include government, education, and culture.

Ireland's 1000 Plus
http://www.itw.ie/Top/topserch.htm
A directory of Ireland's largest companies, the site profiles operations in over 50 industries including construction, electronics, heath care, pharmaceuticals, publishing, and transportation.

Irish Business on the Web
http://homepages.iol.ie/~aidanh/business/
A database of some 1,400 Irish firms, the site is divided into 14 sections including arts and

media, computer hardware, education, tourism, finance, and science and engineering.

Irish Jobs Page
http://www.exp.ie/
An Irish employment service, the site provides a searchable database of Irish jobs and resumes. Features include job-hunting tips, and special job pages for information technology, engineering, and accounting.

Ireland Trade Assistance

Business to Business
http://www.itw.ie/biz2biz/index.html
An online business matchmaking service, the site provides searchable directories of Irish manufacturers seeking foreign distributors, international agents looking for Irish products to distribute, and international companies seeking distributors in Ireland.

Department of Foreign Affairs
http://www.irlgov.ie/iveagh/
Based in Dublin, the site delivers Irish fact sheets, press releases, speeches, foreign policy statements, annual reports, Northern Ireland documents, and European Union-Ireland bulletins.

Irish Exporters Association
http://www.itw.ie/exporter/iea.htm
An Irish export promotion service, the site provides Irish trade news, publication lists, European Union reports, and a directory of export education programs.

Irish Trade Shows and Events
http://www.itw.ie/tradshow.html
A service of Irish Trade Web, the site is a directory of upcoming Irish trade shows, exhibitions, and seminars.

Irish Trade Web
http://www.itw.ie/
A hub of Irish trade information, the site includes Irish business primers, company directories, an online marketplace, event calendar, and web navigation services.

Search for Suppliers
http://www.irish-trade.ie/search_suppliers/ search_by_sector01.html
A searchable directory of Irish companies, the site profiles firms in over 20 industries including aerospace, construction materials, electronics,

agri-food, pharmaceuticals, and printing and packaging.

Southeast European Centre
http://www.amireland.com/waterford_partnership/ partpage/carrefor.html
Part of a network of European Commission information centers, the Center provides European networking and advisory services for businesspeople in Southeast Ireland. The site includes a mission statement and contact information.

Trade Shows in Ireland
http://www.expoguide.com/shows/data/loc_26.htm
Compiled by Expoguide, the site is a directory of upcoming trade shows in Ireland.

Worldwide Office Network
http://www.irish-trade.ie/office_network/ office_locate01.html
A service of Enterprise Ireland, the site is a directory of Irish trade offices in Britain, Continental Europe, North and South America, and Asia.

Ireland Representative Offices

Australia

Irish Australian Business Association
http://www.itw.ie/exporter/iaba.htm
An Australian-Irish trade promotion service, the site lists the mission statement, street address, phone and fax numbers, and e-mail link of the Association in Dublin.

Austria

Austrian Trade Commission in Dublin
http://aw.wk.or.at/awo/ahst-dublin.htm
The site lists the staff, street address, phone and fax numbers, e-mail link, and office hours of the Austrian Trade Commission in Dublin.

Canada

Embassy of Canada in Dublin
http://www.dfait-maeci.gc.ca/english/missions/rep-can2e.htm#ireland
The site provides contact information for the Canadian Embassy in Dublin.

Finland

Finland Trade Center in Dublin
http://www.exports.finland.fi/tradecen.htm
The site lists the staff, street address, phone and fax numbers, and e-mail link of the Finland Trade Center in Dublin.

France

French Trade Commission in Dublin
http://www.dree.org/irlande/
Part of a global network of French trade promotion offices, the site provides Irish market studies, and a directory of export programs for French companies doing business in Ireland.

Germany

German-Irish Chamber of Commerce
http://www.german-irish.ie/
Founded in 1980, the Chamber promotes German-Irish trade. The site features German fact sheets, business guides, Irish bulletins, and a directory of Chamber programs and staff.

Israel

Embassy of Israel in Dublin
http://www.iol.ie/embisrael/
The virtual Embassy delivers Israeli news, fact sheets, staff profiles, cultural bulletins, reports on Irish-Israel trade and relations, and a directory of Embassy programs.

Italy

Embassy of Italy in Dublin
http://homepage.tinet.ie/~italianembassy/
Posted in English and Italian, the site provides Italian news, fact sheets, regional profiles, economic data, tourism guides, and a directory of Embassy programs.

Netherlands

Royal Netherlands Embassy in Dublin
http://indigo.ie/~nethemb/
The online service delivers Dutch fact sheets, travel guides, immigration primers, contact information, and a directory of Dutch government agencies on the web.

Norway

Norwegian Irish Business Council
http://www.iol.ie/~nibc/
Based in Dublin, the Council promotes Irish-Norwegian trade. The site includes Norwegian fact sheets, a member directory, bilateral trade reports, and contact information.

Portugal

Portuguese Trade and Investment Office in Dublin
http://www.portugal.org/geninfo/abouticep/ireland.html
The site lists the staff, street address, phone and fax numbers, and e-mail link of the Portuguese Trade and Investment Office in Dublin.

Spain

Ireland Spain Economic Association
http://www.itw.ie/exporter/isea.htm
An Irish-Spanish trade promotion service, the site lists the mission statement, street address, phone and fax numbers, and e-mail link of the Association in Dublin.

Spanish Commercial Office in Dublin
http://www.icex.es/openURL.html#openURL=/english/infoproyem/ofcomes/ofcomes.html#EU
The site lists the staff, street address, phone and fax numbers, and e-mail link of the Spanish Commercial Office in Dublin.

Sweden

Embassy of Sweden in Dublin
http://www.ud.se/english/mfa/ambassad/irland.htm
The site lists the staff, street address, phone and fax numbers, and e-mail link of the Swedish Embassy in Dublin.

Turkey

Embassy of Turkey in Dublin
http://www.turkey.org/madres.htm
As part of a directory of Turkish diplomatic offices around the world, the site lists the e-mail link of the Turkish Embassy in Dublin.

United Kingdom

Embassy of Britain in Dublin
http://www.fco.gov.uk/directory/posts.asp?IE
The site provides contact information for the British Embassy in Dublin.

United States

Irish American Partnership
http://www.adnet.ie/iap/
With offices in Dublin and Boston, the Partnership promotes economic development in Ireland. The site includes a membership application form, event calendar, and contact information.

United States Embassy in Ireland
http://www.indigo.ie/usembassy-usis/
Along with U.S. fact sheets and visa information, the site features Irish economic bulletins, employment opportunities, and reports on Irish-American trade and relations.

Isle of Man

Isle of Man Market Guides

Department of Trade and Industry
http://www.gov.im/deptindex/dtiinfo.html
Based in Douglas, the Department promotes Isle of Man economic development. The site includes a mission statement, program directory, and contact information.

Isle of Man Business
http://www.isle-of-man.com/business/index.htm
A virtual guide to the Isle of Man, the site provides fact sheets on Isle of Man history, culture, infrastructure, business, geography, climate, tourism, and quality of life.

Isle of Man Government
http://www.gov.im/
The online service provides Isle of Man fact sheets, business primers, parliamentary guides, tourism information, and a directory of government departments, boards, and offices.

Italy

Italy Search Tools

Infoseek Italy
http://www.infoseek.com/
Home?pg=Home.html&sv=IT

Written in Italian, the site provides web navigation, browsing tips, and a searchable directory of Italian resources online.

Infospace Italy
_http://in-135.infospace.com/_1_34407537__info/_
intldb/intl-it.html
A service of Infospace, the Italian search engine includes a travel guide, e-mail directory, and business and people finders.

Lycos Italy
http://www.lycos.it/
Posted in Italian, the search service includes road maps, website reviews, classifieds, shopping guides, and chat forums.

ShinySeek
http://www.shinyseek.it/
A browsable index of Italian resources online, the site is divided into 12 categories including government, business, arts, science, and travel.

Yahoo Italia
http://www.yahoo.it/
A service of Yahoo, the site provides Italian news, web-based personal management tools, and Internet searching.

Italy Media

Italy Media
http://www.mediainfo.com/emediajs/specific-
geo.htm?region=italy
Prepared by Editor and Publisher Interactive, the site is a directory of Italian media sites online, including magazines, newspapers, and radio stations.

Italy Market Guides

Barclays Country Report: Italy
http://www.offshorebanking.barclays.com/
services/economic/yearly/itafeb98/contents.html
Prepared by Barclays Bank, the site reports on Italian economic trends, politics, monetary and fiscal policy, international trade, and U.K.-Italy merchandise trade and investment flows.

Doing Business in Italy
http://www.italyemb.org/chapidx.htm
An Italian business guide, the site provides primers on Italian investments, acquisitions, mergers, distribution agreements, taxation, and business incentives.

General Information about Italy

http://www.italyemb.org/geninfo.htm
A service of the Italian Embassy in Washington, D.C., the site delivers Italian fact sheets, cultural information, commercial guides, business primers, and company directories.

Informest

http://www.informest.it/homei.htm
A service of the Italian government, the site features Italian business opportunities, international trade contacts, company directories, taxation reports, and socioeconomic statistics.

Italia Online

http://www.italyemb.org/chapidx.htm
Written in Italian, the site offers Italian news, business reports, information technology bulletins, web navigation, and a searchable index of Italian online resources.

Italian Chambers of Commerce

http://italchambers.net/
A directory of Italian Chambers of Commerce in 38 countries, the site includes Italian business news, trade leads, company profiles, country reports, and an event calendar.

Italy Business Briefs

http://www.austrade.gov.au/IOOM/Italy/
A service of Austrade, the site offers fact sheets on Italian business etiquette, foreign investment, corporate taxation, marketing, and visas.

Italy Country Profile

http://www.tradenz.govt.nz/intelligence/profiles/italy.html
A service of the New Zealand Trade Development Board, the site provides Italian economic statistics, market information, and business tips.

Italy Country Report

http://www.state.gov/www/issues/economic/trade_reports/europe_canada97/italy97.html
Prepared by the U.S. Department of State, the site delivers information on Italian exchange rates, debt management, trade barriers, and intellectual property protection.

Italy Economy

http://www.italyemb.org/stats.htm
Prepared by the Bank of Italy, the site is a database of Italian economic indicators. The statistics include domestic demand, industrial production, producer and consumer prices, balance of payments, and interest rates.

Italy InfoExport

http://www.infoexport.gc.ca/country-e.asp?continent=Europe&country=23
A service of Foreign Affairs and International Trade Canada, the site provides Italian commercial guides and market reports.

Italy Market Information

http://dtiinfo1.dti.gov.uk/ots/italy/
A service of the London-based Department of Trade and Industry, the site delivers Italian fact sheets, maps, and trade-show information.

Italy Market Research

http://strategis.ic.gc.ca/sc_mrkti/ibinddc/engdoc/1a1b24.html
A service of Industry Canada, the site provides U.S. Department of Commerce reports on Italian business, politics, trade regulations and standards, investment climate, trade and project financing, business travel, and market opportunities.

Italy Patent Information

http://www.european-patent-office.org/it/homepage/homepage.htm
Developed by the Italian Patent and Trademark Office, the site is a searchable directory of Italian patents and trademarks, patent attorneys, European patents, and international trademarks.

Italy Virtual Library

http://www.pitt.edu/~wwwes/italy.nhp.html
A service of the University of Pittsburgh Center for West European Studies, the site is a directory of Italian online resources. Categories include government, education, and culture.

Italy's Industry Directory

http://www.tradenet.it/companies/index.html
A browsable directory of Italian companies, the site profiles companies in 20 categories including agri-food, paper, chemicals, rubber and plastic, machinery, electronics, and transportation equipment.

Pagine Gialle Italy

http://www.paginegialle.it/fe-docs/home/homei.htm
Written in English and Italian, the site is a searchable directory of Italian companies. The database is browsable by company name, industry, province, and region.

Italy Trade Assistance

Emporion On-Line
http://www.emporion.it/English/Indicebig.htm
Based in Roma, the site provides Italian product catalogs, country information, a trade-show database, and a directory of Italian Trade Commission offices around the world.

Italian Customs and Excise Department
http://www.mclink.it/com/makros/dogane/indexi.htm
Posted in English and Italian, the site delivers Italian customs fact sheets, a departmental organization chart, contact information, and a directory of upcoming international trade seminars.

Italian Embassies and Consulates
http://www3.itu.ch/MISSIONS/Italy/rete.htm
A service of the Mission of Italy to the United Nations, the site provides a directory of Italian Embassies, Missions, and Consulates around the world.

Italian Embassy and Consulate Directory
http://www.escapeartist.com/embassy21/embassy21.htm
A service of Escape Artist.Com, the site is a database of Italian Embassies and Consulates in more than 50 countries including Bulgaria, Germany, Malaysia, and South Africa.

Ministry of Foreign Affairs
http://www.esteri.it/
Posted in English and Italian, the site provides Italian fact sheets, press releases, speeches, foreign policy statements, articles, and interviews with leading Ministry officials.

Sistema Italia
http://www.italia.informest.it/ingl/index.htm
A guide to the Italian economy, the site delivers primers on Italian exporting, importing, subcontracting, counter-trade, franchising, leasing, technology transfers, and joint ventures.

Trade.IT
http://www.trade.it/
Posted in English and Italian, the site is a searchable directory of some 5,000 Italian exporters in ten categories including apparel, glasses and optical products, furniture, and industrial ceramics.

Trade Net
http://www.tradenet.it/
A virtual library of Italian business information, the site features Italian company profiles, product finders, agent lists, accommodation directories, and web marketing information.

Trade Shows in Italy
http://www.expoguide.com/shows/data/loc_28.htm
Compiled by Expoguide, the site is a directory of upcoming trade shows in Italy.

Italy Representative Offices

Armenia

Embassy of Armenia in Rome
http://www.armeniaemb.org/forrel/embas2.htm
The site provides contact information for the Armenian Embassy in Rome.

Australia

Austrade in Milan
http://www.austrade.gov.au/Milan/
An Australian export promotion service, the site features business guides, investment primers, and a directory of trade assistance programs for Australian exporters in Italy.

Austria

Austrian Consulate General in Milan
http://www.wk.or.at/wk/aw/atc/italy/indiriz.htm
The site lists the street address, phone and fax numbers, and e-mail link of the Austrian Consulate General in Milan.

Austrian Consulate General in Padova
http://www.wk.or.at/wk/aw/atc/italy/indiriz.htm
The site lists the street address, phone and fax numbers, and e-mail link of the Austrian Consulate in Padova.

Austrian Embassy in Rome
http://www.wk.or.at/wk/aw/atc/italy/
Written in Italian, the site provides Austrian fact sheets, business guides, economic bulletins, travel primers, reports on Austrian-Italian trade, and a directory of Embassy services.

Austrian Trade Commission in Milan
http://aw.wk.or.at/awo/ahst-mailand.htm
The site lists the staff, street address, phone and

fax numbers, e-mail link, and office hours of the Austrian Trade Commission in Milan.

Austrian Trade Commission in Padova
http://aw.wk.or.at/awo/ahst-padua.htm
The site lists the staff, street address, phone and fax numbers, e-mail link, and office hours of the Austrian Trade Commission in Padova.

Austrian Trade Commission in Rome
http://aw.wk.or.at/awo/ahst-rom.htm
The site lists the staff, street address, phone and fax numbers, e-mail link, and office hours of the Austrian Trade Commission in Rome.

Argentina

Embassy of Argentina in Rome
http://www.aconet.it/tur/arg/
Posted in Italian, the site features Argentine fact sheets, maps, Mercosur reports, tourism guides, regional profiles, and visa and passport information.

Canada

Canadian Embassy in Rome
http://www.canada.it/
Along with Canadian fact sheets and foreign policy statements, the site delivers Italian business guides, and market reports for 12 industries including agri-food, packaging, energy, medical equipment, and plastics.

Consulate General of Canada in Milan
http://www.dfait-maeci.gc.ca/english/missions/rep-can2e.htm#italy
The site provides contact information for the Canadian Consulate General in Milan.

China

China Council for the Promotion of International Trade in Milan
http://www.ccpit.org/engVersion/cp_about/cp_over/cp_over.html
A Chinese export promotion service, the site provides contact information for the China Council for the Promotion of International Trade office in Milan.

Colombia

Embassy of Colombia in Rome
http://www.embcolombiaitalia.com/

Posted in Italian and Spanish, the site features Colombian fact sheets, business guides, cultural bulletins, reports on Colombian-Italian trade, and a directory of Embassy programs.

Finland

Embassy of Finland in Rome
http://www.finland.it/
Written in Italian, the site provides Finnish fact sheets, visa and passport information, legal notices, tourism guides, and reports on Finnish-Italian trade and relations.

Finland Trade Center in Milan
http://www.exports.finland.fi/tradecen.htm
The site lists the staff, street address, phone and fax numbers, and e-mail link of the Finland Trade Center in Milan.

France

French Trade Commission in Milan
http://www.dree.org/italie/FRANCAIS/GENERAL/PEE/MILAN.HTM
Posted in French, the site provides contact information, Italian market reports, and a directory of export programs for French companies doing business in Milan and northern Italy.

French Trade Commission in Rome
http://www.dree.org/italie/FRANCAIS/GENERAL/PEE/ROME.HTM
Along with contact information, the site delivers Italian market reports, and a directory of export services for French companies doing business in Rome and southern Italy.

Germany

German Chamber of Commerce in Milan
http://www.ahk.net/en/it/Milano/
The site lists the Chairperson, Chief Executive Officer, street address, phone and fax numbers, and e-mail link of the German Chamber in Milan.

Ghana

Embassy of Ghana in Rome
http://www.juntung.com/ghana-consul-hk/2misabo.htm
The site provides contact information for the Ghanaese Embassy in Rome.

India

Indian Commercial Mission in Rome
http://www.nic.in/commin/ICM.HTM
The site lists the street address, phone and fax numbers, and e-mail link of the Indian Commercial Mission in Rome.

Indonesia

Embassy of Indonesia in Rome
http://indag.dprin.go.id/INGG/trade/atache.HTM
The site provides contact information for the Indonesian Embassy in Rome.

Ireland

Enterprise Ireland in Milan
http://www.irish-trade.ie/office_network/office_locate01.html#milan
The site lists the Manager, street address, and phone and fax numbers of the Enterprise Ireland office in Milan.

Japan

Embassy of Japan in Milan
http://www.ambasciatajp.it/
Written in Italian, the site provides Japanese news, fact sheets, regional profiles, travel guides, reports on Italian-Japanese trade and relations, and a directory of Embassy services.

Madagascar

Embassy of Madagascar in Rome
http://www.madagascar-contacts.com/us/adresse.htm#alext
Along with a directory of Madagascar government agencies, the site provides contact information for the Madagascar Embassy in Rome.

Malaysia

Embassy of Malaysia in Rome
http://www.mnet.com.my/klonline/www/missions/malmiss/mitaly1.htm
The site provides contact information for the Malaysian Embassy in Rome.

Trade Commission of Malaysia in Milan
http://www.mnet.com.my/klonline/www/missions/malmiss/mitaly2.htm
The site provides contact information for the Malaysian Trade Commission in Milan.

Mexico

Consulate General of Mexico in Milan
http://dbweb.agora.stm.it/market/consmex/home.htm
Posted in Italian and Spanish, the site provides Mexican business guides, investment primers, reports on Mexican-Italian trade, and a directory of consular programs and staff.

Embassy of Mexico in Rome
http://www.target.it/messico/
The virtual Embassy delivers Mexican news, political bulletins, visa and passport information, tourism guides, and a directory of Embassy programs and staff.

Trade Commission of Mexico in Milan
http://www.mexico-businessline.com/ingles/ofrepmu3.html#italy
The site lists the street address, phone and fax numbers, and e-mail link of the Mexican Trade Commission in Milan.

New Zealand

Trade New Zealand in Milan
http://www.tradenz.govt.nz/contact/europe.html
An export promotion service, the site provides contact information for the Trade New Zealand office in Milan.

Norway

Norwegian Trade Council in Milan
http://www.ntc.no/cgi-bin/wbch.exe?html=../templates/utekontor2.html&profile=1119
The site lists the staff, street address, phone and fax numbers, and e-mail link of the Norwegian Trade Council in Milan.

Pakistan

Pakistan Trade Office in Rome
http://www.jamal.com/epb/ptoa.htm
The site provides contact information for the Pakistan Trade Office in Rome.

Philippines

Philippine Trade and Investment Promotion Office in Milan
http://www.dti.gov.ph/mil/
The site provides a mission statement, service directory, and contact information for the Philippine Trade Office in Milan.

Portugal

Portuguese Trade and Investment Office in Milan
http://www.portugal.org/geninfo/abouticep/italy.html
The site lists the staff, street address, phone and fax numbers, and e-mail link of the Portuguese Trade and Investment Office in Milan.

South Africa

South Africa Foreign Trade Office in Milan
http://wwwdti.pwv.gov.za/dtiwww/foreign_offices.htm
A service of the South Africa Department of Trade and Industry, the site provides contact information for the South Africa Trade Office in Milan.

South Africa Foreign Trade Office in Rome
http://wwwdti.pwv.gov.za/dtiwww/foreign_offices.htm
A service of the South Africa Department of Trade and Industry, the site provides contact information for the South Africa Trade Office in Rome.

Spain

Spanish Commercial Office in Milan
http://www.icex.es/openURL.html#openURL=/english/infoproyem/ofcomes/ofcomes.html#EU
The site lists the staff, street address, phone and fax numbers, and e-mail link of the Spanish Commercial Office in Milan.

Spanish Commercial Office in Rome
http://www.icex.es/openURL.html#openURL=/english/infoproyem/ofcomes/ofcomes.html#EU
The site lists the staff, street address, phone and fax numbers, and e-mail link of the Spanish Commercial Office in Rome.

Sweden

Embassy of Sweden in Rome
http://www.ud.se/english/mfa/ambassad/italien.htm
The site lists the staff, street address, phone and fax numbers, and e-mail link of the Swedish Embassy in Rome.

Switzerland

Swiss Chamber of Commerce in Milan
http://swisstrade.com/
xicodes2.asp?P1=3&lvl=3&cid=A11
The site lists the street address, phone and fax numbers, and e-mail link of the Swiss Chamber of Commerce in Milan.

Taiwan

Milan Design Center
http://www.cetra.org.tw/english/o_office/indexset.htm
A Taiwanese trade promotion service, the site lists the mission statement and e-mail link of the Milan Design Center.

Taiwan Government Information Office in Rome
http://www.gio.gov.tw/info/ngio/ita-f.html
Posted in Chinese and English, the site lists the street address, phone and fax numbers, and e-mail link of the Taiwan Government Information Office in Rome.

Tanzania

Embassy of Tanzania in Rome
http://www.tanzania-online.gov.uk/visa/envoys.html
The site provides contact information for the Tanzania Embassy in Rome.

Thailand

Royal Thai Embassy in Rome
http://www.mfa.go.th/Embassy/detail/45.htm
The site lists the Ambassador, street address, phone and fax numbers, and e-mail link of the Thai Embassy in Rome.

Thai Trade Center in Milan
http://www.thaitrade.com/wwtto.html
A service of the Thailand Department of Export Promotion, the site lists the street address, phone and fax numbers, and e-mail link of the Thai Trade Center in Milan.

Thailand Office of Commercial Affairs in Rome
http://www.thaitrade.com/thcoaf.html
The site lists the street address, phone and fax numbers, and e-mail link of the Thailand Office of Commercial Affairs in Rome.

Turkey

Embassy of Turkey in Rome
http://www.turkey.org/madres.htm
Part of a directory of Turkish diplomatic offices

around the world, the site lists the e-mail link of the Turkish Embassy in Rome.

United Kingdom

Consulate of Britain in Florence
http://www.fco.gov.uk/directory/posts.asp?IT
The site provides contact information for the British Consulate in Florence.

Consulate General of Britain in Milan
http://www.fco.gov.uk/directory/posts.asp?IT
The site provides contact information for the British Consulate General in Milan.

Embassy of Britain in Rome
http://www.grbr.it/
Posted in Italian, the site provides British fact sheets, business guides, visa and passport information, and a directory of consular and commercial services.

United States

Agricultural Trade Office in Milan
http://www.italcont.com/usda/
Along with primers on exporting food products to Italy, the site features Italian agri-food trade leads, trade-show information, and directories of Italian importers.

United States Consulate General in Florence
http://www.usis.it/mission/florence.htm
The site lists the Consul General, street address, and phone and fax numbers of the American Consulate in Florence.

United States Consulate General in Milan
http://www.usis.it/mission/milan.htm
The site lists the Consul General, street address, and phone and fax numbers of the American Consulate in Milan.

United States Consulate General in Naples
http://www.usis.it/mission/naples.htm
The site lists the Consul General, street address, and phone and fax numbers of the American Consulate in Naples.

United States Embassy in Italy
http://www.usis.it/
Featuring greetings from the Ambassador, the site provides United States fact sheets, speeches, press releases, visa and passport information, foreign policy statements, and government bulletins.

Venezuela

Embassy of Venezuela in Rome
http://www.trade-venezuela.com/EMBVENG.HTM
The site lists the street address, phone and fax numbers, and e-mail link of the Venezuelan Embassy in Rome.

Jersey

Jersey Market Guides

Directory of Jersey Businesses
http://www.jersey.gov.uk/indexes/business.html
A service of the Jersey government, the site is an index of Jersey companies online. Categories include financial services, travel, media, shipping, and electronics.

Island of Jersey
http://www.eyjersey.co.uk/jersey.htm
Prepared by Ernst and Young, the site provides fact sheets on Jersey history, geography, and business.

Jersey Web
http://www.jersey.co.uk/
An online marketplace, the site features Jersey business guides, accommodation directories, travel primers, chat services, sector profiles, and employment opportunities.

States of Jersey
http://www.jersey.gov.uk/
Homepage of the Jersey government, the site delivers Jersey fact sheets, business guides, government profiles, travel information, cultural bulletins, and weather reports.

Liechtenstein

Liechtenstein Media

Liechtenstein Vaterland
http://www.vaterland.li/
An electronic newspaper, the site provides Liechtenstein news, editorials, business reports, and e-mail directories.

Liechtenstein Market Guides

Liechtenstein InfoExport
http://www.infoexport.gc.ca/country-e.asp?continent=Europe&country=25
A service of Foreign Affairs and International

Trade Canada, the site provides fact sheets and statistics on Liechtenstein geography, business, and politics.

Liechtenstein Market Research
http://strategis.ic.gc.ca/sc_mrkti/ibinddc/engdoc/ 1a1b26.html
Posted by Industry Canada, the site provides U.S. Central Intelligence Agency fact sheets on Liechtenstein geography, people, government, economy, communications, and transportation.

Liechtenstein News
http://www.news.li/
A country information hub, the site provides primers on Liechtenstein business, international trade, banking, agriculture, services, taxation, employment, art, and tourism.

WWW Servers in Liechtenstein
http://www.verling.com/fl/
A directory of Liechtenstein online resources, the site is divided into eight categories including newspapers, finance and tax, banks, Internet service providers, and hotels and restaurants.

Luxembourg

Luxembourg Search Tools

Infospace Luxembourg
http://in-114.infospace.com/_1_34407537__info/ intldb/intl-lu.html
A service of Infospace, the site is a Luxembourg online search service. The page includes travel guides, e-mail directories, electronic shopping, and business and people finders.

Luxembourg Media

Luxembourg Media
http://www.mediainfo.com/emediajs/specific-geo.htm?region=luxembourg
Prepared by Editor and Publisher Interactive, the site is a directory of Luxembourg media sites online.

Luxembourg Market Guides

Barclays Country Report: Luxembourg
http://www.offshorebanking.barclays.com/ services/economic/yearly/luxmay97/luxconts.html
Prepared by Barclays Bank, the site reports on Luxembourg economic trends, politics, monetary and fiscal policy, international trade, and U.K.-

Luxembourg merchandise trade and investment flows.

Homepage Luxembourg
http://www.restena.lu/other/luxservers.html
A virtual library of Luxembourg information, the site features primers on Luxembourg government, local authorities, education, tourism, business, and culture.

Luxembourg Business Report
http://italchambers.net/BusinessReports.html
Prepared by the Italian Chamber of Commerce and written in Italian, the site provides Luxembourg fact sheets, market reports, and commercial guides.

Luxembourg InfoExport
http://www.infoexport.gc.ca/country-e.asp?continent=Europe&country=27
A service of Foreign Affairs and International Trade Canada, the site provides fact sheets and statistics on Luxembourg geography, business and politics.

Luxembourg Intellectual Property
http://www.etat.lu/EC/SPI.HTM
A service of the Luxembourg Ministry of the Economy, the site provides information on Luxembourg patents, trade markets, industrial designs, and other intellectual property.

Luxembourg Market Research
http://strategis.ic.gc.ca/sc_mrkti/ibinddc/engdoc/ 1a1b28.html
Posted by Industry Canada, the site provides U.S. Central Intelligence Agency fact sheets on Luxembourg geography, people, government, economy, communications, and transportation.

Luxembourg Virtual Library
http://www.pitt.edu/~wwwes/luxembourg.nhp.html
A service of the University of Pittsburgh Center for West European Studies, the site is a directory of Luxembourg online resources. Categories include government, education, and culture.

Ministries and Administrations of Luxembourg
http://www.etat.lu/
The online service is a directory of Luxembourg government agencies online including the Ministries of Agriculture, Communications, Education, Environment, and Finance.

Survey of Luxembourg
http://www.restena.lu/gover/index_english.html

Posted in English, French, and German, the site provides fact sheets on Luxembourg geography, history, people, languages, business, culture, and food.

Luxembourg Trade Assistance

European Union Presidency Site
http://www.etat.lu/uepres/
The site provides Luxembourg news, press releases, declarations, foreign policy statements, government bulletins, Ministerial profiles, and event information.

Trade Shows in Luxembourg
http://www.expoguide.com/shows/data/loc_36.htm
Compiled by Expoguide, the site is a directory of upcoming trade shows in Luxembourg.

Luxembourg Representative Offices

France

French Trade Commission in Luxembourg
http://www.dree.org/luxembourg/
Posted in French, the site provides Luxembourg maps, fact sheets, market studies, export guides, contact information, and a directory of Commission programs.

Sweden

Embassy of Sweden in Luxembourg
http://www.ud.se/english/mfa/ambassad/luxembur.htm
The site provides contact information for the Swedish Embassy in Luxembourg.

United Kingdom

Embassy of Britain in Luxembourg
http://www.fco.gov.uk/directory/posts.asp?LX
The site provides contact information for the British Embassy in Luxembourg.

United States

American Chamber of Commerce in Luxembourg
http://www.amcham.lu/
A Luxembourg-U.S. trade promotion service, the site delivers U.S. fact sheets, bilateral business opportunities, a Chamber member directory, and business event calendar.

United States Embassy in Luxembourg
http://www.usia.gov/abtusia/posts/LU1/wwwhmain.html
The virtual Embassy provides U.S. fact sheets, foreign policy statements, visa and passport information, Luxembourg guides, and reports on Luxembourg-U.S. trade and relations.

Malta

Malta Media

Malta Media
http://www.mediainfo.com/emediajs/specific-geo.htm?region=malta
Prepared by Editor and Publisher Interactive, the site is a directory of Malta media sites online.

Malta Market Guides

Doing Business in Malta
http://www.metco.com.mt/frame-db.html
A Malta business primer, the site provides fact sheets on Maltese geography, climate, history, language, culture, currency, government, international trade, and tourism.

Malta InfoExport
http://www.infoexport.gc.ca/country-e.asp?continent=Europe&country=29
A service of Foreign Affairs and International Trade Canada, the site provides fact sheets and statistics on Maltese geography, business, and politics.

Malta Market Information
http://dtiinfo1.dti.gov.uk/ots/malta/
A service of the London-based Department of Trade and Industry, the site delivers Maltese fact sheets, maps, and trade-show information.

Malta Market Research
http://strategis.ic.gc.ca/sc_mrkti/ibinddc/engdoc/1a1b30.html
A service of Industry Canada, the site provides U.S. Department of Commerce reports on Maltese business, politics, trade regulations and standards, investment climate, trade and project financing, business travel, and market opportunities.

Ministry of Economy and Finance
http://www.magnet.mt/fac005.htm
A service of the Maltese government, the site provides customs and excise tax regulations,

budget reports, economic surveys, statistics, sector profiles, and a directory of Maltese banks.

Official Website of the Maltese Government
http://www.magnet.mt/
A government information hub, the site delivers Maltese news, fact sheets, executive biographies, departmental profiles, cultural bulletins, and contact information.

Malta Trade Assistance

Malta External Trade Corporation
http://www.u-net.com/metcowww/
Based in San Gwann, the Corporation promotes Maltese exports and international investment. The site includes Maltese business guides, company directories, and international trade news.

Ministry of Foreign Affairs
http://www.magnet.mt/ministries/mfa/index.html
The online service provides Maltese foreign policy statements, press releases, speech archives, staff directories, and interviews with senior Ministry officials.

Trade Point Network
http://www.u-net.com/metcowww/tpm/home.html
Part of the Global Trade Point Network, the site features Maltese trade leads, sector profiles, contact information, and a directory of Network programs and services.

Malta Representative Offices

United Kingdom

High Commission of Britain in Valletta
http://www.fco.gov.uk/directory/posts.asp?MG
The site provides contact information for the British High Commission in Valletta.

United States

United States Embassy in Valletta
http://www.usia.gov/abtusia/posts/MT1/wwwhmain.html
The virtual Embassy provides U.S. fact sheets, press releases, visa and passport information, trade leads, and a directory of commercial services for Maltese and U.S. companies.

Monaco

Monaco Market Guides

Monaco Division of Intellectual Property
*http://www.european-patent-office.org/patlib/country/monaco/*Posted in French, the site delivers information on Monacan patents, trade marks, industrial designs, and other intellectual property.

Monaco InfoExport
http://www.infoexport.gc.ca/country-e.asp?continent=Europe&country=31
A service of Foreign Affairs and International Trade Canada, the site provides fact sheets and statistics on Monacan geography, business, and politics.

Monaco Market Research
http://strategis.ic.gc.ca/sc_mrkti/ibinddc/engdoc/1a1b32.html
Posted by Industry Canada, the site provides U.S. Central Intelligence Agency fact sheets on Monacan geography, people, government, economy, communications, and transportation.

Monaco Online
http://www.monaco.mc/index.html
A hub of country information, the site includes Monacan business directories, classified ads, travel guides, personal home pages, and an event calendar.

Monaco Online Business Directory
http://www.monaco.mc/mod/index.html
A searchable directory of Monacan companies, the site profiles firms in some 20 categories including financial services, import/export, legal services, and accommodation.

Monaco's Economic Situation
http://www.monaco.monte-carlo.mc/us/annu/index.html
A database of Monacan organizations, the site is divided into 20 categories including government, accountants, non-profits, restaurants, hotels, and conference facilities.

Monte-Carlo Online
http://www.monaco.monte-carlo.mc/
Posted in English and French, the site provides Monacan business guides, investment primers, economic statistics, company directories, travel tips, and an event calendar.

Monaco Trade Assistance

Trade Shows in Monaco
http://www.expoguide.com/shows/data/loc_38.htm
Compiled by Expoguide, the site is a directory of upcoming trade shows in Monaco.

Monaco Representative Offices

Foreign Embassies of Monaco
http://www.monaco.monte-carlo.mc/us/annu/ambassade.html
A service of Monaco Monte-Carlo Online, the site lists the Ambassadors, street addresses, and phone and fax numbers of the German, Belgian, Spanish, French, Italian, and Swiss Embassies in Monaco.

United Kingdom

Consulate General of Britain in Monaco
http://www.fco.gov.uk/directory/posts.asp?MN
The site provides contact information for the British Consulate General in Monaco.

Netherlands

Netherlands Search Tools

Dutch Home Page
http://www.dhp.nl/
Written in Dutch, the site is a browsable index of Netherlands resources online. Categories include business, regional, computers, media, transportation, and arts.

Excite Netherlands
http://nl.excite.com/
A personalized web start page, the site features Dutch news, search tips, event finders, and maps and directions.

Infoseek Netherlands
http://www.infoseek.com/Home?pg=Home.html&sv=NL
Written in Dutch, the site provides web navigation, browsing tips, and a searchable directory of Netherlands resources online.

Infospace Netherlands
http://in-128.infospace.com/_1_34407537__info/intldb/intl-nl.html
Part of the Infospace information network, the Dutch search engine provides travel guides, e-mail directories, and business and people finders.

Lycos Netherlands
http://www.lycos.nl/
Posted in Dutch, the search service includes road maps, website reviews, classifieds, shopping guides, and chat forums.

Search NL
http://www.dhp.nl/
Written in Dutch, the site provides web navigation services, browsing tips, and an index of Netherlands resources online.

Netherlands Media

Netherlands Media
http://www.mediainfo.com/emediajs/specific-geo.htm?region=netherlands
Compiled by Editor and Publisher Interactive, the site is a directory of Netherlands media sites online including magazines, newspapers, and radio stations.

Netherlands Market Guides

Dutch Yellow Pages
http://www.markt.nl/dyp/index-en.html
A directory of Dutch companies online, the site profiles firms in 25 categories including computers, consulting, finance, health care, media, real estate, and transportation.

Holland Bulletin
http://www.hollandtrade.com/HBLIST.htm
A service of the Netherlands Foreign Trade Agency, the site provides Dutch news, regional reports, new product reviews, technology bulletins, government communiqués, and economic statistics.

Location Information
http://www.location.info.nl/
Sponsored by the Netherlands Foreign Investment Agency, the site is a Dutch investment primer. The service includes Netherlands fact sheets, sector profiles, quality of life comparisons, and a site location database.

Netherlands.Com
http://www.the-netherlands.com/
A Dutch information hub, the site provides Netherlands fact sheets, regional profiles, travel information, and a directory of Dutch organizations online.

Netherlands Chambers of Commerce and Industry
http://www.kvk.nl/kvk/
kvk.htm?kenmerk=VET&kid=0
A Dutch business primer, the site provides fact sheets on starting a business, legal considerations, human resources, international trade, and market research in the Netherlands.

Netherlands Country Profile
http://www.tradenz.govt.nz/intelligence/profiles/
netherlands.html
A service of the New Zealand Trade Development Board, the site provides Dutch economic statistics, market information, and business tips.

Netherlands Country Report
http://www.state.gov/www/issues/economic/
trade_reports/europe_canada97/
netherlands97.html
Prepared by the U.S. Department of State, the site delivers information on Dutch exchange rates, debt management, trade barriers, and intellectual property protection.

Netherlands Foreign Investment Agency
http://www.nfia.com/
A division of the Dutch Ministry of Economic Affairs, the Agency promotes international investment in the Netherlands. The site includes Dutch fact sheets, industry reports, company profiles, and a site selection database.

Netherlands InfoExport
http://www.infoexport.gc.ca/country-
e.asp?continent=Europe&country=32
A service of Foreign Affairs and International Trade Canada, the site provides Dutch commercial guides and market reports.

Netherlands Market Information
http://dtiinfo1.dti.gov.uk/ots/netherlands/
A service of the London-based Department of Trade and Industry, the site delivers Dutch fact sheets, maps, and trade-show information.

Netherlands Market Research
http://strategis.ic.gc.ca/sc_mrkti/ibinddc/engdoc/
1a1b33.html
A service of Industry Canada, the site provides U.S. Department of Commerce reports on Dutch business, politics, trade regulations and standards, investment climate, trade and project financing, business travel, and market opportunities.

Netherlands Virtual Library
http://www.pitt.edu/~wwwes/netherlands.nhp.html
A service of the University of Pittsburgh Center for West European Studies, the site is a directory of Dutch online resources. Categories include government, education, and culture.

Recruiters Network Nederland
http://www.xs4all.nl/~avotek/recnet.htm
Written in Dutch, the site provides information on Dutch employment opportunities and services. Features include a directory of Netherlands recruiters, headhunters, and job counselors.

Netherlands Trade Assistance

Dutch Export Site
http://www.export.nl/
Along with country profiles and sector reports from around the world, the site features online business matchmaking services, trade leads, and a directory of Dutch exporters.

EVD Partner in Export
http://www.evd.nl/
A Dutch export promotion service, the site provides global business guides, international trade statistics, country profiles, trade leads, and contact information.

Holland Exports
http://www.hollandexports.com/
A service of ABC Business Information Services, the site is a searchable directory of Dutch exporters and export products. The database is browsable by keyword, company name, or product.

Ministry of Foreign Affairs
http://www.bz.minbuza.nl/english/
Posted in English and Dutch, the site provides Dutch news, fact sheets, press releases, foreign policy statements, an event calendar, and organization charts of the Ministry.

Netherlands Embassies and Consulates
http://www.bz.minbuza.nl/english/
f_sumadress14.html
A service of the Dutch Ministry of Foreign Affairs, the site is a directory of Dutch Embassies and Consulates on the Internet. Posts online include Athens, Cape Town, Vienna, and Washington, D.C.

Netherlands Foreign Trade Agency
http://www.hollandtrade.com/
The online service provides Dutch economic bulletins, industrial fact sheets, export statistics, international comparisons, and reports on Netherlands and the European Union.

Trade Shows in the Netherlands
http://www.expoguide.com/shows/data/loc_40.htm
Compiled by Expoguide, the site is a directory of upcoming trade shows in the Netherlands.

Netherlands Representative Offices

Austria

Austrian Trade Commission in The Hague
http://aw.wk.or.at/awo/ahst-denhaag.htm
The site lists the staff, street address, phone and fax numbers, e-mail link, and office hours of the Austrian Trade Commission in The Hague.

Bosnia and Herzegovina

Embassy of Bosnia and Herzegovina in The Hague
http://www.xs4all.nl/~bih/
The virtual Embassy provides Bosnian fact sheets, maps, economic reports, visa and passport information, travel guides, and a directory of Embassy services.

Canada

Canadian Embassy in The Hague
http://www.dfait-maeci.gc.ca/~thehague/
Posted in English and French, the site delivers Canadian fact sheets, travel guides, reports on Dutch-Canadian trade and relations, and a directory of commercial and consular services.

Netherlands-Canada Chamber of Commerce
http://www.dfait-maeci.gc.ca/~thehague/hague-12-e.htm
Based in The Hague, the Chamber promotes Dutch-Canadian trade. The site includes a mission statement, service directory, and contact information.

Finland

Finland Trade Center in The Hague
http://www.exports.finland.fi/tradecen.htm
The site lists the staff, street address, phone and fax numbers, and e-mail link of the Finland Trade Center in The Hague.

France

Embassy of France in The Hague
http://www.ambafrance.nl/
Written in French, the site offers French news, business guides, investment primers, art and culture bulletins, science and technology reports, and language tutorials.

French Trade Commission in The Hague
http://www.dree.org/pays-bas/
Posted in French, the site provides Dutch market reports, and a directory of export programs for French companies doing business in the Netherlands.

Germany

German Chamber of Commerce in The Hague
http://www.ahk.net/en/nl/Den_Haag/
The site lists the Chairperson, Chief Executive Officer, street address, phone and fax numbers, and e-mail link of the German Chamber in The Hague.

India

Indian Commercial Mission in The Hague
http://www.nic.in/commin/ICM.HTM
The site lists the street address, phone and fax numbers, and e-mail link of the Indian Commercial Mission in The Hague.

Indonesia

Embassy of Indonesia in The Hague
http://indag.dprin.go.id/INGG/trade/atache.HTM
The site provides contact information for the Indonesian Embassy in The Hague.

Ireland

Enterprise Ireland in Amsterdam
http://www.irish-trade.ie/office_network/office_locate01.html#anchor1412426
The site lists the Manager, street address, and phone and fax numbers of the Enterprise Ireland office in Amsterdam.

Israel

Embassy of Israel in The Hague
http://www.israel.nl/ambassade/
Posted in Dutch, English, and Hebrew, the site provides Israeli fact sheets, business guides,

travel primers, visa and passport information, and reports on Dutch-Israeli trade and relations.

Italy

Italian Trade Commission in Amsterdam
http://www.wirehub.nl/~iceam/
Posted in English and Italian, the site delivers Italian fact sheets, export catalogs, investment guides, travel information, and reports on Dutch-Italian trade and relations.

Malaysia

Embassy of Malaysia in The Hague
http://www.mnet.com.my/klonline/www/missions/malmiss/mnetherl1.htm
The site provides contact information for the Malaysian Embassy in The Hague.

Trade Commission of Malaysia in Rotterdam
http://www.mnet.com.my/klonline/www/missions/malmiss/mnetherl2.htm
The site provides contact information for the Malaysian Trade Commission in Rotterdam.

Mexico

Trade Commission of Mexico in The Hague
http://www.mexico-businessline.com/ingles/ofrepmu3.html#netherlands
The site lists the street address, phone and fax numbers, and e-mail link of the Mexican Trade Commission in The Hague.

Norway

Norwegian Trade Council in The Hague
http://www.ntc.no/cgi-bin/wbch.exe?html=../templates/utekontor2.html&profile=1106
The site lists the staff, street address, phone and fax numbers, and e-mail link of the Norwegian Trade Council in The Hague.

Palestine

Center for Promotion of Palestinian Products
http://www.ptpo.org/ptpo/
Based in Rotterdam, the Center promotes Palestinian exports. The site includes a mission statement, membership information, Palestinian trade leads, and product catalogs.

Philippines

Philippine Trade and Investment Promotion Office in The Hague
http://www.dti.gov.ph/hag/
The site provides a mission statement, service directory, and contact information for the Philippine Trade Office in The Hague.

Poland

Embassy of Poland in The Hague
http://www.polamb.nl/ambhaga.htm
Posted in Dutch, English, and Polish, the site delivers Polish fact sheets, visa and passport information, cultural bulletins, and a directory of consular and commercial services.

Portugal

Portuguese Trade and Investment Office in The Hague
http://www.portugal.org/geninfo/abouticep/hague.html
The site lists the staff, street address, phone and fax numbers, and e-mail link of the Portuguese Trade and Investment Office in The Hague.

South Africa

South Africa Foreign Trade Office in The Hague
http://wwwdti.pwv.gov.za/dtiwww/foreign_offices.htm
A service of the South Africa Department of Trade and Industry, the site provides contact information for the South Africa Trade Office in The Hague.

Spain

Embassy of Spain in The Hague
http://users.bart.nl/~claboral/
Posted in Dutch and Spanish, the site delivers Spanish news, fact sheets, visa and passport information, travel guides, and a directory of consular and commercial programs.

Sweden

Embassy of Sweden in The Hague
http://www.ud.se/english/mfa/ambassad/nederlan.htm
The site provides contact information for the Swedish Embassy in The Hague.

Taiwan

China External Trade Development Council Office in Rotterdam
http://www.cetra.org.tw/english/o_office/indexset.htm
A Taiwanese trade promotion service, the site lists the mission statement and e-mail link of the China External Trade Development Council Office in Rotterdam.

Taiwan Government Information Office in Amstelveen
http://www.gio.gov.tw/info/ngio/net-f.html
Posted in Chinese and English, the site lists the street address, phone and fax numbers, and e-mail link of the Taiwan Government Information Office in Amstelveen.

Thailand

Royal Thai Embassy in The Hague
http://www.mfa.go.th/Embassy/detail/68.htm
The site lists the Ambassador, street address, and phone and fax numbers of the Thai Embassy in The Hague.

Thailand Office of Commercial Affairs in The Hague
http://www.thaitrade.com/thcoaf.html
The site lists the street address, phone and fax numbers, and e-mail link of the Thailand Office of Commercial Affairs in The Hague.

United Kingdom

Consulate General of Britain in Amsterdam
http://www.fco.gov.uk/directory/posts.asp?NL
The site provides contact information for the British Consulate General in Amsterdam.

Embassy of Britain in The Hague
http://www.fco.gov.uk/directory/posts.asp?NL
The site provides contact information for the British Embassy in The Hague.

United States

American Chamber of Commerce in the Netherlands
http://www.unisys.nl/amcham/
Based in The Hague, the Chamber promotes Dutch-U.S. trade. The site includes a mission statement, membership information, publications lists, and services directory.

State of Indiana European Office in Amsterdam
http://www.case-europe.com/States/in.htm
Along with Indiana fact sheets, the site lists the Trade Specialist, street address, phone and fax numbers, and e-mail link of the Indiana European Office in Amsterdam.

State of Maryland Europe Center in Rotterdam
http://www.mdbusiness.state.md.us/GovSvcs/exp_serv.html
A service of the Maryland Office of International Business, the site lists the street address, phone and fax numbers, and e-mail link of the Maryland Europe Center in Rotterdam.

United States Consulate in Amsterdam
http://www.usemb.nl/consul.htm
The site lists the office hours, street address, phone and fax numbers, and consular services of the American Consulate in Amsterdam.

United States Embassy in the Netherlands
http://www.usemb.nl/
The virtual Embassy provides U.S. news, fact sheets, foreign policy statements, tourism information, reports on Dutch-U.S. trade and relations, and a directory of consular and commercial programs.

Venezuela

Embassy of Venezuela in The Hague
http://www.trade-venezuela.com/EMBVENG.HTM
The site lists the street address, phone and fax numbers, and e-mail link of the Venezuelan Embassy in The Hague.

Norway

Norway Search Tools

Kvasir
http://kvasir.sol.no/no/
Written in Norwegian, the site provides web navigation services, browsing tips, and an index of Norwegian resources online.

Yahoo Norway
http://www.yahoo.no/
Part of the Yahoo search network, the site provides Norwegian news, web-based personal management tools, and Internet browsing.

Norway Media

Norway Daily
http://odin.dep.no/ud/publ/daily/
Compiled by the Royal Ministry of Foreign Affairs, the site provides daily Norwegian news bulletins based on reports and editorials from the major Norwegian daily newspapers.

Norway Media
http://www.mediainfo.com/emediajs/specific-geo.htm?region=norway
Compiled by Editor and Publisher Interactive, the site is a directory of Norwegian media sites online including magazines, newspapers, and television stations.

Norway Post
http://www.norwaypost.no/
Updated daily, the English language site provides Norwegian news, business reports, travel guides, cultural bulletins, community profiles, and education information.

Norway Market Guides

Barclays Country Report: Norway
http://www.offshorebanking.barclays.com/services/economic/yearly/nornov97/index.html
Prepared by Barclays Bank, the site reports on Norwegian trends, politics, monetary and fiscal policy, international trade, and U.K.-Norway merchandise trade and investment flows.

Confederation of Norwegian Business and Industry
http://www.nho.no/
Based in Oslo, the Confederation promotes the interests of more than 15,000 Norwegian enterprises. Written in Norwegian, the site includes a mission statement, contact information, and a program directory.

Hugin Online
http://www.huginonline.com/
A searchable directory of Danish, Finnish, Norwegian, and Swedish companies quoted on Scandinavian Stock Exchanges, the subscription site provides annual reports, quarterly reports, spreadsheets, press releases, prospectus and other financial information.

Norway Business Briefs
http://www.austrade.gov.au/IOOM/Norway/
A service of Austrade, the site offers fact sheets on Norwegian culture, business etiquette, marketing, transportation, travel, and visas.

Norway Country Profile
http://www.tradenz.govt.nz/intelligence/profiles/norway.html
A service of the New Zealand Trade Development Board, the site provides Norwegian economic statistics, market information, and business tips.

Norway Country Report
http://www.state.gov/www/issues/economic/trade_reports/europe_canada97/norway97.html
Prepared by the U.S. Department of State, the site delivers information on Norwegian exchange rates, debt management, trade barriers, and intellectual property protection.

Norway InfoExport
http://www.infoexport.gc.ca/country-e.asp?continent=Europe&country=33
A service of Foreign Affairs and International Trade Canada, the site provides Norwegian commercial guides and market reports.

Norway Market Information
http://dtiinfo1.dti.gov.uk/ots/norway/
A service of the London-based Department of Trade and Industry, the site delivers Norwegian fact sheets, maps, and trade-show information.

Norway Market Research
http://strategis.ic.gc.ca/sc_mrkti/ibinddc/engdoc/1a1b34.html
A service of Industry Canada, the site provides U.S. Department of Commerce reports on Norwegian business, politics, trade regulations and standards, investment climate, trade and project financing, business travel, and market opportunities.

Norway Online Information Service
http://www.norway.org/
A service of the Norwegian Embassy in Washington, D.C., the site provides primers on Norwegian business, government, tourism, culture, and history.

Norwegian Business and Industry
http://odin.dep.no/nhd/publ/naering/
A service of the Ministry of Trade and Industry, the site delivers Norwegian fact sheets, international comparisons, sector profiles, and policy papers.

Norwegian Yellow Pages
http://www.gulesider.no/eng/
A searchable directory of Norwegian companies, the site is browsable by keyword, company name, industry, city, municipality, postal code, post office, and street address.

Official Documentation and Information from Norway
http://odin.dep.no/html/english/
The central web server for the Norwegian government, the site provides Norwegian news, press releases, official publications, and a directory of Norwegian ministries online.

Norway Trade Assistance

Nortrade
http://www.nortrade.com
A virtual library of Norwegian export information, the site features Norwegian fact sheets, export directories, sector profiles, business guides, and investment primers.

Norwegian Trade Council
http://www.ntc.no/
Based in Oslo, the Council promotes Norwegian exports. The site includes a mission statement, contact information, and a directory of the Council's research, networking, and business matchmaking services.

Norwegian Trade Council Offices Abroad
http://www.ntc.no/cgi-bin/wbch.exe?html=../index/profile.html&profile=1061
The site is a directory of Norwegian Trade Council offices in North America, Latin America, Europe, Africa, and Asia.

Trade Shows in Norway
http://www.expoguide.com/shows/data/loc_43.htm
Compiled by Expoguide, the site is a directory of upcoming trade shows in Norway.

Norway Representative Offices

Austria

Austrian Trade Commission in Oslo
http://aw.wk.or.at/awo/ahst-oslo.htm
The site lists the staff, street address, phone and fax numbers, e-mail link, and office hours of the Austrian Trade Commission in Oslo.

Canada

Embassy of Canada in Oslo
http://www.dfait-maeci.gc.ca/english/missions/rep-can3e.htm#norway
The site provides contact information for the Canadian Embassy in Oslo.

Chile

Embassy of Chile in Oslo
http://home.sol.no/~embchile/index.html
Written in English, Norwegian, and Spanish, the site delivers Chilean news, business guides, investment primers, cultural information, region and city profiles, and travel tips.

Denmark

Embassy of Denmark in Oslo
http://www.denmark-embassy.no/
The virtual Embassy provides primers on Danish geography, history, geography, business, and tourism. The service includes contact information and a directory of Danish business resources online.

Finland

Embassy of Finland in Oslo
http://www.finland.no/
The online service provides Finnish news, fact sheets, cultural guides, business primers, visa and passport information, and a directory of consular and commercial services.

France

French Trade Commission in Oslo
http://www.dree.org/norvege/
Written in French, the site provides Norwegian market reports and a directory of export programs for French companies doing business in Norway.

Germany

German Chamber of Commerce in Oslo
http://www.ahk.net/chambers/no/
Posted in English, German, and Norwegian, the site lists the street address, phone and fax numbers, and e-mail link of the German Chamber in Oslo.

Italy

Italian Cultural Institute in Oslo
http://www.sol.no/italcult/
Posted in Italian, the site provides Italian fact sheets, tourism guides, education information, European Union bulletins, and reports on Italian-Norwegian cultural exchanges.

Portugal

Portuguese Trade and Investment Office in Oslo
http://www.portugal.org/geninfo/abouticep/norway.html
The site lists the staff, street address, phone and fax numbers, and e-mail link of the Portuguese Trade and Investment Office in Oslo.

Romania

Embassy of Romania in Oslo
http://home.sol.no/~romemb/
Along with Romanian visa and passport information, the site lists the street address, phone and fax numbers, e-mail link, and office hours of the Romanian Embassy in Oslo.

Spain

Spanish Commercial Office in Oslo
http://www.icex.es/openURL.html#openURL=/english/infoproyem/ofcomes/ofcomes.html#EU
The site lists the staff, street address, phone and fax numbers, and e-mail link of the Spanish Commercial Office in Oslo.

Thailand

Royal Thai Embassy in Oslo
http://thaidip.mfa.go.th/oslo/
Posted in English, the site delivers Thai fact sheets, visa and passport information, tourism guides, business contacts, and a directory of consular and commercial services.

United Kingdom

British Embassy in Oslo
http://home.sol.no/~embassy/
Posted in English and Norwegian, the site offers British fact sheets, business guides, travel information, foreign policy statements, and reports on British-Norwegian trade and relations.

Consulate of Britain in Bergen
http://www.fco.gov.uk/directory/posts.asp?NO
The site provides contact information for the British Consulate in Bergen.

United States

United States Embassy in Norway
http://www.usembassy.no/

The online service features U.S. news, press releases, foreign policy statements, relocation guides, travel information, and reports on American-Norwegian trade and relations.

U.S. Information Service Norway
http://www.usembassy.no/usis/usis.htm
Featuring a daily U.S. policy update, the site includes U.S. electronic journals, government bulletins, travel information, and an e-mail inquiry service.

Venezuela

Embassy of Venezuela in Oslo
http://www.trade-venezuela.com/EMBVENG.HTM
The site lists the street address, phone and fax numbers, and e-mail link of the Venezuelan Embassy in Oslo.

Portugal

Portugal Search Tools

AEIOU
http://www.aeiou.pt/
Written in Portuguese, the site provides web navigation services, browsing tips, and an index of Portuguese resources online.

SAPO
http://sapo.ua.pt/
A searchable directory of Portuguese Internet resources, the site includes news, event finders, and weather bulletins.

Portugal Media

Portugal Media
http://www.mediainfo.com/emediajs/specific-geo.htm?region=portugal
Compiled by Editor and Publisher Interactive, the site is a directory of Portuguese media sites online including magazines, newspapers, and television stations.

Weekly News @ Portugal
http://www.portugaloffer.com/news/index.html
Updated weekly, the site provides the latest Portuguese news, business bulletins, company profiles, government reports, and tourism information.

Portugal Market Guides

Barclays Country Report: Portugal
*http://www.offshorebanking.barclays.com/
services/economic/yearly/poraug97/porcont.html*
Prepared by Barclays Bank, the site reports on
Portuguese economic trends, politics, monetary
and fiscal policy, international trade, and U.K.-
Portugal merchandise trade and investment
flows.

Business Portugal
*http://www.portugal.org/doingbus/investing/
newsletter/newsletter.html*
A quarterly electronic newsletter on Portuguese
business, the site provides sector profiles,
economic statistics, and interviews with leading
corporate and government officials.

Doing Business with Portugal
http://www.portugal.org/doingbus/doingbus.html
A Portuguese investment primer, the site includes Portuguese product catalogs, company
profiles, international trade statistics, business
matchmaking services, and a directory of
business associations.

Portugal Business Report
http://italchambers.net/BusinessReports.html
Prepared by the Italian Chamber of Commerce
and written in Italian, the site provides Portuguese fact sheets, market reports, and commercial guides.

Portugal Country Profile
*http://www.tradenz.govt.nz/intelligence/profiles/
portugal.html*
A service of the New Zealand Trade Development
Board, the site provides Portuguese economic
statistics, market information, and business tips.

Portugal Country Report
*http://www.state.gov/www/issues/economic/
trade_reports/europe_canada97/portugal97.html*
Prepared by the U.S. Department of State, the site
delivers information on Portuguese exchange
rates, debt management, trade barriers, and
intellectual property protection.

Portugal: A Country Study
http://lcweb2.loc.gov/frd/cs/pttoc.html
A service of the U.S. Library of Congress, the site
delivers fact sheets on Portuguese geography,
population, agriculture, mining, manufacturing,
and foreign economic relations.

Portugal InfoExport
*http://www.infoexport.gc.ca/country-
e.asp?continent=Europe&country=35*
A service of Foreign Affairs and International
Trade Canada, the site provides Portugal
commercial guides and market reports.

Portugal Institute of Industrial Property
http://www.inpi.pt/
Written in Portuguese, the site delivers information on Portuguese patents, trade marks,
industrial designs, and other intellectual property.

Portugal Market Information
http://dtiinfo1.dti.gov.uk/ots/portugal/
A service of the London-based Department of
Trade and Industry, the site delivers Portuguese
fact sheets, maps, and trade-show information.

Portugal Market Research
*http://strategis.ic.gc.ca/sc_mrkti/ibinddc/engdoc/
1a1b36.html*
A service of Industry Canada, the site provides
U.S. Department of Commerce reports on
Portuguese business, politics, trade regulations
and standards, investment climate, trade and
project financing, business travel, and market
opportunities.

Portugal Offer
http://www.portugaloffer.com/
Along with Portuguese fact sheets and socioeconomic statistics, the site provides a searchable
directory of Portuguese companies in 49 categories including agri-food, construction, logistics,
and transportation equipment.

Portugal: Selected Issues
*http://www.imf.org/external/pubs/CAT/
longres.cfm?sk=2468.0*
Prepared by the International Monetary Fund, the
site reports on Portuguese production, employment, exchange rates, and financing.

Portugal Virtual Library
http://www.pitt.edu/~wwwes/portugal.nhp.html
A service of the University of Pittsburgh Center for
West European Studies, the site is a directory of
Portuguese online resources. Categories include
government, education, and culture.

Welcome to Portugal
http://www.portugal.org/
A virtual library of Portuguese information, the site
delivers Portuguese fact sheets, business

guides, investment primers, sector profiles, company directories, and economic statistics.

Portugal Trade Assistance

External Trade Statistics
http://www.portugal.org/doingbus/buyingfrom/statistics/statistics.html
A service of Welcome to Portugal, the site provides statistics on Portuguese trade with the European Union, the European Free Trade Association, Eastern Europe, North America, the Middle East, Asia, Africa, and Latin America.

ICEP
http://www.portugal.org/geninfo/abouticep/icep.html
Headquartered in Lisbon, ICEP—Investimentos, Comercio e Turismo de Portugal—is a Portuguese government export promotion service. The site includes a mission statement, program directory, and contact information.

ICEP Offices Around the World
http://www.portugal.org/geninfo/abouticep/about9.html
The site is a directory of Investimentos, Comercio e Turismo de Portugal offices in North America, South America, Europe, the Middle East, Africa, Asia, and Australia.

Portugal's Directory of Exporters
http://www.portugal.org/doingbus/buyingfrom/exportersdb/exportersdb.html
A browsable index of Portuguese exporters, the site is searchable by company name, harmonized system code, trademarks, employment size, sales volume, industry, and target export market.

Portuguese Trade Shows Directory
http://www.portugal.org/doingbus/buyingfrom/tradefairs/tradefairs.html
A searchable index of Portuguese trade shows, the site spotlights events in over 50 categories including computer products, electronics, apparel, and telecommunications.

Trade Shows in Portugal
http://www.expoguide.com/shows/data/loc_48.htm
Compiled by Expoguide, the site is a directory of upcoming trade shows in Portugal.

Portugal Representative Offices

Austria

Austrian Trade Commission in Lisbon
http://aw.wk.or.at/awo/ahst-lissabon.htm
The site lists the staff, street address, phone and fax numbers, e-mail link, and office hours of the Austrian Trade Commission in Lisbon.

Brazil

Consulate General of Brazil in Lisbon
http://www.sectorel.pt/conbrlsp/
Posted in Portuguese, the site provides Brazilian fact sheets, business guides, tourism information, reports on Brazil-Portugal trade, and a directory of Embassy services.

Canada

Embassy of Canada in Lisbon
http://www.dfait-maeci.gc.ca/english/missions/rep-can3e.htm#portugal
The site provides contact information for the Canadian Embassy in Lisbon.

Finland

Finland Trade Center in Lisbon
http://www.exports.finland.fi/tradecen.htm
The site lists the staff, street address, phone and fax numbers, and e-mail link of the Finland Trade Center in Lisbon.

France

Embassy of France in Lisbon
http://www.ip.pt/ambafrance/portugal/
Posted in French and Portuguese, the site features French visa and passport information, tourism guides, and reports on France-Portugal relations and cultural exchanges.

French Trade Commission in Lisbon
http://www.dree.org/portugal/
Written in French, the site provides Portuguese market reports, contact information, and a directory of export programs for French companies doing business in Portugal.

Germany

German Chamber of Commerce in Lisbon
http://www.ahk-germany.de/ahklis/ahklis.htm
Written in German and Portuguese, the site provides Portuguese maps, business guides, investment primers, trade leads, and reports on German-Portugal trade and relations.

Italy

Embassy of Italy in Lisbon
http://www.embital.pt/
Posted in Italian and Portuguese, the site provides Italian fact sheets, tourism guides, Portuguese investment information, a directory of Italian organizations in Portugal, and Portuguese organizations in Italy.

Norway

Norwegian Trade Council in Lisbon
http://www.ntc.no/cgi-bin/wbch.exe?html=../templates/utekontor2.html&profile=1115
The site lists the staff, street address, phone and fax numbers, and e-mail link of the Norwegian Trade Council in Lisbon.

Singapore

Consulate General of Singapore in Lisbon
http://www.gov.sg/mfa/consular/mww_p.htm
The site provides contact information for the Singapore Consulate General in Lisbon.

Spain

Spanish Commercial Office in Lisbon
http://www.icex.es/openURL.html#openURL=/english/infoproyem/ofcomes/ofcomes.html#EU
The site lists the staff, street address, phone and fax numbers, and e-mail link of the Spanish Commercial Office in Lisbon.

Sweden

Embassy of Sweden in Lisbon
http://www.ud.se/english/mfa/ambassad/portugal.htm
The site provides contact information for the Swedish Embassy in Lisbon.

Taiwan

China External Trade Development Council Office in Lisbon
http://www.cetra.org.tw/english/o_office/indexset.htm
A Taiwanese trade promotion service, the site lists the mission statement and e-mail link of the China External Trade Development Council Office in Lisbon.

Thailand

Royal Thai Embassy in Lisbon
http://www.mfa.go.th/Embassy/detail/70.htm
The site lists the Ambassador, street address, and phone and fax numbers of the Thai Embassy in Lisbon.

Turkey

Embassy of Turkey in Lisbon
http://www.turkey.org/madres.htm
As part of a directory of Turkish diplomatic offices around the world, the site lists the e-mail link of the Turkish Embassy in Lisbon.

United Kingdom

Consulate of Britain in Oporto
http://www.fco.gov.uk/directory/posts.asp?PT
The site provides contact information for the British Consulate in Oporto.

Embassy of Britain in Lisbon
http://www.fco.gov.uk/directory/posts.asp?PT
The site provides contact information for the British Embassy in Lisbon.

United States

American Chamber of Commerce in Portugal
http://cca.imediata.pt/
With offices in Lisbon and Porto, the Chamber promotes Portugal-U.S. trade. The site includes a mission statement, contact information, and a directory of Chamber programs and membership categories.

U.S. Commercial Service in Portugal
http://www.portugal.doc.gov/
A service of the U.S. Department of Commerce, the site provides a directory of business counseling, market research, and corporate

matchmaking services for U.S. companies in Portugal.

United States Embassy in Portugal
http://www.american-embassy.pt/
The online service features U.S. news, press releases, foreign policy statements, relocation guides, travel information, and reports on American-Portuguese trade and relations.

United States Information Service in Lisbon
http://www.american-embassy.pt/wwwhusie.html
Along with contact information, the site lists the office hours and services of the U.S. Documentation Center, an American business and cultural library, at the U.S. Embassy in Lisbon.

Venezuela

Embassy of Venezuela in Lisbon
http://www.trade-venezuela.com/EMBVENG.HTM
The site lists the street address, phone and fax numbers, and e-mail link of the Venezuelan Embassy in Lisbon.

San Marino

San Marino Media

San Marino Last News
http://inthenet.sm/rsm/news/news.htm
An electronic newspaper, the site delivers Sammarinese news, business bulletins, education reports, cultural information, and a news archive.

San Marino Market Guides

About San Marino
http://www.omniway.sm/about_e.htm
The online service offers primers on Sammarinese geography, history, people, economy, energy, transportation, communications, tourism, culture, and public administration.

San Marino Market Research
http://strategis.ic.gc.ca/sc_mrkti/ibinddc/engdoc/1a1b39.html
Posted by Industry Canada, the site provides U.S. Central Intelligence Agency fact sheets on Sammarinese geography, people, government, economy, communications, and transportation.

Republic of San Marino Official Website
http://www.omniway.sm/
Sponsored by Intelcom San Marino, the site features Sammarinese fact sheets, tourism guides, event information, shopping directories, and web navigation services.

Welcome to the Republic of San Marino
http://inthenet.sm/rsm/intro.htm
A virtual tour guide, the site provides Sammarinese fact sheets, history lessons, travel tips, accommodation directories, and an index of Sammarinese resources online.

San Marino Trade Assistance

San Marino Virtual Trade Center
http://www.omniway.sm./trade/index_e.htm
Posted in English and Italian, the site is a searchable directory of Sammarinese companies and organizations. Categories include agriculture, banks, engineering, pharmaceuticals, and telecommunications.

San Marino Representative Offices

Thailand

Royal Thai Consulate General in San Marino
http://www.mfa.go.th/Embassy/detail/219.htm
The site lists the Consul General, street address, and phone and fax numbers of the Thai Consulate in San Marino.

United Kingdom

Consulate General of Britain in San Marino
http://www.fco.gov.uk/directory/posts.asp?SA
The site provides contact information for the British Consulate General in San Marino.

Spain

Spain Search Tools

El Indice
http://elindice.com/
Written in Spanish, the site is a browsable index of Spanish resources online. Categories include news, economy, media, geography, science and technology.

Infoseek Spain
http://www.infoseek.com/Home?pg=Home.html&sv=ES
The Spanish site provides web navigation, browsing tips, and a searchable directory of Spanish resources on the web.

Lycos Spain
http://www.es.lycos.de/
Posted in Spanish, the search service includes road maps, website reviews, classifieds, shopping guides, and chat forums.

Olé
http://www.ole.es/
Based in Spain, the site provides web navigation services, browsing tips, and an index of Spanish resources online.

Spain Media

Gaceta de los Negocios
http://56-2.clever.net/tiasa/negocios/edicioni.htm
Updated daily, the site provides Spanish business news, company profiles, international trade reports, real estate bulletins, and a searchable news archive.

Spain Media
http://www.mediainfo.com/emediajs/specific-geo.htm?region=spain
Compiled by Editor and Publisher Interactive, the site is a directory of Spanish media sites online including city guides, magazines, newspapers, and television stations.

Spain Market Guides

Barclays Country Report: Spain
http://www.offshorebanking.barclays.com/services/economic/yearly/spainnov97/spaconts.html
Prepared by Barclays Bank, the site reports on Spanish economic trends, politics, monetary and fiscal policy, international trade, and U.K.-Spain merchandise trade and investment flows.

One-Click Business Guide to Spain
http://malika.iem.csic.es/~grant/vent.html
A directory of Spanish business resources online, the site is divided into ten categories including general search, financial institutions, banks and financial reports, government, and venture capital.

Ministry of Economy
http://www.meh.es/
Homepage of the Spanish Ministry of Economy, the site provides Spanish press releases, economic statistics, sector reports, government bulletins, and a directory of Ministry programs.

Si, Spain
http://www.docuweb.ca/SiSpain/english/index.html
Posted in English, French, German, and Spanish, the site is a virtual library of Spanish information. Modules include geography and population, language and culture, economy and trade, infrastructure and the environment.

Spain Business Briefs
http://www.austrade.gov.au/IOOM/Spain/
A service of Austrade, the site offers fact sheets on Spanish business etiquette, foreign investment, corporate taxation, marketing, and visas.

Spain Business Report
http://italchambers.net/BusinessReports.html
Prepared by the Italian Chamber of Commerce and written in Italian, the site provides Spanish fact sheets, market reports, and commercial guides.

Spain Country Profile
http://www.tradenz.govt.nz/intelligence/profiles/spain.html
A service of the New Zealand Trade Development Board, the site provides Spanish economic statistics, market information, and business tips.

Spain Country Report
http://www.state.gov/www/issues/economic/trade_reports/europe_canada97/spain97.html
Prepared by the U.S. Department of State, the site delivers information on Spanish exchange rates, debt management, trade barriers, and intellectual property protection.

Spain: A Country Study
http://lcweb2.loc.gov/frd/cs/estoc.html
A service of the U.S. Library of Congress, the site delivers fact sheets on Spanish geography, population, agriculture, mining, manufacturing, and foreign economic relations.

Spain Industry
http://www.spaindustry.com/
A searchable directory of some 75,000 companies, the site profiles firms in nine categories including manufacturing, construction, finance, transportation, and communications.

Spain InfoExport
http://www.infoexport.gc.ca/country-e.asp?continent=Europe&country=41
A service of Foreign Affairs and International Trade Canada, the site provides Spanish commercial guides and market reports.

Spain Market Information

http://dtiinfo1.dti.gov.uk/ots/spain/
A service of the London-based Department of Trade and Industry, the site delivers Spanish fact sheets, maps, and trade-show information.

Spain Market Research

http://strategis.ic.gc.ca/sc_mrkti/ibinddc/engdoc/1a1b42.html
A service of Industry Canada, the site provides U.S. Department of Commerce reports on Spanish business, politics, trade regulations and standards, investment climate, trade and project financing, business travel, and market opportunities.

Spanish Companies Directory

http://www.interspain.com/frz_directories_cam.htm
A browsable directory of some two million Spanish companies, the service includes Spanish fact sheets, business guides, investment primers, and travel information.

Spanish Patent Office

http://www.oepm.es/
Written in Spanish, the site delivers primers on Spanish patents, trademarks, industrial designs, and other intellectual property.

Spain Trade Assistance

Economy and Trade

http://www.docuweb.ca/SiSpain/english/economy/
A service of Si, Spain, the site is a directory of Spanish economic and business resources online. Categories include industrial policy, taxation, labor markets, and banking.

ICEX

http://www.icex.es/ministe.html
Based in Madrid, ICEX or the Spanish Institute for Foreign Trade promotes Spanish exports. The site includes Spanish fact sheets, exporter directories, product catalogs, and event information.

Interspain

http://www.interspain.com/home.htm
A virtual library of Spanish business information, the site features Spanish financial news and reports, company directories, relocation primers, statistical information, and a web index.

Spanish Commercial Offices

http://www.icex.es/openURL.html#openURL=/english/conozcanos/present.html
A service of the Spanish Institute for Foreign Trade, the site is a directory of Spanish Embassies, Consulates, and Trade Offices in Europe, North and South America, Asia, Africa, and Australasia.

Trade Shows in Spain

http://www.expoguide.com/shows/data/loc_57.htm
Compiled by Expoguide, the site is a directory of upcoming trade shows in Spain.

Spain Representative Offices

Angola

Embassy of Angola in Madrid

http://195.53.74.3/angola/
Written in Spanish, the site provides Angolan maps, fact sheets, tourism information, arts and cultural bulletins, business guides, regional profiles, and government directories.

Australia

Austrade in Madrid

http://www.austrade.gov.au/Madrid/
An Australian export promotion service, the site features business guides, investment primers, and a directory of trade assistance programs for Australian exporters in Madrid and Spain.

Embassy of Australia in Madrid

http://www.embaustralia.es/
The virtual Embassy provides Australian news, press releases, fact sheets, visa and passport information, business guides, travel primers, and a directory of Embassy services.

Austria

Austrian Trade Commission in Barcelona

http://aw.wk.or.at/awo/ahst-barcelona.htm
The site lists the staff, street address, phone and fax numbers, e-mail link, and office hours of the Austrian Trade Commission in Barcelona.

Austrian Trade Commission in Madrid

http://aw.wk.or.at/awo/ahst-madrid.htm
The site lists the staff, street address, phone and fax numbers, e-mail link, and office hours of the Austrian Trade Commission in Madrid.

Bolivia

Consulate General of Bolivia in Seville
http://www.disbumad.es/consulado/bolivia/
Featuring greetings from the Consul General, the site offers Bolivian fact sheets, visa and passport information, regional profiles, and a directory of Consular programs and staff.

Canada

Canadian Embassy in Madrid
http://www.canada-es.org/
Posted in English, French, and Spanish, the site features Canadian fact sheets, visa and passport information, tourism guides, Spanish market primers, and a directory of Canadian companies doing business in Spain.

Chile

Consulate General of Chile in Bilbao
http://www.bm30.es/socios/consulados/chile_es.html
Along with Chilean maps and economic statistics, the site lists the Consul General, street address, phone and fax numbers, and e-mail link of the Chilean Consulate General in Bilbao.

Finland

Embassy of Finland in Madrid
http://www.finlandia.org/
Posted in Finnish and Spanish, the site provides Finnish news, press releases, business guides, travel information, and a directory of Embassy programs and staff.

France

Embassy of France in Madrid
http://www.nemo.es/embafrancia/
Posted in Spanish, the site features French business guides, cultural bulletins, travel information, government fact sheets, and reports on French-Spanish relations.

French Trade Commission in Barcelona
http://www.dree.org/espagne/francais/general/adbar.htm
Written in French, the site lists the street address, and phone and fax numbers of the French Trade Commission in Barcelona.

French Trade Commission in Bilbao
http://www.dree.org/espagne/francais/general/adbil.htm
Posted in French, the site lists the street address, phone and fax numbers, and e-mail link of the French Trade Commission in Bilbao.

French Trade Commission in Madrid
http://www.dree.org/espagne/francais/general/admad.htm
The site lists the street address, phone and fax numbers, and e-mail link of the French Trade Commission in Madrid.

French Trade Commission in Spain
http://www.dree.org/espagne/sommaire.htm
Written in French, the site provides Spanish market reports, sector profiles, contact information, and a directory of export programs for French companies doing business in Spain.

Germany

German Chamber of Commerce in Madrid
http://www.ahk.net/en/es/Madrid/
The site lists the Chairperson, Chief Executive Officer, street address, phone and fax numbers, and e-mail link of the German Chamber in Madrid.

German Embassy in Madrid
http://www.embajada-alemania.es/
Posted in German and Spanish, the site delivers German fact sheets, press releases, business guides, political bulletins, tourism information, and reports on German-Spanish trade and relations.

Indonesia

Embassy of Indonesia in Madrid
http://indag.dprin.go.id/INGG/trade/atache.HTM
The site provides contact information for the Indonesian Embassy in Madrid.

Ireland

Enterprise Ireland in Madrid
http://www.irish-trade.ie/office_network/office_locate01.html#anchor1416433
The site lists the Manager, street address, and phone and fax numbers of the Enterprise Ireland office in Madrid.

Israel

Embassy of Israel in Madrid
http://www.embajada-israel.es/
Posted in Spanish, the site includes Israeli fact sheets, cultural bulletins, science and technology news, tourism information, and reports on Israeli-Spanish trade and relations.

Italy

Embassy of Italy in Madrid
http://www.area.fi.cnr.it/spagna/ambit.htm
Posted in Italian, the site offers Italian news, regional profiles, political briefs, business guides, economic statistics, cultural primers, and contact information.

Malaysia

Embassy of Malaysia in Madrid
http://www.mnet.com.my/klonline/www/missions/ malmiss/mspain1.htm
The site provides contact information for the Malaysian Embassy in Madrid.

Mexico

Bancomext in Madrid
http://www.bancomext-esp.com/
Written in Spanish, the site features Mexican news, fact sheets, business guides, investment information, regional profiles, and reports on Mexican-Spanish trade and relations.

New Zealand

Trade New Zealand in Madrid
http://www.tradenz.govt.nz/contact/europe.html
An export promotion service, the site provides contact information for the Trade New Zealand office in Madrid.

Norway

Norwegian Trade Council in Madrid
http://www.ntc.no/cgi-bin/wbch.exe?html=../ templates/utekontor2.html&profile=1117
The site lists the staff, street address, phone and fax numbers, and e-mail link of the Norwegian Trade Council in Madrid.

Pakistan

Pakistan Trade Office in Madrid
http://www.jamal.com/epb/ptoa.htm
The site provides contact information for the Pakistan Trade Office in Madrid.

Peru

Consulate General of Peru in Barcelona
http://www.geocities.com/CapitolHill/2145/
The virtual Embassy provides Peruvian fact sheets, contact information, a directory of consular programs and services, and a database of Peruvian Honorary Consuls in Spain.

Philippines

Philippine Trade and Investment Promotion Office in Madrid
http://www.dti.gov.ph/mad/
The site provides a mission statement, service directory, and contact information for the Philippine Trade Office in Madrid.

Portugal

Portuguese Trade and Investment Office in Barcelona
http://www.portugal.org/geninfo/abouticep/ spain.html
The site lists the staff, street address, and phone and fax numbers of the Portuguese Trade and Investment Office in Barcelona.

Portuguese Trade and Investment Office in Madrid
http://www.portugal.org/geninfo/abouticep/ spain.html
The site lists the staff, street address, phone and fax numbers, and e-mail link of the Portuguese Trade and Investment Office in Madrid.

Portuguese Trade and Investment Office in Vigo
http://www.portugal.org/geninfo/abouticep/ spain.html
The site lists the staff, street address, phone and fax numbers, and e-mail link of the Portuguese Trade and Investment Office in Vigo.

South Africa

South Africa Foreign Trade Office in Madrid
http://wwwdti.pwv.gov.za/dtiwww/ foreign_offices.htm
A service of the South Africa Department of Trade and Industry, the site provides contact information for the South Africa Trade Office in Madrid.

Sweden

Embassy of Sweden in Madrid
http://www.embajadasuecia.es/
Posted in English, Spanish, and Swedish, the site features Swedish fact sheets, economic statistics, education bulletins, and a directory of Embassy programs.

Taiwan

China External Trade Development Council Office in Madrid
http://www.cetra.org.tw/english/o_office/ indexset.htm
A Taiwanese trade promotion service, the site lists the mission statement and e-mail link of the China External Trade Development Council Office in Madrid.

Taiwan Government Information Office in Madrid
http://www.gio.gov.tw/info/ngio/spain-f.html
Posted in Chinese and English, the site lists the street address, phone and fax numbers, and e-mail link of the Taiwan Government Information Office in Madrid.

Thailand

Royal Thai Embassy in Madrid
http://thaidip.mfa.go.th/madrid/
The digital Embassy provides Thai fact sheets, visa and passport information, business guides, travel primers, an event calendar, and a directory of Thai government agencies.

Thai Trade Center in Barcelona
http://www.thaitrade.com/wwtto.html
A service of the Thailand Department of Export Promotion, the site lists the street address, phone and fax numbers, and e-mail link of the Thai Trade Center in Barcelona.

Thailand Office of Commercial Affairs in Madrid
http://www.thaitrade.com/thcoaf.html
The site lists the street address, phone and fax numbers, and e-mail link of the Thailand Office of Commercial Affairs in Madrid.

Turkey

Embassy of Turkey in Madrid
http://www.turkey.org/madres.htm
Part of a directory of Turkish diplomatic offices around the world, the site lists the e-mail link of the Turkish Embassy in Madrid.

United Kingdom

Consulate General of Britain in Barcelona
http://www.fco.gov.uk/directory/posts.asp?SM
The site provides contact information for the British Consulate General in Barcelona.

Embassy of Britain in Madrid
http://www.fco.gov.uk/directory/posts.asp?SM
The site provides contact information for the British Embassy in Madrid.

United States

United States Embassy in Madrid
http://www.embusa.es/indexbis.html
Along with United States fact sheets and visa information, the site includes Spanish trade leads, newsletters, commercial guides, and bulletins on Spanish-American trade and relations.

Sweden

Sweden Search Tools

Excite Sweden
http://se.excite.com/
A personalized web start page, the site features Swedish news, search tips, event finders, and online paging.

Infoseek Sweden
http://www.infoseek.com/ Home?pg=Home.html&sv=SE
Written in Swedish, the site provides web navigation, browsing tips, and a searchable directory of Swedish resources online.

Lycos Sweden
http://www.lycos.se/
Posted in Swedish, the search service includes road maps, website reviews, classifieds, shopping guides, and chat forums.

Se
http://www.punkt.se/
A browsable index of Swedish resources online, the site is divided into 12 categories including economy and business, Internet and computer, media, and shopping.

Sweden Media

Affarsvarlden
http://www.afv.se/eng/
Posted in English and Swedish, the site reports on Swedish politics, economic affairs, and capital markets. The service includes a directory of Swedish companies online.

Scandinavia Now Online
http://www.scandinavianow.com/
An English language electronic magazine, the site provides news, business reports, company profiles, and weather bulletins from Denmark, Finland, Iceland, Norway, and Sweden.

Sweden Media
http://www.mediainfo.com/emediajs/specific-geo.htm?region=sweden
Compiled by Editor and Publisher Interactive, the site is a directory of Swedish media sites online including city guides, magazines, and newspapers.

Sweden Market Guides

Barclays Country Guide: Sweden
http://www.offshorebanking.barclays.com/services/economic/yearly/sweapr98/contents.html
Prepared by Barclays Bank, the site reports on Swedish economic trends, politics, monetary and fiscal policy, international trade, and U.K.-Sweden merchandise trade and investment flows.

Country Commercial Guide
http://www.state.gov/www/about_state/business/com_guides/1998/europe_canada/sweden98.html
Prepared by the U.S. Embassy in Stockholm, the site delivers primers on the Swedish economy, political environment, trade regulations and standards, investment climate, trade and project financing, and business travel.

Invest in Sweden Agency
http://www.isa.se/
Posted in five languages, the site provides Swedish news, fact sheets, sector reports, county and municipality profiles, economic statistics, and investment guides.

Statistics Sweden
http://www.scb.se/indexeng.htm
A virtual library of Swedish statistics, the service includes data on Swedish unemployment, consumer prices, production, international trade, and other key indicators.

Sweden Business Briefs
http://www.austrade.gov.au/IOOM/Sweden/
A service of Austrade, the site offers fact sheets on Swedish business etiquette, foreign investment, corporate taxation, marketing, and visas.

Sweden Country Profile
http://www.tradenz.govt.nz/intelligence/profiles/sweden.html
A service of the New Zealand Trade Development Board, the site provides Swedish economic statistics, market information, and business tips.

Sweden Country Report
http://www.state.gov/www/issues/economic/trade_reports/europe_canada97/sweden97.html
Prepared by the U.S. Department of State, the site delivers information on Swedish exchange rates, debt management, trade barriers, and intellectual property protection.

Sweden InfoExport
http://www.infoexport.gc.ca/country-e.asp?continent=Europe&country=42
A service of Foreign Affairs and International Trade Canada, the site provides Swedish commercial guides and market reports.

Sweden Market Information
http://dtiinfo1.dti.gov.uk/ots/sweden/
A service of the London-based Department of Trade and Industry, the site delivers Swedish fact sheets, maps, and trade-show information.

Sweden Market Research
http://strategis.ic.gc.ca/sc_mrkti/ibinddc/engdoc/1a1b44.html
A service of Industry Canada, the site provides U.S. Department of Commerce reports on Swedish business, politics, trade regulations and standards, investment climate, trade and project financing, business travel, and market opportunities.

Swedish Companies Online
http://www.netg.se/Resources/Company/index.html.en
A service of Netguide Scandinavia, the site is a searchable directory of Swedish companies online. Categories include agri-food, electronics, medical, and financial services.

Swedish Patent and Registration Office
http://www.prv.se/prveng/front.htm
Based in Stockholm, the site provides informa-

tion on Swedish patents, trademarks, industrial designs, and other intellectual property.

Sweden Trade Assistance

Ask Sweden Trade
http://www.askswedishtrade.com/default.asp
A service of the Swedish Trade Council, the site allows a user to ask a question regarding Swedish trade, and a response is guaranteed within 24 hours.

Scandinavian Trade Fair Council
http://www.fairlink.se/
The Swedish-based Council is an organization of Scandinavian trade-show organizers. The site includes trade-show news, and a directory of upcoming business events in Denmark, Finland, Norway, and Sweden.

Sweden Online
http://www.swedentrade.com
A virtual library of Swedish trade information, the site includes Swedish export news, international trade primers, online business matchmaking services, and an interactive marketplace.

Sweden Trade Profiles
http://www.swedishtrade.se/tradeprofiles/ index.htm
Developed by the Swedish Trade Council, the site is a searchable database of Swedish international trade statistics.

Swedish Chambers of Commerce
http://www.cci.se/
A directory of Swedish industry associations and chambers of commerce, the site includes Swedish export guides and business matchmaking services.

Swedish Customs
http://www.tullverket.se/engelska/index.htm
The online service provides Swedish customs fact sheets, policies, strategies, and regulations for European Union and non-European Union travelers and products.

Swedish Export Directory
http://www.swedishtrade.se/sed/index.htm
A searchable directory of some 10,000 Swedish companies, the database is browsable by keyword, company name, industry, and target export market.

Swedish Missions Abroad
http://www.ud.se/english/mfa/abroad.htm
A service of the Swedish Ministry of Foreign Affairs, the site is a directory of Swedish Embassies and Consulates in over 100 countries from Afghanistan to Zimbabwe.

Swedish Trade Council International
http://www.swedishtrade.com/
Based in Stockholm, the site is a database of Swedish Trade Council offices and services in over 50 countries including Canada, the United Kingdom, and the United States.

Trade Shows in Sweden
http://www.expoguide.com/shows/data/loc_58.htm
Compiled by Expoguide, the site is a directory of upcoming trade shows in Sweden.

Sweden Representative Offices

Australia

Australian Embassy in Stockholm
http://www.austemb.se/
Along with contact information, the site features Australian fact sheets, visa and passport fact sheets, business guides, travel information, and a directory of Embassy programs and services.

Austria

Austrian Embassy in Stockholm
http://www.wk.or.at/aw/atc/sweden/
Posted in German, the site provides Austrian fact sheets, visa and passport information, and a directory of consular and commercial services.

Austrian Trade Commission in Stockholm
http://aw.wk.or.at/awo/ahst-stockholm.htm
The site lists the staff, street address, phone and fax numbers, e-mail link, and office hours of the Austrian Trade Commission in Stockholm.

Canada

Canadian Embassy in Stockholm
http://www.canadaemb.se/
Posted in English, French, and Swedish, the site includes Canadian fact sheets, visa and passport information, tourism guides, and an event calendar.

Canadian Swedish Business Association
http://www.csba.a.se/
Based in Sweden, the Association promotes Canadian-Swedish trade. The site includes a mission statement, membership information, and a calendar of events.

Virtual Business Corridor: Sweden
http://www.technogate.com/vcorridors/eur/sweden/frame.htm
An alliance of Swedish Science and Technology Parks and the Canadian Embassy in Stockholm, the site is a directory of Swedish and Canadian technology companies seeking partnership opportunities.

Cyprus

Cyprus Trade Center in Stockholm
http://www.cyprustradeny.org/cyny5.html
The site lists the street address, and phone and fax numbers of the Cyprus Trade Center in Stockholm.

Ecuador

Embassy of Ecuador in Stockholm
http://www.embajada-ecuador.se/www.embajada-ecuador.se/
The virtual Embassy provides Ecuadorian fact sheets, press releases, visa regulations, tourism information, international trade guides, and investment primers.

Estonia

Embassy of Estonia in Stockholm
http://www.estemb.se/
Posted in Estonian and Swedish, the site provides Estonian news, press releases, visa and passport information, business guides, and reports on Estonian-Swedish trade and relations.

Ethiopia

Embassy of Ethiopia in Stockholm
http://www.ethemb.se/
The online service provides Ethiopian news, maps, fact sheets, sector profiles, business guides, international trade reports, investment primers, and tourism information.

Finland

Embassy of Finland in Stockholm
http://www.finlandemb.se/

The digital Embassy delivers Finnish visa and passport primers, contact information, and a directory of Embassy staff and programs.

France

French Trade Commission in Stockholm
http://www.dree.org/suede/
Written in French, the site provides Swedish market reports, sector profiles, contact information, and a directory of export programs for French companies doing business in Sweden.

Germany

German Chamber of Commerce in Stockholm
http://www.ahk.net/en/se/Stockholm/
The site lists the Chairperson, Chief Executive Officer, street address, phone and fax numbers, and e-mail link of the German Chamber in Stockholm.

India

Embassy of India in Stockholm
http://www.indianembassy.se/
Along with visa and passport application forms, the site provides Indian fact sheets, business guides, economic statistics, and India-Sweden trade reports.

Ireland

Enterprise Ireland in Stockholm
http://www.irish-trade.ie/office_network/office_locate01.html#anchor1419049
The site lists the Manager, street address, and phone and fax numbers of the Enterprise Ireland office in Stockholm.

Israel

Embassy of Israel in Stockholm
http://home5.swipnet.se/~w-56576/
Written in English and Swedish, the site features Israeli news, fact sheets, cultural bulletins, visa and passport information, business guides, and investment primers.

Italy

Italian Trade Commission in Stockholm
http://www.ice-stoccolma.se/
Written in Italian and Swedish, the site features Italian fact sheets, event information, reports on

Italian-Swedish trade, and a directory of Embassy programs.

Japan

Embassy of Japan in Stockholm
http://www.japansamb.se/
Posted in Japanese and Swedish, the site provides Japanese news, fact sheets, business guides, investment information, and reports on Japanese-Swedish trade and relations.

Japan External Trade Organization in Stockholm
http://www.jetro-stockholm.org/
A Japanese trade promotion service, the site provides Japanese fact sheets, reports on Japan-Sweden trade, and a directory of commercial services.

Laos

Embassy of Laos in Stockholm
http://www.laoembassy.com/news/ embassyabroad.htm
The site provides contact information for the Embassy of Laos in Stockholm.

Malaysia

Embassy of Malaysia in Stockholm
http://www.mnet.com.my/klonline/www/missions/ malmiss/msweden1.htm
The site provides contact information for the Malaysian Embassy in Stockholm.

Namibia

Embassy of Namibia in Stockholm
http://www.republicofnamibia.com/adress.htm
Along with a directory of Namibian companies and government agencies, the site provides contact information for the Namibian Embassy in Stockholm.

Norway

Norwegian Trade Council in Stockholm
http://www.ntc.no/cgi-bin/wbch.exe?html=../ templates/utekontor2.html&profile=1131
The site lists the staff, street address, phone and fax numbers, and e-mail link of the Norwegian Trade Council in Stockholm.

Philippines

Philippine Trade and Investment Promotion Office in Stockholm
http://www.dti.gov.ph/sto/
The site provides a mission statement, service directory, and contact information for the Philippine Trade Office in Stockholm.

Portugal

Portuguese Trade and Investment Office in Stockholm
http://www.portugal.org/geninfo/abouticep/ sweden.html
The site lists the staff, street address, phone and fax numbers, and e-mail link of the Portuguese Trade and Investment Office in Stockholm.

Singapore

Consulate General of Singapore in Stockholm
http://www.gov.sg/mfa/consular/mww_s.htm
The site provides contact information for the Singapore Consulate General in Stockholm.

South Africa

Embassy of South Africa in Stockholm
http://w1.824.telia.com/~u82402049/ sasweden.htm
Featuring an interactive map of South Africa, the site provides South African news, fact sheets, tourism guides, business primers, and visa and passport information.

South Africa Foreign Trade Office in Stockholm
http://wwwdti.pwv.gov.za/dtiwww/ foreign_offices.htm
A service of the South Africa Department of Trade and Industry, the site provides contact information for the South Africa Trade Office in Stockholm.

Spain

Spanish Commercial Office in Stockholm
http://www.icex.es/openURL.html#openURL=/ english/infoproyem/ofcomes/ofcomes.html#EU
The site lists the staff, street address, phone and fax numbers, and e-mail link of the Spanish Commercial Office in Stockholm.

Sri Lanka

Embassy of Sri Lanka in Stockholm
http://www.algonet.se/~slembsto/
The digital Embassy provides Sri Lankan news, fact sheets, cultural bulletins, investment guides, and a directory of Sri Lankan newsgroups.

Taiwan

China External Trade Development Council Office in Stockholm
http://www.cetra.org.tw/english/o_office/indexset.htm
A Taiwanese trade promotion service, the site lists the mission statement and e-mail link of the China External Trade Development Council Office in Stockholm.

Taiwan Government Information Office in Stockholm
http://www.gio.gov.tw/info/ngio/swede-f.html
Posted in Chinese and English, the site lists the street address, phone and fax numbers, and e-mail link of the Taiwan Government Information Office in Stockholm.

Tanzania

Embassy of Tanzania in Stockholm
http://www.tanzania-online.gov.uk/visa/envoys.html
The site provides contact information for the Tanzanian Embassy in Stockholm.

Thailand

Royal Thai Embassy in Stockholm
http://thaidip.mfa.go.th/stockh/
The online service provides Thai fact sheets, visa and passport information, business guides, travel primers, an event calendar, and a directory of Thai government agencies.

United Kingdom

Consulate General of Britain in Gothenburg
http://www.fco.gov.uk/directory/posts.asp?SW
The site provides contact information for the British Consulate General in Gothenburg.

Embassy of Britain in Stockholm
http://www.britishembassy.com/
The site features British fact sheets, visa and passport information, product catalogs, and international trade guides.

United States

United States Embassy in Stockholm
http://www.usis.usemb.se/
Featuring Swedish commercial guides and reports on Swedish-U.S. trade, the site includes U.S. news, press releases, foreign policy statements, relocation guides, and travel information.

United States Information Service in Stockholm
http://www.usis.usemb.se/usis/
A virtual library of U.S. information, the site provides U.S. news, press releases, education bulletins, government directories, Swedish fact sheets, and reports on Swedish-U.S. relations.

Switzerland

Switzerland Search Tools

Net Guide
http://www.netguide.ch/
A browsable index of Swiss resources online, the site is divided into 16 categories including business, computing, media, shopping, and transportation.

Lycos Switzerland
http://www.lycosch.ch/
Posted in French, German, and Italian, the site provides Swiss maps, website reviews, classifieds, shopping guides, and chat forums.

Welcome to Switzerland
http://heiwww.unige.ch/switzerland/
Featuring an interactive map of Switzerland, the site features web navigation services, and a searchable directory of Swiss resources online.

Switzerland Media

Switzerland Media
http://www.mediainfo.com/emediajs/specific-geo.htm?region=switzerland
Compiled by Editor and Publisher Interactive, the site is a directory of Swiss media sites online including city guides, magazines, and newspapers.

Switzerland Market Guides

Barclays Country Guide: Switzerland
http://www.offshorebanking.barclays.com/services/economic/yearly/swiapr98/contents.html

Prepared by Barclays Bank, the site reports on Swiss economic trends, politics, monetary and fiscal policy, international trade, and U.K.-Switzerland merchandise trade and investment flows.

Location Switzerland
http://www.locationswitzerland.ch/
An online investment primer, the site delivers Swiss economic profiles, business guides, financing bulletins, taxation information, and reports on Switzerland-European Union trade and relations.

Swiss Federal Institute of Intellectual Property
http://www.ige.ch/
Posted in English, French, German, and Italian, the site provides information on Swiss patents, trademarks, industry designs, and other intellectual property.

Swiss Home Page
http://www.lib.berkeley.edu/Collections/Romance/swisshpg.html
A service of the University of California, Berkeley, the site provides a directory of Swiss media, business, government culture, and education resources online.

Swiss Marketplace
http://www.swissdir.ch/swisstrade/index.html
A searchable directory of Swiss companies and business opportunities, the site is divided into nine categories including chemicals, electronics, agri-food, machinery, and textiles.

Swiss Web Jobs
http://www.swisswebjobs.ch/exec/index/swj/de
A virtual job bank, the site provides employer profiles, job hunting guides, resume services, and a directory of Swiss employment opportunities.

Swiss Yellow Pages
http://www.swisstelecom.com/gd/web_specials/yellow_pages/yellow_pages-en.html
Written in four languages, the site is a browsable database of Swiss companies, and state and local government agencies. The directory is searchable by organization name and location.

Switzerland Business Report
http://italchambers.net/BusinessReports.html
Prepared by the Italian Chamber of Commerce and written in Italian, the site provides Swiss fact sheets, market reports, and commercial guides.

Switzerland Country Profile
http://www.tradenz.govt.nz/intelligence/profiles/switzerland.html
A service of the New Zealand Trade Development Board, the site provides Swiss economic statistics, market information, and business tips.

Switzerland Country Report
http://www.state.gov/www/issues/economic/trade_reports/europe_canada97/switzerland97.html
Prepared by the U.S. Department of State, the site delivers information on Swiss exchange rates, debt management, trade barriers, and intellectual property protection.

Switzerland InfoExport
http://www.infoexport.gc.ca/country-e.asp?continent=Europe&country=43
A service of Foreign Affairs and International Trade Canada, the site provides Swiss commercial guides and market reports.

Switzerland Market Information
http://dtiinfo1.dti.gov.uk/ots/switzerland/
A service of the London-based Department of Trade and Industry, the site delivers Swiss fact sheets, maps, and trade-show information.

Switzerland Market Research
http://strategis.ic.gc.ca/sc_mrkti/ibinddc/engdoc/1a1b45.html
A service of Industry Canada, the site provides U.S. Department of Commerce reports on Swiss business, politics, trade regulations and standards, investment climate, trade and project financing, business travel, and market opportunities.

Switzerland Trade Assistance

OSEC
http://www.osec.ch/
Based in Zurich, OSEC is the official trade promotion organization of Switzerland. The site includes Swiss market reports, trade fair information, and a directory of Swiss exporters.

Swiss Chambers of Commerce Abroad
http://swisstrade.com/xiunion.asp
Posted in four languages, the site is a directory of Swiss Chamber of Commerce offices in Europe, North America, South America, Asia, Australia, and Asia.

Swiss Trade
http://swisstrade.com/
A searchable directory of Swiss exporters, products, and services, the site includes international trade guides, Swiss manufacturing reports, and investment primers.

Trade Point Geneva
http://www.untpdc.org/incubator/che/tpgva/
Part of the United Nations Global Trade Point Network, the site provides Geneva trade leads, market bulletins, and contact information.

Trade Shows in Switzerland
http://www.expoguide.com/shows/data/loc_59.htm
Compiled by Expoguide, the site is a directory of upcoming trade shows in Switzerland.

Switzerland Representative Offices

Australia

Consulate General of Australia in Geneva
http://www.australia.ch/~australi/
The online diplomatic service includes Australian fact sheets, visa and passport information, economic profiles, international trade reports, and travel guides.

Austria

Austrian Trade Commission in Zurich
http://aw.wk.or.at/awo/ahst-zuerich.htm
The site lists the staff, street address, phone and fax numbers, e-mail link, and office hours of the Austrian Trade Commission in Zurich.

Belgium

Consulate General of Belgium in Geneva
*http://www3.itu.int/consulate/Belgium/*Posted in three languages, the site provides Belgian fact sheets, visa and passport information, economic profiles, and a directory of Belgian organizations in Switzerland.

Canada

Embassy of Canada in Bern
http://www.dfait-maeci.gc.ca/english/missions/rep-can4e.htm#switzerland
The site provides contact information for the Canadian Embassy in Bern.

Denmark

Consulate General of Denmark in Zurich
http://195.141.124.65/
The site lists the street address, phone and fax numbers, and e-mail link of the Danish Consulate in Zurich.

Embassy of Denmark in Bern
http://www.denmark.ch/
The virtual Embassy provides Danish fact sheets, visa and passport information, business guides, travel information, and reports on Denmark-Switzerland trade.

Finland

Finland Trade Center in Zurich
http://www.exports.finland.fi/tradecen.htm
The site lists the staff, street address, phone and fax numbers, and e-mail link of the Finland Trade Center in Zurich.

France

Consulate General of France in Geneva
http://www3.itu.ch/Consulate/France/
Written in French, the site delivers French fact sheets, visa and passport information, reports on French-Swiss trade, and a directory of consular services.

Embassy of France in Bern
http://www3.itu.int/embassy/France/
The site lists the street address, phone and fax numbers, and e-mail link of the French Embassy in Bern.

French Trade Commission in Bern
http://www.dree.org/suisse/
Written in French, the site provides Swiss market reports, sector profiles, contact information, and a directory of export programs for French companies doing business in Switzerland.

Germany

German Chamber of Commerce in Zurich
http://www.ahk.net/en/ch/Zurich/
The site lists the Chairperson, Chief Executive Officer, street address, phone and fax numbers, and e-mail link of the German Chamber in Zurich.

Ghana

Embassy of Ghana in Bern
http://www.juntung.com/ghana-consul-hk/2misabo.htm
The site provides contact information for the Ghanaian Embassy in Bern.

India

Indian Commercial Mission in Bern
http://www.nic.in/commin/ICM.HTM
The site lists the street address, phone and fax numbers, and e-mail link of the Indian Commercial Mission in Bern.

Indian Commercial Mission in Geneva
http://www.nic.in/commin/ICM.HTM
The site lists the street address, phone and fax numbers, and e-mail link of the Indian Commercial Mission in Geneva.

Indonesia

Indonesian Industry and Trade Division in Geneva
http://www.geocities.com/WallStreet/4081/atdagjen.htm
A service of the Indonesian Permanent Mission to the United Nations, the site provides Indonesian trade fact sheets and contact information.

Israel

Embassy of Israel in Bern
http://www.ambassade-israel.ch/
Posted in English, French, and German, the site provides Israeli news, fact sheets, press releases, business guides, economic statistics, and tourism information.

Italy

Consulate General of Italy in Zurich
http://www.consolato-italia-zh.ch/
Written in English, German, and Italian, the site features Italian fact sheets, business guides, tourism information, reports on Italian-Swiss trade, and a directory of consular services.

Japan

Japan Business Association of Geneva
http://www.jetroge.ch/~jetroi/japonais2/jbag.html
Posted in Japanese, the site provides a mission statement, activity reports, event information, and a member directory.

Japan External Trade Organization in Geneva
http://www.jetroge.ch/~jetroi/
Posted in English and Japanese, the site provides a mission statement, reports on Japan-Switzerland trade, and a directory of commercial services.

Malaysia

Trade Commission of Malaysia in Geneva
http://www.mnet.com.my/klonline/www/missions/malmiss/mswitzer2.htm
The site provides contact information for the Malaysian Trade Commission in Geneva.

Pakistan

Consulate General of Pakistan in Zurich
http://www.omnibyte.ch/pakistan/
The site lists the Consul General, street address, phone and fax numbers, and e-mail link of the Pakistani Consulate in Zurich.

Pakistan Trade Promotion Center
http://www.omnibyte.ch/pakistan/paktrade.htm
A Pakistani trade promotion service, the site lists the office hours, street address, phone and fax numbers, and e-mail link of the Pakistan Trade Promotion Center in Zurich. Products on virtual display include food, cotton garments, leatherwear, and sports goods.

Philippines

Philippine Trade and Investment Promotion Office in Geneva
http://www.dti.gov.ph/gen/
The site provides a mission statement, service directory, and contact information for the Philippine Trade Office in Geneva.

Portugal

Consulate General of Portugal in Geneva
http://www3.itu.int/consulate/Portugal/
The site lists the street address, phone and fax numbers, and e-mail link of the Portuguese Consulate in Geneva.

Portuguese Trade and Investment Office in Zurich
http://www.portugal.org/geninfo/abouticep/zurich.html

The site lists the staff, street address, phone and fax numbers, and e-mail link of the Portuguese Trade and Investment Office in Zurich.

South Africa

South Africa Foreign Trade Office in Bern
http://wwwdti.pwv.gov.za/dtiwww/foreign_offices.htm
A service of the South Africa Department of Trade and Industry, the site provides contact information for the South Africa Trade Office in Bern.

Spain

Spanish Commercial Office in Bern
http://www.icex.es/openURL.html#openURL=/english/infoproyem/ofcomes/ofcomes.html#EU
The site lists the staff, street address, phone and fax numbers, and e-mail link of the Spanish Commercial Office in Bern.

Sweden

Embassy of Sweden in Bern
http://www.ud.se/english/mfa/ambassad/schweiz.htm
The site provides contact information for the Swedish Embassy in Bern.

Tanzania

Embassy of Tanzania in Geneva
http://www.tanzania-online.gov.uk/visa/envoys.html
The site provides contact information for the Tanzanian Embassy in Geneva.

Thailand

Royal Thai Embassy in Bern
http://www.mfa.go.th/Embassy/detail/62.htm
The webpage lists the Ambassador, street address, phone and fax numbers, and e-mail link of the Thai Embassy in Bern.

Thailand Office of Commercial Affairs in Geneva
http://www.thaitrade.com/thcoaf.html
The site lists the street address, phone and fax numbers, and e-mail link of the Thailand Office of Commercial Affairs in Geneva.

Turkey

Consulate General of Turkey in Zurich
http://www.access.ch/tuerkei/
Along with contact information, the site provides Turkish fact sheets, cultural guides, foreign policy statements, business opportunities, and tourism information.

United Kingdom

British Swiss Chamber of Commerce
http://www.bscc.co.uk/
Based in Zurich, the Chamber promotes British-Swiss trade. The site includes a mission statement, member directory, event information, and bilateral trade reports.

Consulate of Britain in Geneva
http://www.fco.gov.uk/directory/posts.asp?SX
The site provides contact information for the British Consulate in Geneva.

Embassy of Britain in Bern
http://www.british-embassy-berne.ch/
The virtual Embassy provides British fact sheets, visa and passport information, commercial guides, and a directory of Embassy programs and staff.

United States

America Center of Geneva
http://www.acga.ch/
The online service provides U.S. news, fact sheets, cultural bulletins, business guides, contact information, and reports on U.S.-Swiss trade and relations.

Swiss-American Chamber of Commerce
http://www.amcham.ch/
Based in Zurich, the Chamber promotes Swiss-U.S. trade. The site provides an online mall of members, board and committee directory, and event information.

United States Embassy in Switzerland
http://www3.itu.int/EMBASSY/US-embassy/
Featuring a message from the Ambassador, the site delivers U.S. news, fact sheets, press releases, visa and passport information, and a directory of Swiss-American organizations in Switzerland.

United Kingdom

United Kingdom Search Tools

Excite U.K.
http://www.excite.co.uk/
A personalized web start page, the site features United Kingdom news, business listings, and people finders.

Infoseek United Kingdom
http://www.infoseek.com/
Home?pg=Home.html&sv=UK
Part of the Infoseek search network, the site provides web navigation, browsing tips, and a browsable directory of United Kingdom resources online.

Infospace U.K.
http://in-123.infospace.com/_1_34407537__info/intldb/intl-uk.html
Along with public records and electronic shopping, the search engine provides United Kingdom business and people finders, travel guides, and e-mail directories.

Lycos United Kingdom
http://www.lycos.co.uk/
The search service includes United Kingdom news, website reviews, classifieds, shopping guides, chat forums, and weather bulletins.

Search U.K.
http://www.searchuk.com/
Along with web navigation, the site provides news, browsing tips, and a directory of United Kingdom commercial, academic, government, and non-profit resources online.

U.K. Internet Sites
http://www.hensa.ac.uk/uksites/index.html
A searchable database of U.K. domain names, the site is browsable by web page title, date added, date last changed, site type, and location.

Yahoo U.K. and Ireland
http://www.yahoo.co.uk/
Along with web-based personal management tools, the site provides United Kingdom and Irish news, Internet searching, business directories, and weather bulletins.

United Kingdom Media

England Media
http://www.mediainfo.com/emediajs/specific-geo.htm?region=england
Compiled by Editor and Publisher Interactive, the site is a directory of English media sites online.

Northern Ireland Media
http://www.mediainfo.com/emediajs/specific-geo.htm?region=northernireland
The online service is a database of Northern Ireland magazines, newspapers, and radio stations online.

Scotland Media
http://www.mediainfo.com/emediajs/specific-geo.htm?region=scotland
The online service is a database of Scottish magazines, newspapers, and other media online.

United Kingdom Market Guides

British Council
http://www.britcoun.org/
A virtual library of British information, the site features fact sheets on British economics, business, education, government, law, publishing, science, and technology.

Career Mosaic U.K.
http://www.careermosaic-uk.co.uk/
An online job bank, the site provides employer profiles, resume services, and a browsable index of United Kingdom employment opportunities.

CCTA Government Information Service
http://www.open.gov.uk/
An agency of the U.K. government's Cabinet Office, CCTA or the Central Computer and Telecommunications Agency provides information technology services to the U.K. public. The site includes a searchable directory of U.K. government agencies online.

Competitiveness U.K.
http://www.dti.gov.uk/comp/
A service of the U.K. Board of Trade, the site is a library of articles, speeches, audits, and benchmarking reports on United Kingdom competitiveness and research and development.

Confederation of British Industry
http://www.cbi.org.uk/unregindex.html?location=/
Representing more than 250,000 United Kingdom companies, the Confederation promotes British economic development. The site includes Confederation news, press releases, and trend surveys.

Country Commercial Guide

*http://www.state.gov/www/about_state/business/
com_guides/1998/europe_canada/
unitedkingdom98.html*
Prepared by the U.S. Embassy in London, the
site delivers primers on the United Kingdom
economy, political environment, trade regulations
and standards, investment climate, trade and
project financing, and business travel.

Enterprise Zone

http://www.enterprisezone.org.uk/
A gateway to British business information, the
site features management guides, technology
tips, export primers, company directories, and
online discussion forums.

GB Internet Marketing

http://www.digitalnation.co.uk/gbimd/goalof.htm
Homepage of the Great Britain Internet Marketing
Discussion List, the service provides British
marketing information, strategies, and contacts.

Great Britain Business Reports

http://italchambers.net/BusinessReports.html
Prepared by the Italian Chamber of Commerce
and written in Italian, the site provides British fact
sheets, market reports, and commercial guides.

INbusiness

http://www.inbusiness.co.uk/
A searchable directory of 2.2 million United
Kingdom companies, the database is browsable
by firm name, industry, and location.

Invest in Britain Bureau

http://www.dti.gov.uk/ibb/
Featuring a welcome message from Prime
Minister Tony Blair, the site features British fact
sheets, business news, investment guides, and
contact information.

Queen's Awards

http://www.queensawards.org.uk/
A United Kingdom business awards program,
the site provides a list of past winners, and
background information on the export, technologi-
cal, and environmental award categories.

United Kingdom Business Briefs

http://www.austrade.gov.au/IOOM/UK/
A service of Austrade, the site offers fact sheets
on United Kingdom culture, business etiquette,
marketing, transportation, travel, and visas.

United Kingdom Business Directory

http://www.milfac.co.uk/bisindex.html
A browsable directory of 1.8 million U.K. businesses, the service includes electronic shopping, web navigation, and domain name registration services.

United Kingdom Country Profile

*http://www.tradenz.govt.nz/intelligence/profiles/
united_kingdom.html*
A service of the New Zealand Trade Development
Board, the site provides United Kingdom economic statistics, market information, and business tips.

United Kingdom Country Report

*http://www.state.gov/www/issues/economic/
trade_reports/europe_canada97/
unitedkingdom97.html*
Prepared by the U.S. Department of State, the site
delivers information on United Kingdom exchange rates, debt management, trade barriers,
and intellectual property protection.

United Kingdom InfoExport

*http://www.infoexport.gc.ca/country-
e.asp?continent=Europe&country=45*
A service of Foreign Affairs and International
Trade Canada, the site provides United Kingdom
commercial guides and market reports.

United Kingdom Market Research

*http://strategis.ic.gc.ca/sc_mrkti/ibinddc/engdoc/
1a1b47.html*
A service of Industry Canada, the site provides
U.S. Department of Commerce reports on United
Kingdom business, politics, trade regulations
and standards, investment climate, trade and
project financing, business travel, and market
opportunities.

United Kingdom Patent Office

http://www.patent.gov.uk/
The online service provides information on
United Kingdom patents, trademarks, industrial
designs, copyright, and other intellectual property.
The site includes Patent Office press releases,
notices, and compliance reports.

United Kingdom: Selected Issues

*http://www.imf.org/external/pubs/CAT/
longres.cfm?sk=2489.0*
Prepared by the International Monetary Fund, the
site reports on United Kingdom fiscal plans,
inflation targeting, labor market performance,
employment subsidies, and income distribution.

United Kingdom Trade Assistance

British Diplomatic Missions
http://www.fco.gov.uk/links.asp
A service of the Foreign and Commonwealth Office, the site is a directory of British diplomatic missions online in nearly 30 countries including Canada, South Africa, and the United States.

Committee for Middle East Trade
http://www.comet.org.uk/
A service of the British Overseas Trade Board, the site promotes British-Middle East trade. The site includes a mission statement, event listings, and publication directories.

Department for International Development
http://www.dfid.gov.uk/
Based in London, the Department manages Britain's bilateral and multilateral development programs in developing countries. The site includes news, project reports, and contact information.

Department of Trade and Industry
http://www.dti.gov.uk/
The United Kingdom's lead agency on trade and economic development, the Department of Trade and Industry promotes United Kingdom exports and competitiveness. The site includes business guides, regulatory information, and a directory of Department programs and services.

Development Business Team
http://www.dti.gov.uk/ots/dbt/
A branch of the Department of Trade and Industry, the Team helps British companies compete for World Bank and other international financial institution projects and contracts. The site features a mission statement, staff directory, and contact information.

Export.co.uk
http://www.export.co.uk/frames1.htm
A searchable directory of British exporters, the site is divided into over 20 categories including agri-food, chemicals, wood products, electronics, and transportation products.

Export Credits Guarantee Department
http://www.open.gov.uk/ecgd/
A unit of the United Kingdom government, the Department provides export financing, lines of credit, and export insurance policies. The site delivers Department news, press releases, and program information.

Exports and Investment
http://www.dti.gov.uk/public/frame6.html
Developed by the Department of Trade and Industry, the site reports on United Kingdom export awards, licensing, investment, and international trade library services.

Foreign and Commonwealth Office
http://www.fco.gov.uk/
Headquartered in London, the Office is the British Government department responsible for overseas relations and foreign affairs. The site features British news, export guides, and travel information.

Institute of Export
http://www.export.org.uk/access.html
Based in London, the Institute is a United Kingdom international trade training service. The site includes course listings, contact information, and a directory of export employment opportunities.

National Exporters Database
http://tradeuk.dialog-plc.com/tradeuk-html/ned.htm
A service of Trade U.K., the site is a searchable database of U.K. exporters in over 100 categories including agricultural machinery, office equipment, and wine production.

Overseas Trade Services
http://www.dti.gov.uk/ots/
A service of the Department of Trade and Industry, the site provides a database of country profiles, sector reports, trade leads, and infrastructure projects from around the world.

Overseas Trade Services News
http://www.dti.gov.uk/ots/news/
An electronic magazine on United Kingdom exporting, the site provides country profiles, sector reports, trade leads, and event information from around the world.

Simpler Trade Procedures Board
http://www.sitpro.org.uk/
Based in London, the Board promotes export training and information services to United Kingdom companies. The site includes a staff directory, country fact sheets, and event information.

Trade Development Centre
http://scotexport.org.uk/
Based in Grangemouth, Scotland, the Centre

promotes Scottish exports. The site includes a mission statement, contact information, and a directory of Scottish exporters.

Trade Shows in Britain
http://www.expoguide.com/shows/data/loc_15.htm
Compiled by Expoguide, the site is a directory of upcoming trade shows in Britain.

Trade Shows in Scotland
http://www.expoguide.com/shows/data/loc_53.htm
Compiled by Expoguide, the site is a directory of upcoming trade shows in Scotland.

Trade U.K.
http://www.tradeuk.co.uk/
An online business matchmaking service, the site is a searchable directory of U.K. exporters, importers, and international suppliers. The webpage includes primers on United Kingdom product laws, packaging requirements, and import licenses.

United Kingdom Customs and Excise
http://www.open.gov.uk/customs/c&ehome.htm
Along with information on electronic declarations, duty rates, and value added taxes, the online service provides United Kingdom customs news, fact sheets, and guides.

United Kingdom Representative Offices

Algeria

Embassy of Algeria in London
http://www.consalglond.u-net.com/
The virtual Embassy provides Algerian news, fact sheets, visa and passport information, election results, economic statistics, travel guides, and a directory of Embassy programs and staff.

Argentina

Embassy of Argentina in London
http://easyweb.easynet.co.uk/
~argentineembassy2/homepage/
Along with contact information, the site delivers Argentine fact sheets, visa and passport information, reports on Argentine-U.K. trade and relations, and a directory of Embassy services.

Armenia

Embassy of Armenia in London
http://www.armeniaemb.org/forrel/embas2.htm

The site provides contact information for the Armenian Embassy in London.

Australia

Austrade in London
http://www.austrade.gov.au/london/
An online export promotion service, the site features Australian business guides, investment primers, publication lists, and a database of Australia-U.K. trade statistics.

Austria

Austrian Trade Commission in London
http://aw.wk.or.at/awo/ahst-london.htm
The site lists the staff, street address, phone and fax numbers, e-mail link, and office hours of the Austrian Trade Commission in London.

Bahamas

High Commission of Bahamas in London
http://flamingo.bahamas.net.bs/government/gov8.html
The site provides contact information for the Bahamas High Commission in London.

Belgium

Embassy of Belgium in London
http://www.belgium-embassy.co.uk/
The site provides Belgian news, visa and passport information, travel guides, business guides, investment primers, and a directory of Belgian-U.K. organizations.

Brazil

Brazilian Embassy in London
http://www.brazil.org.uk/
Featuring messages from the Prime Minister and the Ambassador, the site delivers Brazilian news, fact sheets, foreign policy statements, business guides, education bulletins, and a directory of consular services.

Brunei Darussalam

High Commission of Brunei Darussalam in London
http://www.brunet.bn/homepage/gov/bruemb/govemb.htm
The site provides contact information for the Brunei Darussalam High Commission in London.

Canada

Canada-United Kingdom Chamber of Commerce
http://www.canada-uk.org/
Based in London, the Chamber promotes Canada-U.K. trade. The site provides a mission statement, committee directory, event calendar, and contact information.

Canadian High Commission in London
http://www.canada.org.uk/
Posted in English and French, the site provides fact sheets on Canadian visas, passports, immigration, temporary employment, and education programs for international students.

Province of British Columbia Office in London
http://www.ei.gov.bc.ca/directory/bctio/IC98/INTOFF98.htm
A service of the British Columbia Trade and Investment Office, the site lists the street address, phone and fax numbers, and e-mail link of the British Columbia Office in London.

Province of Québec Delegation in London
http://www.mri.gouv.qc.ca/dans_le_monde/europe/londres_an.html
A service of the Québec Ministry of International Affairs, the site lists the Director General, staff, street address, phone and fax numbers, and e-mail link of the Québec Delegation in London.

Chile

Embassy of Chile in London
http://www.demon.co.uk/echileuk/chi0.html
Posted in Spanish, the site provides Chilean fact sheets, press releases, interactive maps, business guides, and United Kingdom market information.

China

China Council for the Promotion of International Trade in London
http://www.ccpit.org/engVersion/cp_about/cp_over/cp_over.html
A Chinese export promotion service, the site provides contact information for the China Council for the Promotion of International Trade office in London.

Embassy of China in London
http://www.chinese-embassy.org.uk/
Along with Chinese language shareware, the site delivers Chinese news, visa and passport information, issue reports, business guides, and science and technology bulletins.

Cyprus

Cyprus Trade Center in London
http://www.cyprustradeny.org/cyny5.html
The site lists the street address, and phone and fax numbers of the Cyprus Trade Center in London.

Czech Republic

Embassy of Czech Republic in London
http://www.czechemb.net/scroll_of_embassies.html
Along with a directory of diplomatic offices in the Czech Republic, the site provides contact information for the Czech Embassy in London.

Denmark

Embassy of Denmark in London
http://www.denmark.org.uk/
The digital Embassy offers Danish news, fact sheets, visa and passport information, and a directory of commercial services for U.K. companies seeking Danish suppliers, and Danish companies interested in doing business in the U.K.

Estonia

Estonian Embassy in London
http://www.estonia.gov.uk/
Featuring interactive maps and contact information, the site provides Estonian fact sheets, visa regulations, business and investment opportunities, and a directory of diplomatic staff.

Fiji

High Commission of Fiji in London
http://fiji.gov.fj/core/fj_mis.html
The site provides contact information for the Fiji High Commission in London.

Finland

Embassy of Finland in London
http://www.finemb.org.uk/
Along with a directory of Honorary Finnish Consuls in the U.K., the site delivers Finnish visa and passport information, an event calendar, and a roster of Embassy personnel.

Finland Trade Center in Edinburgh
http://www.exports.finland.fi/tradecen.htm
The site lists the staff, street address, phone and fax numbers, and e-mail link of the Finland Trade Center in Edinburgh.

Finland Trade Center in London
http://www.exports.finland.fi/tradecen.htm
The site lists the staff, street address, phone and fax numbers, and e-mail link of the Finland Trade Center in London.

France

Embassy of France in London
http://www.ambafrance.org.uk/
Posted in English and French, the site provides French news, fact sheets, media guides, culture and education bulletins, and reports on British-French relations.

French Trade Commission in Edinburgh
http://www.dree.org/grandebretagne/FRANCAIS/ GENERAL/PEE_EDIMBOURG/ORGANIG.HTM
Written in French, the site provides Edinburgh-area market reports, sector profiles, contact information, and a directory of export programs for French companies doing business in the United Kingdom.

French Trade Commission in London
http://www.dree.org/grandebretagne/FRANCAIS/ GENERAL/PEE_LONDRES/ORGANIG.HTM
A French trade promotion service, the site features United Kingdom market studies, sector profiles, and a directory of Commission programs and staff.

Georgia

Embassy of Georgia in London
http://www.darafeev.com/georgia.htm
The virtual Embassy provides Georgian maps, fact sheets, history essays, visa and passport information, government guides, and e-mail directories.

Germany

Embassy of Germany in London
http://www.german-embassy.org.uk/
Along with German press releases, the site delivers primers on German politics, labor, science, law, economics, and media.

German-British Chamber of Commerce in London
http://www.ahk-london.co.uk/
Posted in English and German, the Chamber promotes German-British trade. The site includes a mission statement, membership information, business guides, and a directory of Chamber committee and consulting groups.

Ghana

High Commission of Ghana in London
http://www.juntung.com/ghana-consul-hk/ 2misabo.htm
The site provides contact information for the Ghanaian High Commission in London.

India

Indian Commercial Mission in London
http://www.nic.in/commin/ICM.HTM
The site lists the street address, phone and fax numbers, and e-mail link of the Indian Commercial Mission in London.

Indonesia

Embassy of Indonesia in London
http://indag.dprin.go.id/INGG/trade/atache.HTM
The site provides contact information for the Indonesian Embassy in London.

Iran

Iran Trade Center in London
http://www.neda.net/ibr/tcc.html
An Iranian trade promotion service, the site lists the street address, and phone and fax numbers of the Iran Trade Center in London.

Ireland

Enterprise Ireland in Glasgow
http://www.irish-trade.ie/office_network/ office_locate01.html#anchor1404136
The site lists the Manager, street address, and phone and fax numbers of the Enterprise Ireland office in Glasgow.

Enterprise Ireland in London
http://www.irish-trade.ie/office_network/ office_locate01.html#anchor1404316
The site lists the Director, street address, and phone and fax numbers of the Enterprise Ireland office in London.

Enterprise Ireland in Manchester
*http://www.irish-trade.ie/office_network/
office_locate01.html#anchor1404521*
The site lists the Manager, street address, and phone and fax numbers of the Enterprise Ireland office in Manchester.

Israel

Embassy of Israel in London
http://www.dircon.co.uk/london/
The virtual Embassy provides Israeli news, fact sheets, speeches, visa and passport information, cultural bulletins, and reports on British-Israeli trade and relations.

Italy

Embassy of Italy in London
http://www.embitaly.org.uk/
Featuring an Ambassador's welcome, the site offers Italian news, fact sheets, economic statistics, foreign policy statements, and a directory of Italian cultural events in the United Kingdom.

Japan

Embassy of Japan in London
http://www.embjapan.org.uk/
Along with a primer on Japanese business etiquette, the site provides Japanese news, fact sheets, visa and passport information, cultural bulletins, and reports on Anglo-Japanese relations.

JETRO London
http://www.JETRO.co.uk/
Homepage of the Japan External Trade Organization in London, the site delivers Japanese export and import guides, investment primers, and reports on Japanese-United Kingdom trade.

Malaysia

High Commission of Malaysia in London
*http://www.mnet.com.my/klonline/www/missions/
malmiss/munitedk1.htm*
The site provides contact information for the Malaysian High Commission in London.

Trade Commission of Malaysia in London
*http://www.mnet.com.my/klonline/www/missions/
malmiss/munitedk4.htm*
The site provides contact information for the Malaysian Trade Commission in London.

Mexico

Embassy of Mexico in London
http://www.demon.co.uk/mexuk/
Posted in English and Spanish, the site features Mexican news, fact sheets, speeches, press releases, a staff roster, and a directory of Mexican events in the United Kingdom.

Trade Commission of Mexico in London
*http://www.mexico-businessline.com/ingles/
ofrepmu3.html#england*
The site lists the street address, phone and fax numbers, and e-mail link of the Mexican Trade Commission in London.

Namibia

Embassy of Namibia in London
http://www.republicofnamibia.com/adress.htm
Along with a directory of Namibian companies and government agencies, the site provides contact information for the Namibian Embassy in London.

Nepal

Embassy of Nepal in London
*http://www.info-nepal.com/members/fips/contacts/
nepalese.html*
The site provides contact information for the Nepalese Embassy in London.

New Zealand

New Zealand High Commission in London
http://www.newzealandhc.org.uk/index2.html
Featuring a message from the New Zealand Commissioner in London, the site delivers New Zealand fact sheets, visa and passport information, travel guides, and a directory of consular services.

Trade New Zealand in London
http://www.tradenz.govt.nz/contact/europe.html
An export promotion service, the site provides contact information for the Trade New Zealand office in London.

Norway

Embassy of Norway in London
http://www.norway.org.uk/
The virtual Embassy features Norwegian news, fact sheets, press releases, speeches, educa-

tion and culture reports, business guides, sector profiles, and government directories.

Norwegian Trade Council in London
http://www.norway.org.uk/tra.htm
The site lists the staff, street address, phone and fax numbers, and e-mail link of the Norwegian Trade Council in London.

Organization of Eastern Caribbean States

High Commission of the Organization of Eastern Caribbean States in London
http://www.stkittsnevis.net/offices.html
The site provides contact information for the Organization of Eastern Caribbean States in London.

Pakistan

Pakistan Trade Office in London
http://www.jamal.com/epb/ptoa.htm
The site provides contact information for the Pakistan Trade Office in London.

Philippines

Philippine Trade and Investment Promotion Office in London
http://www.dti.gov.ph/lon/
The site provides a mission statement, service directory, and contact information for the Philippine Trade Office in London.

Poland

Embassy of Poland in London
http://www.poland-embassy.org.uk/
Along with an Embassy staff directory, the site provides Polish fact sheets, visa and passport information, travel guides, and an event calendar.

Polish Business Online
http://www.polishbusiness.co.uk/
Posted in English and Polish, the London-based site offers Polish news, business guides, economic briefings, travel information, and publication lists.

Portugal

Embassy of Portugal in London
http://www.portembassy.gla.ac.uk/
Posted in English and Portuguese, the site

delivers Portuguese news, fact sheets, cultural bulletins, event information, and a directory of Portuguese organizations online.

Portuguese Trade and Investment Office in London
http://www.portugal.org/geninfo/abouticep/london.html
The site lists the staff, street address, phone and fax numbers, and e-mail link of the Portuguese Trade and Investment Office in London.

Saint Vincent and the Grenadines

Saint Vincent and the Grenadines Office in London
http://www.freenet.hamilton.on.ca/~aa462/svgref.html#svgmtd
The site provides contact information for the Saint Vincent and the Grenadines Office in London.

Singapore

High Commission of Singapore in London
http://www.gov.sg/mfa/consular/mww_u.htm
The site provides contact information for the Singapore High Commission in London.

South Africa

South Africa Foreign Trade Office in London
http://wwwdti.pwv.gov.za/dtiwww/foreign_offices.htm
A service of the South Africa Department of Trade and Industry, the site provides contact information for the South Africa Trade Office in London.

Spain

Spanish Commercial Office in London
http://www.mcx.es/polco/londres/london.htm
The site lists the staff, street address, phone and fax numbers, e-mail link, and business matchmaking and research services of the Spanish Commercial Office in London.

Spanish Embassy Education Office in London
http://www.spanishembassy.org.uk/education.office/
Written in Spanish, the site offers information on Spanish language teaching guides, course materials, exams, diploma programs, and Spanish cultural events in the United Kingdom.

Sri Lanka

High Commission of Sri Lanka in London
http://ourworld.compuserve.com/homepages/lanka/
Along with contact information, the site delivers Sri Lankan news, travel guides, business primers, and a directory of Commission consular services.

Sweden

Consulate of Sweden in Belfast
http://www.ud.se/english/mfa/ambassad/storbrit.htm
The site provides contact information for the Swedish Consulate in Belfast.

Embassy of Sweden in London
http://www.ud.se/english/mfa/ambassad/storbrit.htm
The site lists the staff, street address, phone and fax numbers, and e-mail link of the Swedish Embassy in London.

Swedish Trade Council in London
http://www.swedtrade.org.uk/swtc/
A Swedish trade promotion service, the site lists the street address, phone and fax numbers, e-mail link, and staff directory of the Council office in London.

Switzerland

Embassy of Switzerland in London
http://www.swissembassy.org.uk/
Featuring a welcome message from the Swiss Ambassador, the site features Swiss news, fact sheets, economic statistics, business guides, government directories, and reports on Swiss-United Kingdom trade and relations.

Taiwan

China External Trade Development Council Office in London
http://www.cetra.org.tw/english/o_office/indexset.htm
A Taiwanese trade promotion service, the site lists the mission statement and e-mail link of the China External Trade Development Council Office in London.

Taipei Representative Office in London
http://www.roc-taiwan.org.uk/uk/

The online service provides Taiwanese news, fact sheets, electronic magazines, economic statistics, sector profiles, trade-show information, and culture and education bulletins.

Taiwan Government Information Office in London
http://www.gio.gov.tw/info/ngio/uk-f.html
Posted in Chinese and English, the site lists the street address, phone and fax numbers, and e-mail link of the Taiwan Government Information Office in London.

Tanzania

Tanzania High Commission in London
http://www.tanzania-online.gov.uk/
Along with a sound file of the Tanzanian national anthem, the site delivers Tanzanian news, fact sheets, business guides, visa and passport information, and travel primers.

Thailand

Royal Thai Embassy in London
http://www.mfa.go.th/Embassy/detail/205.htm
The site lists the Ambassador, street address, and phone and fax numbers of the Thai Embassy in London.

Thai Trade Center in London
http://www.thaitrade.com/wwtto.html
A service of the Thailand Department of Export Promotion, the site lists the street address, phone and fax numbers, and e-mail link of the Thai Trade Center in London.

Thailand Office of Commercial Affairs in London
http://www.thaitrade.com/thcoaf.html
The site lists the street address, phone and fax numbers, and e-mail link of the Thailand Office of Commercial Affairs in London.

Turkey

Embassy of Turkey in London
http://www.turkey.org/madres.htm
Part of a directory of Turkish diplomatic offices around the world, the site lists the e-mail link of the Turkish Embassy in London.

United States

American Chamber of Commerce in the U.K.
http://www.amcham.org.uk/

Based in London, the Chamber promotes U.K.-U.S. trade. The site includes a mission statement, membership information, publication lists, and a directory of Chamber committees and sector forums.

British American Business Council West of England
http://www.babc.org/west_of_england/
Based in Bristol, the site promotes U.S.-U.K. trade in the west of England. The site includes a newsletter, regional profile, event listings, and membership information.

British American Business Council in Yorkshire
http://www.babc-yorkshire.org.uk/homef.htm
A U.K.-U.S. trade promotion service, the site provides a mission statement and contact information.

British American Business Group in the North West of England
http://www.aits.co.uk/client/babg/
Based in Warrington, the site promotes U.S.-U.K. trade in the northwest of England. The site includes a mission statement, membership guide, and contact information.

Foreign Agricultural Service in London
http://www.usembassy.org.uk/ukfas.html
A branch of the American Embassy in London, the Service promotes the export of U.S. agricultural products to the United Kingdom. The site includes U.K. agricultural fact sheets, trade leads, and business opportunities.

Northern Ireland and the Border Counties of Ireland Homepage
http://www.iep.doc.gov/ire/intro.html
A service of the U.S. Department of Commerce, the site provides Irish news, fact sheets, event information, trade leads, business guides, and investment primers.

Port Authority of New York and New Jersey in London
http://www.case-europe.com/States/nj.htm
Along with New Jersey fact sheets, the site lists the staff, street address, phone and fax numbers, and e-mail link of the Port Authority of New York and New Jersey in London.

State of Arizona Europe Office in London
http://www.commerce.state.az.us/itrade/offices.shtml
The site lists the Trade Representative, street address, phone and fax numbers, and e-mail link of the Arizona Europe Office in London.

State of California Trade Office in London
http://commerce.ca.gov/international/it_off.html#london
A service of the California Trade and Commerce Agency, the site lists the Director, street address, phone and fax numbers, and e-mail link of the California office in London.

State of Colorado Europe Office in London
http://governor.state.co.us/gov_dir/govnr_dir/ITO/abroad.htm#europe
Developed by the Colorado International Trade Office, the site provides a mission statement and contact information for the Colorado Europe Office in London.

State of Florida Trade Office in London
http://www.case-europe.com/States/fl.htm
Along with Florida fact sheets, the site lists the Trade Specialist, street address, phone and fax numbers, and e-mail link of the Florida Trade Office in London.

State of Michigan Trade Office in London
http://www.case-europe.com/States/mi.htm
Along with Michigan fact sheets, the site lists the staff, street address, phone and fax numbers, and e-mail link of the Michigan Trade Office in London.

State of Mississippi European Office in London
http://www.case-europe.com/States/ms.htm
Along with Mississippi fact sheets, the site lists the staff, street address, phone and fax numbers, and e-mail link of the Mississippi European Office in London.

State of Missouri Europe Office in London
http://www.ecodev.state.mo.us/intermark/europe.html
A branch of the Missouri Department of Economic Development, the site posts a mission statement and staff directory for the Missouri Europe Office in London.

State of New York Trade Office in London
http://www.case-europe.com/States/ny.htm
Along with New York fact sheets, the site lists the Director, street address, phone and fax numbers, and e-mail link of the New York Trade Office in London.

State of North Carolina Trade Office in London
http://www.commerce.state.nc.us/commerce/itd/foreign.html
A service of the North Carolina International Trade Division, the site lists the Trade Director,

street address, phone and fax numbers, and e-mail link of the North Carolina Trade Office in London.

State of Pennsylvania Trade Office in London
http://www.case-europe.com/States/pa.htm
Along with Pennsylvania fact sheets, the site lists the staff, street address, phone and fax numbers, and e-mail link of the Pennsylvania Trade Office in London.

State of Utah Trade Office in London
http://www.ce.ex.state.ut.us/international/reps/ reps.htm#United Kingdom
A service of the Utah International Business Development Office, the site lists the Representative, street address, phone and fax numbers, and e-mail link of the Utah Trade Office in London.

U.S. Commercial Service in Belfast
http://www.usembassy.org.uk/ukfcsni.html
The site provides contact information and a directory of export promotion programs for U.S. companies in Belfast including trade missions, conferences, and internship training.

United States Consulate in Edinburgh
http://www.usembassy.org.uk/ ukaddres.html#cgedin
The site lists the Consul General, street address, phone and fax numbers, and office hours of the U.S. Consulate in Edinburgh.

U.S. Commercial Service in London
http://www.usembassy.org.uk/ukfcs.html
The online service provides business primers for U.S. companies seeking to export to the U.K., and U.K. companies interested in representing U.S. firms.

United States Embassy in the United Kingdom
http://www.usembassy.org.uk/
The virtual Embassy provides U.S. news, fact sheets, press releases, speeches, visa and passport information, and a directory of Embassy programs and staff.

United States Information Service in London
http://www.usembassy.org.uk/ukusis.html
The site provides U.S. press releases, fact sheets, media services, cultural bulletins, teaching guides, socioeconomic statistics, and Fulbright scholarship information.

Venezuela

Embassy of Venezuela in London
http://www.demon.co.uk/emb-venuk/
The virtual Embassy provides Venezuelan news, fact sheets, business guides, investment primers, travel information, and reports on United Kingdom-Venezuela trade and relations.

Vatican City

Vatican City Market Guides

The Holy See
http://www.vatican.va/
Posted in six languages, the site provides Vatican City news, Pope profiles, event information, and museum directories.

Vatican City Market Research
http://strategis.ic.gc.ca/sc_mrkti/ibinddc/engdoc/ 1a1b48.html
Posted by Industry Canada, the site provides U.S. Central Intelligence Agency fact sheets on Vatican City geography, people, government, economy, communications, and transportation.

## CHAPTER 7

SLAVIC CYBER-CENTERS: 700+ EASTERN EUROPE AND NEWLY INDEPENDENT STATES BUSINESS RESOURCES ON THE INTERNET

This chapter spotlights more than 700 cross-border business resources online that focus on Eastern Europe and the Newly Independent States. The section profiles regional websites and online hubs for 27 countries and territories including Poland, Russia, and Ukraine. With a population of some 410 million people, the region is in transition from a centrally planned economy to a market economy. While progress to date has been mixed, the region has many economic development assets, including abundant natural resources, and an established industrial base. Leading trade and investment opportunities include transportation, construction, energy, environment, tourism, and infrastructure development. According to NUA Internet Surveys, an estimated two million people in the region—about half of one percent of the total—were online as of January 1999. While this represents a small percentage of the overall population, the segment has considerable purchasing power and business decision-making clout.

Regional Sites

Eastern Europe and Newly Independent States Media

Central Europe Online
http://www.centraleurope.com/
Updated daily, the site delivers Central and Eastern European news, editorials, country profiles, discussion groups, online classifieds, and travel information.

Interfax News Agency
http://www.interfax-news.com/
Based in Moscow, the subscription site delivers news from Russia, the Commonwealth of Independent States, and Baltic Countries. The service includes editorials, sector profiles, and country reports.

NIS News Resources
http://users.aimnet.com/~ksyrah/ekskurs/rusnews.html
A directory of Newly Independent States news resources online, the site is divided into a dozen sections including digests, newspapers, journals, periodicals, and lists.

Eastern Europe and Newly Independent States Market Guides

Business in the Baltic States
http://www.binet.lv/english/database/
A searchable directory of Baltic companies, the database is browsable by company name, executive title, address, phone number, industry, and location.

Eastern Europe Manufacturing Directories
http://www.olvitgroup.ru/business/ibis/bd_main.html
A service of OLVIT, a Russian-based publisher, the site provides manufacturing directories for 15 Eastern European countries including Georgia, Russia, and Ukraine.

EMERGO
http://www.got.kth.se/emergo/
Published by the School of Business at Stockholm University, EMERGO is an academic journal on emerging and transition economies. The site provides a directory of Eastern European scholars and business specialists from around the world.

European Bank for Reconstruction and Development
http://www.ebrd.com/
Established in 1991, the Bank finances economic development projects in countries of Central and Eastern Europe and the Commonwealth of Independent States. The site delivers financing guides, program information, and publication lists.

InfoExport Europe
http://www.infoexport.gc.ca/continent-e.asp?continent=Europe
A service of Foreign Affairs and International Trade Canada, the site provides economic fact sheets and business guides for nearly 40 European countries.

New Independent States of the Former U.S.S.R.
http://www.state.gov/www/regions/nis/index.html
A service of the U.S. State Department, the site provides U.S. press statements, testimony,

briefings, issue reports, and travel information on the Eastern European region and countries.

REESWEB: Russian and East European Studies
http://www.pitt.edu/~cjp/rees.html
A service of the University of Pittsburgh, the site is a directory of Russian and Eastern European resources online. Categories include public affairs, government and politics, business and economics, and media and journalism.

World Bank Group Europe and Central Asia
http://www.worldbank.org/html/extdr/offrep/eca/eca.htm
A database of World Bank projects in Eastern Europe and Central Asia, the site provides press releases, speeches, mission statements, country profiles, and regional economic reports.

Eastern Europe and Independent States Trade Assistance

BISNIS Online
http://www.itaiep.doc.gov/bisnis/bisnis.html
A service of the U.S. Department of Commerce, the site is a virtual library of business information on the Newly Independent States and other countries of the former Soviet Union. The service includes commercial guides, sector profiles, country profiles, trade leads, and event information.

Black Sea Economic Pact
http://www.photius.com/bsec/bsec.html
A regional cooperation agreement, the Pact has 11 member countries: Albania, Armenia, Azerbaijan, Bulgaria, Georgia, Greece, Moldova, Romania, Russia, Ukraine, and Turkey. The site includes a mission statement, country profiles, and contact information.

CEEBICnet
http://www.itaiep.doc.gov/eebic/ceebic.html
A service of the U.S. Department of Commerce, CEEBICnet or the Central and Eastern European Business Information Center provides regional fact sheets, market studies, event information, commercial guides, and a directory of business and procurement opportunities.

Japan's Assistance to New Independent States
http://web.infoweb.ne.jp/scc/
Posted in English, Japanese, and Russian, the site reports on Japanese financial aid and humanitarian assistance to countries of the former Soviet Union.

National Sites

Albania

Albania Media

Albania Media
http://www.mediainfo.com/emediajs/specific-geo.htm?region=albania
Compiled by Editor and Publisher Interactive, the site is a directory of Albanian media sites online, including newspapers and radio stations.

Albanian Daily News
http://www2.AlbanianNews.com/AlbanianNews/
Updated daily, the site provides Albanian news, business reports, online classifieds, a news archive, contact information, and a free e-mail newsletter.

Albania Market Guides

Albania Country Brief
http://www.worldbank.org/cgi-bin/sendoff.cgi?page=%2Fhtml%2Fextdr%2Foffrep%2Feca%2Fal.htm
A service of the World Bank Group, the site provides Albanian population statistics, financial data, development reports, and economic forecasts.

Albania: A Country Study
http://lcweb2.loc.gov/frd/cs/altoc.html
A service of the U.S. Library of Congress, the site delivers fact sheets on Albanian geography, population, agriculture, mining, manufacturing, and foreign economic relations.

Albania Homepage
http://www.albanian.com/main/
A virtual country guide, the site features Albanian news, fact sheets, history lessons, cultural bulletins, travel information, and photo galleries.

Albania Market Research
http://strategis.ic.gc.ca/sc_mrkti/ibinddc/engdoc/1a1b1.html
Posted by Industry Canada, the site provides U.S. Central Intelligence Agency fact sheets on Albanian geography, people, government, economy, communications, and transportation.

Albanian.Com
http://www.albanian.com/
A directory of Albanian resources online, the site

is divided into six sections including news, publications, non-profit organizations, and companies.

Albinfos
http://194.51.140.1/albinfos/
The online service delivers Albanian investment primers, legal guides, economic statistics, sector profiles, business opportunities, and company directories.

Albania Trade Assistance

Albanian Embassies and Missions Abroad
http://www.tirana.al/minjash/embassy.htm
The site lists the staff, street addresses, and phone and fax numbers of Albanian Embassies and Consulates General around the world.

Albanian Ministry of Foreign Affairs
http://www.tirana.al/minjash/ministri.htm
A service of the Albanian government, the webpage provides a directory of conventions and agreements between Albania and other countries and organizations, and a list of countries that maintain diplomatic relations with Albania.

CEEBICnet Albania
http://www.itaiep.doc.gov/eebic/countryr/ albania.htm
A service of the U.S. Department of Commerce Central and Eastern European Business Information Center, the site delivers Albanian fact sheets, market studies, event information, business and procurement opportunities, and a directory of U.S. companies in Albania.

Albania Representative Offices

Diplomatic Representations in Albania
http://www.tirana.al/minjash/diplomat.htm
The site provides a directory of diplomatic posts in Albania. Representatives include Austria, Bulgaria, Czech Republic, Egypt, France, Germany, Hungary, Iran, and Italy.

Sweden

Consulate General of Sweden in Tirana
http://www.ud.se/english/mfa/ambassad/ albanien.htm
The site lists the staff, street address, and phone and fax numbers of the Swedish Consulate General in Tirana.

United Kingdom

Embassy of Britain in Tirana
http://www.fco.gov.uk/directory/posts.asp?AL
The site provides contact information for the British Embassy in Tirana.

Armenia

Armenia Media

Armenia Media
http://www.mediainfo.com/emediajs/specific-geo.htm?region=armenia
Compiled by Editor and Publisher Interactive, the site is a directory of Armenian media sites online.

Armenia Market Guides

Armenia Country Brief
http://www.worldbank.org/cgi-bin/ sendoff.cgi?page=%2Fhtml%2Fextdr%2Foffrep%2 Feca%2Fam.htm
A service of the World Bank Group, the site provides population statistics, financial data, development reports, and economic forecasts.

Armenia: A Country Study
http://lcweb2.loc.gov/frd/cs/amtoc.html
A service of the U.S. Library of Congress, the site delivers fact sheets on Armenian geography, population, agriculture, mining, manufacturing, and foreign economic relations.

Armenia InfoExport
http://www.infoexport.gc.ca/country-e.asp?continent=Europe&country=46
A service of Foreign Affairs and International Trade Canada, the site provides fact sheets and statistics on Armenian geography, business and politics.

Armenia Market Research
_http://strategis.ic.gc.ca/sc_mrkti/ibinddc/engdoc/ 1a1h2.html_
A service of Industry Canada, the site provides U.S. Department of Commerce reports on Armenian business, politics, trade regulations and standards, investment climate, trade and project financing, business travel, and market opportunities.

Armenia: Recent Economic Developments
*http://www.imf.org/external/pubs/CAT/
longres.cfm?sk=2547.0*
Prepared by the International Monetary Fund, the site reports on Armenian prices, wages, employment, tax administration, expenditure control, monetary policies, merchandise trade, and external debt.

Armenia Virtual Library
http://www.arminco.com/ArmeniaVL.html
A service of the Australian National University, the site is a directory of Armenian resources online. Categories include business, government, tourism, and education.

Business Cooperation Offers with Armenian Companies
http://www.arminco.com/Armenia/haikbsn.html
A service of the Haik Institute in Yerevan, the site is a database of Armenian business opportunities. Categories include medical, leather products, and building materials.

Country Commercial Guide
*http://www.state.gov/www/about_state/business/
com_guides/1998/russia_nis/armenia98.html*
Prepared by the U.S. Embassy in Yerevan, the site delivers primers on the Armenian economy, political environment, trade regulations and standards, investment climate, trade and project financing, and business travel.

General Information
*http://www.armeniaemb.org/geninfo/
generalinfo.htm*
Developed by the Armenian Embassy in Washington, D.C., the site reports on Armenian geography, population, history, language, education, science, culture, and business.

Investment Opportunities Guide
*http://www.armeniaemb.org/investment/
inestop.htm*
An online investment primer, the site features fact sheets on Armenian banking, monetary policies, taxation, fiscal policy, foreign trade, natural resources, and agriculture.

Armenia Trade Assistance

Armenia Foreign Trade
*http://www.armeniaemb.org/investment/
fortrade.htm*
Prepared by the Armenian Embassy in Washington, D.C., the site reviews Armenian customs

tariffs, taxes, quotas, licensing, rules of origin, and balance of trade.

Armenian Embassies and Diplomatic Missions
http://www.armeniaemb.org/forrel/embas2.htm
The site lists the staff, street addresses, phone and fax numbers, and e-mail links of Armenian Embassies and Consulates General around the world.

Trade Point Armenia
http://tpa-gw1.amilink.net/
Part of the United Nations Global Trade Point Network, the site provides Armenia trade leads, market bulletins, and contact information.

Armenia Representative Offices

Foreign Embassies and Diplomatic Missions in Armenia
http://www.armeniaemb.org/forrel/embas1.htm
A directory of diplomatic posts in Armenia, the site lists representatives from 12 countries including China, Egypt, France, Germany, Greece, Lebanon, and Ukraine.

Iran

Embassy of the Islamic Republic of Iran in Yerevan
http://www.arminco.com/iran/home.html
The virtual Embassy provides Iranian news, fact sheets, visa and passport information, travel guides, business primers, and a directory of consular services.

Russia

Embassy of Russia in Yerevan
http://www.armeniaemb.org/forrel/embas1.htm
The site lists the Ambassador, street address, phone and fax numbers, and e-mail link of the Russian Embassy in Yerevan.

United Kingdom

Embassy of Britain in Yerevan
http://www.fco.gov.uk/directory/posts.asp?AM
The site provides contact information for the British Embassy in Yerevan.

United States

United States Embassy in Yerevan
http://www.arminco.com/Armenia/CCG/
A country commercial guide, the site reviews

Armenian infrastructure, franchising, joint ventures, pricing, government procurement, trade barriers, dispute settlement, and taxation.

United States Information Service in Yerevan
http://www.arminco.com/homepages/usis/
The site provides U.S. press releases, fact sheets, media services, cultural bulletins, teaching guides, socioeconomic statistics, and Fulbright scholarship information.

Azerbaijan

Azerbaijan Media

Azerbaijan Media
http://www.mediainfo.com/emediajs/specific-geo.htm?region=azerbaijan
Developed by Editor and Publisher Interactive, the site is a directory of Azerbaijani media sites online.

Azerbaijan Market Guides

Azerbaijan Country Brief
http://www.worldbank.org/cgi-bin/sendoff.cgi?page=%2Fhtml%2Fextdr%2Foffrep%2Feca%2Faz.htm
A service of the World Bank Group, the site provides Azerbaijani population statistics, financial data, development reports, and economic forecasts.

Azerbaijan: A Country Study
http://lcweb2.loc.gov/frd/cs/aztoc.html
A service of the U.S. Library of Congress, the site delivers fact sheets on Azerbaijani geography, population, agriculture, mining, and manufacturing.

Azerbaijan InfoExport
http://www.infoexport.gc.ca/country-e.asp?continent=Europe&country=47
A service of Foreign Affairs and International Trade Canada, the site provides fact sheets and statistics on Azerbaijani geography, business and politics.

Azerbaijan Market Research
http://strategis.ic.gc.ca/sc_mrkti/ibinddc/engdoc/1a1h3.html
A service of Industry Canada, the site provides U.S. Department of Commerce reports on Azerbaijani business, politics, trade regulations and standards, investment climate, trade and

project financing, business travel, and market opportunities.

Azerbaijan Pages
http://solar.rtd.utk.edu/oldfriends/azerbaijan/index.html
A directory of Azerbaijani resources online, the site is divided into a dozen categories including business and economy, maps, history, travel, and research.

Azerbaijan Virtual Library
http://scf.usc.edu/~baguirov/azeri.htm
Part of the World Wide Web Virtual Library, the site is a database of Azerbaijani resources online. Categories include business, history, research, media, travel, and reference.

Azerbaijan Representative Offices

France

French Trade Commission in Baku
http://www.co.ru/~peemoscou/peecei/pee_aze.htm
A French trade promotion service, the site lists the Commercial Counselor and contact information for the French Trade Commission in Baku.

Japan

Azerbaijan-Japan Business Link
http://www.mks.or.jp/~genki/azer.index.html
The online service provides Azerbaijani news, fact sheets, maps, business guides, cultural primers, and reports on Azerbaijan-Japan trade and relations.

Russia

Embassy of Russia in Baku
http://intrans.baku.az/embrus/HOMEPAGE.HTM
Posted in Russian, the site provides Russian news, fact sheets, reports on Azerbaijan-Russia trade and relations, and a directory of Embassy services.

Sweden

Consulate General of Sweden in Baku
http://www.ud.se/english/mfa/ambassad/azerbajd.htm
The site lists the staff, street address, phone and fax numbers, and e-mail link of the Swedish Consulate in Baku.

United Kingdom

British Embassy in Baku
http://www.intrans.baku.az/british/
Along with United Kingdom news and fact
sheets, the digital Embassy delivers Azerbaijani
visa information, business guides, and travel
primers.

United States

United States Embassy in Azerbaijan
http://www.usia.gov/abtusia/posts/XA1/
wwwhmain.html
Featuring U.S. fact sheets and passport information, the site provides Azerbaijani city profiles,
maps, business reports, travel guides, and a
photo gallery.

United States Information Service in Baku
http://www.usia.gov/abtusia/posts/XA1/
wwwhusis.html
The site provides U.S. news, press releases, fact
sheets, cultural bulletins, teaching guides,
socioeconomic statistics, electronic journals, and
Fulbright scholarship information.

Belarus

Belarus Media

Belarus Media
http://www.mediainfo.com/emediajs/specific-
geo.htm?region=belarus
Compiled by Editor and Publisher Interactive, the
site is a directory of Belarusian media sites
online.

Belarus Market Guides

Belarus Country Brief
http://www.worldbank.org/cgi-bin/
sendoff.cgi?page=%2Fhtml%2Fextdr%2Foffrep%2
Feca%2Fby.htm
A service of the World Bank Group, the site
provides Belarusian population statistics,
financial data, development reports, and economic forecasts.

Belarus: A Country Study
http://lcweb2.loc.gov/frd/cs/bytoc.html
A service of the U.S. Library of Congress, the site
delivers fact sheets on Belarusian geography,
population, agriculture, mining, manufacturing,
and foreign economic relations.

Belarus Economic Trends
http://www.bettacis.minsk.by/index.htm
A virtual library of Belarusian economic statistics,
the site includes data on prices, wages, inflation,
government finance, privatization, living standards, and other key indicators.

Belarus Market Access Database
http://mkaccdb.eu.int/mkdb/
mkdb.pl?METHOD=COUNTRY
A service of the European Commission, the site
offers briefs on Belarusian trade policy, tariff
barriers, non-tariff barriers, investment-related
measures, and financial services regulations.

Belarus Market Research
http://strategis.ic.gc.ca/sc_mrkti/ibinddc/engdoc/
1a1b7.html
Posted by Industry Canada, the site provides U.S.
Central Intelligence Agency fact sheets on
Belarusian geography, people, government,
economy, communications, and transportation.

Belarus Now
http://www.open.by/belarus-now/
A Belarus electronic magazine, the site features
Belarusian news, business guides, economic
reports, political briefings, investment information, and a news archive.

Belarus: Recent Economic Developments
http://www.imf.org/external/pubs/CAT/
longres.cfm?sk=2427.0
Prepared by the International Monetary Fund, the
site reports on Belarusian economic activity,
output, inflation, price policy, employment, wages,
public finance, monetary policy, and balance of
trade.

Belarusian Business Server
http://www.belbusiness.minsk.by/eng.htm
The online service provides information on the
Belarusian Business Guide, a searchable
directory of some 10,000 Belarusian companies
and organizations.

Internet Business Catalog
http://www.open.by/business/Hello.Eng.html
Posted in English and Russian, the site is a
searchable directory of Belarusian companies.
Categories include banking, computers, construction, law, medicine, publishing, and real
estate.

Republic of Belarus
http://www.undp.org/missions/belarus/
eng_pg01.htm

Posted by the United Nations Development Programme, the site delivers primers on Belarusian history, geography, economy, foreign policy, investment, education, and science.

Belarus Trade Assistance

Trade and Services
http://www.undp.org/missions/belarus/eng_pg01.htm#TRA
An international trade fact sheet, the site reports on Belarusian exports, imports, balance of trade, and major trading partners.

Belarus Representative Offices

Armenia

Embassy of Armenia in Minsk
http://www.armeniaemb.org/forrel/embas2.htm
The site provides contact information for the Armenian Embassy in Minsk.

France

French Trade Commission in Minsk
http://www.co.ru/~peemoscou/peecei/pee_bel.htm
Written in French, the site lists the Commercial Counselors, street address, and phone and fax numbers of the French Trade Commission in Minsk.

United Kingdom

Embassy of Britain in Minsk
http://www.fco.gov.uk/directory/posts.asp?BR
The site provides contact information for the British Embassy in Minsk.

United States

United States Embassy in Minsk
http://www.usis.minsk.by/
Featuring a message from the Ambassador, the site provides U.S. news, fact sheets, press releases, visa and passport information, and reports on U.S.-Belarus trade and relations.

Bosnia and Herzegovina

Bosnia and Herzogovina Media

DANI
http://www.bhdani.com/ehome.htm

Based in Sarajevo, the site provides Bosnian news, editorials, and business reports. The service includes a news archive dating back to 1992.

Bosnia and Herzegovina Market Guides

Bosnia and Herzegovina Country Brief
http://www.worldbank.org/cgi-bin/sendoff.cgi?page=%2Fhtml%2Fextdr%2Foffrep%2Feca%2Fba.htm
A service of the World Bank Group, the site provides Bosnian population statistics, financial data, development reports, and economic forecasts.

Bosnia and Herzegovina Market Research
http://strategis.ic.gc.ca/sc_mrkti/ibinddc/engdoc/1a1b5.html
Posted by Industry Canada, the site provides U.S. Central Intelligence Agency fact sheets on Bosnian geography, people, government, economy, communications, and transportation.

Bosnian/Balkan Reconstruction
http://www.itaiep.doc.gov/eebic/balkan.htm
A service of the U.S. Department of Commerce, the site is a database of Bosnian reconstruction projects managed by the World Bank, the European Bank for Reconstruction and Development, the U.S. government, and other governments and organizations.

Chamber of Commerce of Bosnia and Herzegovina
http://www.komorabih.com/eindex.html
The online service provides Bosnia and Herzegovina business guides, newsletters, investment primers, company directories, sector profiles, and trade-show information.

Welcome to Bosnia and Herzegovina
http://www.bosnianembassy.org/
A service of the Bosnian Embassy in Washington, D.C., the site provides Bosnian fact sheets, history lessons, economic reports, and government bulletins.

Bosnia and Herzegovina Trade Assistance

Bosnian Embassies and Consulates Abroad
http://www.bosnianembassy.org/offices/index.shtml
A directory of Bosnian diplomatic posts abroad,

the site lists representatives in over 30 countries including Albania, Hungary, Libya, Malaysia, Turkey, and the United Arab Emirates.

CEEBICnet Bosnia and Herzegovina
http://www.itaiep.doc.gov/eebic/countryr/ bosniah.htm
A service of the U.S. Department of Commerce Central and Eastern European Business Information Center, the site delivers Bosnian fact sheets, market studies, event information, business and procurement opportunities, and a directory of U.S. companies in Bosnia and Herzegovina.

Bosnia and Herzegovina Representative Offices

Austria

Austrian Trade Commission in Sarajevo
http://www.wk.or.at/aw/atc/bosnien/
The virtual office provides Austrian fact sheets, reports on Austria-Bosnia trade, and contact information.

Canada

Embassy of Canada in Sarajevo
http://www.dfait-maeci.gc.ca/english/missions/rep-can1e.htm#bosnia
The site provides contact information for the Canadian Embassy in Sarajevo.

Malaysia

Embassy of Malaysia in Sarajevo
http://www.mnet.com.my/klonline/www/missions/ malmiss/mbosniah.htm
The site provides contact information for the Malaysian Embassy in Sarajevo.

Norway

Norwegian Trade Council in Sarajevo
http://www.ntc.no/cgi-bin/wbch.exe?html=../ templates/utekontor2.html&profile=1127
The site lists the staff, street address, phone and fax numbers, and e-mail link of the Norwegian Trade Council in Sarajevo.

Sweden

Embassy of Sweden in Sarajevo
http://www.ud.se/english/mfa/ambassad/

bosnienh.htm
The site lists the staff, street address, phone and fax numbers, and e-mail link of the Swedish Embassy in Sarajevo.

United Kingdom

Embassy of Britain in Sarajevo
http://www.fco.gov.uk/directory/posts.asp?BS
The site provides contact information for the British Embassy in Sarajevo.

United States

U.S. Aid Business Development Program
http://www.usaidbf.com.ba/
Established in 1996, the Program provides loans and technical assistance to Bosnian and Herzegovinian companies. The site includes Program news, application forms, and contact information.

Bulgaria

Bulgaria Media

Bulgaria Media
http://www.mediainfo.com/emediajs/specific-geo.htm?region=bulgaria
Compiled by Editor and Publisher Interactive, the site is a directory of Bulgarian media sites online including newspapers and radio stations.

Bulgaria Market Guides

All About Bulgaria
http://www.cs.columbia.edu/~radev/bulginfo.html
A database of some 1,200 Bulgarian resources online, the site is divided into nine categories including news, organizations, people, culture, and frequently asked questions.

Bulgaria.com
http://www.bulgaria.com/
A virtual library of country information, the site delivers Bulgarian news, chat services, personal homepages, business reports, cultural bulletins, and employment opportunities.

Bulgaria Business and Investment Opportunities
http://bgbio.aubg.bg/
A service of the American University in Bulgaria, the site provides Hungarian business guides, company directories, legal primers, investment information, and government bulletins.

Bulgaria Country Brief
http://www.worldbank.org/cgi-bin/
sendoff.cgi?page=%2Fhtml%2Fextdr%2Foffrep%2
Feca%2Fbg.htm
A service of the World Bank Group, the site
provides Bulgarian population statistics, financial
data, development reports, and economic
forecasts.

Bulgaria Country Profile
http://www.tradenz.govt.nz/intelligence/profiles/
bulgaria.html
A service of the New Zealand Trade Development
Board, the site provides Bulgarian economic
statistics, market information, and business tips.

Bulgaria Country Report
http://www.business-europa.co.uk/bsmenu.html
Developed by Business Europa, the site delivers
fact sheets on Bulgarian banking, taxation,
energy, agriculture, transportation, media,
education, travel, and investment.

Bulgaria Country Report
http://www.state.gov/www/issues/economic/
trade_reports/europe_canada97/bulgaria97.html
Prepared by the U.S. Department of State, the site
delivers information on Bulgarian exchange
rates, debt management, trade barriers, and
intellectual property protection.

Bulgaria Market Access Database
http://mkaccdb.eu.int/mkdb/
mkdb.pl?METHOD=COUNTRY
A service of the European Commission, the site
offers briefs on Bulgarian trade policy, tariff
barriers, non-tariff barriers, investment-related
measures, and financial services regulations.

Bulgaria Market Information
http://dtiinfo1.dti.gov.uk/ots/bulgaria/
A service of the London-based Department of
Trade and Industry, the site delivers Bulgarian
fact sheets, maps, and trade-show information.

Bulgaria Market Research
http://strategis.ic.gc.ca/sc_mrkti/ibinddc/engdoc/
1a1b6.html
A service of Industry Canada, the site provides
U.S. Department of Commerce reports on
Bulgarian business, politics, trade regulations
and standards, investment climate, trade and
project financing, business travel, and market
opportunities.

Bulgaria Online
http://www.online.bg/
A hub of country information, the site delivers
Bulgarian biographies, political bulletins,
business reports, and event information.

Bulgarian Digest
http://bulgaria.simplenet.com/digest/
business.htm
The site provides a directory of leading Bulgarian
business resources online. Categories include
privatization, companies, organizations, and
finance and investment.

Bulgarian Industrial Association
http://www.bia-bg.com/
Based in Sofia, the Association promotes
Bulgarian business interests. The site includes a
mission statement, member directory, activity
reports, and investment guides.

Bulgaria Trade Assistance

CEEBICnet Bulgaria
http://www.itaiep.doc.gov/eebic/countryr/
bulgaria.htm
A service of the U.S. Department of Commerce
Central and Eastern European Business
Information Center, the site delivers Bulgarian
fact sheets, market studies, event information,
business and procurement opportunities, and a
directory of U.S. companies in Bulgaria.

Foreign Firms Offer
http://www.pari.bg/doc/engforum.htm
An online marketplace, the site provides a
searchable database of Bulgarian buy and sell
offers. Categories include computers, agri-food,
transportation equipment, electronics, and
building materials.

Trade Point Sofia
http://www.wtcsofia.bg/
Part of the Global Trade Point Network, the site
provides Bulgarian trade contacts and fact
sheets.

Bulgaria Representative Offices

Armenia

Embassy of Armenia in Sofia
http://www.armeniaemb.org/forrel/embas2.htm
The site provides contact information for the
Armenian Embassy in Sofia.

Austria

Austrian Trade Commission in Sofia
http://aw.wk.or.at/awo/ahst-sofia.htm
The site lists the staff, street address, phone and fax numbers, e-mail link, and office hours of the Austrian Trade Commission in Sofia.

France

French Trade Commission in Sofia
http://www.dree.org/bulgarie/
A French trade promotion service, the site features Bulgarian market studies, sector profiles, and a directory of Commission programs and staff.

Germany

German Chamber of Commerce in Sofia
http://www.ahk.net/en/bg/Sofia/
The site lists the Chief Executive Officer, office hours, street address, phone and fax numbers, and e-mail link of the German Chamber in Sofia.

Ghana

Embassy of Ghana in Sofia
http://www.juntung.com/ghana-consul-hk/2misabo.htm
The site provides contact information for the Ghanaian Embassy in Sofia.

India

Indian Commercial Mission in Sofia
http://www.nic.in/commin/ICM.HTM
The site lists the street address, and phone and fax numbers of the Indian Commercial Mission in Sofia.

Italy

Italian Trade Commission in Sofia
http://www.ice.it/estero/sofia/
Written in Italian, the site provides Italian news, fact sheets, business guides, cultural bulletins, reports on Bulgarian-Italian trade and relations, and a directory of consular services.

New Zealand

Trade New Zealand in Sofia
http://www.tradenz.govt.nz/contact/europe.html
An export promotion service, the site provides contact information for the Trade New Zealand office in Sofia.

Spain

Spanish Commercial Office in Sofia
http://www.icex.es/openURL.html#openURL=/english/infoproyem/ofcomes/ofcomes.html#EU
The site lists the staff, street address, and phone and fax numbers of the Spanish Commercial Office in Sofia.

Sweden

Embassy of Sweden in Sofia
http://www.ud.se/english/mfa/ambassad/bulgarie.htm
The site lists the staff, street address, phone and fax numbers, and e-mail link of the Swedish Embassy in Sofia.

United Kingdom

Embassy of Britain in Sofia
http://www.fco.gov.uk/directory/posts.asp?BC
The site provides contact information for the British Embassy in Sofia.

United States

American Chamber of Commerce in Bulgaria
http://www.online.bg/amcham/
Based in Sofia, the Chamber promotes Bulgarian-U.S. trade. The site features a mission statement, members roster, publications list, and contact information.

United States Embassy in Bulgaria
http://www.usis.bg/
The virtual Embassy provides U.S. news, fact sheets, press releases, reports on Bulgarian-U.S. trade and relations, and a directory of Embassy programs and staff.

Venezuela

Embassy of Venezuela in Sofia
http://www.embavenez-sofia.bg/
Along with visa and passport information, the site provides primers on Venezuelan politics, culture, business, energy, tourism, environmental protection, and government.

Croatia

Croatia Search Tools

CROSS: Croatia Search Service
http://cross.carnet.hr/index_en.html
A searchable index of Croatian resources online, the service includes browsing tips, and Internet usage statistics.

Croatia Media

Croatia Media
http://www.mediainfo.com/emediajs/specific-geo.htm?region=croatia
Compiled by Editor and Publisher Interactive, the site is a directory of Croatian media sites online.

Croatia Market Guides

Business and Economy
http://www.croatiaemb.org/base/economy.htm
A service of the Croatian Embassy in Washington, D.C., the site features Croatian business news, statistics, fact sheets, investment guides, and a directory of U.S. companies operating in Croatia.

Croatia Country Brief
http://www.worldbank.org/cgi-bin/ sendoff.cgi?page=%2Fhtml%2Fextdr%2Foffrep%2 Feca%2Fhr.htm
A service of the World Bank Group, the site provides Croatian population statistics, financial data, development reports, and economic forecasts.

Croatia Market Information
http://dtiinfo1.dti.gov.uk/ots/croatia/
A service of the London-based Department of Trade and Industry, the site delivers Croatian fact sheets, maps, and trade-show information.

Croatia Market Research
http://strategis.ic.gc.ca/sc_mrkti/ibinddc/engdoc/ 1a1b8.html
A service of Industry Canada, the site provides U.S. Department of Commerce reports on Croatian business, politics, trade regulations and standards, investment climate, trade and project financing, business travel, and market opportunities.

Croatian Business Pages
http://www.hrvatska.com/
Posted in English and Serbo-Croatian, the site is a browsable index of Croatian companies. Categories include agri-food, computers, electronics, publishing, and pharmaceuticals.

Croatian Chamber of Economy
http://www.hgk.hr/
Based in Zagreb, the Chamber promotes economic development in Croatia. The site includes Croatian commercial guides, a company directory, and an online business opportunities exchange.

Facts on Croatia
http://www.mvp.hr/mvprh-www-eng/10-hrvatska.html
A service of the Croatian Ministry of Foreign Affairs, the site delivers fact sheets on Croatian geography, history, culture, language, business, and government.

Government of the Republic of Croatia
http://www.vlada.hr/eindex.html
Homepage of the Croatian government, the site provides government directories, Cabinet member profiles, press releases, copies of key legislation, and a weekly newsletter on Croatian culture.

Welcome Croatia
http://www.hr/hrvatska/Welcome2Croatia.html
A country primer, the site provides fact sheets on Croatian tourism, history, geography, and science.

Welcome to Croatia
http://tjev.tel.fer.hr/
The online service offers Croatian maps, photos, regional profiles, tourism information, cultural reports, business guides, government bulletins, and accommodation directories.

Croatia Trade Assistance

CEEBICnet Croatia
http://www.itaiep.doc.gov/eebic/countryr/ croatia.htm
A service of the U.S. Department of Commerce Central and Eastern European Business Information Center, the site delivers Croatian fact sheets, market studies, event information, business and procurement opportunities, and a directory of U.S. companies in Croatia.

Diplomatic and Consular Missions of Croatia
http://www.mvp.hr/mvprh-www-eng/6-1predstavnis/6-1hrv-u-svjet.html
A service of the Ministry of Foreign Affairs, the site

provides a directory of Croatian Embassies and Consulates around the world.

Ministry of Foreign Affairs
http://www.mvp.hr/mvprh-www-eng/home-eng.html
Based in Zagreb, the site delivers Croatian news, press releases, speeches, fact sheets, foreign affairs statements, and diplomatic bulletins.

Trade Shows in Croatia
http://194.152.225.1/~perfec/fairs.html
A service of Perfectum, the site is a directory of trade shows and exhibitions in Bjelovar, Osijek, Rijeka, Split, Zagreb, and other Croatian centers.

Croatia Representative Offices

Diplomatic and Consular Missions in Croatia
http://www.mvp.hr/mvprh-www-eng/6-2predstavnis/6-2svijet.html
An index of Embassies, Consulates General, and Trade Offices in Croatia, the database includes representatives from over 30 countries including Albania, Algeria, Korea, and Turkey.

Austria

Austria Trade Commission in Zagreb
http://www.atembassy.hr/atc/
The virtual office provides Austrian fact sheets, reports on Austria-Croatian trade, contact information, and a directory of programs for Austrian companies doing business in Croatia.

Canada

Embassy of Canada in Zagreb
http://www.dfait-maeci.gc.ca/english/missions/rep-can1e.htm#croatia
The site provides contact information for the Canadian Embassy in Zagreb.

France

French Trade Commission in Zagreb
http://www.dree.org/croatie/
Written in French, the site features Croatian market studies, sector profiles, and a directory of export assistance programs for French companies doing business in Croatia.

India

Embassy of India in Zagreb
http://www.ring.net/indija/

Along with Indian fact sheets and visa information, the site lists the street address, phone and fax numbers, and e-mail link of the Indian Embassy in Zagreb.

Italy

Italian Cultural Institute in Zagreb
http://www.jahnke.net/zagabria/
Posted in Italian, the site delivers Italian news, fact sheets, press releases, cultural bulletins, contact information, and a directory of Institute services.

Malaysia

Embassy of Malaysia in Zagreb
http://www.mnet.com.my/klonline/www/missions/malmiss/mcroatia.htm
The site provides contact information for the Malaysian Embassy in Zagreb.

Spain

Spanish Commercial Office in Zagreb
http://www.icex.es/openURL.html#openURL=/english/infoproyem/ofcomes/ofcomes.html#EU
The site lists the staff, street address, and phone and fax numbers of the Spanish Commercial Office in Zagreb.

Sweden

Embassy of Sweden in Zagreb
http://www.ud.se/english/mfa/ambassad/kroatien.htm
The site lists the staff, street address, phone and fax numbers, and e-mail link of the Swedish Embassy in Zagreb.

United Kingdom

Embassy of Britain in Zagreb
http://www.fco.gov.uk/directory/posts.asp?CE
The site provides contact information for the British Embassy in Zagreb.

United States

United States Embassy in Croatia
http://www.open.hr/com/ae_zagreb/
Along with U.S. fact sheets and press releases, the site provides Croatian commercial guides, company directories, investment primers, and reports on U.S.-Croatian trade and relations.

Czech Republic

Czech Republic Media

Czech Happenings
http://www.ctknews.com/
An English language online newspaper, the site provides Czech news, business reports, photo galleries, travel information, classifieds, and language tutorials.

Czech Media
http://www.mediainfo.com/emediajs/specific-geo.htm?region=czechrepublic
Compiled by Editor and Publisher Interactive, the site is a directory of Czech media sites online.

Czech Republic Market Guides

Barclays Country Report: Czech Republic
http://www.offshorebanking.barclays.com/services/economic/yearly/czemay97/index.html
Prepared by Barclays Bank, the site reports on Czech Republic economic trends, politics, monetary and fiscal policy, international trade, and U.K.-Czech merchandise trade and investment flows.

CEEBICnet Czech Republic
http://www.itaiep.doc.gov/eebic/countryr/czechr.htm
A service of the U.S. Department of Commerce Central and Eastern European Business Information Center, the site delivers Czech fact sheets, market studies, event information, business and procurement opportunities, and a directory of U.S. companies in the Czech Republic.

Center for the Regional Development of the Czech Republic
http://www.crr.cz/default_menu_eng.htm
A service of the Czech Ministry for Regional Development, the Center promotes Czech business and economic development. The site provides contact information and a directory of Center programs.

Czech Business Directory
http://www.muselik.com/czech/business/directory/
A searchable database of Czech companies, the site profiles companies in some 30 categories including agricultural machinery, office supplies, toy manufacturing, and transportation.

Czech Companies Looking for Partners
http://www.czech.cz/washington/ekon/profiles.htm
A database of Czech companies seeking U.S. partners, the site lists over 50 firms in 14 industries including chemicals, electronics, machinery, steel, hardware, and travel.

Czech Economic Information
http://www.czech.cz/washington/ekon/ekon.htm
A service of the Czech Embassy in Washington, D.C., the site delivers Czech business news, investment guides, sectoral bulletins, and a directory of U.S. companies in the Czech Republic.

Czech Information Center
http://www.muselik.com/czech/toc.html
A virtual library of country information, the site features Czech fact sheets, business guides, shopping directories, train and bus schedules, travel information, and online bulletin board.

Czech Information System
http://czis.anet.cz/en.htm
Posted in three languages, the site is a searchable directory of Czech companies and organizations. Categories include agriculture, computers, electronics, engineering, and transportation.

Czech Invest
http://www.czechinvest.com/
Developed by the Czech Ministry of Trade and Industry, the site provides Czech fact sheets, press releases, maps, investment guides, sector reports, and case studies.

Czech Republic
http://www.czech.cz/
Written in Czech and English, the site delivers Czech fact sheets, visa and passport information, investment guides, economic reports, cultural bulletins, and travel primers.

Czech Republic: A Case Model
http://www.friends-partners.org/oldfriends/economics/czech.rep.case.study.html
A primer on the Czech economy, the site reports on Czech privatization, investment, banking, unemployment, and international trade.

Czech Republic Country Brief
http://www.worldbank.org/cgi-bin/sendoff.cgi?page=%2Fhtml%2Fextdr%2Foffrep%2Feca%2Fcz.htm
A service of the World Bank Group, the site provides Czech population statistics, financial

data, development reports, and economic forecasts.

Czech Republic Country Profile
http://www.tradenz.govt.nz/intelligence/profiles/czech_republic.html
A service of the New Zealand Trade Development Board, the site provides Czech economic statistics, market information, and business tips.

Czech Republic Country Report
http://www.state.gov/www/issues/economic/trade_reports/europe_canada97/czech97.html
Prepared by the U.S. Department of State, the site delivers information on Czech exchange rates, debt management, trade barriers, and intellectual property protection.

Czech Republic: A Country Study
http://lcweb2.loc.gov/frd/cs/cstoc.html
A service of the U.S. Library of Congress, the site delivers fact sheets on Czech geography, population, agriculture, mining, manufacturing, and foreign economic relations.

Czech Republic InfoExport
http://www.infoexport.gc.ca/country-e.asp?continent=Europe&country=9
A service of Foreign Affairs and International Trade Canada, the site provides Czech commercial guides and market reports.

Czech Republic Market Access Database
http://mkaccdb.eu.int/mkdb/mkdb.pl?METHOD=COUNTRY
A service of the European Commission, the site delivers briefs on Czech trade policy, tariff barriers, non-tariff barriers, investment-related measures, and financial services regulations.

Czech Republic Market Information
http://dtiinfo1.dti.gov.uk/ots/czech_republic/
A service of the London-based Department of Trade and Industry, the site delivers Czech fact sheets, maps, and trade-show information.

Czech Republic Market Research
http://strategis.ic.gc.ca/sc_mrkti/ibinddc/engdoc/1a1b9.html
A service of Industry Canada, the site provides U.S. Department of Commerce reports on Czech business, politics, trade regulations and standards, investment climate, trade and project financing, business travel, and market opportunities.

Doing Business in the Czech Republic
http://www.mpo.cz/english/g/gb/frame.htm
A virtual business primer, the site provides Czech economic forecasts, investment primers, incorporation guides, sector profiles, and a directory of business assistance programs and agencies in the Czech Republic.

Ministry of Industry and Trade
http://www.mpo.cz/english/mpo_uk.htm
Based in Prague, the Ministry administers Czech industrial and trade policy. The site includes Czech fact sheets, economic statistics, key legislation, and business guides.

Czech Republic Trade Assistance

Country Commercial Guide
http://www.state.gov/www/about_state/business/com_guides/1998/europe_canada/czech98.html
Prepared by the U.S. Embassy in Prague, the site delivers primers on Czech business, politics, trade regulations and standards, investment climate, trade and project financing, and business travel.

Czech Embassies Abroad
http://www.czechemb.net/scroll_of_embassies.html
A service of the Czech Republic Embassy in Kuwait, the site provides a directory of Czech Embassies in six countries including Australia, Canada, and Israel.

Czech Trade
http://www.tpo.cz/act1.htm
Based in Prague, the agency promotes Czech exports and international investment. The site includes a quarterly bulletin, global trade fact sheets, economic surveys, and business guides.

Export-Import Express
http://www.icml.com/wbb/export/
A service of the Czech Information Center, the site is a searchable database of Czech and international buy and sell offers. Categories include agri-food, apparel, chemicals, and giftware.

Trade Net
http://www.tradenet.cz/
Posted in English and Czech, the site provides Czech publication lists, company directories, product catalogs, business opportunities, and event information.

Trade Shows in Czech Republic
http://www.expoguide.com/shows/data/loc_12.htm
Compiled by Expoguide, the site is a directory of
upcoming trade shows in the Czech Republic.

Czech Republic Representative Offices

Austria

Austrian Embassy in Prague
http://www.vol.cz/AUSTRIA/
Written in Czech and German, the site provides
Austrian fact sheets, business guides, reports on
Austrian-Czech trade, and a directory of Embassy
programs and staff.

Austrian Trade Commission in Prague
http://aw.wk.or.at/awo/ahst-prag.htm
The site lists the staff, street address, phone and
fax numbers, e-mail link, and office hours of the
Austrian Trade Commission in Prague.

Canada

Canadian Embassy in Prague
http://www.dfait-maeci.gc.ca/~prague/
Posted in four languages, the site delivers
Canadian news, fact sheets, press releases,
visa and passport information, and reports on
Canada-Czech and Canada-Slovakia trade and
relations.

Cyprus

Cyprus Trade Center in Prague
http://www.cyprustradeny.org/cyny5.html
The site lists the street address, and phone and
fax numbers of the Cyprus Trade Center in
Prague.

Finland

Finland Trade Center in Prague
http://www.exports.finland.fi/tradecen.htm
The site lists the staff, street address, phone and
fax numbers, and e-mail link of the Finland Trade
Center in Prague.

Germany

German Chamber of Commerce in Prague
http://www.ahk.net/en/cz/Prague/
The site lists the Chairperson, Chief Executive
Officer, street address, phone and fax numbers,

and e-mail link of the German Chamber in
Prague.

Ghana

Embassy of Ghana in Prague
http://www.juntung.com/ghana-consul-hk/
2misabo.htm
The site provides contact information for the
Ghanaian Embassy in Prague.

India

Indian Commercial Mission in Prague
http://www.nic.in/commin/ICM.HTM
The site lists the street address, phone and fax
numbers, and e-mail link of the Indian Commercial Mission in Prague.

Ireland

Enterprise Ireland in Prague
http://www.irish-trade.ie/office_network/
office_locate01.html#anchor1418627
The site lists the Manager, street address, and
phone and fax numbers of the Enterprise Ireland
office in Prague.

Italy

Embassy of Italy in Prague
http://www.anet.cz/italcult/
Posted in Czech and Italian, the site delivers
Italian fact sheets, cultural bulletins, event
information, and reports on Czech-Italian trade
and relations.

New Zealand

Trade New Zealand in Prague
http://www.tradenz.govt.nz/contact/europe.html
An export promotion service, the site provides
contact information for the Trade New Zealand
office in Prague.

Norway

Norwegian Trade Council in Prague
http://www.ntc.no/cgi-bin/wbch.exe?html=../
templates/utekontor2.html&profile=1124
The site lists the staff, street address, phone and
fax numbers, and e-mail link of the Norwegian
Trade Council in Prague.

Portugal

Portuguese Trade and Investment Office in Prague
http://www.portugal.org/geninfo/abouticep/prague.html
The site lists the staff, street address, phone and fax numbers, and e-mail link of the Portuguese Trade and Investment Office in Prague.

South Africa

South Africa Foreign Trade Office in Prague
http://wwwdti.pwv.gov.za/dtiwww/foreign_offices.htm
A service of the South Africa Department of Trade and Industry, the site provides contact information for the South Africa Trade Office in Prague.

Spain

Spanish Commercial Office in Prague
http://www.icex.es/openURL.html#openURL=/english/infoproyem/ofcomes/ofcomes.html#EU
The site lists the staff, street address, phone and fax numbers, and e-mail link of the Spanish Commercial Office in Prague.

Sweden

Embassy of Sweden in Prague
http://www.ud.se/english/mfa/ambassad/tjeckien.htm
The site lists the staff, street address, phone and fax numbers, and e-mail link of the Swedish Embassy in Prague.

Taiwan

Taiwan Government Information Office in Prague
http://www.gio.gov.tw/info/ngio/cz-f.html
Posted in Chinese and English, the site lists the street address, phone and fax numbers, and e-mail link of the Taiwan Government Information Office in Prague.

Thailand

Royal Thai Embassy in Prague
http://www.thaiemb.cz/
Along with Thai fact sheets and visa information, the site offers Czech business guides, investment primers, and reports on Czech-Thai and Czech-Slovak trade and relations.

Thailand Office of Commercial Affairs in Prague
http://www.thaitrade.com/thcoaf.html
The site lists the street address, phone and fax numbers, and e-mail link of the Thailand Office of Commercial Affairs in Prague.

United Kingdom

British Embassy in Prague
http://www.britain.cz/
The virtual Embassy provides United Kingdom fact sheets, visa and passport information, travel guides, cultural bulletins, and reports on Czech Republic-United Kingdom trade.

United States

United States Embassy in Prague
http://www.usis.cz/
The online service offers United States news, press releases, electronic journals, defense attaché reports, event information, and a directory of Embassy programs and staff.

United States Information Service in Prague
http://www.usis.cz/usis.htm
The site provides United States news, press releases, fact sheets, cultural bulletins, teaching guides, socioeconomic statistics, Fulbright scholarship information, and Czech-American trade mission reports.

Estonia

Estonia Media

Aripaev
http://www.mbp.ee/english.html
An English language e-zine, the site provides Estonian news, business reports, economic statistics, and sector profiles.

Baltic Review
http://www.zzz.ee/tbr/
Based in Tallinn, the site is an English-language e-zine. The service reports on business, law and economics in Estonia, Latvia and Lithuania.

Estonia Media
http://www.mediainfo.com/emediajs/specific-geo.htm?region=estonia
Compiled by Editor and Publisher Interactive, the site is a directory of Estonian media sites.

Estonian News Agency
http://eta.www.ee/
Posted in English and Estonian, the site features Estonian economic news, business reports, and sector profiles.

Estonia Market Guides

CEEBICnet Estonia
http://www.itaiep.doc.gov/eebic/countryr/ estonia.htm
A service of the U.S. Department of Commerce Central and Eastern European Business Information Center, the site delivers Estonian fact sheets, market studies, event information, business and procurement opportunities, and a directory of U.S. companies in Estonia.

Estonia Country Brief
http://www.worldbank.org/cgi-bin/ sendoff.cgi?page=%2Fhtml%2Fextdr%2Foffrep%2 Feca%2Fee.htm
A service of the World Bank Group, the site provides Estonian population statistics, financial data, development reports, and economic forecasts.

Estonia Country Guide
http://www.ciesin.ee/ESTCG/
A virtual library of country information, the site delivers Estonian news, fact sheets, political briefs, economic reports, cultural bulletins, and history lessons.

Estonia InfoExport
http://www.infoexport.gc.ca/country- e.asp?continent=Europe&country=11
A service of Foreign Affairs and International Trade Canada, the site provides fact sheets and statistics on Estonian geography, business and politics.

Estonia Market Access Database
http://mkaccdb.eu.int/mkdb/ mkdb.pl?METHOD=COUNTRY
A service of the European Commission, the site offers briefs on Estonian trade policy, tariff barriers, non-tariff barriers, investment-related measures, and financial services regulations.

Estonia Market Information
http://dtiinfo1.dti.gov.uk/ots/estonia/
A service of the London-based Department of Trade and Industry, the site delivers Estonian fact sheets, maps, and trade-show information.

Estonia Market Research
http://strategis.ic.gc.ca/sc_mrkti/ibinddc/engdoc/ 1a1b11.html
Posted by Industry Canada, the site provides U.S. Central Intelligence Agency fact sheets on Estonian geography, people, government, economy, communications, and transportation.

Estonia: Selected Issues
http://www.imf.org/external/pubs/CAT/ longres.cfm?sk=2497.0
Prepared by the International Monetary Fund, the site reports on Estonian revenues and expenditures, banking, trade policy and protection, and European Union accession.

Estonian Chamber of Commerce and Industry
http://ktk.uninet.ee/
Based in Tallinn, the Chamber promotes Estonian business and economic development. The site features Estonian fact sheets, export directories, and investment guides.

Estonian Investment Agency
http://www.eia.ee/
An online investment primer, the site provides Estonian community profiles, sector reports, economic statistics, and contact information.

Government of the Republic of Estonia
http://www.rk.ee/
Homepage of the Estonian government, the site features policy statements, key legislation, executive profiles, and contact information.

Infoatlas
http://www.hotline.ee/atlas/eng/
A searchable database of Estonian companies, the site is browsable by company name, address, phone number, company director, trademark, and keyword.

Investor's Guide
http://www.estemb.org/pages/business.htm
A service of the Estonian Embassy in Washington, D.C., the site provides fact sheets on Estonian economic policy, taxation, privatization, and international trade.

Estonia Trade Assistance

Estonia Export Directory
http://www.hotline.ee/fair/fair.htm
A searchable directory of Estonian exporters, the site is browsable by company name, product, service, and harmonized system code.

Estonian Customs
http://www.customs.ee/
Posted in English and Estonian, the site provides Estonian customs documents, guides, statistics, definitions, currency exchange rates, and contact information.

Estonian Fairs
http://www.fair.ee/cgi/eng_list.cgi
A database of upcoming trade shows in Estonia, the site lists events in over a dozen industries including electronics, publishing, apparel, computers, medical, environmental, and building materials.

Estonian Ministry of Foreign Affairs
http://www.vm.ee/
Posted in seven languages, the site delivers Estonian news, press releases, foreign policy statements, consular information, economic reports, and government directories.

Estonian Representations around the World
http://www.vm.ee/eng/consularinfo/evmreps.html
A service of the Ministry of Foreign Affairs, the site is a directory of Estonian Embassies and Consulates General in over 40 countries including Argentina, Greece, Spain, and the Ukraine.

Estonian Trade Council
http://www.ee/ETC/
Based in Tallinn, the Council promotes Estonian exports and international investment. The site includes product catalogs, contact information, and a directory of business matchmaking and research services.

Estonian Trade and Investment Review
http://ktk.uninet.ee/tir/index.html
Developed by the Estonian Chamber of Commerce and Industry, the site delivers Estonian business news, economic reports, investment opportunities, and trade-show information.

Trade Shows in Estonia
http://www.expoguide.com/shows/data/loc_16.htm
Compiled by Expoguide, the site is a directory of upcoming trade shows in Estonia.

Estonia Representative Offices

Canada

Embassy of Canada in Tallinn
http://www.dfait-maeci.gc.ca/english/missions/
rep-can2e.htm#estonia

The site provides contact information for the Canadian Embassy in Tallinn.

Denmark

Embassy of Denmark in Tallinn
http://www.denmark.ee/
Written in Danish, English, Estonian, and Russian, the site provides Danish fact sheets, visa and passport information, reports on Danish-Estonian trade and relations, and a directory of Embassy programs and staff.

Finland

Embassy of Finland in Tallinn
http://www.finemb.ee/
Posted in three languages, the site delivers Finnish fact sheets, visa and passport information, cultural bulletins, and a directory of consular and commercial services.

Finland Trade Center in Tallinn
http://www.exports.finland.fi/tradecen.htm
The site lists the staff, street address, phone and fax numbers, and e-mail link of the Finland Trade Center in Tallinn.

Germany

German Chamber of Commerce in Tallinn
http://www.ahk.net/en/ee/Tallinn/
The site lists the Chief Executive Officer, street address, phone and fax numbers, e-mail link, and office hours of the German Chamber in Tallinn.

Norway

Norwegian Trade Council in Tallinn
http://www.ntc.no/cgi-bin/wbch.exe?html=../
templates/utekontor2.html&profile=1133
The site lists the staff, street address, phone and fax numbers, and e-mail link of the Norwegian Trade Council in Tallinn.

Sweden

Embassy of Sweden in Tallinn
*http://www.ud.se/english/mfa/ambassad/
estland.htm*
The site lists the staff, street address, phone and fax numbers, and e-mail link of the Swedish Embassy in Tallinn.

United Kingdom

Embassy of Britain in Tallinn
http://www.fco.gov.uk/directory/posts.asp?ES
The site provides contact information for the British Embassy in Tallinn.

United States

American Chamber of Commerce in Estonia
http://www.acce.ee/
Based in Tallinn, the Chamber promotes Estonian-U.S. trade. The site includes Chamber news, business reports, a calendar of events, and contact information.

United States Embassy in Estonia
http://www.estnet.ee/usislib/
Along with U.S. fact sheets and visa information, the site provides Estonian fact sheets, business guides, investment primers, accommodation directories, and travel tips.

Georgia

Georgia Media

Georgia Media
http://www.mediainfo.com/emediajs/specific-geo.htm?region=georgia-eu
Compiled by Editor and Publisher Interactive, the site is a directory of Georgian newspaper and other media sites online.

Georgia Market Guides

Georgia Country Brief
http://www.worldbank.org/cgi-bin/
sendoff.cgi?page=%2Fhtml%2Fextdr%2Foffrep%2Feca%2Fge.htm
A service of the World Bank Group, the site provides Georgian population statistics, financial data, development reports, and economic forecasts.

Georgia: A Country Study
http://lcweb2.loc.gov/frd/cs/getoc.html
A service of the U.S. Library of Congress, the site delivers fact sheets on Georgian geography, population, agriculture, mining, manufacturing, and foreign economic relations.

Georgia InfoExport
http://www.infoexport.gc.ca/country-e.asp?continent=Europe&country=48
A service of Foreign Affairs and International Trade Canada, the site provides fact sheets and statistics on Georgian geography, business and politics.

Georgia Market Research
http://strategis.ic.gc.ca/sc_mrkti/ibinddc/engdoc/1a1b17.html
A service of Industry Canada, the site provides U.S. Department of Commerce reports on Georgian business, politics, trade regulations and standards, investment climate, trade and project financing, business travel, and market opportunities.

Georgia Virtual Library
http://voyager.rtd.utk.edu/~zlotchen/georgia/
A service of the World Wide Web Virtual Library, the site is a directory of Georgian resources online. Categories include news, software, culture, history, and government.

Georgian Business Centres
http://www.parliament.ge/~nino/inq/busi/buge.html
The site is a database of Georgian business development centers, research institutes, legal firms, translation services, and small business assistance agencies.

Georgian Chamber of Commerce and Industry
http://www.gcci.org.ge/
Based in Tbilisi, the Chamber promotes economic development in Georgia. The site includes Georgian investment primers, culture guides, contact information, and a directory of Chamber services.

Georgian Company Database
http://www.georgia.net.ge/gic/C_D_B/Cover.HTM
A searchable directory of Georgian firms, the site profiles companies in six categories: agriculture, building materials, ceramics, electronics, food and related products, and textiles and garments.

Georgian Investment Center
http://www.georgia.net.ge/gic/
A service of the Georgian Ministry of Trade and Foreign Economic Relations, the site provides Georgian sector profiles, economic fact sheets, privatization reports, taxation information, and a directory of key business contacts.

Parliament of Georgia
http://www.parliament.ge/
Along with parliamentary guides and government

directories, the site delivers Georgian news, fact sheets, travel information, environmental bulletins, and an online message board.

Georgia Trade Assistance

Georgian Government Ministries
http://www.georgia.net.ge/gic/Govcon~1.HTM
A service of the Georgian Investment Center, the site provides a directory of leading economic development and trade agencies in Georgia, diplomatic posts in Georgia, and Georgian Embassies around the world.

International Chamber of Commerce
http://georgia.net.ge/usis/iccg.html
Founded in 1996, the Chamber promotes Georgian exports and international investment. The site includes a mission statement, contact information, and a directory of Chamber programs.

Georgia Representative Offices

Armenia

Embassy of Armenia in Tbilisi
http://www.armeniaemb.org/forrel/embas2.htm
The site provides contact information for the Armenian Embassy in Tbilisi.

European Union

European Commission Delegation in Tbilisi
http://www.eu-delegation.org.ge/
The virtual office posts European Union news, fact sheets, business guides, reports on European Union-Georgia trade and relations, and a directory of Delegation services.

United Kingdom

Embassy of Britain in Tbilisi
http://www.fco.gov.uk/directory/posts.asp?GR
The site provides contact information for the British Embassy in Tbilisi.

United States

United States Embassy in Tbilisi
http://georgia.net.ge/usis/about_mission.html
The site provides U.S. visa and passport information, Georgian travel guides, and a directory of Embassy services including notarization, birth registration, and absentee voting.

United States Information Service in Tbilisi
http://georgia.net.ge/usis/
Along with Georgian economic reports and business opportunities, the site provides U.S. news, press releases, fact sheets, cultural bulletins, and teaching guides.

Hungary

Hungary Media

Hungary Media
http://www.mediainfo.com/emediajs/specific-geo.htm?region=hungary
Compiled by Editor and Publisher Interactive, the site is a directory of Hungarian media sites online.

Hungary Market Guides

Barclays Country Report: Hungary
http://www.offshorebanking.barclays.com/services/economic/yearly/hunsep97/index.html
Prepared by Barclays Bank, the site reports on Hungarian economic trends, politics, monetary and fiscal policy, international trade, and U.K.-Hungary merchandise trade and investment flows.

BusinessWeb Hungary
http://www.businessweb.hu/
A virtual library of country business information, the site features Hungarian news, investment primers, and economic statistics. Access is free with registration.

Hungary Business Briefs
http://www.austrade.gov.au/IOOM/Hungary/
A service of Austrade, the site offers fact sheets on Hungarian culture, business etiquette, marketing, transportation, travel, and visas.

Hungary Business Reports
http://italchambers.net/BusinessReports.html
Prepared by the Italian Chamber of Commerce and written in Italian, the site provides Hungarian fact sheets, market reports, and commercial guides.

Hungary Country Brief
http://www.worldbank.org/cgi-bin/sendoff.cgi?page=%2Fhtml%2Fextdr%2Foffrep%2Feca%2Fhu.htm
A service of the World Bank Group, the site provides Hungarian population statistics,

financial data, development reports, and economic forecasts.

Hungary Country Profile
http://www.tradenz.govt.nz/intelligence/profiles/hungary.html
A service of the New Zealand Trade Development Board, the site provides Hungarian economic statistics, market information, and business tips.

Hungary Country Report
http://www.state.gov/www/issues/economic/trade_reports/europe_canada97/hungary97.html
Prepared by the U.S. Department of State, the site delivers information on Hungarian exchange rates, debt management, trade barriers, and intellectual property protection.

Hungary: A Country Study
http://lcweb2.loc.gov/frd/cs/hutoc.html
A service of the U.S. Library of Congress, the site delivers fact sheets on Hungarian geography, population, agriculture, mining, manufacturing, and foreign economic relations.

Hungary InfoExport
http://www.infoexport.gc.ca/country-e.asp?continent=Europe&country=20
A service of Foreign Affairs and International Trade Canada, the site provides fact sheets and statistics on Hungarian geography, business, trade, and politics.

Hungary Market Access Database
http://mkaccdb.eu.int/mkdb/mkdb.pl?METHOD=COUNTRY
A service of the European Commission, the site delivers briefs on Hungarian trade policy, tariff barriers, non-tariff barriers, investment-related measures, and financial services regulations.

Hungary Market Information
http://dtiinfo1.dti.gov.uk/ots/hungary/
A service of the London-based Department of Trade and Industry, the site provides Hungarian fact sheets, maps, and trade-show information.

Hungary Market Research
http://strategis.ic.gc.ca/sc_mrkti/ibinddc/engdoc/1a1b21.html
A service of Industry Canada, the site provides U.S. Department of Commerce reports on Hungarian business, politics, trade regulations and standards, investment climate, trade and project financing, business travel, and market opportunities.

Hungary Patent Office
http://www.hpo.hu/
Along with fact sheets on Hungarian inventors and inventions, the site provides information on Hungarian trademarks, industrial designs, and other intellectual property.

Hungary: Statistical Annex
http://www.imf.org/external/pubs/CAT/longres.cfm?sk=2420.0
Prepared by the International Monetary Fund, the site reports on Hungarian gross domestic product, aggregate demand, value added by sector, household disposable income, and consumer and producer prices.

Hungary Trade Assistance

CEEBICnet Hungary
http://www.itaiep.doc.gov/eebic/countryr/hungary.htm
A service of the U.S. Department of Commerce Central and Eastern European Business Information Center, the site delivers Hungarian fact sheets, market studies, event information, business and procurement opportunities, and a directory of U.S. companies in Hungary.

Hungarian Investment and Trade Development
http://www.itd.hu/english/index.htm
A virtual investment primer, the site features Hungarian fact sheets, company news, publication lists, business matchmaking services, and *Hungarian Economy*, a quarterly electronic magazine.

Hungary Ministry of Industry, Trade and Tourism
http://www.ikm.iif.hu/english/
Based in Budapest, the Ministry promotes trade and economic development in Hungary. The site delivers Hungarian fact sheets, sector profiles, investment guides, and international trade statistics.

Trade Shows in Hungary
http://www.expoguide.com/shows/data/loc_22.htm
Compiled by Expoguide, the site is a directory of upcoming trade shows in Hungary.

Hungary Representative Offices

Australia

Austrade in Budapest
http://www.austrade.gov.au/budapest/
An online export promotion service, the site

delivers Australian business guides, investment primers, publication lists, contact information, and reports on Australia-Hungary trade.

Austria

Austria Trade Commission in Budapest
http://aw.wk.or.at/awo/ahst-budapest.htm
The site lists the staff, street address, phone and fax numbers, e-mail link, and office hours of the Austrian Trade Commission in Budapest.

Canada

Embassy of Canada in Budapest
http://www.dfait-maeci.gc.ca/english/missions/rep-can2e.htm#hungary
The site provides contact information for the Canadian Embassy in Budapest.

Finland

Finland Trade Center in Budapest
http://www.exports.finland.fi/tradecen.htm
The site lists the staff, street address, phone and fax numbers, and e-mail link of the Finland Trade Center in Budapest.

France

Embassy of France in Budapest
http://ambasfrance.refer.bme.hu/
Posted in French and Hungarian, the site offers French news, fact sheets, business guides, visa information, science and technology reports, and cultural primers.

French Trade Commission in Budapest
http://www.pronet.hu/peebudap/
Written in French, the site provides Hungarian market reports, sector profiles, contact information, and a directory of export programs for French companies doing business in Hungary.

Germany

German Chamber of Commerce in Budapest
http://www.ahk.net/en/hu/Budapest/
The site lists the Chairperson, Chief Executive Officer, street address, phone and fax numbers, office hours, and e-mail link of the German Chamber in Budapest.

India

Indian Commercial Mission in Budapest
http://www.nic.in/commin/ICM.HTM
The site lists the street address, phone and fax numbers, and e-mail link of the Indian Commercial Mission in Budapest.

Ireland

Enterprise Ireland in Budapest
http://www.irish-trade.ie/office_network/office_locate01.html#anchor1414410
The site lists the Manager, street address, and phone and fax numbers of the Enterprise Ireland office in Budapest.

Japan

Embassy of Japan in Budapest
http://www.japan-embassy.hu/
Written in Hungarian and Japanese, the site offers Japanese news, fact sheets, business guides, visa and passport information, and reports on Hungarian-Japanese trade and relations.

Japan External Trade Organization in Budapest
http://www.jetro.hu/
A Japanese trade promotion service, the site provides Japanese fact sheets, business information, and reports on Japan-Hungary trade and relations.

Malaysia

Embassy of Malaysia in Budapest
http://www.mnet.com.my/klonline/www/missions/malmiss/mhungary.htm
The site provides contact information for the Malaysian Embassy in Budapest.

Norway

Norwegian Trade Council in Budapest
http://www.ntc.no/cgi-bin/wbch.exe?html=../templates/utekontor2.html&profile=1104
The site lists the staff, street address, phone and fax numbers, and e-mail link of the Norwegian Trade Council in Budapest.

Pakistan

Pakistan Trade Office in Budapest
http://www.jamal.com/epb/ptoa.htm
The site provides contact information for the Pakistan Trade Office in Budapest.

Portugal

Portuguese Trade and Investment Office in Budapest
http://www.portugal.org/geninfo/abouticep/hungary.html
The site lists the staff, street address, phone and fax numbers, and e-mail link of the Portuguese Trade and Investment Office in Budapest.

Spain

Spanish Commercial Office in Budapest
http://www.mcx.es/budapest/
Written in Spanish, the site provides Spanish fact sheets, export guides, and product catalogs.

Sweden

Embassy of Sweden in Budapest
http://www.ud.se/english/mfa/ambassad/ungern.htm
The site lists the staff, street address, phone and fax numbers, and e-mail link of the Swedish Embassy in Budapest.

Taiwan

China External Trade Development Council Office in Budapest
http://www.cetra.org.tw/english/o_office/indexset.htm
A Taiwanese trade promotion service, the site lists the mission statement and e-mail link of the China External Trade Development Council Office in Budapest.

Taiwan Government Information Office in Budapest
http://www.gio.gov.tw/info/ngio/hung-f.html
Posted in Chinese and English, the site lists the street address, phone and fax numbers, and e-mail link of the Taiwan Government Information Office in Budapest.

Thailand

Royal Thai Embassy in Budapest
http://www.mfa.go.th/Embassy/detail/41.htm
The site lists the Ambassador, street address, and phone and fax numbers of the Thai Embassy in Budapest.

Thailand Office of Commercial Affairs in Budapest
http://www.thaitrade.com/thcoaf.html
The site lists the street address, phone and fax numbers, and e-mail link of the Thailand Office of Commercial Affairs in Budapest.

United Kingdom

Embassy of Britain in Budapest
http://www.fco.gov.uk/directory/posts.asp?HU
The site provides contact information for the British Embassy in Budapest.

United States

American Chamber of Commerce in Hungary
http://www.hungary.com/amcham/
Based in Budapest, the Chamber promotes U.S.-Hungary trade. The site includes a roster of members, event information, and a directory of Chamber programs and services.

State of Illinois Trade Office in Budapest
http://www.commerce.state.il.us/dcca/files/int'l/hungary.htm
A service of the Illinois Department of Commerce and Community Affairs, the site lists the Managing Director, street address, phone and fax numbers, and e-mail link of the Illinois Trade Office in Budapest.

United States Embassy in Budapest
http://www.usis.hu/
Along with U.S. news and fact sheets, the site provides Hungarian sector profiles, economic reports, commercial guides, and a directory of American companies in Hungary.

United States Information Service in Budapest
http://www.usis.hu/usisbp.htm
The site provides U.S. news, press releases, fact sheets, cultural bulletins, teaching guides, socioeconomic statistics, Fulbright scholarship information, and a directory of U.S. Information Service staff in Budapest.

Venezuela

Embassy of Venezuela in Budapest
http://www.trade-venezuela.com/EMBVENG.HTM
The site lists the street address, phone and fax

numbers, and e-mail link of the Venezuelan Embassy in Budapest.

Kazakhstan

Kazakhstan Media

Caravan Weekly Newspaper
http://www.caravan.kz/
Updated weekly, the electronic magazine provides Kazakhstani business news, sector profiles, company information, interviews, socioeconomic statistics, investment guides, and lifestyle reports.

Kazakhstan Media
http://www.mediainfo.com/emediajs/specific-geo.htm?region=kazakhstan
Compiled by Editor and Publisher Interactive, the site is a directory of Kazakhstani radio stations and other media sites online.

Kazakhstan Market Guides

Kazakhstan Business Briefs
http://www.austrade.gov.au/IOOM/Kazakhstan/
A service of Austrade, the site offers fact sheets on Kazakhstani culture, business etiquette, marketing, transportation, travel, and visas.

Kazakhstan Country Brief
http://www.worldbank.org/cgi-bin/
sendoff.cgi?page=%2Fhtml%2Fextdr%2Foffrep%2
Feca%2Fkz.htm
A service of the World Bank Group, the site provides Kazakhstani population statistics, financial data, development reports, and economic forecasts.

Kazakhstan Country Report
http://www.itaiep.doc.gov/bisnis/country/
cntasia.htm#Kazakhstan
A service of the International Trade Administration, the site delivers fact sheets on Kazakhstani politics, banking, trade and investment, customs regulations, and quality and safety standards.

Kazakhstan Market Information
http://dtiinfo1.dti.gov.uk/ots/kazakhstan/
A service of the London-based Department of Trade and Industry, the site delivers Kazakhstani fact sheets, maps, and trade-show information.

Kazakhstan Market Research
http://strategis.ic.gc.ca/sc_mrkti/ibinddc/engdoc/
1a1h7.html
A service of Industry Canada, the site provides

U.S. Department of Commerce reports on Kazakhstani business, politics, trade regulations and standards, investment climate, trade and project financing, business travel, and market opportunities.

Kazakhstan Virtual Library
*http://www.rockbridge.net/personal/bichel/
kazakh.htp*
A service of the World Wide Web Virtual Library, the site is a directory of Kazakhstani resources online. Categories include culture and language, maps and flags, economics, travel, and publications.

Welcome to Kazakhstan
http://www.kz/firsteng.html
Along with information on national cooking and traditional jewelery, the site delivers Kazakhstani maps, fact sheets, city profiles, history lessons, weather bulletins, and economic reports.

Kazakhstan Trade Assistance

Kazakhstan Investment Bank
http://www.nursat.kz/~kib/
Based in Almaty, the Bank promotes international investment in Kazakhstan. The site includes a mission statement, contact information, and a directory of Bank programs and services.

Kazakhstan Representative Offices

Armenia

Embassy of Armenia in Almaty
http://www.armeniaemb.org/forrel/embas2.htm
The site provides contact information for the Embassy of Armenia in Almaty.

Australia

Embassy of Australia in Almaty
http://www.online.ru/people/austemba/
Along with Australian and Kazakhstani travel information, the site lists the street address, phone and fax numbers, and e-mail link of the Australian Embassy in Almaty.

Canada

Embassy of Canada in Almaty
http://www.dfait-maeci.gc.ca/english/missions/
rep-can3e.htm#kazakhstan
The site provides contact information for the Canadian Embassy in Almaty.

France

French Trade Commission in Almaty
*http://www.co.ru/~peemoscou/peecei/
pee_kaz.htm*
Posted in French, the site lists the Commercial
Counselor, street address, and phone and fax
numbers of the French Trade Commission in
Almaty.

Finland

Finland Trade Center in Almaty
http://www.exports.finland.fi/tradecen.htm
The site lists the staff, street address, phone and
fax numbers, and e-mail link of the Finland Trade
Center in Almaty.

Germany

German Chamber of Commerce in Almaty
http://www.ahk.net/en/kz/Almaty/
The site lists the Chief Executive Officer, street
address, phone and fax numbers, office hours,
and e-mail link of the German Chamber in
Almaty.

Malaysia

Embassy of Malaysia in Almaty
http://www.mnet.com.my/klonline/www/missions/
malmiss/mkazakhs.htm
The site provides contact information for the
Malaysian Embassy in Almaty.

United Kingdom

Embassy of Britain in Almaty
http://www.fco.gov.uk/directory/posts.asp?KZ
The site provides contact information for the
British Embassy in Almaty.

Kyrgyzstan

Kyrgyzstan Market Guides

Kyrgyzstan Country Brief
http://www.worldbank.org/cgi-bin/
sendoff.cgi?page=%2Fhtml%2Fextdr%2Foffrep%2
Feca%2Fkg.htm
A service of the World Bank Group, the site
provides Kyrgyzstani population statistics,
financial data, development reports, and economic forecasts.

Kyrgyzstan Country Report
http://www.itaiep.doc.gov/bisnis/country/
cntasia.htm#Kyrgyzstan
A service of the International Trade Administration, the site delivers Kyrgyzstani commercial
guides, socioeconomic statistics, travel information, legal primers, and privatization reports.

Kyrgyzstan Discover the Country
http://www.geocities.com/TheTropics/Shores/7432/
A hub of country information, the site features fact
sheets on Kyrgyzstani business, international
trade, banking, taxation, transportation, communications, tourism, and culture.

Kyrgyzstan Market Information
http://dtiinfo1.dti.gov.uk/ots/kyrgyzstan/
A service of the London-based Department of
Trade and Industry, the site delivers Kyrgyzstani
fact sheets, maps, and trade-show information.

Kyrgyzstan Market Research
http://strategis.ic.gc.ca/sc_mrkti/ibinddc/engdoc/
1a1h8.html
Posted by Industry Canada, the site provides U.S.
Central Intelligence Agency fact sheets on
Kyrgyzstani geography, people, government,
economy, communications, and transportation.

Kyrgyzstan: Recent Economic Developments
http://www.imf.org/external/pubs/CAT/
longres.cfm?sk=2493.0
Prepared by the International Monetary Fund, the
site reports on Kyrgyzstani output, inflation,
wages, prices, taxation, interest rates,
privatization, and pension reform.

Kyrgyzstan Virtual Library
*http://www.rockbridge.net/personal/bichel/
kyrgyz.htp*
A service of the World Wide Web Virtual Library,
the site is a directory of Kyrgyzstani resources
online. Categories include culture and language,
maps and flags, politics, economics, and travel.

Kyrgyzstan Representative Offices

United Kingdom

British Council in Kyrgyzstan
http://www.britcoun.org/kyrgyzstan/index.htm
Along with Kyrgyzstani market profiles, the site
includes British fact sheets, business guides,
event information, and government directories.

Latvia

Latvia Media

Latvia Media
http://www.mediainfo.com/emediajs/specific-geo.htm?region=latvia
Compiled by Editor and Publisher Interactive, the site is a directory of Latvian media sites online.

Latvia Market Guides

Business in Latvia
http://www.virtualglobe.com/latvia/business/
Developed by the Latvian Embassy in Washington, D.C., the site is a directory of Latvian business resources online. Categories include government, partnerships, and investment.

Central Statistical Bureau of Latvia
http://www.csb.lv/
Written in English and Lettish, the site provides statistics on Latvian finance, population, employment, pricing, industry, transportation, and other socioeconomic indicators.

Country Commercial Guide
http://www.state.gov/www/about_state/business/com_guides/1998/europe_canada/latvia98.html
Prepared by the U.S. Embassy in Riga, the site delivers primers on the Latvian economy, political environment, trade regulations and standards, investment climate, trade and project financing, and business travel.

Investment Guide for Latvia
http://www.deloitte.lv/What_new/Guide.htm
Prepared by Deloitte and Touche, the site explains Latvian business organizations, joint-stock companies, accounting and auditing regulations, taxation, and excise duties.

Latvia Country Brief
http://www.worldbank.org/cgi-bin/sendoff.cgi?page=%2Fhtml%2Fextdr%2Foffrep%2Feca%2Flv.htm
A service of the World Bank Group, the site provides Latvian population statistics, financial data, development reports, and economic forecasts.

Latvia InfoExport
http://www.infoexport.gc.ca/country-e.asp?continent=Europe&country=24
A service of Foreign Affairs and International Trade Canada, the site provides fact sheets and statistics on Latvian geography, business, and politics.

Latvia Market Information
http://dtiinfo1.dti.gov.uk/ots/latvia/
A service of the London-based Department of Trade and Industry, the site delivers Latvian fact sheets, maps, and trade-show information.

Latvia Market Access Database
http://mkaccdb.eu.int/mkdb/mkdb.pl?METHOD=COUNTRY
A service of the European Commission, the site offers briefs on Latvian trade policy, tariff barriers, non-tariff barriers, investment-related measures, and financial services regulations.

Latvia Market Research
http://strategis.ic.gc.ca/sc_mrkti/ibinddc/engdoc/1a1b25.html
A service of Industry Canada, the site provides U.S. Department of Commerce reports on Latvian business, politics, trade regulations and standards, investment climate, trade and project financing, business travel, and market opportunities.

Latvia Online
http://www.lda.gov.lv/
Sponsored by the Latvian Development Agency, the site features Latvian investment primers, fact sheets, business guides, statistics, sector profiles, success stories, and project profiles.

Latvian Business Directory
http://www.zl.lv/new1/region-lat.htm
Written in four languages, the site is a searchable directory of Latvian companies. The database is browsable by company name, city, street address, product, and service.

Latvian Chamber of Commerce and Industry
http://sun.lcc.org.lv/
Based in Riga, the Chamber promotes Latvian economic development. The site includes a member directory, event information, project profiles, and business guides.

Latvian Privatization Agency
http://www.lpa.bkc.lv/Lpa02GB.htm
The online service provides a searchable database of privatization opportunities in Latvia. Categories include cattle breeding, construction, food processing, pharmaceuticals, transportation, and wood products.

Welcome to Latvia
http://www.latnet.lv/
A hub of country information, the site delivers fact sheets on Latvian business, communications, transportation, education, science, government, culture, and tourism.

Latvia Trade Assistance

CEEBICnet Latvia
http://www.itaiep.doc.gov/eebic/countryr/latvia.htm
A service of the U.S. Department of Commerce Central and Eastern European Business Information Center, the site delivers Latvian fact sheets, market studies, event information, business and procurement opportunities, and a directory of U.S. companies in Latvia.

Latvia Ministry of Foreign Affairs
http://www.mfa.gov.lv/mfa/pub/public.htm
Written in English and Latvian, the site provides Latvian fact sheets, foreign policy statements, international trade reports, and a directory of Ministry programs and services.

Trade Shows in Latvia
http://www.expoguide.com/shows/data/loc_33.htm
Compiled by Expoguide, the site is a directory of upcoming trade shows in Latvia.

World Trade Center Riga
http://www.iclub.lv/PAGES/WTCR/
A branch of the World Trade Centers Association, the site features Latvian fact sheets, trade leads, economic reports, publication lists, and contact information.

Latvia Representative Offices

Canada

Embassy of Canada in Riga
http://www.dfait-maeci.gc.ca/english/missions/
rep-can3e.htm#latvia
The site provides contact information for the Canadian Embassy in Riga.

Denmark

Embassy of Denmark in Riga
http://vip.latnet.lv/amdkriga/
Featuring a message from the Ambassador, the site provides Danish fact sheets, visa and passport information, business guides, cultural primers, and a directory of Embassy staff and services.

Germany

German Chamber of Commerce in Riga
http://www.ahk.net/en/lv/Riga/
The site lists the Chairperson, Chief Executive Officer, street address, phone and fax numbers, office hours, and e-mail link of the German Chamber in Riga.

Finland

Finland Trade Center in Riga
http://www.exports.finland.fi/tradecen.htm
The site lists the staff, street address, phone and fax numbers, and e-mail link of the Finland Trade Center in Riga.

United Kingdom

Embassy of Britain in Riga
http://www.fco.gov.uk/directory/posts.asp?LV
The site provides contact information for the British Embassy in Riga.

United States

American Chamber of Commerce in Latvia
http://www.amcham.mt.lv/
Based in Riga, the Chamber promotes American-Latvian trade. The site includes a members database, event information, committee directory, and business newsletter.

United States Embassy in Riga
http://www.usis.bkc.lv/
Along with U.S. fact sheets and visa information, the site features Latvian Internet marketing guides, photo galleries, and reports on U.S.-Latvia trade and relations.

Lithuania

Lithuania Media

Lithuania Media
http://www.mediainfo.com/emediajs/specific-geo.htm?region=lithuania
Compiled by Editor and Publisher Interactive, the site is a directory of Latvian newspapers, radio stations, and other media sites online.

Lithuania Market Guides

Advantage Lithuania
http://www.lda.lt/
A service of the Lithuanian Development Agency, the site features Lithuanian investment primers, business guides, economic bulletins, company directories, and event information.

Country Commercial Guide
http://www.state.gov/www/about_state/business/
com_guides/1998/europe_canada/
lithuania98.html
Prepared by the U.S. Embassy in Vilnius, the site delivers primers on the Lithuanian economy, political environment, trade regulations and standards, investment climate, trade and project financing, and business travel.

Lithuania Country Brief
http://www.worldbank.org/cgi-bin/
sendoff.cgi?page=%2Fhtml%2Fextdr%2Foffrep%2
Feca%2Flt.htm
A service of the World Bank Group, the site provides Lithuanian population statistics, financial data, development reports, and economic forecasts.

Lithuania InfoExport
http://www.infoexport.gc.ca/country-
e.asp?continent=Europe&country=26
A service of Foreign Affairs and International Trade Canada, the site provides fact sheets and statistics on Lithuanian geography, business and politics.

Lithuania Market Information
http://dtiinfo1.dti.gov.uk/ots/lithuania/
A service of the London-based Department of Trade and Industry, the site delivers Lithuanian fact sheets, maps, and trade-show information.

Lithuania Market Research
http://strategis.ic.gc.ca/sc_mrkti/ibinddc/engdoc/
1a1b27.html
A service of Industry Canada, the site provides U.S. Department of Commerce reports on Lithuanian business, politics, trade regulations and standards, investment climate, trade and project financing, business travel, and market opportunities.

Lithuanian Business Guide
http://www.lbg.lt/
Written in English and Lithuanian, the site is a searchable directory of Lithuanian companies.

Categories include agriculture, computers, construction, food products, medicine, and tourism.

Lithuanian Companies and Organizations
http://www.is.lt/comp_index.html
A searchable database of Lithuanian firms, the site is browsable by organization name, city, street address, type of company, and year of establishment.

Lithuanian Department of Statistics
http://www.std.lt/
Posted in English and Lithuanian, the site provides contact information, publication lists, and selected Lithuanian socioeconomic statistics.

Lithuanian Patent Office
http://vytautas.is.lt/vpb/engl/
Based in Vilnius, the site provides information on Lithuanian patents, trademarks, industrial designs, and other intellectual property.

Lithuania Trade Assistance

CEEBICnet Lithuania
*http://www.itaiep.doc.gov/eebic/countryr/
lithuani.htm*
A service of the U.S. Department of Commerce Central and Eastern European Business Information Center, the site delivers Lithuanian fact sheets, market studies, event information, business and procurement opportunities, and a directory of U.S. companies in Lithuania.

Customs Tariffs of Lithuania
http://www.ekm.lt/MUITAI/EMUITAI.htm
Posted in English and Lithuanian, the site is a database of Lithuanian duty rates and custom regulations. The service is searchable by keyword and harmonized system code number.

Lithuania Customs Department
http://www.cust.lt/noframe/title.html
The site provides information on Lithuanian customs activities, tariffs, laws, international conventions, antidumping and countervailing duties, and intellectual property rights.

Lithuanian Development Agency Export Department
http://www.lda.lt/home/Exp_d.htm
The site lists the Director, mission statement, street address, phone and fax numbers, and e-mail link of the Lithuanian Export Department in Vilnius.

Trade Shows in Lithuania
_http://www.expoguide.com/shows/data/loc_35.htm_
Compiled by Expoguide, the site is a directory of upcoming trade shows in Lithuania.

Lithuania Representative Offices

Canada

Embassy of Canada in Vilnius
http://www.dfait-maeci.gc.ca/english/missions/
rep-can3e.htm#lithuania
The site provides contact information for the Canadian Embassy in Vilnius.

Finland

Embassy of Finland in Vilnius
http://www.finland.lt/
The virtual Embassy provides Finnish fact sheets, business guides, visa and passport information, press releases, socioeconomic statistics, and a directory of Embassy personnel.

Finland Trade Center in Vilnius
http://www.exports.finland.fi/tradecen.htm
The site lists the staff, street address, phone and fax numbers, and e-mail link of the Finland Trade Center in Vilnius.

Germany

German Chamber of Commerce in Vilnius
http://www.ahk.net/en/lt/Vilnius/
The site lists the Chief Executive Officer, street address, phone and fax numbers, and e-mail link of the German Chamber in Vilnius.

Latvia

Embassy of Latvia in Vilnius
http://www.parks.lv/home/latvijos-ambasada/
Along with fact sheets and business guides, the site features Latvian press releases, visa and passport information, political reports, and government directories.

Sweden

Embassy of Sweden in Vilnius
_http://www.ud.se/english/mfa/ambassad/
litauen.htm_
The site provides contact information for the Swedish Embassy in Vilnius.

United Kingdom

Embassy of Britain in Vilnius
http://www.fco.gov.uk/directory/posts.asp?LT
The site provides contact information for the British Embassy in Vilnius.

Macedonia

Macedonia Media

Macedonia Media
http://www.mediainfo.com/emediajs/specific-
geo.htm?region=macedonia
Compiled by Editor and Publisher Interactive, the site is a directory of Macedonian newspapers and media sites online.

Macedonia Market Guides

Macedonia Market Research
http://strategis.ic.gc.ca/sc_mrkti/ibinddc/engdoc/
1a1b29.html
Posted by Industry Canada, the site provides U.S. Central Intelligence Agency fact sheets on Macedonian geography, people, government, economy, communications, and transportation.

Macedonia Ministry of the Economy
_http://www.gov.mk/en/governme/economy/
e_min.htm_
Along with sector profiles and tourism information, the site offers Macedonian fact sheets, legal primers, economic statistics, business guides, and government directories.

Macedonian Government
http://www.gov.mk/en/governme/index.html
A directory of Macedonian government resources online, the site profiles Macedonian ministries, institutes, agencies, legislation, leading executives, and national symbols.

Macedonian Privatization Agency
http://www.mpa.org.mk/
A virtual investment primer, the site provides Macedonian fact sheets, privatization reports, business guides, partnership opportunities, company profiles, and legal tutorials.

Republic of Macedonia
http://www.soros.org.mk/mk/en/
A service of the Soros Foundations Network, the site delivers Macedonian maps, fact sheets, history lessons, cultural primers, city profiles, and privatization reports.

Virtual Macedonia Network
http://www.vmacedonia.com/index2.html
A hub of country information, the site features modules on Macedonian business, education, science and technology, people, history, politics, travel, health, and media.

Macedonia Trade Assistance

CEEBICnet Macedonia
http://www.itaiep.doc.gov/eebic/countryr/fyrm.htm
A service of the U.S. Department of Commerce Central and Eastern European Business Information Center, the site delivers Macedonian fact sheets, market studies, event information, and business and procurement opportunities.

Macdonia Ministry of Foreign Affairs
http://www.mnr.gov.mk/
The site provides the mission statement, street address, phone and fax numbers, office hours, and e-mail link of the Macedonia Ministry of Foreign Affairs.

Macedonia Representative Offices

United Kingdom

Embassy of Britain in Skopje
http://www.fco.gov.uk/directory/posts.asp?MA
The site provides contact information for the British Embassy in Skopje.

Moldova

Moldova Market Guides

Catalog Moldova
http://www.moldova.net/english/
A directory of Moldovan resources online, the site is divided into 12 categories including politics and government, business and finance, and shopping.

Internet in Moldova
http://www.bnm.org/link/english/sites.htm
A directory of Moldovan resources online, the site is divided into 12 categories including media, education, banks, business, culture and art, computers, international organizations, and tourism.

Moldova Business and Finance
http://www.moldova.net/english/bf/index.jsp
The site is a searchable database of Moldovan companies in 16 categories including banks and finance, electronics, telecommunications, and transportation.

Moldova Country Brief
http://www.worldbank.org/cgi-bin/ sendoff.cgi?page=%2Fhtml%2Fextdr%2Foffrep%2 Feca%2Fmd.htm
A service of the World Bank Group, the site provides Moldovan population statistics, financial data, development reports, and economic forecasts.

Moldova: A Country Study
http://lcweb2.loc.gov/frd/cs/mdtoc.html
A service of the U.S. Library of Congress, the site delivers fact sheets on Moldovan geography, population, agriculture, mining, manufacturing, and foreign economic relations.

Moldova Market Research
http://strategis.ic.gc.ca/sc_mrkti/ibinddc/engdoc/ 1a1b31.html
Posted by Industry Canada, the site provides U.S. Central Intelligence Agency fact sheets on Moldovan geography, people, government, economy, communications, and transportation.

Moldova Ministry of Agriculture
http://www.camib.com/
Written in English and Moldovan, the site features Moldovan agricultural news, market reports, project profiles, company directories, business opportunities, and publication lists.

National Bank of Moldova
http://www.bnm.org/
Along with news on Moldovan balance of payments, foreign trade, and exchange rates, the Chisinau-based site provides Bank news, event information, and annual reports.

Virtual Moldova
http://www.info.polymtl.ca/Moldova/
A hub of country information, the site features Moldovan maps, news, photo galleries, political reports, city profiles, and online discussion groups.

Moldova Trade Assistance

Free Enterprise Zone
http://www.moldova-freezone.com/zone_e.html
Established in 1995, the Free Enterprise Zone consists of four special economic development areas in the Moldovan capital city, Chisinau. The site provides fact sheets on Zone regulations, management, and projects.

Moldova Representative Offices

United States

American Chamber of Commerce in Moldova
http://www.mldnet.com/amcham/ldova
Based in Chisinau, the Chamber promotes U.S.-Moldova trade. The site provides a mission statement, committee directory, executive roster, and contact information.

United States Embassy in Chisinau
http://usis.moldnet.md/
Posted in English, Romanian, and Russian, the site provides U.S. news, press releases, speeches, electronic journals, and reports on U.S.-Moldova trade and relations.

Poland

Poland Search Tools

Polish Home Page
http://plwww.fuw.edu.pl/index.eng.html
Written in English and Polish, the site provides a searchable index of Polish news, economic reports, company profiles, cultural guides, history lessons, and online resources.

Poland Media

Poland Media
http://www.mediainfo.com/emediajs/specific-geo.htm?region=poland
Compiled by Editor and Publisher Interactive, the site is a directory of Polish media sites online.

Warsaw Voice
http://www.warsawvoice.com.pl/Pl-iso/index.html
An English-language weekly online newspaper, the site is divided into seven sections including business, communities, people, society, and opinion.

Poland Market Guides

Barclays Country Report: Poland
http://www.offshorebanking.barclays.com/services/economic/yearly/polmar98/contents.html
Prepared by Barclays Bank, the site reports on Polish economic trends, politics, monetary and fiscal policy, international trade, and U.K.-Poland merchandise trade and investment flows.

Business Polska
http://www.polska.net/
An online guide to Polish business, the site features Polish economic news, company profiles, market studies, sector profiles, investment primers, and trade leads.

Country Commercial Guide
http://www.state.gov/www/about_state/business/com_guides/1998/europe_canada/poland98.html
Prepared by the U.S. Embassy in Warsaw, the site delivers primers on Polish business, politics, trade regulations and standards, investment climate, trade and project financing, and business travel.

Doing Business in Poland
http://www.abcnews.com/sections/travel/DailyNews/biztrav1218.html
A service of ABC News, the site provides Polish maps, business tips, travel information, socioeconomic statistics, and economic reports.

Media and Marketing Poland
http://www.media.com.pl/
Updated daily, the site is a Polish media and marketing electronic magazine. The service includes news, market studies, advertising reviews, and employment opportunities.

Municipal Development Agency
http://www.ark.com.pl/ark/indexe.htm
Based in Warsaw, the Agency develops Polish infrastructure projects. The site includes a mission statement, news, project profiles, and program directories.

Poland: Big Emerging Markets Home Page
http://www.ita.doc.gov/bems/Poland.html
Developed by the U.S. Department of Commerce, the site delivers Polish fact sheets, economic forecasts, export and import statistics, sector profiles, and international trade guides.

Office of Public Procurement
http://www.uzp.gov.pl/a_index.html
The Office provides information on Polish government procurement. The site includes procurement laws, bulletins, and business opportunities.

Official Website of Poland
http://poland.pl/
A hub of country information, the site provides fact sheets on Polish business, government, culture, art, science and education, tourism, and health.

Poland Business Briefs
http://www.austrade.gov.au/IOOM/Poland/
A service of Austrade, the site offers fact sheets on Polish business etiquette, foreign investment, corporate taxation, marketing, and visas.

Poland Country Brief
http://www.worldbank.org/cgi-bin/
sendoff.cgi?page=%2Fhtml%2Fextdr%2Foffrep%2
Feca%2Fpl.htm
A service of the World Bank Group, the site provides Polish population statistics, financial data, development reports, and economic forecasts.

Poland Country Profile
http://www.tradenz.govt.nz/intelligence/profiles/
poland.html
A service of the New Zealand Trade Development Board, the site provides Polish economic statistics, market information, and business tips.

Poland Country Report
http://www.state.gov/www/issues/economic/
trade_reports/europe_canada97/poland97.html
Prepared by the U.S. Department of State, the site delivers information on Polish exchange rates, debt management, trade barriers, and intellectual property protection.

Poland: A Country Study
http://lcweb2.loc.gov/frd/cs/pltoc.html
A service of the U.S. Library of Congress, the site delivers fact sheets on Polish geography, population, agriculture, mining, manufacturing, and foreign economic relations.

Poland InfoExport
http://www.infoexport.gc.ca/country-
e.asp?continent=Europe&country=34
A service of Foreign Affairs and International Trade Canada, the site provides Polish commercial guides and market reports.

Poland Market Access Database
http://mkaccdb.eu.int/mkdb/
mkdb.pl?METHOD=COUNTRY
A service of the European Commission, the site offers briefs on Polish trade policy, tariff barriers, non-tariff barriers, investment-related measures, and financial services regulations.

Poland Market Information
http://dtiinfo1.dti.gov.uk/ots/poland/
A service of the London-based Department of Trade and Industry, the site delivers Polish fact sheets, maps, and trade-show information.

Poland Market Research
http://strategis.ic.gc.ca/sc_mrkti/ibinddc/engdoc/
1a1b35.html
A service of Industry Canada, the site provides U.S. Department of Commerce reports on Polish business, politics, trade regulations and standards, investment climate, trade and project financing, business travel, and market opportunities.

Poland Master Page
http://www.masterpage.com.pl/
Updated daily, the site delivers Polish fact sheets, economic reports, trade leads, travel information, telephone directories, investment guides, and mailing lists.

Poland Now!
http://sarnow.com/poland/BUSINESS/
A virtual library of Polish business information, the site delivers fact sheets on Polish government, taxation, currency rates, companies, trade shows, cities, and media.

Poland '98
http://bmb.ippt.gov.pl/MainFrameE.dbi
Developed by BMB Promotions, the site offers Polish maps, provincial profiles, business guides, travel information, and a searchable directory of Polish companies.

Polish Agency for Foreign Investment
http://www.paiz.gov.pl/frames.htm
Based in Warsaw, the Agency promotes international investment in Poland. The site includes Polish fact sheets, business guides, sector profiles, economic reports, and socioeconomic statistics.

Polish Business Directory
http://www.polish-bus.com/anghome.html
A searchable directory of Polish companies, the site profiles firms in over 30 categories including agriculture, automotive, computers, education, electronics, media, and real estate.

Polish Market Review
http://www.polishmarket.com/
An English-language electronic magazine, the site features Polish economic news, investment

guides, global trade reports, regional profiles, and international comparisons.

Pol-Net
http://www.pol-net.com/inveng.html
A directory of Polish business resources online, the site is divided into four categories: business opportunities, finance, employment, and politics.

Promotion of Poland
http://www.kprm.gov.pl/polska/indexrp.html
A portal of country information, the site delivers fact sheets on Polish business, finance, history, investment, culture, education, agriculture, technology, and tourism.

Poland Trade Assistance

CEEBICnet Poland
http://www.itaiep.doc.gov/eebic/countryr/poland.htm
A service of the U.S. Department of Commerce Central and Eastern European Business Information Center, the site delivers Polish fact sheets, market studies, event information, business and procurement opportunities, and a directory of U.S. companies in Poland.

International Trade Companies in Poland
http://poland.pl/economy/trade.html
A directory of Polish exporters and importers, the site profiles firms in over ten industries including agri-food, electronics, publishing, pharmaceuticals, and automotive.

Trade Shows in Poland
http://www.expoguide.com/shows/data/loc_47.htm
Compiled by Expoguide, the site is a directory of upcoming trade shows in Poland.

Poland Representative Offices

Australia

Austrade in Warsaw
http://www.austrade.gov.au/warsaw/
An online export promotion service, the site features Australian business guides, investment primers, publication lists, contact information, and Polish marketing tips.

Austria

Austrian Trade Commission in Krakow
http://aw.wk.or.at/awo/ahst-krakau.htm

The site lists the staff, street address, phone and fax numbers, e-mail link, and office hours of the Austrian Trade Commission in Krakow.

Austrian Trade Commission in Warsaw
http://aw.wk.or.at/awo/ahst-warschau.htm
The site lists the staff, street address, phone and fax numbers, e-mail link, and office hours of the Austrian Trade Commission in Warsaw.

Canada

Embassy of Canada in Warsaw
http://www.dfait-maeci.gc.ca/english/missions/rep-can3e.htm#poland
The site provides contact information for the Canadian Embassy in Warsaw.

Finland

Finland Trade Center in Warsaw
http://www.exports.finland.fi/tradecen.htm
The site lists the staff, street address, phone and fax numbers, and e-mail link of the Finland Trade Center in Warsaw.

France

French Trade Commission in Warsaw
http://www.dree.org/pologne/
Written in French, the site provides Polish market reports, sector profiles, contact information, and a directory of export programs for French companies doing business in Poland.

Germany

German Chamber of Commerce in Warsaw
http://www.ahk.net/en/pl/Warszawa/
The site lists the Chairpersons, Chief Executive Officer, street address, phone and fax numbers, e-mail link, and office hours of the German Chamber in Warsaw.

India

Indian Commercial Mission in Warsaw
http://www.nic.in/commin/ICM.HTM
The site lists the street address, and phone and fax numbers of the Indian Commercial Mission in Warsaw.

Ireland

Enterprise Ireland in Warsaw
http://www.irish-trade.ie/office_network/
office_locate01.html#anchor1419496
The site lists the Manager, street address, and phone and fax numbers of the Enterprise Ireland office in Warsaw.

Italy

Italian Trade Commission in Warsaw
http://www.medianet.com.pl/~icevar/
Written in English, Italian, and Polish, the site features Italian news, fact sheets, Polish business guides, and reports on Italian-Poland trade and relations.

Laos

Embassy of Laos in Warsaw
http://www.laoembassy.com/news/
embassyabroad.htm
The site provides contact information for the Embassy of Laos in Warsaw.

Malaysia

Embassy of Malaysia in Warsaw
http://www.mnet.com.my/klonline/www/missions/
malmiss/mpoland.htm
The site provides contact information for the Malaysian Embassy in Warsaw.

New Zealand

Trade New Zealand in Warsaw
http://www.tradenz.govt.nz/contact/europe.html
An export promotion service, the site provides contact information for the Trade New Zealand office in Warsaw.

Norway

Norwegian Trade Council in Warsaw
http://www.ntc.no/cgi-bin/wbch.exe?html=../
templates/utekontor2.html&profile=1136
The site lists the staff, street address, phone and fax numbers, and e-mail link of the Norwegian Trade Council in Warsaw.

Portugal

Portuguese Trade and Investment Office in Warsaw
http://www.portugal.org/geninfo/abouticep/
poland.html
The site lists the staff, street address, and phone and fax numbers of the Portuguese Trade and Investment Office in Warsaw.

Spain

Spanish Commercial Office in Warsaw
http://www.icex.es/openURL.html#openURL=/
english/infoproyem/ofcomes/ofcomes.html#EU
The site lists the staff, street address, phone and fax numbers, and e-mail link of the Spanish Commercial Office in Warsaw.

Sweden

Embassy of Sweden in Warsaw
*http://www.ud.se/english/mfa/ambassad/
polen.htm*
The site provides contact information for the Swedish Embassy in Warsaw.

Switzlerland

Swiss Chamber of Commerce in Warsaw
http://swisstrade.com/
xicodes2.asp?P1=3&lvl=3&cid=A13
The site lists the street address, phone and fax numbers, and e-mail link of the Swiss Chamber of Commerce in Warsaw.

Taiwan

China External Trade Development Council Office in Warsaw
*http://www.cetra.org.tw/english/o_office/
indexset.htm*
A Taiwanese trade promotion service, the site lists the mission statement and e-mail link of the China External Trade Development Council Office in Warsaw.

Taiwan Government Information Office in Warsaw
http://www.gio.gov.tw/info/ngio/pol-f.html
Posted in Chinese and English, the site lists the street address, phone and fax numbers, and e-mail link of the Taiwan Government Information Office in Warsaw.

Thailand

Royal Thai Embassy in Warsaw
http://www.mfa.go.th/Embassy/detail/69.htm
The site lists the Ambassador, street address,

and phone and fax numbers of the Thai Embassy in Warsaw.

Thailand Office of Commercial Affairs in Warsaw
http://www.thaitrade.com/thcoaf.html
The site lists the street address, phone and fax numbers, and e-mail link of the Thailand Office of Commercial Affairs in Warsaw.

United Kingdom

British Embassy in Warsaw
http://www.britemb.it.pl/britemb/pierwsza.htm
Posted in Polish, the site provides British fact sheets, business guides, visa and passport information, and a directory of consular and commercial services.

British Chamber of Commerce in Poland
http://www.bccp.org.pl/
Based in Warsaw, the Chamber promotes British-Polish trade. The site includes a bi-monthly electronic magazine, calendar of events, member directory, and committee roster.

Consulate of Britain in Gdansk
http://www.fco.gov.uk/directory/posts.asp?PL
The site provides contact information for the British Consulate in Gdansk.

United States

American Chamber of Commerce in Poland
http://www.amcham.net/
Based in Warsaw, the Chamber promotes U.S.-Polish trade. The site features Chamber news, Polish economic reports, and a directory of over 300 American companies in the Polish market.

State of Illinois Trade Office in Warsaw
http://www.commerce.state.il.us/dcca/files/int'l/poland.htm
A service of the Illinois Department of Commerce and Community Affairs, the site lists the Managing Director, street address, phone and fax numbers, and e-mail link of the Illinois Trade Office in Warsaw.

United States Embassy in Warsaw
http://www.usaemb.pl/
The virtual Embassy provides U.S. news, fact sheets, press releases, electronic journals, Polish business guides, and a directory of consular and commercial services.

United States Information Service in Krakow
http://www.polished.net/usis/index.stm
The site provides U.S. news, press releases, fact sheets, cultural bulletins, teaching guides, socioeconomic statistics, and a directory of U.S.-Polish educational and exchange programs in Krakow.

Romania

Romania Media

Romania Media
http://www.mediainfo.com/emediajs/specific-geo.htm?region=romania
Developed by Editor and Publisher Interactive, the site is a directory of Romanian media sites online.

Romania Market Guides

Chamber of Commerce and Industry of Romania
http://www.ccir.ro/
Based in Bucharest, the Chamber promotes economic development in Romania. The site features Romanian fact sheets, business news, event information, trade leads, and business opportunities.

Invest in Romania
http://www.embassy.org/romania/economic/ir-index.htm
A service of the Romanian Embassy in Washington, D.C., the site delivers fact sheets on Romanian business organizations, international investment, taxation, banking, finance, labor relations, and accounting.

Romania Business Briefs
http://www.austrade.gov.au/IOOM/Romania/
A service of Austrade, the site offers fact sheets on Romanian culture, business etiquette, marketing, transportation, travel, and visas.

Romania Business Economics
http://www.romaniabusiness.com/
The online service delivers Romanian news, economic reports, business guides, investment primers, company profiles, travel information, and government directories.

Romania Country Brief
http://www.worldbank.org/cgi-bin/sendoff.cgi?page=%2Fhtml%2Fextdr%2Foffrep%2Feca%2Fro.htm

A service of the World Bank Group, the site provides Romanian population statistics, financial data, development reports, and economic forecasts.

Romania Country Report

http://www.state.gov/www/issues/economic/ trade_reports/europe_canada97/romania97.html Prepared by the U.S. Department of State, the site delivers information on Romanian exchange rates, debt management, trade barriers, and intellectual property protection.

Romania: A Country Study

http://lcweb2.loc.gov/frd/cs/rotoc.html A service of the U.S. Library of Congress, the site delivers fact sheets on Romanian geography, population, agriculture, mining, manufacturing, and foreign economic relations.

Romania Market Access Database

http://mkaccdb.eu.int/mkdb/ mkdb.pl?METHOD=COUNTRY A service of the European Commission, the site offers briefs on Romanian trade policy, tariff barriers, non-tariff barriers, investment-related measures, and financial services regulations.

Romania Market Information

http://dtiinfo1.dti.gov.uk/ots/romania/ A service of the London-based Department of Trade and Industry, the site delivers Romanian fact sheets, maps, and trade-show information.

Romania Market Research

http://strategis.ic.gc.ca/sc_mrkti/ibinddc/engdoc/ 1a1b37.html A service of Industry Canada, the site provides U.S. Department of Commerce reports on Romanian business, politics, trade regulations and standards, investment climate, trade and project financing, business travel, and market opportunities.

Romania Office for Inventions and Trademarks

http://www.osim.ro/ Written in English and Romanian, the site offers information on Romanian inventions, patents, trademarks, industrial designs, and other intellectual property.

Romania State Ownership Fund

http://www.sof-romania.com/ A guide to privatization in Romania, the site

features investment primers, news, legal information, auction reports, and a directory of companies for sale.

Romanian Companies on the Web

http://www.embassy.org/romania/economic/ trademan.html A service of the Romanian Embassy in Washington, D.C., the site is a directory of Romanian firms online. Categories include automotive, agri-food, apparel, and machinery.

Virtual Romania

http://www.info.polymtl.ca/zuse/tavi/www/ Romania.html A hub of country information, the site features Romanian news, fact sheets, business guides, cultural primers, travel information, and online discussion groups.

Romania Trade Assistance

Breaking Trade and Economic News

http://www.embassy.org/romania/economic/ econ0.html Updated monthly, the site provides the latest Romanian business news. The service includes sector studies, economic reports, company profiles, and event information.

CEEBICnet Romania

http://www.itaiep.doc.gov/eebic/countryr/ romania.htm A service of the U.S. Department of Commerce Central and Eastern European Business Information Center, the site delivers Romanian fact sheets, market studies, event information, business and procurement opportunities, and a directory of U.S. companies in Romania.

Romania Trade and Economy

http://www.embassy.org/romania/economic/ economic.html A directory of Romanian business resources online, the site is divided into seven categories including government, chambers of commerce, banks, companies, and economic media.

Trade Shows in Romania

http://www.expoguide.com/shows/data/loc_49.htm Compiled by Expoguide, the site is a directory of upcoming trade shows in Romania.

Romania Representative Offices

Armenia

Embassy of Armenia in Bucharest
http://www.armeniaemb.org/forrel/embas2.htm
The site provides contact information for the
Armenian Embassy in Bucharest.

Austria

Austria Trade Commission in Bucharest
http://aw.wk.or.at/awo/ahst-bukarest.htm
The site lists the staff, street address, phone and
fax numbers, e-mail link, and office hours of the
Austrian Trade Commission in Bucharest.

Canada

Embassy of Canada in Bucharest
*http://www.dfait-maeci.gc.ca/english/missions/rep-
can4e.htm#romania*
The site provides contact information for the
Canadian Embassy in Bucharest.

Finland

Finland Trade Center in Bucharest
http://www.exports.finland.fi/tradecen.htm
The site lists the staff, street address, and phone
and fax numbers of the Finland Trade Center in
Bucharest.

France

French Trade Commission in Bucharest
http://www.dree.org/roumanie/
Written in French, the site provides Romanian
market reports, sector profiles, contact information, and a directory of export programs for French
companies doing business in Romania.

Germany

German Chamber of Commerce in Bucharest
http://www.ahk.net/en/ro/Bucarest/
The site lists the Chief Executive Officer, street
address, phone and fax numbers, e-mail link,
and office hours of the German Chamber in
Bucharest.

India

Indian Commercial Mission in Bucharest
http://www.nic.in/commin/ICM.HTM

The site lists the street address, phone and fax
numbers, and e-mail link of the Indian Commercial Mission in Bucharest.

Italy

Italian Trade Commission in Bucharest
http://www.ice.it/estero/bucarest/
Written in Italian, the site delivers Italian fact
sheets, business guides, event information,
press releases, statistics, and reports on Italian-
Romanian trade and relations.

Malaysia

Embassy of Malaysia in Bucharest
*http://www.mnet.com.my/klonline/www/missions/
malmiss/mromania.htm*
The site provides contact information for the
Malaysian Embassy in Bucharest.

Mexico

Embassy of Mexico in Bucharest
*http://www.inf.fu-berlin.de:80/~mexico/rum/
rum1.htm*
Written in Spanish, the site features Mexican fact
sheets, investment guides, government directories, and reports on Mexican-Romanian trade
and relations.

Pakistan

Pakistan Trade Office in Bucharest
http://www.jamal.com/epb/ptoa.htm
The site provides contact information for the
Pakistan Trade Office in Bucharest.

Portugal

Portuguese Trade and Investment Office in Bucharest
*http://www.portugal.org/geninfo/abouticep/
bucareste.html*
The site lists the staff, street address, phone and
fax numbers, and e-mail link of the Portuguese
Trade and Investment Office in Bucharest.

Spain

Spanish Commercial Office in Bucharest
*http://www.icex.es/openURL.html#openURL=/
english/infoproyem/ofcomes/ofcomes.html#EU*
The site lists the staff, street address, phone and
fax numbers, and e-mail link of the Spanish
Commercial Office in Bucharest.

Sweden

Embassy of Sweden in Bucharest
http://www.ud.se/english/mfa/ambassad/
rumanien.htm
The site provides contact information for the
Swedish Embassy in Bucharest.

Thailand

Royal Thai Embassy in Bucharest
http://www.mfa.go.th/Embassy/detail/57.htm
The site lists the Ambassador, street address,
and phone and fax numbers of the Thai Embassy
in Bucharest.

United Kingdom

Embassy of Britain in Bucharest
http://www.fco.gov.uk/directory/posts.asp?RO
The site provides contact information for the
British Embassy in Bucharest.

United States

United States Embassy in Bucharest
http://usis.kappa.ro/BEmbassy.html
The virtual Embassy provides U.S. news, fact
sheets, visa and passport information, and a
directory of U.S. Agency for International Development programs in Romania.

U.S. Information Service Bucharest
http://usis.kappa.ro/USIS/BUSIS.html
The site provides U.S. news, press releases, fact
sheets, cultural bulletins, teaching guides,
socioeconomic statistics, Fulbright scholarship
information, and a directory of U.S. assistance
programs in Romania.

Venezuela

Embassy of Venezuela in Bucharest
http://www.trade-venezuela.com/EMBVENG.HTM
The site lists the street address, phone and fax
numbers, and e-mail link of the Venezuelan
Embassy in Bucharest.

Russia

Russia Media

Russia Media
http://www.mediainfo.com/emediajs/specific-
geo.htm?region=russia

Developed by Editor and Publisher Interactive, the
site is a directory of Russian media sites online.

Russia Today
http://www.russiatoday.com/
A service of the European Internet Network, the
site provides Russian news, business reports,
editorials, polls, classifieds, shopping guides,
and online discussion groups.

Russian Story
http://www.russianstory.com/
A directory of Russian newspapers and magazines online, the site is divided into six categories: government and society, business and
economy, culture and arts, science and education, and entertainment and family.

Russia Market Guides

Barclays Country Report: Russia
http://www.offshorebanking.barclays.com/
services/economic/yearly/rusnov97/rusconts.html
Prepared by Barclays Bank, the site reports on
Russian trends, politics, monetary and fiscal
policy, international trade, and U.K.-Russia
merchandise trade and investment flows.

Business Collaboration Center
http://www.cbi.co.ru/
A virtual library of Russian business information,
the site features Russian news, fact sheets,
investment guides, event information, legislative
reviews, and tax primers.

Country Commercial Guide
http://www.state.gov/www/about_state/business/
com_guides/1998/russia_nis/russia98.html
Prepared by the U.S. Embassy in Moscow, the
site delivers primers on the Russian economy,
political environment, trade regulations and
standards, investment climate, trade and project
financing, and business travel.

Gosincor
http://www.gosincor.ru/engl/invite.htm
A state agency based in Moscow, Gosincor
promotes international investment in Russia. The
site provides a mission statement, contact
information, and a directory of investment
opportunities in over 20 industries including agri-
food, electronics, and automotive.

G7 Support Implementation Group
http://www.g7sig.org/
Established by the G7, the Group provides
economic assistance to Russia. The site

includes the Donor Assistance Database, a directory of some 6,000 projects in Russia funded by international agencies and organizations around the world.

InfoArt Computer News

http://www.infoart.ru/it/news/engnews/index.htm
An English-language e-zine, the site covers the Russian information technology industry. The service includes company profiles, product reviews, and Internet reports.

Maximov Online

http://www.maximov.com/index.shtml
A hub of information on Russia and the Newly Independent States, the site features business news, regional profiles, employment opportunities, and publication lists.

REElweb Employment and Funding Opportunities

http://www.indiana.edu/~reeiweb/indemp.html
Developed by Indiana University, the site is a directory of employment, internship, and funding opportunities in Russia and the Newly Independent States.

Ria Novosti

http://www.ria-novosti.com/index.html
Posted in English and Russian, the subscription site provides Russian privatization reports, economic forecasts, company profiles, and business statistics.

Rusline

http://www.rusline.com/
An index of Russian resources online, the site is divided into 16 categories including business and industrial directories, employment opportunities, and finance and investment.

Russia Business Briefs

http://www.austrade.gov.au/IOOM/RussiaCIS/
A service of Austrade, the site offers fact sheets on Russian business etiquette, foreign investment, corporate taxation, marketing, and visas.

Russia/CIS Company Directory

http://www.publications-etc.com/russia/business/directory.html
A searchable directory of Russian companies and business opportunities, the site is divided into some 20 categories including telecommunications, shipping, travel services, and capital goods.

Russia Country Brief

http://www.worldbank.org/cgi-bin/sendoff.cgi?page=%2Fhtml%2Fextdr%2Foffrep%2Feca%2Fru.htm
A service of the World Bank Group, the site provides Russian population statistics, financial data, development reports, and economic forecasts.

Russia Country Report

http://www.state.gov/www/issues/economic/trade_reports/russia_nis97/russia97.html
Prepared by the U.S. Department of State, the site delivers information on Russian exchange rates, debt management, trade barriers, and intellectual property protection.

Russia: A Country Study

http://lcweb2.loc.gov/frd/cs/sutoc.html
A service of the U.S. Library of Congress, the site delivers fact sheets on Russian geography, population, agriculture, mining, manufacturing, and foreign economic relations.

Russia InfoExport

http://www.infoexport.gc.ca/country-e.asp?continent=Europe&country=51
A service of Foreign Affairs and International Trade Canada, the site provides Russian commercial guides and market reports.

Russia Market Access Database

http://mkaccdb.eu.int/mkdb/mkdb.pl?METHOD=COUNTRY
A service of the European Commission, the site offers briefs on Russian trade policy, tariff barriers, non-tariff barriers, investment-related measures, and financial services regulations.

Russia Market Information

http://dtiinfo1.dti.gov.uk/ots/russia/
A service of the London-based Department of Trade and Industry, the site delivers Russian fact sheets, maps, and trade-show information.

Russia Market Research

http://strategis.ic.gc.ca/sc_mrkti/ibinddc/engdoc/1a1b38.html
A service of Industry Canada, the site provides U.S. Department of Commerce reports on Russian business, politics, trade regulations and standards, investment climate, trade and project financing, business travel, and market opportunities.

Russia Net

http://www.russia.net/index.html

Posted in English and Russian, the site offers Russian news, business guides, travel information, cultural bulletins, political updates, history lessons, and an online classifieds.

Russia At Your Fingertips

http://www.publications-etc.com/russia/

A service of the Russian Business and Trade Connections monthly magazine, the site features Russian business news, discussion papers, regional profiles, event information, and company directories.

Russia on the Web

http://www.valley.net/%7Etransnat/

A searchable directory of Russian resources online, the site is divided into 12 categories including Russia-Western projects, business and economy, information and news, education, and culture and art.

Russian Business Law Journal

http://www.spb.su/rulesreg/index.html

A primer on Russian business law, the site provides fact sheets on Russian export regulations, custom tariff rates, listing requirements, and government trade controls.

Russian Company News

http://www.russia-bca.com/

Updated weekly, the site delivers Russian industry news and company profiles. Topics include banking and finance, fuel and energy, metallurgy and mining, and engineering.

Russian Economy: Trends and Perspectives

http://www.online.ru/sp/iet/trends/index.html

A monthly e-zine on the Russian economy, the site provides economic forecasts, budget statements, sub-federal and municipal fiscal reports, and investment bulletins.

Russian Market Weekly Report

http://www.rmg.ru/weekly.html

A service of Rye, Man & Gor Securities, the site delivers weekly updates on Russian business and politics. The service includes a news archive dating back one year.

Russian Far East Update

http://www.russianfareast.com/

Based in Seattle, the subscription site provides Russian business news, sector profiles, and event information. A free sample issue is available with registration.

Russia Trade Assistance

Russia Import-Export Trade Board

http://www.russia-trade.com/

A directory of Russian trade opportunities, the site features buy and sell offers in dozens of categories including machinery, construction, and pharmaceuticals.

Russia Trade Point

http://informves.asn.ru/~tp/

Part of the United Nations Global Trade Point Network, the site provides Russia trade leads, market bulletins, and contact information.

Russian Business and Trade Connections

http://www.publications-etc.com/russia/business/

Updated monthly, the electronic magazine delivers Russian business news, sector profiles, company reports, event information, investment primers, and executive profiles.

Russian Ministry of Foreign Affairs

http://www.diplomat.ru/english/index.html

Posted in English and Russian, the site provides fact sheets on the Ministry, an online discussion forum, and a directory of Russian diplomatic resources online.

Russian Trade Shows

http://www.publications-etc.com/russia/expo/index.html

A browsable directory of Russian trade shows and conferences, the site includes event listings from Belarus, Estonia, Latvia, Turkmenistan, Ukraine, and other Newly Independent States.

St. Petersburg Trade Development Centre

http://tpspb.frinet.org/

Part of the Global Trade Point Network, the site features Russian trade leads, export-import directories, project profiles, and a directory of business opportunities in St. Petersburg.

Shipping Guide to Russia

http://www.itaiep.doc.gov/bisnis/country/ruship.html

Prepared by the U.S. Department of Commerce, the site is a Russian shipping primer. Modules include freight forwarding, export documentation, marking, packing, and customs regulations.

Trade Shows in Russia

http://www.expoguide.com/shows/data/loc_50.htm

Compiled by Expoguide, the site is a directory of upcoming trade shows in Russia.

Tradeinfor
http://www.business.jsc.ru/
Written in Russian, the site provides Russian international trade news, business guides, and investment primers.

Russia Representative Offices

Armenia

Embassy of Armenia in Moscow
http://www.armeniaemb.org/forrel/embas2.htm
The site provides contact information for the Embassy of Armenia in Moscow.

Australia

Austrade in Moscow
http://www.austrade.gov.au/Moscow/
An online export promotion service, the site features Australian fact sheets, investment primers, publication lists, contact information, and Russian business guides.

Austria

Austrian Trade Commission in Moscow
http://aw.wk.or.at/awo/ahst-moskau.htm
The site lists the staff, street address, phone and fax numbers, e-mail link, and office hours of the Austrian Trade Commission in Moscow.

Canada

Consulate General of Canada in St. Petersburg
http://www.dfait-maeci.gc.ca/english/missions/rep-can4e.htm#russia
The site provides contact information for the Canadian Consulate General in St. Petersburg.

Embassy of Canada in Moscow
http://www.dfait-maeci.gc.ca/english/missions/rep-can4e.htm#russia
The site provides contact information for the Canadian Embassy in Moscow.

Chile

Embassy of Chile in Moscow
http://www.chile.sitek.ru/
Written in Russian and Spanish, the site features Chilean fact sheets, visa and passport information, Russian business guides, and reports on Chilean-Russian trade and relations.

China

China Council for the Promotion of International Trade in Moscow
http://www.ccpit.org/engVersion/cp_about/cp_over/cp_over.html
A Chinese export promotion service, the site provides contact information for the China Council for the Promotion of International Trade office in Moscow.

Finland

Embassy of Finland in Moscow
http://www.finemb-moscow.fi/
Posted in English and Russian, the site features Finnish news, fact sheets, press releases, visa and passport information, company directories, and Russian business bulletins.

Finland Trade Center in Moscow
http://www.exports.finland.fi/tradecen.htm
The site lists the staff, street address, phone and fax numbers, and e-mail link of the Finland Trade Center in Moscow.

Finland Trade Center in St. Petersburg
http://www.exports.finland.fi/tradecen.htm
The site lists the staff, street address, phone and fax numbers, and e-mail link of the Finland Trade Center in St. Petersburg.

France

French Trade Commission in Moscow
http://www.co.ru/~peemoscou/peecei/pee_mos.htm
Along with a directory of French commercial officers and their sectoral responsibilities, the site provides Russian market information and business guides.

French Trade Commission in Russia
http://www.dree.org/russie/
Written in French, the site delivers Russian market reports, sector profiles, contact information, and a directory of export programs for French companies doing business in Russia.

French Trade Commission in St. Petersburg
http://www.co.ru/~peemoscou/peecei/pee_stp.htm
The site lists the Commercial Counselor, Assistant Commercial Counselors, street address, and phone and fax numbers of the French Trade Commission in St. Petersburg.

Germany

German Chamber of Commerce in Moscow
http://www.ahk.net/en/ru/Moscow/
The site lists the Chief Executive Officer, street address, phone and fax numbers, e-mail link, and office hours of the German Chamber in Moscow.

German Embassy in Moscow
http://www.Germany.org.ru/
Written in Russian, the site delivers German news, fact sheets, press releases, visa and passport information, Russian business guides, and reports on German-Russian trade and relations.

Ghana

Embassy of Ghana in Moscow
http://www.juntung.com/ghana-consul-hk/2misabo.htm
The site provides contact information for the Ghanaian Embassy in Moscow.

India

Embassy of India in Moscow
http://www.indianembassy.ru/
Posted in Russian, the site provides Indian news, fact sheets, press releases, visa and passport information, Russian business primers, and reports on Indian-Russian trade and relations.

Indonesia

Embassy of Indonesia in Moscow
http://indag.dprin.go.id/INGG/trade/atache.HTM
The site provides contact information for the Indonesian Embassy in Moscow.

Ireland

Enterprise Island in Moscow
http://www.irish-trade.ie/office_network/office_locate01.html#anchor1417621
The site lists the Manager, street address, and phone and fax numbers of the Enterprise Ireland office in Moscow.

Italy

Italian Trade Commission in Moscow
http://www.ice.it/estero/mosca/
Posted in Italian, the site features Italian news, fact sheets, business guides, economic statistics, contact information, and e-mail links to other Italian Trade Commission offices in St. Petersburg and Vladivostok.

Japan

Embassy of Japan in Moscow
http://www.embjapan.ru/
Written in Russian, the site delivers Japanese fact sheets, business guides, reports on Japanese-Russian trade and relations, and a directory of consular and commercial services.

Laos

Embassy of Laos in Moscow
http://www.laoembassy.com/news/embassyabroad.htm
The site provides contact information for the Embassy of Laos in Moscow.

Madagascar

Embassy of Madagascar in Moscow
http://www.madagascar-contacts.com/us/adresse.htm#alext
Along with a directory of Madagascar government agencies, the site provides contact information for the Madagascar Embassy in Moscow.

Malaysia

Embassy of Malaysia in Moscow
http://www.mnet.com.my/klonline/www/missions/malmiss/mrussia1.htm
The site provides contact information for the Malaysian Embassy in Moscow.

Trade Commission of Malaysia in Moscow
http://www.mnet.com.my/klonline/www/missions/malmiss/mrussia2.htm
The site provides contact information for the Malaysian Trade Commission in Moscow.

Namibia

Embassy of Namibia in Moscow
http://www.republicofnamibia.com/adress.htm
Along with a directory of Namibian companies and government agencies, the site provides contact information for the Namibian Embassy in Moscow.

Nepal

Embassy of Nepal in Moscow
http://www.info-nepal.com/members/fips/contacts/
nepalese.html
The site provides contact information for the Embassy of Nepal in Moscow.

Norway

Norwegian Trade Council in Moscow
http://www.ntc.no/cgi-bin/wbch.exe?html=../
templates/utekontor2.html&profile=1120
The site lists the staff, street address, phone and fax numbers, and e-mail link of the Norwegian Trade Council in Moscow.

Norwegian Trade Council in Murmansk
http://www.ntc.no/cgi-bin/wbch.exe?html=../
templates/utekontor2.html&profile=1121
The site lists the staff, street address, phone and fax numbers, and e-mail link of the Norwegian Trade Council in Murmansk.

Norwegian Trade Council in St. Petersburg
http://www.ntc.no/cgi-bin/wbch.exe?html=../
templates/utekontor2.html&profile=1130
The site lists the staff, street address, phone and fax numbers, and e-mail link of the Norwegian Trade Council in St. Petersburg.

Pakistan

Pakistan Trade Office in Moscow
http://www.jamal.com/epb/ptoa.htm
The site provides contact information for the Pakistan Trade Office in Moscow.

Poland

Polish Commercial Office in Moscow
http://www.sbnet.ru/brhmsk/
Written in Russian, the site features Polish fact sheets, visa and passport information, business guides, and reports on Polish-Russian trade and relations.

Portugal

Portuguese Trade and Investment Office in Moscow
http://www.portugal.org/geninfo/abouticep/
russia.html
The site lists the staff, street address, phone and fax numbers, and e-mail link of the Portuguese Trade and Investment Office in Moscow.

Singapore

Embassy of Singapore in Moscow
http://www.gov.sg/mfa/consular/mww_r.htm
The site provides contact information for the Singapore Embassy in Moscow.

South Africa

South Africa Foreign Trade Office in Moscow
http://wwwdti.pwv.gov.za/dtiwww/
foreign_offices.htm
A service of the South Africa Department of Trade and Industry, the site provides contact information for the South Africa Trade Office in Moscow.

Spain

Spanish Commercial Office in Moscow
http://www.icex.es/openURL.html#openURL=/
english/infoproyem/ofcomes/ofcomes.html#EU
The site lists the staff, street address, phone and fax numbers, and e-mail link of the Spanish Commercial Office in Moscow.

Sweden

Consulate General of Sweden in St. Petersburg
http://www.sweden.ru/Konsulstvo.html
Written in Russian, the site lists the staff, street address, phone and fax numbers, e-mail link, office hours, and services of the Swedish Consulate in St. Petersburg.

Embassy of Sweden in Moscow
http://www.sweden.ru/
Posted in English and Russian, the site offers Swedish fact sheets, visa and passport information, cultural bulletins, and reports on Russian-Swedish trade and relations.

Taiwan

China External Trade Development Council Office in Moscow
http://www.cetra.org.tw/english/o_office/
indexset.htm
A Taiwanese trade promotion service, the site lists the mission statement and e-mail link of the China External Trade Development Council Office in Moscow.

Taiwan Government Information Office in Moscow
http://www.gio.gov.tw/info/ngio/mos-f.html
Posted in Chinese and English, the site lists the

street address, phone and fax numbers, and e-mail link of the Taiwan Government Information Office in Moscow.

Tanzania

Embassy of Tanzania in Moscow
http://www.tanzania-online.gov.uk/visa/envoys.html
The site provides contact information for the Tanzania Embassy in Moscow.

Thailand

Royal Thai Embassy in Moscow
http://www.mfa.go.th/Embassy/detail/72.htm
The site lists the Ambassador, street address, and phone and fax numbers of the Thai Embassy in Moscow.

Thailand Office of Commercial Affairs in Moscow
http://www.thaitrade.com/thcoaf.html
The site lists the street address, phone and fax numbers, and e-mail link of the Thailand Office of Commercial Affairs in Moscow.

United Kingdom

Consulate General of Britain in St. Petersburg
http://www.fco.gov.uk/directory/posts.asp?RF
The site provides contact information for the British Consulate General in St. Petersburg.

Embassy of Britain in Moscow
http://www.fco.gov.uk/directory/posts.asp?RF
The site provides contact information for the British Embassy in Moscow.

United States

American Business Centers in Russia and the New Independent States
http://www.ita.doc.gov/abcnis/
A service of the International Trade Administration, the site provides Russian trade leads, business guides, event information, and an online discussion forum.

American Russian Business Council
http://www.russiancouncil.org/
With offices in Moscow, Vladivostok and Irkutsk in Russia and San Diego, Los Angeles, and San Francisco in the U.S., the Council promotes Russia-U.S. trade and relations. The site

includes Russian business guides, trade leads, and event information.

Computer Systems and Software Subgroup of the U.S.-Russia Business Development Committee
http://www.ita.doc.gov/rbdc/
A service of the U.S. International Trade Administration, the organization promotes Russian-U.S. computer and software trade. The site includes Russian commercial guides, meeting minutes, and contact information.

State of Washington Trade Office in Vladivostok
http://www.trade.wa.gov/overseas.htm
A service of Washington State Community, Trade and Economic Development, the site lists the Director, Commercial Director, street address, phone and fax numbers, and e-mail link of the Washington Trade Office in Vladivostok.

United States Consulate in St. Petersburg
http://www.usia.gov/abtusia/posts/RS2/wwwhre1a.html
The site lists the Consul General, principal officers, mission statement, street address, phone and fax numbers, and office hours of the U.S. Consulate in St. Petersburg.

United States Consulate in Vladivostok
http://www.usia.gov/abtusia/posts/RS1/wwwhv000.html
Along with contact information, the site provides a directory of consular and commercial services for U.S. companies doing business in the Vladivostok area.

United States Consulate in Yekaterinburg
http://www.usia.gov/abtusia/posts/RS1/wwwhye.html
Along with U.S. fact sheets and visa information, the service provides a directory of Yekaterinburg-area business contacts in telecommunications, computing, health, and other industries.

United States Embassy in Russia
http://www.usia.gov/posts/moscow.html
The virtual Embassy delivers U.S. fact sheets, press releases, electronic journals, Russian commercial guides, and reports on U.S. government assistance to Russia.

U.S. Information Service in St. Petersburg
http://www.usia.gov/posts/stpetersburg.html
Posted in English and Russian, the site provides U.S. news, fact sheets, press releases, visa and

passport information, and a directory of U.S. government representative agencies in Russia.

Venezuela

Embassy of Venezuela in Moscow
http://www.trade-venezuela.com/EMBVENG.HTM
The site lists the street address, phone and fax numbers, and e-mail link of the Venezuelan Embassy in Moscow.

Serbia and Montenegro

Serbia and Montenegro Media

Serbia Media
http://www.mediainfo.com/emediajs/specific-geo.htm?region=yugoslavia
Developed by Editor and Publisher Interactive, the site is a directory of Serbia and Montenegro media sites online.

Serbia and Montenegro Market Guides

Country Commercial Guide
_http://www.state.gov/www/about_state/business/com_guides/1998/europe_canada/serbia98.html_
Prepared by the U.S. Embassy in Belgrade, the site delivers primers on the Serbian economy, political environment, trade regulations and standards, investment climate, trade and project financing, and business travel.

Former Yugoslavia Country Brief
http://www.worldbank.org/cgi-bin/sendoff.cgi?page=%2Fhtml%2Fextdr%2Foffrep%2Feca%2Fmk.htm
A service of the World Bank Group, the site provides Serbian population statistics, financial data, development reports, and economic forecasts.

Former Yugoslavia: A Country Study
http://lcweb2.loc.gov/frd/cs/yutoc.html
A service of the U.S. Library of Congress, the site delivers fact sheets on Former Yugoslavian geography, population, agriculture, mining, manufacturing, and foreign economic relations.

Former Yugoslavia InfoExport
http://www.infoexport.gc.ca/country-e.asp?continent=Europe&country=53
A service of Foreign Affairs and International Trade Canada, the site provides fact sheets and

statistics on Former Yugoslavian geography, business and politics.

Former Yugoslavia Market Research
_http://strategis.ic.gc.ca/sc_mrkti/ibinddc/engdoc/1a1b49.html_
A service of Industry Canada, the site provides U.S. Department of Commerce reports on Serbian business, politics, trade regulations and standards, investment climate, trade and project financing, business travel, and market opportunities.

Montenegro: A Sovereign and Independent State
http://www.montenegro.org/
A hub of country information, the site provides fact sheets on Montenegrin geography, history, language, culture, music, politics, business, and religion.

Serbia Info
http://www.serbia-info.com/
An online country primer, the site delivers Serbian news, regional profiles, socioeconomic statistics, political bulletins, and cultural guides.

Yugoslavia.Com
http://www.yugoslavia.com/Culture/HTML/yu.html
A hub of country information, the site provides fact sheets on Serbian and Montenegrin people, locations, business, language, and food.

Yurope
http://www.yurope.com/
An e-commerce portal, the site provides a directory of online businesses, magazines, and organizations in the countries of the former Yugoslavia.

Serbia and Montenegro Trade Assistance

CEEBICnet Serbia and Montenegro
http://www.itaiep.doc.gov/eebic/countryr/fyrsm.htm
A service of the U.S. Department of Commerce Central and Eastern European Business Information Center, the site delivers Serbia and Montenegro fact sheets, market studies, and event information.

Trade Shows in Serbia and Montenegro
_http://www.expoguide.com/shows/data/loc_70.htm_
Compiled by Expoguide, the site is a directory of upcoming trade shows in Serbia and Montenegro.

Serbia and Montenegro Representative Offices

Austria

Austrian Trade Commission in Belgrade
http://aw.wk.or.at/awo/ahst-belgrad.htm
The site lists the staff, street address, phone and fax numbers, e-mail link, and office hours of the Austrian Trade Commission in Belgrade.

Canada

Embassy of Canada in Belgrade
http://www.dfait-maeci.gc.ca/english/missions/rep-can4e.htm#yugoslavia
The site provides contact information for the Canadian Embassy in Belgrade.

France

French Trade Commission in Belgrade
http://www.dree.org/yougoslavie/
Written in French, the site delivers Serbian and Montenegrin market reports, sector profiles, contact information, and a directory of export programs for French companies doing business in the countries of the Former Yugoslavia.

India

Indian Commercial Mission in Belgrade
http://www.nic.in/commin/ICM.HTM
The site lists the street address, phone and fax numbers, and e-mail link of the Indian Commercial Mission in Belgrade.

Spain

Embassy of Spain in Belgrade
http://www.spanija.org.yu/
Posted in Serbo-Croatian and Spanish, the site provides Spanish news, fact sheets, press releases, and reports on Serbia and Montenegro-Spain trade and relations.

Sweden

Embassy of Sweden in Belgrade
http://www.ud.se/english/mfa/ambassad/jugoslav.htm
The site provides contact information for the Swedish Embassy in Belgrade.

United Kingdom

Embassy of Britain in Belgrade
http://www.britemb.org.yu/
Posted in English and Serbo-Croatian, the site delivers British press releases, visa and passport information, and Former Yugoslavian commercial guides and sector profiles.

United States

United States Embassy in Belgrade
http://www.amembbg.co.yu/
The virtual Embassy provides U.S. news, fact sheets, press releases, travel guides, visa and passport information, and a directory of Embassy programs and services.

United States Information Service in Belgrade
http://www.amembbg.co.yu/usis.html
The site provides U.S. news, press releases, fact sheets, cultural bulletins, teaching guides, socioeconomic statistics, and Fulbright exchange program information.

Slovakia

Slovakia Media

Slovakia Media
http://www.mediainfo.com/emediajs/specific-geo.htm?region=slovakia
Developed by Editor and Publisher Interactive, the site is a directory of Slovak media sites online including magazines, newspapers, and television stations.

Slovakia Market Guides

Slovak Information Agency
http://www.sia.gov.sk/english/index.htm
A portal of country information, the site features Slovak news, fact sheets, economic reports, government policy statements, and publication lists.

Slovak Republic Frequently Asked Questions
http://photo.net/bp/slovak-FAQ.html
A country travel guide, the site delivers fact sheets on Slovak money, visas, telecommunications, climate, attractions, cities, regions, and accommodations.

Slovakia Country Brief
*http://www.worldbank.org/cgi-bin/
sendoff.cgi?page=%2Fhtml%2Fextdr%2Foffrep%2
Feca%2Fsk.htm*
A service of the World Bank Group, the site
provides Slovak population statistics, financial
data, development reports, and economic
forecasts.

Slovakia Country Profile
*http://www.tradenz.govt.nz/intelligence/profiles/
slovakia.html*
A service of the New Zealand Trade Development
Board, the site provides Slovak economic
statistics, market information, and business tips.

Slovakia InfoExport
*http://www.infoexport.gc.ca/country-
e.asp?continent=Europe&country=39*
A service of Foreign Affairs and International
Trade Canada, the site provides fact sheets and
statistics on Slovak geography, business, trade,
and politics.

Slovakia Market Access Database
*http://mkaccdb.eu.int/mkdb/
mkdb.pl?METHOD=COUNTRY*
A service of the European Commission, the site
offers briefs on Slovak trade policy, tariff barriers,
non-tariff barriers, investment-related measures,
and financial services regulations.

Slovakia Market Information
http://dtiinfo1.dti.gov.uk/ots/slovak_republic/
A service of the London-based Department of
Trade and Industry, the site delivers Slovak fact
sheets, maps, and trade-show information.

Slovakia Market Research
*http://strategis.ic.gc.ca/sc_mrkti/ibinddc/engdoc/
1a1b40.html*
A service of Industry Canada, the site provides
U.S. Department of Commerce reports on Slovak
business, politics, trade regulations and standards, investment climate, trade and project
financing, business travel, and market opportunities.

Slovakia Net
http://slovakia.net/
A searchable directory of Slovak companies, the
site profiles firms in over 20 categories including
electronics, architecture, banking, furniture, and
automotive.

Slovakia Online
http://savba.savba.sk/logos/list-e.html
An index of Slovak resources online, the site is
divided into 15 categories including news,
journals, books, radio, president and government, and exhibitions.

Welcome to Slovakia
http://www.sanet.sk/
Featuring maps and audio clips, the site delivers
Slovak fact sheets, travel information, media
guides, mailing lists, community profiles, and
language primers.

Slovakia Trade Assistance

CEEBICnet Slovakia
*http://www.itaiep.doc.gov/eebic/countryr/
slovakr.htm*
A service of the U.S. Department of Commerce
Central and Eastern European Business
Information Center, the site delivers Slovak fact
sheets, market studies, event information,
business and procurement opportunities, and a
directory of U.S. companies in Slovakia.

Trade Shows in Slovakia
http://www.expoguide.com/shows/data/loc_55.htm
Compiled by Expoguide, the site is a directory of
upcoming trade shows in Slovakia.

Slovakia Representative Offices

Austria

Austrian Trade Commission in Bratislava
http://aw.wk.or.at/awo/ahst-pressburg.htm
The site lists the staff, street address, phone and
fax numbers, e-mail link, and office hours of the
Austrian Trade Commission in Bratislava.

Finland

Finland Trade Center in Bratislava
http://www.exports.finland.fi/tradecen.htm
The site lists the staff, street address, phone and
fax numbers, and e-mail link of the Finland Trade
Center in Bratislava.

France

Embassy of France in Bratislava
http://www.france.sk/
Written in French and Slovak, the site provides

French fact sheets, visa and passport information, cultural bulletins, science and technology reports, and language guides.

French Trade Commission in Bratislava
http://www.dree.org/slovaquie/
Written in French, the site delivers Slovak market reports, sector profiles, contact information, and a directory of export programs for French companies doing business in Slovakia.

Germany

German Chamber of Commerce in Bratislava
http://www.ahk.net/en/sk/Bratislava/
The site lists the Chief Executive Officer, street address, phone and fax numbers, e-mail link, and office hours of the German Chamber in Bratislava.

India

Embassy of India in Bratislava
http://www.eindia.sk/
Written in English and Slovak, the site delivers Indian foreign policy statements and fact sheets on national symbols including the Indian flag, emblem, and anthem.

United Kingdom

Embassy of Britain in Bratislava
http://www.fco.gov.uk/directory/posts.asp?SH
The site provides contact information for the British Embassy in Bratislava.

United States

United States Embassy in Bratislava
http://www.usis.sk/
Along with a directory of consular and commercial services, the site provides U.S. news, press releases, defense attaché reports, Fulbright program information, and Slovak business guides.

United States Information Service in Bratislava
http://www.usis.sk/wwwhusis.html
Featuring a directory of U.S. and Slovak media resources online, the site provides information on the American Reference Center, a U.S. library in Bratislava.

Slovenia

Slovenia Media

Slovenia Media
http://www.mediainfo.com/emediajs/specific-geo.htm?region=slovenia
Developed by Editor and Publisher Interactive, the site is a directory of Slovenian media sites online.

Slovenia Market Guides

Borza Business Opportunities Exchange System
http://www.gzs.si/eng/borza/index.htm
An online marketplace, the site is a searchable database of Slovenian trade leads and business opportunities. Categories include patents, technical cooperation, investment, real estate, and sub-contracting.

Chamber of Commerce and Industry of Slovenia
http://www.gzs.si/eng/index.htm
Based in Ljubljana, the Chamber promotes Slovenian economic development. The site features Slovenian news, fact sheets, business opportunities, and event information.

Slovenia Business Register
http://www.gzs.si/ENG/busopp/register/index.htm
A browsable directory of some 50,000 Slovenian companies and organizations, the site is divided into 17 categories including agriculture, construction, hotels and restaurants, and transportation.

Slovenia Country Brief
http://www.worldbank.org/cgi-bin/ sendoff.cgi?page=%2Fhtml%2Fextdr%2Foffrep%2 Feca%2Fsi.htm
A service of the World Bank Group, the site provides Slovenian population statistics, financial data, development reports, and economic forecasts.

Slovenia: A Guide to Virtual Slovenia
http://www.ijs.si/slo/
Featuring an interactive map of Slovenia, the site delivers Slovenian fact sheets, travel information, city profiles, history lessons, and economic reports.

Slovenia Market Access Database
http://mkaccdb.eu.int/mkdb/ mkdb.pl?METHOD=COUNTRY
A service of the European Commission, the site

offers briefs on Slovenian trade policy, tariff barriers, non-tariff barriers, investment-related measures, and financial services regulations.

Slovenia Market Research
http://strategis.ic.gc.ca/sc_mrkti/ibinddc/engdoc/1a1b41.html
Posted by Industry Canada, the site provides U.S. Central Intelligence Agency fact sheets on Slovenian geography, people, government, economy, communications, and transportation.

Slovenia: Selected Issues
http://www.imf.org/external/pubs/CAT/longres.cfm?sk=2545.0
Prepared by the International Monetary Fund, the site reports on Slovenian privatization, exchange rates, European Union accession, production, and trade.

Slovenian Business Catalog
http://www.kabi.si/si21/SBC/
A virtual library of business information, the site provides Slovenian maps, fact sheets, sector profiles, company directories, and travel guides.

Slovenia Trade Assistance

CEEBICnet Slovenia
http://www.itaiep.doc.gov/eebic/countryr/slovenia.htm
A service of the U.S. Department of Commerce Central and Eastern European Business Information Center, the site delivers Slovenian fact sheets, market studies, event information, business and procurement opportunities, and a directory of U.S. companies in Slovenia.

Embassies and Consulates of Slovenia
http://www.ijs.si/slo/country/economy/embassies/index.html
A service of Virtual Slovenia, the site is a directory of Slovenian Embassies and Consulates in some 40 countries including Canada, China, Italy, Sweden, and the United States.

Fairs and Exhibitions in Slovenia
http://www.gzs.si/ENG/news/fairs.htm
A directory of Slovenian trade shows and conferences, the site profiles events in industries such as electronics, medical, environmental, furniture, and agri-food.

Import/Export Directory of Slovenia
http://www.gzs.si/sloexporta/default.htm
Posted in English and Slovenian, the site is a directory of Slovenian exporters and importers. Categories include manufacturers, banks, transportation, construction and tourism.

Slovenia Customs Administration
http://www.sigov.si/mf/angl/apredmf6.html
Based in Ljubljana, the site describes the administrative structure and duties of the Slovenian Customs Administration. The service includes contact information and a directory of customs offices across Slovenia.

Trade and Investment Promotion Office
http://www.sigov.si/tipo/
A virtual business primer, the site features Slovenian news, fact sheets, investment guides, economic statistics, cost comparisons, and political bulletins.

Trade Point Slovenia
http://www.tradepoint.si/
Along with business and sector studies, the site provides Slovenian company directories, sector profiles, tourism information, and a trade leads bulletin board.

Slovenia Representative Offices

Austria

Austrian Trade Commission in Ljubljana
http://aw.wk.or.at/awo/ahst-laibach.htm
The site lists the staff, street address, phone and fax numbers, e-mail link, and office hours of the Austrian Trade Commission in Ljubljana.

France

French Embassy in Ljubljana
http://www.dree.org/slovenie/
Written in French, the site delivers Slovenian market reports, sector profiles, contact information, and a directory of export programs for French companies doing business in Slovenia.

Germany

German Chamber of Commerce in Ljubljana
http://www.ahk.net/en/si/Ljubljana/
The site lists the Chief Executive Officer, street address, phone and fax numbers, e-mail link, and office hours of the German Chamber in Ljubljana.

Italy

Italian Trade Commission in Ljubljana
http://www.ice.it/estero/lubiana/
Posted in Italian, the site provides Italian news, fact sheets, press releases, business guides, cultural bulletins, event information, and economic statistics.

United Kingdom

Embassy of Britain in Ljubljana
http://www.fco.gov.uk/directory/posts.asp?SI
The site provides contact information for the British Embassy in Ljubljana.

Tajikistan

Tajikistan Market Guides

Doing Business in Tajikistan
http://www.soros.org/tajik/tajkbusi.html
A directory of Tajikistani business resources online, the site includes economic reviews, event information, commercial guides, sector profiles, and travel primers.

Tajikistan Country Brief
http://www.worldbank.org/cgi-bin/
sendoff.cgi?page=%2Fhtml%2Fextdr%2Foffrep%2
Feca%2Ftj.htm
A service of the World Bank Group, the site provides Tajikistani population statistics, financial data, development reports, and economic forecasts.

Tajikistan Country Report
http://www.itaiep.doc.gov/bisnis/country/
cntasia.htm#Tajikistan
A service of the U.S. International Trade Administration, the site provides Tajikistani fact sheets, economic reviews, investment guides, and international trade statistics.

Tajikistan Market Information
http://dtiinfo1.dti.gov.uk/ots/tajikistan/
A service of the London-based Department of Trade and Industry, the site delivers Tajikistani fact sheets, maps, and trade-show information.

Tajikistan Market Research
http://strategis.ic.gc.ca/sc_mrkti/ibinddc/engdoc/
1a1h13.html
Posted by Industry Canada, the site provides U.S. Central Intelligence Agency fact sheets on

Tajikistani geography, people, government, economy, communications, and transportation.

Tajikistan: Recent Economic Developments
http://www.imf.org/external/pubs/CAT/
longres.cfm?sk=2501.0
Prepared by the International Monetary Fund, the site reports on Tajikistani output, employment, prices, wages, public finance, trade policies, privatization, and legal reform.

Tajikistan Resource Page
http://www.soros.org/tajkstan.html
A hub of country information, the site features Tajikistani news, maps, fact sheets, business guides, government directories, travel information, and cultural bulletins.

Tajikistan Update
http://www.angelfire.com/sd/tajikistanupdate/
The online service delivers Tajikistani news, maps, flags, economic reports, history lessons, language primers, travel information, media reports, and photos.

Tajikistan Virtual Library
http://www.rockbridge.net/personal/bichel/tajik.htp
A service of the World Wide Web Virtual Library, the site is a directory of Tajikistani resources online. Categories include culture and language, economics, travel, and politics.

Turkmenistan

Turkmenistan Media

Turkmenistan Media
http://www.mediainfo.com/emediajs/specific-
geo.htm?region=turkmenistan
Compiled by Editor and Publisher Interactive, the site is a directory of Turkmen radio stations and other media sites online.

Turkmenistan Market Guides

Announced Tenders in Turkmenistan
http://www.dc.infi.net/~embassy/tenders.html
A service of the Turkmenistan Embassy in Washington, D.C., the site provides a directory of government procurement opportunities in Turkmenistan. The database includes invitations for bids in energy, telecommunications, and building materials projects.

Business Opportunities Available in Turkmenistan

http://www.dc.infi.net/~embassy/sfp.html
A database of investment, partnership and joint venture opportunities in Turkmenistan, the site is divided into ten categories including transportation, distributorships, energy, and services.

Doing Business in Turkmenistan

http://www.dc.infi.net/~embassy/dbit.html
A virtual business primer, the site provides Turkmen investment guides, international trade statistics, tender announcements, taxation information, and government directories.

Turkmenistan Chaihana

http://hobbes.itc.virginia.edu/~fgl2q/turkmeni.html
The online service provides Turkmen photo galleries, travel information, speeches, articles, language primers, cultural bulletins, and an online message board.

Turkmenistan Country Brief

*http://www.worldbank.org/cgi-bin/
sendoff.cgi?page=%2Fhtml%2Fextdr%2Foffrep%2
Feca%2Ftm.htm*
A service of the World Bank Group, the site provides Turkmen population statistics, financial data, development reports, and economic forecasts.

Turkmenistan Country Report

*http://www.itaiep.doc.gov/bisnis/country/
cntasia.htm#Turkmenistan*
A service of the U.S. International Trade Administration, the site provides Turkmen fact sheets, economic reviews, investment guides, and international trade statistics.

Turkmenistan Information Center

http://www.turkmenistan.com/
A portal of country information, the site features Turkmen fact sheets, maps, photos, travel guides, visa information, history lessons, and executive profiles.

Turkmenistan Market Research

*http://strategis.ic.gc.ca/sc_mrkti/ibinddc/engdoc/
1a1h14.html*
A service of Industry Canada, the site provides U.S. Department of Commerce reports on Turkmen business, politics, trade regulations and standards, investment climate, trade and project financing, business travel, and market opportunities.

Turkmenistan Virtual Library

*http://www.rockbridge.net/personal/bichel/
turkmen.htp*
A service of the World Wide Web Virtual Library, the site is a directory of Turkmen resources online. Categories include economics, culture and language, travel, and politics.

Turkmenistan Trade Assistance

Foreign Trade and Export/Import Statistics

http://www.dc.infi.net/~embassy/dbit.html#dbit2
A service of the Turkmenistan Embassy in Washington, D.C., the site provides Turkmen export, import, and foreign investment statistics by country and commodity.

Trade Shows in Turkmenistan

http://www.expoguide.com/shows/data/loc_64.htm
Compiled by Expoguide, the site is a directory of upcoming trade shows in Turkmenistan.

Turkmenistan Representative Offices

Armenia

Embassy of Armenia in Ashgabat

http://www.armeniaemb.org/forrel/embas2.htm
The site provides contact information for the Armenian Embassy in Ashgabat.

United Kingdom

Embassy of Britain in Ashgabat

http://www.fco.gov.uk/directory/posts.asp?TM
The site provides contact information for the British Embassy in Ashgabat.

United States

United States Embassy in Ashgabat

http://www.usemb-ashgabat.usia.co.at/
Along with U.S. fact sheets and consular information, the site delivers Turkmen business guides, accommodation directories, travel information, and security tips.

United States Information Service in Ashgabat

http://www.usemb-ashgabat.usia.co.at/usis.htm
The site provides U.S. news, press releases, fact sheets, cultural bulletins, teaching guides, socioeconomic statistics, and Fulbright exchange program information.

Ukraine

Ukraine Media

Ukraine Media
http://www.mediainfo.com/emediajs/specific-geo.htm?region=ukraine
Compiled by Editor and Publisher Interactive, the site is a directory of Ukrainian magazines, television stations, and other media sites online.

Ukraine Market Guides

Newbiznet Project
http://dai.kiev.ua/home_engl.html
Sponsored by U.S. AID, the Project promotes the development of Ukrainian small business. The site includes a mission statement, project statistics, and a directory of small business centers across the Ukraine.

Science and Technology Centre of Ukraine
http://www.stcu.kiev.ua/
Sponsored by government agencies in the Ukraine, Canada, Sweden and the U.S., the Center supports Ukrainian scientists and engineers formerly involved in military research. The site provides contact information and a project database.

Ukraine Country Brief
http://www.worldbank.org/cgi-bin/ sendoff.cgi?page=%2Fhtml%2Fextdr%2Foffrep%2 Feca%2Fua.htm
A service of the World Bank Group, the site provides Ukrainian population statistics, financial data, development reports, and economic forecasts.

Ukraine Country Report
http://www.business-europa.co.uk/ukraine/ index.html
A service of Business Europa, the site delivers fact sheets on Ukrainian politics, business, media, geography, transportation, telecommuni-cations, and education.

Ukraine Country Report
http://www.state.gov/www/issues/economic/ trade_reports/russia_nis97/ukraine97.html
Prepared by the U.S. Department of State, the site delivers information on Ukrainian exchange rates, debt management, trade barriers, and intellectual property protection.

Ukraine: FAQ Plus
http://www.tryzub.com/NEW_UKRAINE.html
A hub of country information, the site features primers on Ukrainian business, geography, culture, history, language, law, media, and travel.

Ukraine Home Page
http://www.physics.mcgill.ca/WWW/oleh/ukr-info.html
An index of Ukrainian resources online, the site is divided into 11 categories including general information, media, culture, and travel.

Ukraine InfoExport
http://www.infoexport.gc.ca/country-e.asp?continent=Europe&country=44
A service of Foreign Affairs and International Trade Canada, the site provides fact sheets and statistics on Ukrainian geography, business and politics.

Ukraine Market Access Database
http://mkaccdb.eu.int/mkdb/ mkdb.pl?METHOD=COUNTRY
A service of the European Commission, the site offers briefs on Ukrainian trade policy, tariff barriers, non-tariff barriers, investment-related measures, and financial services regulations.

Ukraine Market Information
http://dtiinfo1.dti.gov.uk/ots/ukraine/
A service of the London-based Department of Trade and Industry, the site delivers Ukrainian fact sheets, maps, and trade-show information.

Ukraine Market Research
http://strategis.ic.gc.ca/sc_mrkti/ibinddc/engdoc/ 1a1b46.html
A service of Industry Canada, the site provides U.S. Department of Commerce reports on Ukrainian business, politics, trade regulations and standards, investment climate, trade and project financing, business travel, and market opportunities.

Ukraine: Recent Economic Developments
http://www.imf.org/external/pubs/CAT/ longres.cfm?sk=2425.0
Prepared by the International Monetary Fund, the site reports on Ukrainian output, competitive-ness, privatization, exchange rates, public finance, trade policies, and investment.

Ukrainian Research Institute
http://www.sabre.org/huri/index.html
Based at Harvard University in Cambridge, the

Institute studies Ukrainian socioeconomic issues. The site includes a mission statement, working papers, and event information.

Ukraine Trade Assistance

Trade Shows in Ukraine
http://www.expoguide.com/shows/data/loc_67.htm
Compiled by Expoguide, the site is a directory of upcoming trade shows in the Ukraine.

Ukraine Trade Opportunities
http://www.brama.com/ua-trade-mission/trade.html
A service of the Trade Mission of Ukraine in New York, the site provides a database of Ukrainian tenders and trade leads. Categories include construction, mining, and building materials.

Ukrainian Industrial Internet Exhibition
http://www.ukrainetrade.com/uiie.htm
A virtual trade show, the site profiles Ukrainian companies and export products. The service includes fact sheets, sector reports, and regional market studies.

Ukraine Representative Offices

Armenia

Embassy of Armenia in Kiev
http://www.armeniaemb.org/forrel/embas2.htm
The site provides contact information for the Armenian Embassy in Kiev.

Austria

Austrian Trade Commission in Kiev
http://aw.wk.or.at/awo/ahst-kiew.htm
The site lists the staff, street address, phone and fax numbers, e-mail link, and office hours of the Austrian Trade Commission in Kiev.

Canada

Embassy of Canada in Kiev
http://www.dfait-maeci.gc.ca/english/missions/rep-can4e.htm#ukraine
The site provides contact information for the Canadian Embassy in Kiev.

Finland

Finland Trade Center in Kiev
http://www.exports.finland.fi/tradecen.htm

The site lists the staff, street address, and phone and fax numbers of the Finland Trade Center in Kiev.

France

French Trade Commission in Kiev
http://www.co.ru/~peemoscou/peecei/pee_ukr.htm
Written in French, the site lists the staff, street address, phone and fax numbers, and e-mail link of the French Trade Commission in Kiev.

Germany

German Chamber of Commerce in Kiev
http://www.ahk.net/en/ua/Kiev/
The site lists the Chief Executive Officer, street address, phone and fax numbers, e-mail link, and office hours of the German Chamber in Kiev.

Sweden

Embassy of Sweden in Kiev
http://www.ud.se/english/mfa/ambassad/ukraina.htm
The site provides contact information for the Swedish Embassy in Kiev.

Turkey

Embassy of Turkey in Kiev
http://www.turkey.org/madres.htm
Part of a directory of Turkish diplomatic offices around the world, the site lists the e-mail link of the Turkish Embassy in Kiev.

United Kingdom

Embassy of Britain in Kiev
http://www.fco.gov.uk/directory/posts.asp?UK
The site provides contact information for the British Embassy in Kiev.

United States

United States Embassy in Kiev
http://www.usemb.kiev.ua/
The virtual Embassy provides U.S. news, fact sheets, press releases, Ukrainian language primers, and a directory of consular and commercial staff and services.

United States Information Service in Kiev
http://www.usis.kiev.ua/
The site provides American news, press re-

leases, fact sheets, cultural bulletins, socioeconomic statistics, and Fulbright exchange program information.

Uzbekistan

Uzbekistan Market Guides

Cyber-Uzbekistan
http://www.cu-online.com/~k_a/uzbekistan/
A hub of country information, the site delivers Uzbekistani news, business guides, travel information, political bulletins, cultural primers, and online classifieds.

Doing Business in Uzbekistan
http://www.abcnews.com/sections/travel/DailyNews/biztrav1204.html
A service of ABC News, the site provides a primer on Uzbekistani business etiquette. One tip: bread should never be placed face down or cut with a knife. Instead, bread should by torn by hand. The reason: the top of a loaf is believed to represent the face of God.

Uzbekistan Country Brief
http://www.worldbank.org/cgi-bin/sendoff.cgi?page=%2Fhtml%2Fextdr%2Foffrep%2Feca%2Fuz.htm
A service of the World Bank Group, the site provides Uzbekistani population statistics, financial data, development reports, and economic forecasts.

Uzbekistan Country Report
http://www.itaiep.doc.gov/bisnis/country/cntasia.htm#Uzbekistan
A service of the U.S. International Trade Administration, the site provides Uzbekistani fact sheets, economic reviews, investment guides, and international trade statistics.

Uzbekistan Market Information
http://dtiinfo1.dti.gov.uk/ots/uzbekistan/
A service of the London-based Department of Trade and Industry, the site delivers Uzbekistani fact sheets, maps, and trade-show information.

Uzbekistan Market Research
http://strategis.ic.gc.ca/sc_mrkti/ibinddc/engdoc/1a1h15.html
Posted by Industry Canada, the site provides U.S. Central Intelligence Agency fact sheets on Uzbekistani geography, people, government, economy, communications, and transportation.

Uzbekistan Virtual Library
http://www.rockbridge.net/personal/bichel/uzbek.htp
A service of the World Wide Web Virtual Library, the site is a directory of Uzbekistani resources online. Categories include economics, culture and language, travel, and politics.

Welcome to Uzbekistan
http://www.gov.uz/
Written in English and Uzbek, the site delivers Uzbekistani business guides, history lessons, city profiles, cultural primers, tourism information, and education reports.

Uzbekistan Representative Offices

Azerbaijan

Embassy of Azerbaijan in Tashkent
http://www.gov.uz/uzi/lst000.html
The site lists the telephone and fax numbers, and e-mail link of the Azerbaijani Embassy in Tashkent.

Finland

Finland Trade Center in Tashkent
http://www.exports.finland.fi/tradecen.htm
The site lists the staff, street address, phone and fax numbers, and e-mail link of the Finland Trade Center in Tashkent.

France

French Trade Commission in Tashkent
http://www.dree.org/pee/bureaux_eurolest.cfm
Written in French, the site lists the Director, street address, phone and fax numbers, and e-mail link of the French Trade Commission in Tashkent.

Germany

German Chamber of Commerce in Tashkent
http://www.ahk.net/en/uz/Tashkent/
The site lists the Chief Executive Officer, street address, phone and fax numbers, and e-mail link of the German Chamber in Tashkent.

Malaysia

Embassy of Malaysia in Tashkent
http://www.mnet.com.my/klonline/www/missions/malmiss/muzbekis.htm
The site provides contact information for the Malaysian Embassy in Tashkent.

Pakistan

Pakistan Trade Office in Tashkent
http://www.jamal.com/epb/ptoa.htm
The site provides contact information for the Pakistan Trade Office in Tashkent.

Ukraine

Embassy of Ukraine in Tashkent
http://www.gov.uz/uzi/lst000.html
The site lists the telephone and fax numbers, and e-mail link of the Ukrainian Embassy in Tashkent.

United Kingdom

Embassy of Britain in Tashkent
http://www.fco.gov.uk/directory/posts.asp?UZ
The site provides contact information for the British Embassy in Tashkent.

United States

United States Embassy in Tashkent
http://www.usis.uz/
The virtual Embassy provides U.S. visa and passport information, taxation guides, a directory of consular and commercial services, and reports on U.S. assistance to Uzbekistan.

U.S. Information Service Tashkent
http://www.usis.uz/wwwhusis.htm
The site provides U.S. news, press releases, fact sheets, cultural bulletins, teaching guides, socioeconomic statistics, and Fulbright exchange program information.

## CHAPTER 8

ARABIAN SEA E-MARTS: 800+ MIDDLE EAST BUSINESS RESOURCES ON THE INTERNET

This chapter profiles more than 800 international business resources online that focus on North Africa, the Middle East, and Southern Asia. The section reviews regional websites and online portals for 24 countries and territories, including Egypt, India, Pakistan, and Turkey. Highly diverse in culture and geography, the region has an estimated 1.5 billion people. While regional conflicts continue, peace and reform initiatives in the area are on the rise, and business opportunities abound. Products and services in growing demand include agri-food items, advanced technology and informatics, civil aviation, medical equipment and services, oil and gas machinery, and forest products. According to NUA Internet Surveys, an estimated 1.3 million people in the region—about one out of every 1,200—were online as of January 1999.

Regional Sites

Middle East Search Tools

ArabSeek
http://www.arabseek.com/
A web navigation service, the site is a searchable index of Middle East and North Africa resources online. Categories include business, government, media, and news.

Middle East Media

Arabia Business
http://www.arabia.com/business/
An online news service, the site provides Arabian business bulletins, country profiles, sector reports, travel information, a currency converter, and online discussion forums.

Middle East Media
http://www.mediainfo.com/emediajs/links-geo.htm?location=mideast
Compiled by Editor and Publisher Interactive, the site is a directory of media sites online in 12 Middle Eastern countries including Bahrain, Lebanon, Turkey, and Yemen.

Middle East Market Guides

Access to Arabia
http://www.accessme.com/
A hub of regional information, the site features Arabian news, country profiles, travel information, cultural primers, and a database of government procurement opportunities.

Arab Business Network
http://www.xroadsme.com/
A searchable database of regional fact sheets,

the site provides country guides, sector profiles, accommodation directories, employment opportunities, and legal primers.

Arab Internet Business Directory
http://www.access2arabia.com/aibd/
Based in Amman, Jordan, the site is a searchable directory of Arabian companies. Categories include banking, computers, engineering, food and beverage, investment, and shipping.

Arab World Online
http://www.awo.net/
A regional information portal, the site delivers Arabian news, country fact sheets, commercial guides, legal primers, travel tips, and event information.

Arab World Online Commercial Directory
http://www.awo.net/awocomdirSearch.asp
A browsable index of Arabian companies and organizations, the site is divided into over 40 categories including aerospace, banking, construction, mining, and packaging.

Arabia Online
http://www.arabiaonline.com/
Updated daily, the site delivers Arabian news, country profiles, business guides, technology reports, shopping directories, cultural primers, and online discussion groups.

ArabNet
http://www.arab.net/welcome.html
An online resource for the Middle East and North Africa, the site delivers Arabian news, country data, business guides, company directories, and travel information.

Bureau of Near Eastern Affairs
http://www.state.gov/www/regions/nea/index.html
A service of the U.S. State Department, the site

provides U.S. press statements, testimony, briefings, issue reports, and travel information on the region and countries of the Middle East.

Country Information
http://www.awo.net/country/
A service of Arab World Online, the site profiles some 20 Middle Eastern countries including Algeria, Egypt, Jordan, Kuwait, Lebanon, Oman, and Syria.

Foreign Governments of the Middle East and North Africa
http://www.lib.umich.edu/libhome/
Documents.center/forme.html
Developed by the University of Michigan Documents Center, the site provides fact sheets on 25 Middle Eastern countries including Armenia, Dubai, Iraq, Israel, and Qatar.

Harvard University Center of Middle Eastern Studies
http://fas-www.harvard.edu:80/~mideast/MESlinks/
MESlinks.html
An index of Middle Eastern resources online, the site includes regional business guides, academic research centers, publications, and bulletin board systems.

InfoExport Middle East
http://www.infoexport.gc.ca/continent-
e.asp?continent=Africa
A service of Foreign Affairs and International Trade Canada, the site provides economic fact sheets and business guides for some 20 Middle Eastern countries.

International Export Connections Library
http://www.teleport.com/~iexportc/library.htm
Based in Beaverton, Oregon, the site provides Middle East business primers. The service includes export quizzes, country fact sheets, and company directories.

Maghreb Net Resources
http://www.maghreb.net/resources/index.html
A browsable directory of Middle Eastern resources online, the site is divided into 12 categories including business, news, science, government, and computing.

Middle East Market Research
http://strategis.ic.gc.ca/sc_mrkti/ibinddc/engdoc/
1a1d.html
A service of Industry Canada, the site is a

database of fact sheets and market studies on over 15 Middle Eastern countries.

Middle East Network Information Center
http://menic.utexas.edu/menic.html
A service of the Center for Middle Eastern Studies at the University of Texas, the site is directory of regional resources online. Categories include business and finance, government and country profiles, and maps and travel.

MidEast Business
http://www.infoprod.co.il/MEB/meb1.htm
A service of Israel-based InfoProd, the site provides weekly briefings on Middle East agriculture, infrastructure, minerals, telecommunications, transportation, and other sectors.

1001 Sites.Com
http://www.1001sites.com/
An Arab Internet directory, the site delivers Middle Eastern news, discussion forums, country profiles, business guides, travel information, and cultural primers.

Rest of Asia Market Research
http://strategis.ic.gc.ca/sc_mrkti/ibinddc/engdoc/
1a1h.html
A service of Industry Canada, the site is a database of fact sheets and market studies on some 20 Middle Eastern and newly independent countries.

World Bank Group Middle East and North Africa
http://www.worldbank.org/html/extdr/offrep/mena/
mena.htm
A database of World Bank projects in the Middle East and North Africa, the site provides press releases, speeches, mission statements, country profiles, and regional economic reports.

Middle East Trade Assistance

Airlines in the Middle East
http://www.freightworld.com/airl_geo.html#8
A service of Freightworld, the site is a directory of Middle Eastern airlines online including El Al Israel Airlines, Kuwait Airways, Pakistan International Airlines, and Turkish Airlines.

Freight Forwarders in the Middle East
http://www.freightworld.com/forw_geo.html#8
A directory of Middle Eastern freight forwarders online, the site links to operations in nine countries including Bahrain, Egypt, Jordan, Lebanon, Saudi Arabia, and Turkey.

Intermodal Carriers in the Middle East
http://www.freightworld.com/intmod_geo.html#8
An index of Middle Eastern intermodal carriers online, the site links to Zim Israel Navigation Company in Israel, and Star International Chartering and Shipping in Turkey.

Maritime Carriers in the Middle East
http://www.freightworld.com/mari_geo.html#8
A directory of Middle Eastern maritime carriers online, the site links to operations in five countries: Egypt, Israel, Kuwait, Lebanon, and Turkey.

Middle East and North Africa Database
http://infoserv2.ita.doc.gov/meweb.nsf
Developed by the U.S. International Trade Administration, the site delivers Middle Eastern country profiles, business guides, export documentation, and event information.

North Africa and Middle East Regional Office of the World Customs Organization
http://www.dxbcustoms.gov.ae/rwco/
Posted in Arabic and English, the site explains the history, mission, and structure of the North Africa and Middle East Regional Office of the World Customs Organization, a global customs organization.

Trucking and Motor Carriers in the Middle East
http://www.freightworld.com/truc_geo.html#8
A service of Freightworld, the site is a directory of Middle Eastern trucking and motor carriers online including Cargomaster in Lebanon, Karas Shipping in Turkey, and Access Tourism and Cargo in the United Arab Emirates.

Middle East Representative Offices

United States

National U.S.-Arab Chamber of Commerce
http://www.nusacc.org/
Based in New York City, the Chamber promotes U.S.-Arab trade. The site includes contact information, sponsorship opportunities, and Arabian business guides.

National Sites

Afghanistan

Afghanistan Media

Afghan Media
http://www.afghani.com/media.htm
Updated daily, the site provides Afghan maps, provincial profiles, business guides, media information, weather bulletins, exchange rates, and a searchable news archive.

Afghan Online Press
http://www.afghan-web.com/aop/
An Afghan news service, the site provides photo essays, political analysis, online discussion groups, and news broadcasts in streaming audio.

Afghanistan Market Guides

Afghanistan Market Research
http://strategis.ic.gc.ca/sc_mrkti/ibinddc/engdoc/1a1h1.html
Posted by Industry Canada, the site provides U.S. Central Intelligence Agency fact sheets on Afghan geography, people, government, economy, communications, and transportation.

Afghanistan Online
http://www.afghan-web.com/
A hub of country information, the site delivers fact sheets on Afghan people, business, culture, geography, language, politics, history, and weather.

Afghanistan Today
http://frankenstein.worldweb.net/afghan/
An online country primer, the site provides Afghan news, maps, city profiles, business guides, political bulletins, cultural primers, and government directories.

Afghanistan Virtual Library
http://www.rockbridge.net/personal/bichel/afghan.htp
A service of the World Wide Web Virtual Library, the site is a directory of Afghan resources online. Categories include economics, culture and language, travel, and politics.

Afghans Business Connection
http://www.afghans.com/
A directory of Afghan businesses online, the site is divided into 15 categories including business, books, restaurants, travel, financial services, and import/export.

Bahrain

Bahrain Media

Bahrain Media
http://www.mediainfo.com/emediajs/specific-geo.htm?region=bahrain
Compiled by Editor and Publisher Interactive, the site is a directory of Bahrain newspapers, television stations, and other media sites online.

Bahrain Market Guides

Bahrain Chamber of Commerce and Industry
http://www.bahchamber.com/
Based in Manama, the Chamber promotes economic development in Bahrain. The site includes news, member profiles, event information, and a directory of Chamber programs and services.

Bahrain Country Brief
http://www.worldbank.org/cgi-bin/ sendoff.cgi?page=%2Fhtml%2Fextdr%2Foffrep%2 Fmena%2Fbh.htm
A service of the World Bank Group, the site provides Bahraini population statistics, financial data, development reports, and economic forecasts.

Bahrain Country Profile
http://www.tradenz.govt.nz/intelligence/profiles/ bahrain.html
A service of the New Zealand Trade Development Board, the site provides Bahraini economic statistics, market information, and business tips.

Bahrain Country Report
http://www.state.gov/www/issues/economic/ trade_reports/neareast97/bahrain97.html
Prepared by the U.S. Department of State, the site delivers information on Bahraini exchange rates, debt management, trade barriers, and intellectual property protection.

Bahrain: A Country Study
http://lcweb2.loc.gov/frd/cs/bhtoc.html
A service of the U.S. Library of Congress, the site delivers fact sheets on Bahraini geography,

population, agriculture, mining, manufacturing, and foreign economic relations.

Bahrain InfoExport
http://www.infoexport.gc.ca/country-e.asp?continent=Africa&country=55
A service of Foreign Affairs and International Trade Canada, the site provides Bahraini commercial guides and market reports.

Bahrain Market Information
http://dtiinfo1.dti.gov.uk/ots/bahrain/
A service of the London-based Department of Trade and Industry, the site delivers Bahraini fact sheets, maps, and trade-show information.

Bahrain Market Research
http://strategis.ic.gc.ca/sc_mrkti/ibinddc/engdoc/ 1a1d1.html
A service of Industry Canada, the site provides U.S. Department of Commerce reports on Bahraini business, politics, trade regulations and standards, investment climate, trade and project financing, business travel, and market opportunities.

Bahrain Promotion and Marketing Board
http://www.bpmb.com/
A hub of country information, the site delivers Bahraini business guides, entry and visa fact sheets, investment primers, accommodation directories, and travel tips.

Bahrain Virtual Library
http://menic.utexas.edu/menic/countries/ bahrain.html
A service of the Center for Middle Eastern Studies at the University of Texas, the site provides a directory of Bahraini resources online. Categories include business and economy, government and politics, and news and current events.

Country Commercial Guide
http://www.state.gov/www/about_state/business/ com_guides/1998/neareast/bahrain98.html
Prepared by the U.S. Embassy in Manama, the site delivers primers on the Bahraini economy, political environment, trade regulations and standards, investment climate, trade and project financing, and business travel.

Bahrain Trade Assistance

Trade Shows in Bahrain
http://www.expoguide.com/shows/data/loc_4.htm
Compiled by Expoguide, the site is a directory of upcoming trade shows in Bahrain.

Bahrain Representative Offices

India

Embassy of India in Manama
http://www.indianembassy-bh.com/
Featuring a message from the Ambassador, the site features Indian news, press releases, fact sheets, business guides, and reports on India-Bahrain trade and relations.

Sweden

Consular Agency of Sweden in Manama
http://www.ud.se/english/mfa/ambassad/bahrain.htm
The site lists the staff, street address, and phone and fax numbers of the Swedish Consular Agency in Manama.

United Kingdom

Embassy of Britain in Manama
http://www.fco.gov.uk/directory/posts.asp?BA
The site provides contact information for the British Embassy in Manama.

United States

United States Embassy in Manama
http://www.usembassy.com.bh/
The virtual Embassy delivers U.S. news, fact sheets, visa and passport information, Internet guides, and a directory of consular and commercial services.

United States Information Service in Manama
http://www.usembassy.com.bh/wwwhusis.htm
The site provides U.S. news, press releases, fact sheets, cultural information, socioeconomic statistics, exchange program primers, and Middle East bulletins.

Bangladesh

Bangladesh Media

Daily Star
http://www.dailystarnews.com/
Based in Dhaka, the site is a Bangladesh online newspaper. The service includes editorials, news highlights, political reports, city profiles, and foreign relation bulletins.

Bangladesh Media
http://www.mediainfo.com/emediajs/specific-geo.htm?region=bangladesh
Developed by Editor and Publisher Interactive, the site is an index of Bangladesh magazines, newspapers, and other media sites online.

Bangladesh Market Guides

Bangladesh Business Briefs
http://www.austrade.gov.au/IOOM/Bangladesh/
A service of Austrade, the site offers fact sheets on Bangladesh business etiquette, foreign investment, corporate taxation, marketing, and visas.

Bangladesh Country Brief
http://www.worldbank.org/cgi-bin/sendoff.cgi?page=%2Fhtml%2Fextdr%2Foffrep%2Fsas%2Fbd.htm
A service of the World Bank Group, the site provides Bangladesh population statistics, financial data, development reports, and economic forecasts.

Bangladesh Country Profile
http://www.tradenz.govt.nz/intelligence/profiles/bangladesh.html
A service of the New Zealand Trade Development Board, the site provides Bangladesh economic statistics, market information, and business tips.

Bangladesh Country Report
http://www.state.gov/www/issues/economic/trade_reports/south_asia97/bangladesh97.html
Prepared by the U.S. Department of State, the site delivers information on Bangladesh exchange rates, debt management, trade barriers, and intellectual property protection.

Bangladesh: A Country Study
http://lcweb2.loc.gov/frd/cs/bdtoc.html
A service of the U.S. Library of Congress, the site delivers fact sheets on Bangladesh geography, population, agriculture, mining, manufacturing, and foreign economic relations.

Bangladesh InfoExport
http://www.infoexport.gc.ca/country-e.asp?continent=Asia&country=5
A service of Foreign Affairs and International Trade Canada, the site provides Bangladesh commercial guides and market reports.

Bangladesh Market Access Database
http://mkaccdb.eu.int/mkdb/
mkdb.pl?METHOD=COUNTRY
A service of the European Commission, the site offers briefs on Bangladesh trade policy, tariff barriers, non-tariff barriers, investment-related measures, and financial services regulations.

Bangladesh Market Research
http://strategis.ic.gc.ca/sc_mrkti/ibinddc/engdoc/
1a1h4.html
A service of Industry Canada, the site provides U.S. Department of Commerce reports on Bangladesh business, politics, trade regulations and standards, investment climate, trade and project financing, business travel, and market opportunities.

Bangladesh Virtual Library
http://asnic.utexas.edu/asnic/countries/bangla/
A service of the World Wide Web Virtual Library, the site is a directory of Bangladesh resources online. Categories include economy, history, and government.

Bdesh
http://www.tuns.ca/~abidmr/bdesh.html
An electronic newsletter, the site provides Bangladesh fact sheets, discussion forums, travel information, language primers, education guides, and weather bulletins.

Commerce Wing
http://members.aol.com/banglaemb/embassy/
commerce/
A service of the Bangladesh Embassy in Washington, D.C., the site delivers reports on Bangladesh-U.S. trade and relations, and a directory of assistance programs for U.S. importers of Bangladeshi goods.

Country Commercial Guide
http://www.state.gov/www/about_state/business/
com_guides/1998/southeast_asia/
bangladesh98.html
Prepared by the U.S. Embassy in Dhaka, the site delivers primers on the Bangladesh economy, political environment, trade regulations and standards, investment climate, trade and project financing, and business travel.

Country Profile
http://members.aol.com/banglaemb/bangladesh/
profile/
The online service delivers background information on Bangladesh business, geography, investment, culture, climate, agriculture, and weather.

Permanent Mission of Bangladesh
http://www.undp.org/missions/bangladesh/
index.htm
Sponsored by the United Nations Development Program, the site features Bangladesh fact sheets, investment opportunities, executive profiles, and government directories.

Bangladesh Representative Offices

Canada

Embassy of Canada in Dhaka
http://www.dfait-maeci.gc.ca/english/missions/rep-
can1e.htm#bangladesh
The site provides contact information for the Canadian Embassy in Dhaka.

Denmark

Embassy of Denmark in Dhaka
http://www.citechco.net/dandhaka/
The site delivers Danish fact sheets, visa and passport information, cultural bulletins, and a directory of consular and commercial services.

France

French Trade Commission in Dhaka
http://www.dree.org/bengladesh/
Written in French, the site delivers Bangladesh market reports, sector profiles, contact information, and a directory of export programs for French companies doing business in Bangladesh.

India

Indian Commercial Mission in Dhaka
http://www.nic.in/commin/ICM.HTM
The site lists the street address, phone and fax numbers, and e-mail link of the Indian Commercial Mission in Dhaka.

Malaysia

High Commission of Malaysia in Dhaka
http://www.mnet.com.my/klonline/www/missions/
malmiss/mbanglad1.htm
The site provides contact information for the Malaysian High Commission in Dhaka.

Nepal

Embassy of Nepal in Dhaka
http://www.info-nepal.com/members/fips/contacts/ nepalese.html
The site provides contact information for the Embassy of Nepal in Dhaka.

Pakistan

Pakistan Trade Office in Dhaka
http://www.jamal.com/epb/ptoa.htm
The site provides contact information for the Pakistan Trade Office in Dhaka.

Singapore

Consulate General of Singapore in Dhaka
http://www.gov.sg/mfa/consular/mww_b.htm
The site provides contact information for the Singapore Consulate General in Dhaka.

Sweden

Embassy of Sweden in Dhaka
http://www.citechco.net/swedhaka/
Featuring a message from the Ambassador, the site provides Swedish fact sheets, and a directory of Swedish companies in Bangladesh.

Thailand

Royal Thai Embassy in Dhaka
http://www.mfa.go.th/Embassy/detail/84.htm
The site lists the Ambassador, street address, and phone and fax numbers of the Thai Embassy in Dhaka.

United Kingdom

High Commission of Britain in Dhaka
http://www.fco.gov.uk/directory/posts.asp?BG
The site provides contact information for the British High Commission in Dhaka.

United States

Bangladesh-U.S.A. Connection
http://www.vmc-world.com/bangladesh-usa/
With offices in Dhaka and Washington, D.C., the Connection promotes Bangladesh-U.S. trade. The site includes contact information and a directory of bilateral business matchmaking services.

United States Information Service in Dhaka
http://www.citechco.net/usdhaka/usis/ usisdhka.htm
The site provides U.S. news, press releases, fact sheets, cultural primers, event information, and a directory of educational and exchange programs.

U.S. Mission in Dhaka
http://www.citechco.net/usdhaka/
The online service provides fact sheets on the U.S. Embassy, U.S. Aid programs to Bangladesh, the U.S. Peace Corps, and mission affiliates such as the American International School.

Bhutan

Bhutan Media

Bhutan Media
http://www.mediainfo.com/emediajs/specific-geo.htm?region=bhutan
Developed by Editor and Publisher Interactive, the site is an index of Bhutanese newspapers and other media sites online.

Kuensel: Bhutan's Newspaper
http://www.kuensel.com/
An English-language electronic newspaper, the site provides Bhutanese news, editorials, company profiles, sector reports, and a searchable archive of past issues.

Bhutan Market Guides

Bhutan Country Brief
http://www.worldbank.org/cgi-bin/ sendoff.cgi?page=%2Fhtml%2Fextdr%2Foffrep%2 Fsas%2Fbt.htm
A service of the World Bank Group, the site provides Bhutanese population statistics, financial data, development reports, and economic forecasts.

Bhutan: A Country Study
http://lcweb2.loc.gov/frd/cs/bttoc.html
A service of the U.S. Library of Congress, the site delivers fact sheets on Bhutanese geography, population, agriculture, mining, manufacturing, and foreign economic relations.

Bhutan Market Research
http://strategis.ic.gc.ca/sc_mrkti/ibinddc/engdoc/ 1a1h5.html
Posted by Industry Canada, the site provides U.S. Central Intelligence Agency fact sheets on

Bhutanese geography, people, government, economy, communications, and transportation.

Bhutan World Wide Web Virtual Library
http://bhutan.org/
A service of the World Wide Web Virtual Library, the site is a directory of Bhutanese resources online. Categories include general reference, commercial information, and government.

Kingdom of Bhutan
http://www.kingdomofbhutan.com/
Homepage of the Bhutan Tourism Corporation, the site provides Bhutanese fact sheets, travel guides, accommodation directories, and contact information.

Cyprus

Cyprus Search Tools

Search Cyprus
http://www.searchcyprus.com/
A directory of Cyprus resources online, the site is divided into over 20 categories including business, education, government, real estate, and shopping.

Cyprus Media

Cyprus Media
http://www.mediainfo.com/emediajs/specific-geo.htm?region=cyprus
Compiled by Editor and Publisher Interactive, the site is an index of Cypriot media sites online.

Cyprus Market Guides

Country Commercial Guide
http://www.state.gov/www/about_state/business/com_guides/1998/europe_canada/cyprus98.html
Prepared by the U.S. Embassy in Nicosia, the site delivers primers on the Cypriot economy, political environment, trade regulations and standards, investment climate, trade and project financing, and business travel.

Cyprus: A Country Study
http://lcweb2.loc.gov/frd/cs/cytoc.html
A service of the U.S. Library of Congress, the site delivers fact sheets on Cypriot geography, population, agriculture, mining, manufacturing, and foreign economic relations.

Cyprus Government
http://www.pio.gov.cy/

A hub of country information, the site delivers Cypriot news, speeches, fact sheets, economic reports, business guides, government directories, and foreign policy statements.

Cyprus Industry Online
http://www.industry.cy.net/
A virtual business library, the site features Cypriot business news, discussion forums, project profiles, sector studies, event information, and a database of management accredited consultants.

Cyprus InfoExport
http://www.infoexport.gc.ca/country-e.asp?continent=Europe&country=50
A service of Foreign Affairs and International Trade Canada, the site provides fact sheets and statistics on Cypriot geography, business and politics.

Cyprus Market Information
http://dtiinfo1.dti.gov.uk/ots/cyprus/
A service of the London-based Department of Trade and Industry, the site delivers Cypriot fact sheets, maps, and trade-show information.

Cyprus Market Research
http://strategis.ic.gc.ca/sc_mrkti/ibinddc/engdoc/1a1d2.html
A service of Industry Canada, the site provides U.S. Department of Commerce reports on Cypriot business, politics, trade regulations and standards, investment climate, trade and project financing, business travel, and market opportunities.

Department of Statistics and Research
http://www.pio.gov.cy/dsr/html/english.html
A service of the Cypriot government, the site provides a database of country statistics on labor, agriculture, consumer prices, international trade, transportation, and other economic indicators.

Cyprus Trade Assistance

Cyprus: A Centre for International Business
http://www.cosmosnet.net/azias/cyprus/bus-main.html
An online business gateway, the site provides Cypriot fact sheets, sector profiles, investment primers, exchange rates, and regulatory information.

Cyprus Trade Centers Worldwide
http://www.cyprustradeny.org/cyny5.html

A service of the Cyprus Trade Center in New York, the site is a directory of Cypriot trade promotion offices in 14 countries including Austria, France, and the United Kingdom.

Foreign Trade
http://www.pio.gov.cy/dsr/html/
foreign_trade_for_1996.html
Developed by the Cyprus Ministry of Finance, the site provides Cypriot export and import data, and trade balance information.

Trade Shows in Cyprus
http://www.expoguide.com/shows/data/loc_11.htm
Compiled by Expoguide, the site is a directory of upcoming trade shows in Cyprus.

Cyprus Representative Offices

Sweden

Consulate General of Sweden in Nicosia
http://www.ud.se/english/mfa/ambassad/
cypern.htm
The site lists the staff, street address, phone and fax numbers, and e-mail link of the Swedish Consulate General in Nicosia.

United Kingdom

High Commission of Britain in Nicosia
http://www.fco.gov.uk/directory/posts.asp?CY
The site provides contact information for the British High Commission in Nicosia.

United States

United States Embassy in Nicosia
http://www.americanembassy.org.cy/
The virtual Embassy delivers U.S. news, press releases, speeches, electronic journals, event information, and a directory of consular and commercial services.

United States Information Service in Nicosia
http://www.americanembassy.org.cy/www2.htm
Featuring a message from the Director, the site provides a mission statement and a directory of U.S. Information Service public affairs and information specialists in Nicosia.

Egypt

Egypt Media

Business Today
http://www.businesstoday-eg.com/
Updated monthly, the subscription news service provides Egyptian business reports, sector profiles, economic forecasts, event information, and tourism information.

Egypt Media
http://www.mediainfo.com/emediajs/specific-geo.htm?region=egypt
Compiled by Editor and Publisher Interactive, the site is an index of Egyptian media sites.

Egypt Today
http://www.egypttoday.com/
Based in Cairo, the subscription service provides Egyptian general news, lifestyle features, food and music reviews, sector profiles, and investigative reports.

Egypt Market Guides

Barclays Country Report: Egypt
http://www.offshorebanking.barclays.com/
services/economic/yearly/egymar98/
contents.html
Prepared by Barclays Bank, the site reports on Egyptian economic trends, politics, monetary and fiscal policy, international trade, and U.K.-Egypt merchandise trade and investment flows.

Country Profile: Egypt
http://www.mbendi.co.za/cyegcy.htm
Developed by Mbendi Information Services, the site provides Egyptian maps, fact sheets, investment primers, business guides, sector profiles, and a management consultant directory.

Egypt Business Briefs
http://www.austrade.gov.au/IOOM/Cairo/
A service of Austrade, the site offers fact sheets on Egyptian culture, business etiquette, marketing, transportation, travel, and visas.

Egypt Business Reports
http://italchambers.net/BusinessReports.html
Prepared by the Italian Chamber of Commerce and written in Italian, the site provides Egypt fact sheets, market reports, and commercial guides.

Egypt Country Brief
*http://www.worldbank.org/cgi-bin/
sendoff.cgi?page=%2Fhtml%2Fextdr%2Foffrep%2
Fmena%2Feg.htm*
A service of the World Bank Group, the site
provides Egyptian population statistics, financial
data, development reports, and economic
forecasts.

Egypt Country Profile
*http://www.tradenz.govt.nz/intelligence/profiles/
egypt.html*
A service of the New Zealand Trade Development
Board, the site provides Egyptian economic
statistics, market information, and business tips.

Egypt Country Report
*http://www.state.gov/www/issues/economic/
trade_reports/neareast97/egypt97.html*
Prepared by the U.S. Department of State, the site
delivers information on Egyptian exchange rates,
debt management, trade barriers, and intellectual
property protection.

Egypt: A Country Study
http://lcweb2.loc.gov/frd/cs/egtoc.html
A service of the U.S. Library of Congress, the site
delivers fact sheets on Egyptian geography,
population, agriculture, mining, manufacturing,
and foreign economic relations.

Egypt Economy
*http://www.sis.gov.eg/egyptinf/economy/html/
econfrm.htm*
Developed by the Egypt State Information Service,
the site delivers Egyptian fact sheets, speeches,
investment guides, business primers, and
tourism information.

Egypt InfoExport
*http://www.infoexport.gc.ca/country-
e.asp?continent=Africa&country=15*
A service of Foreign Affairs and International
Trade Canada, the site provides Egyptian
commercial guides and market reports.

Egypt Market Access Database
*http://mkaccdb.eu.int/mkdb/
mkdb.pl?METHOD=COUNTRY*
A service of the European Commission, the site
offers briefs on Egyptian trade policy, tariff
barriers, non-tariff barriers, investment-related
measures, and financial services regulations.

Egypt Market Information
http://dtiinfo1.dti.gov.uk/ots/egypt/
A service of the London-based Department of
Trade and Industry, the site delivers Egyptian fact
sheets, maps, and trade-show information.

Egypt Market Research
*http://strategis.ic.gc.ca/sc_mrkti/ibinddc/engdoc/
1a1a18.html*
A service of Industry Canada, the site provides
U.S. Department of Commerce reports on
Egyptian business, politics, trade regulations and
standards, investment climate, trade and project
financing, business travel, and market opportunities.

Egypt State Information Service
http://www.sis.gov.eg/
A searchable hub of country information, the site
delivers Egyptian news, press releases, photo
galleries, business guides, cultural bulletins,
history lessons, and travel information.

Egypt Virtual Library
*http://menic.utexas.edu/menic/countries/
egypt.html*
A service of the Center for Middle Eastern Studies
at the University of Texas, the site provides a
directory of Egyptian resources online. Categories include business and economy, government
and politics, and news and media.

Index on Egypt
*http://www.africaindex.africainfo.no/africaindex1/
countries/egypt.html*
A directory of Egyptian resources online, the site
is divided into nine categories including culture,
economy, education, history, news and media,
technology, and tourism.

Investing in Egypt
http://163.121.10.41/invest/
A service of the Egyptian Ministry of International
Cooperation, the site features Egyptian business
guides, investment primers, economic statistics,
and program directories.

Investment Profile: Egypt
http://www.mbendi.co.za/ernsty/cyegeyip.htm
Developed by Ernst and Young, the site provides
fact sheets on Egyptian business establishments, taxation, investment incentives, exchange
controls, entry visas, and work permits.

Technology Development Program
http://its-idsc.gov.eg/tdp/
Established in 1993, the Program promotes high
technology development in Egypt. The site
includes a mission statement, project profiles,
and contact information.

Egypt Trade Assistance

Egyptian Trading Directory
http://www.egtrade.com/
A searchable database of Egyptian companies, the site is divided into six categories including import and export, shipping, insurance, factories, banks, and hotels.

Trade Pages Egypt
http://www.tradepages.com.eg/
A browsable directory of some 60,000 Egyptian companies, the site is searchable by company name, industry, location, and keyword.

Trade Point Egypt
http://www.untpdc.org/incubator/egy/tpcai/
Part of the United Nations Global Trade Point Network, the site provides Egyptian trade leads, market bulletins, and contact information.

Trade Shows in Egypt
http://www.expoguide.com/shows/data/loc_14.htm
Compiled by Expoguide, the site is a directory of upcoming trade shows in Egypt.

Egypt Representative Offices

Austria

Austrian Chamber of Commerce in Cairo
http://aw.wk.or.at/awo/ahst-kairo.htm
The site lists the staff, street address, phone and fax numbers, e-mail link, and office hours of the Austrian Trade Commission in Cairo.

Brunei Darussalam

Embassy of Brunei Darussalam in Cairo
http://www.brunet.bn/homepage/gov/bruemb/govemb.htm
The site provides contact information for the Brunei Darussalam Embassy in Cairo.

Canada

Embassy of Canada in Cairo
http://www.dfait-maeci.gc.ca/english/missions/rep-can2e.htm#egypt
The site provides contact information for the Canadian Embassy in Cairo.

Germany

German Arab Chamber of Commerce
http://www.soficom.com.eg/gacc/
Based in Cairo, the Chamber promotes German-Arab trade. The site provides a mission statement, program directory, and contact information.

German-Arab Chamber of Commerce in Cairo
http://www.gerarcham.com/index1.html
Part of a worldwide network of German bi-national chambers, the site provides German economic news and statistics, sector profiles, event information, publication lists, and Arab procurement opportunities.

German Embassy in Cairo
http://www.german-embassy.org.eg/
Posted in Arabic, English, and German, the site delivers German news, fact sheets, business guides, investment primers, and reports on German-Egyptian trade and relations.

Ghana

Embassy of Ghana in Cairo
http://www.juntung.com/ghana-consul-hk/2misabo.htm
The site provides contact information for the Ghanaian Embassy in Cairo.

India

Indian Commercial Mission in Cairo
http://www.nic.in/commin/ICM.HTM
The site lists the street address, phone and fax numbers, and e-mail link of the Indian Commercial Mission in Cairo.

Indonesia

Embassy of Indonesia in Cairo
http://indag.dprin.go.id/INGG/trade/atache.HTM
The site provides contact information for the Indonesian Embassy in Cairo.

Italy

Italian Trade Commission in Cairo
http://www.ice.it/estero/cairo/
Posted in Italian, the site provides Italian news, fact sheets, press releases, business guides, cultural bulletins, event information, and economic statistics.

Malaysia

Embassy of Malaysia in Cairo
http://www.mnet.com.my/klonline/www/missions/ malmiss/megypt.htm
The site provides contact information for the Malaysian Embassy in Cairo.

Nepal

Embassy of Nepal in Cairo
http://www.info-nepal.com/members/fips/contacts/ nepalese.html
The site provides contact information for the Embassy of Nepal in Cairo.

Singapore

Embassy of Singapore in Cairo
http://www.gov.sg/mfa/consular/mww_e.htm
The site provides contact information for the Singapore Embassy in Cairo.

South Africa

South Africa Foreign Trade Office in Cairo
http://wwwdti.pwv.gov.za/dtiwww/ foreign_offices.htm
A service of the South Africa Department of Trade and Industry, the site provides contact information for the South Africa Trade Office in Cairo.

Spain

Spanish Commercial Office in Cairo
http://www.icex.es/openURL.html#openURL=/ english/infoproyem/ofcomes/ofcomes.html#AF
The site lists the staff, street address, phone and fax numbers, and e-mail link of the Spanish Commercial Office in Cairo.

Sweden

Embassy of Sweden in Cairo
http://www.ud.se/english/mfa/ambassad/ egypten.htm
The site lists the staff, street address, phone and fax numbers, and e-mail link of the Swedish Embassy in Cairo.

Tanzania

Embassy of Tanzania in Cairo
http://www.tanzania-online.gov.uk/visa/ envoys.html
The site provides contact information for the Tanzanian Embassy in Cairo.

Taiwan

China External Trade Development Council Office in Cairo
http://www.cetra.org.tw/english/o_office/ indexset.htm
A Taiwanese trade promotion service, the site lists the mission statement and e-mail link of the China External Trade Development Council Office in Cairo.

Thailand

Royal Thai Embassy in Cairo
http://www.mfa.go.th/Embassy/detail/86.htm
The site lists the Ambassador, street address, and phone and fax numbers of the Thai Embassy in Cairo.

United Kingdom

Embassy of Britain in Cairo
http://www.fco.gov.uk/directory/posts.asp?EG
The site provides contact information for the British Embassy in Cairo.

United States

American Chamber of Commerce in Egypt
http://www.amcham.org.eg/
Based in Cairo, the Chamber promotes American-Egyptian trade. The site includes a members database, trade leads, publication lists, event information, and Egyptian market profiles.

United States Embassy in Egypt
http://www.usis.egnet.net/
The virtual Embassy provides U.S. news, fact sheets, press releases, Egyptian business guides, reports on Egyptian-U.S. trade, and a directory of consular and commercial services.

United States Information Service in Cairo
http://www.usis.egnet.net/usis.htm
The site provides U.S. news, press releases, fact sheets, cultural primers, event information, and a directory of educational and exchange programs.

Venezuela

Embassy of Venezuela in Cairo
http://www.trade-venezuela.com/EMBVENG.HTM
The site lists the street address, phone and fax

numbers, and e-mail link of the Venezuelan Embassy in Cairo.

India

India Search Tools

123India
http://www.123india.com/
A browsable directory of Indian resources online, the site is divided into 14 categories including business and economy, government, news and media, reference, and society and culture.

India Media

Economic Times
http://www.economictimes.com/
An online business newspaper, the site provides Indian business guides, economic surveys, editorials, speeches, statistics, a personal tax calculator, and a currency converter.

Hindu Business Line
http://www.indiaserver.com/bline/bline.html
An Indian business e-zine, the site delivers corporate bulletins, editorials, sector profiles, information technology reports, and a searchable news archive.

India Economic News
http://www.indiaserver.com/embusa/
A service of the Indian Embassy in Washington, D.C., the site provides Indian business news, economic forecasts, investment guides, sector bulletins, and event information.

India Media
http://www.mediainfo.com/emediajs/specific-geo.htm?region=india
Compiled by Editor and Publisher Interactive, the site is an index of Indian media sites online including city guides, magazines, newspapers, and news syndicates.

India Market Guides

Access India
http://www.accessindia.com/snapshot/headline.htm
Updated every business day, the site provides news and fact sheets on Indian banking, finance, foreign relations, international trade, industrial relations, and taxation.

All About India
http://www.indiaintl.com/about.html
A country business guide, the site features Indian fact sheets, consumer and industrial market reports, investment opportunities, international trade bulletins, and state profiles.

All India Association of Industries
http://www.sourceindia.com/aiai/
Based in Bombay, the Association promotes Indian business. The site includes a mission statement, contact information, and Indian economic highlights.

Barclays Country Report: India
http://www.offshorebanking.barclays.com/services/economic/yearly/indjun97/index.html
Prepared by Barclays Bank, the site reports on Indian economic trends, politics, monetary and fiscal policy, international trade, and U.K.-India merchandise trade and investment flows.

Business and Information Technology in India
http://www.brint.com/INDIA.htm
A service of the BizTech Network, the site provides a directory of Indian business resources online. Categories include media, company sites, and technology issues.

Commerce Net India
http://www.commercenetindia.com/
A virtual library of business information, the site includes Indian fact sheets, legal primers, economic statistics, publication lists, budget bulletins, taxation guides, and copyright and patent information.

Confederation of Indian Industry
http://www.indianindustry.com/
Representing over 3,700 companies, the Confederation promotes Indian business. The site includes economic bulletins, event information, electronic commerce guides, export policy highlights, and a searchable members database.

Country Commercial Guide
http://www.state.gov/www/about_state/business/com_guides/1998/southeast_asia/india98.html
Prepared by the U.S. Embassy in New Delhi, the site delivers primers on the Indian economy, political environment, trade regulations and standards, investment climate, trade and project financing, and business travel.

Discover India

http://www.meadev.gov.in/
A service of the Indian Ministry of External Affairs, the site provides Indian fact sheets, foreign relations statements, economic reports, tourism information, science and technology bulletins, and media guides.

Discovery of India

http://www.mahesh.com/india/
An index of Indian resources online, the site is divided into 25 categories including business, education, employment, government, history, and science and technology.

Economic Survey

http://www.nic.in/indiabudget/es97-98/
Prepared by the India Ministry of Finance, the site provides fact sheets on Indian public finance, prices and distribution, international trade, industrial policy, agriculture, and infrastructure.

Explore India

http://www.exploreindia.com/
A hub of country business information, the site delivers fact sheets on Indian financial markets, export associations, business opportunities, real estate, and tourism.

Incore

http://www.incore.com/india.html
An index of Indian resources online, the site is divided into nine categories including business, travel and tourism, history, states, news, community, and entertainment.

India: Big Emerging Markets Homepage

http://www.ita.doc.gov/bems/India.html
Developed by the United States Department of Commerce, the site delivers Indian fact sheets, economic forecasts, export and import statistics, sector profiles, and international trade guides.

India Business Briefs

http://www.austrade.gov.au/IOOM/India/
A service of Austrade, the site offers fact sheets on Indian business etiquette, foreign investment, corporate taxation, marketing, and visas.

India Business Reports

http://italchambers.net/BusinessReports.html
Prepared by the Italian Chamber of Commerce and written in Italian, the site provides Indian fact sheets, market reports, and commercial guides.

India Country Brief

http://www.worldbank.org/cgi-bin/ sendoff.cgi?page=%2Fhtml%2Fextdr%2Foffrep%2 Fsas%2 Fin.htm
A service of the World Bank Group, the site provides Indian population statistics, financial data, development reports, and economic forecasts.

India Country Profile

http://www.tradenz.govt.nz/intelligence/profiles/ india.html
A service of the New Zealand Trade Development Board, the site provides Indian economic statistics, market information, and business tips.

India Country Report

http://www.state.gov/www/issues/economic/ trade_reports/south_asia97/india97.html
Prepared by the U.S. Department of State, the site delivers information on Indian exchange rates, debt management, trade barriers, and intellectual property protection.

India InfoExport

http://www.infoexport.gc.ca/country- e.asp?continent=Asia&country=13
A service of Foreign Affairs and International Trade Canada, the site provides India commercial guides and market reports.

India Invest

http://www.india-invest.com/
A portal of investment information, the site provides Indian business news, event information, strategic alliance opportunities, tender notices, and company profiles.

India Market Access Database

http://mkaccdb.eu.int/mkdb/ mkdb.pl?METHOD=COUNTRY
A service of the European Commission, the site offers briefs on Indian trade policy, tariff barriers, non-tariff barriers, investment-related measures, and financial services regulations.

India Market Information

http://dtiinfo1.dti.gov.uk/ots/india/
A service of the London-based Department of Trade and Industry, the site delivers Indian fact sheets, maps, and trade-show information.

India Market Research

http://strategis.ic.gc.ca/sc_mrkti/ibinddc/engdoc/ 1a1h6.html
A service of Industry Canada, the site provides

U.S. Department of Commerce reports on Indian business, politics, trade regulations and standards, investment climate, trade and project financing, business travel, and market opportunities.

India Monthly Economic Indicators

http://www.nic.in/finmin/ecoind/ecoind.htm
Developed by the Indian Ministry of Finance, the site provides monthly economic updates on the Indian economy. The service reports on agriculture, industrial production, infrastructure, international trade, and banking.

India One-Stop Biz Info Centre

http://indiaonestop.com/
An online marketplace, the site provides Indian trade leads, sector profiles, business news, economic reports, currency rates, company directories, and tender notices.

India: Unlimited Avenues

http://www.indiaintl.com/
Updated weekly, the site delivers Indian business news, trade-show information, online discussion groups, fact sheets, state profiles, business guides, and investment primers.

India Virtual Library

http://webhead.com/WWWVL/India/
A service of the World Wide Web Virtual Library, the site is a directory of Indian resources online. Categories include Indian states, cities and districts, newsgroups, and mailing lists.

Indian Business Directory

http://www.webindia.com/india.html
A browsable database of Indian companies, the site profiles firms in over 50 industries including automotive, banking, electronics, food processing, real estate, and steel.

Indian Corporate Gateway

http://www.owlnet.rice.edu/~ravi/india/index.html
A web-based business forum, the site delivers Indian economic news, company profiles, trade leads, employment opportunities, and an online bulletin board.

India's Infrastructure Investment Opportunities

http://www.nic.in/indiainfra/
Developed by the Indian National Informatics Center, the site is a database of Indian infrastructure investment opportunities. Categories include oil and natural gas, coal, mining, roads, telecommunications, civil aviation, and ports.

IndiaWorld

http://indiaworld.co.in/
An online country gateway, the site provides Indian news, investment information, travel guides, history lessons, currency rates, and sector profiles.

InfoIndia

http://www.infoindia.com/
A searchable archive of Indian business information, the site features company profiles, job postings, online classifieds, procurement opportunities, and web directories.

Locate India

http://www.locateindia.com/
Based in Mumbai, the site provides a searchable database of Indian companies and business organizations in over 20 categories including agri-food, wood products, plastics, publishing, and consulting.

Ministry of Commerce

http://www.nic.in/commin/
Based in New Delhi, the Ministry promotes Indian economic development and international trade. The site provides a directory of Ministry boards and entities including commercial missions abroad.

Ministry of Finance

http://www.nic.in/finmin/
Along with Finance Minister speeches and press releases, the site delivers Indian budget bulletins, business surveys, taxation guides, and economic statistics.

Naukri

http://www.naukri.com/
A resource page for Indian job seekers and recruiters, the site provides employment postings, resume services, hiring surveys, career guides, and scholarship information.

Web India

http://www.webindia.com/
A virtual business exchange, the site provides Indian economic news, event information, online bulletin boards, company profiles, and business opportunities.

India Trade Assistance

Confederation of Indian Industry International Offices
http://www.indianindustry.com/au/
network_main.htm#International Offices
The site is a directory of Confederation of Indian Industry offices in nine countries including China, Germany, Nepal, Singapore, Switzerland, South Africa, and the United Kingdom.

Council for Leather Exports
http://www.leatherindia.com/
Based in Chennai, the Council promotes the export of Indian leather goods. The site includes a member directory, sector profile, investment opportunities, and contact information.

Engineering Export Promotion Council
http://www.eepc.gov.in/
Based in Calcutta, the Council promotes the export of Indian engineering services. The site includes Council news, membership information, trade policy reports, and export award results.

EXIM Policy 1997-2002
http://www.allindia.com/exim98/
The online service reviews the export and import policy of the Indian Department of Commerce. Key issues include duty exemption schemes and export licenses.

Export Credit Guarantee Corporation
http://www.nic.in/commin/
AUTOBODI.HTM#ECGCIL
A branch of the Indian Department of Commerce, the Corporation provides risk management services for Indian exporters. The site provides a mission statement and contact information.

Export Import Trade Flash
http://www.trade-india.com/tflash/
Updated every two weeks, the site provides exporting tips, international trade news, country profiles, customs reports, and business opportunities for Indian exporters.

Export Promotion Cell
http://www.indiagov.org/economy/trade/
expcells.htm
A service of Discover India, the site is a directory of export promotion agencies in India. Organizations include the Agricultural and Processed Food Products Export Development Authority, Apparel Export Promotion Council, and Sports Goods Export Promotion Council.

Exporter's Yellow Pages
http://www.trade-india.com/eyp7/
A searchable database of Indian exporters, the directory is divided into over 50 industrial categories including adhesives, book publishers, marine equipment, and zippers.

Federation of Indian Export Organizations
http://www.fieo.com/
Based in New Delhi, the Federation promotes Indian exports and represents the interests of Indian export associations. The site features press releases, event information, a member directory, and trade leads.

Gems and Jewellery Export Promotion Council
http://www.gjepc.org/
Based in Mumbai, the Council promotes the export of Indian gems and jewelry. The site includes a mission statement, news, event information, a member directory, and export statistics.

India Excise and Customs
http://konark.ncst.ernet.in/customs/index.html
Along with Indian travel guides, the site provides Indian import regulations, duty rates, South Asian Association for Regional Co-operation reports, and contact information.

India Importers Directory
http://www.trade-india.com/iid/
A browsable directory of Indian importers, the site is divided into over 50 industrial categories including automotive, chemicals, printing machinery, and traffic safety.

India Trade Winds
http://www.trade-winds.net/prein.htm
A service of Trade Winds Online, the site is a searchable directory of Indian trade shows, business contacts, tourism information, and media.

Indian Commercial Missions Abroad
http://www.nic.in/commin/ICM.HTM
A service of the Indian Ministry of Commerce, the site is a database of Indian commercial missions in over 60 countries including Bahrain, Russia, Thailand, and the United Kingdom.

Indian Exporters Online
http://www.indianexporters.com/
A hub of Indian international trade information, the site delivers Indian export news, economic reports, export and import statistics, trade policy

reviews, and a directory of India's top 50 exporters.

Indian Institute of Foreign Trade
http://www.nic.in/commin/AUTOBODI.HTM#IIFT
Based in New Delhi, the Institute provides export training to Indian businesspeople. The site lists the mission statement, street address, and phone and fax numbers of the Institute.

Marine Products Export Development Authority
http://www.mpeda.com/
Based in Cochin, the Authority promotes the export of Indian seafood, aquaculture, and other marine products. The site provides a member directory, product catalog, sector profile, and event information.

Ministry of External Affairs
http://www.indiagov.org/economy/trade/mea.htm
The site provides a directory of Ministry divisions and staff who provide trade, economic and investment services on behalf of the Indian government. The divisions include Investment Publicity, Technical Cooperation, and Multilateral Economic Relations.

Missions of India Abroad
http://www.mahesh.com/india/govt/ consulates.html
A service of Discovery of India, the site is a directory of Indian Embassies, High Commissions and Consulates around the world, and foreign diplomatic missions in India.

National Centre for Trade Information
http://www.nic.in/ncti/
Based in New Delhi, the Centre provides Indian international trade information such as tariff rates, country profiles, and trade-show reports. The site includes a mission statement and a directory of Center programs and products.

Overseas Construction Council of India
http://www.exploreindia.com/occi/occi.html
Based in New Delhi, the Council promotes the export of Indian engineering services and building materials for international construction projects. The site includes a mission statement, member directory, and contact information.

Trade Daily Archives
http://www.indianexporters.com/daily/index.html
A service of Indian Exporters Online, the site delivers international business news, and

reports on Indian trade with North America, Latin America, Europe, and Asia Pacific.

Trade India
http://www.trade-india.com/
A portal of global business information, the site provides searchable databases of Indian exporters, importers, trade leads, and strategic alliance opportunities.

Trade India Bulletin Board
http://www.trade-india.com/bbsnew/
Based in New Delhi, the site is a searchable directory of Indian business opportunities including offers to buy, sell, and partner. Categories include agri-food, mining, apparel, and electronics.

Software Technology Parks of India
http://www.soft.net/
A service of the Indian Department of Electronics, the site reports on Indian software exporting, development, training, and certification.

Trade Shows in India
http://www.expoguide.com/shows/data/loc_23.htm
Compiled by Expoguide, the site is a directory of upcoming trade shows in India.

India Representative Offices

Embassies and High Commissions in India
http://www.exploreindia.com/free/ads/tourism/ embassies.html
A service of Explore India, the site provides a directory of the street addresses and phone and fax numbers of the foreign embassies, high commissions, and consulates in India.

Australia

Austrade in India
http://www.austrade.gov.au/india/
An online export promotion service, the site features Australian fact sheets, investment primers, publication lists, contact information, and Indian business guides.

Austria

Austrian Trade Commission in New Delhi
http://aw.wk.or.at/awo/ahst-newdelhi.htm
The site lists the staff, street address, phone and fax numbers, e-mail link, and office hours of the Austrian Trade Commission in New Delhi.

Brunei Darussalam

High Commission of Brunei Darussalam in New Delhi
http://www.brunet.bn/homepage/gov/bruemb/govemb.htm
The site provides contact information for the Brunei Darussalam High Commission in New Delhi.

Canada

Canadian Government Trade Office in Bangalore
http://www.dfait-maeci.gc.ca/english/missions/rep-can2e.htm#india
The site provides contact information for the Canadian Government Trade Office in Bangalore.

Consulate of Canada in Mumbai
http://www.dfait-maeci.gc.ca/english/missions/rep-can2e.htm#india
The site provides contact information for the Canadian Consulate in Mumbai.

Embassy of Canada in New Delhi
http://www.dfait-maeci.gc.ca/english/missions/rep-can2e.htm#india
The site provides contact information for the Canadian Embassy in New Delhi.

Finland

Finland Trade Center in Mumbai
http://www.exports.finland.fi/tradecen.htm
The site lists the staff, street address, phone and fax numbers, and e-mail link of the Finland Trade Center in Mumbai.

Finland Trade Center in New Delhi
http://www.exports.finland.fi/tradecen.htm
The site lists the staff, street address, phone and fax numbers, and e-mail link of the Finland Trade Center in New Delhi.

France

French Trade Commission in India
http://www.dree.org/inde/
Written in French, the site delivers Indian market reports, sector profiles, contact information, and a directory of export programs for French companies doing business in India.

Germany

German Chamber of Commerce
http://www.ahk.net/en/in/Bombay/
The site lists the Chairpersons, street addresses, phone and fax numbers, e-mail links, and office hours of the German Chambers in Bombay, Bangalore, Calcutta, Chennai, and New Delhi.

Embassy of Germany in New Delhi
http://www.germanembassy-india.org/
Along with a directory of consular and commercial services, the virtual Embassy provides German fact sheets, business guides, and reports on Indo-German trade, and German investments in India.

Ghana

High Commission of Ghana in New Delhi
http://www.juntung.com/ghana-consul-hk/2misabo.htm
The site provides contact information for the Ghanaian High Commission in New Delhi.

Indonesia

Embassy of Indonesia in New Delhi
http://indag.dprin.go.id/INGG/trade/atache.HTM
The site provides contact information for the Indonesian Embassy in New Delhi.

Laos

Embassy of Laos in New Delhi
http://www.laoembassy.com/news/embassyabroad.htm
The site provides contact information for the Embassy of Laos in New Delhi.

Malaysia

Consulate General of Malaysia in Bombay
http://www.mnet.com.my/klonline/www/missions/malmiss/mindia2.htm
The site provides contact information for the Malaysian Consulate General in Bombay.

High Commission of Malaysia in New Delhi
http://www.mnet.com.my/klonline/www/missions/malmiss/mindia1.htm
The site provides contact information for the Malaysian High Commission in New Delhi.

Nepal

Embassy of Nepal in New Delhi
http://www.info-nepal.com/members/fips/contacts/nepalese.html
The site provides contact information for the Embassy of Nepal in New Delhi.

New Zealand

Trade New Zealand in New Delhi
http://www.tradenz.govt.nz/contact/measia.html
An export promotion service, the site provides contact information for the Trade New Zealand office in New Delhi.

Pakistan

Pakistan Trade Office in New Delhi
http://www.jamal.com/epb/ptoa.htm
The site provides contact information for the Pakistan Trade Office in New Delhi.

Singapore

Consulate General of Singapore in Chennai
http://www.gov.sg/mfa/consular/mww_i.htm
The site provides contact information for the Singapore Consulate General in Chennai.

Consulate General of Singapore in Mumbai
http://www.gov.sg/mfa/consular/mww_i.htm
The site provides contact information for the Singapore Consulate General in Mumbai.

High Commission of Singapore in New Delhi
http://www.gov.sg/mfa/consular/mww_i.htm
The site provides contact information for the Singapore High Commission in New Delhi.

South Africa

South Africa Foreign Trade Office in Mumbai
http://wwwdti.pwv.gov.za/dtiwww/foreign_offices.htm
A service of the South Africa Department of Trade and Industry, the site provides contact information for the South Africa Foreign Trade Office in Mumbai.

South Africa Foreign Trade Office in New Delhi
http://wwwdti.pwv.gov.za/dtiwww/foreign_offices.htm
A service of the South Africa Department of Trade and Industry, the site provides contact information for the South Africa Foreign Trade Office in New Delhi.

Spain

Spanish Commercial Office in New Delhi
http://www.icex.es/openURL.html#openURL=/english/infoproyem/ofcomes/ofcomes.html#AS
The site lists the staff, street address, phone and fax numbers, and e-mail link of the Spanish Commercial Office in New Delhi.

Sweden

Embassy of Sweden in New Delhi
http://www.ud.se/english/mfa/ambassad/indien.htm
The site lists the staff, street address, and phone and fax numbers of the Swedish Embassy in New Delhi.

Taiwan

China External Trade Development Council Office in New Delhi
http://www.cetra.org.tw/english/o_office/indexset.htm
A Taiwanese trade promotion service, the site lists the mission statement and e-mail link of the China External Trade Development Council Office in New Delhi.

Tanzania

Embassy of Tanzania in New Delhi
http://www.tanzania-online.gov.uk/visa/envoys.html
The site provides contact information for the Tanzania Embassy in New Delhi.

Thailand

Royal Thai Consulate General in Calcutta
http://www.mfa.go.th/Embassy/detail/17.htm
The site lists the Consul General, street address, and phone and fax numbers of the Thai Consulate General in Calcutta.

Royal Thai Consulate General in Mumbai
http://www.mfa.go.th/Embassy/detail/104.htm
The site lists the Consul General, street address, and phone and fax numbers of the Thai Consulate General in Mumbai.

Royal Thai Embassy in New Delhi
http://www.mfa.go.th/Embassy/detail/42.htm
The site lists the Ambassador, street address, and phone and fax numbers of the Thai Embassy in New Delhi.

Thailand Office of Commercial Affairs in New Delhi
http://www.thaitrade.com/thcoaf.html
The site lists the street address, phone and fax numbers, and e-mail link of the Thailand Office of Commercial Affairs in New Delhi.

United Kingdom

High Commission of Britain in New Delhi
http://www.fco.gov.uk/directory/posts.asp?IN
The site provides contact information for the British High Commission in New Delhi.

Trade Office of Britain in Bangalore
http://www.fco.gov.uk/directory/posts.asp?IN
The site provides contact information for the British Trade Office in Bangalore.

United Kingdom in India
http://www.ukinindia.org/
Based in New Delhi, the site provides British fact sheets, business guides, visa and passport information, and a directory of consular and commercial services.

United States

State of Utah Trade Office in Chandigarh
http://www.ce.ex.state.ut.us/international/reps/reps.htm#India
A service of the State of Utah International Business Development Office, the site lists the representative, street address, phone and fax numbers, and e-mail link of the Utah Trade Office in Chandigarh.

U.S. Consulate General in Madras
http://www.sphynx.com/madrasus/
Serving the states of Tamil Nadu, Andhra Pradesh, Karnataka, Kerala, the Union Territory of Pondicherry and the Lakshadweep Islands, the Consulate provides U.S. consular and commercial services. The site includes contact information, frequently asked questions and answers, and a free e-mail newsletter.

United States Consulate in Mumbai
http://www.usia.gov/abtusia/posts/IN3/wwwhmain.html
Along with contact information, the site delivers U.S. news, press releases, foreign policy statements, an Indian trade event calendar, and a directory of consular and commercial services.

United States Embassy in India
http://www.usia.gov/abtusia/posts/IN1/wwwhmain.html
The digital Embassy offers U.S. news, speeches, press releases, electronic journals, visa and passport information, staff profiles, and a directory of consular and commercial programs.

U.S. Information Service Chennai
http://www.usia.gov/posts/chennai/
The site provides U.S. news, press releases, fact sheets, cultural primers, event information, and reports on U.S. Information Service operations in South India.

U.S. Information Service New Delhi
http://www.usia.gov/abtusia/posts/IN1/wwwh5.html
The site provides U.S. news, speeches, press releases, fact sheets, event information, and a directory of Indo-American educational and exchange programs.

Iran

Iran Media

Iran Media
http://www.mediainfo.com/emediajs/specific-geo.htm?region=iran
Compiled by Editor and Publisher Interactive, the site is an index of Iranian media sites online including magazines and newspapers.

Iran Weekly Press Digest
http://www.neda.net/iran-wpd/
A weekly subscription news service, the site provides Iranian political reports, foreign affairs bulletins, business headlines, and a searchable archive of past issues.

Iranian Media
http://www.iranian.com/WebGuide/MediaAZ.html
A directory of Iranian media sites online, the site is divided into five sections: dailies, magazines, periodical, radio, and television.

Iran Market Guides

Iran Business Briefs
http://www.austrade.gov.au/IOOM/Iran/
A service of Austrade, the site offers fact sheets

on Iranian business etiquette, foreign investment, corporate taxation, marketing, and visas.

Iran Business Publications
http://www.neda.net/ibr/publications.html
A directory of Iranian periodicals and directories online, the site includes Iranian business news, export and import reports, company databases, and press bulletins.

Iran Business Resources
http://www.neda.net/ibr/
A service of the Neda Rayaneh Institute, a Tehran-based Internet service provider, the site provides Iranian fact sheets, company directories, publication lists, and event information.

Iran Country Brief
http://www.worldbank.org/cgi-bin/ sendoff.cgi?page=%2Fhtml%2Fextdr%2Foffrep%2 Fmena%2Fir.htm
A service of the World Bank Group, the site provides Iranian population statistics, financial data, development reports, and economic forecasts.

Iran Country Profile
http://www.tradenz.govt.nz/intelligence/profiles/ iran.html
A service of the New Zealand Trade Development Board, the site provides Iranian economic statistics, market information, and business tips.

Iran: A Country Study
http://lcweb2.loc.gov/frd/cs/irtoc.html
A service of the U.S. Library of Congress, the site delivers fact sheets on Iranian geography, population, agriculture, mining, manufacturing, and foreign economic relations.

Iran InfoExport
http://www.infoexport.gc.ca/country- e.asp?continent=Africa&country=56
A service of Foreign Affairs and International Trade Canada, the site provides Iranian commercial guides and market reports.

Iran Market Information
http://dtiinfo1.dti.gov.uk/ots/iran/
A service of the London-based Department of Trade and Industry, the site delivers Iranian fact sheets, maps, and trade-show information.

Iran Market Research
http://strategis.ic.gc.ca/sc_mrkti/ibinddc/engdoc/ 1a1d3.html

Posted by Industry Canada, the site provides U.S. Central Intelligence Agency fact sheets on Iranian geography, people, government, economy, communications, and transportation.

Iran: Recent Economic Developments
http://www.imf.org/external/pubs/CAT/ longres.cfm?sk=2564.0
Prepared by the International Monetary Fund, the site reports on Iranian prices, employment, wages, foreign investment, inflation, government expenditures, and relations with the World Trade Organization.

Iran Virtual Library
http://menic.utexas.edu/menic/countries/iran.html
A service of the Center for Middle Eastern Studies at the University of Texas, the site provides a directory of Iranian resources online. Categories include business and economy, government and politics, and news and media.

Salam Iran Homepage
http://www.salamiran.org/IranInfo/
A service of the Iranian Embassy in Ottawa, the site provides Iranian fact sheets, economic reports, travel information, history lessons, and cultural primers.

Iran Trade Assistance

Calendar of Fairs and Exhibitions in Iran
http://www.neda.net/ibr/calendar.html
A directory of Iranian trade shows, the site lists events from the toy, jewelry, shoe, leather, apparel, furniture, electrical, and household appliance industries.

Export Development Bank of Iran
http://www.neda.net/ibr/edb.html
Based in Tehran, the Bank provides export banking services for Iranian exporters and international buyers. The site provides a mission statement, contact information, and a directory of programs.

Export Guarantee Fund of Iran
http://www.neda.net/ibr/egf.html
Developed by the Iranian Ministry of Commerce, the Fund is a risk management service for Iranian exporters. The site provides contact information and Fund details.

Export Promotion Center of Iran
http://www.neda.net/ibr/epci.html
Based in Tehran, the Center promotes Iranian

exports and conducts international trade research. The site provides contact information and a directory of Center programs and services.

Free Zones in Iran
http://www.neda.net/ibr/freezones.html
The site provides contact information for three Iranian Free Zones: Kish, Qeshm, and Sirjan. The zones are special business development areas managed by the Iranian government.

IRI Trade Centers Corporation
http://www.neda.net/ibr/tcc.html
Based in Tehran, IRI promotes Iranian exports and international investment. The site is a directory of IRI offices in six countries including Germany, Turkey, Syria, and the United Kingdom.

Iran Exports and Imports
http://www.neda.net/iranexports/
Based in Tehran, the subscription site delivers Iranian export news, editorials, international trade reports, sectoral profiles, and executive profiles and interviews.

Iran Representative Offices

Foreign Trade Attachés in Iran
http://www.neda.net/ibr/fta.html
A directory of foreign trade attachés in Iran, the site lists representatives from some 30 countries including Argentina, Denmark, Japan, Poland, Sweden, and Turkey.

Armenia

Embassy of Armenia in Tehran
http://www.armeniaemb.org/forrel/embas2.htm
The site provides contact information for the Armenian Embassy in Tehran.

Austria

Austrian Trade Commission in Tehran
http://aw.wk.or.at/awo/ahst-teheran.htm
The site lists the staff, street address, phone and fax numbers, e-mail link, and office hours of the Austrian Trade Commission in Tehran.

Brunei Darussalam

Embassy of Brunei Darussalam in Tehran
http://www.brunet.bn/homepage/gov/bruemb/govemb.htm
The site provides contact information for the Brunei Darussalam Embassy in Tehran.

Canada

Embassy of Canada in Tehran
http://www.dfait-maeci.gc.ca/english/missions/repcan2e.htm#iran
The site provides contact information for the Canadian Embassy in Tehran.

Denmark

Embassy of Denmark in Tehran
http://inet.uni2.dk/home/ambadane.teheran/
Written in Danish and English, the site provides Danish news, fact sheets, Iranian press bulletins, commercial guides, and reports on Danish-Iranian trade and relations.

Germany

German Chamber of Commerce in Tehran
http://www.ahk.net/en/ir/Teheran/
The site lists the Chairperson, Chief Executive Officer, street address, phone and fax numbers, e-mail link, and office hours of the German Chamber in Tehran.

India

Indian Commercial Mission in Tehran
http://www.nic.in/commin/ICM.HTM
The site lists the street address, phone and fax numbers, and e-mail link of the Indian Commercial Mission in Tehran.

Malaysia

Embassy of Malaysia in Tehran
http://www.mnet.com.my/klonline/www/missions/malmiss/miran.htm
The site provides contact information for the Malaysian Embassy in Tehran.

Pakistan

Pakistan Trade Office in Tehran
http://www.jamal.com/epb/ptoa.htm
The site provides contact information for the Pakistan Trade Office in Tehran.

Portugal

Portuguese Trade and Investment Office in Tehran
http://www.portugal.org/geninfo/abouticep/iran.html

The site lists the staff, street address, phone and fax numbers, and e-mail link of the Portuguese Trade and Investment Office in Tehran.

Spain

Spanish Commercial Office in Tehran
http://www.icex.es/openURL.html#openURL=/ english/infoproyem/ofcomes/ofcomes.html#AS
The site lists the staff, street address, and phone and fax numbers of the Spanish Commercial Office in Tehran.

Sweden

Embassy of Sweden in Tehran
http://www.ud.se/english/mfa/ambassad/iran.htm
The site lists the staff, street address, phone and fax numbers, and e-mail link of the Swedish Embassy in Tehran.

Taiwan

China External Trade Development Council Office in Tehran
http://www.cetra.org.tw/english/o_office/ indexset.htm
A Taiwanese trade promotion service, the site lists the mission statement and e-mail link of the China External Trade Development Council Office in Tehran.

Thailand

Royal Thai Embassy in Tehran
http://www.mfa.go.th/Embassy/detail/83.htm
The site lists the Ambassador, street address, and phone and fax numbers of the Thai Embassy in Tehran.

Thailand Office of Commercial Affairs in Tehran
http://www.thaitrade.com/thcoaf.html
The site lists the street address, phone and fax numbers, and e-mail link of the Thailand Office of Commercial Affairs in Tehran.

United Kingdom

Embassy of Britain in Tehran
http://www.fco.gov.uk/directory/posts.asp?IR
The site provides contact information for the British Embassy in Tehran.

Iraq

Iraq Market Guides

Iraq Business Briefs
http://www.austrade.gov.au/IOOM/Iraq/
A service of Austrade, the site offers fact sheets on Iraqi trade and investment opportunities.

Iraq: A Country Study
http://lcweb2.loc.gov/frd/cs/iqtoc.html
A service of the U.S. Library of Congress, the site delivers fact sheets on Iraqi geography, population, agriculture, mining, manufacturing, and foreign economic relations.

Iraq Market Research
http://strategis.ic.gc.ca/sc_mrkti/ibinddc/engdoc/ 1a1d4.html
Posted by Industry Canada, the site provides U.S. Central Intelligence Agency fact sheets on Iraqi geography, people, government, economy, communications, and transportation.

Iraq Virtual Library
http://menic.utexas.edu/menic/countries/iraq.html
A service of the Center for Middle Eastern Studies at the University of Texas, the site provides a directory of Iraqi resources online. Categories include business and economy, government and politics, and news and current events.

Permanent Mission of Iraq to the United Nations
http://www.iraqi-mission.org/
Based in New York, the site provides Iraqi news, fact sheets, history lessons, leader profiles, cultural information, and reports on Iraqi activities at the United Nations.

Saleh Home Page
http://achilles.net/~sal/
A hub of country information, the site provides Iraqi news, history lessons, language primers, cultural guides, and a directory of United Nations documents on Iraq.

Iraq Trade Assistance

Trade Shows in Iraq
http://www.expoguide.com/shows/data/loc_25.htm
Compiled by Expoguide, the site is a directory of upcoming trade shows in Iraq.

Iraq Representative Offices

Austria

Austrian Trade Commission in Baghdad
http://aw.wk.or.at/awo/ahst-baghdad.htm
The site lists the staff, street address, phone and fax numbers, e-mail link, and office hours of the Austrian Trade Commission in Baghdad.

India

Indian Commercial Mission in Baghdad
http://www.nic.in/commin/ICM.HTM
The site lists the street address, phone and fax numbers, and e-mail link of the Indian Commercial Mission in Baghdad.

Malaysia

Embassy of Malaysia in Baghdad
http://www.mnet.com.my/klonline/www/missions/malmiss/miraq.htm
The site provides contact information for the Malaysian Embassy in Baghdad.

Spain

Spanish Commercial Office in Baghdad
http://www.icex.es/openURL.html#openURL=/english/infoproyem/ofcomes/ofcomes.html#AS
The site lists the staff, street address, and phone and fax numbers of the Spanish Commercial Office in Baghdad.

Thailand

Royal Thai Embassy in Baghdad
http://www.mfa.go.th/Embassy/detail/43.htm
The site lists the street address, and phone and fax numbers of the Thai Embassy in Baghdad.

Israel

Israel Media

Israel Media
http://www.mediainfo.com/emediajs/specific-geo.htm?region=israel
Compiled by Editor and Publisher Interactive, the site is an index of Israeli media sites online.

Israel's Business Arena
http://www.globes.co.il/
An English-language electronic newspaper, the site delivers Israeli business news, company profiles, high technology reports, trade leads, and employment opportunities.

The Jerusalem Post
http://www.jpost.co.il/
Updated daily, the site provides Israeli news, editorials, business reports, lifestyle features, tourism information, weather bulletins, and searchable archives of past issues.

Israel Market Guides

Barclays Country Report: Israel
http://www.offshorebanking.barclays.com/services/economic/yearly/isrmay97/index.html
Prepared by Barclays Bank, the site reports on Israeli economic trends, politics, monetary and fiscal policy, international trade, and U.K.-Israel merchandise trade and investment flows.

DunsTrade
http://dunstrade.dundb.co.il/index.html
A service of Dun and Bradstreet Israel, the site provides a searchable directory of Israeli companies in 12 categories including manufacturing, retail, wholesale, services, import, and export.

Government of Israel Economic Mission
http://204.140.231.199/iem/
A service of the Israeli government, the site provides Israeli business news, economic fact sheets, event information, and a directory of key business contacts.

Federation of Israeli Chambers of Commerce
http://www.chamber.org.il/
Based in Tel Aviv, the Federation promotes Israeli business and international trade. The site includes a member directory, newsletter, publications list, and business proposals.

Israel: Background Studies
http://www.imf.org/external/pubs/CAT/longres.cfm?sk=2565.0
Prepared by the International Monetary Fund, the site provides fact sheets and statistics on Israeli output, taxation, interest rates, investment, privatization, and international trade.

Israel Business Briefs
http://www.austrade.gov.au/IOOM/Israel/
A service of Austrade, the site offers fact sheets on Israeli business etiquette, foreign investment, corporate taxation, marketing, and visas.

Israel Country Profile
*http://www.tradenz.govt.nz/intelligence/profiles/
israel.html*
A service of the New Zealand Trade Development
Board, the site provides Israeli economic
statistics, market information, and business tips.

Israel Country Report
*http://www.state.gov/www/issues/economic/
trade_reports/neareast97/israel97.html*
Prepared by the U.S. Department of State, the site
delivers information on Israeli exchange rates,
debt management, trade barriers, and intellectual
property protection.

Israel: A Country Study
http://lcweb2.loc.gov/frd/cs/iltoc.html
A service of the U.S. Library of Congress, the site
delivers fact sheets on Israeli geography,
population, agriculture, mining, manufacturing,
and foreign economic relations.

Israel Economic Mission Country Offices
http://204.140.231.199/iem/office.htm
A directory of Israeli Economic Missions in North
America, the site lists representatives in New
York, Georgia, California, Illinois, Massachusetts,
and Ontario.

Israel InfoExport
*http://www.infoexport.gc.ca/country-
e.asp?continent=Africa&country=58*
A service of Foreign Affairs and International
Trade Canada, the site provides Israel commercial guides and market reports.

Israel Market Access Database
*http://mkaccdb.eu.int/mkdb/
mkdb.pl?METHOD=COUNTRY*
A service of the European Commission, the site
offers briefs on Israeli trade policy, tariff barriers,
non-tariff barriers, investment-related measures,
and financial services regulations.

Israel Market Information
http://dtiinfo1.dti.gov.uk/ots/israel/
A service of the London-based Department of
Trade and Industry, the site delivers country fact
sheets, maps, and trade-show information.

Israel Market Research
*http://strategis.ic.gc.ca/sc_mrkti/ibinddc/engdoc/
1a1d5.html*
A service of Industry Canada, the site provides
U.S. Department of Commerce reports on Israeli
business, politics, trade regulations and stan-

dards, investment climate, trade and project
financing, business travel, and market opportunities.

Israel Virtual Library
*http://menic.utexas.edu/menic/countries/
israel.html*
A service of the Center for Middle Eastern Studies
at the University of Texas, the site provides a
directory of Israeli resources online. Categories
include business and economy, government and
politics, and news and media.

Israel Yellow Pages
http://www.yellowpages.co.il/cgi-bin/main.pl
A searchable directory of Israeli companies, the
site is divided into over 100 industry categories
including aerospace, machinery, telecommunications, and water treatment.

Israeli Industry Center for R&D
http://www.matimop.org.il/
Based in Tel Aviv, the Center promotes Israeli
research and development. The site includes a
mission statement, event information, and a
directory of Israeli research and development
opportunities in 20 categories including agriculture, information technology, and construction.

Manufacturers Association of Israel
http://www.industry.org.il/frameeng.html
Representing over 1,700 companies, the
Association promotes the interests of Israeli
manufacturers. The site includes a members
database, sector report, publications list, and
program directory.

Ministry of Finance
http://www.mof.gov.il/englishframe.htm
Written in English and Hebrew, the site provides
Israeli fact sheets, economic forecasts, budget
statements, executive profiles, and a directory of
Ministry programs and services.

Israel Trade Assistance

Embassies and Consulates Abroad
http://www.israel-mfa.gov.il/mfa/embsites.html
A service of the Israel Ministry of Foreign Affairs,
the site is a directory of Israeli Embassies and
Consulates online around the world.

Israel Export Institute
http://www.export.gov.il/english.html
Based in Tel Aviv, the Institute promotes Israeli
exports. The site includes an Israeli exporter

database, sector profiles, economic fact sheets, and a directory of trade leads and business opportunities.

Israel Ministry of Foreign Affairs
http://www.israel.org/
Posted in English, French, Hebrew, and Spanish, the site provides Israeli cultural primers, economic fact sheets, and directories of Israeli Embassies and Consulates abroad, and foreign embassies and consulates in Israel.

Israel Trade and Investment
http://www.std.com/neicc/
A service of the Association of America-Israel Chambers of Commerce, the site is a searchable directory of Israeli business resources online. Categories include trade assistance, technology, business finance, and statistics.

Trade Point Tel Aviv
http://www.untpdc.org/incubator/isr/tptel/
Part of the United Nations Global Trade Point Network, the site provides Tel Aviv trade leads, market bulletins, and contact information.

Trade Shows in Israel
http://www.expoguide.com/shows/data/loc_27.htm
Compiled by Expoguide, the site is a directory of upcoming trade shows in Israel.

Israel Representative Offices

Austria

Austrian Trade Commission in Tel Aviv
http://aw.wk.or.at/awo/ahst-telaviv.htm
The site lists the staff, street address, phone and fax numbers, e-mail link, and office hours of the Austrian Trade Commission in Tel Aviv.

Canada

Canadian Embassy in Tel Aviv
http://www.canada-embassy.org.il/embassy/welcome3.htm
Posted in English and French, the site provides Canadian visa and passport information, Israeli fact sheets and business guides, and marketing tips for the Canadian exporter.

Cyprus

Cyprus Trade Center in Tel Aviv
http://www.cyprustradeny.org/cyny5.html

The site lists the street address, and phone and fax numbers of the Cyprus Trade Center in Tel Aviv.

Czech Republic

Embassy of Czech Republic in Tel Aviv
http://www.grapho.net/embassy/cz.htm
The site lists the street address, and phone and fax numbers of the Czech Embassy in Tel Aviv.

Denmark

Embassy of Denmark in Tel Aviv
http://www.dk-embassy.org.il/
Written in Danish and English, the site provides Danish fact sheets, visa and passport information, Israeli commercial guides, and reports on Denmark-Israel trade and relations.

El Salvador

Embassy of El Salvador in Israel
http://www.el-salvador.org.il/
Posted in English and Spanish, the site features Salvadoran news, fact sheets, business guides, economic reports, travel information, and a directory of El Salvador-Israel exchange programs.

Finland

Embassy of Finland in Tel Aviv
http://www.finemb.org.il/
Written in English and Finnish, the site provides Finnish fact sheets, visa and passport information, business guides, and a directory of Finnish-Israel twin city agreements.

France

Embassy of France in Tel Aviv
http://www.ifta.co.il/
Written in French, the site delivers French fact sheets, business guides, science and technology bulletins, and reports on French-Israeli trade and relations.

Israel-France Chamber of Commerce
http://www.ifta.co.il/cciif/
An Israeli-French trade promotion service, the site includes a member directory, French business guides, Israeli fact sheets, and a directory of Chamber programs.

Germany

German Chamber of Commerce in Tel Aviv
http://www.ahk.net/en/il/Tel_Aviv/
The site lists the Chairperson, Chief Executive Officer, street address, phone and fax numbers, e-mail link, and office hours of the German Chamber in Tel Aviv.

Philippines

Philippine Trade and Investment Promotion Office in Tel Aviv
http://www.dti.gov.ph/tlv/
The site provides a mission statement, service directory, and contact information for the Philippine Trade and Investment Promotion Office in Tel Aviv.

Portugal

Portuguese Trade and Investment Office in Tel Aviv
http://www.portugal.org/geninfo/abouticep/israel.html
The site lists the staff, street address, phone and fax numbers, and e-mail link of the Portuguese Trade and Investment Office in Tel Aviv.

South Africa

South Africa Foreign Trade Office in Tel Aviv
http://wwwdti.pwv.gov.za/dtiwww/foreign_offices.htm
A service of the South Africa Department of Trade and Industry, the site provides contact information for the South Africa Foreign Trade Office in Tel Aviv.

Spain

Spanish Commercial Office in Tel Aviv
http://www.icex.es/openURL.html#openURL=/english/infoproyem/ofcomes/ofcomes.html#AS
The site lists the staff, street address, phone and fax numbers, and e-mail link of the Spanish Commercial Office in Tel Aviv.

Sweden

Embassy of Sweden in Tel Aviv
http://www.ud.se/english/mfa/ambassad/israel.htm
The site lists the staff, street address, phone and fax numbers, and e-mail link of the Swedish Embassy in Tel Aviv.

Taiwan

Taiwan Government Information Office in Tel Aviv
http://www.gio.gov.tw/info/ngio/israel-f.html
Posted in Chinese and English, the site lists the street address, phone and fax numbers, and e-mail link of the Taiwan Government Information Office in Tel Aviv.

Thailand

Royal Thai Embassy in Tel Aviv
http://www.mfa.go.th/Embassy/detail/166.htm
The site lists the Ambassador, street address, and phone and fax numbers of the Thai Embassy in Tel Aviv.

Thailand Office of Commercial Affairs in Tel Aviv
http://www.thaitrade.com/thcoaf.html
The site lists the street address, phone and fax numbers, and e-mail link of the Thailand Office of Commercial Affairs in Tel Aviv.

United Kingdom

Embassy of Britain in Tel Aviv
http://www.fco.gov.uk/directory/posts.asp?IL
The site provides contact information for the British Embassy in Tel Aviv.

United States

Israel-America Chamber of Commerce and Industry
http://www.amcham.co.il/
Based in Tel Aviv, the Chamber promotes Israeli-U.S. trade. The site includes Israeli business guides, legal primers, trade leads, and a members database.

State of California Trade Office in Jerusalem
http://commerce.ca.gov/international/it_off.html#israel
A service of the California Office of Trade and Investment, the site lists the Director, street address, phone and fax numbers, and e-mail link of the California Trade Office in Jerusalem.

State of Massachusetts Trade Office in Jerusalem
http://www.case-europe.com/States/ma.htm
Along with Massachusetts fact sheets, the site lists the Director, street address, phone and fax numbers, and e-mail link of the Massachusetts Trade Office in Jerusalem.

State of Ohio Trade Office in Ramat Gan
http://ohiotrade.tpusa.com/offices.htm
Posted by the Ohio Department of Development, the site lists the street address, phone and fax numbers, and e-mail link of the Ohio Trade Office in Ramat Gan.

State of Utah Trade Office in Tel Aviv
http://www.ce.ex.state.ut.us/international/reps/reps.htm#Israel
A service of the Utah International Business Development Office, the site lists the representative, street address, phone and fax numbers, and e-mail link of the Utah Trade Office in Tel Aviv.

U.S. Mission in Tel Aviv
http://www.usis-israel.org.il/publish/mission.htm
Along with U.S. visa and passport information, the site features U.S. news, press releases, speeches, reports on U.S.-Israel trade, and a directory of consular and commercial services.

United States Information Service in Tel Aviv
http://www.usis-israel.org.il/
The site provides U.S. news, speeches, press releases, fact sheets, event information, electronic journals, and a directory of U.S.-Israeli educational and exchange programs.

Jordan

Jordan Media

Jordan Media
http://www.mediainfo.com/emediajs/specific-geo.htm?region=jordan
Developed by Editor and Publisher Interactive, the site is an index of Jordanian magazines, newspapers, and other media sites online.

Jordan Today
http://corp.arabia.com/JordanToday/
Based in Amman, the site provides Jordanian news, business guides, lifestyle reports, cultural bulletins, travel information, and accommodation directories.

The Star
http://star.arabia.com/
Updated weekly, the site delivers Jordanian political bulletins, business news, sector profiles, technology reports, and cultural information.

Jordan Market Guides

Country Commercial Guide
http://www.state.gov/www/about_state/business/com_guides/1998/neareast/jordan98.html
Prepared by the U.S. Embassy in Amman, the site delivers primers on Jordanian business, politics, trade regulations and standards, investment climate, trade and project financing, and business travel.

Federation of Jordanian Chambers of Commerce
http://www.fjcc.com/
Based in Amman, the Chamber promotes Jordanian economic development and trade. The site includes a member directory, event information, and trade leads.

Industrial Development Bank
http://www.indevbank.com/english/index.html
Based in Amman, the Bank finances economic development projects in Jordan. The site includes executive profiles, program directories, and loan information.

Jordan Business Briefs
http://www.austrade.gov.au/IOOM/Jordan/
A service of Austrade, the site offers fact sheets on Jordanian business etiquette, foreign investment, corporate taxation, marketing, and visas.

Jordan Business Directory
http://nic.gov.jo/jbd/index.htm
A searchable database of Jordanian companies online, the site is divided into some 30 categories including communications, computers, office equipment, and tourism.

Jordan Country Brief
http://www.worldbank.org/cgi-bin/sendoff.cgi?page=%2Fhtml%2Fextdr%2Foffrep%2Fmena%2Fjo.htm
A service of the World Bank Group, the site provides Jordanian population statistics, financial data, development reports, and economic forecasts.

Jordan Country Profile
http://www.tradenz.govt.nz/intelligence/profiles/jordan.html
A service of the New Zealand Trade Development Board, the site provides Jordanian economic statistics, market information, and business tips.

Jordan Country Report
http://www.state.gov/www/issues/economic/trade_reports/neareast97/jordan97.html
Prepared by the U.S. Department of State, the site delivers information on Jordanian exchange rates, debt management, trade barriers, and intellectual property protection.

Jordan: A Country Study
http://lcweb2.loc.gov/frd/cs/jotoc.html
A service of the U.S. Library of Congress, the site delivers fact sheets on Jordanian geography, population, agriculture, mining, manufacturing, and foreign economic relations.

Jordan Government Ministries
http://amon.nic.gov.jo/nic/owa/get_ministry
A directory of Jordanian Ministries, the site links to over 25 organizations including the Ministries of Agriculture, Defense, Education, Planning, Transport, and Water and Irrigation.

Jordan InfoExport
http://www.infoexport.gc.ca/country-e.asp?continent=Africa&country=59
A service of Foreign Affairs and International Trade Canada, the site provides Jordanian commercial guides and market reports.

Jordan Market Information
http://dtiinfo1.dti.gov.uk/ots/jordan/
A service of the London-based Department of Trade and Industry, the site delivers country fact sheets, maps, and trade-show information.

Jordan Market Research
http://strategis.ic.gc.ca/sc_mrkti/ibinddc/engdoc/1a1d6.html
A service of Industry Canada, the site provides U.S. Department of Commerce reports on Jordanian business, politics, trade regulations and standards, investment climate, trade and project financing, business travel, and market opportunities.

Jordan Virtual Library
http://menic.utexas.edu/menic/countries/jordan.html
A service of the Center for Middle Eastern Studies at the University of Texas, the site provides a directory of Jordanian resources online. Categories include business and economy, government and politics, and news and media.

National Information System
http://www.nic.gov.jo/
A hub of country information, the site delivers fact sheets on Jordanian agriculture, economics, geography, science and technology, transportation, industry, and government and politics.

Jordan Trade Assistance

Amman World Trade Center
http://www.arab-business.net/wtcnn/
Part of the New York-based World Trade Center Association, the site delivers director profiles, membership information, and a searchable database of trade leads.

Export and Finance Bank
http://www.access2arabia.com/efbank/
Based in Amman, the Bank provides export financing services to Jordanian exporters and international buyers. The site includes a mission statement, financial statements, and contact information.

Jordan Customs Department
http://www.customs.gov.jo/
Posted in Arabic and English, the site provides fact sheets on Jordanian customs law, tariff rates, and border regulations.

Jordan Customs Law
http://www.multitasking.com/jordanbiz/customs.html
Published by the Official Gazette of the Hashemite Kingdom of Jordan, the site provides primers on Jordanian border tariffs, customs clearance stages, and other export and import regulations.

Jordan Trade Association
http://www.arab-business.net/jta/
Based in Amman, the Association promotes Jordanian exports. The site includes a mission statement, member directory, director roster, and program directory.

Jordan Representative Offices

Austria

Austria Trade Commission in Amman
http://aw.wk.or.at/awo/ahst-amman.htm
The site lists the staff, street address, phone and fax numbers, e-mail link, and office hours of the Austrian Trade Commission in Amman.

Canada

Embassy of Canada in Amman
http://www.cns.com.jo/directory/embassy/canada/index.htm
Along with visa and passport information, the site provides Canadian fact sheets, cultural guides, international trade reports, and a directory of consular and commercial services.

France

French Trade Commission in Amman
http://www.dree.org/jordanie/
Written in French, the site delivers Jordanian market reports, sector profiles, contact information, and a directory of export programs for French companies doing business in Jordan.

Germany

German Chamber of Commerce in Amman
http://www.ahk.net/en/jo/amman/
Part of an international network of German chambers, the site provides Chamber contact information and member profiles, along with Jordanian fact sheets and company directories.

India

Indian Commercial Mission in Amman
http://www.nic.in/commin/ICM.HTM
The site lists the street address, phone and fax numbers, and e-mail link of the Indian Commercial Mission in Amman.

Spain

Spanish Commercial Office in Amman
http://www.icex.es/openURL.html#openURL=/english/infoproyem/ofcomes/ofcomes.html#AS
The site lists the staff, street address, phone and fax numbers, and e-mail link of the Spanish Commercial Office in Amman.

Sweden

Embassy of Sweden in Amman
http://www.ud.se/english/mfa/ambassad/jordanie.htm
The site provides contact information for the Swedish Embassy in Amman.

United Kingdom

Embassy of Britain in Amman
http://www.fco.gov.uk/directory/posts.asp?JO
The site provides contact information for the British Embassy in Amman.

United States

United States Embassy in Amman
http://www.usembassy-amman.org.jo/
The virtual Embassy provides U.S. news, press releases, speeches, Middle East fact sheets, Jordanian commercial guides, and a directory of environmental business opportunities in the region.

United States Information Service in Amman
http://www.usembassy-amman.org.jo/wwwhusis.html
A public relations service of the U.S. Embassy, the site provides U.S. news, press releases, cultural primers, language guides, and a directory of teaching and translation programs.

Kuwait

Kuwait Search Tools

Kuwala
http://www.kuwala.com/
A web navigation service, the site provides a searchable index of Kuwaiti resources online. Categories include business, computers, education, news, reference, and people.

Kuwait Media

Kuwait Media
http://www.mediainfo.com/emediajs/specific-geo.htm?region=kuwait
Developed by Editor and Publisher Interactive, the site is an index of Kuwaiti newspapers and other media sites online.

Kuwait Times
http://www.paaet.edu.kw/Info/HomePage/shaheen/kt/current/kutoday.htm

Based in Safat, the English-language site delivers Kuwaiti news, editorials, business reports, cultural bulletins, and an archive of previous issues.

Kuwait Market Guides

Kuwait Book
http://www.kuwaitbook.com/
A searchable directory of Kuwait companies, the site is divided into some 50 industry categories including automotive, banking, printing, office equipment, and transportation.

Kuwait Country Brief
http://www.worldbank.org/cgi-bin/ sendoff.cgi?page=%2Fhtml%2Fextdr%2Foffrep%2 Fmena%2Fkw.htm
A service of the World Bank Group, the site provides Kuwait population statistics, financial data, development reports, and economic forecasts.

Kuwait Country Profile
http://www.tradenz.govt.nz/intelligence/profiles/ kuwait.html
A service of the New Zealand Trade Development Board, the site provides Kuwaiti economic statistics, market information, and business tips.

Kuwait Country Report
http://www.state.gov/www/issues/economic/ trade_reports/neareast97/kuwait97.html
Prepared by the U.S. Department of State, the site delivers information on Kuwaiti exchange rates, debt management, trade barriers, and intellectual property protection.

Kuwait InfoExport
http://www.infoexport.gc.ca/country- e.asp?continent=Africa&country=60
A service of Foreign Affairs and International Trade Canada, the site provides Kuwaiti commercial guides and market reports.

Kuwait Investment Authority
http://www.kia.gov.kw/
Based in Safat, the Authority promotes international investment in Kuwait. The site features Kuwaiti news, fact sheets, business guides, economic reports, and event information.

Kuwait Market Information
http://dtiinfo1.dti.gov.uk/ots/kuwait/
A service of the London-based Department of

Trade and Industry, the site delivers Kuwait fact sheets, maps, and trade-show information.

Kuwait Market Research
http://strategis.ic.gc.ca/sc_mrkti/ibinddc/engdoc/ 1a1d7.html
A service of Industry Canada, the site provides U.S. Department of Commerce reports on Kuwaiti business, politics, trade regulations and standards, investment climate, trade and project financing, business travel, and market opportunities.

Kuwait: A Market Study
http://lcweb2.loc.gov/frd/cs/kwtoc.html
A service of the U.S. Library of Congress, the site delivers fact sheets on Kuwait geography, population, agriculture, mining, manufacturing, and foreign economic relations.

Kuwait Ministry of Information
http://www.info-kuwait.org/
A hub of country information, the site delivers Kuwaiti news, fact sheets, government directories, economic reports, education bulletins, and arts and cultural reports.

Kuwait Net
http://www.kuwait.net/
An index of Kuwaiti resources online, the site is divided into ten categories including newsgroups, companies, education, and government.

Kuwait Virtual Library
http://menic.utexas.edu/menic/countries/ kuwait.html
A service of the Center for Middle Eastern Studies at the University of Texas, the site provides a directory of Kuwaiti resources online. Categories include business and economy, government and politics, and news and current events.

Kuwait Yellow Pages
http://www.kuwait-yellow-pages.com/
Along with Kuwait fact sheets and sector profiles, the site provides a browsable index of Kuwaiti companies. Categories include communications, consumer products, and shipping.

Kuwait's Toplist
http://www.kuwait-toplist.com/
A virtual handbook of Kuwait's largest corporations, the site profiles over 5,000 companies in some 400 industries including earth-moving equipment, hydraulic machinery, and packaging.

Kuwait Trade Assistance

Kuwait Ministry of Foreign Affairs
http://www.mofa.gov.kw/
The site provides Kuwaiti fact sheets, press releases, foreign policy statements, executive profiles, and government directories.

Kuwaiti Embassies Abroad
http://www.mofa.gov.kw/mofa/www.nsf/ByKeyword2?OpenView
A service of the Kuwait Ministry of Foreign Affairs, the site is a directory of Kuwaiti Embassies in Africa, Europe, North and South America, and the Middle East.

Trade Shows in Kuwait
http://www.expoguide.com/shows/data/loc_32.htm
Compiled by Expoguide, the site is a directory of upcoming trade shows in Kuwait.

Kuwait Representative Offices

Canada

Embassy of Canada in Kuwait
http://www.dfait-maeci.gc.ca/english/missions/rep-can3e.htm#kuwait
The site provides contact information for the Canadian Embassy in Kuwait.

Czech Republic

Embassy of the Czech Republic in Kuwait
http://www.czechemb.net/
Featuring a sound file of the Czech national anthem, the site delivers Czech fact sheets, company directories, travel information, statistics, and a directory of consular and commercial services.

India

Indian Commercial Mission in Kuwait
http://www.nic.in/commin/ICM.HTM
The site lists the street address, phone and fax numbers, and e-mail link of the Indian Commercial Mission in Kuwait.

Malaysia

Embassy of Malaysia in Kuwait
http://www.mnet.com.my/klonline/www/missions/malmiss/mkuwait1.htm
The site provides contact information for the Malaysian Embassy in Kuwait.

Trade Commission of Malaysia in Kuwait
http://www.mnet.com.my/klonline/www/missions/malmiss/mkuwait2.htm
The site provides contact information for the Malaysian Trade Commission in Kuwait.

Philippines

Philippine Trade and Investment Promotion Office in Kuwait
http://www.dti.gov.ph/kwt/
The site provides a mission statement, service directory, and contact information for the Philippine Trade Office in Kuwait.

Thailand

Royal Thai Embassy in Kuwait
http://www.mfa.go.th/Embassy/detail/71.htm
The site lists the Ambassador, street address, and phone and fax numbers of the Thai Embassy in Kuwait.

United Kingdom

Embassy of Britain in Kuwait
http://www.fco.gov.uk/directory/posts.asp?KW
The site provides contact information for the British Embassy in Kuwait.

Lebanon

Lebanon Media

Lebanon Media
http://www.mediainfo.com/emediajs/specific-geo.htm?region=lebanon
Developed by Editor and Publisher Interactive, the site is an index of Lebanese media sites online including magazines, newspapers, and television stations.

Lebanon Market Guides

Beirut Chamber of Commerce and Industry
http://www.ccib.org.lb/
The online service provides Lebanese commercial guides, economic data, legal primers, product catalogs, contact information, and *Lebanese and Arab Economy*, a monthly electronic business magazine.

Country Commercial Guide
http://www.state.gov/www/about_state/business/com_guides/1998/neareast/lebanon98.html
Prepared by the U.S. Embassy in Beirut, the site

delivers primers on Lebanese business, politics, trade regulations and standards, investment climate, trade and project financing, and business travel.

Investment Development Authority of Lebanon
http://www.IDAL.com.lb/
Established in 1994, the Authority promotes Lebanese economic development and international investment. The site includes Lebanese fact sheets, investment opportunities, project profiles, and contact information.

Lebanon Business Briefs
http://www.austrade.gov.au/IOOM/Lebanon/
A service of Austrade, the site offers fact sheets on Lebanese business etiquette, foreign investment, corporate taxation, marketing, and visas.

Lebanon.Com
http://www.lebanon.com/index.htm
A virtual country gateway, the site provides Lebanese news, company profiles, travel information, reconstruction reports, business directories, and online discussion groups.

Lebanon Country Brief
http://www.worldbank.org/cgi-bin/ sendoff.cgi?page=%2Fhtml%2Fextdr%2Foffrep%2 Fmena%2Flb.htm
A service of the World Bank Group, the site provides Lebanese population statistics, financial data, development reports, and economic forecasts.

Lebanon: A Country Study
http://lcweb2.loc.gov/frd/cs/lbtoc.html
A service of the U.S. Library of Congress, the site delivers fact sheets on Lebanese geography, population, agriculture, mining, manufacturing, and foreign economic relations.

Lebanon InfoExport
http://www.infoexport.gc.ca/country- e.asp?continent=Africa&country=61
A service of Foreign Affairs and International Trade Canada, the site provides Lebanese commercial guides and market reports.

Lebanon Mall
http://www.lebanonmall.com/
The online service features Lebanese photos, fact sheets, city guides, economic reports, tourism information, weather bulletins, business directories, and company profiles.

Lebanon Market Information
http://dtiinfo1.dti.gov.uk/ots/lebanon/
A service of the London-based Department of Trade and Industry, the site delivers Lebanese fact sheets, maps, and trade-show information.

Lebanon Market Research
http://strategis.ic.gc.ca/sc_mrkti/ibinddc/engdoc/ 1a1d8.html
A service of Industry Canada, the site provides U.S. Department of Commerce reports on Lebanese business, politics, trade regulations and standards, investment climate, trade and project financing, business travel, and market opportunities.

Lebanon Ministry of Economy and Trade
http://www.economy.gov.lb/
Featuring a message from the Minister, the site provides Lebanese fact sheets, policy statements, economic statistics, event information, and a directory of key business contacts.

Lebanon Virtual Library
http://menic.utexas.edu/menic/countries/ lebanon.html
A service of the Center for Middle Eastern Studies at the University of Texas, the site provides a directory of Lebanese resources online. Categories include business and economy, government and politics, and news and current events.

Lebanon Web
http://www.lebanonweb.com/
A browsable directory of Lebanese companies, the site is divided into 11 categories including banks, tourism, insurance, classified, real estate, and exhibitions.

Lebanon Trade Assistance

Trade Information Center
http://www.economy.gov.lb/tic.htm
Based in Beirut, the Center promotes Lebanese exports and international business. The site includes fact sheets, trade statistics, and bilateral agreements.

Trade Shows in Lebanon
http://www.expoguide.com/shows/data/loc_34.htm
Compiled by Expoguide, the site is a directory of upcoming trade shows in Lebanon.

Lebanon Representative Offices

Armenia

Embassy of Armenia in Beirut
http://www.armeniaemb.org/forrel/embas2.htm
The site provides contact information for the Armenian Embassy in Beirut.

Australia

Embassy of Australia in Beirut
http://www.austemb.org.lb/
The online service delivers Australian news, fact sheets, press releases, visa and passport information, business guides, and a directory of consular and commercial services.

Austria

Austrian Trade Commission in Beirut
http://aw.wk.or.at/awo/ahst-beirut.htm
The site lists the staff, street address, phone and fax numbers, e-mail link, and office hours of the Austrian Trade Commission in Beirut.

Canada

Embassy of Canada in Beirut
http://www.dfait-maeci.gc.ca/english/missions/rep-can3e.htm#lebanon
The site provides contact information for the Canadian Embassy in Beirut.

Germany

Delegate of German Industry and Trade
http://www.kleudge.com/dihtddwb/
A representation office of the Association of German Chambers of Industry and Commerce, the Delegate promotes German-Lebanese trade. The site includes a mission statement, service directory, and contact information.

German Chamber of Commerce in Beirut
http://www.ahk.net/en/lb/Beirut/
The site lists the Delegate, street address, phone and fax numbers, e-mail link, and office hours of the German Chamber in Beirut.

Lebanese German Business Council
http://www.kleudge.com/lgbc/
Founded in 1997, the Council promotes Lebanese-German trade. The site includes a mission statement, program directory, executive roster, and contact information.

Iran

Iran Trade Center in Beirut
http://www.neda.net/ibr/tcc.html
An Iranian trade promotion service, the site lists the street address and phone and fax numbers of the Iran Trade Center in Beirut.

Singapore

Consulate General of Singapore in Beirut
http://www.gov.sg/mfa/consular/mww_l.htm
The site provides contact information for the Singapore Consulate General in Beirut.

United Kingdom

Embassy of Britain in Beirut
http://www.fco.gov.uk/directory/posts.asp?LE
The site provides contact information for the British Embassy in Beirut.

United States

United States Embassy in Beirut
http://www.usembassy.com.lb/
Posted in Arabic and English, the site provides U.S. news, press releases, speeches, travel advisories, U.S. AID information, and a directory of Embassy programs and staff.

United States Information Service in Beirut
http://www.usembassy.com.lb/wwwhusis.htm
Posted in Arabic, English, and French, the site provides U.S. news, press releases, electronic journals, foreign policy statements, Middle East reports, and a directory of teaching and translation programs.

Libya

Libya Media

Libyan Affairs
http://www.libyanaffairs.com/
Written in Arabic and English, the site features Libyan news, economic reports, political bulletins, cultural information, book reviews, and online discussion forums.

Libya Market Guides

Country Profile: Libya
http://www.mbendi.co.za/cylbcy.htm
Developed by MBendi, the site provides Libyan

fact sheets, maps, sector profiles, exchange rates, travel information, and business contacts.

Index on Libya
http://www.africaindex.africainfo.no/africaindex1/ countries/libya.html
A service of the Norwegian Council for Africa, the site is a directory of Libyan resources online. Categories include culture, economy, news, and tourism.

Libya: A Country Study
http://lcweb2.loc.gov/frd/cs/lytoc.html
A service of the U.S. Library of Congress, the site delivers fact sheets on Libyan geography, people, agriculture, mining, manufacturing, and foreign economic relations.

Libya Market Research
http://strategis.ic.gc.ca/sc_mrkti/ibinddc/engdoc/ 1a1d9.html
Posted by Industry Canada, the site provides U.S. Central Intelligence Agency fact sheets on Libyan geography, people, government, economy, communications, and transportation.

Libya Virtual Library
http://menic.utexas.edu/menic/countries/ libya.html
A service of the Center for Middle Eastern Studies at the University of Texas, the site is a directory of Libyan resources online. Categories include business and economy, government and politics, and news and current events.

Libya Representative Offices

Austria

Austrian Trade Commission in Tripoli
http://aw.wk.or.at/awo/ahst-tripolis.htm
The site lists the staff, street address, phone and fax numbers, e-mail link, and office hours of the Austrian Trade Commission in Tripoli.

Ghana

Embassy of Ghana in Tripoli
http://www.juntung.com/ghana-consul-hk/ 2misabo.htm
The site provides contact information for the Ghanaian Embassy in Tripoli.

India

Indian Commercial Mission in Tripoli
http://www.nic.in/commin/ICM.HTM
The site lists the street address, phone and fax numbers, and e-mail link of the Indian Commercial Mission in Tripoli.

Malaysia

Embassy of Malaysia in Tripoli
http://www.mnet.com.my/klonline/www/missions/ malmiss/mlibya.htm
The site provides contact information for the Malaysian Embassy in Tripoli.

Spain

Spanish Commercial Office in Tripoli
http://www.icex.es/openURL.html#openURL=/ english/infoproyem/ofcomes/ofcomes.html#AF
The site lists the staff, street address, phone and fax numbers, and e-mail link of the Spanish Commercial Office in Tripoli.

Oman

Oman Media

Oman Daily Observer
http://www.omanobserver.com/
An English-language electronic newspaper, the site provides Omani headlines, business reports, investment bulletins, company profiles, and oil price information.

Oman Media
http://www.mediainfo.com/emediajs/specific- geo.htm?region=oman
Developed by Editor and Publisher Interactive, the site is an index of Omani newspaper and other media sites online.

Oman Market Guides

Oman Chamber of Commerce and Industry
http://www.omanchamber.com/
Established in 1973, the Chamber promotes economic development in Oman. The site includes Omani fact sheets, business guides, and investment primers.

Oman Country Brief
*http://www.worldbank.org/cgi-bin/
sendoff.cgi?page=%2Fhtml%2Fextdr%2Foffrep%2
Fmena%2Fom.htm*
A service of the World Bank Group, the site
provides population statistics, financial data,
development reports, and economic forecasts.

Oman: A Country Study
http://lcweb2.loc.gov/frd/cs/omtoc.html
A service of the U.S. Library of Congress, the site
delivers fact sheets on Omani geography,
population, agriculture, mining, manufacturing,
and foreign economic relations.

Oman Country Profile
*http://www.tradenz.govt.nz/intelligence/profiles/
oman.html*
A service of the New Zealand Trade Development
Board, the site provides Omani economic
statistics, market information, and business tips.

Oman Country Report
*http://www.state.gov/www/issues/economic/
trade_reports/neareast97/oman97.html*
Prepared by the U.S. Department of State, the site
delivers information on Omani exchange rates,
debt management, trade barriers, and intellectual
property protection.

Oman InfoExport
*http://www.infoexport.gc.ca/country-
e.asp?continent=Africa&country=62*
A service of Foreign Affairs and International
Trade Canada, the site provides Omani commercial guides and market reports.

Oman Market Information
http://dtiinfo1.dti.gov.uk/ots/oman/
A service of the London-based Department of
Trade and Industry, the site delivers country fact
sheets, maps, and trade-show information.

Oman Market Research
*http://strategis.ic.gc.ca/sc_mrkti/ibinddc/engdoc/
1a1d10.html*
A service of Industry Canada, the site provides
U.S. Department of Commerce reports on Omani
business, politics, trade regulations and standards, investment climate, trade and project
financing, business travel, and market opportunities.

Oman Ministry of Information
http://www.omanet.com/
A hub of country information, the site provides fact
sheets on Omani history, geography, business,
people, government, culture, foreign affairs, and
oil production.

Oman Ministry of National Economy
http://www.modevelop.com/
Based in Muscat, the Ministry promotes Omani
economic development. The site includes Omani
fact sheets, investment plans, socioeconomic
statistics, and executive profiles.

Oman Virtual Library
*http://menic.utexas.edu/menic/countries/
oman.html*
A service of the Center for Middle Eastern Studies
at the University of Texas, the site provides a
directory of Omani resources online. Categories
include business and economy, government and
politics, and news and current events.

Oman Yellow Pages
http://www.omanyellowpages.com/
A searchable directory of Omani operations, the
site is divided into over 200 industry categories
including bottle cap manufacturers, landscape
architects, and wooden furniture.

Oman Trade Assistance

Oman Foreign Affairs
http://www.omanet.com/moi_for.htm
A service of the Omani Ministry of Information, the
site provides fact sheets on the Middle East
peace process, desalination research, World
Trade Organization, and Oman-Yemen border
demarcation.

Oman International Trade and Exhibitions
http://www.oite.com/
A database of Omani trade shows and conferences, the site lists events from over a dozen
industries including computers, electronics, and
energy.

Omzest Group
http://www.omzest.com/
Along with Omani fact sheets and business
guides, the site profiles 60 leading Omani
exporters and importers in five categories

including manufacturing, shipping, banking, and construction.

Oman Representative Offices

Brunei Darussalam

Embassy of Brunei Darussalam in Muscat
http://www.brunet.bn/homepage/gov/bruemb/govemb.htm
The site provides contact information for the Brunei Darussalam Embassy in Muscat.

France

French Trade Commission in Muscat
http://www.dree.org/oman/
Written in French, the site delivers Omani market reports, sector profiles, contact information, and a directory of export programs for French companies doing business in Oman.

India

Indian Commercial Mission in Muscat
http://www.nic.in/commin/ICM.HTM
The site lists the street address, phone and fax numbers, and e-mail link of the Indian Commercial Mission in Muscat.

Japan

Embassy of Japan in Muscat
http://www.embjapan-om.org/
Written in Arabic, English, and Japanese, the site features an address from the Japanese Ambassador, Japanese visa and passport information, and reports on Japan-Oman trade and relations.

Malaysia

Embassy of Malaysia in Muscat
http://www.mnet.com.my/klonline/www/missions/malmiss/moman.htm
The site provides contact information for the Malaysian Embassy in Muscat.

Netherlands

Royal Netherlands Embassy in Muscat
http://www.hollandpromo.com/oman/embassy/
Along with Dutch news and fact sheets, the site provides Omani business guides, company directories, tender notices, project profiles, and investment opportunities.

Pakistan

Pakistan Trade Office in Muscat
http://www.jamal.com/epb/ptoa.htm
The site provides contact information for the Pakistan Trade Office in Muscat.

Thailand

Royal Thai Embassy in Muscat
http://www.mfa.go.th/Embassy/detail/54.htm
The site lists the Ambassador, street address, and phone and fax numbers of the Thai Embassy in Muscat.

United Kingdom

Embassy of Britain in Muscat
http://www.fco.gov.uk/directory/posts.asp?OM
The site provides contact information for the British Embassy in Muscat.

United States

United States Embassy in Muscat
http://www.usia.gov/posts/muscat/
The virtual Embassy provides staff profiles, U.S. fact sheets, a directory of consular and commercial services, and reports on U.S.-Omani trade and relations.

United States Information Service in Muscat
http://www.usia.gov/abtusia/posts/MU1/wwwhusis.html
Posted in Arabic and English, the site delivers U.S. news, press releases, electronic journals, foreign policy statements, Middle East reports, and a directory of teaching and translation programs.

Pakistan

Pakistan Media

Dawn
http://www.xiber.com/dawn/
Based in Karachi, the site is an English language Pakistani newspaper. The service provides local and national news, editorials, business reports, and a searchable archive of past issues.

Pakistan Media
http://www.mediainfo.com/emediajs/specific-geo.htm?region=pakistan
Developed by Editor and Publisher Interactive, the

site is an index of Pakistani media sites online including magazines, newspapers, and television stations.

Pakistan Market Guides

Country Commercial Guide
http://www.state.gov/www/about_state/business/ com_guides/1998/southeast_asia/ pakistan98.html
Prepared by the U.S. Embassy in Karachi, the site delivers primers on Pakistani business, politics, trade regulations and standards, investment climate, trade and project financing, and business travel.

Federation of Pakistani Chambers of Commerce and Industry
http://www.g77tin.org/fpccihp.html
Based in Karachi, the Federation promotes Pakistani business and economic development. The site includes a mission statement, member directory, industry reports, and an online marketplace.

Government of Pakistan
http://www.pak.gov.pk/
Homepage of the Pakistani government, the site is a hub of country information. Modules include basic facts, history, tourism, land and people, economy, government, and Ministries.

Jamal's Yellow Pages of Pakistan
http://www.jamal.com/
A browsable index of some 125,000 Pakistan companies, the site is searchable by city and by over 2,500 industry categories including carbon products, management consultants, and telecommunications equipment.

Pakistan Business Briefs
http://www.austrade.gov.au/IOOM/Pakistan/
A service of Austrade, the site offers fact sheets on Pakistani business etiquette, foreign investment, corporate taxation, marketing, and visas.

Pakistan Business Network
http://www.pak-economist.com/
Updated weekly, the site provides Pakistani business news, trade and investment opportunities, industry profiles, company directories, tourism information, and online discussion forums.

Pakistan Country Brief
http://www.worldbank.org/cgi-bin/
sendoff.cgi?page=%2Fhtml%2Fextdr%2Foffrep%2 Fsas%2Fpk.htm
A service of the World Bank Group, the site provides Pakistani population statistics, financial data, development reports, and economic forecasts.

Pakistan Country Profile
http://www.tradenz.govt.nz/intelligence/profiles/ pakistan.html
A service of the New Zealand Trade Development Board, the site provides Pakistani economic statistics, market information, and business tips.

Pakistan Country Report
http://www.state.gov/www/issues/economic/ trade_reports/south_asia97/pakistan97.html
Prepared by the U.S. Department of State, the site delivers information on Pakistani exchange rates, debt management, trade barriers, and intellectual property protection.

Pakistan: A Country Study
http://lcweb2.loc.gov/frd/cs/pktoc.html
A service of the U.S. Library of Congress, the site delivers fact sheets on Pakistani geography, population, agriculture, mining, manufacturing, and foreign economic relations.

Pakistan InfoExport
http://www.infoexport.gc.ca/country-e.asp?continent=Asia&country=32
A service of Foreign Affairs and International Trade Canada, the site provides Pakistani commercial guides and market reports.

Pakistan Market Access Database
http://mkaccdb.eu.int/mkdb/ mkdb.pl?METHOD=COUNTRY
A service of the European Commission, the site offers briefs on Pakistan trade policy, tariff barriers, non-tariff barriers, investment-related measures, and financial services regulations.

Pakistan Market Information
http://dtiinfo1.dti.gov.uk/ots/pakistan/
A service of the London-based Department of Trade and Industry, the site delivers Pakistani fact sheets, maps, and trade-show information.

Pakistan Market Research
http://strategis.ic.gc.ca/sc_mrkti/ibinddc/engdoc/ 1a1h11.html
A service of Industry Canada, the site provides U.S. Department of Commerce reports on Pakistani business, politics, trade regulations

and standards, investment climate, trade and project financing, business travel, and market opportunities.

Pakistan: Recent Economic Developments
http://www.imf.org/external/pubs/CAT/longres.cfm?sk=2467.0
Developed by the International Monetary Fund, the site provides fact sheets and statistics on Pakistani foreign direct investment, privatization, monetary developments, and consumer and wholesale prices.

Pakistan Virtual Library
http://www.clas.ufl.edu/users/gthursby/pak/
A service of the World Wide Web Virtual Library, the site is an index of Pakistani resources online. Categories include business and commerce, government and law, and e-mail discussion lists.

Pakistan's Business World
http://www.PakistanBiz.com/
Along with country news and fact sheets, the site delivers Pakistani company directories, bulletin board services, business rankings, and government directories.

Pakistan Trade Assistance

Commerce Division
http://www.pakistan-embassy.com/pakcommerce.html
A service of the Pakistani Embassy in Washington, D.C., the site offers Pakistani trade leads, investment opportunities, product catalogs, and a directory of leading national business associations.

Export Promotion Bureau
http://www.epb.jamal.com/
A portal of international trade information, the site provides Pakistani trade leads, statistics, trade policy reports, product catalogs, exporter directories, and tariff information.

Ideal Business
http://www.idealbusiness.com/
A browsable index of Pakistani exporters and importers, the site is divided into 12 categories, including garments, carpets, textile mills, building products, freight forwarders, and distributors.

Pakistan Trade Offices Abroad
http://www.jamal.com/epb/ptoa.htm
A service of the Pakistani Export Promotion

Bureau, the site is a directory of Pakistani Trade Offices in some 40 countries including Australia, Iran, Singapore, and Uzbekistan.

Trade Shows in Pakistan
http://www.expoguide.com/shows/data/loc_45.htm
Compiled by Expoguide, the site is a directory of upcoming trade shows in Pakistan.

Pakistan Representative Offices

Austria

Austrian Trade Commission in Karachi
http://aw.wk.or.at/awo/ahst-karachi.htm
The site lists the staff, street address, phone and fax numbers, e-mail link, and office hours of the Austrian Trade Commission in Karachi.

Brunei Darussalam

High Commission of Brunei Darussalam in Islamabad
http://www.brunet.bn/homepage/gov/bruemb/govemb.htm
The site provides contact information for the Brunei Darussalam High Commission in Islamabad.

Canada

High Commission of Canada in Islamabad
http://www.dfait-maeci.gc.ca/english/missions/rep-can3e.htm#pakistan
The site provides contact information for the Canadian High Commission in Islamabad.

India

Indian Commercial Mission in Islamabad
http://www.nic.in/commin/ICM.HTM
The site lists the street address, phone and fax numbers, and e-mail link of the Indian Commercial Mission in Islamabad.

Japan

Embassy of Japan in Karachi
http://www.japanemb.org.pk/
Posted in English, the site provides Japanese fact sheets, press releases, culture and education bulletins, visa and passport information, and reports on Japan-Pakistan trade and relations.

Malaysia

High Commission of Malaysia in Islamabad
*http://www.mnet.com.my/klonline/www/missions/
malmiss/mpakista1.htm*
The site provides contact information for the
Malaysian High Commission in Islamabad.

New Zealand

Trade New Zealand in Karachi
http://www.tradenz.govt.nz/contact/measia.html
An export promotion service, the site provides
contact information for the Trade New Zealand
office in Karachi.

Singapore

Consulate General of Singapore in Karachi
http://www.gov.sg/mfa/consular/mww_p.htm
The site provides contact information for the
Singapore Consulate General in Karachi.

Spain

Spanish Commercial Office in Islamabad
*http://www.icex.es/openURL.html#openURL=/
english/infoproyem/ofcomes/ofcomes.html#AS*
The site lists the staff, street address, phone and
fax numbers, and e-mail link of the Spanish
Commercial Office in Islamabad.

Sweden

Embassy of Sweden in Islamabad
*http://www.ud.se/english/mfa/ambassad/
pakistan.htm*
The site provides contact information for the
Swedish Embassy in Islamabad.

Thailand

Royal Thai Consulate General in Karachi
http://www.mfa.go.th/Embassy/detail/25.htm
The site lists the Consul General, street address,
and phone and fax numbers of the Thai Consulate General in Karachi.

Royal Thai Embassy in Islamabad
http://www.mfa.go.th/Embassy/detail/55.htm
The site lists the Ambassador, street address,
and phone and fax numbers of the Thai Embassy
in Islamabad.

United Kingdom

High Commission of Britain in Islamabad
http://www.britcoun.org.pk/bol/bol.htm
The site provides British fact sheets, press
releases, company directories, and visa and
passport information.

Trade Office of Britain in Lahore
http://www.fco.gov.uk/directory/posts.asp?PK
The site provides contact information for the
British Trade Office in Lahore.

United States

United States Consulate in Karachi
*http://www.usia.gov/abtusia/posts/PK2/
wwwhamcn.html*
The virtual Consulate provides U.S. news, press
releases, fact sheets, event bulletins, visa and
passport information, and a directory of consular
and commercial services.

United States Information Service in Karachi
*http://www.usia.gov/abtusia/posts/PK2/
wwwhmain.html*
The site delivers U.S. news, press releases,
electronic journals, event information, foreign
policy statements, and a directory of teaching and
translation programs.

Palestinian Authority

Palestinian Authority Market Guides

Complete Guide to Palestine's Websites
http://www.birzeit.edu/links/index.html
A service of the World Wide Web Virtual Library,
the site is an index of Palestinian resources
online. Categories include business and
economy, government and services, and organizations and associations.

Palestine Chamber of Commerce
http://www.g77tin.org/pccghp.html
Based in Gaza, the Chamber promotes Palestinian economic development and trade. The site
provides Palestinian news, business guides,
market reports, and contact information.

Palestinian Business Directory
http://www.pal-chambers.com/business/top.htm
A browsable directory of Palestinian

businesspeople and companies, the site is divided into six categories including trade, agriculture, services, and construction.

Palestinian Central Bureau of Statistics
http://www.pcbs.org/
Posted in Arabic and English, the site is a database of Palestinian statistics on population, wages, labor, international trade, construction, consumer prices, and other economic indicators.

Palestinian Chambers of Commerce, Industry and Agriculture
http://www.pal-chambers.com/
An index of Palestinian Chambers of Commerce, the site lists offices in 11 centers, including Bethlehem, Hebron, Jericho, Nablus, Ramallah, and Tulkarem.

Palestinian Development InfoNet
http://www.arts.mcgill.ca/MEPP/PDIN/pdfront.html
Sponsored in part by the World Bank, the site provides information on development assistance and reconstruction in the West Bank and Gaza. The service includes economic reports, discussion lists, and bulletin boards.

Palestinian Economic Council for Development and Reconstruction
http://www.pecdar.org/
Established in 1993, the Council manages economic development in Palestine. The site includes activity reports, project profiles, speeches, and contact information.

Palestinian National Authority
http://www.pna.net/
Featuring a statement by Yasser Arafat, the online service provides Palestinian fact sheets, speeches, press releases, peace process reports, and United Nations Security Council bulletins.

Program of Assistance to the Palestinian People
http://www.papp.undp.org/
A service of the United Nations Development Program, the site provides information on infrastructure, training, and other assistance projects in Palestine in recent years.

Palestinian Authority Trade Assistance

Palestinian Trade Development Center
http://www.paltrade.org/
Based in Ramallah, the Center promotes Palestinian exports. The site provides Palestinian business guides, buy and sell offers, international trade leads, and membership information.

Palestinian Trade Promotion Organization
http://www.ptpo.org/ptpo/
Established in 1992, the organization promotes Palestinian exports and international business. The site features a mission statement, contact information, Palestinian trade leads, and product catalogs.

Palestinian Authority Representative Offices

Germany

German Chamber of Commerce for Palestinian Territories
http://www.ahk.net/en/pal/Ramallah/
The site lists the Chairperson, Chief Executive Officer, street address, phone and fax numbers, and e-mail link of the German Chamber in Ramallah.

Qatar

Qatar Media

Qatar Media
http://www.mediainfo.com/emediajs/specific-geo.htm?region=qatar
Developed by Editor and Publisher Interactive, the site is an index of Qatari newspaper and other media sites online.

Qatar Market Guides

Country Commercial Guide
http://www.state.gov/www/about_state/business/com_guides/1998/neareast/qatar98.html
Prepared by the U.S. Embassy in Doha, the site delivers primers on Qatari business, politics, trade regulations and standards, investment climate, trade and project financing, and business travel.

Qatar Country Brief
http://www.worldbank.org/cgi-bin/sendoff.cgi?page=%2Fhtml%2Fextdr%2Foffrep%2Fmena%2Fqa.htm
A service of the World Bank Group, the site provides population statistics, financial data, development reports, and economic forecasts.

Qatar: A Country Study
http://lcweb2.loc.gov/frd/cs/qatoc.html
A service of the U.S. Library of Congress, the site delivers fact sheets on Qatari geography, population, agriculture, mining, manufacturing, and foreign economic relations.

Qatar InfoExport
http://www.infoexport.gc.ca/country-e.asp?continent=Africa&country=63
A service of Foreign Affairs and International Trade Canada, the site provides Qatar commercial guides and market reports.

Qatar Market Information
http://dtiinfo1.dti.gov.uk/ots/qatar/
A service of the London-based Department of Trade and Industry, the site delivers Qatari fact sheets, maps, and trade-show information.

Qatar Market Research
http://strategis.ic.gc.ca/sc_mrkti/ibinddc/engdoc/1a1d11.html
A service of Industry Canada, the site provides U.S. Department of Commerce reports on Qatari business, politics, trade regulations and standards, investment climate, trade and project financing, business travel, and market opportunities.

Qatar Online
http://www.qatar-online.com/index-e.htm
A browsable index of Qatari resources online, the site is divided into 12 categories including news, business, technology, culture, education, tourism, and information.

Qatar Virtual Library
http://menic.utexas.edu/menic/countries/qatar.html
A service of the Center for Middle Eastern Studies at the University of Texas, the site provides a directory of Qatari resources online. Categories include business and economy, government and politics, and news and current events.

Qatar Trade Assistance

Diplomatic Pouch
http://www.mofa.gov.qa/embassies/index-e.htm
A directory of Qatari Embassies, Consulates, and Permanent Missions, the site lists offices in over 30 countries including Canada, Korea, Italy, Norway, and the United States.

Ministry of Foreign Affairs
http://www.mofa.gov.qa/
Posted in Arabic and English, the site delivers Qatari news, fact sheets, foreign policy statements, government directories, executive profiles, and employment opportunities.

Qatar Representative Offices

India

Embassy of India in Doha
http://qatar.net.qa/indian-embassy/
Featuring a message from the Ambassador, the site provides Indian fact sheets, visa and passport information, and a directory of consular and commercial services.

United Kingdom

Embassy of Britain in Doha
http://www.fco.gov.uk/directory/posts.asp?QA
The site provides contact information for the British Embassy in Doha.

United States

United States Embassy in Doha
http://qatar.net.qa/usisdoha/wwwhemb.htm
Along with a profile of the Ambassador, the site provides U.S. visa and passport information, and a directory of consular and commercial services.

United States Information Service in Doha
http://qatar.net.qa/usisdoha/fram.htm
The site delivers U.S. news, press releases, electronic journals, event information, foreign policy statements, and a directory of teaching and translation programs.

Saudi Arabia

Saudi Arabia Media

Al Madina
http://www.almadinah.com/
Posted in Arabic, the site provides Saudi news, regional bulletins, business reports, editorials, interviews, cultural guides, company profiles, and weather information.

Saudi Arabia Media

http://www.mediainfo.com/emediajs/specific-geo.htm?region=saudiarabia
Developed by Editor and Publisher Interactive, the site is an index of Saudi media sites online.

Saudi Arabia Market Guides

Barclays Country Report: Saudi Arabia

http://www.offshorebanking.barclays.com/services/economic/yearly/sauoct97/index.html
Prepared by Barclays Bank, the site reports on Saudi Arabian economic trends, politics, monetary and fiscal policy, international trade, and U.K.-Saudi merchandise trade and investment flows.

Economic Offset Program

http://www.saudioffset.com/
A procurement reinvestment initiative, the Program promotes economic development in Saudi Arabia in cooperation with foreign multinational contractors. The site includes a mission statement, investment guides, and contact information.

Saudi Arabia Business Briefs

http://www.austrade.gov.au/IOOM/Riyadh/
A service of Austrade, the site offers fact sheets on Saudi culture, business etiquette, marketing, transportation, travel, and visas.

Saudi Arabia Country Brief

http://www.worldbank.org/cgi-bin/sendoff.cgi?page=%2Fhtml%2Fextdr%2Foffrep%2Fmena%2Fsa.htm
A service of the World Bank Group, the site provides Saudi population statistics, financial data, development reports, and economic forecasts.

Saudi Arabia Country Profile

http://www.tradenz.govt.nz/intelligence/profiles/kingdom_of_saudi_arabia.html
A service of the New Zealand Trade Development Board, the site provides Saudi economic statistics, market information, and business tips.

Saudi Arabia Country Report

http://www.state.gov/www/issues/economic/trade_reports/neareast97/saudiarabia97.html
Prepared by the U.S. Department of State, the site delivers information on Saudi exchange rates, debt management, trade barriers, and intellectual property protection.

Saudi Arabia: A Country Study

http://lcweb2.loc.gov/frd/cs/satoc.html
A service of the U.S. Library of Congress, the site delivers fact sheets on Saudi geography, population, agriculture, mining, manufacturing, and foreign economic relations.

Saudi Arabia InfoExport

http://www.infoexport.gc.ca/country-e.asp?continent=Africa&country=64
A service of Foreign Affairs and International Trade Canada, the site provides Saudi commercial guides and market reports.

Saudi Arabia Market Access Database

http://mkaccdb.eu.int/mkdb/mkdb.pl?METHOD=COUNTRY
A service of the European Commission, the site offers briefs on Saudi trade policy, tariff barriers, non-tariff barriers, investment-related measures, and financial services regulations.

Saudi Arabia Market Information

http://dtiinfo1.dti.gov.uk/ots/saudi_arabia/
A service of the London-based Department of Trade and Industry, the site delivers Saudi fact sheets, maps, and trade-show information.

Saudi Arabia Market Research

http://strategis.ic.gc.ca/sc_mrkti/ibinddc/engdoc/1a1d12.html
A service of Industry Canada, the site provides U.S. Department of Commerce reports on Saudi business, politics, trade regulations and standards, investment climate, trade and project financing, business travel, and market opportunities.

Saudi Arabia Virtual Library

http://www.arablink.com/saudi-arabia/
A service of the World Wide Web Virtual Library, the site is a directory of Saudi resources online. Categories include business and economy, computers and communications, and news and media.

Saudi Business Park

http://dspace.dial.pipex.com/town/square/ed84/index.htm
A country business gateway, the site provides Saudi fact sheets, project profiles, investment opportunities, economic forecasts, company directories, and international trade statistics.

Saudi View
http://www.arabview.net/SaudiView/
A hub of country information, the site delivers backgrounders on Saudi business, education, media, art and culture, and government. The service includes a Saudi currency converter and commercial guide.

Top 100 Saudi Companies
http://www.arab.net/saudi100/welcome.html
Compiled by Arab News, the site is a searchable directory of leading Saudi companies. The profiles include data on assets, profits, number of employees, and turnover.

Saudi Arabia Trade Assistance

Saudi Arabia Trade Show
http://www.mentorweb.net/tradeshow/
A virtual trade show, the site showcases Saudi companies and products in over 50 categories including medical products, machinery, electronics, engineering, and construction.

Trade Shows in Saudi Arabia
http://www.expoguide.com/shows/data/loc_52.htm
Compiled by Expoguide, the site is a directory of upcoming trade shows in Saudi Arabia.

Saudi Arabia Representative Offices

Austria

Austrian Trade Commission in Jeddah
http://aw.wk.or.at/awo/ahst-jeddah.htm
The site lists the staff, street address, phone and fax numbers, e-mail link, and office hours of the Austrian Trade Commission in Jeddah.

Austrian Trade Commission in Riyadh
http://aw.wk.or.at/awo/ahst-riyadh.htm
The site lists the staff, street address, phone and fax numbers, e-mail link, and office hours of the Austrian Trade Commission in Riyadh.

Brunei Darussalam

Consulate General of Brunei Darussalam in Jeddah
http://www.brunet.bn/homepage/gov/bruemb/govemb.htm
The site provides contact information for the Brunei Darussalam Consulate General in Jeddah.

Embassy of Brunei Darussalam in Riyadh
http://www.brunet.bn/homepage/gov/bruemb/govemb.htm
The site provides contact information for the Brunei Darussalam Embassy in Riyadh.

Canada

Consulate of Canada in Jeddah
http://www.dfait-maeci.gc.ca/english/missions/rep-can4e.htm#saudi arabia
The site provides contact information for the Canadian Consulate in Jeddah.

Embassy of Canada in Riyadh
http://www.dfait-maeci.gc.ca/english/missions/rep-can4e.htm#saudi arabia
The site provides contact information for the Canadian Embassy in Riyadh.

Finland

Finland Trade Center in Riyadh
http://www.exports.finland.fi/tradecen.htm
The site lists the staff, street address, phone and fax numbers, and e-mail link of the Finland Trade Center in Riyadh.

Germany

German Chamber of Commerce in Riyadh
http://www.ahk.net/en/sa/Riyadh/
The site lists the Delegate, street address, phone and fax numbers, e-mail link, and office hours of the German Chamber in Riyadh.

Ghana

Embassy of Ghana in Riyadh
http://www.juntung.com/ghana-consul-hk/2misabo.htm
The site provides contact information for the Ghanaian Embassy in Riyadh.

India

Indian Commercial Mission in Jeddah
http://www.nic.in/commin/ICM.HTM
The site lists the street address, phone and fax numbers, and e-mail link of the Indian Commercial Mission in Jeddah.

Indian Commercial Mission in Riyadh
http://www.nic.in/commin/ICM.HTM
The site lists the street address, phone and fax

numbers, and e-mail link of the Indian Commercial Mission in Riyadh.

Indonesia

Embassy of Indonesia in Riyadh
http://indag.dprin.go.id/INGG/trade/atache.HTM
The site provides contact information for the Indonesian Embassy in Riyadh.

Ireland

Enterprise Ireland in Riyadh
http://www.irish-trade.ie/office_network/
office_locate01.html#anchor1441434
The site lists the Manager, street address, and phone and fax numbers of the Enterprise Ireland office in Riyadh.

Malaysia

Consulate General of Malaysia in Jeddah
http://www.mnet.com.my/klonline/www/missions/
malmiss/msaudia2.htm
The site provides contact information for the Malaysian Consulate General in Jeddah.

Embassy of Malaysia in Riyadh
http://www.mnet.com.my/klonline/www/missions/
malmiss/msaudia1.htm
The site provides contact information for the Malaysian Embassy in Riyadh.

Trade Commission of Malaysia in Jeddah
http://www.mnet.com.my/klonline/www/missions/
malmiss/msaudia3.htm
The site provides contact information for the Malaysian Trade Commission in Jeddah.

Nepal

Embassy of Nepal in Riyadh
http://www.info-nepal.com/members/fips/contacts/
nepalese.html
The site provides contact information for the Embassy of Nepal in Riyahd.

New Zealand

Trade New Zealand in Riyadh
http://www.tradenz.govt.nz/contact/measia.html
An export promotion service, the site provides contact information for the Trade New Zealand office in Riyadh.

Pakistan

Pakistan Trade Office in Jeddah
http://www.jamal.com/epb/ptoa.htm
The site provides contact information for the Pakistan Trade Office in Jeddah.

Philippines

Philippine Trade and Investment Promotion Office in Jeddah
http://www.dti.gov.ph/jed/
The site provides a mission statement, service directory, and contact information for the Philippine Trade Office in Jeddah.

Singapore

Consulate General of Singapore in Jeddah
http://www.gov.sg/mfa/consular/mww_s.htm
The site provides contact information for the Singapore Consulate General in Jeddah.

Embassy of Singapore in Riyadh
http://www.gov.sg/mfa/consular/mww_s.htm
The site provides contact information for the Singapore Embassy in Riyadh.

Spain

Spanish Commercial Office in Riyadh
http://www.icex.es/openURL.html#openURL=/
english/infoproyem/ofcomes/ofcomes.html#AS
The site lists the staff, street address, phone and fax numbers, and e-mail link of the Spanish Commercial Office in Riyadh.

Sweden

Consulate General of Sweden in Jeddah
http://www.ud.se/english/mfa/ambassad/
saudiara.htm
The site provides contact information for the Swedish Embassy in Jeddah.

Embassy of Sweden in Riyadh
http://www.ud.se/english/mfa/ambassad/
saudiara.htm
The site provides contact information for the Swedish Embassy in Riyadh.

Taiwan

Taiwan Government Information Office in Riyadh
http://www.gio.gov.tw/info/ngio/sau-f.html
Posted in Chinese and English, the site lists the street address, phone and fax numbers, and e-mail link of the Taiwan Government Information Office in Riyadh.

Tanzania

Embassy of Tanzania in Riyadh
http://www.tanzania-online.gov.uk/visa/envoys.html
The site provides contact information for the Tanzanian Embassy in Riyadh.

Thailand

Royal Thai Consulate General in Jeddah
http://www.mfa.go.th/Embassy/detail/30.htm
The site lists the Consul General, street address, and phone and fax numbers of the Thai Consulate in Jeddah.

Royal Thai Embassy in Riyadh
http://www.mfa.go.th/Embassy/detail/81.htm
The site lists the street address, and phone and fax numbers of the Thai Embassy in Riyadh.

Thailand Office of Commercial Affairs in Jeddah
http://www.thaitrade.com/thcoaf.html
The site lists the street address, phone and fax numbers, and e-mail link of the Thailand Office of Commercial Affairs in Jeddah.

United Kingdom

Consulate General of Britain in Jeddah
http://www.fco.gov.uk/directory/posts.asp?SC
The site provides contact information for the British Consulate General in Jeddah.

Embassy of Britain in Riyadh
http://www.fco.gov.uk/directory/posts.asp?SC
The site provides contact information for the British Embassy in Riyadh.

United States

U.S.-Saudi Arabian Business Council
http://www.us-saudi-business.org/index.html
With offices in Riyadh and Washington, D.C., the Council promotes U.S.-Saudi trade. The site

includes Saudi fact sheets, business guides, joint venture opportunities, and contact information.

Sri Lanka

Sri Lanka Media

Sri Lanka Media
http://www.mediainfo.com/emediajs/specific-geo.htm?region=srilanka
Developed by Editor and Publisher Interactive, the site is an index of Sri Lankan media sites online including magazines, newspapers, and television stations.

Sri Lanka Market Guides

Board of Investment
http://www.BOIsrilanka.org/boihome/boi.htm
Established in 1993, the Board promotes foreign investment in Sri Lanka. The site includes Sri Lankan investment incentives, project approval procedures, and contact information.

Bureau of Infrastructure Investment
http://www.boisrilanka.org/boihome/bii.htm
A unit of the Board of Investment, the Bureau promotes private investment in Sri Lankan infrastructure projects. The site provides a database of infrastructure investment opportunities, incentives, and recent projects.

Census Statistics
http://www.lk/national/census/sl_figures95.html
A service of Sri Lanka Web Window, the site is a database of statistics on Sri Lankan population, labor force, health, agriculture, forestry, public finance, and other key economic indicators.

Ceylon Chamber of Commerce
http://www.lanka.net/chamber/
Based in Colombo, the Chamber promotes Sri Lankan economic development and trade. The site provides Sri Lankan fact sheets, international trade statistics, and business matchmaking services.

Foreign Investing in Sri Lanka
http://www.boisrilanka.org/boihome/invest.htm
A virtual country gateway, the site delivers Sri Lankan news, business guides, quality of life comparisons, investment opportunities, and budget highlights.

Lanka Business Web
http://www.lanka.net/lisl2/yellow/
A directory of Sri Lankan companies online, the site is divided into over 50 categories including accounting, food and beverages, electronics, hardware products, and pharmaceuticals.

Lanka Super Pages
http://lankasuperpages.LSPLK.com/
A browsable database of some 22,000 Sri Lankan business listings, the site is divided into 200 categories including advertising, public notaries, and welding equipment.

Sri Lanka Business Briefs
http://www.austrade.gov.au/IOOM/SriLanka/
A service of Austrade, the site offers fact sheets on Sri Lankan culture, business etiquette, marketing, transportation, travel, and visas.

Sri Lanka Country Brief
http://www.worldbank.org/cgi-bin/ sendoff.cgi?page=%2Fhtml%2Fextdr%2Foffrep%2 Fsas%2Flk.htm
A service of the World Bank Group, the site provides Sri Lankan population statistics, financial data, development reports, and economic forecasts.

Sri Lanka Country Profile
http://www.tradenz.govt.nz/intelligence/profiles/ sri_lanka.html
A service of the New Zealand Trade Development Board, the site provides Sri Lankan economic statistics, market information, and business tips.

Sri Lanka: A Country Study
http://lcweb2.loc.gov/frd/cs/lktoc.html
A service of the U.S. Library of Congress, the site delivers fact sheets on Sri Lankan geography, population, agriculture, mining, manufacturing, and foreign economic relations.

Sri Lanka InfoExport
http://www.infoexport.gc.ca/country- e.asp?continent=Asia&country=39
A service of Foreign Affairs and International Trade Canada, the site provides fact sheets and statistics on Sri Lankan geography, business, trade, and politics.

Sri Lanka Market Information
http://dtiinfo1.dti.gov.uk/ots/sri_lanka/
A service of the London-based Department of Trade and Industry, the site delivers Sri Lankan fact sheets, maps, and trade-show information.

Sri Lanka Market Research
http://strategis.ic.gc.ca/sc_mrkti/ibinddc/engdoc/ 1a1h12.html
A service of Industry Canada, the site provides U.S. Department of Commerce reports on Sri Lankan economic trends, politics, trade regulations and standards, investment climate, trade and project financing, business travel, and market opportunities.

Sri Lanka Virtual Library
http://laf.cioe.com/~lanka/wlib/
A service of the World Wide Web Virtual Library, the site is a directory of Sri Lankan resources online. Categories include business and investments, food and beverages, and government and embassies.

Sri Lanka Web Window
http://www.lk/
Homepage of the Sri Lankan government, the site provides fact sheets on Sri Lankan history, business, education, science and technology, travel, culture, and media.

Sri Lanka Trade Assistance

Embassies and Consulates Abroad
http://www.lk/DipMissionF.html
A service of the Sri Lankan Ministry of Foreign Affairs, the site is a database of Sri Lankan Embassies and High Commissions around the world.

Government and Embassies
http://laf.cioe.com/~lanka/wlib/gov.html
A service of the Sri Lanka Virtual Library, the site is a directory of Sri Lankan Embassies and High Commissions in over 40 countries including Australia, France, India, and the United States.

Tradenet Sri Lanka
http://www.tradenetsl.lk/
Developed by the Sri Lanka Export Development Board, the site delivers Sri Lankan fact sheets, trade leads, event information, and export and import statistics.

Sri Lanka Representative Offices

Diplomatic Missions in Sri Lanka
http://www.lk/DipMission.html
A service of Sri Lanka Web Window, the site is a directory of foreign diplomatic missions in Sri Lanka. Representatives include Bangladesh, Cuba, France, Iraq, and the United Kingdom.

Canada

High Commission of Canada in Colombo
http://www.dfait-maeci.gc.ca/english/missions/rep-can4e.htm#sri lanka
The site provides contact information for the Canadian High Commission in Colombo.

France

French Trade Commission in Colombo
http://www.dree.org/srilanka/
Written in French, the site delivers Sri Lankan market reports, sector profiles, contact information, and a directory of export programs for French companies doing business in Sri Lanka.

India

Indian Commercial Mission in Colombo
http://www.nic.in/commin/ICM.HTM
The site lists the street address, phone and fax numbers, and e-mail link of the Indian Commercial Mission in Colombo.

Malaysia

High Commission of Malaysia in Colombo
http://www.mnet.com.my/klonline/www/missions/malmiss/msrilank.htm
The site provides contact information for the Malaysian High Commission in Colombo.

Nepal

Embassy of Nepal in Colombo
http://www.info-nepal.com/members/fips/contacts/nepalese.html
The site provides contact information for the Embassy of Nepal in Colombo.

Pakistan

Pakistan Trade Office in Colombo
http://www.jamal.com/epb/ptoa.htm
The site provides contact information for the Pakistan Trade Office in Colombo.

Singapore

Consulate General of Singapore in Colombo
http://www.gov.sg/mfa/consular/mww_s.htm
The site provides contact information for the Singapore Consulate General in Colombo.

Thailand

Royal Thai Embassy in Colombo
http://www.mfa.go.th/Embassy/detail/61.htm
The site lists the Ambassador, street address, and phone and fax numbers of the Thai Embassy in Colombo.

United Kingdom

High Commission of Britain in Colombo
http://www.fco.gov.uk/directory/posts.asp?SN
The site provides contact information for the British High Commission in Colombo.

United States

American Chamber of Commerce in Sri Lanka
http://www.lanka.net/amcham/
Based in Colombo, the Chamber promotes U.S.-Sri Lankan trade. The site includes a mission statement, newsletter, calendar of events, and contact information.

United States Embassy in Colombo
http://www.usia.gov/posts/sri_lanka/
Along with Sri Lankan country reports, the site delivers U.S. news, press releases, visa and passport information, and a directory of consular and commercial services.

United States Information Service in Colombo
http://www.usia.gov/abtusia/posts/CE1/wwwhusis.html
The site delivers U.S. news, press releases, electronic journals, event information, foreign policy statements, and a directory of U.S.-Sri Lankan exchange programs.

Syria

Syria Market Guides

Business in Syria
http://www.visit-syria.com/bis/index2.html
A hub of country information, the site provides Syrian fact sheets, history lessons, investment guides, legal primers, and company directories.

Country Commercial Guide
http://www.state.gov/www/about_state/business/com_guides/1998/neareast/syria98.html
Prepared by the U.S. Embassy in Damascus, the site delivers primers on Syrian business, politics, trade regulations and standards, investment

climate, trade and project financing, and business travel.

Syria Country Report
http://www.state.gov/www/issues/economic/ trade_reports/neareast97/syria97.html
Prepared by the U.S. Department of State, the site delivers information on Syrian exchange rates, debt management, trade barriers, and intellectual property protection.

Syria: A Country Study
http://lcweb2.loc.gov/frd/cs/sytoc.html
A service of the U.S. Library of Congress, the site delivers fact sheets on Syrian geography, population, agriculture, mining, manufacturing, and foreign economic relations.

Syria InfoExport
http://www.infoexport.gc.ca/country-e.asp?continent=Africa&country=65
A service of Foreign Affairs and International Trade Canada, the site provides Syrian commercial guides and market reports.

Syria Market Information
http://dtiinfo1.dti.gov.uk/ots/syria/
A service of the London-based Department of Trade and Industry, the site delivers Syrian fact sheets, maps, and trade-show information.

Syria Market Research
http://strategis.ic.gc.ca/sc_mrkti/ibinddc/engdoc/ 1a1d13.html
A service of Industry Canada, the site provides U.S. Department of Commerce reports on Syrian business, politics, trade regulations and standards, investment climate, trade and project financing, business travel, and market opportunities.

Syria Net
http://www.syria-net.com/
A directory of Syrian resources online, the site is divided into ten categories including news, business, science, education, and tourism.

Syria Virtual Library
http://menic.utexas.edu/menic/countries/ syria.html
A service of the Center for Middle Eastern Studies at the University of Texas, the site provides a directory of Syrian resources online. Categories include business and economy, government and politics, and news and current events.

Syria Trade Assistance

Traders and Businessmen in Syria
http://www.visit-syria.com/bis/business.html
A searchable directory of Syrian companies, the site is divided into 12 industry categories including food products, textiles, import/export offices, restaurants, and hotels.

Syria Representative Offices

Armenia

Embassy of Armenia in Damascus
http://www.armeniaemb.org/forrel/embas2.htm
The site provides contact information for the Armenian Embassy in Damascus.

Austria

Austrian Trade Commission in Damascus
http://aw.wk.or.at/awo/ahst-damaskus.htm
The site lists the staff, street address, phone and fax numbers, e-mail link, and office hours of the Austrian Trade Commission in Damascus.

Canada

Embassy of Canada in Damascus
http://www.dfait-maeci.gc.ca/english/missions/rep-can4e.htm#syria
The site provides contact information for the Canadian Embassy in Damascus.

Germany

German Arab Chamber of Commerce in Aleppo
http://www.kleudge.com/dihtalep/
The site lists the contact person, mission statement, street address, phone and fax numbers, and e-mail link of the German Chamber in Aleppo.

India

Indian Commercial Mission in Damascus
http://www.nic.in/commin/ICM.HTM
The site lists the street address, phone and fax numbers, and e-mail link of the Indian Commercial Mission in Damascus.

Iran

Iran Trade Center in Damascus
http://www.neda.net/ibr/tcc.html
An Iranian trade promotion service, the site lists the street address and phone and fax numbers of the Iran Trade Center in Damascus.

Pakistan

Pakistan Trade Office in Damascus
http://www.jamal.com/epb/ptoa.htm
The site provides contact information for the Pakistan Trade Office in Damascus.

Spain

Spanish Commercial Office in Damascus
http://www.icex.es/openURL.html#openURL=/ english/infoproyem/ofcomes/ofcomes.html#AS
The site lists the staff, street address, phone and fax numbers, and e-mail link of the Spanish Commercial Office in Damascus.

Sweden

Embassy of Sweden in Damascus
http://www.ud.se/english/mfa/ambassad/ syrien.htm
The site provides contact information for the Swedish Embassy in Damascus.

United Kingdom

Embassy of Britain in Damascus
http://www.fco.gov.uk/directory/posts.asp?SY
The site provides contact information for the British Embassy in Damascus.

Turkey

Turkey Media

Dunya Online
http://www.dunya.com/
Updated daily, the site is a Turkish electronic newspaper. The service includes Turkish news summaries, political and economic bulletins, exchange rates, and art and culture guides.

Turkey Media
http://www.mediainfo.com/emediajs/specific-geo.htm?region=turkey
Developed by Editor and Publisher Interactive, the site is an index of Turkish media sites online including city guides, magazines, and newspapers.

Turkish Daily News Online
http://www.turkishdailynews.com/
An English-language electronic newspaper, the site provides Turkish news, business guides, economic reports, government bulletins, classifieds, and cultural information.

Turkey Market Guides

Barclays Country Report: Turkey
http://www.offshorebanking.barclays.com/ services/economic/yearly/tursep97/index.html
Prepared by Barclays Bank, the site reports on Turkish economic trends, politics, monetary and fiscal policy, and U.K.-Turkey merchandise trade and investment flows.

Business Turkey
http://www.btimg.com/
An interactive guide to Turkish business, the site provides Turkish economic news, investment and marketing primers, and a company directory.

Central Bank of the Republic of Turkey
http://www.tcmb.gov.tr/
Posted in English and Turkish, the site delivers Turkish exchange rates, press bulletins, banking surveys, economic discussion papers, and international trade statistics.

Dost Net Turkish Business Directory
http://www.dost.net/business/
Written in English and Turkish, the site features Turkish business news, company directories, an online discussion board, employment opportunities, and website reviews.

Internet Sites in Turkey
http://www.ozemail.com.au/~turkembs/sites.htm
An index of Turkish Internet resources online, the site is divided into 12 categories including commercial, government, education, organizations, and media.

Republic of Turkey Homepage
http://www.turkey.org/
Homepage of the Turkish government, the site is a hub of country information. Modules include business and economy, politics and policy, tourism, and calendar of events.

State Institute of Statistics
http://www.die.gov.tr/ENGLISH/index.html
A virtual library of socioeconomic statistics, the site provides data on Turkish gross domestic product, international trade, industrial production, and other key indicators.

Turkey: Big Emerging Markets Homepage
http://www.ita.doc.gov/bems/Turkey.html
Developed by the United States Department of Commerce, the site delivers Turkish fact sheets, economic forecasts, export and import statistics, sector profiles, and international trade guides.

Turkey Business Briefs
http://www.austrade.gov.au/IOOM/Turkey/
A service of Austrade, the site offers fact sheets on Turkish business etiquette, foreign investment, corporate taxation, marketing, and visas.

Turkey Business and Economy
http://www.mfa.gov.tr/GRUPC/GRUPC.HTM
A service of the Turkish Ministry of Foreign Affairs, the site delivers Turkish international trade statistics, economic forecasts, investment guides, and business opportunities.

Turkey Business Report
http://italchambers.net/BusinessReports.html
Prepared by the Italian Chamber of Commerce and written in Italian, the site provides Turkish fact sheets, market reports, and commercial guides.

Turkey Country Brief
http://www.worldbank.org/cgi-bin/ sendoff.cgi?page=%2Fhtml%2Fextdr%2Foffrep% 2Feca%2Ftr.htm
A service of the World Bank Group, the site provides Turkish population statistics, financial data, development reports, and economic forecasts.

Turkey Country Profile
http://www.tradenz.govt.nz/intelligence/profiles/ turkey.html
A service of the New Zealand Trade Development Board, the site provides Turkish economic statistics, market information, and business tips.

Turkey Country Report
http://www.state.gov/www/issues/economic/ trade_reports/europe_canada97/turkey97.html
Prepared by the U.S. Department of State, the site delivers information on Turkish exchange rates, debt management, trade barriers, and intellectual property protection.

Turkey: A Country Study
http://lcweb2.loc.gov/frd/cs/trtoc.html
A service of the U.S. Library of Congress, the site delivers fact sheets on Turkish geography, population, agriculture, mining, manufacturing, and foreign economic relations.

Turkey InfoExport
http://www.infoexport.gc.ca/country- e.asp?continent=Europe&country=49
A service of Foreign Affairs and International Trade Canada, the site provides Turkish commercial guides and market reports.

Turkey Market Information
http://dtiinfo1.dti.gov.uk/ots/turkey/
A service of the London-based Department of Trade and Industry, the site delivers Turkish fact sheets, maps, and trade-show information.

Turkey Market Research
http://strategis.ic.gc.ca/sc_mrkti/ibinddc/engdoc/ 1a1d14.html
A service of Industry Canada, the site provides U.S. Department of Commerce reports on Turkish business, politics, trade regulations and standards, investment climate, trade and project financing, business travel, and market opportunities.

Turkey: Recent Economic Developments
http://www.imf.org/external/pubs/CAT/ longres.cfm?sk=2426.0
Developed by the International Monetary Fund, the site delivers fact sheets and statistics on Turkish output, demand, income distribution, prices, trade policy, interest rates, and wage costs.

Turkey Virtual Library
http://menic.utexas.edu/menic/countries/ turkey.html
A service of the Center for Middle Eastern Studies at the University of Texas, the site provides a directory of Turkish resources online. Categories include business and economy, government and politics, and news and current events.

Turkindex
http://www.turkindex.com/
A directory of some 300,000 Turkish companies, the site is divided into 14 categories including agriculture, construction, electronics, export-import, transportation, and tourism.

Turkey Trade Assistance

Business and Economics
http://www.turkey.org/business.htm
A service of the Turkish government, the site offers fact sheets and statistics on Turkish international trade, banking, construction, agriculture, and privatization.

Business and Trade Index in Turkey
http://www.businessturkey.com/
Along with a searchable directory of Turkish companies, the site provides a browsable index of Turkish business opportunities including offers to sell, buy, and joint venture.

Consular Information
http://www.mfa.gov.tr/grupf/konsolos/default.htm
Posted by the Ministry of Foreign Affairs, the site is an e-mail directory of Turkish Embassies, Consulates, Permanent Representatives, and commercial counselors around the world.

Dost BBS
http://www.dost.net/bbs/impex.html
Posted in English and Turkish, the site is a virtual marketplace. The service includes online message boards with buy and sell offers, and a directory of employment opportunities.

Export Promotion Center of Turkey
http://www.foreigntrade.gov.tr/ENGLISH/IGEME/IGEME.HTM
Based in Ankara, the Center promotes Turkish exports. The site provides a directory of Center export training programs, publications, and promotion services.

Foreign Trade of Turkey
http://www.turkey.org/globebiz.htm
Prepared by the Turkish Undersecretary of Foreign Trade, the site delivers international trade statistics, sectoral export-import reports, and trade forecasts.

Foreign Trade Statistics
http://www.foreigntrade.gov.tr/English/Ftrade/EKO/fmenu2.htm
A virtual library of international trade statistics, the site includes data on Turkish exports and imports by sector, commodity, country, country groups, and continent.

IGEME
http://www.igeme.org.tr/english/maineng.htm
Along with Turkish trade leads and business opportunities, the site features fact sheets on Turkish international trade, foreign investment, banking, tourism, and free zones.

Ministry of Foreign Affairs
http://www.mfa.gov.tr/
Posted in English and Turkish, the site delivers Ministry press releases, foreign policy statements, economic reports, tourism information, and history lessons.

Trade Point Ankara
http://www.tpankara.org.tr/
Written in English and Turkish, the site provides a virtual exhibition of Turkish export products, fact sheets on Turkish foreign investment and free zones, and reports on Turkey-European Union trade.

TurkEx
http://www.turkex.com/
Along with a browsable directory of Turkish exporters and importers, the site features a database of Turkish trade leads and business opportunities in 24 categories including footware, textiles, food and beverage, and plastics.

Turkish Exporters Directory
http://www.foreigntrade.gov.tr/english/director/turkihr/trexp.htm
A service of the Undersecretariat of Foreign Trade, the site is a searchable database of Turkish exporters. The index is browsable by company name, product, and target market.

Turkish Missions Abroad
http://www.turkey.org/madres.htm
A directory of Turkish Embassies, Permanent Representatives and Consulates General, the site lists representatives in over 70 countries including Brazil, Germany, Japan, and the United States.

Turkish Trade Shows
http://www.turkex.com/fairs/
A service of TurkEx, the site is a database of international trade shows and conferences in Turkey. Key events include the Clothing Machines and Accessories Fair, Istanbul Packaging, and International Leather Days.

TurkTrade
http://turktrade.com/
A database of Turkish trade leads and business opportunities, the site is divided into 20 categories including automotive, clothing and textiles, electronics, and professional services.

Undersecretariat of Foreign Trade
http://www.foreigntrade.gov.tr/menueng.htm
The online service provides Turkish trade reports, export and import statistics, free trade zone bulletins, and fact sheets on Turkey-European Union trade and relations.

Turkey Representative Offices

Australia

Austrade in Istanbul
http://www.austrade.gov.au/Istanbul/
An online export promotion service, the site features Australian fact sheets, investment primers, publication lists, contact information, and Turkish business guides.

Austria

Austria Trade Commission in Turkey
http://www.austria.org.tr/
Posted in English, German, and Turkish, the site provides Austrian fact sheets, business guides, economic statistics, trade leads, and a directory of Austrian-Turkish flight connections.

Austrian Trade Commission in Ankara
http://aw.wk.or.at/awo/ahst-ankara.htm
Written in Turkish, the site lists the Director, street address, phone and fax numbers, e-mail link and office hours of the Austrian Trade Commission in Ankara.

Austrian Trade Commission in Istanbul
http://aw.wk.or.at/awo/ahst-istanbul.htm
Posted in Turkish, the site lists the Director, street address, phone and fax numbers, e-mail link and office hours of the Austrian Trade Commission in Istanbul.

Canada

Embassy of Canada in Ankara
http://www.dfait-maeci.gc.ca/english/missions/rep-can4e.htm#turkey
The site provides contact information for the Canadian Embassy in Ankara.

Finland

Finland Trade Center in Ankara
http://www.exports.finland.fi/tradecen.htm
The site lists the staff, street address, phone and fax numbers, and e-mail link of the Finland Trade Center in Ankara.

France

Embassy of France in Ankara
http://www.raksnet.com.tr/ambassadefrance/
Written in French, the site delivers French fact sheets, science and technology bulletins, contact information, and a directory of consular and commercial services.

French Trade Commission in Ankara
http://www.dree.org/turquie/
Posted in French, the site delivers Turkish market reports, sector profiles, contact information, and a directory of export programs for French companies doing business in Turkey.

Iran

Iran Trade Center in Ankara
http://www.neda.net/ibr/tcc.html
An Iranian trade promotion service, the site lists the street address and phone and fax numbers of the Iran Trade Center in Ankara.

Italy

Italian Cultural Institute in Ankara
http://www.iic.org.tr/
Posted in Italian and Turkish, the site provides Italian fact sheets, cultural bulletins, and contact information.

Malaysia

Embassy of Malaysia in Ankara
http://www.mnet.com.my/klonline/www/missions/malmiss/mturkey1.htm
The site provides contact information for the Malaysian Embassy in Ankara.

New Zealand

Trade New Zealand in Ankara
http://www.tradenz.govt.nz/contact/measia.html
An export promotion service, the site provides contact information for the Trade New Zealand office in Ankara.

Norway

Norwegian Trade Council in Istanbul
http://www.ntc.no/cgi-bin/wbch.exe?html=../templates/utekontor2.html&profile=1111
The site lists the staff, street address, phone and fax numbers, and e-mail link of the Norwegian Trade Council in Istanbul.

Pakistan

Pakistan Trade Office in Istabul
http://www.jamal.com/epb/ptoa.htm
The site provides contact information for the Pakistan Trade Office in Istanbul.

Singapore

Consulate General of Singapore in Istanbul
http://www.gov.sg/mfa/consular/mww_t.htm
The site provides contact information for the Singapore Consulate General in Istanbul.

South Africa

Embassy of South Africa in Ankara
http://www.southafrica.org.tr/
The site features South African fact sheets, tourism guides, visa and passport information, and a directory of South African Chambers of Commerce.

Spain

Spanish Commercial Office in Ankara
http://www.icex.es/openURL.html#openURL=/english/infoproyem/ofcomes/ofcomes.html#EU
The site lists the staff, street address, phone and fax numbers, and e-mail link of the Spanish Commercial Office in Ankara.

Spanish Commercial Office in Istanbul
http://www.icex.es/openURL.html#openURL=/english/infoproyem/ofcomes/ofcomes.html#EU
The site lists the staff, street address, phone and fax numbers, and e-mail link of the Spanish Commercial Office in Istanbul.

Sweden

Embassy of Sweden in Ankara
http://www.ud.se/english/mfa/ambassad/turkiet.htm
The site provides contact information for the Swedish Embassy in Ankara.

Taiwan

China External Trade Development Council Office in Istanbul
http://www.cetra.org.tw/english/o_office/indexset.htm
A Taiwanese trade promotion service, the site lists the mission statement and e-mail link of the

China External Trade Development Council Office in Istanbul.

Thailand

Royal Thai Embassy in Ankara
http://www.mfa.go.th/Embassy/detail/63.htm
The site lists the Ambassador, street address, and phone and fax numbers of the Thai Embassy in Ankara.

Thai Trade Center in Istanbul
http://www.thaitrade.com/wwtto.html
A service of the Thailand Department of Export Promotion, the site lists the street address, phone and fax numbers, and e-mail link of the Thai Trade Center in Istanbul.

United Kingdom

Consulate General of Britain in Istanbul
http://www.fco.gov.uk/directory/posts.asp?TK
The site provides contact information for the British Consulate General in Istanbul.

Embassy of Britain in Ankara
http://www.fco.gov.uk/directory/posts.asp?TK
The site provides contact information for the British Embassy in Ankara.

United States

United States Consulate in Istanbul
http://www.usisist.org.tr/
The digital Consulate delivers information on the U.S. Foreign Commercial Service, Foreign Agricultural Service, and American Information Resource Center operations in Turkey.

United States Embassy in Ankara
http://www.usis-ankara.org.tr/
The virtual Embassy delivers U.S. news, press releases, visa and passport information, a staff roster, and a directory of consular and commercial services.

United States Information Service in Ankara
http://www.usis-ankara.org.tr/usis/usis.htm
The site delivers U.S. press releases, electronic journals, event information, foreign policy statements, and a directory of U.S.-Turkey exchange programs.

United States Information Service in Istanbul
http://www.usisist.org.tr/libopen2.html
Along with contact information, the site provides

U.S. electronic journals, Voice of America information, and a directory of U.S.-Turkey educational programs in Istanbul.

United Arab Emirates

United Arab Emirates Media

Khaleej Times Online
http://www.khaleejtimes.com/index.html
Along with regional and world news, the site delivers Emiri headlines, editorials, business reports, employment opportunities, and a browsable archive of past issues.

United Arab Emirates Media
http://www.mediainfo.com/emediajs/specific-geo.htm?region=unitedarabemirates
Developed by Editor and Publisher Interactive, the site is an index of Emiri magazines, newspapers and other media sites online.

United Arab Emirates Market Guides

Abu Dhabi Chamber of Commerce and Industry
http://www.adcci-uae.com/
Along with Emiri fact sheets, the site delivers Abu Dhabi commercial guides, tender bulletins, event information, and business matchmaking services.

Barclays Country Guide: United Arab Emirates
http://www.offshorebanking.barclays.com/services/economic/yearly/uaedec97/uaecont.html
Prepared by Barclays Bank, the site reports on Emiri economic trends, politics, monetary and fiscal policy, and United Kingdom-United Arab Emirates merchandise trade and investment flows.

Buy Dubai
http://www.buydubai.com/BuyDubai/buydubai.nsf
A searchable directory of Emiri companies, the site is divided into over 50 categories including beverages, building materials, environmental services, and office equipment.

Ministry of Finance and Industry
http://www.uae.gov.ae/mofi/engheads.htm
Posted in English, the site provides Emiri fact sheets, business guides, investment primers, tourism information, and government directories.

Tenders, Auctions and General Announcements
http://www.uae.gov.ae/mofi/tendann.htm
The online service is a directory of tenders and auctions sponsored by six Emiri government agencies including the Ministries of Finance and Industry, Health, and Water and Electricity.

United Arab Emirates Business Briefs
http://www.austrade.gov.au/IOOM/UAE/
A service of Austrade, the site offers fact sheets on Emiri culture, business etiquette, marketing, transportation, travel, and visas.

United Arab Emirates Country Brief
http://www.worldbank.org/cgi-bin/sendoff.cgi?page=%2Fhtml%2Fextdr%2Foffrep%2Fmena%2Fae.htm
A service of the World Bank Group, the site provides Emiri population statistics, financial data, development reports, and economic forecasts.

United Arab Emirates Country Profile
http://www.tradenz.govt.nz/intelligence/profiles/united_arab_emirates.html
A service of the New Zealand Trade Development Board, the site provides Emiri economic statistics, market information, and business tips.

United Arab Emirates: A Country Study
http://lcweb2.loc.gov/frd/cs/aetoc.html
A service of the U.S. Library of Congress, the site delivers fact sheets on Emiri geography, population, agriculture, mining, manufacturing, and foreign economic relations.

United Arab Emirates InfoExport
http://www.infoexport.gc.ca/country-e.asp?continent=Africa&country=66
A service of Foreign Affairs and International Trade Canada, the site provides Emiri commercial guides and market reports.

United Arab Emirates Interact
http://www.uaeinteract.com/front.shtml
An online country guide, the site delivers Emiri news, fact sheets, government directories, tourism information, sector profiles, and economic forecasts.

United Arab Emirates Internet Yellow Pages
http://uae-ypages.com/html/1.htm
A browsable directory of Emiri companies and organizations, the site is divided into over 50 industry categories including air carriers, hotels, and textile merchants.

United Arab Emirates Market Access Database
http://mkaccdb.eu.int/mkdb/mkdb.pl?METHOD=COUNTRY

A service of the European Commission, the site offers briefs on Emiri trade policy, tariff barriers, non-tariff barriers, investment-related measures, and financial services regulations.

United Arab Emirates Market Information
http://dtiinfo1.dti.gov.uk/ots/abu_dhabi/
A service of the London-based Department of Trade and Industry, the site delivers Emiri fact sheets, maps, and trade-show information.

United Arab Emirates Market Research
http://strategis.ic.gc.ca/sc_mrkti/ibinddc/engdoc/1a1d15.html
A service of Industry Canada, the site provides U.S. Department of Commerce reports on Emiri business, politics, trade regulations and standards, investment climate, trade and project financing, business travel, and market opportunities.

United Arab Emirates Ministry of Economy and Commerce
http://www.economy.gov.ae/
Based in Abu Dhabi, the Ministry promotes Emiri economic development. The site features a mission statement, publication lists, and commercial laws and regulations.

United Arab Emirates Pages
http://www.uae.org.ae/
Featuring fact sheets on the seven Emirates of the United Arab Emirates, the site delivers Emiri country maps, history lessons, tourism information, and culture guides.

United Arab Emirates Virtual Library
http://menic.utexas.edu/menic/countries/uae.html
A service of the Center for Middle Eastern Studies at the University of Texas, the site provides a directory of Emiri resources online. Categories include business and economy, government and politics, and news and current events.

United Arab Emirates Yellow Pages
http://uae-ypages.com/
Along with a browsable index of Emiri companies, the site delivers country fact sheets, and a directory of government departments and offices.

United Arab Emirates Trade Assistance

Ajman Free Zone
http://www.ajmanfreezone.com/
Homepage of the Ajman Free Zone, a special economic development enclave, the site provides Zone fact sheets, customs clearance information, cost information, and a directory of companies located in the Zone.

Dubai Ports and Customs
http://www.dxbcustoms.gov.ae/
Posted in Arabic and English, the site provides Emiri port and customs news, statistics, and downloadable forms such as an electronic manifest and other customs documentation.

Dubai World Trade Center
http://www.dwtc.com/
Featuring trade-show listings and exhibition reports, the site features Emiri accommodation directories, shopping guides, and travel information.

Hamriyah Free Zone
http://www.hamriyahfz.com/index1.htm
A primer on the Hamriyah Free Trade Zone, the site provides Zone press reviews, incentive information, facility guides, a company directory, and frequently asked questions and answers.

Ras Al Khaimah Free Trade Zone
http://www.rakiftz.com/
Featuring a welcome from the Zone Chairperson, the site provides Zone fact sheets, news, application forms, incentive information, and employment opportunities.

Sharjah Customs Department
http://www.sharjahcustoms.gov.ae/
A virtual primer on customs regulations, the site explains Emiri border registration procedures, required documents, payment methods, and other customs issues.

Trade Shows in United Arab Emirates
http://www.expoguide.com/shows/data/loc_65.htm
Compiled by Expoguide, the site is a directory of upcoming trade shows in the United Arab Emirates.

United Arab Emirates Representative Offices

Consulates in Dubai
http://uae-ypages.com/html/dxbce.htm
A service of the United Arab Emirates Internet Yellow Pages, the site is a directory of Consulates in Dubai. The service lists representatives from over 30 countries including Finland, India, and Lebanon.

Embassies in Abu Dhabi
http://uae-ypages.com/html/auhemb.htm
A service of the United Arab Emirates Internet Yellow Pages, the site is a directory of Embassies in Abu Dhabi. The service lists representatives from over 60 countries including Belize, Croatia, and Ukraine.

Austria

Austrian Trade Commission in Abu Dhabi
http://aw.wk.or.at/awo/ahst-abudhabi.htm
The site lists the staff, street address, phone and fax numbers, and e-mail link of the Austrian Trade Commission in Abu Dhabi.

Brunei Darussalam

Embassy of Brunei Darussalam in Abu Dhabi
http://www.brunet.bn/homepage/gov/bruemb/govemb.htm
The site provides contact information for the Brunei Darussalam Embassy in Abu Dhabi.

Canada

Consulate of Canada in Dubai
http://www.dfait-maeci.gc.ca/english/missions/rep-can4e.htm#united arab emirates
The site provides contact information for the Canadian Consulate in Dubai.

Embassy of Canada in Abu Dhabi
http://www.canada.org.ae/
Along with a directory of Emiri resources online, the site features fact sheets on Canadian economic and commercial affairs, tourism, immigration, and national defense.

China

China Council for the Promotion of International Trade in Abu Dhabi
http://www.ccpit.org/engVersion/cp_about/cp_over/cp_over.html
A Chinese export promotion service, the site provides contact information for the China Council for the Promotion of International Trade office in Abu Dhabi.

Cyprus

Cyprus Trade Center in Dubai
http://www.cyprustradeny.org/cyny5.html
The site lists the street address, and phone and fax numbers of the Cyprus Trade Center in Dubai.

Finland

Embassy of Finland in Abu Dhabi
http://www.finemb-abu.com/
Written in Arabic and English, the site provides Finnish news, press releases, fact sheets, business guides, economic reports, government directories, and travel information.

Finland Trade Center in Abu Dhabi
http://www.finemb-abu.com/files/ftc.htm
The site lists the Trade Officer, street address, phone and fax numbers, and e-mail link of the Finland Trade Center in Abu Dhabi.

France

French Trade Commission in Abu Dhabi
http://www.dree.org/emirats/
Written in French, the site delivers Emiri market reports, sector profiles, contact information, and a directory of export programs for French companies doing business in the area.

India

Embassy of India in Abu Dhabi
http://indembassyuae.org/ind/
Posted in Arabic and English, the site provides Indian fact sheets, business guides, press releases, reports on India-United Arab Emirates trade and relations, and a directory of consular and commercial services.

Malaysia

Consulate General of Malaysia in Dubai
http://www.mnet.com.my/klonline/www/missions/malmiss/muniteda2.htm
The site provides contact information for the Malaysian Consulate General in Dubai.

Embassy of Malaysia in Abu Dhabi
http://www.mnet.com.my/klonline/www/missions/malmiss/muniteda1.htm
The site provides contact information for the Malaysian Embassy in Abu Dhabi.

Trade Commission of Malaysia in Dubai
http://www.mnet.com.my/klonline/www/missions/malmiss/muniteda3.htm
The site provides contact information for the Malaysian Trade Commission in Dubai.

New Zealand

Trade New Zealand in Dubai
http://www.tradenz.govt.nz/contact/measia.html
An export promotion service, the site provides contact information for the Trade New Zealand office in Dubai.

Norway

Embassy of Norway in Abu Dhabi
http://www.ntc.no/cgi-bin/wbch.exe?html=../templates/utekontor2.html&profile=1100
The site lists the staff, street address, phone and fax numbers, and e-mail link of the Norwegian Embassy in Abu Dhabi.

Pakistan

Pakistan Trade Office in Dubai
http://www.jamal.com/epb/ptoa.htm
The site provides contact information for the Pakistan Trade Office in Dubai.

Philippines

Philippine Trade and Investment Promotion Office in Dubai
http://www.dti.gov.ph/dub/
The site provides a mission statement, service directory, and contact information for the Philippine Trade Office in Dubai.

Singapore

Consulate General of Singapore in Dubai
http://www.gov.sg/mfa/consular/mww_u.htm
The site provides contact information for the Singapore Consulate General in Dubai.

Spain

Spanish Commercial Office in Dubai
http://www.icex.es/openURL.html#openURL=/english/infoproyem/ofcomes/ofcomes.html#AS
The site lists the staff, street address, phone and fax numbers, and e-mail link of the Spanish Commercial Office in Dubai.

Sweden

Consulate General of Sweden in Dubai
http://www.ud.se/english/mfa/ambassad/arabemir.htm
The site provides contact information for the Swedish Consulate in Dubai.

Taiwan

China External Trade Development Council Office in Dubai
http://www.cetra.org.tw/english/o_office/indexset.htm
A Taiwanese trade promotion service, the site lists the mission statement and e-mail link of the China External Trade Development Council Office in Dubai.

Thailand

Royal Thai Consulate General in Dubai
http://www.mfa.go.th/Embassy/detail/24.htm
The site lists the Consul General, street address, and phone and fax numbers of the Thai Consulate General in Dubai.

Royal Thai Embassy in Abu Dhabi
http://www.mfa.go.th/Embassy/detail/73.htm
The site lists the Ambassador, street address, and phone and fax numbers of the Thai Embassy in Abu Dhabi.

United Kingdom

Embassy of Britain in Abu Dhabi
http://www.fco.gov.uk/directory/posts.asp?UA
The site provides contact information for the British Embassy in Abu Dhabi.

United States

American Business Council of Dubai
http://www.abcdubai.com/
A U.S.-United Arab Emirates trade promotion service, the site features Council news, a board of directors roster, member directory, and Emiri fact sheets and business guides.

United States Embassy in Abu Dhabi
http://www.usembabu.gov.ae/
Along with Emiri fact sheets, the virtual Embassy delivers U.S. news, event information, a staff roster, and a directory of consular and commercial services.

United States Information Service in Abu Dhabi
http://www.usembabu.gov.ae/abusis.html
The site delivers U.S. press releases, electronic journals, event information, foreign policy

statements, Gulf security reports, and a directory of U.S.-United Arab Emirates exchange and educational programs.

Yemen

Yemen Market Guides

General Investment Authority
http://www.giay.gov.ye/
Posted in Arabic and English, the site provides Yemeni investment guides, business primers, fact sheets, government directories, and contact information.

Yemen Country Brief
http://www.worldbank.org/cgi-bin/ sendoff.cgi?page=%2Fhtml%2Fextdr%2Foffrep%2 Fmena%2Fye.htm
A service of the World Bank Group, the site provides Yemeni population statistics, financial data, development reports, and economic forecasts.

Yemen InfoExport
http://www.infoexport.gc.ca/country- e.asp?continent=Africa&country=67
A service of Foreign Affairs and International Trade Canada, the site provides Yemeni commercial guides and market reports.

Yemen Investment
http://www.yemen-investments.com/
Based in Mukalla, the site provides a directory of Yemeni investment projects and proposals. Priority industries include mining, free trade zones, travel tours, and waterfront beach resorts.

Yemen Market Research
http://strategis.ic.gc.ca/sc_mrkti/ibinddc/engdoc/ 1a1d16.html
A service of Industry Canada, the site provides U.S. Department of Commerce reports on Yemeni business, politics, trade regulations and standards, investment climate, trade and project financing, business travel, and market opportunities.

Yemen Virtual Library
http://menic.utexas.edu/menic/countries/ yemen.html
A service of the Center for Middle Eastern Studies at the University of Texas, the site provides a directory of Yemeni resources online. Categories include business and economy, government and politics, and news and current events.

Yemen's Information Ministry
http://www.yemeninfo.gov.ye/
Written in Arabic and English, the site delivers Yemeni news, business guides, investment primers, economic reports, privatization bulletins, and cultural information.

Yemen Representative Offices

France

French Trade Commission in Sana'a
http://www.dree.org/yemen/
Written in French, the site delivers Yemeni market reports, sector profiles, contact information, and a directory of programs for French exporters.

India

Indian Commercial Mission in Sana'a
http://www.nic.in/commin/ICM.HTM
The site lists the street address, phone and fax numbers, and e-mail link of the Indian Commercial Mission in Sana'a.

Sweden

Consulate General of Sweden in Sana'a
http://www.ud.se/english/mfa/ambassad/ yemen.htm
The site provides contact information for the Swedish Consulate General in Sana'a.

United Kingdom

Embassy of Britain in Sana'a
http://www.fco.gov.uk/directory/posts.asp?YE
The site provides contact information for the British Embassy in Sana'a.

United States

United States Embassy in Sana'a
http://www.usembassy-usis.ye/
Featuring a biography of the Ambassador, the virtual Embassy delivers U.S. visa and passport fact sheets, contact information, and a directory of consular and commercial services.

United States Information Service in Sana'a
http://www.usembassy-usis.ye/usis.htm
Along with a directory of cultural and exchange programs, the site provides U.S. news, press releases, publication lists, and electronic journals.

## CHAPTER 9

SUB-SAHARA WEB-HUBS: 850+ AFRICA BUSINESS RESOURCES ON THE INTERNET

This chapter spotlights more than 850 international business resources online that focus on Sub-Saharan Africa. The section reviews regional websites and online hubs for 55 countries and territories, including Kenya, Nigeria, and South Africa. Although severe poverty and political strife persist, growing political and economic openness in recent years have boosted prospects for the region's 700 million people. Leading trade and investment opportunities include mining, transportation, telecommunications, energy, health, and professional services. According to NUA Internet Surveys, an estimated one million people in the region—about one of every 700—were online as of January 1999. Of these, over 90 percent were concentrated in South Africa. While Internet development has been slowed by poor infrastructure, high telephone charges, and low literacy levels, e-mail use is increasing throughout the region and is becoming a key communications medium.

Regional Sites

Africa Search Tools

Infospace Africa
http://in-114.infospace.com/_1_34407537__info/intl/africa.html
An online content aggregator, the site provides chat services and a searchable directory of residences and companies online in Egypt, Mauritius, and South Africa.

Africa Media

Africa Media
http://www.mediainfo.com/emediajs/links-geo.htm?location=africa
Developed by Editor and Publisher Interactive, the site is an index of media sites online in over 20 African countries including Algeria, Benin, Morocco, and Uganda.

Africa Online
http://www.africaonline.com/
Updated daily, the site provides African news, business and financial reports, country guides, travel information, chat services, online discussion groups, and weather bulletins.

Africa Market Guides

Africa Business Information Services
http://www.afbis.com/
A United Kingdom-based information service, the site provides African country bulletins, economic reports, editorials, political analysis, leader profiles, and Nigerian business guides.

Africa Business Network
http://www.ifc.org/abn/
A regional investment primer, the site features African news, country fact sheets, maps, publication lists, business guides, socioeconomic statistics, and travel information.

Africa Chambers of Commerce and Industry
http://mipa.malawi.net/chambers.htm
A service of the Malawi Investment Promotion Agency, the site provides a directory of leading chambers of commerce in 20 African countries including Botswana, Ethiopia, and Uganda.

Africa Intelligence
http://www.indigo-net.com/africa.html
A database of some 18,000 articles, the subscription service provides African news, leader profiles, country fact sheets, sector reports, and privatization bulletins.

Africa International Business Resources
http://ciber.bus.msu.edu/busres/africa.htm
A service of Michigan State University, the site provides a directory of African international trade resources online including business guides, investment primers, and company databases.

Africa Market Research
http://strategis.ic.gc.ca/sc_mrkti/ibinddc/engdoc/1a1a.html
A service of Industry Canada, the site is a database of fact sheets and market studies on over 40 African countries.

Africa Recovery Online
http://www.un.org/ecosocdev/geninfo/afrec/
Posted in English and French, the site reports on United Nations economic development initiatives

in Africa. The service includes country profiles, donor reports, and briefing papers.

Africa Studies at Penn
http://www.sas.upenn.edu/African_Studies/ AS.html
A service of the African Studies Center at the University of Pennsylvania, the site is a directory of African resources online. Categories include statistics, country-specific, and multimedia.

Africa Today
http://www.africa.co.uk/
A regional electronic journal, the site delivers African business news, economic reports, mining guides, privatization bulletins, company directories, and socioeconomic statistics.

African Club for Research and Initiatives
http://www.africaserv.com/main.htm
Based in Washington, D.C., the Club is a forum for African research and economic development professionals. The site offers fact sheets on African countries, history, and culture.

African Conferences and Exhibitions
http://www.mbendi.co.za/a_sndmsg/ event_srch.asp?P=0&C=1
A service of MBendi, the site provides a searchable directory of African-related trade shows, conferences, and other events in over 20 industries including agriculture, construction, and waste management.

African Development Bank
http://www.afdb.org/
Based in Abidjan, Côte d'Ivoire, the Bank finances economic development projects in Africa. The site delivers Bank program information and a database of loan and grant approvals by sector and country.

Africasia
http://dialspace.dial.pipex.com/icpubs/index.htm
The site is the homepage of IC Publications, publishers of *African Business* and *New African* magazines. Updated monthly, the service delivers magazine highlights and excerpts.

Bureau of African Affairs
http://www.state.gov/www/regions/africa/index.html
A service of the U.S. State Department, the site provides U.S. press statements, testimony, briefings, issue reports, and travel information on the region and countries of Africa.

Common Market for Eastern and Southern Africa
http://www.comesa.int/
Based in Lusaka, Zambia, COMESA—the Common Market for Eastern and Southern Africa—is a trading block of 21 African countries. The site provides COMESA news, fact sheets, business guides, and customs information.

Companies of Africa
http://www.mbendi.co.za/coaf.htm
A searchable directory of African companies, the site is divided into some 30 industry categories including agriculture and forestry, electrical power, food and beverage, and packaging.

Ernst & Young Guide to Investing in Africa
http://www.mbendi.co.za/ernsty/eycyprof.htm
A service of Ernst & Young, the site is a database of business guides and investment primers for over 20 African countries including Angola, Morocco, Namibia, and Tunisia.

Global Coalition for Africa
http://www.gca-cma.org/
Based in Washington, D.C., the Coalition is an African policy and economic development forum. The site includes annual reports, press releases, committee bulletins, and discussion papers on African political and economic developments.

Greater Horn Information Exchange
http://198.76.84.1/HORN/
Sponsored in part by U.S. Aid, the site reports on countries in the Horn of Africa including Eritrea, Ethiopia, Kenya, Somalia, Sudan, and Tanzania. The service includes situation reports and socioeconomic statistics.

Harambee Africa
http://ourworld.compuserve.com/homepages/ Harambee/
Based in London, the organization is a business club for companies doing business in eastern, central and southern Africa. The site includes a member directory, event listings, and an online discussion forum.

InfoExport Africa
http://www.infoexport.gc.ca/continent-e.asp?continent=Africa
A service of Foreign Affairs and International Trade Canada, the site provides economic fact sheets and business guides for some 20 African countries.

MBendi: Information for Africa
http://www.mbendi.co.za/cyaf.htm
A hub of regional information, the site provides fact sheets and business guides for over 50 African countries including Benin, Ethiopia, Kenya, Rwanda, Sudan, and Togo.

Multilateral Investment Guarantee Agency in Africa
http://www.ipanet.net/region/mia.htm
A service of the World Bank, the site reports on the activities of the Multilateral Investment Guarantee Agency in Africa.

Lex Africa Business Guides
http://mbendi.co.za/werksmns/lexaf/#Members
Developed by Lex Africa, a regional law firm network, the site is a virtual library of business and legal guides for 16 African countries including Botswana, Ghana, South Africa, and Swaziland.

Solid Africa
http://humanism.org/SolidAfrica/Welcome.html
Based in New York, Solid Africa promotes economic development in Africa. The site includes a mission statement, project reports, maps, event information, and a directory of advisory board members and volunteers.

South African Development Community
http://www.sadc-usa.net/
Based in Gaberone, Botswana, the Community is an economic development alliance of 14 member countries including Angola, Botswana, Lesotho, Malawi, and Mauritius. The site features Community fact sheets, country profiles, and investment information.

U.S. AID Leland Initiative
http://www.info.usaid.gov/regions/afr/leland/
Sponsored by the U.S. Agency for International Development, the Leland Initiative is a five-year, $15 million initiative to connect some 20 African countries to the Internet. The site includes a mission statement, project business opportunities, and contact information.

West Africa Enterprise Network
http://www.waen.com/
Created in 1993, the Network promotes economic development in 13 West African countries including Benin, Burkina Faso, Chad, Gambia, and Ghana. The site provides a directory of key contacts and business opportunities.

World Bank Group Sub-Saharan Africa
http://www.worldbank.org/html/extdr/offrep/afr/afr.htm
A database of World Bank projects in Africa, the site provides press releases, speeches, mission statements, country profiles, and regional economic reports.

WWW Virtual Library Africa Studies
http://www.vibe.com/History/AfricanStudies/africanWWW.html
A service of the World Wide Web Virtual Library, the site is a directory of African resources online. Categories include education, business, and connectivity.

Africa Trade Assistance

Airlines in Africa
http://www.freightworld.com/airl_geo.html#5
A service of Freightworld, the site is a directory of African airlines online including Trans Africa Air Express in Ethiopia, Ghana Airways in Ghana, and Africargo Airlines in South Africa.

Airports in Africa
http://www.freightworld.com/airptgeo.html#5
An index of African airports online, the site links to one airport in Uganda, and 22 in South Africa including Cape Town International, and Johannesburg International.

Buy-Afrika
http://www.buy-africa.com/home.html
A browsable directory of African companies and export products, the site is divided into six categories including art, crafts, industrial, and lifestyle products.

Freight Forwarders in Africa
http://www.freightworld.com/forw_geo.html#5
A database of African freight forwarders online, the site links to operations in eight countries including Happy World Cargo in Mauritius and Hellmann International Forwarders in South Africa.

Maritime Carriers in Africa
http://www.freightworld.com/mari_geo.html#5
An index of African maritime carriers online, the site links to two companies: Egytrans in Egypt, and Thrutainers International in South Africa.

Package Carriers in Africa
http://www.freightworld.com/exp_geo.html#5
A directory of African package carriers online, the

site links to operations in 11 countries including Trans Africa Air Express in Ethiopia, and Streamline Air Charter in South Africa.

Railroads in Africa
http://www.freightworld.com/railroads.html#5
A database of African railroads online, the site links to one operation: Spoornet in South Africa.

Trade and Policy Development for Africa
http://www.ustr.gov/reports/africa/1997/index.html
Developed by the U.S. Trade Representative, the site reports on African economic reform, trade liberalization and promotion, investment trends, and private sector development.

U.S.-Africa Business On-Line
http://www.usafricabusiness.com/
A U.S.-Africa trade promotion service, the site provides African news, investment opportunities, commercial guides, classifieds, and event information for U.S. businesspeople.

Africa Representative Offices

United States

Africa Regional Services
http://www.usia.gov/abtusia/posts/FR2/wwwhhars.html
A unit of the U.S. Embassy in Paris, Africa Regional Services is the primary source of French language program materials for U.S. Information Service posts at American embassies throughout francophone Africa. The service includes African news, publication lists, and speaker and artist directories.

U.S. Information Agency Africa
http://www.usia.gov/regional/af/af.htm
Posted in English and French, the site provides U.S. news, press releases, fact sheets, electronic journals, mission briefings, and Africa human rights reports.

National Sites

Algeria

Algeria Media

Algeria Media
http://www.mediainfo.com/emediajs/specific-geo.htm?region=algeria
Developed by Editor and Publisher Interactive, the

site is an index of Algerian newspaper and other media sites online.

Algeria Market Guides

Algeria Country Brief
http://www.worldbank.org/cgi-bin/sendoff.cgi?page=%2Fhtml%2Fextdr%2Foffrep%2Fmena%2Fdz.htm
A service of the World Bank Group, the site provides population statistics, financial data, development reports, and economic forecasts.

Algeria Country Profile
http://www.tradenz.govt.nz/intelligence/profiles/algeria.html
A service of the New Zealand Trade Development Board, the site provides Algerian economic statistics, market information, and business tips.

Algeria Country Report
http://www.state.gov/www/issues/economic/trade_reports/neareast97/algeria97.html
Prepared by the U.S. Department of State, the site delivers information on Algerian exchange rates, debt management, trade barriers, export subsidies, intellectual property protection, worker rights, and foreign investment.

Algeria: A Country Study
http://lcweb2.loc.gov/frd/cs/dztoc.html
A service of the U.S. Library of Congress, the site delivers fact sheets on Algerian geography, people, agriculture, mining, manufacturing, and foreign economic relations.

Algeria InfoExport
http://www.infoexport.gc.ca/country-e.asp?continent=Africa&country=1
A service of Foreign Affairs and International Trade Canada, the site provides Algerian commercial guides and market reports.

Algeria Market Research
http://strategis.ic.gc.ca/sc_mrkti/ibinddc/engdoc/1a1a1.html
A service of Industry Canada, the site provides U.S. Department of Commerce reports on Algerian economic trends, trade regulations and standards, investment climate, trade and project financing, business travel, and market opportunities.

Algeria Page
http://www.sas.upenn.edu/African_Studies/Country_Specific/Algeria.html
A service of the African Studies Center at the

University of Pennsylvania, the site is a directory of Algerian resources online. Categories include mailing lists, languages, and energy.

Country Commercial Guide
http://www.state.gov/www/about_state/business/com_guides/1998/neareast/algeria98.html
Prepared by the U.S. Embassy in Algiers, the site delivers primers on Algerian business, politics, trade regulations and standards, investment, and business travel.

Country Profile: Algeria
http://www.mbendi.co.za/cyalcy.htm
Developed by Claremont, South Africa-based MBendi, the site provides Algerian fact sheets, maps, sector profiles, exchange rates, and travel information.

Window on Algeria
http://www.geocities.com/CapitolHill/1078/index10.html
A hub of country information, the site provides Algeria statistics, maps, business guides, government directories, and reports on Algeria-U.S. trade and relations.

Algeria Representative Offices

Austria

Austrian Trade Commission in Algiers
http://aw.wk.or.at/awo/ahst-algier.htm
The site lists the staff, street address, phone and fax numbers, e-mail link and office hours of the Austrian Trade Commission in Algiers.

Canada

Embassy of Canada in Algiers
http://www.dfait-maeci.gc.ca/english/missions/rep-can1e.htm#algeria
The site provides contact information for the Canadian Embassy in Algiers.

Ghana

Embassy of Ghana in Algiers
http://www.juntung.com/ghana-consul-hk/2misabo.htm
The site provides contact information for the Ghanaian Embassy in Algiers.

India

Indian Commercial Mission in Algiers
http://www.nic.in/commin/ICM.HTM
The site lists the street address, phone and fax numbers, and e-mail link of the Indian Commercial Mission in Algiers.

Madagascar

Embassy of Madagascar in Algiers
http://www.madagascar-contacts.com/us/adresse.htm#alext
Along with a directory of Madagascar government agencies, the site provides contact information for the Madagascar Embassy in Algiers.

Portugal

Portuguese Trade and Investment Office in Algiers
http://www.portugal.org/geninfo/abouticep/argel.html
The site lists the staff, street address, phone and fax numbers, and e-mail link of the Portuguese Trade and Investment Office in Algiers.

Spain

Spanish Commercial Office in Algiers
http://www.icex.es/openURL.html#openURL=/english/infoproyem/ofcomes/ofcomes.html#AF
The site lists the staff, street address, phone and fax numbers, and e-mail link of the Spanish Commercial Office in Algiers.

Sweden

Embassy of Sweden in Algiers
http://www.ud.se/english/mfa/ambassad/algeriet.htm
The site lists the staff, street address, phone and fax numbers, and e-mail link of the Swedish Embassy in Algiers.

United Kingdom

Embassy of Britain in Algiers
http://www.fco.gov.uk/directory/posts.asp?AK
The site provides contact information for the British Embassy in Algiers.

Angola

Angola Media

Angola Media
http://www.mediainfo.com/emediajs/specific-geo.htm?region=angola
Developed by Editor and Publisher Interactive, the site is an index of Angolan television stations and other media sites online.

Angola News Index
http://www.angola.org/news/index.htm
An Angolan news archive, the site provides headlines, government press releases, a bimonthly newsletter, electronic journals, and reports on U.S.-Angola trade and relations.

Angola Market Guides

Angola Business Opportunities Bulletin Board
http://www.angola.org/business/opportunity/index.html
A service of the Angolan Embassy in Washington, D.C., the site is a database of Angolan trade leads and business opportunities in 22 categories including agriculture, construction, forestry, franchising, and telecommunications.

Angola Country Brief
http://www.worldbank.org/cgi-bin/sendoff.cgi?page=%2Fhtml%2Fextdr%2Foffrep%2Fafr%2Fao.htm
A service of the World Bank Group, the site provides Angolan population statistics, financial data, development reports, and economic forecasts.

Angola: A Country Study
http://lcweb2.loc.gov/frd/cs/aotoc.html
A service of the U.S. Library of Congress, the site delivers fact sheets on Angolan geography, people, agriculture, mining, manufacturing, and foreign economic relations.

Angola Economy
http://195.53.74.3/angola/economia.html
A service of the Angolan Embassy in Madrid, the site provides fact sheets on Angolan energy production, agriculture, forestry, and fishing.

Angola InfoExport
http://www.infoexport.gc.ca/country-e.asp?continent=Africa&country=2
A service of Foreign Affairs and International

Trade Canada, the site provides fact sheets and statistics on Angolan geography, business and politics.

Angola Market Research
http://strategis.ic.gc.ca/sc_mrkti/ibinddc/engdoc/1a1a2.html
Posted by Industry Canada, the site provides U.S. Central Intelligence Agency fact sheets on Angolan geography, people, government, economy, communications, and transportation.

Angola Page
http://www.sas.upenn.edu/African_Studies/Country_Specific/Angola.html
A service of the African Studies Center at the University of Pennsylvania, the site is a directory of Angolan resources online. Categories include maps, languages, energy, and country guides.

Angola: Recent Economic Developments
http://www.imf.org/external/pubs/CAT/longres.cfm?sk=2428.0
Prepared by the International Monetary Fund, the site provides fact sheets and statistics on Angolan output, prices, licensing, tariffs, international trade, and taxation.

Country Profile: Angola
http://www.mbendi.co.za/cyancy.htm
Developed by MBendi, the site provides Angolan fact sheets, maps, sector profiles, exchange rates, and travel information.

Index on Angola
http://www.africaindex.africainfo.no/africaindex1/countries/angola.html
A service of the Norwegian Council for Africa, the site is a directory of Angolan resources online. Categories include economy, education, politics, and tourism.

Investment Profile: Angola
http://www.mbendi.co.za/ernsty/cyaneyip.htm
A service of Ernst & Young, the site provides fact sheets on Angolan business establishments, taxation, exchange controls, visa requirements, foreign investment regulations, and work permits.

Republic of Angola Official Page
http://www.angola.org/
A portal of country information, the site features Angolan news, business guides, investment opportunities, an event calendar, cultural bulletins, and reports on U.S.-Angola trade and relations.

Angola Trade Assistance

Guide to Investment and Trade Opportunities
http://www.angola.org/business/guide97/
index.html
Developed by the Angolan Embassy in Washington, D.C., the site delivers U.S.-Angola trade statistics, Angolan investment opportunities, and a directory of U.S. companies in Angola.

Angola Representative Offices

Canada

Consulate of Canada in Luanda
http://www.dfait-maeci.gc.ca/english/missions/rep-can1e.htm#angola
The site provides contact information for the Canadian Embassy in Luanda.

Ghana

Embassy of Ghana in Luanda
http://www.juntung.com/ghana-consul-hk/
2misabo.htm
The site provides contact information for the Ghanaian Embassy in Luanda.

Namibia

Embassy of Namibia in Luanda
http://www.republicofnamibia.com/adress.htm
Along with a directory of Namibian companies and government agencies, the site provides contact information for the Namibian Embassy in Luanda.

Portugal

Portuguese Trade and Investment Office in Luanda
http://www.portugal.org/geninfo/abouticep/
luanda.html
The site lists the staff, street address, phone and fax numbers, and e-mail link of the Portuguese Trade and Investment Office in Luanda.

Spain

Spanish Commercial Office in Luanda
http://www.icex.es/openURL.html#openURL=/
english/infoproyem/ofcomes/ofcomes.html#AF
The site lists the staff, street address, phone and fax numbers, and e-mail link of the Spanish Commercial Office in Luanda.

Sweden

Embassy of Sweden in Luanda
http://www.ud.se/english/mfa/ambassad/
angola.htm
The site lists the staff, street address, phone and fax numbers, and e-mail link of the Swedish Embassy in Luanda.

United Kingdom

Embassy of Britain in Luanda
http://www.fco.gov.uk/directory/posts.asp?AN
The site provides contact information for the British Embassy in Luanda.

Benin

Benin Media

Benin Media
http://www.mediainfo.com/emediajs/specific-geo.htm?region=benin
A service of Editor and Publisher Interactive, the site is an index of Beninese television stations and other media sites online.

Benin Market Guides

Benin Country Brief
http://www.worldbank.org/cgi-bin/
sendoff.cgi?page=%2Fhtml%2Fextdr%2Foffrep%2
Fafr%2Fbj.htm
A service of the World Bank Group, the site provides Beninese population statistics, financial data, development reports, and economic forecasts.

Benin Market Research
http://strategis.ic.gc.ca/sc_mrkti/ibinddc/engdoc/
1a1a4.html
A service of Industry Canada, the site provides U.S. Department of Commerce reports on Beninese economic trends, trade regulations and standards, investment climate, trade and project financing, business travel, and market opportunities.

Benin Page
http://www.sas.upenn.edu/African_Studies/
Country_Specific/Benin.html
A service of the African Studies Center at the University of Pennsylvania, the site is a directory of Beninese resources online including fact sheets, language information, and maps.

Country Profile: Benin
http://www.mbendi.co.za/cybecy.htm
Developed by MBendi, the site provides Beninese fact sheets, maps, sector profiles, exchange rates, and travel information.

Index on Benin
http://www.africaindex.africainfo.no/africaindex1/countries/benin.html
A service of the Norwegian Council for Africa, the site is a directory of Beninese resources online. Categories include culture, economy, news, and tourism.

Benin Representative Offices

Ghana

Embassy of Ghana in Cotonou
http://www.juntung.com/ghana-consul-hk/2misabo.htm
The site provides contact information for the Ghanaian Embassy in Cotonou.

Sweden

Consulate of Sweden in Cotonou
http://www.ud.se/english/mfa/ambassad/benin.htm
The site lists the staff, street address, and phone and fax numbers of the Swedish Consulate in Cotonou.

United States

United States Information Service in Cotonou
http://eit.intnet.bj/cca/ccaeng.htm
Posted in English and French, the site provides U.S. news, press releases, electronic journals, and a directory of U.S.-Benin cultural and exchange programs.

Botswana

Botswana Market Guides

Botswana Country Brief
http://www.worldbank.org/cgi-bin/sendoff.cgi?page=%2Fhtml%2Fextdr%2Foffrep%2Fafr%2Fbw.htm
A service of the World Bank Group, the site provides Botswana population statistics, financial data, development reports, and economic forecasts.

Botswana InfoExport
http://www.infoexport.gc.ca/country-e.asp?continent=Africa&country=4
A service of Foreign Affairs and International Trade Canada, the site provides fact sheets and statistics on Botswana geography, business and politics.

Botswana Market Research
http://strategis.ic.gc.ca/sc_mrkti/ibinddc/engdoc/1a1a5.html
A service of Industry Canada, the site provides U.S. Department of Commerce reports on Botswana economic trends, trade regulations and standards, investment climate, trade and project financing, business travel, and market opportunities.

Botswana Page
http://www.sas.upenn.edu/African_Studies/Country_Specific/Botswana.html
A service of the African Studies Center at the University of Pennsylvania, the site is a directory of Botswana resources online. Categories include maps, news, languages, and country guides.

Country Profile: Botswana
http://mbendi.co.za/cybocy.htm
A virtual library of country information, the site provides Botswana business opportunities, economic reports, sector profiles, travel information, and legal advice.

Doing Business in Botswana
http://mbendi.co.za/werksmns/lexaf/busbo.htm
Written by Armstrongs Attorneys, the site delivers fact sheets on Botswana business formation, taxation, foreign investment, exchange controls, and intellectual property.

Country Commercial Guide
http://www.state.gov/www/about_state/business/com_guides/1998/africa/botswana98.html
Prepared by the U.S. Embassy in Gaborone, the site delivers primers on Botswana business, politics, trade regulations and standards, investment, and travel.

Index on Botswana
http://www.africaindex.africainfo.no/africaindex1/countries/botswana.html
A service of the Norwegian Council for Africa, the site is a directory of Botswana resources online. Categories include culture, economy, news, and tourism.

Investment Profile: Botswana

http://www.mbendi.co.za/ernsty/cyboeyip.htm
Developed by Ernst & Young, the site reviews
Botswana business law, taxation, incentive
policies, exchange controls, and visa requirements.

Botswana Representative Offices

France

French Trade Commission in Gaborone

http://www.dree.org/botswana/
Written in French, the site delivers Botswana
market reports, sector profiles, contact information, and a directory of export programs for French
companies doing business in the area.

Sweden

Embassy of Sweden in Gaborone

*http://www.ud.se/english/mfa/ambassad/
botswana.htm*
The site lists the staff, street address, phone and
fax numbers, and e-mail link of the Swedish
Embassy in Gaborone.

United Kingdom

High Commission of Britain in Gaborone

http://www.fco.gov.uk/directory/posts.asp?BW
The site provides contact information for the
British High Commission in Gaborone.

United States

United States Embassy in Gaborone

*http://www.usia.gov/abtusia/posts/BC1/
wwwhmain.html*
Along with a biography of the Ambassador, the
virtual Embassy delivers Botswana fact sheets,
U.S. visa and passport information, and a
directory of consular and commercial services.

United States Information Service in Gaborone

*http://www.usia.gov/abtusia/posts/BC1/
wwwhusis.html*
Part of a global network of U.S. Information
Service offices, the site provides U.S. news,
press releases, fact sheets, electronic journals,
and educational program information for
Botswana students.

Burkina Faso

Burkina Faso Market Guides

Burkina Faso Country Brief

*http://www.worldbank.org/cgi-bin/
sendoff.cgi?page=%2Fhtml%2Fextdr%2Foffrep%2
Fafr%2Fbf.htm*
A service of the World Bank Group, the site
provides Burkinabe population statistics, financial data, development reports, and economic
forecasts.

Burkina Faso InfoExport

*http://www.infoexport.gc.ca/country-
e.asp?continent=Africa&country=5*
A service of Foreign Affairs and International
Trade Canada, the site provides Burkinabe
commercial guides and market reports.

Burkina Faso Market Research

*http://strategis.ic.gc.ca/sc_mrkti/ibinddc/engdoc/
1a1a8.html*
A service of Industry Canada, the site provides
U.S. Department of Commerce reports on
Burkinabe economic trends, trade regulations
and standards, investment climate, trade and
project financing, business travel, and market
opportunities.

Burkina Faso Page

*http://www.sas.upenn.edu/African_Studies/
Country_Specific/Burkina.html*
A service of the African Studies Center at the
University of Pennsylvania, the site is a directory
of Burkinabe resources online. Categories
include country guides, languages, and travel.

Country Profile: Burkina Faso

http://mbendi.co.za/cybfcy.htm
Developed by MBendi, the site provides
Burkinabe fact sheets, maps, sector profiles,
exchange rates, travel information, and business
contacts.

Index on Burkina Faso

*http://www.africaindex.africainfo.no/africaindex1/
countries/burkinafaso.html*
A service of the Norwegian Council for Africa, the
site is a directory of Burkinabe resources online.
Categories include culture, economy, news,
telecommunications, and tourism.

Burkina Faso Representative Offices

Canada

Embassy of Canada in Ouagadougou
http://www.dfait-maeci.gc.ca/english/missions/rep-can1e.htm#burkina
The site provides contact information for the Canadian Embassy in Ouagadougou.

France

French Trade Commission in Ouagadougou
http://www.dree.org/burkina/
Written in French, the site delivers Burkinabe market reports, sector profiles, contact information, and a directory of export programs for French companies doing business in the area.

Ghana

Embassy of Ghana in Ouagadougou
http://www.juntung.com/ghana-consul-hk/2misabo.htm
The site provides contact information for the Ghanaian Embassy in Ouagadougou.

Sweden

Consulate of Sweden in Ouagadougou
http://www.ud.se/english/mfa/ambassad/burkina.htm
The site lists the staff, street address, phone and fax numbers, and e-mail link of the Swedish Consulate in Ouagadougou.

United Kingdom

Consulate of Britain in Ouagadougou
http://www.fco.gov.uk/directory/posts.asp?BK
The site provides contact information for the British Consulate in Ouagadougou.

Burundi

Burundi Market Guides

Burundi Country Brief
http://www.worldbank.org/cgi-bin/sendoff.cgi?page=%2Fhtml%2Fextdr%2Foffrep%2Fafr%2Fbi.htm
A service of the World Bank Group, the site provides Burundi population statistics, financial data, development reports, and economic forecasts.

Burundi Country Profile
http://198.76.84.1/HORN/burundi/burundi.html
A service of the Greater Horn Information Exchange, the site provides Burundi situation reports, fact sheets, socioeconomic statistics, health and nutrition bulletins, and crop and food supply assessments.

Burundi Market Research
http://strategis.ic.gc.ca/sc_mrkti/ibinddc/engdoc/1a1a9.html
Posted by Industry Canada, the site provides U.S. Central Intelligence Agency fact sheets on Burundi geography, people, government, economy, communications, and transportation.

Burundi Page
http://www.sas.upenn.edu/African_Studies/Country_Specific/Burundi.html
A service of the African Studies Center at the University of Pennsylvania, the site is a directory of Burundi resources online. Categories include country guides, languages, and travel.

Burundi: Recent Economic Developments
http://www.imf.org/external/pubs/CAT/longres.cfm?sk=2461.0
Prepared by the International Monetary Fund, the site provides fact sheets and statistics on Burundi money and banking, coffee sector reform, interest rates, and central government revenue and expenditure.

Country Profile: Burundi
http://www.mbendi.co.za/cybucy.htm
Developed by MBendi, the site provides Burundi fact sheets, maps, sector profiles, exchange rates, travel information, and business contacts.

Index on Burundi
http://www.africaindex.africainfo.no/africaindex1/countries/burundi.html
A service of the Norwegian Council for Africa, the site is a directory of Burundi resources online. Categories include culture, economy, news, environment, and tourism.

Burundi Representative Offices

Sweden

Consulate of Sweden in Bujumbura
http://www.ud.se/english/mfa/ambassad/burundi.htm
The site lists the staff, street address, phone and fax numbers, and e-mail link of the Swedish Consulate in Bujumbura.

Cameroon

Cameroon Media

Mbengwi News Network
http://everest.hunter.cuny.edu/~kerstine/
Along with Cameroonian fact sheets and language information, the site provides country bulletins and a directory of African news organizations online.

Cameroon Market Guides

Cameroon Country Brief
http://www.worldbank.org/cgi-bin/
sendoff.cgi?page=%2Fhtml%2Fextdr%2Foffrep%2
Fafr%2Fcm.htm
A service of the World Bank Group, the site provides Cameroonian population statistics, financial data, development reports, and economic forecasts.

Cameroon Market Research
http://strategis.ic.gc.ca/sc_mrkti/ibinddc/engdoc/
1a1a10.html
A service of Industry Canada, the site provides U.S. Department of Commerce reports on Cameroonian economic trends, trade regulations and standards, investment climate, trade and project financing, business travel, and market opportunities.

Cameroon: Statistical Appendix
http://www.imf.org/external/pubs/CAT/
longres.cfm?sk=2542.0
Prepared by the International Monetary Fund, the site provides fact sheets and statistics on Cameroonian gross domestic product, expenditure, income, savings, food production, and prices.

Complete Guide to Cameroon
http://www.cameroon.net/
An online country gateway, the site provides Cameroonian discussion rooms, chat services, fact sheets, classifieds, business reports, photo galleries, and travel information.

Country Profile: Cameroon
http://www.mbendi.co.za/cycacy.htm
Developed by MBendi, the site provides Cameroonian fact sheets, maps, sector profiles, exchange rates, travel information, and business contacts.

Home Page of the Republic of Cameroon
http://www.compufix.demon.co.uk/camweb/
A personal webpage maintained by Michael Fosong, the site provides Cameroonian travel information, heath reports, cultural guides, and media bulletins.

Index on Cameroon
http://www.africaindex.africainfo.no/africaindex1/
countries/cameroon.html
A service of the Norwegian Council for Africa, the site is a directory of Cameroonian resources online. Categories include culture, economy, news, and tourism.

Cameroon Representative Offices

Canada

High Commission of Canada in Yaoundé
http://www.dfait-maeci.gc.ca/english/missions/rep-
can1e.htm#cameroon
The site provides contact information for the Canadian High Commission in Yaoundé.

France

French Trade Commission in Yaoundé
http://www.dree.org/cameroun/
Written in French, the site delivers Cameroonian market reports, sector profiles, contact information, and a directory of export programs for French companies doing business in the area.

Sweden

Consulate of Sweden in Yaoundé
http://www.ud.se/english/mfa/ambassad/
kamerun.htm
The site lists the staff, street address, phone and fax numbers, and e-mail link of the Swedish Consulate in Yaoundé.

United Kingdom

High Commission of Britain in Yaoundé
http://www.fco.gov.uk/directory/posts.asp?CM
The site provides contact information for the British High Commission in Yaoundé.

Cape Verde

Cape Verde Market Guides

Cape Verde Country Brief
*http://www.worldbank.org/cgi-bin/
sendoff.cgi?page=%2Fhtml%2Fextdr%2Foffrep
%2Fafr%2Fcv.htm*
A service of the World Bank Group, the site
provides Cape Verdean population statistics,
financial data, development reports, and economic forecasts.

Cape Verde Homepage
*http://www.umassd.edu/SpecialPrograms/
caboverde/capeverdean.html*
Hosted at the University of Massachusetts in
Dartmouth, the site delivers Cape Verdean fact
sheets, business contacts, travel information,
government directories, and history lessons.

Cape Verde Market Research
*http://strategis.ic.gc.ca/sc_mrkti/ibinddc/engdoc/
1a1a11.html*
A service of Industry Canada, the site provides
U.S. Department of Commerce reports on Cape
Verdean economic trends, trade regulations and
standards, investment climate, trade and project
financing, business travel, and market opportunities.

Country Profile: Cape Verde
http://www.mbendi.co.za/cycvcy.htm
Developed by MBendi, the site provides Cape
Verdean fact sheets, maps, sector profiles,
exchange rates, travel information, and business
contacts.

Index on Cape Verde
*http://www.africaindex.africainfo.no/africaindex1/
countries/capeverde.html*
A service of the Norwegian Council for Africa, the
site is a directory of Cape Verdean resources
online. Categories include culture, economy,
news, and tourism.

Cape Verde Representative Offices

Portugal

Portuguese Trade and Investment Office in Praia
*http://www.portugal.org/geninfo/abouticep/
verde.html*
The site lists the staff, street address, phone and
fax numbers, and e-mail link of the Portuguese
Trade and Investment Office in Praia.

Sweden

Consulate of Sweden in São Vicente
*http://www.ud.se/english/mfa/ambassad/
kapverde.htm*
The site lists the staff, street address, phone and
fax numbers, and e-mail link of the Swedish
Consulate in São Vicente.

United Kingdom

Consulate of Britain in São Vicente
http://www.fco.gov.uk/directory/posts.asp?CV
The site provides contact information for the
British Consulate in São Vicente.

Central African Republic

Central African Republic Market Guides

Central African Republic Country Brief
*http://www.worldbank.org/cgi-bin/
sendoff.cgi?page=%2Fhtml%2Fextdr%2Foffrep%
2Fafr%2Fcf.htm*
A service of the World Bank Group, the site
provides Central African population statistics,
financial data, development reports, and economic forecasts.

Central African Republic Market Research
*http://strategis.ic.gc.ca/sc_mrkti/ibinddc/engdoc/
1a1a12.html*
Posted by Industry Canada, the site provides U.S.
Central Intelligence Agency fact sheets on
Central African geography, people, government,
economy, communications, and transportation.

Central African Republic Page
*http://www.sas.upenn.edu/African_Studies/
Country_Specific/CAR.html*
A service of the African Studies Center at the
University of Pennsylvania, the site is a directory
of Central African resources online. Categories
include country guides, languages, and travel.

Country Profile: Central African Republic
http://www.mbendi.co.za/cycrcy.htm
Developed by MBendi, the site provides Central
African fact sheets, maps, sector profiles,
exchange rates, travel information, and business
contacts.

Index on Central African Republic
http://www.africaindex.africainfo.no/africaindex1/countries/car.html
A service of the Norwegian Council for Africa, the site is a directory of Central African resources online. Categories include culture, economy, news, and tourism.

Navel of Africa
http://www.venus.dti.ne.jp/~tee/index.e.html
A portal of country information, the site delivers Central African fact sheets, socioeconomic statistics, history lessons, travel information, and weather bulletins.

Central African Republic Representative Offices

Sweden

Consulate of Sweden in Bangui
http://www.ud.se/english/mfa/ambassad/centrafr.htm
The site lists the staff, street address, phone and fax numbers, and e-mail link of the Swedish Consulate in Bangui.

Chad

Chad Market Guides

Chad Country Brief
http://www.worldbank.org/cgi-bin/sendoff.cgi?page=%2Fhtml%2Fextdr%2Foffrep%2Fafr%2Ftd.htm
A service of the World Bank Group, the site provides Chadian population statistics, financial data, development reports, and economic forecasts.

Chad: A Country Study
http://lcweb2.loc.gov/frd/cs/tdtoc.html
A service of the U.S. Library of Congress, the site delivers fact sheets on Chadian geography, people, agriculture, mining, manufacturing, and foreign economic relations.

Chad Market Research
http://strategis.ic.gc.ca/sc_mrkti/ibinddc/engdoc/1a1a13.html
A service of Industry Canada, the site provides U.S. Department of Commerce reports on Chadian economic trends, trade regulations and standards, investment climate, trade and project

financing, business travel, and market opportunities.

Chad Page
http://www.sas.upenn.edu/African_Studies/Country_Specific/Chad.html
A service of the African Studies Center at the University of Pennsylvania, the site is a directory of Chadian resources online. Categories include country guides, languages, and travel.

Country Profile: Chad
http://www.mbendi.co.za/cychcy.htm
Developed by MBendi, the site provides Chad fact sheets, maps, sector profiles, exchange rates, travel information, and business contacts.

Index on Chad
http://www.africaindex.africainfo.no/africaindex1/countries/chad.html
A service of the Norwegian Council for Africa, the site is a directory of Chadian resources online. Categories include culture, economy, news, and tourism.

Chad Representative Offices

Sweden

Consulate of Sweden in N'Djamena
http://www.ud.se/english/mfa/ambassad/tchad.htm
The site lists the staff, street address, phone and fax numbers, and e-mail link of the Swedish Consulate in N'Djamena.

Comoros

Comoros Market Guides

Comoros Country Brief
http://www.worldbank.org/cgi-bin/sendoff.cgi?page=%2Fhtml%2Fextdr%2Foffrep%2Fafr%2Fkm.htm
A service of the World Bank Group, the site provides Comoran population statistics, financial data, development reports, and economic forecasts.

Comoros: A Country Study
http://lcweb2.loc.gov/frd/cs/kmtoc.html
A service of the U.S. Library of Congress, the site delivers fact sheets on Comoran geography, people, agriculture, mining, manufacturing, and foreign economic relations.

Comoros InfoExport

*http://www.infoexport.gc.ca/country-
e.asp?continent=Africa&country=11*
A service of Foreign Affairs and International
Trade Canada, the site provides fact sheets and
statistics on Comoran geography, business and
politics.

Comoros Market Research

*http://strategis.ic.gc.ca/sc_mrkti/ibinddc/engdoc/
1a1a14.html*
Posted by Industry Canada, the site provides U.S.
Central Intelligence Agency fact sheets on
Comoran geography, people, government,
economy, communications, and transportation.

Comoros: Statistical Annex

*http://www.imf.org/external/pubs/CAT/
longres.cfm?sk=2462.0*
Prepared by the International Monetary Fund, the
site provides fact sheets and statistics on
Comoran gross domestic product, food crop
production, tourism activity, and interest rates.

Country Profile: Comoros

http://www.mbendi.co.za/cycmcy.htm
Developed by MBendi, the site provides Comoran
fact sheets, maps, sector profiles, exchange
rates, travel information, and business contacts.

Index on Comoros

*http://www.africaindex.africainfo.no/africaindex1/
countries/comoros.html*
A service of the Norwegian Council for Africa, the
site is a directory of Comoran resources online.
Categories include culture, economy, news, and
tourism.

Côte d'Ivoire

Côte d'Ivoire Media

Côte d'Ivoire Media

*http://www.mediainfo.com/emediajs/specific-
geo.htm?region=ivorycoast*
Developed by Editor and Publisher Interactive, the
site is an index of Ivorian newspapers and other
media sites online.

Le Jour

*http://www.africaonline.co.ci/AfricaOnline/infos/
lejour/lejour.html*
Updated daily, the French language electronic
newspaper delivers Ivorian headlines, business
reports, sector profiles, interviews, editorials, and
cultural bulletins.

Côte d'Ivoire Market Guides

Côte d'Ivoire Country Brief

*http://www.worldbank.org/cgi-bin/
sendoff.cgi?page=%2Fhtml%2Fextdr%2Foffrep%2
Fafr%2Fci.htm*
A service of the World Bank Group, the site
provides Ivorian population statistics, financial
data, development reports, and economic
forecasts.

Côte d'Ivoire: A Country Study

http://lcweb2.loc.gov/frd/cs/citoc.html
A service of the U.S. Library of Congress, the site
delivers fact sheets on Ivorian geography, people,
agriculture, mining, manufacturing, and foreign
economic relations.

Côte d'Ivoire Economic Bureau

http://w3.cotedivoire.com/sommaus.htm
Posted in English and French, the site features
Ivorian economic reports, commercial guides,
key business contacts, investment primers, and
privatization bulletins.

Côte d'Ivoire InfoExport

*http://www.infoexport.gc.ca/country-
e.asp?continent=Africa&country=13*
A service of Foreign Affairs and International
Trade Canada, the site provides Ivorian commercial guides and market reports.

Côte d'Ivoire Market Research

*http://strategis.ic.gc.ca/sc_mrkti/ibinddc/engdoc/
1a1a16.html*
A service of Industry Canada, the site provides
U.S. Department of Commerce reports on Ivorian
economic trends, trade regulations and standards, investment climate, trade and project
financing, business travel, and market opportunities.

Country Profile: Côte d'Ivoire

http://mbendi.co.za/cycicy.htm
Developed by MBendi, the site provides Ivorian
fact sheets, maps, sector profiles, exchange
rates, travel information, and business contacts.

Doing Business in Côte d'Ivoire

http://mbendi.co.za/werksmns/lexaf/busci.htm
Written by the law firm of Fadika-Chauveau-
Kacoutié, the site delivers fact sheets on Ivorian
business formation, taxation, foreign investment,
exchange controls, and intellectual property.

Index on Côte d'Ivoire
*http://www.africaindex.africainfo.no/africaindex1/
countries/civ.htm*
A service of the Norwegian Council for Africa, the site is a directory of Ivorian resources online. Categories include culture, economy, news, and tourism.

Investment Profile: Côte d'Ivoire
http://www.mbendi.co.za/ernsty/cycieyip.htm
A service of Ernst & Young, the site provides fact sheets on Ivorian business establishments, taxation, exchange controls, visa requirements, foreign investment regulations, and work permits.

Côte d'Ivoire Representative Offices

Canada

Embassy of Canada in Abidjan
*http://www.dfait-maeci.gc.ca/english/missions/rep-
can1e.htm#Côte d'Ivoire*
The site provides contact information for the Canadian Embassy in Abidjan.

Québec Trade Office in Abidjan
*http://www.mri.gouv.qc.ca/dans_le_monde/
afrique_moy_orient/abidjan_an.html*
A service of the Québec Ministry of International Relations, the site lists the street address, phone and fax numbers, e-mail link, and territorial responsibility of the Québec Trade Office in Abidjan.

France

French Trade Commission in Abidjan
http://www.dree.org/cotedivoire/
Written in French, the site delivers Ivorian market reports, sector profiles, contact information, and a directory of export programs for French companies doing business in the region.

South Africa

South Africa Foreign Trade Office in Abidjan
*http://wwwdti.pwv.gov.za/dtiwww/
foreign_offices.htm*
A service of the South Africa Department of Trade and Industry, the site provides contact information for the South Africa Trade Office in Abidjan.

Spain

Spanish Commercial Office in Abidjan
http://www.icex.es/openURL.html#openURL=/

english/infoproyem/ofcomes/ofcomes.html#AF
The site lists the staff, street address, phone and fax numbers, and e-mail link of the Spanish Commercial Office in Abidjan.

Sweden

Embassy of Sweden in Abidjan
*http://www.ud.se/english/mfa/ambassad/
elfenben.htm*
The site lists the staff, street address, phone and fax numbers, and e-mail link of the Swedish Embassy in Abidjan.

United Kingdom

Embassy of Britain in Abidjan
http://www.fco.gov.uk/directory/posts.asp?IV
The site provides contact information for the British Embassy in Abidjan.

United States

Embassy of the U.S. in Abidjan
*http://www.usia.gov/abtusia/posts/IV1/
wwwhmiss.html*
Along with Ivorian fact sheets and commercial guides, the site provides U.S. visa and passport information, and a directory of consular and commercial services.

United States Information Service in Abidjan
*http://www.usia.gov/abtusia/posts/IV1/
wwwhusis.html*
Written in English and French, the site delivers U.S. electronic bulletins, fact sheets, economic reports, cultural information, and a directory of U.S.- Côte d'Ivoire educational and exchange programs.

Democratic Republic of Congo (formerly Zaire)

Democratic Republic of Congo Market Guides

Democratic Republic of Congo
http://drcongo.org/frames/index.html
A hub of country information, the site provides Democratic Republic of Congo fact sheets, maps, press releases, economic reports, socioeconomic statistics, and government directories.

Democratic Republic of Congo Country Brief
*http://www.worldbank.org/cgi-bin/
sendoff.cgi?page=%2Fhtml%2Fextdr%2Foffrep%2
Fafr%2Fcd.htm*
A service of the World Bank Group, the site provides Democratic Republic of Congo population statistics, financial data, development reports, and economic forecasts.

Democratic Republic of Congo Page
*http://www.sas.upenn.edu/African_Studies/
Country_Specific/Zaire.html*
A service of the African Studies Center at the University of Pennsylvania, the site is a directory of Democratic Republic of Congo resources online. Categories include country guides, languages, and travel.

Index on Democratic Republic of Congo
*http://www.africaindex.africainfo.no/africaindex1/
countries/zaire.html*
A service of the Norwegian Council for Africa, the site is a directory of Democratic Republic of Congo resources online. Categories include culture, economy, news, and tourism.

Democratic Republic of Congo Representative Offices

Canada

Embassy of Canada in Kinshasa
*http://www.dfait-maeci.gc.ca/english/missions/rep-
can1e.htm#kinshasa*
The site provides contact information for the Canadian Embassy in Kinshasa.

South Africa

South Africa Foreign Trade Office in Kinshasa
*http://wwwdti.pwv.gov.za/dtiwww/
foreign_offices.htm*
A service of the South Africa Department of Trade and Industry, the site provides contact information for the South Africa Trade Office in Kinshasa.

Sweden

Embassy of Sweden in Kinshasa
*http://www.ud.se/english/mfa/ambassad/
kongo2.htm*
The site lists the staff, street address, phone and fax numbers, and e-mail link of the Swedish Embassy in Kinshasa.

United Kingdom

Embassy of Britain in Kinshasa
http://www.fco.gov.uk/directory/posts.asp?DC
The site provides contact information for the British Embassy in Kinshasa.

Djibouti

Djibouti Market Guides

Country Profile: Djibouti
http://www.mbendi.co.za/cydjcy.htm
Developed by MBendi, the site provides Djiboutian fact sheets, maps, sector profiles, exchange rates, travel information, and business contacts.

Djibouti Country Brief
*http://www.worldbank.org/cgi-bin/
sendoff.cgi?page=%2Fhtml%2Fextdr%2Foffrep%2
Fafr%2Fdj.htm*
A service of the World Bank Group, the site provides Djiboutian population statistics, financial data, development reports, and economic forecasts.

Djibouti InfoExport
*http://www.infoexport.gc.ca/country-
e.asp?continent=Africa&country=14*
A service of Foreign Affairs and International Trade Canada, the site provides fact sheets and statistics on Djiboutian geography, business, and politics.

Djibouti International Chamber of Commerce
http://www.intnet.dj/cicid/index.html
A searchable directory of Djiboutian companies, the site is divided into 16 categories including food and beverage, electronics, automotive, pharmaceuticals, textiles, and transportation.

Djibouti Market Research
*http://strategis.ic.gc.ca/sc_mrkti/ibinddc/engdoc/
1a1a17.html*
Posted by Industry Canada, the site provides U.S. Central Intelligence Agency fact sheets on Djiboutian geography, people, government, economy, communications, and transportation.

Djibouti Page
*http://www.sas.upenn.edu/African_Studies/
Country_Specific/Djibouti.html*
A service of the African Studies Center at the University of Pennsylvania, the site is a directory

of Djiboutian resources online. Categories include country guides, languages, and travel.

Index on Djibouti
http://www.africaindex.africainfo.no/africaindex1/
countries/djibouti.html
A service of the Norwegian Council for Africa, the site is a directory of Djiboutian resources online. Categories include culture, economy, news, and tourism.

Djibouti Representative Offices

Sweden

Consulate of Sweden in Djibouti
http://www.ud.se/english/mfa/ambassad/
djibouti.htm
The site lists the staff, street address, and phone and fax numbers of the Swedish Consulate in Djibouti.

United Kingdom

Consulate of Britain in Djibouti
http://www.fco.gov.uk/directory/posts.asp?DJ
The site provides contact information for the British Consulate in Djibouti.

Equatorial Guinea

Equatorial Guinea Market Guides

Country Profile: Equatorial Guinea
http://www.mbendi.co.za/cyeqcy.htm
Developed by MBendi, the site provides Equatorial Guinean fact sheets, maps, sector profiles, exchange rates, travel information, and business contacts.

Equatorial Guinea Country Brief
http://www.worldbank.org/cgi-bin/
sendoff.cgi?page=%2Fhtml%2Fextdr%2Foffrep%2
Fafr%2Fgq.htm
A service of the World Bank Group, the site provides Equatorial Guinean population statistics, financial data, development reports, and economic forecasts.

Equatorial Guinea Market Research
_http://strategis.ic.gc.ca/sc_mrkti/ibinddc/engdoc/_
1a1a19.html
Posted by Industry Canada, the site provides U.S. Central Intelligence Agency fact sheets on

Equatorial Guinean geography, people, government, economy, communications, and transportation.

Equatorial Guinea Page
_http://www.sas.upenn.edu/African_Studies/_
_Country_Specific/Eq_Guinea.html_
A service of the African Studies Center at the University of Pennsylvania, the site is a directory of Equatorial Guinean resources online. Categories include country guides, languages, and travel.

Index on Equatorial Guinea
http://www.africaindex.africainfo.no/africaindex1/
countries/equatorial.html
A service of the Norwegian Council for Africa, the site is a directory of Equatorial Guinean resources online. Categories include culture, economy, news, and tourism.

Eritrea

Eritrea Market Guides

Country Profile: Eritrea
http://www.mbendi.co.za/cyercy.htm
Developed by MBendi, the site provides Eritrean fact sheets, maps, sector profiles, exchange rates, travel information, and business contacts.

Eritrea Business Guide
http://www.usia.gov/abtusia/posts/ET9/
wwwhe01a.html
A service of the U.S. Mission to Eritrea, the site delivers Eritrean fact sheets, commercial guides, government directories, investment primers, tourism information, and business contacts.

Eritrea Country Brief
http://www.worldbank.org/cgi-bin/
sendoff.cgi?page=%2Fhtml%2Fextdr%2Foffrep%2
Fafr%2Fer.htm
A service of the World Bank Group, the site provides Eritrean population statistics, financial data, development reports, and economic forecasts.

Eritrea Country Profile
http://198.76.84.1/HORN/eritrea/eritrea.html
A service of the Greater Horn Information Exchange, the site provides Eritrean fact sheets, human rights reports, socioeconomic statistics, health and nutrition bulletins, and crop and food supply assessments.

Eritrea InfoExport
http://www.infoexport.gc.ca/country-e.asp?continent=Africa&country=17
A service of Foreign Affairs and International Trade Canada, the site provides fact sheets and statistics on Eritrean geography, business, and politics.

Eritrea Net
http://eritrea.net/
A web-based country gateway, the site offers Eritrean news, business guides, travel tips, investment primers, fact sheets, cultural bulletins, and a photo gallery.

Eritrean Government Homepage
http://www.NetAfrica.org/eritrea/index.html
A hub of country information, the site delivers fact sheets of Eritrean government, agriculture, cities, education, energy, health, history, tourism, transportation, and international trade.

Eritrean Network Information Center
http://eritrea.org/
A virtual library of country reports, the site provides Eritrean economic profiles, commercial guides, socioeconomic statistics, tourism information, and culture and arts primers.

Index on Eritrea
http://www.africaindex.africainfo.no/africaindex1/countries/eritrea.html
A service of the Norwegian Council for Africa, the site is a directory of Eritrean resources online. Categories include culture, economy, news, and tourism.

Eritrea Trade Assistance

Eritrean Embassies and Consulates
http://www.netafrica.org/eritrea/embassies.html
Along with visa and passport information, the site provides a directory of Eritrean Embassies and Consulates in some 15 countries including Australia, Belgium, China, and France.

Eritrea Representative Offices

Sweden

Consulate of Sweden in Asmara
http://www.ud.se/english/mfa/ambassad/eritrea.htm
The site lists the staff, street address, and phone and fax numbers of the Swedish Consulate in Asmara.

United Kingdom

Embassy of Britain in Asmara
http://www.fco.gov.uk/directory/posts.asp?ER
The site provides contact information for the British Embassy in Asmara.

United States

American Business Council in Asmara
http://www.usia.gov/abtusia/posts/ET9/wwwhabc.html
Formed in 1997, the Council promotes U.S.-Eritrea trade. The site includes a mission statement, member directory, and contact information.

United States Embassy in Asmara
http://www.usia.gov/abtusia/posts/ET9/wwwhmemb.html
Along with Eritrean business guides and sector profiles, the site lists the key officers, street address, phone and fax numbers, and e-mail link of the U.S. Embassy in Asmara.

United States Information Service in Asmara
http://www.usia.gov/abtusia/posts/ET9/wwwhsusi.html
Along with contact information, the site provides U.S. electronic bulletins, fact sheets, economic reports, cultural information, and a directory of U.S.- Eritrea educational and exchange programs

U.S. Mission to Eritrea
http://www.usia.gov/posts/eritrea/
A service of the U.S. State Department, the site delivers fact sheets on U.S. government operations in Eritrea including the U.S. Agency for International Development, the Peace Corps, and the U.S. Department of Defense.

Ethiopia

Ethiopia Media

Addis Tribune
http://AddisTribune.EthiopiaOnline.Net/
Updated weekly, the site provides Ethiopian headlines, editorials, economic reports, cultural information, weather information, and a searchable archive of past issues.

Daily Home News
http://www.nicom.com/~ethiopia/daily.htm
A service of the Ethiopian Ministry of Foreign Affairs, the site delivers Ethiopian news, eco-

nomic bulletins, business reports, and government press releases.

Ethiopia Media
http://www.mediainfo.com/emediajs/specific-geo.htm?region=ethiopia
Developed by Editor and Publisher Interactive, the site is an index of Ethiopian newspaper and other media sites online.

Ethiopian Weekly Press Digest
http://pressdigest.phoenixuniversal.com/
Updated every week, the English-language electronic newspaper provides Ethiopian news, editorials, special reports, regional headlines, and political bulletins.

Ethiopia Market Guides

Country Commercial Guide
http://www.state.gov/www/about_state/business/com_guides/1998/africa/ethiopia98.html
Prepared by the U.S. Embassy in Addis Ababa, the site delivers primers on Ethiopian business, politics, trade regulations and standards, investment, and travel.

Country Profile: Ethiopia
http://www.mbendi.co.za/cyetcy.htm
Developed by MBendi, the site provides Ethiopian fact sheets, maps, sector profiles, exchange rates, travel information, and business contacts.

Ethiopia Country Brief
http://www.worldbank.org/cgi-bin/sendoff.cgi?page=%2Fhtml%2Fextdr%2Foffrep%2Fafr%2Fet.htm
A service of the World Bank Group, the site provides Ethiopian population statistics, financial data, development reports, and economic forecasts.

Ethiopia Country Profile
http://198.76.84.1/HORN/ethiopia/index.html
A service of the Greater Horn Information Exchange, the site provides Ethiopian situation reports, fact sheets, socioeconomic statistics, health profiles, and crop and food supply assessments.

Ethiopia: A Country Study
http://lcweb2.loc.gov/frd/cs/ettoc.html
A service of the U.S. Library of Congress, the site delivers fact sheets on Ethiopian geography, people, agriculture, mining, manufacturing, and foreign economic relations.

Ethiopia InfoExport
http://www.infoexport.gc.ca/country-e.asp?continent=Africa&country=18
A service of Foreign Affairs and International Trade Canada, the site provides Ethiopian commercial guides and market reports.

Ethiopia Investment
http://www.nicom.com/~ethiopia/invest.htm
A service of the Ethiopian Embassy in Washington, D.C., the site provides Ethiopian investment guides, a list of state-owned enterprises to be privatized, and a database of Ethiopian companies seeking foreign joint venture partners.

Ethiopia Market Information
http://dtiinfo1.dti.gov.uk/ots/ethiopia/
A service of the London-based Department of Trade and Industry, the site delivers Ethiopian fact sheets, maps, and trade-show information.

Ethiopia Market Research
http://strategis.ic.gc.ca/sc_mrkti/ibinddc/engdoc/1a1a20.html
A service of Industry Canada, the site provides U.S. Department of Commerce reports on Ethiopian economic trends, trade regulations and standards, investment climate, trade and project financing, business travel, and market opportunities.

Ethiopia: Statistical Appendix
http://www.imf.org/external/pubs/CAT/longres.cfm?sk=2491.0
Prepared by the International Monetary Fund, the site provides fact sheets and statistics on Ethiopian gross domestic product, agricultural production, exchange rates, and international trade.

Index on Ethiopia
http://www.africaindex.africainfo.no/africaindex1/countries/ethiopia.html
A service of the Norwegian Council for Africa, the site is a directory of Ethiopian resources online. Categories include culture, economy, news, and tourism.

Ethiopia Trade Assistance

Ethiopia Trade and Industry
http://www.nicom.com/~ethiopia/trdinv.htm
Prepared by the Ethiopian Embassy n Washington, D.C., the site provides situation reports on Ethiopian manufacturing, trade policy, labor standards, competition policy, environmental regulations, and international trade.

Ethiopia Representative Offices

Canada

Embassy of Canada in Addis Ababa
http://www.dfait-maeci.gc.ca/english/missions/rep-can2e.htm#ethiopia
The site provides contact information for the Canadian Embassy in Addis Ababa.

France

French Trade Commission in Addis Ababa
http://www.dree.org/ethiopie/
Written in French, the site delivers Ethiopian market reports, sector profiles, contact information, and a directory of export programs for French companies doing business in the region. .

Ghana

Embassy of Ghana in Addis Ababa
http://www.juntung.com/ghana-consul-hk/2misabo.htm
The site provides contact information for the Ghanaian Embassy in Addis Ababa.

India

Indian Commercial Mission in Addis Ababa
http://www.nic.in/commin/ICM.HTM
The site lists the street address, phone and fax numbers, and e-mail link of the Indian Commercial Mission in Addis Ababa.

Madagascar

Embassy of Madagascar in Addis Ababa
http://www.madagascar-contacts.com/us/adresse.htm#alext
Along with a directory of Madagascar government agencies, the site provides contact information for the Madagascar Embassy in Addis Ababa.

Namibia

Embassy of Namibia in Addis Ababa
http://www.republicofnamibia.com/adress.htm
Along with a directory of Namibian companies and government agencies, the site provides contact information for the Namibian Embassy in Addis Ababa.

Sweden

Embassy of Sweden in Addis Ababa
http://www.ud.se/english/mfa/ambassad/etiopien.htm
The site lists the staff, street address, phone and fax numbers, and e-mail link of the Swedish Embassy in Addis Ababa.

Tanzania

Embassy of Tanzania in Addis Ababa
http://www.tanzania-online.gov.uk/visa/envoys.html
The site provides contact information for the Tanzanian Embassy in Addis Ababa.

United Kingdom

Embassy of Britain in Addis Ababa
http://www.fco.gov.uk/directory/posts.asp?ET
The site provides contact information for the British Embassy in Addis Ababa.

Gabon

Gabon Market Guides

Country Profile: Gabon
http://www.mbendi.co.za/cygacy.htm
Developed by MBendi, the site provides Gabonese fact sheets, maps, sector profiles, exchange rates, travel information, and business contacts.

Economy General Data
http://www.presidence-gabon.com/a/data/eco/generaleco.html
A service of the Gabon Ministry of Finance, the site delivers Gabonese fact sheets, socioeconomic statistics, legal guides, sector profiles, and investment primers.

Gabon Country Brief
http://www.worldbank.org/cgi-bin/sendoff.cgi?page=%2Fhtml%2Fextdr%2Foffrep%2Fafr%2Fga.htm
A service of the World Bank Group, the site provides Gabonese population statistics, financial data, development reports, and economic forecasts.

Gabon Market Research
http://strategis.ic.gc.ca/sc_mrkti/ibinddc/engdoc/1a1a22.html
A service of Industry Canada, the site provides U.S. Department of Commerce reports on Gabonese economic trends, trade regulations and standards, investment climate, trade and project financing, business travel, and market opportunities.

Gabon Page
http://www.sas.upenn.edu/African_Studies/Country_Specific/Gabon.html
A service of the African Studies Center at the University of Pennsylvania, the site is a directory of Gabonese resources online. Categories include country guides, languages, and travel.

Index on Gabon
http://www.africaindex.africainfo.no/africaindex1/countries/gabon.html
A service of the Norwegian Council for Africa, the site is a directory of Gabonese resources online. Categories include culture, economy, news, and tourism.

Investment Profile: Gabon
http://www.mbendi.co.za/ernsty/cygaeyip.htm
A service of Ernst & Young, the site provides fact sheets on Gabonese business establishments, taxation, exchange controls, visa requirements, foreign investment regulations, and work permits.

Welcome to Gabon
http://www.presidence-gabon.com/index-a.html
Posted in English and French, the site provides Gabon fact sheets, event information, leader profiles, socioeconomic statistics, and government directories.

Gabon Trade Assistance

External Trade
http://www.presidence-gabon.com/a/data/eco/commerce.html
A service of the Gabonese government, the site provides Gabonese international trade statistics, export forecasts, and reports on crude oil, manganese, and uranium production.

Gabon Representative Offices

Canada

Embassy of Canada in Libreville
http://www.dfait-maeci.gc.ca/english/missions/rep-can2e.htm#gabon
The site provides contact information for the Canadian Embassy in Libreville.

France

French Trade Commission in Libreville
http://www.dree.org/gabon/
Written in French, the site delivers Gabonese market reports, sector profiles, contact information, and a directory of French export promotion services in the region.

Sweden

Consulate General of Sweden in Libreville
http://www.ud.se/english/mfa/ambassad/gabon.htm
The site lists the staff, street address, and phone and fax numbers of the Swedish Consulate General in Libreville.

United Kingdom

Consulate of Britain in Libreville
http://www.fco.gov.uk/directory/posts.asp?GO
The site provides contact information for the British Consulate in Libreville.

Gambia

Gambia Market Guides

Banjul Freeport
http://www.gambia.com/freeport/index.html
A primer on Banjul Freeport, a Gambian seaport, the site features facility fact sheets, transportation guides, West African maps, and contact information.

Country Profile: Gambia
http://www.mbendi.co.za/cygmcy.htm
Developed by MBendi, the site provides Gambian fact sheets, maps, sector profiles, exchange rates, travel information, and business contacts.

Gambia Country Brief
http://www.worldbank.org/cgi-bin/sendoff.cgi?page=%2Fhtml%2Fextdr%2Foffrep%2Fafr%2Fgm.htm
A service of the World Bank Group, the site provides Gambian population statistics, financial data, development reports, and economic forecasts.

Gambia Market Research
http://strategis.ic.gc.ca/sc_mrkti/ibinddc/engdoc/1a1a23.html
Posted by Industry Canada, the site provides U.S. Central Intelligence Agency fact sheets on Gambian geography, people, government, economy, communications, and transportation.

Gambia: Statistical Annex
http://www.imf.org/external/pubs/CAT/longres.cfm?sk=2463.0
Prepared by the International Monetary Fund, the site provides fact sheets and statistics on Gambian gross domestic product, savings, agricultural production, tourism, energy, prices, and international trade.

Gambia's Economic Development
http://www.gambia.com/econ/econ.html
A directory of major economic projects in Gambia, the site profiles initiatives in seven categories including infrastructure, communications, education, health, and agriculture.

Gambia's Investment Opportunities
http://www.gambia.com/invest/invest.html
Along with a business-start up guide, the site provides a directory of investment incentives in Gambia. Priority industries include agriculture, fishing, tourism, manufacturing, and financial services.

Index on Gambia
http://www.africaindex.africainfo.no/africaindex1/countries/gambia.html
A service of the Norwegian Council for Africa, the site is a directory of Gambian resources online. Categories include culture, economy, news, and tourism.

Republic of Gambia Webpage
http://www.gambia.com/
Homepage of the Gambian Republic, the site is a hub of country information. Modules include history and geography, government, investment opportunities, economic development, and tourism.

Gambia Representative Offices

Sweden

Consulate of Sweden in Banjul
http://www.ud.se/english/mfa/ambassad/gambia.htm
The site lists the staff, street address, phone and fax numbers, and e-mail link of the Swedish Consulate in Banjul.

United Kingdom

High Commission of Britain in Banjul
http://www.fco.gov.uk/directory/posts.asp?GA
The site provides contact information for the British High Commission in Banjul.

Ghana

Ghana Media

Ghana Media
http://www.mediainfo.com/emediajs/specific-geo.htm?region=ghana
Developed by Editor and Publisher Interactive, the site is an index of Ghanaian newspapers, radio stations, and other media sites online.

Ghana Market Guides

Barclays Country Guide: Ghana
http://www.offshorebanking.barclays.com/services/economic/yearly/ghanamay98/contents.html
Prepared by Barclays Bank, the site reports on Ghanaian economic trends, politics, monetary and fiscal policy, and U.K.-Ghana merchandise trade and investment flows.

Business Guide to Ghana
http://www.ghana-embassy.org/trade/gateway/index.html
A country business guide, the site provides Ghanaian fact sheets, business guides, international trade opportunities, travel tips, and visa and work permit information.

Country Profile: Ghana
http://mbendi.co.za/cyghcy.htm
Developed by MBendi, the site provides Ghanaian fact sheets, maps, sector profiles, exchange rates, travel information, business contacts, and leader profiles.

Doing Business in Ghana
http://mbendi.co.za/werksmns/lexaf/busgh.htm
Written by the law firm of Fugar & Company, the site delivers fact sheets on Ghanaian business formation, taxation, foreign investment, exchange controls, and intellectual property.

Ghana Classifieds
http://www.ghanaclassifieds.com/

Along with a chat and streaming audio service, the site provides Ghanaian news, political bulletins, employment opportunities, and media guides.

Ghana Country Brief

http://www.worldbank.org/cgi-bin/ sendoff.cgi?page=%2Fhtml%2Fextdr%2Foffrep%2 Fafr%2Fgh.htm
A service of the World Bank Group, the site provides Ghanaian population statistics, financial data, development reports, and economic forecasts.

Ghana Country Report

http://www.state.gov/www/issues/economic/ trade_reports/africa97/ghana97.html
Prepared by the U.S. Department of State, the site delivers information on Ghanaian exchange rates, debt management, trade barriers, export subsidies, intellectual property protection, worker rights, and foreign investment.

Ghana: A Country Study

http://lcweb2.loc.gov/frd/cs/ghtoc.html
A service of the U.S. Library of Congress, the site delivers fact sheets on Ghanaian geography, people, agriculture, mining, manufacturing, and foreign economic relations.

Ghana Market Information

http://dtiinfo1.dti.gov.uk/ots/ghana/
A service of the London-based Department of Trade and Industry, the site delivers Ghanaian fact sheets, maps, and trade-show information.

Ghana Market Research

http://strategis.ic.gc.ca/sc_mrkti/ibinddc/engdoc/ 1a1a24.html
A service of Industry Canada, the site provides U.S. Department of Commerce reports on Ghanaian economic trends, trade regulations and standards, investment climate, trade and project financing, business travel, and market opportunities.

Ghana: Statistical Annex

http://www.imf.org/external/pubs/CAT/ longres.cfm?sk=2487.0
Prepared by the International Monetary Fund, the site provides fact sheets and statistics on Ghanaian gross domestic product, savings, investment, mining, manufacturing, fishing, and energy.

Index on Ghana

http://www.africaindex.africainfo.no/africaindex1/ countries/ghana.html
A service of the Norwegian Council for Africa, the site is a directory of Ghanaian resources online. Categories include culture, economy, news, and tourism.

Investor's Guide to Ghana

http://www.ghana-embassy.org/trade/ investors_guide/index.html
Developed by the Ghana Investment Promotion Centre, the site provides Ghanaian business guides, investment primers, economic reports, and work permit information.

Investment Profile: Ghana

http://www.mbendi.co.za/ernsty/cygheyip.htm
A service of Ernst & Young, the site provides fact sheets on Ghanaian business establishments, taxation, exchange controls, visa requirements, and foreign investment regulations.

Profile of Ghana

http://www.ghana-embassy.org/profile/index.html
Prepared by the Ghana Embassy in Washington, D.C., the site delivers briefs on Ghanaian history, geography, people, government, and climate.

Welcome to Ghana

http://www.ghana.gov.gh/
Homepage of the Ghanaian government, the site is a portal of country information. Modules include business opportunities, international missions, culture and traditions, and visas and passports.

Ghana Trade Assistance

Ghana Trade and Investment

http://www.ghana-embassy.org/trade/index.html
A virtual library of country business information, the site provides Ghanaian investment guides, free trade zone reports, and joint venture opportunities.

Ghana's Diplomatic Missions Abroad

http://www.juntung.com/ghana-consul-hk/ 2misabo.htm
A service of the Honorary Consul of Ghana in Hong Kong, the site provides a directory of Ghanaian Embassies and High Commissions in over 20 countries including Angola, Brazil, Cuba, and Libya.

Ghana Representative Offices

Foreign Representatives in Accra
http://www.juntung.com/ghana-consul-hk/2dipacra.htm
A service of the Honorary Consul of Ghana in Hong Kong, the site provides a directory of foreign embassies in Ghana. Representatives from over 20 countries are listed, including Algeria, Bulgaria, Egypt, and India.

Canada

High Commission of Canada in Accra
http://www.dfait-maeci.gc.ca/english/missions/rep-can2e.htm#ghana
The site provides contact information for the Canadian High Commission in Accra.

India

Indian Commercial Mission in Accra
http://www.nic.in/commin/ICM.HTM
The site lists the street address, phone and fax numbers, and e-mail link of the Indian Commercial Mission in Accra.

Netherlands

Royal Netherlands Embassy in Accra
http://wworks.com/~Truuk/
Written in English, the site provides Dutch maps, fact sheets, business guides, reports on Netherlands-Ghana trade and relations, and a directory of Embassy staff.

United Kingdom

High Commission of Britain in Accra
http://www.fco.gov.uk/directory/posts.asp?GH
The site provides contact information for the British High Commission in Accra.

United States

United States Embassy in Accra
http://www.usembassy.org.gh/
Featuring a welcome from the Ambassador, the virtual Embassy delivers Ghanaian fact sheets, trade leads, and a directory of U.S. consular and commercial services.

United States Information Service in Accra
http://www.usembassy.org.gh/usis.htm
The site provides U.S. electronic bulletins, fact sheets, economic reports, cultural information, and a directory of U.S.-Ghana educational and exchange programs

Guinea

Guinea Market Guides

Core Data on Guinea
http://www.mirinet.net.gn/opip/opipe.html
A country fact sheet, the site delivers Guinean economic statistics, work permit information, business contacts, cost comparisons, and investment reports.

Country Profile: Guinea
http://www.mbendi.co.za/cygucy.htm
Developed by MBendi, the site provides Guinean fact sheets, maps, sector profiles, exchange rates, travel information, and business contacts.

Guinea Country Brief
http://www.worldbank.org/cgi-bin/sendoff.cgi?page=%2Fhtml%2Fextdr%2Foffrep%2Fafr%2Fgn.htm
A service of the World Bank Group, the site provides Guinean population statistics, financial data, development reports, and economic forecasts.

Guinea Market Research
http://strategis.ic.gc.ca/sc_mrkti/ibinddc/engdoc/1a1a26.html
A service of Industry Canada, the site provides U.S. Department of Commerce reports on Guinean economic trends, trade regulations and standards, investment climate, trade and project financing, business travel, and market opportunities.

Guinea Page
http://www.sas.upenn.edu/African_Studies/Country_Specific/Guinea.html
A service of the African Studies Center at the University of Pennsylvania, the site is a directory of Guinean resources online. Categories include country guides, languages, and travel.

Index on Guinea
http://www.africaindex.africainfo.no/africaindex1/countries/guinea.html
A service of the Norwegian Council for Africa, the site is a directory of Guinean resources on the web. Categories include culture, economy, news, and tourism.

Guinea Representative Offices

Canada

Embassy of Canada in Conakry
http://www.dfait-maeci.gc.ca/english/missions/rep-can2e.htm#guinea
The site provides contact information for the Canadian Embassy in Conakry.

France

French Trade Commission in Conakry
http://www.dree.org/guinee/
Written in French, the site delivers Guinean market reports, sector profiles, contact information, and a directory of French export promotion services.

Ghana

Embassy of Ghana in Conakry
http://www.juntung.com/ghana-consul-hk/2misabo.htm
The site provides contact information for the Ghanaian Embassy in Conakry.

United Kingdom

Consulate of Britain in Conakry
http://www.fco.gov.uk/directory/posts.asp?GI
The site provides contact information for the British Consulate in Conakry.

United States

United States Embassy in Conakry
http://www.eti-bull.net/USEMBASSY/embassy.htm
The virtual Embassy delivers U.S. fact sheets, visa and passport information, a staff e-mail directory, and a list of consular and commercial services.

United States Information Service in Conakry
http://www.eti-bull.net/USEMBASSY/usis.htm
The site lists the street address, and phone and fax numbers of the American Cultural Center in Conakry. The Center is a U.S. research library and meeting center.

United States Mission in the Republic of Guinea
http://WWW.ETI-BULL.NET/USEMBASSY/
Featuring biographies of the U.S. Ambassador and Deputy Chief of Mission, the site is a directory of U.S. government operations in Guinea, including the U.S. Agency for International Development and the U.S. Peace Corps.

Guinea-Bissau

Guinea-Bissau Market Guides

Country Profile: Guinea Bissau
http://www.mbendi.co.za/cygbcy.htm
Developed by MBendi, the site provides Guinea Bissauan fact sheets, maps, sector profiles, exchange rates, travel information, and business contacts.

Guinea-Bissau Country Brief
http://www.worldbank.org/cgi-bin/sendoff.cgi?page=%2Fhtml%2Fextdr%2Foffrep%2Fafr%2Fgw.htm
A service of the World Bank Group, the site provides Guinea-Bissauan population statistics, financial data, development reports, and economic forecasts.

Guinea-Bissau Market Research
http://strategis.ic.gc.ca/sc_mrkti/ibinddc/engdoc/1a1a25.html
Posted by Industry Canada, the site provides U.S. Central Intelligence Agency fact sheets on Guinea-Bissauan geography, people, government, economy, communications, and transportation.

Guinea-Bissau Page
http://www.sas.upenn.edu/African_Studies/Country_Specific/G_Bissau.html
A service of the African Studies Center at the University of Pennsylvania, the site is a directory of Guinea-Bissauan resources online. Categories include country guides, languages, and travel.

Guinea-Bissau Trade Assistance

Index on Guinea-Bissau
http://www.africaindex.africainfo.no/africaindex1/countries/guinea-bissau.html
A service of the Norwegian Council for Africa, the site is a directory of Guinea-Bissauan resources online. Categories include culture, economy, news, and tourism.

Guinea-Bissau Representative Offices

Sweden

Embassy of Sweden in Bissau
http://www.ud.se/english/mfa/ambassad/guineabi.htm
The site lists the staff, street address, phone and fax numbers, and e-mail link of the Swedish Embassy in Bissau.

United Kingdom

Consulate of Britain in Bissau
http://www.fco.gov.uk/directory/posts.asp?GB
The site provides contact information for the British Consulate in Bissau.

Kenya

Kenya Media

Kenya Media
http://www.mediainfo.com/emediajs/specific-geo.htm?region=kenya
Developed by Editor and Publisher Interactive, the site is an index of Kenyan magazines, newspapers, and other media sites online.

Kenya Market Guides

Barclays Country Report: Kenya
http://www.offshorebanking.barclays.com/services/economic/yearly/kenfeb98/index.html
Prepared by Barclays Bank, the site reports on Kenyan economic trends, politics, monetary and fiscal policy, foreign debt, and U.K.-Kenya merchandise trade and investment flows.

Country Profile: Kenya
http://mbendi.co.za/cykecy.htm
Developed by MBendi, the site provides Kenyan fact sheets, maps, sector profiles, exchange rates, travel information, and business contacts.

Doing Business in Kenya
http://mbendi.co.za/werksmns/lexaf/buske.htm
Written by the law firm of Kaplan & Stratton, the site delivers fact sheets on Kenyan business formation, taxation, foreign investment, exchange controls, and intellectual property.

Index on Kenya
http://www.africaindex.africainfo.no/africaindex1/countries/kenya.html
A service of the Norwegian Council for Africa, the site is a directory of Kenyan resources online. Categories include culture, economy, news, and tourism.

Investment Profile: Kenya
http://www.mbendi.co.za/ernsty/cykeeyip.htm
A service of Ernst & Young, the site provides fact sheets on Kenyan business establishments, taxation, exchange controls, visa requirements, and foreign investment regulations.

Kenya Country Brief
http://www.worldbank.org/cgi-bin/sendoff.cgi?page=%2Fhtml%2Fextdr%2Foffrep%2Fafr%2Fke.htm
A service of the World Bank Group, the site provides Kenyan population statistics, financial data, development reports, and economic forecasts.

Kenya InfoExport
http://www.infoexport.gc.ca/country-e.asp?continent=Africa&country=24
A service of Foreign Affairs and International Trade Canada, the site provides Kenyan commercial guides and market reports.

Kenya Market Information
http://dtiinfo1.dti.gov.uk/ots/kenya/
A service of the London-based Department of Trade and Industry, the site delivers Kenyan fact sheets, maps, and trade-show information.

Kenya Market Research
http://strategis.ic.gc.ca/sc_mrkti/ibinddc/engdoc/1a1a27.html
A service of Industry Canada, the site provides U.S. Department of Commerce reports on Kenyan economic trends, trade regulations and standards, investment climate, trade and project financing, business travel, and market opportunities.

KenyaWeb
http://www.kenyaweb.com/
A searchable index of Kenyan resources online, the site is divided into ten categories including government, business, economy, education, land, history, and tourism.

Kenya Representative Offices

Belgium

Embassy of Belgium in Nairobi
http://www.cais.com/usa/nairobi/index.html
Featuring a greeting from the Ambassador, the site provides Belgian news, fact sheets, business guides, visa and passport information, and a directory of consular and commercial services.

Canada

Embassy of Canada in Nairobi
http://www.dfait-maeci.gc.ca/english/missions/rep-can3e.htm#kenya
The site provides contact information for the Canadian Embassy in Nairobi.

France

French Trade Commission in Nairobi
http://www.dree.org/kenya/anglais/index.htm#top
Written in French, the site delivers Kenyan market reports, sector profiles, contact information, and a directory of French export promotion services.

India

Indian Commercial Mission in Nairobi
http://www.nic.in/commin/ICM.HTM
The site lists the street address, phone and fax numbers, and e-mail link of the Indian Commercial Mission in Nairobi.

Iran

Iran Trade Center in Nairobi
http://www.neda.net/ibr/tcc.html
An Iranian trade promotion service, the site lists the street address and phone and fax numbers of the Iran Trade Center in Nairobi.

Malaysia

Trade Commission of Malaysia in Nairobi
http://www.mnet.com.my/klonline/www/missions/malmiss/mkenya.htm
The site provides contact information for the Malaysian Trade Commission in Nairobi.

Pakistan

Pakistan Trade Office in Nairobi
http://www.jamal.com/epb/ptoa.htm
The site provides contact information for the Pakistan Trade Office in Nairobi.

Sweden

Embassy of Sweden in Nairobi
http://www.ud.se/english/mfa/ambassad/kenya.htm
The site provides contact information for the Swedish Embassy in Nairobi.

Tanzania

Embassy of Tanzania in Nairobi
http://www.tanzania-online.gov.uk/visa/envoys.html
The site provides contact information for the Tanzanian Embassy in Nairobi.

South Africa

South Africa Foreign Trade Office in Nairobi
http://wwwdti.pwv.gov.za/dtiwww/foreign_offices.htm
A service of the South Africa Department of Trade and Industry, the site provides contact information for the South Africa Trade Office in Nairobi.

Thailand

Royal Thai Embassy in Nairobi
http://www.mfa.go.th/Embassy/detail/76.htm
The site lists the Ambassador, street address, and phone and fax numbers of the Thai Embassy in Nairobi.

United Kingdom

High Commission of Britain in Nairobi
http://www.fco.gov.uk/directory/posts.asp?KY
The site provides contact information for the British High Commission in Nairobi.

Lesotho

Lesotho Market Guides

Country Profile: Lesotho
http://mbendi.co.za/cylecy.htm
Developed by MBendi, the site provides Lesotho fact sheets, maps, sector profiles, exchange rates, travel information, and business contacts.

Doing Business in Lesotho
http://mbendi.co.za/werksmns/lexaf/busle.htm
Written by the law firm of Webber Newdigate, the site delivers fact sheets on Lesotho business formation, taxation, foreign investment, exchange controls, and intellectual property.

Index on Lesotho
http://www.africaindex.africainfo.no/africaindex1/countries/lesotho.html
A service of the Norwegian Council for Africa, the site is a directory of Lesotho resources online. Categories include culture, economy, news, and tourism.

Investment Profile: Lesotho
http://www.mbendi.co.za/ernsty/cyleeyip.htm
A service of Ernst & Young, the site provides fact sheets on Lesotho business establishments, taxation, exchange controls, visa requirements, and foreign investment regulations.

Lesotho Country Brief
http://www.worldbank.org/cgi-bin/sendoff.cgi?page=%2Fhtml%2Fextdr%2Foffrep%2Fafr%2Fls.htm
A service of the World Bank Group, the site provides Lesotho population statistics, financial data, development reports, and economic forecasts.

Lesotho InfoExport
http://www.infoexport.gc.ca/country-e.asp?continent=Africa&country=25
A service of Foreign Affairs and International Trade Canada, the site provides Lesotho fact sheets and statistics on Lesotho geography, business and politics.

Lesotho Market Research
http://strategis.ic.gc.ca/sc_mrkti/ibinddc/engdoc/1a1a28.html
A service of Industry Canada, the site provides U.S. Department of Commerce reports on Lesotho economic trends, trade regulations and standards, investment climate, trade and project financing, business travel, and market opportunities.

Lesotho Page
http://www.sas.upenn.edu/African_Studies/Country_Specific/Lesotho.html
A service of the African Studies Center at the University of Pennsylvania, the site is a directory of Lesotho resources online. Categories include country guides, languages, and travel.

Lesotho: Statistical Annex
http://www.imf.org/external/pubs/CAT/longres.cfm?sk=2566.0
Prepared by the International Monetary Fund, the site provides fact sheets and statistics on Lesotho interest rates, balance of payments, mining, taxation, and international trade.

Lesotho Representative Offices

United Kingdom

High Commission of Britain in Maseru
http://www.lesoff.co.za/bhcmaseru/
The site lists the staff, street address, phone and fax numbers, and consular and commercial services of the British High Commission in Maseru.

Liberia

Liberia Market Guides

Country Profile: Liberia
http://www.mbendi.co.za/cylicy.htm
Developed by MBendi, the site provides Liberian fact sheets, maps, sector profiles, exchange rates, travel information, and business contacts.

Index on Liberia
http://www.africaindex.africainfo.no/africaindex1/countries/liberia.html
A service of the Norwegian Council for Africa, the site is a directory of Liberian resources online. Categories include culture, economy, news, and tourism.

Liberia Country Brief
http://www.worldbank.org/cgi-bin/sendoff.cgi?page=%2Fhtml%2Fextdr%2Foffrep%2Fafr%2Flr.htm
A service of the World Bank Group, the site provides Liberian population statistics, financial data, development reports, and economic forecasts.

Liberia Market Research
http://strategis.ic.gc.ca/sc_mrkti/ibinddc/engdoc/1a1a29.html
Posted by Industry Canada, the site provides U.S. Central Intelligence Agency fact sheets on Liberian geography, people, government, economy, communications, and transportation.

Liberia Pages
http://groove.mit.edu/LiberiaPages/index.htm
An online country gateway, the site features Liberian news, photos, history lessons, cultural information, a discussion forum, political bulletins, and web guides.

Liberia Representative Offices

Ghana

Embassy of Ghana in Monrovia
http://www.juntung.com/ghana-consul-hk/2misabo.htm
The site provides contact information for the Ghanaian Embassy in Monrovia.

Madagascar

Madagascar Media

Madagascar Media
http://www.mediainfo.com/emediajs/specific-geo.htm?region=madagascar
Developed by Editor and Publisher Interactive, the site is a directory of Madagascar newspapers and other media sites online.

Midi Madagascar
http://dts.dts.mg/midi/
Posted in French, the site provides Madagascar news, political bulletins, economic reports, cultural information, and a searchable archive of past issues.

Madagascar Market Guides

Country Profile: Madagascar
http://www.mbendi.co.za/cymdcy.htm
Developed by MBendi, the site provides Madagascar fact sheets, maps, sector profiles, exchange rates, travel information, and business contacts.

Index on Madagascar
http://www.africaindex.africainfo.no/africaindex1/countries/madagascar.html
A service of the Norwegian Council for Africa, the site is a directory of Madagascar resources online. Categories include culture, economy, news, and environment.

Madagascar Contacts
http://www.madagascar-contacts.com/us/index.html

Written in English and French, the site features Madagascar news, maps, history lessons, fact sheets, travel guides, and online discussion forums.

Madagascar Country Brief
http://www.worldbank.org/cgi-bin/sendoff.cgi?page=%2Fhtml%2Fextdr%2Foffrep%2Fafr%2Fmg.htm
A service of the World Bank Group, the site provides Madagascar population statistics, financial data, development reports, and economic forecasts.

Madagascar: A Country Study
http://lcweb2.loc.gov/frd/cs/mgtoc.html
A service of the U.S. Library of Congress, the site delivers fact sheets on Madagascar geography, people, agriculture, mining, manufacturing, and foreign economic relations.

Madagascar InfoExport
http://www.infoexport.gc.ca/country-e.asp?continent=Africa&country=28
A service of Foreign Affairs and International Trade Canada, the site provides Madagascar commercial guides and market reports.

Madagascar Market Research
http://strategis.ic.gc.ca/sc_mrkti/ibinddc/engdoc/1a1a30.html
A service of Industry Canada, the site provides U.S. Department of Commerce reports on Madagascar economic trends, trade regulations and standards, investment climate, trade and project financing, business travel, and market opportunities.

Madagascar: Recent Economic Developments
http://www.imf.org/external/pubs/CAT/longres.cfm?sk=2422.0
Prepared by the International Monetary Fund, the site provides fact sheets and statistics on Madagascar public finance, population trends, civil service reform, and export processing zones.

Madagascar Trade Assistance

Madagascar Consulates and Embassies Abroad
http://www.madagascar-contacts.com/us/adresse.htm#alext
A service of Madagascar Contacts, the site is a directory of Madagascar Embassies and Consulates in over 15 countries including Algeria, Ethiopia, Germany, and Japan.

Madagascar Representative Offices

Foreign Consulates and Embassies in Madagascar
http://www.madagascar-contacts.com/us/ adresse.htm#amada
A service of Madagascar Contacts, the site is an index of foreign embassies and consulates in Madagascar. The service lists representatives from 15 countries including Belgium, Indonesia, and Canada.

France

French Trade Commission in Antananarivo
http://www.dree.org/madagascar/
Written in French, the site delivers Madagascar market reports, sector profiles, contact information, and a directory of French export promotion services.

United Kingdom

Embassy of Britain in Antananarivo
http://www.fco.gov.uk/directory/posts.asp?MB
The site provides contact information for the British Embassy in Antananarivo.

Malawi

Malawi Market Guides

Country Profile: Malawi
http://mbendi.co.za/cymacy.htm
Developed by MBendi, the site provides Malawian fact sheets, maps, sector profiles, exchange rates, travel information, and business contacts.

Doing Business in Malawi
http://mbendi.co.za/werksmns/lexaf/busma.htm
Written by the law firm of Sacranie, Gow & Co., the site delivers fact sheets on Malawian business formation, taxation, foreign investment, exchange controls, and intellectual property.

Index on Malawi
http://www.africaindex.africainfo.no/africaindex1/ countries/malawi.html
A service of the Norwegian Council for Africa, the site is a directory of Malawian resources online. Categories include culture, economy, news, and tourism.

Investment Profile: Malawi
http://www.mbendi.co.za/ernsty/cymaeyip.htm
A service of Ernst & Young, the site provides fact sheets on Malawian business establishments, taxation, exchange controls, visa requirements, and foreign investment regulations.

Malawi
http://www.math.unh.edu/~llk/
An online country gateway, the site features Malawian news, fact sheets, travel information, political bulletins, and frequently asked questions and answers.

Malawi Country Brief
http://www.worldbank.org/cgi-bin/ sendoff.cgi?page=%2Fhtml%2Fextdr%2Foffrep%2 Fafr%2Fmw.htm
A service of the World Bank Group, the site provides Malawian population statistics, financial data, development reports, and economic forecasts.

Malawi InfoExport
http://www.infoexport.gc.ca/country-e.asp?continent=Africa&country=29
A service of Foreign Affairs and International Trade Canada, the site provides fact sheets and statistics on Malawian geography, business, and politics.

Malawi Investment Promotion Agency
http://mipa.malawi.net/
Established in 1991, the Agency promotes foreign investment in Malawi. The site provides a mission statement, business guides, consultant directory, and contact information.

Malawi Market Research
http://strategis.ic.gc.ca/sc_mrkti/ibinddc/engdoc/ 1a1a31.html
A service of Industry Canada, the site provides U.S. Department of Commerce reports on Malawian economic trends, trade regulations and standards, investment climate, trade and project financing, business travel, and market opportunities.

Malawi Net
http://www.malawi.net/
A hub of country information, the site provides Malawian news, maps, fact sheets, education bulletins, cultural guides, government directories, and statistics.

Malawi: Recent Economic Developments
http://www.imf.org/external/pubs/CAT/ longres.cfm?sk=2423.0
Prepared by the International Monetary Fund, the site provides fact sheets and statistics on

Malawian public finance, gross domestic product, agricultural production, interest rates, and international trade.

Malawi Trade Assistance

Export Processing Zones
http://mipa.malawi.net/EPZ.htm
A service of the Malawi Investment Promotion Agency, the site delivers fact sheets on Malawian export process zones, international trade regulations, and investment incentives.

Malawi Representative Offices

Taiwan

Taiwan Government Information Office in Lilongwe
http://www.gio.gov.tw/info/ngio/malaw-f.html
Posted in Chinese and English, the site lists the street address, phone and fax numbers, and e-mail link of the Taiwan Government Information Office in Lilongwe.

United Kingdom

High Commission of Britain in Lilongwe
http://www.fco.gov.uk/directory/posts.asp?MC
The site provides contact information for the British High Commission in Lilongwe.

Mali

Mali Market Guides

Country Profile: Mali
http://mbendi.co.za/cymlcy.htm
Developed by MBendi, the site provides Malian fact sheets, maps, sector profiles, exchange rates, travel information, and business contacts.

Index on Mali
http://www.africaindex.africainfo.no/africaindex1/countries/mali.html
A service of the Norwegian Council for Africa, the site is a directory of Malian resources online. Categories include culture, economy, news, and tourism.

Mali Country Brief
http://www.worldbank.org/cgi-bin/sendoff.cgi?page=%2Fhtml%2Fextdr%2Foffrep%2Fafr%2Fml.htm
A service of the World Bank Group, the site

provides Malian population statistics, financial data, development reports, and economic forecasts.

Mali InfoExport
http://www.infoexport.gc.ca/country-e.asp?continent=Africa&country=30
A service of Foreign Affairs and International Trade Canada, the site provides Malian commercial guides and market reports.

Mali Market Research
http://strategis.ic.gc.ca/sc_mrkti/ibinddc/engdoc/1a1a32.html
A service of Industry Canada, the site provides U.S. Department of Commerce reports on Malian economic trends, trade regulations and standards, investment climate, trade and project financing, business travel, and market opportunities.

Mali Page
http://www.sas.upenn.edu/African_Studies/Country_Specific/Mali.html
A service of the African Studies Center at the University of Pennsylvania, the site is a directory of Malian resources online. Categories include country guides, languages, and travel.

Mali: Statistical Annex
http://www.imf.org/external/pubs/CAT/longres.cfm?sk=2499.0
Prepared by the International Monetary Fund, the site provides fact sheets and statistics on Malian gross domestic product, agricultural production, consumer prices, interest rates, and international trade.

Mali Representative Offices

Canada

Embassy of Canada in Bamako
http://www.dfait-maeci.gc.ca/english/missions/rep-can3e.htm#mali
The site provides contact information for the Canadian Embassy in Bamako.

Mauritania

Mauritania Market Guides

Country Profile: Mauritania
http://www.mbendi.co.za/cymucy.htm
Developed by MBendi, the site provides Mauritanian fact sheets, maps, sector profiles,

exchange rates, travel information, and business contacts.

Index on Mauritania
http://www.africaindex.africainfo.no/africaindex1/ countries/mauritania.html
A service of the Norwegian Council for Africa, the site is a directory of Mauritanian resources online. Categories include culture, economy, news, and tourism.

Mauritania
http://i-cias.com/m.s/mauritan/index.htm
A virtual country gateway, the site provides Mauritanian travel guides, regional profiles, fact sheets, visa and passport information, and weather bulletins.

Mauritania Country Brief
http://www.worldbank.org/cgi-bin/ sendoff.cgi?page=%2Fhtml%2Fextdr%2Foffrep%2 Fafr%2Fmr.htm
A service of the World Bank Group, the site provides Mauritanian population statistics, financial data, development reports, and economic forecasts.

Mauritania: A Country Guide
http://lcweb2.loc.gov/frd/cs/mrtoc.html
A service of the U.S. Library of Congress, the site delivers fact sheets on Mauritanian geography, people, agriculture, mining, manufacturing, and foreign economic relations.

Mauritania Market Research
http://strategis.ic.gc.ca/sc_mrkti/ibinddc/engdoc/ 1a1a33.html
A service of Industry Canada, the site provides U.S. Department of Commerce reports on Mauritanian economic trends, trade regulations and standards, investment climate, trade and project financing, business travel, and market opportunities.

Mauritania Page
http://www.sas.upenn.edu/African_Studies/ Country_Specific/Mauritania.html
A service of the African Studies Center at the University of Pennsylvania, the site is a directory of Mauritanian resources online. Categories include country guides, languages, and travel.

Mauritania Virtual Library
http://menic.utexas.edu/menic/countries/ mauritania.html
A service of the Center for Middle Eastern Studies at the University of Texas, the site is an index of

Mauritanian resources on the web. Sections include education, government, and politics.

Mauritania Representative Offices

France

French Trade Commission in Nouakchott
http://www.dree.org/mauritanie/anglais/ index.htm#top
Written in French, the site delivers Mauritanian market reports, sector profiles, contact information, and a directory of French export promotion services.

Mauritius

Mauritius Media

Mauritius Media
http://www.mediainfo.com/emediajs/specific- geo.htm?region=mauritius
Developed by Editor and Publisher Interactive, the site is an index of Mauritian magazines, newspapers, and other media sites online.

L'Express
http://www.lexpress-net.com/
Updated daily and written in French, the site features Mauritius news, editorials, business reports, interviews, sector profiles, and employment opportunities.

Mauritius Market Guides

Country Commercial Guide
http://www.state.gov/www/about_state/business/ com_guides/1998/africa/mauritius98.html
Prepared by the U.S. Embassy in Port Louis, the site delivers primers on Mauritian business, politics, trade regulations and standards, investment, and travel.

Country Profile: Mauritius
http://www.mbendi.co.za/cymrcy.htm
Developed by MBendi, the site provides Mauritian fact sheets, maps, sector profiles, exchange rates, travel information, and business contacts.

Doing Business in Mauritius
http://mbendi.co.za/werksmns/lexaf/busmr.htm
Written by the law firm of De Comarmond Koenig, the site delivers fact sheets on Mauritian business formation, taxation, foreign investment, exchange controls, and intellectual property.

Government of Mauritius
http://ncb.intnet.mu/govt/house.htm
Homepage of the Mauritius government, the site delivers fact sheets on the Mauritian Constitution, leading Ministers, and organizations such as the Ministry of Urban and Rural Development, and the Ministry of Finance.

Index on Mauritius
http://www.africaindex.africainfo.no/africaindex1/countries/mauritius.html
A service of the Norwegian Council for Africa, the site is a directory of Mauritian resources online. Categories include culture, economy, news, and tourism.

Investment Profile: Mauritius
http://www.mbendi.co.za/ernsty/cymreyip.htm
A service of Ernst & Young, the site provides fact sheets on Mauritian business establishments, taxation, exchange controls, visa requirements, and foreign investment regulations.

Mauritius Business Briefs
http://www.austrade.gov.au/IOOM/PortLouis/
A service of Austrade, the site offers fact sheets on Mauritian culture, business etiquette, marketing, transportation, travel, and visas.

Mauritius Country Brief
http://www.worldbank.org/cgi-bin/sendoff.cgi?page=%2Fhtml%2Fextdr%2Foffrep%2Fafr%2Fmu.htm
A service of the World Bank Group, the site provides Mauritian population statistics, financial data, development reports, and economic forecasts.

Mauritius: A Country Guide
http://lcweb2.loc.gov/frd/cs/mutoc.html
A service of the U.S. Library of Congress, the site delivers fact sheets on Mauritian geography, people, agriculture, mining, manufacturing, and foreign economic relations.

Mauritius InfoExport
http://www.infoexport.gc.ca/country-e.asp?continent=Africa&country=32
A service of Foreign Affairs and International Trade Canada, the site provides fact sheets and statistics on Mauritian geography, business and politics.

Mauritius Information
http://www.mauritius-info.com/
A virtual library of country information, the site features Mauritian news, event information, business guides, company directories, tourism guides, and investment primers.

Mauritius Market Information
http://dtiinfo1.dti.gov.uk/ots/mauritius/
A service of the London-based Department of Trade and Industry, the site delivers Mauritian fact sheets, maps, and trade-show information.

Mauritius Market Research
http://strategis.ic.gc.ca/sc_mrkti/ibinddc/engdoc/1a1a34.html
A service of Industry Canada, the site provides U.S. Department of Commerce reports on Mauritian economic trends, trade regulations and standards, investment climate, trade and project financing, business travel, and market opportunities.

Mauritius Ministry of Industry and Commerce
http://ncb.intnet.mu/mic.htm
Based in Port Louis, the Ministry regulates Mauritian business activity. The site includes fact sheets on Mauritius business permits, industrial incentives, and technology programs.

Mauritius Online Business Directory
http://www.mauritius.co.uk/
A searchable directory of Mauritian companies, the site is divided into 16 categories including banks, information technology, financial services, manufacturing, and textiles.

Mauritius Yellow Pages
http://www.mauritiusyellowpages.com/
Along with country news and shopping guides, the site is a browsable database of Mauritian companies in over 100 categories including architects, plastics, and transportation.

Ministry of Economic Development
http://ncb.intnet.mu/medrc.htm
A virtual library of socioeconomic statistics, the site provides data on Mauritian international trade, tourism, employment and earnings, agricultural and fish production, and other economic indicators.

Mauritius Trade Assistance

Apparel Network
http://epzda.intnet.mu/ApparelN/apparelf.htm
An online forum for Mauritian apparel and textile manufacturers, the site provides design and fashion reports, technology bulletins, company directories, and trade statistics.

Export Processing Zones Development Authority
http://epzda.intnet.mu/
A primer on Mauritian free trade zones, the site delivers facility fact sheets, incentive guides, productivity comparisons, event information, and discussion forums.

Mauritius Export Development and Investment Authority
http://ncb.intnet.mu/media/home.htm
Based in Port Louis, the Authority promotes Mauritian exports and international investment. The service features a Mauritian business guide and exporters directory.

Ministry of Foreign Affairs and International Trade
http://ncb.intnet.mu/mfa.htm
Posted in English and French, the site lists the executive, street address, phone and fax numbers, and e-mail links of the Ministry of Foreign Affairs and International Trade in Port Louis.

Mauritius Representative Offices

France

French Trade Commission in Port Louis
http://www.dree.org/maurice/anglais/index.htm#top
Posted in French, the site delivers Mauritian market reports, sector profiles, contact information, and a directory of French export promotion services.

India

Indian Commercial Mission in Port Louis
http://www.nic.in/commin/ICM.HTM
The site lists the street address, phone and fax numbers, and e-mail link of the Indian Commercial Mission in Port Louis.

South Africa

South Africa Foreign Trade Office in Port Louis
http://wwwdti.pwv.gov.za/dtiwww/foreign_offices.htm
A service of the South Africa Department of Trade and Industry, the site provides contact information for the South Africa Trade Office in Port Louis.

United Kingdom

High Commission of Britain in Port Louis
http://www.fco.gov.uk/directory/posts.asp?MJ
The site provides contact information for the British High Commission in Port Louis.

United States

United States Embassy in Port Louis
http://usis.intnet.mu/embassy.htm
Featuring a biography of the Ambassador, the site provides U.S. fact sheets, publication lists, visa and passport information, and a directory of consular and commercial services.

U.S. Information Service Mauritius
http://usis.intnet.mu/
The site provides U.S. electronic bulletins, fact sheets, economic reports, cultural information, and a directory of U.S.- Mauritius educational and exchange programs

Mayotte

Mayotte Market Guides

About Mayotte
http://www.worldwidenews.net/TRAVEL/PLACES/AFRICA/MAYOTTE/COUNTRY.HTM
A service of TravelWorld, the site provides Mahoran fact sheets, maps, and travel information.

Mayotte
http://travel.epicurious.com/bin/where-to.cgi?path=africa/Mayotte
A virtual travel guide, the site delivers Mahoran tourism information, maps, accommodation directories, weather bulletins, and transportation guides.

Mayotte Travel Documents
http://www.traveldocs.com/yt/govern.htm
Developed by Washington, D.C.-based Travel Documents Systems, the site provides Mahoran fact sheets, government directories, political bulletins, and contact information.

Morocco

Morocco Media

Morocco Media
http://www.mediainfo.com/emediajs/specific-geo.htm?region=morocco
Developed by Editor and Publisher Interactive, the site is a directory of Moroccan radio stations and other media sites online.

Morocco Today
http://www.morocco-today.com/
An English-language electronic newspaper, the site delivers Moroccan news, editorials, business guides, travel information, online discussion forums, and regional headlines.

Morocco Market Guides

Country Profile: Morocco
http://www.mbendi.co.za/cymocy.htm
Developed by MBendi, the site provides Moroccan fact sheets, maps, sector profiles, exchange rates, travel information, and business contacts.

Index on Morocco
http://www.africaindex.africainfo.no/africaindex1/countries/morocco.html
A service of the Norwegian Council for Africa, the site is a directory of Moroccan resources online. Categories include culture, economy, news, and tourism.

Investment Profile: Morocco
http://www.mbendi.co.za/ernsty/cymoeyip.htm
A service of Ernst & Young, the site provides fact sheets on Moroccan business, taxation, exchange controls, visa requirements, and foreign investment regulations.

Kingdom of Morocco
http://www.mincom.gov.ma/
Posted in English and French, the site provides Moroccan news, investment guides, city profiles, fact sheets, cultural information, and a directory of government ministers.

Morocco Business Report
http://italchambers.net/BusinessReports.html
Prepared by the Italian Chamber of Commerce and written in Italian, the site provides Moroccan fact sheets, market reports, and commercial guides.

Morocco Country Brief
http://www.worldbank.org/cgi-bin/sendoff.cgi?page=%2Fhtml%2Fextdr%2Foffrep%2Fmena%2Fma.htm
A service of the World Bank Group, the site provides Moroccan population statistics, financial data, development reports, and economic forecasts.

Morocco Country Profile
http://www.tradenz.govt.nz/intelligence/profiles/morocco.html
A service of the New Zealand Trade Development Board, the site provides Moroccan economic statistics, market information, and business tips.

Morocco Country Report
http://www.state.gov/www/issues/economic/trade_reports/neareast97/morocco97.html
Prepared by the U.S. Department of State, the site delivers information on Moroccan exchange rates, debt management, trade barriers, export subsidies, intellectual property protection, worker rights, and foreign investment.

Morocco InfoExport
http://www.infoexport.gc.ca/country-e.asp?continent=Africa&country=33
A service of Foreign Affairs and International Trade Canada, the site provides Moroccan commercial guides and market reports.

Morocco Market Access Database
http://mkaccdb.eu.int/mkdb/mkdb.pl?METHOD=COUNTRY
A service of the European Commission, the site offers briefs on Moroccan trade policy, tariff barriers, non-tariff barriers, investment-related measures, and financial services regulations.

Morocco Market Information
http://dtiinfo1.dti.gov.uk/ots/morocco/
A service of the London-based Department of Trade and Industry, the site delivers Moroccan fact sheets, maps, and trade-show information.

Morocco Market Research
http://strategis.ic.gc.ca/sc_mrkti/ibinddc/engdoc/1a1a35.html
A service of Industry Canada, the site provides U.S. Department of Commerce reports on Moroccan economic trends, trade regulations and standards, investment climate, trade and project financing, business travel, and market opportunities.

Morocco Virtual Library
http://menic.utexas.edu/menic/countries/morocco.html
A service of the Center for Middle Eastern Studies at the University of Texas, the site is an index of Moroccan resources online. Categories include business and economy, government and politics, and news and current events.

Morocco Web
http://www.moroccoweb.com/en/index.html
Posted in English and French, the site is a virtual country gateway. The service provides Moroccan business guides, economic statistics, investment primers, political bulletins, and tourism information.

Morocco Trade Assistance

Foreign Trade
http://www.mincom.gov.ma/english/generalities/trade/trade.html
A service of the Moroccan government, the site delivers international trade statistics, export and import regulations, and a directory of trade promotion agencies in Morocco.

Morocco Ministry of Trade and Industry
http://www.mcinet.gov.ma/engindex.htm
A virtual library of Moroccan trade information, the site features an exporter directory, international trade statistics, product catalogs, and investment guides.

Morocco Foreign Trade
http://194.204.216.224/mce.htm
Written in French, the site delivers Moroccan export statistics, international business reports, sector profiles, and a directory of Moroccan trade pacts and agreements with the European Union and other trading blocs and countries.

Moroccan Centre for Export Promotion
http://www.cmpe.org.ma/
Part of the United Nations Global Trade Point Network, the site provides Moroccan trade leads, market bulletins, and contact information.

Morocco Representative Offices

Foreign Embassies in Morocco
http://www.council.org.ma/foreign.htm
A service of the Morocco-U.S. Council on Trade and Investment, the site is a directory of over 60 foreign embassies and consulates in Morocco.

Austria

Austria Trade Commission in Casablanca
http://aw.wk.or.at/awo/ahst-casablanca.htm
The site lists the staff, street address, phone and fax numbers, e-mail link, and office hours of the Austrian Trade Commission in Casablanca.

Canada

Embassy of Canada in Rabat
http://www.dfait-maeci.gc.ca/english/missions/repcan3e.htm#morocco
The site provides contact information for the Canadian Embassy in Rabat.

France

Consulate General of France in Casablanca
http://www.consulatfr-casa.org/
Posted in French, the site delivers French fact sheets, business guides, visa and passport information, and a directory of consular and commercial services.

Embassy of France in Rabat
http://www.ambafrance-ma.org/
Along with Morocco commercial guides and event information, the site provides French news, science and technology bulletins, and reports on France-Morocco trade and relations.

French Trade Commission in Casablanca
http://www.dree.org/maroc/
Written in French, the site lists the street address, phone and fax numbers, and e-mail links of the French Trade Commission offices in Casablanca and Rabat.

Germany

German Chamber of Commerce in Casablanca
http://www.ahk.net/en/ma/Casablanca/
The site lists the Chairperson, Chief Executive Officer, street address, phone and fax numbers, and e-mail link of the German Chamber in Casablanca.

Malaysia

Embassy of Malaysia in Rabat
http://www.mnet.com.my/klonline/www/missions/malmiss/mmorocco.htm
The site provides contact information for the Malaysian Embassy in Rabat.

Netherlands

Royal Netherlands Embassy in Rabat
http://users.mtds.com/~nlgovrab/
Along with Dutch visa and passport information, the site lists the street address, phone and fax numbers, and e-mail link of the Netherlands Embassy in Rabat.

Portugal

Portuguese Trade and Investment Office in Rabat
http://www.portugal.org/geninfo/abouticep/morocco.html
The site lists the staff, street address, and phone and fax numbers of the Portuguese Trade and Investment Office in Rabat.

Spain

Spanish Commercial Office in Casablanca
http://www.icex.es/openURL.html#openURL=/english/infoproyem/ofcomes/ofcomes.html#AF
The site lists the staff, street address, and phone and fax numbers of the Spanish Commercial Office in Casablanca.

Spanish Commercial Office in Rabat
http://www.icex.es/openURL.html#openURL=/english/infoproyem/ofcomes/ofcomes.html#AF
The site lists the staff, street address, phone and fax numbers, and e-mail link of the Spanish Commercial Office in Rabat.

Taiwan

China External Trade Development Council Office in Casablanca
http://www.cetra.org.tw/english/o_office/indexset.htm
A Taiwanese trade promotion service, the site lists the mission statement and e-mail link of the China External Trade Development Council Office in Casablanca.

Thailand

Royal Thai Embassy in Rabat
http://www.mfa.go.th/Embassy/detail/48.htm
The site lists the Ambassador, street address, and phone and fax numbers of the Thai Embassy in Rabat.

United Kingdom

Embassy of Britain in Rabat
http://www.fco.gov.uk/directory/posts.asp?MR
The site provides contact information for the British Embassy in Rabat.

United States

Morocco-U.S. Council on Trade and Investment
http://www.council.org.ma/
With offices in Casablanca, New York, and Washington, D.C., the site promotes Morocco-U.S. trade. The site includes a mission statement, contact information, and Moroccan business opportunities and sector profiles.

Mozambique

Mozambique Media

Mozambique News Agency
http://www.poptel.org.uk/mozambique-news/
Updated twice a month, the English language electronic newspaper provides Mozambican headlines, business reports, editorials, and a searchable archive of past issues.

Mozambique Market Guides

Country Profile: Mozambique
http://www.mbendi.co.za/cymzcy.htm
Developed by MBendi, the site provides Mozambican fact sheets, maps, sector profiles, exchange rates, travel information, and business contacts.

Index on Mozambique
http://www.africaindex.africainfo.no/africaindex1/countries/mozambique.html
A service of the Norwegian Council for Africa, the site is a directory of Mozambican resources online. Categories include culture, economy, news, and tourism.

Investment Profile: Mozambique
http://www.mbendi.co.za/ernsty/cymzeyip.htm
A service of Ernst & Young, the site provides fact sheets on Mozambican business establishments, taxation, exchange controls, visa requirements, and foreign investment regulations.

Mozambique Country Brief
*http://www.worldbank.org/cgi-bin/
sendoff.cgi?page=%2Fhtml%2Fextdr%2Foffrep%2
Fafr%2Fmz.htm*
A service of the World Bank Group, the site
provides Mozambican population statistics,
financial data, development reports, and economic forecasts.

Mozambique Economy
http://www.mozambique.mz/economy/eindex.htm
Posted in English and Portuguese, the site
provides Mozambican investment guides,
economic reports, socioeconomic statistics,
privatization bulletins, and banking information.

Mozambique InfoExport
*http://www.infoexport.gc.ca/country-
e.asp?continent=Africa&country=34*
A service of Foreign Affairs and International
Trade Canada, the site provides fact sheets and
statistics on Mozambican geography, business,
and politics.

Mozambique Market Research
*http://strategis.ic.gc.ca/sc_mrkti/ibinddc/engdoc/
1a1a36.html*
A service of Industry Canada, the site provides
U.S. Department of Commerce reports on
Mozambican economic trends, trade regulations
and standards, investment climate, trade and
project financing, business travel, and market
opportunities.

Mozambique Official Homepage
http://www.mozambique.mz/eindex.htm
A hub of country information, the site provides fact
sheets on Mozambican business, people,
regions, culture, tourism, elections, and health.

World Bank Mozambique Mission
http://www.worldbank.mz/
Along with contact information, the English
language site reports on World Bank economic
development programs and projects in
Mozambique and Africa.

Mozambique Trade Assistance

Mozambique Export Promotion Institute
*http://www.mozambique.mz/economy/ipex/
eindex.htm*
Based in Maputo, the Institute promotes
Mozambican exports and international investment. The site includes a mission statement,
exporters directory, and contact information.

Mozambique Representative Offices

Canada

Embassy of Canada in Maputo
*http://www.dfait-maeci.gc.ca/english/missions/rep-
can3e.htm#mozambique*
The site provides contact information for the
Canadian Embassy in Maputo.

France

French Trade Commission in Maputo
http://www.dree.org/mozambique/
Posted in French, the site delivers Mozambican
market reports, sector profiles, contact information, and a directory of French export promotion
services.

Portugal

**Portuguese Trade and Investment Office in
Maputo**
*http://www.portugal.org/geninfo/abouticep/
mozambique.html*
The site lists the staff, street address, phone and
fax numbers, and e-mail link of the Portuguese
Trade and Investment Office in Maputo.

South Africa

South Africa Foreign Trade Office in Maputo
*http://wwwdti.pwv.gov.za/dtiwww/
foreign_offices.htm*
A service of the South Africa Department of Trade
and Industry, the site provides contact information
for the South Africa Trade Office in Maputo.

Tanzania

Embassy of Tanzania in Maputo
*http://www.tanzania-online.gov.uk/visa/
envoys.html*
The site provides contact information for the
Tanzanian Embassy in Maputo.

United Kingdom

High Commission of Britain in Maputo
http://www.fco.gov.uk/directory/posts.asp?MZ
The site provides contact information for the
British High Commission in Maputo.

Namibia

Namibia Media

Namibia Media
http://www.mediainfo.com/emediajs/specific-geo.htm?region=namibia
Developed by Editor and Publisher Interactive, the site is an index of Namibian newspapers and other media sites online.

Namibia News
http://www.republicofnamibia.com/news.htm
Posted in English, the site provides Namibia headlines, political bulletins, business reports, editorials, interviews, tourism information, and book and movie reviews.

Namibia Market Guides

Country Profile: Namibia
http://www.mbendi.co.za/cynacy.htm
Developed by MBendi, the site provides Namibian fact sheets, maps, sector profiles, exchange rates, travel information, and business contacts.

Doing Business in Namibia
http://mbendi.co.za/werksmns/lexaf/busna.htm
Written by the law firm of Lorentz & Bone, the site delivers fact sheets on Namibian business formation, taxation, foreign investment, exchange controls, and intellectual property.

Index on Namibia
http://www.africaindex.africainfo.no/africaindex1/countries/namibia.html
A service of the Norwegian Council for Africa, the site is a directory of Namibian resources online. Categories include culture, economy, news, and tourism.

Investment Profile: Namibia
http://www.mbendi.co.za/ernsty/cynaeyip.htm
A service of Ernst & Young, the site provides fact sheets on Namibian business, taxation, exchange controls, visa requirements, and foreign investment regulations.

Namibia Country Brief
http://www.worldbank.org/cgi-bin/sendoff.cgi?page=%2Fhtml%2Fextdr%2Foffrep%2Fafr%2Fna.htm
A service of the World Bank Group, the site provides Namibian population statistics, financial data, development reports, and economic forecasts.

Namibia Economy
http://www.republicofnamibia.com/eco.htm
Along with investment guides and sector profiles, the site features Namibian economic statistics, oil production reports, and United Nations aid bulletins.

Namibia InfoExport
http://www.infoexport.gc.ca/country-e.asp?continent=Africa&country=35
A service of Foreign Affairs and International Trade Canada, the site provides fact sheets and statistics on Namibian geography, business, and politics.

Namibia Market Research
http://strategis.ic.gc.ca/sc_mrkti/ibinddc/engdoc/1a1a37.html
A service of Industry Canada, the site provides U.S. Department of Commerce reports on Namibian economic trends, trade regulations and standards, investment climate, trade and project financing, business travel, and market opportunities.

Namibia: Recent Economic Developments
http://www.imf.org/external/pubs/CAT/longres.cfm?sk=2466.0
Prepared by the International Monetary Fund, the site provides fact sheets and statistics on Namibian mining, agriculture, fishing, manufacturing, construction, energy, and tourism.

Republic of Namibia
http://www.republicofnamibia.com/
An online country gateway, the site features fact sheets on Namibian people, politics, business, international relations, tourism, and transportation.

Namibia Trade Assistance

Namibia Export Processing Zone
http://www.republicofnamibia.com/export.htm
Featuring a roster of leading banking and government contacts, the site provides fact sheets on Namibian free trade zones, taxation, business licensing, and export markets.

Namibian Trade Representatives and Diplomatic Missions
http://www.republicofnamibia.com/adress.htm
Along with a directory of leading business

contacts, the site lists Namibian Embassies and Consulates in 15 countries including Belgium, Cuba, Germany, and the United Kingdom.

Namibia Representative Offices

Finland

Embassy of Finland in Windhoek
http://www.apple.com.na/finland/
Along with contact information, the site provides a staff roster and a directory of Finnish poverty reduction and environmental projects in Namibia.

Malaysia

Embassy of Malaysia in Windhoek
http://www.mnet.com.my/klonline/www/missions/ malmiss/mnamibia.htm
The site provides contact information for the Malaysian Embassy in Windhoek.

Sweden

Embassy of Sweden in Windhoek
http://www.ud.se/english/mfa/ambassad/ namibia.htm
The site provides contact information for the Swedish Embassy in Windhoek.

United Kingdom

High Commission of Britain in Windhoek
http://www.fco.gov.uk/directory/posts.asp?NA
The site provides contact information for the British High Commission in Windhoek.

Venezuela

Embassy of Venezuela in Windhoek
http://www.trade-venezuela.com/EMBVENG.HTM
The site lists the street address, phone and fax numbers, and e-mail link of the Venezuelan Embassy in Windhoek.

Niger

Niger Media

Niger News
http://www.txdirect.net/users/jmayer/cet.html
Updated weekly and posted in English and French, the site delivers Nigerien headlines, editorials, political bulletins, business reports, and cultural news.

Niger Market Guides

Country Profile: Niger
http://www.mbendi.co.za/cynicy.htm
Developed by MBendi, the site provides Nigerien fact sheets, maps, sector profiles, exchange rates, travel information, and business contacts.

Focus on Niger
http://www.txdirect.net/users/jmayer/fon.html
A directory of Nigerien resources online, the site is divided into eight modules including country guides, photos, maps and flags, travel, and regional information.

Index on Niger
http://www.africaindex.africainfo.no/africaindex1/ countries/niger.html
A service of the Norwegian Council for Africa, the site is a directory of Nigerien resources on the web. Categories include culture, economy, news, and tourism.

Niger Country Brief
http://www.worldbank.org/cgi-bin/ sendoff.cgi?page=%2Fhtml%2Fextdr%2Foffrep%2 Fafr%2Fne.htm
A service of the World Bank Group, the site provides Nigerien population statistics, financial data, development reports, and economic forecasts.

Niger Market Research
http://strategis.ic.gc.ca/sc_mrkti/ibinddc/engdoc/ 1a1a39.html
A service of Industry Canada, the site provides U.S. Department of Commerce reports on Nigerien economic trends, trade regulations and standards, investment climate, trade and project financing, business travel, and market opportunities.

Niger-Net
http://www.txdirect.net/users/jmayer/nnform.html
The online service is an e-mail network of Nigeriens, Peace Corps volunteers, and other current and former residents of Niger. The site provides a mission statement and contact information.

Welcome to Niamey
http://www.gsi-niger.com/cca-usis/wwwhclo.htm
An unofficial publication of the U.S. Embassy, the site provides background information about life in Niamey, Niger. Modules include travel, telecommunications, and shopping.

Niger Representative Offices

Canada

Embassy of Canada in Niamey
http://www.dfait-maeci.gc.ca/english/missions/rep-can3e.htm#niger
The site provides contact information for the Canadian Embassy in Niamey.

United States

American Embassy in Niamey
http://www.gsi-niger.com/cca-usis/wwwhemb.htm
Featuring a biography of the U.S. Ambassador, the virtual Embassy delivers American visa and passport information, and a directory of consular and commercial services.

United States Information Service in Niamey
http://www.gsi-niger.com/cca-usis/wwwhusis.htm
Posted in English and French, the site provides U.S. electronic bulletins, fact sheets, economic reports, cultural information, and a directory of U.S.-Niger educational and exchange programs.

Nigeria

Nigeria Media

Nigeria Media
http://www.mediainfo.com/emediajs/specific-geo.htm?region=nigeria
Developed by Editor and Publisher Interactive, the site is an index of Nigerian newspapers and other media sites online.

Nigeria Media Monitor
http://www.kilima.com/mediamonitor/
A service of the Independent Journalism Centre in Lagos, Nigeria, the site delivers Nigerian headlines, editorial, political bulletins, and business reports.

Post Express
http://www.postexpresswired.com/
Updated daily, the electronic newspaper delivers Nigerian news, editorials, business reports, economic indicators, political bulletins, and arts and culture features.

Nigeria Market Guides

Barclays Country Report: Nigeria
http://www.offshorebanking.barclays.com/
services/economic/yearly/nigfeb98/index.html
Prepared by Barclays Bank, the site reports on Nigerian economic trends, politics, monetary and fiscal policy, and U.K.-Nigeria merchandise trade and investment flows.

Country Profile: Nigeria
http://www.mbendi.co.za/cyngcy.htm
Developed by MBendi, the site provides Nigerian fact sheets, maps, sector profiles, exchange rates, travel information, and business contacts.

Index on Nigeria
http://www.africaindex.africainfo.no/africaindex1/countries/nigeria.html
A service of the Norwegian Council for Africa, the site is a directory of Nigerian resources online. Categories include culture, economy, news, and tourism.

Investment Profile: Nigeria
http://www.mbendi.co.za/ernsty/cyngeyip.htm
A service of Ernst & Young, the site provides fact sheets on Nigerian business, taxation, exchange controls, visa requirements, and foreign investment regulations.

Nigeria.Com
http://www.nigeria.com/
A hub of country information, the site delivers Nigerian news, fact sheets, discussion forums, chat services, and shopping guides.

Nigeria Country Brief
http://www.worldbank.org/cgi-bin/sendoff.cgi?page=%2Fhtml%2Fextdr%2Foffrep%2Fafr%2Fng.htm
A service of the World Bank Group, the site provides Nigerian population statistics, financial data, development reports, and economic forecasts.

Nigeria: A Country Study
http://lcweb2.loc.gov/frd/cs/ngtoc.html
A service of the U.S. Library of Congress, the site delivers fact sheets on Nigerian geography, people, agriculture, mining, manufacturing, and foreign economic relations.

Nigeria Country Report
http://www.state.gov/www/issues/economic/trade_reports/africa97/nigeria97.html
Prepared by the U.S. Department of State, the site delivers information on Nigerian exchange rates, debt management, trade barriers, export subsidies, intellectual property protection, worker rights, and foreign investment.

Nigeria Market Information
http://dtiinfo1.dti.gov.uk/ots/nigeria/
A service of the London-based Department of Trade and Industry, the site delivers Nigerian fact sheets, maps, and trade-show information.

Nigeria Market Research
http://strategis.ic.gc.ca/sc_mrkti/ibinddc/engdoc/1a1a38.html
A service of Industry Canada, the site provides U.S. Department of Commerce reports on Nigerian economic trends, trade regulations and standards, investment climate, trade and project financing, business travel, and market opportunities.

Nigeria Online
http://www.afrocaribbean.com/nigeria/nigeria.html
An index of Nigerian companies, the site profiles operations in ten categories including banking, building materials, office equipment, and food and beverage products.

Nigerian Business Galleria
http://www.nigeriangalleria.com/home.htm
A hub of country business information, the site delivers Nigerian economic headlines, fact sheets, international trade opportunities, travel guides, and cultural reports.

Nigeria Trade Assistance

Nigerian Embassies and Consulates Abroad
http://WWW.rain.org/~ananet/missions.html
A service of the Association of Nigerians Abroad, the site is a directory of Nigerian Embassies and Consulates in over 60 countries, including Angola, Denmark, and Sweden.

Trade Shows in Nigeria
http://www.expoguide.com/shows/data/loc_42.htm
Compiled by Expoguide, the site is a directory of upcoming trade shows in Nigeria.

Nigeria Representative Offices

Bilateral Chambers of Commerce in Nigeria
http://www.nigeriangalleria.com/business/chambers.htm
A service of the Nigerian Business Galleria, the site lists 20 bilateral chambers of commerce in Nigeria including the African-American Institute, the Nigerian-Brazilian Chamber of Commerce and Industry, and the Nigerian British Chamber of Commerce.

Austria

Austrian Trade Commission in Lagos
http://aw.wk.or.at/awo/ahst-lagos.htm
The site lists the staff, street address, phone and fax numbers, e-mail link, and office hours of the Austrian Trade Commission in Lagos.

France

French Trade Commission in Lagos
http://www.dree.org/nigeria/
Along with Nigerian market reports and business opportunities, the site lists the street address, phone and fax numbers, and e-mail links of the French Trade Commission offices in Abuja and Lagos.

Ghana

High Commission of Ghana in Lagos
http://www.juntung.com/ghana-consul-hk/2misabo.htm
The site provides contact information for the Ghanaian High Commission in Lagos.

Germany

German Chamber of Commerce in Lagos
http://www.ahk.net/chambers/ng/english/firsten.htm
Written in English, the site provides a mission statement, staff directory, activity reports, event information, and bulletins on German-Nigerian trade and relations.

India

Indian Commercial Mission in Lagos
http://www.nic.in/commin/ICM.HTM
The site lists the street address, phone and fax numbers, and e-mail link of the Indian Commercial Mission in Lagos.

Malaysia

High Commission of Malaysia in Lagos
http://www.mnet.com.my/klonline/www/missions/malmiss/mnigeria.htm
The site provides contact information for the Malaysian High Commission in Lagos.

Spain

Spanish Commercial Office in Lagos
http://www.icex.es/openURL.html#openURL=/english/infoproyem/ofcomes/ofcomes.html#AF

The site lists the staff, street address, phone and fax numbers, and e-mail link of the Spanish Commercial Office in Lagos.

Tanzania

Embassy of Tanzania in Lagos
http://www.tanzania-online.gov.uk/visa/ envoys.html
The site provides contact information for the Tanzanian Embassy in Lagos.

Thailand

Royal Thai Embassy in Lagos
http://www.mfa.go.th/Embassy/detail/52.htm
The site lists the street address, and phone and fax numbers of the Thai Embassy in Lagos.

United Kingdom

High Commission of Britain in Lagos
http://www.fco.gov.uk/directory/posts.asp?NG
The site provides contact information for the British High Commission in Lagos.

Republic of Congo

Republic of Congo Market Guides

Republic of Congo Country Brief
http://www.worldbank.org/cgi-bin/ sendoff.cgi?page=%2Fhtml%2Fextdr%2Foffrep%2 Fafr%2Fcg.htm
A service of the World Bank Group, the site provides Republic of Congo population statistics, financial data, development reports, and economic forecasts.

Republic of Congo Geography
http://geography.tqn.com/library/maps/ blcongo.htm
A service of the Mining Company, the site provides a directory of Republic of Congo resources online. Categories include maps, geography, and statistics.

Reunion

Reunion Market Guides

Reunion Market Research
http://strategis.ic.gc.ca/sc_mrkti/ibinddc/engdoc/ 1a1a40.html

Posted by Industry Canada, the site provides U.S. Central Intelligence Agency fact sheets on Reunionese geography, people, government, economy, communications, and transportation.

Reunion Page
http://www.sas.upenn.edu/African_Studies/ Country_Specific/Reunion.html
A service of the African Studies Center at the University of Pennsylvania, the site is a directory of Reunionese resources online. Categories include country guides, languages, and maps.

Rwanda

Rwanda Market Guides

Business and Economy
http://www.rwandemb.org/business/business.htm
A service of the Rwandan Embassy in Washington, D.C., the site provides Rwandan economic policy statements, balance of payment information, and economic forecasts.

Country Profile: Rwanda
http://www.mbendi.co.za/cyrwcy.htm
Developed by MBendi, the site provides Rwandan fact sheets, maps, sector profiles, exchange rates, travel information, and business contacts.

Index on Rwanda
http://www.africaindex.africainfo.no/africaindex1/ countries/rwanda.html
A service of the Norwegian Council for Africa, the site is a directory of Rwandan resources online. Categories include culture, economy, news, and tourism.

Rwanda Country Brief
http://www.worldbank.org/cgi-bin/ sendoff.cgi?page=%2Fhtml%2Fextdr%2Foffrep%2Fafr %2Frw.htm
A service of the World Bank Group, the site provides Rwandan population statistics, financial data, development reports, and economic forecasts.

Rwanda Information Exchange
http://www.rwanda.net/
A hub of country information, the site provides fact sheets on Rwandan geography, history, economy, government, tourism, and employment opportunities.

Rwanda Market Research
http://strategis.ic.gc.ca/sc_mrkti/ibinddc/engdoc/
1a1a41.html
Posted by Industry Canada, the site provides U.S. Central Intelligence Agency fact sheets on Rwandan geography, people, government, economy, communications, and transportation.

Rwanda Trade Assistance

External Sector Policies
http://www.rwandemb.org/business/
business.htm#External sector
Prepared by the Rwandan Embassy in Washington, D.C., the site provides Rwandan international trade statistics, export forecasts, and multilateral assistance reports.

Rwanda Representative Offices

Canada

Embassy of Canada in Kigali
http://www.dfait-maeci.gc.ca/english/missions/rep-
can4e.htm#rwanda
The site provides contact information for the Canadian Embassy in Kigali.

United Kingdom

Embassy of Britain in Kigali
http://www.fco.gov.uk/directory/posts.asp?RW
The site provides contact information for the British Embassy in Kigali.

Saint Helena

Saint Helena Market Guides

Saint Helena Market Research
http://strategis.ic.gc.ca/sc_mrkti/ibinddc/engdoc/
1a1a48.html
Posted by Industry Canada, the site provides U.S. Central Intelligence Agency fact sheets on Saint Helenian geography, people, government, economy, communications, and transportation.

São Tomé and Príncipe

São Tomé and Príncipe Market Guides

Country Profile: São Tomé and Príncipe
http://www.mbendi.co.za/cyspcy.htm
Developed by MBendi, the site provides São Toméan fact sheets, maps, sector profiles,

exchange rates, travel information, and business contacts.

Index on São Tomé and Príncipe
http://www.africaindex.africainfo.no/africaindex1/
countries/saotome.html
A service of the Norwegian Council for Africa, the site is a directory of São Toméan resources online. Categories include culture, economy, news, and tourism.

São Tomé and Príncipe Country Brief
http://www.worldbank.org/cgi-bin/
sendoff.cgi?page=%2Fhtml%2Fextdr%2Foffrep%2
Fafr%2Fst.htm
A service of the World Bank Group, the site provides São Toméan population statistics, financial data, development reports, and economic forecasts.

São Tomé and Príncipe Market Research
http://strategis.ic.gc.ca/sc_mrkti/ibinddc/engdoc/
1a1a42.html
Posted by Industry Canada, the site provides U.S. Central Intelligence Agency fact sheets on São Toméan geography, people, government, economy, communications, and transportation.

São Tomé and Príncipe Page
http://www.sas.upenn.edu/African_Studies/
Country_Specific/Sao_Tome.html
A service of the African Studies Center at the University of Pennsylvania, the site is a directory of São Toméan resources online. Categories include country guides, languages, and maps.

São Tomé and Príncipe Representative Offices

United Kingdom

Consulate of Britain in São Tomé
http://www.fco.gov.uk/directory/posts.asp?SB
The site provides contact information for the British Consulate in São Tomé.

Senegal

Senegal Media

Senegal Media
http://www.mediainfo.com/emediajs/specific-
geo.htm?region=senegal
Developed by Editor and Publisher Interactive, the site is an index of Senegalese radio stations and other media sites online.

Senegal Market Guides

Country Profile: Senegal
http://www.mbendi.co.za/cysncy.htm
Developed by MBendi, the site provides
Senegalese fact sheets, maps, sector profiles,
exchange rates, travel information, and business
contacts.

Index on Senegal
*http://www.africaindex.africainfo.no/africaindex1/
countries/senegal.html*
A service of the Norwegian Council for Africa, the
site is a directory of Senegalese resources
online. Categories include culture, economy,
news, and tourism.

Investment Profile: Senegal
http://www.mbendi.co.za/ernsty/cysneyip.htm
A service of Ernst & Young, the site provides fact
sheets on Senegalese business establishments, taxation, exchange controls, visa requirements, and foreign investment regulations.

Official Home Page of the Republic of Senegal
http://www.earth2000.com/senegal/
Posted in English and French, the site provides
Senegalese company directories, travel information, city guides, and leader profiles.

Republic of Senegal
http://www.primature.sn/
Posted in French, the site delivers Senegalese
government directories, leader biographies,
travel guides, investment primers, infrastructure
reports, and technology bulletins.

Senegal Country Brief
*http://www.worldbank.org/cgi-bin/
sendoff.cgi?page=%2Fhtml%2Fextdr%2Foffrep%
2Fafr%2Fsn.htm*
A service of the World Bank Group, the site
provides Senegalese population statistics,
financial data, development reports, and economic forecasts.

Senegal Market Research
*http://strategis.ic.gc.ca/sc_mrkti/ibinddc/engdoc/
1a1a43.html*
A service of Industry Canada, the site provides
U.S. Department of Commerce reports on
Senegalese economic trends, trade regulations
and standards, investment climate, trade and

project financing, business travel, and market
opportunities.

Senegal Online
http://www.teranga.com/uk/index.html
Posted in English and French, the site delivers
Senegalese fact sheets, maps, and city profiles
of Dakar, Kaolack, Saint Louis, Tambacounda,
and Touba.

Who's Doing Business in Senegal
http://www.earth2000.com/senegal/bi/firms.html
A directory of local and international companies
in Senegal, the site lists over 50 operations
including Exxon, IBM, Philip Mobil Oil, Morris, 3M
Company, and Xerox.

Senegal Trade Assistance

Trade Point Dakar
*http://www.untpdc.org/incubator/sen/tpdkr/
welcome.html*
Part of the United Nations Global Trade Point
Network, the site provides Dakar trade leads,
market bulletins, and contact information.

Senegal Representative Offices

Canada

Embassy of Canada in Dakar
*http://www.dfait-maeci.gc.ca/english/missions/rep-
can4e.htm#senegal*
The site provides contact information for the
Canadian Embassy in Dakar.

France

French Trade Commission in Dakar
http://www.dree.org/senegal/
Posted in French, the site delivers Senegalese
market reports, sector profiles, contact information, and a directory of French export promotion
services.

India

Indian Commercial Mission in Dakar
http://www.nic.in/commin/ICM.HTM
The site lists the street address, phone and fax
numbers, and e-mail link of the Indian Commercial Mission in Dakar.

Malaysia

Embassy of Malaysia in Dakar
http://www.mnet.com.my/klonline/www/missions/malmiss/msenegal.htm
The site provides contact information for the Malaysian Embassy in Dakar.

Spain

Spanish Commercial Office in Dakar
http://www.icex.es/openURL.html#openURL=/english/infoproyem/ofcomes/ofcomes.html#AF
The site lists the staff, street address, phone and fax numbers, and e-mail link of the Spanish Commercial Office in Dakar.

Taiwan

Taiwan Government Information Office in Dakar
http://www.gio.gov.tw/info/ngio/seneg-f.html
Posted in Chinese and English, the site lists the street address, phone and fax numbers, and e-mail link of the Taiwan Government Information Office in Dakar.

Thailand

Royal Thai Embassy in Dakar
http://www.mfa.go.th/Embassy/detail/58.htm
The site lists the Ambassador, street address, and phone and fax numbers of the Thai Embassy in Dakar.

United Kingdom

Embassy of Britain in Dakar
http://www.fco.gov.uk/directory/posts.asp?SD
The site provides contact information for the British Embassy in Dakar.

United States

Doing Business in Senegal: Facilitation Page
http://www.dakarcom.com/
Prepared by the U.S. Embassy, the site delivers Senegalese business guides, investment primers, tender bulletins, and a directory of U.S. companies in Senegal.

United States Embassy in Dakar
http://www.usia.gov/abtusia/posts/SG1/wwwhemb.html
Along with Senegal market reports and business contacts, the virtual Embassy provides U.S. fact sheets, visa and passport information, and a directory of consular and commercial services.

United States Information Service in Senegal
http://www.usia.gov/abtusia/posts/SG1/wwwhusis.html
Posted in English and French, the site offers U.S. electronic bulletins, fact sheets, economic reports, cultural information, and a directory of U.S.-Senegal educational and exchange programs

Seychelles

Seychelles Market Guides

Country Profile: Seychelles
http://www.mbendi.co.za/cysecy.htm
Developed by MBendi, the site provides Seychelles fact sheets, maps, sector profiles, exchange rates, travel information, and business contacts.

Index on Seychelles
http://www.africaindex.africainfo.no/africaindex1/countries/seychelles.html
A service of the Norwegian Council for Africa, the site is a directory of Seychelles resources online. Categories include culture, economy, news, and tourism.

Seychelles Country Brief
http://www.worldbank.org/cgi-bin/sendoff.cgi?page=%2Fhtml%2Fextdr%2Foffrep%2Fafr%2Fsc.htm
A service of the World Bank Group, the site provides Seychelles population statistics, financial data, development reports, and economic forecasts.

Seychelles: A Country Study
http://lcweb2.loc.gov/frd/cs/sctoc.html
A service of the U.S. Library of Congress, the site delivers fact sheets on Seychelles geography, people, agriculture, mining, manufacturing, and foreign economic relations.

Seychelles InfoExport
http://www.infoexport.gc.ca/country-e.asp?continent=Africa&country=41
A service of Foreign Affairs and International Trade Canada, the site provides fact sheets and statistics on Seychelles geography, business and politics.

Seychelles Market Research
http://strategis.ic.gc.ca/sc_mrkti/ibinddc/engdoc/1a1a44.html
Posted by Industry Canada, the site provides U.S. Central Intelligence Agency fact sheets on Seychelles geography, people, government, economy, communications, and transportation.

Seychelles Trade Assistance

Seychelles International Business Authority
http://www.seychelles.net/siba/index.html
A virtual library of business information, the site features Seychelles transportation guides, infrastructure bulletins, investment primers, and free trade zone information.

Seychelles International Trade Zone
http://www.seychelles.net/siba/seyfut.html
A guide to the Seychelles free trade zone, the site includes facility reports, taxation information, incentive guides, and license fee schedules.

United Kingdom

High Commission of Britain in Victoria
http://www.fco.gov.uk/directory/posts.asp?SE
The site provides contact information for the British High Commission in Victoria.

Sierra Leone

Sierra Leone Market Guides

Country Profile: Sierra Leone
http://www.mbendi.co.za/cyslcy.htm
Developed by MBendi, the site provides Sierra Leonean fact sheets, maps, sector profiles, exchange rates, travel information, and business contacts.

Index on Sierra Leone
http://www.africaindex.africainfo.no/africaindex1/countries/sierraleone.html
A service of the Norwegian Council for Africa, the site is a directory of Sierra Leonean resources online. Categories include culture, economy, news, and tourism.

Sierra Leone Country Brief
http://www.worldbank.org/cgi-bin/sendoff.cgi?page=%2Fhtml%2Fextdr%2Foffrep%2Fafr%2Fsl.htm
A service of the World Bank Group, the site provides Sierra Leonean population statistics, financial data, development reports, and economic forecasts.

Sierra Leone Market Research
http://strategis.ic.gc.ca/sc_mrkti/ibinddc/engdoc/1a1a45.html
Posted by Industry Canada, the site provides U.S. Central Intelligence Agency fact sheets on Sierra Leonean geography, people, government, economy, communications, and transportation.

Sierra Leone Page
http://www.sas.upenn.edu/African_Studies/Country_Specific/S_Leone.html
A service of the African Studies Center at the University of Pennsylvania, the site is a directory of Sierra Leonean resources online. Categories include country guides, languages, and maps.

Sierra Leone Representative Offices

Ghana

High Commission of Ghana in Freetown
http://www.juntung.com/ghana-consul-hk/2misabo.htm
The site provides contact information for the Ghanaian High Commission in Freetown.

United Kingdom

High Commission of Britain in Freetown
http://www.fco.gov.uk/directory/posts.asp?SF
The site provides contact information for the British High Commission in Freetown.

Somalia

Somalia Media

Somali News Page
http://www.etek.chalmers.se/~e3hassan/news.html
Along with world and regional headlines, the site provides Somali news, editorials, photos, political bulletins, weather information, and a searchable archive of past issues.

Somalia Market Guides

Country Profile: Somalia
http://www.mbendi.co.za/cysocy.htm
Developed by MBendi, the site provides Somali fact sheets, maps, sector profiles, exchange rates, travel information, and business contacts.

Index on Somolia

http://www.africaindex.africainfo.no/africaindex1/
countries/somalia.html
A service of the Norwegian Council for Africa, the site is a directory of Somali resources online. Categories include culture, economy, news, and tourism.

Somali Net

http://somalinet.com/
Posted in English and Somali, the site delivers Somali headlines, business reports, company directories, arts and culture bulletins, online discussion forums, and mailing lists.

Somalia Country Brief

http://www.worldbank.org/cgi-bin/
sendoff.cgi?page=%2Fhtml%2Fextdr%2Foffrep%2
Fafr%2Fso.htm
A service of the World Bank Group, the site provides Somali population statistics, financial data, development reports, and economic forecasts.

Somalia Country Profile

http://198.76.84.1/HORN/somalia/somalia.html
A service of the Greater Horn Information Exchange, the site provides Somali situation reports, fact sheets, socioeconomic statistics, health profiles, and crop and food supply assessments.

Somalia: A Country Study

http://lcweb2.loc.gov/frd/cs/sotoc.html
A service of the U.S. Library of Congress, the site delivers fact sheets on Somali geography, people, agriculture, mining, manufacturing, and foreign economic relations.

Somalia InfoExport

http://www.infoexport.gc.ca/country-
e.asp?continent=Africa&country=43
A service of Foreign Affairs and International Trade Canada, the site provides fact sheets and statistics on Somali geography, business, and politics.

Somalia Market Research

http://strategis.ic.gc.ca/sc_mrkti/ibinddc/engdoc/
1a1a46.html
Posted by Industry Canada, the site provides U.S. Central Intelligence Agency fact sheets on Somali geography, people, government, economy, communications, and transportation.

South Africa

South Africa Search Tools

Ananzi

http://www.ananzi.co.za/
A web navigation service, the site is a searchable directory of South African resources online. Categories include business and commerce, environment and agriculture, and politics and government.

South Africa Media

Business Day

http://www.bday.co.za/
Updated daily, the site offers South African business headlines, sector profiles, exchange rates, editorials, a news archive, and reports in streaming audio.

Business Times Online

http://www.btimes.co.za/
Updated weekly, the electronic newspaper delivers South African business news, company reports, executive profiles, labor guides, and personal calculators.

South Africa Media

http://www.mediainfo.com/emediajs/specific-
geo.htm?region=southafrica
Developed by Editor and Publisher Interactive, the site is an index of South African media sites online including city guides, magazines, newspapers, news services, and radio and television stations.

South Africa Market Guides

Africa.Com

http://africa.com/
A virtual library of country and regional information, the site provides South African news, business reports, political bulletins, history lessons, travel information, and web guides.

Barclays Country Report: South Africa

http://www.offshorebanking.barclays.com/
services/economic/yearly/safoct97/index.html
Prepared by Barclays Bank, the site reports on South African economic trends, politics, monetary and fiscal policy, and U.K.-South Africa merchandise trade and investment flows.

Best South African Manufactured Products
http://www.expo.co.za/
A directory of South African manufacturers and products, the site is divided into 14 categories including agriculture, chemicals, electronics, engineering, machinery, mining, and safety and security.

Business and Economy
http://www.southafrica.net/economy/default.html
A service of the South African Embassy in Washington, D.C., the site delivers South African sector profiles, investment guides, and an opportunities bulletin board.

Central Statistical Service
http://www.css.gov.za/
Along with publication lists and user guides, the site provides fact sheets and statistics on South African people, tourism, housing, manufacturing, mining, international trade, and other economic indicators.

Country Profile: South Africa
http://www.mbendi.co.za/cysacy.htm
Developed by MBendi, the site provides South African fact sheets, maps, sector profiles, exchange rates, travel information, international trade reports, and business contacts.

Council for Scientific and Industrial Research
http://www.csir.co.za/
Based in Pretoria, the Council is a South African research and development network. The site includes press releases, technology bulletins, mining research news, and contact information.

Doing Business in South Africa
http://mbendi.co.za/werksmns/lexaf/bussa.htm
Written by the Werksmans law firm, the site delivers fact sheets on South African business formation, taxation, foreign investment, exchange controls, and intellectual property.

Executives Association of Southern Africa
http://www.grg.pix.za/business/exas/index.html
A South African networking forum, the site includes a mission statement, member directory, event information, and a speaker roster.

Index on South Africa
http://www.africaindex.africainfo.no/africaindex1/countries/rsa.html
A service of the Norwegian Council for Africa, the site is a directory of South African resources online. Categories include culture, economy, news, tourism, and politics.

Investment Profile: South Africa
http://www.mbendi.co.za/ernsty/cysaeyip.htm
A service of Ernst & Young, the site provides fact sheets on South African business establishments, taxation, exchange controls, visa requirements, and foreign investment regulations.

Investment South Africa
http://www.isa.org.za/
A virtual investment primer, the site provides South African business guides, incentive information, company profiles, international comparisons, and a directory of investment opportunities.

National Economic Development and Labour Council
http://www.nedlac.org.za/
Founded in 1995, the Council promotes economic development in South Africa. The site includes news, annual reports, event information, and a virtual library of labor and business legislation.

South Africa: Big Emerging Markets Homepage
http://www.ita.doc.gov/bems/Safrica.html
Developed by the United States Department of Commerce, the site delivers South African fact sheets, economic forecasts, export and import statistics, sector profiles, and international trade guides.

South Africa Business Briefs
http://www.austrade.gov.au/IOOM/SthAfrica/
A service of Austrade, the site offers fact sheets on South African business etiquette, foreign investment, corporate taxation, marketing, and visas.

South Africa Country Brief
http://www.worldbank.org/cgi-bin/sendoff.cgi?page=%2Fhtml%2Fextdr%2Foffrep%2Fafr%2Fza.htm
A service of the World Bank Group, the site provides South African population statistics, financial data, development reports, and economic forecasts.

South Africa Country Profile
http://www.tradenz.govt.nz/intelligence/profiles/south_africa.html
A service of the New Zealand Trade Development Board, the site provides South African economic statistics, market information, and business tips.

South Africa Country Report

http://www.state.gov/www/issues/economic/ trade_reports/africa97/south_africa97.html
Prepared by the U.S. Department of State, the site delivers information on South African exchange rates, debt management, trade barriers, export subsidies, intellectual property protection, worker rights, and foreign investment.

South Africa InfoExport

http://www.infoexport.gc.ca/country- e.asp?continent=Africa&country=44
A service of Foreign Affairs and International Trade Canada, the site provides South African commercial guides and market reports.

South Africa Market Access Database

http://mkaccdb.eu.int/mkdb/ mkdb.pl?METHOD=COUNTRY
A service of the European Commission, the site offers briefs on South African trade policy, tariff barriers, non-tariff barriers, investment-related measures, and financial services regulations.

South Africa Market Information

http://dtiinfo1.dti.gov.uk/ots/south_africa/
A service of the London-based Department of Trade and Industry, the site delivers South African fact sheets, maps, and trade-show information.

South Africa Market Research

http://strategis.ic.gc.ca/sc_mrkti/ibinddc/engdoc/ 1a1a47.html
A service of Industry Canada, the site provides U.S. Department of Commerce reports on South African economic trends, trade regulations and standards, investment climate, trade and project financing, business travel, and market opportunities.

South African Business Directory

http://os2.iafrica.com/w3/bus_dir.htm
A directory of South African companies, the site profiles operations in over 30 categories including food and beverage products, manufacturing, retail, and transportation.

South African Investors Library

http://sunsite.sut.ac.jp/embassy/jasanet/eco- nomic/ilibrary.htm
A service of the South African Embassy in Tokyo, the site is a searchable library of South African business guides, investment primers, magazines, and newspapers.

Welcome to South Africa

http://www.southafrica.net/
A service of the South African Embassy in Washington, D.C., the site provides fact sheets on South African business, government, tourism, and arts and culture.

South Africa Trade Assistance

Are You Export Ready?

http://wwwdti.pwv.gov.za/export/Questionnaire.htm
A self-assessment test for exporters, the service rates the export readiness of South African businesspeople based on a series of questions related to exporting and international business management.

Department of Trade and Industry

http://wwwdti.pwv.gov.za/dtiwww/
Based in Pretoria, the Department promotes South African exports and international investment. The site includes export guides, incentive information, and international trade statistics.

ExiNet Business and Trade Opportunities

http://www.exinet.co.za/exinet.html
Along with employment opportunities and a virtual marketplace of buy and sell offers, the site provides a directory of South African companies in ten categories including international trade, environment, and publishing.

Export Help Desk

http://wwwdti.pwv.gov.za/export/Export_HD.asp
Sponsored by the Department of Trade and Industry, the service allows a user to submit questions about exporting goods and services from South Africa. Export specialists review the questions and provide answers by e-mail.

Foreign Offices

http://wwwdti.pwv.gov.za/dtiwww/ foreign_offices.htm
The site is a directory of South African Embassies, High Commissions, and Consulates in over 40 countries including Argentina, Australia, India, Mexico, and Spain.

Export Information Exchange

http://wwwdti.pwv.gov.za/export/EIE.asp
A virtual library of international trade information, the site features fact sheets and discussion forums on export finance, freight and shipping, and other global business topics.

Global Trade Centre

http://www.gtrade.co.za/
An international trade gateway, the site is a directory of South African exporters and importers in over 20 categories including construction, education and training, financial services, and manufacturing.

Seaports in South Africa

http://www.freightworld.com/port_geo.html#5
A service of Freightworld, the site is a directory of seven South African seaports online including Cape Town, Durban, East London, Mossel Bay, and Port Elizabeth.

South African Trade Center

http://www.satcis.com/
Along with investment guides and travel information, the site is a directory of South African business opportunities including companies for sale, equity partners sought, and venture capital funding required.

Trade Page South Africa

http://www.tradepage.co.za/
A browsable index of South African exporters and importers, the site profiles operations in over 30 industries including electronics, printing, tourism, packaging, and steel.

Trade Shows in South Africa

http://www.expoguide.com/shows/data/loc_56.htm
Compiled by Expoguide, the site is a directory of upcoming trade shows in South Africa.

South Africa Representative Offices

Australia

Austrade in Johannesburg

http://www.austrade.gov.au/Johannesburg/
An Australian trade promotion service, the site provides a mission statement, market reports, and contact information for Austrade in Johannesburg.

Austria

Austrian Trade Commission in Johannesburg

http://aw.wk.or.at/awo/ahst-johannesburg.htm
The site lists the staff, street address, phone and fax numbers, e-mail link, and office hours of the Austrian Trade Commission in Johannesburg.

Belgium

Consulate of Belgium in Port Elizabeth

http://users.iafrica.com/j/jv/jvds/consulwelcome.html
Posted in English and Flemish, the site delivers Belgian fact sheets, business reports, visa and passport information, travel primers, and web guides.

Canada

Canadian Government Trade Office in Johannesburg

http://www.dfait-maeci.gc.ca/southafrica/indextrd.htm
Written in English and French, the site provides Canadian news, fact sheets, investment primers, reports on Canada-South Africa trade and relations, and a directory of commercial services.

Canadian High Commission in Pretoria

http://www.canada.co.za/index.htm
Featuring a message from the High Commissioner, the site features Canadian fact sheets, visa and passport information, and South Africa travel guides.

Finland

Finland Trade Center in Johannesburg

http://www.finland.co.za/
Along with contact information, the site provides Finnish fact sheets, international trade statistics, and a directory of commercial services.

France

French Trade Commission in Cape Town

http://www.dree.org/afriquedusud/francais/general/pee/lecap.htm
The site lists the mission statement, street address, phone and fax numbers, and e-mail link of the French Trade Commission in Cape Town.

French Trade Commission in Johannesburg

http://www.dree.org/afriquedusud/francais/general/pee/joburg.htm
The site lists the mission statement, street address, phone and fax numbers, and e-mail link of the French Trade Commission in Johannesburg.

French Trade Commission in Pretoria
*http://www.dree.org/afriquedusud/francais/general/
pee/pretoria.htm*
The site lists the mission statement, street
address, phone and fax numbers, and e-mail link
of the French Trade Commission in Pretoria.

French Trade Commission in South Africa
http://www.dree.org/afriquedusud/
Posted in French, the site delivers South African
market reports, sector profiles, contact information, and a directory of French export promotion
services.

Germany

German Chamber of Commerce in Johannesburg
http://www.ahk.net/en/za/Johannesburg/
The site lists the Chairperson, Chief Executive
Officer, street address, phone and fax numbers,
e-mail link, and office hours of the German
Chamber of Commerce in Johannesburg.

India

Consulate General of India in Johannesburg
http://www.indconjoburg.co.za/
Along with fact sheets and maps, the site delivers
Indian news, visa and passport information,
business guides, and reports on India-South
Africa trade and relations.

Italy

Italian Trade Commission in Johannesburg
http://www.ice.it/estero/johannesburg/
Posted in Italian, the site features Italian fact
sheets, government directories, business
guides, travel information, and reports on Italy-
South Africa trade and relations.

Japan

Japan External Trade Organization in Johannesburg
http://www.jetro.co.za/
A Japanese trade promotion service, the site
features Japanese news, fact sheets, event
information, publications, and reports on Japan-
South Africa trade and relations.

Malaysia

High Commission of Malaysia in Pretoria
*http://www.mnet.com.my/klonline/www/missions/
malmiss/msouthaf1.htm*
The site provides contact information for the
Malaysian High Commission in Pretoria.

Trade Commission of Malaysia in Johannesburg
*http://www.mnet.com.my/klonline/www/missions/
malmiss/msouthaf2.htm*
The site provides contact information for the
Malaysian Trade Commission in Johannesburg.

Namibia

High Commission of Namibia in Pretoria
http://www.republicofnamibia.com/adress.htm
Along with a directory of Namibian companies
and government agencies, the site provides
contact information for the Namibian Embassy in
Pretoria.

Netherlands

Royal Netherlands Consulate in Cape Town
http://users.iafrica.com/n/nl/nlgovkaa/
Along with press releases and visa information,
the site features Dutch business guides, economic bulletins, and reports on Dutch-South
Africa trade and relations.

South Africa Netherlands Chamber of Commerce
*http://users.iafrica.com/n/nl/nlgovkaa/pages/
economy%20trade/c_sanec.html*
Established in 1992, the Chamber promotes
Dutch-South Africa trade. The site includes a
mission statement, activity reports, and contact
information.

New Zealand

Trade New Zealand in Johannesburg
http://www.tradenz.govt.nz/contact/pacific.html
An export promotion service, the site provides
contact information for the Trade New Zealand
office in Johannesburg.

Norway

Norwegian Trade Council in Johannesburg
*http://www.ntc.no/cgi-bin/wbch.exe?html=../
templates/utekontor2.html&profile=1113*
The site lists the staff, street address, phone and
fax numbers, and e-mail link of the Norwegian
Trade Council in Johannesburg.

Pakistan

Pakistan Trade Office in Johannesburg
http://www.jamal.com/epb/ptoa.htm
The site provides contact information for the Pakistan Trade Office in Johannesburg.

Philippines

Philippine Trade and Investment Promotion Office in Johannesburg
http://www.dti.gov.ph/jnb/
The site provides a mission statement, service directory, and contact information for the Philippine Trade Office in Johannesburg.

Portugal

Portuguese Trade and Investment Office in Johannesburg
http://www.portugal.org/geninfo/abouticep/joanesburgo.html
The site lists the staff, street address, phone and fax numbers, and e-mail link of the Portuguese Trade and Investment Office in Johannesburg.

Singapore

High Commission of Singapore in Pretoria
http://www.gov.sg/mfa/consular/mww_s.htm
The site provides contact information for the Singapore High Commission in Pretoria.

Spain

Spanish Commercial Office in Johannesburg
http://www.icex.es/openURL.html#openURL=/english/infoproyem/ofcomes/ofcomes.html#AF
The site lists the staff, street address, phone and fax numbers, and e-mail link of the Spanish Commercial Office in Johannesburg.

Sweden

Swedish Business Association in South Africa
http://www.swedishtrade.org.za/sba.htm
Based in Johannesburg, the Association promotes Swedish-South African trade. The site includes a mission statement and contact information.

Taiwan

Taiwan Government Information Office in Johannesburg
http://www.gio.gov.tw/info/ngio/south-f.html

Posted in Chinese and English, the site lists the street address, phone and fax numbers, and e-mail link of the Taiwan Government Information Office in Johannesburg.

Tanzania

Embassy of Tanzania in Johannesburg
http://www.tanzania-online.gov.uk/visa/envoys.html
The site provides contact information for the Tanzanian Embassy in Johannesburg.

Thailand

Royal Thai Embassy in Pretoria
http://www.mfa.go.th/Embassy/detail/80.htm
The site lists the Ambassador, street address, and phone and fax numbers of the Thai Embassy in Pretoria.

Thailand Office of Commercial Affairs in Pretoria
http://www.thaitrade.com/thcoaf.html
The site lists the street address, phone and fax numbers, and e-mail link of the Thailand Office of Commercial Affairs in Pretoria.

United Kingdom

Britain in South Africa
http://www.britain.org.za/
Along with economic news and event information, the site delivers British fact sheets, press releases, investment guides, and a directory of consular and commercial services.

British Consulate General in Johannesburg
http://www.britain.org.za/mission/jhb.html
Along with contact information and a staff roster, the site provides a directory of British commercial services including export counseling and business matchmaking.

British Consulate in Durban
http://www.britain.org.za/mission/bc_durb.html
Along with a directory of British consular and commercial services, the site lists the staff, street address, and phone and fax numbers of the British Consulate in Durban.

British High Commission in Cape Town
http://www.britain.org.za/mission/bhc_cape.html
The site lists the High Commissioner, street address, and phone and fax numbers of the British High Commission in Cape Town.

British High Commission in Pretoria

http://www.britain.org.za/mission/
bhc_pretoria.html
The site lists the High Commissioner, Deputy High Commissioner, street address, and phone and fax numbers of the British High Commission in Pretoria.

United States

California Office of Trade and Investment in South Africa

http://www.cotisa.co.za/
Based in Johannesburg, the Office promotes California products and services in South Africa. The site provides South African market reports, and a directory of California companies in South Africa.

United States Mission to South Africa

http://www.usia.gov/abtusia/posts/SF1/
wwwhmain.html
Along with South African commercial guides and sector profiles, the site provides U.S. visa and passport information, reports on U.S.-South Africa trade and relations, and a directory of consular and commercial services.

United States Information Service in Pretoria

http://www.usia.gov/abtusia/posts/SF1/
wwwhis1.html
The site offers U.S. news, press releases, fact sheets, electronic journals, economic reports, cultural information, and a directory of U.S.-South Africa educational and exchange programs.

Sudan

Sudan Market Guides

Country Profile: Sudan

http://www.mbendi.co.za/cysucy.htm
Developed by MBendi, the site provides Sudanese fact sheets, maps, sector profiles, exchange rates, travel information, and business contacts.

Index on Sudan

http://www.africaindex.africainfo.no/africaindex1/
countries/sudan.html
A service of the Norwegian Council for Africa, the site is a directory of Sudanese resources online. Categories include culture, economy, news, and tourism.

Republic of Sudan

http://www.columbia.edu/~tm146/sudan.html
A country fact sheet, the site provides Sudanese maps, climate information, travel guides, photo galleries, music samples, education bulletins, and web guides.

Sudan Country Brief

http://www.worldbank.org/cgi-bin/
sendoff.cgi?page=%2Fhtml%2Fextdr%2Foffrep%2
Fafr%2Fsd.htm
A service of the World Bank Group, the site provides Sudanese population statistics, financial data, development reports, and economic forecasts.

Sudan Country Profile

http://198.76.84.1/HORN/sudan/sudan/
sudan.html
A service of the Greater Horn Information Exchange, the site provides Sudanese situation reports, fact sheets, socioeconomic statistics, health profiles, and crop and food supply assessments.

Sudan: A Country Study

http://lcweb2.loc.gov/frd/cs/sdtoc.html
A service of the U.S. Library of Congress, the site delivers fact sheets on Sudanese geography, people, agriculture, mining, manufacturing, and foreign economic relations.

Sudan InfoExport

http://www.infoexport.gc.ca/country-
e.asp?continent=Africa&country=45
A service of Foreign Affairs and International Trade Canada, the site provides fact sheets and statistics on Sudanese geography, business and politics.

Sudan Market Research

http://strategis.ic.gc.ca/sc_mrkti/ibinddc/engdoc/
1a1a49.html
Posted by Industry Canada, the site provides U.S. Central Intelligence Agency fact sheets on Sudanese geography, people, government, economy, communications, and transportation.

Sudan Page

http://www.sudan.net/
A virtual library of country information, the site delivers Sudanese news, maps, fact sheets, company directories, history lessons, language primers, discussion forums, weather information, and a list of Sudanese Embassies.

Sudan Virtual Library
http://menic.utexas.edu/menic/countries/
sudan.html
Developed by the Center for Middle Eastern Studies at the University of Texas, the site is a directory of Sudanese resources online. Categories include education, general information, and news and current events.

Sudan Representative Offices

United Kingdom

Embassy of Britain in Khartoum
http://www.fco.gov.uk/directory/posts.asp?SS
The site provides contact information for the British Embassy in Khartoum.

Swaziland

Swaziland Media

Swaziland Media
http://www.mediainfo.com/emediajs/specific-geo.htm?region=swaziland
Developed by Editor and Publisher Interactive, the site is an index of Swazi city guides, newspapers, and other media sites online.

Swazi Observer
http://www.swaziobserver.sz/
Updated daily, the site provides Swazi headlines, editorials, photos, business reports, letters to the editor, and a searchable archive of past issues.

Swaziland Market Guides

Country Profile: Swaziland
http://www.mbendi.co.za/cyswcy.htm
Developed by MBendi, the site provides Swazi fact sheets, maps, sector profiles, exchange rates, travel information, and business contacts.

Doing Business in Swaziland
http://mbendi.co.za/werksmns/lexaf/bussw.htm
Written by the law firm of Robinson Bertram, the site delivers fact sheets on Swazi business formation, taxation, foreign investment, exchange controls, and intellectual property.

Index on Swaziland
http://www.africaindex.africainfo.no/africaindex1/
countries/swaziland.html
A service of the Norwegian Council for Africa, the site is a directory of Swazi resources online.

Categories include culture, economy, news, and tourism.

Investment Profile: Swaziland
http://www.mbendi.co.za/ernsty/cysweyip.htm
A service of Ernst & Young, the site provides fact sheets on Swazi business, taxation, exchange controls, visa requirements, and foreign investment regulations.

Swaziland Business Internet Directory
http://www.realnet.co.sz/real/business.html
An index of Swazi companies online, the site is divided into 20 categories including computing, electronics, transportation, construction, education, and international trade.

Swaziland Business Today
http://www.realnet.co.sz/businessday/
szbtoday.html
A virtual library of business information, the site provides Swazi company directories, economic reports, exchange rates, annual reports, and development plans.

Swaziland Business Yearbook
http://www.realnet.co.sz/real/sbyb/sbyb.html
A virtual commercial guide, the site delivers Swazi fact sheets, government directories, cost of living comparisons, investment guides, and city profiles.

Swaziland Country Brief
http://www.worldbank.org/cgi-bin/
sendoff.cgi?page=%2Fhtml%2Fextdr%2Foffrep%0
2Fafr%2Fsz.htm
A service of the World Bank Group, the site provides Swazi population statistics, financial data, development reports, and economic forecasts.

Swaziland E-mail Directory
http://www.directory.sz/email/
A directory of over 800 Swazi e-mail addresses, the site is searchable by family name and organization. Users may add their name to the database at no charge.

Swaziland InfoExport
http://www.infoexport.gc.ca/country-
e.asp?continent=Africa&country=46
A service of Foreign Affairs and International Trade Canada, the site provides fact sheets and statistics on Swazi geography, business and politics.

Swaziland Market Research
http://strategis.ic.gc.ca/sc_mrkti/ibinddc/engdoc/1a1a50.html
A service of Industry Canada, the site provides U.S. Department of Commerce reports on Swazi economic trends, trade regulations and standards, investment climate, trade and project financing, business travel, and market opportunities.

Swaziland on the Internet
http://www.realnet.co.sz/
A virtual country gateway, the site provides Swazi business contacts, tourism information, culture guides, classifieds, government directories, and tender notices.

Swaziland Representative Offices

Diplomatic Offices
http://www.realnet.co.sz/real/sbyb/diplomat.html
A service of the Swaziland Business Year Book, the site is a directory of foreign embassies and consulates in Swaziland, and Swaziland Embassies and Consulates around the world.

United Kingdom

High Commission of Britain in Mbabane
http://www.fco.gov.uk/directory/posts.asp?SV
The site provides contact information for the British High Commission in Mbabane.

Tanzania

Tanzania Media

Tanzania Media
http://www.mediainfo.com/emediajs/specific-geo.htm?region=tanzania
Developed by Editor and Publisher Interactive, the site is an index of Tanzanian newspapers, radio stations, and other media sites online.

Tanzania Market Guides

Country Profile: Tanzania
http://www.mbendi.co.za/cytacy.htm
Developed by MBendi, the site provides Tanzanian fact sheets, maps, sector profiles, exchange rates, travel information, and business contacts.

Index on Tanzania
http://www.africaindex.africainfo.no/africaindex1/countries/tanzania.html
A service of the Norwegian Council for Africa, the site is a directory of Tanzanian resources online. Categories include culture, economy, news, and tourism.

Investment Profile: Tanzania
http://www.mbendi.co.za/ernsty/cytaeyip.htm
A service of Ernst & Young, the site provides fact sheets on Tanzanian business establishments, taxation, exchange controls, visa requirements, and foreign investment regulations.

Tanzania Country Brief
http://www.worldbank.org/cgi-bin/sendoff.cgi?page=%2Fhtml%2Fextdr%2Foffrep%2Fafr%2Ftz.htm
A service of the World Bank Group, the site provides Tanzanian population statistics, financial data, development reports, and economic forecasts.

Tanzania InfoExport
http://www.infoexport.gc.ca/country-e.asp?continent=Africa&country=47
A service of Foreign Affairs and International Trade Canada, the site provides Tanzanian commercial guides and market reports.

Tanzania Market Information
http://dtiinfo1.dti.gov.uk/ots/tanzania/
A service of the London-based Department of Trade and Industry, the site delivers Tanzanian fact sheets, maps, and trade-show information.

Tanzania Market Research
http://strategis.ic.gc.ca/sc_mrkti/ibinddc/engdoc/1a1a51.html
A service of Industry Canada, the site provides U.S. Department of Commerce reports on Tanzanian economic trends, trade regulations and standards, investment climate, trade and project financing, business travel, and market opportunities.

Tanzania: Statistical Appendix
http://www.imf.org/external/pubs/CAT/longres.cfm?sk=2490.0
Prepared by the International Monetary Fund, the site provides fact sheets and statistics on Tanzanian gross domestic product, food production, international trade, interest rates, and consumer prices.

Tanzania Trade Assistance

Tanzania Envoys Abroad
http://www.tanzania-online.gov.uk/visa/envoys.html

Posted by the Tanzania High Commission in London, the site is a directory of Tanzanian Embassies and diplomatic posts in more than 20 countries including China, Germany, Egypt, and Japan.

Tanzania Representative Offices

Diplomatic Corps in Tanzania
http://www.tanzania-online.gov.uk/profile/ missions.html
A service of the Tanzania High Commission in London, the site is a directory of foreign diplomatic offices, embassies, high commissions, and consulates in Tanzania.

Canada

High Commission of Canada in Dar Es Salaam
http://www.dfait-maeci.gc.ca/english/missions/rep- can4e.htm#tanzania
The site provides contact information for the Canadian High Commission in Dar Es Salaam.

India

Indian Commercial Mission in Dar Es Salaam
http://www.nic.in/commin/ICM.HTM
The site lists the street address, phone and fax numbers, and e-mail link of the Indian Commercial Mission in Dar Es Salaam.

Sweden

Embassy of Sweden in Dar Es Salaam
http://www.ud.se/english/mfa/ambassad/ tanzania.htm
The site provides contact information for the Swedish Embassy in Dar Es Salaam.

United Kingdom

High Commission of Britain in Dar Es Salaam
http://www.fco.gov.uk/directory/posts.asp?TZ
The site provides contact information for the British High Commission in Dar Es Salaam.

United States

United States Embassy in Dar Es Salaam
http://www.cats-net.com/amemb/main.htm
Along with Tanzania travel guides, the virtual Embassy delivers U.S. fact sheets, visa and passport information, reports on U.S.-Tanzania

trade and relations, and a directory of U.S. companies in Tanzania.

Togo

Togo Market Guides

Country Profile: Togo
http://www.mbendi.co.za/cytocy.htm
Developed by MBendi, the site provides Togolese fact sheets, maps, sector profiles, exchange rates, travel information, and business contacts.

Index on Togo
http://www.africaindex.africainfo.no/africaindex1/ countries/togo.html
A service of the Norwegian Council for Africa, the site is a directory of Togolese resources online. Categories include culture, economy, news, and tourism.

Republic of Togo
http://www.republicoftogo.com/english/home.html
A portal of country information, the site provides Togolese fact sheets, economic reports, presidential statements, travel guides, and an event calendar.

Togo Country Brief
http://www.worldbank.org/cgi-bin/ sendoff.cgi?page=%2Fhtml%2Fextdr%2Foffrep%2 Fafr%2Ftg.htm
A service of the World Bank Group, the site provides Togolese population statistics, financial data, development reports, and economic forecasts.

Togo Market Research
http://strategis.ic.gc.ca/sc_mrkti/ibinddc/engdoc/ 1a1a52.html
A service of Industry Canada, the site provides U.S. Department of Commerce reports on Togolese economic trends, trade regulations and standards, investment climate, trade and project financing, business travel, and market opportunities.

Togo: Selected Issues
http://www.imf.org/external/pubs/CAT/ longres.cfm?sk=2546.0
Prepared by the International Monetary Fund, the site provides fact sheets and statistics on Togolese civil service employment, gross domestic product, manufacturing value added, and international trade.

Togo Trade Assistance

Togo Free Trade Zone
http://www.republicoftogo.com/english/ecozone.html
Along with contact information, the site provides fact sheets on the Togo Free Trade Zone, a business development area offering tax and tariff abatements for eligible companies.

Togo Representative Offices

Ghana

Embassy of Ghana in Lomé
http://www.juntung.com/ghana-consul-hk/2misabo.htm
The site provides contact information for the Ghanaian Embassy in Lomé .

Sweden

Consulate General of Sweden in Lomé
http://www.ud.se/english/mfa/ambassad/togo.htm
The site provides contact information for the Swedish Embassy in Lomé.

Tunisia

Tunisia Media

Tunisia Media
http://www.mediainfo.com/emediajs/specific-geo.htm?region=tunisia
Developed by Editor and Publisher Interactive, the site is an index of Tunisian radio stations and other media sites online.

Tunisia Market Guides

Country Profile: Tunisia
http://www.mbendi.co.za/cytucy.htm
Developed by MBendi, the site provides Tunisian fact sheets, maps, sector profiles, exchange rates, travel information, and business contacts.

Index on Tunisia
http://www.africaindex.africainfo.no/africaindex1/countries/tunisia.html
A service of the Norwegian Council for Africa, the site is a directory of Tunisian resources online. Categories include culture, economy, news, and tourism.

Invest in Tunisia
http://www.investintunisia.tn/
Along with maps and climate information, the site delivers Tunisian investment guides, privatization reports, and a database of business opportunities in 12 categories including food and beverage, pharmaceuticals, packaging, and transportation.

Investment Profile: Tunisia
http://www.mbendi.co.za/ernsty/cytueyip.htm
A service of Ernst & Young, the site provides fact sheets on Tunisian business, taxation, exchange controls, visa requirements, and foreign investment regulations.

Stelfair Tunisia
http://www.stelfair.com/tunisia/fairvirt.htm
A directory of Tunisian products and companies, the site is divided into 12 categories including retail, tourism, textiles, plastics, real estate, and transportation.

Tunisia Country Brief
http://www.worldbank.org/cgi-bin/sendoff.cgi?page=%2Fhtml%2Fextdr%2Foffrep%2Fmena%2Ftn.htm
A service of the World Bank Group, the site provides Tunisian population statistics, financial data, development reports, and economic forecasts.

Tunisia Country Profile
http://www.tradenz.govt.nz/intelligence/profiles/tunisia.html
A service of the New Zealand Trade Development Board, the site provides Tunisian economic statistics, market information, and business tips.

Tunisia Economy
http://www.tunisiaonline.com/html/economy.html
The site provides Tunisian development plans, banking reports, and statistics on gross domestic product, investment, international trade, and other economic indicators.

Tunisia Market Information
http://dtiinfo1.dti.gov.uk/ots/tunisia/
A service of the London-based Department of Trade and Industry, the site delivers Tunisian fact sheets, maps, and trade-show information.

Tunisia Market Research
http://strategis.ic.gc.ca/sc_mrkti/ibinddc/engdoc/1a1a53.html
A service of Industry Canada, the site provides

U.S. Department of Commerce reports on Tunisian economic trends, trade regulations and standards, investment climate, trade and project financing, business travel, and market opportunities.

Tunisia Online
http://www.tunisiaonline.com/
A digital country gateway, the site delivers Tunisian fact sheets, history lessons, government directories, economic bulletins, tourism information, and culture guides.

Tunisia Virtual Library
http://menic.utexas.edu/menic/countries/ tunisia.html
A service of the Center for Middle Eastern Studies at the University of Texas, the site is a directory of Tunisian resources online. Categories include country guides, education, and general information.

Tunisinfo
http://www.tunisinfo.com/homeengl.htm
A hub of country information, the site provides Tunisian sector profiles, investment guides, tender notices, accommodation directories, and event information.

Tunisia Trade Assistance

Tunisia and the World
http://www.tunisiaworld.com/
Posted in English and French, the site features Tunisian foreign policy statements, and reports on diplomatic initiatives in Asia, the Middle East, Africa, and North and South America.

Tunisia Representative Offices

Austria

Austrian Trade Commission in Tunis
http://aw.wk.or.at/awo/ahst-tunis.htm
The site lists the staff, street address, phone and fax numbers, e-mail link, and office hours of the Austrian Trade Commission in Tunisia.

Canada

Embassy of Canada in Tunis
http://www.dfait-maeci.gc.ca/english/missions/ rep-can4e.htm#tunisia
The site provides contact information for the Canadian Embassy in Tunis.

Germany

German Chamber of Commerce in Tunis
http://www.ahk.net/en/tn/Tunis/
The site lists the Chairperson, Chief Executive Officer, street address, phone and fax numbers, and e-mail link of the German Chamber in Tunis.

India

Indian Commercial Mission in Tunis
http://www.nic.in/commin/ICM.HTM
The site lists the street address, and phone and fax numbers of the Indian Commercial Mission in Tunis.

Portugal

Portuguese Trade and Investment Office in Tunis
http://www.portugal.org/geninfo/abouticep/ tunisia.html
The site lists the staff, street address, phone and fax numbers, and e-mail link of the Portuguese Trade and Investment Office in Tunis.

Spain

Spanish Commercial Office in Tunis
http://www.icex.es/openURL.html#openURL=/ english/infoproyem/ofcomes/ofcomes.html#AF
The site lists the staff, street address, and phone and fax numbers of the Spanish Commercial Office in Tunis.

Sweden

Embassy of Sweden in Tunis
http://www.ud.se/english/mfa/ambassad/ tunisien.htm
The site provides contact information for the Swedish Embassy in Tunis.

United Kingdom

British Embassy in Tunis
http://www.british-emb.intl.tn/
Posted in English and French, the site delivers Tunisian trade-show bulletins, British visa and passport information, and a directory of consular and commercial services.

Uganda

Uganda Media

The Monitor
http://www.africanews.com/monitor/
Updated daily, the site delivers Ugandan headlines, editorials, business reports, lifestyle
features, employment opportunities, and a
searchable archive of past issues.

Uganda Media
http://www.mediainfo.com/emediajs/specific-
geo.htm?region=uganda
Developed by Editor and Publisher Interactive, the
site is an index of Ugandan newspapers and
other media sites online.

Uganda Market Guides

Country Profile: Uganda
http://www.mbendi.co.za/cyugcy.htm
Developed by MBendi, the site provides Ugandan
fact sheets, maps, sector profiles, exchange
rates, travel information, and business contacts.

Government of Uganda
http://www.uganda.co.ug/Govern.htm
A directory of Ugandan government agencies
online, the site lists some 20 organizations
including the Ministries of Foreign Affairs, Trade
and Industry, and Energy and Minerals.

Index on Uganda
http://www.africaindex.africainfo.no/africaindex1/
countries/uganda.html
A service of the Norwegian Council for Africa, the
site is a directory of Ugandan resources online.
Categories include culture, economy, news, and
tourism.

Investment Profile: Uganda
http://www.mbendi.co.za/ernsty/cyugeyip.htm
A service of Ernst & Young, the site provides fact
sheets on Ugandan business establishments,
taxation, exchange controls, visa requirements,
and foreign investment regulations.

Privatization in Uganda
http://www.uganda.co.ug/perds/
A service of the Ministry of Finance, the site
delivers Ugandan fact sheets, privatization plans,
telecommunications market reports, and a
directory of multinationals in Uganda.

Uganda Country Brief
*http://www.worldbank.org/cgi-bin/
sendoff.cgi?page=%2Fhtml%2Fextdr%2Foffrep%2
Fafr%2Fug.htm*
A service of the World Bank Group, the site
provides Ugandan population statistics, financial
data, development reports, and economic
forecasts.

Uganda Country Profile
http://198.76.84.1/HORN/uganda/uganda.html
A service of the Greater Horn Information Exchange, the site provides Ugandan situation
reports, fact sheets, socioeconomic statistics,
health profiles, and crop and food supply assessments.

Uganda: A Country Study
http://lcweb2.loc.gov/frd/cs/ugtoc.html
A service of the U.S. Library of Congress, the site
delivers fact sheets on Ugandan geography,
people, agriculture, mining, manufacturing, and
foreign economic relations.

Uganda InfoExport
http://www.infoexport.gc.ca/country-
e.asp?continent=Africa&country=50
A service of Foreign Affairs and International
Trade Canada, the site provides fact sheets and
statistics on Ugandan geography, business, and
politics.

Uganda Manufacturers Association
http://www.nic.ug/tradepoint/html/uma.html
Based in Kampala, the Association promotes the
interests of Ugandan manufacturers. The site
includes a mission statement, membership
information, and a committee directory.

Uganda Market Research
http://strategis.ic.gc.ca/sc_mrkti/ibinddc/engdoc/
1a1a54.html
A service of Industry Canada, the site provides
U.S. Department of Commerce reports on
Ugandan economic trends, trade regulations and
standards, investment climate, trade and project
financing, business travel, and market opportunities.

Uganda National Chamber of Commerce and Industry
http://www.nic.ug/tradepoint/html/uncc.html
Created in 1978, the Chamber promotes economic development in Uganda. The site reviews
the history, objectives, and international affilia-
tions of the organization.

Uganda Online National Information Center
http://www.nic.ug/
An online country gateway, the site delivers Ugandan news, fact sheets, investment guides, company directories, tourism information, and education bulletins.

Uganda Pages
http://www.ugandapages.com/
A web hosting service, the site features Ugandan classifieds, chat services, event information, and Internet tutorials.

Uganda: Pearl of Africa
http://www.uganda.co.ug/
A hub of country information, the site delivers Ugandan news, company directories, sector profiles, tourism guides, political bulletins, and presidential speeches.

Uganda Trade Assistance

Uganda Clearing and Forwarding Agents Association
http://www.nic.ug/tradepoint/html/ucfa.html
An online alliance of Ugandan customs brokers and freight forwarders, the site provides a member directory, and fee schedules for the clearance of surface traffic, air freight, and exports.

Uganda Export Promotion Board
http://www.nic.ug/tradepoint/html/uepb.html
Established in 1983, the Board promotes Ugandan exports and international investment. The service includes Ugandan trade statistics, product catalogs, and export forecasts.

Uganda Ministry of Foreign Affairs
http://www.uganda.co.ug/govt9.htm
A directory of leading Ministry officials, the site lists the Ministers of State, and the Directors of Protocol, Multilateral Organizations, and Legal Treaties.

Uganda Ministry of Tourism, Trade and Industry
http://www.uganda.co.ug/govt18.htm
A directory of leading Ministry officials, the site lists the Directors of foreign trade, industry and technology, training, tourism, and economics.

Uganda Representative Offices

France

French Trade Commission in Kampala
http://www.dree.org/ouganda/
Posted in French, the site delivers Ugandan market reports, sector profiles, contact information, and a directory of French export promotion services.

India

Indian Commercial Mission in Kampala
http://www.nic.in/commin/ICM.HTM
The site lists the street address, phone and fax numbers, and e-mail link of the Indian Commercial Mission in Kampala.

Sweden

Embassy of Sweden in Kampala
http://www.ud.se/english/mfa/ambassad/uganda.htm
The site provides contact information for the Swedish Embassy in Kampala.

Tanzania

Embassy of Tanzania in Kampala
http://www.tanzania-online.gov.uk/visa/envoys.html
The site provides contact information for the Tanzanian Embassy in Kampala.

United Kingdom

High Commission of Britain in Kampala
http://www.fco.gov.uk/directory/posts.asp?UG
The site provides contact information for the British High Commission in Kampala.

Western Sahara

Western Sahara Market Guides

Country Profile: Western Sahara
http://www.mbendi.co.za/cywscy.htm
Developed by MBendi, the site provides Sahrawian fact sheets, maps, sector profiles, exchange rates, travel information, and business contacts.

Index on Western Sahara
http://www.africaindex.africainfo.no/africaindex1/countries/westsaha.html
A service of the Norwegian Council for Africa, the site is a directory of Sahrawian resources online. Categories include culture, economy, news, and tourism.

Western Sahara
http://www.arso.org//
Posted in five languages, the site provides Sahrawian fact sheets, electronic newspapers, human rights reports, and United Nations bulletins.

Western Sahara Market Research
http://strategis.ic.gc.ca/sc_mrkti/ibinddc/engdoc/1a1a55.html
Posted by Industry Canada, the site provides U.S. Central Intelligence Agency fact sheets on Sahrawian geography, people, government, economy, communications, and transportation.

Zambia

Zambia Media

Zambia Media
http://www.mediainfo.com/emediajs/specific-geo.htm?region=zambia
Developed by Editor and Publisher Interactive, the site is an index of Zambian newspapers and other media sites online.

Zambia Daily Mail
http://www.zamnet.zm/zamnet/zadama/zadama.html
Along with regional and world news, the English language newspaper provides Zambian headlines, business reports, editorials, and political bulletins.

Zambia Market Guides

Barclay's Country Report: Zambia
http://www.offshorebanking.barclays.com/services/economic/yearly/zamaug97/zamcont.html
Prepared by Barclays Bank, the site reports on Zambian economic trends, politics, monetary and fiscal policy, and U.K.-Zambia merchandise trade and investment flows.

Country Commercial Guide
http://www.state.gov/www/about_state/business/com_guides/1998/africa/zambia98.html

Prepared by the U.S. Embassy in Lusaka, the site delivers primers on Zambian business, politics, trade regulations and standards, investment, and travel.

Country Profile: Zambia
http://www.mbendi.co.za/cyzacy.htm
Developed by MBendi, the site provides Zambian fact sheets, maps, sector profiles, exchange rates, travel information, and business contacts.

Index on Zambia
http://www.africaindex.africainfo.no/africaindex1/countries/zambia.html
A service of the Norwegian Council for Africa, the site is a directory of Zambian resources online. Categories include culture, economy, news, and tourism.

Investment Profile: Zambia
http://www.mbendi.co.za/ernsty/cyzaeyip.htm
A service of Ernst & Young, the site provides fact sheets on Zambian business establishments, taxation, exchange controls, visa requirements, and foreign investment regulations.

Zambia Country Brief
http://www.worldbank.org/cgi-bin/sendoff.cgi?page=%2Fhtml%2Fextdr%2Foffrep%2Fafr%2Fzm.htm
A service of the World Bank Group, the site provides Zambian population statistics, financial data, development reports, and economic forecasts.

Zambia InfoExport
http://www.infoexport.gc.ca/country-e.asp?continent=Africa&country=53
A service of Foreign Affairs and International Trade Canada, the site provides Zambian commercial guides and market reports.

Zambia Investment Center
http://www.zamnet.zm/zamnet/zambus/zic/zichome.html
Based in Lusaka, the Center promotes international investment in Zambia. The site includes a newsletter, incentive information, business guides, and employment opportunities.

Zambia Market Information
http://dtiinfo1.dti.gov.uk/ots/zambia/
A service of the London-based Department of Trade and Industry, the site delivers Zambian fact sheets, maps, and trade-show information.

Zambia Market Research
http://strategis.ic.gc.ca/sc_mrkti/ibinddc/engdoc/1a1a57.html
A service of Industry Canada, the site provides U.S. Department of Commerce reports on Zambian business, trade regulations and standards, investment climate, trade and project financing, business travel, and market opportunities.

Zambia: Selected Issues
http://www.imf.org/external/pubs/CAT/longres.cfm?sk=2465.0
Prepared by the International Monetary Fund, the site provides fact sheets and statistics on Zambian civil service reform, privatization, bank restructuring, and trade liberalization.

Zambia Today
http://www.zamnet.zm/zamnet/zana/zamtoday.html
The site is a compilation of news stories published by the Zambian Media including the *Times of Zambia*, *Sunday Times of Zambia*, the *Zambia Daily Mail*, and the *Zambian News Agency*.

Zambian Business WWW Pages
http://www.zamnet.zm/zamnet/zambus/zambushome.html
Posted by Zamnet, the site is a directory of leading business organizations in Zambia. The database includes banks, consultants, transportation companies, and industry associations.

Zambian National WWW Server
http://www.zamnet.zm/newpage.html
A hub of country information, the site delivers Zambian fact sheets, business guides, legal primers, discussion forums, company directories, and event reports.

Zambia Trade Assistance

Export Board of Zambia
http://www.zamnet.zm/zamnet/zambus/ebz/ebz.htm
Established in 1985, the Board promotes Zambian exports. The site provides contact information and a directory of Zambian exporters in 18 categories including building materials, mining equipment, and wood products.

Zambia Export and Import Bank
http://www.zamnet.zm/zamnet/zambus/zpa/exim.html
Based in Lusaka, the Bank provides export

finance services. The site includes a mission statement, program directory, staff roster, and contact information.

Zambia Representative Offices

Canada

High Commission of Canada in Lusaka
http://www.dfait-maeci.gc.ca/english/missions/rep-can4e.htm#zambia
The site provides contact information for the Canadian High Commission in Lusaka.

Finland

Embassy of Finland in Lusaka
http://www.zamnet.zm/zamnet/diplomatic/finland/finhome.htm
The site provides Finnish news, fact sheets, visa and passport information, business guides, and a directory of consular and commercial services.

India

Indian Commercial Mission in Lusaka
http://www.nic.in/commin/ICM.HTM
The site lists the street address, phone and fax numbers, and e-mail link of the Indian Commercial Mission in Lusaka.

Namibia

Embassy of Namibia in Lusaka
http://www.republicofnamibia.com/adress.htm
Along with a directory of Namibian companies and government agencies, the site provides contact information for the Namibian Embassy in Lusaka.

Sweden

Embassy of Sweden in Lusaka
http://www.ud.se/english/mfa/ambassad/zambia.htm
The site provides contact information for the Swedish Embassy in Lusaka.

Tanzania

Embassy of Tanzania in Lusaka
http://www.tanzania-online.gov.uk/visa/envoys.html
The site provides contact information for the Tanzanian Embassy in Lusaka.

United Kingdom

High Commission of Britain in Lusaka
http://www.fco.gov.uk/directory/posts.asp?ZA
The site provides contact information for the British High Commission in Lusaka.

United States

United States Embassy in Lusaka
http://www.zamnet.zm/zamnet/usemb/Welcome.html
Featuring a message from the Ambassador, the site delivers U.S. aid reports, visa and passport information, and a directory of consular and commercial services.

United States Information Service in Lusaka
http://www.zamnet.zm/zamnet/usemb/wwwhusis.htm
The site offers U.S. news, press releases, fact sheets, electronic journals, economic reports, and a directory of U.S.-Zambia educational and exchange programs.

Zimbabwe

Zimbabwe Media

Financial Gazette
http://www.africaonline.co.zw/fingaz/
Based in Harare, the electronic newspaper provides Zimbabwean news, company profiles, real estate reports, agricultural bulletins, and reader forums.

Zimbabwe Independent
http://www.samara.co.zw/zimin/
Updated weekly, the site provides Zimbabwean headlines, economic reports, editorials, classifieds, letters to the editor, and a searchable archive of past issues.

Zimbabwe Media
http://www.mediainfo.com/emediajs/specific-geo.htm?region=zimbabwe
Developed by Editor and Publisher Interactive, the site is an index of Zimbabwean magazines, newspapers, and other media sites online.

Zimbabwe Market Guides

Barclays Country Report: Zimbabwe
http://www.offshorebanking.barclays.com/services/economic/yearly/zimjul97/zimcont.html

Prepared by Barclays Bank, the site reports on Zimbabwe economic trends, politics, monetary and fiscal policy, and U.K.-Zimbabwe merchandise trade and investment flows.

Country Profile: Zimbabwe
http://www.mbendi.co.za/cyzicy.htm
Developed by MBendi, the site provides Zimbabwean fact sheets, maps, sector profiles, exchange rates, travel information, and business contacts.

Doing Business in Zimbabwe
http://mbendi.co.za/werksmns/lexaf/buszi.htm
Written by the law firm of Scanlen & Holderness, the site delivers fact sheets on Zimbabwean business, taxation, foreign investment, exchange controls, and intellectual property.

Index on Zimbabwe
http://www.africaindex.africainfo.no/africaindex1/countries/zimbabwe.html
A service of the Norwegian Council for Africa, the site is a directory of Zimbabwean resources online. Categories include culture, economy, news, and tourism.

Investing in Zimbabwe
http://www.africaonline.co.zw/zfic/investments.html
A virtual library of business information, the site delivers fact sheets on Zimbabwean taxation, financial institutions, immigration, and incentive programs.

Investment Profile: Zimbabwe
http://www.mbendi.co.za/ernsty/cyzieyip.htm
A service of Ernst & Young, the site provides fact sheets on Zimbabwean business, taxation, visa requirements, and foreign investment.

Virtual Zimbabwe
http://www.mediazw.com/index.shtml
A digital country gateway, the site features Zimbabwean company directories, product catalogs, tourism information, city guides, photo galleries, and discussion forums.

Zimbabwe Business Briefs
http://www.austrade.gov.au/IOOM/Zimbabwe/
A service of Austrade, the site offers fact sheets on Zimbabwean culture, business etiquette, marketing, transportation, travel, and visas.

Zimbabwe Country Brief
http://www.worldbank.org/cgi-bin/

sendoff.cgi?page=%2Fhtml%2Fextdr%2Foffrep%2Fafr%2Fzw.htm
A service of the World Bank Group, the site provides Zimbabwean population statistics, financial data, development reports, and economic forecasts.

Zimbabwe InfoExport
http://www.infoexport.gc.ca/country-e.asp?continent=Africa&country=54
A service of Foreign Affairs and International Trade Canada, the site provides fact sheets and statistics on Zimbabwean geography, business and politics.

Zimbabwe Market Information
http://dtiinfo1.dti.gov.uk/ots/zimbabwe/
A service of the London-based Department of Trade and Industry, the site delivers Zimbabwean fact sheets, maps, and trade-show information.

Zimbabwe Market Research
http://strategis.ic.gc.ca/sc_mrkti/ibinddc/engdoc/1a1a58.html
A service of Industry Canada, the site provides U.S. Department of Commerce reports on Zimbabwean economic trends, trade regulations and standards, investment climate, trade and project financing, business travel, and market opportunities.

Zimbabwe Network
http://www.zimbabwe.net/
Along with fact sheets, city guides, and travel information, the site provides a directory of Zimbabwe companies in 15 categories including financial services, medical, and wood products.

ZimWeb
http://www.mother.com/~zimweb/
An online country forum, the site features Zimbabwean discussion groups, interviews, mailing lists, education directories, travel information, and Internet reports.

Zimbabwe Trade Assistance

Shipping and Forwarding Agents' Association of Zimbabwe
http://www.zimtrade.co.zw/TPHARARE/shipping.html
A service of Trade Point Harare, the site is a directory of over 20 cargo, freight, and storage companies in Zimbabwe including Air Express International, Cheston Cargo, and Mercan Shipping.

Trade Point Harare
http://www.zimtrade.co.zw/TPHARARE/index.html
A portal of international trade information, the site provides Zimbabwean trade leads, business guides, socioeconomic statistics, and transportation bulletins.

ZimTrade
http://www.zimtrade.co.zw/
A service of the National Trade Development Organization of Zimbabwe, the site provides Zimbabwean trade and investment opportunities, investment guides, and city profiles.

Zimbabwe Representative Offices

Australia

Zimbabwe Australia Business Council
http://www.zabc.com/
Established in 1994, the Council promotes Australia-Zimbabwe trade. The site provides a mission statement, member directory, and trade leads.

Austria

Austrian Trade Commission in Harare
http://aw.wk.or.at/awo/ahst-harare.htm
The site lists the staff, street address, phone and fax numbers, e-mail link, and office hours of the Austrian Trade Commission in Harare.

Canada

High Commission of Canada in Harare
http://www.dfait-maeci.gc.ca/english/missions/rep-can4e.htm#zimbabwe
The site provides contact information for the Canadian High Commission in Harare.

France

French Trade Commission in Harare
http://www.dree.org/zimbabwe/
Posted in French, the site delivers Zimbabwean market reports, sector profiles, contact information, and a directory of French export promotion services.

Ghana

Embassy of Ghana in Harare
http://www.juntung.com/ghana-consul-hk/2misabo.htm
The site provides contact information for the Ghanaian Embassy in Harare.

Malaysia

High Commission of Malaysia in Harare
http://www.mnet.com.my/klonline/www/missions/malmiss/mzimbabw.htm
The site provides contact information for the Malaysian High Commission in Harare.

Namibia

Embassy of Namibia in Harare
http://www.republicofnamibia.com/adress.htm
Along with a directory of Namibian companies and government agencies, the site provides contact information for the Namibian Embassy in Harare.

Norway

Embassy of Norway in Harare
http://www.ntc.no/cgi-bin/wbch.exe?html=../templates/utekontor2.html&profile=1109
The site lists the staff, street address, phone and fax numbers, and e-mail link of the Norwegian Embassy in Harare.

South Africa

South Africa Foreign Trade Office in Harare
http://wwwdti.pwv.gov.za/dtiwww/foreign_offices.htm
A service of the South Africa Department of Trade and Industry, the site provides contact information for the South Africa Trade Office in Harare.

Sweden

Embassy of Sweden in Harare
http://www.ud.se/english/mfa/ambassad/zimbabwe.htm
The site provides contact information for the Swedish Embassy in Harare.

Tanzania

Embassy of Tanzania in Harare
http://www.tanzania-online.gov.uk/visa/envoys.html
The site provides contact information for the Tanzanian Embassy in Harare.

United Kingdom

High Commission of Britain in Harare
http://www.fco.gov.uk/directory/posts.asp?ZI
The site provides contact information for the British High Commission in Harare.

CHAPTER 10

FAR EAST POWER PORTALS: 1,500+ ASIA PACIFIC BUSINESS RESOURCES ON THE INTERNET

This chapter reviews more than 1,500 global business resources online that focus on the Asia Pacific area. The section reviews regional websites and online hubs for 44 countries and territories, including Australia, China, Japan, and South Korea. Home to over two billion people, the region has faced severe economic challenges in recent years, although political reforms and market adjustments are positioning the region for a major comeback. Leading trade and investment opportunities include fish and food products, forest and building products, information technologies, power and energy equipment, transportation, environment, and oil and gas equipment. According to NUA Internet Surveys, an estimated 26 million people in the region—about one out of every 75—were online as of January 1999. Based on projections by IDC Research, the Asia Pacific Internet population is expected to grow to 45 million by 2002.

Regional Sites

Asia Pacific Search Tools

AltaVista Asia
http://altavista.skali.com.my/
Part of the AltaVista search network, the site is a browsable index of Asian resources online. The service provides web navigation using Korean, Japanese, Vietnamese, and other international character sets.

Infospace Asia
http://in-114.infospace.com/_1_34407537__info/ intl/asia.html
A regional search service, the site includes Asian business and people finders, home listings, personals, city profiles, and travel guides for 12 countries including China, Hong Kong, and Japan.

Yahoo in Asia
http://www.yahoo.com.sg/
A network of web navigation and programming services, the site delivers Asian news, country profiles, message boards, exchange rates, and shopping guides.

Asia Pacific Media

Asia, Inc. Online
http://www.asia-inc.com/
Along with a directory of who's who in Asia, the site delivers Asian business briefings, management models, executive interviews, technology guides, and online conference rooms.

Asia Business Magazine
http://web3.asia1.com.sg/timesnet/navigatn/text/ ab.html

Based in Hong Kong, the monthly magazine reviews Asian business trends and issues. The site contains the complete archive of stories published by the periodical since January, 1996 in 20 categories including marketing, trade, and information technology.

Asia Media
http://www.mediainfo.com/emediajs/links-geo.htm?location=asia
A service of Editor and Publisher Interactive, the site is a directory of media sites in over 20 Asian countries including Bangladesh, Singapore, and Vietnam.

Asia Pacific Economic Review
http://www.moshix2.net/APER/
Based in the United States, the site provides Asian business news, country guides, a regional company directory, and reports on 20 industries including tourism, electronics, finance, and agriculture.

Oceania Media
http://www.mediainfo.com/emediajs/links-geo.htm?location=oceania
Developed by Editor and Publisher Interactive, the site is an index of media sites in Oceania including Australia, Guam, New Zealand, and Papua New Guinea.

Asia Pacific Market Guides

Access Asia
http://www.accessasia.com/
A hub of regional information, the subscription site provides a searchable directory of companies in 10 Asian countries including China, Indonesia, Malaysia, and Thailand.

Asia Business Connection
http://asiabiz.com/
A directory of Asian business resources online, the site is searchable by country and by subject, such as news, travel, shopping, manufacturing, or exporting.

Asia Business Network
http://infomanage.com/asia/abn/contactsdata.html
A virtual marketplace, the site is a browsable database of buy and sell offers and alliance opportunities from across Asia and around the world.

Asia-Europe Meeting Connect
http://www.asemconnect.com.sg/
An online meeting place for Asian and European companies, Asia-Europe Meeting or ASEM Connect provides Asian and European business news, notice boards, and web guides.

Asia International Business Resources
http://ciber.bus.msu.edu/busres/asia.htm
A service of Michigan State University, the site provides a directory of Asia Pacific international trade resources online including business guides, investment primers, and company databases.

Asia Pacific Chamber of Commerce
http://oneworld.wa.com/apcc/apcc.html
Based in Seattle, Washington, the Chamber promotes Asian economic growth and cross-cultural understanding. The site includes a mission statement, product catalog, and contact information.

Asia and the Pacific Database
http://infoserv2.ita.doc.gov/apweb.nsf
A service of the United States International Trade Administration, the site provides business information and commercial guides for over 30 Asian countries including China, Indonesia, and Taiwan.

Asia Pacific Economic Cooperation Homepage
http://www.apecsec.org.sg/
A regional economic forum with 18 member countries, Asia Pacific Economic Cooperation or APEC promotes economic development and trade liberalization in the Asian region. The site delivers country profiles, press releases, action plans, declarations, statistics, and web guides.

Asia Pacific Management Forum
http://www.apmforum.com/
A hub of regional business information, the site delivers Asian economic news, editorials, discussion forums, travel information, online tutorials, and employment opportunities.

Asia's Marketplace
http://www.asiatrade.com/Mkt.html
A digital marketplace, the site is a searchable database of joint ventures and buy and sell offers in over 20 categories including electronics, apparel, food and beverage, and transportation.

Asian Business Watch
http://www.asianbusinesswatch.com/
A virtual library of regional business information, the site features Asian economic news, company directories, special reports, slide shows, and rankings.

Asian Development Bank
http://www.asiandevbank.org/
Headquartered in Manila, the Bank finances economic development projects in Asian developing countries. The site includes press releases, speeches, publications, and project profiles.

Asian Development Bank Business Opportunities
http://www.asiandevbank.org/adbbo/adbbo.html
Updated monthly, the site is a database of Asian Development Bank proposed projects, procurement notices, contract awards, pre-qualified contractors, and project profiles.

Asian Economic Survey
http://interactive.wsj.com/public/current/summaries/aes98.htm
A service of Wall Street Journal Interactive, the site provides Asian country profiles, economic forecasts, reform updates, company reviews, and executive interviews.

Asian Internet Marketing Group
http://www.aim.apic.net/
A forum for Asian Internet marketers, the site includes online discussion groups, a member directory, and a searchable archive of Asian marketing news and reports.

Asian Sources Online
http://www.asiansources.com/
A resource for volume buyers, the site features Asian product catalogs, supplier directories, excess stock listings, and a free e-mail alert service which notifies users about new sourcing opportunities.

Association of Southeast Asian Nations: Big Emerging Markets Homepage
http://www.ita.doc.gov/bems/aseanlft.htm
Developed by the United States Department of Commerce, the site delivers Association of Southeast Asian Nation fact sheets, economic forecasts, export and import statistics, sector profiles, and international trade guides.

Association of Southeast Asian Nations Secretariat Home Page
http://www.aseansec.org/
Based in Jakarta, the Association of Southeast Asian Nations promotes economic development and political stability in Southeast Asia. The site includes Asian country profiles, statistics, publications, event information, and electronic commerce reports.

Association of Southeast Asian Nations Standards
http://www.aseansec.org/accsq/sqmain.htm
The site provides fact sheets on Association of Southeast Asian Nations quality agreements, national standards, environmental regulations, and technical requirements.

Bureau of East Asian and Pacific Affairs
http://www.state.gov/www/regions/eap/index.html
A service of the U.S. State Department, the site provides U.S. press statements, testimony, briefings, issue reports, and travel information on the East Asian region.

Bureau of South Asian Affairs
http://www.state.gov/www/regions/sa/index.html
Developed by the U.S. State Department, the site provides United States press statements, testimony, briefings, issue reports, and travel information on the South Asian region.

Far East Business Directory
http://www.net-trade.com/
A database of Asian companies, the site is divided into 14 categories including electronics, fashion, jewelry, machinery, optical products, toys and gifts, and watches.

InfoExport Asia Pacific
http://www.infoexport.gc.ca/continent-e.asp?continent=Asia
A service of Foreign Affairs and International Trade Canada, the site provides economic fact sheets and business guides for over 30 Asia Pacific countries.

Northeast Asia Market Research
http://strategis.ic.gc.ca/sc_mrkti/ibinddc/engdoc/1a1f.html
A service of Industry Canada, the site is a database of fact sheets and market studies on eight Northeast Asian countries.

Southeast Asia Market Research
http://strategis.ic.gc.ca/sc_mrkti/ibinddc/engdoc/1a1i.html
A service of Industry Canada, the site is a database of fact sheets and market studies on over 40 Southeast Asian countries.

World Bank Group East Asia and the Pacific
http://www.worldbank.org/html/extdr/offrep/eap/eap.htm
A database of World Bank projects in Eastern Asia and the Asia Pacific region, the site provides press releases, speeches, mission statements, country profiles, and regional economic reports.

World Bank Group South Asia
http://www.worldbank.org/html/extdr/offrep/sas/sas.htm
A database of World Bank projects in South Asia, the site provides press releases, speeches, mission statements, country profiles, and regional economic reports.

Asia Pacific Trade Assistance

Airlines in Asia
http://www.freightworld.com/airl_geo.html#6
A service of Freightworld, the site is a directory of Asian Airlines online in eight countries including China, Japan, Malaysia, South Korea, Taiwan, and Thailand.

Airports in Asia
http://www.freightworld.com/airptgeo.html#6
An index of Asian airports online, the site connects to two operations: Hong Kong International Airport at Chek Lap Kok, and Singapore Changi Airport.

Airlines in Oceania
http://www.freightworld.com/airl_geo.html#9
A directory of Oceania airlines online, the site links to six operations in Australia including Qantas and Alliance Air, and three airlines in New Zealand including Air New Zealand, and Mount Cook Airline.

Asia Pacific Regional Perspectives
http://www.dfait-maeci.gc.ca/asia/menu-e.asp?name=Asia
A service of the Department of Foreign Affairs and International Trade, the site provides fact sheets and reports on Canadian trade and relations with some 40 Asian countries.

Asia Trade
http://www.asiatrade.com/
Along with Asian business news and business opportunities, the site offers a directory of Asian companies in 12 categories including manufacturers, exporters, wholesalers, and financial services.

Asian Net
http://www.asiannet.com/
A searchable database of Asian business opportunities, the service includes trade leads, buy and sell offers, agents wanted notices, company profiles, and employment opportunities.

Asian Trade Shows
http://www.asiansources.com/TRADESHW/TRDSHFRM.HTM
Hosted by Asian Sources Online, the site provides Asian trade-show listings and reviews. The reports include attendance figures, attendee interviews, and exhibitor reports.

Freight Forwarders in Asia
http://www.freightworld.com/forw_geo.html#6
A database of Asian freight forwarders online, the site links to over 50 operations in the region including Oriental Air Transport in Hong Kong, Cho Yang Shipping in South Korea, and YCH Group in Singapore.

Intermodal Carriers in Asia
http://www.freightworld.com/intmod_geo.html#6
A directory of Asian intermodal carriers online, the site connects to operations in four countries including Jardine Logistics in Hong Kong, Seino in Japan, and Ace Containers in Sri Lanka.

Maritime Carriers in Asia
http://www.freightworld.com/mari_geo.html#6
A database of Asian maritime carriers online, the site links to operations in 10 countries including Bangladesh, China, Indonesia, Japan, South Korea, Malaysia, and Singapore.

Pacific Business Center
http://www.cba.hawaii.edu/pbcp/
Based at the University of Hawaii, the Center promotes economic development in the Pacific Islands. The site includes project profiles, planning kits, and contact information.

Package Carriers in Asia
http://www.freightworld.com/exp_geo.html#6
An index of Asian package carriers online, the site links to seven operations in the region including Trans Asia Air Express in Bangladesh, and Express Systems International in Singapore.

Postal Services in Asia
http://www.freightworld.com/postal.html#6
A database of Asian postal services online, the site connects to four operations in the region including the Shanghai Posts and Telecommunications in China, and the Ministry of Posts and Telecommunications in Japan.

Railroads in Asia
http://www.freightworld.com/railroads.html#6
A directory of Asian railroads online, the site links to one operation in Malaysia: Keretapi Tanah Melayu Berhad.

Seaports in Asia
http://www.freightworld.com/port_geo.html#6
An index of Asian seaports online, the site connects to over 20 operations in the region including Nagoya in Japan, Kelang in Malaysia, and Pohang in South Korea.

Trade Net
http://www.trade.net.hk/
Based in Hong Kong, the site is a directory of Asian manufacturers and suppliers. Categories include consumer electronics, food products, footwear, apparel, toys, and watches.

Trade Winds
http://www.trade-winds.net/
Based in Taipei, the site is a directory of Asian product catalogs, company profiles, industry reports, trade-show information, shipping guides, and electronic publications.

Trucking and Motor Carriers in Asia
http://www.freightworld.com/truc_geo.html#6
A database of Asian trucking and motor carriers online, the site links to operations in two countries: Piff Shipping in China, and Brink's in Thailand.

Asia Pacific Representative Offices

United States

United States and Asia Pacific Economic Cooperation
http://www.usia.gov/regional/ea/apec/apec.htm
Based in Kuala Lumpur, the site provides United States-Asia Pacific Economic Cooperation Forum speeches, fact sheets, documents, action plans, and event information.

National Sites

American Samoa

American Samoa Market Guides

American Samoa
http://www.ipacific.com/samoa/samoa.html
The electronic journal provides American Samoan news, travel guides, medical bulletins, sound files, folk stories, language primers, and cultural information.

American Samoa Business Briefs
http://www.austrade.gov.au/IOOM/AmericanSamoa/
A service of Austrade, the site offers fact sheets on American Samoan culture, business etiquette, marketing, transportation, travel, and visas.

American Samoa Market Research
http://strategis.ic.gc.ca/sc_mrkti/ibinddc/engdoc/1a1i1.html
Posted by Industry Canada, the site provides U.S. Central Intelligence Agency fact sheets on American Samoan geography, people, government, business, and transportation.

American Samoa Profile
http://www.tradenz.govt.nz/intelligence/profiles/american_samoa.html
A service of the New Zealand Trade Development Board, the site provides American Samoan economic statistics, market information, and business tips.

Australia

Australia Search Tools

AltaVista Australia
http://www.altavista.yellowpages.com.au/cgi-bin/telstra?
Part of the AltaVista search network, the site is a browsable index of Australian resources online. Categories include business and finance, computer and Internet, and shopping and services.

Australian Internet Directories
http://www.sofcom.com/Directories/
Along with e-mail and newsgroup services, the site provides a searchable database of Australian resources online. Topics include events, shopping, and professional organizations.

Excite Australia
http://au.excite.com/
A personalized webstart page, the site features Australian news, business listings, people finders, Internet tutorials, and virtual shopping and technology channels.

Infospace Australia
http://in-114.infospace.com/_1_34407537__info/intl/australia.html
Along with travel guides and chat services, the site delivers Australian business directories, people finders, city profiles, and online shopping information.

WebWombat
http://www2.webwombat.com.au/
An Australian web navigation service, the site includes a company directory, trademark database, classified ads, Internet guides, and travel resources.

Yahoo Australia
http://www.yahoo.com.au/
Part of the Yahoo search network, the site provides Australian news, web-based personal management tools, shopping guides, event information, and people finders.

Australia Media

Australian Financial Review
http://www.afr.com.au/index.html
Updated daily, the site provides Australian business news, editorials, employment opportunities, and special reports on topics such as global sourcing and leasing.

Australia Media
http://www.mediainfo.com/emediajs/specific-geo.htm?region=australia
Developed by Editor and Publisher Interactive, the site is an index of Australian media sites online

including city guides, magazines, newspapers, and radio and television stations.

Business Review Weekly
http://www.brw.com.au/
The electronic magazine provides Australian business briefs, editorials, surveys, online discussion forums, company rankings, and a loan simulator.

Australia Market Guides

AusIndustry
http://www.ausindustry.gov.au/
An online gateway to Australian government business assistance programs and services, the site provides industry surveys, best practice reports, and research and development scoreboards.

Aussie Pages
http://aussie.com.au/index.html
A searchable directory of 1.2 million Australian businesses and organizations, the site is divided into a dozen subject areas, including business and finance, construction and engineering, and infrastructure and utilities.

Australia Business Reports
http://italchambers.net/BusinessReports.html
Prepared by the Italian Chamber of Commerce and written in Italian, the site provides Australian fact sheets, market reports, and commercial guides.

Australia Country Profile
http://www.tradenz.govt.nz/intelligence/profiles/australia.html
A service of the New Zealand Trade Development Board, the site provides Australian economic statistics, market information, and business tips.

Australia Country Report
http://www.state.gov/www/issues/economic/trade_reports/eastasia97/australia97.html
Prepared by the U.S. Department of State, the site reports on Australian exchange rates, debt management, trade barriers, export subsidies, intellectual property protection, worker rights, and foreign investment.

Australia Economic Views
http://www.norwich.com.au/monrep/curmon.htm
A service of Norwich Union Australia, the site provides Australian economic forecasts, global financial reports, and Australia-United States exchange rate bulletins.

Australia InfoExport
http://www.infoexport.gc.ca/country-e.asp?continent=Asia&country=50
A service of Foreign Affairs and International Trade Canada, the site provides Australia commercial guides and market reports.

Australia: An Introduction
http://www.apecsec.org.sg/member/apecaust.html
A service of the Asia Pacific Economic Cooperation, the site provides fact sheets on Australian geography, climate, population, language, religion and government.

Australia Market Access Database
http://mkaccdb.eu.int/mkdb/mkdb.pl?METHOD=COUNTRY
A service of the European Commission, the site offers briefs on Australian trade policy, tariff barriers, non-tariff barriers, investment-related measures, and financial services regulations.

Australia Market Information
http://dtiinfo1.dti.gov.uk/ots/australia/
A service of the London-based Department of Trade and Industry, the site delivers Australian fact sheets, maps, and trade-show information.

Australia Market Research
http://strategis.ic.gc.ca/sc_mrkti/ibinddc/engdoc/1a1i2.html
A service of Industry Canada, the site provides U.S. Department of Commerce reports on Australian economic trends, trade barriers, investment climate, business travel, and market opportunities.

Australia Virtual Library
http://www.austudies.org/vl/
A service of the World Wide Web Virtual Library, the site is a directory of Australian resources online. Categories include business, government, and information technology.

Australian Business Guide
http://www.ausmanufacturers.com.au/
Along with a database of buy and sell offers, the site features a browsable directory of Australian manufacturers and distributors in over 20 categories including food and beverage, electronics, and wood products.

Australian Chamber of Commerce and Industry
http://www.acci.asn.au/
Representing over 350,000 companies nationwide, the Chamber promotes Australian business interests. The service includes press

releases, project reports, and international trade briefs.

Australia's Cultural Network
http://www.acn.net.au/
An initiative of the Australian Federal Department of Communications, the site is an online gateway to Australian cultural organizations, resources, and news.

Barclays Country Report: Australia
http://www.offshorebanking.barclays.com/ services/economic/yearly/ausmay97/ auscont.html
Prepared by Barclays Bank, the site reports on Australian economic trends, politics, monetary and fiscal policy, exchange rates, international trade, and investment flows.

Business Centre
http://www.buscentre.com.au/
A digital library of business information, the site features Australian daily news, company directories, management advice, Asia market reports, and employment opportunities.

Employment Opportunities Australia
http://www.employment.com.au/
Along with career guides and resume services, the site provides a searchable database of Australian employment opportunities in over 25 categories including banking and finance, logistics, and engineering and mining.

IP Australia
http://www.ipaustralia.gov.au/
Along with a directory of intellectual property conventions and treaties, the Canberra-based site provides information on Australian patents, trademarks, industrial designs, and other intellectual property.

Telstra Transigo
http://www.transigo.net.au/wci/home
Hosted by the Australian federal government, the site is a database of Australian government procurement projects, business opportunities, and requests for quotes.

Australia Trade Assistance

AusAid
http://www.ausaid.gov.au/
Based in Canberra, AusAid provides financing and technical assistance to developing countries.

The service features press releases, country profiles, and tender opportunities.

Austrade Online
http://www.austrade.gov.au/
Austrade is the export promotion agency of the Australian government. The service includes export guides, country briefs, event information, and international trade fact sheets.

Austrade Regional Offices
http://www.austrade.gov.au/RegionalOffices/ index.asp
The online service is a directory of Austrade offices and export promotion services in North America, Central and South America, Asia, Europe, Africa, and Asia Pacific.

Australia On Display
http://www.austrade.gov.au/AOD/index.asp
A service of Austrade, the site is a directory of Australian exporters in 20 categories including agriculture and forestry, mining and energy, telecommunications, and multimedia.

Australian Customs Service
http://www.customs.gov.au/
Along with press releases, speeches, and notices, the site provides primers on Australian importing, exporting, travel, and customs regulations and documentation.

Australian Department of Foreign Affairs and Trade
http://www.dfat.gov.au/index.html
Based in Canberra, the Department is responsible for the Australian Government's international relations and trade programs. The service includes annual reports, country fact sheets, policy papers, and trade and economic statistics.

Australian Diplomatic and Trade Offices Worldwide
http://www.dfat.gov.au/directories/offices.html
A service of the Australian Department of Foreign Affairs and Trade, the site is a directory of Australian diplomatic offices in Asia Pacific, the Americas, Europe, Middle East, and Africa.

Australian Federation of International Forwarders
http://www.afif.org/
Created in 1996, the Federation promotes the interests of Australian air and sea freight handlers. The site includes news, activity reports, a member directory, and contact information.

Australian Yellow Pages
http://www.yellowpages.com.au/
A searchable directory of Australian companies and organizations, the site is divided into 20 categories including building and construction, finance, trades people, and utilities.

Business Entry Point
http://www.business.gov.au/
A service of the Australian federal government, the site provides guides and fact sheets on doing business in Australia. Topics include international trade, investment, education and training, and licensing and registrations.

Customs Brokers Council of Australia
http://www.cbca.org.au/
An online forum for Australian customs brokers, the site provides a mission statement, news, a member directory, event information, and training bulletins.

Export Centre
http://www.theexportcentre.com.au/
Based in North Parramatta, the site provides advice to New South Wales exporters. The site includes news, program directories, and contact information.

Export Finance and Insurance Corporation
http://www.efic.gov.au/
Hosted by the Australian government, the Corporation provides export financing and risk management services for Australian exporters. The service includes press releases, success stories, and country risk ratings.

Freight Forwarders in Australia
http://www.freightworld.com/forw_geo.html#9
A service of Freightworld, the site is a directory of Australian freight forwarders online including All Ports International Logistics, Republic Freight Systems, and Seawings Shipping.

Intermodal Carriers in Australia
http://www.freightworld.com/intmod_geo.html#9
An index of Australian intermodal carriers online, the site lists two operations: BHP Transport, and Plimsoll Shipping.

Maritime Carriers in Australia
http://www.freightworld.com/mari_geo.html#9
A database of Australian maritime carriers online, the site lists four operations including Owens International Freight, and Tradexpress.

Package Carriers in Australia
http://www.freightworld.com/exp_geo.html#9
A directory of Australian package carriers online, the site connects to two operations: Barnetts Couriers and Bonds Couriers.

Postal Services in Australia
http://www.freightworld.com/postal.html#9
An index of Australian postal services online, the site links to two operations: the Croydon Post Office, and Queensland Post Office.

Promote Yourself Online
http://www.austrade.gov.au/AOD/index.asp
A service of Austrade, the site is a searchable directory of Australian exporters in 20 categories including mining and energy, textiles and clothing, telecommunications, and multimedia.

Railways in Australia
http://www.freightworld.com/railroads.html#9
A directory of Australian railways online, the site connects to two operations: National Rail Corporation and Westrail.

Seaports in Australia *http://www.freightworld.com/port_geo.html#9*
A database of Australian seaports online, the site links to 15 facilities including Adelaide, Hobart, Melbourne, Port Lincoln, Thevenard, and Wallaroo.

South Pacific Trade Commission
http://www.sptc.gov.au/
Based in Sydney, the Commission promotes economic development in the South Pacific Islands. The site includes news, country profiles, business opportunities, and investment information.

Trade Point Melbourne
http://www.tpmel.com.au/
Part of the United Nations Global Trade Point Network, the site features Australian export guides, company directories, business matchmaking services, and international trade news.

Trade Shows in Australia
http://www.expoguide.com/shows/data/loc_2.htm
Compiled by Expoguide, the site is a directory of upcoming trade shows in Australia.

Tradegate
http://www.tradegate.org.au/
A consortium of over 400 companies and

government agencies, the organization promotes electronic commerce in Australia. The site includes news, event information, and a member directory.

Trucking and Motor Carriers in Australia
http://www.freightworld.com/truc_geo.html#9
A directory of Australian trucking and motor carriers online, the site connects to three operations: BHP Transport, Mainfreight, and Owens International Freight.

Australia Representative Offices

Argentina

Consulate General of Argentina in Sydney
http://www.consarsydney.org.au/
Posted in English and Spanish, the site delivers Argentine fact sheets, economic reports, statistics, visa and passport information, and a directory of consular and commercial services.

Austria

Austrian Trade Commission in Sydney
http://aw.wk.or.at/awo/ahst-sydney.htm
The site lists the staff, street address, phone and fax numbers, e-mail link, and office hours of the Austrian Trade Commission in Sydney.

Brunei Darussalam

Embassy of Brunei Darussalam in Canberra
http://www.brunet.bn/homepage/gov/bruemb/govemb.htm
The site provides contact information for the Brunei Darussalam Embassy in Canberra.

Canada

Consulate General of Canada in Sydney
http://www.dfait-maeci.gc.ca/english/missions/rep-can1e.htm#australia
The site provides contact information for the Canadian Consulate in Sydney.

Embassy of Canada in Canberra
http://www.dfait-maeci.gc.ca/english/missions/rep-can1e.htm#australia
The site provides contact information for the Canadian Embassy in Canberra.

Chile

Asia Pacific-Chile Online
http://www.ozemail.com.au/~pibu/asiapac/index.htm
A service of Prochile, the Spanish language site reports on business and trade opportunities in China, Malaysia, Vietnam, and other Asia Pacific countries.

Australia-Chile Chamber of Commerce
http://www.ozemail.com.au/~pibu/accc/index.htm
Based in Sydney, the Chamber promotes Australia-Chile trade. The site includes Chamber news, event information, bilateral trade opportunities, and Chilean business guides.

Embassy of Chile in Canberra
http://users.netinfo.com.au/chile/
Featuring a message from the Ambassador, the site provides Chilean fact sheets, event information, and a directory of Chilean diplomatic posts in Australia.

China

China Council for the Promotion of International Trade in Sydney
http://www.ccpit.org/engVersion/cp_about/cp_over/cp_over.html
A Chinese export service, the site provides contact information for the China Council for the Promotion of International Trade office in Sydney.

Czech Republic

Embassy of Czech Republic in Canberra
http://www.czechemb.net/scroll_of_embassies.html
Along with a directory of diplomatic offices in the Czech Republic, the site provides contact information for the Czech Embassy in Canberra.

Denmark

Consulate General of Denmark in Sydney
http://www.dkconsul-sydney.org.au/
Written in English and Danish, the site provides Danish news, fact sheets, business guides, visa and passport information, travel tips, and a primer on how to trace Danish ancestors.

European Union

Delegation of the European Commission to Australia
http://www.ecdel.org.au/
Established in 1981, the Delegation is responsible for the conduct of official relations between Australia and the European Community. The site includes European Unions news, documents, and contact information.

Fiji

High Commission of Fiji in Canberra
http://fiji.gov.fj/core/fj_mis.html
The site provides contact information for the Fijian High Commission in Canberra.

Finland

Finland Trade Center in Sydney
http://www.exports.finland.fi/tradecen.htm
The site lists the staff, street address, phone and fax numbers, and e-mail link of the Finland Trade Center in Sydney.

France

Embassy of France in Canberra
http://www.france.net.au/official/
Posted in English and French, the site delivers French fact sheets, press releases, reports on Australia-France trade and relations, and a directory of consular and commercial services.

French Trade Commission in Australia
http://www.dree.org/australie/
Posted in French, the site delivers Australian market reports, sector profiles, contact information, and a directory of French export promotion services.

French Trade Commission in Canberra
http://www.dree.org/australie/FRANCAIS/LesPEE/canberra.htm
The site lists the staff, street address, phone and fax numbers, and e-mail link of the French Trade Commission in Canberra.

French Trade Commission in Melbourne
http://www.dree.org/australie/FRANCAIS/LesPEE/melbourn.htm
The site lists the staff, street address, phone and fax numbers, and e-mail link of the French Trade Commission in Melbourne.

French Trade Commission in Sydney
http://www.dree.org/australie/FRANCAIS/LesPEE/sydney.htm
The site lists the staff, street address, phone and fax numbers, and e-mail link of the French Trade Commission in Sydney.

Germany

German-Australia Chamber of Commerce
http://www.ahk.net/en/au/Sydney/
The site lists the Chairperson, Chief Executive Officer, street address, phone and fax numbers, and e-mail link of the German Chambers in Sydney and Melbourne.

Ghana

Consulate of Ghana in Sydney
http://www.juntung.com/ghana-consul-hk/2misabo.htm
The site provides contact information for the Ghanaian Consulate in Sydney.

India

Australia-India Council
http://www.dfat.gov.au/aic/aichome.html
Established in 1992, the Council promotes Australia-India trade and cultural exchanges. The site includes a mission statement, member directory, and program information.

Indian Commercial Mission in Sydney
http://www.nic.in/commin/ICM.HTM
The site lists the street address, and phone and fax numbers of the Indian Commercial Mission in Sydney.

Indonesia

Australia-Indonesia Institute
http://www.dfat.gov.au/aii/aii_home.html
Created in 1989, the Institute promotes Australia-Indonesia trade and relations. The site features a mission statement, member directory, and financial assistance information.

Embassy of Indonesia in Canberra
http://indag.dprin.go.id/INGG/trade/atache.HTM
The site provides contact information for the Indonesian Embassy in Canberra.

Israel

Australia-Israel Chamber of Commerce
http://www.aicc.org.au/
With offices in Sydney, Melbourne, Adelaide, Brisbane, Perth, and Tel Aviv, the Chamber promotes Australia-Israel trade. The site includes event information and a directory of bilateral business opportunities.

Italy

Italian Cultural Institute in Sydney
http://www.geocities.com/Baja/Dunes/3023/
Posted in Italian, the site provides Italian fact sheets, cultural guides, language information, and a directory of Italian-related lectures, seminars, and other events in Australia.

Laos

Embassy of Laos in Canberra
*http://www.laoembassy.com/news/
embassyabroad.htm*
The site provides contact information for the Embassy of Laos in Canberra.

Malaysia

Consulate of Malaysia in Adelaide
*http://www.mnet.com.my/klonline/www/missions/
malmiss/maustra4.htm*
The site provides contact information for the Malaysian Consulate in Adelaide.

Consulate of Malaysia in Melbourne
*http://www.mnet.com.my/klonline/www/missions/
malmiss/maustra3.htm*
The site provides contact information for the Malaysian Consulate in Melbourne.

Consulate of Malaysia in Perth
*http://www.mnet.com.my/klonline/www/missions/
malmiss/maustra5.htm*
The site provides contact information for the Malaysian Consulate in Perth.

High Commission of Malaysia in Canberra
*http://www.mnet.com.my/klonline/www/missions/
malmiss/maustra1.htm*
The site provides contact information for the Malaysian High Commission in Canberra.

Trade Commission of Malaysia in Sydney
http://www.mnet.com.my/klonline/www/missions/

malmiss/maustra10.htm
The site provides contact information for the Malaysian Trade Commission in Sydney.

Netherlands

Australian Netherlands Chamber of Commerce
http://www.ancoc.com.au/
Based in Sydney, the Chamber promotes Australian-Dutch trade. The site includes a mission statement, member directory, trade leads, and a business matchmaking service.

New Zealand

Trade New Zealand in Sydney
http://www.tradenz.govt.nz/contact/pacific.html
An export promotion service, the site provides contact information for the Trade New Zealand office in Sydney.

Pakistan

Pakistan Trade Office in Sydney
http://www.jamal.com/epb/ptoa.htm
The site provides contact information for the Pakistan Trade Office in Sydney.

Philippines

Philippine Trade and Investment Promotion Office in Sydney
http://www.dti.gov.ph/syd/
The site provides a mission statement, service directory, and contact information for the Philippine Trade Office in Sydney.

Singapore

High Commission of Singapore in Canberra
http://www.gov.sg/mfa/consular/mww_a.htm
The site provides contact information for the Singapore High Commission in Canberra.

South Africa

Australia-Southern Africa Business Council
http://www.asabc.asn.au/
Created in 1990, the Council promotes Australia-South Africa trade. The site features a mission statement, membership database, business opportunities, and contact information.

South Africa Foreign Trade Office in Canberra
*http://wwwdti.pwv.gov.za/dtiwww/
foreign_offices.htm*
A service of the South Africa Department of Trade
and Industry, the site provides contact information
for the South Africa Trade Office in Canberra.

South Korea

Australia-Korea Foundation
http://www.dfat.gov.au/akf/akf_home.html
Established in 1989, the Foundation promotes
Australia-Korea trade and cultural exchanges.
The site includes a mission statement, grant
application guidelines, and contact information.

Spain

Spanish Commercial Office in Sydney
*http://www.icex.es/openURL.html#openURL=/
english/infoproyem/ofcomes/ofcomes.html#OC*
The site lists the staff, street address, phone and
fax numbers, and e-mail link of the Spanish
Commercial Office in Sydney.

Sweden

Swedish-Australian Chamber of Commerce
http://www.swedishtrade.org.au/chamber.htm
Based in Sydney, the Chamber promotes
Swedish-Australian trade and investment. The
site features a mission statement, activity reports,
and contact information.

Swedish-Australian Mining Group
http://www.swedishtrade.org.au/samg.htm
Founded in 1994, the Group is an association of
nine Australian mining companies with Swedish
technology or market interests. The site includes
a member directory and contact information.

Swedish Embassy and Consulates
*http://www.ud.se/english/mfa/ambassad/
australi.htm*
A service of the Swedish Ministry of Foreign
Affairs, the site lists the street address, phone
and fax numbers, and e-mail links of the Swedish
Embassy in Canberra, and the Swedish Consulates General in Adelaide, Brisbane, Cairns,
Darwin, Hobart, Melbourne, Perth, and Sydney.

Swedish Trade Council in Australia
http://www.swedishtrade.org.au/
Based in Sydney, the online service provides
Swedish fact sheets, trade leads, company

directories, sector profiles, event information, and
export guides.

Switzerland

Swiss Chamber of Commerce in Sydney
*http://swisstrade.com/
xicodes2.asp?P1=3&lvl=3&cid=D01*
The site lists the street address, phone and fax
numbers, and e-mail link of the Swiss Chamber
of Commerce in Sydney.

Taiwan

Australia-Taiwan Business Council
*http://www.australia.org.tw/commerce/council-
eng.html*
Founded in 1984, the Council promotes the
interests of Australian companies doing business with Taiwan. The site features executive
profiles, activity reports, and contact information.

**China External Trade Development Council
Office in Sydney**
*http://www.cetra.org.tw/english/o_office/
indexset.htm*
A Taiwanese trade promotion service, the site
lists the mission statement and e-mail link of the
China External Trade Development Council Office
in Sydney.

**Taiwan Government Information Office in
Sydney**
http://www.gio.gov.tw/info/ngio/austr-f.html
Posted in Chinese and English, the site lists the
street address, phone and fax numbers, and e-
mail link of the Taiwan Government Information
Office in Sydney.

Taiwanese Australian Business Association
*http://www.australia.org.tw/commerce/taba-
eng.html*
The Association promotes Taiwan-Australia trade
and relations. The site includes a mission
statement, executive profiles, contact information,
and a directory of programs and services.

Thailand

Royal Thai Consulate General in Sydney
http://www.mfa.go.th/Embassy/detail/27.htm
The site lists the Consul General, street address,
and phone and fax numbers of the Thai Consulate in Sydney.

Royal Thai Embassy in Canberra
http://www.mfa.go.th/Embassy/detail/32.htm
The site lists the Ambassador, street address, and phone and fax numbers of the Thai Embassy in Canberra.

Thai Trade Center in Auckland
http://www.thaitrade.com/wwtto.html
A service of the Thailand Department of Export Promotion, the site lists the street address, phone and fax numbers, and e-mail link of the Thai Trade Center in Auckland.

Thai Trade Center in Sydney
http://www.thaitrade.com/wwtto.html
A service of the Thailand Department of Export Promotion, the site lists the street address, phone and fax numbers, and e-mail link of the Thai Trade Center in Sydney.

Thailand Office of Commercial Affairs in Canberra
http://www.thaitrade.com/thcoaf.html
The site lists the street address, phone and fax numbers, and e-mail link of the Thailand Office of Commercial Affairs in Canberra.

Turkey

Embassy of the Republic of Turkey in Canberra
http://www.ozemail.com.au/~turkembs/
Posted in English and Turkish, the site delivers Turkish fact sheets, commercial guides, visa and passport information, and a directory of Turkish businesspeople in Australia.

Turkish Commercial Counsellor's Office in Sydney
http://www.geocities.com/CapitolHill/Senate/8919/
Along with contact information, the site delivers Turkish export guides, product catalogs, tradeshow schedules, investment bulletins, and Australian customs primers.

United Kingdom

British Consulate General in Adelaide
http://www.uk.emb.gov.au/contact/bcg_adel.htm
The site lists the street address, phone and fax numbers, and e-mail link of the British Consulate General in Adelaide.

British Consulate General in Brisbane
http://www.uk.emb.gov.au/contact/bcg_brisb.htm
The site lists the street address, phone and fax numbers, and e-mail link of the British Consulate General in Brisbane.

British Consulate General in Melbourne
http://www.uk.emb.gov.au/contact/bcg_melb.htm
The site lists the street address, phone and fax numbers, and e-mail link of the British Consulate General in Melbourne.

British Consulate General in Perth
http://www.uk.emb.gov.au/contact/bcg_perth.htm
The site lists the street address, phone and fax numbers, and e-mail link of the British Consulate General in Perth.

British Consulate General in Sydney
http://www.uk.emb.gov.au/contact/bcg_syd.htm
The site lists the street address, phone and fax numbers, and e-mail link of the British Consulate General in Sydney.

British Information Services Australia
http://www.uk.emb.gov.au/
The online service delivers British news, fact sheets, export guides, investment primers, travel tips, visa information, chat services, and education bulletins.

United States

American Chamber of Commerce in Australia
http://www.amcham.com.au/
Founded in 1961, the Chamber promotes Australia-United States trade. The site includes activity reports, a member directory, trade leads, and contact information.

State of Kansas Trade Office in Sydney
http://www.kansascommerce.com/0306-04why.html#WE WELCOME
A service of the Kansas Department of Commerce and Housing, the site lists the representative, street address, phone and fax numbers, and e-mail link of the Kansas Trade Office in Sydney.

United States Consulate General in Melbourne
http://www.usis-australia.gov/melbourne/index.html
The site features United States visa and passport information, taxation guides, and reports on Defense Contract Management Command Pacific-Australia, an organization responsible for management of United States government contracts in Australia and New Zealand.

United States Consulate General in Perth
http://www.usis-australia.gov/perth/
The digital Consulate delivers United States fact sheets, visa and passport information, taxation guides, and a directory of consular and commercial services.

United States Consulate General in Sydney
http://www.usconsydney.org/
Along with visa and passport information, the site provides U.S. news, fact sheets, travel tips, business guides, and a directory of consular and commercial services.

United States Embassy in Australia
http://www.usis-australia.gov/embassy.html
The virtual Embassy provides United States news, economic reports, travel guides, business primers, and updates on the Asia Pacific Economic Cooperation process.

Venezuela

Embassy of Venezuela in Canberra
http://www.trade-venezuela.com/EMBVENG.HTM
The site lists the street address, phone and fax numbers, and e-mail link of the Venezuelan Embassy in Canberra.

Western Samoa

Western Samoa High Commission in Canberra
http://www.interwebinc.com/samoa/missoz.html
The site lists the street address and phone and fax numbers of the Western Samoa High Commission in Canberra.

Brunei Darussalam

Brunei Darussalam Media

Borneo Bulletin On-Line
http://www.brunet.bn/news/bb/front.htm
Along with world and regional headlines, the English-language site delivers Bruneian news, editorials, business reports, lifestyle features, and employment opportunities.

Brunei Darussalam Media
http://www.mediainfo.com/emediajs/specific-geo.htm?region=bruneidarussalam
Developed by Editor and Publisher Interactive, the site is an index of Bruneian newspapers, television stations, and other media sites online.

Brunei Darussalam Market Guides

Brunei Business Guide
http://www.brunet.bn/homepage/bus_com/guide/busguid.htm
A hub of country business information, the site delivers fact sheets on Bruneian telecommunications, banking, taxation, investment, and intellectual property.

Brunei Business Listing
http://web3.asia1.com.sg/borneo/tamu.htm
Along with country fact sheets and flight schedules, the site is a directory of Bruneian companies and organizations. Categories include construction, finance, manufacturing, and tourism.

Brunei Darussalam Business Briefs
http://www.austrade.gov.au/IOOM/Brunei/
A service of Austrade, the site offers fact sheets on Bruneian culture, business etiquette, marketing, transportation, travel, and visas.

Brunei Darussalam InfoExport
http://www.infoexport.gc.ca/country-e.asp?continent=Asia&country=7
A service of Foreign Affairs and International Trade Canada, the site provides fact sheets and statistics on Bruneian geography, business, trade, and politics.

Brunei Darussalam: An Introduction
http://www.apecsec.org.sg/member/apecbrun.html
A service of the Asia Pacific Economic Cooperation, the site provides fact sheets on Bruneian geography, climate, population, language, vegetation, and water resources.

Brunei Darussalam Market Information
http://dtiinfo1.dti.gov.uk/ots/brunei/
A service of the London-based Department of Trade and Industry, the site delivers Bruneian fact sheets, maps, and trade-show information.

Brunei Darussalam Market Research
http://strategis.ic.gc.ca/sc_mrkti/ibinddc/engdoc/1a1i3.html
Posted by Industry Canada, the site provides U.S. Central Intelligence Agency fact sheets on Bruneian geography, people, government, business, and transportation.

Brunei Small and Medium Enterprises Homepage

http://www.brunet.bn/org/bsmehp/bsmehp.htm
A virtual business library, the site features Bruneian commercial guides, investment primers, taxation information, and a directory of government programs and services for small business.

Brunei Darussalam: Statistical Appendix

http://www.imf.org/external/pubs/CAT/ longres.cfm?sk=2460.0
Prepared by the International Monetary Fund, the site reports on Bruneian gross domestic product, oil and gas production, employment, consumer prices, and exports.

Brunei Darussalam Virtual Library

http://iias.leidenuniv.nl/wwwvl/southeas/ brunei.html
A service of the Asian Studies World Wide Web Virtual Library, the site is a directory of Bruneian resources online. Categories include business, government, and travel.

Government of Brunei Darussalam

http://www.brunet.bn/homepage/gov/mibhom.htm
Homepage of the Brunei Darussalam government, the site delivers maps, speeches, fact sheets, executive profiles, government directories, travel information, and business guides.

Brunei Darussalam Trade Assistance

Brunei Darussalam Indonesia Malaysia Philippines East ASEAN Business Council

http://www.brunet.bn/org/bimpeabc/index.htm
Founded in 1994, the Council promotes economic development and trade among members of the Association of Southeast Asian Nations. The service includes a company directory, sector profiles, and event information.

Brunei Darussalam Embassies Abroad

http://www.brunet.bn/homepage/gov/bruemb/ govemb.htm
The site is a directory of Bruneian Embassies and Consulates in over 20 countries including Australia, Germany, India, Thailand, and the United States.

Brunei Darussalam Representative Offices

Diplomatic Missions in Brunei Darussalam

http://www.brunet.bn/homepage/tourism/formiss/ formiss.htm
A directory of foreign embassies and consulates in Brunei Darussalam, the site lists representatives from over 20 countries including Austria, France, Iran, and Vietnam.

Australia

Austrade in Bandar Seri Begawan

http://www.austrade.gov.au/Brunei/
The online service provides Australian export guides, company directories, product catalogs, success stories, investment primers, and contact information.

Canada

High Commission of Canada in Bandar Seri Begawan

http://www.dfait-maeci.gc.ca/english/missions/rep-can1e.htm#brunei
The site provides contact information for the Canadian High Commission in Bandar Seri Begawan.

France

French Trade Commission in Bandar Seri Begawan

http://www.dree.org/brunei/
Posted in French, the site delivers Bruneian market reports, sector profiles, contact information, and a directory of French export promotion services.

India

High Commission of India to Brunei

http://www.brunet.bn/gov/emb/india/
Along with reports on India-Brunei trade and relations, the site provides Indian fact sheets, press releases, visa and passport information, and a directory of consular and commercial services.

Malaysia

High Commission of Malaysia in Bandar Seri Begawan

http://www.mnet.com.my/klonline/www/missions/ malmiss/mbruneid.htm
The site provides contact information for the Malaysian High Commission in Bandar Seri Begawan.

Pakistan

Embassy of Pakistan in Bandar Seri Begawan
*http://www.brunet.bn/gov/emb/pakistan/
welcome.htm*
Featuring a virtual greeting from the High Commissioner, the site delivers Pakistani news, fact
sheets, visa and passport information, business
guides, and travel tips.

Singapore

High Commission of Singapore in Bandar Seri Begawan
http://www.gov.sg/mfa/consular/mww_n.htm
The site provides contact information for the
Singapore High Commission in Bandar Seri
Begawan.

Sweden

Consulate of Sweden in Bandar Seri Begawan
*http://www.ud.se/english/mfa/ambassad/
brunei.htm*
The site lists the staff, street address, and phone
and fax numbers of the Swedish Consulate in
Bandar Seri Begawan.

Thailand

Royal Thai Embassy in Bandar Seri Begawan
http://www.mfa.go.th/Embassy/detail/66.htm
The site lists the Ambassador, street address,
and phone and fax numbers of the Thai Embassy
in Bandar Seri Begawan.

Thailand Office of Commercial Affairs in Bandar Seri Begawan
http://www.thaitrade.com/thcoaf.html
The site lists the street address, phone and fax
numbers, and e-mail link of the Thailand Office of
Commercial Affairs in Bandar Seri Begawan.

United Kingdom

High Commission of Britain in Bandar Seri Begawan
http://www.fco.gov.uk/directory/posts.asp?BU
The site provides contact information for the
British High Commission in Bandar Seri
Begawan.

Cambodia

Cambodia Media

Cambodia Media
*http://www.mediainfo.com/emediajs/specific-
geo.htm?region=cambodia*
Developed by Editor and Publisher Interactive, the
site is an index of Cambodian newspapers and
other media sites online.

Phnom Penh Post
http://www.newspapers.com.kh/PhnomPenhPost/
The English language electronic newspaper
provides Cambodian news, editorials,
classifieds, letters to the editor, reader surveys,
and a searchable archive of past issues.

Cambodia Market Guides

Cambodia Country Brief
*http://www.worldbank.org/cgi-bin/
sendoff.cgi?page=%2Fhtml%2Fextdr%2Foffrep%2Feap
%2Fkh.htm*
A service of the World Bank Group, the site
provides Cambodian population statistics,
financial data, development reports, and economic forecasts.

Cambodia: A Country Study
http://lcweb2.loc.gov/frd/cs/khtoc.html
A service of the U.S. Library of Congress, the site
delivers fact sheets on Cambodian geography,
people, agriculture, mining, manufacturing, and
foreign economic relations.

Cambodia InfoExport
*http://www.infoexport.gc.ca/country-
e.asp?continent=Asia&country=9*
A service of Foreign Affairs and International
Trade Canada, the site provides fact sheets and
statistics on Cambodian geography, business,
trade, and politics.

Cambodia Market Research
*http://strategis.ic.gc.ca/sc_mrkti/ibinddc/engdoc/
1a1i4.html*
A service of Industry Canada, the site provides
U.S. Department of Commerce reports on
Cambodian economic trends, trade barriers,
investment climate, business travel, and market
opportunities.

Cambodia: Open for Business
http://www.embassy.org/cambodia/business.htm
A service of the Cambodian Embassy in Washington, D.C., the site provides Cambodian investment guides, incentive information, and international trade bulletins.

Cambodia Virtual Library
http://iias.leidenuniv.nl/wwwvl/southeas/cambodia.html
Hosted by the Asian Studies World Wide Web Virtual Library, the site is a directory of Cambodian resources online. Categories include business, government, news, and travel.

Cambodian Information Center
http://www.cambodia.org/
An online country gateway, the site connects to Cambodian web guides, academic papers, language primers, homepages, news, and cultural information.

Cambodia Representative Offices

Australia

Austrade in Phnom Pehn
http://www.austrade.gov.au/GreaterMekongRegion/
The online service provides Australian export guides, company profiles, product catalogs, success stories, investment primers, and contact information for the Austrade office in Phnom Pehn.

Canada

Embassy of Canada in Phnom Pehn
http://www.dfait-maeci.gc.ca/english/missions/rep-can1e.htm#cambodia
The site provides contact information for the Canadian Embassy in Phnom Pehn.

France

French Trade Commission in Phnom Pehn
http://www.dree.org/cambodge/
Posted in French, the site delivers Cambodian market reports, sector profiles, contact information, and a directory of French export promotion services.

Laos

Embassy of Laos in Phnom Pehn
http://www.laoembassy.com/news/embassyabroad.htm
The site provides contact information for the Embassy of Laos in Phnom Pehn.

Malaysia

Embassy of Malaysia in Phnom Pehn
http://www.mnet.com.my/klonline/www/missions/malmiss/mcambodi.htm
The site provides contact information for the Malaysian Embassy in Phnom Pehn.

Singapore

Embassy of Singapore in Phnom Pehn
http://www.gov.sg/mfa/consular/mww_c.htm
The site provides contact information for the Singapore Embassy in Phnom Pehn.

Sweden

Embassy of Sweden in Phnom Pehn
http://www.ud.se/english/mfa/ambassad/kambodja.htm
The site lists the staff, street address, phone and fax numbers, and e-mail link of the Swedish Embassy in Phnom Pehn.

Thailand

Royal Thai Embassy in Phnom Penh
http://www.mfa.go.th/Embassy/detail/165.htm
The site lists the Ambassador, street address, and phone and fax numbers of the Thai Embassy in Phnom Penh.

Thailand Office of Commercial Affairs in Phnom Penh
http://www.thaitrade.com/thcoaf.html
The site lists the street address, phone and fax numbers, and e-mail link of the Thailand Office of Commercial Affairs in Phnom Penh.

United Kingdom

Embassy of Britain in Phnom Penh
http://www.fco.gov.uk/directory/posts.asp?CD
The site provides contact information for the British Embassy in Phnom Penh.

China

China Search Tools

GlobePage
http://www.globepage.com/
A web navigation service, the site provides a searchable directory of Chinese resources online in 14 categories including business, government, organizations, news, and computers.

Hong Kong Search Engine
http://www.chkg.com/
Along with weather bulletins and travel information, the site offers Internet search services, personal management tools, and website reviews.

WhatSite
http://www.whatsite.com/
Posted in English and Chinese, the site provides Internet searching, web guides, and an index of Chinese resources online in a dozen categories including business, shopping, education, and science.

Yahoo Chinese
http://chinese.yahoo.com/docs/info/bridge.html
Posted in traditional and simplified Chinese, the site delivers web navigation services, country and world news, message boards, and web reviews.

China Media

China Daily
http://www.chinadaily.net/
Along with world and regional headlines, the site delivers Chinese news, editorials, business guides, lifestyle features, and travel information.

China Media
http://www.mediainfo.com/emediajs/specific-geo.htm?region=china
Developed by Editor and Publisher Interactive, the site is an index of Chinese media sites online including magazines, newspapers, and television stations.

China News Service
http://www.chinanews.com/
Posted in English and Chinese, the site delivers Chinese headlines, photos, business news, economic reports, cultural information, and media guides.

Hong Kong Media
http://www.mediainfo.com/emediajs/specific-geo.htm?region=hongkong
A service of Editor and Publisher Interactive, the site is an index of Hong Kong media sites on the web.

Hong Kong Standard
http://www.hkstandard.com/online/finance/001/hksfin.htm
Updated daily, the site delivers Hong Kong and Chinese news, computer reports, tourism guides, employment opportunities, and personal webpages.

Inside China Today
http://www.insidechina.com/
Along with online classifieds and discussion groups, the site provides Chinese headlines, opinion, business news, photo galleries, and shopping directories.

China Market Guides

All China Federation of Industry and Commerce
http://www.asiawww.com/acfic/index.htm
Founded in 1953, the Federation promotes Chinese business interests. The site includes a mission statement, executive profiles, and activity reports.

Barclays Country Report: China
http://www.offshorebanking.barclays.com/services/economic/yearly/chifeb97/chiconts.html
Prepared by Barclays Bank, the site reports on Chinese economic trends, politics, monetary and fiscal policy, exchange rates, international trade, and investment flows.

Barclays Country Report: Hong Kong
http://www.offshorebanking.barclays.com/services/economic/yearly/hondec97/index.html
Prepared by Barclays Bank, the site reports on Hong Kong economic trends, politics, monetary and fiscal policy, exchange rates, international trade, and investment flows.

Career China
http://www.globalvillager.com/villager/CC.html
An online employment center, the site provides a directory of job openings in China, Hong Kong, and Taiwan. The service includes resume guides, interview tips, and chat services.

China Big

http://www.chinabig.com/

Posted in Chinese and English, the site is a searchable directory of Chinese organizations in some 20 categories including building materials, agriculture, and health.

China: Big Emerging Markets Homepage

http://www.ita.doc.gov/bems/China.html

Developed by the United States Department of Commerce, the site delivers Chinese fact sheets, economic forecasts, export and import statistics, sector profiles, and international trade guides.

China Business Briefs

http://www.austrade.gov.au/IOOM/China/

A service of Austrade, the site offers fact sheets on Chinese culture, business etiquette, marketing, transportation, travel, and visas.

China Business Net Pages

http://www.business-china.com/index.htm

Along with country fact sheets, the site provides Chinese investment guides, product catalogs, company directories, trade-show information, and business opportunities.

China.Com

http://china.com/english/

Along with news, city guides, and e-mail services, the site provides a directory of Chinese resources online in eight categories including business, finance, computers, and shopping.

China Country Brief

http://www.worldbank.org/cgi-bin/ sendoff.cgi?page=%2Fhtml%2Fextdr%2Foffrep%2 Feap%2Fcn.htm

A service of the World Bank Group, the site provides Chinese population statistics, financial data, development reports, and economic forecasts.

China Country Profile

http://www.tradenz.govt.nz/intelligence/profiles/ china.html

A service of the New Zealand Trade Development Board, the site provides Chinese economic statistics, market information, and business tips.

China Country Report

http://www.state.gov/www/issues/economic/ trade_reports/eastasia97/china97.html

Prepared by the U.S. Department of State, the site reports on Chinese exchange rates, debt management, trade barriers, export subsidies, intellectual property protection, worker rights, and foreign investment.

China: A Country Study

http://lcweb2.loc.gov/frd/cs/cntoc.html

A service of the U.S. Library of Congress, the site delivers fact sheets on Chinese geography, people, agriculture, mining, manufacturing, and foreign economic relations.

China Economic Information Network

http://www.cei.gov.cn/

Posted in Chinese and English, the site delivers Chinese business guides, economic reports, real estate bulletins, employment opportunities, legal primers, and investment information.

China InfoExport

http://www.infoexport.gc.ca/country- e.asp?continent=Asia&country=10

A service of Foreign Affairs and International Trade Canada, the site provides Chinese commercial guides and market reports.

China Internet Information Center

http://www.chinanews.org/

Along with national news, the site delivers discussion papers on Chinese human rights, penal reform, Tibet, Taiwan, family planning, arms control, environmental protection, and other issues.

China: An Introduction

http://www.apecsec.org.sg/member/apecchin.html

A service of the Asia Pacific Economic Cooperation, the site provides fact sheets on Chinese geography, climate, population, language, business, and international trade.

China Invest

http://www.china-invest.com/

Along with sector profiles and business guides, the site provides a directory of investment projects in over 30 Chinese provinces and cities including Beijing, Tianjin, and Shanghai.

China Market Access Database

http://mkaccdb.eu.int/mkdb/ mkdb.pl?METHOD=COUNTRY

A service of the European Commission, the site offers briefs on Chinese trade policy, tariff barriers, non-tariff barriers, investment-related measures, and financial services regulations.

China Market Information
http://dtiinfo1.dti.gov.uk/ots/china/
A service of the London-based Department of Trade and Industry, the site delivers Chinese fact sheets, maps, and trade-show information.

China Market Research
http://strategis.ic.gc.ca/sc_mrkti/ibinddc/engdoc/1a1f1.html
A service of Industry Canada, the site provides U.S. Department of Commerce reports on Chinese economic trends, trade barriers, investment regulations, business travel, and market opportunities.

China Net
http://www.bta.net.cn/
Written in Chinese, the site provides Chinese news, business guides, employment opportunities, cultural information, government directories, and free downloads.

China Public Procurement and Bidding
http://www.chinabidding.gov.cn/indexe.html
Posted in English and Chinese, the subscription service provides information on Chinese government procurement opportunities and bidding regulations.

China Standardization
http://www.csicci.gov.cn/
A service of the China Standardization and Information Classifying and Coding Institute, the site provides fact sheets on Chinese product and environmental standards.

China Torch Program
http://www.chinatorch.com/
Created in 1988, the Program promotes high technology development in China. The site includes project profiles, contact information, and a directory of Chinese companies in biotechnology, electronics, environmental protection, and other technology industries.

China Virtual Library
http://sun.sino.uni-heidelberg.de/igcs/
A service of the World Wide Web Virtual Library, the site is an index of Chinese resources online. Categories include online journals, news media, business and economy, culture, and mailing lists.

China Window
http://china-window.com/
An online country gateway, the site provides an index of Chinese resources on the web in six categories including business and economy, investments, and news and analysis.

Chinese Finance Association
http://www.aimhi.com/VC/tcfa/
An online forum for Chinese accounting and banking professionals, the site provides member profiles, working papers, and event information.

Chinese General Chamber of Commerce
http://www.cgcc.org.hk/
Based in Hong Kong, the Chamber promotes Chinese and Hong Kong international trade. The site includes a member directory, Chinese economic news, and a database of Chinese provincial and municipal representative trading offices in Hong Kong.

Chinese Manufacturers' Association of Hong Kong
http://www.cma.org.hk/
An online forum for Hong Kong manufacturers, the site provides a mission statement, event reports, trade leads, investment guides, and membership information.

Chinese Patent Office
http://www.cpo.cn.net/
Based in Beijing, the site delivers fact sheets on Chinese patents, trademarks, industrial designs, and other intellectual property. The service includes contact information and annual reports.

Country Commercial Guide Hong Kong
http://www.state.gov/www/about_state/business/com_guides/1998/eastasia/hongkong98.html
Prepared by the United States Consulate General in Hong Kong, the site delivers primers on Hong Kong business, politics, trade regulations and standards, investment, and travel.

Economy and Development
http://www.chinese-embassy.org.uk/Economy/economy.htm
A service of the Chinese Embassy in London, the site provides fact sheets on Chinese agriculture, international trade, foreign investment, financial services, transportation, and economic development programs.

Federation of Hong Kong Industries
http://www.fhki.org.hk/
Established in 1960, the Federation promotes the interests of Hong Kong business. The service includes a mission statement, training information, and a directory of industry councils.

Guide to China Investment

http://www.chinainvest.net.cn/eindex.htm

A virtual library of Chinese investment information, the site includes development zone guides, a strategic alliance newsletter, and procurement and bidding bulletins.

Hong Kong Business Briefs

http://www.austrade.gov.au/IOOM/HongKong/

A service of Austrade, the site offers fact sheets on Hong Kong business etiquette, foreign investment, corporate taxation, marketing, and visas.

Hong Kong Country Report

http://www.state.gov/www/issues/economic/ trade_reports/eastasia97/hongkong97.html

Prepared by the U.S. Department of State, the site reports on Hong Kong exchange rates, debt management, trade barriers, export subsidies, intellectual property protection, worker rights, and foreign investment.

Hong Kong Government Information Centre

http://www.info.gov.hk/

The online service delivers Hong Kong government speeches, press releases, fact sheets, departmental guides, statistics, tender notices, and business directories.

Hong Kong Government Supplies Department

http://www.info.gov.hk/gsd/tender.htm

Homepage of the Hong Kong government central purchasing authority, the site posts tender notices, supplier application forms, purchase forecasts, and procurement regulations.

Hong Kong Intellectual Property Department

http://www.houston.com.hk/hkgipd/

Posted in Chinese and English, the site delivers information on Hong Kong patents, trademarks, industrial designs, and other intellectual property. The service includes news, circulars, and a staff roster.

Hong Kong: An Introduction

http://www.apecsec.org.sg/member/apechk1.html

A service of the Asia Pacific Economic Cooperation, the site provides fact sheets on Hong Kong geography, climate, population, language, business, and international trade.

Hong Kong Market Access Database

http://mkaccdb.eu.int/mkdb/ mkdb.pl?METHOD=COUNTRY

A service of the European Commission, the site

offers briefs on Hong Kong trade policy, tariff barriers, non-tariff barriers, investment-related measures, and financial services regulations.

Hong Kong Market Information

http://dtiinfo1.dti.gov.uk/ots/hong_kong/

A service of the London-based Department of Trade and Industry, the site delivers Hong Kong fact sheets, maps, and trade-show information.

Hong Kong Market Research

http://strategis.ic.gc.ca/sc_mrkti/ibinddc/engdoc/ 1a1f2.html

A service of Industry Canada, the site provides U.S. Department of Commerce reports on Hong Kong economic trends, trade barriers, investment regulations, business travel, and market opportunities.

Hong Kong Virtual Library

http://www.asiawind.com/hkwwwvl/

A service of the World Wide Web Virtual Library, the site is an index of Hong Kong resources online. Categories include government, finance and economy, and science and technology.

Info China

http://www.info-china.com/

A virtual archive of Chinese macroeconomic statistics, the site includes data on Chinese gross domestic product, investment, and consumer and producer prices.

Law Online

http://www.lawhk.hku.hk/

A service of the University of Hong Kong, the site provides a database of Chinese national laws and regulations. Categories include cases, customs law, civil aviation law, and import and export regulations.

Market Profile on Mainland China

http://www.tdc.org.hk/main/china.htm

A service of the Hong Kong Trade Development Council, the site provides a Mainland China market profile. Modules include economic indicators, foreign trade, and investment policies.

Regent Commerce Network of China

http://www.china-inc.com/index.shtml

Along with fact sheets and travel guides, the site features a searchable directory of Chinese companies in eight categories including technology, textiles, international trade, transportation, and real estate.

Shanghai Science and Technology Network
http://www.stn.sh.cn/
Along with fact sheets and trade-show information, the site delivers Shanghai company directories, technology transfer opportunities, and research reports.

Shanghai Windows
http://china-window.com/shanghai/elink/eindex.html
Posted in Chinese and English, the site provides Shanghai news, investment opportunities, international trade reports, government directories, and tourism information.

Western China Products on the Web
http://www.sichuan-china.com/sichuan-china/scpages/F_Products_List.htm
The site is a directory of products from Sichuan, a Chinese province. Categories include medical instruments, furniture, and vegetables.

World Chinese Business Network
http://wcbn.com.sg/cgi-bin/multi/index_eng_ascii.htm?language=en&encoding=eng_ascii
A service of the Singapore Chinese Chamber of Commerce, the site is a directory of business associations, trade opportunities, and events in China, and Chinese communities around the world.

Xiamen Foreign Investment Executive Committee
http://209.41.56.40/
The site provides business fact sheets on Xiamen, a seaport in southeastern China. The service includes an investment guide, development zone reports, and project profiles.

China Trade Assistance

China Council for the Promotion of International Trade
http://www.ccpit.org/
Based in Beijing, the Council promotes Chinese exports and international investment. The site delivers Chinese economic news, business guides, trade-show information, trade leads, and legal primers.

China Council Jilin
http://www.jl.org/
The Council promotes exports and international investment in Jilin, a Chinese province. The site includes company directories, project profiles, and trade leads.

China Council Shanghai
http://www.china-collection.com/shanghai/ccpit/ccpit.htm
A forum for promoting Shanghai exports and foreign investment, the site features Shanghai fact sheets, company directories, and buy and sell offers.

China Council Tianjin
http://www.chinainfornet.com/ccpit/
Part of the China Council for the Promotion of International Trade, the organization promotes exports and international investment in Tianjin, a Chinese city. The service includes a member directory, company profiles, and contact information.

China Customs Statistics
http://www.chinanews.com/project/eiac/a1.htm
Posted in Chinese and English, the site provides information on how to order Chinese import and export data from China Customs Statistics, a Hong Kong-based trade information agency.

China Fair for International Investment and Trade
http://www.chinafair.org.cn/
Along with a database of investment projects in China, the Chinese and English language site provides Chinese business news, commercial guides, and an online bulletin board.

China Market
http://www.chinamarket.com.cn/
Posted in Chinese and English, the site is a searchable directory of Chinese companies and products. Categories include apparel, chemicals, electronics, and food.

China Trade Winds
http://www.trade-winds.net/prech.htm
A service of Trade Winds Online, the site is a searchable directory of Chinese trade shows, business contacts, tourism information, and media.

China Trading
http://www.chinatrading.com/
Along with investment bulletins and web guides, the site provides a directory of Chinese manufacturers and international traders in over 30 categories including electronics, apparel, pharmaceuticals, and plastics.

Fairs and Conferences in Hong Kong
http://www.tdc.org.hk/exh-con/

A database of Hong Kong trade shows and exhibitions, the site is searchable by organizer, event name, venue, date, and keyword.

Hong Kong Associations in Mainland China and Overseas Countries

http://www.tdc.org.hk/global/assoc.htm
A service of the Hong Kong Trade Development Council, the site is a database of Hong Kong associations and bilateral chambers of commerce in Europe, North America, and Asia.

Hong Kong Export Credit Insurance Corporation

http://www.hkecic.com/
The Corporation provides export finance and risk management services for Hong Kong exporters. The site includes press releases, annual reports, and a directory of Corporation programs and services.

Hong Kong Shipping Directory

http://www.info.gov.hk/mardep/sdfiles/shipdir.htm
A directory of Hong Kong shipping operations, the site is divided into more than 30 categories including freight forwarders, maritime insurance, passenger ferry services, and pilots.

Hong Kong Trade Development Council

http://www.tdc.org.hk/
Posted in Chinese and English, the site delivers Chinese and Hong Kong news, commercial guides, trade leads, business matching services, economic statistics, and a cyber campus.

Hong Kong Trade Winds

http://www.trade-winds.net/prehk.htm
A service of Trade Winds Online, the site is a searchable directory of Hong Kong trade shows, business contacts, tourism information, and media.

Hong Kong Trader

http://www.tdc.org.hk/hktrader/
Updated monthly, the site delivers Hong Kong business news, interviews, sector profiles, investment bulletins, and a searchable archive of past issues.

Ministry of Foreign Affairs

http://www.fmprc.gov.cn/
Posted in Chinese and English, the site is the official homepage of the Chinese Ministry of Foreign Affairs. The service provides press releases, foreign policy statements, and event information.

Ministry of Foreign Trade and Economic Cooperation

http://www.moftec.gov.cn/
A virtual library of country business information, the site features Chinese fact sheets, company directories, investment guides, trade leads, import and export statistics, rankings, and technology bulletins.

Overseas Organization

http://www.moftec.gov.cn/moftec/official/overseas_organization.html
A service of the Ministry of Foreign Trade and Economic Cooperation, the site is a directory of Chinese economic counselors in Asia, Oceania, Europe, the Americas, and Africa.

Trade Development Council Global Network

http://www.tdc.org.hk/global/offices.htm
The site is a directory of Hong Kong Trade Development Corporation offices around the world.

Trade Point Beijing

http://www.tpbjc.gov.cn/
Part of the United Nations Global Trade Point Network, the site provides Beijing trade leads, market bulletins, and contact information.

Trade Point Shanghai

http://www.tpsha.gov.cn/
Posted in Chinese and English, the site provides Shanghai trade leads, market bulletins, and contact information.

Trade Shows in China

http://www.expoguide.com/shows/data/loc_44.htm
Compiled by Expoguide, the site is a directory of upcoming trade shows in China.

Trade Shows in Hong Kong

http://www.expoguide.com/shows/data/loc_21.htm
Compiled by Expoguide, the site is a directory of upcoming trade shows in Hong Kong.

World Trade Database

http://www.wtdb.com/
An online marketplace, the site provides a Chinese company directory, trade leads, credit reports, investment guides, trade-show information, and marketing reports.

China Representative Offices

Argentina

Consulate General of Argentina in Hong Kong
http://home.netvigator.com/~consarhk/index.htm
Posted in English and Spanish, the site delivers Argentine fact sheets, business guides, visa and passport information, travel tips, and a database of Spanish translation services in Hong Kong.

Australia

Austrade in China
http://www.austrade.gov.au/China/
Featuring Australian product catalogs, success stories, and investment guides, the site provides a directory of Austrade offices in Beijing, Dalian, Guangzhou, Hangzhou, Nanjing, and Shanghai.

Austrade in Hong Kong
http://www.austrade.gov.au/HongKong/
The online service provides Australian export guides, company directories, product catalogs, success stories, investment primers, and contact information.

Austrade in Shanghai
http://www.aus-in-shanghai.com/austrade/sh_e.html
Along with fact sheets and trade statistics, the site delivers Australian product catalogs, investment guides, and profiles of the Australian trade commissioners in Shanghai.

Australia's Hong Kong Site
http://www.australia.org.hk/
The online service features Australian fact sheets, travel information, government guides, and a directory of Australian organizations in Hong Kong.

Australian Chamber of Commerce in Hong Kong
http://www.austcham.com.hk/
Representing over 500 companies, the Chamber promotes Australian-Hong Kong trade. The site includes news, classifieds, a calendar of events, and contact information.

Consulate General of Australia in Hong Kong
http://www.australia.org.hk/auscon/consulate.html
Featuring a welcome by the Consul General, the site provides Australian fact sheets, visa and passport information, customs guides, and media contacts.

Consulate General of Australia in Shanghai
http://www.aus-in-shanghai.com/
Posted in Chinese, the site provides Australian fact sheets, business guides, visa and passport information, and reports on Australia-China trade.

Embassy of Australia in Beijing
http://www.austemb.org.cn/
Posted in English and Chinese, the delivers Australian commercial guides, travel information, and a directory of consular and commercial services.

Northern Territory Government Office
http://www.australia.org.hk/state/north/north.html
Along with fact sheets and maps, the site provides a directory of Northern Territory commercial services in Hong Kong.

Queensland Government Office in Hong Kong
http://www.australia.org.hk/state/queens/queens.html
The state government site provides Queensland fact sheets, statistics, tourism guides, investment primers, and contact information.

South Australian Government Commercial Representative Office in Hong Kong
http://www.australia.org.hk/state/south/south.html
Established in 1976, the Office promotes trade and investment between South Australia and Hong Kong, Macau and Taiwan.

Austria

Austrian Trade Commission in Beijing
http://aw.wk.or.at/awo/ahst-peking.htm
The site lists the staff, street address, phone and fax numbers, e-mail link, and office hours of the Austrian Trade Commission in Beijing.

Austrian Trade Commission in Hong Kong
http://aw.wk.or.at/awo/ahst-hongkong.htm
The site lists the staff, street address, phone and fax numbers, e-mail link, and office hours of the Austrian Trade Commission in Hong Kong.

Austrian Trade Commission in Shanghai
http://aw.wk.or.at/awo/ahst-shanghai.htm
The site lists the staff, street address, phone and fax numbers, e-mail link, and office hours of the Austrian Trade Commission in Shanghai.

Belgium

Consulate General of Belgium in Hong Kong
http://consubel.org/hk/hkhome.html
The digital Consulate delivers Belgian fact sheets, news, travel guides, visa and passport information, and a directory of consular and commercial services.

Brunei Darussalam

Embassy of Brunei Darussalam in Beijing
http://www.brunet.bn/homepage/gov/bruemb/govemb.htm
The site provides contact information for the Brunei Darussalam Embassy in Beijing.

Canada

Canadian Chamber of Commerce in Hong Kong
http://www.cancham.com.hk/
Founded in 1977, the Chamber promotes Canada-Hong Kong trade. The service includes a mission statement, executive profiles, a calendar of events, and membership information.

Canadian Consulate General in Chongqing
http://www.canada.org.hk/english/p1115.html
The site lists the Consul General, staff, street address, and phone and fax numbers of the Canadian Consulate General in Chongqing.

Canadian Consulate General in Guangzhou
http://www.canada.org.hk/english/p1114.html
The site lists the Consul General, staff, street address, phone and fax numbers, and office hours of the Canadian Consulate General in Guangzhou.

Canadian Consulate General in Hong Kong
http://www.canada.org.hk/
Posted in English and French, the site features Canadian fact sheets, visa and passport information, travel guides, and reports on Chinese business opportunities in 12 industries including agri-food, electric power, transportation, and health.

Canadian Consulate General in Shanghai
http://www.canada.org.hk/english/p1113.html
The site lists the Consul General, staff, street address, phone and fax numbers, and e-mail link of the Canadian Consulate General in Shanghai.

Canadian Embassy in Beijing
http://www.canada.org.hk/english/p1111.html
The site lists the Ambassador, staff, street address, phone and fax numbers, and office hours of the Canadian Embassy in Beijing.

China Alberta Petroleum Center
http://www.altabjo.cn.net/
Based in Beijing, the Center promotes the export of advanced petroleum science and technology from Alberta to China. The site includes a staff roster, event information, market reports, and photos.

Province of Alberta Office in Hong Kong
http://www.alberta.org.hk/
Established in 1980, the Office coordinates Alberta trade, investment and business immigration related activities in China and Hong Kong. The service features a mission statement, event calendar, and trade opportunities.

Denmark

Consulate General of Denmark in Shanghai
http://www.dk-embassy-cn.org/gkltask.html
Along with Danish fact sheets, the site provides Chinese market reports, and a directory of Danish companies in the Shanghai area.

Embassy of Denmark in Beijing
http://www.dk-embassy-cn.org/
Posted in Chinese and English, the site provides Danish fact sheets, business guides, visa and passport information, and reports on China-Denmark trade and relations.

Finland

Embassy of Finland in Beijing
http://www.finland-in-china.com/home.htm
Posted in Chinese and English, the site provides Finnish fact sheets, visa and passport information, company profiles, and a directory of consular and commercial services.

Finland Trade Center in Beijing
http://www.exports.finland.fi/tradecen.htm
The site lists the staff, street address, phone and fax numbers, and e-mail link of the Finland Trade Center in Beijing.

Finland Trade Center in Hong Kong
http://www.exports.finland.fi/tradecen.htm
The site lists the staff, street address, phone and fax numbers, and e-mail link of the Finland Trade Center in Hong Kong.

Finland Trade Center in Shanghai
http://www.exports.finland.fi/tradecen.htm
The site lists the staff, street address, phone and fax numbers, and e-mail link of the Finland Trade Center in Shanghai.

France

French Trade Commission in China
http://www.dree.org/chine/
Posted in Chinese and French, the site delivers Chinese market reports, sector profiles, contact information, and a directory of French export promotion services.

French Trade Commission in Beijing
http://www.dree.org/chine/FRANCAIS/GENERAL/MEF/pekin.htm
The site lists the staff, street address, phone and fax numbers, and e-mail link of the French Trade Commission in Beijing.

French Trade Commission in Guangzhou
http://www.dree.org/chine/FRANCAIS/GENERAL/MEF/canton.htm
The site lists the staff, street address, phone and fax numbers, and e-mail link of the French Trade Commission in Guangzhou.

French Trade Commission in Hong Kong
http://www.dree.org/hongkong/
Posted in French, the site delivers Hong Kong market reports, sector profiles, contact information, and a directory of French export promotion services.

French Trade Commission in Shanghai
http://www.dree.org/chine/FRANCAIS/GENERAL/MEF/shanghai.htm
The site lists the staff, street address, phone and fax numbers, and e-mail link of the French Trade Commission in Shanghai.

French Trade Commission in Wuhan
http://www.dree.org/chine/FRANCAIS/GENERAL/MEF/wuhan.htm
The site lists the staff, street address, phone and fax numbers, and e-mail link of the French Trade Commission in Wuhan.

Germany

German Chamber of Commerce in Beijing
http://www.ahk.net/en/cn/Beijing/
The site lists the Executive, street address, phone and fax numbers, and e-mail link of the German Chamber in Beijing.

German Chamber of Commerce in Guangzhou
http://www.ahk.net/en/cn/Canton/
The site lists the Executive, street address, phone and fax numbers, and e-mail link of the German Chamber in Guangzhou.

German Chamber of Commerce in Hong Kong
http://www.ahk.net/en/cn/HongKong/
The site lists the Executive, street address, phone and fax numbers, and e-mail link of the German Chamber in Hong Kong.

German Chamber of Commerce in Shanghai
http://www.ahk.net/en/cn/Shanghai/
The site lists the Executive, street address, phone and fax numbers, and e-mail link of the German Chamber in Shanghai.

Ghana

Embassy of Ghana in Beijing
http://www.juntung.com/ghana-consul-hk/2misabo.htm
The site provides contact information for the Ghanaian Embassy in Beijing.

Honorary Consul of Ghana in Hong Kong
http://www.juntung.com/ghana-consul-hk/
Featuring a message from the Honorary Consul, the site provides Ghanaian fact sheets, cultural guides, visa and passport information, and a sound file of the national anthem.

India

Confederation of Indian Industry in China
http://www.indianindustry.com/au/cii_china.htm
An online forum for Indian businesspeople in China, the site provides Chinese market reports, action plans, and a directory of Confederation partners in China including the China Council for Promotion of International trade.

Consulate General of India in Hong Kong
http://www.hk.super.net/~comind1/
Along with Indian news and maps, the site features Indian commercial guides, investment primers, visa and passport information, and trade-show bulletins.

Consulate General of India in Shanghai
http://www.shanghai-ed.com/india/index.html
Featuring Indian news, fact sheets, and visa information, the site offers Chinese market guides, trade-show bulletins, and *Shanghai-India Business*, a monthly electronic magazine.

Embassy of India in Beijing
http://www.gcinfo.com/indembch/
The digital Embassy provides Indian fact sheets, sector profiles, and company directories, along with Chinese market reports, web guides, and business primers.

Indonesia

Embassy of Indonesia in Beijing
http://indag.dprin.go.id/INGG/trade/atache.HTM
The site provides contact information for the Indonesian Embassy in Beijing.

Ireland

Enterprise Ireland in Beijing
*http://www.irish-trade.ie/office_network/
office_locate01.html#anchor1439051*
The site lists the Manager, street address, and phone and fax numbers of the Enterprise Ireland office in Beijing.

Enterprise Ireland in Hong Kong
*http://www.irish-trade.ie/office_network/
office_locate01.html#anchor1439554*
The site lists the Manager, street address, and phone and fax numbers of the Enterprise Ireland office in Hong Kong.

Enterprise Ireland in Shanghai
*http://www.irish-trade.ie/office_network/
office_locate01.html#shanghai*
The site lists the Manager, street address, and phone and fax numbers of the Enterprise Ireland office in Shanghai.

Israel

Consulate General of Israel in Hong Kong
http://www.cgis.com.hk/
Posted in Chinese and English, the virtual Consulate provides Israeli fact sheets, economic reports, government guides, and reports on Hong Kong-Israel trade and relations.

Consulate General of Israel in Shanghai
*http://www.uninet.com.cn/consulate/israel/
index_en.htm*
The site lists the mission statement, street address, phone and fax numbers, and e-mail link of the Israeli Consulate General in Shanghai.

Italy

Consulate General of Italy in Hong Kong
http://home.netvigator.com/~itconshk/
Featuring a welcome from the Consul General, the service provides Italian fact sheets, business guides, visa and passport information, and a directory of Italian organizations in Hong Kong.

Japan

Consulate General of Japan in Hong Kong
http://www.japan.org.hk/
Posted in English and Japanese, the site delivers Japanese news, economic facts, education bulletins, visa information, and reports on Hong Kong-Japan trade and relations.

Laos

Embassy of Laos in Beijing
*http://www.laoembassy.com/news/
embassyabroad.htm*
The site provides contact information for the Embassy of Laos in Beijing.

Madagascar

Embassy of Madagascar in Beijing
*http://www.madagascar-contacts.com/us/
adresse.htm#alext*
Along with a directory of Madagascar government agencies, the site provides contact information for the Madagascar Embassy in Beijing.

Malaysia

Commission of Malaysia in Hong Kong
*http://www.mnet.com.my/klonline/www/missions/
malmiss/mhongkon1.htm*
The site provides contact information for the Malaysian Commission in Hong Kong.

Consulate General of Malaysia in Guangzhou
*http://www.mnet.com.my/klonline/www/missions/
malmiss/mchina2.htm*
The site provides contact information for the Malaysian Consulate General in Guangzhou.

Embassy of Malaysia in Beijing
*http://www.mnet.com.my/klonline/www/missions/
malmiss/mchina1.htm*
The site provides contact information for the Malaysian Embassy in Beijing.

Trade Commission of Malaysia in Beijing
*http://www.mnet.com.my/klonline/www/missions/
malmiss/mchina4.htm*
The site provides contact information for the
Malaysian Trade Commission in Beijing.

Trade Commission of Malaysia in Hong Hong
*http://www.mnet.com.my/klonline/www/missions/
malmiss/mhongkon2.htm*
The site provides contact information for the
Malaysian Trade Commission in Hong Kong.

Marshall Islands

Embassy of the Marshall Islands in Beijing
http://www.rmiembassyus.org/address.html
The site lists the street, phone and fax numbers,
and e-mail link of the Marshall Islands Embassy
in Beijing.

Mexico

Trade Commission of Mexico in Hong Kong
*http://www.mexico-businessline.com/ingles/
ofrepmu3.html#hong*
The site lists the street address, phone and fax
numbers, and e-mail link of the Trade Commission of Mexico in Hong Kong.

Nepal

Embassy of Nepal in Beijing
*http://www.info-nepal.com/members/fips/contacts/
nepalese.html*
The site provides contact information for the
Embassy of Nepal in Beijing.

New Zealand

Trade New Zealand in Beijing
http://www.tradenz.govt.nz/contact/northasia.html
An export promotion service, the site provides
contact information for the Trade New Zealand
office in Beijing.

Trade New Zealand in Hong Kong
http://www.tradenz.govt.nz/contact/northasia.html
The site provides contact information for the
Trade New Zealand office in Hong Kong.

Trade New Zealand in Shanghai
http://www.tradenz.govt.nz/contact/northasia.html
The site provides contact information for the
Trade New Zealand office in Shanghai.

Norway

Embassy of Norway in Beijing
*http://www.ntc.no/cgi-bin/wbch.exe?html=../
templates/utekontor2.html&profile=1102*
The site lists the staff, street address, phone and
fax numbers, and e-mail link of the Norwegian
Embassy in Beijing.

Pakistan

Pakistan Trade Office in Beijing
http://www.jamal.com/epb/ptoa.htm
The site provides contact information for the
Pakistan Trade Office in Beijing.

Pakistan Trade Office in Hong Kong
http://www.jamal.com/epb/ptoa.htm
The site provides contact information for the
Pakistan Trade Office in Hong Kong.

Peru

Embassy of Peru in China
http://www.embperu.cn.net/
Posted in Chinese and English, the site provides
Peruvian fact sheets, investment primers, cultural
guides, photo galleries, and a staff roster.

Philippines

**Philippine Trade and Investment Promotion
Office in Guangzhou**
http://www.dti.gov.ph/gzh/
The site provides a mission statement, service
directory, and contact information for the Philippine Trade Office in Guangzhou.

**Philippine Trade and Investment Promotion
Office in Hong Kong**
http://www.dti.gov.ph/HK/
The site provides a mission statement, service
directory, and contact information for the Philippine Trade Office in Hong Kong.

Portugal

**Portuguese Trade and Investment Office in
Beijing**
*http://www.portugal.org/geninfo/abouticep/
china.html*
The site lists the staff, street address, phone and
fax numbers, and e-mail link of the Portuguese
Trade and Investment Office in Beijing.

Singapore

Consulate General of Singapore in Hong Kong
http://www.gov.sg/mfa/consular/mww_c.htm
The site provides contact information for the Singapore Consulate General in Hong Kong.

Consulate General of Singapore in Shanghai
http://www.gov.sg/mfa/consular/mww_c.htm
The site provides contact information for the Singapore Consulate General in Shanghai.

Consulate General of Singapore in Xiamen
http://www.gov.sg/mfa/consular/mww_c.htm
The site provides contact information for the Singapore Consulate General in Xiamen.

Embassy of Singapore in Beijing
http://www.gov.sg/mfa/consular/mww_c.htm
The site provides contact information for the Singapore Embassy in Beijing.

South Africa

South Africa Foreign Trade Office in Beijing
http://wwwdti.pwv.gov.za/dtiwww/foreign_offices.htm
A service of the South Africa Department of Trade and Industry, the site provides contact information for the South Africa Trade Office in Beijing.

South Africa Foreign Trade Office in Hong Kong
http://wwwdti.pwv.gov.za/dtiwww/foreign_offices.htm
A service of the South Africa Department of Trade and Industry, the site provides contact information for the South Africa Trade Office in Hong Kong.

South Korea

Korean International Trade Association in Beijing
http://www.kita.or.kr/eng/national.html
The site provides contact information for the Korean International Trade Association in Beijing.

Korean International Trade Association in Hong Kong
http://www.kita.or.kr/eng/national.html
The site provides contact information for the Korean International Trade Association in Hong Kong.

Spain

Spanish Commercial Office in Beijing
http://www.icex.es/openURL.html#openURL=/english/infoproyem/ofcomes/ofcomes.html#AS
The site lists the staff, street address, phone and fax numbers, and e-mail link of the Spanish Commercial Office in Beijing.

Spanish Commercial Office in Hong Kong
http://www.icex.es/openURL.html#openURL=/english/infoproyem/ofcomes/ofcomes.html#AS
The site lists the staff, street address, phone and fax numbers, and e-mail link of the Spanish Commercial Office in Hong Kong.

Sweden

Consulate General of Sweden in Hong Kong
http://www.ud.se/english/mfa/ambassad/kina.htm
The site lists the staff, street address, phone and fax numbers, and e-mail link of the Swedish Consulate General in Hong Kong.

Consulate General of Sweden in Shanghai
http://www.swedcons-shanghai.com/
Posted in Chinese, English, and Swedish, the site provides Swedish fact sheets, event information, and a directory of consular and commercial services.

Embassy of Sweden in Beijing
http://www.ud.se/english/mfa/ambassad/kina.htm
The site lists the staff, street address, phone and fax numbers, and e-mail link of the Swedish Embassy in Beijing.

Taiwan

China External Trade Development Council Office in Hong Kong
http://www.cetra.org.tw/english/o_office/indexset.htm
A Taiwanese trade promotion service, the site lists the mission statement and e-mail link of the China External Trade Development Council Office in Hong Kong.

Taiwan Government Information Office in Hong Kong
http://www.gio.gov.tw/info/ngio/hong-f.html
Posted in Chinese and English, the site lists the street address, phone and fax numbers, and e-

mail link of the Taiwan Government Information Office in Hong Kong.

Tanzania

Embassy of Tanzania in Beijing
http://www.tanzania-online.gov.uk/visa/ envoys.html
The site provides contact information for the Tanzania Embassy in Beijing.

Thailand

Royal Thai Consulate General in Guangzhou
http://www.mfa.go.th/Embassy/detail/26.htm
The site lists the Consul General, street address, and phone and fax numbers of the Thai Consulate General in Guangzhou.

Royal Thai Consulate in Hong Kong
http://www.mfa.go.th/Embassy/detail/201.htm
The site lists the Consul General, street address, and phone and fax numbers of the Thai Consulate General in Hong Kong.

Royal Thai Consulate General in Kunming
http://www.mfa.go.th/Embassy/detail/13.htm
The site lists the Consul General, street address, and phone and fax numbers of the Thai Consulate General in Kunming.

Royal Thai Consulate General in Shanghai
http://www.mfa.go.th/Embassy/detail/209.htm
The site lists the Consul General, street address, and phone and fax numbers of the Thai Consulate General in Shanghai.

Royal Thai Embassy in Beijing
http://www.mfa.go.th/Embassy/detail/85.htm
The site lists the Ambassador, street address, and phone and fax numbers of the Thai Embassy in Beijing.

Thailand Office of Commercial Affairs in Beijing
http://www.thaitrade.com/thcoaf.html
The site lists the street address, phone and fax numbers, and e-mail link of the Thailand Office of Commercial Affairs in Beijing.

Thailand Office of Commercial Affairs in Hong Kong
http://www.thaitrade.com/thcoaf.html
The site lists the street address, phone and fax numbers, and e-mail link of the Thailand Office of Commercial Affairs in Hong Kong.

Turkey

Consulate General of Turkey in Hong Kong
http://www.turkey.org/madres.htm
As part of a directory of Turkish diplomatic offices around the world, the site lists the e-mail link of the Turkish Consulate General in Hong Kong.

United Kingdom

British Chamber of Commerce in China
http://www.bcchina.org/
A forum for British-China trade promotion, the site includes a newsletter, event calendar, training bulletins, a committee directory, and contact information.

British Chamber of Commerce in Hong Kong
http://www.britcham.com/core.html
Representing over 500 companies, the Chamber promotes British business interests in Hong Kong and China. The site includes a member directory, event calendar, and activity reports.

British Council of Hong Kong
http://www.britcoun.org.hk/index.htm
The British Council promotes educational, cultural and technical cooperation between Britain and countries around the world. The service includes a directory of British organizations and training programs in Hong Kong.

Consulate General of Britain in Guangzhou
http://www.fco.gov.uk/directory/posts.asp?CN
The site provides contact information for the British Embassy in Guangzhou.

Consulate General of Britain in Hong Kong
http://www.webhk.com/bcghk/
The digital Consulate delivers British fact sheets, business guides, cultural bulletins, visa and passport information, and a directory of consular and commercial services.

Consulate General of Britain in Shanghai
http://www.fco.gov.uk/directory/posts.asp?CN
The site provides contact information for the British Embassy in Shanghai.

Embassy of Britain in Beijing
http://www.fco.gov.uk/directory/posts.asp?CN
The site provides contact information for the British Embassy in Beijing.

Invest in Britain Bureau in Hong Kong
http://www.webhk.com/ibbasia/

A British investment promotion service, the site includes United Kingdom fact sheets, economic statistics, regional profiles, and business matchmaking services.

United States

American Chamber of Commerce in Hong Kong
http://www.amcham.org.hk/
Established in 1968, the Chamber promotes Hong Kong-United States trade. The site features press releases, position papers, business surveys, and event information.

China Commercial Brief
http://www.usembassy-china.gov/english/commercial/ccb.htm
A daily e-mail newsletter prepared by the United States and Foreign Commercial Service in Beijing, the Brief provides a compilation of Chinese and international media articles on Chinese business.

State of California Trade Office in Hong Kong
http://commerce.ca.gov/international/it_off.html#hongkong
A service of the California Trade and Commerce Agency, the site lists the Director, street address, phone and fax numbers, and e-mail link of the California Trade Office in Hong Kong.

State of Illinois Trade Office in Hong Kong
http://www.commerce.state.il.us/dcca/files/int'l/hongkong.htm
A service of the Illinois Department of Commerce and Community Affairs, the site lists the Managing Director, street address, phone and fax numbers, and e-mail link of the Illinois Trade Office in Hong Kong.

State of Michigan Trade Office in Shanghai
http://www.state.mi.us/mjc/ceo/business/inbd.htm
A service of the Michigan Jobs Commission, the site lists the street address and phone and fax numbers of the Michigan Trade Office in Shanghai.

State of North Carolina Trade Office in Hong Kong
http://www.commerce.state.nc.us/commerce/itd/foreign.html
A service of the North Carolina International Trade Division, the site lists the staff, street address, phone and fax numbers, and e-mail link of the North Carolina Trade Office in Hong Kong.

State of Ohio Trade Office in Hong Kong
http://ohiotrade.tpusa.com/offices.htm
A service of the Ohio Department of Commerce, the site lists the street address, phone and fax numbers, and e-mail link of the Ohio Trade Office in Hong Kong.

State of Utah Trade Office in Beijing
http://www.ce.ex.state.ut.us/international/reps/reps.htm#China
A service of the Utah International Business Development Office, the site lists the Vice President, street address, phone and fax numbers, and e-mail link of the Utah Trade Office in Beijing.

State of Washington Trade Office in Shanghai
http://www.trade.wa.gov/overseas.htm
Part of Washington State Community, Trade and Economic Development, the site lists the Executive Director, street address, phone and fax numbers, and e-mail link of the Washington Trade Office in Shanghai.

United States Agricultural Trade Office in Shanghai
http://www.usembassy-china.gov/english/agriculture/ATOS/index.html
Along with a mission statement and staff roster, the site includes reports on Chinese consumers, agri-food market trends, distribution systems, and domestic and third country competition.

United States-China Management and Education Training
http://www.ita.doc.gov/region/china/
A resource center for United States companies training Chinese managers, the site provides a directory of management training tools online. Categories include business schools, news, and management information hubs.

United States Commercial Center in Shanghai
http://www.ita.doc.gov/uscs/ccshnghi.html
The site lists the trade promotion services, street address, and e-mail link of the United States Commercial Center in Shanghai.

United States Consulate General in Chengdu
http://www.usembassy-china.gov/english/home/consulate-info.html#Chengdu
The site lists the street address and phone and fax numbers of the United States Consulate General in Chengdu.

United States Consulate General in Hong Kong

http://www.usconsulate.org.hk/
Along with reports on United States trade and relations with China and Hong Kong, the site delivers United States fact sheets, press releases, and a directory of consular and commercial services.

United States Consulate General in Guangzhou

http://www.usembassy-china.gov/english/home/ consulate-info.html#Guangzhou
The site lists the street address and phone and fax numbers of the United States Consulate General in Guangzhou.

United States Consulate General in Shanghai

http://www.usembassy-china.gov/english/home/ consulate-info.html#Shanghai
The site lists the street address and phone and fax numbers of the United States Consulate General in Shanghai.

United States Consulate General in Shenyang

http://www.usembassy-china.gov/english/home/ consulate-info.html#Shenyang
The site lists the street address and phone and fax numbers of the United States Consulate General in Shenyang.

United States Embassy in Beijing

http://www.usembassy-china.gov/
Featuring a message from the Ambassador, the site delivers Chinese commercial guides, electronic commerce reports, Internet regulations, and economic statistics.

United States Information Service in Beijing

http://www.usembassy-china.gov/english/press/ index.html
The site provides United States fact sheets, speeches, press releases, electronic journals, East Asian reports, and cultural and exchange program information.

Cook Islands

Cook Islands Media

Cook Islands News Online

http://www.cinews.co.ck/
Updated weekly, the electronic newspaper delivers Cook Islander news, business reports, editorials, and letters to the editor.

Cook Islands Market Guides

Cook Islands

http://www.cook-islands.com/
A virtual travel primer, the site delivers Cook Islander fact sheets, maps, history and culture lessons, sightseeing information, accommodation guides, and a directory of airline connections.

Cook Islands Business

http://cookpages.com/
Along with an event calendar and weather bulletins, the site offers a directory of Cook Islander organizations in 10 industries including media, marine, retail, and accommodation.

Cook Islands Country Profile

http://www.tradenz.govt.nz/intelligence/profiles/ cook_islands.html
A service of the New Zealand Trade Development Board, the site provides Cook Islander economic statistics, market information, and business tips.

Cook Islands InfoExport

http://www.infoexport.gc.ca/country-e.asp?continent=Asia&country=51
A service of Foreign Affairs and International Trade Canada, the site provides fact sheets and statistics on Cook Islander geography, business, and politics.

Cook Islands Market Research

http://strategis.ic.gc.ca/sc_mrkti/ibinddc/engdoc/ 1a1i7.html
Posted by Industry Canada, the site provides U.S. Central Intelligence Agency fact sheets on Cook Islander geography, people, government, business, and transportation.

Cook Islands Trade Assistance

Cook Islands Development Investment Board

http://www.cookislands-invest.com/
Based in Rarotonga, the Board promotes economic development in the Cook Islands. The site includes commercial guides, trade and investment opportunities, a staff directory, and contact information.

Fiji

Fiji Market Guides

Fiji Business Briefs
http://www.austrade.gov.au/IOOM/Fiji/
A service of Austrade, the site offers fact sheets on Fijian business etiquette, foreign investment, corporate taxation, marketing, and visas.

Fiji Country Brief
http://www.worldbank.org/cgi-bin/ sendoff.cgi?page=%2Fhtml%2Fextdr%2Foffrep%2 Feap%2Ffj.htm
A service of the World Bank Group, the site provides Fijian population statistics, financial data, development reports, and economic forecasts.

Fiji Country Profile
http://www.tradenz.govt.nz/intelligence/profiles/ fiji.html
A service of the New Zealand Trade Development Board, the site provides Fijian economic statistics, market information, and business tips.

Fiji Government
http://fiji.gov.fj/core/home.html
Homepage of the Fijian Government, the site provides press releases, news briefs, fact sheets, maps, government directories, sector profiles, and a photo gallery.

Fiji InfoExport
http://www.infoexport.gc.ca/country- e.asp?continent=Asia&country=53
A service of Foreign Affairs and International Trade Canada, the site provides fact sheets and statistics on Fijian geography, business and politics.

Fiji Market Research
http://strategis.ic.gc.ca/sc_mrkti/ibinddc/engdoc/ 1a1i8.html
A service of Industry Canada, the site provides U.S. Department of Commerce reports on Fijian economic trends, trade barriers, investment regulations, business travel, and market opportunities.

Fiji Online
http://www.fiji-online.com.fj/
A virtual country gateway, the site delivers Fiji news, fact sheets, weather bulletins, travel information, and a directory of Fijian companies in ten categories including engineering, medical, manufacturing, telecommunications, and trade.

Fiji Trade Assistance

Fiji Ministry of Foreign Affairs and External Trade
http://fiji.gov.fj/m_forgn/index.html
Based in Suva, the Ministry is responsible for Fijian external relations and trade promotion. The site includes a mission statement, executive profiles, and contact information.

Fiji Missions Overseas
http://fiji.gov.fj/core/fj_mis.html
An index of Fijian Embassies and High Commissions abroad, the site lists offices in 10 countries including Belgium, Malaysia, New Zealand, and the United States.

Fiji Trade and Investment Board
http://computech.ftib.org.fj/
A virtual library of business information, the site provides Fijian investment opportunities, trade leads, business guides, legal primers, sector profiles, and incentive information.

Fiji Representative Offices

Diplomatic Missions in Fiji
http://fiji.gov.fj/core/for_mis.html
A directory of diplomatic missions in Suva, the site lists representatives from 15 countries including Australia, China, France, and Japan.

Malaysia

Embassy of Malaysia in Suva
http://www.mnet.com.my/klonline/www/missions/ malmiss/mfiji.htm
The site provides contact information for the Malaysian Embassy in Suva.

Marshall Islands

Embassy of the Marshall Islands in Suva
http://www.rmiembassyus.org/address.html
The site lists the street, phone and fax numbers, and e-mail link of the Marshall Islands Embassy in Fiji.

New Zealand

Trade New Zealand in Suva
http://www.tradenz.govt.nz/contact/pacific.html
An export promotion service, the site provides contact information for the Trade New Zealand office in Suva.

Sweden

Consulate of Sweden in Suva
http://www.ud.se/english/mfa/ambassad/fiji.htm
The site lists the staff, street address, phone and fax numbers, and e-mail link of the Swedish Consulate in Suva.

United Kingdom

Britain in the Pacific Region
http://www.bhc.org.fj/
The site provides information on British diplomatic offices in the Oceania region.

High Commission of Britain in Suva
http://www.fco.gov.uk/directory/posts.asp?FJ
The site provides contact information for the British High Commission in Suva.

French Polynesia

French Polynesia Market Guides

French Polynesia
http://www.cd-enterprises.com/french_polynesia/
Developed by Chris Davis, the site provides a directory of French Polynesian resources online. Categories include news, travel, and weather.

French Polynesia Country Profile
http://www.tradenz.govt.nz/intelligence/profiles/french_polynesia.html
A service of the New Zealand Trade Development Board, the site provides French Polynesian economic statistics, market information, and business tips.

French Polynesia Market Research
http://strategis.ic.gc.ca/sc_mrkti/ibinddc/engdoc/1a1i9.html
Posted by Industry Canada, the site provides U.S. Central Intelligence Agency fact sheets on French Polynesian geography, people, government, business, and transportation.

Guam

Guam Media

Guam Media
http://www.mediainfo.com/emediajs/specific-geo.htm?region=guam
Developed by Editor and Publisher Interactive, the site is an index of Guamanian newspapers and other media sites online.

Pacific Daily News
http://www.pdnguam.com/
The site is homepage of *Pacific Daily News*, a daily newspaper published on Guam and circulated throughout Micronesia. The service includes Guamanian news and contact information.

Guam Market Guides

Guam Country Profile
http://www.tradenz.govt.nz/intelligence/profiles/guam.html
A service of the New Zealand Trade Development Board, the site provides Guamanian economic statistics, market information, and business tips.

Guam Economic Development Authority
http://www.iftech.net/c/geda/home.html
The online service delivers fact sheets on Guamanian geography, climate, politics, business, culture, tourism, education, health care, housing, and recreation.

Guam Market Research
http://strategis.ic.gc.ca/sc_mrkti/ibinddc/engdoc/1a1i10.html
Posted by Industry Canada, the site provides U.S. Central Intelligence Agency fact sheets on Guamanian geography, people, government, business, and transportation.

Guam Representative Offices

Australia

Austrade in Guam
http://www.austrade.gov.au/Manila/index.asp?PageID=20424
Along with Australian product catalogs, success stories and investment guides, the site provides Australia-Guam trade reports, and contact information.

Japan

Consulate General of Japan in Guam
http://www.embjapan.org/agana/
The virtual Consulate delivers Japanese fact sheets, business guides, visa and passport information, reports on Guam-Japan relations, and a directory of consular and commercial services.

Micronesia

Micronesia Consulate in Tamuning
http://www.fsmembassy.org/guam.htm
The site lists the Consul General, staff, street address, phone and fax numbers, and e-mail link of the Federated States of Micronesia Consulate in Tamuning.

Indonesia

Indonesia Media

Indonesia Media
http://www.mediainfo.com/emediajs/specific-geo.htm?region=indonesia
Developed by Editor and Publisher Interactive, the site is an index of Indonesian media sites online including magazines, newspapers, and television stations.

Indonesia Market Guides

Access Indonesia Online
http://www.accessindo.com/
An online country gateway, the site provides Indonesian fact sheets, company directories, discussion forums, a buy and sell exchange, and a directory of leading business organizations.

Central Bureau of Statistics
http://www.bps.go.id/
A virtual library of statistics, the site provides data on Indonesian employment, wages, agriculture, manufacturing, mining, public finance, international trade, and other economic indicators.

Commerce Net Indonesia
http://www.commerce.net.id/
Along with news, exchange rates, and weather bulletins, the site provides Indonesian discussion forums, interactive quizzes, employment opportunities, and company directories.

Country Commercial Guide
http://www.state.gov/www/about_state/business/com_guides/1998/eastasia/indonesia98.html
Prepared by the United States Embassy in Jakarta, the site delivers primers on Indonesian business, politics, trade regulations and standards, investment, and travel.

Guide to Indonesian Products
http://www.prica.org/commerce/guide/
Featuring country fact sheets and web guides, the site offers a directory of Indonesian products and companies in nine categories including textiles, ceramics, furniture, and fish.

Indonesia Business Briefs
http://www.austrade.gov.au/IOOM/Indonesia/
A service of Austrade, the site offers fact sheets on Indonesian business etiquette, foreign investment, corporate taxation, marketing, and visas.

Indonesia Business Center Online
http://www.indobiz.com/
A hub of business information, the site features Indonesian company directories, trade leads, news, travel information, classified ads, and employment opportunities.

Indonesia Business Contacts
http://www.indobiz.com/board/contact.htm
A directory of Indonesian buy and sell offers, the site is divided into 10 categories including technology, professional services, raw materials, food products, and consumer goods.

Indonesian Business Directory
http://www.cyberdia.com/business.htm
A searchable database of Indonesian companies and organizations, the site is divided into 14 categories including computers, food products, real estate, textiles, and travel.

Indonesia Country Brief
http://www.worldbank.org/cgi-bin/sendoff.cgi?page=%2Fhtml%2Fextdr%2Foffrep%2Feap%2Fid.htm
A service of the World Bank Group, the site provides Indonesian population statistics, financial data, development reports, and economic forecasts.

Indonesia Country Profile
http://www.tradenz.govt.nz/intelligence/profiles/indonesia.html
A service of the New Zealand Trade Development Board, the site provides Indonesian economic statistics, market information, and business tips.

Indonesia Country Report
http://www.state.gov/www/issues/economic/trade_reports/eastasia97/indonesia97.html
Prepared by the U.S. Department of State, the site reports on Indonesian exchange rates, debt management, trade barriers, export subsidies, intellectual property protection, worker rights, and foreign investment.

Indonesia: A Country Study
http://lcweb2.loc.gov/frd/cs/idtoc.html
A service of the U.S. Library of Congress, the site delivers fact sheets on Indonesian geography, people, agriculture, mining, manufacturing, and foreign economic relations.

Indonesia InfoExport
http://www.infoexport.gc.ca/country-e.asp?continent=Asia&country=14
A service of Foreign Affairs and International Trade Canada, the site provides Indonesian commercial guides and market reports.

Indonesia: An Introduction
http://www.apecsec.org.sg/member/apecindo.html
A service of the Asia Pacific Economic Cooperation, the site provides fact sheets on Indonesian geography, climate, population, language, business, and currency.

Indonesia Market Access Database
http://mkaccdb.eu.int/mkdb/mkdb.pl?METHOD=COUNTRY
A service of the European Commission, the site offers briefs on Indonesian trade policy, tariff barriers, non-tariff barriers, investment-related measures, and financial services regulations.

Indonesia Market Information
http://dtiinfo1.dti.gov.uk/ots/indonesia/
A service of the London-based Department of Trade and Industry, the site delivers Indonesian fact sheets, maps, and trade-show information.

Indonesia Market Research
http://strategis.ic.gc.ca/sc_mrkti/ibinddc/engdoc/1a1i12.html
A service of Industry Canada, the site provides U.S. Department of Commerce reports on Indonesian economic trends, trade barriers, investment regulations, business travel, and market opportunities.

Indonesia Virtual Library
http://coombs.anu.edu.au/WWWVLPages/IndonPages/WWWVL-Indonesia.html
A service of the World Wide Web Virtual Library, the site is a directory of Indonesian resources online. Categories include news and media, government, travel, and education.

Indonesian Macro Economic Statistics
http://www.bps.go.id/execsum/
An online statistical archive, the site provides data on Indonesian inflation rates, consumer and wholesale prices, oil and gas production, international trade, and tourism.

Indonesian Yellow Pages
http://www.yellowpages.co.id/
Along with employment opportunities and web guides, the site features a browsable index of Indonesian companies and organizations in over 100 categories.

Indonesia Trade Assistance

Export Support Board of Indonesia
http://www.inaweb.co.id/esb-dpe
Established by the Government of Indonesia, the Board promotes Indonesian exports. The site provides a product catalog, company directory, and contact information.

InaWeb Home Page
http://www.inaweb.co.id/
A service of the Indonesian Ministry of Industry and Trade, the site delivers Indonesian trade-show information, exporter directories, and product catalogs.

Indonesia Export Directory
http://www.accessindo.com/business/html/export.html
A directory of Indonesian exporters and products, the site is divided into 20 categories including agriculture, furniture, plastics, steel, textiles, and toys.

Indonesia Global Promotion
http://www.igpweb.com/
Along with news and travel information, the site features a searchable index of Indonesian business associations and companies in over 100 industries including aerospace, metals, electronics, and food products.

Indonesian Trade Representative Offices
http://indag.dprin.go.id/INGG/trade/atache.HTM
A database of Indonesia Missions and Embassies abroad, the site lists offices in over 20 countries including Austria, China, Philippines, and the United States.

Indonesia Trade Winds
http://www.trade-winds.net/preid.htm
A service of Trade Winds Online, the site is a searchable directory of Indonesian trade shows, business contacts, tourism information, and media.

Ministry of Industry and Trade
http://indag.dprin.go.id/
Along with economic fact sheets and trade statistics, the site delivers Indonesian sector profiles, standards regulations, and government directories.

National Agency for Export Development
http://www.inaweb.co.id/nafed/
Established in 1971, the Agency promotes Indonesian exports. The site includes an organization directory, export news, event information, and international business guides.

Pusdata Online
http://www.dprin.go.id/index.html
A service of the Indonesian Ministry of Industry and Trade of the Republic, the site provides discussion groups, bulletin boards, chat services, and web guides.

Trade Shows in Indonesia
_http://www.expoguide.com/shows/data/loc_24.htm_
Compiled by Expoguide, the site is a directory of upcoming trade shows in Indonesia.

Indonesia Representative Offices

Embassies and Consulates in Jakarta
_http://www.travel.com.hk/consulat/con_id.htm_
A directory of foreign diplomatic posts in Jakarta, the site lists representative offices from over 20 countries including Afghanistan, Egypt, Iraq, Kuwait, Sweden, and Vietnam.

Australia

Austrade in Jakarta
http://www.austrade.gov.au/Jakarta/
The online service provides Australian export guides, company directories, product catalogs, success stories, investment primers, and contact information.

Austria

Austrian Trade Commission in Jakarta
http://aw.wk.or.at/awo/ahst-jakarta.htm
The site lists the staff, street address, phone and fax numbers, e-mail link, and office hours of the Austrian Trade Commission in Jakarta.

Brunei Darussalam

Embassy of Brunei Darussalam in Jakarta
http://www.brunet.bn/homepage/gov/bruemb/
govemb.htm
The site provides contact information for the Brunei Darussalam Embassy in Jakarta.

Canada

Canada-Indonesia Business Development Office
http://www.dfait-maeci.gc.ca/jakarta/menu-e.htm?trade-e.htm
Based in Jakarta, the Office promotes Canada-Indonesia trade and technology transfer. The site includes a mission statement, staff roster, and contact information.

Embassy of Canada in Jakarta
http://www.dfait-maeci.gc.ca/jakarta/
Posted in English and French, the site provides Canadian fact sheets, travel guides, visa and passport information, Indonesian business primers, and a database of Canadian companies in Indonesia.

Finland

Finland Trade Center in Jakarta
http://www.exports.finland.fi/tradecen.htm
The site lists the staff, street address, phone and fax numbers, and e-mail link of the Finland Trade Center in Jakarta.

France

French Trade Commission in Jakarta
http://www.dree.org/indonesie/
Posted in French, the site delivers Indonesian market reports, sector profiles, contact information, and a directory of French export promotion services.

Germany

German-Indonesian Chamber of Commerce
http://www.io.com/ekonid/
Established in 1970, the Chamber promotes German-Indonesian trade. The site includes news, a member directory, business guides, and contact information.

India

Indian Commercial Mission in Jakarta
http://www.nic.in/commin/ICM.HTM
The site lists the street address, phone and fax numbers, and e-mail link of the Indian Commercial Mission in Jakarta.

Japan

Embassy of Japan in Jakarta
http://www.rad.net.id/eojind/
Posted in English and Japanese, the site provides Japanese fact sheets, press releases, economic reports, media guides, and visa and passport information.

Laos

Embassy of Laos in Jakarta
http://www.laoembassy.com/news/ embassyabroad.htm
The site provides contact information for the Embassy of Laos in Jakarta.

Malaysia

Embassy of Malaysia in Jakarta
http://www.mnet.com.my/klonline/www/missions/ malmiss/mindone1.htm
The site provides contact information for the Malaysian Embassy in Jakarta.

Trade Commission of Malaysia in Jakarta
http://www.mnet.com.my/klonline/www/missions/ malmiss/mindone6.htm
The site provides contact information for the Malaysian Trade Commission in Jakarta.

Netherlands

Royal Netherlands Embassy in Jakarta
http://www.neth-embassy-jakarta.org/
The online service delivers Dutch fact sheets, press releases, commercial guides, legal primers, sector profiles, web guides, and visa and passport information.

New Zealand

Trade New Zealand in Jakarta
http://www.tradenz.govt.nz/contact/seasia.html
An export promotion service, the site provides contact information for the Trade New Zealand office in Jakarta.

Norway

Embassy of Norway in Jakarta
http://www.ntc.no/cgi-bin/wbch.exe?html=../ templates/utekontor2.html&profile=1112
The site lists the staff, street address, phone and fax numbers, and e-mail link of the Norwegian Embassy in Jakarta.

Pakistan

Pakistan Trade Office in Jakarta
http://www.jamal.com/epb/ptoa.htm
The site provides contact information for the Pakistan Trade Office in Jakarta.

Philippines

Philippine Trade and Investment Promotion Office in Jakarta
http://www.dti.gov.ph/jkt/
The site provides a mission statement, service directory, and contact information for the Philippine Trade Office in Jakarta.

Singapore

Consulate General of Singapore in Medan
http://www.gov.sg/mfa/consular/mww_i.htm
The site provides contact information for the Singapore Consulate General in Medan.

Embassy of Singapore in Jakarta
http://www.gov.sg/mfa/consular/mww_i.htm
The site provides contact information for the Singapore Embassy in Jakarta.

South Africa

South Africa Foreign Trade Office in Jakarta
http://wwwdti.pwv.gov.za/dtiwww/ foreign_offices.htm
A service of the South Africa Department of Trade and Industry, the site provides contact information for the South Africa Trade Office in Jakarta.

Spain

Spanish Commercial Office in Jakarta
http://www.icex.es/openURL.html#openURL=/ english/infoproyem/ofcomes/ofcomes.html#AS
The site lists the staff, street address, phone and fax numbers, and e-mail link of the Spanish Commercial Office in Jakarta.

Sweden

Embassy of Sweden in Jakarta
http://www.swedemb-jakarta.com/
The site provides Swedish fact sheets, visa and passport information, and a directory of consular and commercial services.

Taiwan

China External Trade Development Council Office in Jakarta
http://www.cetra.org.tw/english/o_office/ indexset.htm
A Taiwanese trade promotion service, the site lists the mission statement and e-mail link of the China External Trade Development Council Office in Jakarta.

Taiwan Government Information Office in Jakarta
http://www.gio.gov.tw/info/ngio/indo-f.html
Posted in Chinese and English, the site lists the street address, phone and fax numbers, and e-mail link of the Taiwan Government Information Office in Jakarta.

Thailand

Royal Thai Embassy in Jakarta
http://www.mfa.go.th/Embassy/detail/82.htm
The site lists the Ambassador, street address, and phone and fax numbers of the Thai Embassy in Jakarta.

Thailand Office of Commercial Affairs in Jakarta
http://www.thaitrade.com/thcoaf.html
The site lists the street address, phone and fax numbers, and e-mail link of the Thailand Office of Commercial Affairs in Jakarta.

United Kingdom

Consulate of Britain in Medan
http://www.fco.gov.uk/directory/posts.asp?IS
The site provides contact information for the British Consulate in Medan.

Consulate of Britain in Surabaya
http://www.fco.gov.uk/directory/posts.asp?IS
The site provides contact information for the British Consulate in Surabaya.

Embassy of Britain in Jakarta
http://www.british-emb-jakarta.or.id/
The site provides British fact sheets, business guides, visa and passport information, event bulletins, and a directory of consular and commercial services.

United States

State of California Trade Office in Jakarta
http://commerce.ca.gov/international/ it_off.html#jakarta
A service of the California Trade and Commerce Agency, the site lists the street address, phone and fax numbers, and e-mail link of the California Trade Office in Jakarta.

United States Commercial Center in Jakarta
http://www.ita.doc.gov/uscs/ccjakrta.html
The site lists the trade promotion services, street address, and e-mail link of the United States Commercial Center in Jakarta.

United States Consulate General in Surabaya
http://www.usembassyjakarta.org/surabaya.html
The site lists the Principal Officer, street address, phone and fax numbers, e-mail link, and office hours of the United States Consulate General in Surabaya.

United States Embassy in Jakarta
http://www.usembassyjakarta.org/
Along with Indonesian commercial guides, the virtual Embassy delivers United States news, visa and passport information, and a directory of consular and commercial services.

United States Foreign Agricultural Service in Jakarta
http://www.usembassyjakarta.org/fas/
A unit of the United States Department of Agriculture, the Service promotes the export of United States agricultural products to Indonesia. The site provides activity reports and a directory of commercial services.

United States Information Service in Jakarta
http://www.usembassyjakarta.org/usis.html
The site provides United States fact sheets, speeches, press releases, English language training information, Voice of America schedules, and Fulbright scholarship bulletins.

Japan

Japan Search Tools

EasySearch
http://www.aist.go.jp/NIBH/~honda/EasySEARCH/
A metasearch engine, the web navigation service

scans some 30 online search tools simulta-neously, and returns a consolidated list of responses in English and Japanese.

Excite Japan
http://jp.excite.com/
A personalized webstart page, the English and Japanese language site features Japanese news, business listings, people finders, Internet tutorials, and shopping channels.

Infoseek Japan
http://japan.infoseek.com/
Written in Japanese, the site provides web navigation services, browsing tips, and a search-able directory of Japanese resources online.

Lycos Japan
http://www.lycos.co.jp/
Posted in Japanese, the search service includes road maps, website reviews, classifieds, shopping guides, and chat forums.

Yahoo Japan
http://www.yahoo.co.jp/
A service of Yahoo, the site provides Japanese news, web-based personal management tools, and Internet searching.

Japan Media

Jam Jam
http://www.mainichi.co.jp/index-e.html
Posted in English and Japanese, the site provides Japanese headlines, editorials, business reports, high technology bulletins, and cultural information.

Japan Media
http://www.mediainfo.com/emediajs/specific-geo.htm?region=japan
Compiled by Editor and Publisher Interactive, the site is an index of Japanese media sites online including magazines, newspapers, and radio and television stations.

NIKKEI Net
http://www.nikkei.co.jp/enews/
Updated daily, the English and Japanese language site delivers Japanese news, eco-nomic reports, regional bulletins, and a search-able archive of back issues.

Japan Market Guides

Access to Japan
http://www.keidanren.or.jp/A2J/index.html

A service of the Japan Federation of Economic Organizations, the site provides a directory of procurement contacts for more than 400 major Japanese companies.

Barclays Country Report: Japan
http://www.offshorebanking.barclays.com/ services/economic/yearly/japsep97/index.html
Prepared by Barclays Bank, the site reports on Japanese economic trends, politics, monetary and fiscal policy, exchange rates, international trade, and investment flows.

Business of Japan
http://www.iijnet.or.jp/press/boj/index.e.html
A browsable database of Japanese companies, the site is divided into more than 20 categories including food products, interior design, apparel, architecture, cosmetics, and multimedia.

Career Mosaic Japan
http://www.careermosaic.or.jp/
Part of the Career Mosaic global network, the site provides Japanese employer profiles, resume posting services, online job fairs, career primers, and a searchable job database.

Chambers Information Network
http://www.jcci.or.jp/home-e.html
A service of the Japan Chamber of Commerce and Industry, the site provides a directory of chamber of commerce organizations in Japan, and a browsable database of Japanese compa-nies seeking international partners.

Daiwa Institute of Research
http://www.dir.co.jp/welcome.html
Homepage of a Japanese think tank, the site delivers Japanese economic forecasts, invest-ment bulletins, sector profiles, and Asia Pacific business reports.

Global Window
http://www.anderson.ucla.edu/research/japan/
Co-sponsored by Meikai and Asahi Universities in Japan, the site is a primer on how to conduct business in Japan. Modules include understand-ing your counterpart, legal considerations, and tips for the business traveler.

Invest in Japan
http://www.JETRO.go.jp/INVEST/index.html
A service of the Japan External Trade Organiza-tion, the site delivers Japanese investment guides, regional profiles, taxation primers, and business start-up tips.

Japan Business Briefs

http://www.austrade.gov.au/IOOM/Japan/
A service of Austrade, the site offers fact sheets on Japanese business etiquette, foreign investment, corporate taxation, marketing, and visas.

Japan Business Report

http://italchambers.net/BusinessReports.html
Prepared by the Italian Chamber of Commerce and written in Italian, the site provides Japanese fact sheets, market reports, and commercial guides.

Japan Country Profile

http://www.tradenz.govt.nz/intelligence/profiles/japan.html
A service of the New Zealand Trade Development Board, the site provides Japanese economic statistics, market information, and business tips.

Japan Country Report

http://www.state.gov/www/issues/economic/trade_reports/eastasia97/japan97.html
Prepared by the U.S. Department of State, the site reports on Japanese exchange rates, debt management, trade barriers, export subsidies, intellectual property protection, worker rights, and foreign investment.

Japan: A Country Study

http://lcweb2.loc.gov/frd/cs/jptoc.html
A service of the U.S. Library of Congress, the site delivers fact sheets on Japanese geography, people, agriculture, mining, manufacturing, and foreign economic relations.

Japan Development Bank

http://www.jdb.go.jp/index_e.html
Founded in 1951, the Bank finances economic development projects in Japan. The site includes a mission statement, activity reports, Japanese economic articles, and loan information.

Japan Directory

http://www.jinjapan.org/jd/
A hub of country information, the site provides a searchable directory of Japanese resources online. Categories include industry and economy, media and publishing, and culture.

Japan Economic Foundation

http://www.jef.or.jp/index.html
Based in Tokyo, the Foundation promotes communication and economic cooperation with Japanese trading partners. The site provides a mission statement, news, event information, and Japanese business reports.

Japan Foundation

http://www.jpf.go.jp/
Established in 1972, the Foundation organizes Japanese cultural exchanges with countries around the world. The site includes activity reports, program information, and Japanese culture guides.

Japanese Economic Reports

http://www.dkb.co.jp/english/market/index.html
A service of the Dai-Ichi Kangyo Bank, the site offers global and Japanese economic reports, currency bulletins, business forecasts, and sector profiles.

Japanese Government Procurement Database

http://www.JETRO.go.jp/cgi-bin/gov/govinte.cgi
A searchable database of Japanese procurement notices, the site posts tender information for some 100 Japanese agencies, and over 70 industry categories including pharmaceuticals, machinery, and market research services.

Japan InfoExport

http://www.infoexport.gc.ca/country-e.asp?continent=Asia&country=18
A service of Foreign Affairs and International Trade Canada, the site provides Japanese commercial guides and market reports.

Japan Information Network

http://www.jinjapan.org/
An online country gateway, the site provides Japanese maps, city profiles, business guides, travel tips, event information, government directories, and photo galleries.

Japan Information Network Statistics

http://jin.jcic.or.jp/stat/
Posted in English and Japanese, the site provides data on Japanese politics, economics, labor, living standards, housing, education, research and development, and other economic indicators.

Japan: An Introduction

http://www.apecsec.org.sg/member/apecjp.html
A service of the Asia Pacific Economic Cooperation, the site provides fact sheets on Japanese geography, climate, population, language, business, and international trade.

Japan: An International Comparison

http://www.keidanren.or.jp/KKC/english/journal/aic.html
A virtual country guide, the site offers Japanese fact sheets and statistics. Categories include

land and population, national economy, industries, and international trade.

Japan Market Access Database
http://mkaccdb.eu.int/mkdb/
mkdb.pl?METHOD=COUNTRY
A service of the European Commission, the site offers briefs on Japanese trade policy, tariff barriers, non-tariff barriers, investment-related measures, and financial services regulations.

Japan Market Information
http://dtiinfo1.dti.gov.uk/ots/japan/
A service of the London-based Department of Trade and Industry, the site delivers Japanese fact sheets, maps, and trade-show information.

Japan Market Research
http://strategis.ic.gc.ca/sc_mrkti/ibinddc/engdoc/
1a1f3.html
A service of Industry Canada, the site provides U.S. Department of Commerce reports on Japanese economic trends, trade barriers, investment regulations, business travel, and market opportunities.

Japan Patent Office
http://www.jpo-miti.go.jp/
Along with press releases and policy papers, the English and Japanese language site provides a searchable database of Japanese patents, trademarks, and other intellectual property.

J-Guide
http://fuji.stanford.edu/JGUIDE/
Presented by the Stanford University United States-Japan Technology Management Center, the site is a directory of Japanese resources information. Categories include search engines, business and economics, and government and politics.

Journal of Japanese Trade and Industry
http://www.jef.or.jp/over/index_jti.html
A service of the Japan Economic Foundation, the site provides Japanese business news, industrial surveys, sector profiles, and macro-economic reports.

Keidanren
http://www.keidanren.or.jp/
Established in 1946, the Japan Federation of Economic Organizations—abbreviated in Japanese as "Keidanren"—is a nationwide business association. The site includes fact sheets on Japanese economic policy, business law, and taxation.

Ministry of Search
http://st.jr.chiba-u.ac.jp/mos/index-e.html
Posted in English and Japanese, the site is a searchable index of Japanese government agencies online from the Ministry of Finance to the Maritime Safety Agency to the Audit Board.

Nihongo Yellow Pages
http://www.nyp.com/
A searchable directory of Japanese companies and organizations, the site is divided into ten categories, including business, education, finance, health, and technology.

Research for Business Competition
http://www.rbc.co.jp/english/
Homepage of a Japanese marketing firm, the site provides a free report on the Japanese retail and wholesale food market.

Small and Medium Enterprises in Japan
http://www.sme.ne.jp/japane.html
Along with government policy papers and program information, the site provides a browsable database of Japanese small and medium-sized enterprises in over 30 categories including publishing, plastics, and transportation equipment.

Statistics Bureau
http://www.stat.go.jp/1.htm
Based in Tokyo, the site delivers Japanese census and statistical information. Categories include family income, consumer prices, and population estimates.

Japan Trade Assistance

Japan Customs
http://www.mof.go.jp/~customs/conte-e.htm
The site provides fact sheets on Japanese import and export clearance procedures, quarantine regulations, prohibited articles, and other customs laws and regulations.

Japan Embassies and Consulates Abroad
http://www.mofa.go.jp/about/emb_cons/
mofaserv.html
A service of the Ministry of Foreign Affairs of Japan, the site is a directory of Japanese Embassies and Consulates online in Asia, North America, South America, Europe, and the Middle East.

Japan External Trade Organization

http://www.JETRO.go.jp/top/index.html
Headquartered in Tokyo, the Japan External Trade Organization or JETRO promotes Japanese exports and international business. The service includes press releases, investment guides, and procurement information.

Japan Trade Winds

http://www.trade-winds.net/prejp.htm
A service of Trade Winds Online, the site is a searchable directory of Japan trade shows, business contacts, tourism information, and media.

Japan Yellow Pages

http://www.jetc.com/jyp.html
A searchable directory of Japanese companies and organizations, the English and Japanese language site is divided into over 100 industry categories including food products, electronics, and pharmaceuticals.

JETRO Websites

http://www.JETRO.go.jp/HOMEPAGE/05.html
The site is a directory of Japan External Trade Organization offices online in the United States, Canada, Central and South America, Europe, the Middle East, and Africa.

Ministry of Foreign Affairs

http://www.mofa.go.jp/
Along with press releases and foreign policy statements, the site provides a virtual library of reports on Japanese economic and political relations with over 50 countries and international organizations.

Ministry of International Trade and Industry

http://www.miti.go.jp/index-e.html
Based in Tokyo, the Ministry promotes Japanese business and exports. The site includes press releases, policy statements, and special reports on topics including import barriers, electronic commerce, and the World Trade Organization.

Ministry of International Trade and Industry Statistics

http://www.miti.go.jp/stat-e/h-menu-e.html
Along with Japanese business surveys, the site delivers fact sheets and statistics on a dozen leading Japanese industries including iron and steel, plastics, machinery, textiles, and petroleum.

Towards the Age of the Digital Economy

http://www.miti.go.jp/intro-e/a228101e.html
Prepared by the Ministry of International Trade and Industry, the site is a virtual discussion paper on Japanese electronic commerce policy. Topics include commercial transactions, intellectual property rights, and personal data and privacy.

Trade Shows in Japan

http://www.expoguide.com/shows/data/loc_30.htm
Compiled by Expoguide, the site is a directory of upcoming trade shows in Japan.

Trade Shows in Japan

http://www.jetc.com/TradeShows.html
A service of Oregon-based Japan Export and Trade Consultants, the site provides a directory of Japanese trade shows in seven areas including high technology, medical, and industrial.

Japan Representative Offices

Embassy Avenue

http://embassy.kcom.ne.jp/index-e.htm
Posted in English and Japanese, the site is a directory of foreign Embassies and Consulates in Japan. The service includes a newsletter and online resources for foreigners living in Japan.

Foreign Governments in Japan

http://jin.jcic.or.jp/navi/category_11.html
A service of the Japan Information Network, the site is a directory of foreign diplomatic posts in Japan. The list includes representatives from over 20 countries including Mongolia, Philippines, and Russia.

Argentina

Embassy of Argentina in Tokyo

http://embassy.kcom.ne.jp/argentina/index.htm
Written in English and Japanese, the site delivers Argentine news, fact sheets, maps, economic reports, trade regulations, and visa and passport information.

Association of Southeast Asian Nations

ASEAN Center

http://www.asean.or.jp/
Created in 1981, the Center promotes Japanese trade with member countries of ASEAN, the Association of Southeast Asian Nations. The site includes a directory of trade, investment, and tourism programs and opportunities.

Australia

Austrade in Japan

http://www.austrade.gov.au/japan/
The online service provides Australian export guides, company directories, product catalogs, success stories, investment primers, and contact information.

Australian Business Centre

http://www2.gol.com/users/anzccj/abc.html
Based in Tokyo, the Centre promotes Australian exports to Japan. The site includes a mission statement, contact information, and a directory of tenants that include Australia's key federal and state export, investment and tourism organizations.

Australia-Japan Society in Fukuoka

http://www2.gol.com/users/cflynn/koala/ajf.html
An online forum for promoting Australia-Japan relations, the Japanese language site provides a mission statement, event calendar, program directory, and contact information.

Australian and New Zealand Chamber of Commerce in Japan

http://www2.gol.com/users/anzccj/
Based in Tokyo, the Chamber promotes trade between Japan and Australia and New Zealand. The site includes activity reports, event information, and a committee directory.

Embassy of Australia in Tokyo

http://www.australia.or.jp/cgi-bin/qweb/nph-qweb.pl/english/index.htm
Posted in English and Japanese, the site features Australian news, chat services, a virtual art gallery, event information, and an online visa application.

Japan Australia New Zealand Society Homepage

http://www.jade.dti.ne.jp/~janznet/
The Society promotes cultural exchanges and relations between Japan and Australia and New Zealand. The site includes a mission statement, activity reports, and contact information.

Austria

Austrian Trade Commission in Japan

http://www.osk.threewebnet.or.jp/~atcosaka/
Posted in English and Japanese, the site delivers Austrian news, fact sheets, company directories, business opportunities, sector profiles, and event information.

Austrian Trade Office in Osaka

http://www.osk.3web.ne.jp/~atcosaka/english.htm
The site lists the Trade Commissioner, street address, phone and fax numbers, and e-mail link of the Austrian Trade Office in Osaka.

Belgium

Flanders Investment Office in Tokyo

http://www.japan.co.jp/flanders/
The online service provides fact sheets on Flanders investment opportunities, business incentives, labor force, infrastructure, technology, and quality of life.

Bulgaria

Embassy of Bulgaria in Tokyo

http://www.infotrans.or.jp/~rose/bulgaria/
Posted in Japanese, the site delivers Bulgarian fact sheets, business guides, visa and passport information, and reports on Bulgaria-Japan trade and relations.

Brazil

Consulate General of Brazil in Tokyo

http://www2.gol.com/users/consbras/
Posted in English and Spanish, the digital Consulate offers Brazilian news, business guides, travel tips, media bulletins, and visa and passport information.

Consulate General of Brazil in Nagoya

http://www2.gol.com/users/cgnagoya/
Written in Spanish, the site delivers Brazilian news, culture guides, travel primers, media bulletins, procurement bulletins, and visa and passport information.

Embassy of Brazil in Tokyo

http://www.brasemb.or.jp/frame1.html
Posted in Japanese, the site offers Brazilian fact sheets, business guides, travel information, and reports on Brazil-Japan trade and relations.

Brunei Darussalam

Embassy of Brunei Darussalam in Tokyo

http://www.brunet.bn/homepage/gov/bruemb/govemb.htm
The site provides contact information for the Bruneian Embassy in Tokyo.

Cambodia

Embassy of Cambodia in Tokyo
http://iac.co.jp/~kpnarin/
Posted in English and French, the site offers Cambodian news, fact sheets, history lessons, culture guides, travel information, city profiles, and weather bulletins.

Cameroon

Embassy of Cameroon in Tokyo
http://africa.himeji-du.ac.jp/cameroun/home.html
Posted in Japanese, the site delivers Cameroon news, fact sheets, commercial guides, travel information, and reports on Cameroon-Japan trade and relations.

Canada

Canadian Chamber of Commerce in Japan
http://www.cccj.or.jp/
Established in 1975, the Chamber promotes Canada-Japan trade. The site includes a mission statement, committee directory, publications list, and event information.

Canadian Consulate General in Fukuoka
http://www.dfait-maeci.gc.ca/ni-ka/offices/fukuoka/menu-e.asp
Along with a regional fact sheet, the site lists the staff, street address, phone and fax numbers, and e-mail link of Canadian Consulate General in Fukuoka.

Canadian Consulate General in Nagoya
http://www.dfait-maeci.gc.ca/ni-ka/offices/nagoya/menu-e.asp
Posted in English and French, the site provides Consul General speeches, contact information, Japanese cultural guides, and Nagoya-region fact sheets and market reports.

Canadian Consulate General in Osaka
http://www.dfait-maeci.gc.ca/ni-ka/offices/osaka/menu-e.asp
The online service delivers fact sheets on the Kansai region and Osaka economy. Topics include export and investment opportunities, business travel, and distribution.

Canadian Embassy in Tokyo
http://www.dfait-maeci.gc.ca/ni-ka/offices/tokyo/menu-e.asp
Posted in English and French, the site delivers Embassy speeches, a staff roster, visa and passport information, and a directory of Canadian cultural events in Japan.

Directory of Canadian Business in Japan
http://www.dcbj.com/
A browsable database of Canadian companies doing business in Japan, the site profiles firms in nine categories including biotechnology, energy and metals, and high technology products.

Ni-Ka Online
http://www.dfait-maeci.gc.ca/ni-ka/menu.asp
A service of Foreign Affairs and International Trade Canada, the site provides Japanese market reports, and bulletins on Canada-Japan trade and relations.

Province of Alberta Office in Tokyo
http://www.altanet.or.jp/index.htm
Established in 1970, the Office promotes Alberta exports to Japan. The site includes a mission statement, event calendar, and contact information.

Province of British Columbia Trade Office in Tokyo
http://www.ei.gov.bc.ca/directory/bctio/IC98/INTOFF98.htm
A service of the British Columbia Trade and Investment Office, the site lists the street address, phone and fax numbers, and e-mail link of the British Columbia Trade Office in Tokyo.

Province of Québec General Delegation in Tokyo
http://www.mri.gouv.qc.ca/tokyo/index.html
A service of the Québec Ministry of International Relations, the French language site provides Québec fact sheets, event information, and reports on Japan-Québec trade and relations.

Chile

Embassy of Chile in Tokyo
http://www.oficom-chile.gol.com/
Posted in Japanese, the site delivers Chilean fact sheets, business guides, travel tips, visa and passport information, and reports on Chile-Japan trade and relations.

China

China Council for the Promotion of International Trade in Tokyo
http://www.ccpit.org/engVersion/cp_about/cp_over/cp_over.html
A Chinese export promotion service, the site

provides contact information for the China Council for the Promotion of International Trade office in Tokyo.

Embassy of China in Tokyo
http://embassy.kcom.ne.jp/embnet/china.htm
The site lists the street address, phone and fax numbers, e-mail link, and consular and commercial services of the Chinese Embassy in Tokyo.

Hong Kong Economic and Trade Office in Tokyo
http://www.hketotyo.or.jp/
A Hong Kong trade promotion service, the English and Japanese language site delivers Hong Kong fact sheets, investment primers, and business guides.

Colombia

Embassy of Colombia in Tokyo
http://embassy.kcom.ne.jp/colombia/index.htm
Posted in English and Japanese, the site delivers Colombian fact sheets, cultural guides, company directories, export reports, and visa information.

Embassy of Colombia Commercial Office in Tokyo
http://embassy.kcom.ne.jp/colombia/indeco.htm
The online service delivers Colombian economic fact sheets, investment guides, event information, export statistics, and a directory of Japanese companies in Colombia.

Croatia

Embassy of Croatia in Tokyo
http://embassy.kcom.ne.jp/embnet/croatia.htm
Posted in Japanese, the site provides Croatian news, fact sheets, business guides, travel tips, and a directory of consular and commercial services.

Cyprus

Cyprus Trade Center in Tokyo
http://www.cyprustradeny.org/cyny5.html
The site lists the street address, and phone and fax numbers of the Cyprus Trade Center in Tokyo.

Czech Republic

Embassy of the Czech Republic in Tokyo
http://embassy.kcom.ne.jp/czech/index.htm

Posted in English and Japanese, the site delivers Czech news, fact sheets, culture reports, travel primers, web guides, and visa and passport information.

Denmark

Embassy of Denmark in Tokyo
http://www.twics.com/~dkembtok/
Posted in Danish and Japanese, the site offers Danish fact sheets, investment guides, travel information, and reports on Denmark-Japan trade and relations.

Djibouti

Embassy of Djibouti
http://www.sfc.keio.ac.jp/~adesso/country/Djibouti/index-e.html
Along with a map to the Embassy, the site features fact sheets on Djiboutian geography, history, culture, politics, government, foreign policy, and economic development.

Ecuador

Embassy of Ecuador in Tokyo
http://www.teleserve.co.jp/embassy/embassy/ecu/
Posted in English and Japanese, the digital Embassy delivers Ecuadorian news, visa and passport information, business guides, travel primers, and economic reports.

Egypt

Embassy of Egypt in Tokyo
http://embassy.kcom.ne.jp/egypt/index.htm
Along with news and visa information, the site provides fact sheets on Egyptian geography, history, climate, politics, foreign policy, business, investment, and tourism.

Ethiopia

Embassy of Ethiopia
http://www.crisscross.com/users/ethio-embtok/main.html
Featuring a greeting from the Ambassador, the site offers Ethiopian statistics, visa and passport information, international trade reports, investment guides, and travel primers.

European Union

Delegation of the European Commission in Japan
http://jpn.cec.eu.int/english/
Posted in English and Japanese, the site provides European Union fact sheets, press releases, event information, and reports on European Union-Japan trade and relations.

European Business Community in Japan
http://www.access-plannet.com/EBC/
Based in Tokyo, the Community represents European business interests in Japan. The site includes a mission statement, activity reports, and committee directory.

European Union-Japan Center for Industrial Cooperation
http://www.eu.japan.co.jp/
With offices in Brussels and Tokyo, the Center operates training programs in Japan for European Union managers. The site includes a newsletter, program directory, and contact information.

Fiji

Embassy of Fiji in Tokyo
http://fiji.gov.fj/core/fj_mis.html
The site provides contact information for the Fijian Embassy in Tokyo.

Finland

Embassy of Finland in Tokyo
http://www.finland.or.jp/
Posted in English, the site provides Finnish press releases, economic reports, visa and passport information, an event calendar, and a directory of Finnish companies in Japan.

Finland Technology Development Centre
http://www.finland.or.jp/tekes.html
Based in Tokyo, the Centre promotes technology alliances between Finnish and Japanese companies. The site includes a mission statement, staff directory, and publications list.

France

French Chamber of Commerce and Industry in Japan
http://www.ccifj.or.jp/
Established in 1918, the Chamber promotes

French business interests in Japan. The site provides a mission statement, member directory, event calendar, and contact information.

French Trade Commission in Fukuoka
http://www.dree.org/japon/francais/PEE/pee/mapfukuo.htm
Posted in French, the site lists the street address and phone and fax numbers of the French Trade Commission in Fukuoka.

French Trade Commission in Japan
http://www.dree.org/japon/
Written in French, the site delivers Japanese market reports, sector profiles, contact information, and a directory of French export promotion services.

French Trade Commission in Nagoya
http://www.dree.org/japon/francais/PEE/pee/mapnagoy.htm
The site lists the street address and phone and fax numbers of the French Trade Commission in Nagoya.

French Trade Commission in Osaka
http://www.dree.org/japon/francais/PEE/PEE/OSAKA.HTM
The site lists the staff, street address, phone and fax numbers, and e-mail link of the French Trade Commission in Osaka.

French Trade Commission in Tokyo
http://www.dree.org/japon/francais/PEE/PEE/TOKYO.HTM
Posted in French, the site lists the staff, street address, phone and fax numbers, and e-mail link of the French Trade Commission in Tokyo.

Germany

German Chamber of Commerce in Tokyo
http://www.ahk.net/en/jp/Tokyo/
The site lists the Chairperson, Chief Executive Officer, street address, phone and fax numbers, e-mail link, and office hours of the German Chamber in Tokyo.

Embassy of Germany in Tokyo
http://www.germanembassy-japan.org/
Posted in German and Japanese, the site delivers German news, fact sheets, web guides, economic reports, investment primers, and reports on German-Japanese trade and relations.

Ghana

Embassy of Ghana in Tokyo
http://www.juntung.com/ghana-consul-hk/
2misabo.htm
The site provides contact information for the
Ghanaian Embassy in Tokyo.

Greece

Embassy of Greece in Tokyo
http://embassy.kcom.ne.jp/embnet/greece.htm
Written in Japanese, the site delivers Greek
news, fact sheets, travel guides, economic
reports, and a directory of consular and commercial services.

Hungary

Embassy of Hungary in Tokyo
http://www2.gol.com/users/huembtio/
The English and Japanese language site
provides Hungarian news, fact sheets, economic
reports, investment guides, travel tips, and visa
and passport information.

Hungarian Trade Office in Tokyo
http://www2.gol.com/users/kiss/
Along with Japanese economic news and web
guides, the site provides Hungarian legal guides,
travel information, and reports on Hungarian-
Japanese trade and relations.

India

Embassy of India in Tokyo
http://embassy.kcom.ne.jp/embnet/india.htm
Written in Japanese, the site delivers Indian fact
sheets, business guides, travel tips, visa and
passport information, and reports on India-Japan
trade and relations.

Japan-India Technology Network
http://sunsite.sut.ac.jp/asia/india/jitnet/
A forum for promoting India-Japan technology
collaboration, the site includes a mission
statement, activity reports, technology bulletins,
and contact information.

Indonesia

Embassy of Indonesia in Tokyo
http://indag.dprin.go.id/INGG/trade/atache.HTM
The site provides contact information for the
Indonesian Embassy in Tokyo.

Iran

Embassy of Iran in Tokyo
http://embassy.kcom.ne.jp/iran/index.htm
Featuring a biweekly newsletter, the site provides
Iranian fact sheets, economic reports, culture
guides, travel primers, and visa and passport
information.

Ireland

Embassy of Ireland in Tokyo
http://embassy.kcom.ne.jp/ireland/index.htm
Posted in English and Japanese, the site
delivers Irish news, fact sheets, economic
reports, travel guides, cultural primers, and visa
and passport information.

Enterprise Ireland in Tokyo
http://www.irish-trade.ie/office_network/
office_locate01.html#anchor1441818
The site lists the Manager, street address, and
phone and fax numbers of the Enterprise Ireland
office in Tokyo.

Israel

Embassy of Israel in Tokyo
http://www.israelembassy-tokyo.com/
Posted in English and Japanese, the site
provides Israeli fact sheets, history lessons,
government directories, foreign policy statements, and web guides.

Italy

Embassy of Italy in Tokyo
http://sunsite.sut.ac.jp/embitaly/
Featuring a message from the Ambassador, the
site delivers Italian fact sheets, travel tips,
socioeconomic statistics, and a directory of
Italian activities in Japan.

Italian Chamber of Commerce in Japan
http://www.iccj.or.jp/index.html
Established in 1972, the Chamber promotes
Italian-Japanese trade. The site includes a
mission statement, member directory, event
information, and an online bulletin board.

Italian Trade Commission in Tokyo
http://www.ice-tokyo.or.jp/
Along with Japanese news and business guides,
the Italian and Japanese language site offers
Italian economic reports, international trade
statistics, and travel information.

Jordan

Jordan Embassy in Tokyo
http://www2.giganet.net/private/users/emb-jord/
Written in English and Japanese, the site features Jordanian fact sheets, commercial guides, sector profiles, investment reports, and government directories.

Kenya

Embassy of Kenya in Tokyo
http://www.teleserve.co.jp/embassy/embassy/kenya/index.htm
Featuring a message from the Ambassador, the site provides Kenyan press releases, visa and passport information, economic reports, and event information.

Laos

Embassy of Laos in Tokyo
http://embassy.kcom.ne.jp/embnet/lao.htm
The site lists the street address, phone and fax numbers, e-mail link, and consular and commercial services of the Laos Embassy in Tokyo.

Madagascar

Embassy of Madagascar in Tokyo
http://www.madagascar-contacts.com/us/adresse.htm#alext
Along with a directory of Madagascar government agencies, the site provides contact information for the Madagascar Embassy in Tokyo.

Malaysia

Embassy of Malaysia in Tokyo
http://www.mnet.com.my/klonline/www/missions/malmiss/mjapan1.htm
The site provides contact information for the Malaysian Embassy in Tokyo.

Trade Commission of Malaysia in Tokyo
http://www.mnet.com.my/klonline/www/missions/malmiss/mjapan4.htm
The site provides contact information for the Malaysian Trade Commission in Tokyo.

Marshall Islands

Embassy of the Marshall Islands in Tokyo
http://www.rmiembassyus.org/address.html
The site lists the street address, phone and fax numbers, and e-mail link of the Marshall Islands in Tokyo.

Mexico

Embassy of Mexico in Tokyo
http://embassy.kcom.ne.jp/mexico/index.htm
The online service offers Mexican science and technology bulletins, economic reports, cultural and tourism guides, and visa and passport information.

Trade Commission of Mexico in Tokyo
http://www.mexico-businessline.com/ingles/ofrepmu3.html#japan
The site lists the street address, phone and fax numbers, and e-mail link of the Trade Commission of Mexico in Tokyo.

Micronesia

Embassy of Micronesia
http://embassy.kcom.ne.jp/embnet/micronesia.htm
The site lists the street address, phone and fax numbers, e-mail link, and consular and commercial services of the Micronesian Embassy in Tokyo.

Mongolia

Embassy of Mongolia in Tokyo
http://embassy.kcom.ne.jp/mongolia/index.htm
Written in English and Japanese, the site provides a Mongolian country profile, history lessons, business guides, travel tips, and visa and passport information.

Nepal

Embassy of Nepal in Tokyo
http://www.info-nepal.com/members/fips/contacts/nepalese.html
The site provides contact information for the Embassy of Nepal in Tokyo.

New Zealand

Embassy of New Zealand in Tokyo
http://embassy.kcom.ne.jp/newzealand/index.htm
The English and Japanese language site provides New Zealand news, fact sheets, economic reports, sector profiles, business guides, and a directory of consular and commercial services.

Trade New Zealand in Tokyo

http://www.tradenz.govt.nz/contact/northasia.html
An export promotion service, the site provides
contact information for the Trade New Zealand
office in Tokyo.

Norway

Embassy of Norway in Tokyo

*http://www.ntc.no/cgi-bin/wbch.exe?html=../
templates/utekontor2.html&profile=1134*
The site lists the staff, street address, phone and
fax numbers, and e-mail link of the Norwegian
Embassy in Tokyo.

Pakistan

Pakistan Trade Office in Tokyo

http://www.jamal.com/epb/ptoa.htm
The site provides contact information for the
Pakistan Trade Office in Tokyo.

Panama

Embassy of Panama in Tokyo

http://embassy.kcom.ne.jp/panama/top.htm
Along with bulletins on the Panama Canal, the
site delivers Panamanian news, fact sheets,
business guides, cultural reports, and a virtual art
gallery.

Paraguay

Embassy of Paraguay in Tokyo

http://embassy.kcom.ne.jp/paraguay/index.htm
The digital Embassy provides Paraguayan news,
country profiles, economic reports, sector
profiles, culture guides, and visa and passport
information.

Peru

Embassy of Peru in Tokyo

http://embassy.kcom.ne.jp/peru/index-j.htm
Posted in Japanese, the site delivers Peruvian
visa and passport information, country fact
sheets, economic reports, business guides, and
a directory of consular and commercial services.

Philippines

Embassy of the Philippines in Tokyo

http://www2.gol.com/users/jjpgim/
The English and Japanese language site
provides Philippine news, a staff roster, visa and
passport information, and reports on Philippine-
Japan trade and relations.

Philippine International Trading Corporation in Tokyo

http://www.dti.gov.ph/pitc/pitc1.htm#Directory
The site provides contact information for the
Philippine International Trading Corporation in
Tokyo.

Philippine Trade and Investment Promotion Office in Fukuoka

http://www.dti.gov.ph/fuk/
The site provides a mission statement, service
directory, and contact information for the Philippine Trade Office in Fukuoka.

Philippine Trade and Investment Promotion Office in Osaka

http://www.dti.gov.ph/osk/
The site provides a mission statement, service
directory, and contact information for the Philippine Trade Office in Osaka.

Philippine Trade and Investment Promotion Office in Tokyo

http://www.dti.gov.ph/tyo/
The site provides a mission statement, service
directory, and contact information for the Philippine Trade Office in Tokyo.

Portugal

Embassy of Portugal in Tokyo

http://www.pnsnet.co.jp/users/cltembpt/
Featuring a message from the Ambassador, the
site offers Portuguese fact sheets, government
directories, event information, and reports on
Portugal-Japan trade and relations.

Portuguese Trade and Investment Office in Tokyo

*http://www.portugal.org/geninfo/abouticep/
japan.html*
The site lists the staff, street address, phone and
fax numbers, and e-mail link of the Portuguese
Trade and Investment Office in Tokyo.

Romania

Embassy of Romania in Tokyo

http://iac.co.jp/~romembjp/
Along with a staff directory and visa information,
the site provides fact sheets on Romanian
politics, business, history, culture, and foreign
relations.

Russia

Embassy of Russia in Tokyo
http://embassy.kcom.ne.jp/russia/index.htm
Posted in English and Japanese, the site provides Russian news, fact sheets, visa and passport information, business guides, economic reports, and cultural bulletins.

Japan's Assistance to New Independent States
http://web.infoweb.ne.jp/scc/
Posted in English, Japanese, and Russian, the site reports on Japanese financial and technical assistance to the newly independent states of the former Soviet Union.

Singapore

Consulate General of Singapore in Nagoya
http://www.gov.sg/mfa/consular/mww_j.htm
The site provides contact information for the Singapore Consulate General in Nagoya.

Consulate General of Singapore in Osaka
http://www.gov.sg/mfa/consular/mww_j.htm
The site provides contact information for the Singapore Consulate General in Osaka.

Embassy of Singapore in Tokyo
http://www.gov.sg/mfa/consular/mww_j.htm
The site provides contact information for the Singapore Embassy in Tokyo.

Slovakia

Embassy of Slovakia in Tokyo
http://embassy.kcom.ne.jp/slovakia/index.html
Written in English and Japanese, the site delivers Slovakian news, fact sheets, economic reports, business guides, travel bulletins, and visa and passport information.

South Africa

Economic Office of South Africa in Tokyo
http://SunSITE.sut.ac.jp/embassy/jasanet/economic/
The site provides South African commercial guides, publication lists, government directories, Japanese media guides, and contact information.

Japan-South Africa Network
http://sunsite.sut.ac.jp/embassy/jasanet/
Along with maps and web guides, the site offers South African headlines, commercial guides,

cultural reports, and a directory of South African non-profit organizations and community projects.

South Africa Foreign Trade Office in Tokyo
http://wwwdti.pwv.gov.za/dtiwww/foreign_offices.htm
A service of the South Africa Department of Trade and Industry, the site provides contact information for the South Africa Trade Office in Tokyo.

South Korea

Korean International Trade Association in Tokyo
http://www.kita.or.kr/eng/national.html
The site provides contact information for the Korean International Trade Association in Tokyo.

South Korean Embassy in Tokyo
http://embassy.kcom.ne.jp/korea/index.htm
Written in English and Japanese, the site delivers South Korean fact sheets, commercial guides, investment primers, travel tips, and visa and passport information.

Spain

Embassy of Spain in Tokyo
http://embassy.kcom.ne.jp/embnet/spain.htm
Posted in Japanese, the site provides Spanish news, fact sheets, business guides, travel tips, and a directory of consular and commercial services.

Spanish Commercial Office in Tokyo
http://www.icex.es/openURL.html#openURL=/english/infoproyem/ofcomes/ofcomes.html#AS
The site lists the staff, street address, phone and fax numbers, and e-mail link of the Spanish Commercial Office in Tokyo.

Sri Lanka

Embassy of Sri Lanka in Tokyo
http://embassy.kcom.ne.jp/embnet/srilanka.htm
The site lists the street address, phone and fax numbers, e-mail link, and consular and commercial services of the Sri Lankan Embassy in Tokyo.

Sweden

Embassy of Sweden in Tokyo
http://www.ud.se/english/mfa/ambassad/japan.htm
The site provides contact information for the Swedish Embassy in Tokyo.

Investment Sweden in Tokyo
http://www.twics.com/~isatyo/
Posted in Japanese, the site delivers Swedish investment guides, commercial primers, incentive information, and reports on Japan-Sweden trade and relations.

Swedish Chamber of Commerce and Industry in Japan
http://www.sccj.org/
An online forum for Swedish businesspeople in Japan, the site includes a mission statement, member directory, activity reports, event information, and web guides.

Switzerland

Swiss Chamber of Commerce and Industry in Japan
http://www.gol.com/swiss/
Based in Tokyo, the Chamber promotes Japan-Switzerland land. The site features a mission statement, member directory, resume database, and event information.

Taiwan

China External Trade Development Council Office in Tokyo
http://www.cetra.org.tw/english/o_office/indexset.htm
A Taiwanese trade promotion service, the site lists the mission statement and e-mail links of the China External Trade Development Council Offices in Fukuoka, Osaka, and Tokyo.

Osaka Design Center
http://www.cetra.org.tw/english/o_office/indexset.htm
A Taiwanese trade promotion service, the site lists the mission statement and e-mail link of the Osaka Design Center.

Taiwan Government Information Office in Tokyo
http://www.gio.gov.tw/info/ngio/jap-f.html
Posted in Chinese and English, the site lists the street address, phone and fax numbers, and e-mail link of the Taiwan Government Information Office in Tokyo.

Tanzania

Embassy of Tanzania in Tokyo
http://www.tanzania-online.gov.uk/visa/envoys.html

The site provides contact information for the Tanzania Embassy in Tokyo.

Thailand

Royal Thai Consulate General in Osaka
http://www.mfa.go.th/Embassy/detail/18.htm
The site lists the Consul General, street address, and phone and fax numbers of the Thai Consulate General in Osaka.

Royal Thai Embassy in Tokyo
http://www.mfa.go.th/Embassy/detail/46.htm
The site lists the Ambassador, street address, and phone and fax numbers of the Thai Embassy in Tokyo.

Thai Trade Center in Fukuoka
http://www.thaitrade.com/wwtto.html
A service of the Thailand Department of Export Promotion, the site lists the street address, phone and fax numbers, and e-mail link of the Thai Trade Center in Fukuoka.

Thai Trade Center in Osaka
http://www.thaitrade.com/wwtto.html
A service of the Thailand Department of Export Promotion, the site lists the street address, phone and fax numbers, and e-mail link of the Thai Trade Center in Osaka.

Thailand Office of Commercial Affairs in Tokyo
http://www.thaitrade.com/thcoaf.html
The site lists the street address, phone and fax numbers, and e-mail link of the Thailand Office of Commercial Affairs in Tokyo.

Turkey

Embassy of Turkey in Tokyo
http://www.turkey.org/madres.htm
Part of a directory of Turkish diplomatic offices around the world, the site lists the e-mail link of the Turkish Embassy in Tokyo.

United Kingdom

British Chamber of Commerce in Japan
http://www.iac.co.jp:80/bccj/bccjhome.html
Based in Tokyo, the Chamber promotes British business interests in Japan. The site includes a mission statement, contact information, and bulletins on the Science and Technology Action Group, a Chamber subcommittee that promotes British-Japanese technical cooperation.

Consulate of Britain in Fukuoka
http://www.fco.gov.uk/directory/posts.asp?JP
The site provides contact information for the British Consulate in Fukuoka.

Consulate General of Britain in Osaka
http://www.fco.gov.uk/directory/posts.asp?JP
The site provides contact information for the British Consulate General in Osaka.

Embassy of Britain in Tokyo
http://www.gate-uk.co.jp/embassy/top.html
Written in Japanese, the digital Embassy provides British fact sheets, investment guides, travel information, and a directory of consular and commercial services.

Gate U.K.
http://www.gate-uk.co.jp/
A hub of country information, the English and Japanese language site delivers British news, business guides, shopping directories, cultural bulletins, and event information.

Trade and Investment Office of Britain in Nagoya
http://www.fco.gov.uk/directory/posts.asp?JP
The site provides contact information for the British Trade and Investment Office in Nagoya.

United States

American Chamber of Commerce in Japan
http://www.accj.or.jp/
Based in Tokyo, the Chamber promotes United States business interests in Japan. The site includes a member directory, event information, and committee reports.

American Consulate General in Fukuoka
http://www.city.kitakyushu.jp/amconsul/
Posted in English and Japanese, the site provides United States visa and passport information, emergency and disaster instructions, and lists of English-speaking doctors, lawyers, and other professionals in the region.

American Consulate General in Sapporo
http://plaza12.mbn.or.jp/~AmConGenSapporo/
Along with a list of United States-Japan sister-state and sister-city relationships in the region, the site provides United States visa and passport information, and a directory of consular and commercial services.

American Consulate in Nagoya
http://www.japan-net.or.jp/~amconngo/
Featuring a message from the Principal Officer, the site delivers Japanese market reports, procurement opportunities, trade mission reports, and reports on United States-Japan trade and relations.

American Consulate General in Osaka-Kobe
http://www.senri-I.or.jp/amcon/usa_01.htm
Along with Japanese maps, the site provides United States visa and passport information, legal primers, and a directory of consular and commercial services.

American State Offices Association
http://www.venture-web.or.jp/asoa/e-asoa1.html
Established in 1980, the Association promotes the interests of United States state offices located in Japan. The site includes a mission statement, member directory, and contact information.

Commercial Service Japan
http://www.csjapan.doc.gov/
A unit of the American Embassy in Tokyo, the site provides online product exhibitions, reports on United States trade missions and events in Japan, and Japanese commercial guides and market reports.

Enterprise Florida Japan Office
http://www.venture-web.or.jp/florida/
Based in Tokyo, the Office promotes Florida business interests in Japan. Written in Japanese, the site provides a state fact sheet, and a directory of Florida-Japan trade and investment opportunities.

Enterprise Indiana Japan Office
http://www.venture-web.or.jp/indiana/menu.html
Posted in English and Japanese, the site delivers Indiana fact sheets, investment guides, Asian trade mission reports, and a database of Indiana companies seeking agents and distributors worldwide.

Fairfax County Trade Office in Tokyo
http://www.venture-web.or.jp/asoa/e-directory.html#1
The site lists the staff, street address, and phone and fax numbers of the Fairfax County Trade Office in Tokyo.

Missouri-Japan Office
*http://www.ecodev.state.mo.us/intermark/
japan.html*
Opened in 1983, the Office promotes Missouri business interests in Japan. The site includes a mission statement, staff directory, and activity reports.

National Science Foundation in Tokyo
http://www.twics.com/~nsftokyo/home.html
The Foundation promotes United States science and technology interests in Japan. The site includes a mission statement, staff roster, and a directory of research fellowship opportunities in Japan.

Office of Japan
http://www.ita.doc.gov/region/japan/japan.html
Part of the United States International Trade Administration, the Office assists American companies which are encountering trade barriers and market access difficulties in Japan. The site provides a mission statement and contact information.

Port Authority of New York and New Jersey Trade Office in Tokyo
http://www.venture-web.or.jp/asoa/e-directory.html#1
The site lists the staff, street address, and phone and fax numbers of the Port Authority of New York and New Jersey Trade Office in Tokyo.

San Bernardino County Trade Office in Tokyo
http://www.venture-web.or.jp/asoa/e-directory.html#1
The site lists the staff, street address, and phone and fax numbers of the San Bernardino County Trade Office in Tokyo.

State of Alabama Trade Office in Tokyo
http://www.venture-web.or.jp/asoa/e-directory.html#1
The site lists the staff, street address, and phone and fax numbers of the Alabama Trade Office in Tokyo.

State of Alaska Trade Office in Tokyo
http://www.venture-web.or.jp/asoa/e-directory.html#1
The site lists the staff, street address, phone and fax numbers, and e-mail links of the Alaska Trade Office in Tokyo.

State of Arizona Trade Office in Tokyo
http://www.venture-web.or.jp/asoa/e-directory.html#1

The site lists the staff, street address, and phone and fax numbers of the Arizona Trade Office in Tokyo.

State of Arkansas Trade Office in Tokyo
http://www.venture-web.or.jp/asoa/e-directory.html#1
The site lists the staff, street address, phone and fax numbers, and e-mail link of the Arkansas Trade Office in Tokyo.

State of California Trade Office in Tokyo
http://www.venture-web.or.jp/asoa/e-directory.html#1
The site lists the staff, street address, phone and fax numbers, and e-mail link of the California Trade Office in Tokyo.

State of Colorado Trade Office in Osaka
*http://governor.state.co.us/gov_dir/govnr_dir/ITO/
abroad.htm#japan*
A unit of the Colorado International Trade Office, the site lists the mission statement and trade promotion services of the Colorado Trade Office in Osaka.

State of Colorado Trade Office in Tokyo
http://www.venture-web.or.jp/asoa/e-directory.html#1
The site lists the contact, street address, phone and fax numbers, and e-mail link of the Colorado Trade Office in Tokyo.

State of Georgia Trade Office in Tokyo
http://www.venture-web.or.jp/asoa/e-directory.html#1
The site lists the Managing Director, street address, phone and fax numbers, and e-mail link of the Georgia Trade Office in Tokyo.

State of Hawaii Trade Office in Tokyo
http://www.venture-web.or.jp/asoa/e-directory.html#1
The site lists the Director of Operations, street address, phone and fax numbers, and e-mail link of the Hawaii Trade Office in Tokyo.

State of Idaho Trade Office in Tokyo
http://www.venture-web.or.jp/asoa/e-directory.html#1
The site lists the representative, street address, and phone and fax numbers of the Idaho Trade Office in Tokyo.

State of Illinois Trade Office in Tokyo
*http://www.commerce.state.il.us/dcca/files/int'l/
japan.htm*

A service of the Illinois Department of Commerce and Community Affairs, the site lists the Managing Director, street address, phone and fax numbers, and e-mail link of the Illinois Trade Office in Tokyo.

State of Iowa Trade Office in Tokyo
http://www.venture-web.or.jp/asoa/e-directory.html#1
The site lists the staff, street address, phone and fax numbers, and e-mail link of the Iowa Trade Office in Tokyo.

State of Kansas Trade Office in Tokyo
http://www.kansascommerce.com/0306-04why.html#WE%20WELCOME
A service of the Kansas Department of Commerce and Housing, the site lists the staff, street address, phone and fax numbers, and e-mail link of the Kansas Trade Office in Tokyo.

State of Kentucky Trade Office in Tokyo
http://www.venture-web.or.jp/asoa/e-directory.html#1
The site lists the staff, street address, phone and fax numbers, and e-mail link of the Kentucky Trade Office in Tokyo.

State of Maryland Business Center in Tokyo
http://www.venture-web.or.jp/asoa/e-directory.html#1
The site lists the staff, street address, phone and fax numbers, and e-mail link of the Maryland Business Center in Tokyo.

State of Michigan Trade Office in Tokyo
http://www.venture-web.or.jp/asoa/e-directory.html#1
The site lists the staff, street address, phone and fax numbers, and e-mail link of the Michigan Trade Office in Tokyo.

State of Minnesota Trade Office in Tokyo
http://www.venture-web.or.jp/asoa/e-directory.html#1
The site lists the staff, street address, and phone and fax numbers of the Minnesota Trade Office in Tokyo.

State of Mississippi Trade Office in Tokyo
http://www.venture-web.or.jp/asoa/e-directory.html#1
The site lists the staff, street address, phone and fax numbers, and e-mail link of the Mississippi Trade Office in Tokyo.

State of New Jersey Trade Office in Tokyo
http://www.venture-web.or.jp/asoa/e-directory.html#1
The site lists the staff, street address, and phone and fax numbers of the New Jersey Trade Office in Tokyo.

State of New York Trade Office in Tokyo
http://www.venture-web.or.jp/asoa/e-directory.html#1
The site lists the staff, street address, phone and fax numbers, and e-mail link of the New York Trade Office in Tokyo.

State of North Carolina Trade Office in Tokyo
http://www.commerce.state.nc.us/commerce/itd/foreign.html
A service of the North Carolina International Trade Division, the site lists the staff, street address, phone and fax numbers, and e-mail link of the North Carolina Trade Office in Tokyo.

State of Ohio Trade Office in Tokyo
http://ohiotrade.tpusa.com/offices.htm
A service of the Ohio Department of Development, the site lists the street address and e-mail link of the Ohio Trade Office in Tokyo.

State of Oregon Trade Office in Tokyo
http://www.venture-web.or.jp/asoa/e-directory.html#1
The site lists the staff, street address, phone and fax numbers, and e-mail link of the Oregon Trade Office in Tokyo.

State of Pennsylvania Trade Office in Tokyo
http://www.venture-web.or.jp/asoa/e-directory.html#1
The site lists the staff, street address, phone and fax numbers, and e-mail link of the Pennsylvania Trade Office in Tokyo.

State of South Carolina Trade Office in Tokyo
http://www.state.sc.us/commerce/trade2.htm
A service of the South Carolina Department of Commerce, the site lists the Director, street address, and phone and fax numbers of the South Carolina Trade Office in Tokyo.

State of Texas Trade Office in Tokyo
http://www.venture-web.or.jp/asoa/e-directory.html#1
The site lists the staff, street address, and phone and fax numbers of the Texas Trade Office in Tokyo.

State of Utah Trade Office in Tokyo

http://www.ce.ex.state.ut.us/international/reps/reps.htm#Japan

A service of the Utah International Business Development Office, the site lists the representative, street address, phone and fax numbers, and e-mail link of the Utah Trade Office in Tokyo.

State of Virginia Trade Office in Tokyo

http://www.venture-web.or.jp/virginia/

Posted in English and Japanese, the site provides fact sheets on Virginia trade, investment, and quality of life.

State of Washington Housing and Building Materials for Japan

http://www.trade.wa.gov/jpn_housing/

Co-sponsored by Washington Community, Trade, and Economic Development, the site reports on the Japanese housing industry, and includes a directory of building supply exporters in the state of Washington.

State of Washington Trade Office in Tokyo

http://www2.gol.com/users/tt/

Posted in English and Japanese, the site delivers Washington state fact sheets, sector profiles, trade leads, investment guides, and a directory of business matchmaking services.

State of West Virginia Trade Office in Tokyo

http://www.wvdo.org/international/offices.htm

A service of the West Virginia Development Office, the site lists the e-mail link of the West Virginia Trade Office in Tokyo.

State of Wisconsin Trade Office in Tokyo

http://www.venture-web.or.jp/asoa/e-directory.html#1

The site lists the staff, street address, phone and fax numbers, and e-mail link of the Wisconsin Trade Office in Tokyo.

United States Agricultural Trade Service in Tokyo

http://www.usato.or.jp/

Part of the United States Department of Agriculture, the Service promotes American agricultural exports to Japan. The site includes Japanese food market reports and trade opportunities.

United States Embassy in Tokyo

http://www.usia.gov/posts/japan/

Posted in English and Japanese, the virtual Embassy provides United States fact sheets, speeches, visa and passport information, and reports on American-Japanese trade and relations.

United States Information Service in Tokyo

http://www.usia.gov/posts/tokyo.html

Written in English and Japanese, the site delivers United States fact sheets, electronic journals, Asian and Japanese economic reports, and a directory of American and Japanese foundations and grants.

United States Trade Center in Tokyo

http://www.csjapan.doc.gov/ustc/

Operated by the United States Commercial Service, the Center is a venue for American trade exhibitions in Japan. The site includes facility fact sheets, sample floor plans, and event information.

Venezuela

Embassy of Venezuela in Tokyo

http://sunsite.sut.ac.jp/venemb/embvenez.html

Posted in Spanish, the site lists the staff, services, street address, phone and fax numbers, and e-mail link of the Venezuelan Embassy in Tokyo.

Japan-Venezuela Network

http://sunsite.sut.ac.jp/embassy/venemb/

Based in Tokyo, the Network promotes Japan-Venezuela trade and technical collaboration. The site includes a mission statement, activity reports, and contact information.

Vietnam

Embassy of Vietnam in Tokyo

http://embassy.kcom.ne.jp/embnet/vietnam.htm

The site lists the street address, phone and fax numbers, e-mail link, and consular and commercial services of the Vietnamese Embassy in Tokyo.

Western Samoa

Honorary Consulate General of Western Samoa in Tokyo

http://www.interwebinc.com/samoa/missjp.html

The site lists the street address, and phone and fax numbers of the Western Samoan Honorary Consulate General in Tokyo.

Kiribati

Kiribati Market Guides

Kiribati
http://www.hideawayholidays.com.au/trw_.htm
The online service provides Kiribati history lessons, fact sheets, accommodation directories, transportation guides, and contact information.

Kiribati Country Brief
http://www.worldbank.org/cgi-bin/ sendoff.cgi?page=%2Fhtml%2Fextdr%2Foffrep%2 Feap%2Fki.htm
A service of the World Bank Group, the site provides population statistics, financial data, development reports, and economic forecasts.

Kiribati Country Profile
http://www.tradenz.govt.nz/intelligence/profiles/ kiribati.html
A service of the New Zealand Trade Development Board, the site provides Kiribati economic statistics, market information, and business tips.

Kiribati Market Research
http://strategis.ic.gc.ca/sc_mrkti/ibinddc/engdoc/ 1a1i13.html
Posted by Industry Canada, the site provides U.S. Central Intelligence Agency fact sheets on Kiribati geography, people, government, business, and transportation.

Laos

Laos Media

Vientiane Times
http://www.vientianetimes.com/Headlines.html
Published twice a week, the English language site provides Lao news, business reports, weather bulletins, currency information, and a searchable archive of past issues.

Laos Market Guides

Laos Country Brief
http://www.worldbank.org/cgi-bin/ sendoff.cgi?page=%2Fhtml%2Fextdr%2Foffrep%2 Feap%2Fla.htm
A service of the World Bank Group, the site provides Lao population statistics, financial data, development reports, and economic forecasts.

Laos InfoExport
http://www.infoexport.gc.ca/country- e.asp?continent=Asia&country=25
A service of Foreign Affairs and International Trade Canada, the site provides fact sheets and statistics on Lao geography, business, trade, and politics.

Laos Infosite
http://users.vmicro.com/laosinfosite/
Written in English, the site delivers Lao news, maps, fact sheets, history lessons, cultural guides, travel information, language primers, and an online message board.

Laos Market Research
http://strategis.ic.gc.ca/sc_mrkti/ibinddc/engdoc/ 1a1i14.html
Posted by Industry Canada, the site provides U.S. Central Intelligence Agency fact sheets on Lao geography, people, government, business, and transportation.

Laos: A Market Study
http://lcweb2.loc.gov/frd/cs/latoc.html
A service of the U.S. Library of Congress, the site delivers fact sheets on Lao geography, people, agriculture, mining, manufacturing, and foreign economic relations.

LaoSearch
http://www.angelfire.com/ca/laoscom/
A searchable index of Lao resources online, the site is divided into 14 categories including business and economy, science and research, and news and media.

Laos Virtual Library
http://www.global.lao.net/laoVL.html
A service of the Asian Studies World Wide Web Virtual Library, the site is a directory of Lao resources online. Categories include networking, research, publications, and photos and maps.

Laos Trade Assistance

Lao Embassies
http://www.laoembassy.com/news/ embassyabroad.htm
A service of the Laos Embassy in Washington, D.C., the site is a directory of Lao Embassies in over 15 countries including Cambodia, China, India, and Myanmar.

Laos Representative Offices

Australia

Austrade in Vientiane
http://www.austrade.gov.au/ GreaterMekongRegion/
The online service provides Australian export guides, company profiles, product catalogs, success stories, investment primers, and contact information for the Austrade office in Vientiane.

Malaysia

Embassy of Malaysia in Vientiane
http://www.mnet.com.my/klonline/www/missions/ malmiss/mlaos.htm
The site provides contact information for the Malaysian Embassy in Vientiane.

Singapore

Embassy of Singapore in Vientiane
http://www.gov.sg/mfa/consular/mww_l.htm
The site provides contact information for the Singapore Embassy in Vientiane.

Thailand

Royal Thai Consulate General in Savannakhet
http://www.mfa.go.th/Embassy/detail/19.htm
The site lists the Consul General, street address, and phone and fax numbers of the Thai Consulate General in Savannakhet.

Royal Thai Embassy in Vientiane
http://www.mfa.go.th/Embassy/detail/78.htm
The site lists the Ambassador, street address, and phone and fax numbers of the Thai Embassy in Vientiane.

Thailand Office of Commercial Affairs in Vientiane
http://www.thaitrade.com/thcoaf.html
The site lists the street address, phone and fax numbers, and e-mail link of the Thailand Office of Commercial Affairs in Vientiane.

United Kingdom

Embassy of Britain in Vientiane
http://www.fco.gov.uk/directory/posts.asp?LA
The site provides contact information for the British Embassy in Vientiane.

United States

United States Embassy in Vientiane
http://www.inet.co.th/org/usis/laos.htm
Along with reports on the United States-Laos Trade Agreement, the site delivers an Ambassador profile, staff roster, and a directory of consular and commercial services.

Macau

Macau Market Guides

Macau Census and Statistics Department
http://www.dsec.gov.mo/
Posted in Chinese, English, and Portuguese, the site provides Macau press releases, fact sheets, socioeconomic statistics, a publications list, and contact information.

Macau Economic Services
http://www.economia.gov.mo/
Along with a quarterly economic bulletin, the site provides data on Macau gross domestic product, foreign trade, exchange rates, and other economic indicators.

Macau Market Research
http://strategis.ic.gc.ca/sc_mrkti/ibinddc/engdoc/ 1a1f6.html
Posted by Industry Canada, the site provides U.S. Central Intelligence Agency fact sheets on Macau geography, people, government, business, and transportation.

Macau Productivity and Technology Transfer Center
http://www.cpttm.org.mo/
Co-sponsored by the Macau government, the Center provides technology consulting and training. The site includes a mission statement, staff roster, activity reports, and course directory.

Macau Trade Assistance

Macau Trade and Investment Promotion Institute
http://www.ipim.gov.mo/
Posted in Chinese, the site provides Macau business guides, investment primers, international trade leads, company directories, employment opportunities, and contact information.

World Trade Center in Macau
http://www.wtca.org/wtc/macau.html

The site lists the Managing and Executive Directors, services, street address, phone and fax numbers, and e-mail link of the World Trade Center in Macau.

Malaysia

Malaysia Media

Malaysia Media
http://www.mediainfo.com/emediajs/specific-geo.htm?region=malaysia
Developed by Editor and Publisher Interactive, the site is an index of Malaysian media sites online including city guides, magazines, newspapers, and television stations.

Star Online
http://www1.jaring.my:80/~star/
Launched in 1995, the site provides Malaysian news, editorials, business reports, technology bulletins, weather information, and a searchable archive of past issues.

Malaysia Market Guides

Barclays Country Report: Malaysia
http://www.offshorebanking.barclays.com/services/economic/yearly/maldec97/index.html
Prepared by Barclays Bank, the site reports on Malaysian economic trends, politics, monetary and fiscal policy, exchange rates, international trade, and investment flows.

Federation of Malaysian Manufacturers
http://www.fmm.org.my/
Established in 1968, the Federation promotes the interests of Malaysian manufacturers. The site includes press releases, trade opportunities, a member directory, and a product showcase.

Kuala Lumpur Online
http://www.mnet.com.my/klonline/www/klomain.htm
A hub of city information, the site delivers Kuala Lumpur company profiles, maps, travel information, shopping guides, government directories, and weather bulletins.

Malaysia Business Briefs
http://www.austrade.gov.au/IOOM/Malaysia/
A service of Austrade, the site offers fact sheets on Malaysian business etiquette, foreign investment, corporate taxation, marketing, and visas.

Malaysia Country Brief
http://www.worldbank.org/cgi-bin/sendoff.cgi?page=%2Fhtml%2Fextdr%2Foffrep%2Feap%2Fmy.htm
A service of the World Bank Group, the site provides Malaysian population statistics, financial data, development reports, and economic forecasts.

Malaysia Country Profile
http://www.tradenz.govt.nz/intelligence/profiles/malaysia.html
A service of the New Zealand Trade Development Board, the site provides Malaysian economic statistics, market information, and business tips.

Malaysia Country Report
http://www.state.gov/www/issues/economic/trade_reports/eastasia97/malaysia97.html
Prepared by the U.S. Department of State, the site reports on Malaysian exchange rates, debt management, trade barriers, export subsidies, intellectual property protection, worker rights, and foreign investment.

Malaysia Homepage
http://www.jaring.my/~webmster/msia-new/
A hub of country information, the site delivers Malaysian news, fact sheets, economic reports, research and development bulletins, legal primers, and tourism information.

Malaysia InfoExport
http://www.infoexport.gc.ca/country-e.asp?continent=Asia&country=27
A service of Foreign Affairs and International Trade Canada, the site provides Malaysian commercial guides and market reports.

Malaysia: An Introduction
http://www.apecsec.org.sg/member/apecmy.html
A service of the Asia Pacific Economic Cooperation, the site provides fact sheets on Malaysian geography, climate, population, language, business, and international trade.

Malaysia Market Access Database
http://mkaccdb.eu.int/mkdb/mkdb.pl?METHOD=COUNTRY
A service of the European Commission, the site offers briefs on Malaysian trade policy, tariff barriers, non-tariff barriers, investment-related measures, and financial services regulations.

Malaysia Market Information
http://dtiinfo1.dti.gov.uk/ots/malaysia/
A service of the London-based Department of Trade and Industry, the site delivers Malaysian fact sheets, maps, and trade-show information.

Malaysia Market Research
http://strategis.ic.gc.ca/sc_mrkti/ibinddc/engdoc/ 1a1i15.html
A service of Industry Canada, the site provides U.S. Department of Commerce reports on Malaysian economic trends, trade barriers, investment regulations, business travel, and market opportunities.

Malaysia Online
http://www.asiadragons.com/malaysia/
A virtual country gateway, the site delivers Malaysian news, company directories, employment opportunities, travel information, and arts and culture bulletins.

Malaysia: Your Profit Centre in Asia
http://www.jaring.my/mida/
A service of the Malaysian Industrial Development Authority, the site provides Malaysian fact sheets, investment guides, sector profiles, incentive information, and manufacturing statistics.

Malaysia: Recent Economic Developments
http://www.imf.org/external/pubs/CAT/ longres.cfm?sk=2494.0
Prepared by the International Monetary Fund, the site reports on Malaysian savings and investment, consumer and producer prices, trade policies, interest rates, and balance of payments.

Malaysia Virtual Library
http://www.mtc.com.my/Virtual-Library/ Malaysia.html
A service of the World Wide Web Virtual Library, the site is a directory of Malaysian resources online. Categories include networking, education, government, and online forums.

Malaysian Business Page
http://www.jaring.my/~mbp/welcome.html
Along with world headlines and exchange rates, the site delivers Malaysian business news, company directories, travel information, chat services, and an online bulletin board.

Putrajaya
http://www.jaring.my/~webmster/msia-new/govt/ putrajaya/put-main.html
Featuring a message from the Prime Minister, the site provides fact sheets on Putrajaya, a new high-technology city near Kuala Lumpur. The service includes maps, design plans, and contact information.

Malaysia Trade Assistance

Malaysia Electronic Publication
http://www.asiaep.com/my/malays.htm
Featuring a message from the Minister of International Trade and Industry, the site provides Malaysian company directories, product catalogs, and a directory of international buyers.

Malaysia Export Exhibition Centre
http://www.matrade.gov.my/meec.html
A service of Matrade or the Malaysia External Trade Development Corporation, the Centre is a display facility in Kuala Lumpur that promotes Malaysian products and services. The site provides a service directory and contact information.

Malaysia Trade Figures and Services
http://miti.gov.my/trade.htm
Along with reports on Malaysian anti-dumping cases, the site provides fact sheets and statistics on Malaysian international trade by major global region.

Malaysia Trade Winds
http://www.trade-winds.net/premy.htm
A service of Trade Winds Online, the site is a searchable directory of Malaysian trade shows, business contacts, tourism information, and media.

Malaysian Missions Overseas
http://www.mnet.com.my/klonline/www/missions/ malmiss/mmcountr.htm
A service of Kuala Lumpur Online, the site is a directory of Malaysian embassies, high commissions, consulates, trade commissions and representative offices around the world.

Matrade
http://www.matrade.gov.my/
A Malaysian trade promotion service, the site includes a Malaysian product showcase, event information, exchange control reports, and a program and services directory.

Ministry of International Trade and Industry
http://miti.gov.my/
Based in Kuala Lumpur, the Ministry promotes Malaysian trade and economic development. The

site includes trade statistics, organization charts, a program and service directory, and a sound file of the Ministry theme song.

Trade Shows in Malaysia
http://www.expoguide.com/shows/data/loc_37.htm
Compiled by Expoguide, the site is a directory of upcoming trade shows in Malaysia.

Malaysia Representative Offices

Foreign Missions in Malaysia
http://www.mnet.com.my/klonline/www/missions/formiss/formiss.htm
A service of Kuala Lumpur Online, the site is a directory of foreign embassies, high commissions, consulates, trade commissions, United Nations agencies, and other international organizations in Malaysia.

Australia

Austrade in Kuala Lumpur
http://www.austrade.gov.au/malaysia/
The online service provides Australian export guides, company directories, product catalogs, success stories, investment primers, and contact information.

Austria

Austrian Trade Commission in Kuala Lumpur
http://aw.wk.or.at/awo/ahst-kualalumpur.htm
The site lists the staff, street address, phone and fax numbers, e-mail link, and office hours of the Austrian Trade Commission in Kuala Lumpur.

Brunei Darussalam

High Commission of Brunei Darussalam in Kuala Lumpur
http://www.brunet.bn/homepage/gov/bruemb/govemb.htm
The site provides contact information for the Bruneian High Commission in Kuala Lumpur.

Canada

Embassy of Canada in Kuala Lumpur
http://www.dfait-maeci.gc.ca/english/missions/rep-can3e.htm#malaysia
The site provides contact information for the Canadian Embassy in Kuala Lumpur.

Malaysia Canada Business Council
http://www.cmysys.com/mcbc/
With offices in Kuala Lumpur, Toronto, and Vancouver, the Council promotes Malaysia-Canada trade and investment. The site features a mission statement, membership guidelines, and contact information.

Chile

Embassy of Chile in Kuala Lumpur
http://www.bjweb.com/prochile/
The site delivers Chilean fact sheets, economic reports, cultural information, and bulletins on Chile-Malaysia trade and relations.

Denmark

Danish Consulates in Malaysia
http://www.jaring.my/denmark/consulates.htm
The site lists the Consul Generals, street addresses, phone and fax numbers, and office hours of the Danish Consulates in the Malaysian states of Pulau Pinang, Sabah, Sarawak, and Selangor.

Embassy of Denmark in Kuala Lumpur
http://www.jaring.my/denmark/
Featuring a welcome from the Ambassador, the site provides Danish fact sheets, trade statistics, a business publications list, Embassy activity plans, and a directory of consular and commercial services.

Malaysian Danish Business Council
http://www.jaring.my/denmark/mdbc.htm
Established in 1992, the Council promotes Danish business interests in Malaysia. The site includes a mission statement, program directory, and contact information.

Fiji

High Commission of Fiji in Kuala Lumpur
http://fiji.gov.fj/core/fj_mis.html
The site provides contact information for the Fijian High Commission in Kuala Lumpur.

Finland

Finland Trade Center in Kuala Lumpur
http://www.exports.finland.fi/tradecen.htm
The site lists the staff, street address, phone and fax numbers, and e-mail link of the Finland Trade Center in Kuala Lumpur.

France

French Trade Commission in Kuala Lumpur
http://www.dree.org/malaisie/
Written in French, the site delivers Malaysian market reports, sector profiles, contact information, and a directory of French export promotion services.

Germany

German Chamber of Commerce in Kuala Lumpur
http://www.ahk.net/en/my/Kuala_Lumpur/
The site lists the Chairperson, street address, phone and fax numbers, e-mail link, and office hours of the German Chamber in Kuala Lumpur.

Ireland

Enterprise Ireland in Kuala Lumpur
http://www.irish-trade.ie/office_network/
office_locate01.html#anchor1440012
The site lists the Manager, street address, and phone and fax numbers of the Enterprise Ireland office in Kuala Lumpur.

Italy

Embassy of Italy in Kuala Lumpur
http://www.italyembassy.org.my/italyembassy/
Along with Malaysian fact sheets, the site delivers Italian country profiles, media guides, socioeconomic statistics, travel information, and reports on Italy-Malaysia trade and relations.

Japan

Embassy of Japan in Kuala Lumpur
http://www.embjapan.org.my/
Posted in English, the site provides Japanese fact sheets, press releases, visa and passport information, reports on Japan-Malaysia trade, and a directory of consular and commercial services.

Laos

Embassy of Laos in Kuala Lumpur
http://www.laoembassy.com/news/
embassyabroad.htm
The site provides contact information for the Embassy of Laos in Kuala Lumpur.

Mexico

Trade Commission of Mexico in Kuala Lumpur
http://www.mexico-businessline.com/ingles/
ofrepmu3.html#malasia
The site lists the street address, phone and fax numbers, and e-mail link of the Mexican Trade Commission in Kuala Lumpur.

New Zealand

Trade New Zealand in Kuala Lumpur
http://www.tradenz.govt.nz/contact/seasia.html
An export promotion service, the site provides contact information for the Trade New Zealand office in Kuala Lumpur.

Norway

Norwegian Trade Council in Kuala Lumpur
http://www.norway.org.my/tra.htm
The site delivers Norwegian fact sheets, government directories, business and economic reports, product catalogs, travel guides, event information, and culture bulletins.

Pakistan

Pakistan Trade Office in Kuala Lumpur
http://www.jamal.com/epb/ptoa.htm
The site provides contact information for the Pakistan Trade Office in Kuala Lumpur.

Philippines

Philippine Trade and Investment Promotion Office in Kuala Lumpur
http://www.dti.gov.ph/KL/
The site provides a mission statement, service directory, and contact information for the Philippine Trade Office in Kuala Lumpur.

Singapore

High Commission of Singapore in Kuala Lumpur
http://www.gov.sg/mfa/consular/mww_m.htm
The site provides contact information for the Singapore High Commission in Kuala Lumpur.

South Africa

South Africa Foreign Trade Office in Kuala Lumpur
http://wwwdti.pwv.gov.za/dtiwww/
foreign_offices.htm

A service of the South Africa Department of Trade and Industry, the site provides contact information for the South Africa Trade Office in Kuala Lumpur.

Spain

Spanish Commercial Office in Kuala Lumpur
http://www.icex.es/openURL.html#openURL=/ english/infoproyem/ofcomes/ofcomes.html#AS
The site lists the staff, street address, phone and fax numbers, and e-mail link of the Spanish Commercial Office in Kuala Lumpur.

Sweden

Embassy of Sweden in Kuala Lumpur
http://www.ud.se/english/mfa/ambassad/ malaysia.htm
The site provides contact information for the Swedish Embassy in Kuala Lumpur.

Taiwan

Taiwan Government Information Office in Kuala Lumpur
http://www.gio.gov.tw/info/ngio/mal-f.html
Posted in Chinese and English, the site lists the street address, phone and fax numbers, and e-mail link of the Taiwan Government Information Office in Kuala Lumpur.

Thailand

Royal Thai Consulate General in Kota Bharu
http://www.mfa.go.th/Embassy/detail/20.htm
The site lists the Consul General, street address, and phone and fax numbers of the Thai Consulate General in Kota Bharu.

Royal Thai Consulate General in Penang
http://www.mfa.go.th/Embassy/detail/31.htm
The site lists the Consul General, street address, and phone and fax numbers of the Thai Consulate General in Penang.

Royal Thai Embassy in Kuala Lumpur
http://www.mfa.go.th/Embassy/detail/162.htm
The site lists the Ambassador, street address, and phone and fax numbers of the Thai Embassy in Kuala Lumpur.

Thailand Office of Commercial Affairs in Kuala Lumpur
http://www.thaitrade.com/thcoaf.html
The site lists the street address, phone and fax numbers, and e-mail link of the Thailand Office of Commercial Affairs in Kuala Lumpur.

Turkey

Embassy of Turkey in Kuala Lumpur
http://www.turkey.org/madres.htm
As part of a directory of Turkish diplomatic offices around the world, the site lists the e-mail link of the Turkish Embassy in Kuala Lumpur.

United Kingdom

Consulate of Britain in Kuching
http://www.fco.gov.uk/directory/posts.asp?MD
The site provides contact information for the British Consulate in Kuching.

High Commission of Britain in Kuala Lumpur
http://www.fco.gov.uk/directory/posts.asp?MD
The site provides contact information for the British High Commission in Kuala Lumpur.

United States

American Malaysian Chamber of Commerce
http://www.jaring.my/amcham/
Based in Kuala Lumpur, the Chamber promotes United States-Malaysia trade. The site includes a member directory, business briefings, and contact information.

United States Embassy in Malaysia
http://www.jaring.my/usiskl/
The virtual Embassy provides United States news, press releases, speeches, reports on America-Malaysia trade, and a directory of consular and commercial services.

United States Foreign Agriculture Service in Malaysia
http://www.jaring.my/usiskl/embassy/klfas.html
Part of the American Embassy, the Service promotes United States agricultural exports to Malaysia. The service includes a mission statement, contact information, and reports on Malaysian credit guarantees.

United States Information Service in Kuala Lumpur
http://www.jaring.my/usiskl/embassy/klusis.html
The site lists the staff, media and public affairs services, street address, and phone and fax numbers of the United States Information Service in Kuala Lumpur.

Venezuela

Embassy of Venezuela in Kuala Lumpur
http://www.trade-venezuela.com/EMBVENG.HTM
The site lists the street address, phone and fax numbers, and e-mail link of the Venezuelan Embassy in Kuala Lumpur.

Maldives

Maldives Media

Haveeru Daily
http://haveeru.com/
The electronic newspaper provides Maldivian news, editorials, business reports, exchange rate information, lifestyle reports, letters to the editor, and photos.

Maldives Media
http://www.mediainfo.com/emediajs/specific-geo.htm?region=maldives
Developed by Editor and Publisher Interactive, the site is an index of Maldivian newspapers and other media sites online.

Maldives Market Guides

Maldives Country Brief
http://www.worldbank.org/cgi-bin/ sendoff.cgi?page=%2Fhtml%2Fextdr%2Foffrep%2 Fsas%2Fmv.htm
A service of the World Bank Group, the site provides Maldivian population statistics, financial data, development reports, and economic forecasts.

Maldives: A Country Study
http://lcweb2.loc.gov/frd/cs/mvtoc.html
A service of the U.S. Library of Congress, the site delivers fact sheets on Maldivian geography, people, agriculture, mining, manufacturing, and foreign economic relations.

Maldives Market Research
http://strategis.ic.gc.ca/sc_mrkti/ibinddc/engdoc/ 1a1h9.html
Posted by Industry Canada, the site provides U.S. Central Intelligence Agency fact sheets on Maldivian geography, people, government, business, and transportation.

Maldives Virtual Library
http://library.berkeley.edu/SSEAL/SouthAsia/ WWWVL/maldives.html

A service of the World Wide Web Virtual Library, the site is a directory of Maldivian resources online. Categories include country profiles, maps, and news.

Marshall Islands

Marshall Islands Market Guides

Marshall Islands Country Brief
http://www.worldbank.org/cgi-bin/ sendoff.cgi?page=%2Fhtml%2Fextdr%2Foffrep% 2Feap%2Fmh.htm
A service of the World Bank Group, the site provides Marshallese population statistics, financial data, development reports, and economic forecasts.

Marshall Islands Country Profile
http://www.tradenz.govt.nz/intelligence/profiles/ marshall_islands.html
A service of the New Zealand Trade Development Board, the site provides Marshallese economic statistics, market information, and business tips.

Republic of the Marshall Islands Online
http://www.rmiembassyus.org/index.html
A service of the Marshall Islands Embassy in Washington, D.C., the site provides fact sheets on Marshallese people, geography, history, culture, business and travel.

Marshall Islands Trade Assistance

Marshall Islands Embassies, Missions, and Consulates
http://www.rmiembassyus.org/address.html
The site lists the street addresses, phone and fax numbers, and e-mail links of Marshallese diplomatic offices in the United States, China, Fiji, and Japan.

Marshall Islands Foreign Trade Statistics
http://www.rmiembassyus.org/tradstat.html
An archive of international trade statistics, the site includes data on Marshall Islands exports and imports by product and trading partner.

Micronesia

Micronesia Media

Island Tribune
http://www.islandtribune.com/
The electronic newspaper delivers Micronesian

news, editorials, press releases, letters to the editor, business reports, and lifestyle features.

Micronesia Market Guides

Federated States of Micronesia
http://www.fsmgov.org/
A hub of country information, the site delivers fact sheets on Micronesian geography, history, people, business, culture, language, education, and investment.

Investing in Micronesia
http://www.fsminvest.fm/
A service of the Micronesia Department of Economic Affairs, the site provides Micronesian investment guides, sector profiles, and a directory of business resources.

Micronesia Country Brief
http://www.worldbank.org/cgi-bin/ sendoff.cgi?page=%2Fhtml%2Fextdr%2Foffrep%2 Feap%2Ffm.htm
A service of the World Bank Group, the site provides Micronesian population statistics, financial data, development reports, and economic forecasts.

Micronesia Market Research
http://strategis.ic.gc.ca/sc_mrkti/ibinddc/engdoc/ 1a1i17.html
Posted by Industry Canada, the site provides U.S. Central Intelligence Agency fact sheets on Micronesian geography, people, government, business, and transportation.

Micronesia Zone
http://darkwing.uoregon.edu/~robertsr/ micronesia_zone/index.html
An index of Micronesia resources online, the site includes links to Micronesian fact sheets, business guides, travel information, statistics, and photos.

Micronesia Trade Assistance

Micronesia Embassies and Consulates Abroad
http://www.fsmgov.org/ovmis.html
A service of the Micronesia Department of External Affairs, the site is a directory of Micronesian embassies, consulates, and missions around the world.

Mongolia

Mongolia Media

Mongolia Media
http://www.mediainfo.com/emediajs/specific- geo.htm?region=mongolia
Developed by Editor and Publisher Interactive, the site is an index of Mongolian newspapers and other media sites online.

Mongolia Market Guides

Foreign Direct Investment
http://www.mongolnet.com/invest.htm
A primer on foreign investment, the site provides fact sheets on Mongolian business laws, incentive programs, project approval procedures, and dispute resolution.

Government of Mongolia
http://www.pmis.gov.mn/MAINPGE/Defengg.htm
A directory of Mongolian government resources online, the site connects to over 20 agencies, including the Ministries of Finance, Environment, Defense, and Education.

Investment and Business Opportunities
http://www.mol.mn/mri/sector.htm
A service of the Mongolia Market Research Institute, the site is a directory of state-owned enterprises that are scheduled to be privatized.

Mongolia Business Development Agency
http://www.mol.mn/mbda/a1.htm
Established in 1994, the Agency promotes economic development and foreign investment in Mongolia. The site includes a mission statement, activity reports, and contact information.

Mongolia Country Brief
http://www.worldbank.org/cgi-bin/ sendoff.cgi?page=%2Fhtml%2Fextdr%2Foffrep%2 Feap%2Fmn.htm
A service of the World Bank Group, the site provides Mongolian population statistics, financial data, development reports, and economic forecasts.

Mongolia: A Country Study
http://lcweb2.loc.gov/frd/cs/mntoc.html
A service of the U.S. Library of Congress, the site

delivers fact sheets on Mongolian geography, people, agriculture, mining, manufacturing, and foreign economic relations.

Mongolia Market Research
http://strategis.ic.gc.ca/sc_mrkti/ibinddc/engdoc/1a1f7.html
A service of Industry Canada, the site provides U.S. Department of Commerce reports on Mongolian economic trends, trade barriers, investment regulations, business travel, and market opportunities.

Mongolia Online
http://www.mongoliaonline.mn/english/
A virtual country gateway, the site provides Mongolian fact sheets, news, economic reports, government directories, sector profiles, and domain name databases.

Mongolian Chamber of Commerce and Industry
http://www.mol.mn/mcci/mlogo.htm
The online service provides Mongolian economic reports, commercial guides, company directories, investment primers, taxation bulletins, and visa information.

State Property Committee
http://www.spc.gov.mn/
An agency of the Mongolian government, the Committee is responsible for managing and privatizing state-owned assets. The site includes privatization reports, investment guides, and a list of upcoming state auctions.

Mongolia Trade Assistance

Market Research Institute
http://www.mol.mn/mri/dmc.htm
Along with foreign trade applications and customs guide, the site provides a directory of Mongolian companies in eight categories including construction, mining, agriculture, and telecommunications.

Ministry of External Relations
http://www.pmis.gov.mn/external/
The Ministry homepage delivers Mongolian fact sheets, history lessons, foreign policy statements, business guides, foreign investment primers, and visa and passport information.

Mongolia Foreign Trade
http://www.mongolnet.com/trade.htm
Along with export and import statistics, the online service provides briefs on Mongolian customs

duties and valuation, non-tariff measures, and other international trade regulations.

Mongolian Trade and Industry Promotion Agency
http://www.magicnet.mn/mri/motra.htm
Based in Ulaanbaatar, the Agency promotes Mongolian exports and international investment. The service includes a mission statement, investment guides, and contact information.

Mongolia Representative Offices

Laos

Embassy of Laos in Ulaanbaatar
http://www.laoembassy.com/news/embassyabroad.htm
The site provides contact information for the Embassy of Laos in Ulaanbaatar.

United Kingdom

Embassy of Britain in Ulaanbaatar
http://www.fco.gov.uk/directory/posts.asp?MO
The site provides contact information for the British Embassy in Ulaanbaatar.

Myanmar

Myanmar Market Guides

Investment in Myanmar
http://www.myanmar.com/gov/trade/inv.htm
A virtual library of country information, the site provides Myanmar fact sheets, investment guides, export and import primers, socioeconomic statistics, and incentive information.

Myanmar Country Brief
http://www.worldbank.org/cgi-bin/sendoff.cgi?page=%2Fhtml%2Fextdr%2Foffrep%2Feap%2Fmm.htm
A service of the World Bank Group, the site provides Myanmar population statistics, financial data, development reports, and economic forecasts.

Myanmar Country Profile
http://www.tradenz.govt.nz/intelligence/profiles/myanmar_(burma).html
A service of the New Zealand Trade Development Board, the site provides Myanmar economic statistics, market information, and business tips.

Myanmar Home Page
http://www.myanmar.com/
Posted in English, French, German, and Japanese, the site provides Myanmar commercial guides, tourist bulletins, cultural reports, and event information.

Myanmar InfoExport
http://www.infoexport.gc.ca/country-e.asp?continent=Asia&country=8
A service of Foreign Affairs and International Trade Canada, the site provides fact sheets and statistics on Myanmar geography, business and politics.

Myanmar Market Research
http://strategis.ic.gc.ca/sc_mrkti/ibinddc/engdoc/1a1i18.html
A service of Industry Canada, the site provides U.S. Department of Commerce reports on Myanmar economic trends, trade barriers, investment regulations, business travel, and market opportunities.

Myanmar Virtual Library
http://iias.leidenuniv.nl/wwwvl/southeas/MM_Info.html
A service of the Asian Studies World Wide Web Virtual Library, the site is a directory of Myanmar resources online. Categories include business, government, news, and travel.

Myanmar Trade Assistance

Trade Shows in Myanmar
http://www.expoguide.com/shows/data/loc_39.htm
Compiled by Expoguide, the site is a directory of upcoming trade shows in Myanmar.

Myanmar Representative Offices

Australia

Austrade in Rangoon
http://www.austrade.gov.au/GreaterMekongRegion/
The online service provides Australian export guides, company profiles, product catalogs, success stories, investment primers, and contact information for the Austrade office in Rangoon.

Laos

Embassy of Laos in Rangoon
http://www.laoembassy.com/news/
embassyabroad.htm
The site provides contact information for the Laotian Embassy in Rangoon.

Malaysia

Embassy of Malaysia in Rangoon
http://www.mnet.com.my/klonline/www/missions/malmiss/mmyanmar.htm
The site provides contact information for the Malaysian Embassy in Rangoon.

Nepal

Embassy of Nepal in Rangoon
http://www.info-nepal.com/members/fips/contacts/nepalese.html
The site provides contact information for the Nepalese Embassy in Rangoon.

Singapore

Embassy of Singapore in Rangoon
http://www.gov.sg/mfa/consular/mww_m.htm
The site provides contact information for the Singapore Embassy in Rangoon.

Thailand

Thailand Office of Commercial Affairs in Rangoon
http://www.thaitrade.com/thcoaf.html
The site lists the street address, phone and fax numbers, and e-mail link of the Thailand Office of Commercial Affairs in Rangoon.

United Kingdom

Embassy of Britain in Rangoon
http://www.fco.gov.uk/directory/posts.asp?BM
The site provides contact information for the British Embassy in Rangoon.

Nauru

Nauru Market Guides

Nauru Country Profile
http://www.tradenz.govt.nz/intelligence/profiles/nauru.html
A service of the New Zealand Trade Development Board, the site provides Nauruan economic statistics, market information, and business tips.

Nauru Market Research
http://strategis.ic.gc.ca/sc_mrkti/ibinddc/engdoc/
1a1i19.html
Posted by Industry Canada, the site provides U.S.
Central Intelligence Agency fact sheets on
Nauruan geography, people, government,
business, and transportation.

Nauru: Nations of the Commonwealth
http://www.tbc.gov.bc.ca/cwgames/country/Nauru/
nauru.html
The online service provides fact sheets on
Nauruan climate, population, language, currency,
exports, imports, culture, and agriculture.

Nepal

Nepal Media

Nepal Media
http://www.mediainfo.com/emediajs/specific-
geo.htm?region=nepal
Developed by Editor and Publisher Interactive, the
site is an index of Nepalese media sites online
including magazines, newspapers, and radio
stations.

People's Review
http://www.info-nepal.com/p-review/
The electronic magazine provides Nepalese
news, editorials, business reports, lifestyle
features, and a searchable archive of back
issues for the past two years.

Nepal Market Guides

Country Commercial Guide
http://www.state.gov/www/about_state/business/
com_guides/1998/southeast_asia/nepal98.html
Prepared by the United States Embassy in
Kathmandu, the site delivers primers on
Nepalese business, politics, trade regulations
and standards, investment, and travel.

Nepal Country Brief
http://www.worldbank.org/cgi-bin/
sendoff.cgi?page=%2Fhtml%2Fextdr%2Foffrep%2
Fsas%2Fnp.htm
A service of the World Bank Group, the site
provides Nepalese population statistics, financial
data, development reports, and economic
forecasts.

Nepal: A Country Study
http://lcweb2.loc.gov/frd/cs/nptoc.html
A service of the U.S. Library of Congress, the site

delivers fact sheets on Nepalese geography,
people, agriculture, mining, manufacturing, and
foreign economic relations.

Nepal Foreign Investment Board
http://www.info-nepal.com/fips/
A service of the Nepal Ministry of Industry, the site
provides briefs on Nepalese investment opportunities, international trade, infrastructure, labor,
and taxation.

Nepal Home Page
http://www.info-nepal.com/
A virtual country gateway, the site provides a
directory of Nepalese resources online in 11
categories including business, education,
economy and development, and government and
politics.

Nepal InfoExport
http://www.infoexport.gc.ca/country-
e.asp?continent=Asia&country=30
A service of Foreign Affairs and International
Trade Canada, the site provides fact sheets and
statistics on Nepalese geography, business and
politics.

Nepal Market Research
http://strategis.ic.gc.ca/sc_mrkti/ibinddc/engdoc/
1a1h10.html
A service of Industry Canada, the site provides
U.S. Department of Commerce reports on
Nepalese economic trends, trade barriers,
investment regulations, business travel, and
market opportunities.

Nepal Privatization
http://www.privat.gov.np/
A service of the Nepal Ministry of Finance, the site
delivers Nepalese fact sheets, economic reports,
privatization reports, and investment opportunities.

Nepal Virtual Library
http://www.catmando.com/wwwvlnp.htm
A service of the World Wide Web Virtual Library,
the site is a directory of Nepalese resources
online. Categories include business, travel, and
culture and art.

South-Asia Com
http://www.south-asia.com/
An index of Nepalese sites online, the site is
divided into 17 categories including publications,
embassies, products, finance, courier and cargo,
and science and technology.

Nepal Trade Assistance

Major Export Organizations
*http://www.info-nepal.com/epb/exportdir/firm/
firmlist1.html*
A service of the Nepal Export Promotion Board,
the site is a directory of leading Nepalese
exporters in over 20 categories including beverages, confectionery, footwear, and steel products.

Nepal Export Promotion Board
http://www.info-nepal.com/epb/
Based in Kathmandu, the Board promotes
Nepalese exports and foreign investment. The
service includes Nepalese trade statistics, trade
and investment policies, export directories, and a
directory of bilateral trade agreements.

Nepalese Missions Abroad
*http://www.info-nepal.com/members/fips/contacts/
nepalese.html*
A directory of Nepalese Embassies around the
world, the site lists offices in over 15 countries
including Belgium, China, Egypt, Thailand, and
the United Kingdom.

Nepal Representative Offices

Residential Diplomatic Missions
*http://www.info-nepal.com/members/fips/contacts/
residential.html*
A directory of foreign diplomatic offices in Nepal,
the site lists representatives from over 20
countries including Australia, Bangladesh,
Pakistan, and Russia.

Finland

Embassy of Finland in Kathmandu
http://www.south-asia.com/embassy-Finland/
Posted in English and Finnish, the site provides
Finnish fact sheets, sector profiles, visa and
passport information, and reports on Finland-
Nepal trade and relations.

India

Embassy of India in Kathmandu
*http://www.indiaexpress.com/embassy/
indemb.html*
Posted in English, the site provides Indian news,
fact sheets, government guides, reports on
Nepal-India trade and relations, and a directory of
consular and commercial services.

Thailand

Royal Thai Embassy in Kathmandu
http://www.mfa.go.th/Embassy/detail/50.htm
The site lists the Ambassador, street address,
and phone and fax numbers of the Thai Embassy
in Kathmandu.

United Kingdom

Embassy of Britain in Kathmandu
http://www.fco.gov.uk/directory/posts.asp?NP
The site provides contact information for the
British Embassy in Kathmandu.

United States

United States Embassy in Kathmandu
http://www.south-asia.com/USA/
Along with a directory of consular and commercial services, the virtual Embassy delivers
Nepalese business guides, procurement
opportunities, and reports on United States-
Nepal trade and relations.

**United States Information Service in
Kathmandu**
http://www.south-asia.com/USA/usispage.htm
The online service provides United States news,
press releases, fact sheets, electronic journals,
foreign policy statements, and a directory of
educational and exchange programs.

New Caledonia

New Caledonia Market Guides

New Caledonia Business Briefs
http://www.austrade.gov.au/IOOM/NewCaledonia/
A service of Austrade, the site offers fact sheets
on New Caledonian culture, business etiquette,
marketing, transportation, travel, and visas.

New Caledonia Country Profile
*http://www.tradenz.govt.nz/intelligence/profiles/
new_caledonia.html*
A service of the New Zealand Trade Development
Board, the site provides New Caledonian
economic statistics, market information, and
business tips.

New Caledonia Market Research
http://strategis.ic.gc.ca/sc_mrkti/ibinddc/engdoc/1a1i20.html
Posted by Industry Canada, the site provides U.S. Central Intelligence Agency fact sheets on New Caledonian geography, people, government, business, and transportation.

Welcome to New Caledonia
http://www.new-caledonia.com/eng.htm
An online travel gateway, the site provides New Caledonian tourism guides, shopping directories, event information, photos, and an online discussion forum.

New Caledonia Representative Offices

New Zealand

Trade New Zealand in New Caledonia
http://www.tradenz.govt.nz/contact/pacific.html
An export promotion service, the site provides contact information for the Trade New Zealand office in New Caledonia.

New Zealand

New Zealand Search Tools

Search NZ
http://www.searchnz.co.nz/
A browsable index of New Zealand resources online, the site includes a new sites guide, web reviews, search tips, and domain name searching.

New Zealand Media

New Zealand Media
http://www.mediainfo.com/emediajs/specific-geo.htm?region=newzealand
Developed by Editor and Publisher Interactive, the site is an index of New Zealand media sites online including magazines, newspapers, and news syndicates.

New Zealand Market Guides

Business Development News
http://www.moc.govt.nz/cae/bd/news/index.html
Published ten times a year by the New Zealand Ministry of Commerce, the site provides New Zealand business news, surveys, checklists, and regulatory updates.

Companies Office
http://www.companies.govt.nz/search/cad/DBSSITEN.Main
A service of the Ministry of Commerce, the site is a searchable database of New Zealand business registrations, insolvencies, trademarks, and motor vehicles.

Intellectual Property Office of New Zealand
http://www.iponz.govt.nz/
A unit of the Ministry of Commerce, the site provides information on New Zealand trademarks, patents, industrial designs, and other intellectual property.

Introduction to Investment in New Zealand
http://www.rmmb.co.nz/investnz/Welcome.html
A service of Auckland-based Russell McVeagh McKenzie Bartleet and Company law firm, the site delivers fact sheets on New Zealand investment, immigration, and intellectual property laws.

JobNet NZ
http://www.jobnetnz.co.nz/
An online job service, the site provides a searchable directory of New Zealand employment opportunities in 15 categories including banking, education, engineering, and management.

New Zealand Business Briefs
http://www.austrade.gov.au/IOOM/NewZealand/
A service of Austrade, the site offers fact sheets on New Zealand business etiquette, foreign investment, corporate taxation, marketing, and visas.

New Zealand Business Directory
http://www.nzbd.co.nz/
A directory of New Zealand companies online, the site is divided into some 30 categories including agriculture, consultancy and business services, retailers and online shopping, and security products.

New Zealand Business Links
http://www.govt.nz/nz_info/business_links.shtml
The site provides a directory of New Zealand government ministries and agencies which provide programs and services to business.

New Zealand Government Online
http://www.govt.nz/
Along with a searchable database of government programs and services, the site includes New Zealand news, press releases, socioeconomic statistics, and employment opportunities.

New Zealand InfoExport

http://www.infoexport.gc.ca/country-e.asp?continent=Asia&country=61
A service of Foreign Affairs and International Trade Canada, the site provides New Zealand commercial guides and market reports.

New Zealand: An Introduction

http://www.apecsec.org.sg/member/apecnzea1.html
A service of the Asia Pacific Economic Cooperation, the site provides fact sheets on New Zealand geography, climate, population, language, business, and international trade.

New Zealand Manufacturers Federation

http://www.manufacturers.org.nz/
Based in Wellington, the Federation promotes the interests of New Zealand manufacturers. The site includes a member directory, tender notices, and an online discussion group.

New Zealand Market Access Database

http://mkaccdb.eu.int/mkdb/mkdb.pl?METHOD=COUNTRY
A service of the European Commission, the site offers briefs on New Zealand trade policy, tariff barriers, non-tariff barriers, investment-related measures, and financial services regulations.

New Zealand Market Information

http://dtiinfo1.dti.gov.uk/ots/new_zealand/
A service of the London-based Department of Trade and Industry, the site delivers New Zealand fact sheets, maps, and trade-show information.

New Zealand Market Research

http://strategis.ic.gc.ca/sc_mrkti/ibinddc/engdoc/1a1i21.html
A service of Industry Canada, the site provides U.S. Department of Commerce reports on New Zealand economic trends, trade barriers, investment regulations, business travel, and market opportunities.

New Zealand Ministry of Commerce

http://www.moc.govt.nz/
Based in Wellington, the Ministry promotes economic development and business performance in New Zealand. The site includes business regulation and registration information.

New Zealand: Selected Issues

http://www.imf.org/external/pubs/CAT/longres.cfm?sk=2488.0
Prepared by the International Monetary Fund, the site reports on New Zealand saving and investment trends, pension reform, taxation, government expenditures, and demographic projections.

New Zealand Virtual Library

http://austudies.org/nzvl/
A service of the World Wide Web Virtual Library, the site is a directory of New Zealand resources online. Categories include business, government, information technology, and news.

New Zealand Yellow Pages

http://www.yellowpages.co.nz/
A searchable database of New Zealand companies and organizations online, the site is divided into 20 categories including business services, health, and storage and distribution.

Statistics New Zealand

http://www.stats.govt.nz/statsweb.nsf
A virtual archive of New Zealand statistics, the site features data on the national economy, business activity, household spending, labor, and international trade.

New Zealand Trade Assistance

Export Institute of New Zealand

http://www.nzwwa.com/business/ex-importers/export/index.htm
Based in Wellington, the Institute provides export education services to New Zealand businesspeople. The site provides a newsletter, member directory, activity reports, and course information.

Freight Forwarders in New Zealand

http://www.freightworld.com/forw_geo.html#9
A service of Freightworld, the site is a directory of New Zealand freight forwarders online including Fast Cargo International, International Freight Management, and Mainfreight Limited.

Maritime Carriers in New Zealand

http://www.freightworld.com/mari_geo.html#9
A database of New Zealand maritime carriers online, the site connects to four operations including Barbican Line, Oceantranz Limited, and Sofrana Unilines.

Ministry of Foreign Affairs and Trade

http://www.mft.govt.nz/
The online site provides New Zealand foreign policy statements, press releases, trade policy reports, event information, travel guides, and international trade statistics.

Ministry of Foreign Affairs and Trade Overseas Representation
http://www.mft.govt.nz/Overseas/index.htm
A service of the Ministry of Foreign Affairs and Trade, the site is a directory of New Zealand diplomatic offices in Africa, the Americas, Asia, Europe, the Middle East, and Asia Pacific.

New Zealand Customs
http://www.customs.govt.nz/
Along with traveler's information, the site delivers fact sheets on New Zealand exchange rates, export and import restrictions, rules of origin, trade permits, and other customs regulations.

New Zealand Importer/Exporter Directory
http://www.nzexporters.co.nz/
A searchable index of New Zealand importers and exporters, the site is divided into over 20 industry categories including agri-food, chemicals, wood products, and electronics.

New Zealand Marine Exporters
http://www.marex.org.nz/
A directory of New Zealand marine exporters, the site lists ship builders, marine engine manufacturers, dockage and berthage service providers, and publishers.

New Zealand Trade Centre
http://nztc.co.nz/nztc/index.htm
Based in Auckland, the Centre is an exhibition of over 2,000 New Zealand products for export. The site includes a mission statement, service directory, and contact information.

New Zealand Trade Development Board
http://www.tradenz.govt.nz/
Based in Wellington, the Board promotes New Zealand exports. The site includes New Zealand fact sheets, international trade guides, statistics, and sector profiles.

New Zealand Trade Offices
http://www.tradenz.govt.nz/contact/index.html
A directory of New Zealand Trade offices around the world, the site lists operations in Asia Pacific, Europe, the Middle East, and North and South America.

Railways in New Zealand
http://www.freightworld.com/railroads.html#9
An index of New Zealand railways online, the site links to one operation: Tranz Rail.

Trade Shows in New Zealand
http://www.expoguide.com/shows/data/loc_41.htm
Compiled by Expoguide, the site is a directory of upcoming trade shows in New Zealand.

Trucking and Motor Carriers in New Zealand
http://www.freightworld.com/truc_geo.html#9
A database of New Zealand motor carriers online, the site connects to one operation: Mainfreight Limited.

New Zealand Representative Offices

Diplomatic and Consular Representatives
http://www.mft.govt.nz/Publications/Dip/index.htm
A service of the New Zealand Ministry of Foreign Affairs and Trade, the site is a directory of foreign diplomatic posts and international organizations in New Zealand.

Australia

Austrade in Auckland
http://www.austrade.gov.au/Auckland/
An Australian trade promotion service, the site provides a mission statement, market reports, and contact information for Austrade in Auckland.

Canada

High Commission of Canada in Wellington
http://www.dfait-maeci.gc.ca/english/missions/rep-can3e.htm#new zealand
The site provides contact information for the Canadian High Commission in Wellington.

Chile

Embassy of Chile in Wellington
http://www.prochinz.co.nz/
Along with visa and passport information, the online service provides Chilean fact sheets, government directories, media guides, company databases, and trade leads.

European Union

Delegation of the European Commission to New Zealand
http://www.ecdel.org.au/
Established in 1984, the Delegation represents the European Community in New Zealand. The site includes European Union news, documents, and contact information.

Fiji

High Commission of Fiji in Wellington
http://fiji.gov.fj/core/fj_mis.html
The site provides contact information for the Fijian High Commission in Wellington.

France

French Trade Commission in Auckland
http://www.dree.org/nouvellezelande/FRANCAIS/ Nous%20contacter/Auckland.htm
The site lists the street address, phone and fax numbers, and e-mail link of the French Trade Commission in Auckland.

French Trade Commission in New Zealand
http://www.dree.org/nouvellezelande/
Written in French, the site delivers New Zealand market reports, sector profiles, contact information, and a directory of French export promotion services.

French Trade Commission in Wellington
http://www.dree.org/nouvellezelande/FRANCAIS/ Nous%20contacter/Wellington.htm
The site lists the street address, phone and fax numbers, and e-mail link of the French Trade Commission in Wellington.

Germany

German Chamber of Commerce in Auckland
http://www.ahk.net/en/nz/Auckland/
The site lists the Chief Executive Officer, street address, phone and fax numbers, and e-mail link of the German Chamber in Auckland.

Israel

Embassy of Israel in Wellington
http://www.webnz.com/israel/
The online service delivers Israeli fact sheets, visa and passport information, reports on Israel-New Zealand trade, and a directory of consular and commercial services.

Israel Trade Commission
http://www.wej.com.au/itc/itc_home.html
Based in Sydney, the Commission promotes Israeli exports to Australia. The site includes a mission statement, activity reports, and contact information.

New Zealand-Israel Trade Association
http://webnz.com/israel/nzita.htm
Established in 1994, the Association promotes New Zealand-Israel trade. The site includes a mission statement, newsletter, activity reports, and contact information.

Malaysia

High Commission of Malaysia in Wellington
http://www.mnet.com.my/klonline/www/missions/ malmiss/mnewzeal1.htm
The site provides contact information for the Malaysian High Commission in Wellington.

Netherlands

Royal Netherlands Embassy in Wellington
http://canterbury.cyberplace.co.nz/community/d-embass.html
The site lists the street address and phone and fax numbers of the Dutch Embassy in Wellington, and the Dutch Consulates in Auckland and Christchurch.

Singapore

High Commission of Singapore in Wellington
http://www.gov.sg/mfa/consular/mww_n.htm
The site provides contact information for the Singapore High Commission in Wellington.

South Korea

Korea New Zealand Business Council
http://www.koreanz.co.nz/
Based in Auckland, the Council promotes Korea-New Zealand trade. The site includes event information, activity reports, and Korean business news and guides.

Thailand

Royal Thai Embassy in Wellington
http://www.mfa.go.th/Embassy/detail/51.htm
The site lists the Ambassador, street address, and phone and fax numbers of the Thai Embassy in Wellington.

United Kingdom

ANZLink
http://www.anzlink.com/
An Australia-New Zealand-United Kingdom trade promotion service, the site includes business guides, investment primers, and trade-show information for the three countries.

British Consulate General in Auckland
http://www.brithighcomm.org.nz/
office.html#consulate
The site lists the commercial services, street address, phone and fax numbers, and e-mail link of the British Consulate General in Auckland.

British High Commission in Wellington
http://www.brithighcomm.org.nz/
A virtual library of country information, the site provides British fact sheets, business guides, visa and passport information, and a directory of consular and commercial services.

British-New Zealand Trade Council
http://www.anzlink.com/Nzland/Helpadv/
bnztc.htm
Established in 1917, the Council promotes British-New Zealand trade. The site features a mission statement, activity reports, and membership information.

United States

United States Consulate in Auckland
http://homepages.ihug.co.nz/~amcongen/
Along with New Zealand trade guides, the digital Consulate delivers United States fact sheets, visa information, and a directory of consular and commercial services.

United States Embassy in Wellington
http://www.usia.gov/abtusia/posts/NZ1/
wwwhemb.html
Featuring a welcome from the Ambassador, the virtual Embassy provides United States fact sheets, visa and passport information, and a directory of consular and commercial services.

United States Foreign Agricultural Service in Wellington
http://www.usia.gov/abtusia/posts/NZ1/
wwwhfas.html
A branch of the United States Embassy, the Service promotes American agricultural exports to New Zealand. The site includes contact information and agri-food trade leads.

United States Information Service in Wellington
http://www.usia.gov/abtusia/posts/NZ1/
wwwhusis.html
The online service provides United States news, press releases, fact sheets, electronic journals, foreign policy statements, and a directory of United States-New Zealand educational and exchange programs.

Western Samoa

Consulate General of Western Samoa in Auckland
http://www.interwebinc.com/samoa/
missnz.html#consul
The site lists the street address, and phone and fax numbers of the Western Samoan Consulate General in Auckland.

Western Samoa High Commission in Wellington
http://www.interwebinc.com/samoa/missnz.html
The site lists the street address, and phone and fax numbers of the Western Samoan High Commission in Wellington.

Niue

Niue Market Guides

Niue Country Profile
http://www.tradenz.govt.nz/intelligence/profiles/
niue.html
A service of the New Zealand Trade Development Board, the site provides Niuean economic statistics, market information, and business tips.

Niue Island
http://www.hideawayholidays.com.au/niue_.htm
The online service provides fact sheets on Niuean Islands people, government, climate, currency, customs, transportation, shopping, telecommunications, and travel.

Niue Market Research
http://strategis.ic.gc.ca/sc_mrkti/ibinddc/engdoc/
1a1i22.html
Posted by Industry Canada, the site provides U.S. Central Intelligence Agency fact sheets on Niuean geography, people, government, business, and transportation.

Norfolk Island

Norfolk Island Market Guides

Norfolk Island Market Research
http://strategis.ic.gc.ca/sc_mrkti/ibinddc/engdoc/
1a1i23.html
Posted by Industry Canada, the site provides U.S. Central Intelligence Agency fact sheets on Norfolk Islander geography, people, government, business, and transportation.

Norfolk Island on the Net
http://www.nf/

A hub of area information, the site includes Norfolk Islander fact sheets, travel guides, shopping directories, weather bulletins, census statistics, and an event calendar.

Norfolk Island Website
http://www.ozemail.com.au/~jbp/pds/contents.html
Along with maps and history lessons, the site delivers Norfolk Islander government directories, visitor information, a virtual tour, and reports on relations with Australia and the United Nations.

North Korea

North Korea Media

North Korea News
http://darkwing.uoregon.edu/~felsing/kstuff/nknews.html
A service of the University of Oregon, the site provides a directory of North Korean media sources including the North Korean News and the Korean Central News Agency.

North Korea Market Guides

Democratic People's Republic of Korea Unofficial Page
http://www.dpr-korea.com/english.html
Posted in English and Japanese, the Japanese-based site provides North Korean business reports, accommodation directories, travel information, and cultural guides.

Handbook on North Korea
http://203.255.151.12/nkbook/hbindex.html
A service of the Korea Herald, the site delivers fact sheets on North Korean history, geography, politics, government, foreign relations, culture, and leaders.

North Korea: A Country Study
http://lcweb2.loc.gov/frd/cs/kptoc.html
A service of the U.S. Library of Congress, the site delivers fact sheets on North Korean geography, people, agriculture, mining, manufacturing, and foreign economic relations.

North Korea InfoExport
http://www.infoexport.gc.ca/country-e.asp?continent=Asia&country=21
A service of Foreign Affairs and International Trade Canada, the site provides fact sheets and statistics on North Korean geography, business and politics.

North Korea Market Research
http://strategis.ic.gc.ca/sc_mrkti/ibinddc/engdoc/1a1f4.html
Posted by Industry Canada, the site provides U.S. Central Intelligence Agency fact sheets on North Korean geography, people, government, business, and transportation.

North Korea Subject Guide
http://darkwing.uoregon.edu/~felsing/kstuff/nkshelf.html
A directory of North Korean resources online, the site is divided into over 30 categories including business, geography, infrastructure, and science and technology.

North Korea Virtual Library
http://www.duke.edu/~myhan/b_NK.html
A service of the World Wide Web Virtual Library, the site is an index of North Korean resources on the web. Categories include economy, history, media, and science and technology.

Northern Mariana Islands

Northern Mariana Islands Media

Saipan Tribune Online
http://www.tribune.co.mp/
An electronic newspaper, the site offers Northern Mariana Islander news, editorials, business reports, lifestyle features, and a searchable archive of past issues.

Northern Mariana Islands Market Guides

Business Directory
http://www.saipan.com/business/index.htm
A directory of Northern Mariana Islander companies and organizations online, the site is divided into over 20 categories including construction, government, and shipping.

Commonwealth of the Northern Mariana Islands Home Page
http://www.saipan.com/
An online country gateway, the site includes Northern Marian Islander tourism information, business guides, education reports, weather bulletins, and government directories.

General Information
http://www.saipan.com/gov/general/
A virtual country primer, the site delivers fact sheets on Northern Mariana Islander history,

geography, customs, politics, housing, education, and taxation.

Palau

Palau Market Guides

Country Book of Palau
http://www.theodora.com/wfb/palau_government.html
A virtual country profile, the site provides briefs on Palauan geography, people, government, economy, transportation, communications, defense, culture, and business.

Palau Briefing
http://www.odci.gov/cia/publications/factbook/ps.html
Written by the United States Central Intelligence Agency, the site offers fact sheets on Palauan geography, people, government, business, and transportation.

Palau Market Research
http://strategis.ic.gc.ca/sc_mrkti/ibinddc/engdoc/1a1i24.html
Posted by Industry Canada, the site provides U.S. Central Intelligence Agency fact sheets on Palauan geography, people, government, business, and transportation.

Papua New Guinea

Papua New Guinea Media

National Online
http://www.wr.com.au/national/
An electronic newspaper, the site provides Papua New Guinean news, business reports, editorials, letters to the editor, and a browsable archive of back issues.

Papua New Guinea Media
http://www.mediainfo.com/emediajs/specific-geo.htm?region=papuanewguinea
Developed by Editor and Publisher Interactive, the site is an index of Papua New Guinean newspapers, television stations, and other media sites online.

Papua New Guinea Market Guides

International Business Practices in Papua New Guinea
http://www.smartbiz.com/sbs/arts/bpr60.htm

A service of the University of Missouri at St. Louis, the site features fact sheets on Papua New Guinean business organizations, exporting, commercial policies, and foreign investment.

Investment Promotion Authority
http://www.ipa.gov.pg/
A Papua New Guinean investment promotion service, the site includes a newsletter, discussion papers, and a directory of business opportunities in 15 industries including agriculture, wood, and printing.

Papua New Guinea Business Briefs
http://www.austrade.gov.au/IOOM/PNG/
A service of Austrade, the site offers fact sheets on Papua New Guinean business etiquette, foreign investment, corporate taxation, marketing, and visas.

Papua New Guinea Country Brief
http://www.worldbank.org/cgi-bin/sendoff.cgi?page=%2Fhtml%2Fextdr%2Foffrep%2Feap%2Fpg.htm
A service of the World Bank Group, the site provides Papua New Guinean population statistics, financial data, development reports, and economic forecasts.

Papua New Guinea Country Profile
http://www.tradenz.govt.nz/intelligence/profiles/papua_new_guinea.html
A service of the New Zealand Trade Development Board, the site provides Papua New Guinean economic statistics, market information, and business tips.

Papua New Guinea InfoExport
http://www.infoexport.gc.ca/country-e.asp?continent=Asia&country=33
A service of Foreign Affairs and International Trade Canada, the site provides fact sheets and statistics on Papua New Guinean geography, business and politics.

Papua New Guinea Information Site
http://ww3.datec.com.pg/png/
An online country gateway, the site provides Papua New Guinean media guides, e-mail directories, travel information, regional profiles, and language primers.

Papua New Guinea: An Introduction
http://www.apecsec.org.sg/member/apecpnewg.html
A service of the Asia Pacific Economic Coopera-

tion, the site provides fact sheets on Papua New Guinean geography, climate, population, language, business, and international trade.

Papua New Guinea Market Research
http://strategis.ic.gc.ca/sc_mrkti/ibinddc/engdoc/1a1i25.html
A service of Industry Canada, the site provides U.S. Department of Commerce reports on Papua New Guinean economic trends, trade barriers, investment regulations, business travel, and market opportunities.

Papua New Guinea: Recent Economic Developments
http://www.imf.org/external/pubs/CAT/longres.cfm?sk=2543.0
Prepared by the International Monetary Fund, the site reports on Papua New Guinean gross domestic product, government debt, price controls, interest rates, and balance of payments.

Papua New Guinea Virtual Library
http://coombs.anu.edu.au/SpecialProj/PNG/WWWVL-PNG.html
A service of the World Wide Web Virtual Library, the site is a directory of Papua New Guinean resources online. Categories include economy, development, media, and culture.

Papua New Guinea Representative Offices

Fiji

High Commission of Fiji in Port Moresby
http://fiji.gov.fj/core/fj_mis.html
The site provides contact information for the Fijian Embassy in Port Moresby.

Malaysia

High Commission of Malaysia in Port Moresby
http://www.mnet.com.my/klonline/www/missions/malmiss/mpapuane.htm
The site provides contact information for the Malaysian High Commission in Port Moresby.

New Zealand

Trade New Zealand in Port Moresby
http://www.tradenz.govt.nz/contact/pacific.html
An export promotion service, the site provides contact information for the Trade New Zealand office in Port Moresby.

Singapore

Consulate General of Singapore in Port Moresby
http://www.gov.sg/mfa/consular/mww_p.htm
The site provides contact information for the Singapore Consulate General in Port Moresby.

United Kingdom

High Commission of Britain in Port Moresby
http://www.fco.gov.uk/directory/posts.asp?PP
The site provides contact information for the British High Commission in Port Moresby.

Philippines

Philippines Search Tools

EDSA
http://www.edsa.com.ph/
Along with search tips and personal webpages, the site features a searchable index of Philippine resources online in eight categories including business and economy, government, and society and culture.

G-Spot
http://www.gsilink.com/gspot/
Established in 1995, the site is a Philippine web navigation service. The site includes search tips and web guides.

Yehey
http://www.yehey.com.ph/
Along with news and weather bulletins, the site offers a browsable index of Philippine resources online in a dozen categories including business and economy, computers and technology, and government.

Philippines Media

BusinessWorld
http://www.bworld.com.ph/current/today.html
An electronic magazine, the site provides Philippine business news, editorials, economic reports, exchange rate bulletins, executive profiles, and arts and leisure features.

Manila Bulletin
http://www.mb.com.ph/frntpage.asp
Updated daily, the site delivers Philippine news, business reports, editorials, information technology briefs, weather bulletins, online papers, and a back issues archive.

Philippines Media

http://www.mediainfo.com/emediajs/specific-geo.htm?region=philippines
Developed by Editor and Publisher Interactive, the site is an index of Philippine media online including city guides, magazines, and newspapers.

Philippines Market Guides

Barclays Country Report: Philippines

http://www.offshorebanking.barclays.com/services/economic/yearly/philnov97/index.html
Prepared by Barclays Bank, the site reports on Philippine economic trends, politics, monetary and fiscal policy, exchange rates, international trade, and investment flows.

National Economic and Development Authority

http://www.neda.gov.ph/
Created in 1972, the Authority promotes and manages Philippine economic development. The site includes press releases, speeches, planning studies, and economic forecasts.

National Statistics Office

http://www.census.gov.ph/
An archive of statistical information, the site includes data on Philippine prices and inflation, foreign trade, energy consumption, labor and employment, and other economic indicators.

Philippine Business Briefs

http://www.austrade.gov.au/IOOM/Philippines/
A service of Austrade, the site offers fact sheets on Philippine business etiquette, foreign investment, corporate taxation, marketing, and visas.

Philippines Country Brief

http://www.worldbank.org/cgi-bin/sendoff.cgi?page=%2Fhtml%2Fextdr%2Foffrep%2Feap%2Fph.htm
A service of the World Bank Group, the site provides Philippine population statistics, financial data, development reports, and economic forecasts.

Philippines Country Profile

http://www.tradenz.govt.nz/intelligence/profiles/philippines.html
A service of the New Zealand Trade Development Board, the site provides Philippine economic statistics, market information, and business tips.

Philippines Country Report

http://www.state.gov/www/issues/economic/trade_reports/eastasia97/philippines97.html
Prepared by the U.S. Department of State, the site reports on Philippine exchange rates, debt management, trade barriers, export subsidies, intellectual property protection, worker rights, and foreign investment.

Philippines: A Country Study

http://lcweb2.loc.gov/frd/cs/phtoc.html
A service of the U.S. Library of Congress, the site delivers fact sheets on Philippine geography, people, agriculture, mining, manufacturing, and foreign economic relations.

Philippines InfoExport

http://www.infoexport.gc.ca/country-e.asp?continent=Asia&country=34
A service of Foreign Affairs and International Trade Canada, the site provides Philippine commercial guides and market reports.

Philippines: An Introduction

http://www.apecsec.org.sg/member/apecphil.html
A service of the Asia Pacific Economic Cooperation, the site provides fact sheets on Philippine transportation, population, language, business, and international trade.

Philippines Market Access Database

http://mkaccdb.eu.int/mkdb/mkdb.pl?METHOD=COUNTRY
A service of the European Commission, the site offers briefs on Philippine trade policy, tariff barriers, non-tariff barriers, investment-related measures, and financial services regulations.

Philippines Market Information

http://dtiinfo1.dti.gov.uk/ots/philippines/
A service of the London-based Department of Trade and Industry, the site delivers country fact sheets, maps, and trade-show information.

Philippines Market Research

http://strategis.ic.gc.ca/sc_mrkti/ibinddc/engdoc/1a1i27.html
A service of Industry Canada, the site provides U.S. Department of Commerce reports on Philippine economic trends, trade barriers, investment regulations, business travel, and market opportunities.

Philippines Virtual Library

http://iias.leidenuniv.nl/wwwvl/southeas/philippi.html
A service of the Asian Studies World Wide Web Virtual Library, the site is a directory of Philippine

resources online. Categories include business, government, and news.

Philippines Trade Assistance

Bureau of Export Trade Promotion
http://www.dti.gov.ph/betp/
A service of the Department of Trade and Industry, the Bureau promotes Philippine exports. The site includes a mission statement, program directory, and contact information.

Department of Trade and Industry
http://www.dti.gov.ph/
A virtual library of business information, the site provides Philippine press releases, speeches, export guides, investment primers, and international and domestic commercial reports.

Export Assistance Network
http://www.dti.gov.ph/exponet/
An online assistance center for Philippine exporters, the site provides export guides, activity reports, a members roster, and a directory of information and financing programs.

Export Development Council
http://www.dti.gov.ph/edc/
Created in 1994, the Council promotes Philippine exports. The site includes a mission statement, staff roster, committee directory, and rankings of top Philippine exporters by sector and sales category.

Foreign Trade Service Corps
http://www.dti.gov.ph/ftscmnl/
Based in Manila, the Corps promotes Philippine exports and international investment. The site features a directory of 36 Corps offices in the United States, Canada, Europe, Asia, the Middle East, and Africa.

Garments and Textile Export Board
http://www.dti.gov.ph/gteb/
A trade promotion service for Philippine garment and textile manufacturers, the site provides a member directory, activity reports, export statistics, and trade mission bulletins.

PhilExport
http://www.philexport.org/
An online export forum, the site features a searchable database of over 3,000 Philippine exporters in over 20 categories including agriculture, electronics, pharmaceuticals, and transportation.

Philippine International Trading Corporation
http://www.dti.gov.ph/pitc/
A government-owned trading company, the organization provides general trading, countertrade, and other export services for Philippine exporters. The site includes a mission statement, program directory, and contact information.

Philippine International Trading Corporation Overseas Offices
http://www.dti.gov.ph/pitc/pitc1.htm#Directory
The site lists the street addresses, and phone and fax numbers of the Philippine International Trading Corporation offices in Japan and Vietnam.

Philippine Shippers' Bureau
http://www.dti.gov.ph/psb/
Created in 1973, the Bureau promotes the interests of Philippine ship users. The site includes a mission statement, activity reports, and a directory of accredited Philippine freight forwarders.

Philippine Trade Training Center
http://www.dti.gov.ph/pttc/
A service of the Department of Trade and Industry, the Center provides export and management training. The site includes a staff roster, curriculum directory, and contact information.

Philippine Trade Winds
http://www.trade-winds.net/preph.htm
A service of Trade Winds Online, the site is a searchable directory of Philippine trade shows, business contacts, tourism information, and media.

Trade Shows in Philippines
http://www.expoguide.com/shows/data/loc_46.htm
Compiled by Expoguide, the site is a directory of upcoming trade shows in the Philippines.

Philippines Representative Offices

Australia

Austrade in Manila
http://www.austrade.gov.au/manila/
The online service provides Australian export guides, company profiles, product catalogs, success stories, investment primers, and contact information for the Austrade office in Manila.

Austria

Austrian Trade Commission in Manila
http://aw.wk.or.at/awo/ahst-manila.htm
The site lists the staff, street address, phone and fax numbers, e-mail link, and office hours of the Austrian Trade Commission in Manila.

Brunei Darussalam

Embassy of Brunei Darussalam in Manila
http://www.brunet.bn/homepage/gov/bruemb/govemb.htm
The site provides contact information for the Bruneian Embassy in Manila.

Canada

Canadian Chamber of Commerce of the Philippines
http://www.designet.net/canchamphil/
Based in Manila, the Chamber promotes Canada-Philippines trade and relations. The site includes a mission statement, membership guidelines, and event information.

Embassy of Canada in Manila
http://www.dfait-maeci.gc.ca/manila/
Featuring a message from the Ambassador, the English and French language site delivers a staff directory, visa and passport information, and reports on Canada-Philippine trade and relations.

European Union

Philippine-European Business Page
http://www.eccp.com/
A service of the Manila-based European Chamber of Commerce of the Philippines, the site provides Philippine-Europe trade news, business bulletins, and investment opportunities.

Finland

Finland Trade Center in Manila
http://www.exports.finland.fi/tradecen.htm
The site lists the staff, street address, phone and fax numbers, and e-mail link of the Finland Trade Center in Manila.

France

French Trade Commission in Manila
http://www.dree.org/philippines/

Written in French, the site delivers Philippine market reports, sector profiles, contact information, and a directory of French export promotion services.

Germany

German Chamber of Commerce in Manila
http://www.ahk.net/en/ph/Makati/
The site lists the Chairperson, Chief Executive Officer, street address, phone and fax numbers, and e-mail link of the German Chamber in Manila.

India

Indian Commercial Mission in Manila
http://www.nic.in/commin/ICM.HTM
The site lists the street address, phone and fax numbers, and e-mail link of the Indian Commercial Mission in Manila.

Indonesia

Embassy of Indonesia in Manila
http://indag.dprin.go.id/INGG/trade/atache.HTM
The site provides contact information for the Indonesian Embassy in Manila.

Philippine-Indonesia Business Council
http://www.asiaonline.net.ph/business/partners/mbc/business/phindo.htm
Based in Manila, the Council promotes Philippine-Indonesia trade. The site includes an executive roster, activity reports, trade statistics, and investment bulletins.

Malaysia

Consulate General of Malaysia in Davao City
http://www.mnet.com.my/klonline/www/missions/malmiss/mphilipp2.htm
The site provides contact information for the Malaysian Consulate General in Davao City.

Embassy of Malaysia in Manila
http://www.mnet.com.my/klonline/www/missions/malmiss/mphilipp1.htm
The site provides contact information for the Malaysian Embassy in Manila.

Philippine-Malaysia Business Council
http://www.asiaonline.net.ph/business/partners/mbc/business/phmalay.htm
Launched in 1996, the Council promotes

Philippine-Malaysia trade. The site includes an executive roster, economic reports, legislative bulletins, and contact information.

Trade Office of Malaysia in Manila
http://www.mnet.com.my/klonline/www/missions/malmiss/mphilipp3.htm
The site provides contact information for the Malaysian Trade Office in Manila.

New Zealand

Trade New Zealand in Manila
http://www.tradenz.govt.nz/contact/seasia.html
An export promotion service, the site provides contact information for the Trade New Zealand office in Manila.

Norway

Norwegian Trade Council in Manila
http://www.ntc.no/cgi-bin/wbch.exe?html=../templates/utekontor2.html&profile=1118
The site lists the staff, street address, phone and fax numbers, and e-mail link of the Norwegian Trade Council in Manila.

Pakistan

Pakistan Trade Office in Manila
http://www.jamal.com/epb/ptoa.htm
The site provides contact information for the Pakistan Trade Office in Manila.

Singapore

Philippine-Singapore Business Council
http://www.asiaonline.net.ph/business/partners/mbc/business/phsing.htm
Established in 1994, the Council promotes Philippine-Singapore trade. The site includes an executive roster, activity reports, trade statistics, and investment bulletins.

Embassy of Singapore in Manila
http://www.gov.sg/mfa/consular/mww_p.htm
The site provides contact information for the Singapore Embassy in Manila.

Spain

Spanish Commercial Office in Manila
http://www.icex.es/openURL.html#openURL=/english/infoproyem/ofcomes/ofcomes.html#AS
The site lists the staff, street address, phone and fax numbers, and e-mail link of the Spanish Commercial Office in Manila.

Sweden

Embassy of Sweden in Manila
http://www.swedemb-manila.com/
The site delivers Swedish fact sheets, visa and passport information, and a directory of consular and commercial services.

Taiwan

Taiwan Government Information Office in Manila
http://www.gio.gov.tw/info/ngio/phi-f.html
Posted in Chinese and English, the site lists the street address, phone and fax numbers, and e-mail link of the Taiwan Government Information Office in Manila.

Thailand

Royal Thai Embassy in Manila
http://www.mfa.go.th/Embassy/detail/207.htm
The site lists the Ambassador, street address, and phone and fax numbers of the Thai Embassy in Manila.

Thailand Office of Commercial Affairs in Manila
http://www.thaitrade.com/thcoaf.html
The site lists the street address, phone and fax numbers, and e-mail link of the Thailand Office of Commercial Affairs in Manila.

Turkey

Embassy of Turkey in Manila
http://www.turkey.org/madres.htm
As part of a directory of Turkish diplomatic offices around the world, the site lists the e-mail link of the Turkish Embassy in Manila.

United Kingdom

Embassy of Britain in Manila
http://www.fco.gov.uk/directory/posts.asp?PH
The site provides contact information for the British Embassy in Manila.

Philippine-British Business Council
http://www.asiaonline.net.ph/business/partners/mbc/business/phbrt.htm
Launched in 1995, the Council promotes Philippine-British trade. The site includes an executive roster, activity reports, trade statistics, and investment bulletins.

United States

Philippine-United States Business Council
http://www.asiaonline.net.ph/business/partners/
mbc/business/phus.htm
Based in Manila, the Council promotes Philippine-United States trade. The site includes an executive roster, activity reports, trade statistics, and investment bulletins.

United States Embassy in Manila
http://www.usia.gov/abtusia/posts/RP1/
wwwh3007.html
Along with Philippine economic forecasts and market guides, the virtual Embassy provides United States visa and passport information, and a directory of consular and commercial services.

United States Foreign Agricultural Service in Manila
http://www.usia.gov/abtusia/posts/RP1/
wwwh3011.html
A branch of the United States Embassy, the Service promotes American agricultural exports to the Philippines. The site provides a mission statement and contact information.

United States Information Service in Manila
http://www.usia.gov/abtusia/posts/RP1/
wwwhmain.html
The online service provides United States news, press releases, fact sheets, electronic journals, and a directory of United States-Philippine educational and exchange programs.

Venezuela

Embassy of Venezuela in Manila
http://www.trade-venezuela.com/EMBVENG.HTM
The site lists the street address, phone and fax numbers, and e-mail link of the Venezuelan Embassy in Manila.

Pitcairn Islands

Pitcairn Islands Market Guides

Pitcairn Islands Government
http://users.iconz.co.nz/pitcairn/
Official homepage of the Pitcairn Islands Government, the site includes tourism guides, immigration regulations, history lessons, stamp bulletins, and contact information.

Pitcairn Island Website
http://www.wavefront.com/~pjlareau/pitc1.html

A hub of Pitcairn Islander information, the site includes maps, fact sheets, government bulletins, photos, history lessons, travel information, and web guides.

Pitcairn Islands Market Research
http://strategis.ic.gc.ca/sc_mrkti/ibinddc/engdoc/
1a1i28.html
Posted by Industry Canada, the site provides U.S. Central Intelligence Agency fact sheets on Pitcairn Islander geography, people, government, business, and transportation.

Singapore

Singapore Media

Singapore Business Times Online
http://biztimes.asia1.com/
Along with global and regional headlines, the site delivers Singapore news, editorials, interviews, business reports, company profiles, and shipping schedules.

Singapore Media
http://www.mediainfo.com/emediajs/specific-
geo.htm?region=singapore
Developed by Editor and Publisher Interactive, the site is an index of Singapore media sites online.

Singapore Market Guides

Barclays Country Report: Singapore
http://www.offshorebanking.barclays.com/
services/economic/yearly/singmar98/
contents.html
Prepared by Barclays Bank, the site reports on Singapore economic trends, politics, monetary and fiscal policy, exchange rates, international trade, and investment flows.

Business Customs in Singapore
http://www.abcnews.com/sections/travel/
DailyNews/biztrav1106.html
A service of ABC News, the site provides a primer on Singapore business etiquette. Tips include speaking calmly and quietly, and praising your company, not yourself.

Government Internet Tendering Information System
http://wwwdb1.gov.sg/gitis/
A database of Singapore government tender notices and procurement fact sheets, the site is searchable by the awarding entity, and tender publication and closing date.

Singapore Business Briefs
http://www.austrade.gov.au/IOOM/Singapore/
A service of Austrade, the site offers fact sheets on Singapore business etiquette, foreign investment, corporate taxation, marketing, and visas.

Singapore Country Profile
http://www.tradenz.govt.nz/intelligence/profiles/singapore.html
A service of the New Zealand Trade Development Board, the site provides Singapore economic statistics, market information, and business tips.

Singapore Business Opportunities
http://www.tdb.gov.sg/singbiz/sb_menu.html
A directory of Singapore companies and organizations, the site is divided into over 40 industry categories including building materials, fashion and textiles, and telecommunications.

Singapore Company Profiles
http://www.tdb.gov.sg/coyprof/scp.html
A service of the Singapore Trade Development Board, the site provides a browsable index of some 5,000 Singapore companies. Categories include construction, electronics, and industrial machinery.

Singapore Country Report
http://www.state.gov/www/issues/economic/trade_reports/eastasia97/singapore97.html
Prepared by the U.S. Department of State, the site reports on Singapore exchange rates, debt management, trade barriers, export subsidies, intellectual property protection, worker rights, and foreign investment.

Singapore: A Country Study
http://lcweb2.loc.gov/frd/cs/sgtoc.html
A service of the U.S. Library of Congress, the site delivers fact sheets on Singapore geography, people, agriculture, mining, manufacturing, and foreign economic relations.

Singapore Government
http://www.gov.sg/
From committee reports to environmental permits to employment opportunities, the site provides a directory of Singapore government programs, services, and bulletins.

Singapore Inc.
http://www.singapore-inc.com/home.html
A hub of country business information, the site includes Singapore company profiles, investment primers, industrial facility reports, and science and technology bulletins.

Singapore InfoExport
http://www.infoexport.gc.ca/country-e.asp?continent=Asia&country=38
A service of Foreign Affairs and International Trade Canada, the site provides Singapore commercial guides and market reports.

Singapore: An Introduction
http://www.apecsec.org.sg/member/apecsing.html
A service of the Asia Pacific Economic Cooperation, the site provides fact sheets on Singapore geography, climate, population, language, business, and international trade.

Singapore Market Access Database
http://mkaccdb.eu.int/mkdb/mkdb.pl?METHOD=COUNTRY
A service of the European Commission, the site offers briefs on Singapore trade policy, tariff barriers, non-tariff barriers, investment-related measures, and financial services regulations.

Singapore Market Information
http://dtiinfo1.dti.gov.uk/ots/singapore/
A service of the London-based Department of Trade and Industry, the site delivers Singapore fact sheets, maps, and trade-show information.

Singapore Market Research
http://strategis.ic.gc.ca/sc_mrkti/ibinddc/engdoc/1a1i29.html
A service of Industry Canada, the site provides U.S. Department of Commerce reports on Singapore economic trends, trade barriers, investment regulations, business travel, and market opportunities.

Singapore Online
http://www.singapore.com/
A virtual country gateway, the site provides Singapore product catalogs, company profiles, travel guides, government directories, and a database of international buyers.

Singapore Phone Book
http://www.phonebook.com.sg/
A searchable database of Singapore business and residential phone numbers, the site is browsable by name, number, street address, and industry.

Singapore Virtual Library

http://www.univie.ac.at/Sinologie/sg-wwwvl.htm
A service of the World Wide Web Virtual Library, the site is a directory of Singapore resources online. Categories include business and economy, society and culture, and electronic journals.

Statistics Singapore

http://www.singstat.gov.sg/
A virtual archive of Singapore statistics, the site delivers data on population, literacy, newspaper circulation, crime, employment, productivity, and other social and economic indicators.

Singapore Trade Assistance

GlobalLink

http://www.tdb.gov.sg/index.html
Homepage of the Singapore Trade Development Board, the site provides annual reports, press releases, trade briefs, success stories, and a database of international buy and sell opportunities.

Ministry of Foreign Affairs

http://www.gov.sg/mfa/
Along with Ministry speeches and press releases, the site includes foreign policy statements, Singapore fact sheets, and reports on the World Trade Organization and other international organizations.

Ministry of Trade and Industry

http://www.gov.sg/mti/
Featuring data on economic growth, foreign trade, and exchange rates, the site delivers Singapore competitive reports, business surveys, and Ministry press releases.

Shipping Times Singapore

http://shiptimes.asia1.com.sg/
An electronic journal, the site provides global and regional shipping news, editorials, and a database of vessels coming to and departing from Singapore.

Singapore Connect

http://sgconnect.asia1.com.sg/
A virtual marketplace, the site provides Singapore company directories, sector profiles, and business opportunities in six categories including electronics, consumer products, and investment.

Singapore Customs

http://www.gov.sg/customs/
The online service provides fact sheets on Singapore customs documentation, valuation, taxation, clearance procedures, security requirements, and other border regulations.

Singapore Missions Wordwide

http://www.gov.sg/mfa/consular/mwwmain.htm#List of Overseas Missions
A service of the Ministry of Foreign Affairs, the site is a directory of Singapore Embassies, High Commissions, Consulate Generals, and other representative offices around the world.

Singapore Trade News

http://www.tdb.gov.sg/stn/stn_main.html
A bi-monthly publication of the Singapore Trade Development Board, the site delivers Singapore international trade reports, exporter profiles, trade-show reviews, and a back issues archive.

Singapore Trade Winds

http://www.trade-winds.net/presg.htm
A service of Trade Winds Online, the site is a searchable directory of Singapore trade shows, business contacts, tourism information, and media.

Trade Shows in Singapore

http://www.expoguide.com/shows/data/loc_54.htm
Compiled by Expoguide, the site is a directory of upcoming trade shows in Singapore.

Singapore Representative Offices

Embassies and Consulates in Singapore

http://www.gov.sg/mfa/consular/fdmsmain.htm
A service of the Singapore Ministry of Foreign Affairs, the site is a directory of embassies, high commissions, and other representative offices in Singapore.

Australia

Austrade in Singapore

http://www.austrade.gov.au/Singapore/
The online service provides Australian export guides, company profiles, product catalogs, success stories, investment primers, and contact information for the Austrade office in Singapore.

Singapore Australian Business Council

http://www2.sabc.org.sg/sabc/
A bi-national networking organization, the Council promotes Australian business interests in Singapore. The site includes news, a member directory, event information, and Australian commercial guides.

Austria

Austrian Trade Commission in Singapore
http://aw.wk.or.at/awo/ahst-singapur.htm
The site lists the staff, street address, phone and fax numbers, e-mail link, and office hours of the Austrian Trade Commission in Singapore.

Belgium

Embassy of Belgium in Singapore
http://www.embelsing.org.sg/
Featuring a message from the Ambassador, the site delivers Belgian news, fact sheets, travel guides, visa and passport information, and a calendar of events.

Brazil

Embassy of Brazil in Singapore
http://sunflower.singnet.com.sg/~cinbrem/
Posted in English and Portuguese, the site provides Brazilian fact sheets, economic bulletins, event information, and reports on Brazil-Singapore trade and relations.

Brunei Darussalam

High Commission of Brunei Darussalam in Singapore
http://www.brunet.bn/homepage/gov/bruemb/govemb.htm
The site provides contact information for the Bruneian High Commission in Singapore.

Canada

High Commission of Canada in Singapore
http://www.dfait-maeci.gc.ca/english/missions/rep-can4e.htm#singapore
The site provides contact information for the Canadian High Commission in Singapore.

China

Singapore Shandong Business Council
http://ssbc.tdb.gov.sg/
Established in 1993, the Council promotes trade between Singapore and Shandong, a Chinese province. The site features a mission statement, member profiles, and Shandong fact sheets and statistics.

Denmark

Embassy of Denmark in Singapore
http://www.denmark.com.sg/
Along with Singapore web guides, the site provides Danish commercial primers, fact sheets, visa and passport information, and a directory of consular and commercial services.

Finland

Finland Trade Center in Singapore
http://www.exports.finland.fi/tradecen.htm
The site lists the staff, street address, phone and fax numbers, and e-mail link of the Finland Trade Center in Singapore.

France

Embassy of France in Singapore
http://www.france.org.sg/france/
Posted in English and French, the site offers French fact sheets, regional profiles, travel information, science and technology bulletins, and cultural guides.

French Business Association
http://www.fba.org.sg/
Based in Singapore, the Association promotes French business interests in Singapore. The site includes a member 0roster, committee directory, and contact information.

French Business Centre
http://sunflower.singnet.com.sg/~fbafbc/
Launched in 1995, the Center is a French trade promotion facility in Singapore. The site features a mission statement, activity reports, and contact information.

French Trade Commission in Singapore
http://www.dree.org/singapour/
Written in French, the site delivers Singapore market reports, sector profiles, contact information, and a directory of French export promotion services.

Germany

Asia Business Coordinator
http://diht.vitnet.com.sg/
Along with Asian country profiles and company directories, the site lists the commercial services,

street address, phone and fax numbers, and e-mail link of the German Industry and Commerce Delegate in Singapore.

Embassy of Germany in Singapore
http://www.commerceasia.com/germanembassy/
Posted in English and German, the site delivers German fact sheets, business guides, science and technology reports, travel tips, and visa and passport information.

German Chamber of Commerce in Singapore
http://www.ahk.net/en/sg/Singapore/
The site lists the Delegate, street address, phone and fax numbers, e-mail link, and office hours of the German Chamber in Singapore.

India

High Commission of India in Singapore
http://www.allindia.com/hcisin/
Posted in English, the site provides passport fact sheets, and application forms for Indian transit, tourist, business, and student visas.

India Watch
http://www.tdb.gov.sg/country/india/inwatch.html
A service of the Singapore Trade Development Board, the site provides statistics on Singapore-India trade, and reports on Indian investment, infrastructure, and electronics.

Indonesia

Embassy of Indonesia in Singapore
http://indag.dprin.go.id/INGG/trade/atache.HTM
The site provides contact information for the Indonesian Embassy in Singapore.

Ireland

Enterprise Ireland in Singapore
http://www.irish-trade.ie/office_network/office_locate01.html#anchor1441079
The site lists the Director, street address, and phone and fax numbers of the Enterprise Ireland office in Singapore.

Japan

Embassy of Japan in Singapore
http://www.japan-emb.org.sg/
Posted in English and Japanese, the site provides Japanese news, commercial guides, visa and passport information, an event calendar, and reports on Singapore-Japan trade and relations.

Japanese Chamber of Commerce and Industry in Singapore
http://www.jcci.org.sg/
Established in 1969, the Chamber promotes Japanese business interests in Singapore. The site features activity reports, a member roster, and committee directory.

Malaysia

High Commission of Malaysia in Singapore
http://www.mnet.com.my/klonline/www/missions/malmiss/msingapo1.htm
The site provides contact information for the Malaysian High Commission in Singapore.

Trade Commission of Malaysia in Singapore
http://www.mnet.com.my/klonline/www/missions/malmiss/msingapo3.htm
The site provides contact information for the Malaysian Trade Commission in Singapore.

New Zealand

High Commission of New Zealand in Singapore
http://www.nz-high-com.org.sg/
Along with media, the site provides New Zealand visa and passport information, travel guides, and a directory of consular programs and services.

New Zealand-Singapore Business Council
http://www.nz-high-com.org.sg/nzsbc.html
Based in Singapore, the Council promotes New Zealand business interests in Singapore. The site includes a president's message, membership information, and a calendar of events.

Trade New Zealand in Singapore
http://www.tradenz.govt.nz/contact/seasia.html
An export promotion service, the site provides contact information for the Trade New Zealand office in Singapore.

Norway

Norwegian Trade Council in Singapore
http://www.ntc.org.sg/
Along with contact information, the site provides Norwegian fact sheets, and reports on Norway-Singapore trade and relations.

Pakistan

Pakistan Trade Office in Singapore
http://www.jamal.com/epb/ptoa.htm
The site provides contact information for the Pakistan Trade Office in Singapore.

Philippines

Philippine Trade and Investment Promotion Office in Singapore
http://www.dti.gov.ph/sin/
The site provides a mission statement, service directory, and contact information for the Philippine Trade Office in Singapore.

South Africa

South Africa Foreign Trade Office in Singapore
http://wwwdti.pwv.gov.za/dtiwww/foreign_offices.htm
A service of the South Africa Department of Trade and Industry, the site provides contact information for the South Africa Trade Office in Singapore.

South African High Commission in Singapore
http://sunflower.singnet.com.sg/~satrade2/
Featuring a monthly newsletter on South African trade and investment opportunities, the service includes South African commercial guides, customs information, and Singapore fact sheets.

Spain

Spanish Commercial Office in Singapore
http://www.icex.es/openURL.html#openURL=/english/infoproyem/ofcomes/ofcomes.html#AS
The site lists the staff, street address, phone and fax numbers, and e-mail link of the Spanish Commercial Office in Singapore.

Sweden

Embassy of Sweden in Singapore
http://www.ud.se/english/mfa/ambassad/singapor.htm
The site provides contact information for the Swedish Embassy in Singapore.

Switzerland

Swiss Chamber of Commerce in Singapore
http://swisstrade.com/xicodes2.asp?P1=3&lvl=3&cid=D09
The site lists the street address, phone and fax numbers, and e-mail link of the Swiss Chamber of Commerce in Singapore.

Taiwan

Taiwan Government Information Office in Singapore
http://www.gio.gov.tw/info/ngio/sing-f.html
Posted in Chinese and English, the site lists the street address, phone and fax numbers, and e-mail link of the Taiwan Government Information Office in Singapore.

Thailand

Royal Thai Embassy in Singapore
http://www.mfa.go.th/Embassy/detail/59.htm
The site lists the Ambassador, street address, and phone and fax numbers of the Thai Embassy in Singapore.

Thailand Office of Commercial Affairs in Singapore
http://www.thaitrade.com/thcoaf.html
The site lists the street address, phone and fax numbers, and e-mail link of the Thailand Office of Commercial Affairs in Singapore.

Turkey

Embassy of Turkey in Singapore
http://www.turkey.org/madres.htm
As part of a directory of Turkish diplomatic offices around the world, the site lists the e-mail link of the Turkish Embassy in Singapore.

United Kingdom

High Commission of Britain in Singapore
http://www.britain.org.sg/
Featuring a message from the High Commissioner, the site provides British fact sheets, business guides, visa and passport information, and a directory of consular and commercial services.

United States

American Chamber of Commerce in Singapore
http://www.amcham.org.sg/
Launched in 1973, the Chamber promotes American business interests in Singapore. The site features a mission statement, calendar of events, and membership information.

State of Utah Trade Office in Singapore
*http://www.ce.ex.state.ut.us/international/reps/
reps.htm#Singapore*
A service of the Utah International Business Development Office, the site lists the representative, street address, phone and fax numbers, and e-mail link of the Utah Trade Office in Singapore.

United States Embassy in Singapore
http://sunsite.nus.sg/usis/Embassy/
The virtual Embassy provides United States fact sheets, business guides, visa and passport information, and a directory of consular and commercial services.

United States Foreign Agricultural Service in Singapore
http://www.atosingapore.org.sg/
A unit of the United States Department of Agriculture, the Service promotes American agricultural exports to Singapore. The site includes agri-food trade leads, buyer alerts, and program information.

United States Information Service in Singapore
http://sunsite.nus.edu.sg/usis/
The online service provides United States news, press releases, fact sheets, electronic journals, and a directory of United States-Singapore educational and exchange programs.

Solomon Islands

Solomon Islands Market Guides

Solomon Islands Business Briefs
http://www.austrade.gov.au/IOOM/SolomonIs/
A service of Austrade, the site offers fact sheets on Solomon Islander culture, business etiquette, marketing, transportation, travel, and visas.

Solomon Islands Country Brief
*http://www.worldbank.org/cgi-bin/
sendoff.cgi?page=%2Fhtml%2Fextdr%2Foffrep%2
Feap%2Fsb.htm*
A service of the World Bank Group, the site provides Solomon Islander population statistics, financial data, development reports, and economic forecasts.

Solomon Islands InfoExport
*http://www.infoexport.gc.ca/country-
e.asp?continent=Asia&country=67*
A service of Foreign Affairs and International Trade Canada, the site provides fact sheets and statistics on Solomon Islander geography, business and politics.

Solomon Islands Market Research
*http://strategis.ic.gc.ca/sc_mrkti/ibinddc/engdoc/
1a1i30.html*
Posted by Industry Canada, the site provides U.S. Central Intelligence Agency fact sheets on Solomon Islander geography, people, government, business, and transportation.

Solomonesia Sojourn
http://www.geocities.com/RainForest/4665/
The online service provides Soloman Islander maps, travel guides, cultural information, recipes, web guides, and contact information.

Solomon Islands Representative Offices

United Kingdom

High Commission of Britain in Honiara
http://www.fco.gov.uk/directory/posts.asp?SJ
The site provides contact information for the British High Commission in Honiara.

South Korea

South Korea Search Tools

Kor-seek
http://www.kor-seek.com/cgi-bin/korea
Posted in Korean, the site provides a searchable index of South Korean resources online. Categories include business, science and technology, government, and culture.

Yahoo Korea
http://www.yahoo.co.kr/
A service of Yahoo, the Korean language site provides South Korean news, web-based personal management tools, and Internet searching.

South Korea Media

Korea Economic Daily
http://www.ked.co.kr/
Posted in Korean, the site delivers Korean business news, editorials, economic reports, company profiles, executive interviews, and exchange rate bulletins.

South Korea Media
http://www.mediainfo.com/emediajs/specific-geo.htm?region=southkorea
Developed by Editor and Publisher Interactive, the site is an index of South Korean media sites online.

South Korea Market Guides

Access Korea
http://www.accesskorea.com/
Along with business news and editorials, the site provides South Korean commercial guides, company directories, product catalogs, sector profiles, and trade liberalization reports.

Barclays Country Report: South Korea
http://www.offshorebanking.barclays.com/services/economic/yearly/skormar98/contents.html
Prepared by Barclays Bank, the site reports on South Korean economic trends, politics, monetary and fiscal policy, exchange rates, international trade, and investment flows.

Business in Korea
http://korea.emb.washington.dc.us/new/business/business.htm
A service of the Korean Embassy in Washington, D.C., the site delivers South Korean fact sheets, economic forecasts, investment guides, taxation primers, and socioeconomic statistics.

Business Korea Plaza
http://www.bizkorea.com/
Posted in English, the site provides South Korean trade leads, company directories, and virtual catalogs for jewelry, headgear, apparel, medical equipment, and other products.

Electronics Mall of Korea
http://www.enet.co.kr/
A virtual catalog of South Korean electronic products, the site is divided into eight categories including video, audio, motors, capacitors, filters, and printed circuit boards.

Invest in Korea
http://sp09a.etri.re.kr/attract/
An online investment primer, the site delivers briefs on South Korean business regulations, incentives, taxation, trade barriers, exchange rates, and exhibitions.

Korea.Com
http://korea.com/
A hub of business information, the site provides South Korean company directories, product catalogs, shopping guides, chat services, event information, and an online discussion board.

Korean Industrial Property Office
http://www.kipo.go.kr/
Along with annual reports and contact information, the site provides fact sheets on South Korean patents, trademarks, industrial designs, and other intellectual property.

Ministry of Information and Communication
http://www.mic.go.kr/
Posted in English and Korean, the site offers discussion papers on South Korean telecommunications, broadcasting, information technology, and foreign investment.

Small and Medium Enterprises of Korea
http://www.smipc.or.kr/
Featuring product catalogs and economic reports, the site provides a searchable directory of South Korean small and medium-sized enterprises in 20 categories including plastics, base metals, and machinery.

South Korea: Big Emerging Markets Homepage
http://www.ita.doc.gov/bems/Korea.html
Developed by the United States Department of Commerce, the site delivers South Korean fact sheets, economic forecasts, export and import statistics, sector profiles, and international trade guides.

South Korea Business Briefs
http://www.austrade.gov.au/IOOM/Korea/
A service of Austrade, the site offers fact sheets on South Korean business etiquette, foreign investment, corporate taxation, marketing, and visas.

South Korea Country Profile
http://www.tradenz.govt.nz/intelligence/profiles/republic_of_south_korea.html
A service of the New Zealand Trade Development Board, the site provides South Korean economic statistics, market information, and business tips.

South Korea Country Report
http://www.state.gov/www/issues/economic/trade_reports/eastasia97/korea97.html
Prepared by the U.S. Department of State, the site reports on South Korean exchange rates, debt management, trade barriers, export subsidies, intellectual property protection, worker rights, and foreign investment.

South Korea: A Country Study

http://lcweb2.loc.gov/frd/cs/krtoc.html
A service of the U.S. Library of Congress, the site delivers fact sheets on South Korean geography, people, agriculture, mining, manufacturing, and foreign economic relations.

South Korea InfoExport

http://www.infoexport.gc.ca/country-e.asp?continent=Asia&country=22
A service of Foreign Affairs and International Trade Canada, the site provides South Korean commercial guides and market reports.

South Korea: An Introduction

http://www.apecsec.org.sg/member/apeckore.html
A service of the Asia Pacific Economic Cooperation, the site provides fact sheets on South Korean geography, climate, population, language, business, and international trade.

South Korea Market Access Database

http://mkaccdb.eu.int/mkdb/mkdb.pl?METHOD=COUNTRY
A service of the European Commission, the site offers briefs on South Korean trade policy, tariff barriers, non-tariff barriers, investment-related measures, and financial services regulations.

South Korea Market Information

http://dtiinfo1.dti.gov.uk/ots/south_korea/
A service of the London-based Department of Trade and Industry, the site delivers South Korean fact sheets, maps, and trade-show information.

South Korea Market Research

http://strategis.ic.gc.ca/sc_mrkti/ibinddc/engdoc/1a1f5.html
A service of Industry Canada, the site provides U.S. Department of Commerce reports on South Korean economic trends, trade barriers, investment regulations, business travel, and market opportunities.

South Korea Virtual Library

http://www.duke.edu/~myhan/b_SK.html
A service of the World Wide Web Virtual Library, the site is a directory of South Korean resources online. Categories include science and technology, politics, media, and environment.

Welcome to Korea

http://www.gcc.go.kr/
Homepage of the South Korean government, the site delivers fact sheets on Korean history, climate, population, education, business, culture, and politics.

South Korea Trade Assistance

Cyber Commerce World

http://www.cybercc.com/
Based in Seoul, the site is a searchable database of South Korean buy and sell offers and strategic alliance opportunities. The service includes South Korean fact sheets and product catalogs.

EC Market

http://www.eckorea.net/ECMarket/
An online marketplace, the site is a browsable database of South Korean business and trade opportunities in over 50 categories including agrifood, chemicals, metals, and transportation.

Global Commerce System

http://www.tradepost-chat.com/
Posted in English and Korean, the site provides a South Korean product catalog, mailing list, international trade bulletin board, online discussion forums, currency converter, and an automatic buyer and seller matching system.

Korea International Trade Association

http://www.kita.or.kr/
Based in Seoul, the Association promotes South Korean exports. The site includes a chairperson's message, member directory, and a directory of programs and services.

Korea International Trade Association National and Overseas Branches

http://www.kita.or.kr/eng/national.html
The site is a directory of Korea International Trade Association branches in six cities around the world including Beijing, Brussels, Hong Kong, New York, and Tokyo.

Korea Trade Information Services

http://www.kotis.net/
Posted in Korean, the service is an online forum for South Korean exporters and traders. The service includes a company directory, product catalog, and buy and sell offers.

Korea Trade and Investment Promotion Agency

http://www.kotra.co.kr/
Based in Seoul, the Agency promotes South Korean exports and international investment. The site includes a newsletter, cyber exhibitions, economic updates, and business guides.

Korea Trade Network
http://www.ktnet.co.kr/enghome/index.html
Founded in 1992, the Network promotes South
Korean exports. The site features a newsletter,
trade leads, electronic commerce fact sheets,
and a directory of programs and services.

Korea World Trade Center
http://www.kwtc.com/
Based in Seoul, the Center is a business
exhibition and meeting facility. The site includes
floor plans, fee schedules, and a directory of
information and event services.

South Korea Trade Winds
http://www.trade-winds.net/prekr.htm
A service of Trade Winds Online, the site is a
searchable directory of South Korean trade
shows, business contacts, tourism information,
and media.

Trade Point Seoul
http://www.tpseoul.org/index.html
Managed by the Korea International Trade
Association, the site provides South Korean trade
leads, economic statistics, product catalogs, and
business matchmaking services.

Trade Shows in South Korea
http://www.expoguide.com/shows/data/loc_31.htm
Compiled by Expoguide, the site is a directory of
upcoming trade shows in South Korea.

South Korea Representative Offices

Australia

Austrade in Seoul
http://www.austrade.gov.au/korea/
The online service provides Australian export
guides, company profiles, product catalogs,
success stories, investment primers, and contact
information for the Austrade office in Seoul.

Australian Embassy in Seoul
http://www.australia.or.kr/
Posted in English and Korean, the site delivers
Australian business guides, science and
technology bulletins, foreign affairs statements,
and visa and passport information.

Austria

Austrian Trade Commission in South Korea
http://aw.wk.or.at/awo/ahst-seoul.htm
The site lists the staff, street address, phone and

fax numbers, e-mail link, and office hours of the
Austrian Trade Commission in Seoul.

Brunei Darussalam

Embassy of Brunei Darussalam in Seoul
*http://www.brunet.bn/homepage/gov/bruemb/
govemb.htm*
The site provides contact information for the
Bruneian Embassy in Seoul.

Canada

Canadian Education Centre in Seoul
http://cec.or.kr/
Part of a global network of offices, the Centre
markets Canadian educational and training
institutions to international students. The service
includes scholarship and program information.

Canadian Embassy in Seoul
http://cec.or.kr/canada/
Written in English, French, and Korean, the site
provides Canadian fact sheets, visa and passport information, travel guides, and Korean high
technology news.

China

**China Council for the Promotion of International
Trade in Seoul**
*http://www.ccpit.org/engVersion/cp_about/
cp_over/cp_over.html*
A Chinese export promotion service, the site
provides contact information for the China
Council for the Promotion of International Trade
office in Seoul.

European Union

**European Union Chamber of Commerce in
Korea**
http://www.eucck.org/
Founded in 1986, the Chamber promotes
European Union-South Korea trade. The site
includes daily business news, a publication list,
event information, and a technology partnering
service.

Finland

Finland Trade Center in Seoul
http://www.exports.finland.fi/tradecen.htm
The site lists the staff, street address, phone and
fax numbers, and e-mail link of the Finland Trade
Center in Seoul.

France

Embassy of France in Seoul
http://ambassade.france.or.kr/
Written in French and Korean, the site provides French fact sheets, science and technology bulletins, cultural information, and a directory of consular and commercial services.

French Trade Commission in Seoul
http://www.dree.org/coree/
Written in French, the site delivers South Korean market reports, sector profiles, contact information, and a directory of French export promotion services.

Germany

German Chamber of Commerce in Seoul
http://www.ahk.net/en/kr/Seoul/
A German trade promotion service, the site lists the Chairperson, Chief Executive Officer, street address, phone and fax numbers, e-mail link, and office hours of the German Chamber in Seoul.

India

Indian Commercial Mission in Seoul
http://www.nic.in/commin/ICM.HTM
The site lists the street address, and phone and fax numbers of the Indian Commercial Mission in Seoul.

Indonesia

Embassy of Indonesia in Seoul
http://indag.dprin.go.id/INGG/trade/atache.HTM
The site provides contact information for the Indonesian Embassy in Seoul.

Japan

Embassy of Japan in Seoul
http://www.japanem.or.kr/
Posted in Japanese, the site delivers Japanese fact sheets, business guides, travel tips, visa and passport information, and reports on Japan-South Korea trade.

Malaysia

Embassy of Malaysia in Seoul
http://www.mnet.com.my/klonline/www/missions/malmiss/mkoreaso1.htm
The site provides contact information for the Malaysian Embassy in Seoul.

Trade Commission of Malaysia in Seoul
http://www.mnet.com.my/klonline/www/missions/malmiss/mkoreaso2.htm
The site provides contact information for the Malaysian Trade Commission in Seoul.

Mexico

Trade Commission of Mexico in Seoul
http://www.mexico-businessline.com/ingles/ofrepmu3.html#korea
A Mexican trade promotion service, the site lists the street address, phone and fax numbers, and e-mail link of the Mexican Trade Commission in Seoul.

New Zealand

Trade New Zealand in Seoul
http://www.tradenz.govt.nz/contact/northasia.html
An export promotion service, the site provides contact information for the Trade New Zealand office in Seoul.

Norway

Embassy of Norway in Seoul
http://www.ntc.no/cgi-bin/wbch.exe?html=../templates/utekontor2.html&profile=1128
The site lists the staff, street address, phone and fax numbers, and e-mail link of the Norwegian Embassy in Seoul.

Pakistan

Pakistan Trade Office in Seoul
http://www.jamal.com/epb/ptoa.htm
The site provides contact information for the Pakistan Trade Office in Seoul.

Philippines

Philippine Trade and Investment Promotion Office in Seoul
http://www.dti.gov.ph/seo/
The site provides a mission statement, service directory, and contact information for the Philippine Trade Office in Seoul.

Portugal

Portuguese Trade and Investment Office in Seoul

http://www.portugal.org/geninfo/abouticep/
korea.html
The site lists the staff, street address, phone and
fax numbers, and e-mail link of the Portuguese
Trade and Investment Office in Seoul.

Singapore

Embassy of Singapore in Seoul
http://www.gov.sg/mfa/consular/mww_k.htm
The site provides contact information for the
Singapore Embassy in Seoul.

South Africa

South Africa Foreign Trade Office in Seoul
http://wwwdti.pwv.gov.za/dtiwww/
foreign_offices.htm
A service of the South Africa Department of Trade
and Industry, the site provides contact information
for the South Africa Trade Office in Seoul.

Spain

Spanish Commercial Office in Seoul
http://www.icex.es/openURL.html#openURL=/
english/infoproyem/ofcomes/ofcomes.html#AS
The site lists the staff, street address, phone and
fax numbers, and e-mail link of the Spanish
Commercial Office in Seoul.

Sweden

Embassy of Sweden in Seoul
http://www.swedemb.or.kr/
The site provides Swedish fact sheets, visa and
passport information, and a directory of consular
and commercial services.

Switzerland

Embassy of Switzerland in Seoul
http://www.elim.net/~swissemb/
Featuring a welcome from the Ambassador, the
site provides Swiss news, fact sheets, business
guides, science and technology bulletins, and a
directory of consular and commercial services.

Taiwan

Taiwan Government Information Office in Seoul
http://www.gio.gov.tw/info/ngio/korea-f.html
Posted in Chinese and English, the site lists the
street address, phone and fax numbers, and e-
mail link of the Taiwan Government Information
Office in Seoul.

Thailand

Royal Thai Embassy in Seoul
http://www.mfa.go.th/Embassy/detail/47.htm
The site lists the Ambassador, street address,
and phone and fax numbers of the Thai Embassy
in Seoul.

Thailand Office of Commercial Affairs in Seoul
http://www.thaitrade.com/thcoaf.html
The site lists the street address, phone and fax
numbers, and e-mail link of the Thailand Office of
Commercial Affairs in Seoul.

Turkey

Embassy of Turkey in Seoul
http://www.turkey.org/madres.htm
As part of a directory of Turkish diplomatic offices
around the world, the site lists the e-mail link of
the Turkish Embassy in Seoul.

United Kingdom

Embassy of Britain in Seoul
http://www.fco.gov.uk/directory/posts.asp?[A
The site provides contact information for the
British Embassy in Seoul.

Trade Office of Britain in Pusan
http://www.fco.gov.uk/directory/posts.asp?[A
The site provides contact information for the
British Trade Office in Pusan.

United States

American Chamber of Commerce in Korea
http://www.amchamkorea.org/
Based in Seoul, the Chamber promotes American business interests in Korea. The site
includes a committee directory, trade briefings,
and event information.

State of California Trade Office in Seoul
http://commerce.ca.gov/international/
it_off.html#seoul
A service of the California Trade and Investment
Agency, the site lists the Trade Representative,
street address, phone and fax numbers, and e-
mail link of the California Trade Office in Seoul.

State of Missouri Trade Office in Seoul
http://www.ecodev.state.mo.us/intermark/
korea.html
A service of the Missouri Office of International
Marketing, the site lists the staff, mission state-

ment, and street address of the Missouri Trade Office in Seoul.

State of Utah Trade Office in Seoul
http://www.ce.ex.state.ut.us/international/reps/reps.htm#Korea
A service of the Utah International Business Development Office, the site lists the representative, street address, phone and fax numbers, and e-mail link of the Utah Trade Office in Seoul.

United States Agricultural Trade Office in Seoul
http://www.atoseoul.com/atoseoul.htm
A service of the United States Department of Agriculture, the site provides Korean agri-food trade leads, importer lists, customs and quarantine information, and trade-show bulletins.

United States Embassy in Seoul
http://www.usia.gov/abtusia/posts/KS1/wwwhmain.html
Posted in English and Korean, the virtual Embassy delivers United States fact sheets, business guides, visa and passport information, and a directory of consular and commercial services.

United States Information Service in Seoul
http://www.usia.gov/abtusia/posts/KS1/wwwhus.html
The online service provides United States press releases, speeches, fact sheets, electronic journals, and a directory of United States-South Korea educational and exchange programs.

Western Samoa

Consulate General of Western Samoa in Seoul
http://www.interwebinc.com/samoa/misskr.html
The site lists the street address of the Consulate General of Western Samoa in Seoul.

Tahiti

Tahiti Media

La Dépêche de Tahiti
http://www.tahiti-news.com/
Updated daily and posted in French, the site provides Tahitian news, editorials, business reports, cultural bulletins, shopping guides, and photos.

Tahiti Representative Office

New Zealand

Trade New Zealand in Tahiti
http://www.tradenz.govt.nz/contact/pacific.html
An export promotion service, the site provides contact information for the Trade New Zealand office in Tahiti.

Taiwan

Taiwan Search Tools

YamWeb Navigator
http://taiwan.iis.sinica.edu.tw/en/yam
A searchable index of Taiwanese resources online, the site is divided into 12 categories including companies, government and state, and news and information.

Taiwan Media

China Times Web
http://www.chinatimes.com.tw/
Posted in Chinese and based in Taipei, the site delivers Taiwanese headlines, business reports, editorials, interviews, lifestyle features, and cultural information.

Taiwan Business Media
http://www.cens.com/
Updated daily, the site provides Taiwanese business news, company profiles, economic bulletins, product catalogs, publication directories, and trade-show information.

Taiwan Media
http://www.mediainfo.com/emediajs/specific-geo.htm?region=taiwan
Compiled by Editor and Publisher Interactive, the site is an index of Taiwanese media sites online.

Taiwan Market Guides

Barclays Country Report: Taiwan
http://www.offshorebanking.barclays.com/services/economic/yearly/taioct97/index.html
Prepared by Barclays Bank, the site reports on Taiwan economic trends, politics, monetary and fiscal policy, exchange rates, international trade, and investment flows.

Council for Economic Planning and Development

http://cepd.spring.org.tw/
Based in Taipei, the Council promotes economic development in Taiwan. The site includes a mission statement, speeches, statistics, and economic forecasts.

Chinese Taipei: An Introduction

http://www.apecsec.org.sg/member/apectaip.html
A service of the Asia Pacific Economic Cooperation, the site provides fact sheets on Taiwanese geography, climate, population, language, business, and international trade.

Doing Business with Taiwan

http://www.tptaiwan.org.tw/conte01.htm
A hub of country business information, the site delivers Taiwanese economic fact sheets, product catalogs, media guides, trade-show information, and travel tips.

Economic Situation and Outlook

http://cepd.spring.org.tw/English/situation/index.html
A service of the Council for Economic Planning and Development in Taipei, the site provides forecasts for Taiwanese economic growth, foreign trade, and domestic investment.

Government Information Office

http://www.gio.gov.tw/
Posted in seven languages including German, Russian, and Spanish, the site delivers Taiwanese news, fact sheets, speeches, government directories, and cultural information.

Taiwan: Big Emerging Markets Homepage

http://www.ita.doc.gov/bems/Taiwan.html
Developed by the United States Department of Commerce, the site delivers Taiwanese fact sheets, economic forecasts, export and import statistics, sector profiles, and international trade guides.

Taiwan Business Briefs

http://www.austrade.gov.au/IOOM/Taiwan/
A service of Austrade, the site offers fact sheets on Taiwanese business etiquette, foreign investment, corporate taxation, marketing, and visas.

Taiwan Business Directory

http://tbdo.anjes.com.tw/
A searchable directory of Taiwanese companies and organizations, the site is divided into 14 categories including electronics, furniture, plastics, and medical instruments.

Taiwan Business Guide

http://203.66.210.8/english/business/indexset.htm
A service of the China External Trade Development Council, the site provides fact sheets on Taiwanese visas, work permits, housing, business etiquette, culture, and travel.

Taiwan Commerce

http://www.commerce.com.tw/
Posted in Chinese and English, the site delivers Taiwanese news, trade leads, company directories, technology reports, event information, and media guides.

Taiwan Country Profile

http://www.tradenz.govt.nz/intelligence/profiles/taiwan.html
A service of the New Zealand Trade Development Board, the site provides Taiwanese economic statistics, market information, and business tips.

Taiwan Country Report

http://www.state.gov/www/issues/economic/trade_reports/eastasia97/taiwan97.html
Prepared by the U.S. Department of State, the site reports on Taiwanese exchange rates, debt management, trade barriers, export subsidies, intellectual property protection, worker rights, and foreign investment.

Taiwan InfoExport

http://www.infoexport.gc.ca/country-e.asp?continent=Asia&country=41
A service of Foreign Affairs and International Trade Canada, the site provides Taiwanese commercial guides and market reports.

Taiwan Manufacturers of Products

http://www.commerce.com.tw/manufacture/
A browsable index of Taiwan manufacturers, the site is divided into ten categories including chemicals, optical, toys, sporting goods, and transportation equipment.

Taiwan Market Access Database

http://mkaccdb.eu.int/mkdb/mkdb.pl?METHOD=COUNTRY
A service of the European Commission, the site offers briefs on Taiwanese trade policy, tariff barriers, non-tariff barriers, investment-related measures, and financial services regulations.

Taiwan Market Information

http://dtiinfo1.dti.gov.uk/ots/taiwan/
A service of the London-based Department of Trade and Industry, the site delivers Taiwanese fact sheets, maps, and trade-show information.

Taiwan Market Research

http://strategis.ic.gc.ca/sc_mrkti/ibinddc/engdoc/1a1f8.html
A service of Industry Canada, the site provides U.S. Department of Commerce reports on Taiwanese economic trends, trade barriers, investment regulations, business travel, and market opportunities.

Taiwan Products Online

http://manufacture.com.tw/
Along with buy and sell offers, the site provides a searchable directory of Taiwanese companies in over 20 categories including construction materials, machine tools, and educational supplies.

Taiwan Virtual Library

http://peacock.tnjc.edu.tw/taiwan-wwwvl.html
A service of the World Wide Web Virtual Library, the site is a directory of Taiwanese resources online. Categories include news, politics, reference, and information technology.

Taiwan Trade Assistance

China External Trade Development Council

http://www.cetra.org.tw/
Founded in 1970, the Council promotes Taiwanese exports. The site includes a mission statement, product catalog, company directory, and trade inquiry service.

China External Trade Development Council Overseas Offices

http://www.cetra.org.tw/english/o_office/indexset.htm
The site is a directory of the Chinese External Trade Development Council offices in Asia, the Middle East, Africa, Europe, and North and South America.

Fair Trade Commission

http://www.ftc.gov.tw/
Established in 1992, the Commission regulates Taiwanese international trade and imports. The site includes a mission statement, organization fact sheets, statistics, and a publications list.

Government Information Offices Abroad

http://www.gio.gov.tw/info/ngio/e_gio-1.html
The site is a directory of Taiwan Government Information Offices in over 40 countries including Argentina, Honduras, Japan, Panama, Saudi Arabia, and Thailand.

International Trade Association of Taiwan

http://www.itac.org.tw/
Founded in 1962 and based in Taipei, the Association promotes international business in Taiwan. The site includes news, activity reports, and executive profiles.

Purchase Directly from Taiwan

http://www.netperfect.com/taiwan/taiwan.htm
A searchable index of Taiwanese suppliers, the site is divided into 15 categories including apparel, automotive, information technology, office equipment, and sporting goods.

Taipei Trade Shows

http://www.taipeitradeshows.org/
The site provides a directory of upcoming trade shows and exhibitions in Taipei. The service includes event profiles and contact information.

Taipei World Trade Center

http://twtc.cetra.org.tw/english/index.htm
Opened in 1986, the Center is a trade exhibition facility. The site features a newsletter, floor plans, product catalogs, event bulletins, and travel information.

Taiwan Chamber of Commerce

http://www.tcoc.com.tw/
Established in 1946, the Chamber promotes Taiwanese business interests. The site includes fact sheets, activity reports, event information, and an executive directory.

Taiwan Conferences and Trade Exhibitions

http://tradepoint.cybertaiwan.com/events/
A service of Trade Point Taiwan, the site provides a directory of upcoming trade shows, conferences, and other business events in Taiwan.

Taiwan Export Express

http://www.cens.com/cens/express.html
An electronic export journal, the site delivers Taiwanese international trade news, economic forecasts, trade-show reports, company directories, and product catalogs.

Taiwan Foreign Trade Statistics
http://tptaiwan.org.tw/st/pst.htm
A virtual library of international trade statistics, the site provides data on Taiwanese exports and imports by global region, country, and commodity.

Taiwan Import-Export Bulletin Board
http://yellowpage.com.tw/trade/main.htm
A virtual marketplace, the site is a searchable database of Taiwanese buy and sell offers and other business opportunities in over 20 industry categories including automotive, electronics, and plastics.

Taiwan Ministry of Foreign Affairs
http://www.mofa.gov.tw/
Posted in Chinese and English, the site provides Taiwan fact sheets, press releases, and foreign policy statements.

Taiwan Trade Opportunities
http://tbdo.cybertaiwan.com/tradeop/
Posted in Chinese and English, the site is a database of Taiwanese buy and sell offers in 14 categories including automotive, furniture, machinery, and plastics.

Taiwan Trade Opportunities
http://tptaiwan.org.tw/tto/tto.htm
The site provides a searchable index of Taiwanese suppliers, buyers, and agents in over 20 categories including chemicals, packaging, electronics, and aerospace.

Taiwan Trade Opportunity
http://manufacture.com.tw/trade.htm
A virtual marketplace, the site is a database of Taiwanese buy and sell offers and business opportunities. Categories include chemicals, steel, electronics, machinery, and wood products.

Taiwan Trade Winds
http://www.trade-winds.net/pretw.htm
A service of Trade Winds Online, the site is a searchable directory of Taiwan trade shows, business contacts, tourism information, and media.

Taiwan's Leading Manufacturers and Exporters
http://www.cens.com/biz/directory.html
Posted in English, Japanese, and Spanish, the site provides searchable directories of Taiwanese manufacturers and exporters in 15 industries including machinery, lighting, and furniture.

Trade Shows in Taiwan
http://www.expoguide.com/shows/data/loc_60.htm
Compiled by Expoguide, the site is a directory of upcoming trade shows in Taiwan.

Taiwan Representative Offices

Embassies and International Organizations in Taiwan
http://www.commerce.com.tw/embass.htm
A directory of embassies and international organizations in Taipei, the site lists offices from over 30 countries including Austria, France, Haiti, and the Netherlands.

Australia

Australia Commerce and Industry Office in Taipei
http://www.australia.org.tw/
Posted in Chinese and English, the site provides Australian fact sheets, business guides, travel information, and reports on Australia-Taiwan trade and relations.

Australian and New Zealand Business Association in Taiwan
http://www.australia.org.tw/commerce/anzba-eng.html
Formed in 1991, the Association promotes the interests of Australian and New Zealand businesspeople in Taiwan. The site includes activity reports and contact information.

ROC-Australia Business Council
http://www.australia.org.tw/commerce/rocaus-eng.html
Based in Taipei, the Council promotes Taiwan-Australia trade. The site includes a mission statement, executive roster, activity reports, and contact information.

Austria

Austrian Trade Commission in Taipei
http://www.austria.org.tw/
Posted in five languages, the site delivers Austrian fact sheets, business guides, company directories, interactive maps, product catalogs, and event information.

Canada

Canadian Trade Office in Taipei
http://www.ctot.org.tw/
Posted in Chinese, English, and French, the site provides Canadian fact sheets, Taiwanese sector profiles, and reports on Canada-Taiwan trade and relations.

Province of British Columbia Trade Office in Taipei
http://www.ei.gov.bc.ca/directory/bctio/taiwan/taiwan.htm
A British Columbia export and investment promotion service, the site provides a mission statement, contact information, and a directory of programs and services.

European Community

European Council of Commerce and Trade in Taipei
http://www.ecct.com.tw/ici.html
Established in 1988, the Council promotes European business interests in Taiwan. The site includes press releases, position papers, a committee directory, and an online bulletin board.

Fiji

Fiji Trade Office in Taipei
http://fiji.gov.fj/core/fj_mis.html
The site provides contact information for the Fijian Trade Office in Taipei.

Finland

Finland Trade Center in Taipei
http://www.exports.finland.fi/tradecen.htm
The site lists the staff, street address, phone and fax numbers, and e-mail link of the Finland Trade Center in Taipei.

France

French Trade Commission in Taipei
http://www.dree.org/taiwan/
Written in French, the site delivers Taiwanese market reports, sector profiles, contact information, and a directory of French export promotion services.

Guatemala

Embassy of Guatemala in Taipei
http://www.geocities.com/WallStreet/Floor/8227/
The site delivers Guatemalan fact sheets, commercial guides, investment primers, government directories, travel information, cultural bulletins, and weather reports.

Germany

German Chamber of Commerce in Taipei
http://www.ahk.net/en/tw/Taipei/
The site lists the Chairperson, Chief Executive Officer, street address, phone and fax numbers, and e-mail link of the German Chamber in Taipei.

Indonesia

Embassy of Indonesia in Taipei
http://indag.dprin.go.id/INGG/trade/atache.HTM
The site provides contact information for the Indonesian Embassy in Taipei.

Israel

Israel Economic and Cultural Office in Taipei
http://mail.tpe.wownet.net/~iseco/
Posted in Chinese and English, the site delivers Israeli news, fact sheets, visa and passport information, travel guides, and a business matchmaking service.

Malaysia

Trade Commission of Malaysia in Taipei
http://www.mnet.com.my/klonline/www/missions/malmiss/mtaiwan2.htm
The site provides contact information for the Malaysian Trade Commission in Taipei.

Mexico

Trade Commission of Mexico in Taipei
http://www.mexico-businessline.com/ingles/ofrepmu3.html#taiwan
The site lists the street address, phone and fax numbers, and e-mail link of the Mexican Trade Commission in Taipei.

New Zealand

Trade New Zealand in Taipei

http://www.tradenz.govt.nz/contact/northasia.html
An export promotion service, the site provides contact information for the Trade New Zealand office in Taipei.

Norway

Norwegian Trade Council in Taipei

http://www.ntc.no/cgi-bin/wbch.exe?html=../ templates/utekontor2.html&profile=1132
The site lists the staff, street address, phone and fax numbers, and e-mail link of the Norwegian Trade Council in Taipei.

Peru

Commercial Office of Peru in Taipei

http://www.peru.org.tw/
Posted in Chinese and English, the site features Peruvian news, fact sheets, economic forecasts, trade statistics, sector profiles, and travel information.

Philippines

Philippine Trade and Investment Promotion Office in Taipei

http://www.dti.gov.ph/tai/
The site provides a mission statement, service directory, and contact information for the Philippine Trade Office in Taipei.

Singapore

Trade Mission of Singapore in Taipei

http://www.gov.sg/mfa/consular/mww_t.htm
The site provides contact information for the Singapore Trade Mission in Taipei.

South Africa

South Africa Foreign Trade Office in Taipei

http://wwwdti.pwv.gov.za/dtiwww/ foreign_offices.htm
A service of the South Africa Department of Trade and Industry, the site provides contact information for the South Africa Trade Office in Taipei.

Thailand

Thailand Trade and Economic Office in Taipei

http://www.mfa.go.th/Embassy/detail/214.htm

Posted in Chinese, the site lists the Executive Director, street address, and phone and fax numbers of the Thailand Trade and Economic Office in Taipei.

United States

Agricultural Trade Office in Taipei

http://ait.org.tw/ait/AGRI/ato.htm
A service of the United States Department of Agriculture, the Office promotes United States agricultural exports to Taiwan. The site includes a staff roster, program directory, and contact information.

American Chamber of Commerce in Taipei

http://www.amcham.com.tw/
Representing over 500 companies, the Chamber promotes American business interests in Taiwan. The site includes a member directory, activity reports, and Taiwanese fact sheets.

American Institute in Taiwan

http://www.ait.org.tw/
A non-profit, private corporation, the Institute promotes American commercial and cultural interests in Taiwan. Posted in Chinese and English, the site includes United States visa and passport information, and Taiwanese fact sheets.

State of Arizona Trade Office in Taipei

http://www.commerce.state.az.us/itrade/ offices.shtml
A service of the Arizona Department of Commerce, the site lists the Trade Representative, street address, phone and fax numbers, and e-mail link of the Arizona Trade Office in Taipei.

State of California Trade Office in Taipei

http://commerce.ca.gov/international/ it_off.html#taiwan
A service of the California Trade and Commerce Agency, the site lists the Director, street address, phone and fax numbers, and e-mail link of the California Trade Office in Taipei.

State of Idaho Trade Office in Taipei

http://www.idoc.state.id.us/Information/exportinfo/ overseas.html
A service of the Idaho Department of Commerce, the site lists the Manager, street address, phone and fax numbers, and e-mail link of the Idaho Trade Office in Taipei.

State of Missouri Office in Taipei
http://www.ecodev.state.mo.us/intermark/taiwan.html
Hosted by the Missouri Department of Economic Development, the site lists the mission statement and Manager of the Missouri Trade Office in Taipei.

State of Utah Trade Office in Taipei
http://www.ce.ex.state.ut.us/international/reps/reps.htm#Taiwan
A service of the Utah International Business Development Office, the site lists the Representative, street address, phone and fax numbers, and e-mail link of the Utah Trade Office in Taipei.

State of Washington Trade Office in Taipei
http://www.trade.wa.gov/overseas.htm
A service of Washington Community, Trade and Economic Development, the site lists the Director, street address, phone and fax numbers, and e-mail link of the Washington Trade Office in Taipei.

State of West Virginia Trade Office in Taipei
http://www.wvdo.org/international/offices.htm
A service of the West Virginia Development Office, the site lists the location and e-mail link of the West Virginia Trade Office in Taipei.

Thailand

Thailand Search Tools

Thai Search
http://www.cnet.net.th/
Posted in English and Thai, the site provides a searchable directory of Thai resources online. The service includes web reviews and company directories.

Thailand Media

Bangkok Post
http://www.bangkokpost.net/
Updated daily, the site delivers Thai and Bangkok news, business reports, economic forecasts, cultural bulletins, and a searchable archive of back issues.

Business Day
http://bday.net/
An electronic business newspaper, the site delivers Thai economic news, corporate profiles, editorials, event information, and a browsable index of past issues.

The Nation
http://www.nationmultimedia.com/
Along with regional and national breaking news, the site provides Thai political bulletins, editorials, lifestyle features, online polls, and chat services.

Thailand Media
http://www.mediainfo.com/emediajs/specific-geo.htm?region=thailand
Developed by Editor and Publisher Interactive, the site is a directory of Thai media sites online including magazines, newspapers, and television stations.

Thailand Market Guides

Barclay's Country Report: Thailand
http://www.offshorebanking.barclays.com/services/economic/yearly/taifeb98/contents.html
Prepared by Barclays Bank, the site reports on Thai economic trends, politics, monetary and fiscal policy, exchange rates, international trade, and investment flows.

Commercial Directory of Thailand
http://www.sino.net/thai/commerce/thaiprod.html
The site is a directory of Thai companies and organizations in over 50 categories including aerospace, beverages, hardware, steel, and textile machinery.

Federation of Thai Industries Online
http://www.fti.or.th/
Representing more than 4,500 members, the Federation promotes business interests in Thailand. The site includes news, a member directory, and trade-show information.

Office of Thailand Board of Investment
http://www.boi.go.th/
Posted in English, French, Japanese, and Thai, the site provides Thailand business news, investment guides, event information, and merger and acquisition bulletins.

Royal Thai Government
http://www.thaigov.go.th/
Posted in English and Thai, the site provides Thai fact sheets, press releases, speeches, policy statements, government directories, and executive profiles.

Thai Chamber of Commerce
http://www.thaicommerce.com/
Based in Bangkok, the Chamber promotes Thai business and international trade. The site

includes economic forecasts, executive profiles, and an online bulletin board.

Thai E-Commerce
http://www.thaiecommerce.net/
Along with regional and national news, the site delivers Thai business reports, e-commerce bulletins, travel guides, and cultural information.

Thai Government Tender
http://www.siamweb.com/tender/
The site is a directory of government procurement tenders in Thailand. Products in demand include chemicals, electronics, measuring apparatus, base metals, and medical equipment.

Thailand: The Big Picture
http://www.nectec.or.th/index.html
A virtual country gateway, the site provides Thai fact sheets, telephone directories, economic reports, cultural information, weather bulletins, and web guides.

Thailand Business Briefs
http://www.austrade.gov.au/IOOM/Thailand/
A service of Austrade, the site offers fact sheets on Thai business etiquette, foreign investment, corporate taxation, marketing, and visas.

Thailand Business Report
http://italchambers.net/BusinessReports.html
Prepared by the Italian Chamber of Commerce and written in Italian, the site provides Thai fact sheets, market reports, and commercial guides.

Thailand Country Brief
http://www.worldbank.org/cgi-bin/ sendoff.cgi?page=%2Fhtml%2Fextdr%2Foffrep%2 Feap%2Fth.htm
A service of the World Bank Group, the site provides Thai population statistics, financial data, development reports, and economic forecasts.

Thailand Country Profile
http://www.tradenz.govt.nz/intelligence/profiles/ thailand.html
A service of the New Zealand Trade Development Board, the site provides Thai economic statistics, market information, and business tips.

Thailand Country Report
http://www.state.gov/www/issues/economic/ trade_reports/eastasia97/thailand97.html
Prepared by the U.S. Department of State, the site reports on Thai exchange rates, debt management, trade barriers, export subsidies, intellectual

property protection, worker rights, and foreign investment.

Thailand: A Country Study
http://lcweb2.loc.gov/frd/cs/thtoc.html
A service of the U.S. Library of Congress, the site delivers fact sheets on Thai geography, people, agriculture, mining, manufacturing, and foreign economic relations.

Thailand Department of Employment
http://www.doe.go.th/
Posted in English and Thai, the site provides Thai job databases, resume services, career guides, an event calendar, and work permit information.

Thailand Department of Intellectual Property
http://www.dbe.moc.go.th/DIP/index.html
Posted in English and Thai, the site provides fact sheets on Thai patents, trademarks, industrial designs, and other intellectual property.

Thailand InfoExport
http://www.infoexport.gc.ca/country- e.asp?continent=Asia&country=43
A service of Foreign Affairs and International Trade Canada, the site provides Thai commercial guides and market reports.

Thailand: An Introduction
http://www.apecsec.org.sg/member/apecthai.html
A service of the Asia Pacific Economic Cooperation, the site provides fact sheets on Thai geography, climate, population, language, business, and international trade.

Thailand Market Access Database
http://mkaccdb.eu.int/mkdb/ mkdb.pl?METHOD=COUNTRY
A service of the European Commission, the site offers briefs on Thai trade policy, tariff barriers, non-tariff barriers, investment-related measures, and financial services regulations.

Thailand Market Information
http://dtiinfo1.dti.gov.uk/ots/thailand/
A service of the London-based Department of Trade and Industry, the site delivers Thai fact sheets, maps, and trade-show information.

Thailand Market Research
http://strategis.ic.gc.ca/sc_mrkti/ibinddc/engdoc/ 1a1i32.html
A service of Industry Canada, the site provides U.S. Department of Commerce reports on Thai

economic trends, trade barriers, investment regulations, business travel, and market opportunities.

Thailand Ministry of Commerce
http://www.moc.go.th/
Based in Bangkok, the Ministry promotes economic development and international trade in Thailand. The site includes government directories, press releases, and executive profiles.

Thailand Update
http://www.boi.go.th/thailandupdate/index.html
Published by the Thai government and updated monthly, the site provides Thai economic reports and forecasts, statistics, government press releases, and business briefs.

Thailand Trade Assistance

International Trade Training Institute
http://www.dep.moc.go.th/itti/index.htm
Based in Bangkok, the Institute provides international trade training to Thailand businesspeople. The site includes news, activity reports, and contact information.

Overseas Business Opportunity
http://www.moc.go.th/ctrprofile/
A service of the Thailand Ministry of Commerce, the site provides fact sheets and market studies on Eastern Europe, the European Union, Japan, and the United States.

Thai Trade Fair
http://www.thaitradefair.com/
A virtual trade exhibition, the site features Thai company profiles, product catalogs, press releases, digital meeting rooms, and an online discussion board.

Thailand Commercial Affairs Offices
http://www.thaitrade.com/thcoaf.html
A directory of Thailand Commercial Affairs offices around the world, the site lists representatives in over 20 countries including Australia, Hungary, and Vietnam.

Thailand Customs Department
http://www.customs.go.th/
Along with export and import statistics, the English and Thai language site delivers Thailand customs tariffs, regulations, documentation, and exchange rates.

Thailand Department of Export Promotion
http://www.thaitrade.com/
Based in Bangkok, the Department promotes Thai exports and international investment. The site includes company directories, trade leads, and trade-show information.

Thailand Department of Export Promotion On-Line Business Opportunities
http://www.thaitrade.com/postmsg.html
A digital marketplace, the site is a database of Thai buy and sell offers and strategic alliance opportunities. Categories include consumer products, agri-food, and base metals.

Thailand Export Mart
http://www.thaitrade.com/mart.htm
Based in Bangkok, the Mart is a virtual exhibition center and product showcase. The site includes floor plans, a services directory, and contact information.

Thailand Exporters for E-Commerce
http://www.exporter.moc.go.th/
A virtual library of international trade information, the site includes export and import statistics, and a searchable database of Thai manufacturers, buyers, and products.

Thailand Exporters Search Engine
http://203.151.17.16/mainsearch.htm
A service of the Ministry of Commerce, the site is a searchable database of Thai exporters in 17 categories including automotive, building materials, and household products.

Thailand Ministry of Foreign Affairs
http://www.mfa.go.th/
Based in Bangkok, the site delivers Thai fact sheets, foreign policy statements, press releases, visa and passport information, and a Ministry directory.

Thailand Trade Information System
http://www.exporter.moc.go.th/thaitrade/
Posted in English and Thai, the site is a virtual library of Thai international trade statistics. The data includes Thai exports and imports by commodity and country.

Thailand Trade Offices
http://www.thaitrade.com/wwtto.html
A directory of Thai Trade Centers around the world, the site lists offices in some 20 countries including Brazil, Canada, Germany, Italy, and the United States.

Thailand Trade Winds
http://www.trade-winds.net/preth.htm
A service of Trade Winds Online, the site is a searchable directory of Thai trade shows, business contacts, tourism information, and media.

Trade On-Line
http://www.sino.net/
A virtual business exchange, the site is a browsable database of Thai buy, sell, and joint venture offers. Categories include exports, imports, franchises, and distributors.

Trade Shows in Thailand
http://www.expoguide.com/shows/data/loc_61.htm
Compiled by Expoguide, the site is a directory of upcoming trade shows in Thailand.

Virtual Trade Embassy
http://www.thaiecommerce.net/discus/virtual.htm
A service of the Thailand government, the site provides international trade discussion forums. Topics include the Association of Southeast Asian Nations, the European Union, and the United States.

Thailand Representative Offices

Embassies and Missions in Thailand
http://www.mfa.go.th/foreign/default.htm
A service of the Ministry of Foreign Affairs, the site is a database of foreign embassies, high commissions, consulates, and other diplomatic posts in Thailand.

Australia

Austrade in Bangkok
http://www.austrade.gov.au/ GreaterMekongRegion/
The online service provides Australian export guides, company profiles, product catalogs, success stories, investment primers, and contact information for the Austrade office in Bangkok.

Embassy of Australia in Bangkok
http://www.austembassy.or.th/
Featuring a welcome from the Ambassador, the site provides Australian fact sheets, visa and passport information, and a directory of consular staff and services.

Austria

Austrian Trade Commission in Bangkok
http://www.austriaemb.or.th/
Posted in five languages, the site delivers Austrian fact sheets, business guides, company directories, interactive maps, product catalogs, and event information.

Brunei Darussalam

Embassy of Brunei Darussalam in Bangkok
http://www.brunet.bn/homepage/gov/bruemb/ govemb.htm
The site provides contact information for the Bruneian Embassy in Bangkok.

Canada

Embassy of Canada in Bangkok
http://www.dfait-maeci.gc.ca/english/missions/rep-can4e.htm#thailand
The site provides contact information for the Canadian Embassy in Bangkok.

Thai Canadian Chamber of Commerce
http://www.thai-canadian-chamber.org/
Based in Bangkok, the Chamber promotes Canada-Thailand trade. The site includes a mission statement, member directory, committee directory, and contact information.

Chile

Embassy of Chile in Bangkok
http://www.chile-thai.com/
Featuring a welcome from the Consul, the English and Thai language site provides Chilean fact sheets, visa and passport information, and web guides.

China

Thai Chinese Chamber
http://www.thai-chinese-chamber.com/ mainpage.htm
Based in Bangkok, the Chamber promotes Thai-Chinese trade and relations. The site includes a mission statement, newsletter, commercial guide, and contact information.

European Union

European Business Information Centre in Thailand
http://www.ebicbkk.org/
Based in Bangkok, the Centre promotes European Union business interests in Thailand. The site includes European Union fact sheets, statistics, publications, and business opportunities.

European Union Chambers of Commerce in Thailand
http://www.ebicbkk.org/html/eu_chambers.html
The site is a directory of European Union bilateral chambers of commerce in Thailand. Organizations include the Thai-Danish, Thai-Finnish, Franco-Thai, and German-Thai Chambers of Commerce.

Finland

Finland Trade Center in Bangkok
http://www.exports.finland.fi/tradecen.htm
The site lists the staff, street address, phone and fax numbers, and e-mail link of the Finland Trade Center in Bangkok.

France

French Trade Commission in Bangkok
http://www.dree.org/thailande/
Written in French, the site delivers Thai market reports, sector profiles, contact information, and a directory of French export promotion services.

Germany

German Chamber of Commerce in Bangkok
http://www.ahk.net/en/th/
Along with Thai fact sheets, the site lists the Chairperson, Chief Executive Officer, street address, phone and fax numbers, e-mail link, and office hours of the German Chamber in Bangkok.

India

Embassy of India in Bangkok
http://www.indiaemb.or.th/
The online service provides Indian news, fact sheets, press releases, economic reports, government directories, and reports on India-Thailand trade and relations.

Indonesia

Embassy of Indonesia in Bangkok
http://indag.dprin.go.id/INGG/trade/atache.HTM
The site provides contact information for the Indonesian Embassy in Bangkok.

Italy

Italian Trade Commission in Bangkok
http://www.nondhas.com/icebkkth/
Posted in Italian, the site provides Italian fact sheets, economic reports, statistics, investment guides, and reports on Italian-Thai trade and relations.

Thai Italian Chamber of Commerce
http://www.thaitch.org/
Posted in English and Italian, the Chamber promotes Thai-Italian trade. The site features news, a member directory, activity reports, and contact information.

Laos

Embassy of Laos in Bangkok
http://www.laoembassy.com/news/embassyabroad.htm
The site provides contact information for the Embassy of Laos in Bangkok.

Malaysia

Consulate General of Malaysia in Songkla
http://www.mnet.com.my/klonline/www/missions/malmiss/mthailan3.htm
The site provides contact information for the Malaysian Consulate General in Songkla.

Embassy of Malaysia in Bangkok
http://www.mnet.com.my/klonline/www/missions/malmiss/mthailan1.htm
The site provides contact information for the Malaysian Embassy in Bangkok.

Trade Commission of Malaysia in Bangkok
http://www.mnet.com.my/klonline/www/missions/malmiss/mthailan2.htm
The site provides contact information for the Malaysian Trade Commission in Bangkok.

Nepal

Embassy of Nepal in Bangkok
http://www.info-nepal.com/members/fips/contacts/nepalese.html
The site provides contact information for the Embassy of Nepal in Bangkok.

Netherlands

Embassy of Netherlands in Bangkok
http://www.thai-info.net/netherlands/
Posted in Dutch and English, the site provides Dutch fact sheets, visa and passport information, travel guides, and a directory of consular and commercial services.

New Zealand

Trade New Zealand in Bangkok
http://www.tradenz.govt.nz/contact/seasia.html
An export promotion service, the site provides contact information for the Trade New Zealand office in Bangkok.

Norway

Embassy of Norway in Bangkok
http://www.ntc.no/cgi-bin/wbch.exe?html=../templates/utekontor2.html&profile=1101
The site lists the staff, street address, phone and fax numbers, and e-mail link of the Norwegian Embassy in Bangkok.

Pakistan

Pakistan Trade Office in Bangkok
http://www.jamal.com/epb/ptoa.htm
The site provides contact information for the Pakistan Trade Office in Bangkok.

Philippines

Philippine Trade and Investment Promotion Office in Bangkok
http://www.dti.gov.ph/bkk/
The site provides a mission statement, service directory, and contact information for the Philippine Trade Office in Bangkok.

Singapore

Embassy of Singapore in Bangkok
http://www.gov.sg/mfa/consular/mww_t.htm

The site provides contact information for the Singapore Embassy in Bangkok.

South Africa

South Africa Foreign Trade Office in Bangkok
http://wwwdti.pwv.gov.za/dtiwww/foreign_offices.htm
A service of the South Africa Department of Trade and Industry, the site provides contact information for the South Africa Trade Office in Bangkok.

Spain

Spanish Commercial Office in Bangkok
http://www.icex.es/openURL.html#openURL=/english/infoproyem/ofcomes/ofcomes.html#AS
The site lists the staff, street address, phone and fax numbers, and e-mail link of the Spanish Commercial Office in Bangkok.

Sweden

Embassy of Sweden in Bangkok
http://www.ud.se/english/mfa/ambassad/thailand.htm
The site provides contact information for the Swedish Embassy in Bangkok.

Taiwan

Taiwan Government Information Office in Bangkok
http://www.gio.gov.tw/info/ngio/tha-f.html
Posted in Chinese and English, the site lists the street address, phone and fax numbers, and e-mail link of the Taiwan Government Information Office in Bangkok.

Turkey

Embassy of Turkey in Bangkok
http://www.turkey.org/madres.htm
As part of a directory of Turkish diplomatic offices around the world, the site lists the e-mail link of the Turkish Embassy in Bangkok.

United Kingdom

British Chamber of Commerce in Bangkok
http://www.bccthai.com/
Founded in 1946, the Chamber promotes British business interests in Thailand. The site includes a member directory, staff roster, publications list, and event information.

Consulate of Britain in Chiang Mai
http://www.fco.gov.uk/directory/posts.asp?TH
The site provides contact information for the British Consulate in Chiang Mai.

Embassy of Britain in Bangkok
http://www.fco.gov.uk/directory/posts.asp?TH
The site provides contact information for the British Embassy in Bangkok.

United States

United States Consulate in Chiang Mai
http://www.inet.co.th/org/usis/chiang.htm
The site lists the mission statement, staff, geographic responsibility, street address, phone and fax numbers, and office hours of the United States Consulate in Chiang Mai.

United States Embassy in Bangkok
http://www.inet.co.th/org/usis/embindex.htm
Posted in English and Thai, the virtual Embassy delivers United States fact sheets, visa and passport information, and a directory of consular and commercial services.

United States Foreign Agricultural Service in Bangkok
http://www.inet.co.th/org/usis/fas.htm
A unit of the United States Department of Agriculture, the Service promotes American agricultural exports to Thailand. The site includes a staff directory, activity reports, and contact information.

United States Information Service in Bangkok
http://usa.or.th/
The online service provides United States press releases, speeches, fact sheets, electronic journals, and a directory of United States-Thailand educational and exchange programs.

Tonga

Tonga Market Guides

Business and Investments in Tonga
http://www.tongaonline.com/business/business.htm
Along with currency rate bulletins, the site provides fact sheets on Tongan investment regulations, government incentives, taxation, and business permits.

Kingdom of Tonga
http://www.tongatapu.net.to/
A hub of country information, the site delivers Tongan news, history lessons, government directories, travel guides, event information, and photos.

Tonga Business Briefs
http://www.austrade.gov.au/IOOM/Tonga/
A service of Austrade, the site offers fact sheets on Tongan culture, business etiquette, marketing, transportation, travel, and visas.

Tonga Country Brief
http://www.worldbank.org/cgi-bin/sendoff.cgi?page=%2Fhtml%2Fextdr%2Foffrep%2Feap%2Fto.htm
A service of the World Bank Group, the site provides Tongan population statistics, financial data, development reports, and economic forecasts.

Tonga Country Profile
http://www.tradenz.govt.nz/intelligence/profiles/tonga.html
A service of the New Zealand Trade Development Board, the site provides Tongan economic statistics, market information, and business tips.

Tonga Market Research
http://strategis.ic.gc.ca/sc_mrkti/ibinddc/engdoc/1a1i34.html
Posted by Industry Canada, the site provides U.S. Central Intelligence Agency fact sheets on Tongan geography, people, government, business, and transportation.

Tonga Online
http://www.tongaonline.com/
A virtual country gateway, the site provides Tongan news, commercial guides, language resources, cultural information, weather bulletins, and chat services.

Tonga Representative Offices

Sweden

Consulate of Sweden in Nuku'alofa
http://www.ud.se/english/mfa/ambassad/tonga.htm
The site provides contact information for the Swedish Consulate in Nuku'alofa.

United Kingdom

High Commission of Britain in Nuku'alofa
http://www.fco.gov.uk/directory/posts.asp?TN
The site provides contact information for the British High Commission in Nuku'alofa.

Tuvalu

Tuvalu Market Guides

Tuvalu Country Profile
http://www.tradenz.govt.nz/intelligence/profiles/ tuvalu.html
A service of the New Zealand Trade Development Board, the site provides Tuvaluan economic statistics, market information, and business tips.

Tuvalu Factbook
http://www.odci.gov/cia/publications/factbook/ tv.html
The site delivers briefs on Tuvaluan geography, maritime claims, climate, natural resources, natural hazards, environment, language, religion, government, and economy.

Tuvalu Market Research
http://strategis.ic.gc.ca/sc_mrkti/ibinddc/engdoc/ 1a1i35.html
Posted by Industry Canada, the site provides U.S. Central Intelligence Agency fact sheets on Tuvaluan geography, people, government, business, and transportation.

Vanuatu

Vanuatu Market Guides

Vanuatu Business Briefs
http://www.austrade.gov.au/IOOM/Vanuatu/
A service of Austrade, the site offers fact sheets on Vanuatu culture, business etiquette, marketing, transportation, travel, and visas.

Vanuatu Country Brief
http://www.worldbank.org/cgi-bin/ sendoff.cgi?page=%2Fhtml%2Fextdr%2Foffrep%2 Feap%2Fvu.htm
A service of the World Bank Group, the site provides Vanuatu population statistics, financial data, development reports, and economic forecasts.

Vanuatu Country Profile
http://www.tradenz.govt.nz/intelligence/profiles/ vanuatu.html

A service of the New Zealand Trade Development Board, the site provides Vanuatu economic statistics, market information, and business tips.

Vanuatu InfoExport
http://www.infoexport.gc.ca/country-e.asp?continent=Asia&country=71
A service of Foreign Affairs and International Trade Canada, the site provides fact sheets and statistics on Vanuatu geography, business and politics.

Vanuatu Market Research
http://strategis.ic.gc.ca/sc_mrkti/ibinddc/engdoc/ 1a1i37.html
Posted by Industry Canada, the site provides U.S. Central Intelligence Agency fact sheets on Vanuatu geography, people, government, business, and transportation.

Vanuatu Online
http://www.vanuatu.net.vu/pages/Vanuatu.html
A digital country gateway, the site delivers Vanuatu business guides, sector profiles, travel primers, event information, cultural bulletins, and geography lessons.

Vanuatu Representative Offices

Sweden

Consulate of Sweden in Port Vila
http://www.ud.se/english/mfa/ambassad/ vanuatu.htm
The site provides contact information for the Swedish Consulate in Port Vila.

United Kingdom

High Commission of Britain in Port Vila
http://www.fco.gov.uk/directory/posts.asp?VA
The site provides contact information for the British High Commission in Port Vila.

Vietnam

Vietnam Media

Vietnam Business Journal
http://www.viam.com/
Updated monthly, the site provides Vietnamese business news, editorials, economic reports, interviews, company directories, sector profiles, and investment and trade statistics.

Vietnam Economy

http://www.vneconomy.com.vn/
Updated daily, the English and Vietnamese language site provides Vietnamese business news, economic reports, legal guides, and international trade bulletins.

Vietnam Media

http://www.mediainfo.com/emediajs/specific-geo.htm?region=vietnam
Compiled by Editor and Publisher Interactive, the site is a directory of Vietnamese magazines, newspapers, and other media sites online.

Vietnam News Agency

http://www.vnagency.com.vn/
Official news service of the Vietnamese government, the site provides country news, government press releases, economic reports, cultural information, and photos.

Vietnam Market Guides

Representative Offices in Vietnam

http://home.vnn.vn/english/office/
A database of international companies in Vietnam, the service lists operations from over 20 countries including Canada, China, Germany, and Taiwan.

VietGate

http://www.vietgate.net/
An online country gateway, the site provides Vietnamese news, web navigation services, company directories, mailing lists, cultural information, and media guides.

Vietnam Business

http://www.cgtd.com/global/directory/veconomy.htm
A service of the Center for Global Trade Development, the site provides Vietnamese business news, economic reports, political bulletins, and company profiles.

Vietnam Business Briefs

http://www.austrade.gov.au/IOOM/Vietnam/
A service of Austrade, the site offers fact sheets on Vietnamese culture, business etiquette, marketing, transportation, travel, and visas.

Vietnam Country Brief

http://www.worldbank.org/cgi-bin/sendoff.cgi?page=%2Fhtml%2Fextdr%2Foffrep%2Feap%2Fvn.htm
A service of the World Bank Group, the site provides Vietnamese population statistics,

financial data, development reports, and economic forecasts.

Vietnam Country Profile

http://www.tradenz.govt.nz/intelligence/profiles/viet_nam.html
A service of the New Zealand Trade Development Board, the site provides Vietnamese economic statistics, market information, and business tips.

Vietnam: A Country Study

http://lcweb2.loc.gov/frd/cs/vntoc.html
A service of the U.S. Library of Congress, the site delivers fact sheets on Vietnamese geography, people, agriculture, mining, manufacturing, and foreign economic relations.

Vietnam Economy

http://www.vietnamembassy-usa.org/frcont02.htm
A service of the Vietnamese Embassy in Washington, D.C., the site provides bulletins on Vietnamese business law, financial reporting, international trade, and advertising.

Vietnam InfoExport

http://www.infoexport.gc.ca/country-e.asp?continent=Asia&country=48
A service of Foreign Affairs and International Trade Canada, the site provides Vietnamese commercial guides and market reports.

Vietnam Market Access Database

http://mkaccdb.eu.int/mkdb/mkdb.pl?METHOD=COUNTRY
A service of the European Commission, the site offers briefs on Vietnamese trade policy, tariff barriers, non-tariff barriers, investment-related measures, and financial services regulations.

Vietnam Market Research

http://strategis.ic.gc.ca/sc_mrkti/ibinddc/engdoc/1a1i38.html
A service of Industry Canada, the site provides U.S. Department of Commerce reports on Vietnamese economic trends, trade barriers, investment regulations, business travel, and market opportunities.

Vietnam Online

http://www.Vietnamonline.net/
Based in Hanoi, the site provides Vietnamese commercial guides, company directories, investment reports, legal primers, travel information, and cultural bulletins.

Vietnam: Selected Issues

http://www.imf.org/external/pubs/CAT/

longres.cfm?sk=2567.0
Prepared by the International Monetary Fund, the site reports on Vietnamese banking and money markets, state enterprise reform, export restrictions, import controls, and taxation.

Vietnam Virtual Library
http://coombs.anu.edu.au/WWWVLPages/
VietPages/WWWVL-Vietnam.html
A service of the World Wide Web Virtual Library, the site is a directory of Vietnamese resources online. Categories include economics, government, travel, and jobs.

Vietnam Web
http://home.vnn.vn/
Posted in English and Vietnamese, the site provides Vietnamese news, fact sheets, economic reports, company directories, travel information, and web guides.

VNN Company Whitepage
http://home.vnn.vn/english/company/
search_com.html
A directory of Vietnamese companies and organizations, the site is browsable by company name, business activity, street address, and city.

Vietnam Trade Assistance

Trade Shows in Vietnam
http://www.expoguide.com/shows/data/loc_69.htm
Compiled by Expoguide, the site is a directory of upcoming trade shows in Vietnam.

Vietnam Trade Winds
http://www.trade-winds.net/prevn.htm
A service of Trade Winds Online, the site is a searchable directory of Vietnamese trade shows, business contacts, tourism information, and media.

Vietnam Trade Show Calendar
http://www.viam.com/calendar.html
A service of Vietnam Business Journal, the site is a directory of Vietnamese trade shows and business events in over ten categories including energy, construction, and telecommunications.

Vietnam Representative Offices

Foreign Embassies in Vietnam
http://home.vnn.vn/english/embassy/
A directory of foreign embassies and consulates in Vietnam, the site lists representatives from

over 50 countries including Argentina, Egypt, Malaysia, and the Netherlands.

Brunei Darussalam

Embassy of Brunei Darussalam in Hanoi
http://www.brunet.bn/homepage/gov/bruemb/
govemb.htm
The site provides contact information for the Bruneian Embassy in Hanoi.

Canada

Embassy of Canada in Hanoi
http://www.dfait-maeci.gc.ca/english/missions/rep-
can4e.htm#viet nam
The site provides contact information for the Canadian Embassy in Hanoi.

Finland

Finland Trade Center in Hanoi
http://www.exports.finland.fi/tradecen.htm
The site lists the staff, street address, phone and fax numbers, and e-mail link of the Finland Trade Center in Hanoi.

France

French Trade Commission in Hanoi
http://www.dree.org/vietnam/
Written in French, the site delivers Vietnamese market reports, sector profiles, contact information, and a directory of French export promotion services.

Germany

German Chamber of Commerce in Hanoi
http://www.ahk.net/en/vn/Hanoi/
A German export promotion service, the site lists the Chairperson, Chief Executive Officer, street address, phone and fax numbers, and e-mail link of the German Chamber in Hanoi.

Laos

Embassy of Laos in Ho Chi Minh City
http://www.laoembassy.com/news/
embassyabroad.htm
The site provides contact information for the Embassy of Laos in Ho Chi Minh City.

Malaysia

Consulate General of Malaysia in Ho Chi Minh City
http://www.mnet.com.my/klonline/www/missions/ malmiss/mvietna2.htm
The site provides contact information for the Malaysian Consulate General in Ho Chi Minh City.

Embassy of Malaysia in Hanoi
http://www.mnet.com.my/klonline/www/missions/ malmiss/mvietna1.htm
The site provides contact information for the Malaysian Embassy in Hanoi.

Trade Commission of Malaysia in Ho Chi Minh City
http://www.mnet.com.my/klonline/www/missions/ malmiss/mvietna3.htm
The site provides contact information for the Malaysian Trade Commission in Ho Chi Minh City.

New Zealand

Trade New Zealand in Ho Chi Minh City
http://www.tradenz.govt.nz/contact/seasia.html
An export promotion service, the site provides contact information for the Trade New Zealand office in Ho Chi Minh City.

Philippines

Philippine International Trading Corporation in Ho Chi Minh City
http://www.dti.gov.ph/pitc/pitc1.htm#Directory
The site provides contact information for the Philippine International Trading Corporation in Ho Chi Minh City.

Singapore

Consulate General of Singapore in Ho Chi Minh City
http://www.gov.sg/mfa/consular/mww_v.htm
The site provides contact information for the Singapore Consulate General in Ho Chi Minh City.

Embassy of Singapore in Hanoi
http://www.gov.sg/mfa/consular/mww_v.htm
The site provides contact information for the Singapore Embassy in Hanoi.

Spain

Spanish Commercial Office in Ho Chi Minh City
http://www.icex.es/openURL.html#openURL=/ english/infoproyem/ofcomes/ofcomes.html#AS
The site lists the staff, street address, phone and fax numbers, and e-mail link of the Spanish Commercial Office in Ho Chi Minh City.

Sweden

Consulate of Sweden in Ho Chi Minh City
http://www.ud.se/english/mfa/ambassad/ vietnam.htm
The site provides contact information for the Swedish Embassy in Ho Chi Minh City.

Embassy of Sweden in Hanoi
http://www.ud.se/english/mfa/ambassad/ vietnam.htm
The site provides contact information for the Swedish Embassy in Hanoi.

Taiwan

China External Trade Development Council Office in Ho Chi Minh City
http://www.cetra.org.tw/english/o_office/ indexset.htm
A Taiwanese trade promotion service, the site lists the mission statement and e-mail link of the China External Trade Development Council Office in Ho Chi Minh City.

Thailand

Royal Thai Consulate General in Ho Chi Minh City
http://www.mfa.go.th/Embassy/detail/28.htm
The site lists the Consul General, street address, and phone and fax numbers of the Thai Consulate General in Ho Chi Minh City.

Royal Thai Embassy in Hanoi
http://www.mfa.go.th/Embassy/detail/65.htm
The site lists the Ambassador, street address, and phone and fax numbers of the Thai Embassy in Hanoi.

Thai Trade Center in Ho Chi Minh City
http://www.thaitrade.com/wwtto.html
A service of the Thailand Department of Export Promotion, the site lists the street address,

phone and fax numbers, and e-mail link of the Thai Trade Center in Ho Chi Minh City.

Thailand Office of Commercial Affairs in Hanoi
http://www.thaitrade.com/thcoaf.html
The site lists the street address, phone and fax numbers, and e-mail link of the Thailand Office of Commercial Affairs in Hanoi.

United Kingdom

Consulate General of Britain in Ho Chi Minh City
http://www.fco.gov.uk/directory/posts.asp?VM
The site provides contact information for the British Consulate General in Ho Chi Minh City.

Embassy of Britain in Hanoi
http://www.fco.gov.uk/directory/posts.asp?VM
The site provides contact information for the British Embassy in Hanoi.

United States

United States Consulate General in Ho Chi Minh City
http://members.aol.com/nomhawj/embassy/general.htm
The site lists the staff, mission statement, street address, and phone and fax numbers of the American Consulate General in Ho Chi Minh City.

United States Embassy in Hanoi
http://members.aol.com/nomhawj/embassy/home.htm
Along with Vietnamese photos and market reports, the site delivers United States visa and passport information, travel guides, and a directory of consular and commercial services.

Wallis and Futuna

Wallis and Futuna Market Guides

Wallis and Futuna Islands
http://wallis-islands.com/index2.htm
A hub of territory information, the site provides fact sheets on Wallis and Futuna Islander geography, history, people, transportation, travel, and business.

Wallis and Futuna Market Research
http://strategis.ic.gc.ca/sc_mrkti/ibinddc/engdoc/1a1i39.html
Posted by Industry Canada, the site provides U.S. Central Intelligence Agency fact sheets on Wallis

and Futuna Islander geography, people, government, business, and transportation.

Western Samoa

Western Samoa Market Guides

Samoa Business Briefs
http://www.austrade.gov.au/IOOM/Samoa/
A service of Austrade, the site offers fact sheets on Western Samoan culture, business etiquette, marketing, transportation, travel, and visas.

Samoa Country Brief
http://www.worldbank.org/cgi-bin/sendoff.cgi?page=%2Fhtml%2Fextdr%2Foffrep%2Feap%2Fws.htm
A service of the World Bank Group, the site provides Western Samoan population statistics, financial data, development reports, and economic forecasts.

Samoa Country Profile
http://www.tradenz.govt.nz/intelligence/profiles/samoa.html
A service of the New Zealand Trade Development Board, the site provides Western Samoan economic statistics, market information, and business tips.

Government of Western Samoa
http://www.interwebinc.com/samoa/
Featuring photos and maps, the site delivers Western Samoan fact sheets, history lessons, travel guides, event information, government directories, and cultural bulletins.

Western Samoa InfoExport
http://www.infoexport.gc.ca/country-e.asp?continent=Asia&country=73
A service of Foreign Affairs and International Trade Canada, the site provides fact sheets and statistics on Western Samoan geography, business and politics.

Western Samoa Market Research
http://strategis.ic.gc.ca/sc_mrkti/ibinddc/engdoc/1a1i40.html
Posted by Industry Canada, the site provides U.S. Central Intelligence Agency fact sheets on Western Samoan geography, people, government, business, and transportation.

Western Samoa Trade Assistance

Western Samoa Overseas Missions
http://www.interwebinc.com/samoa/missions.html
A directory of Western Samoan Embassies, Consulates, and High Commissions worldwide, the site lists offices in seven countries including Australia, Belgium, Japan, and New Zealand.

APPENDIX A: E-CUSTOMER PROFILER

Use this questionnaire to profile your ideal e-business customer(s).

Which Customers Do You Want to Reach Online?

#	Questions	Your Response
1	Which products or services will you sell online?	
2	What are the competitive advantages of your product or service? Why should a customer buy from you?	
3	Which industries will you target (e.g., auto manufacturers, travel agents)	
4	What size of operation are you targeting? (e.g., 1-10 employees, 500+ employees)	
5	Which decision-maker in the firm do you wish to target? (e.g., President, Owner, CFO, Vice President)	

Exercise #1

1. In 100 words or less, write out your online **selling** mission statement. Describe what you want to sell and to whom and why.
2. Write out 20 keywords or phrases that could be used in your online searches for your ideal customers. Include the names of the products or services you wish to sell, the solutions you provide, the industries you wish to target, and the job titles of those whom you wish to reach.
3. Using the resources in this book and your keywords, scan the web. Compile a list of ten organizations that could potentially buy what you sell, and write down their names and details in the form below.
4. Write each of these ten organizations a brief e-mail no more than 200 words in length. Introduce yourself and explain how the two of you could potentially work together in the future.
5. Follow up with those who respond.

Top E-Customer Prospects

#	Organization	URL	E-mail Address	Key Contact	Opportunity
1					
2					
3					
4					
5					
6					
7					
8					
9					
10					

APPENDIX B: E-SUPPLIER PROFILER

Use this questionnaire to profile your ideal e-business supplier(s).

Which Suppliers Do You Want to Reach Online?

#	Questions	Your Response
1	Which products or services will you source online?	
2	What competitive advantages are you seeking (e.g., low price, high quality, wide selection)?	
3	What are your delivery requirements (e.g., batch size, order frequency)?	
4	What are your after-sales service requirements?	
5	Do you require any special warranties or performance guarantees? If so, what are they?	

Exercise #2

1. In 100 words or less, write out your online **buying** mission statement. Describe what you want to buy at what price and on what terms.
2. Write out 20 keywords or phrases that could be used in your online searches for your ideal suppliers. Include the names of the products or services you wish to buy, the solutions they provide, and detailed descriptions of the items or services you require.
3. Using the resources in this book and your keywords, scan the web. Compile a list of ten organizations that could potentially supply what you require, and write down their names in the form below.
4. Write each of these ten organizations a brief e-mail no more than 200 words in length. Introduce yourself, explain your sourcing requirements, and inquire if they'd be interested in submitting a quotation or information on any or all of the products or services you need.
5. Follow up with those who respond.

Top E-Supplier Prospects

#	Organization	URL	E-mail Address	Key Contact	Opportunity
1					
2					
3					
4					
5					
6					
7					
8					
9					
10					

APPENDIX C: E-PARTNER PROFILER

Use this questionnaire to profile your ideal e-business partner(s).

Which Partners Do You Want to Reach Online?

#	Questions	Your Response
1	What solutions are you seeking (e.g., expanded dealer network, enhanced R&D capability)?	
2	Which region(s) or countries are you targeting?	
3	What products or services should your ideal partner provide?	
4	How much competitive clout and experience should they have?	
5	What type of partnership arrangement are you seeking (e.g., joint venture, franchising)?	

Exercise #3

1. In 100 words or less, write out your online **partnering** mission statement. Describe what type of partnership you are seeking and why.
2. Write out 20 keywords or phrases that could be used in your online searches for your ideal partners. Include the solutions you are seeking, the geographic areas you are targeting, and the type of partnership arrangements you prefer.
3. Using the resources in this book and your keywords, scan the web. Compile a list of ten organizations that could potentially partner with you, and write down their names in the form below.
4. Write each of these ten organizations a brief e-mail no more than 200 words in length. Introduce yourself, explain your partnering requirements, and inquire if they'd be interested in working together in the future.
5. Follow up with those who respond.

Top E-Partnering Prospects

#	Organization	URL	E-mail Address	Key Contact	Opportunity
1					
2					
3					
4					
5					
6					
7					
8					
9					
10					

APPENDIX D: E-MAIL TEMPLATES

Use these templates to help draft your initial correspondence to your leading online customer, supplier, and partner prospects.

For Potential Customers

To: idealcustomer@business.com
From: Mr. Lance Brett
Subject: Greetings from Transcona, Canada

Dear Ms. Valerie Joseph, Vice President,

My name is Lance Brett, Vice President of Lockport Enterprises in Transcona, Manitoba, Canada. I recently visited your website and was particularly intrigued by your product X. Exactly what materials and machinery do you use to manufacture this item? I ask this because my firm—company AA—is a leading supplier in your industry, and we offer a variety of products, services, and solutions that may save you time and money in the production of item X.

I have a few ideas on how we could possibly work together in the future. If you wish, I'll forward you more detailed information about our company and products. I also have a list of Internet links from our industry that I could pass along for your information.

Thanks ahead of time for your interest, and I look forward to your response in the next few days.

Regards,
Mr. Lance Brett
Vice President
Lockport Enterprises
Transcona, Manitoba

For Potential Suppliers

To: idealsupplier@business.com
From: Mr. Lance Brett
Subject: Greetings from Transcona, Canada

Dear Ms. Valerie Joseph, Vice President,

My name is Lance Brett, Vice President of Lockport Enterprises in Transcona, Manitoba, Canada. I recently visited your website and was particularly intrigued by your service Y. Our company regularly purchases this service, and I was wondering if you could provide more information and a quotation.

I have a few ideas on how we could possibly work together in the future. If you wish, I'll forward you more detailed information about myself, my company, and our supply requirements.

Thanks ahead of time for your interest, and I look forward to your response in the next few days.

Regards,
Mr. Lance Brett
Vice President
Lockport Enterprises
Transcona, Manitoba

For Potential Partners

To: idealparnter@business.com
From: Mr. Lance Brett
Subject: Greetings from Transcona, Canada

Dear Ms. Valerie Joseph, Vice President,

My name is Lance Brett, Vice President of Lockport Enterprises in Transcona, Manitoba, Canada. I recently visited your website and was particularly intrigued by your research capabilities. Our company is seeking a development partner, and I was wondering if you could provide more information about your scientific activities.

I have a few ideas on how we could possibly work together in the future, and would welcome the opportunity to discuss a number of strategic alliance opportunities. If you wish, I'll forward you more detailed information about myself, my company, and our products. I also have a list of Internet links from our industry that I could pass along for your information.

Thanks ahead of time for your interest, and I look forward to your response in the next few days.

Regards,
Mr. Lance Brett
Vice President
Lockport Enterprises
Transcona, Manitoba

APPENDIX E: RESEARCH NODES CHECKLISTS

Use these checklists to identify research nodes on the web, and guide your information gathering online.

Home Nation Nodes

Home Nation: _____

#	Research Nodes	Resource Availability		Resource Name	URL	Information Provided
		Available	Not Available			
1	National Trade Agencies					
2	State/Provincial Trade Agencies					
3	City Trade Agencies					
4	Trade Training Programs					
5	Trade Mentor Programs					
6	Export Guides					
7	Geographic Guides					
8	Trade Finance Organizations					
9	National Representative Offices in Target Market					
10	National Representative Offices in Target Market Regions					
11	State/Provincial Offices in Target Market					
12	City Offices in Target Market					
13	National Export Associations in Home Market					
14	National Sector-Focused Export Associations					
15	National Geographic-Focused Export Associations					
16	State/Provincial Export Associations					
17	City Export Associations					
18	Bilateral Chambers of Commerce in Home Market					
19	Industry Associations					
20	Outgoing Trade Missions to Target Market					
21	Incoming Trade Missions from Target Market					
22	Business Events on Target Market					
23	Export Directories in Home Market					
24	International Trade Statistics					
25	Media in Home Market					

Target Market Nodes

Target Market: _____

#	Research Nodes	Resource Availability		Resource Name	URL	Information Provided
		Available	Not Available			
1	National Trade Agencies					
2	Customs Agency					
3	State/Provincial Economic Development Agencies					
4	City Economic Development Agencies					
5	National Representative Offices in Home Nation					
6	National Representative Offices in Home Region					
7	National Representative Offices in Home City					
8	National Representative Offices in Third Countries					
9	State/Provincial Representative Offices in Home Nation					
10	City Representative Offices in Home Nation					
11	Export Associations in Target Market					
12	Bilateral Chambers in Target Market					
13	Industry Associations in Target Market					
14	Statistical Agency in Target Market					
15	Credit Agencies in Target Market					
16	Stock Exchanges in Target Market					
17	Patent and Trademark Authority in Target Market					
18	Business Events in Target Market					
19	Company Directories in Target Market					
20	Internet Newsgroups on Target Market					
21	Employment Databases on Target Market					
22	Procurement Agencies in Target Market					
23	Business and Investment Guides on Target Market					
24	Trade Leads in Target Market					
25	Internet Search Engines on Target Market					
26	Media in Target Market					

Third Country Nodes

Third Countries: _____

_____

_____

_____

_____

#	Research Nodes	Resource Availability		Resource Name	URL	Information Provided
		Available	Not Available			
1	National Trade Agencies in Third Countries					
2	Representative Offices in Target Market					
3	Export Guides					
4	Geographic Guides					
5	Trade Finance Organizations					
6	Export Associations					
7	Bilateral Chambers in Target Market					
8	Bilateral Chambers in Third Countries					
9	Industry Associations					
10	Outgoing Trade Missions to Target Market					
11	Incoming Trade Missions from Target Market					
12	Business Events on Target Market					
13	Trade Leads					
14	Media in Third Countries					

APPENDIX F: NAVIGATION CHECKLIST

Use this checklist to trouble-shoot broken links, and find sites that may have moved.

#	To Do		Tips
1	Check own Internet connection.		Local ISP may be down. Wait until service is restored.
2	Check that URL is copied exactly.		Ensure that every alpha-numeric character is typed exactly as indicated and in the precise order.
3	Watch Number One's and Letter L's.		Verify that number one (1) and letter L (l) characters are not reversed.
4	Watch Number Zero's and Letter O's.		Check that zero (0) and letter O (o) characters are not reversed.
5	Fiddle with ending.		Dropping or adding a period (.) or forward slash (/) at end of URL could trigger connection.
6	Wait it out.		Be patient. Depending on speed of Internet connection, access may take 90 seconds or more.
7	Hit Enter key again.		First connection attempt may have been aborted by network error. Try again.
8	Open another browser window, retype URL and hit enter.		In some cases, entering the URL in another browser window will make connection.
9	Use different browser.		If using Navigator, try Explorer, and vice-versa. Some sites are browser finicky.
10	Connect during off-peak hours.		During peak periods—usually early evening—access to a site may be temporarily suspended.
11	Try again tomorrow, the day after, and next week.		Website could be down for temporary repairs or upgrades.
12	Slash after the slash. From right to left, delete portion of URL to next forward slash (/).		In some cases, this allows a user to return to home page of website, and search for new location of target site.
13	Search Dogpile at http://www.dogpile.com/.		Site may have moved. This search engine of search engines may identify new location.
14	Search Virtual International Search at http://www.dreamscape.com/frankvad/search.international.html.		Site may have moved, and be listed on a regional search engine, not a popular U.S.-based search service.
15	Search AltaVista at http://www.altavista.com/.		AltaVista is one of the largest and most powerful online search services. May identify new location.
16	Search with quotes (" ") on AltaVista.		Enter name of site in quotes on AltaVista. This will do search for that specific phrase.
17	Search title in AltaVista.		Type *title:name of site*. This searches for specific phrase in browser title bars on web.
18	Search text in AltaVista.		Type *text:name of site*. This searches for phrase in actual text of websites.
19	Search URL in AltaVista.		Type *url:original url*. This searches for pages with original URL. New information may be uncovered.
20	Search link in AltaVista.		Type *link:original url*. This searches for pages that link to original URL. New information may be uncovered.
21	Search DejaNews at http://www.dejanews.com.		A database of discussion groups, the service may provide updates on site's status or new location.
22	Post message.		Using DejaNews, find discussion groups related to target site. Post message to groups inquiring about status of site, or where similar information could be found online.
23	Contact other nationals.		Contact related websites in same country. They may provide a status report or suggest alternatives.

APPENDIX G: INTERNET COUNTRY CODES

Many web and e-mail addresses contain a two-letter code that indicates the country location of the website and e-mail service. An example is the Yemeni General Investment Authority at http://www.giay.gov.ye/. The *ye* in http://www.giay.gov.*ye*/ is the country code, and indicates that the website is located in Yemen. Another example is the author's e-mail address at gwasny@direct.ca. The *ca* in gwasny@direct.*ca* is the country code, and notes that the e-mail service is located in Canada. The following is a directory of Internet Country Codes for nations around the world. Use the codes to help identify the physical location of websites and e-mail services.

Afghanistan: af
Albania: al
Algeria: dz
American Samoa: as
Andorra: ad
Angola: ao
Anguilla: ai
Antarctica: aq
Antigua and Barbuda: ag
Argentina: ar
Armenia: am
Aruba: aw
Australia: au
Austria: at
Azerbaijan: az
Bahamas: bs
Bahrain: bh
Bangladesh: bd
Barbados: bb
Belarus: by
Belgium: be
Belize: bz
Benin: bj
Bermuda: bm
Bhutan: bt
Bolivia: bo
Bosnia and Herzegovina: ba
Botswana: bw
Bouvet Island: bv
Brazil: br
British Indian Ocean Territory: io
Brunei Darussalam: bn
Bulgaria: bg
Burkina Faso: bf
Burundi: bi
Cambodia: kh
Cameroon: cm120
Canada: ca
Cape Verde: cv
Cayman Islands: ky

Central African Republic: cf
Chad: td
Chile: cl
China: cn
Christmas Island: cx
Cocos (Keeling) Islands: cc
Colombia: co
Comoros: km
Congo: cg
Congo, the Democratic Republic of the: cd
Cook Islands: ck
Costa Rica: cr
Côte d'Ivoire: ci
Croatia (local name: Hrvatska): hr
Cuba: cu
Cyprus: cy
Czech Republic: cz
Denmark: dk
Djibouti: dj
Dominica: dm
Dominican Republic: do
East Timor: tp
Ecuador: ec
Egypt: eg
El Salvador: sv
Equatorial Guinea: gq
Eritrea: er
Estonia: ee
Ethiopia: et
Falkland Islands: fk
Faroe Islands: fo
Fiji: fj
Finland: fi
France: fr
France, metropolitan: fx
French Guiana: gf
French Polynesia: pf
French Southern Territories: tf
Gabon: ga
Gambia: gm
Georgia: ge

Germany: de
Ghana: gh
Gibraltar: gi
Greece: gr
Greenland: gl
Grenada: gd
Guadeloupe: gp
Guam: gu
Guatemala: gt
Guinea: gn
Guinea-Bissau: gw
Guyana: gy
Haiti: ht
Holy See (Vatican City State): va
Honduras: hn
Hong Kong: hk
Hungary: hu
Iceland: is
India: in
Indonesia: id
Iran: ir
Iraq: iq
Ireland: ie
Israel: il
Italy: it
Jamaica: jm
Japan: jp
Jordan: jo
Kazakhstan: kz
Kenya: ke
Kiribati: ki
Korea, North: kp
Korea, South: kr
Kuwait: kw
Kyrgyzstan: kg
Laos: la
Latvia: lv
Lebanon: lb
Lesotho: ls
Liberia: lr
Libya: ly
Liechtenstein: li
Lithuania: lt

Luxembourg: lu
Macau: mo
Macedonia: mk
Madagascar: mg
Malawi: mw
Malaysia: my
Maldives: mv
Mali: ml
Malta: mt
Marshall Islands: mh
Martinique: mq
Mauritania: mr
Mauritius: mu
Mayotte: yt
Mexico: mx
Micronesia: fm
Moldova: md
Monaco: mc
Mongolia: mn
Montserrat: ms
Morocco: ma
Mozambique: mz
Myanmar: mm
Namibia: na
Nauru: nr
Nepal: np
Netherlands: nl
Netherlands Antilles: an
New Caledonia: nc
New Zealand: nz
Nicaragua: ni
Niger: ne
Nigeria: ng
Niue: nu
Norfolk Island: nf
Northern Mariana Islands: mp
Norway: no
Oman: om
Pakistan: pk
Palau: pw

Panama: pa
Papua New Guinea: pg
Paraguay: py
Peru: pe
Philippines: ph
Pitcairn Islands: pn
Poland: pl
Portugal: pt
Puerto Rico: pr
Qatar: qa
Reunion: re
Romania: ro
Russia: ru
Rwanda: rw
Saint Kitts and Nevis: kn
Saint Lucia: lc
Saint Vincent and the Grenadines: vc
Samoa: ws
San Marino: sm
São Tomé and Príncipe: st
Saudi Arabia: sa
Senegal: sn
Seychelles: sc
Sierra Leone: sl
Singapore: sg
Slovakia: sk
Slovenia: si
Solomon Islands: sb
Somalia: so
South Africa: za
Spain: es
Sri Lanka: lk
St. Helena: sh
St. Pierre and Miquelon: pm
Sudan: sd
Suriname: sr
Swaziland: sz
Sweden: se
Switzerland: ch
Syria: sy

Taiwan: tw
Tajikistan: tj
Tanzania: tz
Thailand: th
Togo: tg
Tonga: to
Trinidad and Tobago: tt
Tunisia: tn
Turkey: tr
Turkmenistan: tm
Turks and Caicos Islands: tc
Tuvalu: tv
Uganda: ug
Ukraine: ua
United Arab Emirates: ae
United Kingdom: gb
United States: us
Uruguay: uy
Uzbekistan: uz
Vanuatu: vu
Venezuela: ve
Vietnam: vn
Virgin Islands (British): vg
Virgin islands (U.S.): vi
Wallis and Futuna Islands: wf
Western Sahara: eh
Yemen: ye
Zambia: zm
Zimbabwe: zw

Source: Network Wizards at http://nw.com/zone/iso-country-codes.

ABOUT THE AUTHOR

Garrett Wasny, CMC (Certified Management Consultant) is an award-winning international trade writer, webmaster, and trainer in Vancouver, Canada. Author of more than 100 published articles on global business and Internet topics, he is the principal contributor to *Using the Web to Compete in a Global Marketplace* (http://www.ginfo.net/book/), published in 1998 by John Wiley and Sons.

A prize-winning speaker, Mr. Wasny delivers a series of *How to Conquer the World* seminars and workshops to develop international business. Informative and entertaining, the presentations have been delivered to over 100 international trade organizations and multinationals in dozens of cities across North America and Europe, including New York, Los Angeles, Chicago, Washington, D.C., Atlanta, Cleveland, Dallas, San Francisco, Tampa, Toronto, Vancouver, and Oslo.

To contact Mr. Wasny:

E-mail: webmaster@howtoconquertheworld.com

Web: http://www.howtoconquertheworld.com/

Telephone: 604/878-4555

Fax: 604/689-1653